USING COMPUTERS IN THE

LAW OFFICE

SEVENTH EDITION

USING COMPUTERS IN THE LAW OFFICE

SEVENTH EDITION

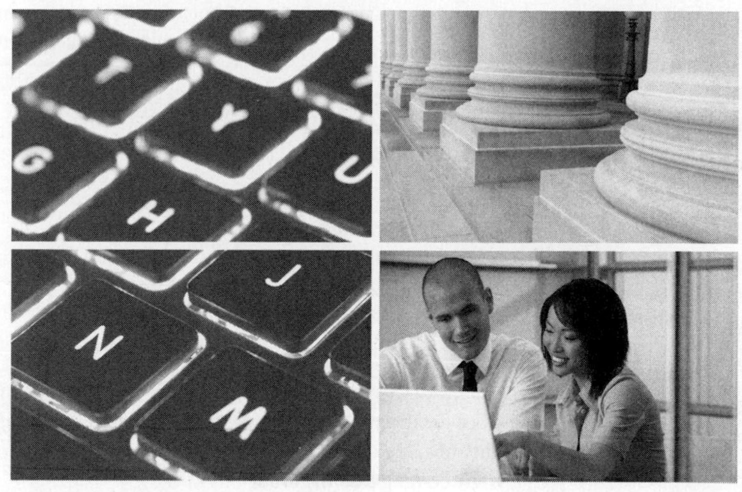

Matthew S. Cornick, J.D.
Clayton State University

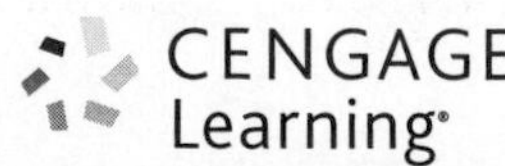

Australia • Brazil • Mexico • Singapore • United Kingdom • United States

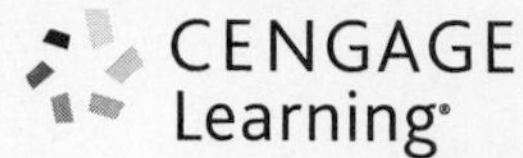

Using Computers in the Law Office, Seventh Edition
Matthew S. Cornick

Senior Vice President, General Manager for Skills and Global Product Management: Dawn Gerrain

Product Manager: Paul Lamond

Senior Director, Development/Global Product Management, Skills: Marah Bellegarde

Senior Product Development Manager: Larry Main

Senior Content Developer: Melissa Riveglia

Senior Product Assistant: Diane E. Chrysler

Vice President Marketing Services: Jennifer Baker

Marketing Manager: Scott Chrysler

Senior Production Director: Wendy Troeger

Production Director: Andrew Crouth

Senior Content Project Manager: Betty L. Dickson

Art Director: Brenda Carmichael, Lumina Datamatics, Inc.

Senior Technology Project Manager: Joe Pliss

Cover image(s):
Business colleagues working
Copyright: © Nicole Waring/istockphoto.com

Illuminated keyboard
Copyright: © Pierre Mentz/Shutterstock

Pillars
Copyright: © SNEHIT/Shutterstock

WCN: 01-100-101

Library of Congress Control Number: 2013958137

ISBN: 978-1-285-18959-8

Cengage Learning
20 Channel Center Street,
Boston, MA 02210
USA

Cengage Learning is a leading provider of customized learning solutions with office locations around the globe, including Singapore, the United Kingdom, Australia, Mexico, Brazil, and Japan. Locate your local office at:
www.cengage.com/global

Cengage Learning products are represented in Canada by Nelson Education, Ltd.

To learn more about Cengage Learning, visit **www.cengage.com**

Purchase any of our products at your local college store or at our preferred online store **www.cengagebrain.com**

Printed in the United States of America
Print Number: 02 Print Year: 2015

For Renda, Peter, and Julia

BRIEF CONTENTS

CONTENTS

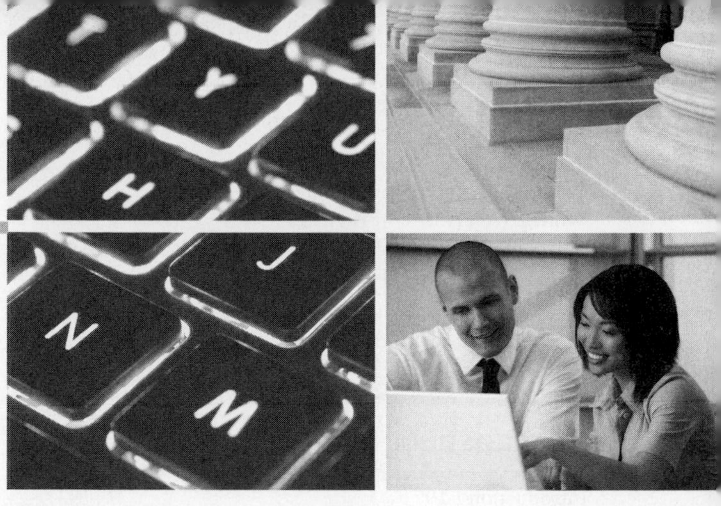

CHAPTER 3

Spreadsheet Software | 197

CHAPTER 4

Legal Timekeeping and Billing Software | 323

CHAPTER 5

Databases, Case Management, and Docket Control Software | 382

CHAPTER 6

The Cloud and Social Media | 447

CHAPTER 7

Electronic Discovery | 480

CHAPTER 8

Litigation Support Software | 519

CHAPTER 9

The Internet, Computer-Assisted Legal Research, and Electronic Mail | 619

PREFACE

I should make a confession. There was a time (many years ago) when I believed that I could be successful in the law office without knowing much about computers. That was then. This is now. Let me state this as plainly as I can: a successful legal professional *must* know how to use a computer and the applications commonly used in a law office. With the advent of all things "e"—e-mail, e-discovery, e-filing, and so on—it is essential that you gain the skills this text seeks to impart. The 21st century is well under way and computer literacy is a basic competency in law offices. *Using Computers in the Law Office*, Seventh Edition, is designed to give students both theoretical understanding and practical experience with common law-office computer applications. These include both widely used applications, such as Microsoft Word, Excel, PowerPoint, and HotDocs; and programs specific to the law office, such as Tabs3, AbacusLaw, Clio, Discover FY, CaseMap, TimeMap, Westlaw, LexisNexis, and TrialDirector. I hope that students will learn not only the specific uses of these programs, but also that they should not doubt their abilities or fear the prospect of working with computers.

TO THE STUDENT

If I could give you only one piece of advice, it would be this: *be patient*. Do not rush through the Hands-On Exercises. I can tell you from personal experience that haste is a sure path to mistakes and frustration. If you are a novice to these applications, I hope (and expect) that you will find you can do far more than you ever thought possible.

If I could give you a second piece of advice, it would be to *keep learning*. Technology is always evolving. Never more so than today, knowledge is power. For years, I have been telling my students that the surest way to make themselves invaluable to their employers is to know how to do something the employer does not know. Learn the skills emphasized throughout this text and then keep learning, and your success is almost a certainty.

ORGANIZATION OF THE TEXT

This textbook is organized into ten chapters. The first chapter introduces students to computers with a discussion of the importance of computers to the legal field and a review of computer hardware and software terms. The objective is to give students a rudimentary understanding of basic computer terminology and systems on which the rest of the book can build.

The next nine chapters represent the heart of the book. They cover word processing, spreadsheets, timekeeping and billing, case management/docket control, electronic discovery, the cloud and social media, litigation support, the Internet and electronic mail, computer-assisted research, and the electronic courthouse/automated courtroom and presentation graphics. Each topic is presented in a clear and organized manner and includes many examples of how the relevant software is actually used by paralegals in legal organizations.

Since the publication of the last edition, three new buzzwords have dominated the world of law office technology. These are "cloud computing," "social media," and "predictive coding." The cloud and social media are discussed briefly throughout the text and extensively in a new chapter—Chapter 6 (The Cloud and Social Media). Predictive Coding is discussed in Chapter 7 (Electronic Discovery). The only certainty in this area of the law is change. And to that end, I am pleased that all of the software applications and data files needed to complete the Hands-On Exercises are available online at the Premium Website. Please be sure to check the website before beginning any exercises to check for the latest updates to the exercises and the software applications.

CHANGES TO THE SEVENTH EDITION

Technology in the legal field continues to grow at an astounding rate. In particular, the increasing use of the cloud and social media has, and will continue to have, a dramatic impact on the way legal professionals practice law. Accordingly, this edition features a new chapter on "The Cloud and Social Media." Some of the changes include

- A new cloud-based software application (Clio).
- Each of these new applications is accompanied by new Hands-On Exercises designed to impart the practical skills required in a modern law office.

- For the first time, all of the software applications can be installed directly from downloadable links via the Premium Website.
- Almost every set of Hands-On Exercises includes a basic, intermediate, and advanced section. The exercises have been revised and updated.
- All of the screen shots have been updated.
- There are over 575 screen shots in this edition; more than ever before.
- Expanded discussion of electronic discovery, metadata, and electronically stored information has been added.
- The latest developments in computer-assisted legal research (WestlawNext, and Lexis Advance) are introduced.

LEARNING FEATURES

Chapter features include the following:

- **Chapter objectives** open each chapter to focus the student's attention on the main elements of the chapter.
- **Internet sites** are referenced, and useful and relevant ones are listed near the end of each chapter.
- **Key terms** are boldfaced in the body of the text, and definitions appear in the margin for easy review and reference. (A comprehensive glossary appears at the end of the book.)
- **Numerous illustrations,** including screen shots, legal documents, tables, and other graphics, are included throughout the text.
- **Test your Knowledge exercises** are included in each chapter.
- **On the Web exercises** are included in each chapter.
- **Questions and Exercises** are included in each chapter to challenge students to apply the information learned in the chapter.
- An **Ethics Question** is included for each chapter.
- **Hands-On Exercises** are included for most chapters to give students actual experience on a computer.

HANDS-ON EXERCISES

Hands-On Exercises are included for 22 different applications; there are 150 exercises in all. These exercises assume that the student has access to a computer and to application software, but no prior computer experience is necessary to complete the tutorials.

The Hands-On Exercises include step-by-step instructions that guide the student through the application. There are literally hundreds of screen shots to guide the student and act as reference points. All of the Hands-On Exercises are completely interactive, allowing the student to gain hands-on experience with the software. In addition, all of the Hands-On Exercises are specifically related to legal organizations and legal applications, so the student not only learns how to operate the computer and software, but also learns how to use them in the legal environment.

Full tutorials are included for the following applications:

- Microsoft Word 2013 (NEW)
- Microsoft Word 2010
- Microsoft Word 2007
- HotDocs (v.11)
- Microsoft Excel 2013 (NEW)
- Microsoft Excel 2010
- Microsoft Excel 2007
- Tabs3 (v.17)
- AbacusLaw (v.22)
- Clio (NEW)
- Discover FY (v.6.3.9)
- LexisNexis CaseMap (v.10)
- LexisNexis TimeMap (v.5)
- Westlaw
- WestlawNext (NEW)
- Lexis
- Lexis Advance (NEW)
- Microsoft PowerPoint 2013 (NEW)
- Microsoft PowerPoint 2010
- Microsoft PowerPoint 2007
- TrialDirector (v.6.5)

To help students complete some of the Hands-On Exercises, data files are available on the Premium Website.

- Excel
- HotDocs
- PowerPoint
- Word Processing

EDUCATIONAL SOFTWARE

Access to the following demonstration software is included with the text via the Premium Website. Use the Access Code included on the Premium Website card included with your text to activate your free online access. Please visit http://www.CengageBrain.com to create your account, log in, and access the Premium Website.

Please do not download the software programs until your instructor tells you to do so. Please note that many of the programs expire, and will not work after a certain number of days elapse from when the program was first loaded; other limitations may also apply to certain demonstration software:

- **HotDocs.** HotDocs 11 is a registered trademark of HotDocs, Ltd. HotDocs expires 120 days after it is first installed.
- **Tabs3.** Tabs3 is a registered trademark of Software Technology, Inc. Tabs3 does not expire, however the following features are disabled: run data file integrity check, run reindex data files, run advance current reporting month, run credit card authorization.
- **AbacusLaw.** AbacusLaw is a registered trademark of Abacus Data Systems, Inc. AbacusLaw expires 120 days after it is first installed.
- **Clio.** Clio runs on any operating system. The demo expires 365 days after it is first installed.
- **Discover FY.** Discover FY is the intellectual property of Webig Development, LLC. Discover FY does not expire; however, the ability to process data other than the provided content is disabled.
- **LexisNexis CaseMap.** CaseMap is a registered trademark of CaseSoft, a division of LexisNexis. CaseMap expires 120 days after it is first installed.
- **LexisNexis TimeMap.** TimeMap is a registered trademark of CaseSoft, a division of LexisNexis. TimeMap expires 120 days after it is first installed.
- **TrialDirector.** TrialDirector is a registered trademark of inData Corporation. TrialDirector expires 140 days after it is first installed.

NOTE:

- Access to Microsoft Office applications (Word; Excel; PPT) is not included with the text.
- Access to the Westlaw and LexisNexis research databases (described in Chapter 9, with hands-on exercises) is not included with the text.

SUPPLEMENTAL TEACHING AND LEARNING MATERIALS

Premium Website

The Premium Website includes resources for instructors and students. The card in the text includes an access code for this book's Premium Website. Go to login.cengagebrain.com to access the downloadable software demos and updates to the text.

INSTRUCTOR COMPANION SITE 

The online Instructor Companion Site provides the following resources:

Instructor's Manual

The Instructor's Manual provides comprehensive teaching support. The Instructor's Manual contains the following:

- Syllabus and lesson plans
- Chapter objectives and outlines
- Teaching suggestions and class discussion ideas
- Sample grading rubrics
- Answers to exercises in the text
- Testbank and answer key

PowerPoint Presentations

Customizable Microsoft PowerPoint® Presentations focus on key points for each chapter. (Microsoft PowerPoint® is a registered trademark of the Microsoft Corporation.)

Cengage Learning Testing Powered by Cognero is a flexible, online system that allows you to:

- author, edit, and manage test bank content from multiple Cengage Learning solutions
- create multiple test versions in an instant
- deliver tests from your LMS, your classroom or wherever you want

Start right away!

Cengage Learning Testing Powered by Cognero works on any operating system or browser.

- No special installs or downloads needed
- Create tests from school, home, the coffee shop—anywhere with Internet access

What will you find?

- Simplicity at every step. A desktop-inspired interface features drop-down menus and familiar, intuitive tools that take you through content creation and management with ease.
- Full-featured test generator. Create ideal assessments with your choice of 15 question types (including true/false, multiple choice, opinion scale/likert, and essay). Multi-language support, an equation editor, and unlimited metadata help ensure your tests are complete and compliant.
- Cross-compatible capability. Import and export content into other systems.

MINDTAP 

MindTap for Cornick/Using Computers in the Law Office is a highly personalized fully online learning platform of authoritative content, assignments, and services offering you a tailored presentation of course curriculum created by your instructor. MindTap for Cornick/Using Computers in the Law Office guides you through the course curriculum via an innovative learning path where you will complete reading assignments, annotate your readings, complete homework, and engage with quizzes and assessments. MindTap includes a variety of web-apps known as "MindApps" – allowing functionality, like having the text read aloud to you as well as MindApps that allow you to synchronize your notes with your personal Evernote account. MindApps are tightly woven into the MindTap platform and enhance your learning experience.

How MindTap helps students succeed?

- Use the Progress App to see where you stand at all times—individually and compared to highest performers in your class
- ReadSpeaker reads the course material to you
- MyNotes provides the ability to highlight text and take notes—that link back to the MindTap material for easy reference when you are studying for an exam or working on a project
- *Merriam-Webster Dictionary* and a glossary are only a click away
- Flashcards are pre-created to help you memorize the key terms

Not using MindTap in your course?

- It's an online destination housing ALL your course material and assignments . . . neatly organized to match your syllabus
- It's loaded with study tools that help you learn the material more easily
- To learn more go to www.cengage.com/mindtap or ask your instructor to try it out

Supplements At-A-Glance

Supplement:	What it is:	What's in it:
Premium Website	Resources for instructor and students Access card included with textbook Go to login.cengage.com	• Downloadable software demo links • Data files • Updates to the text
Online Instructor Companion Site	Resources for the instructor, via Cengage SSO	• Instructor's Manual with syllabus and lesson plans, chapter objectives and outlines, teaching suggestions, grading rubrics answers to text questions, testbank, and answer key • Computerized Testbank in Cognero, with many questions and styles to choose from to create customized assessments for your students • PowerPoint® presentations

ACKNOWLEDGMENTS

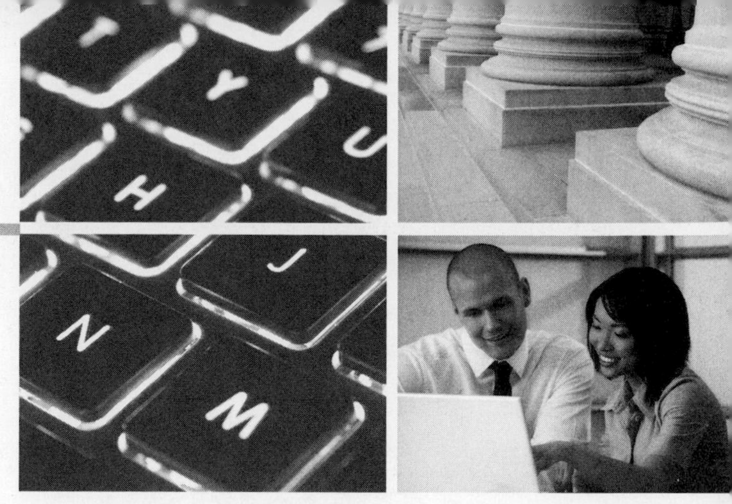

This book was made possible by many individuals. This book required an enormous amount of work from a superb team of talented professionals. To all of you, many thanks.

REVIEWERS

Special thanks go to the reviewers of the text for their ideas and suggestions:

Janice Hollman
Portland Community College
Portland, OR

Judith Quinby
Kennesaw State University
Kennesaw, GA

Chuck Splawn
Horry-Georgetown Technical College
Myrtle Beach, SC

Marc Vallen
University of Hartford
West Hartford, CT

Diane Yohe
Bristol Community College
Fall River, MA

Cengage Learning

I am deeply indebted to my editors at Cengage Learning. Shelley Esposito was my Acquisitions Editor. Melissa Riveglia, the Senior Product Manager, had the unenviable task of making sure all the T's were crossed and the I's dotted. This text would not exist without her assistance. So many other folks had the responsibility of double-checking the accuracy of the text and the Hands-On Exercises. This project would not have been possible without their support and encouragement.

My Family

I am so grateful to my family. By necessity, writing is a solitary task and there have been more than a few missed dinners and vacations not taken in the past five years. I love you all very much and appreciate your patience and encouragement. This is for you.

Please note that the Internet resources are of a time-sensitive nature and URL addresses may often change or be deleted.

CHAPTER 1

Overview of Computers in the Law Office

CHAPTER OBJECTIVES

After completing this chapter, you should be able to do the following:

1. Identify how computers are being used in legal organizations.
2. Identify the various computer-system components.
3. Distinguish among the various forms of computer software.
4. Understand the concept of metadata.
5. Recognize the ethical issues raised by the use of computers in the law office.

INTRODUCTION

Computers are an important part of our society. They are used in nearly every facet of our lives, including our jobs, to automate services and products; our health, to enhance medical treatment; our government, to maintain, organize, and analyze information; our education, to help children read and write; our financial institutions, to track and maintain our banking, credit, and investment-related information; our entertainment, including the Internet, movies, music, and the arts; and our transportation, to control the electronic systems in cars and public transportation systems such as subways.

Just as the use of computers in our society has grown, so has the use of computers in the practice of law. The application of computers in large, medium, and small law firms, corporate law departments, and government offices has increased dramatically over the past few decades. It is imperative for paralegals entering the job market to have an understanding of computers, because computers and computer skills (1) allow a paralegal to be more productive and efficient, (2) can give an attorney and paralegal a competitive advantage in court, (3) simplify complicated tasks, and (4) allow the user to stay competitive in the job market.

INTRODUCTION TO COMPUTERS AND THE LAW

Prior to the early 1980s, computers had little effect on the practice of law. A few extremely large firms used them for "back-office" functions such as accounting or billing, but other than that, computers were not used much in legal organizations. A legal professional's tools of the trade were pen, legal pad, law books, typewriter, and copy machine. After the introduction of personal computers in the mid-1980s, all of that began to change. Now computers are involved in nearly every facet of a legal professional's job. Virtually all legal professionals use a desktop, laptop, and/or handheld computer with DVD drives, Internet and email access, and a printer. It is now possible—indeed, often required—to stay in contact with colleagues no matter where they are.

A computer revolution has taken place in the legal industry. An industry that started out rejecting technology has now embraced it. Much of the rise in computer use in legal organizations is due to the increased power, decreased cost, and increased ease of use and efficiency of computers, all of which contribute to the competitive advantage that they give the user. Computers are being used for everything from word processing, timekeeping, and billing to legal research on the Internet to website management. This holds true for all types and sizes of law firms, whether a solo practitioner, a thousand-attorney global law firm, or a corporate or government legal department. In prior years, solo practitioners and small law offices lagged far behind larger law offices when it came to technology. This is generally no longer true. Technology is no longer a tool just for the large law firm. The cost of technology has decreased so much that even solo practitioners, small law offices, and legal aid offices can afford state-of-the-art computers.

Computers are used to organize documents, not just in large cases involving tens of thousands of documents, but in smaller cases as well. Computers are used to communicate with clients, often via email, and to exchange documents. Attorneys take depositions of witnesses by using videoconferencing. Laptop computers are used in the courtroom to search for documents, track exhibits, and make presentations to juries. Laptop or handheld computers are used in the courtroom to conduct legal research right at the counsel table. Later in this chapter, we will discuss some more recent and emerging technologies.

Internet
One of the world's largest computer networks; actually a "network of networks." It allows hundreds of millions of users around the world to share information.

The Internet has had a profound impact on the practice of law and on how paralegals perform their jobs. The **Internet** is one of the world's largest computer networks; actually, it is a "network of networks." It connects hundreds of millions of computers around the world and allows them to share information. Legal organizations and paralegals in particular can send and receive electronic messages, research both legal and nonlegal information, send documents, and do much more. The pervasive use of the Internet is clearly driving some of the need for paralegals to have good computer skills.

Computers are also being used by courts in a variety of ways. Many courts allow parties to file documents electronically, using the Internet, and allow attorneys and paralegals online access to the courts' computer systems. Courts use computers to track currently pending cases. Such systems can automatically set scheduling deadlines for each case and alert judges to scheduling concerns or problems, particularly for criminal cases in which defendants have the right to a speedy trial. In some courts, court reporters can store information electronically, within seconds of it being presented, so that it can be displayed immediately for jurors, judges, and parties to view the information.

In short, all types of legal organizations and legal professionals, including paralegals, are using computers on a daily basis in a variety of ways. Given this overwhelming move toward technology use and computerization, all types of legal organizations are looking for legal professionals who not only have good legal skills, but also have the skills to use the organization's computer systems with little additional training.

ELEMENTARY COMPUTER CONCEPTS

This text is not concerned with imparting technical and scientific information on how a computer operates; rather, its focus is on how paralegals can use computers in a practical way to carry out their duties. Nevertheless, it is necessary to cover some basic computer concepts as background for users. The following sections introduce most of the terms and concepts that a paralegal will encounter on the job.

SYSTEM COMPONENTS

A **computer** is an electronic device that accepts, processes, outputs, and stores information. Information that is entered into a computer is called **input**. Information that comes out of a computer is called **output**. **Hardware** is the actual physical components of a computer system. **Software** refers to instructions that make the computer hardware function. A computer system works together with peripheral devices, such as auxiliary storage and input, output, and communication devices (hardware), to accomplish the information-handling tasks. The system contains a central processing unit and a main memory.

Central Processing Unit

The **central processing unit (CPU)** organizes and processes information. It is the "brain" of the computer. It performs logical operations—in accordance with the operating system software—and coordinates and communicates with auxiliary storage devices and input, output, and communication devices (see Exhibit 1–1).

At the heart of the CPU is the **processor chip** (see Exhibit 1–1). One or more processor chips perform the actual arithmetic computations and logic functions. The speed of the processor, and thus of the computer, is determined by how many bits or bytes of information the chip can process at a time and how fast it acts to process the information. The more bits that can be processed in one cycle, the faster the computer will be. For example, a processor that processes 64 bits at a time is considerably faster than one that processes only 16 bits. How fast a computer works to process information is also characterized in **gigahertz (GHz)**, which refers to the "clock speed" of a computer. The faster the clock speed is, the faster the computer processes information.

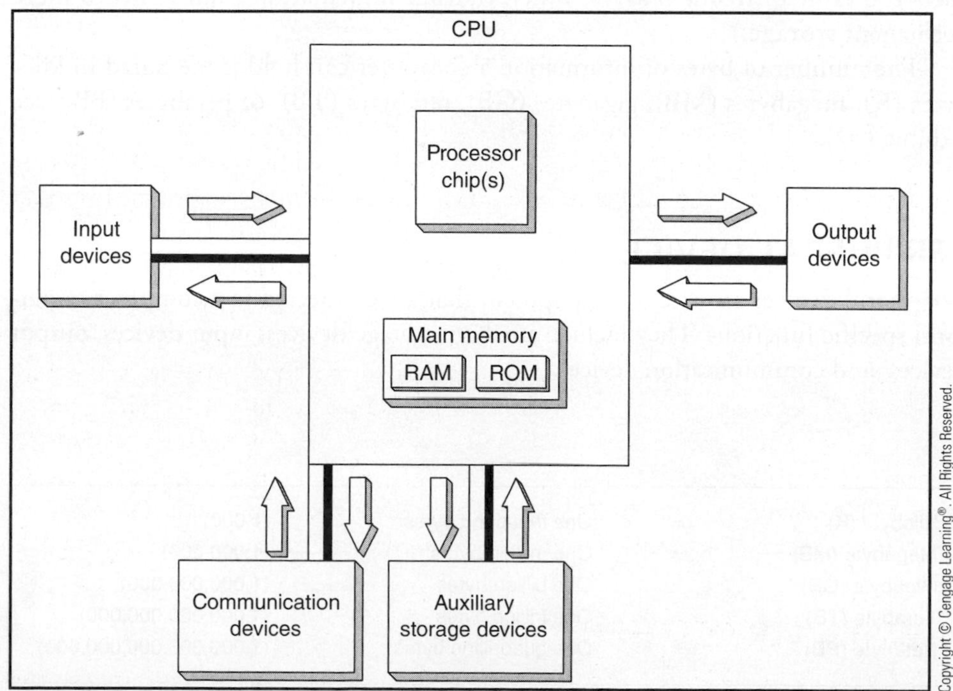

EXHIBIT 1–1
Central processing unit (CPU)

computer
An electronic device that accepts input data, processes data, outputs data, and stores data electronically; types include desktop, laptop, handheld, tablet, and file server.

input
Data or information that is entered or transferred into a computer (including by keyboard, mouse, scanner, voice, etc.).

output
Information or computer results that are produced or transmitted from a computer to a user as a result of the computer's operations (including to monitor, printer, etc.).

hardware
The physical equipment of a computer system, as opposed to programs or software.

software
Computer programs that instruct the computer hardware how to function and perform tasks.

central processing unit (CPU)
The part of a computer that contains the processor chip and main memory. The CPU organizes and manipulates information, in addition to coordinating with peripheral devices.

processor chip
The part of the computer that performs the actual arithmetic computations and logic functions.

gigahertz (GHz)
Measure of the clock speed of a computer.

Main Memory

The function of the **main memory** is to hold or store information that the computer is processing. This is accomplished through memory chips. **Memory chips**, like processor chips, are made up of tiny electronic circuits, but instead of processing information, they store or hold information. Main memory comes in one of two types: read-only and random-access.

main memory
The part of the CPU that stores information that the computer is processing. Main memory consists of read-only memory and random-access memory.

memory chips
Parts of a computer that store or hold information.

Read-Only Memory

Read-only memory (ROM) is permanent, unchanging memory that a computer uses internally to operate itself. It is permanently installed by the manufacturer and cannot be changed or altered; hence the name "read-only." A computer reads ROM, but you cannot enter information into ROM or change the data in it. The data contained in ROM are not lost when the computer is turned off. Practically speaking, you never even become aware that ROM exists.

read-only memory (ROM)
A part of main memory that contains permanent information a computer uses to operate itself. ROM can be read, but cannot be written to.

Random-Access Memory

Random-access memory (RAM) is temporary memory that is used when the computer is turned on. Unlike ROM, it is erased when the computer is turned off. RAM is used to temporarily store programs "on the computer screen" when the programs are loaded. For example, when a person is using a word-processing program, that program is in RAM. As words are typed into the word processor, the words are also stored in RAM. To save the information when the computer is turned off, the user must save the information from RAM to an auxiliary storage device such as a hard disk. An auxiliary storage device stores data so it can be retrieved later. One of the most frustrating experiences in computer use occurs when one is working with information in RAM and power is interrupted, such as when the lights flicker from an interruption in power transmission. When power to the computer is lost, even if just for a fraction of a second, the computer turns off and any information in RAM is lost. (This quickly teaches users the value of frequent saves, which transfer information from RAM to more permanent **storage**.)

The number of bytes of information a computer can hold is measured in kilobytes (K), megabytes (MB), gigabytes (GB), terabytes (TB), or petabytes (PB) (see Exhibit 1–2).

random-access memory (RAM)
A part of main memory that is temporary and volatile in nature; it is erased every time the computer's power is turned off. Application programs and data are loaded into RAM when the computer is processing the data.

storage
Retention of electronic information for future use (using storage devices such as hard disks, DVDs, flash drives, and other media).

PERIPHERAL DEVICES

Peripheral devices are pieces of equipment that are connected to a computer to perform specific functions. They include auxiliary storage devices, input devices, output devices, and communication devices.

peripheral devices
Pieces of equipment that are connected to a computer to perform specific functions, such as storing information (auxiliary storage devices), inputting information (input devices), outputting information (output devices), and communicating with other computers (communication devices).

Kilobyte (K)	=	One thousand bytes	(1,000)
Megabyte (MB)	=	One million bytes	(1,000,000)
Gigabyte (GB)	=	One billion bytes	(1,000,000,000)
Terabyte (TB)	=	One trillion bytes	(1,000,000,000,000)
Petabyte (PB)	=	One quadrillion bytes	(1,000,000,000,000,000)

EXHIBIT 1–2
Storage capacities

Auxiliary Storage Devices

An **auxiliary storage device** is used to permanently store information. Auxiliary storage devices and RAM are sometimes confused with one another, because they both use megabytes and gigabytes to refer to their respective **storage capacities**, and they both store information, albeit for different purposes. RAM is where information is stored temporarily, while the user is working with it, and is erased every time the computer is turned off. In contrast, an auxiliary storage device stores information permanently.

auxiliary storage device
A device that stores information so that it can be retrieved for later use. Auxiliary storage devices retain data after power to the computer has been turned off. Auxiliary storage devices include flash drives, hard disk drives, and others.

storage capacity
The maximum amount of data that can be stored on a device.

Hard Disk For permanent storage, most personal computers contain a rigid magnetic disk or **hard disk drive**. Hard disks are very reliable and have fast **access times**. They can also read and write data. It is possible, however, for them to crash if they are handled roughly (e.g., if the computer is dropped) or if they are defective or old. When a crash occurs, some or all of the information on the hard disk is lost or destroyed. Crashing often causes physical damage to the surface of the disk, making data retrieval difficult even for experts. Sometimes, it seems that hard drives crash for no reason at all. This alone is a good reason to get in the habit of backing up your data on a regular basis.

At least one hard disk drive is usually mounted inside the computer; usually a small light turns on when information is either accessed from or saved to the drive. Most hard disks are permanently sealed and are fixed inside the drive; thus, they cannot be removed. Large-capacity hard disks are standard equipment on most computers produced today. Many people use external hard drives for backup purposes; these auxiliary devices are literally freestanding hard disk drive units.

hard disk drive
A reliable and fast auxiliary storage device that stores data on a rigid magnetic disk; may be built into the computer (internal) or a freestanding peripheral device (external).

access times
The amount of time it takes to transfer data between a storage device and RAM.

Removable Drives A large amount of data can be stored using **removable drives**. Removable drives include zip drives and flash drives. Zip drives are about the size of an audio cassette and are relatively slow; they are a somewhat dated technology. Flash drives have largely replaced them. Flash drives, thumb drives (so called because they are about the size of a human thumb), or sticks are extremely small and portable, and are also fairly fast. A flash drive simply plugs into a computer's USB port and is immediately accessible by the computer once it has been loaded. Flash drives are typically used to move large files from one system to another. Many MP3 players also use this technology.

removable drives
A small portable device that stores a large amount of data; often used to transfer information between computers.

Magnetic Tape In a **magnetic tape system**, data are written to and stored on a spool of magnetic tape. The magnetic tape can be stored either on large tape reels or in tape cartridges.

Magnetic tape systems store data sequentially. (This is similar to an old VHS tape: if you wanted to access a particular section of the tape, you typically had to fast-forward or rewind the tape to the desired section.) For this reason, access times are quite slow. This is why magnetic tape is usually used only for making backup copies of information residing on other storage devices. However, although their access times are slow, they have large capacities, up to a terabyte or more.

magnetic tape system
Storage device that records data on magnetic tape.

optical storage devices
Devices that use laser beams to write data onto small plastic disks. Optical storage devices can record hundreds of megabytes of data on a single disk.

Optical Storage Devices Using laser beams, **optical storage devices** can record data on and retrieve data from small plastic disks, such as CDs and DVDs. Optical storage devices can store hundreds of megabytes of data on a single disk. This has allowed manufacturers to store everything from music and video/multimedia presentations to large software programs on a single disk. The space saving made possible by these technologies has been immensely beneficial to law offices, which often must keep large numbers of records for long periods of time. And while the trend may now be to store data in the cloud (computer storage accessible through the Internet), many legal professionals still prefer to use these more tangible storage devices.

Input Devices

input devices
Devices used to enter information into a computer; include the mouse, keyboards, scanners, voice recognition devices, digital cameras, and others.

Input devices are used to enter information into a computer. Input devices include the mouse, keyboards, scanners (including bar code and imaging scanners), voice recognition devices, digital cameras, and others.

Computer Keyboard Most computer keyboards are similar to the keyboard of an ordinary typewriter, with a few additions. They are made up of alphanumeric keys, function keys, cursor movement keys, special keys, and a numeric keypad. Keyboards are inexpensive and come in a variety of types and styles.

Scanners A scanner has the ability to bring hard-copy documents into a computer. Many scanners look like small office copiers. Scanners shine light on the document and translate the reflected light into digital signals that a computer can recognize and store. The scanner allows the image of a document, such as a photograph or a microfilm frame, to be put into a computer; this is called imaging.

imaging
Scanning a document into a computer so the user can see an exact picture of the document on the computer.

More specifically, **imaging** refers to the ability to scan a document into a computer so the user can see the exact image of the original document on the computer. Imaging is similar to taking a photograph of a document: you can see the image of the document, but you cannot change it or edit the text. To edit the text of a document, you would need optical character recognition software (see below).

With document imaging, the paper is handled only once, when it is scanned into the computer. Document images can be reviewed, copied, sorted, and filed electronically. Document imaging gives users immediate access to documents, saves storage space, and keeps originals from being lost or damaged. Imaging software allows law offices to track and manage scanned images. Imaging and OCR technologies are used quite frequently in litigation support to track and search for documents in litigation.

optical character recognition (OCR)
A technology that allows the text of documents to be read or scanned into a computer so the text of the document can be searched or brought into a word processor to be edited.

Scanners can also translate the text of a document into an electronic format so that the text can then be electronically searched or manipulated with a word processor. This is called **optical character recognition (OCR)**. Using a scanner and OCR software, users can "read" printed material into a computer so the text of the document can be searched (like searching in Westlaw or LexisNexis databases) or brought into a word processor for text editing. In OCR, the scanner reflects light onto the printed text, compares the shapes of the letters in the text to the letters in the scanner/computer memory, and writes the information into the computer. Through the use of OCR technology, it is possible to scan printed information into a computer much faster than a keyboard operator could enter the information. Large OCR scanners can scan thousands of pages of text into a computer in a relatively short time.

However, if the printed text that is being scanned does not exactly match the letters in the scanner's memory, an error will occur, and the right letter will not be entered. This potential for inaccuracy can be a problem. Even if a document is scanned in with 99 percent accuracy, that can still leave plenty of errors in the scanned version of the document. For example, if a user scans in a 10,000-word document, that would leave 100 errors in the document. The accuracy rating drops dramatically if a document is not clear or has nonstandard type. OCR scanners can be very useful, but accuracy must be checked carefully.

Imaging and OCR are similar yet different. Imaging allows the user to see the document in its original state, but the user cannot search for words using imaging. OCR allows the user to search for words and word patterns, but not to see the exact image of the original document, only the text it contained.

Some law firms use **bar code scanner** systems to track documents in litigation. This is the same technology used in nearly all retail stores. Once a bar code is applied to a document, the bar code scanner or reader can read the special lines on the bar codes and recognize which document it identifies.

bar code scanner
Device that reads the special lines of bar codes. Can be used to track documents in litigation, or physical objects such as office furniture and equipment.

Many multifunction devices are currently on the market that combine OCR scanning, imaging, faxing, copying, and printing. The prices of all of these technologies have decreased significantly in recent years, making these useful devices extremely popular.

Mouse The cursor on a monitor is moved with a **mouse**. This input device is approximately the same size as the palm of your hand. As the mouse is moved, it transmits to the computer a signal that correspondingly moves the cursor in the same direction. For example, if the mouse is moved to the right, the cursor moves to the right, and so on. There are a variety of other devices that perform functions similar to those of a mouse. These include trackballs, trackpoints, and touch pads.

mouse
An input device used to move the cursor on the monitor. The cursor moves in the same direction as the mouse is moved.

Speech Recognition The ability of a computer to understand spoken words is called **speech recognition**. The user speaks into a microphone that is connected to the computer. Using sophisticated software, the computer is able to interpret the speech and translate it into computer commands and into text for use with word processors, email, and other software. Typically, speech recognition software leads the user through exercises that are designed to teach the software the nuances of that particular person's voice.

speech recognition
The ability of a computer to understand spoken words.

Voice input systems have a number of advantages. Most people can speak faster and more naturally than they can write or type, and they need little or no training to use such a system. It also frees the hands to perform other tasks. Speech recognition systems are very popular in offices where they augment or take the place of some secretarial functions such as transcribing dictation. Some users also prefer to use speech recognition instead of typing, as it increases their productivity.

Although speech recognition accuracy is quite good—typically greater than 95 percent—it is still absolutely necessary to proofread the text created by the software. For this reason, among others, many legal organizations do not make much use of speech recognition technology.

Digital Cameras Digital cameras allow the user to take photographs or full-motion video and sound and download or transfer them directly into a computer or upload them to the Internet. The software accompanying these devices also allows the user to easily edit, enhance, and view the information. Many legal organizations are using these devices to cut and paste data directly into presentation graphics programs for displaying evidence to juries. Many legal organizations are rediscovering the old adage that "a picture is worth a thousand words." Video evidence can be extremely persuasive to juries and factfinders.

Output Devices

Output devices provide a user with the data that a computer has generated or stored. Like input devices, they come in many different types. The type you select depends on the application you are using.

output devices
Peripheral device that provides a user with the data a computer has generated, accessed, or manipulated.

Computer output is displayed on a **monitor**. It is important to recognize that the quality of the picture on the monitor is in part determined by the **video adapter card**, which acts as an interface between the monitor and the computer. The number of colors that a color monitor can display also depends on the video adapter card. Because of the graphical nature of the Internet and the rise in multimedia and video, manufacturers now produce graphics accelerators, video card memory, and other hardware to make graphics appear on the monitor faster.

monitor
Screen that displays computer output.

video adapter card
Piece of hardware that acts as an interface between the monitor and the computer.

sound card
A device that enhances the sounds that come out of a computer and/or enables speakers attached to a computer to function. Nearly all computers now come with a sound card.

Much data is still output on paper (sometimes called hard copy) with a printer. Nearly all computers now come with a sound card and speakers. A **sound card** enhances the sounds that come out of the computer and/or enables speakers attached to a computer to function.

A portable projector allows a user to display the image from a computer to an audience. Portable projectors are often used in trials in conjunction with laptop computers or tablets to display presentations and computer-generated evidence to juries.

Communication Devices

modem
A device that allows computers in different locations to communicate using a telephone line.

A communication device, such as a modem, allows computers to exchange information. Such a device is technically both an input and an output device, as it can receive data from other computers (input) and also send data to other computers (output).

cable modem
A data modem that is designed to work over cable TV lines.

DSL (Digital Subscriber Line)
A type of digital phone line that allows both data and voice to be transmitted on the same line, simultaneously if desired. Transmission speed is fairly fast.

A **modem** allows computers in different locations to communicate using a telephone line. Although a modem acting through a dial-up connection allows users to exchange information with each other over long distances, this type of connection is very slow compared to other types of technology. This is particularly true regarding most World Wide Web sites on the Internet, which are graphically based. Cable, T1, and DSL are alternatives to standard analog phone lines and modems, and are increasingly popular because of the much speedier communication they enable. These and other technologies are making standard modems obsolete. The main advantages that dial-up connections have over cable, T1, and DSL are their much lower cost and almost universal availability. However, these advantages seldom compensate for the extended time required for information transfer via dial-up.

A **cable modem** is a data modem that is designed to work over cable television lines (increasingly, these lines are fiber-optic). The primary advantage of cable modems over dial-up modems is their much faster data-transmission speed, made possible by cable's far greater bandwidth.

DSL (Digital Subscriber Line) is a type of digital phone line that is hundreds of times faster than a dial-up connection. This type of connection also allows data and voice to be transmitted on the same line.

wireless modems
Modems that many mobile phones and handheld computers now use to connect to the Internet.

Wireless Modem

Many mobile phones and handheld computers now use **wireless modems** to connect to the Internet. A wireless modem typically is either built into the device or slides into an open slot on a laptop or handheld computer; in either case, it allows the user to access email, the Internet, and other mobile devices without hardwired connections.

Videoconferencing
A private broadcast between two or more remote locations, with live image transmission, display, and sound. Uses data communications to conduct long-distance, face-to-face meetings.

Videoconferencing

Videoconferencing is a private broadcast between two or more remote locations, with live image transmission, display, and sound. This technology uses data communications to conduct long-distance, face-to-face meetings. Because of the huge amounts of sound and image data transferred with this technology, it requires audiovisual equipment and special communication lines. Videoconferencing is very useful in a legal organization for meeting with clients, interviewing job candidates, meeting with co-counsel, taking depositions, and other applications.

Voice over Internet Protocol (VoIP)
Functionality that allows users to make telephone calls using a broadband Internet connection instead of a regular phone line.

Voice over Internet Protocol

Voice over Internet Protocol (VoIP) allows users to make telephone calls using a broadband Internet connection instead of a regular (analog) phone line. Most VoIP service providers allow the user to call anyone who has a telephone number, including local, long-distance, mobile, and international numbers. VoIP allows a user to make a call directly from a computer, a special VoIP phone, or a traditional telephone using an adapter. Cost savings over long-distance telephone charges can be substantial, because most VoIP providers charge a flat fee for unlimited call time. Some systems can support multiparty conference calls, and can integrate voice mail and faxes with email.

A major disadvantage is VoIP's dependence on electrical power: if the power goes out, so do the phones, unless there is a backup system. VoIP is also dependent on proper operation of both the broadband connection and the network; if they go down, so do the phones.

Communication Devices in Legal Organizations Most legal organizations have long since moved from slower, dial-up modems to faster communication technologies such as cable, DSL, and T1. This is primarily due to the overwhelming use of the Internet in law offices and the need for fast connections to email.

Tablets and Smartphones Look around your classroom. Chances are that many students are not using laptop computers; instead they are using tablet computers (or just "tablets"). A tablet is a light, slim, portable computer that uses a touchscreen as its primary input device, such as the Apple iPad. When your class takes a break, how many students reach for a smartphone, such as the Apple iPhone? These small mobile devices are simple to use, yet they can have extraordinary computing capability. Internet access is available via the device's cellular capability and Wi-Fi.

LOCAL AND WIDE AREA NETWORKS

Networks connect a multitude of computers and allow them to work together. Law offices may use local area and/or wide area networks.

Virtual Private Networks (VPN)

You have probably logged onto numerous private networks without even thinking about it. For example, when you are online in your classroom, you are probably connected to your school's network. These private networks used by universities and corporations usually take advantage of sophisticated security systems to protect the data sent on the network. On the other hand, when you use the Internet provided by a hotel or a coffee shop, that is a public network and does not offer the same level of security as a private network. That creates the potential for all kinds of trouble as confidential client information is essentially streaming through the air available to anyone with the means and desire to intercept it.

A Virtual Private Network, or VPN, is a technology that lets people access their office's computer network over the Internet while at home or traveling. One way to think of a VPN is to think of it as a tunnel. Inside this "tunnel" information may travel safely. While in this "tunnel," information is encrypted. The end result is that the tunnel protects the information and even if it is intercepted, since it is encrypted, it is not of any use to the hacker. Accessing a network via a VPN is sometimes referred to as remote access.

So why would you want to use VPN for remote access? Let's say you want to be able to work from home. Or maybe you need to retrieve a file while traveling. Without a VPN, in order to make resources on the office network available to users, the network administrator would have to weaken the security of your network by opening holes in your firewall—which isn't usually a good idea.

With VPN, the integrity of your office network remains intact, but you can allow remote users to act as part of the office network. After connecting over VPN, remote users can access files, print documents, and generally do anything with their computers that they would be able to do in the office.

Still, using VPN is not the same as being in the office. Most office networks are pretty fast. Most Internet connections are not. Even the fastest DSL and cable connections are around one-tenth the speed of your average office LAN. This means that accessing resources on the LAN will be much slower over VPN. It would also depend on the "upstream" or upload speed of your office's network connection. As opposed to working on files directly over the VPN connection, it is often more time-efficient to copy them to your computer over the VPN connection. When you are done working with them, you would copy them back to the file server.

single-user system A computer that can accommodate only one person at a time and is not linked to other systems or computers.

local area network (LAN) A multiuser system linking computers that are in close proximity for the purpose of communication.

Local Area Networks

Computers started as single-user systems. A **single-user system** can accommodate only one person at a time and is not linked to other systems or computers. A **local area network (LAN)** is a multiuser system that links computers that are in close proximity for the purpose of communication. Two primary reasons for installing a LAN are to share data and software among multiple computers and to share peripheral devices such as printers, optical storage devices, and communication devices (see Exhibit 1–3).

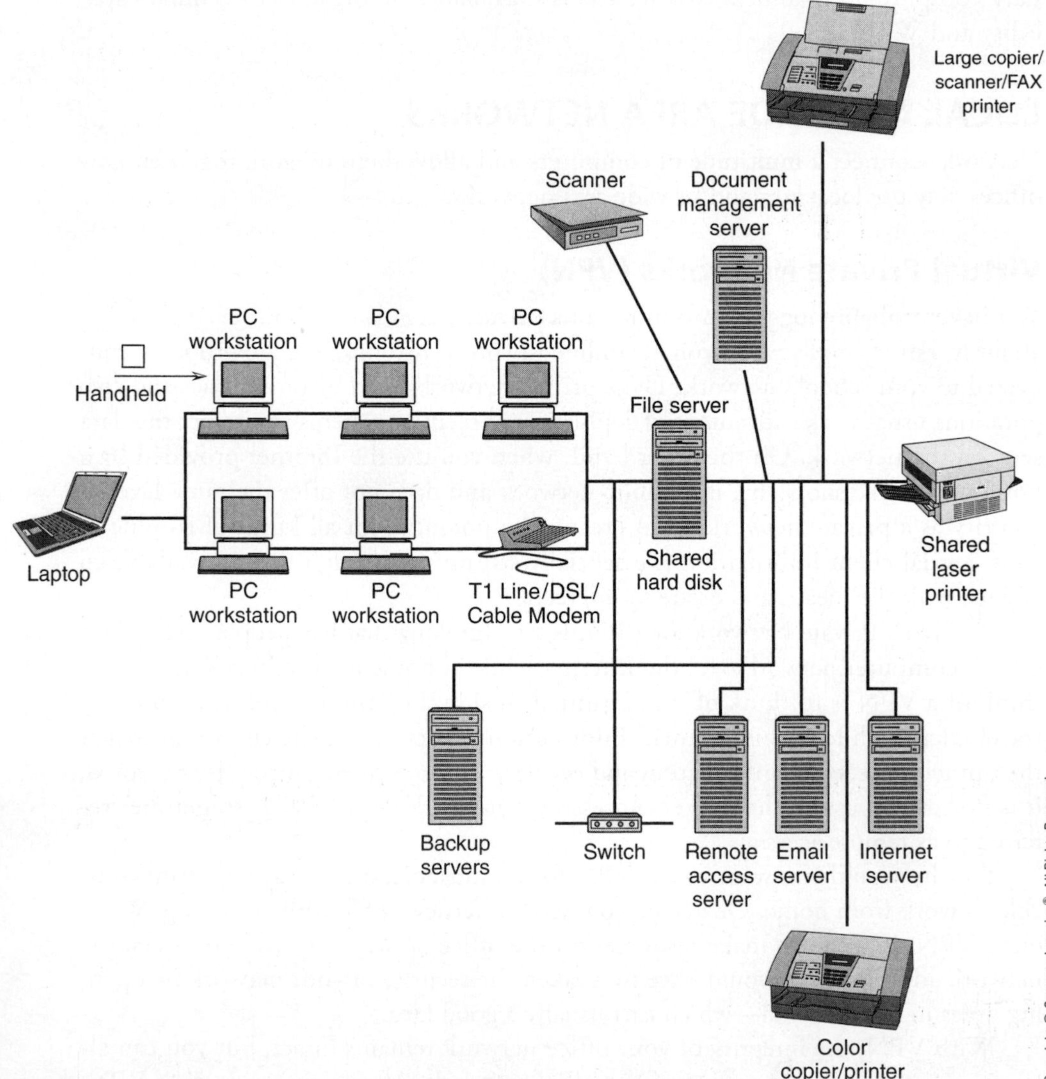

EXHIBIT 1–3
A local area network (LAN) allows users to share hardware and software

Consider how a LAN could be used in a law office. Suppose a law office has 20 staff members who need access to each other's word-processing files, docket control data, and time and billing information, and who also need to communicate via email with one another. Using stand-alone computers, the staff members would not be able to share information effectively. However, using a LAN, each staff member has access to all the information residing on any computer in the network. Another advantage is that different types of computers (e.g., personal computers (PCs), Apple Macintosh computers, tablets, and others) can be linked together to share data in many LAN configurations.

Nearly all legal organizations now have a LAN, and most software that is purchased for legal organizations is a networked version of a single-user program. Primary network software used in a legal organization typically includes word processing, database management, spreadsheets, timekeeping and billing, accounting, calendar/docket control/case management, electronic mail, document management, litigation support, client files/records, and specialized legal-specific programs. With a network, attorneys and paralegals who are traveling can connect to the network and exchange messages, access files, and do other tasks.

There are different types of LANs, including client/server and peer-to-peer networks.

Client/Server Networks **Client/server networks** use a server or servers to enhance the functionality of the other computers on the network. Network servers are computers that meet the needs of the other computers on the network, which are called *workstations* or *clients* (see Exhibit 1–3). The server stores program files and data files, and hosts email and remote access platforms used by the workstations, among other possible applications. Some servers are dedicated, meaning that they cannot be used for any other purpose. Other servers, depending on how the LAN is configured, are nondedicated, meaning that they can also be used as workstations. Most LANs in legal organizations are the client/server type.

client/server networks
A network that uses a server (or servers) to enhance the function and meet the needs of the other computers on the network.

Servers are generally high-powered machines with large memories that can support or even perform some of the computing functions of many workstations. Servers can be devoted to specific network operating functions and can be connected together on the network. For example, a legal organization could have separate electronic mail servers, file servers, print servers, web servers, and remote access servers (for giving staff access to the office network from remote locations such as a staff member's house, hotel room, or a courtroom).

In years past, most networks were hardwired. Today, an alternative to hardwired networks that require cables is **wireless networking**. Wireless networks are extremely popular in law offices, because they nearly eliminate the necessity to install long cable runs throughout an office.

wireless networking
System that allows computers on the network to communicate with each other using wireless antennas coordinated through a wired access point.

Peer-to-Peer Networks **Peer-to-peer networks** do not use a server; instead, each computer on the network acts as both a server and a client. Because the computers are performing two tasks—running an application program, such as a word processor, and acting as a server—they are not as fast as the workstations on a client/server network. However, they still offer the ability to share printers, files, and other resources. Peer-to-peer networks are less expensive, because they do not require a separate server.

Peer-to-peer networks
A computer network in which each computer acts both as a server and a client.

Web-Based Networks: Internet, Intranet, and Extranet

Many legal organizations have expanded their networks to include intranets and extranets. An **intranet** is an internal network designed to provide and disseminate

intranet
An internal network designed to provide and disseminate information to internal staff; most mimic the look and feel of the World Wide Web.

information to internal staff; most such systems use a web browser and mimic the look and feel of the World Wide Web. In much the same way as the Internet provides information to the public, an intranet provides information to internal users. An intranet can be walled off from the Internet to provide security from Internet users. An intranet is part of a legal organization's networked computer system and in some cases the organization has a server dedicated to supporting the intranet. Information that a legal organization typically places on an intranet includes office policies and procedures, links to law-related websites, training materials, contact lists, and access to the firm's extranet. The use of intranets is growing substantially in legal organizations.

extranet
A secure web-based site that allows clients to access information about their cases and collaborate with the legal professionals who are providing legal services to them.

An **extranet** is a network designed to provide, disseminate, and share confidential information with clients. A client with a web browser can tap into the legal organization's extranet, after going through security and identification/password protections, to access his or her case plans, documents, case strategies, billing information, and other information. This is also extremely helpful when a law office must communicate with multiple clients or co-counsel on one case. Exhibit 1–4 notes the similarities and differences between intranets and extranets.

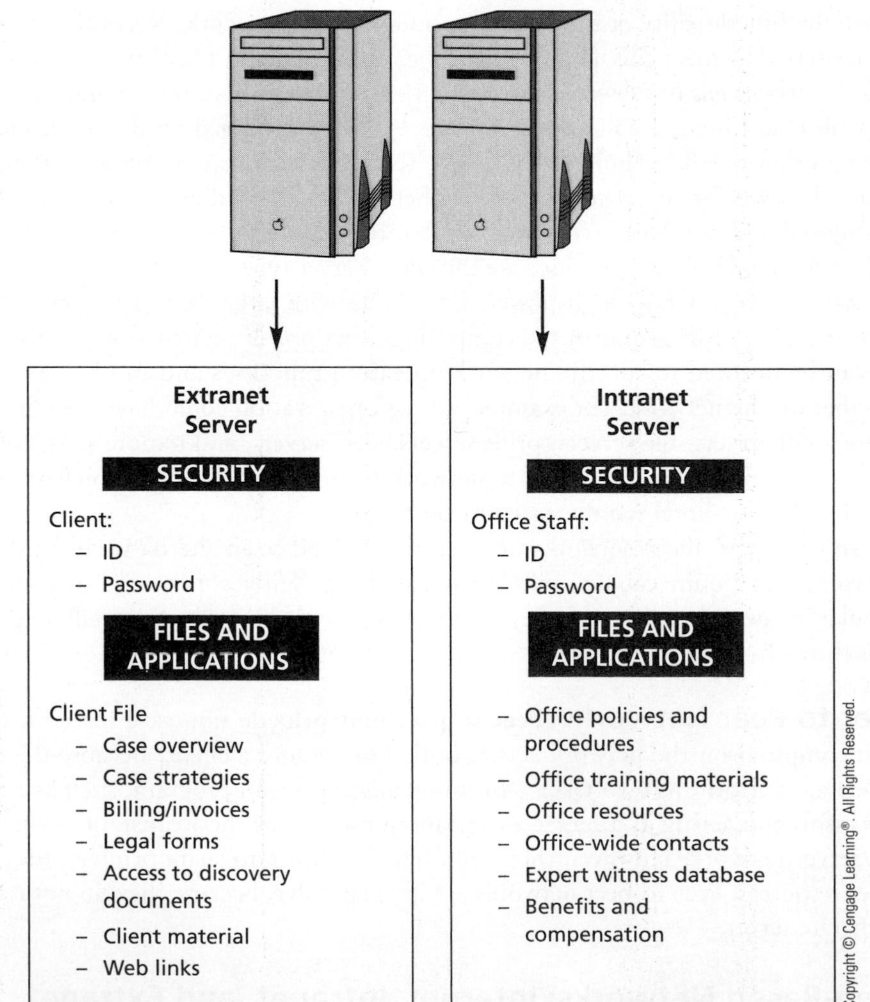

EXHIBIT 1–4
Extranet and intranet

Wide Area Networks

Wide area networks take up where LANs stop. A **wide area network (WAN)** is a multiuser system linking computers that may be located thousands of miles apart. Large law firms that have offices located across the country or across the world can use WANs to allow their offices to communicate with each other as if they were next door. LANs and WANs can also be used together. A law firm's offices located in New York and Los Angeles may each have a LAN, but be connected to each other using a WAN. LANs and WANs allow law offices to share information in the same location, across town, or across the globe.

wide area network (WAN)
A multiuser system linking computers that may be located thousands of miles apart.

Networks in Legal Organizations

LANs, WANs, intranets, and extranets are now commonly found in legal organizations. As technology continues to expand, so will the use of all types of networks in the legal industry. Although it is not necessary for a paralegal to have detailed knowledge of the ins and outs of office networks, it is helpful to have a general overview of how they function, because of the importance of networks to the practice of law in the 21st century.

INTRODUCTION TO COMPUTER SOFTWARE

Computer hardware is useless without computer software to make it operate. Computer software (i.e., a computer program) is a set of step-by-step instructions that direct a computer how to function and perform tasks. Three basic types of software are available: operating system software, utility software, and application software.

The **operating system software (program)** instructs the computer hardware how to operate its internal circuitry and how to communicate with input, output, and auxiliary storage devices; this program also allows the user to manage the computer. Operating system software ties the computer hardware and software together. Using operating system software, users can delete old or unwanted files, obtain a directory of the files on a disk, and manage the resources of a computer. Some type of operating system software comes free with nearly all computers.

operating system software (program)
A set of instructions that tell the computer how to operate its own circuitry and manage its components; also controls how the computer communicates with input, output, and auxiliary storage devices. Allows the user to manage the computer.

Utility software helps users with the housekeeping and maintenance tasks that a computer requires. Thousands of utility programs are available. Utility programs can back up a hard disk, recover data that have been accidentally deleted, protect computers from viruses, and carry out many other tasks.

utility software
Instructions that help users with the housekeeping and maintenance tasks a computer requires; helps manage either the hardware or software aspects of a computer.

Application software instructs the computer to perform a specific function or task, such as word processing. Practically speaking, when people use the word *software*, they are usually referring to application software. A word-processing program, a spreadsheet program, and a database program are all examples of application software, because they each tell the computer how to perform a specific task or set of tasks.

application software
Instructions (programs) that tell the computer to perform a specific function or task, such as word processing.

Relax, You've Done This Before: Specific Law Office Uses of Computer Software

Take comfort in the fact that most paralegal students are already competent in and comfortable with performing basic computer functions. You may have used a software program to "clean" your computer by removing unwanted files. That is an example of a utility program. It is likely that you have prepared documents (e.g., a term paper) using a word-processing program. That is an example of application software. It follows, then, that you probably already have many of the essential skills required to use a computer in a modern law office.

license agreement
Contract setting out the user's rights and restrictions on how a piece of software can be used.

Software Licensing

Most software is purchased subject to a **license agreement**. The license agreement sets out the terms under which the person or group is allowed to use the software; it specifies the purchaser's rights to and restrictions on use of the software. Some license agreements are based on the number of computers that the software can be loaded on, whereas others are based on the number of people who can use the software. Use of software in a manner that violates the license agreement, such as loading software onto additional computers beyond the number of licenses that have been purchased, can constitute copyright infringement. The licensor may revoke a violator's license(s) and/or may bring a civil suit against the violator.

Operating System Software

When the computer is turned on, or "booted up," the operating system is loaded into RAM. The operating system is necessary to the basic functioning of a computer; the computer cannot even turn itself on properly without such a system.

Operating systems are usually unique to each type of computer. For example, an Apple Macintosh computer uses a different operating system than do Windows-based computers. The manufacturer of a computer usually supplies the operating system, though this is not always the case. Some computer manufacturers now offer a choice of the operating system to be used.

Duties of the Operating System The operating system is a cross between a traffic officer who directs the flow of data between the computer and different input, output, and auxiliary storage devices and a housekeeper who organizes and maintains the system. Operating systems manage main memory; control input, output, and auxiliary storage devices (including addition of new devices and deletion of old ones); manage the CPU; give the user tools with which to perform maintenance on the computer; and manage the computer's files. From a user's viewpoint, file management is one of the most important things the operating system software does. File management includes copying files, deleting files, and renaming files, as well as maintaining and accessing stored files.

Windows
A graphical operating system developed by Microsoft. Various versions of Windows include Windows XP and Windows 8.

The Windows Operating System **Windows** is a graphical operating system developed by Microsoft. Every few years Microsoft updates Windows to add more features.

All versions of Windows use a graphical user interface (GUI). The graphical interface allows users to enter commands and work with programs using a mouse, pull-down menus, and icons (pictures that appear on the screen to represent applications or documents) instead of requiring users to learn a complicated and exacting command structure. Windows is also a multitasking environment that allows users to run several programs at the same time.

Tens of thousands of programs are currently available for the Windows operating system. It is the predominant operating system and it commands most of the computer software market share in the United States. Windows applications have similar menus and appearances, and can share information quite easily. This similarity among programs allows users to learn programs more quickly than if they had to learn a new command structure for each program. More than 95 percent of all legal organizations use some version of the Windows operating system. Microsoft Windows, in its various versions, dominates the legal market for computer operating systems.

Network Operating Systems Local area networks require special **network operating systems** to handle communications among the computers on a network. Regular operating systems such as Windows XP and Windows 8 may work with file server networks. However, more complex client/server networks require network operating systems such as Windows NT.

network operating systems
System that handles communication tasks between the computers on a network.

Utility Software Utility software helps manage either the hardware or the software aspects of a computer. Some utility programs come as part of the operating system; others are separate programs. There is a huge amount of utility software, including utilities that compress files, back up files, and protect a computer from viruses or other "malware."

compression utilities
Program that reorganizes a file so that the file takes up less room when it is saved. Many large files that are downloaded from the Internet are routinely compressed to reduce the time needed for the download.

Compression Utilities **Compression utilities**, such as WinZip, reconfigure (compress) a file so that it takes up less room when it is saved or transmitted. This is particularly important when one is sending or receiving extremely large files (files containing graphics or video are often huge, and can take a long time to download or upload). Many large files that are downloaded from the Internet are routinely compressed.

backup utility
Program that creates a copy of a user's hard disk or other storage device. The backup copy can be restored if the hard disk is damaged or lost.

Backup Utilities **Backup utility** programs create a copy of a user's hard disk or other storage device. The backup copy can be restored if the hard disk is damaged or lost. Some backup utilities allow users to schedule specific times to back up their files (e.g., every Wednesday and Friday, or every morning at 2:00 A.M.).

antivirus and antispyware utilities
Programs that attempt to prevent virus and spyware programs from getting into the computer system; most also function to locate and remove any viruses or spyware that do manage to get into the computer.

Antivirus and Antispyware Utilities **Antivirus and antispyware utilities** attempt to prevent viruses and spyware programs from getting into a computer system, and also locate and remove any viruses that do manage to get into the computer. Because new viruses and spyware appear almost daily, many antivirus software manufacturers allow users to update their software from the Internet. Exhibit 1–5 lists some important things that users can do to prevent or lessen the chance of getting

- Make backup copies of data on a regular schedule.
- Use passwords on your computer system.
- Turn your computer off when you are not using it.
- Do not let other people install programs on your computer or use your computer without expressly telling you how they will use it.
- Avoid downloading games, shareware, and other information from the Internet or other sources if you are not certain that the site is reputable and virus-free.
- Do not loan or pass your software programs on to others.
- Install antivirus and antispyware programs and run them frequently.
- Update your antivirus and antispyware programs regularly.
- Do not open files that are attached to emails unless you know the sender of the email and that the attached file is safe. An email scanner, which may be part of your antivirus/antispyware program package, is an excellent first line of defense.
- Read license agreements and installation instructions carefully to avoid installing spyware.
- Try to restrict your Internet surfing to known, reputable sites.

EXHIBIT 1–5
How to protect your electronic data from a computer virus

a computer virus or spyware. Once a virus or spyware gets onto a user's computer system, it can be extremely difficult to completely remove it (depending on the program). The best solution is to prevent it from attaching to or "infecting" the computer in the first place.

Application Software

Thousands of different kinds of application software (applications or apps) have been developed. This text focuses on the application programs that are widely used in legal organizations, including word processing, PDF creation and document assembly (Chapter 2), spreadsheets (Chapter 3), timekeeping and billing (Chapter 4), databases, case management and docket control (Chapter 5), cloud-based software applications (Chapter 6), electronic discovery (Chapter 7), litigation support (Chapter 8), computer-assisted legal research and electronic mail (Chapter 9), presentation graphics/trial software (Chapter 10). Following is a brief description of several other types of application software used in legal organizations.

project management software
Application program that allows the user to track the sequence and timing of the separate activities of a larger project or task.

Project Management **Project management software** uses the computer to track the sequence and timing of the separate activities of a larger project or task. Complex projects or jobs consist of many smaller activities that must be completed before the overall project is finished. Some activities must be performed in a certain sequence, whereas others must be completed concurrently. Project management software tracks all of this information. For example, a paralegal might use a project manager to track all the tasks that must be completed before a case is ready for trial.

Accounting Accounting software uses a computer to track and maintain the financial data and records of a business. Accounting information is crucial to any business or organization. It is required for income tax purposes, to obtain loans, to help in the operation and control of an organization, and more. Computerized accounting programs are often less time-consuming to use, introduce fewer errors, and usually produce final reports better and faster than manual methods. Accounting software used by a legal organization might include a general ledger, accounts payable, accounts receivable, payroll, and trust accounting.

document management software
Program that organizes, controls, distributes, and allows for extensive searching of electronic documents, typically in a networked environment.

Document Management **Document management software** organizes, controls, distributes, and allows for extensive searching of electronic documents, typically in a networked environment. Document management software allows a legal organization to file documents electronically so that they can be found by anyone in the organization, even when there are hundreds of users spread across offices located throughout the country. Document management software goes far beyond the file management capabilities built into operating system software. It is the electronic equivalent of a file room with rows and rows of filing cabinets. As the legal community moves to the "paperless office," each legal organization will most likely have to use a document management program to manage electronic files. Document management software also provides extensive searching capabilities and allows users to add a profile of every document, which can be easily searched on later.

application service provider (ASP)
A company that provides software or a service application through the Internet directly to the user's computer.

Application Service Providers and Internet-Based Programs

An **application service provider (ASP)** is a company that supplies software or a service application through the Internet directly to the user's computer. The software is not retained on the user's computer, but instead resides on the software company's computer/server at a remote location and is "rented" to the user as needed. This is sometimes referred to as *hosted software*. The advantages of ASPs are that the user does not have to purchase the software, install the software, upgrade the software, or maintain the software in any way. The user still has access to the software 24 hours a day, 7 days a week, globally, wherever there is an Internet connection.

Two of the best known ASPs in the legal industry are Westlaw and LexisNexis. Other common law-office ASP applications include timekeeping and billing, document management, and litigation support.

HOW COMPUTERS CAN HELP THE PARALEGAL

A paralegal's job is information intensive. A paralegal using a computer can both gather and organize data many times faster than one using manual methods.

The Internet

The availability of the Internet has had a profound impact on how legal professionals practice law and how paralegals do their jobs. The Internet is used in countless ways by paralegals: sending and receiving electronic mail (email); sending instant messages; conducting factual and legal research; uploading information to and downloading information from the "cloud"; accessing listservs, blogs, and newsgroups to gather information and communicate with groups of people; maintaining a legal organization's website; purchasing legal-related services; and gaining continuing education.

Electronic Mail Paralegals use email to exchange information and documents via the Internet with clients, attorneys, other paralegals, courts, co-counsel, vendors, and many others in a manner that is quick, convenient, and cost-effective. Many courts now accept electronic filing of documents in lieu of hard copy, so email is used to submit documents to many court clerks.

Instant Messaging Instant messaging allows users who are connected to the Internet to communicate immediately with one another. Using instant messaging, paralegals or attorneys in court can communicate in real time with colleagues at their office for assistance, legal research, or other needs that may affect the outcome of a case or a hearing.

General and Factual Research Paralegals use the Internet for a wide variety of research, including:

- Conducting background information research on parties to cases
- Locating expert witnesses throughout the world
- Finding newspaper, online, and technical articles related to cases
- Locating the current whereabouts of people for service of process
- Researching information about witnesses
- Discovering financial information about corporations, including accessing Securities and Exchange Commission filings
- Finding public records about people or businesses
- Finding co-counsel in another jurisdiction

Legal Research Many paralegals perform legal research. In the past, the only option for legal research was the law library with its law books, periodicals, statutes, indexes, and digests. Nowadays, legal research can be conducted for free using the Internet. Sites such as www.findlaw.com and hundreds of others provide access to federal and state cases and statutes, provide a portal to other legal research sites on the Internet, and generally offer a wealth of free legal-related information. Fee-based computer-assisted legal research sites, including Westlaw and LexisNexis, allow users to electronically search the full text of cases, statutes, and documents.

Listservs and Electronic Mailing Lists Listservs are like electronic mailing lists. They send email messages to people whose names are on a list. They are a simple way for groups of people to communicate with one another through email. There are thousands of listservs on the Internet. Paralegals use these to communicate with other paralegals, to communicate with other legal professionals who practice in their legal specialty, and to communicate with others who have similar interests in other areas. Examples include:

LawTech—for legal professionals who want to discuss legal technology issues (see www.americanbar.org)

Paralegal Today—specifically for paralegals who want to share information about paralegal issues, ideas, and experiences or who have questions about practice issues (see www.paralegaltoday.com)

To find more listservs about the practice of law or the paralegal profession, you can use an Internet browser and a general search engine to search for "paralegal listservs," or whatever specific topic you are interested in.

Blogs A blog (originally short for "weblog") is a website with information contained in posts that are arranged in reverse chronological order. Blogs resemble diary or journal entries, and they may contain links to other websites or articles. There are many law-related blogs (sometimes referred to as "blawgs") on the Internet, including blogs on specific areas of law, such as immigration or tax.

Litigation Support Software Many paralegals are involved in litigation support tasks. This means that they help attorneys organize, store, retrieve, and summarize the information that is gathered for the conduct of a lawsuit. During the course of any lawsuit, numerous documents and pieces of information are gathered, and must be organized for use at the time of trial or in support of settlement negotiations. For example, suppose your case has 10,000 documents associated with it, and you are requested to find all the documents that refer to a person named John Doe. Manual methods, such as looking through all 10,000 documents, could take weeks. Computerized litigation support software automates this process so that you can do such a search in seconds. In addition, using the Internet or an extranet, your firm can make litigation support databases available to staff, clients, or co-counsel, so that they can access the information from remote locations such as other offices, a courthouse, or a client's office. Litigation support software is crucial in large cases, but even small cases can benefit from this technology.

Collecting and Organizing Data: Database Management Software

Paralegals are often required to collect and organize data. For example, a paralegal might be asked to prepare a list of the names of witnesses and their probable testimony in a case; generate a list of all the documents in a case; prepare a chronological listing of major events in a case; or put together a current list of all the cases being handled by the firm, including name of client, adverse party, case number, court, and name of the presiding judge.

A *database management system* is a computer program that stores, searches, sorts, and organizes data. Database management systems allow users to manipulate information in many different formats. For example, a paralegal can easily create a current case list database that shows all active cases for the firm in alphabetical order. Once the data are entered, users can produce many different types of reports in many different formats without having to reenter the data. In our example, the paralegal could then use the same current-case database to produce a list of all the firm's cases in a specific court or before a particular judge or to produce a numerical listing by case number of all the firm's cases. Databases are covered in detail in Chapter 5.

Performing Mathematical Calculations: Spreadsheet Software

Paralegals may be required to perform mathematical calculations as part of their jobs. The calculations might be relatively simple, such as adding up the amount of damages a party has asked for in a case or preparing a case budget for a client; or more complicated, such as calculating principal and interest payments in a real estate transaction, analyzing statistics for trends, or calculating lost wages in a workers' compensation case.

A spreadsheet program calculates and manipulates numbers. Spreadsheet programs allow numerical data to be added, subtracted, multiplied, and divided automatically. They also allow users to edit, copy, and move numerical data; perform complex calculations quickly and accurately; graph numerical data automatically; save and retrieve information; and recalculate totals if any numbers in the spreadsheet change. Spreadsheet programs are easy to use and can greatly expedite work with numerical data.

Performing Timekeeping and Billing Functions: Timekeeping and Billing Software

In some law firms, paralegals record and track attorney and paralegal time and then send out bills to clients based on the amount of time spent on a case. Using a word processor for timekeeping and billing functions is tedious and time-consuming. Manual billing methods are so slow, in fact, that billings done manually tend to be generated infrequently, and in many cases bills are late getting to clients. Both of these consequences hurt the cash flow of a law office. In addition, bills prepared manually are more likely to contain errors, as numerous calculations must be performed for many bills.

When set up correctly, computerized legal timekeeping and billing programs are simple and easy to use. Information, such as the client's name, address, and billing rates, is entered into the system once. Then, as an attorney or paralegal spends time on a case, the time is entered into the system. If all entries are accurate, at the end of a billing period—one week, two weeks, one month, and so on—the computer automatically calculates and generates invoices, so they are produced and mailed on time with no calculation errors. This is covered in detail in Chapter 4.

Tracking Appointments and Deadlines: Computerized Docket Control and Case Management Software

Some paralegals must track appointments, deadlines, hearings, and other important dates to ensure that events get scheduled and then are not forgotten. This function is referred to as *docket control*, or sometimes as *case management*.

Although scheduling and tracking appointments and deadlines in a legal organization may seem at first glance like unimportant or merely clerical tasks, controlling an attorney's schedule and legal docket is, in fact, critical to his or her practice. Every year, thousands of ethical complaints are filed against attorneys. A primary reason clients file ethical complaints against their attorneys is the attorneys' failure to properly follow up on client matters. Many legal malpractice claims are also filed every year for the same reason. The importance of an effective docket control system in a legal organization should not be underestimated.

Although the terms *docket control* and *case management* are sometimes used interchangeably, there is a difference. Docket control software is fairly limited in nature, and primarily tracks appointments and deadlines in legal matters. Case management programs typically control the docketing of a case, but they usually also help the legal professional track and control the entire case, not just the scheduling aspects. Many case management programs include the ability to track a client's name, address, and telephone numbers; make notes about each phone conversation a legal professional has with the client; track appointments and deadlines by case; automatically schedule deadlines by type of case (typically where court rules mandate deadlines); perform conflict-of-interest searches when new cases are entered; produce letters and notices depending on the type of case; and more.

Presentation Graphics/Trial Software

High-quality, professional presentations can be created using presentation graphics software. Paralegals use presentation graphics programs to prepare charts, tables, video clips, evidence, and other information for juries and factfinders; to present information to clients; and to present information to colleagues, such as an in-house training program, a marketing plan for the law office, a proposed budget, or a new initiative. Each page of a presentation can contain many elements, including color, images of documents, text, charts, shapes, video, clip art, photos, and sound. Presentation graphics programs can produce the information on paper, overhead transparencies, 35-mm slides, or electronic on-screen presentations. This is covered in detail in Chapter 10.

LEGAL TECHNOLOGY TRENDS

Legal technology is continuing to move forward. Following are some general technology trends that are significantly changing how legal professionals will be performing their jobs in the future.

Mobile Computing, Instant Wireless Access, and Remote Access

Laptop, tablet, netbook, smartphones and tablet computers, are changing the way legal professionals communicate. All of these technologies are being merged in small, extremely powerful, fully connected mobile machines. These machines, no matter what you call them, operate as mobile phones, allow the user to send and receive email, have instant-messaging features, act as pagers, access the Internet, send and receive faxes, allow the user to edit and send documents, and synchronize with a user's desktop system. Small laptops or tablet computers can store millions of pages of documents electronically, fully access online legal databases such as Westlaw and LexisNexis on the go, and remotely access law-firm and service provider databases nearly globally. Users can connect to networks and the Internet allows legal professionals to access nearly all the same information and tools as if they were sitting at a desk in the office. This kind of mobile and immediate access to information will continue to change and drive the way legal professionals practice law.

Electronic Discovery

Electronic discovery is the process of producing litigation documents in an electronic format. The Federal Rules of Civil Procedure and many state court rules now require electronic discovery. This fact is forcing legal organizations to develop internal systems that can produce, store, search, and handle the production of electronic information in a variety of formats and across multiple computing platforms (desktops, servers, laptops, etc.). Electronic discovery will continue to have a profound impact on the practice of law for many years to come, especially as more and more courts and legal professionals make effective use of it. Electronic discovery is discussed more fully in Chapter 7.

Electronic Filing

With **electronic filing**, courts accept (and may even require) electronic versions of legal documents to be submitted, via the Internet or other electronic means, instead of requiring a hard copy of the document. Although this might sound easy, in reality it can be quite complicated. Issues concerning standardization, control, security, and the establishment of hardware and software systems to support electronic filing have all had to be overcome. Nevertheless, many states, courts, federal agencies, and other regulatory bodies have successfully implemented electronic filing, and many others are currently entering the implementation stage.

electronic filing
Supplying electronic versions of legal documents to a court, via the Internet or other electronic means, when the court does not require the hard copy of the document.

The Paperless Office

Just as courts have been working to implement electronic filing and require electronic discovery, many law offices have begun to implement the **paperless office**. This refers to converting all information into an electronic form for storage, processing, distribution, and use. Typically, this is done by scanning all hard-copy documents that come into the office and saving all computer-generated documents electronically without a hard copy. Some advantages of the paperless office include (1) significant reduction in paper usage and copying costs, (2) reduction of storage and lease space (the cost of office lease space now far exceeds the cost of electronic storage space), (3) increased portability, (4) increased collaboration (because digital information can be shared by multiple users via a network or the Internet), and (5) quicker search and retrieval of documents than with manual methods. As with electronic filing, there are implementation issues regarding the paperless office, including putting the hardware and software systems in place to support it, training staff, and other issues. Some law offices have fully implemented this concept and many others are taking steps toward this goal.

paperless office
Firm in which all hard-copy documents are converted into electronic form(s) for storage, processing, and distribution.

Cloud Computing

In recent years there has been much talk of "the cloud" and "cloud" computing. **Cloud computing** refers to the ability to use one computer to access information stored on a different computer or server. Although the term *cloud computing* may be relatively new, the concept is as old as the Internet. For example, Westlaw is a form of cloud computing. So is web-based email such as Google's Gmail.

cloud computing
The ability to use one computer to access information stored on a different computer or server.

Cloud computing has affected law offices in several ways. One is the use of hosted software applications. These are software applications that are not downloaded onto the user's computer; rather, users access the software via the Internet. This allows each user to store information on the host's computers, ensures that the user is always using the latest version of the software, and eliminates the need to download and install applications. Another use of the cloud is as a place to store documents and other data. This raises ethical issues: How secure are the data stored with a third party, and what is the law firm's liability for any breaches of confidentiality? There are more questions than answers as the law struggles to keep up with emerging technologies.

That said, there are several principles legal professionals should follow when working in the cloud environment:

1. Encryption—look for the lock icon to indicate use of Secure Sockets Layer (SSL), an industry-standard encryption technology used for Internet commerce
2. Server security—there must be evidence that a competent third party has audited the service provider's security
3. Client security—legal professionals need to be sure that their computers are properly secured (firewalls, current antivirus protection, etc.)
4. Password security—make sure all users have good passwords

Microsoft Office 2013/Office 365

The evolution of the Microsoft Office suite (Word, Excel, PowerPoint, etc.) continues with Office 2013 and Office 365. Office 2010 replaced the Office Button with the File Tab, which gives users access to a full-window file menu, which Microsoft calls "Backstage View." From here, users can easily access functions such as Open, Save, Save As, and Print. The most noticeable changes in Office 2013 result from the interface of Office and the cloud. Office 2013 may be purchased as a stand-alone product or users may buy a license that permits them to install Office 2013 on as many as five devices. This license allows users to download the software from the cloud (as opposed to using a disk). In addition, when users save a file, the default location is not a drive on the user's computer; it is the cloud. To be more specific, files are saved to Microsoft SkyDrive. (Users may choose to save files on their computers as they always have, too.) This means that a file that is created in one office and saved to SkyDrive may be accessed from any other device connected to the Internet. There are many other similar cloud products (e.g., Google Drive, Dropbox), but the fact that SkyDrive is not only integrated into the Office suite, but is the default location for saved files demonstrates how the cloud has become an acceptable, perhaps even preferable, location for storage of electronic files.

The Hands-On Exercises for the 2013 versions of Word, Excel, and PowerPoint will highlight the other changes in these well-known applications.

Social Media

social media
Online platforms that enable people to communicate easily to share information and resources, including text, audio, video, and images.

What is social media? Definitions may vary, but **social media** may generally be defined as online platforms that enable people to communicate easily to share information and resources, including text, audio, video, and images. Examples include blogs and well-known websites such as Facebook, Twitter, LinkedIn, Foursquare, and Wikipedia. Social media allows a community of users to create the content that is then viewed and commented on by other users. For legal professionals, social media is the new frontier. On the one hand, social media provides a vast source of original material (Facebook status updates, photographs, tweets, etc.). Nevertheless, this new frontier is not without its challenges, both practical and ethical.

Practical challenges include:

- The need to authenticate the material discovered on social media. It is necessary to prove that the comments made on a Facebook page were actually made by the person alleged to have made them.
- It may not be possible to get the material from the social media provider. Companies like Facebook and Twitter may be governed by the Stored Communications Act (18 U.S.C. § 2701), which prevents certain Internet

companies from responding to formal discovery requests. Case law in this area is still evolving, but a leading case in this area as of this writing is *Crispin v. Christian Audigier*, 717 F. Supp. 2d 965 (C.D. Cal. 2010). In this case, the Court ruled that whether an Internet company is compelled to comply with a subpoena depends on the user's privacy settings. For example, if the Facebook user sets the privacy settings so that only invited "friends" have access to the user's page and "wall posts" (essentially an electronic bulletin board), that material is deemed private and is not subject to formal discovery. However, if the privacy settings allow the general public to view the material, the Internet company/host would have to comply with the discovery request. In any event, any material sent as a private message would not be subject to a formal discovery request sent to the Internet company/host. A better option may be to try to get the information directly from the user.

Ethical challenges include:

- Legal professionals have the duty to maintain the confidences and secrets of clients as well as information relating to the representation of a client. In several instances, an attorney has been sanctioned for a blog post that revealed information about a case or expressed the attorney's less-than-temperate opinions of a judge.
- Legal professionals also have the duty to act competently and diligently on behalf of a client. Recently, family law attorneys have been using social media sites such as Facebook as a source of incriminating information. Legal professionals who do not know how to use social media, or who fail to do so, are not acting ethically. Furthermore, diligent representation requires attorneys to help their clients avoid legal problems in the first place. Thus, it could be argued that law firms should work with clients to help them create and implement social media policies to teach their employees the dangers posed by careless use of social media.

The Automated Courtroom

Many courts have installed sophisticated electronic equipment in their courtrooms, including evidence display systems and real-time court reporting. An evidence display system is a computerized system that shows evidence, via monitors, to the judge, jurors, counsel, and the public simultaneously. It also displays this information to the court reporter and clerks.

The master controls are located at the judge's bench so that he or she can control all monitors, sound systems, and cameras in the courtroom. The attorneys and/or judge can use the evidence display system to display properly admitted evidence in the courtroom, whether by means of video images, animation, photographic images, hard copy, or other media.

Many evidence display systems also support videoconferencing. For example, with the judge's approval, an out-of-state witness can testify at a trial without actually being present in the courtroom. It may also be possible to receive real-time text of the transcript in addition to the audio and video feeds.

Another type of courtroom technology is real-time court reporting. A witness's testimony is transcribed by a court reporter within a few seconds and can be displayed on the courtroom monitors or given to the judge, jurors, or attorneys on a real-time basis. This gives parties instant written and electronic access to witness testimony and can eliminate the need to read back a witness's testimony when there is a question.

LEGAL ETHICS AND COMPUTER TECHNOLOGY

At first it may appear that legal ethics and computers have little to do with one another. In fact, the opposite is true. In addition to known, existing ethical issues (which do not disappear with computerization), many legal ethical issues arise specifically from the proliferation of computers and computer use in legal organizations. Many of these ethical concerns revolve around two key issues: competence or negligence of a legal professional and client confidentiality. In recent years, the rules of professional responsibility have explicitly addressed the need for legal professionals to become (and remain) competent in technology. Today's legal professionals cannot provide competent legal representation without also understanding how to use all that the computer and Internet have to offer.

Attorney Competence

Attorneys have a duty to perform legal services in a competent manner. Computers, though incredibly helpful, can also be a vehicle for incompetence and legal malpractice. Computer-related legal malpractice and ethical breaches can take place in a variety of ways:

- Legal research performed with a computer may be inadequate and less than thorough.
- New documents are prepared using previously saved word-processing documents, but are inadequately proofread and contain old information (from the previous client).
- Typographical errors are made (especially when the person preparing the document relies on a spell checker rather than intelligent proofreading).
- Improper computerized forms or templates are used.
- A user generally fails to understand how a computer or a piece of software works, and thus fails to anticipate or discover an error.
- Automated legal or spreadsheet software is used with formula errors, logic errors, or lack of oversight or proofreading/review by the supervising attorney or other legal professionals.

Attorneys are responsible for their work product. It does not matter whether it was prepared by or with the assistance of a computer: if the end product has errors in it or is incompetently prepared, the attorney is still ultimately responsible for the work product. If the error or incompetent work product causes harm to the client, the attorney may be subject to attorney discipline charges and a legal malpractice claim.

Client Confidentiality

Attorneys have a duty to safeguard and keep confidential all client-related information, including information that is contained on computers. Every state has rules requiring attorneys to maintain the confidentiality of client information, no matter where that information resides.

This represents an enormous responsibility, given the technological advances in society generally and in legal organizations in particular. Although computers yield tremendous benefits to legal organizations in terms of efficiency, productivity, and delivery of high-quality legal services to clients, they also create substantial ethical and security issues. The threat of confidential client information being released either by mistake or by intrusion is very real, and can happen in a wide variety of ways, including:

- Interception of electronic mail by a third party (whether inadvertent or intentional)
- Interception of word-processing documents and other attachments to electronic mail by outsiders

- A breach of legal organization computer security, such as:
  - passwords not being appropriately maintained
  - computer hackers gaining access to confidential legal organization computers via the Internet or other online means
  - computer viruses deleting, accessing, or corrupting confidential client information
  - laptop and handheld computers holding confidential client information being stolen or inadvertently left for third parties to find
  - computer disks holding confidential client information being left or misplaced for third parties to find
  - computer hardware and storage devices not being sufficiently cleaned, so that client data are not destroyed before outdated equipment is disposed of

General Law Office Security

Law office computer systems in general are vulnerable to ordinary security threats, such as theft, sabotage, and natural disasters. It is important for all legal organizations to maintain adequate security measures, including having security and alarm systems to protect computer equipment from being stolen or damaged.

passwords
Code entered into a computer system or software that acts as a key, allowing the user to access the system and the information it contains.

Passwords

Passwords are codes entered into a computer system or software that act as a key and allow the user to access the system and the information it contains. Passwords are very important and are usually a good first line of defense against intrusion into a computer system, but they are not invulnerable.

It is important to choose strong passwords. Hacker software programs on the Internet contain tens of thousands of common passwords that can be used to break into a computer system. Here are some rules for selecting and using strong passwords:

- Passwords should be a minimum of eight characters.
- They should be non-dictionary words.
- They should combine uppercase and lowercase characters.
- They should use at least one symbol (e.g., $ or :).
- They should use at least one number.
- They should be changed every 90 days.
- They should not contain or be based on personal information such as birthdates, names of family members, or other easily attainable pieces of information.

An example of a strong password would be something such as: RD10$Tk# or XP358LIN!.

access rights
Network security measure that limits a user's access to only those directories and programs that the user is authorized to use.

Access Rights

All network operating systems for LANs and WANs and even some sophisticated application programs allow an administrator to limit the access rights of users. **Access rights** determine which computer directories, programs, or functions a user can get to and use, and are usually granted on a need-to-know basis. Users should be given only the access rights they absolutely need to have—never more than they need. For example, if John needed to use only general word-processing and litigation support files, his access rights could be limited to only those files and directories; he would thus not be able to access other directories and programs.

Limiting users' access rights limits the number of people who can access computer files, information, and programs, so the exposure of the legal organization is less than it would be if everyone were given access to everything. It is important that access rights be closely controlled and monitored regularly.

backing up
Making a copy of a user's computer files.

Backing Up **Backing up** refers to making a copy of a computer file or program. Backups are absolutely necessary in the event the legal organization's file server or other storage device crashes; files are accidentally deleted; files become corrupted; the computer system becomes infected with a virus or other malware; or fire, theft, or a natural disaster occurs. If a legal organization has a good plan for regular, timely backup of its data, and a disaster does happen, the data can be restored with no loss of information.

Backing up data is easier than ever before. A number of hardware tools are available for performing backups, including high-capacity, highly reliable data backup units; secondary servers that back up data throughout the day or at the end of the day. Also, there are Internet-based companies that will back up a legal organization's data automatically at predetermined times.

Whatever method is chosen, it is important that the information be maintained securely offsite, that backup be done regularly, and that the backup be reliable and usable. Legal organizations should verify on a regular basis that their backups are actually working; a good way to do this is by restoring some of the saved data to make sure it is usable.

metadata
Electronically stored information that may identify the origin, date, author, usage, comments, or other information about a file; "data about data."

The Dangers of Metadata **Metadata** is electronically stored information that may identify the origin, date, author, usage, comments, or other information about an electronic file. Metadata is often described as "data about data." For example, in Microsoft Office files (such as Word or Excel files), you can see metadata that identifies the original author of a document, company name, subject, previous authors, date created, date last modified, editing time, and other information. You can see this for yourself by simply loading a file and clicking on File Properties. Metadata is usually not visible when a document is printed, but if one knows where to look it is often easy to find.

Other, more dangerous metadata includes things like the comments and tracked changes in a Word document. In several instances, Word files were produced and tracked changes or comments were enabled to show the various stages of revisions of the document, including who saw the document and when and exactly what changes were made to the document. This kind of metadata allows subsequent users to infer things about the thinking of original creators.

Subsequent chapters will detail the specific dangers posed by metadata for specific law office computer applications and how best to mitigate those dangers.

Electronic Mail

Electronic mail is an incredibly popular means of communication. Millions of Americans use email and collectively we send hundreds of millions of messages each day. Although it is extremely convenient, email can pose a large security risk due to a lack of privacy and security. The problem is that email sent over the Internet is not secure; it may pass through many other networks before it gets to the intended recipient. As it passes through the networks, others have the potential to see or read the message. Email can be encrypted to ensure that no one except the intended recipient can read the contents of the message while it is in transit. **Encryption** runs the message through an encoder that uses an encrypting key to alter the characters in the message. Unless a person has the correct encryption (decryption) key needed to decode it, the message appears unreadable.

encryption
Process of running a message through an encoder that uses an encrypting key to alter the characters in the message. Unless the person wanting to read the message has the encryption key needed to decode it, the message appears unreadable.

There are many other security issues with email, including sending email to the wrong person, sending email to distribution lists (many email recipients) by mistake, and much more. These problems can become quite acute and complicated when the message contains confidential client information. Unless encryption or similar methods are used, it is safest not to send confidential client information via email, given the potential for abuse. These issues are discussed further later in this text.

Viruses Email also presents a threat because computer viruses can be attached to emails. A **computer virus** is a computer program that is destructive in nature. When the attachment containing the virus is opened, the virus is brought or allowed into the receiver's computer system. Users should never open an attachment from an unknown source. Most legal organizations run antivirus programs that prevent or at least alert users to potential viruses. However, because hackers are constantly updating their technology, legal organizations must regularly update their antivirus programs at least weekly (preferably daily), using the Internet. Most software suppliers issue patches and updates to their programs to respond to new threats. In addition to updating virus definitions regularly, many software companies update their programs to include new security measures. Users should regularly update their operating systems and application programs and take advantage of the latest security measures they provide.

computer virus
A destructive computer program that may be designed to delete data, corrupt files, or do other damage; may also be self-replicating, using an "infected" computer to transmit itself to other computers.

Spyware **Spyware** is a general term used for software that tracks your movement on the Internet for advertising and marketing purposes, collects personal information about the user, or changes the configuration of the user's computer without the user's consent. Spyware commonly gets onto a user's computer when the user downloads or installs a program. Spyware may be included with the program software, although that information may be buried in the licensing agreement—or the user may not be warned about it at all. Whenever you install programs on your computer, it is important to carefully read the disclosures, the license agreement, and the privacy statement. A number of antispyware programs are available that can detect and remove installed spyware.

spyware
A general term for software that tracks a user's movement on the Internet for advertising and marketing purposes, collects personal information about the user, or changes the configuration of the user's computer without the user's consent.

Computer Hackers and Firewalls Nearly all legal organizations now provide access to the Internet for their staff. Many of these organizations use DSL, T1, cable modems, or other communication technologies that are "always connected" to the Internet. Computer hackers can use such connections to access the office computer system unless there is a firewall that cuts off this access. A **firewall** allows users from inside an organization to access the Internet but keeps outside users from entering a computer or the organization's LAN.

firewall
Security measure that allows users from inside an organization to access the Internet but keeps outside users from entering the computer or LAN.

Mobile Computing and Wi-Fi Dangers The security threats associated with mobile computers and wireless networks are substantial. Because laptop computers now rival the power and versatility of desktop computers, they can contain literally tens of thousands of client records. The potential for harm to a client cannot be exaggerated. One way to protect data on laptops and handheld computers is to install a power-on password. With a **power-on password**, the computer immediately prompts the user to enter a password after the machine has been turned on, but before the computer has completely booted the operating system software. If the user does not know the password, the system will not start and the computer will be unusable. Nearly all laptops and handhelds have this feature, but it must be activated. This type of system is very effective in the event a computer is stolen.

Encryption software can also be loaded onto a laptop. If the user loses the laptop or it is stolen, the data on the laptop remains safe because it cannot be accessed without the encryption key.

Wi-Fi computing allows users to access wireless LANs. A Wi-Fi–enabled device allows a user to connect to the Internet when in proximity to an access point

power-on password
Password that the computer immediately prompts the user to enter after the machine has been turned on, but before the computer has completely booted the operating system software. If the user does not know the password, the system will not start and the computer will be unusable.

(sometimes referred to as *hotspots*). The problem is that in crowded and public spaces, there are increased security risks, including easier anonymous hacking, inadvertent transmission diversion, and intentional hijacking of signals and access points. For example, using a Wi-Fi connection in a hotel may let the person in the next room hack into your computer through its own wireless connection. It would be better, in these circumstances, to use an Ethernet or other hardwired system.

"Delete" Is Not Permanent Many users mistakenly believe that when a file is "deleted," it is permanently deleted. This is usually not the case. Simply erasing or deleting does not permanently delete files even if you have emptied the recycle bin. In many instances, files can be retrieved by hackers and others from hard drives and flash drives. It is critical to physically destroy a storage device such as a flash drive to ensure that the data on it cannot be retrieved. In addition, in Windows, deleted files are typically not deleted at all, but are sent to the recycle bin, so it is important to empty that utility from time to time.

Disaster Recovery Plans

disaster recovery plan A prewritten plan of action to be followed if a disaster befalls the legal organization.

A **disaster recovery plan** is a plan of action that can be followed in case a disaster (whether of natural or human origin) befalls the legal organization. For example, what would happen if a legal organization suffered a total loss to its computer systems from a fire, hurricane, flood, earthquake, tornado, bomb, power failure, theft, hard disk crash, or virus? Disaster recovery plans are prepared in advance of a disaster (typically multiple plans are prepared for different types of disasters) when there is plenty of time to think through alternative courses of action, anticipate problems, and design appropriate solutions.

Disaster recovery plans include a wide variety of information, such as who will be in charge, what services are the most vital, what steps will be taken first, what each department will require in terms of resources (computers, software, data, etc.), how to contact vendors, and how to contact employees. Many organizations make offsite data and backup storage an integral part of disaster recovery planning.

SUMMARY

A few years ago, it was important for a paralegal entering the job market to have computer skills. Now it is imperative. Computer use in law offices has grown substantially and will continue to grow in the future. Computers are currently used in the legal field for a wide variety of purposes.

A computer is an electronic device that accepts, processes, outputs, and stores information. Information that is entered into a computer is called input. Information that comes out of a computer is called output. Hardware is the actual, physical components of a computer system. Software refers to instructions to the computer hardware that make the computer function. Computers can be used to help paralegals perform many of their functions, including communicating with clients and other legal professionals using electronic mail; drafting documents using word-processing software; collecting and organizing data using database management software; performing mathematical calculations using spreadsheet software; performing timekeeping and billing functions using timekeeping and billing software; tracking appointments and deadlines using docket control and case management software; providing litigation support using litigation support software; preparing electronic discovery requests using electronic discovery software; conducting legal and factual research using the Internet and fee-based online services; and creating presentations with presentation graphics software.

Every computer has a system unit, which contains the CPU and main memory. The CPU, which is the "brain" of the computer, organizes and processes information in addition to coordinating functions of peripheral devices. The main memory is made up of ROM, which is permanent memory, and RAM, which is volatile memory.

Auxiliary storage devices, such as hard disks and optical storage devices, store information so that it can be retrieved later. Removable drives such as flash or "thumb" drives are small and portable, but can still hold up to several gigabytes of information.

Input devices enter information into a computer. Scanning and imaging both refer to importing a picture of a hard-copy document into a computer. Making an image of a document is similar to taking a photograph of the document. A related functionality is optical character recognition. When a user scans a document into a computer using OCR, the result is a file that contains the text of the document, which can be edited or manipulated with a word processor or other application.

Output devices provide the user with the data that the computer has generated or received. They include monitors, printers, portable projectors, and soundboards.

Communication devices allow computers to exchange information with other users via the Internet and other channels. Communication technology uses dial-up modems, cable modems, DSL and T1 lines, wireless modems, VoIP, and videoconferencing, among others.

A local area network is a multiuser system that links mainframes or computers that are in close proximity for the purpose of communication. LANs can be either client/server or peer-to-peer networks. A wide area network is a multiuser system that links computers that may be located thousands of miles apart.

Operating system software instructs the computer hardware how to operate its circuitry and how to communicate with input, output, and auxiliary storage devices. It allows the user to manage the computer. Microsoft Windows is the most common operating system in the legal environment.

Utility software helps to manage the hardware and software of a computer. Popular utility programs include antivirus and antispyware programs.

Legal organizations use many types of application programs, and the list grows longer every day. Document management software organizes, controls, distributes, and allows for extensive searching of electronic documents, typically in a networked environment. An application service provider is a company that provides software or a service application through the Internet directly to the user's computer.

Current and future technology trends that will affect the way legal professionals provide services to clients include mobile computing and instant wireless access, automated courtrooms, electronic filing of court documents, the paperless office, cloud computing, the use of social media, and heightened security and confidentiality concerns.

Many security and ethical issues surround the use of technology in legal organizations. The underlying principle is that legal professionals must safeguard and keep client information confidential. Current security concerns include passwords, access rights to files, data backup, release of client information, security surrounding electronic mail, viruses, spyware, firewalls, mobile computing problems with lost or stolen laptops or handhelds, disaster recovery, and metadata. Metadata is electronically stored information that may identify the origin, date, author, usage, comments, or other information about a file.

KEY TERMS

access rights
access time
antivirus and antispyware utilities
application service provider (ASP)
application software
auxiliary storage device
backing up
backup utility
bar code scanner
cable modem
central processing unit (CPU)
client/server network
cloud computing
compression utility
computer
computer virus
disaster recovery plan
document management software
DSL (Digital Subscriber Line)
electronic filing
encryption
extranet
firewall
gigahertz (GHz)
hard disk drive
hardware
imaging
input
input devices
Internet
intranet
license agreement
local area network (LAN)
magnetic tape system
main memory
memory chips
metadata
modem
monitor

mouse
network operating system
operating system software (program)
optical character recognition (OCR)
optical storage devices
output
output device
paperless office
password
peer-to-peer network
peripheral devices
power-on password
processor chip
project management software
random-access memory (RAM)
read-only memory (ROM)
removable drive
single-user system
social media
software
sound card
speech recognition
spyware
storage
storage capacity
utility software
video adapter card
videoconferencing
Voice over Internet Protocol (VoIP)
wide area network (WAN)
Windows
wireless modem
wireless networking

INTERNET SITES

Internet sites for this chapter include:

GENERAL PARALEGAL SITES ON THE INTERNET

ORGANIZATION	PRODUCT/SERVICE	WORLD WIDE WEB ADDRESS
American Bar Association	Products/services for legal professionals	www.americanbar.org
National Federation of Paralegal Associations	Products/information for paralegals	www.paralegals.org
National Association of Legal Assistants	Products/information for paralegals	www.nala.org
International Paralegal Management Association	Products/information for paralegals	www.paralegalmanagement.org
Paralegal magazine	Magazine for paralegals	www.paralegaltoday.com
Technolawyer.com	Email newsletter on legal technology issues	www.technolawyer.com
American Bar Association, Legal Technology Resource Center	Legal technology issues	www.lawtechnology.org
Findlaw's Legal Technology Center	Legal technology issues	technology.findlaw.com

COMPUTER HARDWARE

ORGANIZATION	PRODUCT/SERVICE	WORLD WIDE WEB ADDRESS
AMD	Microprocessors	www.amd.com
Apple	Hardware/software for Apple computers	www.apple.com
BlackBerry	Smartphones	www.rim.net
Cisco	Network operating system peripherals	www.cisco.com
Dell Computers	Computer hardware/software	www.dell.com

Hewlett-Packard	Computer hardware/peripherals	www.hp.com
Intel	Microprocessors	www.intel.com
Lenovo	Computer hardware	www.lenovo.com
NEC	Computer hardware/software	www.nec.com
Toshiba	Computer hardware/peripherals	www.toshiba.com

COMPUTER SOFTWARE

ORGANIZATION	PRODUCT/SERVICE	WORLD WIDE WEB ADDRESS
Business Software Alliance	Antipiracy information	www.bsa.org
LexisNexis	Research databases and document assembly software	www.lexisnexis.com
Microsoft	Computer software	www.microsoft.com
Mozilla	Browser software	www.mozilla.com
Network Associates	Antivirus/spyware software	www.mcafee.com
Novell	Network operating systems	www.novell.com
Software and Information Industry	Antipiracy information	www.siia.com
Symantec Corp.	Antivirus and other application programs	www.symantec.com

TEST YOUR KNOWLEDGE

1. Why is it imperative for paralegals to have an understanding of computers?
2. True or False: The Internet has only had a mild impact on practicing paralegals, because many of their day-to-day activities have not changed.
3. Distinguish between intranets, extranets, and the Internet.
4. True or False: Manual billing systems are typically slow and impede a legal organization's cash flow.
5. In the legal field, another name for a calendaring system software is __________.
6. Name two ways in which computer technology affects an attorney's ethical duties.
7. True or False: The central processing unit is the "brain" of a computer.
8. The memory that is cleared when a user turns the machine off is called __________.
9. Name three auxiliary storage devices.
10. Differentiate between imaging and optical character recognition.
11. What is VoIP?
12. Why are software access rights important?
13. What is an alternative to backing up software using hardware components such as tape backup and secondary servers?
14. Define metadata.
15. What are some of the ethical dangers of mobile computing?
16. What is the federal statute that governs whether an Internet company may comply with a formal discovery request?

ON THE WEB EXERCISES

1. Using the Internet and a general search engine, such as www.yahoo.com or www.google.com, or using one or more of the websites listed at the end of this chapter, research one of the following topics and write a one- to two-page paper on the topic. Update the information contained in this chapter and give a general overview of the topic.
   - Automated courtroom
   - Videoconferencing
   - Electronic filing
   - The paperless office
2. Using the Internet and a general search engine, such as www.yahoo.com or www.google.com, identify at least one free source of online access to your state's statutes.
3. Identify a minimum of five potential security threats that could affect a law office. For each, identify ways in which a legal organization can mitigate the threat.
4. Using a general search engine on the Internet, such as www.google.com or www.yahoo.com, write a one-page summary of what metadata is. If possible, list examples of how mistakes or problems arise from the use of metadata for unintended purposes.
5. As a paralegal in a small law office, you have been asked for your input regarding replacing your current computer, which is now outdated. Go to www.pcmagazine.com, www.pcworld.com, http://practice.findlaw.com, www.dell.com, www.gateway.com, www.toshiba.com, and www.compaq.com and research the following:
   a. What common microprocessors are being used
   b. How much RAM is usually included with the machines
   c. How much hard disk storage is typically being included
   d. What types and sizes of monitors are common
   e. What common peripherals are sold with the computers
   f. What choices you have among handheld, laptop, tablet, or desktop machines

   What would you choose, and why?
6. Using the Internet, determine what is the largest-capacity flash drive you can find and what it costs. Approximately how many hard-copy pages of documents could be stored on the flash drive by an employee who decided to steal documents from your law firm?
7. As a paralegal in a corporate legal department, you are responsible for tracking hundreds of real estate transactions throughout the United States every year. Keeping the paperwork organized and on track is beginning to overwhelm you. Because you work with attorneys and corporate staff all over the country, it would be nice to be able to forward electronic versions of real estate records, title searches, and other records. Because many of the documents are in hard-copy format, you would have to convert the documents to images. Using www.lawofficecomputing.com, www.lawtechnology.org, www.technolawyer.com, and www.practice.findlaw.com, write a short paper on imaging. Answer the following questions:
   a. How much do high-speed scanners cost?
   b. How accurate is imaging?
   c. Do many legal organizations use imaging?
   d. In the end, would you recommend the move to imaging?
8. As a paralegal in a solo practitioner's office, you have approached the attorney about purchasing handheld computers for both of you so that you can communicate more easily with each other and with clients. The attorney is concerned about security regarding handheld computers. He would like to know answers to the following questions:
   a. If the device gets lost, can just anyone pick it up and have access to the information (and if so, are there any precautions that can be taken to reduce this risk)?
   b. How secure is information when using wireless services such as wireless email?
   c. Assuming that the security issues can be solved, what are the latest features being offered in these devices?
9. Microsoft is continually updating its Windows operating system software and Office application programs. Go to its website at www.microsoft.com and comment on the latest version(s) of the program that it is releasing.
10. Go to www.facebook.com and www.twitter.com and read the privacy policies. What options are available on these platforms, and how do they differ?

QUESTIONS AND EXERCISES

1. Are you surprised to see the extent to which paralegals use computers in their jobs? What conclusions can you draw regarding the paralegal computer user?
2. Knowing that some legal research can be done free of charge on the Internet, and that other information is best found using a fee-based system, what approach would you use in conducting legal research?
3. You work as a paralegal for a small law firm that handles collection matters. The firm is currently representing a furniture store that loaned money to a number of customers who now have disappeared. Unless you find the whereabouts of the customers, the furniture store will not be able to collect its money. What computer resource would you use to try to find the customers, and why?
4. What policies and procedures could be put in place to limit an employee's ability to download and subsequently successfully use large amounts of client data when the employee leaves a law firm to practice elsewhere?
5. Write a two-page memorandum regarding the ethical rules in your state regarding a law firm's duty to safeguard client information that is stored electronically. What are the rules that might apply? Are there any exceptions for accidental disclosure?

ETHICS QUESTION

A client of your firm is engaged in complex litigation. She has just purchased the latest must-have mobile Wi-Fi device. The client plans on using this device for email and voice communication. What ethical issues are raised by this scenario?

CHAPTER 2

Word Processing and Document Assembly

CHAPTER OBJECTIVES

After completing this chapter, you should be able to do the following:

1. Explain how legal organizations and paralegals use word processors.
2. Describe major features found in word-processing programs.
3. Explain what document assembly is and how it works.
4. Discuss ethical problems related to word processing.

INTRODUCTION

word-processing software
Program used to edit, manipulate, and revise text to create documents.

document assembly software
Powerful computer program that creates standardized templates and forms.

This chapter introduces the fundamentals of word processing and document assembly. **Word-processing software** is used to edit, manipulate, and revise text to create documents. It is one of the most widely used types of application software in legal organizations. Paralegals use word processors to prepare memos, correspondence, form letters, discovery documents, and many other legal documents.

Document assembly software creates powerful standardized templates and forms. Once a template or form has been set up, users respond to a series of questions and prompts to fill in data. The document assembly program then merges the form or template with the answers and builds a new, completed document. Many legal organizations incorporate document assembly into their practices, particularly in areas for which well-structured forms and templates have been created and are routinely used.

CENTRALIZED AND DECENTRALIZED WORD PROCESSING

centralized word-processing system
A system in which all the word-processing documents for an organization are input or typed in a single location or by one department (i.e., a word-processing department).

Legal organizations use various approaches to word processing, including centralized, decentralized, or a combination of both.

Centralized Word Processing

With a **centralized word-processing system**, a legal organization has a separate word-processing department where correspondence, memorandums, and other documents in the office are input (typed). For example, a large firm with a centralized word-processing system might require its litigation, tax, and corporate law departments to send all their major word-processing projects to the word-processing department.

Most word-processing departments, sometimes called word-processing centers, have trained staff that do nothing but type in documents and data. Usually, the firm uses a standardized form for requesting services from this department. When a document has been input and printed, it is then sent back to the originating party for correction and for distribution. Such centralized word-processing departments are most often found in large firms.

Decentralized Word Processing

With a **decentralized word-processing system**, individuals perform word processing for themselves, for another person, or for a small group. For example, it is common for paralegals, law clerks, legal secretaries, and attorneys to perform some or all of their own word processing. Many law firms are now able to place relatively inexpensive personal computers on the desks of most staff, thus creating a decentralized system. In the past, attorneys rarely, if ever, did their own typing or word processing. Now it is very common.

decentralized word-processing system
A system in which individuals or separate departments in an organization perform their own word processing.

Today, many small law firms use a decentralized word-processing system. Even large firms, which have traditionally used centralized word processing, may now use a combination of the two systems. It is common for large firms to maintain a word-processing center while still allowing legal professionals to do some of their own word processing.

LEGAL WORD-PROCESSING PROGRAMS: MICROSOFT WORD VS. COREL WORDPERFECT

The leading word-processing program for legal organizations is Microsoft Word, but some firms prefer to use Corel WordPerfect. Microsoft offers several versions of Word, which are all popular in the legal field: Word 2013, Word 2010, and Word 2007. Word 2007 implemented a major change in the Word interface. Microsoft Word uses a "ribbon" (see Exhibit 2–1) packed with tools that the user can change based on what the user is doing. These newer versions of Word also include a "quick access toolbar" that the user can customize (see Exhibit 2–1). Word 2007 introduced the Office button, which provided quick access to a series of common commands (such as New, Open, Close, Save, Save As, and Print). Word 2010 replaced the Office button with the File tab. See Exhibit 2–1A. One of the major differences between the newer versions and earlier versions of Word is that the drop-down menus that have been a staple of Word were eliminated. Word 2003, like earlier versions of Word, used an interface that includes drop-down menus and a static toolbar.

Another major change beginning with Word 2007 is that the file format in which documents are saved was revised. The default file format in Word 2007 is ".docx" (e.g., "letter.docx"). For many years, Word saved documents with the ".doc" file extension (e.g., "letter.doc"). Word 2007, Word 2010 and Word 2013 offer users the option of saving documents in the older ".doc" file format, but at the cost of sacrificing some options that are not available or do not work in the older file format.

All Microsoft Office 2010 and 2013 applications, including Word 2010 and Word 2013, introduced yet another new feature, the File tab. The File tab replaces the Office button used in the 2007 versions. Microsoft describes the File tab as the place "you do everything *to* a file that you don't do *in* a file." In other words, this is where you access the Open, Save, and Print features (among many others). See Exhibit 2–1A. Extensive hands-on exercises, which can be done in Word 2013, Word 2010, or Word 2007, appear at the end of this chapter.

EXHIBIT 2–1
Microsoft Word 2007

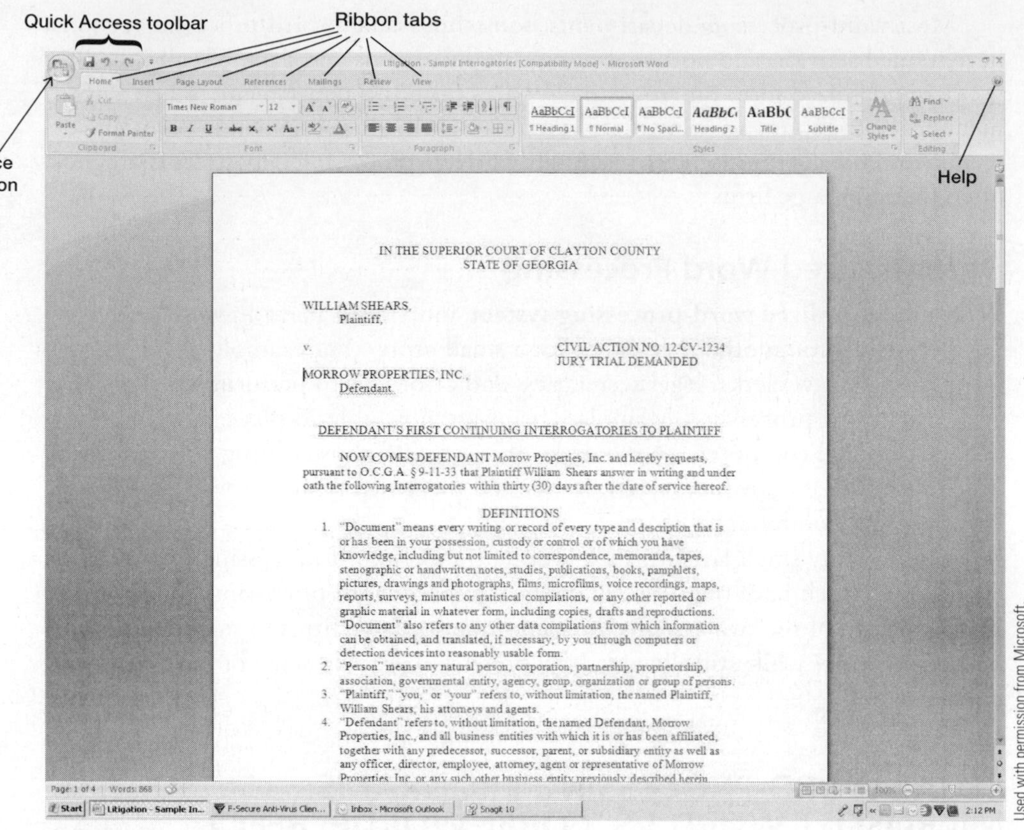

EXHIBIT 2–1A
Microsoft Word 2010

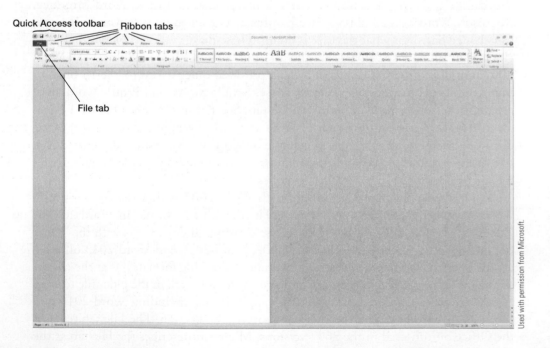

See Exhibits 2–2, 2–2A and 2–2B for quick reference guides to Word.

Word 2007 Quick Reference Guide

HOME RIBBON

Office button; Dialog box launcher; Help; Cut, Copy, Paste; Font format; Paragraph format; Styles; Find/Replace

NAVIGATION

Up 1 Screen	[Page Up]	Beginning of Document	[Ctrl]+[Home]
Down 1 Screen	[Page Down]	End of Document	[Ctrl]+[End]
Beginning of a Line	[Home]	Go To	[F5]
End of a Line	[End]		

KEYBOARD SHORTCUTS

Copy Text	[Ctrl]+[C]	Undo a Command	[Ctrl]+[Z]
Paste Text	[Ctrl]+[V]	Redo / Repeat	[Ctrl]+[Y]
Cut Text	[Ctrl]+[X]	Print a Document	[Ctrl]+[P]
Bold Text	[Ctrl]+[B]	Save a Document	[Ctrl]+[S]
Underline Text	[Ctrl]+[U]	Select Everything	[Ctrl]+[A]
Italics Text	[Ctrl]+[I]	Open File	[Ctrl]+[O]
Find / Replace	[Ctrl]+[F]	New File	[Ctrl]+[N]
Go To	[Ctrl]+[G]	Reveal Formatting	[Shift]+[F1]
Spell, Grammar Check	[F7]	Hide Ribbon	[Ctrl]+[F1]

WORD FEATURE	COMMAND STRUCTURE
Attach Document to an Email	Office Button, Send, Email
Change Case of Text	Home, Font, Change Case
Clear all Formatting of Text	Home, Font, Clear Formatting
Clip Art from Internet (Inserting)	Insert, Illustrations, Clip Art, Clip Art on Office Online
Clip Art / Files / Charts, Shapes (Inserting)	Insert, Illustrations
Compare Documents	Review, Compare
Find / Replace	Home, Editing, Find / Replace
Font Control	Home, Font
Footnotes / Endnotes	References, Footnotes, Insert Footnotes
Header / Footer	Insert, Header & Footer, Header or Footer
Indent text	Home, Paragraph, Dialog Box Launcher
Line Spacing Changes	Home, Paragraph, Line Spacing
Macros	View, Macros
Mail Merge	Mailings, Start Mail Merge
Margins, Paper Orientation	Page Layout, Page Setup, Margins
Shading	Home, Paragraph, Shading
Styles	Home, Styles
Tables (Inserting)	Home, Insert, Tables
Tabs	Home, Paragraph, Dialog Box Launcher, Indents and Spacing, Tabs
Track Changes	Review, Tracking, Track Changes
New Document	Office Button, New
Open (Existing) document	Office Button, Open
Save a document	Office Button, Save
Print and Print Preview	Office Button, Print
Table of Authorities	References, Table of Authorities

EXHIBIT 2–2
Word 2007 Quick Reference Guide

Word 2010 Quick Reference Guide

HOME RIBBON

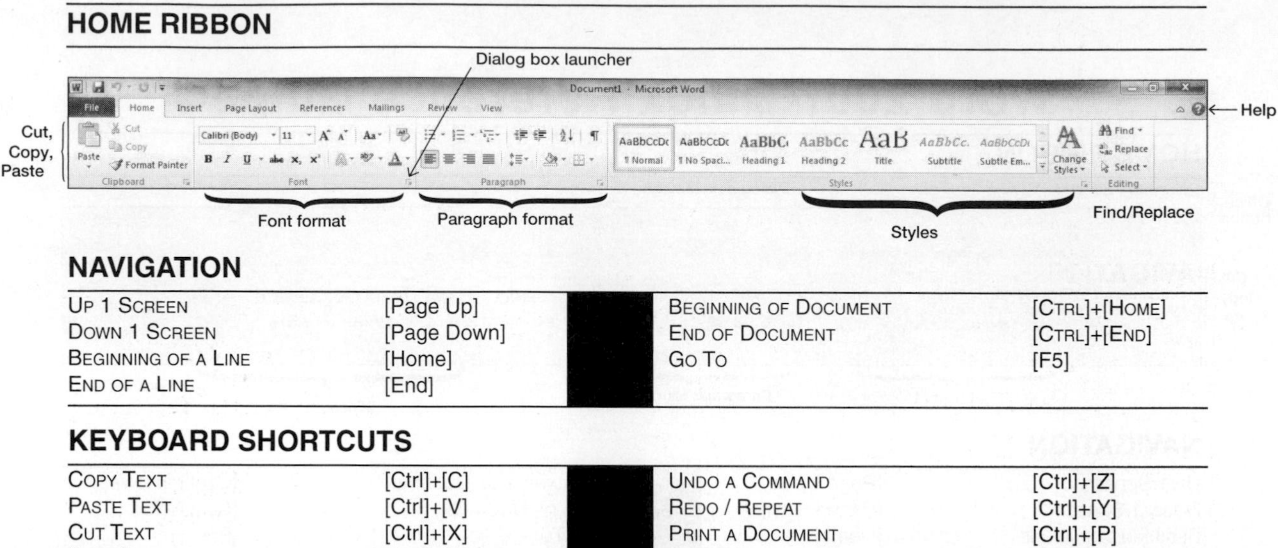

NAVIGATION

Up 1 Screen	[Page Up]	Beginning of Document	[Ctrl]+[Home]
Down 1 Screen	[Page Down]	End of Document	[Ctrl]+[End]
Beginning of a Line	[Home]	Go To	[F5]
End of a Line	[End]		

KEYBOARD SHORTCUTS

Copy Text	[Ctrl]+[C]	Undo a Command	[Ctrl]+[Z]
Paste Text	[Ctrl]+[V]	Redo / Repeat	[Ctrl]+[Y]
Cut Text	[Ctrl]+[X]	Print a Document	[Ctrl]+[P]
Bold Text	[Ctrl]+[B]	Save a Document	[Ctrl]+[S]
Underline Text	[Ctrl]+[U]	Select Everything	[Ctrl]+[A]
Italics Text	[Ctrl]+[I]	Open File	[Ctrl]+[O]
Find / Replace	[Ctrl]+[F]	New File	[Ctrl]+[N]
Go To	[Ctrl]+[G]	Reveal Formatting	[Shift]+[F1]
Spell, Grammar Check	[F7]	Hide Ribbon	[Ctrl]+[F1]

WORD FEATURE	COMMAND STRUCTURE
Attach Document to an Email	File Tab, Send, Email
Change Case of Text	Home, Font, Change Case
Clear all Formatting of Text	Home, Font, Clear Formatting
Clip Art from Internet (Inserting)	Insert, Illustrations, Online Pictures
Clip Art / Files / Charts, Shapes (Inserting)	Insert, Illustrations
Compare Documents	Review, Compare
Find / Replace	Home, Editing, Find / Replace
Font Control	Home, Font
Footnotes / Endnotes	References, Footnotes, Insert Footnotes
Header / Footer	Insert, Header & Footer, Header or Footer
Indent text	Home, Paragraph, Dialog Box Launcher
Line Spacing Changes	Home, Paragraph, Line Spacing
Macros	View, Macros
Mail Merge	Mailings, Start Mail Merge
Margins, Paper Orientation	Page Layout, Page Setup, Margins
Shading	Home, Paragraph, Shading
Styles	Home, Styles
Tables (Inserting)	Home, Insert, Tables
Tabs	Home, Paragraph Dialog Box Launcher, Indents and Spacing, Tabs
Track Changes	Review, Tracking, Track Changes
New Document	File Tab, New
Open (Existing) document	File Tab, Open
Save a document	File Tab, Save
Print and Print Preview	File Tab, Print
Table of Authorities	References, Table of Authorities

EXHIBIT 2–2A
Word 2010 Quick Reference Guide

Word 2013 Quick Reference Guide

HOME RIBBON

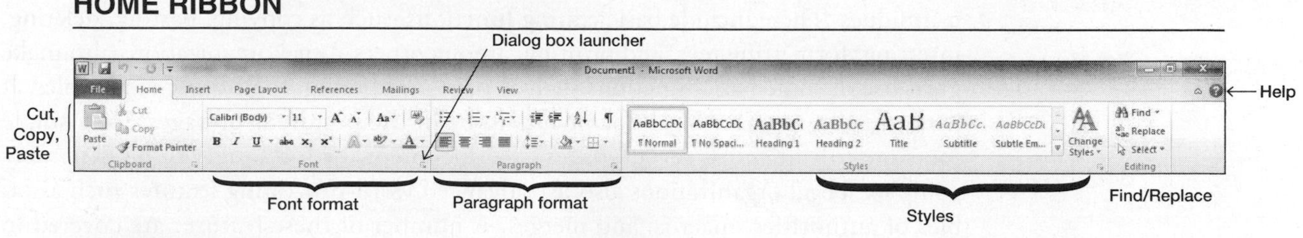

NAVIGATION

Up 1 Screen	[Page Up]	Beginning of Document	[Ctrl]+[Home]
Down 1 Screen	[Page Down]	End of Document	[Ctrl]+[End]
Beginning of a Line	[Home]	Go To	[F5]
End of a Line	[End]		

KEYBOARD SHORTCUTS

Copy Text	[Ctrl]+[C]	Undo a Command	[Ctrl]+[Z]
Paste Text	[Ctrl]+[V]	Redo / Repeat	[Ctrl]+[Y]
Cut Text	[Ctrl]+[X]	Print a Document	[Ctrl]+[P]
Bold Text	[Ctrl]+[B]	Save a Document	[Ctrl]+[S]
Underline Text	[Ctrl]+[U]	Select Everything	[Ctrl]+[A]
Italics Text	[Ctrl]+[I]	Open File	[Ctrl]+[O]
Find / Replace	[Ctrl]+[F]	New File	[Ctrl]+[N]
Go To	[Ctrl]+[G]	Reveal Formatting	[Shift]+[F1]
Spell, Grammar Check	[F7]	Hide Ribbon	[Ctrl]+[F1]

WORD FEATURE	COMMAND STRUCTURE
Attach Document to an Email	File Tab, Share, Email
Change Case of Text	Home, Font, Change Case
Clear all Formatting of Text	Home, Font, Clear Formatting
Clip Art from Internet (Inserting)	Insert, Illustrations, Online Pictures
Clip Art / Files / Charts, Shapes (Inserting)	Insert, Illustrations
Compare Documents	Review, Compare
Find / Replace	Home, Editing, Find / Replace
Font Control	Home, Font
Footnotes / Endnotes	References, Footnotes, Insert Footnote
Header / Footer	Insert, Header & Footer, Header or Footer
Indent text	Home, Paragraph, Dialog Box Launcher
Line Spacing Changes	Home, Paragraph, Line Spacing
Macros	View, Macros
Mail Merge	Mailings, Start Mail Merge
Margins, Paper Orientation	Page Layout, Page Setup, Margins
Shading	Home, Paragraph, Shading
Styles	Home, Styles
Tables (Inserting)	Insert, Tables
Tabs	Home, Paragraph Dialog Box Launcher, Indents and Spacing, Tabs
Track Changes	Review, Tracking, Track Changes
New Document	File Tab, New
Open (Existing) document	File Tab, Open
Save a document	File Tab, Save
Print and Print Preview	File Tab, Print
Table of Authorities	References, Table of Authorities

EXHIBIT 2–2B

Word 2013 Quick Reference Guide

LEGAL WORD-PROCESSING FUNDAMENTALS

Legal organizations use a variety of basic and advanced word-processing features and techniques. These include basic editing functions, such as copying, pasting, deleting, inserting, formatting text, and printing, among others. Legal organizations also make great use of some basic functions such as page numbering, footnoting, and tables. It is not uncommon for legal documents to be in the hundreds of pages, for a single footnote to run across several pages in a document, or for a table to be extremely complex. Legal organizations also use advanced word-processing features such as tables of authorities, macros, and merges. A number of these features are covered in this chapter.

Whole-Paragraph Functions

Automatic Paragraph Numbering Most word processors have an automatic paragraph numbering feature that allows users to have paragraphs and lists of information numbered automatically by the software. This feature is used extensively in legal organizations because information is routinely presented in a hierarchical format (e.g., 1, 2, 3 or A, B, C). With the automatic paragraph numbering feature, the program will automatically renumber a list when you add or delete material. If you had not used the numbering function, you would have had to renumber the whole list manually each time you added information to or deleted material from the list. For example, notice in Exhibit 2–3 that the headings "A. Introduction" and "B. Jurisdiction" are in a hierarchical format, as is the list with items "1)," "2)," and "3)." If, for example, after "A. Introduction" you created a new topic, "B. Venue," the program would automatically renumber "Jurisdiction" to be "C. Jurisdiction."

In addition to improving accuracy, this feature saves huge amounts of time for legal organizations, because motions and briefs can be extremely long and complex and have many levels of hierarchical information. Users can even set up custom paragraph numbering schemes, including setting custom margins to comply with local court rules and employing a variety of numbering formats and sublevels (including numeric, alphanumeric, alphabetical, and others).

style
A named set of formatting characteristics that users can apply to text.

Styles A **style** is a named set of formatting characteristics that users apply to text. Using styles, users can quickly apply multiple formatting to text. For example, notice the different styles used in Exhibit 2–3. The style applied to "A. Introduction" and "B. Jurisdiction" is titled "Heading 2." Any material styled "Heading 2" is bolded, underlined, set in small caps, and automatically numbered. Instead of having to go to each section heading and then enter the font command and the automatic numbering command, you can simply use the Style command to have all the formatting automatically applied, all at once.

Styles can also be automatically changed and updated. Suppose that the user who created Exhibit 2–3 has 40 section headings and now needs to change the format of all of these headings so that they are not underlined. If the user had not used the Style feature, he or she would have had to go to each of the 40 headings and manually make the desired changes. Using the Style feature, the user can simply invoke the Style command, click "Heading 2," use the Select All feature to automatically select all text with the "Heading 2" style, and then make the desired changes. The format of all "Heading 2" text is then automatically updated.

The Style feature is particularly helpful in long and complex documents that have recurring elements and where consistency is important. Styles are covered in detail in Lesson 6 of the Hands-On Exercises found at the end of this chapter.

EXHIBIT 2–3
Word processing: Header, footer, Styles, footnotes, Auto Number, Automatic Page Numbering in Word 2007

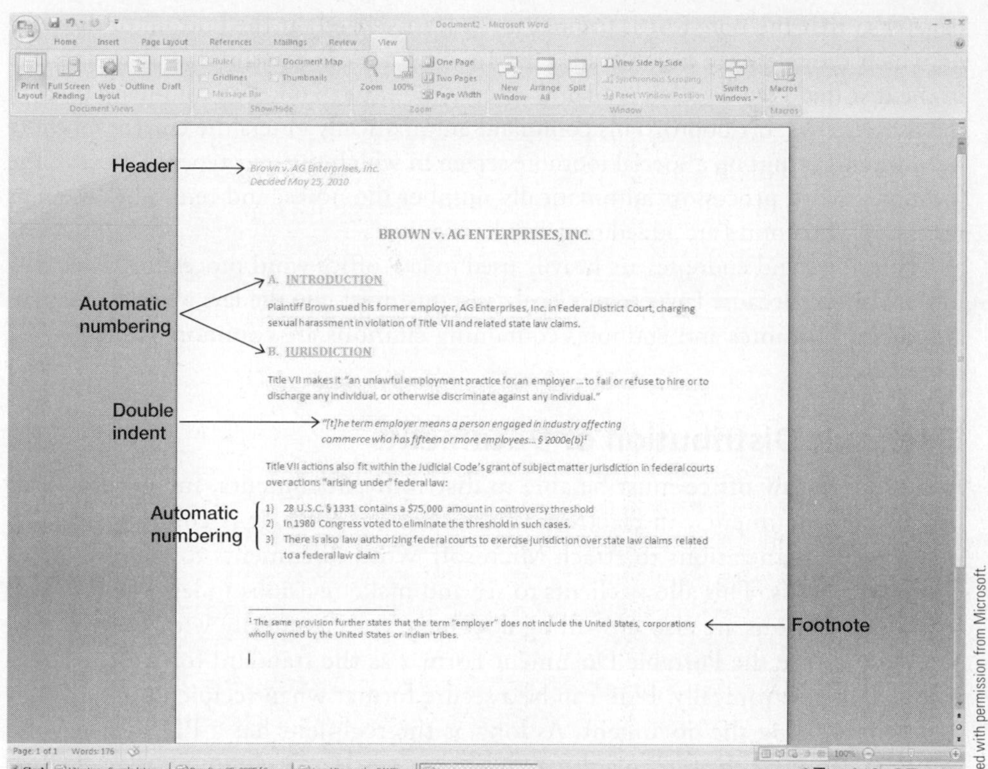

Headers and Footers A **header** is a title or heading that appears at the top of each page of a document. A **footer** is text that appears at the bottom of each page of a document. For example, a footer may indicate the current page number and the total number of pages of the document. The program can automatically calculate both the current page number and the total number of pages using an automatic page numbering feature.

Automatic Page Numbering An **automatic page numbering** feature automatically calculates the appropriate page number for each page of a document. In most word processors, you can specify where the page number should be placed on the page (e.g., centered at the bottom of the page in a footer or in the upper right corner of the header). With the automatic page numbering feature, new page numbers are automatically recalculated and inserted when text is added to, moved or reformatted, or deleted from a page.

Double Indenting Text is indented an equal distance from the left and right margins by using **double indenting**. Paralegals and attorneys use the double-indent feature frequently when including quotations from primary authorities. To use the double-indent feature, go to where the double indent should start, enter the Double Indent command, and type in the appropriate text. The text is automatically indented the same distance from the left and right margins.

Footnotes and Endnotes A **footnote** is material that is printed at the bottom of a page on which a numbered reference appears in text. An **endnote**, like a footnote, has a numbered reference in the text, but instead of appearing at the bottom of a page, the note material appears at the end of a chapter or document. Footnotes and endnotes are easy to produce with a word processor. Most word processors have an automatic footnote feature that tracks the current footnote number and formats the

header
A title or heading that appears at the top of each page of a document.

footer
Text that appears at the bottom of each page of a document.

automatic page numbering
Word-processor feature that automatically numbers the pages of a document for the user; also renumbers pages as material is moved, added, or deleted.

double indenting
Word-processor feature (also found in other types of programs) that indents text an equal distance from the left and right margins.

footnote
Material that is printed at the bottom of a page; marked in text by a numbered referent.

endnote
Material that is printed at the end of a chapter or document; marked in text by a numbered referent.

page(s) so that the note text is printed (or at least started) at the bottom of the page on which the reference number appears. To enter a footnote, simply go to the place in the text that is to be referenced and execute the Insert Footnote command (within the References tab/ribbon). This command automatically enters the correct footnote number and brings up a special footnote screen in which the user types the text of the footnote. Word processors automatically number the notes, and renumber them as necessary when notes are added or deleted.

Footnotes and endnotes are heavily used in law-office word processing, especially in legal briefs. Because lawyers and legal assistants must cite the law when making an argument, footnotes and endnotes containing citations are common—and may be quite lengthy.

Electronic Distribution of Documents

Any modern law office must be able to distribute documents, including word-processing documents, in electronic form. For example, it is commonplace in many legal organizations to attach Microsoft Word documents to emails sent to corporate clients. This allows clients to see and make revisions to legal work. Most legal organizations are also now filing documents electronically with court clerks. Most courts use the Portable Document Format as the standard format for documents filed electronically. PDF can be a secure format when recipients are prohibited from editing the document. As long as the recipient has a PDF viewer, the recipient can view the file on a different type or version of computer than the one on which the document was created. Some word processors can export to a PDF file from within the word-processing program. Users can also purchase a separate program, such as Adobe Acrobat, to convert word-processing and other documents to PDF files.

Printing

Even with the prevalence of electronic document distribution, the ability to print hard copies of documents is still important. Word processors are extremely flexible when it comes to printing documents. Users can print single pages, whole documents, specific pages (e.g., pages 67 to 74), color, one- or two-sided pages, and much more. Many legal organizations have moved to digital printing, using multifunction printers that can print, copy, scan, add tabs, collate, and staple. Most word processors also have a "print layout" view or a Print Preview command that allows the user to see exactly how the document will look when printed.

Tables

The table feature in a word processor allows you to create a table of information using rows and columns. You can then quickly organize information into columns and rows without using tabs. Exhibit 2–4 shows a basic table. Grid lines divide the table into rows and columns (although you can adjust the settings so the lines are not displayed). Tables can include text, numbers, and even formulas.

Tables are very easy to set up in most word processors. You simply enter the Table command and tell the program how many rows and columns to start with. You can also change the size of the columns or rows, add and delete columns or rows, split columns or rows, add color, add graphics, and include calculations. Tables are frequently used in legal word processing for many purposes. Tables are covered in detail in Lesson 4 of the Hands-On Exercises found at the end of this chapter.

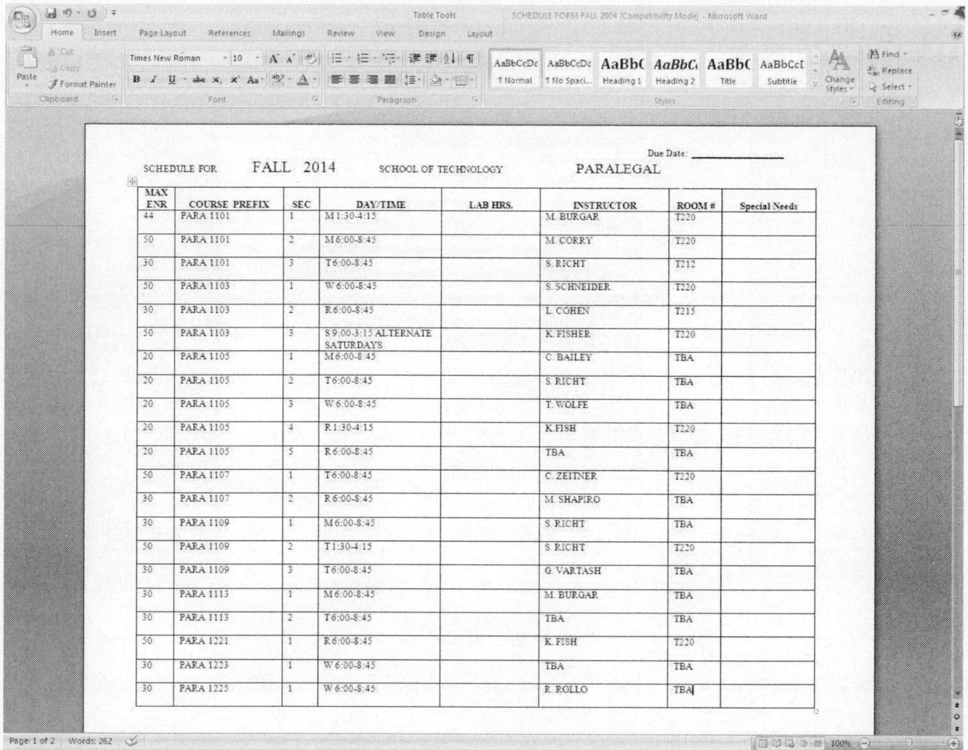

Due Date: ___________

SCHEDULE FOR FALL 2014 SCHOOL OF TECHNOLOGY PARALEGAL

MAX ENR	COURSE PREFIX	SEC	DAY/TIME	LAB HRS.	INSTRUCTOR	ROOM #	Special Needs
44	PARA 1101	1	M 1:30-4:15		M. BURGAR	T220	
50	PARA 1101	2	M 6:00-8:45		M. CORRY	T220	
30	PARA 1101	3	T 6:00-8:45		S. RICHT	T212	
50	PARA 1103	1	W 6:00-8:45		S. SCHNEIDER	T220	
30	PARA 1103	2	R 6:00-8:45		L. COHEN	T215	
50	PARA 1103	3	S 9:00-3:15 ALTERNATE SATURDAYS		K. FISHER	T220	
20	PARA 1105	1	M 6:00-8:45		C. BAILEY	TBA	
20	PARA 1105	2	T 6:00-8:45		S. RICHT	TBA	
20	PARA 1105	3	W 6:00-8:45		T. WOLFE	TBA	
20	PARA 1105	4	R 1:30-4:15		K.FISH	T220	
20	PARA 1105	5	R 6:00-8:45		TBA	TBA	
50	PARA 1107	1	T 6:00-8:45		C. ZEITNER	T220	
30	PARA 1107	2	R 6:00-8:45		M. SHAPIRO	TBA	
30	PARA 1109	1	M 6:00-8:45		S. RICHT	TBA	
50	PARA 1109	2	T 1:30-4:15		S. RICHT	T220	
30	PARA 1109	3	T 6:00-8:45		G. VARTASH	TBA	
30	PARA 1113	1	M 6:00-8:45		M. BURGAR	TBA	
30	PARA 1113	2	T 6:00-8:45		TBA	TBA	
50	PARA 1221	1	R 6:00-8:45		K. FISH	T220	
30	PARA 1223	1	W 6:00-8:45		TBA	TBA	
30	PARA 1225	1	W 6:00-8:45		R. ROLLO	TBA	

EXHIBIT 2–4
A table in Word 2007

Macros

A **macro** records a user's keystrokes, saves those keystrokes, and then allows the user to play those keystrokes back. For example, you might create a macro for the legal organization's name or to close a letter. Notice in the first screen of Exhibit 2–5 that the user has created a macro entitled "PleadSignBlock." When it was created, the macro recorded the keystrokes that produce the standard signature block for a pleading. From then on, you never have to retype that signature block. At the end of a pleading, such as the second screen of Exhibit 2–5, you simply run the macro: the macro does the rest by quickly and sequentially replaying the recorded keystrokes.

macro
Word-processor feature that records the user's keystrokes, saves those keystrokes, and then allows the user to play those keystrokes back.

Macros can also be created to perform word-processing commands or even series of commands (e.g., applying a style, then applying a double indent). Macros increase productivity, efficiency, and accuracy, because users do not have to keep keying in repetitious material or going through long sequences of commands. Macros can be created by invoking the New Macro command; with the recording feature, the user's keystrokes and commands are recorded in the order in which they are executed, and then saved under whatever file name the user has assigned to the macro. To play the macro, the user simply invokes the Play Macro command and enters the name of the macro or clicks on the name in a list. (For even quicker access, macros that are used frequently can be assigned to a keyboard stroke combination, such as Ctrl-Alt-P; this means the user need not even go to the Macros menu or take hands off the keyboard.)

Macros are an extremely handy and time-saving feature. Macros are covered in detail in Lesson 12 of the Hands-On Exercises found at the end of this chapter.

EXHIBIT 2–5
Macro in Word 2010

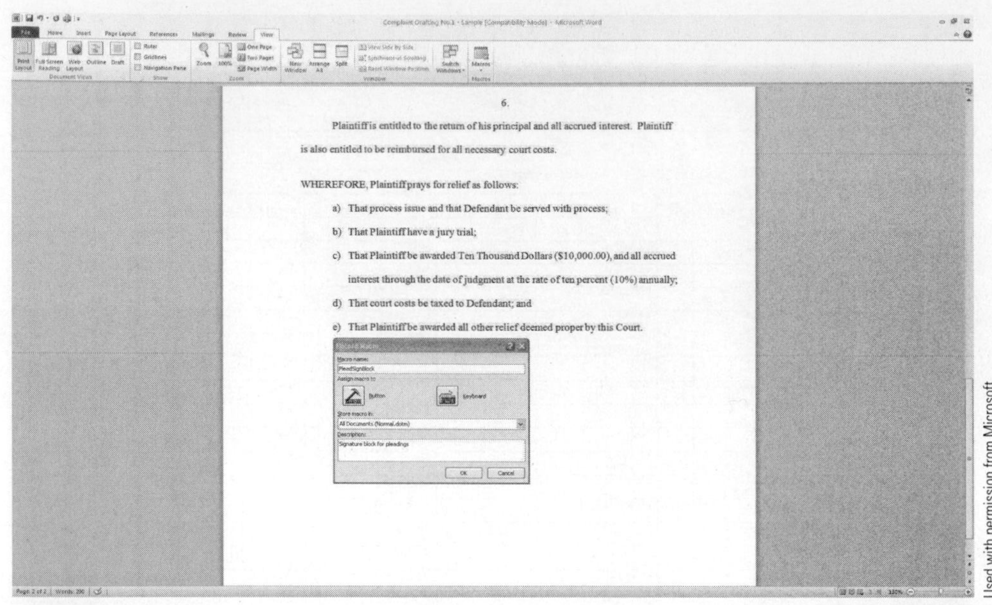

Used with permission from Microsoft.

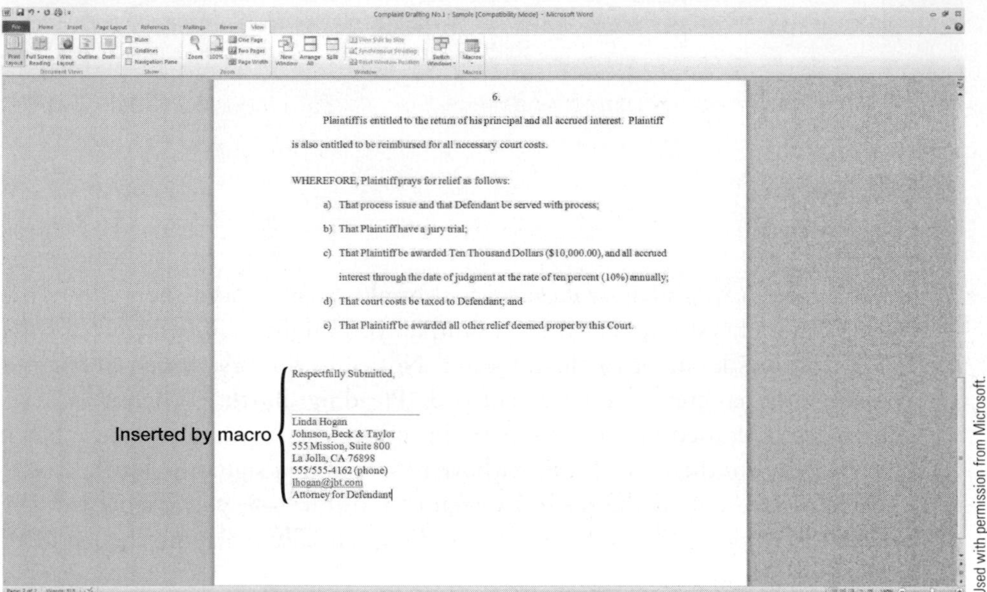

Used with permission from Microsoft.

comment
Word-processor feature that allows a user to annotate and create notes in a document without changing the text of the document.

compare documents
Word-processor feature that allows a user to compare and contrast two documents, either side by side or by blacklining (usually through the creation of a third document showing differences).

Comments, Comparing Documents, and Track Changes

Word processors allow groups of people to collaborate effectively using a number of features and tools, including comments, compare documents, and track changes. The **comment** feature allows a user to annotate and make notes or comments in a document without actually changing it. Notice in Exhibit 2–6 that the reviewer has inserted a comment, which includes questions, in the user's document. The original user can then make changes and delete the comment or respond to the reviewer by editing the comment with his or her own opinion.

A **compare documents** feature allows you to compare two separate word-processing files. Most word processors can do this in a couple of ways, including allowing simultaneous viewing of the two files or by producing a third document

Review ribbon

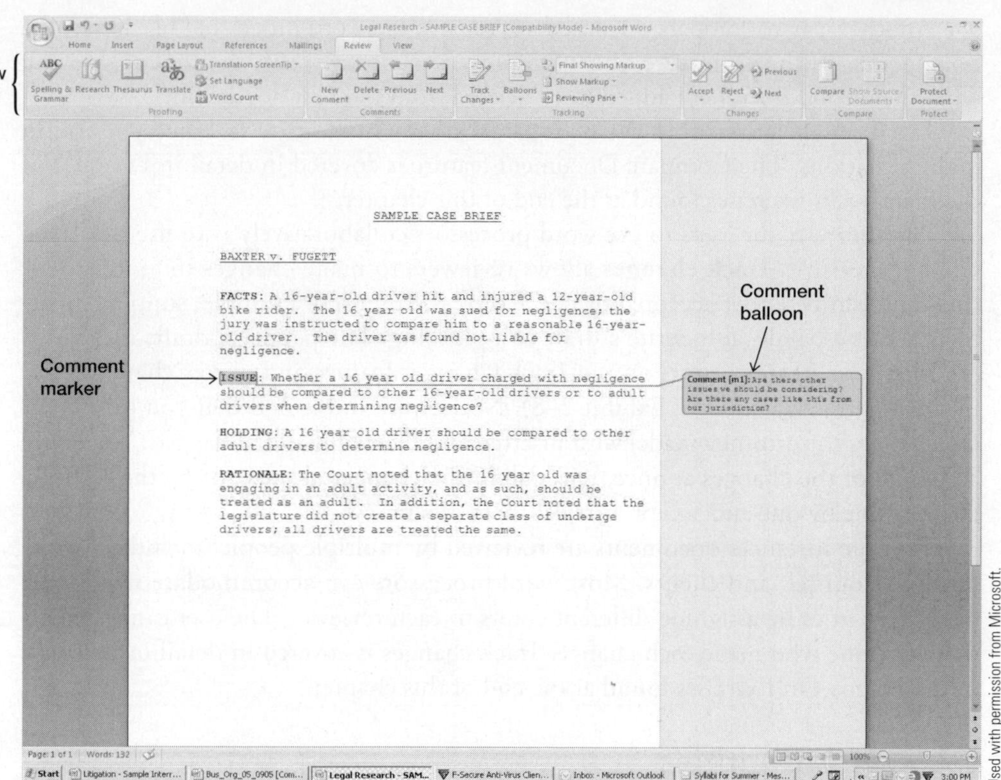

EXHIBIT 2–6
Adding a comment to a document in Word 2007

that shows the differences between the two versions. Notice in Exhibit 2–7 that two similar but different documents are being viewed. The second document adds some verbiage to paragraph 1 (Term of Employment), but other than that it is substantially similar to the first. Using this method, you can view two documents at the same time to find the differences. You can also set the word processor to synchronize the documents so that they scroll side by side as you move through the documents.

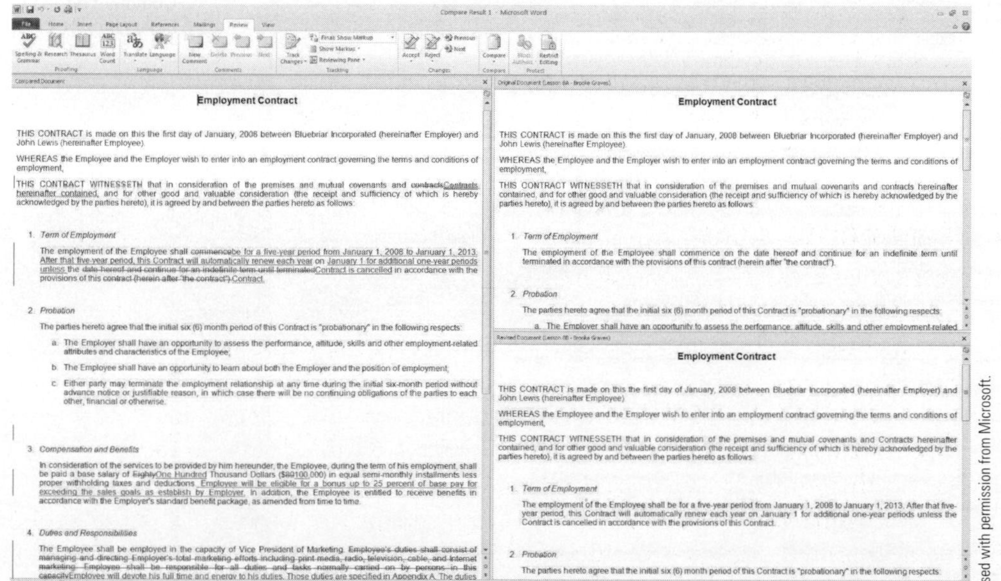

EXHIBIT 2–7
Comparing documents: Simultaneous viewing and blacklining in Word 2010

Another way to compare documents is to have the word processor "blackline" the documents. With this feature, the word processor creates a new document showing what the second document added to or deleted from the first document.

Legal organizations find the Compare Documents feature to be very useful in many situations. The Compare Document feature is covered in detail in Lesson 8 of the Hands-On Exercises found at the end of this chapter.

track changes
Word-processor feature that allows reviewers to make or recommend changes to a document; these changes can later be either accepted or rejected by the original author.

Another way for users to use word processors collaboratively is to use the Track Changes feature. **Track changes** allows reviewers to make changes to a document that later can be either accepted or rejected by the user. For example, suppose an attorney asks a paralegal to write a draft of a pleading. The paralegal drafts the pleading; then the attorney turns on the Track Changes feature and makes changes right in the document itself (see Exhibit 2–8). Notice in Exhibit 2–8 that you can see all the changes the attorney made, with inserted and deleted material flagged. You could accept all of the changes at once, reject all of the changes at once, or go through the changes one by one and accept or reject them separately.

In some instances documents are reviewed by multiple people, including attorneys, co-counsel, and clients. Most word processors can accommodate reviews by multiple parties by assigning different colors to each reviewer. The user can then easily determine who made each change. Track changes is covered in detail in Lesson 9 of the Hands-On Exercises found at the end of this chapter.

Table of Authorities

table of authorities
Automated word-processor feature that allows the program to generate an accurate list of case and statute citations (authorities), along with the page number(s) on which each cite appears.

Most word processors have automated features for creating a table of authorities (commonly referred to as a TOA or TA). A **table of authorities** is a section in a legal document or brief that lists the cases, statutes, and other authorities referenced in that legal document or brief. A table of authorities is similar to a table of contents except that it lists cases and other reference materials, along with the page numbers on which they appear in the document. Tables of authorities are typically created by marking all of the case citations and other authorities and then generating the table itself near the beginning of the document (see Exhibit 2–9).

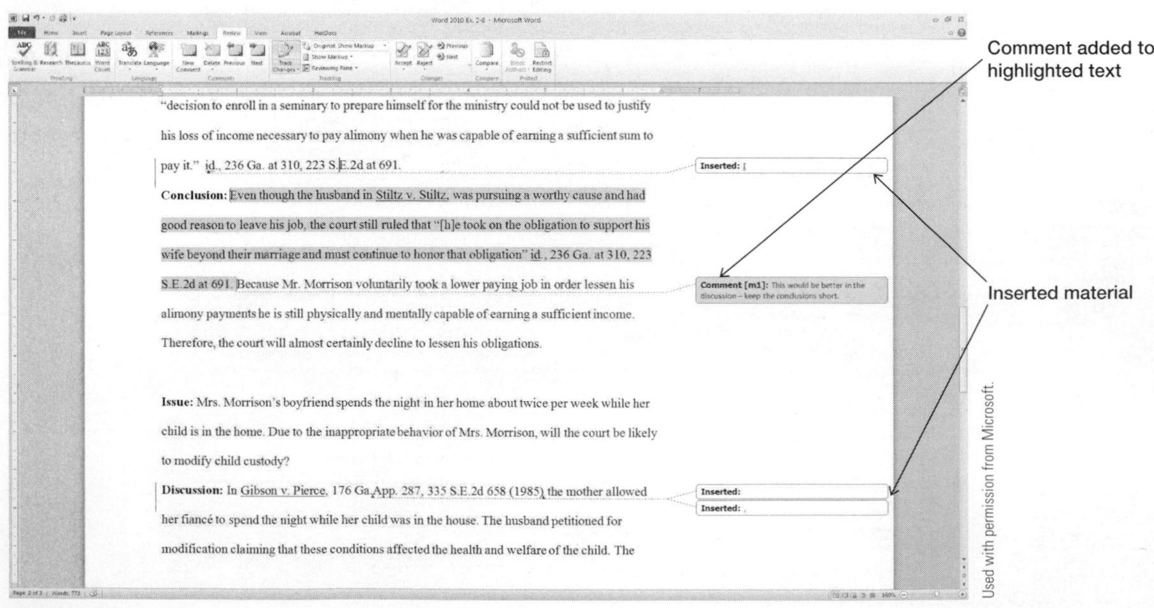

EXHIBIT 2–8
Track changes in Word 2010

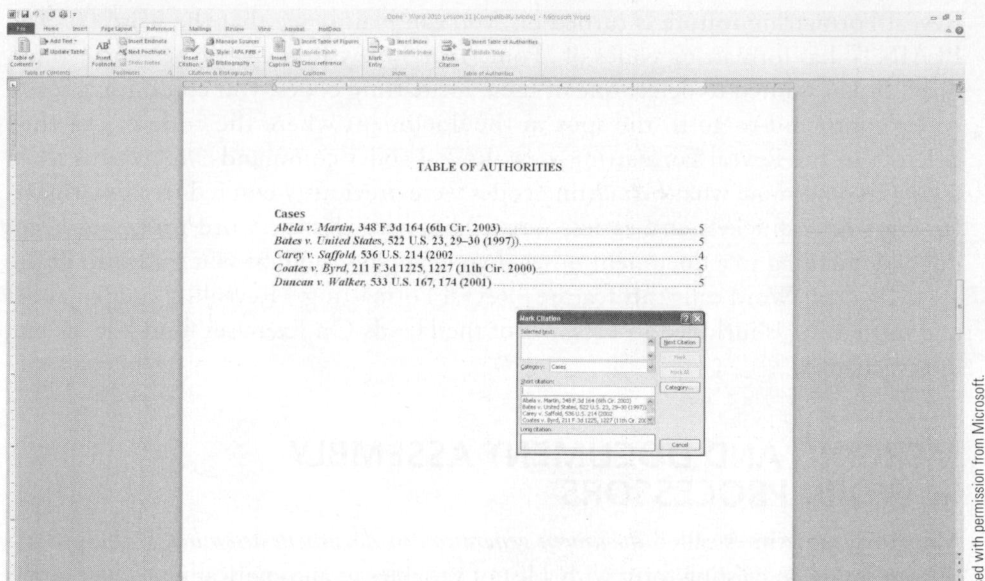

EXHIBIT 2–9
Table of authorities in Word 2010

The Table of Authorities feature in a word processor is very important because manual creation of a TOA is an extremely time-consuming process, particularly if revisions are made after the table has been generated. With the automated feature, even if changes are made to a document after a table of authorities has been created, the user can regenerate the table; that is, the program will automatically recreate the table with all of the new items and page numbers. Tables of authorities are covered in detail in Lesson 11 of the Hands-On Exercises found at the end of this chapter.

Revealing Hidden Codes

When text is typed into a word processor, all the user sees on the screen is the actual text. However, most word processors have a command that allows the user to see the "invisible" codes that indicate things such as word spaces, boldfacing, and margin changes.

Revealing the hidden codes makes it easier to delete, edit, or change the formatting of a document (see Exhibit 2–10). For example, in Exhibit 2–10, when the

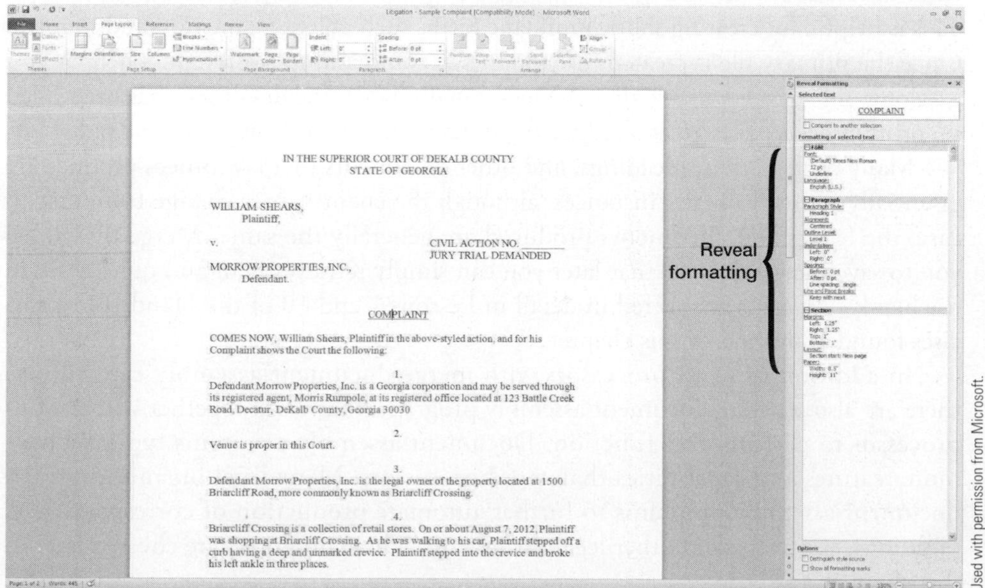

EXHIBIT 2–10
Styles and formatting revealed in Word 2010

Reveal Formatting feature is turned on, you can plainly see that the word "COMPLAINT" has formatting codes of "Font: Times New Roman, 12 pt., and Underline." If you wanted to delete one of these formatting codes, you could use a reveal codes command to go to the spot in the document where the code is and then delete it in the Reveal Formatting view. Reveal codes commands are helpful when trying to determine what formatting codes were previously entered in a document. (It can be the quickest and easiest way to discover why the word processor keeps doing something to a document other than what you thought you told it to do!)

Microsoft Word calls this feature "Reveal Formatting." Revealing hidden codes and formatting is included in Lesson 5 of the Hands-On Exercises found at the end of this chapter.

MERGING AND DOCUMENT ASSEMBLY IN WORD PROCESSORS

merging
The process of combining a form with a list of variables to automatically produce a document; sometimes called document generation.

Merging, sometimes called *document generation* or *document assembly*, is the process of combining an existing form with a list of variables to automatically produce a new document. For instance, if you want to send the same letter to a number of clients, but you want each letter to be personalized, you can use the Merge feature found in most word processors to do this quickly. The body of each letter remains the same; the only information that changes is the name and address of the client. The information that remains the same in each letter (in this example, the body of the text) is called a *constant*. The information that changes in each letter (here, the name and address of the client) is called a *variable*.

primary file
A file that contains the information that remains the same (the constant) in a document that is used more than once; usually referred to as a *form* or *template* in a merge document.

secondary file
The file that contains the information that varies (the *variable*) in a merge document.

The first step in the merge process is to create the primary file. The **primary file** (also called a *main document*) contains the constant information and is usually referred to as a *form* or *template* in a merge document. The second step is to create the list of names and addresses. This is called the secondary file. The **secondary file** (also called a *data file*) contains the variable information in a merge document. In this example, the secondary file contains the names and addresses of the clients. The third step is to merge or combine the primary file with the secondary file, thus creating a separate letter for each client, using the Merge command. The final step is to print the document(s).

Another way to use a merge file is to create a primary file or template and then enter information into the form as you go along, without using a secondary file at all. This is helpful for creating short, mundane forms such as letters, memos, and so forth. Once the primary file is created, use the merge command to retrieve it. Then, as you go along, fill in each variable that changes. Finally, when the document has been filled in, print it. Merge files greatly reduce the time it takes to perform repetitive tasks.

Many of the letters, pleadings, and other documents that law offices produce are essentially forms. In many instances, although the client names change from case to case, the letters and documents produced are generally the same. Merge files allow you to save these forms, so that later you can simply retrieve them and quickly fill in the blanks. Merging is covered in detail in Lessons 7 and 10 of the Hands-On Exercises found at the end of this chapter.

In addition to word processors with merge/document assembly capabilities, there are also separate document assembly programs that work together with a word processor to perform this function. Document assembly programs typically have more features and capabilities than word processors. Many legal organizations use document assembly programs to further automate production of correspondence, pleadings, contracts, and other legal documents. These programs are covered later in this chapter.

MICROSOFT WORD ONLINE TRAINING AND WORD TEMPLATES

Microsoft provides free online training courses for Microsoft Word on its website. More than 20 courses are available for each version. To find the online training courses, use a general search engine (such as www.google.com or www.yahoo.com) and use the search terms "Microsoft Word 2010 Courses" or "Microsoft Word 2007 Courses."

The Microsoft website also provides a wide variety of free Word templates. In Word 2007, the online templates can be accessed by selecting the Office button, selecting New, and then clicking on any of the available templates. In Word 2013 and Word 2010, the online templates can be accessed by clicking the File tab, selecting New, and then clicking on any of the available templates.

PDF FILES

As noted earlier, many courts now allow—and in fact require—legal organizations to file documents electronically. Most courts use PDF as the standard for filing documents electronically. The federal courts in particular have standardized filing around the PDF format. Thousands of attorneys have filed documents for millions of cases using the federal courts' Case Management and Electronic Case File system.

The PDF standard was created by Adobe Systems. PDF can be made a secure format, meaning that recipients cannot edit the document and that the look and format of the document are locked. For electronic filing of documents with a court, this is crucial.

Another advantage of PDF is that as long as the recipient has a PDF viewer (which is free), the recipient can view the file on a different type of computer than the one on which the document was created. Thus, if a court system used a Windows-based operating system and an attorney used an Apple Macintosh computer, it would not matter. As long as the attorney saved the document to be filed as a PDF, the court could still use and access the document, even though it was created on a computer with a completely different operating system.

PDF/A

Imagine that you are rummaging through an old file cabinet and coming across a couple of floppy disks. You would like to see what information the disks contain, but you cannot find a computer with a slot for floppy disks. And even if you did, there is no guarantee that your computer would be able to read the files on the disks. That is the problem that the PDF/A seeks to avoid. The "A" in PDF/A stands for "archive". PDF/A was created to provide a platform for electronic information that would remain accessible for years to come. Federal courts now require that all filings be made as a PDF/A.

What makes a PDF/A different than a regular PDF? In a PDF/A:

- All fonts must be embedded in the PDF/A and the file must be completely self-contained with no reliance on external players or links.
- PDF/A does not allow: Cross-document links (e.g., links to a different PDF file); media files, including movies or sounds; links to websites; any level of security.

Adobe Acrobat

Adobe Acrobat is a PDF conversion utility. Acrobat can convert many types of files to PDF. Adobe Acrobat has several versions, which may be confusing. Acrobat has a Reader program that can be downloaded for free from the Internet. However, to create PDF files, you need either the Standard or Professional version of Adobe Acrobat.

Adobe Acrobat is an output program; it is essentially a glorified digital printer. As a matter of fact, when Acrobat is downloaded, it adds an option to your list of available printers; images may now be sent to the PDF printer. This can be useful for saving images from web pages (receipts, travel information, etc.). Also, even though Acrobat is essentially a print utility, you can "print" a copy of something as a PDF without actually creating a hard copy; instead, you can just save a copy of a document as a PDF.

DOCUMENT ASSEMBLY PROGRAMS

Document assembly software creates powerful standardized templates and forms. Users create forms and templates and then respond to a series of questions and prompts. The document assembly program then merges the selected template or form with the answers and builds a completed document. Document assembly programs work best, and are most useful, when the user has well-structured templates and forms that must be completed often and in a routine manner.

Word processors have some document assembly functions, but stand-alone document assembly programs are much more powerful. Text templates are based on text documents (e.g., a simple will or articles of incorporation) and are initially created with the user's word-processing program. Form templates create forms (e.g., an IRS tax form or credit application). At most law firms, text templates are much more common than form templates.

Suppose that a law firm routinely drafts employment contracts for a large client. Instead of using a word processor to slowly edit the document for every new employee the client hires, the law firm would like to use a document assembly program to automate the process.

Exhibit 2–11 shows a template for an employment agreement, which was built in a document assembly program. The document assembly program is running inside of the user's word processor; notice the special document assembly toolbar in Exhibit 2–11. Notice also that a number of variables are listed in Exhibit 2–11, including <Employee Name>, <Agreement Date>, <Job Title>, and others.

A *variable* is something that will change in the document. Notice that the variable <Employee Name> in Exhibit 2–11 is included more than once in the document. The beauty of a document assembly program is that once the text for the variable <Employee Name> has been entered (e.g., "Cynthia Jones"), the computer automatically

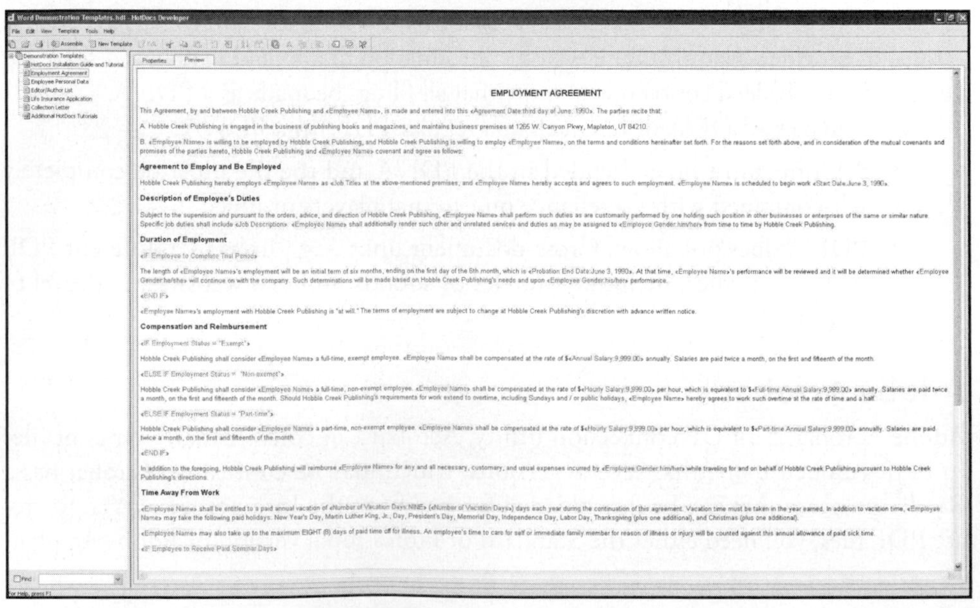

EMPLOYMENT AGREEMENT

This Agreement, by and between Hobble Creek Publishing and «Employee Name», is made and entered into this «Agreement Date:third day of June, 1990». The parties recite that:

A. Hobble Creek Publishing is engaged in the business of publishing books and magazines, and maintains business premises at 1265 W. Canyon Pkwy, Mapleton, UT 84210.

B. «Employee Name» is willing to be employed by Hobble Creek Publishing, and Hobble Creek Publishing is willing to employ «Employee Name», on the terms and conditions hereinafter set forth. For the reasons set forth above, and in consideration of the mutual covenants and promises of the parties hereto, Hobble Creek Publishing and «Employee Name» covenant and agree as follows:

Agreement to Employ and Be Employed

Hobble Creek Publishing hereby employs «Employee Name» as «Job Title» at the above-mentioned premises, and «Employee Name» hereby accepts and agrees to such employment. «Employee Name» is scheduled to begin work «Start Date:June 3, 1990».

Description of Employee's Duties

Subject to the supervision and pursuant to the orders, advice, and direction of Hobble Creek Publishing, «Employee Name» shall perform such duties as are customarily performed by one holding such position in other businesses or enterprises of the same or similar nature. Specific job duties shall include «Job Description». «Employee Name» shall additionally render such other and unrelated services and duties as may be assigned to «Employee Gender:him/her» from time to time by Hobble Creek Publishing.

Duration of Employment

«IF Employee to Complete Trial Period»

The length of «Employee Name»'s employment will be an initial term of six months, ending on the first day of the 6th month, which is «Probation End Date:June 3, 1990». At that time, «Employee Name»'s performance will be reviewed and it will be determined whether «Employee Gender:he/she» will continue on with the company. Such determinations will be made based on Hobble Creek Publishing's needs and upon «Employee Gender:his/her» performance.

«END IF»

«Employee Name»'s employment with Hobble Creek Publishing is "at will." The terms of employment are subject to change at Hobble Creek Publishing's discretion with advance written notice.

Compensation and Reimbursement

«IF Employment Status = "Exempt"»

Hobble Creek Publishing shall consider «Employee Name» a full-time, exempt employee. «Employee Name» shall be compensated at the rate of $«Annual Salary:9,999.00» annually. Salaries are paid twice a month, on the first and fifteenth of the month.

«ELSE IF Employment Status = "Non-exempt"»

Hobble Creek Publishing shall consider «Employee Name» a full-time, non-exempt employee. «Employee Name» shall be compensated at the rate of $«Hourly Salary:9,999.00» per hour, which is equivalent to $«Full-time Annual Salary:9,999.00» annually. Salaries are paid twice a month, on the first and fifteenth of the month. Should Hobble Creek Publishing's requirements for work extend to overtime, including Sundays and / or public holidays, «Employee Name» hereby agrees to work such overtime at the rate of time and a half.

«ELSE IF Employment Status = "Part-time"»

Hobble Creek Publishing shall consider «Employee Name» a part-time, non-exempt employee. «Employee Name» shall be compensated at the rate of $«Hourly Salary:9,999.00» per hour, which is equivalent to $«Part-time Annual Salary:9,999.00» annually. Salaries are paid twice a month, on the first and fifteenth of the month.

«END IF»

In addition to the foregoing, Hobble Creek Publishing will reimburse «Employee Name» for any and all necessary, customary, and usual expenses incurred by «Employee Gender:him/her» while traveling for and on behalf of Hobble Creek Publishing pursuant to Hobble Creek Publishing's directions.

Time Away From Work

«Employee Name» shall be entitled to a paid annual vacation of «Number of Vacation Days:NINE» («Number of Vacation Days») days each year during the continuation of this agreement. Vacation time must be taken in the year earned. In addition to vacation time, «Employee Name» may take the following paid holidays: New Year's Day, Martin Luther King, Jr., Day, President's Day, Memorial Day, Independence Day, Labor Day, Thanksgiving (plus one additional), and Christmas (plus one additional).

«Employee Name» may also take up to the maximum EIGHT (8) days of paid time off for illness. An employee's time to care for self or immediate family member for reason of illness or injury will be counted against this annual allowance of paid sick time.

«IF Employee to Receive Paid Seminar Days»

EXHIBIT 2–11
Document assembly program: Employment agreement—Completed template

fills it in anywhere the variable <Employee Name> appears. This software also allows the form to correctly enter "he" or "she" depending on the gender of the employee.

Once a template has been built, the user executes the template in the document assembly program (creates a custom document from a generic form). The document assembly program takes the answers the user gives and opens a new word-processing document. The next step is for the user to answer the questions the template asks. When all of the questions have been answered, the finished template document is displayed in the user's word-processing program so that the finished document can be edited as needed.

Document assembly programs are extremely powerful and have many advanced features that make them great time-savers in many legal organizations. You will have the opportunity to assemble a text template and create a new text template in the HotDocs Hands-On Exercises at the end of this chapter (HotDocs 11).

ETHICAL CONSIDERATIONS

Although word processing has done wonders for the legal profession in terms of efficiency and ease of use, it has a downside that raises important ethical issues. Word processors can make users lazy. For instance, users may misspell words because they assume that the spell checker will catch any errors. Users can use poor grammar because the grammar checker will fix it. Users do not have to start from scratch to prepare a will or other legal documents because form wills, templates, and other documents that can easily be modified are available on the computer or on the Internet. Users do not have to go back and do legal research over and over again every time a new legal document is filed, because they can copy legal research from one client's documents to another's.

Finally, even if a document's content is poor, users can make it look pretty with fancy fonts, justified margins, tables, and many other features. And that is the problem: potential lack of content. An attorney has an ethical duty to provide competent representation. Lawyers and paralegals must make sure that their word-processing documents are competently and thoroughly prepared. That is, they should not only look good, but also be proofread well, contain up-to-date and accurate cites, and be the best documents the attorney or paralegal can produce.

The following are a few common ethical issues related to the use of word processors.

Leaving Metadata in Documents

As you may recall from Chapter 1, *metadata* is electronically stored information that may identify the origin, date, author, usage, comments, or other information about a file. It is important that a legal organization delete or remove the metadata from any document before that document leaves the firm.

In Word 2007, a user can inspect all parts of a document for metadata. If metadata is discovered in the document, the user can choose to remove it. In addition, Adobe Acrobat now has strong security enhancements that can remove metadata from PDF files and permanently delete the redacted information.

It should be noted that while legal organizations do not want documents going out of the office with metadata still present in them, some courts have held that in the context of discovery (production of documents during the discovery stage of a lawsuit), opposing parties are entitled to metadata. Note here the major difference between documents prepared by attorneys for their clients (e.g., word-processing documents), where security is of the utmost importance, and discovery documents produced by clients for the opposing parties in a case. In the latter, some courts have said that the parties have the right to see the metadata, including the origin of documents and other information. This is another reason to make sure, as an important matter of practice, that a word-processing document has no metadata attached to it before it leaves the legal organization.

Old Client Data Left in New Document

It is common, when preparing a new document, to retrieve an old document and use it as the basis of the new one. For instance, when preparing a new real estate contract, the user might pull up an old real estate contract from a few months ago as a place to start. The trouble is that it is easy to leave the old data (i.e., old property description, old client names, old prices, wrong pronouns) in the new document. This problem is a strong argument for both excellent proofreading and the creation and use of fill-in templates or forms.

Typographical Errors That Spell Checkers Will Not Catch

Some typographical errors will not be caught by a spell checker; they can be picked up only by careful proofreading of the document. Common errors of this sort include insertion or retention of the wrong case facts, and misuse of a correctly spelled word. For example, a complaint should demand a jury *trial*, not a jury *trail*. In one well-publicized case, a paralegal mistakenly left out the last three zeros on a mortgage used to secure a $92,885,000 loan to a company that eventually went into bankruptcy. Because of the mistake, the company the paralegal worked for had only a $92,885 lien. Going by the provisions of the mortgage, that left $92,792,115 unsecured.

It is absolutely critical that all documents be carefully proofread even if the user is using a word processor, and a spell checker, and a grammar checker. Some mistakes can be caught only by the user. Supervising attorneys cannot afford to become careless about these matters, no matter how good or trustworthy the paralegal is.

Improper Form Selected; Leaving in or Deleting Wrong Paragraphs

It is very easy to select the wrong form when creating new documents. Unfortunately, this can have a devastating impact. Another very common error is to either leave in inappropriate material or delete a wrong paragraph from the form. If you are using a form, it is important to know and understand every paragraph in the form so you can make appropriate decisions about what stays and what goes.

Not Following Court Rules

Many courts have document preparation rules, especially regarding the kind of font or typeface to be used, the font size, margin widths, and paper sizes. It is important that these rules be followed exactly. In one case, a corporate legal department repeatedly filed appellate briefs using a 10-point Times New Roman font instead of the 12-point Courier required by court rules. The law department did this because another court rule limited briefs to 30 pages, and they could get in 50 percent more verbiage using the smaller font. The court finally dismissed the appeal because the law office did not follow the court's rules.

Preparing Legal Documents without the Supervision of an Attorney (Unauthorized Practice of Law)

Most states have a criminal statute that prohibits a layperson from practicing law. In addition to criminal laws, there are also ethical prohibitions that proscribe a nonlawyer from practicing law. Simply put, paralegals cannot draft legal documents, such as wills, briefs, motions, pleadings, or contracts, without the supervision of an attorney. Paralegals routinely draft these types of documents; the distinction is that they do so properly, under the direction and supervision of a member of the bar. The attorney is ultimately responsible for the legal documents.

What happens if an attorney does not look at a document a paralegal has prepared using a word processor or document assembly program? Assume that the paralegal has been working hard on a motion and has taken cases and arguments from past documents prepared by the supervising attorney, but the document is due by 5:00 p.m. and there is no time for the attorney to review it. This is how unauthorized practice of law issues regarding word processing and drafting documents arise in real life.

The reason for the rule is that legal documents affect the legal rights of clients and parties and therefore require the attention of an attorney. As long as a paralegal is actively working under the supervision of an attorney, and the attorney maintains a relationship with the client, the paralegal may interview witnesses or prospective clients, perform legal research, draft pleadings and briefs, and investigate the facts of cases without being accused of the unauthorized practice of law. However, the moment the paralegal prepares a legal document on her own, without the review of an attorney, a breach of the rule has most likely occurred.

No matter how routine the legal document is, always have an attorney review it. Never let an attorney approve your work without reading it. If the attorney says, "I don't have time to review it; I'll sign it and you just send it out, I trust you," bring the document back at another time or find a tactful way to suggest to the attorney that the document must be approved in the correct way.

Overlooking Prudent Practices

Competent representation of a client requires more than just competence regarding knowledge of the law and the quality of the legal services provided. It requires competence in all aspects of the law office, including the following areas.

Use Full-Function Spell and Grammar Checkers Certainly, you should not rely on the spell checker/grammar checker to do your only review of documents. However, you should by all means use these functions on every document you prepare. There is nothing more embarrassing than finding obvious typographical or grammatical errors in a document that has gone out—particularly when it has been sent out under the signature of your supervising attorney. Never assume that the automatic spell/grammar checking that occurs as you type your document (where problems are flagged by being underlined with colored squiggly lines) is enough. *It is not.* It is extremely easy to fail to see these errors when drafting. Always go back and run the full-function spell/grammar checker to make sure you have not missed any obvious mistakes.

Always Validate Cases/Citations and Factual References Before a paralegal cites a case or references a fact in a legal document that he is unsure about, it is imperative that he double-check and validate the case or fact to make sure it is still good law or that the "fact" actually happened. Never throw something into a word processor with the thought that you will get back to it and verify it—what happens if you forget? The answer is that the client can be harmed, the attorney's reputation can be harmed, your reputation certainly will be harmed, and serious ethical ramifications could arise for your supervising attorney or the law office. Do not take the chance; always double-check your work.

Password-Protect Confidential Word-Processing Documents That Will Be Emailed It is always a good idea, out of an abundance of caution, to password-protect confidential documents that will be emailed through an Internet provider or sent over large networks. Most word-processing programs have the capability to do this; for example, Microsoft Word can password-protect word-processing files. It is very easy to do and does not cost anything. It is just one more layer of protection to maintain the confidentiality of client or case-related data.

SUMMARY

Word processors are computer programs that are used to edit, manipulate, and revise text to create documents. A law office with a centralized word-processing system has a separate word-processing department that inputs all documents for an organization, as opposed to a decentralized word-processing system in which individuals perform word processing for themselves or a small group. The primary word-processing program in law offices is Microsoft Word, though some still use Corel WordPerfect.

Modern legal organizations use a variety of word-processing functions and features, including, among others, automatic paragraph numbering, styles, footnotes and endnotes, tables, macros, comments, multiple-document comparisons, track changes, creation of tables of authorities, and document merging.

Document assembly software creates powerful templates for form documents. Once the user answers the questions in the template, the answers are then merged with the template and a new, final document is output. Document assembly software is extremely sophisticated and serves many functions in legal organizations.

When preparing legal documents, it is important for users to carefully review their work to ensure that old information is not left in documents, metadata is deleted, research is updated and current, and there are no typographical errors.

KEY TERMS

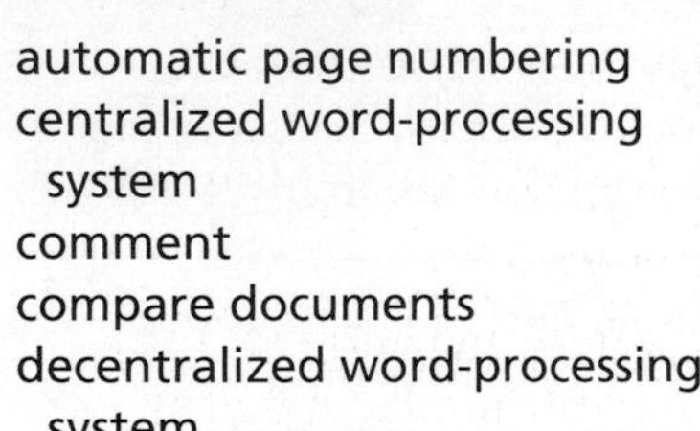

automatic page numbering
centralized word-processing system
comment
compare documents
decentralized word-processing system
document assembly software
double indenting
endnote
footer
header
macro
merging
Portable Document Format (PDF)
primary file
secondary file
style
table of authorities
track changes
word-processing software

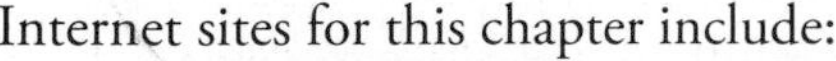

INTERNET SITES

Internet sites for this chapter include:

ORGANIZATION	PRODUCT/SERVICE	INTERNET ADDRESS
HotDocs	HotDocs document assembly program	www.hotdocs.com
Corel Corporation	WordPerfect	www.corel.com
Findlaw.com	Online legal forms	www.findlaw.com
Microsoft	Microsoft Word	www.microsoft.com/word
ProDoc	ProDoc document assembly program	www.prodoc.com
Adobe Systems, Inc.	Adobe Acrobat PDF file creation	www.adobe.com
Nitro PDF, Inc.	Free PDF creator software	www.primopdf.com

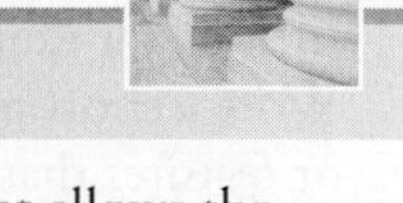

TEST YOUR KNOWLEDGE

1. What does "PDF" stand for?
2. Compare and contrast centralized and decentralized word processing.
3. True or False: The automatic paragraph numbering feature numbers the pages in a document.
4. True or False: A style is a named set of formatting characteristics that users apply to text.
5. Text that is indented an equal distance from the left and right margin is called __________.
6. True or False: A word-processing feature that combines a primary and secondary file is called a macro.
7. A word-processing feature that allows the reviewer to make annotations in the document without actually changing the document is called a __________.
8. Distinguish between primary and secondary merge files.
9. What standard document type do most courts use to allow attorneys to file documents electronically?
10. True or False: Word-processing merge files have exactly the same features as stand-alone document assembly programs.

ON THE WEB EXERCISES

1. Using the "Internet Sites" listed in this chapter and a general Internet search engine (such as www.google.com or www.yahoo.com), research the current versions of Microsoft Word. Prepare a summary of the differences, similarities, and reviews of the products. Which product would you rather use in the legal environment and why?
2. Using the "Internet Sites" listed in this chapter and a general Internet search engine (such as www.google.com or www.yahoo.com), research the Case Management and Electronic Filing System for the U.S. federal courts. Write a two-page summary of your findings, including how it works, what the standard is, and other relevant information about the system.
3. Using the "Internet Sites" listed in this chapter and a general Internet search engine (such as www.google.com or www.yahoo.com), find a word-processing template for a simple last will and testament for your state. How hard or easy was it to find? Were you able to find fee-based forms, free forms, or both?
4. Using http://forms.lp.findlaw.com, find a recent United States Supreme Court opinion under "Cases and Codes." Copy and paste the opinion into your word processor. How easy was this to do? Can you manipulate and edit the document? Describe why using the Internet and your word processor in this way might be an important feature for a legal organization.
5. Using the "Internet Sites" listed in this chapter and a general Internet search engine (such as www.google.com or www.yahoo.com), research document assembly programs. What programs did you find? What features do they have? What are their advantages? How are they different from the merge capabilities in word processors? Do they have any disadvantages?
6. Using the "Internet Sites" listed in this chapter and a general Internet search engine (such as www.google.com or www.yahoo.com), research what a PDF file is and what advantages PDFs have over other file formats.

QUESTIONS AND EXERCISES

1. Contact a law office, legal organization, paralegal, or attorney you know and ask what word processor they use and why. Ask what features they like about it, what features they wish they had, whether the program is fulfilling their basic needs, and whether they are looking to change word processors. Also, ask who does word processing at the firm, and if there is a centralized or decentralized system. Type a one-page summary of your conversations.

2. Word processors have developed over time to include hundreds of features and functions. Write a short paper on the top 10 functions or features that you use when you do word processing. Explain what each function is and why you use it.
3. On your own computer, open any word-processing document in your word processor. Point and click File and then on Properties. What metadata was included in the "Properties" section of the document?
4. In Microsoft Word, open a new document and do the following:
   - **a.** Type the following phrases: This is secret text no one should see. This is text that is open to the public.
   - **b.** Turn on Track Changes by going to "Tools" on the menu bar and then clicking on "Track Changes."
   - **c.** Now, using the delete key, delete the sentence "This is secret text no one should see." Notice that to the right it now shows the text is deleted.
   - **d.** Point and click with your mouse on the down arrow next to "Final Showing Markup" in the "Tracking" item on the Review toolbar. Then click "Final." Notice that you cannot see "This is secret text no one should see." Assume for the purposes of this exercise that you sent this document to the opposing party in a case.
   - **e.** Now, assume that you are the opposing party in the case. Select the down arrow next to "Final" in the "Tracking" item on the Review toolbar and select "Original." Notice that you can perfectly see "This is secret text no one should see." Point and click with your mouse on the down arrow next to "Original" in the "Final Showing Markup" item on the Review toolbar and select "Original Showing Markup." You can now see all of the changes in the document.

   What confidentiality issues might arise with use of the Track Changes feature? Suggest some ways to avoid these problems.

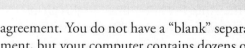

ETHICS QUESTION

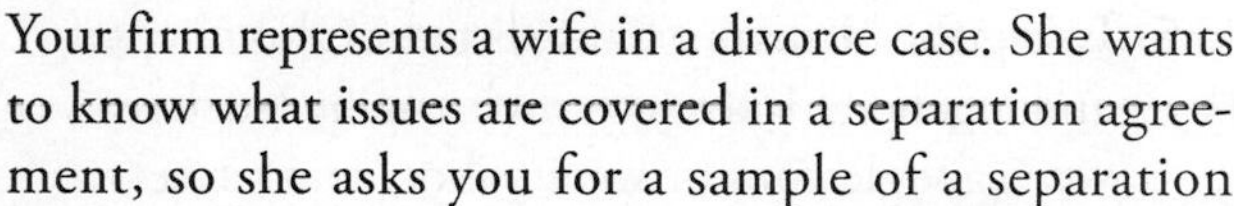

Your firm represents a wife in a divorce case. She wants to know what issues are covered in a separation agreement, so she asks you for a sample of a separation agreement. You do not have a "blank" separation agreement, but your computer contains dozens of examples. What ethical issues are raised by this scenario?

FEATURED SOFTWARE
Microsoft Word 2013
Microsoft Word 2010
Microsoft Word 2007
HotDocs

WORD PROCESSING HANDS-ON EXERCISES

READ THIS FIRST!

1. Microsoft Word 2013
2. Microsoft Word 2010
3. Microsoft Word 2007

I. DETERMINING WHICH TUTORIAL TO COMPLETE

To use the Word Processing Hands-On Exercises, you must already own or have access to Microsoft Word 2013, Microsoft Word 2010, or Microsoft Word 2007. If you have one of the programs but do not know the version you are using, it is easy to find out (e.g., whether your version is Word 2013, Word 2010, Word 2007, or some other version of Word). For Word 2007, click the Office button, and then click "Word Options," and look under the title "Resources." For Word 2010, click the File tab, then click "Help." For Word 2013, click the File tab, then click "Account." You must know the version of the program you are using and select the correct tutorial version or the tutorials will not work correctly. For example, if you have Word 2010 but try to use the Word 2007 tutorial, the tutorial will not work correctly.

II. USING THE WORD PROCESSING HANDS-ON EXERCISES

The Word Processing Hands-On Exercises in this section are easy to use and contain step-by-step instructions. They start with basic word-processing skills and proceed to intermediate and advanced levels. If you already have a good working knowledge of your word processor, you may be able to proceed directly to the intermediate and advanced exercises. To truly be ready for word processing in a legal environment, you must be able to accomplish the tasks and exercises in the advanced exercises.

III. ACCESSING THE HANDS-ON EXERCISE FILES

Some of the intermediate and advanced Word Processing Hands-On Exercises use documents on the Premium Website.

To access these files, go to your CengageBrain account and click the link for Premium Website for Cornick's *Using Computers in the Law Office, 7th Edition.* A new window will open. Under Book Level Resources, click the Data Files: Word Processing tab, then click the link to the desired lesson. When prompted, click "Open."

IV. INSTALLATION QUESTIONS

If you have installation questions regarding loading the word-processing file from the Premium Website, you may contact Technical Support at http://cengage.com/support.

HANDS-ON EXERCISES

MICROSOFT WORD 2013 FOR WINDOWS

Number	Lesson Title	Concepts Covered
BASIC LESSONS		
Lesson 1	Typing a Letter	Using word wrap, Tab key, cursor keys, underline, bold, italics; saving and printing a document
Lesson 2	Editing a Letter	Retrieving a file, block moving/deleting, and spell/grammar checking
Lesson 3	Typing a Pleading	Centering, changing margins, changing line spacing, adding a footnote, double indenting, and automatic page numbering
Lesson 4	Creating a Table	Creating a table, entering data in a table, using automatic numbering, adjusting columns in a table, and using the Table AutoFormat command
INTERMEDIATE LESSONS		
Lesson 5	Tools and Techniques	Editing an employment policy using the Format Painter tool, revealing document formatting, using the Beginning of Document command, clearing formatting, changing case, using Search and Replace, using the Go To command, creating a section break, and changing the orientation of the page to Landscape
Lesson 6	Using Styles	Using, modifying, and creating styles to maintain consistent and uniform formatting of documents
Lesson 7	Creating a Template (office letterhead/letter)	Finding ready-made templates in Word, creating a new office letterhead and letter template, filling in/completing a template, and adding a command to the Quick Access toolbar
Lesson 8	Comparing Documents (multiple versions of an employment contract)	Comparing documents using the simultaneous viewing method and merging the documents into a separate annotated blacklined document
Lesson 9	Using Track Changes	Turning on Track Changes, making revisions, and accepting and rejecting revisions
ADVANCED LESSONS		
Lesson 10	Creating a Mail Merge Document	Creating and entering a list of recipients for a mail merge, creating a mail merge document, and merging the list with the document
Lesson 11	Creating a Table of Authorities	Finding and marking cases in a brief and generating an actual table of authorities for the brief
Lesson 12	Creating a Macro (pleading signature block)	Creating and executing a pleading signature block macro
Lesson 13	Drafting a Will	Using Word to draft a will

GETTING STARTED

Introduction

Throughout these lessons and exercises, information you need to type into the program will be designated in several different ways:

- Keys to be pressed on the keyboard are designated in brackets, in all caps, and in bold (e.g., press the **[ENTER]** key).

- Movements with the mouse pointer are designated in bold and italics (e.g., ***point to File and click***).
- Words or letters that should be typed are designated in bold (e.g., type **Training Program**).
- Information that is or should be displayed on your computer screen is shown in bold, with quotation marks (e.g., "**Press ENTER to continue.**").
- Specific menu items and commands are designated with an initial capital letter (e.g., click Open).

OVERVIEW OF MICROSOFT WORD 2013

Here are some tips on using Microsoft Word 2013 that will help you complete these exercises:

I. General Rules for Microsoft Word 2013

A. *Word Wrap.* You do not need to press the **[ENTER]** key after each line of text as you would with a typewriter.

B. *Double-Spacing.* If you want to double-space, do not hit the **[ENTER]** key twice. Instead, change the line spacing by ***clicking on the HOME ribbon tab, then clicking on the Line and Paragraph Spacing icon in the Paragraph group and selecting 2.0*** (see Word 2013 Exhibit 1).

C. *Moving through Already Entered Text.* If you want to move the mouse pointer to various positions within already entered text, ***use the cursor (arrow) keys or point and click.***

D. *Moving the Pointer Where No Text Has Been Entered.* You cannot use the cursor keys to move the pointer where no text has been entered. Said another way, you cannot move any further in a document than where you have typed text or pressed the **[ENTER]** key. You must use the **[ENTER]** key or first type text.

E. *Saving a Document.* To save a document, ***click the File tab in the upper left corner of the screen and then click Save*** (see Word 2013 Exhibit 1A–Backstage).

F. *New Document.* To get a new, clean document, ***click the File tab, then click New, and then click Blank document*** (see Word 2013 Exhibit 1A–Backstage).

G. *Help.* To get help, press **[F1]** or ***click the ? icon in the upper right corner of the screen*** (see Word 2013 Exhibit 1).

II. Editing a Document

A. *Pointer Movement*

One space to left	**[LEFT ARROW]**
One space to right	**[RIGHT ARROW]**
Beginning of line	**[HOME]**
End of line	**[END]**
One line up	**[UP ARROW]**
One line down	**[DOWN ARROW]**
One screen up	**[PAGE UP]**
One screen down	**[PAGE DOWN]**
Beginning of document	**[CTRL]+[HOME]**
End of document	**[CTRL]+[END]**

WORD 2013 EXHIBIT 1
Word 2013 screen

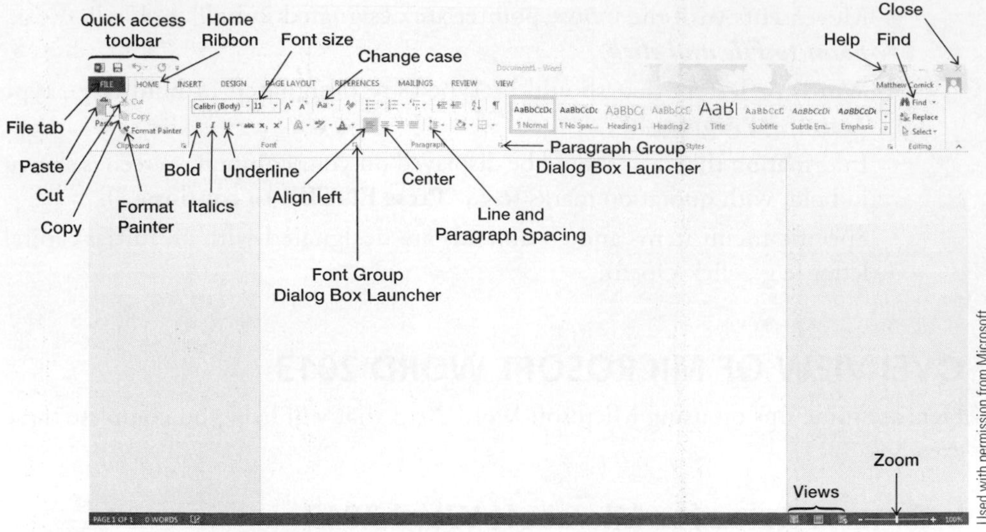

WORD 2013 EXHIBIT 1A
Microsoft office Backstage

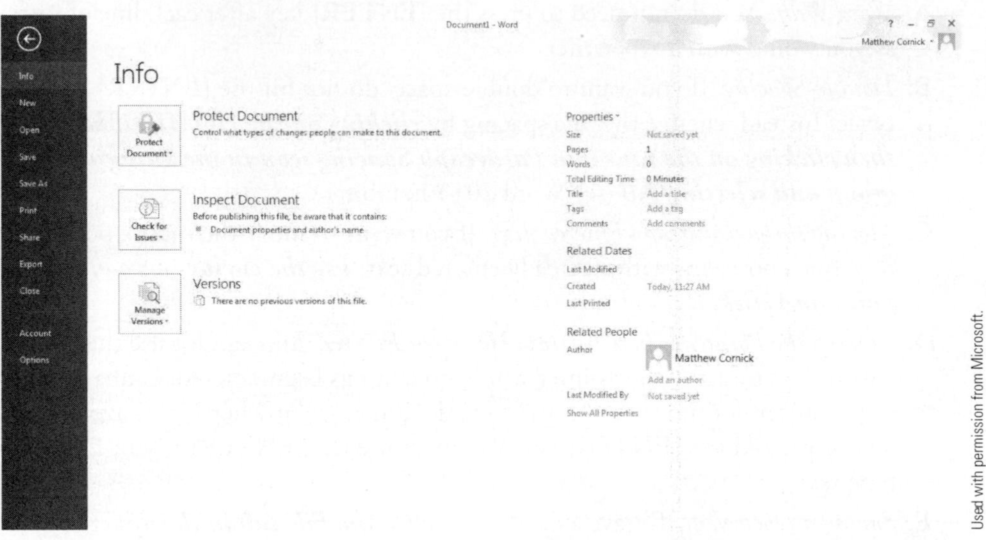

B. *Deleting Text*

Delete the text under the pointer or to the right	**[DEL]**
Delete the text to the left of the pointer	**[BACKSPACE]**
Delete the whole word to the left of the pointer	**[CTRL]+[BACKSPACE]**
Delete the whole word to the right of the pointer	**[CTRL]+[DEL]**

C. *Delete Blocked Text.* ***Drag the mouse pointer to select or highlight text,*** and press **[DEL]** or ***from the HOME ribbon tab, select the Cut icon from the Clipboard group*** (see Word 2013 Exhibit 1). Another way to select or highlight text is ***to press the [SHIFT] key and keep it depressed while you use the cursor keys to mark/highlight the desired text.***

D. *Undoing/Undeleting Text.* If you delete text and immediately want it back, ***click the Undo icon on the Quick Access toolbar.*** This can also be done by pressing **[CTRL]+[Z]**. Press **[CTRL]+[Z]** or ***click the Undo icon*** until your desired text reappears. The Undo feature works on many other activities in Word, but not all. So, if something goes wrong, at least try pressing **[CTRL]+[Z]** to undo whatever you did.

E. *Moving Text.* ***Drag the mouse pointer to highlight or select the text. Then, from the HOME ribbon tab, select the Cut icon from the Clipboard group***

(see Word 2013 Exhibit 1), ***move the mouse pointer to where the text should be moved, and from the HOME ribbon tab, select Paste from the Clipboard group.*** Another way to do this is to ***drag the mouse pointer to highlight the area and then right-click.*** This brings up a menu that includes the Cut, Copy, and Paste commands. Yet another way to do this is to use the drag-and-drop method: ***Drag the mouse pointer to highlight the area, release the mouse button, click the highlighted area, drag the text to the new location, and release the mouse button.***

F. *Copying Text.* ***Drag the mouse pointer to highlight or select the area. From the HOME ribbon tab, click the Copy icon from the Clipboard group*** (see Word 2013 Exhibit 1). ***Then, move the mouse pointer to where the text should be copied, and from the HOME ribbon tab, click Paste.*** Another way to do this is to use the drag-and-drop method: ***Drag the pointer to highlight the area, release the mouse button, click the highlighted area, drag the text to the new location while pressing [CTRL], and release the mouse button.*** The text is then copied to the new location.

III. Formatting

A. *Centering Text.* ***Move the pointer to the line with the text that should be centered. From the HOME ribbon tab, click the Paragraph Group Dialog Box Launcher*** (see Word 2013 Exhibit 1). ***In the Indents and Spacing tab, click the down arrow key next to Alignment and select Centered, then click OK and begin typing.*** If the text has already been typed, move the pointer to the paragraph where the text is and then issue the command. Alternatively, ***from the HOME ribbon tab, click the Center icon in the Paragraph group*** (see Word 2013 Exhibit 1).

B. *Bold Type.* To type in bold, ***from the HOME ribbon tab, click the Font Group Dialog Box Launcher*** (see Word 2013 Exhibit 1), ***and then, in the Font tab, click Bold under Font Style. Then, click OK.*** Alternatively, ***from the HOME ribbon tab, click the Bold icon in the Font group.*** Another way is to press **[CTRL]+[B].**

C. *Underlining.* To underline, ***from the HOME ribbon tab, click the Font Group Dialog Box Launcher*** (see Word 2013 Exhibit 1). ***Then, in the Font tab, click the down arrow under Underline style, select the underline style you would like, and then click OK.*** Alternatively, ***from the HOME ribbon tab, click the Underline icon in the Font group.*** Another way is to press **[CTRL]+[U].**

D. *Margins.* Margins can be set by ***clicking the PAGE LAYOUT ribbon tab and then clicking on Margins from the Page Setup group.***

E. *Line Spacing.* Line spacing can be changed by ***clicking the HOME ribbon tab and then clicking the Line and Paragraph Spacing icon in the Paragraph group*** (see Word 2013 Exhibit 1).

F. *Justification.* Move the pointer to the line where the text should be justified. Then, ***from the HOME ribbon tab, click the Paragraph Group Dialog Box Launcher*** (see Word 2013 Exhibit 1). ***In the Indents and Spacing tab, click the down arrow key next to Alignment and select Justified; then click OK and begin typing.*** If the text has already been typed, move the cursor to the paragraph where the text is and then issue the command. Alternatively, ***from the HOME ribbon tab, click the Justify icon in the Paragraph group*** (see Word 2013 Exhibit 1).

G. *Header/Footer.* ***From the INSERT ribbon tab, click Header or Footer from the Header & Footer group.***

H. *Hard Page Break.* To force the addition of a new page in the current document by using the Hard Page Break command, press **[CTRL]+[ENTER]** or ***from the INSERT ribbon tab, click Blank Page from the Pages group.*** Page breaks also occur automatically when the current page is full of text.

I. *Indent.* ***From the HOME ribbon tab, click the Paragraph Group Dialog Box Launcher*** (see Word 2013 Exhibit 1). ***In the Indents and Spacing tab under Indentation, click the up arrow next to Left or Right to set the indentation amount; then click OK and begin typing.*** Alternatively, ***from the HOME ribbon tab, point to the Decrease Indent or Increase Indent icon in the Paragraph group.***

IV. Other Functions

A. *Printing.* To print, ***click the File tab and then click Print*** (see Word 2013 Exhibit 1A–Backstage).

B. *Spell Check.* To turn on the spell-checking function, ***from the REVIEW ribbon tab, click Spelling & Grammar in the Proofing group.*** Additionally, a red squiggly line will appear under each word that is not recognized. If you ***right-click the word,*** the program will suggest possible spellings.

C. *Open Files.* To open a file, ***click the File tab then click Open*** (see Word 2013 Exhibit 1A–Backstage).

D. *Tables.* ***From the INSERT ribbon tab, click Table from the Tables group.*** You can move between cells in the table by pressing the **[TAB]** and the **[SHIFT]+[TAB]** keys.

MICROSOFT OFFICE BACKSTAGE

As you can see from the above, several key functions now are accessible through what Microsoft refers to as "Backstage." When you click the File tab, the default screen is the "Info" screen. See Exhibit 1A–Backstage. On the right side of the screen, you can see some of the metadata associated with the file (e.g., Properties, Related Dates, Related People). You could also control who can (and cannot) see the document (Protect Document), inspect it for metadata (Inspect Document), and see other versions of the document (Versions). See Exhibit 1A–Backstage.

Backstage is where you can open a new (New) or existing file (Open), save a file (Save) and (Save As), print a file (Print), share a file (Share), export a file to another application (Export), and close a file (Close). Backstage is also where you can access information about your account (Account) and customize your options for working with Word 2013 (Options). See Exhibit 1A–Backstage.

BASIC LESSONS

LESSON 1: TYPING A LETTER

This lesson shows you how to type the letter shown in Word 2013 Exhibit 2. It explains how to use the word wrap feature; the **[TAB]** key; the cursor (or arrow) keys; the underline, bold, and italics features; the save document function; and the print document function. Keep in mind that if at any time you make a mistake in this

WORD 2013 EXHIBIT 2
Letter

October 1, 2013

Steven Matthews
Matthews, Smith & Russell
P.O. Box 12341
Boston, MA 59920

Subject: Turner v. Smith
Case No. CV-13-0046

Dear Mr. Matthews:

In line with our recent conversation, the deposition of the defendant, Jonathan R. Smith, will be taken in your office on **November 15 at 9:00 a.m.** Please find enclosed a *"Notice of Deposition."*

I expect that I will be able to finish this deposition on November 15 and that discovery will be finished, in line with the Court's order, by December 15.

I will be finishing answers to your interrogatories this week and will have them to you by early next week.

If you have any questions, please feel free to contact me.

Kindest regards,

Mirabelle Watkinson
For the Firm

MW:db
Enclosures (as indicated)
cc

lesson, you may press **[CTRL]+[Z]** to undo what you have done. Also remember that any time you would like to see the name of an icon on the ribbon tabs, just ***point to the icon for a second or two*** and the name will be displayed.

1. Open Windows. When it has loaded, ***double-click the Microsoft Office Word 2013 icon on the desktop*** to open Word 2013 for Windows. Alternatively, ***click the Start button, point to Programs or All Programs, and then click the Microsoft Word 2013 icon*** (or ***point to Microsoft Office and then click Microsoft Office Word 2013***). You should now be in a clean, blank document. If you are not in a blank document, ***click the File tab, click New, and then click Blank document.***
2. At this point you cannot move the pointer around the screen by pushing the cursor keys (also called arrow keys). Text must first be entered before the pointer can be moved using the cursor keys. The pointer can only move through text. ***On the HOME ribbon tab, click the Paragraph Group Dialog Box Launcher. In the "Paragraph" window, click the down arrow below "Line spacing" and select "Single." Make sure the "Before" and "After" spacing are both 0 point. Then, click OK.***

3. Press the **[ENTER]** key four times. (Watch the status line in the lower left-hand corner of the screen, which tells you what page of your document you are on.)
4. Type the date of the letter as shown in Word 2013 Exhibit 2. Notice as you type the word "October" that Auto Text may anticipate that you are typing "October" and give you the following prompt: **"October (Press ENTER to Insert)."** You can either press the **[ENTER]** key and let Auto Text finish typing the word for you, or you can ignore it and continue typing the word yourself.
5. Press the **[ENTER]** key three times.
6. Type the inside address as shown in Word 2013 Exhibit 2. Press the **[ENTER]** key after each line of the inside address. When you finish the line with "Boston, MA 59920," press the **[ENTER]** key three times.
7. Press the **[TAB]** key one time. (Word automatically sets default tabs every five spaces.) The pointer will move five spaces to the right.
8. Type **Subject:** and then press the **[TAB]** key. ***On the HOME ribbon tab, click the Underline icon in the Font group*** (it looks like a "U"). Alternatively, you can press **[CTRL]+[U]** to turn the underline feature on and off, or ***point to the Font Group Dialog Box Launcher*** (see Word 2013 Exhibit 1) and select the Underline style. Then, type **Turner v. Smith**. ***On the HOME ribbon tab in the Font group, click the Underline icon*** to turn the underline feature off.
9. Press the **[ENTER]** key one time.
10. Press the **[TAB]** key three times and then type **Case No. CV-15-0046**.
11. Press the **[ENTER]** key three times.
12. Type the salutation **Dear Mr. Matthews:**
13. Press the **[ENTER]** key twice.
14. Type **In line with our recent conversation, the deposition of the defendant, Jonathan R. Smith, will be taken in your office on.** *Note:* You should not press the **[ENTER]** key at the end of the line. Word will automatically "wrap" the text down to the next line. Be sure to press the **[SPACEBAR]** once after the word "on."
15. ***Turn on the Bold feature by clicking the Bold icon*** (a capital "B") ***in the Font group in the HOME ribbon tab*** (see Word 2013 Exhibit 1). Alternatively, you can press **[CTRL]+[B]** to turn bold on and off. Type **November 15 at 9:00 a.m.** Turn off the Bold feature either by pressing **[CTRL]+[B]**, or by ***clicking the Bold icon in the Font group in the HOME ribbon tab.*** Press the **[SPACEBAR]** twice.
16. Type **Please find enclosed a** and then press **[SPACEBAR]**.
17. ***Turn on the Italics feature by clicking the Italics icon*** (it looks like an "I") ***in the Font group in the HOME ribbon tab*** (see Word 2013 Exhibit 1). Alternatively, you can press **[CTRL]+[I]** to turn italics on and off. Type **Notice to Take Deposition.** Turn off the Italics feature either by pressing **[CTRL]+[I]** or by ***clicking the Italics icon in the Font group in the HOME ribbon tab.***
18. Press the **[ENTER]** key twice.
19. Type the second paragraph of the letter and then press the **[ENTER]** key twice.
20. Type the third paragraph of the letter and then press the **[ENTER]** key twice.
21. Type the fourth paragraph of the letter and then press the **[ENTER]** key twice.
22. Type **Kindest regards,** and then press the **[ENTER]** key four times.
23. Type **Mirabelle Watkinson** and then press the **[ENTER]** key.
24. Type **For the Firm** and then press the **[ENTER]** key twice.

25. Finish the letter by typing the author's initials, enclosures, and copy abbreviation (cc) as shown in Word 2013 Exhibit 2.
26. To print the document, ***click the File tab, click Print, and then click Print.***
27. To save the document, ***click the File tab and then click Save.*** The default location for saved Word 2013 files is OneDrive, Microsoft's cloud storage facility. You also have the option of saving files to your computer. If you downloaded Microsoft Office 2013, you should have created a OneDrive account. If you have not, follow the on-screen directions for doing so. For this lesson, you will save the file to your OneDrive. Then, type **Letter1** next to **"File name."** ***Click Save*** to save the letter to OneDrive. (*Note:* In Lesson 2, you will edit this letter, so it is important that you save it.)
28. ***Click the File tab and then click Close*** to close the document, or to exit Word 2013, ***click the small x in the upper right corner of the screen*** to exit the program.

This concludes Lesson 1.

LESSON 2: EDITING A LETTER

This lesson shows you how to retrieve and edit the letter you typed in Lesson 1. It explains how to retrieve a file, perform block moves and deletes, and spell-/grammar-check your document. Keep in mind that if at any time you make a mistake in this lesson, you may press **[CTRL]+[Z]** to undo what you have done. Also remember that any time you would like to see the name of an icon on the ribbon tab, just ***point to the icon for a second or two*** and the name will be displayed.

1. Open Windows. When it has loaded, ***double-click the Microsoft Office Word 2013 icon on the desktop*** to open Word 2013 for Windows. Alternatively, ***click the Start button, point to Programs or All Programs, and then click the Microsoft Word 2013 icon*** (or ***point to Microsoft Office and then click Microsoft Office Word 2013***), ***then click the [ESC] key.*** You should now be in a clean, blank document. If you are not in a blank document, ***click the File tab, click New, and then click Blank document.***
2. In this lesson, you will begin by retrieving the document you created in Lesson 1. To open the file, ***click the File tab, then click Open, then click your OneDrive account.*** Then type **Letter1** and ***click Open.*** Alternatively, ***scroll using the horizontal scroll bar until you find the file, click it, and then click Open.***
3. Notice in Word 2013 Exhibit 3 that some changes have been made to the letter. You will spend the rest of this lesson making these changes.
4. Use your cursor keys or mouse to go to the salutation line, "Dear Mr. Matthews:" With the pointer to the left of the first "M" in "Mr. Matthews," press the **[DEL]** key 12 times until "Mr. Matthews" is deleted.
5. Type **Steve**. The salutation line should now read "Dear Steve:"
6. Using your cursor keys or mouse, ***move the pointer to the left of the comma following the word "conversation" in the first paragraph.*** Press the **[SPACEBAR]**, then type **of September 30**. The sentence now reads:
   A. In line with our recent conversation of September 30, the deposition of the defendant . . .
7. The next change you will make is to move the second paragraph so that it becomes part of the first paragraph. Although this can be accomplished in more than one way, this lesson uses the Cut command.
8. Using your cursor keys or mouse, ***move the pointer to the beginning of the second paragraph of Word 2013 Exhibit 2.***

HANDS-ON EXERCISES

WORD 2013 EXHIBIT 3
Corrections to a letter

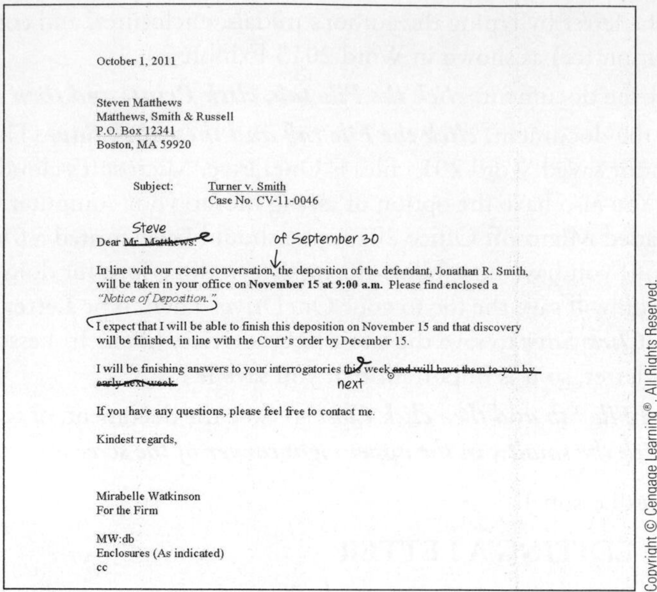

October 1, 2011

Steven Matthews
Matthews, Smith & Russell
P.O. Box 12341
Boston, MA 59920

Subject: Turner v. Smith
Case No. CV-11-0046

Dear ~~Mr. Matthews~~: Steve

In line with our recent conversation of September 30, the deposition of the defendant, Jonathan R. Smith, will be taken in your office on **November 15 at 9:00 a.m.** Please find enclosed a *"Notice of Deposition."*

I expect that I will be able to finish this deposition on November 15 and that discovery will be finished, in line with the Court's order by December 15.

I will be finishing answers to your interrogatories ~~this~~ next week ~~and will have them to you by early next week.~~

If you have any questions, please feel free to contact me.

Kindest regards,

Mirabelle Watkinson
For the Firm

MW:db
Enclosures (As indicated)
cc

9. ***Click and drag the mouse pointer*** (hold the left mouse button down, and move the mouse) ***until the entire second paragraph is highlighted, and then release the mouse button.***
10. ***From the HOME ribbon tab, click the Cut icon in the Clipboard group*** (see Word 2013 Exhibit 1). An alternative is to right-click anywhere in the highlighted area, and then ***click Cut.*** The text is no longer on the screen, but it is not deleted—it has been temporarily placed on the Office Clipboard.
11. Move the pointer to the end of the first paragraph. Press the **[SPACEBAR]** twice. If the pointer appears to be in italics mode, ***from the HOME ribbon tab, click the Italics icon in the Font group,*** or press **[CTLR]+[I]** to turn the Italics feature off.
12. ***From the HOME ribbon tab, click Paste from the Clipboard group*** (see Word 2013 Exhibit 1). Notice that the text has now been moved. Also, you may notice that a small icon in the shape of a clipboard has appeared where you pasted the text. ***Click the down arrow of the Paste Options icon.*** Notice that you are given the option to keep the source formatting or change the formatting so that the text matches the destination formatting (i.e., the formatting of the place you are copying it to). In this example, both formats are the same, so it does not matter, but if the text you are copying is a different format, you may or may not want to change it to the destination format. Press the **[ESC]** key to make the Paste Options menu disappear.
13. Move the pointer to the line below the newly expanded first paragraph, and use the **[DEL]** key to delete any unnecessary blank lines.
14. Using your cursor keys or mouse, ***move the pointer to what is now the second paragraph and place it to the left of the*** **"t"** ***in*** **"this week."**
15. Use the **[DEL]** key to delete the word **"this,"** and then type **next**.
16. We will now delete the rest of the sentence in the second paragraph. ***Drag the pointer until*** **"and will have them to you by early next week."** ***is highlighted.*** Press the **[DEL]** key. Type a period at the end of the sentence.
17. You have now made all of the changes that need to be made. To be sure the letter does not have misspelled words or grammar errors, we will use the Spelling and Grammar command.

18. ***Click the REVIEW ribbon tab and then click Spelling & Grammar in the Proofing group.***
19. If an error is found, it will be highlighted. You have the choice of ignoring it once, ignoring it completely, accepting one of the suggestions listed, or changing or correcting the problem yourself. Correct any spelling or grammar errors. When the spell and grammar check is done, ***click OK.***
20. To print the document, ***click the File tab, click Print, and then click Print.***
21. To save the document, ***click the File tab and then select Save As. Click your OneDrive account, then*** type **Letter2** in the "File name" box, ***and then click Save*** to save the document to OneDrive.
22. ***Click the File tab and then click Close*** to close the document, or ***click the small x in the upper right corner of the screen*** to exit the program.

This concludes Lesson 2.

HANDS-ON EXERCISES

LESSON 3: TYPING A PLEADING

This lesson shows you how to type a pleading, as shown in Word 2013 Exhibit 4. It expands on the items presented in Lessons 1 and 2. It also explains how to center text, change margins, change line spacing, add a footnote, double-indent text, and use automatic page numbering. Keep in mind that if at any time you make a mistake, you may press **[CTRL]+[Z]** to undo what you have done.

1. Open Windows. When it has loaded, ***double-click the Microsoft Office Word 2013 icon on the desktop*** to open Word 2013 for Windows. Alternatively, ***click the Start button, point to Programs or All Programs, and then click the Microsoft Word 2013 icon*** (or ***point to Microsoft Office and then click Microsoft Office Word 2013***), ***then click the [ESC] key.*** You should now be in a clean, blank document. If you are not in a blank document, ***click the File tab, click New, and then click Blank document.*** Remember, any time you would like to see the name of an icon on the ribbon tabs, just ***point to the icon for a second or two*** and the name will be displayed.
2. You will be creating the document shown in Word 2013 Exhibit 4. The first thing you will need to do is to change the margins so that the left margin is 1.5 inches and the right margin is 1 inch. To change the margins, ***click the PAGE LAYOUT ribbon tab and then click Margins in the Page Setup group. Next, click Custom Margins at the bottom of the drop-down menu. In the Page Setup window, change the left margin to 1.5 inches and the right margin to 1 inch. Then, click OK.*** Also, ***on the HOME ribbon tab, click the Paragraph Group Dialog Box Launcher. In the "Paragraph" window, click the down arrow below Line Spacing and select Single. Make sure the Before and After spacing are both 0 point. Then, click OK.***
3. Notice in Word 2013 Exhibit 4 that there is a page number at the bottom of the page. Word can automatically number your pages for you.
4. ***Click the INSERT ribbon tab, and then click Page Number in the Header & Footer group*** (see Word 2013 Exhibit 5).
5. ***Next, point to Bottom of Page*** (see Word 2013 Exhibit 5) and notice that a number of options are displayed. ***Click the down arrow in the lower right*** for additional options (see Word 2013 Exhibit 5). Notice that many page-number options are available. ***Scroll back up to the top of the option list and click the second option, Plain Number 2.***

WORD 2013 EXHIBIT 4
A pleading

IN THE DISTRICT COURT OF
ORANGE COUNTY, MASSACHUSETTS

JIM TURNER,

Plaintiff,

vs. Case No. CV-13-0046

JONATHAN R. SMITH,

Defendant.

NOTICE TO TAKE DEPOSITION

COMES NOW the plaintiff and pursuant to statute[1] hereby gives notice that the deposition of Defendant, Jonathan R. Smith, will be taken as follows:

Monday, November 15, 2013, at 9:00 a.m. at the law offices of Matthews, Smith & Russell, 17031 W. 69th Street, Boston, MA.

Said deposition will be taken before a court reporter and is not expected to take more than one day in duration.

____
Mirabelle Watkinson
Attorney for Plaintiff

[1] Massachusetts Statutes Annotated 60-2342(a)(1).

6. Your pointer should now be in the area marked "Footer." Specifically, your pointer should be to the left of the number 1. Type **Page** and then press **[SPACEBAR].**
7. ***Click the HOME ribbon tab. Then, click the vertical scroll bar*** (see Word 2013 Exhibit 1) ***or use the [UP ARROW] key to go back to the beginning of the document.***
8. ***Double-click just below the header.***
9. On the first line of the document, ***from the HOME ribbon tab, click the Center icon in the Paragraph group***. Type **IN THE DISTRICT COURT OF**. Press the **[ENTER]** key. Type **ORANGE COUNTY, MASSACHUSETTS.**

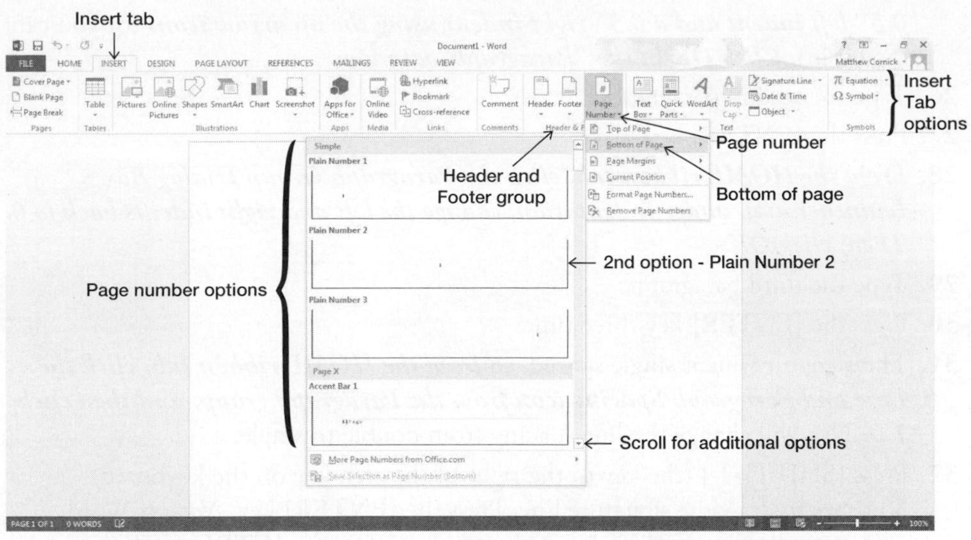

WORD 2013 EXHIBIT 5
Adding a page number

HANDS-ON EXERCISES

10. Press the [ENTER] key five times. ***From the HOME ribbon tab, click the Align Left icon in the Paragraph group.***
11. Type **JIM TURNER,** and press the [ENTER] key twice.
12. Press the [TAB] key three times and type **Plaintiff,** then press the [ENTER] key twice.
13. Type **vs.** (Note - when you type "vs.", Word 2013 may automatically change it to "Vs."; if that happens, just type **vs.** again.) Then, press the [TAB] key six times, and type **Case No. CV-15-0046**.
14. Press the [ENTER] key twice.
15. Type **JONATHAN R. SMITH,** and press the [ENTER] key twice.
16. Press the [TAB] key three times and type **Defendant.** Press the [ENTER] key four times.
17. ***From the HOME ribbon tab, click the Center icon in the Paragraph group.***
18. ***From the HOME ribbon tab, click the Bold icon and the Underline icon, both found in the Font group.*** Type **NOTICE TO TAKE DEPOSITION**. ***Click the Bold and Underline icons*** to turn them off.
19. Press the [ENTER] key three times. ***From the HOME ribbon tab, click the Align Left icon in the Paragraph group.***
20. ***From the HOME ribbon tab, click the Line and Paragraph Spacing icon from the Paragraph group*** (see Word 2013 Exhibit 1), ***and then click 2.0.*** This will change the line spacing from single to double.
21. Type **COMES NOW the plaintiff and pursuant to statute**. Notice that a footnote follows the word *statute* in Word 2013 Exhibit 4.
22. With the pointer just to the right of the "e" in "statute," ***from the REFERENCES ribbon tab, click Insert Footnote from the Footnotes group.*** The cursor should now be at the bottom of the page in the footnote window.
23. Type **Massachusetts Statutes Annotated 60-2342(a)(1).**
24. To move the pointer back to the body of the document, simply ***click to the right of the word "statute" (and the superscript number 1) in the body of the document.*** Now, continue to type the rest of the first paragraph. Once the paragraph is typed, press the [ENTER] key twice.
25. To double-indent the second paragraph, ***from the HOME ribbon tab, click the Paragraph Group Dialog Box Launcher*** (see Word 2013 Exhibit 1). The "Paragraph" window should now be displayed. ***Under Indentation, add a***

0.5" left indent and a 0.5" right indent using the up arrow icons (or you can type it in). ***Click OK in the "Paragraph" window.***

26. Type the second paragraph.
27. Press the **[ENTER]** key twice.
28. ***From the HOME ribbon tab, click the Paragraph Group Dialog Box Launcher and, under Indentation, change the left and right indents back to 0. Then, click OK.***
29. Type the third paragraph.
30. Press the **[ENTER]** key three times.
31. The signature line is single spaced, so ***from the HOME ribbon tab, click the Line and Paragraph Spacing icon from the Paragraph group, and then click 1.0.*** This will change the line spacing from double to single.
32. Press **[SHIFT]+[-]** (the key to the right of the zero key on the keyboard) 30 times to draw the signature line. Press the **[ENTER]** key. *Note:* If Word automatically inserts a line across the whole page, press **[CTRL]+[Z]** to undo the Auto Correct line. Alternatively, you can ***click the down arrow in the Auto Correct Options icon*** (it looks like a lightning bolt and should be just over the line that now runs across the page) and ***select Undo Border Line.***
33. Type **Mirabelle Watkinson**, and then press the **[ENTER]** key.
34. Type **Attorney for Plaintiff**.
35. To print the document, ***click the File tab, click Print, and then click Print.***
36. ***To save the document, click the File tab, click Save As, and then double-click Computer. Select the drive or folder you would like to save the document in.*** Type **Pleading1** in the "File name" box ***and then click Save*** to save the document in the default directory.
37. ***Click the File tab and then Close*** to close the document, or ***click the small x in the upper right corner of the screen*** to exit the program.

This concludes Lesson 3.

LESSON 4: CREATING A TABLE

This lesson shows you how to create the table shown in Word 2013 Exhibit 6. It expands on the items presented in Lessons 1, 2, and 3 and explains how to change a font size, create a table, enter data into a table, add automatic numbering, adjust column widths, and use the Table AutoFormat command. Keep in mind that if at any time you make a mistake, you may press **[CTRL]+[Z]** to undo what you have done.

1. Open Windows. When it has loaded, ***double-click the Microsoft Office Word 2013 icon on the desktop*** to open Word 2013 for Windows. Alternatively, ***click the Start button, point to Programs or All Programs, and then click the Microsoft Word 2013 icon*** (or ***point to Microsoft Office and then click Microsoft Office Word 2013***), ***then click the [ESC] key.*** You should be in a clean, blank document. If you are not in a blank document, ***click the File tab, click New, and then click Blank document.***
2. ***From the HOME ribbon tab, click the Center icon in the Paragraph group, and then click the Bold icon in the Font group.***
3. ***From the HOME ribbon tab, click the Font Size drop-down arrow in the Font group*** and change the font size to 14 either by typing **14** in the box or by ***choosing 14 from the drop-down menu.*** Alternatively, you can both turn on bold and change the font size by ***clicking the Font Group Dialog Box Launcher from the HOME ribbon tab*** (see Word 2013 Exhibit 1).

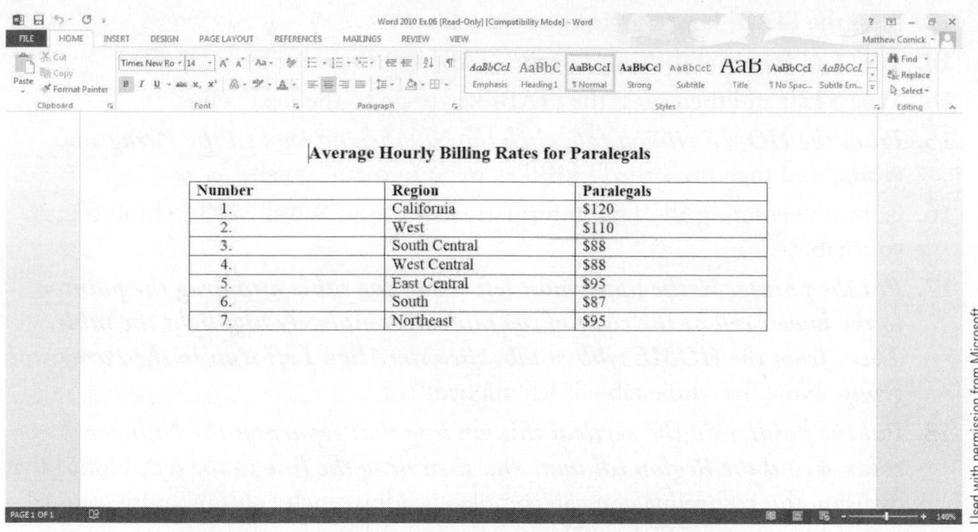

Average Hourly Billing Rates for Paralegals

Number	Region	Paralegals
1.	California	$120
2.	West	$110
3.	South Central	$88
4.	West Central	$88
5.	East Central	$95
6.	South	$87
7.	Northeast	$95

WORD 2013 EXHIBIT 6
Creating a table

4. Type **Average Hourly Billing Rates for Paralegals** (see Word 2013 Exhibit 6). Press the **[ENTER]** key once, and then ***click the Font Size icon and change the type back to 12 point. Click the Bold icon*** to turn bold off.
5. Press the **[ENTER]** key once.
6. ***From the INSERT ribbon tab, click Table.*** Notice that a number of columns and rows of boxes are displayed. This allows you to graphically depict your table.
7. ***Point within the Table menu so that three columns are highlighted, and then point and click so that eight rows are highlighted*** (e.g., 3 × 8 Table). Notice that as you point, the table is temporarily shown in your document. This is called a *live preview*. When you click the cell that is three columns over and eight cells down, the table (as opposed to the live preview) will be displayed permanently in your document.
8. The blank table should now be displayed and the cursor should be in the first column of the first row of the table. ***If the cursor is not in the first column of the first row, click in this cell to place the cursor there. Click the Bold icon on the HOME ribbon tab.*** Type **Number** and then press the **[TAB]** key once to go to the next cell in the table.
9. ***Click the Bold icon.*** Type **Region** and then press the **[TAB]** key once to go to the next cell in the table. (*Note:* If you need to go back to a previous cell, you can either use the mouse or the cursor keys, or you can press **[SHIFT]+[TAB]**. Also, if you accidentally hit the **[ENTER]** key instead of the **[TAB]** key, you can either press the **[BACKSPACE]** key to delete the extra line, or you can press **[CTRL]+[Z]** to undo it.
10. ***Click the Bold icon.*** Type **Paralegals** and then press the **[TAB]** key to go to the next cell.
11. We will now use the automatic paragraph numbering feature to number our rows. ***From the HOME ribbon tab, click the Numbering icon in the Paragraph group*** (see Word 2013 Exhibit 1—it is the icon that has the numbers 1, 2, 3 in a column, with a short line next to each number). Notice that the number 1 was automatically entered in the cell. ***From the HOME ribbon tab, point on the down arrow next to the Numbering icon in the Paragraph group.*** Under Numbering Library, look at the different formats that are available. The default format is fine, so press **[ESC]** to make the menu disappear.

12. Press the **[TAB]** key to go to the next cell.
13. Type **California** and then press the **[TAB]** key to go to the next cell.
14. Type **$120** and then press the **[TAB]** key to go to the next cell.
15. ***From the HOME ribbon tab, click the Numbering icon in the Paragraph group,*** and then press the **[TAB]** key to go to the next cell.
16. Continue entering all of the information shown in Word 2013 Exhibit 6 into your table.
17. ***Put the pointer in the uppermost left cell of the table and drag the pointer to the lowest cell at the right of the table to completely highlight the table. Then, from the HOME ribbon tab, click the Align Left icon in the Paragraph group.*** Now the whole table is left aligned.
18. ***Put the pointer on the vertical column line that separates the Number column and the Region column, and then drag the line to the left.*** Notice that by using this technique you can completely adjust each column width as much as you like. Press **[CTRL]+[Z]** to undo the column move, because the current format is fine.
19. ***Click any cell in the table.*** Notice that just above the ribbon tab, new options are now shown; under the new heading Table Tools, two more tabs (Design and Layout) appear. ***Click the DESIGN ribbon tab.*** Notice that the ribbon tab now shows six table styles. ***Point (don't click) on one of the tables;*** notice that the Live Preview feature shows you exactly what your table will look like with this design. ***Click the down arrow in the Table Styles group*** and browse to see many more table styles. ***Click a table style that you like.*** The format of the table has been completely changed.
20. To print the document, ***click the File tab, click Print, and then click Print.***
21. ***To save the document, click the File tab, click Save As, and then double-click Computer. Select the drive or folder you would like to save the document in.*** Type **Table1** in the "File name" box, ***and then click Save*** to save the document in the default directory.
22. ***Click the File tab and then on Close*** to close the document, or ***click the small x in the upper right corner of the screen*** to exit the program.

This concludes Lesson 4.

INTERMEDIATE LESSONS

LESSON 5: TOOLS AND TECHNIQUES

This lesson shows you how to edit an employment policy (from the Premium Website), use the Format Painter tool, reveal formatting, clear formatting, change the case of text, use the Find and Replace feature, use the Go To command, create a section break, and change the orientation of a page from Portrait to Landscape. This lesson assumes that you have completed Lessons 1 through 4 and that you are generally familiar with Word 2013.

1. Open Windows. When it has loaded, ***double-click the Microsoft Office Word 2013 icon on the desktop*** to open Word 2013 for Windows. Alternatively, ***click the Start button, point the pointer to Programs or All Programs, and then click the Microsoft Word 2013 icon*** (or ***point to Microsoft Office and then click Microsoft Office Word 2013***), ***then click the [ESC] key.*** You should

be in a clean, blank document. If you are not in a blank document, ***click the File tab, click New, and then click Blank document.***

2. The first thing you will do is to open the "Lesson 5" file from the Premium Website. On the Premium Website, click the Data Files: Word Processing tab, then under Word 2013, click the "Lesson 5" file. The file entitled "World Wide Technology, Inc. alcohol and drug policy" should now be displayed on your screen. If the document appears in Protected View, ***click Enable Editing*** to continue with the lesson. In this lesson, you will be editing this policy for use by another client. The next thing you need to do is to go to section 3, "Definitions," and change the subheadings so that they all have the same format. You will use the Format Painter tool to do this.
3. Use the cursor keys or the mouse and the horizontal scroll bars to scroll to section 3, "Definitions" (see Word 2013 Exhibit 7). Notice that the first definition, "Alcohol or alcoholic beverages," is bold and in a different font from the rest of the definitions in section 3. You will use the Format Painter feature to quickly copy the formatting from "Alcohol or alcoholic beverages" to the other four definitions in section 3.
4. ***Click anywhere in the text* "Alcohol or alcoholic beverages:"** This tells the Format Painter feature the formatting you want to copy.
5. ***From the HOME ribbon tab, click the Format Painter icon in the Clipboard group.*** It looks like a paintbrush (see Word 2013 Exhibit 7). Remember, if you hover your mouse pointer over an icon for a second or two, the name of the icon will appear.
6. Notice that your mouse pointer now turns to a paintbrush. ***Drag the pointer*** (hold the left mouse button down and move the mouse) ***until the heading* "Legal drugs:" *is highlighted*** (see Word 2013 Exhibit 7), ***and then let go of the mouse button.*** Notice that the paintbrush on your cursor is now gone. ***Click the left mouse button once anywhere in the screen to make the highlight go away.*** Notice that **"Legal drugs"** now has the same formatting as **"Alcohol or alcoholic beverages."** The Format Painter command is a quick way to make formatting changes.
7. You will now use the Format Painter command to copy the formatting to the remaining three definitions, with one additional trick. ***Click anywhere in the text* "Legal drugs."**

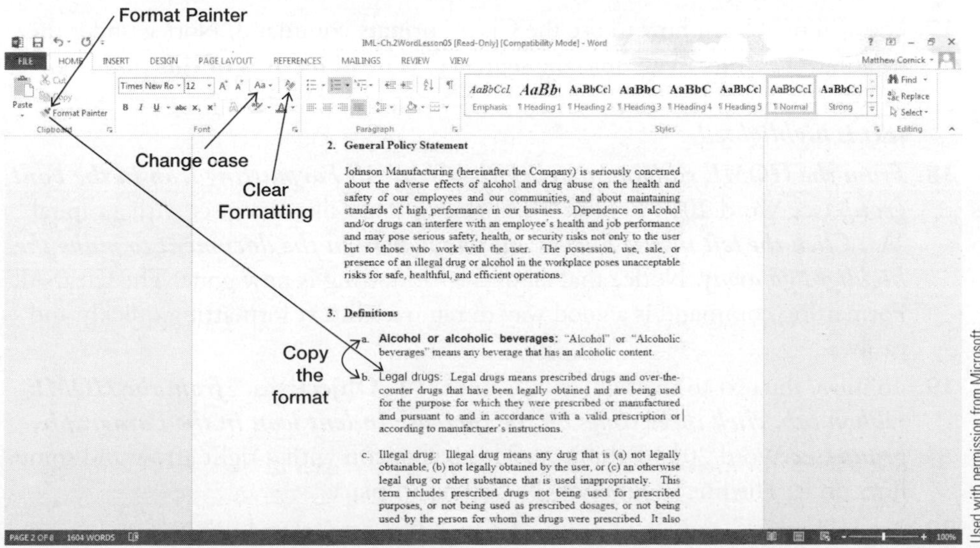

WORD 2013 EXHIBIT 7
The Format Painter tool

8. Next, ***from the HOME ribbon tab, double-click the Format Painter icon in the Clipboard group.*** (Your pointer should now have a paintbrush attached to it.) The double-click tells Format Painter that you are going to copy this format to multiple locations, instead of just one location. This is a great time-saving feature if you need to copy formatting to several places, because it keeps you from having to click the Format Painter icon each time you copy the same formatting to a new location.
9. ***Drag the pointer until the heading*** **"Illegal drug:"** ***is highlighted, and then let go of the mouse button.*** Notice that the paintbrush is still attached to your pointer.
10. ***Drag the pointer until the heading*** **"Controlled substance:"** ***is highlighted, and then let go of the mouse button.***
11. ***Drag the pointer until the heading*** **"Prescription drug:"** ***is highlighted, and then let go of the mouse button.***
12. To turn the Format Painter off, press the **[ESC]** button on the keyboard. ***Click the left mouse button once anywhere in the document to make the highlight go away.*** Notice that all of the headings are now uniform.
13. You will now learn to use the Reveal Formatting command. ***Click the heading*** **"Prescription drug:"**
14. Press **[SHIFT]+[F1]** on the keyboard. Notice that the Reveal Formatting task pane has opened on the right side of the screen. The Reveal Formatting task pane lists all format specifications for the selected text. The items are divided into several groups, including Font, Paragraph, Bullets and Numbering, and Section. You can make formatting changes to the text directly from the Reveal Formatting task pane by simply clicking on the format setting you want to change (the links are shown in blue, underlined text). For example, ***click the blue underlined word "Font" in the Reveal Formatting task pane.*** Notice that the "Font" window opens. You can now select a new font if you so desire. The Reveal Formatting task pane allows you to quickly see all formatting attached to specific text and, if necessary, to change it.
15. ***Click Cancel in the "Font" window.*** To close the Reveal Formatting task pane, ***click the "x" (the Close button) at the top of the Reveal Formatting task pane.*** It is just to the right of the words **"Reveal Formatting."** The Reveal Formatting task pane should now be gone.
16. Press **[CTRL]+[HOME]** to go to the beginning of the document.
17. You will now learn how to use the Clear Formats command. Notice under the heading **"1. Objectives"** that the sentence **"The objectives of this policy are as follows:"** is in bold and italics; this is a mistake. ***Drag the pointer until this text is highlighted.***
18. ***From the HOME ribbon tab, click the Clear All Formatting icon in the Font group*** (see Word 2013 Exhibit 7). This icon looks like an eraser with a capital "A". ***Click the left mouse button once anywhere in the document to make the highlight go away.*** Notice that all of the formatting is now gone. The Clear All Formatting command is a good way to remove all text formatting quickly and easily.
19. To move the text to the right so it is under **"1. Objectives,"** ***from the HOME ribbon tab, click three times on the Increase Indent icon in the Paragraph group*** (see Word 2013 Exhibit 7). This is the icon with a right arrow and some lines on it. The line should now be back in its place.
20. You will now learn how to use the Change Case command. Press **[CTRL]+[HOME]** on the keyboard to go to the beginning of the document.

21. ***Drag the pointer until* "World Wide Technology, Inc."** ***in the document's title is highlighted.***
22. ***From the HOME ribbon tab, click the Change Case icon in the Font group. Click UPPERCASE.*** Notice that the text is now in all capitals. ***Click anywhere in the document to make the highlighting disappear.***
23. ***Drag the pointer until the subtitle* "alcohol and drug policy"** ***is highlighted. From the HOME ribbon tab, click the Change Case icon in the Font group. Click "Capitalize Each Word."*** Notice that the text is now in title case. ***Click the left mouse button once anywhere in the document to make the highlighting go away.*** The Change Case command is a convenient way to change the case of text without having to retype it.
24. Highlight the subtitle "Alcohol And Drug Policy" again. From the Review Ribbon tab, click Spelling and Grammar. The Spelling and Grammar: English U.S. dialog box will open. Click Change to accept the change to "and" (with a lower case "a"). When asked whether you want to continue checking the remainder of the document, click No.
25. Press **[CTRL]+[HOME]** on the keyboard to go to the beginning of the document.
26. You will now learn how to use the Find and Replace command. ***From the HOME ribbon tab, click the Replace icon in the Editing group.*** Alternatively, you could press **[CTRL]+[H]**, and then click Replace.
27. In the "Find and Replace" window, in the white box next to **"Find what,"** type **World Wide Technology, Inc.** Then, in the white box next to **"Replace with,"** type **Johnson Manufacturing.** ***Now, click the Replace All button in the "Find and Replace" window.*** The program will respond by stating that it made four replacements. ***Click OK.***
28. ***Click the Close button in the "Find and Replace" window to close the window.*** Notice that World Wide Technology, Inc. has now been changed to Johnson Manufacturing.
29. You will now learn how to use the Go To command. The Go To command is an easy way to navigate through large and complex documents. Press **[F5].** Notice that the "Find and Replace" window is again displayed on the screen, but this time the Go To tab is selected. In the white box directly under **"Enter page number,"** type **7** from the keyboard and then ***click Go To in the "Find and Replace" window.*** Notice that page 7, **"**REASONABLE SUSPICION REPORT,**"** is now displayed. (*Note:* If the "Find and Replace" window blocks your view of the document, point at the blue box in the "Find and Replace" window and drag the window lower so you can see the document text). ***Click Close in the "Find and Replace" window.***
30. Suppose that you would like to change the orientation of only one page in a document from Portrait (where the length is greater than the width) to Landscape (where the width is greater than the length). In this example, you will change the layout of only the REASONABLE SUSPICION REPORT to Landscape while keeping the rest of the document in Portrait orientation. To do this in Word, you must enter a section break.
31. Your cursor should be on page 7 just above **"Johnson Manufacturing REASONABLE SUSPICION REPORT."** ***From the PAGE LAYOUT ribbon tab, click Breaks in the Page Setup group.***
32. ***Under Section Breaks, click Next Page.***
33. In the View tab, ***click Draft in the Views group;*** this will permit you to view the document in Draft view. Press the **[UP ARROW]** key two times. Notice that a double-dotted line that says **"Section Break (Next Page)"** is now displayed.

HANDS-ON EXERCISES

34. The Word 2013 interface allows you to switch views by clicking on one of the view layouts in the lower right of the screen (see Word 2013 Exhibit 7). Print Layout is the default mode of viewing documents. Other choices include Read Mode and Web Layout. ***Click Read Mode and then Web Layout*** to see different views of your document. In addition, the Zoom tool just to the right of the Web Layout view allows you to zoom in or out of your document.
35. With the section break in place, you can now change the format of the page from Portrait to Landscape without changing the orientation of previous pages.
36. ***With the cursor on the*** **"Johnson Manufacturing REASONABLE SUSPICION REPORT"** ***page, from the PAGE LAYOUT ribbon tab, click Orientation in the Page Setup group. Click Landscape.*** Notice that the layout of the page has changed.
37. ***Click the Print Layout icon in the lower right of the screen*** (see Word 2013 Exhibit 7).
38. To confirm that the layout has changed, ***click the File tab, then click Print.*** On the right side of the screen you can see that the layout is now Landscape (the width is greater than the length). Press the **[PAGE UP]** key until you are back to the beginning of the document. Notice that all of the other pages in the document are still in Portrait orientation.
39. To print the document, ***click the File tab, click Print, and then click Print.***
40. To save the document, ***click the File tab, click Save As, and then double-click Computer. Select the drive or folder*** you would like to save the document in. Then, next to File name, type **Done—Word 2013 Lesson 5 Document** and ***click Save*** to save the document.
41. ***Click the File tab, and then click Close*** to close the document, or ***click the small x in the upper right corner of the screen*** to exit the program.

This concludes Lesson 5.

LESSON 6: USING STYLES

This lesson gives you an introduction to styles. Styles are particularly helpful when you are working with long documents that must be formatted uniformly.

1. Open Windows. When it has loaded, ***double-click the Microsoft Office Word 2013 icon on the desktop*** to open Word 2013 for Windows. Alternatively, ***click the Start button, point to Programs or All Programs, and then click the Microsoft Word 2013 icon*** (or ***point to Microsoft Office and then click Microsoft Office Word 2013***), ***then click the [ESC] key.*** You should now be in a clean, blank document. If you are not in a blank document, ***click the File tab, click New, and then click Blank document.***
2. The first thing you will do is to open the "Lesson 6" file from the Premium Website. On the Premium Website, click the Data Files: Word Processing tab, then under Word 2013, click the "Lesson 6" file. ***Double-click the Word Processing File folder. Double-click the Word 2013 folder. Double-click the "Lesson 6" file.*** If the document appears in Protected View, ***click Enable Editing*** to continue with the lesson.
3. The text "SARBANES-OXLEY ACT OF 2002" should now be displayed on your screen (see Word 2013 Exhibit 8). In this lesson you will use styles to add uniform formatting to this document. In the HOME ribbon tab, notice the Styles group. ***Click any text on the page.*** Notice in the Styles group on the HOME ribbon tab that the "Normal" box is highlighted (see Word 2013 Exhibit 8). Currently, all text in the document is in the Normal style.

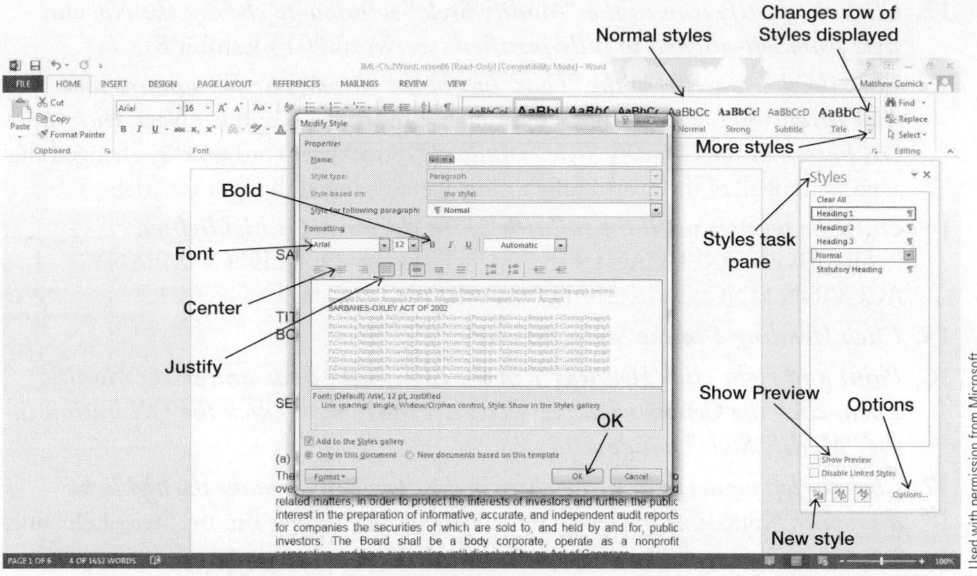

WORD 2013 EXHIBIT 8
Styles

4. Using your cursor keys or the horizontal scroll bar, scroll down through the document. Notice that all of the paragraphs are left-aligned and that the right edge of all the paragraphs is jagged (e.g., not justified).
5. ***From the HOME ribbon tab, click the Styles Group Dialog Box Launcher.*** Notice that the Styles task pane now appears on the right side of the screen (see Word 2013 Exhibit 8). In the Styles task pane, ***if the white box next to "Show Preview" is not marked, click the box so a check mark appears*** (see Word 2013 Exhibit 8). Notice that a few styles in the Styles task pane are currently being displayed (e.g., Heading 1, Heading 2, and Normal). Also notice that the Normal style has a blue box around it, indicating that your cursor is on text with the Normal style. Finally, notice that there is a paragraph sign after each of these heading names, indicating that these are paragraph styles.
6. Notice at the bottom of the Styles task pane the word "Options" in blue; ***click Options.*** The "Style Pane Options" window should now be displayed.
7. ***In the "Style Pane Options" window, under Select styles to show, click the down arrow and click All styles. Then, in the "Style Pane Options" window, click OK.***
8. Notice that the Styles task pane is now full of additional styles. These are all of the styles that are automatically available in Word 2013. ***Click the down arrow in the Styles task pane*** to see the full list of styles.
9. To return to the list of just a few styles, ***click Options in the lower right of the Styles task pane. Under Select styles to show, click the down arrow and click In current document. Then, in the "Style Pane Options" window, click OK.***
10. Notice that the short list of styles is again displayed. To access other styles from the Styles group on the HOME ribbon tab, ***click the down arrow in the Styles group.*** If you ***click the More icon*** (the icon that shows a down arrow with a line over it) in the Styles group, you can see all of the styles at one time. Press the **[ESC]** key to close the list.
11. Styles are extremely useful. Assume now that you would like to have all of the text in the document justified. ***Point and right-click Normal in the Styles task pane. Then, point and left-click Modify.*** The "Modify Style" window should now be displayed (see Word 2013 Exhibit 8). Using the "Modify Style" window, you can completely change the formatting for any style.

12. ***Click the Justify icon in the "Modify Style" window to change the Normal style from left-aligned to fully justified*** (see Word 2013 Exhibit 8).
13. ***Click the down arrow in the "Font" box in the "Modify Style" window and click Arial*** (you may have to scroll through some fonts to find it). ***Next, click the OK button in the "Modify Style" window.*** Notice that Word quickly changed the alignment of all of the text to fully justified and changed the font to Arial.
14. ***Drag the pointer until the full title of the document is highlighted*** (SARBANES-OXLEY ACT OF 2002 TITLE I—PUBLIC COMPANY ACCOUNTING OVERSIGHT BOARD).
15. ***Click Heading 1 in the Styles task pane.***
16. ***Point and right-click Heading 1 in the Styles task pane and select Modify. Then, click the Center icon.*** See Word 2013 Exhibit 8. ***Click the OK button in the "Modify Style" window.***
17. ***Click the left mouse button anywhere in the document to make the highlight disappear.*** Notice that the text of the title shows as Heading 1 in the Styles task pane.
18. ***Click anywhere in* "SEC. 101. ESTABLISHMENT; ADMINISTRATIVE PROVISIONS."** ***Then, click Heading 2 in the Styles task pane.*** Notice that the heading has now changed.
19. ***Click anywhere in the subheading* "(a) ESTABLISHMENT OF BOARD."** ***Then, click the New Style icon at the bottom of the Styles task pane*** (see Word 2013 Exhibit 8).
20. The "Create New Style from Formatting" window should now be displayed. Under Properties, next to Name, type **Heading 3A**, and then under Formatting, ***click the Bold icon. Then, click OK in the "Create New Style from Formatting" window.***
21. Now, go to the following subheadings and format them as Heading 3A by ***clicking on them and selecting Heading 3A from the Styles task pane:***

    (b) STATUS

    (c) DUTIES OF THE BOARD

    (d) COMMISSION DETERMINATION

    (e) BOARD MEMBERSHIP

    (f) POWERS OF THE BOARD

    (g) RULES OF THE BOARD

    (h) ANNUAL REPORT TO THE COMMISSION

    Press **[CTRL]+[HOME]** to go to the beginning of the document. Your document is now consistently formatted. Using styles, your documents can also easily be uniformly changed. For example, if you read in your local rules that subheadings for pleadings must be in 15-point Times New Roman font, you could quickly change the subheadings in your document by modifying the heading styles, rather than highlighting each subheading and changing the format manually.
22. To print the document, ***click the File tab, click Print, and then click Print.***
23. To save the document, ***click the File tab, click Save As, and then double-click Computer. Select the drive or folder*** you would like to save the document in. Then, next to File name, type **Done—Word 2013 Lesson 6 Document** ***and click Save*** to save the document.
24. ***Click the File tab, and then on Close*** to close the document, or ***click the small x in the upper right corner of the screen*** to exit the program.

This concludes Lesson 6.

LESSON 7: CREATING A TEMPLATE

This lesson shows you how to create the template shown in Word 2013 Exhibit 9. It explains how to create a template of a letter, how to insert fields, and how to fill out and use a finished template. You will also learn how to add a command to the Quick Access toolbar. The information that will be merged into the letter will be entered from the keyboard. Keep in mind that if at any time you make a mistake, you may press **[CTRL]+[Z]** to undo what you have done.

1. Open Windows. When it has loaded, ***double-click the Microsoft Office Word 2013 icon on the desktop*** to open Word 2013 for Windows. Alternatively, ***click the Start button, point to Programs or All Programs, and then click the Microsoft Word 2013 icon*** (or ***point to Microsoft Office and then click Microsoft Office Word 2013***), ***then click the [ESC] key***. You should be in a clean, blank document. If you are not in a blank document, ***click the File tab, click New, and then click Blank document.***
2. ***Click the File tab, then click New, and then next to Suggested Searches:, click Blank. Several sample templates will appear, click Classic (blank). (See Word 2013 Exhibit 10).***

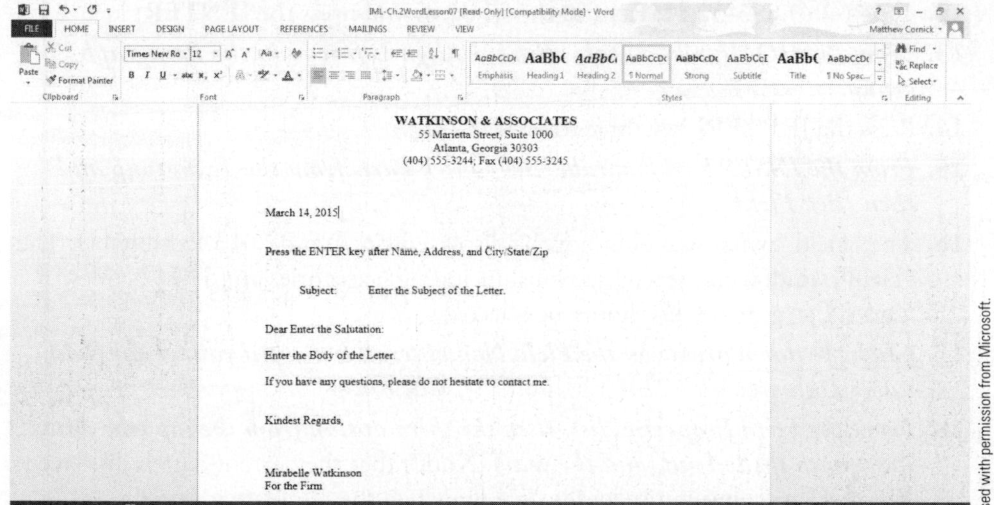

WORD 2013 EXHIBIT 9
Office Letter template

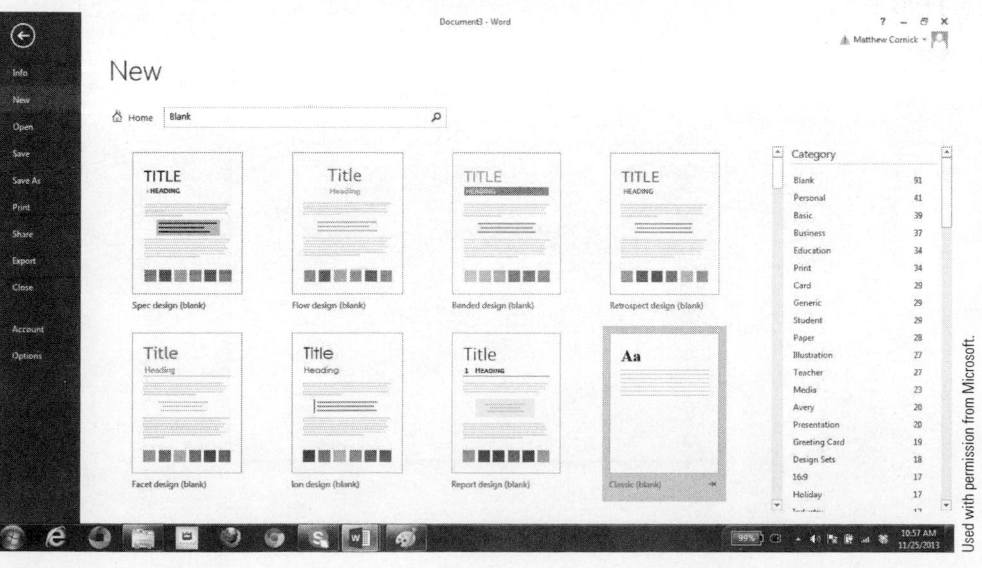

WORD 2013 EXHIBIT 10
Creating a New field

3. A new dialog box will open with details of the selected template. ***Click Create.***
4. You should now have a blank document on your screen. You will now build the template shown in Word 2013 Exhibit 9.
5. Also, ***on the HOME ribbon tab, click the Paragraph Group Dialog Box Launcher. In the "Paragraph" window, click the down arrow below Line Spacing and select Single. Make sure the Before and After spacing are both 0 point. Then, click OK.***
6. ***From the HOME ribbon tab, click the Center icon in the Paragraph group. Then, from the HOME ribbon tab, click the Bold icon in the Font group.***
7. ***From the HOME ribbon tab, click the Font Size drop-down arrow from the Font group and select 14 from the list. Then, click the "Font" box and select Times New Roman.***
8. Type **WATKINSON & ASSOCIATES** and then, ***from the HOME ribbon tab, click the Font Size icon and select 12 from the list. Click the Bold icon from the Font group*** to turn off bolding.
9. Press the **[ENTER]** key.
10. Type **55 Marietta Street, Suite 1000** and press the **[ENTER]** key.
11. Type **Atlanta, Georgia 30303** and press the **[ENTER]** key.
12. Type **(404) 555-3244; Fax (404) 555-3245** and press the **[ENTER]** key.
13. ***From the HOME ribbon tab, click the Align Left icon in the Paragraph group.***
14. Press the **[ENTER]** key three times.
15. ***From the INSERT ribbon tab, click Quick Parts from the Text group and then click Field.***
16. The "Field" window should now be displayed (see Word 2013 Exhibit 11). The "Field" window has several sections, including Categories and Field Names. Under Categories, *(All)* should be selected.
17. ***Click the down arrow on the Field Names scroll bar until you see the field name Date*** (see Word 2013 Exhibit 11). ***Click it.***
18. ***From the Field Properties list, click the third option from the top (the date, the month spelled out, and the year).*** Notice that the current date is displayed. This field will always display the date on which the template is actually

WORD 2013 EXHIBIT 11
Inserting fields in a template

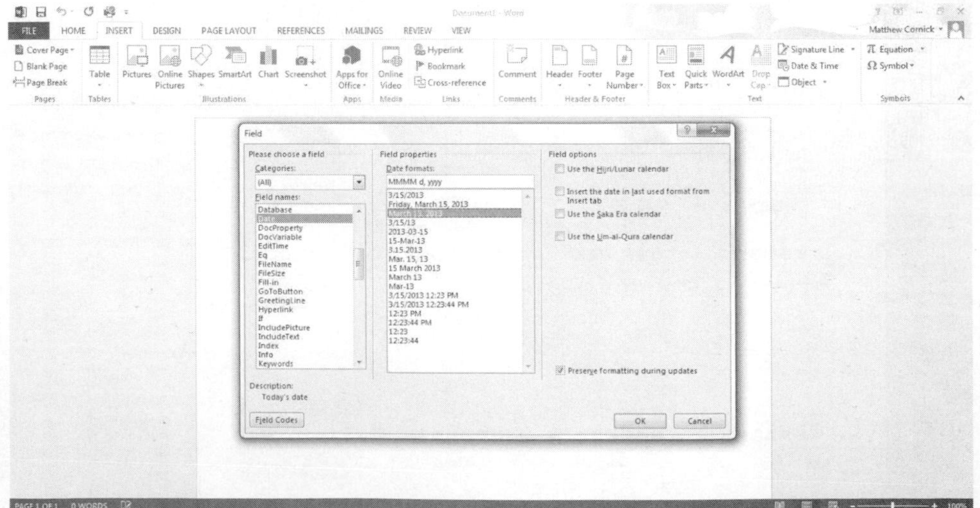

executed, so if the template is executed on January 1, January 1 will be the date shown on the letter. ***Click OK in the "Field" window.***

19. Press the **[ENTER]** key three times.
20. ***From the INSERT ribbon tab, click Quick Parts from the Text group and then click Field.***
21. ***Click the down arrow on the Field names scroll bar until you see Fill-in in the Field Name area*** (see Word 2013 Exhibit 11). ***Click Fill-in.***
22. In the "Prompt:" box under Field Properties, type **"Type the Name and Address of the Recipient."** *Note:* You must type the quotation marks.
23. ***Click OK in the "Field" window.***
24. You will now see a window on your screen that says **"Type the Name and Address of the Recipient."** Type **Press the ENTER key after Name, Address, and City/State/Zip** (see Word 2013 Exhibit 12). ***Then, click OK.***
25. Press the **[ENTER]** key three times.
26. Press the **[TAB]** key.
27. Type **Subject:**.
28. Press the **[TAB]** key.
29. ***From the INSERT ribbon tab, click Quick Parts from the Text group and then click Field.***
30. ***Click the down arrow on the Field names scroll bar until you see Fill-in in the Field Name area. Click Fill-in.***
31. In the "Prompt:" box under Field Properties, type **"Type the Subject of the Letter."** *Note:* You must type the quotation marks. ***Click OK.***
32. You will now see a window on your screen that says **"Type the Subject of the Letter."** Type **Enter the Subject of the Letter**. ***Click OK.***
33. Press the **[ENTER]** key three times.
34. Type **Dear**, press the **[SPACEBAR]**; ***from the INSERT ribbon tab, click Quick Parts from the Text group, and then click Field.***
35. ***Click the down arrow on the Field names scroll bar until you see Fill-in in the Field Name area. Click Fill-in.***
36. In the "Prompt:" box under Field Properties, type **"Salutation."** *Note:* You must type the quotation marks. ***Click OK.***

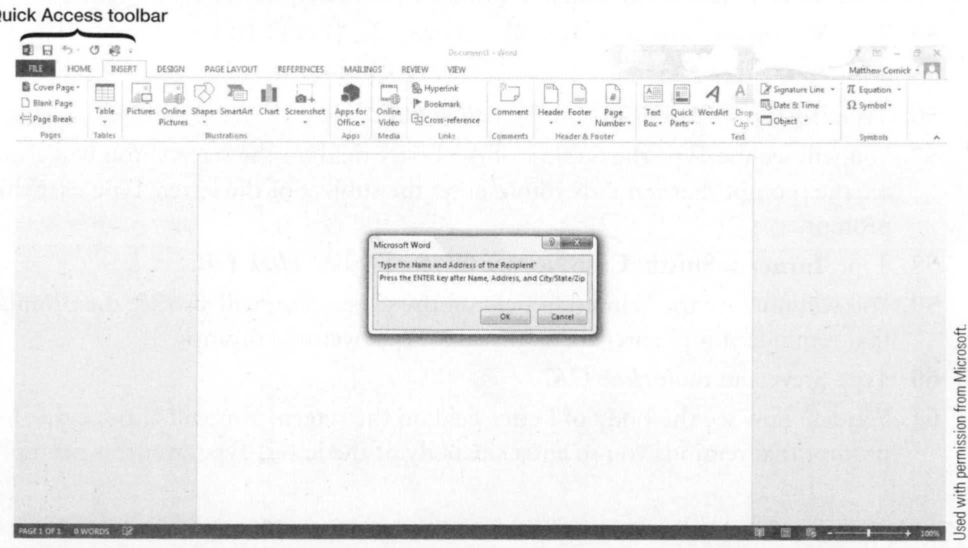

WORD 2013 EXHIBIT 12
Entering a "Fill-in" field

37. You will now see a window on your screen that says **"Salutation."** Type **Enter the Salutation.** ***Then, click OK.***
38. Type **:** (a colon).
39. Press the **[ENTER]** key twice.
40. ***From the INSERT ribbon tab, click Quick Parts from the Text group and then click Field.***
41. ***Click the down arrow on the Field names scroll bar until you see Fill-in in the Field Name area. Click Fill-in.***
42. In the "Prompt:" box under Field Properties, type **"Body of Letter."** *Note:* You must type the quotation marks. ***Click OK.***
43. You will now see a window on your screen that says **"Body of Letter."** Type **Enter the Body of the Letter**. ***Then, click OK.***
44. Press the **[ENTER]** key twice.
45. Type **If you have any questions, please do not hesitate to contact me.** Press the **[ENTER]** key three times.
46. Type **Kindest Regards,** and press the **[ENTER]** key four times.
47. Type **Mirabelle Watkinson** and press the **[ENTER]** key once.
48. Type **For the Firm**.
49. ***Click the File tab, then point to Save As and double-click Computer to save the file to your computer.*** Then, next to File name:, type **Watkinson Letter Template.** Then in the Save As dialog box, next to Save as type:, ***scroll down and select Word Template. Click Save.*** (*Note:* If you do not save this as a Word template, you will not be able to finish the lesson.) Word will save the template to a special template folder; if you save it to another folder you will not be able to run the template in the next portion of this exercise.
50. ***Click the File tab and then on Close.*** You are now ready to type a letter using the template.
51. ***Click the File tab, then click New. Next, click Personal, then double-click Watkinson Letter Template.***
52. The template letter is now running. You will see the "Type the Name and Address of the Recipient" field on the screen. You will also see the prompt that reminds you to press the **[ENTER]** key after the name, address, and city/state/zip. Type over this prompt.
53. Type **Steven Matthews, Esq.** and press the **[ENTER]** key.
54. Type **Matthews, Smith & Russell** and press the **[ENTER]** key.
55. Type **P.O. Box 12341** and press the **[ENTER]** key.
56. Type **Boston, MA 59920** and then ***click OK.***
57. You will see the Type the Subject of the Letter field on the screen. You will also see the prompt that reminds you to enter the subject of the letter. Type over this prompt.
58. Type **Turner v. Smith, Case No. 15-0046** and then ***click OK.***
59. You will now see the Salutation field on the screen. You will also see the prompt that reminds you to enter the salutation. Type over this prompt.
60. Type **Steve** and then ***click OK.***
61. You will now see the Body of Letter field on the screen. You will also see the prompt that reminds you to enter the body of the letter. Type over this prompt.

62. Type **This will confirm our conversation of this date. You indicated that you had no objection to us requesting an additional ten days to respond to your Motion for Summary Judgment.** ***Click OK.*** You are now through typing the letter. The completed letter should now be displayed. (*Note:* If another window displays, prompting you for the name and address of the recipient, simply ***click cancel***; the completed letter should then be displayed.)
63. You are now ready to print the document. First, you will create a Quick Print icon on the Quick Access toolbar. Instead of going to the File tab each time to print, you will be able to print a document from the Quick Access toolbar (see Word 2013 Exhibit 12).
64. ***Click the down arrow to the right of the Quick Access Toolbar.***
65. ***Click Quick Print.***
66. Notice that a Quick Print icon is now displayed in the Quick Access toolbar.
67. ***Click the Quick Print icon on the Quick Access toolbar,*** or ***click the File tab, click Print, and then click Print.***
68. To save the document, ***click the File tab, click Save As, and then double-click Computer. Select the drive or folder*** you would like to save the document in. Then, next to File name, type **Done—Word 2013 Lesson 7 Document** ***and click Save*** to save the document. *Note:* You just saved the output of your template to a separate file named "Done—Word Lesson 7 Document." Your original template ("Watkinson Letter Template") is unaffected by the Lesson 7 document, and is still a clean template ready to be used again and again for any case.
69. ***Click the File tab, and then on Close*** to close the document, or ***click the small x in the upper right corner of the screen*** to exit the program.

This concludes Lesson 7.

LESSON 8: COMPARING DOCUMENTS

This lesson shows you how to compare documents by simultaneously viewing two documents and by creating a separate blacklined document with the changes. There will be times in a law office when you send someone a digital file for revision, and find that when the file is returned, the revisions are not apparent. Using these tools in Word 2013, you can see what has changed in the document.

1. Open Windows. When it has loaded, ***double-click the Microsoft Office Word 2013 icon on the desktop*** to open Word 2013 for Windows. Alternatively, ***click the Start button, point to Programs or All Programs, and then click the Microsoft Word 2013 icon*** (or ***point to Microsoft Office and then click Microsoft Office Word 2013), then click the [ESC] key.*** You should now be in a clean, blank document. If you are not in a blank document, ***click the File tab, click New, and then click Blank document.***
2. For the purpose of this lesson, we will assume that your firm drafted an employment contract for a corporate client named Bluebriar Incorporated. Bluebriar is in negotiations with an individual named John Lewis, whom they would like to hire as their vice president of marketing. Your firm is negotiating with John Lewis's attorney regarding the terms and language of the employment contract. The file "Lesson 8A" is the original document you sent to John Lewis's attorney. The file "Lesson 8B" is the new file sent to you by John Lewis's attorney.

HANDS-ON EXERCISES

3. You will now open both of these files from the Premium Website and then compare them side by side. ***On the Premium Website, click the Data Files: Word Processing tab, then under Word 2013, click the "Lesson 8A" file.*** Follow the same directions to open the "Lesson 8B" file. If the documents appear in Protected View, ***click Enable Editin***g to continue with the lesson.
4. ***From the VIEW ribbon tab, click View Side by Side in the Window group.*** Both documents should now be displayed side by side (see Word 2013 Exhibit 13).
5. Keep pushing the **[DOWN ARROW]** key to scroll down through the document. Notice that both documents scroll simultaneously.
6. From the VIEW ribbon tab, notice that the Synchronous Scrolling icon in the Window group is highlighted (see Word 2013 Exhibit 13). To turn off this feature, you would click this icon. The Synchronous Scrolling icon toggles Synchronous Scrolling on and off. If you turn off Synchronous Scrolling and wish to turn it back on, simply realign the windows where you want them, and ***click the Synchronous Scrolling icon.*** (*Note:* If the VIEW ribbon tab shows the Window group collapsed, ***click the Window Group, and click Synchronous Scrolling.***)
7. You will now learn how to merge the changes into one document. ***Click anywhere in Lesson 8A.doc; then click the File tab and then on Close.***
8. You should now have one document open.
9. ***From the REVIEW ribbon tab, click Compare in the Compare group. Then, click Compare.***
10. The "Compare Documents" window should now be displayed (see Word 2013 Exhibit 14). ***Under Original document, click the down arrow, use the Browse feature to find Lesson 8A.doc, and then double-click it*** (see Word 2013 Exhibit 14).
11. ***Under Revised document, click the down arrow, use the Browse feature to find Lesson 8B.doc, and then double-click it*** (see Word 2013 Exhibit 14).
12. Next to **"Label changes with,"** type **John Lewis' Attorney** and then ***click OK in the "Compare Documents" window. If a new dialog box opens asking if all track changes should be accepted, click OK.***
13. Notice that a new document has been created that merges the documents (see Word 2013 Exhibit 15). Scroll through the new document and review all of the changes.

WORD 2013 EXHIBIT 13
Comparing documents side by side

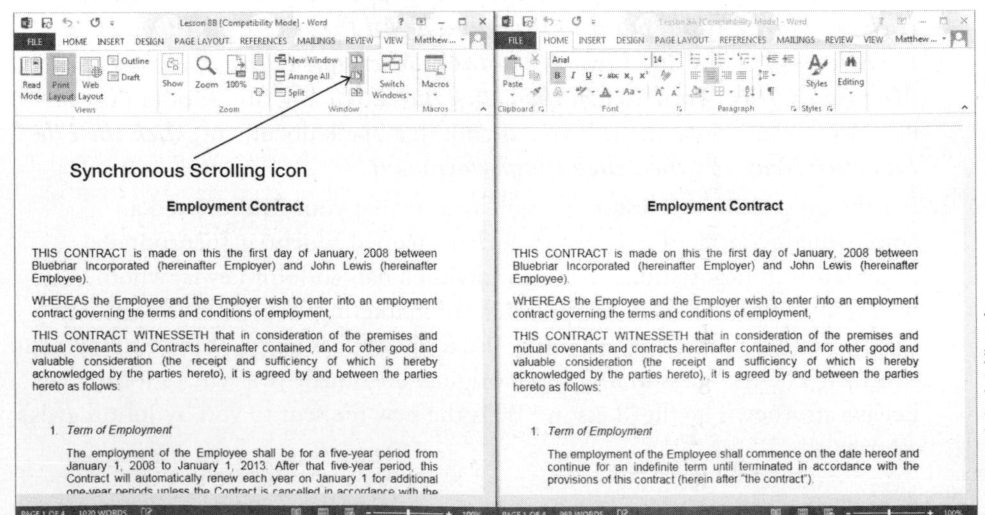

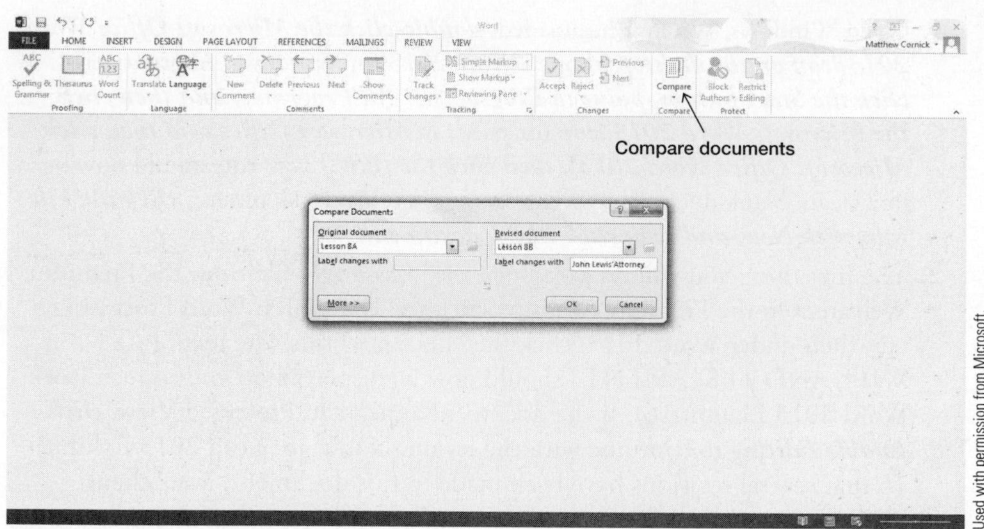

Used with permission from Microsoft.

WORD 2013 EXHIBIT 14
Comparing documents—Legal blackline settings

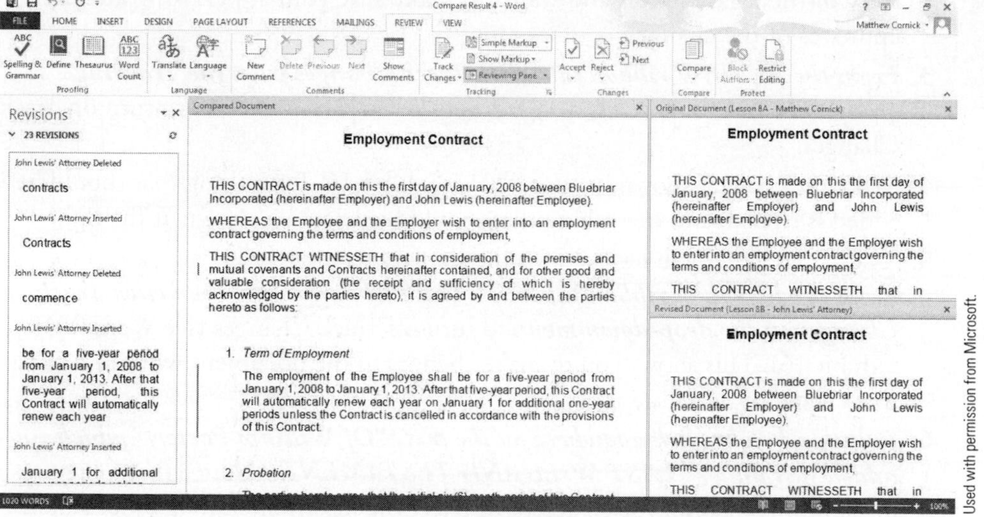

Used with permission from Microsoft.

WORD 2013 EXHIBIT 15
Completed blackline documents

14. The Compare feature is extremely helpful when you are comparing multiple versions of the same file. By right-clicking on any of the additions or deletions, you can accept or reject the change. This is called Track Changes, and you will learn how to do this in more detail in the next lesson.
15. To print the document, ***click the Quick Print icon on the Quick Access toolbar,*** or ***click the File tab, click Print, and then click Print.***
16. To save the document, ***click the File tab, click Save As, and then double-click Computer. Select the drive or folder*** you would like to save the document in. Next to File name:, type **Done—Word 2013 Lesson 8 Merged Doc** and then ***click Save*** to save the document.
17. ***Click the File tab, and then on Close*** to close the document, or ***click the small x in the upper right corner of the screen*** to exit the program.

This concludes Lesson 8.

LESSON 9: USING TRACK CHANGES

In this lesson, you will learn how to use the Track Changes feature by editing a will, and then accepting and/or rejecting the changes.

1. Open Windows. When it has loaded, ***double-click the Microsoft Office Word 2013 icon on the desktop*** to open Word 2013 for Windows. Alternatively, ***click the Start button, point to Programs or All Programs, and then click the Microsoft Word 2013 icon*** (or ***point to Microsoft Office and then click Microsoft Office Word 2013***), ***then click the [ESC] key.*** You should now be in a clean, blank document. If you are not in a blank document, ***click the File tab, click New, and then click Blank document.***
2. The first thing you will do is to open the "Lesson 9" file from the Premium Website. On the Premium Website, click the Data Files: Word Processing tab, then under Word 2013, click the "Lesson 9" file. The text "LAST WILL AND TESTAMENT" should now be displayed on your screen (see Word 2013 Exhibit 16). If the document appears in Protected View, ***click Enable Editing*** to continue with the lesson. Notice in Word 2013 Exhibit 16 that several revisions have been made to this document. Your client, William Porter, has asked you to use the Track Changes feature to show your supervising attorney the changes he would like to make. Mr. Porter is rather leery of the legal process and wants to make sure your supervising attorney approves of the changes.
3. ***From the REVIEW ribbon tab, click Track Changes from the Tracking group. Then, click Track Changes from the drop-down menu*** to turn on Track Changes.
4. Make the changes shown in Word 2013 Exhibit 16. Everything that should be added is circled, and everything that should be deleted is shown at the right
5. Assume now that you have shown the changes to your supervising attorney. ***From the REVIEW ribbon tab, click Track Changes, and then click Track Changes on the drop-down menu*** to turn off Track Changes (see Word 2013 Exhibit 16). This allows you to make changes to the document without having them show up as revisions.
6. ***Point and right-click anywhere on the text, "Of William Porter," which you added just under "LAST WILL AND TESTAMENT."*** Notice that a menu is displayed that allows you to accept or reject the insertion, among other actions. ***Click Accept Insertion.*** The revision has now been accepted.
7. ***From the REVIEW ribbon tab, click Next in the Changes group*** (see Word 2013 Exhibit 16). This should take you to the next change. ***From the REVIEW***

WORD 2013 EXHIBIT 16
Using Track Changes

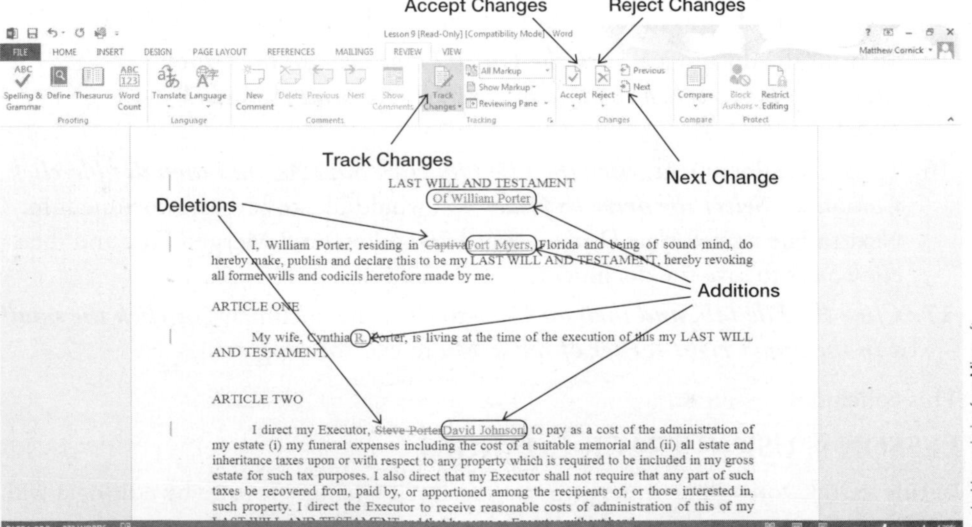

ribbon tab, click Accept down arrow in the Changes group, then click Accept and Move to Next (see Word 2013 Exhibit 16) to accept the change. Notice that one of the options is "Accept All Changes." Do not select it. This is a quick way to accept all changes in a document without going through each one of them.

8. Use the Next feature to continue to go to each change and accept the revisions. The only revision you will *not* accept is changing the executor from Steve Porter to David Johnson; reject this change. Assume that the supervising attorney has learned that Mr. Johnson is terminally ill and most likely will not be able to serve as executor, so the client has decided to keep Steve Porter as the executor.
9. To print the document, ***click the Quick Print icon on the Quick Access toolbar,*** or ***click the File tab, click Print, and then click Print.***
10. To save the document, ***click the File tab, click Save As, and then double-click Computer. Select the drive or folder*** you would like to save the document in. Next to File name, type **Done—Word 2013 Lesson 9 Document** ***and then click Save*** to save the document.
11. ***Click the File tab, and then on Close*** to close the document, or ***click the small x in the upper right corner of the screen*** to exit the program.

This concludes Lesson 9.

ADVANCED LESSONS

LESSON 10: CREATING A MAIL MERGE DOCUMENT

In this lesson, you will create a merge document for an open house that you will send to three clients (see Word 2013 Exhibit 17). First, you will create the data file that will be merged into the letter. You will then create the letter itself; finally, you will merge the two together. Keep in mind that if at any time you make a mistake, you may press **[CTRL]+[Z]** to undo what you have done.

1. Open Windows. When it has loaded, ***double-click the Microsoft Office Word 2013 icon on the desktop*** to open Word 2013 for Windows. Alternatively,

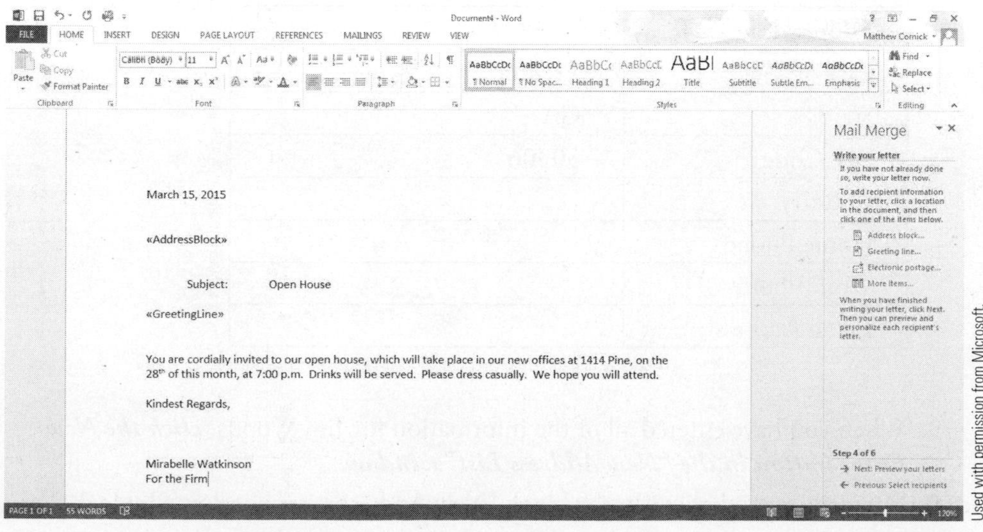

WORD 2013 EXHIBIT 17
Mail merge letter

click the Start button, point to Programs or All Programs, and then click the Microsoft Word 2013 icon (or ***point to Microsoft Office and then click Microsoft Office Word 2013***), ***then click the [ESC] key.*** You should now be in a clean, blank document. If you are not in a blank document, ***click the File tab, click New, and then click Blank document.***

2. ***From the MAILINGS ribbon tab, click Start Mail Merge. Then, from the drop-down menu, select Step-by-Step Mail Merge Wizard.*** The Mail Merge task pane is now shown on the task pane to the right of your document.
3. The bottom of the Mail Merge task pane shows that you are on step 1 of 6. You are asked to **"Select document type."** You are typing a letter, so the default selection, Letters, is fine. To continue to the next step, ***click Next: Starting document at the bottom of the Mail Merge task pane under Step 1 of 6.***
4. The bottom of the Mail Merge task pane shows that you are on step 2 of 6. You are asked to **"Select starting document."** You will be using the current document to type your letter, so the default selection, Use the current document, is fine. To continue to the next step, ***click Next: Select recipients at the bottom of the Mail Merge task pane under Step 2 of 6.***
5. The bottom of the Mail Merge task pane shows that you are on step 3 of 6. You are asked to **"Select recipients."** You will be typing a new list, so ***click Type a new list.***
6. ***Under the Type a new list section of the Mail Merge task pane, click "Create."***
7. The "New Address List" window is now displayed. You will now fill in the names of the three clients to whom you want to send your open house letter.
8. Type the following (Table 2–1). (*Note:* You can use the **[TAB]** key to move between the fields, or you can use the mouse.) Only complete the fields below; skip the fields in the "New Address List" window that we will not be using.

TABLE 2–1	
First Name	Jim
Last Name	Woods
Company Name	
Address Line 1	2300 Briarcliff Road
Address Line 2	
City	Atlanta
State	GA
ZIP Code	30306
Country	
Home Phone	
Work Phone	
Email Address	

9. When you have entered all of the information for Jim Woods, ***click the New Entry button in the "New Address List" window.***
10. Enter the second client in the blank "New Address List" window (Table 2–2).

HANDS-ON EXERCISES

TABLE 2–2	
First Name	Jennifer
Last Name	John
Company Name	
Address Line 1	3414 Peachtree Road
Address Line 2	
City	Atlanta
State	GA
ZIP Code	30314
Country	
Home Phone	
Work Phone	
Email Address	

11. When you have entered all of the information for Jennifer John, ***click the New Entry button in the "New Address List" window.***
12. Enter the third client in the blank "New Address List" window (Table 2–3).

TABLE 2–3	
First Name	Jonathan
Last Name	Phillips
Company Name	
Address Line 1	675 Clifton Road
Address Line 2	
City	Atlanta
State	GA
ZIP Code	30030
Country	
Home Phone	
Work Phone	
Email Address	

13. When you have entered all of the information for Jonathan Phillips, ***click OK in the "New Address List" window.***
14. The "Save Address List" window is now displayed. You need to save the address list so that it can later be merged with the open-house letter. In the "Save Address List" window, next to File name, type **Open House List** and then ***click Save in the "Save Address List" window*** to save the file to the default directory.
15. The "Mail Merge Recipients" window is now displayed (see Word 2013 Exhibit 18). ***Click the "Last Name" field in the "Mail Merge Recipients" window to sort the list by last name*** (see Word 2013 Exhibit 18). Notice that the order of the list is now sorted by last name.
16. ***Click OK in the "Mail Merge Recipients" window.*** You are now back at a blank document with the Mail Merge task pane open to the right. The bottom

WORD 2013 EXHIBIT 18
Entering mail merge recipients

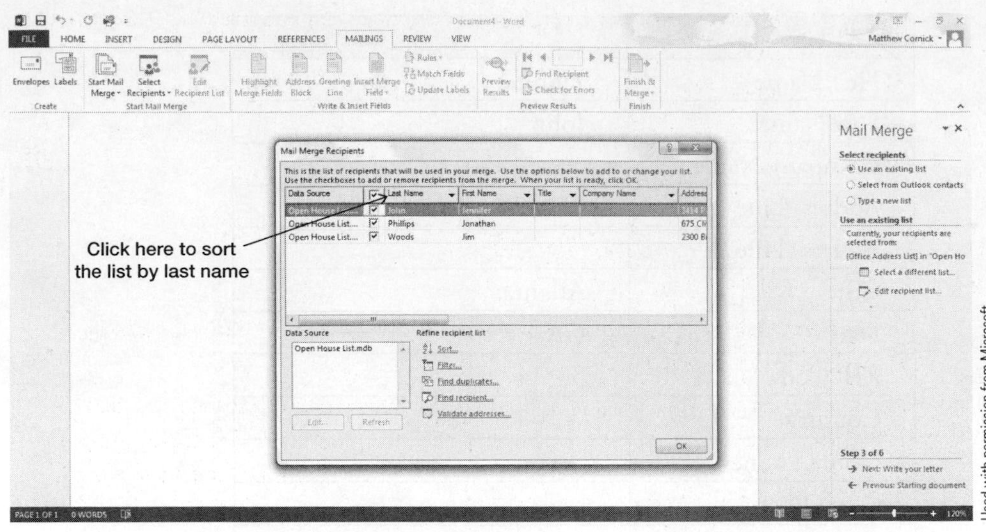

of the Mail Merge task pane indicates that you are still at step 3 of 6. ***Click Next: Write your letter at the bottom of the Mail Merge task pane under Step 3 of 6*** to continue to the next step.

17. The bottom of the Mail Merge task pane indicates that you are on step 4 of 6. In the Mail Merge task pane, **"Write your letter"** is displayed. You are now ready to write the letter. ***On the HOME ribbon tab, click the Paragraph Group Dialog Box Launcher. In the "Paragraph" window, click the down arrow below Line Spacing and select Single. Make sure the Before and After spacing are both 0 point. Then, click OK.***
18. Press the **[ENTER]** key four times.
19. Type the current date and press the **[ENTER]** key three times.
20. ***Click Address Block in the Mail Merge task pane under the Write your letter option.***
21. The "Insert Address Block" window is now displayed. You will now customize how the address block will appear in the letters.
22. ***In the "Insert Address Block" window, click "Joshua Randall Jr."*** Then, ***click Insert company name to deselect it, because we did not include company names in our data list*** (see Word 2013 Exhibit 19).

WORD 2013 EXHIBIT 19
Insert address block

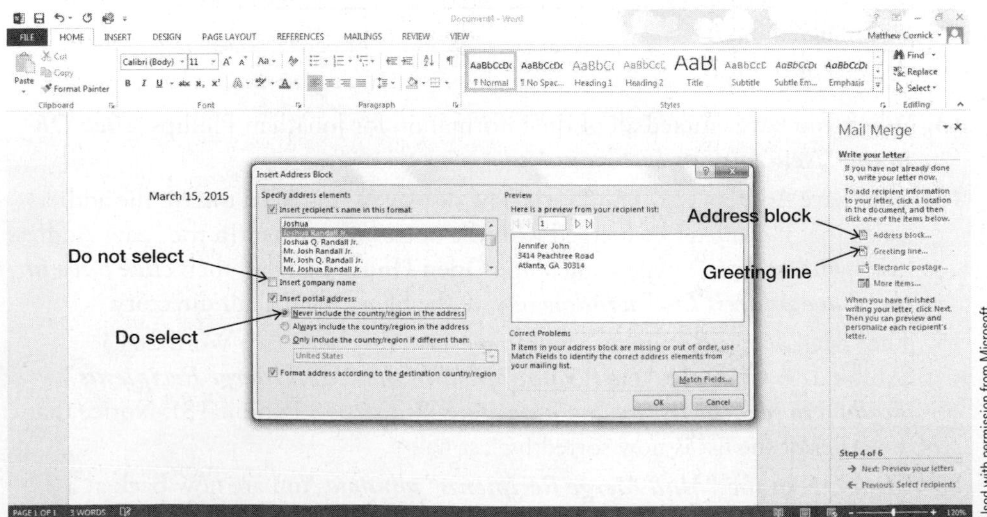

23. ***Under Insert postal address, click Never include the country/region in the address*** (see Word 2013 Exhibit 19).
24. ***Click OK in the "Insert Address Block" window.***
25. The words "**<<AddressBlock>>**" are now displayed in your document.
26. Press the **[ENTER]** key three times.
27. Press the **[TAB]** key once and then type **Subject:**.
28. Press the **[TAB]** key and then type **Open House.**
29. Press the **[ENTER]** key twice.
30. ***In the Mail Merge task pane, under "Write your letter," click Greeting line*** (see Word 2013 Exhibit 19).
31. The "Insert Greeting Line" window is now displayed. You will now customize how the greeting or salutation will appear in the letter. ***In the "Insert Greeting Line" window, click the down arrow next to "Mr. Randall" and then scroll down and click "Josh." Click OK in the "Insert Greeting Line" window.***
32. The words "**<<GreetingLine>>**" are now displayed in your document.
33. Press the **[ENTER]** key three times.
34. Type **You are cordially invited to our open house, which will take place in our new office at 1414 Pine Street, on the 28th of this month, at 7:00 p.m. Drinks will be served. Please dress casually. We hope you will attend.**
35. Press the **[ENTER]** key twice.
36. Type **Kindest Regards,**.
37. Press the **[ENTER]** key four times.
38. Type **Mirabelle Watkinson**.
39. Press the **[ENTER]** key once and type **For the Firm**.
40. You are now done typing the letter. Your letter should look similar to Word 2013 Exhibit 17. The only thing left to do is to merge the recipient list with the form.
41. ***Under Step 4 of 6 at the bottom of the Mail Merge task pane, click Next: Preview your letters*** to continue to the next step.
42. Your first letter is now displayed. ***In the Mail Merge task pane, under Preview your letters, click the button showing two arrows pointing to the right to see the rest of your letters.***
43. To continue to the next step, ***click Next: Complete the merge at the bottom of the Mail Merge task pane under Step 5 of 6.***
44. The Mail Merge task pane now will display **"Complete the merge."** ***Click Print in the Mail Merge task pane under Merge. At the "Merge to Printer" window, click OK*** to print your letters.
45. ***Click Edit individual letters in the Mail Merge task pane under Merge.*** In the "Merge to New Document" window, ***click OK.*** Word has now opened a new document with all of the letters in it. (*Note:* Here you can edit and personalize each letter if you would like.)
46. To save the document, ***click the File tab, click Save As, and then double-click Computer. Select the drive or folder*** you would like to save the Word document in. Then, next to File name:, type **Open House Letters** ***and then click Save*** to save the document.
47. ***If they do not close automatically, click the File tab and then on Close*** to close the personalized letters.
48. You should be back at the mail merge letter. To save the document, ***click the File tab, click Save As, and then double-click Computer. Select the drive or***

HANDS-ON EXERCISES

folder you would like to save the document in. Then, next to File name:, type **Open House Mail Merge; *click Save*** to save the document.

49. ***Click the File tab, and then on Close*** to close the document, or ***click the small x in the upper right corner of the screen*** to exit the program.

This concludes Lesson 10.

LESSON 11: CREATING A TABLE OF AUTHORITIES

In this lesson, you will prepare a table of authorities for a reply brief (see Word 2013 Exhibit 22). You will learn how to find cases, mark cases, and then automatically generate a table of authorities.

1. Open Windows. When it has loaded, ***double-click the Microsoft Office Word 2013 icon on the desktop*** to open Word 2013 for Windows. Alternatively, ***click the Start button, point to Programs or All Programs, and then click the Microsoft Word 2013 icon*** (or ***point to Microsoft Office and then click Microsoft Office Word 2013***), ***then click the [ESC] key.*** You should now be in a clean, blank document. If you are not in a blank document, ***click the File tab, click New, and then click Blank document.***
2. The first thing you will do is to open the "Lesson 11" file from the Premium Website. On the Premium Website, click the Data Files: Word Processing tab, then under Word 2013, click the "Lesson 11" file. The text "***In the Supreme Court of the United States–TED SUTTON, Petitioner v. STATE OF ALASKA, Respondent***" should now be displayed on your screen. If the document appears in Protected View, ***click Enable Editing*** to continue with the lesson.
3. In this exercise you will build the case section of the table of authorities for this reply brief. There are five cases to be included and they are all shown in bold so that you can easily identify them. Your first task will be to mark each of the cases so that Word knows they are the cases to be included; then you will execute the command for Word to build the table.
4. If you are not at the beginning of the document, press **[CTRL]+[HOME]** to go to the beginning.
5. You will now mark the cases. ***From the REFERENCES ribbon tab, click Mark Citations from the Table of Authorities group.***
6. The "Mark Citation" window should now be displayed (see Word 2013 Exhibit 20). Notice, next to Category:, that Cases is displayed. This indicates that you will

WORD 2013 EXHIBIT 20
Marking a citation for inclusion in a table of authorities

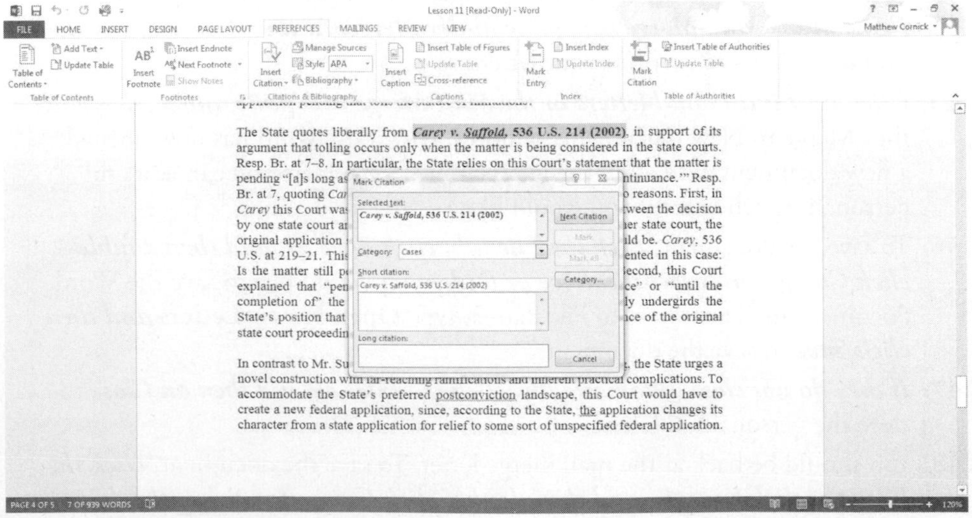

be marking case citations. ***Click the down arrow next to Cases*** to see that you can also mark citations to be included for Statutes, Rules, Treatises, Regulations, and Other Authorities.

7. ***Click Cases again;*** you will now start marking cases to be included in the TABLE OF AUTHORITIES.
8. ***In the "Mark Citation" window, click Next Citation.*** Word looks for terms such as "vs" or "v." when finding citations. The cursor should now be on the "v." in *Ted Sutton v. State of Alaska.* Because this is the caption of the current case, we do not want to mark it. *Note:* If the "Mark Citation" window gets in the way of your seeing the brief, put the pointer on the blue title bar of the "Mark Citation" window and drag it out of your way.
9. ***Click Next Citation in the "Mark Citation" window.*** Again, this is the caption of the current case, *Ted Sutton v. State of Alaska,* so we do not want to mark it.
10. ***Click again on Next Citation in the "Mark Citation" window.*** Word has now found the case *Carey v. Saffold.* We want to mark this case so that it will be included in the table of authorities.
11. ***Click once on the* Carey v. Saffold *case.***
12. ***Drag the pointer to highlight* "Carey v. Saffold, 536 U.S. 214 (2002)" *and then click in the white box under Selected text: in the "Mark Citation" window.*** The case is automatically copied there (see Word 2013 Exhibit 20).
13. ***Click Mark in the "Mark Citation" window.*** *Note:* When you mark a citation, Word changes your view to the Show/Hide paragraph view. It shows you that you have embedded table of authorities formatting codes in the document. To switch out of Show/Hide view, ***from the HOME ribbon tab, click the Show/ Hide icon in the Paragraph group.*** (It looks like a paragraph sign.)
14. ***Click Next Citation in the "Mark Citation" window.***
15. ***Click once on the* "Duncan v. Walker" *case.***
16. ***Drag the mouse to highlight* "Duncan v. Walker, 533 U.S. 167, 174 (2001)" *and then click in the white box under Selected text: in the "Mark Citation" window.*** The case is automatically copied there.
17. ***Click Mark in the "Mark Citation" window.*** Notice under Short Citation in the "Mark Citation" window that the *Carey* and *Duncan* cases are listed. Again, if at any time the "Mark Citation" window prevents you from seeing the case

HANDS-ON EXERCISES

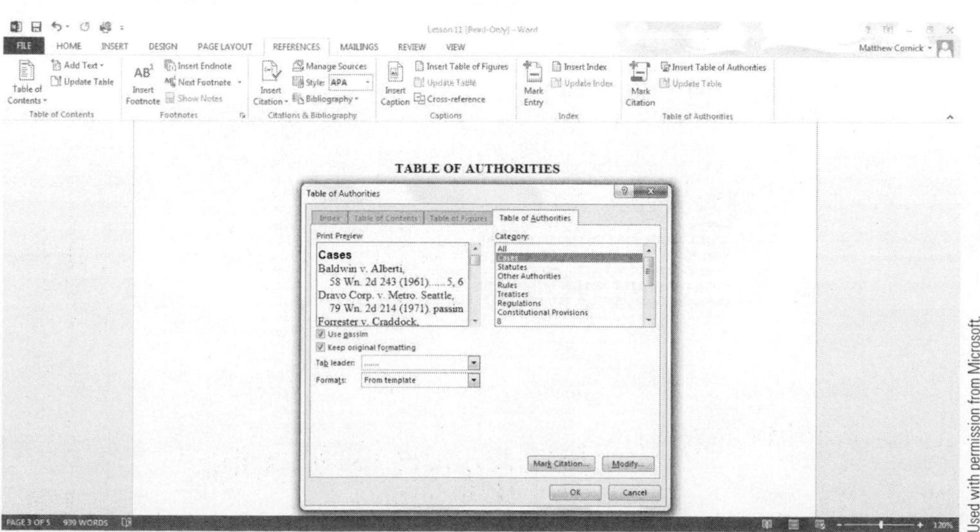

WORD 2013 EXHIBIT 21
Inserting a table of authorities

you need to highlight, just ***click the blue bar at top of the "Mark Citation" window and drag to the left or the right*** to move the window out of your way.

18. To switch out of Show/Hide view, ***from the HOME tab on the ribbon, click the Show/Hide icon in the Paragraph group.***
19. ***Click Next Citation in the "Mark Citation" window.***
20. ***Click once on the* "Bates v. United States" *case.***
21. ***Drag the pointer to highlight* " Bates v. United States, 522 U.S. 23, 29–30 (1997)," *and then click in the white box under Selected text: in the "Mark Citation" window.*** The case is automatically copied there.
22. ***Click Mark in the "Mark Citation" window.***
23. ***Click Next Citation in the "Mark Citation" window.***
24. ***Click once on the* "Abela v. Martin" *case.***
25. ***Drag to highlight* "Abela v. Martin, 348 F.3d 164 (6th Cir. 2003)" *and then click in the white box under Selected text: in the "Mark Citation" window.*** The case is automatically copied there.
26. ***Click Mark in the "Mark Citation" window.***
27. ***Click Next Citation in the "Mark Citation" window.***
28. ***Click once on the* "Coates v. Byrd" *case.***
29. ***Drag the mouse to highlight* "Coates v. Byrd, 211 F.3d 1225, 1227 (11th Cir. 2000)," *and then click in the white box under Selected text: in the "Mark Citation" window.*** The case is automatically copied there.
30. ***Click Mark in the "Mark Citation" window.***
31. ***Click Close in the "Mark Citation" window to close it.***
32. ***On the HOME ribbon tab, click the Show/Hide paragraph icon to make the paragraph marks disappear.***
33. Using the cursor keys or the horizontal scroll bar, place the cursor on page 3 of the document two lines under the title **"TABLE OF AUTHORITIES"** (see Word 2013 Exhibit 22). You are now ready to generate the table.
34. ***From the REFERENCES ribbon tab, click the Insert Table of Authorities icon in the Table of Authorities group*** (see Word 2013 Exhibit 21).
35. ***The "Table of Authorities" window should now be displayed*** (see Word 2013 Exhibit 21). ***Click Cases under Category and then click OK.***

WORD 2013 EXHIBIT 22
Completed table of authorities

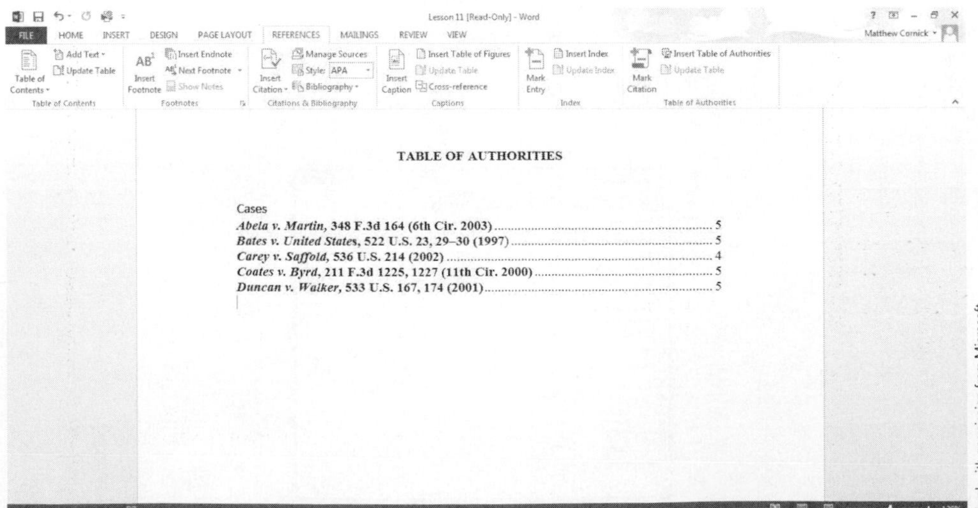

36. Notice that the table of authorities has been prepared and completed, and that the cases and the page numbers where they appear in the document have been included (see Word 2013 Exhibit 22).
37. To print the document, ***click the Quick Print icon on the Quick Access toolbar,*** or ***click the File tab, click Print, and then click Print.***
38. To save the document, ***click the File tab, click Save As, and then double-click Computer. Select the drive or folder*** you would like to save the document in. Then, next to File name:, type **Done—Word 2013 Lesson 11 Document** ***and click Save*** to save the document.
39. ***Click the File tab, and then on Close*** to close the document, or ***click the small x in the upper right corner of the screen*** to exit the program.

This concludes Lesson 11.

LESSON 12: CREATING A MACRO

In this lesson you will prepare a macro that will automatically type the signature block for a pleading (see Word 2013 Exhibit 23). You will then execute the macro to make sure that it works properly.

1. Open Windows. When it has loaded, ***double-click the Microsoft Office Word 2013 icon on the desktop*** to open Word 2013 for Windows. Alternatively, ***click the Start button, point to Programs or All Programs, and then click the Microsoft Word 2013 icon*** (or ***point to Microsoft Office and then click Microsoft Office Word 2013***). You should now be in a clean, blank document. If you are not in a blank document, ***click the File tab, click New, and then click Blank document.***
2. The first thing you need to do to create a new macro is to name the macro and then turn on the Record function. ***From the VIEW ribbon tab, click the down arrow under Macros in the Macros group*** (see Word 2013 Exhibit 23).
3. ***Click Record Macro on the drop-down menu.***
4. The "Record Macro" window should now be displayed (see Word 2013 Exhibit 23). In the "Record Macro" window, under Macro Name:, type **Pleadingsignblock** ***and then click OK*** (see Word 2013 Exhibit 23).
5. Notice that your cursor has a cassette tape on it. The cassette tape on your cursor indicates that Word is now recording all of your keystrokes and commands.

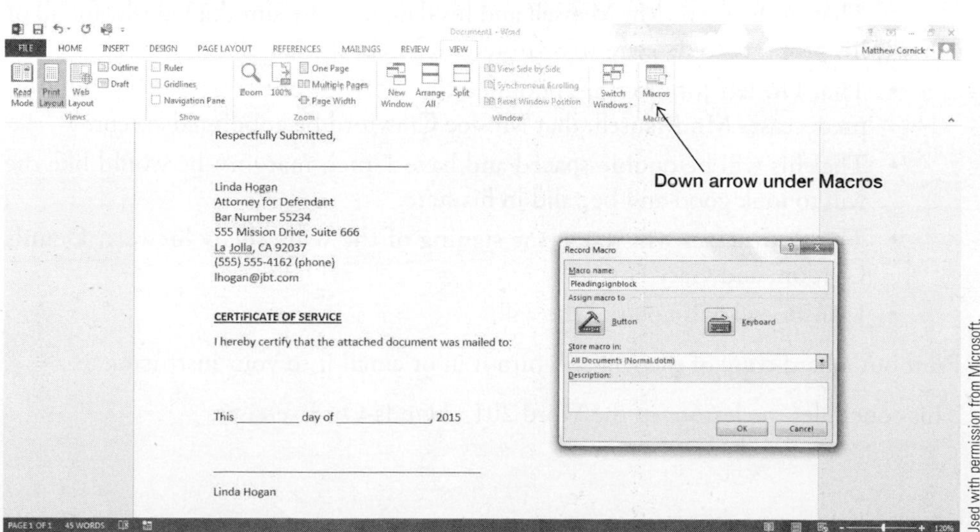

WORD 2013 EXHIBIT 23
Creating a pleading signature block macro

6. Type the information shown in Word 2013 Exhibit 23. When you have completed typing the information, ***from the VIEW ribbon tab, click the down arrow under Macros in the Macros group*** (see Word 2013 Exhibit 23).
7. ***Click Stop Recording on the drop-down menu.***
8. You will now test your macro to see if it works properly. ***Click the File tab and then on Close*** to close the document. At the prompt **"Do you want to save the changes to Document?"** ***click Don't Save.***
9. To open a blank document, ***click the File tab, click New, and then click Blank document.***
10. To run the macro, ***from the VIEW ribbon tab, click the down arrow under Macros in the Macros group*** (see Word 2013 Exhibit 23).
11. ***Click View Macros.***
12. ***In the "Macros" window, click*** **Pleadingsignblock** ***and then click Run.*** Your pleading signature block should now appear in your document.
13. To print the document, ***click the Quick Print icon on the Quick Access toolbar,*** or ***click the File tab, click Print, and then click Print.***
14. To save the document, ***click the File tab, click Save As, and then double-click Computer. Select the drive or folder*** you would like to save the document in. Then, next to File name:, type **Done—Word 2013 Lesson 12 Document** ***and click Save*** to save the document.
15. ***Click the File tab, and then on Close*** to close the document, or ***click the small x in the upper right corner of the screen*** to exit the program.

This concludes Lesson 12.

LESSON 13: DRAFTING A WILL

Using the websites at the end of the chapter or a form book from a law library, draft a simple will that would be valid in your state. You will be drafting the will for Thomas Mansell, who is a widower. The will should be dated July 1 of the current year. Mr. Mansell requests the following:

- That his just debts and funeral expenses be paid.
- That his lifelong friend, Dr. Jeff Johnson, receive $20,000 in cash.
- That his local YMCA receive his 100 shares of stock in IBM.
- That all of his remaining property (real or personal) descend to his daughter Sharon Mansell.
- That in the event Mr. Mansell and his daughter die simultaneously, for all of his property to descend to Sharon's son Michael Mansell.
- That Dr. Jeff Johnson be appointed the executor of the will; if Dr. Johnson predeceases Mr. Mansell, that Mr. Joe Crawford be appointed executor.
- That his will be double-spaced and have 1-inch margins; he would like the will to look good and be valid in his state.
- Three witnesses will watch the signing of the will: Shelly Stewart, Dennis Gordon, and Gary Fox.
- John Boesel will notarize the will.

Print out a hard copy of the will and turn it in or email it to your instructor.

This concludes the lessons in the Word 2013 Hands-On Exercises.

HANDS-ON EXERCISES

MICROSOFT WORD 2010 FOR WINDOWS

Number	Lesson Title	Concepts Covered
BASIC LESSONS		
Lesson 1	Typing a Letter	Using word wrap, Tab key, cursor keys, underline, bold, italic, and saving and printing a document
Lesson 2	Editing a Letter	Retrieving a file, block moving/deleting, and spell/grammar checking
Lesson 3	Typing a Pleading	Centering, changing margins, changing line spacing, adding a footnote, double indenting, and automatic page numbering
Lesson 4	Creating a Table	Creating a table, entering data in a table, using automatic numbering, adjusting columns in a table, and using the Table Auto Format command
INTERMEDIATE LESSONS		
Lesson 5	Tools and Techniques	Editing an employment policy, using the Format Painter tool, revealing formatting, using Beginning of Document command, clearing formatting, changing case, using Search and Replace, using Go To command, creating a section break, and changing the orientation of the page to Landscape
Lesson 6	Using Styles	Using, modifying, and creating styles to maintain consistent and uniform formatting of documents
Lesson 7	Creating a Template (office letterhead/letter)	Finding ready-made templates in Word, creating a new office letterhead and letter template, filling in/completing a template, and adding a command to the Quick Access toolbar
Lesson 8	Comparing Documents (multiple versions of an employment contract)	Comparing documents using the simultaneous viewing method and merging the documents into a separate, annotated, blacklined document
Lesson 9	Using Track Changes	Turning on Track Changes, making revisions, and then accepting and rejecting revisions
ADVANCED LESSONS		
Lesson 10	Creating a Mail Merge Document	Creating and entering a list of recipients for a mail merge, creating a mail merge document, and merging the list with the document
Lesson 11	Creating a Table of Authorities	Finding and marking cases in a reply brief, and then generating an actual table of authorities for the brief
Lesson 12	Creating a Macro (pleading signature block)	Creating and executing a pleading signature block macro
Lesson 13	Drafting a Will	Using Word to draft a will

GETTING STARTED

Introduction

Throughout these lessons and exercises, information you need to type into the program will be designated in several different ways:

- Keys to be pressed on the keyboard are designated in brackets, in all caps, and in bold (e.g., press the **[ENTER]** key).
- Movements with the mouse pointer are designated in bold and italics (e.g., ***point to File and click***).
- Words or letters that should be typed are designated in bold (e.g., type **Training Program**).
- Information that is or should be displayed on your computer screen is shown in bold, with quotation marks (e.g., "**Press ENTER to continue.**").
- Specific menu items and commands are designated with an initial capital letter (e.g., click Open).

OVERVIEW OF MICROSOFT WORD 2010

Here are some tips on using Microsoft Word 2010 that will help you complete these exercises:

I. General Rules for Microsoft Word 2010

A. *Word Wrap.* You do not need to press the **[ENTER]** key after each line of text as you would with a typewriter.

B. *Double-Spacing.* If you want to double-space, do not hit the **[ENTER]** key twice. Instead, change the line spacing by ***clicking on the Home ribbon tab, then clicking on the Line and Paragraph Spacing icon in the Paragraph group and selecting 2.0*** (see Word 2010 Exhibit 1).

C. *Moving through Already Entered Text.* If you want to move the mouse pointer to various positions within already entered text, ***use the cursor (arrow) keys or point and click.***

D. *Moving the Pointer Where No Text Has Been Entered.* You cannot use the cursor keys to move the pointer where no text has been entered. Said another way, you cannot move any further in a document than where you have typed text or pressed the **[ENTER]** key. You must use the **[ENTER]** key or first type text.

E. *Saving a Document.* To save a document, ***click the File tab in the upper left corner of the screen and then click Save*** (see Word 2010 Exhibit 1).

F. *New Document.* To get a new, clean document, ***click the File tab, then click New, and then double-click "Blank document"*** (see Word 2010 Exhibit 1).

G. *Help.* To get help, press **[F1]** or ***click the ? icon in the upper right corner of the screen*** (see Word 2010 Exhibit 1).

II. Editing a Document

A. *Pointer Movement*

One space to left	**[LEFT ARROW]**
One space to right	**[RIGHT ARROW]**
Beginning of line	**[HOME]**
End of line	**[END]**
One line up	**[UP ARROW]**
One line down	**[DOWN ARROW]**

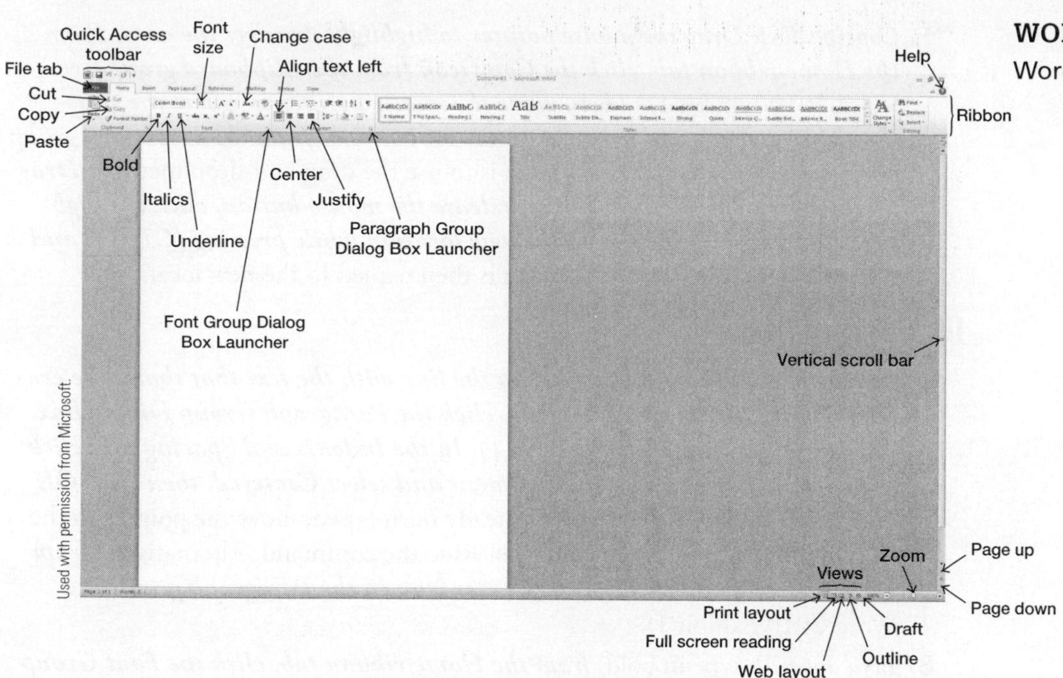

WORD 2010 EXHIBIT 1
Word 2010 screen

One screen up	**[PAGE UP]**
One screen down	**[PAGE DOWN]**
Beginning of document	**[CTRL]+[HOME]**
End of document	**[CTRL]+[END]**

B. *Deleting Text*

Delete the text under the pointer or to the right	**[DEL]**
Delete the text to the left of the pointer	**[BACKSPACE]**
Delete the whole word to the left of the pointer	**[CTRL]+[BACKSPACE]**
Delete the whole word to the right of the pointer	**[CTRL]+[DEL]**

C. *Delete Blocked Text.* ***Drag the mouse pointer to select or highlight text,*** and press **[DEL]**, or ***drag the mouse pointer and then from the Home ribbon tab, select the Cut icon from the Clipboard group*** (see Word 2010 Exhibit 1). Another way to select or highlight text is ***to press the [SHIFT] key and keep it depressed while you use the cursor keys to mark/highlight the desired text.***

D. *Undoing/Undeleting Text.* If you delete text and immediately want it back, ***click the Undo icon on the Quick Access toolbar.*** This can also be done by pressing **[CTRL]+[Z]**. Press **[CTRL]+[Z]** or ***click the Undo icon*** until your desired text reappears. The Undo feature works on many other activities in Word, but not all. So, if something goes wrong, at least try pressing **[CTRL]+[Z]** to undo whatever you did.

E. *Moving Text.* ***Drag the mouse pointer to highlight or select the text. Then, from the Home ribbon tab, select the Cut icon from the Clipboard group*** (see Word 2010 Exhibit 1)***, move the mouse pointer to where the text should be moved, and from the Home ribbon tab, select Paste from the Clipboard group.*** Another way to do this is to ***drag the mouse pointer to highlight the area and then right-click.*** This brings up a menu that includes the Cut, Copy, and Paste commands. Yet another way to do this is to use the drag-and-drop method: ***Drag the mouse pointer to highlight the area, release the mouse button, click the highlighted area, drag the text to the new location, and release the mouse button.***

F. *Copying Text.* ***Drag the mouse pointer to highlight or select the area. From the Home ribbon tab, click the Copy icon from the Clipboard group*** (see Word 2010 Exhibit 1). ***Then, move the mouse pointer to where the text should be copied, and from the Home ribbon tab, from the Clipboard group click Paste.*** Another way to do this is to use the drag-and-drop method: ***Drag the pointer to highlight the area, release the mouse button, click the highlighted area, drag the text to the new location while pressing [CTRL], and release the mouse button.*** The text is then copied to the new location.

III. Formatting

A. *Centering Text.* ***Move the pointer to the line with the text that should be centered. From the Home ribbon tab, click the Paragraph Group Dialog Box Launcher*** (see Word 2010 Exhibit 1). ***In the Indents and Spacing tab, click the down arrow key next to Alignment and select Centered, then click OK and begin typing.*** If the text has already been typed, move the pointer to the paragraph where the text is and then issue the command. Alternatively, ***from the Home ribbon tab, click the Center icon in the Paragraph group*** (see Word 2010 Exhibit 1).

B. *Bold Type.* To type in bold, ***from the Home ribbon tab, click the Font Group Dialog Box Launcher*** (see Word 2010 Exhibit 1), ***and then, in the Font tab, click Bold under Font style. Then, click OK.*** Alternatively, ***from the Home ribbon tab, click the Bold icon in the Font group.*** Another way is to press **[CTRL]+[B].**

C. *Underlining.* To underline, ***from the Home ribbon tab, click the Font Group Dialog Box Launcher*** (see Word 2010 Exhibit 1). ***Then, in the Font tab, click the down arrow under Underline style, select the underline style you would like, and then click OK.*** Alternatively, ***from the Home ribbon tab, click the Underline icon in the Font group.*** Another way is to press **[CTRL]+[U].**

D. *Margins.* Margins can be set by ***clicking the Page Layout ribbon tab and then clicking on Margins from the Page Setup group.***

E. *Line Spacing.* Line spacing can be changed by ***clicking the Home ribbon tab and then clicking the Line and Paragraph Spacing icon in the Paragraph group*** (see Word 2010 Exhibit 1).

F. *Justification.* Move the pointer to the line where the text should be justified. Then, ***from the Home ribbon tab, click the Paragraph Group Dialog Box Launcher*** (see Word 2010 Exhibit 1). ***In the Indents and Spacing tab, click the down arrow key next to Alignment and select Justified; then click OK and begin typing.*** If the text has already been typed, move the cursor to the paragraph where the text is and then issue the command. Alternatively, ***from the Home ribbon tab, click the Justify icon in the Paragraph group*** (see Word 2010 Exhibit 1).

G. *Header/Footer.* ***From the Insert ribbon tab, click Header or Footer from the Header & Footer group.***

H. *Hard Page Break.* To force the addition of a new page in the current document by using the Hard Page Break command, press **[CTRL]+[ENTER]** or ***from the Insert ribbon tab, click Blank Page from the Pages group.*** Page breaks also occur automatically when the current page is full of text.

I. *Indent.* ***From the Home ribbon tab, click the Paragraph Group Dialog Box Launcher*** (see Word 2010 Exhibit 1). ***In the Indents and Spacing tab under Indentation, click the up arrow next to Left or Right to set the indentation amount; then click OK and begin typing.*** Alternatively, ***from the Home ribbon tab, point to the Decrease Indent or Increase Indent icon in the Paragraph group.***

IV. Other Functions

A. *Printing.* To print, ***click the File tab and then click Print*** (see Word 2010 Exhibit 1).

B. *Spell Check.* To turn on the spell-checking function, ***from the Review ribbon tab, click Spelling & Grammar in the Proofing group.*** Additionally, a red squiggly line will appear under each word that is not recognized. If you ***right-click the word,*** the program will suggest possible spellings.

C. *Open Files.* To open a file, ***click the File tab then click Open*** (see Word 2010 Exhibit 1).

D. *Tables.* ***From the Insert ribbon tab, click Table from the Tables group.*** You can move between cells in the table by pressing the **[TAB]** and the **[SHIFT]+[TAB]** keys.

BASIC LESSONS

LESSON 1: TYPING A LETTER

This lesson shows you how to type the letter shown in Word 2010 Exhibit 2. It explains how to use the word wrap feature; the **[TAB]** key; the cursor (or arrow) keys; the underline, bold, and italics features; the save document function; and the print document function. Keep in mind that if at any time you make a mistake in this lesson, you may press **[CTRL]+[Z]** to undo what you have done. Also remember that any time you would like to see the name of an icon on the ribbon tabs, just ***point to the icon for a second or two*** and the name will be displayed.

1. Open Windows. When it has loaded, ***double-click the Microsoft Office Word 2010 icon on the desktop*** to open Word 2010 for Windows. Alternatively, ***click the Start button, point to Programs or All Programs, and then click the Microsoft Word 2010 icon*** (or ***point to Microsoft Office and then click Microsoft Office Word 2010***). You should now be in a clean, blank document. If you are not in a blank document, ***click the File tab, click New, and then double-click Blank document.***
2. At this point you cannot move the pointer around the screen by pushing the cursor keys (also called arrow keys). Text must first be entered before the pointer can be moved using the cursor keys. The pointer can only move through text. ***On the Home ribbon tab, click the Paragraph Group Dialog Box Launcher. In the "Paragraph" window, click the down arrow below*** **"Line spacing"** ***and select*** **"Single."** ***Make sure the*** **"Before"** ***and*** **"After"** ***spacing are both 0 point. Then, click OK.***
3. Press the **[ENTER]** key four times. (Watch the status line in the lower left-hand corner of the screen, which tells you what page of your document you are on.)
4. Type the date of the letter as shown in Word 2010 Exhibit 2. Notice as you type the word "October" that Auto Text may anticipate that you are typing "October" and give you the following prompt: **"October (Press ENTER to Insert)."** You can either press the **[ENTER]** key and let Auto Text finish typing the word for you, or you can ignore it and continue typing the word yourself.
5. Press the **[ENTER]** key three times.
6. Type the inside address as shown in Word 2010 Exhibit 2. Press the **[ENTER]** key after each line of the inside address. When you finish the line with "Boston, MA 59920," press the **[ENTER]** key three times.

HANDS-ON EXERCISES

WORD 2010 EXHIBIT 2
Letter

October 1, 2013

Steven Matthews
Matthews, Smith & Russell
P.O. Box 12341
Boston, MA 59920

Subject: Turner v. Smith
Case No. CV-13-0046

Dear Mr. Matthews:

In line with our recent conversation, the deposition of the defendant, Jonathan R. Smith, will be taken in your office on **November 15 at 9:00 a.m.** Please find enclosed a *"Notice of Deposition."*

I expect that I will be able to finish this deposition on November 15 and that discovery will be finished, in line with the Court's order, by December 15.

I will be finishing answers to your interrogatories this week and will have them to you by early next week.

If you have any questions, please feel free to contact me.

Kindest regards,

Mirabelle Watkinson
For the Firm

MW:db
Enclosures (as indicated)
cc

7. Press the **[TAB]** key one time. (Word automatically sets default tabs every five spaces.) The pointer will move five spaces to the right.
8. Type **Subject:** and then press the **[TAB]** key. ***On the Home ribbon tab, click the Underline icon in the Font group*** (it looks like a "U"). Alternatively, you can press **[CTRL]+[U]** to turn the underline feature on and off, or ***point to the Font Group Dialog Box Launcher*** (see Word 2010 Exhibit 1) and select the Underline style. Then, type **Turner v. Smith**. ***On the Home ribbon tab in the Font group, click the Underline icon*** to turn the underline feature off.
9. Press the **[ENTER]** key one time.
10. Press the **[TAB]** key three times and then type **Case No. CV-13-0046**.
11. Press the **[ENTER]** key three times.
12. Type the salutation **Dear Mr. Matthews:**
13. Press the **[ENTER]** key twice.
14. Type **In line with our recent conversation, the deposition of the defendant, Jonathan R. Smith, will be taken in your office on**. *Note:* You should not press the **[ENTER]** key at the end of the line. Word will automatically "wrap" the text down to the next line. Be sure to press the **[SPACEBAR]** once after the word "on."

15. ***Turn on the Bold feature by clicking the Bold icon*** (a capital "B") ***in the Font group in the Home ribbon tab*** (see Word 2010 Exhibit 1). Alternatively, you can press **[CTRL]+[B]** to turn bold on and off. Type **November 15 at 9:00 a.m.** Turn off the Bold feature either by pressing **[CTRL]+[B]**, or by ***clicking the Bold icon in the Font group in the Home ribbon tab.*** Press the **[SPACEBAR]** twice.
16. Type **Please find enclosed a** and then press **[SPACEBAR]**.
17. ***Turn on the Italics feature by clicking the Italics icon*** (it looks like an "I") ***in the Font group in the Home ribbon tab*** (see Word 2010 Exhibit 1). Alternatively, you can press **[CTRL]+[I]** to turn italics on and off. Type **"Notice of Deposition."** Turn off the Italics feature either by pressing **[CTRL]+[I]** or by ***clicking the Italics icon in the Font group in the Home ribbon tab.***
18. Press the **[ENTER]** key twice.
19. Type the second paragraph of the letter and then press the **[ENTER]** key twice.
20. Type the third paragraph of the letter and then press the **[ENTER]** key twice.
21. Type the fourth paragraph of the letter and then press the **[ENTER]** key twice.
22. Type **Kindest regards,** and then press the **[ENTER]** key four times.
23. Type **Mirabelle Watkinson** and then press the **[ENTER]** key.
24. Type **For the Firm** and then press the **[ENTER]** key twice.
25. Finish the letter by typing the author's initials, enclosures, and copy abbreviation (cc) as shown in Word 2010 Exhibit 2.
26. To print the document, ***click the File tab, click Print, and then click Print.***
27. To save the document, ***click the File tab and then click Save.*** Then, type **Letter1** next to **"File name."** ***Click Save*** to save the letter to the default directory. (*Note:* In Lesson 2, you will edit this letter, so it is important that you save it.)
28. ***Click the File tab and then click Close*** to close the document, or to exit Word 2010, ***click the File tab and then click Exit*** to exit the program.

This concludes Lesson 1.

LESSON 2: EDITING A LETTER

This lesson shows you how to retrieve and edit the letter you typed in Lesson 1. It explains how to retrieve a file, perform block moves and deletes, and spell-/grammar-check your document. Keep in mind that if at any time you make a mistake in this lesson, you may press **[CTRL]+[Z]** to undo what you have done. Also remember that any time you would like to see the name of an icon on the Ribbon tab, just ***point to the icon for a second or two*** and the name will be displayed.

1. Open Windows. When it has loaded, ***double-click the Microsoft Office Word 2010 icon on the desktop*** to open Word 2010 for Windows. Alternatively, ***click the Start button, point to Programs or All Programs, and then click the Microsoft Word 2010 icon*** (or ***point to Microsoft Office and then click Microsoft Office Word 2010***). You should now be in a clean, blank document. If you are not in a blank document, ***click the File tab, click New, and then double-click Blank document.***
2. In this lesson, you will begin by retrieving the document you created in Lesson 1. To open the file, ***click the File tab and click Open.*** Then type in the File name textbox **Letter1** and ***click Open.*** Alternatively, ***scroll using the horizontal scroll bar until you find the file, click it, and then click Open.***

3. Notice in Word 2010 Exhibit 3 that some changes have been made to the letter. You will spend the rest of this lesson making these changes.
4. Use your cursor keys or mouse to go to the salutation line, "Dear Mr. Matthews:" With the pointer to the left of the "M" in "Mr. Matthews," press the **[DEL]** key 12 times until "Mr. Matthews" is deleted.
5. Type **Steve**. The salutation line should now read "Dear Steve:"
6. Using your cursor keys or mouse, ***move the pointer to the left of the comma following the word "conversation" in the first paragraph.*** Press the **[SPACEBAR]**, then type **of September 30**. The sentence now reads:

   In line with our recent conversation of September 30, the deposition of the defendant . . .
7. The next change you will make is to move the second paragraph so that it becomes part of the first paragraph. Although this can be accomplished in more than one way, this lesson uses the Cut command.
8. Using your cursor keys or mouse, ***move the pointer to the beginning of the second paragraph of Word 2010 Exhibit 2.***
9. ***Click and drag the mouse pointer*** (hold the left mouse button down, and move the mouse) ***until the entire second paragraph is highlighted, and then release the mouse button.***
10. ***From the Home ribbon tab, click the Cut icon in the Clipboard group*** (see Word 2010 Exhibit 1). An alternative is to right-click anywhere in the highlighted area, and then ***click Cut.*** The text is no longer on the screen, but it is not deleted—it has been temporarily placed on the Office Clipboard.
11. Move the pointer to the end of the first paragraph. Press the **[SPACEBAR]** twice. If the pointer appears to be in italics mode, ***from the Home ribbon tab, click the Italics icon in the Font group,*** or press **[CTLR]+[I]** to turn the Italics feature off.
12. ***From the Home ribbon tab, click Paste from the Clipboard group*** (see Word 2010 Exhibit 1). Notice that the text has now been moved. Also, you may notice that a small icon in the shape of a clipboard has appeared where you pasted the text. ***Click the down arrow of the Paste Options icon.*** Notice

WORD 2010 EXHIBIT 3
Corrections to a letter

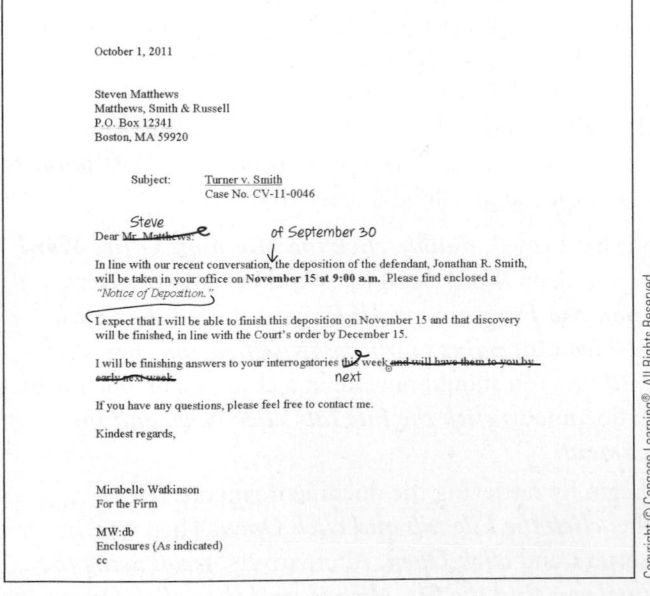
October 1, 2011

Steven Matthews
Matthews, Smith & Russell
P.O. Box 12341
Boston, MA 59920

Subject: Turner v. Smith
Case No. CV-11-0046

Dear ~~Mr. Matthews~~: Steve

In line with our recent conversation, [of September 30] the deposition of the defendant, Jonathan R. Smith, will be taken in your office on **November 15 at 9:00 a.m.** Please find enclosed a *"Notice of Deposition."*

I expect that I will be able to finish this deposition on November 15 and that discovery will be finished, in line with the Court's order by December 15.

I will be finishing answers to your interrogatories ~~this~~ next week ~~and will have them to you by early next week~~.

If you have any questions, please feel free to contact me.

Kindest regards,

Mirabelle Watkinson
For the Firm

MW:db
Enclosures (As indicated)
cc

that you are given the option to keep the source formatting or change the formatting so that the text matches the destination formatting (i.e., the formatting of the place you are copying it to). In this example, both formats are the same, so it does not matter, but if the text you are copying is a different format, you may or may not want to change it to the destination format. Press the **[ESC]** key to make the Paste Options menu disappear.

13. Move the pointer to the line below the newly expanded first paragraph, and use the **[DEL]** key to delete any unnecessary blank lines.
14. Using your cursor keys or mouse, ***move the pointer to what is now the second paragraph and place it to the left of the*** "**t**" ***in*** **"this week."**
15. Use the **[DEL]** key to delete the word **"this,"** and then type **next**.
16. We will now delete the rest of the sentence in the second paragraph. ***Drag the pointer until*** **"and will have them to you by early next week."** ***is highlighted.*** Press the **[DEL]** key. Type a period at the end of the sentence.
17. You have now made all of the changes that need to be made. To be sure the letter does not have misspelled words or grammar errors, we will use the Spelling and Grammar command.
18. ***Click the Review ribbon tab and then click Spelling & Grammar in the Proofing group.***
19. If an error is found, it will be highlighted. You have the choice of ignoring it once, ignoring it completely, accepting one of the suggestions listed, or changing or correcting the problem yourself. Correct any spelling or grammar errors. When the spell and grammar check is done, ***click OK.***
20. To print the document, ***click the File tab, click Print, and then click Print.***
21. To save the document, ***click the File tab and then select Save As.*** Type **Letter2** in the "File name" box, ***and then click Save*** to save the document in the default directory.
22. ***Click the File tab and then click Close*** to close the document, or ***click the File tab and then click Exit*** to exit the program.

This concludes Lesson 2.

LESSON 3: TYPING A PLEADING

This lesson shows you how to type a pleading, as shown in Word 2010 Exhibit 4. It expands on the items presented in Lessons 1 and 2. It also explains how to center text, change margins, change line spacing, add a footnote, double-indent text, and use automatic page numbering. Keep in mind that if at any time you make a mistake, you may press **[CTRL]+[Z]** to undo what you have done.

1. Open Windows. When it has loaded, ***double-click the Microsoft Office Word 2010 icon on the desktop*** to open Word 2010 for Windows. Alternatively, ***click the Start button, point to Programs or All Programs, and then click the Microsoft Word 2010 icon*** (or ***point to Microsoft Office and then click Microsoft Office Word 2010***). You should now be in a clean, blank document. If you are not in a blank document, ***click the File tab, click New, and then double-click Blank document.*** Remember, any time you would like to see the name of an icon on the ribbon tabs, just ***point to the icon for a second or two*** and the name will be displayed.
2. You will be creating the document shown in Word 2010 Exhibit 4. The first thing you will need to do is to change the margins so that the left margin is 1.5 inches and the right margin is 1 inch. To change the margins, ***click the Page***

HANDS-ON EXERCISES

WORD 2010 EXHIBIT 4
A pleading

IN THE DISTRICT COURT OF
ORANGE COUNTY, MASSACHUSETTS

JIM TURNER,

Plaintiff,

vs. Case No. CV-13-0046

JONATHAN R. SMITH,

Defendant.

NOTICE TO TAKE DEPOSITION

COMES NOW the plaintiff and pursuant to statute[1] hereby gives notice that the deposition of Defendant, Jonathan R. Smith, will be taken as follows:

Monday, November 15, 2013, at 9:00 a.m. at the law offices of Matthews, Smith & Russell, 17031 W. 69th Street, Boston, MA.

Said deposition will be taken before a court reporter and is not expected to take more than one day in duration.

____
Mirabelle Watkinson
Attorney for Plaintiff

[1] Massachusetts Statutes Annotated 60-2342(a)(1).

Layout ribbon tab and then click Margins in the Page Setup group. Next, click Custom Margins at the bottom of the drop-down menu. In the "Page Setup" window, change the left margin to 1.5 inches and the right margin to 1 inch. Then, click OK. Also, ***on the Home ribbon tab, click the Paragraph Group Dialog Box Launcher. In the "Paragraph" window, click the down arrow below Line Spacing and select Single. Make sure the Before and After spacing are both 0 point. Then, click OK.***

3. Notice in Word 2010 Exhibit 4 that there is a page number at the bottom of the page. Word will automatically number your pages for you.

4. ***Click the Insert ribbon tab, and then click Page Number in the Header & Footer group*** (see Word 2010 Exhibit 5).
5. ***Next, point to Bottom of Page*** (see Word 2010 Exhibit 5) and notice that a number of options are displayed. ***Click the down arrow in the lower right*** for additional options (see Word 2010 Exhibit 5). Notice that many page-number options are available. ***Scroll back up to the top of the option list and click the second option, Plain Number 2.***
6. Your pointer should now be in the area marked "Footer." Specifically, your pointer should be to the left of the number 1. Type **Page** and then press **[SPACEBAR]**.
7. ***Click the Home ribbon tab. Then, click the vertical scroll bar*** (see Word 2010 Exhibit 1) ***or use the [UP ARROW] key to go back to the beginning of the document.***
8. ***Double-click just below the header.***
9. On the first line of the document, ***from the Home ribbon tab, click the Center icon in the Paragraph group.*** Type **IN THE DISTRICT COURT OF.** Press the **[ENTER]** key. Type **ORANGE COUNTY, MASSACHUSETTS.**
10. Press the **[ENTER]** key five times. ***From the Home ribbon tab, click the Align Text Left icon in the Paragraph group.***
11. Type **JIM TURNER,** and press the **[ENTER]** key twice.
12. Press the **[TAB]** key three times and type **Plaintiff,** then press the **[ENTER]** key twice.
13. Type **vs.** Then, press the **[TAB]** key six times, and type **Case No. CV-13-0046.**
14. Press the **[ENTER]** key twice.
15. Type **JONATHAN R. SMITH,** and press the **[ENTER]** key twice.
16. Press the **[TAB]** key three times and type **Defendant.** Press the **[ENTER]** key four times.
17. ***From the Home ribbon tab, click the Center icon in the Paragraph group.***

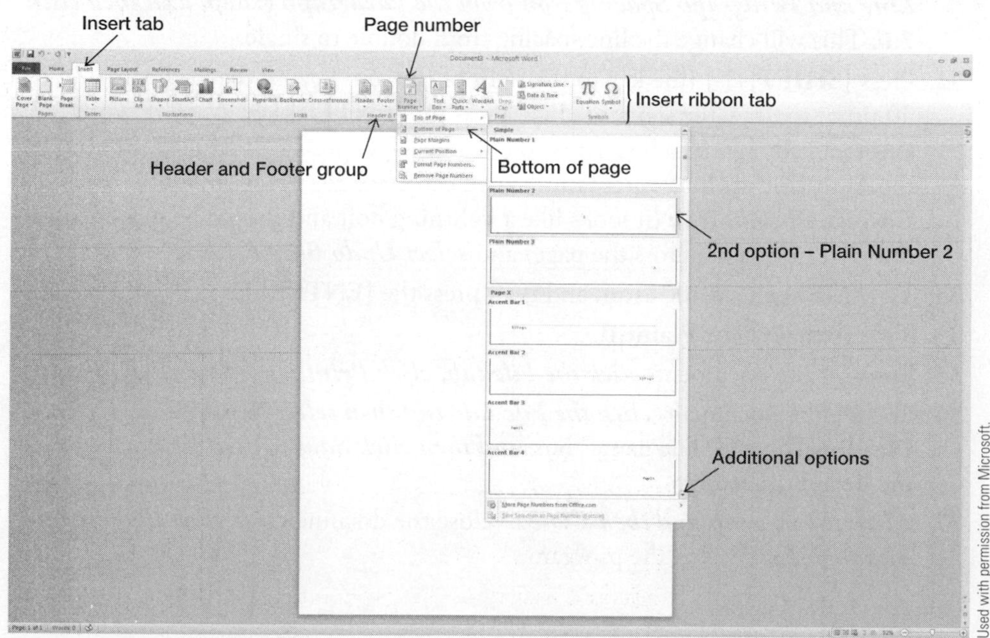

WORD 2010 EXHIBIT 5
Adding a page number

HANDS-ON EXERCISES

18. ***From the Home ribbon tab, click the Bold icon and the Underline icon, both found in the Font group.*** Type **NOTICE TO TAKE DEPOSITION**. ***Click the Bold and Underline icons*** to turn them off.
19. Press the **[ENTER]** key three times. ***From the Home ribbon tab, click the Align Text Left icon in the Paragraph group.***
20. ***From the Home ribbon tab, click the Line and Paragraph Spacing icon from the Paragraph group*** (see Word 2010 Exhibit 1), ***and then click 2.0.*** This will change the line spacing from single to double.
21. Type **COMES NOW the plaintiff and pursuant to statute**. Notice that a footnote follows the word *statute* in Word 2010 Exhibit 4.
22. With the pointer just to the right of the "e" in "statute," ***from the References ribbon tab, click Insert Footnote from the Footnotes group.*** The cursor should now be at the bottom of the page in the footnote window.
23. Type **Massachusetts Statutes Annotated 60-2342(a)(1).**
24. To move the pointer back to the body of the document, simply ***click to the right of the word "statute" (and the superscript number 1) in the body of the document.*** Now, continue to type the rest of the first paragraph. Once the paragraph is typed, press the **[ENTER]** key twice.
25. To double-indent the second paragraph, ***from the Home ribbon tab, click the Paragraph Group Dialog Box Launcher*** (see Word 2010 Exhibit 1). The "Paragraph" window should now be displayed. ***Under Indentation, add a 0.5" left indent and a 0.5" right indent using the up arrow icons*** (or you can type it in). ***Click OK in the "Paragraph" window.***
26. Type the second paragraph.
27. Press the **[ENTER]** key twice.
28. ***From the Home ribbon tab, click the Paragraph Group Dialog Box Launcher and, under Indentation, change the left and right indents back to 0. Then, click OK.***
29. Type the third paragraph.
30. Press the **[ENTER]** key three times.
31. The signature line is single spaced, so ***from the Home ribbon tab, click the Line and Paragraph Spacing icon from the Paragraph group, and then click 1.0.*** This will change the line spacing from double to single.
32. Press **[SHIFT]+[-]** (the key to the right of the zero key on the keyboard) 30 times to draw the signature line. Press the **[ENTER]** key. *Note:* If Word automatically inserts a line across the whole page, press **[CTRL]+[Z]** to undo the Auto Correct line. Alternatively, you can ***click the down arrow in the Auto Correct Options icon*** (it looks like a lightning bolt and should be just over the line that now runs across the page) and ***select Undo Border Line.***
33. Type **Mirabelle Watkinson**, and then press the **[ENTER]** key.
34. Type **Attorney for Plaintiff**.
35. To print the document, ***click the File tab, click Print, and then click Print.***
36. To save the document, ***click the File tab and then select Save As.*** Type **Pleading1** in the "File name" box ***and then click Save*** to save the document in the default directory.
37. ***Click the File tab and then Close*** to close the document, or ***click the File tab, and then Exit*** to exit the program.

This concludes Lesson 3.

HANDS-ON EXERCISES

LESSON 4: CREATING A TABLE

This lesson shows you how to create the table shown in Word 2010 Exhibit 6. It expands on the items presented in Lessons 1, 2, and 3 and explains how to change a font size, create a table, enter data into a table, add automatic numbering, adjust column widths, and use the Table AutoFormat command. Keep in mind that if at any time you make a mistake, you may press **[CTRL]+[Z]** to undo what you have done.

1. Open Windows. When it has loaded, ***double-click the Microsoft Office Word 2010 icon on the desktop*** to open Word 2010 for Windows. Alternatively, ***click the Start button, point to Programs or All Programs, and then click the Microsoft Word 2010 icon*** (or ***point to Microsoft Office and then click Microsoft Office Word 2010***). You should be in a clean, blank document. If you are not in a blank document, ***click the File tab, click New, and then double-click Blank document.***
2. ***From the Home ribbon tab, click the Center icon in the Paragraph group, and then click the Bold icon in the Font group.***
3. ***From the Home ribbon tab, click the Font Size icon in the Font group*** and change the font size to 14 either by typing **14** in the box or by ***choosing 14 from the drop-down menu.*** Alternatively, you can both turn on bold and change the font size by ***clicking the Font Group Dialog Box Launcher from the Home ribbon tab*** (see Word 2010 Exhibit 1).
4. Type **Average Hourly Billing Rates for Paralegals** (see Word 2010 Exhibit 6). Press the **[ENTER]** key once, and then from the Home Ribbon tab ***click the Font Size icon and change the type back to 12 point. Click the Bold icon*** to turn bold off.
5. Press the **[ENTER]** key once.
6. ***From the Insert ribbon tab, click Table.*** Notice that a number of columns and rows of boxes are displayed. This allows you to graphically depict your table.
7. ***Point within the Table menu so that three columns are highlighted, and then point and click so that eight rows are highlighted*** (e.g., 3 × 8 Table). Notice that as you point, the table is temporarily shown in your document.

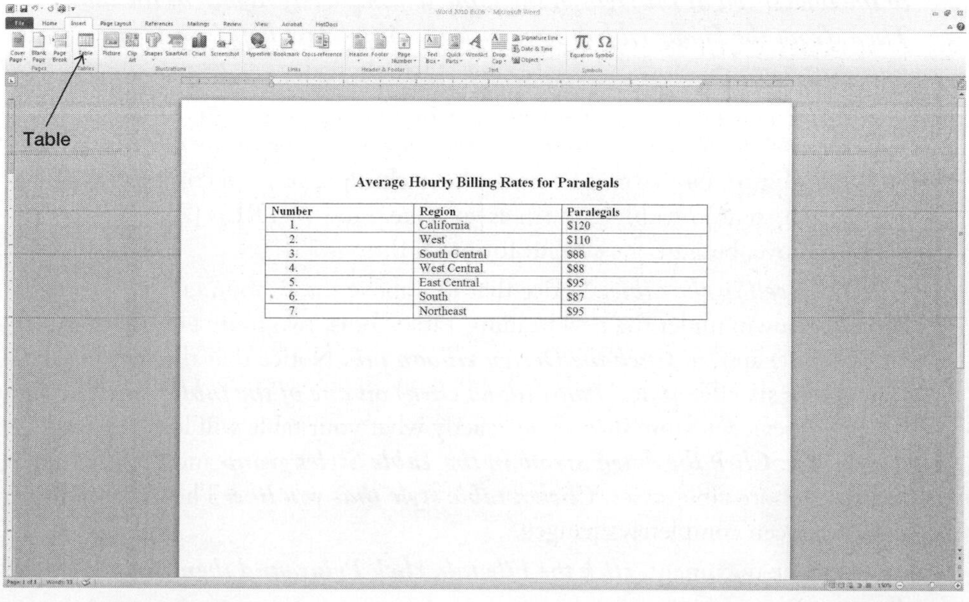
Table
Average Hourly Billing Rates for Paralegals
Number | Region | Paralegals
1. | California | $120
2. | West | $110
3. | South Central | $88
4. | West Central | $88
5. | East Central | $95
6. | South | $87
7. | Northeast | $95

WORD 2010 EXHIBIT 6
Creating a table

HANDS-ON EXERCISES

This is called a *live preview*. When you click the cell that is three columns over and eight cells down, the table (as opposed to the live preview) will be displayed permanently in your document.

8. The blank table should now be displayed and the cursor should be in the first column of the first row of the table. ***If the cursor is not in the first column of the first row, click in this cell to place the cursor there. Click the Bold icon on the Home ribbon tab.*** Type **Number** and then press the **[TAB]** key once to go to the next cell in the table.
9. ***Click the Bold icon.*** Type **Region** and then press the **[TAB]** key once to go to the next cell in the table. (*Note:* If you need to go back to a previous cell, you can either use the mouse or the cursor keys, or you can press **[SHIFT]+[TAB]**. Also, if you accidentally hit the **[ENTER]** key instead of the **[TAB]** key, you can either press the **[BACKSPACE]** key to delete the extra line, or you can press **[CTRL]+[Z]** to undo it.
10. ***Click the Bold icon.*** Type **Paralegals** and then press the **[TAB]** key to go to the next cell.
11. We will now use the automatic paragraph numbering feature to number our rows. ***From the Home ribbon tab, click the Numbering icon in the Paragraph group*** (see Word 2010 Exhibit 1—it is the icon that has the numbers 1, 2, 3 in a column, with a short line next to each number). Notice that the number 1 was automatically entered in the cell. ***From the Home ribbon tab, point on the down arrow next to the Numbering icon in the Paragraph group.*** Under Numbering Library, look at the different formats that are available. The default format is fine, so press **[ESC]** to make the menu disappear.
12. Press the **[TAB]** key to go to the next cell.
13. Type **California** and then press the **[TAB]** key to go to the next cell.
14. Type **$120** and then press the **[TAB]** key to go to the next cell.
15. ***From the Home ribbon tab, click the Numbering icon in the Paragraph group,*** and then press the **[TAB]** key to go to the next cell.
16. Continue entering all of the information shown in Word 2010 Exhibit 6 into your table.
17. ***Put the pointer in the uppermost left cell of the table and drag the pointer to the lowest cell at the right of the table to completely highlight the table. Then, from the Home ribbon tab, click the Align Text Left icon in the Paragraph group.*** Now the whole table is left aligned.
18. ***Put the pointer on the vertical column line that separates the Number column and the Region column, and then drag the line to the left*** (see Word 2010 Exhibit 6). Notice that by using this technique you can completely adjust each column width as much as you like. Press **[CTRL]+[Z]** to undo the column move, because the current format is fine.
19. ***Click any cell in the table.*** Notice that just above the Ribbon tab, new options are now shown; under the new heading Table Tools, two more tabs (Design and Layout) appear. ***Click the Design ribbon tab.*** Notice that the ribbon tab now shows six table styles. ***Point (don't click) on one of the tables;*** notice that the Live Preview feature shows you exactly what your table will look like with this design. ***Click the down arrow in the Table Styles group*** and browse to see many more table styles. ***Click a table style that you like.*** The format of the table has been completely changed.
20. To print the document, ***click the File tab, click Print, and then click Print.***

HANDS-ON EXERCISES

21. To save the document, ***click the File tab and then select Save As.*** Type **Table1** in the "File name" box, ***and then click Save*** to save the document in the default directory.
22. ***Click the File tab and then on Close*** to close the document, or ***click the File tab and then on Exit*** to exit the program.

This concludes Lesson 4.

INTERMEDIATE LESSONS

LESSON 5: TOOLS AND TECHNIQUES

This lesson shows you how to edit an employment policy (from the Premium Website), use the Format Painter tool, reveal formatting, clear formatting, change the case of text, use the Find and Replace feature, use the Go To command, create a section break, and change the orientation of a page from Portrait to Landscape. This lesson assumes that you have completed Lessons 1 through 4 and that you are generally familiar with Word 2010.

1. Open Windows. When it has loaded, ***double-click the Microsoft Office Word 2010 icon on the desktop*** to open Word 2010 for Windows. Alternatively, ***click the Start button, point the pointer to Programs or All Programs, and then click the Microsoft Word 2010 icon*** (or ***point to Microsoft Office and then click Microsoft Office Word 2010***). You should be in a clean, blank document. If you are not in a blank document, ***click the File tab, click New, and then double-click Blank document.***
2. The first thing you will do is to open the "Lesson 5" file from the Premium Website. On the Premium Website, ***click the Data Files: Word Processing tab,*** then under Word 2010, ***click the "Lesson 5" file.***
3. The file entitled "World Wide Technology, Inc. alcohol and drug policy" should now be displayed on your screen. If the document appears in Protected View, ***click Enable Editing*** to continue with the lesson. In this lesson, you will be editing this policy for use by another client. The next thing you need to do is to go to section 3, "Definitions," and change the subheadings so that they have all have the same format. You will use the Format Painter tool to do this.
4. Use the cursor keys or the mouse and the horizontal scroll bars to scroll to section 3, "Definitions" (see Word 2010 Exhibit 7). Notice that the first definition, "Alcohol or alcoholic beverages," is bold and in a different font from the rest of the definitions in section 3. You will use the Format Painter feature to quickly copy the formatting from "Alcohol or alcoholic beverages" to the other four definitions in section 3.
5. ***Click anywhere in the text*** **"Alcohol or alcoholic beverages:"** This tells the Format Painter feature the formatting you want to copy.
6. ***From the Home ribbon tab, click the Format Painter icon in the Clipboard group.*** It looks like a paintbrush (see Word 2010 Exhibit 7). Remember, if you hover your mouse pointer over an icon for a second or two, the name of the icon will appear.
7. Notice that your mouse pointer now turns to a paintbrush. ***Drag the pointer*** (hold the left mouse button down and move the mouse) ***until the heading*** **"Legal drugs:"** ***is highlighted*** (see Word 2010 Exhibit 7), ***and then let go of the mouse button.*** Notice that the paintbrush on your cursor is now gone. ***Click the left mouse button once anywhere in the screen to make the***

HANDS-ON EXERCISES

WORD 2010 EXHIBIT 7
The Format Painter tool

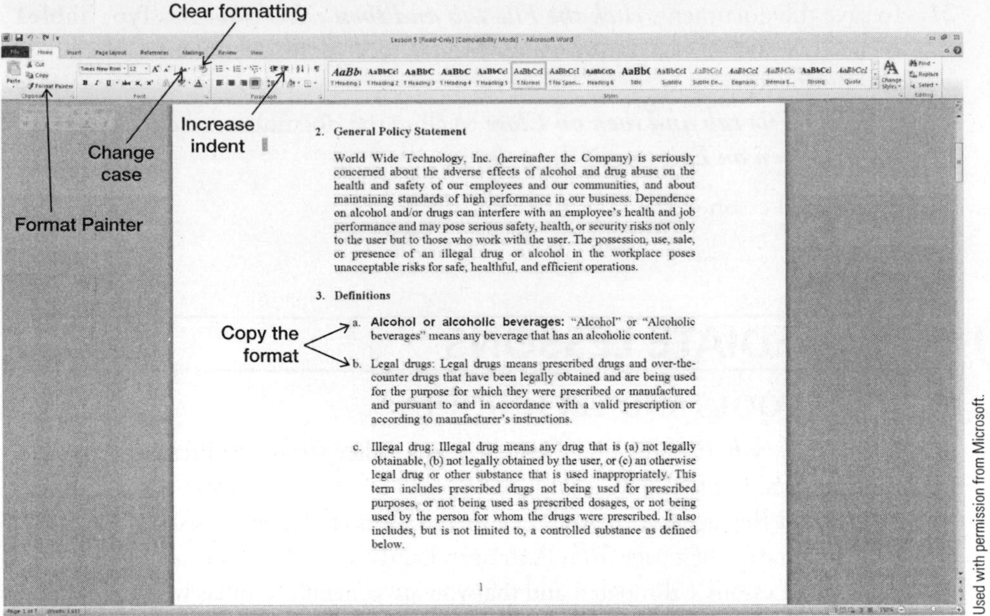

highlight go away. Notice that **"Legal drugs"** now has the same formatting as **"Alcohol or alcoholic beverages."** The Format Painter command is a quick way to make formatting changes.

8. You will now use the Format Painter command to copy the formatting to the remaining three definitions, with one additional trick. ***Click anywhere in the text* "Legal drugs."**
9. Next, ***from the Home ribbon tab, double-click the Format Painter icon in the Clipboard group.*** (Your pointer should now have a paintbrush attached to it.) The double-click tells Format Painter that you are going to copy this format to multiple locations, instead of just one location. This is a great time-saving feature if you need to copy formatting to several places, because it keeps you from having to click the Format Painter icon each time you copy the same formatting to a new location.
10. ***Drag the pointer until the heading* "Illegal drug:" *is highlighted, and then let go of the mouse button.*** Notice that the paintbrush is still attached to your pointer.
11. ***Drag the pointer until the heading* "Controlled substance:" *is highlighted, and then let go of the mouse button.***
12. ***Drag the pointer until the heading* "Prescription drug:" *is highlighted, and then let go of the mouse button.***
13. To turn the Format Painter off, press the **[ESC]** button on the keyboard. ***Click the left mouse button once anywhere in the document to make the highlight go away.*** Notice that all of the headings are now uniform.
14. You will now learn to use the Reveal Formatting command. ***Click the heading* "Prescription drug:"**
15. Press **[SHIFT]+[F1]** on the keyboard. Notice that the Reveal Formatting task pane has opened on the right side of the screen. The Reveal Formatting task pane lists all format specifications for the selected text. The items are divided into several groups, including Font, Paragraph, Bullets and Numbering, and Section. You can make formatting changes to the text directly from the Reveal Formatting task pane by simply clicking on the format setting you want to change (the links are shown in blue, underlined text). For example, ***click the blue underlined word* "Font" *in the Reveal Formatting task pane.*** Notice

that the "Font" window opens. You can now select a new font if you so desire. The Reveal Formatting task pane allows you to quickly see all formatting attached to specific text and, if necessary, to change it.

16. ***Click Cancel in the Font window.*** To close the Reveal Formatting task pane, ***click the "x" (the Close button) at the top of the Reveal Formatting task pane.*** It is just to the right of the words **"Reveal Formatting."** The Reveal Formatting task pane should now be gone.
17. Press **[CTRL]+[HOME]** to go to the beginning of the document.
18. You will now learn how to use the Clear Formats command. Notice under the heading **"1. Objectives"** that the sentence **"The objectives of this policy are as follows:"** is in bold and italics; this is a mistake. ***Drag the pointer until this text is highlighted.***
19. ***From the Home ribbon tab, click the Clear Formatting icon in the Font group*** (see Word 2010 Exhibit 7). This icon looks like an eraser next to a capital "A" and a lowercase "a." ***Click the left mouse button once anywhere in the sentence to make the highlight go away.*** Notice that all of the formatting is now gone. The Clear Formats command is a good way to remove all text formatting quickly and easily.
20. To move the text to the right so it is under **"1. Objectives,"** ***from the Home ribbon tab, click three times on the Increase Indent icon in the Paragraph group*** (see Word 2010 Exhibit 7). This is the icon with a right arrow and some lines on it. The line should now be back in its place.
21. You will now learn how to use the Change Case command. Press **[CTRL]+[HOME]** on the keyboard to go to the beginning of the document.
22. ***Drag the pointer until* "World Wide Technology, Inc." *in the document's title is highlighted.***
23. ***From the Home ribbon tab, click the Change Case icon in the Font group. Click UPPERCASE.*** Notice that the text is now in all capitals. ***Click anywhere in the document to make the highlighting disappear.***
24. ***Drag the pointer until the subtitle* "alcohol and drug policy" *is highlighted. From the Home ribbon tab, click the Change Case icon in the Font group. Click "Capitalize Each Word."*** Notice that the text is now in title case. ***Click the left mouse button once anywhere in the document to make the highlighting go away.*** The Change Case command is a convenient way to change the case of text without having to retype it.
25. ***Highlight the subtitle "Alcohol And Drug Policy" again. From the Review Ribbon tab, click Spelling and Grammar. The Spelling and Grammar: English U.S. dialog box will open. Click Change to accept the change to "and" (with a lower case "a"). When asked whether you want to continue checking the remainder of the document, click No.***
26. Press **[CTRL]+[HOME]** on the keyboard to go to the beginning of the document.
27. You will now learn how to use the Find and Replace command. ***From the Home ribbon tab, click the Replace icon in the Editing group.*** Alternatively, you could press **[CTRL]+[H]**, and then click Replace.
28. In the "Find and Replace" window, in the white box next to **"Find what,"** type **World Wide Technology, Inc.** Then, in the white box next to **"Replace with,"** type **Johnson Manufacturing.** ***Now, click the Replace All button in the "Find and Replace" window.*** The program will respond by stating that it made four replacements. ***Click OK.***

HANDS-ON EXERCISES

29. ***Click the Close button in the "Find and Replace" window to close the window.*** Notice that World Wide Technology, Inc. has now been changed to Johnson Manufacturing.
30. You will now learn how to use the Go To command. The Go To command is an easy way to navigate through large and complex documents. Press **[F5]**. Notice that the "Find and Replace" window is again displayed on the screen, but this time the Go To tab is selected. In the white box directly under **"Enter page number,"** type 7 from the keyboard and then ***click Go To in the Find and Replace window.*** Notice that page 7, "REASONABLE SUSPICION REPORT," is now displayed. (*Note:* If the "Find and Replace" window blocks your ability to see the text of the document, point at the blue box in the "Find and Replace" window and drag the window lower so you can see the document text.) ***Click Close in the "Find and Replace" window.***
31. Suppose that you would like to change the orientation of only one page in a document from Portrait (where the length is greater than the width) to Landscape (where the width is greater than the length). In this example, you will change the layout of only the REASONABLE SUSPICION REPORT to Landscape while keeping the rest of the document in Portrait orientation. To do this in Word, you must enter a section break.
32. Your cursor should be on page 7 just above **"Johnson Manufacturing REASONABLE SUSPICION REPORT."** ***From the Page Layout ribbon tab, click Breaks in the Page Setup group.***
33. ***Under Section Breaks, click Next Page.***
34. In the lower right of the screen, ***click the Draft icon*** (see Word 2010 Exhibit 1). Press the **[UP ARROW]** key two times. Notice that a double-dotted line that says **"Section Break (Next Page)"** is now displayed.
35. The Word 2010 interface allows you to switch views by clicking on one of the view layouts in the lower right of the screen (see Word 2010 Exhibit 7). Print Layout and Draft are two of the most popular layouts. In addition, the Zoom tool just to the right of the Draft view allows you to zoom in or out of your document.
36. With the section break in place, you can now change the format of the page from Portrait to Landscape without changing the orientation of previous pages.
37. ***With the cursor on the*** **"Johnson Manufacturing REASONABLE SUSPICION REPORT"** ***page, from the Page Layout ribbon tab, click Orientation in the Page Setup group. Click Landscape.*** Notice that the layout of the page has changed.
38. ***Click the Print Layout icon in the lower right of the screen*** (see Word 2010 Exhibit 1).
39. To confirm that the layout has changed, ***click the File tab and then click Print.*** On the left side of the screen you can see that the layout is now Landscape (the width is greater than the length). Press the **[PAGE UP]** key until you are back to the beginning of the document. Notice that all of the other pages in the document are still in Portrait orientation.
40. To print the document, ***click the File tab, click Print, and then click Print.***
41. To save the document, ***click the File tab, click Save As, and then click "Word 97-2003 Document." Under Save in, select the drive or folder*** you would like to save the document in. Then, next to File name, type **Done—Word 2010 Lesson 5 Document** and ***click Save*** to save the document.
42. ***Click the File tab, and then click Close*** to close the document, or ***click the File tab, and then on Exit*** to exit the program.

This concludes Lesson 5.

LESSON 6: USING STYLES

This lesson gives you an introduction to styles. Styles are particularly helpful when you are working with long documents that must be formatted uniformly.

1. Open Windows. When it has loaded, ***double-click the Microsoft Office Word 2010 icon on the desktop*** to open Word 2010 for Windows. Alternatively, ***click the Start button, point to Programs or All Programs, and then click the Microsoft Word 2010 icon*** (or ***point to Microsoft Office and then click Microsoft Office Word 2010***). You should now be in a clean, blank document. If you are not in a blank document, ***click the File tab, click New, and then double-click Blank document.***
2. The first thing you will do is to open the "Lesson 6" file from the Premium Website. On the Premium Website, click the Data Files: Word Processing tab, then under Word 2010, click the "Lesson 6" file.
3. The text "SARBANES-OXLEY ACT OF 2002" should now be displayed on your screen (see Word 2010 Exhibit 8). If the document appears in Protected View, ***click Enable Editing*** to continue with the lesson. In this lesson you will use styles to add uniform formatting to this document. In the Home ribbon tab, notice the Styles group. ***Click any text on the page.*** Notice in the Styles group on the Home ribbon tab that the "Normal" box is highlighted in yellow (see Word 2010 Exhibit 8). Currently, all text in the document is in the Normal style.
4. Using your cursor keys or the horizontal scroll bar, scroll down through the document. Notice that all of the paragraphs are left-aligned and that the right edge of all the paragraphs is jagged (e.g., not justified).
5. ***From the Home ribbon tab, click the Styles Group Dialog Box Launcher.*** Notice that the Styles task pane now appears on the right side of the screen (see Word 2010 Exhibit 8). In the Styles task pane, ***if the white box next to "Show Preview" is not marked, click the box so a green check mark appears*** (see Word 2010 Exhibit 8). Notice that a few styles in the Styles task pane are currently being displayed (e.g., Heading 1, Heading 2, and Normal). Also notice that the Normal style has a blue box around it, indicating that your cursor is on text with the Normal style. Finally, notice that there is a paragraph sign after each of these heading names, indicating that these are paragraph styles.

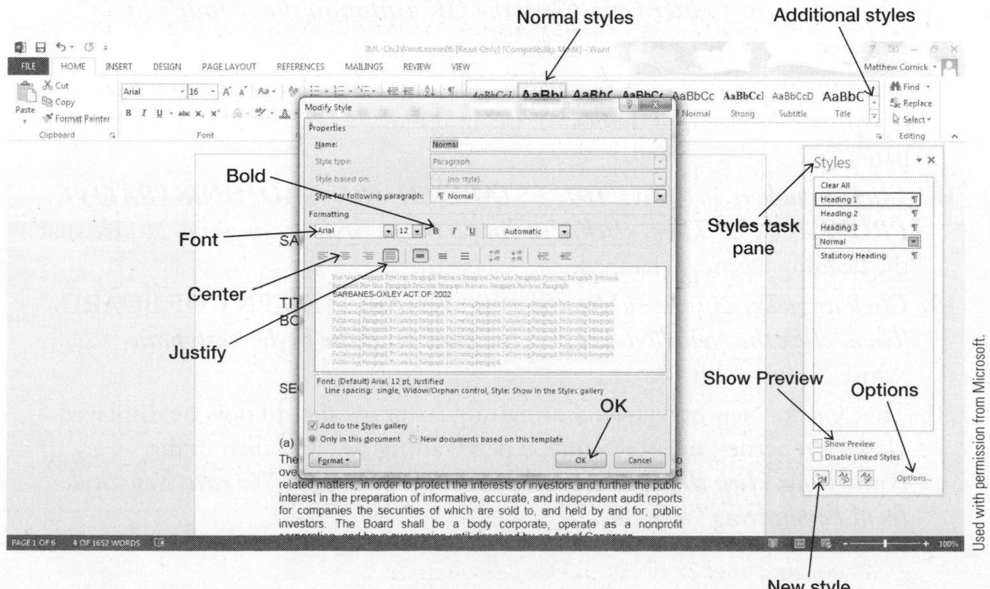

WORD 2010 EXHIBIT 8
Styles

6. Notice at the bottom of the Styles task pane the word "**Options**" in blue; ***click Options.*** The "Style Pane Options" window should now be displayed.
7. ***In the "Style Pane Options" window, under Select styles to show, click the down arrow and click All styles. Then, in the "Style Pane Options" window, click OK.***
8. Notice that the Styles task pane is now full of additional styles. These are all of the styles that are automatically available in Word 2010. ***Click the down arrow in the Styles task pane*** to see the full list of styles.
9. To return to the list of just a few styles, ***click Options in the lower right of the Styles task pan. Under Select styles to show, click the down arrow and click In current document. Then, in the "Style Pane Options" window, click OK.***
10. Notice that the short list of styles is again displayed. To access a longer list of styles from the Styles group **on the Home ribbon tab,** ***click the down arrow in the Styles group.*** If you select the More icon (the icon that shows a down arrow with a line over it) in the Styles group, you can see all of the styles at one time. Press the **[ESC]** key to close the list.
11. Styles are extremely useful. Assume now that you would like to have all of the text in the document justified. ***Point and right-click Normal in the Styles task pane. Then, point and left-click Modify.*** The "Modify Style" window should now be displayed (see Word 2010 Exhibit 8). Using the "Modify Style" window, you can completely change the formatting for any style.
12. ***Click the Justify icon in the "Modify Style" window to change the Normal style from left-aligned to fully justified*** (see Word 2010 Exhibit 8).
13. ***Click the down arrow in the "Font" box under Formatting in the "Modify Style" window and click Arial*** (you may have to scroll through some fonts to find it). ***Next, click the OK button in the "Modify Style" window.*** Notice that Word quickly changed the alignment of all of the text to fully justified and changed the font to Arial.
14. ***Drag the pointer until the full title of the document is highlighted*** (SARBANES-OXLEY ACT OF 2002 TITLE I—PUBLIC COMPANY ACCOUNTING OVERSIGHT BOARD).
15. ***Click Heading 1 in the Styles task pane.***
16. ***Point and right-click Heading 1 in the Styles task pane and select Modify. Then, click the Center icon. Click the OK button in the "Modify Style" window.***
17. ***Click the left mouse button anywhere in the title to make the highlight disappear.*** Notice that the text of the title shows as Heading 1 in the Styles task pane.
18. ***Click anywhere in "SEC. 101. ESTABLISHMENT; ADMINISTRATIVE PROVISIONS." Then, click Heading 2 in the Styles task pane.*** Notice that the heading has now changed.
19. ***Click anywhere in the subheading*** "**(a) ESTABLISHMENT OF BOARD.**" ***Then, click the New Style icon at the bottom of the Styles task pane*** (see Word 2010 Exhibit 8).
20. The "Create New Style from Formatting" window should now be displayed. Under Properties, next to Name, type **Heading 3A**, and then under Formatting, ***click the Bold icon. Then, click OK in the "Create New Style from Formatting" window.***

21. Now, go to the following subheadings and format them as Heading 3A by ***clicking on them and selecting Heading 3A from the Styles task pane:***
    (b) STATUS
    (c) DUTIES OF THE BOARD
    (d) COMMISSION DETERMINATION
    (e) BOARD MEMBERSHIP
    (f) POWERS OF THE BOARD
    (g) RULES OF THE BOARD
    (h) ANNUAL REPORT TO THE COMMISSION
    Press **[CTRL]+[HOME]** to go to the beginning of the document. Your document is now consistently formatted. Using styles, your documents can also easily be uniformly changed. For example, if you read in your local rules that subheadings for pleadings must be in 15-point Times New Roman font, you could quickly change the subheadings in your document by modifying the heading styles, rather than highlighting each subheading and changing the format manually.
22. To print the document, ***click the File tab, click Print, and then click Print.***
23. To save the document, ***click the File tab and click Save As. Then click "Word 97-2003 Document." Under Save in, select the drive or folder*** you would like to save the document in. Then, next to File name, type **Done—Word 2010 Lesson 6 Document *and click Save*** to save the document.
24. ***Click the File tab, and then on Close*** to close the document, or ***click the File tab, and then on Exit*** to exit the program.

This concludes Lesson 6.

LESSON 7: CREATING A TEMPLATE

This lesson shows you how to create the template shown in Word 2010 Exhibit 9. It explains how to create a template of a letter, how to insert fields, and how to fill out and use a finished template. You will also learn how to add a command to the Quick Access toolbar. The information that will be merged into the letter will be entered from the keyboard. Keep in mind that if at any time you make a mistake, you may press **[CTRL]+[Z]** to undo what you have done.

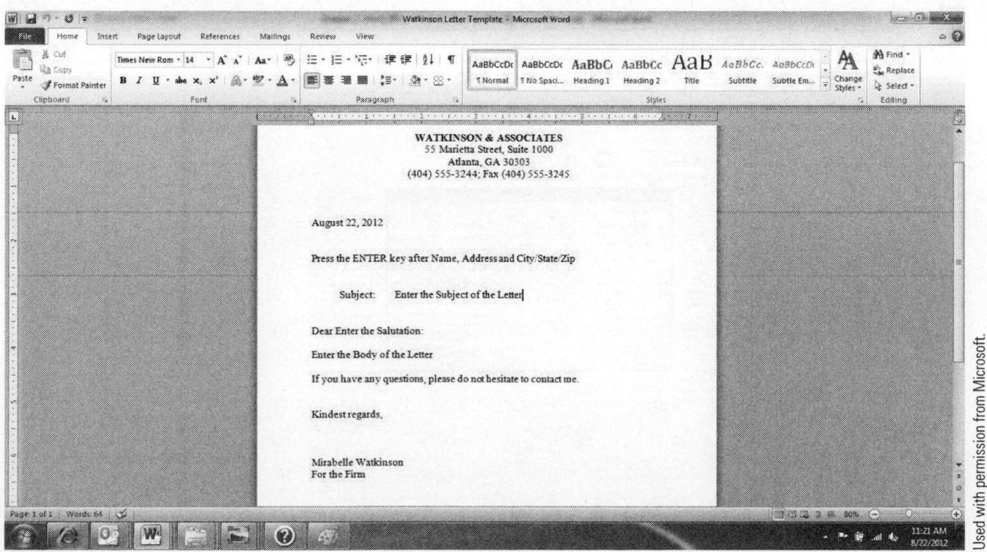

WORD 2010 EXHIBIT 9
Office Letter template

1. Open Windows. When it has loaded, ***double-click the Microsoft Office Word 2010 icon on the desktop*** to open Word 2010 for Windows. Alternatively, ***click the Start button, point to Programs or All Programs, and then click the Microsoft Word 2010 icon*** (or ***point to Microsoft Office and then click Microsoft Office Word 2010***). You should be in a clean, blank document. If you are not in a blank document, ***click the File tab, click New, and then double-click Blank document.***
2. ***Click the File tab, then click New, and then under Available Templates click My templates.***
3. ***Click Template under the Create New field in the lower right of the "New" window*** (see Word 2010 Exhibit 10).
4. ***Click Blank Document.*** Blank Document should now be highlighted. ***Then, click OK*** (see Word 2010 Exhibit 10).
5. You should now have a blank template on your screen. The Windows title should say **"Template1—Microsoft Word"** in the upper middle of the screen. You will now build the template shown in Word 2010 Exhibit 9.
6. Also, ***on the Home ribbon tab, click the Paragraph Group Dialog Box Launcher. In the "Paragraph" window, click the down arrow below Line Spacing and select Single. Make sure the Before and After spacing are both 0 point. Then, click OK.***
7. ***From the Home ribbon tab, click the Center icon in the Paragraph group. Then, from the Home ribbon tab, click the Bold icon in the Font group.***
8. ***From the Home ribbon tab, click the Font Size icon from the Font group and select 14 from the list. Then, click the "Font" box and select Times New Roman.***
9. Type **WATKINSON & ASSOCIATES** and then, ***from the Home ribbon tab, click the Font Size icon and select 12 from the list. Click the Bold icon from the Font group*** to turn off bolding.
10. Press the **[ENTER]** key.
11. Type **55 Marietta Street, Suite 1000** and press the **[ENTER]** key.
12. Type **Atlanta, Georgia 30303** and press the **[ENTER]** key.

WORD 2010 EXHIBIT 10
Creating a new template

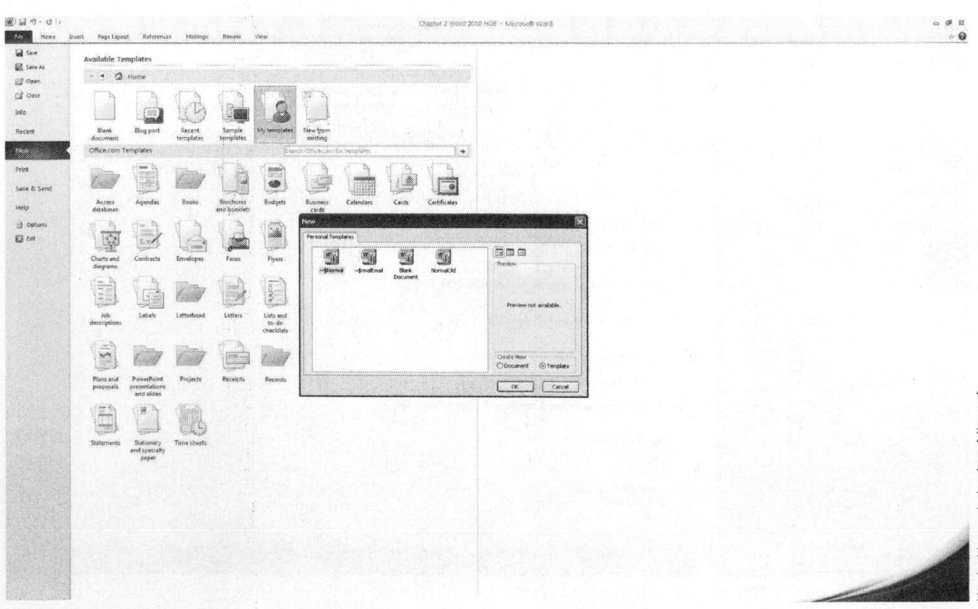

13. Type **(404) 555-3244; Fax (404) 555-3245** and press the **[ENTER]** key.
14. ***From the Home ribbon tab, click the Align Text Left icon in the Paragraph group.***
15. Press the **[ENTER]** key three times.
16. ***From the Insert ribbon tab, click Quick Parts from the Text group and then click Field.***
17. The "Field" window should now be displayed (see Word 2010 Exhibit 11). The "Field" window has several sections, including Categories and Field names. Under Categories, *(All)* should be selected.
18. ***Click the down arrow on the Field Names scroll bar until you see the field name Date*** (see Word 2010 Exhibit 11). ***Click it.***
19. ***From the Field Properties list, click the third option from the top (the date, the month spelled out, and the year).*** Notice that the current date is displayed. This field will always display the date on which the template is actually executed, so if the template is executed on January 1, January 1 will be the date shown on the letter. ***Click OK in the "Field" window.***
20. Press the **[ENTER]** key three times.
21. ***From the Insert ribbon tab, click Quick Parts from the Text group and then click Field.***
22. ***Click the down arrow on the Field names scroll bar until you see Fill-in in the Field Name area*** (see Word 2010 Exhibit 11). ***Click Fill-in.***
23. In the "Prompt:" box under Field Properties, type **"Type the Name and Address of the Recipient."** *Note:* You must type the quotation marks.
24. ***Click OK in the "Field" window.***
25. You will now see a window on your screen that says **"Type the Name and Address of the Recipient."** Type **Press the ENTER key after Name, Address, and City/State/Zip** (see Word 2010 Exhibit 12). ***Then, click OK.***
26. Press the **[ENTER]** key three times.
27. Press the **[TAB]** key.
28. Type **Subject:**.
29. Press the **[TAB]** key.

HANDS-ON EXERCISES

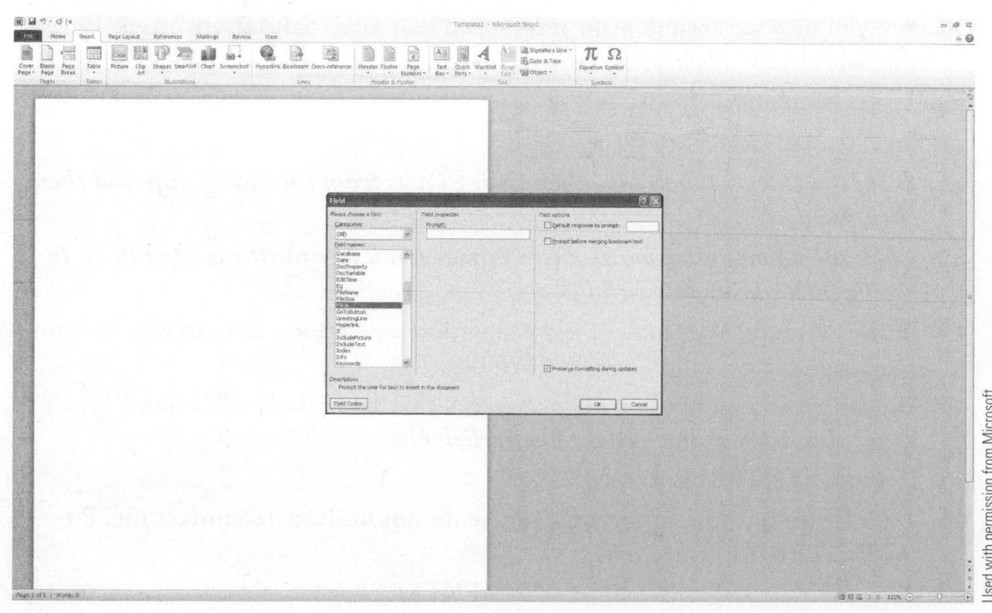

WORD 2010 EXHIBIT 11
Inserting fields in a template

WORD 2010 EXHIBIT 12
Entering a "Fill-in" field

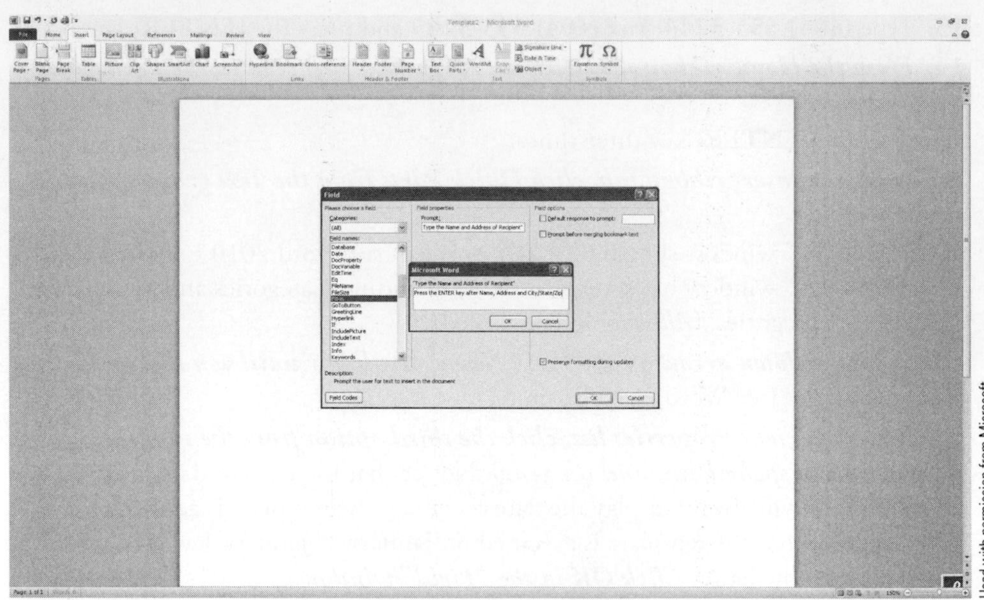

30. ***From the Insert ribbon tab, click Quick Parts from the Text group and then click Field.***
31. ***Click the down arrow on the Field names scroll bar until you see Fill-in in the Field names area. Click Fill-in.***
32. In the "Prompt:" box under Field Properties, type **"Type the Subject of the Letter."** *Note:* You must type the quotation marks. ***Click OK.***
33. You will now see a window on your screen that says **"Type the Subject of the Letter."** Type **Enter the Subject of the Letter**. ***Click OK.***
34. Press the **[ENTER]** key three times.
35. Type **Dear**, press the **[SPACEBAR]**; ***from the Insert ribbon tab, click Quick Parts from the Text group, and then click Field.***
36. ***Click the down arrow on the Field names scroll bar until you see Fill-in in the Field Name area. Click Fill-in.***
37. In the "Prompt:" box under Field Properties, type **"Salutation."** *Note:* You must type the quotation marks. ***Click OK.***
38. You will now see a window on your screen that says **"Salutation."** Type **Enter the Salutation.** ***Then, click OK.***
39. Type **:** (a colon).
40. Press the **[ENTER]** key twice.
41. ***From the Insert ribbon tab, click Quick Parts from the Text group and then click Field.***
42. ***Click the down arrow on the Field names scroll bar until you see Fill-in in the Field Name area. Click Fill-in.***
43. In the "Prompt:" box under Field Properties, type **"Body of Letter."** *Note:* You must type the quotation marks. ***Click OK.***
44. You will now see a window on your screen that says **"Body of Letter."** Type **Enter the Body of the Letter**. ***Then, click OK.***
45. Press the **[ENTER]** key twice.
46. Type **If you have any questions, please do not hesitate to contact me.** Press the **[ENTER]** key three times.
47. Type **Kindest Regards,** and press the **[ENTER]** key four times.
48. Type **Mirabelle Watkinson** and press the **[ENTER]** key once.

49. Type **For the Firm**.
50. ***Click the File tab, then click Save As and click Word Template next to Save as type.*** (*Note:* If you do not save this as a Word template, you will not be able to finish the lesson.) Then, next to File name:, type **Watkinson Letter Template.** Word will save the template to a special template folder; if you save it to another folder you will not be able to run the template in the next portion of this exercise. ***Next to Save as type:, click the down arrow button, select Word 97-2003 Template, and then click Save*** to save the document.
51. ***Click the File tab and then on Close.*** You are now ready to type a letter using the template.
52. ***Click the File tab, then click New. Next, under Available Templates click My templates.*** In the "New" window, under the Personal Templates tab, ***double-click Watkinson Letter Template.***
53. The template letter is now running. You will see the "Type the Name and Address of the Recipient" field on the screen. You will also see the prompt that reminds you to press the **[ENTER]** key after the name, address, and city/state/zip. Type over this prompt.
54. Type **Steven Matthews, Esq.** and press the **[ENTER]** key.
55. Type **Matthews, Smith & Russell** and press the **[ENTER]** key.
56. Type **P.O. Box 12341** and press the **[ENTER]** key.
57. Type **Boston, MA 59920** and then ***click OK.***
58. You will see the Type the Subject of the Letter field on the screen. You will also see the prompt that reminds you to enter the subject of the letter. Type over this prompt.
59. Type **Turner v. Smith, Case No. 13-0046** and then ***click OK.***
60. You will now see the Salutation field on the screen. You will also see the prompt that reminds you to enter the salutation. Type over this prompt.
61. Type **Steve** and then ***click OK.***
62. You will now see the Body of Letter field on the screen. You will also see the prompt that reminds you to enter the body of the letter. Type over this prompt.
63. Type **This will confirm our conversation of this date. You indicated that you had no objection to us requesting an additional ten days to respond to your Motion for Summary Judgment.** ***Click OK.*** You are now through typing the letter. The completed letter should now be displayed. (*Note:* If another window displays, prompting you for the name and address of the recipient, simply ***click cancel***; the completed letter should then be displayed.)
64. You are now ready to print the document. First, you will create a Quick Print icon on the Quick Access toolbar. Instead of going to the File tab each time to print, you will be able to print a document from the Quick Access toolbar (see Word 2010 Exhibit 12).
65. ***Point and right-click anywhere in the ribbon. Click Customize Quick Access Toolbar.***
66. The "Word Options" window should now be displayed. ***Double-click Quick Print on the left side of the screen (under Popular Commands). Click Add and then click OK in the "Word Options" window.***
67. Notice that a Quick Print icon is now displayed in the Quick Access toolbar.
68. ***Click the Quick Print icon on the Quick Access toolbar,*** or ***click the File tab, click Print, and then click Print.***
69. To save the document, ***click the File tab, click Save As, and then click Word 97-2003 Document next to Save as type. Under Save in, select the drive or folder*** you would like to save the document in. Then, next to File name,

type **Done—Word 2010 Lesson 7 Document** ***and click Save*** to save the document. *Note:* You just saved the output of your template to a separate file named "Done—Word Lesson 7 Document." Your original template ("Watkinson Letter Template") is unaffected by the Lesson 7 document, and is still a clean template ready to be used again and again for any case.

70. ***Click the File tab, and then on Close*** to close the document, or ***click the File tab, and then on Exit*** to exit the program.

This concludes Lesson 7.

LESSON 8: COMPARING DOCUMENTS

This lesson shows you how to compare documents by simultaneously viewing two documents and by creating a separate blacklined document with the changes. There will be times in a law office when you send someone a digital file for revision, and find that when the file is returned, the revisions are not apparent. Using these tools in Word 2010, you can see what has changed in the document.

1. Open Windows. When it has loaded, ***double-click the Microsoft Office Word 2010 icon on the desktop*** to open Word 2010 for Windows. Alternatively, ***click the Start button, point to Programs or All Programs, and then click the Microsoft Word 2010 icon*** (or ***point to Microsoft Office and then click Microsoft Office Word 2010***). You should now be in a clean, blank document. If you are not in a blank document, ***click the File tab, click New, and then double-click Blank document.***
2. For the purpose of this lesson, we will assume that your firm drafted an employment contract for a corporate client named Bluebriar Incorporated. Bluebriar is in negotiations with an individual named John Lewis, whom they would like to hire as their vice president of marketing. Your firm is negotiating with John Lewis's attorney regarding the terms and language of the employment contract. The file "Lesson 8A" on the Premium Website is the original document you sent to John Lewis's attorney. The file "Lesson 8B" on the Premium Website is the new file sent to you by John Lewis's attorney.
3. You will now open both of these files from the Premium Website and then compare them side by side. On the Premium Website, click the Data File: Word Processing tab, then under Word 2010, click the "Lesson 8A" file.
4. Follow the same directions to open the "Lesson 8B"file. If the documents appear in Protected View, ***click Enable Editing*** to continue with the lesson.
5. ***From the View ribbon tab, click View Side by Side in the Window group.*** Both documents should now be displayed side by side (see Word 2010 Exhibit 13).
6. Keep pushing the **[DOWN ARROW]** key to scroll down through the document. Notice that both documents scroll simultaneously.
7. From the View ribbon tab, notice that the Synchronous Scrolling icon in the Window group is highlighted (see Word 2010 Exhibit 13). To turn off this feature, you would click this icon. The Synchronous Scrolling icon toggles Synchronous Scrolling on and off. If you turn off Synchronous Scrolling and wish to turn it back on, simply realign the windows where you want them, and ***click the Synchronous Scrolling icon.*** (*Note:* If the View ribbon tab shows the Window group collapsed, ***click the Window Group, and click Synchronous Scrolling.***)
8. You will now learn how to merge the changes into one document. ***Click anywhere in Lesson 8A.doc; then click the File tab and then on Close.***
9. Do the same for Word Lesson 8B.doc.
10. You should now have no documents open.

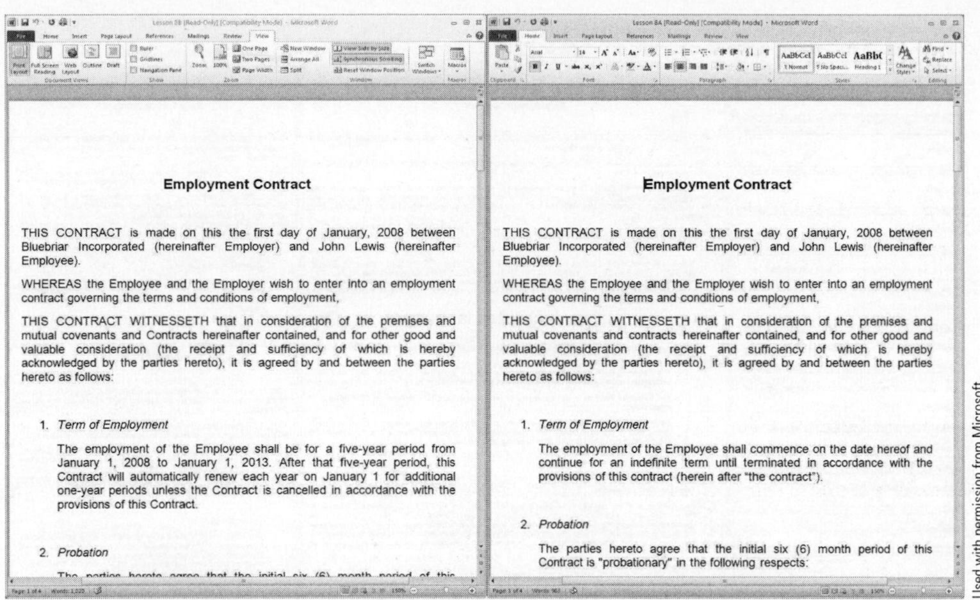

WORD 2010 EXHIBIT 13
Comparing documents side by side

11. ***From the Review ribbon tab, click Compare in the Compare group. Then, click Compare.***
12. The "Compare Documents" window should now be displayed (see Word 2010 Exhibit 14). ***Under Original document, click the down arrow, use the Browse feature to find Lesson 8A.doc, and then double-click it*** (see Word 2010 Exhibit 14).
13. ***Under Revised document, click the down arrow, use the Browse feature to find Lesson 8B.doc, and then double-click it*** (see Word 2010 Exhibit 14).
14. Next to **"Label Changes with,"** type **John Lewis' Attorney** and then ***click OK in the "Compare Documents" window.***
15. Notice that a new document has been created that merges the documents (see Word 2010 Exhibit 15). Scroll through the new document and review all of the changes.
16. The Compare feature is extremely helpful when you are comparing multiple versions of the same file. By right-clicking on any of the additions or deletions,

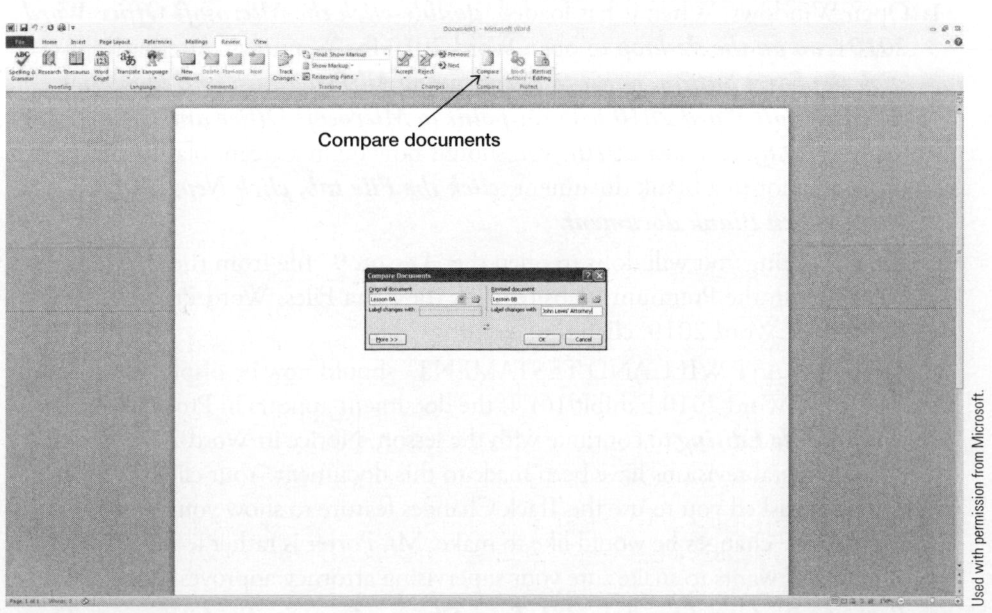

WORD 2010 EXHIBIT 14
Comparing documents—Legal blackline settings

WORD 2010 EXHIBIT 15
Completed blackline documents

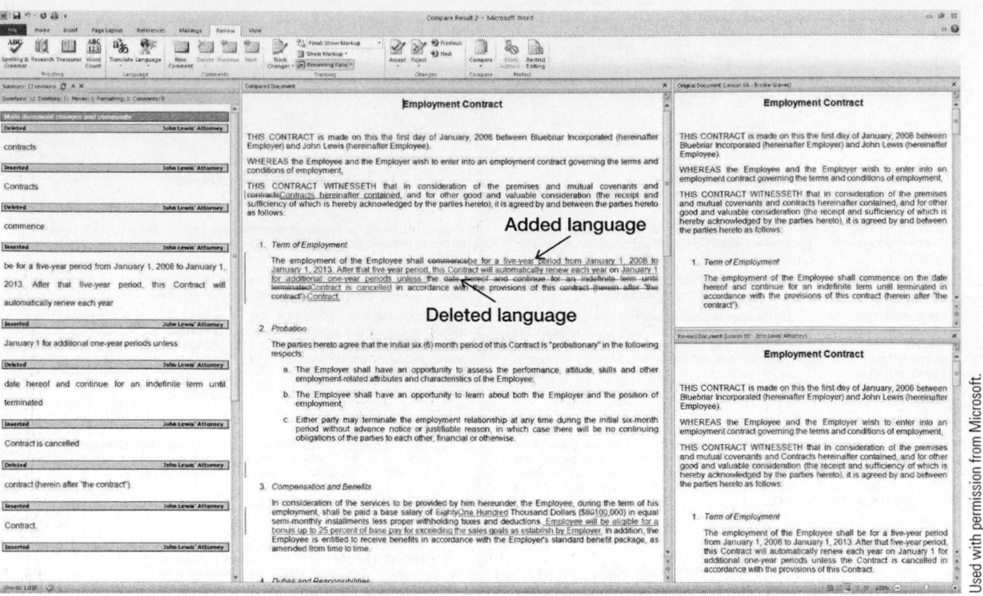

you can accept or reject the change. This is called Track Changes, and you will learn how to do this in more detail in the next lesson.

17. To print the document, ***click the Quick Print icon on the Quick Access toolbar,*** or ***click the File tab, click Print, and then click Print.***
18. To save the document, ***click the File tab, click Save As, and then click "Word 97-2003 Document." Under Save in, select the drive or folder*** you would like to save the document in. Next to File name:, type **Done—Word 2010 Lesson 8 Merged Doc** and then ***click Save*** to save the document.
19. ***Click the File tab, and then on Close*** to close the document, or ***click the File tab, and then on Exit*** to exit the program.

This concludes Lesson 8.

LESSON 9: USING TRACK CHANGES

In this lesson, you will learn how to use the Track Changes feature by editing a will, and then accepting and/or rejecting the changes.

1. Open Windows. When it has loaded, ***double-click the Microsoft Office Word 2010 icon on the desktop*** to open Word 2010 for Windows. Alternatively, ***click the Start button, point to Programs or All Programs, and then click the Microsoft Word 2010 icon*** (or ***point to Microsoft Office and then click Microsoft Office Word 2010***). You should now be in a clean, blank document. If you are not in a blank document, ***click the File tab, click New, and then double-click Blank document.***
2. The first thing you will do is to open the "Lesson 9" file from the Premium Website. On the Premium Website, click the Data Files: Word Processing tab, then under Word 2010, click the "Lesson 9" file.
3. The text "LAST WILL AND TESTAMENT" should now be displayed on your screen (see Word 2010 Exhibit 16). If the document appears in Protected View, ***click Enable Editing*** to continue with the lesson. Notice in Word 2010 Exhibit 16 that several revisions have been made to this document. Your client, William Porter, has asked you to use the Track Changes feature to show your supervising attorney the changes he would like to make. Mr. Porter is rather leery of the legal process and wants to make sure your supervising attorney approves of the changes.
4. ***From the Review ribbon tab, click Track Changes from the Tracking group. Then, click Track Changes from the drop-down menu*** to turn on Track Changes.

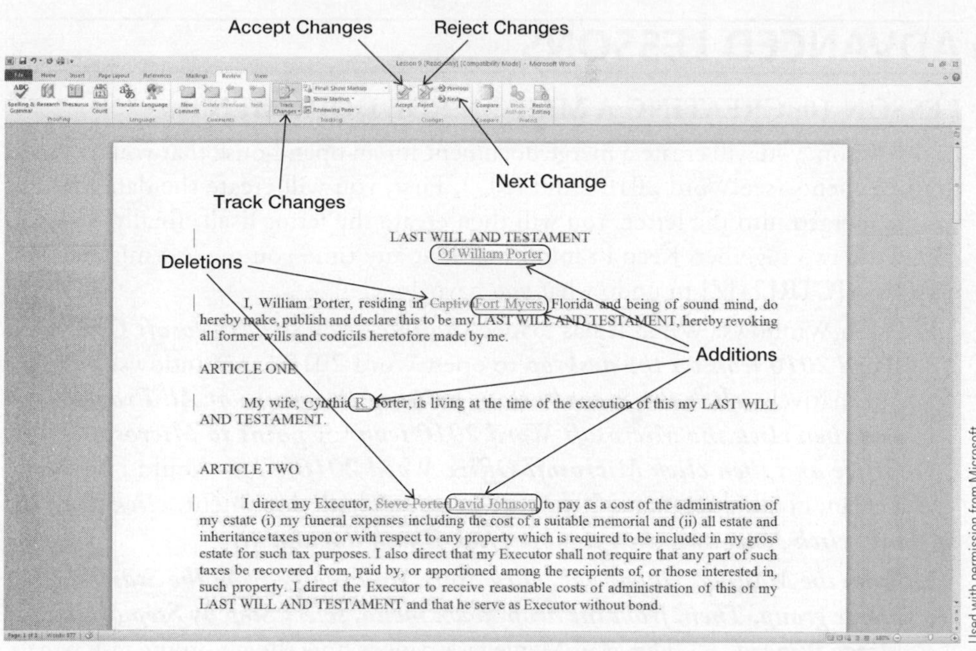

WORD 2010 EXHIBIT 16
Using Track Changes

5. Make the changes shown in Word 2010 Exhibit 16. Everything that should be added is circled, and everything that should be deleted is crossed out.
6. Assume now that you have shown the changes to your supervising attorney. ***From the Review ribbon tab, click Track Changes, and then click Track Changes on the drop-down menu*** to turn off Track Changes (see Word 2010 Exhibit 16). This allows you to make changes to the document without having them show up as revisions.
7. ***Point and right-click anywhere on the text, "Of William Porter," which you added just under "LAST WILL AND TESTAMENT."*** Notice that a menu is displayed that allows you to accept or reject the insertion, among other actions. ***Click Accept Change.*** The revision has now been accepted.
8. ***From the Review ribbon tab, click Next in the Changes group*** (see Word 2010 Exhibit 16). This should take you to the next change. ***From the Review ribbon tab, click Accept in the Changes group, then click Accept and Move to Next*** (see Word 2010 Exhibit 16) to accept the change. Notice that one of the options is "Accept All Changes in Document." Do not select it. This is a quick way to accept all changes in a document without going through each one of them.
9. Use the Next feature to continue to go to each change and accept the revisions. The only revision you will *not* accept is changing the executor from Steve Porter to David Johnson; reject this change. Assume that the supervising attorney has learned that Mr. Johnson is terminally ill and most likely will not be able to serve as executor, so the client has decided to keep Steve Porter as the executor.
10. To print the document, ***click the Quick Print icon on the Quick Access toolbar,*** or ***click the File tab, click Print, and then click Print.***
11. To save the document, ***click the File tab, click Save As, and then click "Word 97-2003 Document." Under Save in, select the drive or folder*** you would like to save the document in. Next to File name, type **Done—Word 2010 Lesson 9 Document** ***and then click Save*** to save the document.
12. ***Click the File tab, and then on Close*** to close the document, or ***click the File tab, and then on Exit*** to exit the program.

This concludes Lesson 9.

ADVANCED LESSONS

LESSON 10: CREATING A MAIL MERGE DOCUMENT

In this lesson, you will create a merge document for an open house that you will send to three clients (see Word 2010 Exhibit 17). First, you will create the data file that will be merged into the letter. You will then create the letter itself; finally, you will merge the two together. Keep in mind that if at any time you make a mistake, you may press **[CTRL]+[Z]** to undo what you have done.

1. Open Windows. When it has loaded, ***double-click the Microsoft Office Word 2010 icon on the desktop*** to open Word 2010 for Windows. Alternatively, ***click the Start button, point to Programs or All Programs, and then click the Microsoft Word 2010 icon*** (or ***point to Microsoft Office and then click Microsoft Office Word 2010***). You should now be in a clean, blank document. If you are not in a blank document, ***click the File tab, click New, and then double-click Blank document.***
2. ***From the Mailings ribbon tab, click Start Mail Merge from the Start Mail Merge group. Then, from the drop-down menu, select Step by Step Mail Merge Wizard. . . .*** The Mail Merge task pane is now shown on the task pane to the right of your document.
3. The bottom of the Mail Merge task pane shows that you are on step 1 of 6. You are asked to **"Select document type."** You are typing a letter, so the default selection, Letters, is fine. To continue to the next step, ***click Next: Starting document at the bottom of the Mail Merge task pane under Step 1 of 6.***
4. The bottom of the Mail Merge task pane shows that you are on step 2 of 6. You are asked to **"Select starting document."** You will be using the current document to type your letter, so the default selection, Use the current document, is fine. To continue to the next step, ***click Next: Select recipients at the bottom of the Mail Merge task pane under Step 2 of 6.***

HANDS-ON EXERCISES

WORD 2010 EXHIBIT 17
Mail merge letter

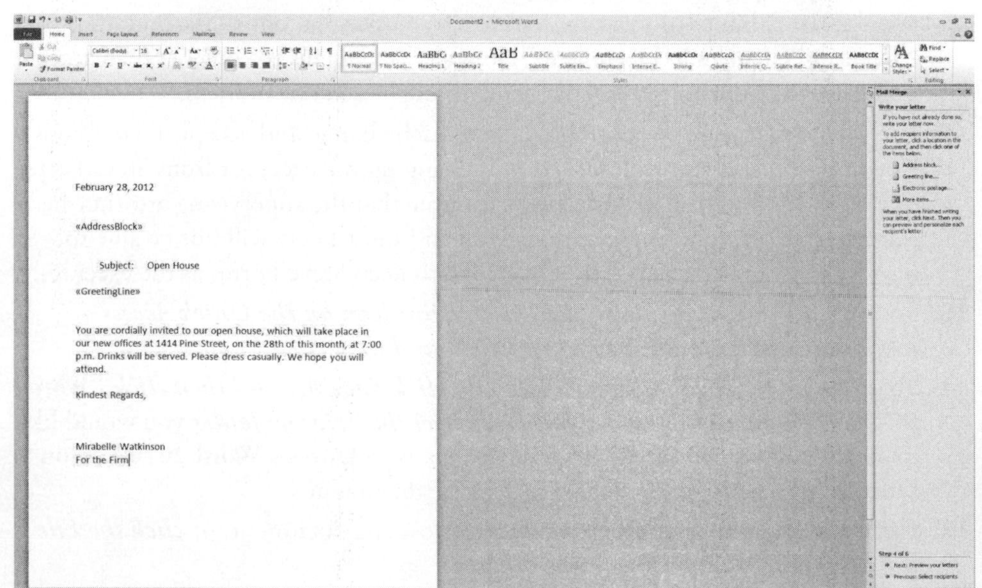

Used with permission from Microsoft.

5. The bottom of the Mail Merge task pane shows that you are on step 3 of 6. You are asked to **"Select recipients."** You will be typing a new list, so ***click Type a new list.***
6. ***Under the Type a new list section of the Mail Merge task pane, click "Create. . . ."***
7. The "New Address List" window is now displayed. You will now fill in the names of the three clients to whom you want to send your open-house letter.
8. Type the following (Table 2–4). (*Note:* You can use the **[TAB]** key to move between the fields, or you can use the mouse.) Only complete the fields below; skip the fields in the "New Address List" window that we will not be using.

TABLE 2–4	
First Name	Jim
Last Name	Woods
Company Name	
Address Line 1	2300 Briarcliff Road
Address Line 2	
City	Atlanta
State	GA
ZIP Code	30306
Country	
Home Phone	
Work Phone	
Email Address	

9. When you have entered all of the information for Jim Woods, ***click the New Entry button in the "New Address List" window.***
10. Enter the second client in the blank "New Address List" window (Table 2–5).

TABLE 2–5	
First Name	Jennifer
Last Name	John
Company Name	
Address Line 1	3414 Peachtree Road
Address Line 2	
City	Atlanta
State	GA
ZIP Code	30314
Country	
Home Phone	
Work Phone	
Email Address	

11. When you have entered all of the information for Jennifer John, ***click the New Entry button in the "New Address List" window.***
12. Enter the third client in the blank "New Address List" window (Table 2–6).

TABLE 2–6	
First Name	Jonathan
Last Name	Phillips
Company Name	
Address Line 1	675 Clifton Road
Address Line 2	
City	Atlanta
State	GA
ZIP Code	30030
Country	
Home Phone	
Work Phone	
Email Address	

13. When you have entered all of the information for Jonathan Phillips, ***click OK in the "New Address List" window.***
14. The "Save Address List" window is now displayed. You need to save the address list so that it can later be merged with the open-house letter. In the "Save Address List" window, next to File name, type **Open House List** and then ***click Save in the "Save Address List" window*** to save the file to the default directory.
15. The "Mail Merge Recipients" window is now displayed (see Word 2010 Exhibit 18). ***Click the "Last Name" field in the "Mail Merge Recipients" window to sort the list by last name*** (see Word 2010 Exhibit 18). Notice that the order of the list is now sorted by last name.

WORD 2010 EXHIBIT 18
Entering mail merge recipients

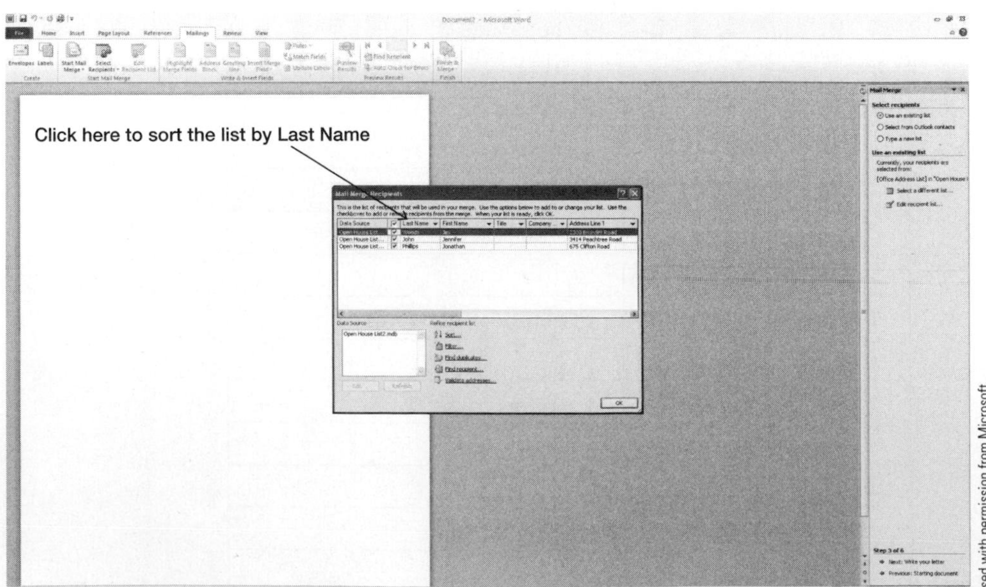

16. ***Click OK in the "Mail Merge Recipients" window.*** You are now back at a blank document with the Mail Merge task pane open to the right. The bottom of the Mail Merge task pane indicates that you are still at step 3 of 6. ***Click Next: Write your letter at the bottom of the Mail Merge task pane under Step 3 of 6*** to continue to the next step.
17. The bottom of the Mail Merge task pane indicates that you are on step 4 of 6. In the Mail Merge task pane, **"Write your letter"** is displayed. You are now ready to write the letter. ***On the Home ribbon tab, click the Paragraph Group Dialog Box Launcher. In the "Paragraph" window, click the down arrow below Line Spacing and select Single. Make sure the Before and After spacing are both 0 point. Then, click OK.***
18. Press the **[ENTER]** key four times.
19. Type the current date and press the **[ENTER]** key three times.
20. ***Click Address Block . . . in the Mail Merge task pane under the Write your letter option.***
21. The "Insert Address Block" window is now displayed. You will now customize how the address block will appear in the letters.
22. ***In the "Insert Address Block" window, click "Joshua Randall Jr."*** Then, ***click Insert company name to deselect it, because we did not include company names in our data list*** (see Word 2010 Exhibit 19).
23. ***Under Insert postal address, click Never include the country/region in the address*** (see Word 2010 Exhibit 19).
24. ***Click OK in the "Insert Address Block" window.***
25. The words **"<<AddressBlock>>"** are now displayed in your document.
26. Press the **[ENTER]** key three times.
27. Press the **[TAB]** key once and then type **Subject:**.
28. Press the **[TAB]** key and then type **Open House.**
29. Press the **[ENTER]** key twice.
30. ***In the Mail Merge task pane, under "Write your letter," click Greeting line. . .*** (see Word 2010 Exhibit 19).

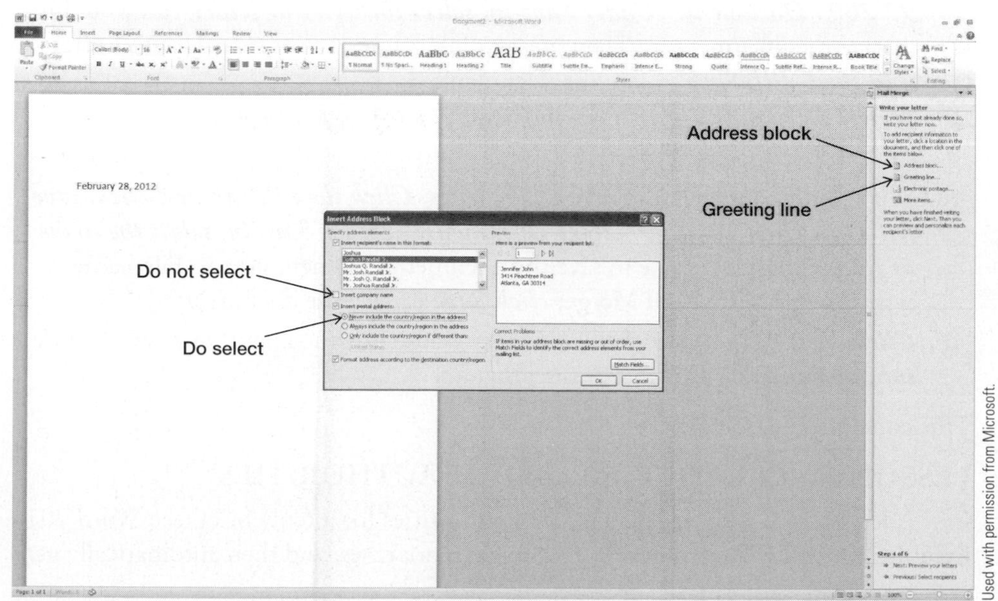

WORD 2010 EXHIBIT 19
Insert address block

31. The "Insert Greeting Line" window is now displayed. You will now customize how the greeting or salutation will appear in the letter. ***In the "Insert Greeting Line" window, click the down arrow next to "Mr. Randall" and then scroll down and click "Josh." Click OK in the "Insert Greeting Line" window.***
32. The words **"<<GreetingLine>>"** are now displayed in your document.
33. Press the **[ENTER]** key three times.
34. Type **You are cordially invited to our open house, which will take place in our new offices at 1414 Pine Street, on the 28th of this month, at 7:00 p.m. Drinks will be served. Please dress casually. We hope you will attend.**
35. Press the **[ENTER]** key twice.
36. Type **Kindest Regards,**.
37. Press the **[ENTER]** key four times.
38. Type **Mirabelle Watkinson**.
39. Press the **[ENTER]** key once and type **For the Firm**.
40. You are now done typing the letter. Your letter should look similar to Word 2010 Exhibit 17. The only thing left to do is to merge the recipient list with the form.
41. ***Under Step 4 of 6 at the bottom of the Mail Merge task pane, click Next: Preview your letters*** to continue to the next step.
42. Your first letter is now displayed. ***In the Mail Merge task pane, under Preview your letters, click the button showing two arrows pointing to the right to see the rest of your letters.***
43. To continue to the next step, ***click Next: Complete the merge at the bottom of the Mail Merge task pane under Step 5 of 6.***
44. The Mail Merge task pane now will display **"Complete the merge."** ***Click Print. . . in the Mail Merge task pane under Merge, and then click OK. At the "Merge to Printer" window, click OK*** to print your letters.
45. ***Click Edit individual letters. . . in the Mail Merge task pane under Merge.*** In the "Merge to New Document" window, ***click OK.*** Word has now opened a new document with all of the letters in it. (*Note:* Here you can edit and personalize each letter if you would like.)
46. To save the document, ***click the File tab, click Save As, and then click "Word 97-2003 Document." Under Save in, select the drive or folder*** you would like to save the document in. Then, next to File name:, type **Open House Letters *and then click Save*** to save the document.
47. ***If they do not close automatically, click the File tab and then on Close*** to close the personalized letters.
48. You should be back at the mail merge letter. ***Click the File tab and click Save As. Then click "Word 97-2003 Document." Under Save in, select the drive or folder*** you would like to save the document in. Then, next to File name:, type **Open House Mail Merge; *click Save*** to save the document.
49. ***Click the File tab, and then on Close*** to close the document, or ***click the File tab, and then on Exit*** to exit the program.

This concludes Lesson 10.

LESSON 11: CREATING A TABLE OF AUTHORITIES

In this lesson, you will prepare a table of authorities for a reply brief (see Word 2010 Exhibit 22). You will learn how to find cases, mark cases, and then automatically generate a table of authorities.

HANDS-ON EXERCISES

1. Open Windows. When it has loaded, ***double-click the Microsoft Office Word 2010 icon on the desktop*** to open Word 2010 for Windows. Alternatively, ***click the Start button, point to Programs or All Programs, and then click the Microsoft Word 2010 icon*** (or ***point to Microsoft Office and then click Microsoft Office Word 2010***). You should now be in a clean, blank document. If you are not in a blank document, ***click the File tab, click New, and then double-click Blank document.***
2. The first thing you will do is to open the "Lesson 11" file from the Premium Website. On the Premium Website, click the Data Files: Word Processing tab, then under Word 2010, click the "Lesson 11" file.
3. The text ***"In the Supreme Court of the United States–TED SUTTON, Petitioner v. STATE OF ALASKA, Respondent"*** should now be displayed on your screen. If the document appears in Protected View, ***click Enable Editing*** to continue with the lesson.
4. In this exercise you will build the case section of the table of authorities for this reply brief. There are five cases to be included and they are all shown in bold so that you can easily identify them. Your first task will be to mark each of the cases so that Word knows they are the cases to be included; then you will execute the command for Word to build the table.
5. If you are not at the beginning of the document, press **[CTRL]+[HOME]** to go to the beginning.
6. You will now mark the cases. ***From the References ribbon tab, click Mark Citation from the Table of Authorities group.***
7. The "Mark Citation" window should now be displayed (see Word 2010 Exhibit 20). Notice, next to Category:, that Cases is displayed. This indicates that you will be marking case citations. ***Click the down arrow next to Cases*** to see that you can also mark citations to be included for Statutes, Rules, Treatises, Regulations, and Other Authorities.
8. ***Click Cases again;*** you will now start marking cases to be included in the TABLE OF AUTHORITIES.
9. ***In the "Mark Citation" window, click Next Citation.*** Word looks for terms such as "vs" or "v." when finding citations. The cursor should now be on the

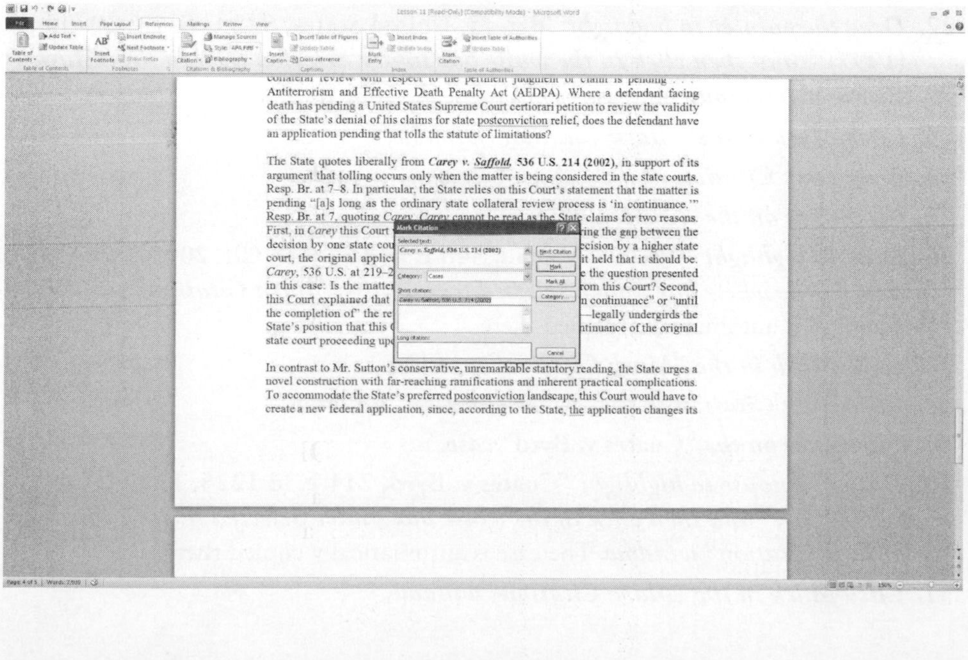

WORD 2010 EXHIBIT 20
Marking a citation for inclusion in a table of authorities

"v." in *Ted Sutton v. State of Alaska*. Because this is the caption of the current case, we do not want to mark it. *Note:* If the "Mark Citation" window gets in the way of your seeing the brief, put the pointer on the blue title bar of the "Mark Citation" window and drag it out of your way.

10. ***Click Next Citation in the "Mark Citation" window.*** Again, this is the caption of the current case, *Ted Sutton v. State of Alaska,* so we do not want to mark it.
11. ***Click again on Next Citation in the "Mark Citation" window.*** Word has now found the case *Carey v. Saffold.* We want to mark this case so that it will be included in the table of authorities.
12. ***Click once on the* Carey v. Saffold *case.***
13. ***Drag the pointer to highlight* "Carey v. Saffold, 536 U.S. 214 (2002)" *and then click in the white box under Selected text: in the "Mark Citation" window.*** The case is automatically copied there (see Word 2010 Exhibit 20).
14. ***Click Mark in the "Mark Citation" window.*** *Note:* When you mark a citation, Word changes your view to the Show/Hide paragraph view. It shows you that you have embedded table of authorities formatting codes in the document. To switch out of Show/Hide view, ***from the Home ribbon tab, click the Show/Hide icon in the Paragraph group.*** (It looks like a paragraph sign.)
15. ***Click Next Citation in the "Mark Citation" window.***
16. ***Click once on the* "Duncan v. Walker" *case.***
17. ***Drag the mouse to highlight* "Duncan v. Walker, 533 U.S. 167, 174 (2001)" *and then click in the white box under Selected text: in the "Mark Citation" window.*** The case is automatically copied there.
18. ***Click Mark in the "Mark Citation" window.*** Notice under Short Citation in the "Mark Citation" window that the *Carey* and *Duncan* cases are listed. Again, if at any time the "Mark Citation" window prevents you from seeing the case you need to highlight, just ***click the blue bar at top of the "Mark Citation" window and drag to the left or the right*** to move the window out of your way.
19. To switch out of Show/Hide view, ***from the Home tab on the ribbon, click the Show/Hide icon in the Paragraph group.***
20. ***Click Next Citation in the "Mark Citation" window.***
21. ***Click once on the* "Bates v. United States" *case.***
22. ***Drag the pointer to highlight* "Bates v. United States, 522 U.S. 23, 29–30 (1997)," *and then click in the white box under Selected text: in the "Mark Citation" window.*** The case is automatically copied there.
23. ***Click Mark in the "Mark Citation" window.***
24. ***Click Next Citation in the "Mark Citation" window.***
25. ***Click once on the* "Abela v. Martin" *case.***
26. ***Drag to highlight* "Abela v. Martin, 348 F.3d 164 (6th Cir. 2003)" *and then click in the white box under Selected text: in the "Mark Citation" window.*** The case is automatically copied there.
27. ***Click Mark in the "Mark Citation" window.***
28. ***Click Next Citation in the "Mark Citation" window.***
29. ***Click once on the* "Coates v. Byrd" *case.***
30. ***Drag the mouse to highlight* "Coates v. Byrd, 211 F.3d 1225, 1227 (11th Cir. 2000)," *and then click in the white box under Selected text: in the "Mark Citation" window.*** The case is automatically copied there.
31. ***Click Mark in the "Mark Citation" window.***

32. ***Click Close in the "Mark Citation" window to close it.***
33. ***On the Home ribbon tab, click the Show/Hide paragraph icon to make the paragraph marks disappear.***
34. Using the cursor keys or the horizontal scroll bar, place the cursor on page 3 of the document two lines under the title **"TABLE OF AUTHORITIES"** (see Word 2010 Exhibit 22). You are now ready to generate the table.
35. ***From the References ribbon tab, click the Insert Table of Authorities icon in the Table of Authorities group*** (see Word 2010 Exhibit 21).
36. ***The "Table of Authorities" window should now be displayed*** (see Word 2010 Exhibit 21). ***Click Cases under Category and then click OK.***
37. Notice that the table of authorities has been prepared and completed, and that the cases and the page numbers where they appear in the document have been included (see Word 2010 Exhibit 22).

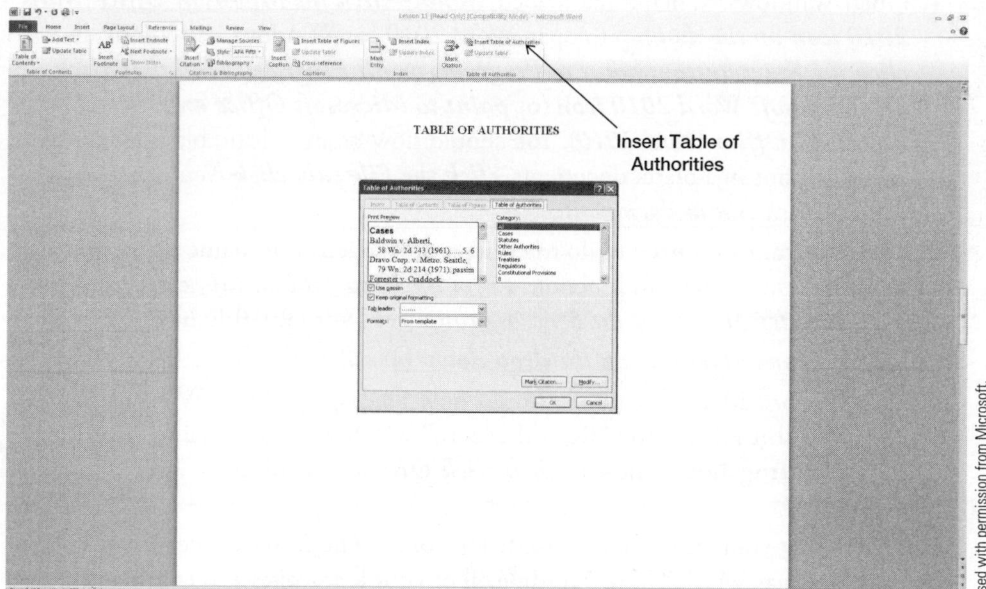

WORD 2010 EXHIBIT 21
Inserting a table of authorities

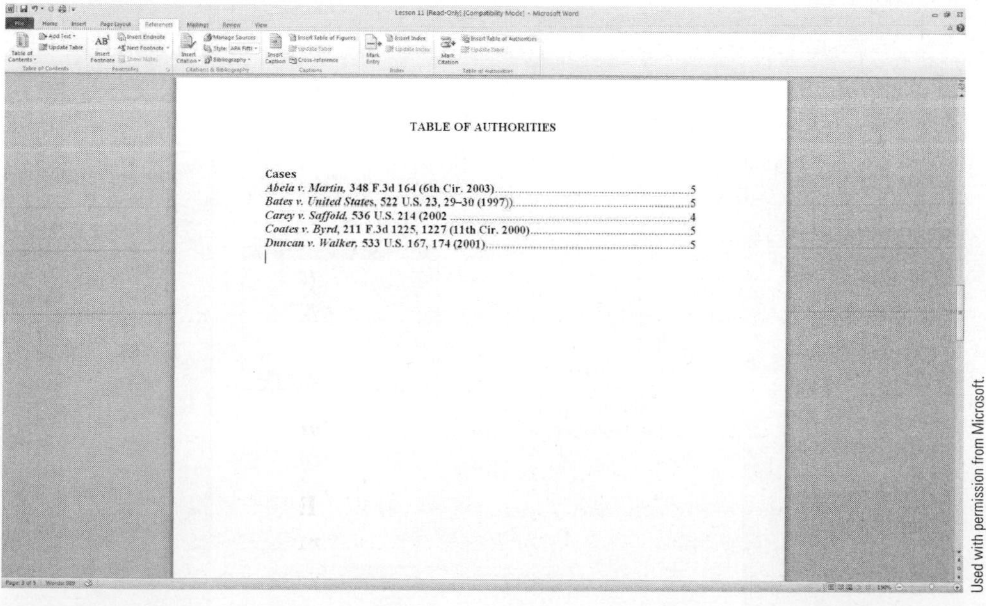

WORD 2010 EXHIBIT 22
Completed table of authorities

38. To print the document, ***click the Quick Print icon on the Quick Access toolbar,*** or ***click the File tab, click Print, and then click Print.***
39. To save the document, ***click the File tab and click Save As, then click "Word 97-2003 Document." Under Save in, select the drive or folder*** you would like to save the document in. Then, next to File name:, type **Done—Word 2010 Lesson 11 Document *and click Save*** to save the document.
40. ***Click the File tab, and then on Close*** to close the document, or ***click the File tab, and then on Exit*** to exit the program.

This concludes Lesson 11.

LESSON 12: CREATING A MACRO

In this lesson you will prepare a macro that will automatically type the signature block for a pleading (see Word 2010 Exhibit 23). You will then execute the macro to make sure that it works properly.

1. Open Windows. When it has loaded, ***double-click the Microsoft Office Word 2010 icon on the desktop*** to open Word 2010 for Windows. Alternatively, ***click the Start button, point to Programs or All Programs, and then click the Microsoft Word 2010 icon*** (or ***point to Microsoft Office and then click Microsoft Office Word 2010***). You should now be in a clean, blank document. If you are not in a blank document, ***click the File tab, click New, and then double-click Blank document.***
2. The first thing you need to do to create a new macro is to name the macro and then turn on the Record function. ***From the View ribbon tab, click the down arrow under Macros in the Macros group*** (see Word 2010 Exhibit 23).
3. ***Click Record Macro. . . on the drop-down menu.***
4. The "Record Macro" window should now be displayed (see Word 2010 Exhibit 23). In the "Record Macro" window, under Macro name:, type **Pleadingsignblock *and then click OK*** (see Word 2010 Exhibit 23).
5. Notice that your cursor has a cassette tape on it. The cassette tape on your cursor indicates that Word is now recording all of your keystrokes and commands.

WORD 2010 EXHIBIT 23
Creating a pleading signature block macro

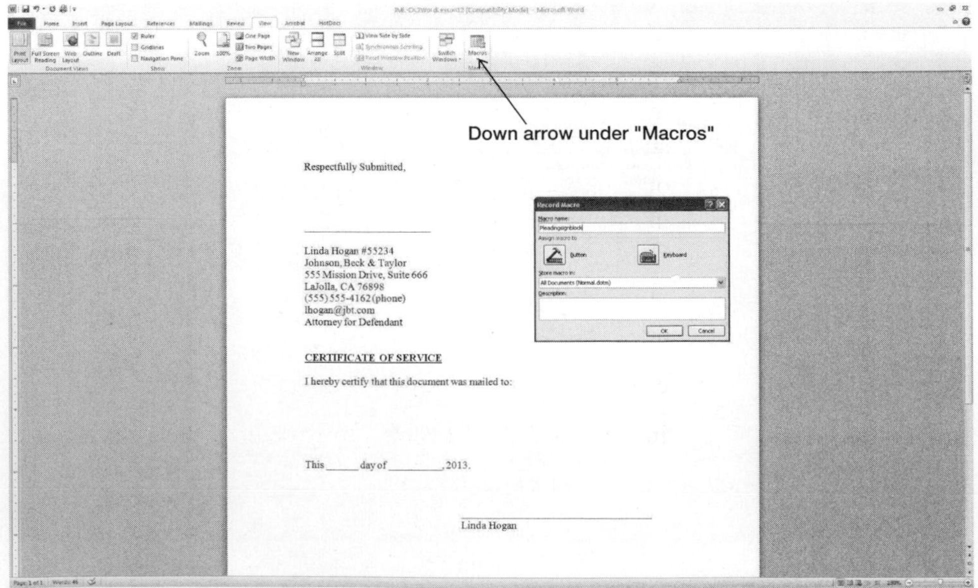

6. Type the information shown in Word 2010 Exhibit 23. When you have completed typing the information, ***from the View ribbon tab, click the down arrow under Macros in the Macros group*** (see Word 2010 Exhibit 23).
7. ***Click Stop Recording on the drop-down menu.***
8. You will now test your macro to see if it works properly. ***Click the File tab and then on Close*** to close the document. At the prompt **"Do you want to save the changes to Document?"** ***click Don't Save.***
9. To open a blank document, ***click the File tab, click New, and then double-click Blank document.***
10. To run the macro, ***from the View ribbon tab, click the down arrow under Macros in the Macros group*** (see Word 2010 Exhibit 23).
11. ***Click View Macros.***
12. ***In the "Macros" window, click* Pleadingsignblock *and then click Run.*** Your pleading signature block should now appear in your document.
13. To print the document, ***click the Quick Print icon on the Quick Access toolbar,*** or ***click the File tab, click Print, and then click Print.***
14. To save the document, ***click the File tab, click Save As, and then click "Word 97-2003 Document." Under Save in, select the drive or folder*** you would like to save the document in. Then, next to File name:, type **Done—Word 2010 Lesson 12 Document** ***and click Save*** to save the document.
15. ***Click the File tab, and then on Close*** to close the document, or ***click the File tab, and then on Exit*** to exit the program.

This concludes Lesson 12.

LESSON 13: DRAFTING A WILL

Using the websites at the end of the chapter or a form book from a law library, draft a simple will that would be valid in your state. You will be drafting the will for Thomas Mansell, who is a widower. The will should be dated July 1 of the current year. Mr. Mansell requests the following:

- That his just debts and funeral expenses be paid.
- That his lifelong friend, Dr. Jeff Johnson, receive $20,000 in cash.
- That his local YMCA receive his 100 shares of stock in IBM.
- That all of his remaining property (real or personal) descend to his daughter Sharon Mansell.
- That in the event Mr. Mansell and his daughter die simultaneously, for all of his property to descend to Sharon's son Michael Mansell.
- That Dr. Jeff Johnson be appointed the executor of the will; if Dr. Johnson predeceases Mr. Mansell, that Mr. Joe Crawford be appointed executor.
- That his will be double-spaced and have 1-inch margins; he would like the will to look good and be valid in his state.
- Three witnesses will watch the signing of the will: Shelly Stewart, Dennis Gordon, and Gary Fox.
- John Boesel will notarize the will.

Print out a hard copy of the will and turn it in or email it to your instructor.

This concludes the lessons in the Word 2010 Hands-On Exercises.

HANDS-ON EXERCISES

MICROSOFT WORD 2007 FOR WINDOWS

Number	Lesson Title	Concepts Covered
BASIC LESSONS		
Lesson 1	Typing a Letter	Using word wrap, Tab key, cursor keys, underline, bold, italics; saving and printing a document
Lesson 2	Editing a Letter	Retrieving a file, block moving/deleting, and spell/grammar checking
Lesson 3	Typing a Pleading	Centering, changing margins, changing line spacing, adding a footnote, double indenting, and automatic page numbering
Lesson 4	Creating a Table	Creating a table, entering data in a table, using automatic numbering, adjusting columns in a table, and using the Table AutoFormat command
INTERMEDIATE LESSONS		
Lesson 5	Tools and Techniques	Editing an employment policy using the Format Painter tool, revealing document formatting, using the Beginning of Document command, clearing formatting, changing case, using Search and Replace, using the Go To command, creating a section break, and changing the orientation of the page to Landscape
Lesson 6	Using Styles	Using, modifying, and creating styles to maintain consistent and uniform formatting of documents
Lesson 7	Creating a Template (office letterhead/letter)	Finding ready-made templates in Word, creating a new office letterhead and letter template, filling in/completing a template, and adding a command to the Quick Access toolbar
Lesson 8	Comparing Documents (multiple versions of an employment contract)	Comparing documents using the simultaneous viewing method and merging the documents into a separate annotated blacklined document
Lesson 9	Using Track Changes	Turning on Track Changes, making revisions, and accepting and rejecting revisions
ADVANCED LESSONS		
Lesson 10	Creating a Mail Merge Document	Creating and entering a list of recipients for a mail merge, creating a mail merge document, and merging the list with the document
Lesson 11	Creating a Table of Authorities	Finding and marking cases in a brief and generating an actual table of authorities for the brief
Lesson 12	Creating a Macro (pleading signature block)	Creating and executing a pleading signature block macro
Lesson 13	Drafting a Will	Using Word to draft a will

GETTING STARTED

Introduction

Throughout these lessons and exercises, information you need to type into the program will be designated in several different ways:

- Keys to be pressed on the keyboard are designated in brackets, in all caps, and in bold (e.g., press the **[ENTER]** key). A key combination, where two or more keys are pressed at once, is designated with a plus sign between the key names (e.g., **[CTRL]+[BACKSPACE]**). You should not type the plus sign.
- Movements with the mouse are designated in bold and italics (e.g., ***point to File on the menu bar and click***).
- Words or letters that should be typed are designated in bold (e.g., type **Training Program**).
- Information that is or should be displayed on your computer screen is shown in bold, with quotation marks (e.g., **"Press ENTER to continue."**).

OVERVIEW OF MICROSOFT WORD 2007

The following tips on using Microsoft Word will help you complete these exercises.

I. General Rules for Microsoft Word 2007

A. *Word Wrap:* You do not need to press the **[ENTER]** key after each line of text, as you would with a typewriter.

B. *Double Spacing:* If you want to double-space, do not hit the **[ENTER]** key twice. Instead, change the line spacing (***click the Home ribbon tab, then click the Line spacing icon in the Paragraph group and select 2.0).*** See Word 2007 Exhibit 1.

C. *Moving Through Already-Entered Text:* If you want to move the cursor to various positions within already-entered text, use the cursor (arrow) keys, or ***point and click.***

D. *Moving the Pointer Where No Text Has Been Entered:* You cannot use the cursor keys to move the pointer where no text has been entered. Said another way, you cannot move any further in a document than where you have typed text or pressed the **[ENTER]** key. You must use the **[ENTER]** key or first type text.

E. *Saving a Document:* To save a document, ***click the Office button in the upper left corner of the screen and then click Save*** (see Word 2007 Exhibit 1).

F. *New Document:* To get a new, clean document, ***click the Office button, then click New, then double-click Blank document*** (see Word 2007 Exhibit 1).

G. *Help:* To get help, press **[F1]** or ***click the ? icon in the upper right corner of the screen*** (see Word 2007 Exhibit 1).

II. Editing a Document

A. Pointer Movement

One space to left	**[LEFT ARROW]**
One space to right	**[RIGHT ARROW]**
Beginning of line	**[HOME]**
End of line	**[END]**
One line up	**[UP ARROW]**

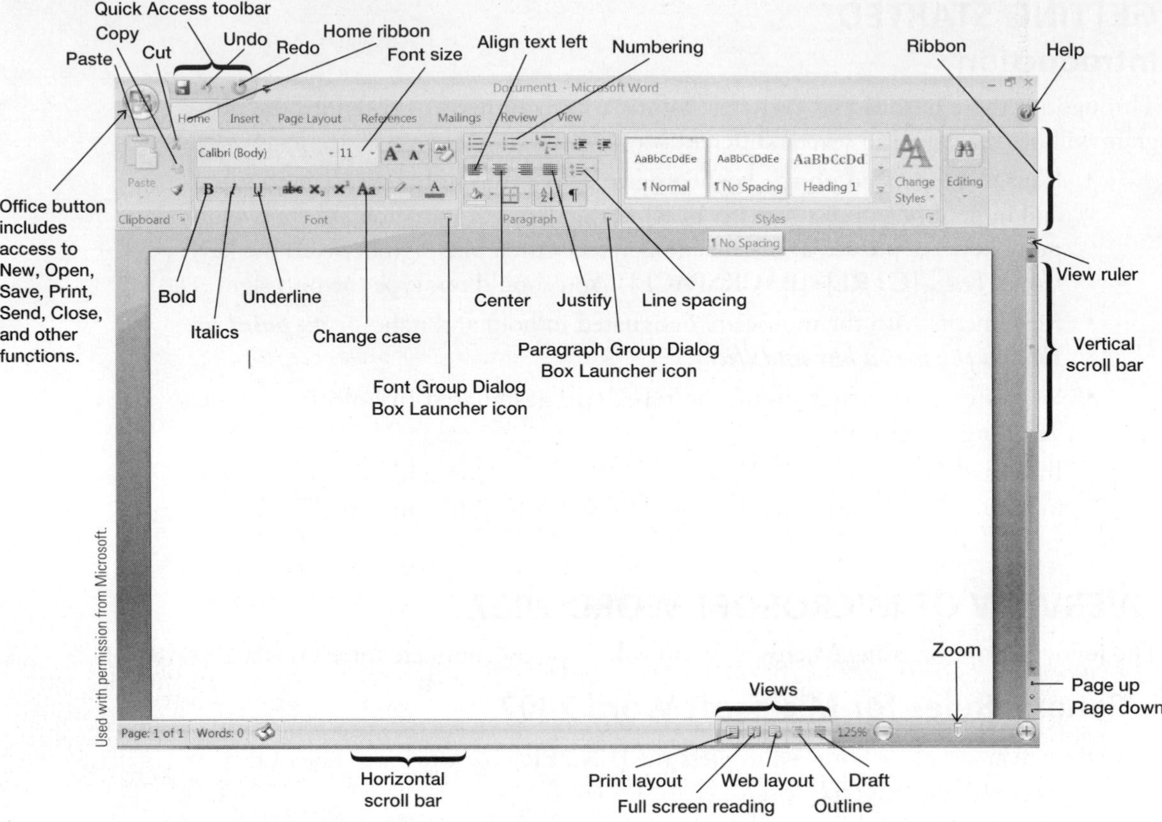

WORD 2007 EXHIBIT 1
Word 2007 screen

One line down **[DOWN ARROW]**
One screen up **[PAGE UP]**
One screen down **[PAGE DOWN]**
Beginning of document **[CTRL]+[HOME]**
End of document **[CTRL]+[END]**

B. Deleting Text
Delete the text under the cursor or to the right of it **[DEL]**
Delete the text to the left of the cursor **[BACKSPACE]**
Delete the whole word to the left of the cursor **[CTRL]+[BACKSPACE]**
Delete the whole word to the right of the cursor **[CTRL]+[DEL]**

C. *Delete Blocked Text*—***Drag the mouse pointer to select or highlight text,*** and then press **[DEL]**; or ***drag the mouse pointer to select or highlight text, and then from the Home ribbon tab, select the Cut icon from the Clipboard group*** (see Word 2007 Exhibit 1). Another way to select or highlight text is to press and hold the **[SHIFT]** key while using the cursor keys to mark/highlight the desired text.

D. *Undoing/Undeleting Text*—If you delete text and immediately want it back, ***click the Undo icon on the Quick Access toolbar.*** This can also be done by pressing **[CTRL]+[Z]**. Press **[CTRL]+[Z]** or ***click the Undo icon*** until your desired text reappears. The Undo feature also works on many other activities in Word, but not all. So, if something goes wrong, at least try pressing **[CTRL]+[Z]** to undo whatever you did.

E. *Moving Text*—***Drag the mouse pointer to highlight or select the text. Then, from the Home ribbon tab, select the Cut icon from the Clipboard group*** (see Word 2007 Exhibit 1). ***Move the cursor to where the text should be inserted, and, from the Home ribbon tab, select Paste from the Clipboard group.*** Another way to do this is to ***drag the mouse pointer to highlight the area and then right-click.*** This brings up a menu that includes the Cut, Copy, and Paste commands. Yet another way to do this is to use the drag-and-drop method: ***Drag the mouse pointer to highlight the area, release the mouse button, click the highlighted area, drag the text to the new location, and release the mouse button.***

F. *Copying Text*—***Drag the mouse pointer to highlight or select the area. From the Home ribbon tab, click the Copy icon from the Clipboard group*** (see Word 2007 Exhibit 1). ***Move the cursor to where the text should be copied, and, from the Home ribbon tab, click Paste.*** Another way to do this is to ***drag the pointer to highlight the area and then right-click Copy. Then move the cursor to where you want to copy the text and right-click Paste.*** Still another way to do this is to use the drag-and-drop method: ***Drag the cursor to highlight the area, release the mouse button, click the highlighted area*** while pressing **[CTRL]**, ***drag the text to the new location, and release the mouse button.*** The text is then copied to the new location.

III. Formatting

A. *Centering Text*—***Move the pointer to the line where the text should be centered. From the Home ribbon tab, click the Paragraph Group Dialog Box Launcher*** (see Word 2007 Exhibit 1). ***In the Indents and Spacing tab, click the down arrow key next to Alignment and select Centered; then click OK and begin typing.*** If the text has already been typed, move the pointer to the paragraph where the text is and then issue the command. Alternatively, ***from the Home ribbon tab, click the Center icon in the Paragraph group*** (see Word 2007 Exhibit 1).

B. *Bold Type*—To type in bold, ***from the Home ribbon tab, click the Font Group Dialog Box Launcher*** (see Word 2007 Exhibit 1); ***in the Font tab, click Bold under Font style. Click OK.*** Alternatively, ***from the Home ribbon tab, click the Bold icon in the Font group.*** Another way is to press **[CTRL]+[B].**

C. *Underlining*—To underline, ***from the Home ribbon tab, click the Font Group Dialog Box Launcher*** (see Word 2007 Exhibit 1); ***in the Font tab, click the down arrow under Underline style, select the underline style you would like, then click OK.*** Alternatively, ***from the Home ribbon tab, click the Underline icon in the Font group.*** Another way is to press **[CTRL]+[U].**

D. *Margins*—Margins can be set by ***clicking the Page Layout ribbon tab and then clicking on Margins from the Page Setup group.***

E. *Line Spacing*—Line spacing can be changed by ***clicking the Home ribbon tab, then clicking the Line Spacing icon in the Paragraph group*** (see Word 2007 Exhibit 1).

F. *Justification*—***Move the pointer to the line where the text should be justified.*** Then, ***from the Home ribbon tab, click the Paragraph Group Dialog Box Launcher*** (see Word 2007 Exhibit 1). ***In the Indents and Spacing tab, click the down arrow key next to Alignment and select Justified; then click OK and begin typing.*** If the text has already been typed, move the cursor to the paragraph where the text is and then issue the command. Alternatively, *from the Home ribbon tab, click the Justify icon in the Paragraph group* (see Word 2007 Exhibit 1).

G. *Header/Footer*—***From the Insert ribbon tab, click Header or Footer from the Header & Footer group.***

H. *Hard Page Break*—To force the addition of a new page in the current document by using the Hard Page Break command, press **[CTRL]+[ENTER]**, or ***from the Insert ribbon tab, click Blank Page from the Pages group.*** Page breaks also occur automatically when the current page is full of text.

I. *Indent*—***From the Home ribbon tab, click the Paragraph Group Dialog Box Launcher*** (see Word 2007 Exhibit 1). ***In the Indents and Spacing tab under Indentation, click the up arrow next to Left or Right to set the indentation amount; then click OK and begin typing.*** Alternatively, ***from the Home ribbon tab, point to the Decrease Indent or Increase Indent icon in the Paragraph group.***

IV. Other Functions

A. *Printing*—To print, ***click the Office button, and then click Print*** (see Word 2007 Exhibit 1).

B. *Spell Check*—To turn on the spell-checking function, ***from the Review ribbon tab, click Spelling & Grammar in the Proofing group.*** Additionally, a red squiggly line will appear under each word that the computer's dictionary does not recognize. If you right-click the word, the program will suggest possible spellings.

C. *Open Files*—To open a file, ***click the Office button, and then click Open*** (see Word 2007 Exhibit 1).

D. *Tables*—***From the Insert ribbon tab, click Table from the Tables group.*** You can move between cells in the table by pressing the **[TAB]** and the **[SHIFT]+[TAB]** keys.

BASIC LESSONS

LESSON 1: TYPING A LETTER

This lesson shows you how to type the letter shown in Word 2007 Exhibit 2. It explains how to use the word wrap feature; the [TAB] key; the cursor (or arrow) keys; the underline, bold, and italics features; the save document function; and the print document function. Keep in mind that if you make a mistake in this lesson at any time, you may press **[CTRL]+[Z]** to undo what you have done. Also remember that any time you would like to see the name of an icon on the ribbon tabs, just ***point to the icon for a second or two*** and the name will be displayed.

1. Open Windows. After it has loaded, ***double-click the Microsoft Office Word 2007 icon on the desktop*** to open Word 2007 for Windows. Alternatively, ***click the Start button, point to Programs or All Programs, then click the Microsoft Word 2007 icon,*** or ***point to Microsoft Office and then click Microsoft Office Word 2007.*** You should now be in a new, clean, blank document. If you are not in a blank document, ***click the Office button, click New, then double-click Blank document.***
2. At this point you cannot move the pointer around the screen by pressing the cursor keys (also called arrow keys). This is because text must first be entered;

WORD 2007 EXHIBIT 2
Letter

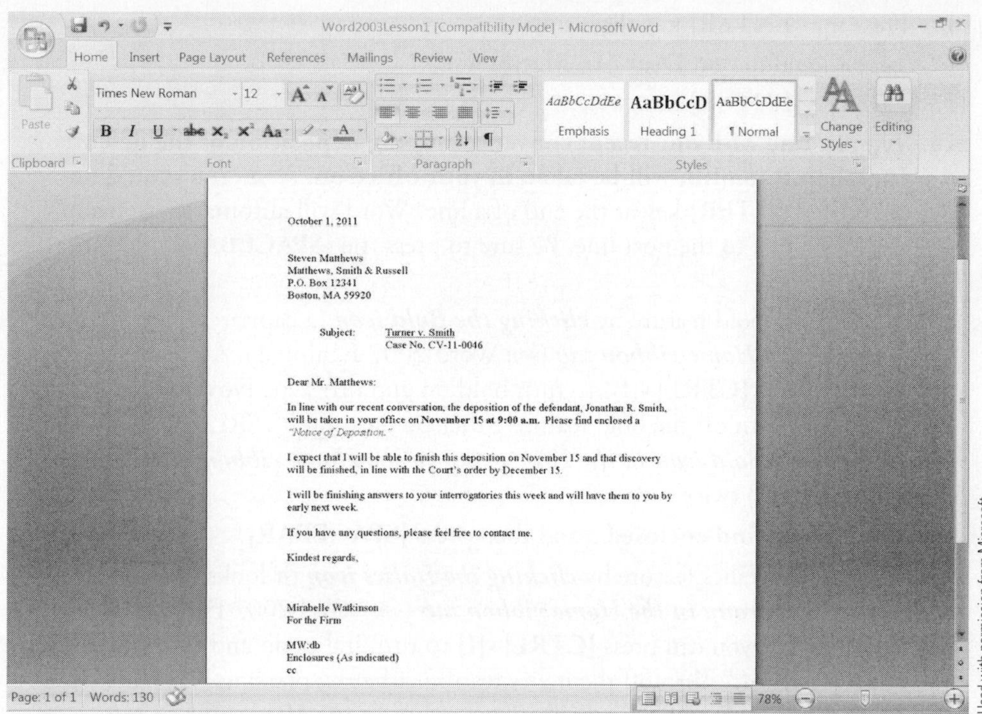

October 1, 2011

Steven Matthews
Matthews, Smith & Russell
P.O. Box 12341
Boston, MA 59920

Subject: Turner v. Smith
Case No. CV-11-0046

Dear Mr. Matthews:

In line with our recent conversation, the deposition of the defendant, Jonathan R. Smith, will be taken in your office on **November 15 at 9:00 a.m.** Please find enclosed a *"Notice of Deposition."*

I expect that I will be able to finish this deposition on November 15 and that discovery will be finished, in line with the Court's order by December 15.

I will be finishing answers to your interrogatories this week and will have them to you by early next week.

If you have any questions, please feel free to contact me.

Kindest regards,

Mirabelle Watkinson
For the Firm

MW:db
Enclosures (As indicated)
cc

HANDS-ON EXERCISES

the pointer can only move through text, so the cursor keys will not function if no text exists. ***On the Home ribbon tab, click the Paragraph Group Dialog Launcher. In the "Paragraph" window, click the down arrow below Line spacing and select Single.*** Make sure the "Before" and "After" spacing boxes are both 0 point. ***Click OK.***

3. Press the **[ENTER]** key four times. Watch the status line in the lower left-hand corner of the screen, which tells you what page of your document you are on.
4. Type the date of the letter as shown in Word 2007 Exhibit 2. Notice that as you type the word "October," AutoText may anticipate that you are typing "October" and give you the following prompt: **"October (Press ENTER to Insert)."** If you press the **[ENTER]** key, AutoText will finish typing the word for you. You can also ignore it and just continue typing the word yourself.
5. Press the **[ENTER]** key three times.
6. Type the inside address as shown in Word 2007 Exhibit 2. Press the **[ENTER]** key after each line of the inside address. When you finish the line with "Boston, MA 59920," press the **[ENTER]** key three times.
7. Press the **[TAB]** key one time (Word automatically sets default tabs every five spaces). The pointer will move five spaces to the right.
8. Type **Subject:** and then press the **[TAB]** key twice. ***On the Home ribbon tab, click the Underline icon in the Font group*** (it looks like a "U" with a thin line under it). Alternatively, you can press **[CTRL]+[U]** to turn the underline feature on and off, or ***point to the Font Group Dialog Box Launcher*** (see Word 2007 Exhibit 1) and ***select the Underline style.*** Then, type **Turner v. Smith.** ***On the Home ribbon tab in the Font group, click the Underline icon*** to turn the underline feature off.
9. Press the **[ENTER]** key one time.
10. Press the **[TAB]** key three times, and then type **Case No. CV-11-0046.**

11. Press the **[ENTER]** key three times.
12. Type the salutation **Dear Mr. Matthews:**
13. Press the **[ENTER]** key twice.
14. Type **In line with our recent conversation, the deposition of the defendant, Jonathan R. Smith, will be taken in your office on**. *Note:* You should not press the **[ENTER]** key at the end of a line. Word will automatically "wrap" the text down to the next line. Be sure to press the **[SPACEBAR]** once after the word "on."
15. Turn on the bold feature by ***clicking the Bold icon*** (a capital "B") ***in the Font group in the Home ribbon tab*** (see Word 2007 Exhibit 1). Alternatively, you can press **[CTRL]+[B]** to turn bold on and off. Type **November 15 at 9:00 a.m.** Turn off the bold feature either by pressing **[CTRL]+[B]**, or ***by clicking the Bold icon in the Font group in the Home ribbon tab.*** Press the **[SPACEBAR]** twice.
16. Type **Please find enclosed a** and then press **[SPACEBAR]**.
17. Turn on the italics feature by ***clicking the Italics icon*** (it looks like an "I") ***in the Font group in the Home ribbon tab*** (see Word 2007 Exhibit 1). Alternatively, you can press **[CTRL]+[I]** to turn italics on and off. Type **"Notice of Deposition."** Turn off the italics feature either by pressing **[CTRL]+[I],** or ***by clicking the Italics icon in the Font group in the Home ribbon tab.***
18. Press the **[ENTER]** key twice.
19. Type the second paragraph of the letter and then press the **[ENTER]** key twice.
20. Type the third paragraph of the letter and then press the **[ENTER]** key twice.
21. Type the fourth paragraph of the letter and then press the **[ENTER]** key twice.
22. Type **Kindest regards,** and then press the **[ENTER]** key four times.
23. Type **Mirabelle Watkinson** and then press the **[ENTER]** key.
24. Type **For the Firm** and then press the **[ENTER]** key twice.
25. Finish the letter by typing the author's initials, enclosures, and copy abbreviation (cc) as shown in Word 2007 Exhibit 2.
26. To print the document, ***click the Office button, then click Print, then click OK.***
27. To save the document, ***click the Office button and then click Save.*** Type **Letter1** next to File name:. ***Click Save*** to save the letter to the default directory. *Note:* You will edit this letter in Lesson 2, so it is important that you save it.
28. ***Click the Office button and then Close*** to close the document, or, to exit Word 2007, ***click the Office button and then click Exit Word.***

This concludes Lesson 1.

LESSON 2: EDITING A LETTER

This lesson shows you how to retrieve and edit the letter you typed in Lesson 1. It explains how to retrieve a file, perform block moves and deletes, and spell-/grammar-check your document. Keep in mind that if you make a mistake in this lesson at any time, you may press **[CTRL]+[Z]** to undo what you have done. Also remember that any time you would like to see the name of an icon on the ribbon tab, just ***point to the icon for a second or two*** and the name will be displayed.

1. Open Windows. ***Double-click the Microsoft Office Word 2007 icon on the desktop*** to open Word 2007 for Windows. Alternatively, ***click the Start button, point to Programs or All Programs, then click the Microsoft Word 2007 icon.*** (You can also ***point to Microsoft Office and then click Microsoft Office Word***

HANDS-ON EXERCISES

WORD 2007 EXHIBIT 3
Corrections to a letter

October 1, 2011

Steven Matthews
Matthews, Smith & Russell
P.O. Box 12341
Boston, MA 59920

Subject: Turner v. Smith
Case No. CV-11-0046

Steve
Dear ~~Mr. Matthews~~:

of September 30

In line with our recent conversation, the deposition of the defendant, Jonathan R. Smith, will be taken in your office on **November 15 at 9:00 a.m.** Please find enclosed a *"Notice of Deposition."*

I expect that I will be able to finish this deposition on November 15 and that discovery will be finished, in line with the Court's order by December 15.

I will be finishing answers to your interrogatories ~~this~~ week ~~and will have them to you by early next week.~~
next

If you have any questions, please feel free to contact me.

Kindest regards,

Mirabelle Watkinson
For the Firm

MW:db
Enclosures (As indicated)
cc
Mirabelle Watkinson

2007). You should now be in a new, clean, blank document. If you are not in a blank document, ***click the Office button, click New, then double-click Blank document.***

2. In this lesson, you will begin by retrieving the document you created in Lesson 1. To open the file, ***click the Office button and click Open.*** Then type **Letter1** and ***click Open.*** Alternatively, ***scroll using the horizontal scroll bar until you find the file, then click it, then click Open.***
3. Notice in Word 2007 Exhibit 3 that some editing changes have been made to the letter. You will spend the rest of this lesson making these changes.
4. Use your cursor keys or mouse to go to the salutation line, "Dear Mr. Matthews:" With the pointer to the left of the "M" in "Mr. Matthews," press the **[DEL]** key 12 times until "Mr. Matthews" is deleted.
5. Type **Steve**. The salutation line should now read "Dear Steve:"
6. Using your cursor keys or mouse, ***move the pointer to the left of the comma following the word "conversation" in the first paragraph.*** Press the **[SPACEBAR]**, then type **of September 30**. The sentence now reads:

In line with our recent conversation of September 30, the deposition of the defendant, . . .

7. The next change you will make is to move the second paragraph so that it becomes part of the first paragraph. Although this can be accomplished in more than one way, this lesson uses the Cut command.
8. Using your cursor keys or mouse, ***move the pointer to the beginning of the second paragraph of Word 2007 Exhibit 3.***
9. ***Click and drag the cursor*** (hold the left mouse button down and move the mouse) ***until the entire second paragraph is highlighted, and then release the mouse button.***
10. ***From the Home ribbon tab, click the Cut icon in the Clipboard group*** (see Word 2007 Exhibit 1). An alternative is to ***right-click anywhere in the highlighted area and then click Cut.*** The text is no longer on the screen, but it is not deleted—it has been temporarily placed on the Office Clipboard.

HANDS-ON EXERCISES

HANDS-ON EXERCISES

11. Move the pointer to the end of the first paragraph. Press the **[SPACEBAR]** twice. If the pointer appears to be in italics mode, ***from the Home ribbon tab, click the Italics icon in the Font group,*** or press **[CTLR]+[I]** to turn the italics feature off.
12. ***From the Home ribbon tab, click Paste from the Clipboard group*** (see Word 2007 Exhibit 1). Notice that the text has now been moved. Also, you may notice that a small icon in the shape of a clipboard has appeared where you pasted the text. Click the down arrow of the Paste Options icon. Notice that you are given the option to keep the source formatting or change the formatting so that the text matches the destination formatting (i.e., the formatting of the place you are copying it to). In this example, both formats are the same, so it does not matter, but if the text you are copying is a different format, you can choose whether or not to change it to the destination format. Press the **[ESC]** key to make the Paste Options menu disappear.
13. Move the pointer to the line below the first paragraph, and use the **[DEL]** key to delete any unnecessary blank lines.
14. Using your cursor keys or mouse, ***move the pointer to what is now the second paragraph and place the pointer to the left of the "t" in "this week."***
15. Use the **[DEL]** key to delete the word "this," and then type **next**.
16. We will now delete the rest of the sentence in the second paragraph. ***Drag the pointer until "and will have them to you by early next week." is highlighted.*** Press the **[DEL]** key. Type a period at the end of the sentence.
17. You have now made all of the necessary changes. To be sure the letter does not have misspelled words or grammar errors, you will use the Spelling and Grammar command.
18. ***Point on the Review ribbon tab, then click Spelling & Grammar in the Proofing group.***
19. If an error is found, it will be highlighted. You have the options of ignoring it once, ignoring it completely, accepting one of the suggestions listed, or changing/correcting the problem yourself. Correct any spelling or grammar errors. When the spell and grammar check is done, ***click OK.***
20. To print the document, ***click the Office button, click Print, then click OK.***
21. To save the document, ***click the Office button and then select Save As.*** Type **Letter2** in the "File name:" box, ***then click Save*** to save the document in the default directory.
22. ***Click the Office button and then click Close*** to close the document, or ***click the Office button and then click Exit Word*** to exit the program.

This concludes Lesson 2.

LESSON 3: TYPING A PLEADING

This lesson shows you how to type a pleading, as shown in Word 2007 Exhibit 4. It expands on the items presented in Lessons 1 and 2. It also explains how to center text, change margins, change line spacing, add a footnote, double-indent text, and use automatic page numbering. Keep in mind that if you make a mistake at any time, you may press **[CTRL]+[Z]** to undo what you have done.

1. Open Windows. ***Double-click the Microsoft Office Word 2007 icon on the desktop*** to open Word 2007 for Windows. Alternatively, ***click the Start button, point to Programs or All Programs, then click the Microsoft Word 2007 icon.*** (You can also ***point to Microsoft Office and then click Microsoft Office Word***

IN THE DISTRICT COURT OF
ORANGE COUNTY, MASSACHUSETTS

JIM TURNER,

Plaintiff,

vs. Case No. CV-11-0046

JONATHAN R. SMITH,

Defendant.

NOTICE TO TAKE DEPOSITION

COMES NOW, the plaintiff and pursuant to statute[1] hereby gives notice that the deposition of Defendant, Jonathan R. Smith, will be taken as follows:

Monday, November 15, 2012, at 9:00 a.m. at the law offices of Matthews, Smith & Russell, 17031 W. 69th Street, Boston, MA.

Said deposition will be taken before a court reporter and is not expected to take more than one day in duration.

____
Mirabelle Watkinson
Attorney for Plaintiff

[1] Massachusetts Statutes Annotated 60-2342(a)(1).

Page 1

WORD 2007 EXHIBIT 4
A pleading

2007.) You should now be in a new, clean, blank document. If you are not in a blank document, ***click the Office button, click New, then double-click Blank document.*** Remember, any time you would like to see the name of an icon on the ribbon tabs, just ***point to the icon for a second or two*** and the name will be displayed.

2. You will be creating the document shown in Word 2007 Exhibit 4. The first thing you will need to do is change the margins so that the left margin is 1.5 inches and the right margin is 1 inch. To change the margins, ***click the Page Layout ribbon tab and then click Margins in the Page Setup group. Next, click Custom Margins at the bottom of the drop-down menu. In the "Page Setup" window in the Margins tab, change the left margin to 1.5 inches and the right margin to 1 inch. Click OK.*** Also, ***on the Home ribbon tab, click the Paragraph Group dialog launcher. In the "Paragraph" window in the***

Indents and Spacing tab, click the down arrow below Line spacing and select Single. Make sure the "Before" and "After" spacing boxes are both 0 point; then ***click OK.***

3. Notice in Word 2007 Exhibit 4 that there is a page number at the bottom of the page. Word will automatically number your pages for you.
4. ***Click the Insert ribbon tab, then click Page Number in the Header & Footer group*** (see Word 2007 Exhibit 5).
5. ***Point to Bottom of Page*** (see Word 2007 Exhibit 5) and notice that a number of options are displayed. ***Click the down arrow in the lower right for additional options*** (see Word 2007 Exhibit 5). Notice that many page number options are available. ***Scroll back up to the top of the option list and click the second option, Plain Number 2.***
6. Your pointer should now be in the area marked "Footer." Specifically, your pointer should be to the left of the number 1. Type **Page** and then press **[SPACEBAR].**
7. ***Click the Home ribbon tab. Then, click the vertical scroll bar*** (see Word 2007 Exhibit 1) ***or use the [UP ARROW] key to go back to the beginning of the document.***
8. ***Point and double-click just below the header.***
9. On the first line of the document, ***from the Home ribbon tab, click the Center icon in the Paragraph group.*** Type **IN THE DISTRICT COURT OF**. Press the **[ENTER]** key. Type **ORANGE COUNTY, MASSACHUSETTS.**
10. Press the **[ENTER]** key five times. ***From the Home ribbon tab, click the Align Text Left icon in the Paragraph group.***
11. Type **JIM TURNER,** and press the **[ENTER]** key twice.
12. Press the **[TAB]** key three times and type **Plaintiff,** then press the **[ENTER]** key twice.

WORD 2007 EXHIBIT 5
Adding a page number

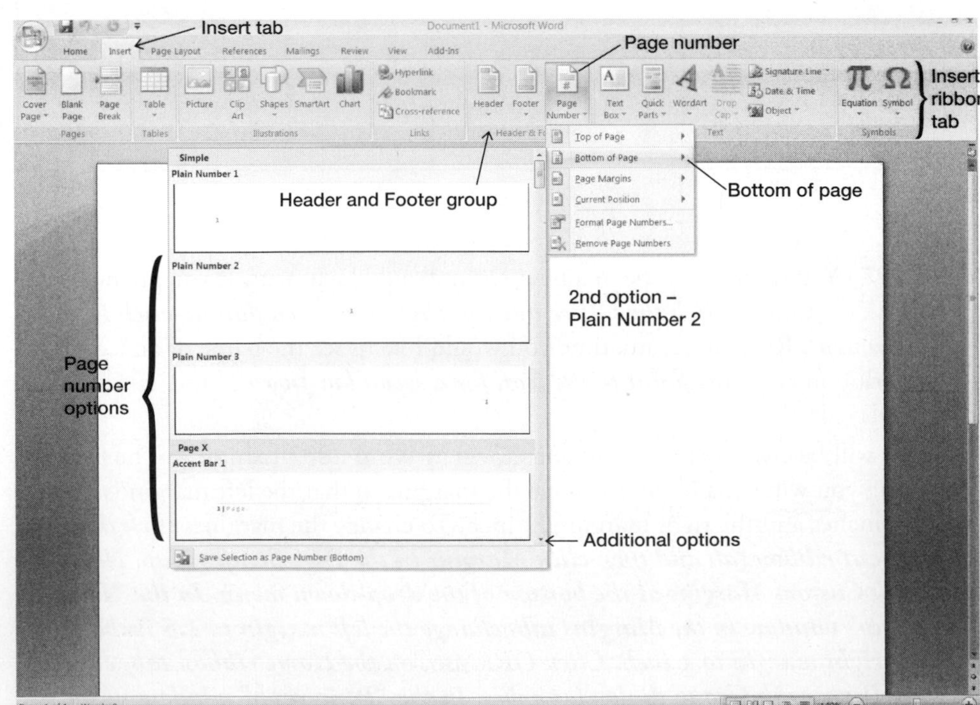

13. Type **vs.** Then press the **[TAB]** key six times, and type **Case No. CV-11-0046**.
14. Press the **[ENTER]** key twice.
15. Type **JONATHAN R. SMITH,** and press the **[ENTER]** key twice.
16. Press the **[TAB]** key three times and type **Defendant.** Press the **[ENTER]** key four times.
17. ***From the Home ribbon tab, click the Center icon in the Paragraph group.***
18. ***From the Home ribbon tab, click the Bold icon and the Underline icon, both found in the Font group.*** Type **NOTICE TO TAKE DEPOSITION**. ***Click the Bold and Underline icons*** to turn them off.
19. Press the **[ENTER]** key three times. ***From the Home ribbon tab, click the Align Text Left icon in the Paragraph group.***
20. ***From the Home ribbon tab, click the Line spacing icon from the Paragraph group*** (see Word 2007 Exhibit 1), ***then click 2.0.*** This will change the line spacing from single to double.
21. Type **COMES NOW, the plaintiff and pursuant to statute**. Notice that a footnote follows the word *statute* in Word 2007 Exhibit 4.
22. With the pointer just to the right of the e in "statute," ***from the References ribbon tab, click Insert Footnote from the Footnotes group.*** The cursor should now be at the bottom of the page in the footnote window.
23. Type **Massachusetts Statutes Annotated 60–2342(a)(1).**
24. To move the pointer back to the body of the document, simply ***click to the right of the word "statute" and the superscript number 1 in the body of the document.*** Now, continue to type the rest of the first paragraph. Once the paragraph is typed, press the **[ENTER]** key twice.
25. To double-indent the second paragraph, ***from the Home ribbon tab, click the Paragraph Group Dialog Box Launcher*** (see Word 2007 Exhibit 1). The "Paragraph" window should now be displayed. ***In the Indents and Spacing tab under Indentation, add a 0.5-inch left indent and a 0.5-inch right indent using the up arrow icons*** (or you can type in **.5**). ***Click OK in the "Paragraph" window.***
26. Type the second paragraph.
27. Press the **[ENTER]** key twice.
28. ***From the Home ribbon tab, click the Paragraph Group dialog launcher and, under Indentation, change the left and right indents back to 0. Click OK.***
29. Type the third paragraph.
30. Press the **[ENTER]** key three times.
31. The signature line is single spaced, so ***from the Home ribbon tab, click the Line spacing icon from the Paragraph group, then click 1.0.*** This will change the line spacing from double to single.
32. Press **[SHIFT]+[-]** (the key to the right of the zero key on the top row of the keyboard) 30 times to draw the signature line. Press the **[ENTER]** key. *Note:* If Word automatically inserts a line across the whole page, press **[CTRL]+[Z]** to undo the AutoCorrect line.
33. Type **Mirabelle Watkinson** and then press the **[ENTER]** key.
34. Type **Attorney for Plaintiff.**
35. To print the document, ***click the Office button, click Print, then click OK.***
36. To save the document, ***click the Office button and then select Save As.*** Type **Pleading1** in the "File name:" box, ***then click Save*** to save the document in the default directory.

37. ***Click the Office button and then click Close*** to close the document, or ***click the Office button and then click Exit Word*** to exit the program.

This concludes Lesson 3.

LESSON 4: CREATING A TABLE

This lesson shows you how to create the table shown in Word 2007 Exhibit 6. It expands on the items presented in Lessons 1, 2, and 3 and explains how to change a font size, create a table, enter data into a table, add automatic numbering, adjust column widths, and use the Table AutoFormat command. Keep in mind that if you make a mistake at any time, you may press **[CTRL]+[Z]** to undo what you have done.

1. Open Windows. ***Double-click the Microsoft Office Word 2007 icon on the desktop*** to open Word 2007 for Windows. Alternatively, ***click the Start button, point to Programs or All Programs, then click the Microsoft Word 2007 icon,*** or ***point to Microsoft Office and then click Microsoft Office Word 2007.*** You should be in a new, clean, blank document. If you are not in a blank document, ***click the Office button, click New, then double-click Blank document.***
2. ***From the Home ribbon tab, click the Center icon in the Paragraph group, and then click the Bold icon in the Font group.***
3. ***From the Home ribbon tab, click the Font Size icon in the Font group*** and change the font size to 14 by either typing **14** in the box or ***choosing 14 from the drop-down menu.*** Alternatively, you can both turn on bold and change the font size by ***clicking the Font Group Dialog Box Launcher from the Home ribbon tab*** (see Word 2007 Exhibit 1).
4. Type **Average Hourly Billing Rates for Paralegals** (see Word 2007 Exhibit 6). Press the **[ENTER]** key once, and then ***click the Font Size icon and change the type back to 12 point. Click the Bold icon*** to turn bold off.

HANDS-ON EXERCISES

WORD 2007 EXHIBIT 6
Creating a table

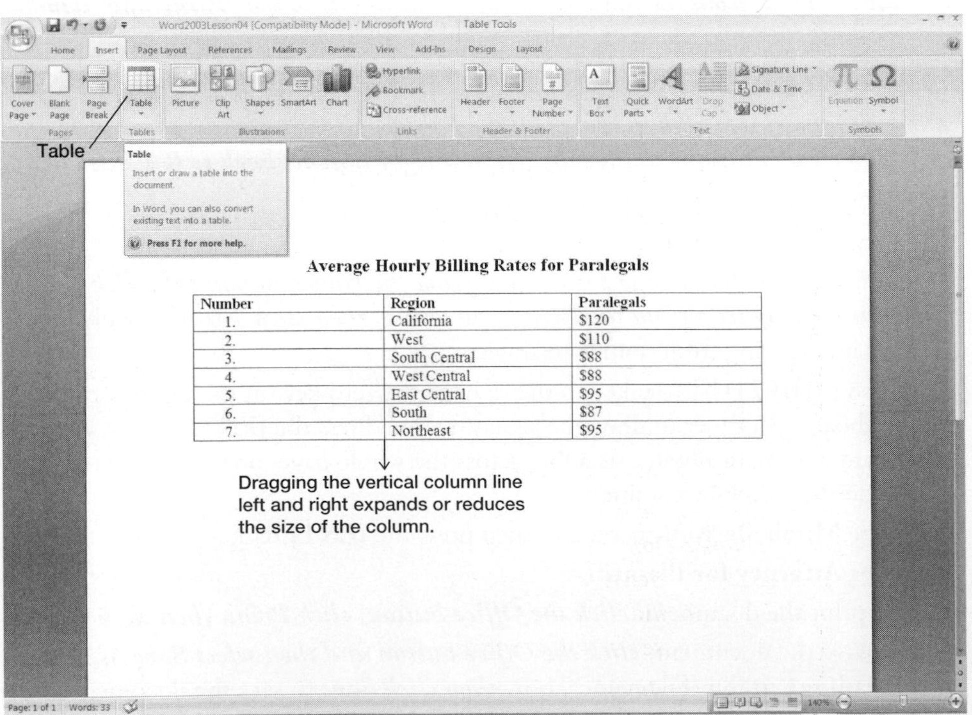

Average Hourly Billing Rates for Paralegals

Number	Region	Paralegals
1.	California	$120
2.	West	$110
3.	South Central	$88
4.	West Central	$88
5.	East Central	$95
6.	South	$87
7.	Northeast	$95

Used with permission from Microsoft.

5. Press the **[ENTER]** key once.
6. ***From the Insert ribbon tab, click Table from the Tables group.*** Notice that a number of columns and rows of boxes are displayed. This allows you to choose the graphic style of your table.
7. ***Point within the Table menu so that three columns are highlighted, then point and click so that eight rows are highlighted*** (e.g., 3 × 8 Table). Notice that as you point, the table is temporarily shown in your document. This is called a *live preview*. When you point and click the cell that is three columns over and eight cells down, the table (as opposed to the live preview) will be displayed permanently in your document.
8. The blank table should now be displayed and the cursor should be in the first column of the first row of the table. If the cursor is not in the first column of the first row, ***click in this cell to place the cursor there. From the Home ribbon tab, click the Bold icon on the Font group.*** Type **Number** and then press the **[TAB]** key once to go to the next cell in the table.
9. ***Click the Bold icon.*** Type **Region** and then press the **[TAB]** key once to go to the next cell in the table. *Note:* If you need to go back to a previous cell, you can use either the mouse or the cursor keys, or you can press **[SHIFT]+[TAB]**. Also, if you accidentally hit the **[ENTER]** key instead of the **[TAB]** key, you can either press the **[BACKSPACE]** key to delete the extra line, or you can press **[CTRL]+[Z]** to undo it.
10. ***Click the Bold icon.*** Type **Paralegals** and then press the **[TAB]** key to go to the next cell.
11. You will now use the automatic paragraph numbering feature to number the rows. ***From the Home ribbon tab, click the Numbering icon in the Paragraph group*** (see Word 2007 Exhibit 1—it is the icon that has the numbers 1, 2, 3 in a column, with a short line next to each number). Notice that the number 1 was automatically entered in the cell. ***From the Home ribbon tab, point on the down arrow next to the Numbering icon in the Paragraph group.*** Under Numbering Library, look at the different formats that are available. The default format is fine, so press **[ESC]** to make the menu disappear.
12. Press the **[TAB]** key to go to the next cell.
13. Type **California** and then press the **[TAB]** key to go to the next cell.
14. Type **$120** and then press the **[TAB]** key to go to the next cell.
15. ***From the Home ribbon tab, click the Numbering icon in the Paragraph group,*** and then press the **[TAB]** key to go to the next cell.
16. Continue entering all of the information shown in Word 2007 Exhibit 6 into your table.
17. ***Put the pointer in the uppermost left cell of the table and drag the pointer to the lowest cell at the right of the table to completely highlight the table. Then, from the Home ribbon tab, click the Align Text Left icon in the Paragraph group.*** Now the whole table is left-aligned.
18. ***Put the pointer on the vertical column line that separates the Number column and the Region column, and then drag the line to the left*** (see Word 2007 Exhibit 6). Notice that by using this technique you can completely adjust each column width as much as you like. Press **[CTRL]+[Z]** to undo the column move, because the current format is fine.
19. ***Click any cell in the table.*** Notice that just above the ribbon tab, new options are now shown; two more tabs, Design and Layout, appear under the new

heading "Table Tools." ***Click the Design ribbon tab.*** Notice that the ribbon tab now shows seven table styles. ***Point (don't click) on one of the tables;*** notice that the Live Preview feature shows you exactly what your table will look like with this design. ***Point and click the down arrow in the Table Styles group and browse to see many more table styles. Point and click a table style that you like.*** The format of the table changes completely.

20. To print the document, ***click the Office button, click Print, then click OK.***
21. To save the document, ***click the Office button and then select Save As.*** Type **Table1** in the "File name:" box, ***then point and click Save*** to save the document in the default directory.
22. ***Click the Office button and then on Close*** to close the document, or ***click the Office button and then on Exit Word*** to exit the program.

This concludes Lesson 4.

INTERMEDIATE LESSONS

LESSON 5: TOOLS AND TECHNIQUES

This lesson shows you how to edit an employment policy, use the Format Painter tool, reveal formatting, clear formatting, change the case of text, use the Find and Replace feature, use the Go To command, create a section break, and change the orientation of a page from portrait to landscape. This lesson assumes that you have completed Lessons 1 through 4 and that you are generally familiar with Word 2007.

1. Open Windows. ***Double-click the Microsoft Office Word 2007 icon on the desktop*** to open Word 2007 for Windows. Alternatively, ***click the Start button, point the pointer to Programs or All Programs, then click the Microsoft Word 2007 icon.*** You also may ***point to Microsoft Office and then click Microsoft Office Word 2007.*** You should be in a new, clean, blank document. If you are not in a blank document, ***click the Office button, click New, then double-click Blank document.***
2. The first thing you will do is open the "Lesson 5" file from the Premium Website. On the Premium Website, click the Data Files: Word Processing tab, the under Word 2007, click the "Lesson 5" file.
3. The file entitled "World Wide Technology, Inc. alcohol and drug policy" should now be displayed on your screen. In this lesson, you will be editing this policy for use by another client. The next thing you need to do is to go to section 3, "Definitions," and change the subheadings so that they all have the same format. You will use the Format Painter tool to do this.
4. Use the cursor keys or the mouse and the scroll bars to scroll to section 3, "Definitions" (see Word 2007 Exhibit 7). Notice that the first definition, "Alcohol or alcoholic beverages:," is bold and in a different font from the rest of the definitions in section 3. You will use the Format Painter tool to quickly copy the formatting from "Alcohol or alcoholic beverages:" to the other four definitions in section 3.
5. ***Point and click anywhere in the text "Alcohol or alcoholic beverages:"*** This tells the Format Painter tool the formatting you want to copy.

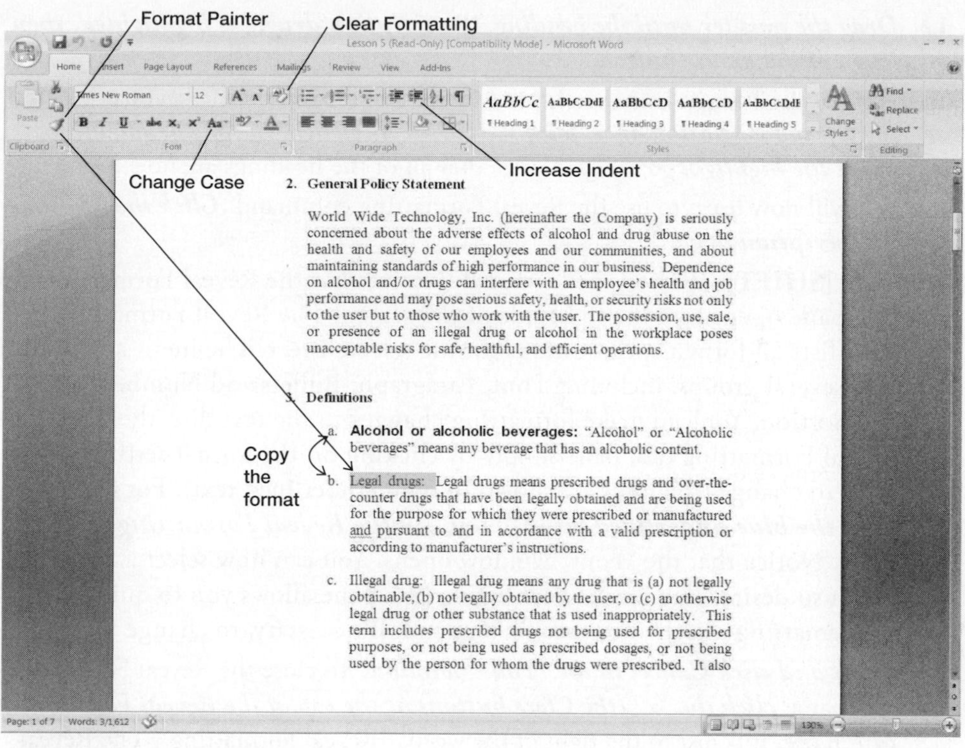

WORD 2007 EXHIBIT 7
The Format Painter tool

6. Next, ***from the Home ribbon tab, point and click the Format Painter icon in the Clipboard group.*** It looks like a paintbrush (see Word 2007 Exhibit 7). Remember, if you hover your cursor over an icon for a second or two, the name of the icon will appear.
7. Notice that your cursor now turns to a paintbrush. ***Drag the pointer*** (hold the left mouse button down and move the mouse) ***until the heading "Legal drugs:" is highlighted*** (see Word 2007 Exhibit 7), ***then let go of the mouse button.*** Notice that the paintbrush on your cursor is now gone. ***Click the left mouse button once anywhere in the screen to make the highlight go away.*** Notice that "Legal drugs:" now has the same formatting as "Alcohol or alcoholic beverages:" The Format Painter command is a quick way to make formatting changes.
8. You will now use the Format Painter command to copy the formatting to the remaining three definitions, with one additional trick. ***Click anywhere in the text "Legal drugs:"***
9. Next, ***from the Home ribbon tab, double-click the Format Painter icon in the Clipboard group.*** (Your pointer should now have a paintbrush attached to it.) The double-click tells Format Painter that you are going to copy this format to multiple locations, instead of just one location. This is a great time-saving feature if you need to copy formatting to several places, because it keeps you from having to click the Format Painter icon each time you copy the same formatting to a new location.
10. ***Drag the pointer until the heading "Illegal drug:" is highlighted, then let go of the mouse button.*** Notice that the paintbrush is still attached to your pointer.
11. ***Drag the pointer until the heading "Controlled substance:" is highlighted, then let go of the mouse button.***

12. ***Drag the pointer until the heading "Prescription drug:" is highlighted, then let go of the mouse button.***
13. To turn the Format Painter off, press the **[ESC]** button on the keyboard. ***Click the left mouse button once, with the cursor anywhere in the document, to make the highlight go away.*** Notice that all of the headings are now uniform.
14. You will now learn to use the Reveal Formatting command. ***Click the heading "Prescription drug:"***
15. Press **[SHIFT]+[F1]** on the keyboard. Notice that the Reveal Formatting task pane opened on the right side of the screen. The Reveal Formatting task pane lists all format specifications for the selected text. The items are divided into several groups, including Font, Paragraph, Bullets and Numbering, and Section. You can make formatting changes to the text directly from the Reveal Formatting task pane simply by clicking on the format setting you want to change (the links are shown in blue, underlined text). For example, ***click the blue underlined word*** **"Font"** ***in the Reveal Formatting task pane.*** Notice that the "Font" window opens. You can now select a new font if you so desire. The Reveal Formatting task pane allows you to quickly see all formatting attached to specific text and, if necessary, to change it.
16. ***Point and click Cancel in the "Font" window.*** To close the Reveal Formatting task pane, ***click the "x" (the Close button) at the top of the Reveal Formatting task pane.*** It is just to the right of the words "Reveal Formatting." The Reveal Formatting task pane should now be gone.
17. Press **[CTRL]+[HOME]** to go to the beginning of the document.
18. You will now learn how to use the Clear Formats command. Notice under the heading "1. Objectives" that the sentence "The objectives of this policy are as follows:" is bold and italics; this is a mistake. ***Drag the pointer until this text is highlighted.***
19. ***From the Home ribbon tab, click the Clear Formatting icon in the Font group*** (see Word 2007 Exhibit 7). This icon looks like an eraser next to a capital "A" and a lowercase "a." Then, ***move the pointer to anywhere in the sentence and click the left mouse button once to make the highlight go away.*** Notice that all of the formatting is now gone. The Clear Formats command is a good way to remove all text formatting quickly and easily.
20. To move the text to the right so it is under "1. Objectives," ***from the Home ribbon tab, click three times on the Increase Indent icon in the Paragraph group*** (see Word 2007 Exhibit 7). This is the icon with a right arrow and some lines on it. The line should now be back in its place.
21. You will now learn how to use the Change Case command. Press **[CTRL]+[HOME]** on the keyboard to go to the beginning of the document.
22. ***Drag the pointer until "World Wide Technology, Inc." in the document's title is highlighted.***
23. ***From the Home ribbon tab, point and click the Change Case icon in the Font group. Click UPPERCASE.*** Notice that the text is now in all capitals. ***Click the left mouse button once anywhere in the document to make the highlighting disappear.***
24. ***Drag the pointer until the subtitle "alcohol and drug policy" is highlighted. From the Home ribbon tab, click the Change Case icon in the Font group. Click "Capitalize Each Word."*** Notice that the text is now in title case. ***Click the left mouse button once anywhere in the document to make the highlighting go away.*** The Change Case command is a convenient way to

change the case of text without having to retype it. *Note:* Retyping always increases the risk of introducing errors!

25. ***Highlight the subtitle "Alcohol And Drug Policy" again. From the Review Ribbon tab, click Spelling and Grammar. The Spelling and Grammar: English U.S. dialog box will open. Click Change to accept the change to "and" (with a lower case "a"). When asked whether you want to continue checking the remainder of the document, click No.***
26. Press **[CTRL]+[HOME]** on the keyboard to go to the beginning of the document.
27. You will now learn how to use the Find and Replace command. ***From the Home ribbon tab, point and click the Replace icon in the Editing group.*** Alternatively, you could press **[CTRL]+[H]**, then ***click Replace.***
28. In the "Find and Replace" window, in the white box next to "Find what:" type **World Wide Technology, Inc.** Then, in the white box next to "Replace with:" type **Johnson Manufacturing.** ***Click the Replace All button in the "Find and Replace" window.*** The program will respond by stating that it made four replacements. ***Click OK in that notification window.***
29. ***Click the Close button in the "Find and Replace" window to close the window.*** Notice that "World Wide Technology, Inc." has now been changed to "Johnson Manufacturing."
30. You will now learn how to use the Go To command. The Go To command is an easy way to navigate through large and complex documents. Press **[F5].** Notice that the "Find and Replace" window is again displayed on the screen, but this time the Go To tab is selected. In the white box directly under "Enter page number:" type 7 using the keyboard and then ***click Go To in the "Find and Replace" window.*** Notice that on page 7, "Reasonable Suspicion Report," is now displayed. (*Note:* If the "Find and Replace" window blocks your view of the text of the document, point at the blue box in the "Find and Replace" window and drag the window lower so you can see the document.) ***Click Close in the "Find and Replace" window.***
31. Suppose that you would like to change the orientation of only one page in a document from Portrait (where the length is greater than the width) to Landscape (where the width is greater than the length). In this example, you will change the layout of only the Reasonable Suspicion Report to Landscape while keeping the rest of the document in Portrait orientation. To do this in Word, you must enter a section break.
32. Your cursor should be on page 7, just above "Johnson Manufacturing Reasonable Suspicion Report." ***From the Page Layout ribbon tab, click Breaks in the Page Setup group.***
33. ***Under Section Breaks, click Next Page.***
34. ***Click the Draft icon*** in the lower right area of the screen (see Word 2007 Exhibit 7). ***Press the [UP ARROW] key two times.*** Notice that a double dotted line that says "Section Break (Next Page)" is now displayed.
35. The Word 2007 interface allows you to switch views by clicking on one of the view layouts in the lower right of the screen (see Word 2007 Exhibit 7). Print and Draft are two of the most popular layouts. In addition, the Zoom tool just to the right of the Draft view allows you to zoom in or out (increase or decrease the magnification) of your document.
36. With the section break in place, you can now change the format of the page from Portrait to Landscape without changing the orientation of previous pages.

37. ***With the cursor on the "Johnson Manufacturing Reasonable Suspicion Report" page, from the Page Layout ribbon tab, click Orientation in the Page Setup group. Click Landscape.*** Notice that the layout of the page has changed.
38. ***Click the Print Layout icon*** in the lower right of the screen (see Word 2007 Exhibit 7).
39. To confirm that the layout has changed, ***click the Office button, then point to Print, then click Print Preview.*** Notice that the layout is now Landscape (the width is greater than the length). Press the **[PAGE UP]** key until you are back to the beginning of the document. Notice that all of the other pages in the document are still in Portrait orientation.
40. ***From the Print Preview ribbon tab, click the Close Print Preview icon in the preview group*** (this icon is a red X at the far right of the ribbon tab).
41. To print the document, ***click the Office button, click Print, then click OK.***
42. To save the document, ***click the Office button, point to Save As, then click Word 97-2003 Document. Under Save in, select the drive or folder*** you would like to save the document in. Then, next to File name:, type **Done—Word 2007 Lesson 5 Document** ***and click Save*** to save the document.
43. ***Click the Office button, then click Close*** to close the document, or ***click the Office button and then on Exit Word*** to exit the program.

This concludes Lesson 5.

LESSON 6: USING STYLES

This lesson gives you an introduction to styles. Styles are particularly helpful when you are working with long documents that must be formatted uniformly.

1. Open Windows. ***Double-click the Microsoft Office Word 2007 icon on the desktop*** to open Word 2007 for Windows. Alternatively, ***click the Start button, point the cursor to Programs or All Programs, then click the Microsoft Word 2007 icon.*** (You may also ***point to Microsoft Office and then click Microsoft Office Word 2007.***) You should now be in a new, clean, blank document. If you are not in a blank document, ***click the Office button, click New, then double-click Blank document.***
2. The first thing you will do is open the "Lesson 6" file from the Premium Website. On the Premium Website, click the Data Files: Word Processing tab, then under Word 2007, click the "Lesson 6" file.
3. The text "SARBANES-OXLEY ACT OF 2002" should now be displayed on your screen (see Word 2007 Exhibit 8). In this lesson you will use styles to add uniform formatting to this document. In the Home ribbon tab, notice the Styles group. ***Point and click any text on the page.*** Notice in the Styles group on the Home ribbon tab that the Normal box is highlighted in yellow (see Word 2007 Exhibit 8). Currently, all text in this document is in the Normal style.
4. Using your cursor keys or the scroll bar, scroll down through the document. Notice that all of the paragraphs are left-aligned and that the right edge of all the paragraphs is ragged (not justified).
5. ***From the Home ribbon tab, click the Styles Group Dialog Box Launcher.*** Notice that the Styles task pane now appears on the right side of the screen (see Word 2007 Exhibit 8). In the Styles task pane, ***if the white box next to Show Preview is not marked, click the box so that a green check mark appears*** (see Word 2007 Exhibit 8). Notice that a few styles in the Styles task

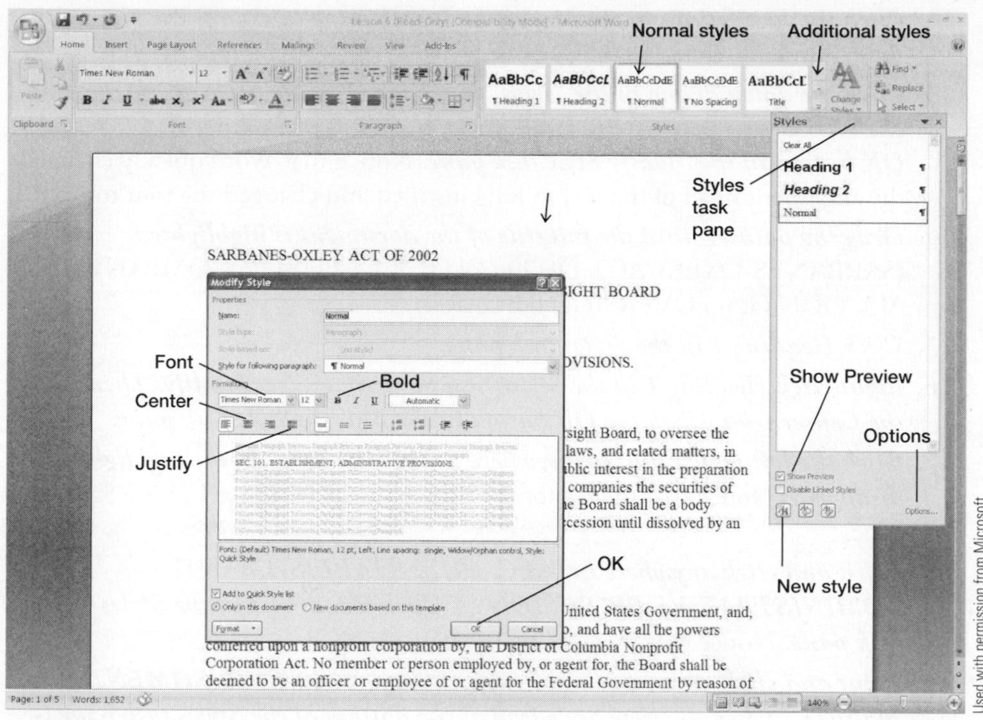

WORD 2007 EXHIBIT 8
Styles

pane are currently being displayed (e.g., Heading 1, Heading 2, and Normal). Also notice that the Normal style has a blue box around it, indicating that your cursor is on text with the Normal style. Finally, notice that there is a paragraph sign after each of these heading names, indicating that these are paragraph styles.

6. Notice at the bottom of the Styles task pane the word Options. . . in blue; ***click Options.*** The "Style Pane Options" window should now be displayed.
7. ***In the "Style Pane Options" window under Select styles to show, click the down arrow next to "In current document" and click "All styles." Then, in the "Style Pane Options" window, click OK.***
8. Notice that the Styles task pane is now full of additional styles. These are all of the styles that are automatically available in Word 2007. ***Click the down arrow in the Styles task pane to see the full list of styles.***
9. To return to the list of just a few styles, ***click Options in the lower right of the Styles task pane. Under Select styles to show:, click the down arrow and click "In current document." Then, in the "Style Pane Options" window, click OK.***
10. Notice that the short list of styles is again displayed. To access a longer list of styles from the Styles group on the Home ribbon tab, ***click the down arrow in the Styles group.*** If you select the More icon (the icon that shows a down arrow with a line over it) in the Styles group, you can see all of the styles at one time. Press the **[ESC]** key to close the list.
11. Styles are extremely useful. Assume now that you would like to have all of the text in the document justified. ***Right-click Normal in the Styles task pane. Left-click Modify.*** The Modify Style task pane should now be displayed (see Word 2007 Exhibit 8). Using the Modify Style task pane, you can completely change the formatting for any style.

12. ***Click the Justify icon in the Modify Style task pane*** to change the Normal style from left-aligned to fully justified (see Word 2007 Exhibit 8).
13. ***Click the down arrow in the "Font" box in the Modify Style task pane and click Arial*** (you may have to scroll through some fonts to find it). ***Click the OK button in the Modify Style task pane.*** Notice that Word quickly changed the alignment of all of the text to fully justified and changed the font to Arial.
14. ***Drag the pointer until the full title of the document is highlighted*** (SARBANES-OXLEY ACT OF 2002 TITLE I—PUBLIC COMPANY ACCOUNTING OVERSIGHT BOARD).
15. ***Click Heading 1 in the Styles task pane.***
16. ***Right-click Heading 1 in the Styles task pane and select Modify. Then, click the Center icon. Click the OK button in the Modify Style task pane.***
17. ***Click the left mouse button anywhere in the title to make the highlight disappear.*** Notice that the text of the title shows as Heading 1 in the Styles task pane.
18. ***Point and click anywhere in "SEC. 101. ESTABLISHMENT; ADMINISTRATIVE PROVISIONS." Click Heading 2 in the Styles task pane.*** Notice that the heading has now changed.
19. ***Point and click anywhere in the subheading "(a) ESTABLISHMENT OF BOARD." Click the New Style icon at the bottom of the Styles task pane*** (see Word 2007 Exhibit 8).
20. The "Create New Style from Formatting" window should now be displayed. Under Properties, next to Name, type **Heading 3A**; then, ***under Formatting, click the Bold icon. Click OK in the "Create New Style from Formatting" window.***
21. Now, go to the following subheadings and format them as Heading 3A by clicking on them and selecting Heading 3A from the Styles task pane:

    (b) STATUS.

    (c) DUTIES OF THE BOARD.

    (d) COMMISSION DETERMINATION.

    (e) BOARD MEMBERSHIP.

    (f) POWERS OF THE BOARD.

    (g) RULES OF THE BOARD.

    (h) ANNUAL REPORT TO THE COMMISSION.

    Press **[CTRL]+[HOME]** to go to the beginning of the document. Your document is now consistently formatted. Using styles, your documents can also easily be uniformly changed. For example, if you read in your local rules that subheadings for pleadings must be in 15-point Times New Roman font, you could quickly change the subheadings in your document by modifying the heading styles, rather than highlighting each subheading and changing the format manually.
22. To print the document, ***click the Office button, click Print, then click OK.***
23. To save the document, ***click the Office button and point to Save As. Then click Word 97-2003 Document. Under Save in, select the drive or folder*** in which you would like to save the document. Then, next to File name:, type **Done—Word 2007 Lesson 6 Document** ***and click Save*** to save the document.

24. ***Click the Office button and then on Close*** to close the document, or ***click the Office button and then on Exit Word*** to exit the program.

This concludes Lesson 6.

LESSON 7: CREATING A TEMPLATE

This lesson shows you how to create the template shown in Word 2007 Exhibit 9. It explains how to create a template of a letter, how to insert fields, and how to fill out and use a finished template. You will also learn how to add a command to the Quick Access toolbar. The information that will be merged into the letter will be entered from the keyboard. Keep in mind that if you make a mistake at any time, you may press **[CTRL]+[Z]** to undo what you have done.

1. Open Windows. ***Double-click the Microsoft Office Word 2007 icon on the desktop*** to open Word 2007 for Windows. Alternatively, ***click the Start button, point the cursor to Programs or All Programs, then click the Microsoft Word 2007 icon.*** (You can also ***point to Microsoft Office and then click Microsoft Office Word 2007.***) You should be in a new, clean, blank document. If you are not in a blank document, ***click the Office button, click New, then double-click Blank document.***
2. ***Click the Office button, then click New. Under Templates, click My templates.***
3. ***Click Template under the Create New field in the lower right of the "New" window*** (see Word 2007 Exhibit 10).
4. ***Click Blank Document.*** Blank Document should now be highlighted. ***Click OK*** (see Word 2007 Exhibit 10).
5. You should now have a blank template on your screen. The Windows title should say ***Template1—Microsoft Word*** in the upper middle of the screen. You will now build the template shown in Word 2007 Exhibit 9.

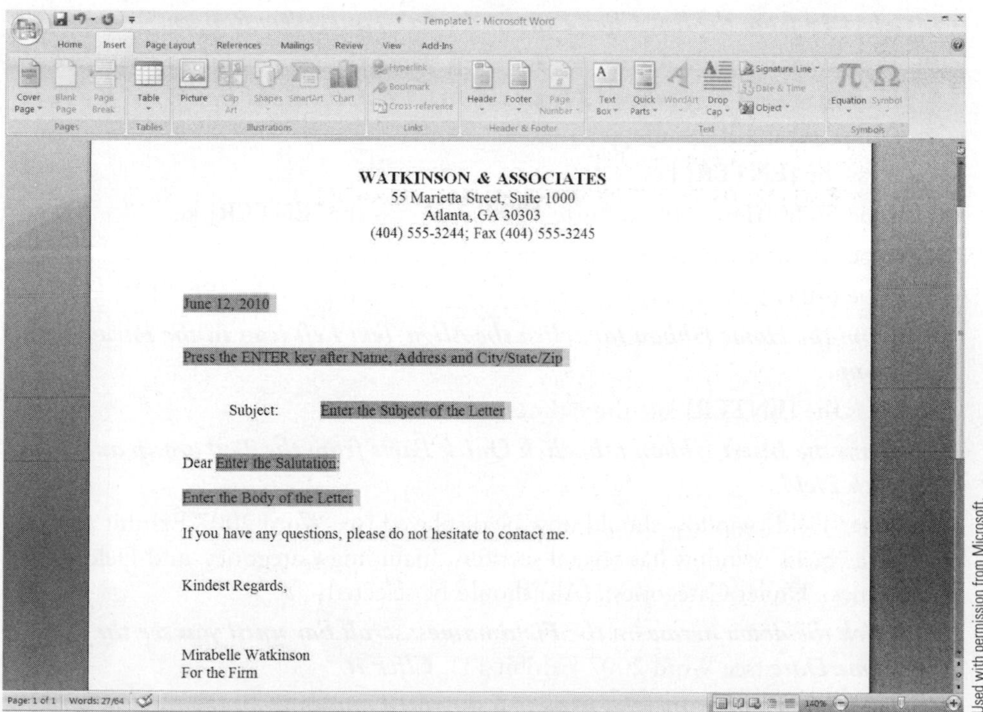

WORD 2007 EXHIBIT 9
Office Letter template

WORD 2007 EXHIBIT 10
Creating a new template

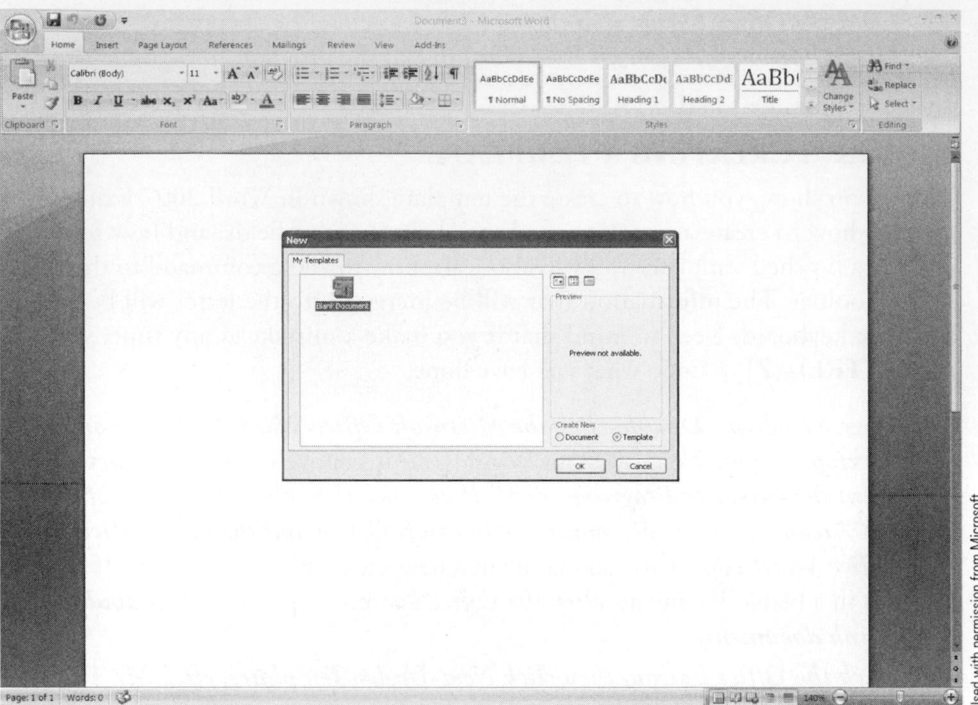

6. ***Also, on the Home ribbon tab, click the Paragraph Group dialog launcher. In the "Paragraph" window, in the Indents and Spacing tab, click the down arrow below Line spacing and select Single.*** Make sure the Before and After spacing are both 0 point. Then, ***click OK.***
7. ***From the Home ribbon tab, click the Center icon in the Paragraph group. From the Home ribbon tab, click the Bold icon in the Font group.***
8. ***From the Home ribbon tab, click the Font Size icon from the Font group and select 14 from the list. Click Font and select Times New Roman.***
9. Type **Watkinson & Associates** and then, ***from the Home ribbon tab, click the Font Size icon and select 12 from the list. Click the Bold icon from the Font group*** to turn off bolding.
10. Press the **[ENTER]** key.
11. Type **55 Marietta Street, Suite 1000** and press the **[ENTER]** key.
12. Type **Atlanta, GA, 30303** and press the **[ENTER]** key.
13. Type **(404) 555–3244; Fax (404) 555–3245** and press the **[ENTER]** key.
14. ***From the Home ribbon tab, click the Align Text Left icon in the Paragraph group.***
15. Press the **[ENTER]** key three times.
16. ***From the Insert ribbon tab, click Quick Parts from the Text group and then click Field.***
17. The "Field" window should now be displayed (see Word 2007 Exhibit 11). The "Field" window has several sections, including Categories: and Field names:. Under Categories:, (All) should be selected.
18. ***Click the down arrow on the Field names: scroll bar until you see the field name Date*** (see Word 2007 Exhibit 11). ***Click it.***
19. ***From the Field properties list, click the third option from the top*** (the month spelled out, the date, and the year). Notice that the current

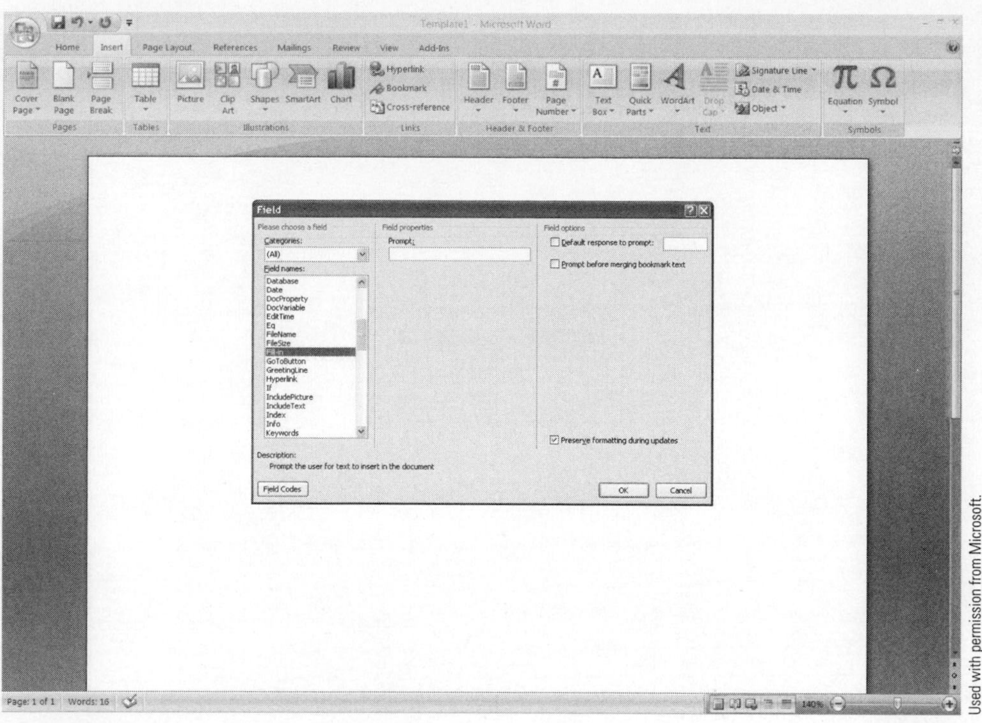

WORD 2007 EXHIBIT 11
Inserting fields in a template

date is displayed. This field will always display the date on which the template is actually executed, so if the template is executed on January 1, January 1 will be the date shown on the letter. ***Click OK in the "Field" window.***

20. Press the **[ENTER]** key three times.

21. ***From the Insert ribbon tab, click Quick Parts from the Text group and then click Field.***

22. ***Click the down arrow on the Field names: scroll bar until you see "Fill-in" in the Field names: area*** (see Word 2007 Exhibit 11). ***Click Fill-in.***

23. In the "Prompt:" box under Field properties:, type **"Type the Name and Address of the Recipient."** *Note:* You must include the quotation marks.

24. ***Click OK in the "Field" window.***

25. You will now see a window on your screen that says **"Type the Name and Address of Recipient."** ***Press the ENTER key after Name, Address and City/State/Zip*** (see Word 2007 Exhibit 12). ***Click OK.***

26. Press the **[ENTER]** key three times.

27. Press the **[TAB]** key.

28. Type **Subject:**.

29. Press the **[TAB]** key.

30. ***From the Insert ribbon tab, click Quick Parts from the Text group and then click Field.***

31. ***Click the down arrow on the Field names: scroll bar until you see "Fill-in" in the Field names: area. Click Fill-in.***

32. In the "Prompt:" box, under Field properties:, type **"Type the Subject of the Letter."** *Note:* You must include the quotation marks. ***Point and click OK.***

33. You will now see a window on your screen that says **"Type the Subject of the Letter."** Type **Enter the Subject of the Letter**. ***Click OK.***

34. Press the **[ENTER]** key three times.

WORD 2007 EXHIBIT 12
Entering a "Fill-in" field

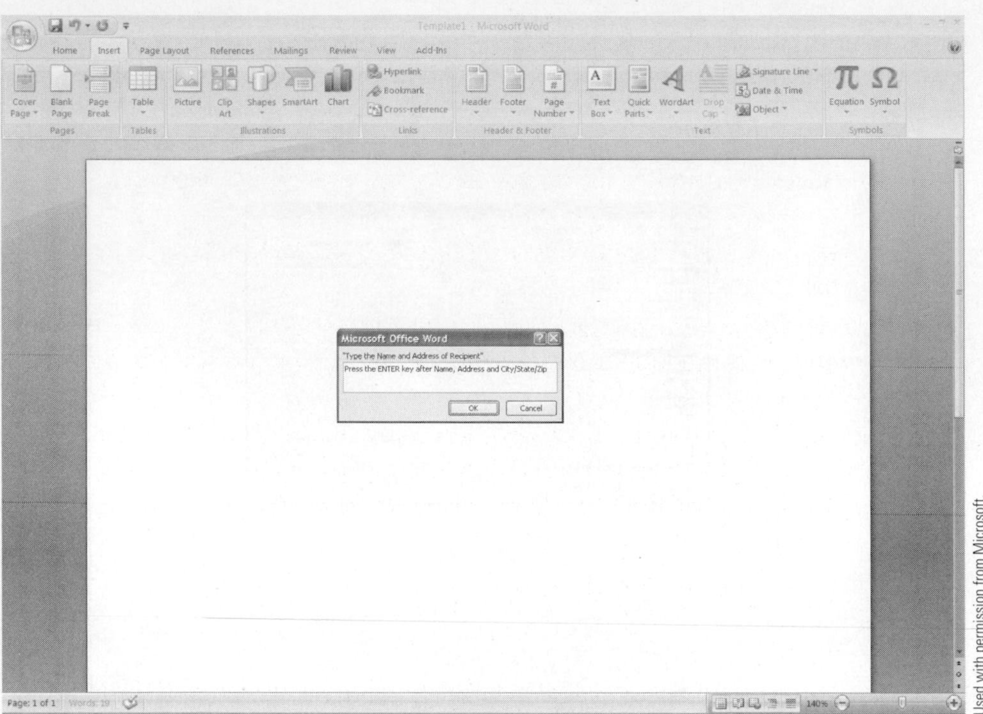

35. Type **Dear** and press the **[SPACEBAR].** Then, ***from the Insert ribbon tab, click Quick Parts from the Text group, then click Field.***
36. ***Click the down arrow on the Field names: scroll bar until you see "Fill-in" in the Field names: area. Click Fill-in.***
37. In the "Prompt:" box under Field properties:, type **"Salutation"** (*Note:* You must include the quotation marks). ***Click OK.***
38. You will now see a window on your screen that says **"Salutation."** Type **Enter the Salutation. *Click OK.***
39. Type **:** [a colon].
40. Press the **[ENTER]** key twice.
41. ***From the Insert ribbon tab, click Quick Parts from the Text group and then click Field.***
42. ***Click the down arrow on the Field names: scroll bar until you see "Fill-in" in the Field names: area. Click Fill-in.***
43. In the "Prompt:" box under Field properties:, type **"Body of Letter."** *Note:* You must include the quotation marks. ***Click OK.***
44. You will now see a window on your screen that says **"Body of Letter."** Type **Enter the Body of the Letter**. ***Click OK.***
45. Press the **[ENTER]** key twice.
46. Type **If you have any questions, please do not hesitate to contact me.** Press the **[ENTER]** key three times.
47. Type **Kindest regards,** and press the **[ENTER]** key four times.
48. Type **Mirabelle Watkinson** and press the **[ENTER]** key once.
49. Type **For the Firm.**
50. ***Click the Office button, then point to Save As and click Word Template.*** (*Note:* If you do not save this as a Word Template, you will

not be able to finish the lesson.) Then, next to File name:, type **Watkinson Letter Template.** Word will save the template to a special template folder; if you save it to another folder, you will not be able to run the template in the next portion of this exercise. ***Next to "Save as type:," click the down arrow button, select Word 97-2003 Template(*.dot), then click Save*** to save the document.

51. ***Click the Office button and then on Close.*** You are now ready to type a letter using the template.
52. ***Click the Office button, then click New. Under Templates, click My templates. In the "New" window, under the My Templates tab, double-click Watkinson Letter Template.***
53. The template letter is now running. You will see the Type the Name and Address of the Recipient field on the screen. You will also see the prompt that reminds you to press ENTER after the name, address, and city/state/zip. Type over this prompt.
54. Type **Steven Matthews, Esq.** and press the **[ENTER]** key.
55. Type **Matthews, Smith & Russell** and press the **[ENTER]** key.
56. Type **P.O. Box 12341** and press the **[ENTER]** key.
57. Type **Boston, MA 59920** and then ***click OK.***
58. You will see the Type the Subject of the Letter field on the screen. You will also see the prompt that reminds you to enter the subject of the letter. Type over this prompt.
59. Type **Turner v. Smith, Case No. CV-11-0046** and then ***click OK.***
60. You will now see the Salutation field on the screen. You will also see the prompt that reminds you to enter the salutation. Type over this prompt.
61. Type **Steve** and then ***click OK.***
62. You will now see the Body of Letter field on the screen. You will also see the prompt that reminds you to enter the body of the letter. Type over this prompt.
63. Type **This will confirm our conversation of this date. You indicated that you had no objection to us requesting an additional ten days to respond to your Motion for Summary Judgment.** ***Click OK.*** You are now through typing the letter. The completed letter should now be displayed. (*Note:* If another window is displayed prompting you for the name and address of the recipient, simply ***click Cancel***; the completed letter should then be displayed.)
64. You are now ready to print the document. First, you will create a Quick Print icon on the Quick Access toolbar. Instead of going to the Office button each time to print, you will be able to print a document from the Quick Access toolbar (see Word 2007 Exhibit 12).
65. ***Point and right-click anywhere in the ribbon. Click Customize Quick Access Toolbar. . . .***
66. The "Word Options" window should now be displayed. ***Double-click Quick Print on the left side of the screen (under Popular Commands), then click Add. Click OK in the "Word Options" window.***
67. Notice that a Quick Print icon is now displayed in the Quick Access toolbar.
68. ***Click the Quick Print icon on the Quick Access toolbar,*** or ***click the Office button, click Print, then click OK.***

69. To save the document, ***click the Office button, point to Save As, then click Word 97-2003 Document. Under Save in, select the drive or folder*** in which you would like to save the document. Next to File name:, type **Done—Word 2007 Lesson 7 Document** and ***click Save*** to save the document. *Note:* You just saved the output of your template to a separate file named "Done—Word Lesson 7 Document." Your original template ("Watkinson Letter Template") is unaffected by the Lesson 7 document, and is still a clean template ready to be used again and again for any correspondence.
70. ***Click the Office button and then on Close*** to close the document, or ***click the Office button and then on Exit Word*** to exit the program.

This concludes Lesson 7.

LESSON 8: COMPARING DOCUMENTS

This lesson shows you how to compare documents by simultaneously viewing two documents and by creating a separate blacklined document with the changes. In your law-office career, you will often send someone a digital file for revision, only to find that when the file is returned, the revisions are not apparent. Using the comparison tools in Word 2007, you can see what has changed in the document.

1. Open Windows. ***Double-click the Microsoft Office Word 2007 icon on the desktop*** to open Word 2007 for Windows. Alternatively, ***click the Start button, point the cursor to Programs or All Programs, then click the Microsoft Word 2007 icon.*** (You can also ***point to Microsoft Office and then click Microsoft Office Word 2007.***) You should now be in a new, clean, blank document. If you are not in a blank document, ***click the Office button, click New, then double-click Blank document.***
2. For the purpose of this lesson, we will assume that your firm drafted an employment contract for a corporate client named Bluebriar Incorporated. Bluebriar is in negotiations with an individual named John Lewis, whom they would like to hire as their vice president of marketing. Your firm is negotiating with John Lewis's attorney regarding the terms and language of the employment contract. The "Lesson 8A" file on the Premium Website is the original document you sent to John Lewis's attorney. The "Lesson 8B" file on the Premium Website is the new file sent back to you by John Lewis's attorney.
3. You will now open both of these files from the Premium Website and then compare them side by side. On the Premium Website, click the Data Files: Word Processing tab, then under Word 2010, click the "Lesson 8A" file.
4. Follow the same directions to open the "Lesson 8B" file.
5. ***From the View ribbon tab, click View Side by Side in the Window group.*** Both documents should now be displayed side by side (see Word 2007 Exhibit 13).
6. Push the **[DOWN ARROW]** key to scroll down through the document. Notice that both documents simultaneously scroll.
7. From the View ribbon tab, notice that the Synchronous Scrolling icon in the Window group is highlighted (see Word 2007 Exhibit 13). To turn this feature off, you would click this icon. The Synchronous Scrolling icon toggles synchronous scrolling on and off. If you turn off synchronous scrolling and wish to turn it back on, simply realign the windows where you want them, and ***click the Synchronous Scrolling icon.*** (*Note:* If the View ribbon tab looks like Word 2007 Exhibit 13, with the Window group collapsed, ***point and click the Window group, and click Synchronous Scrolling.***)

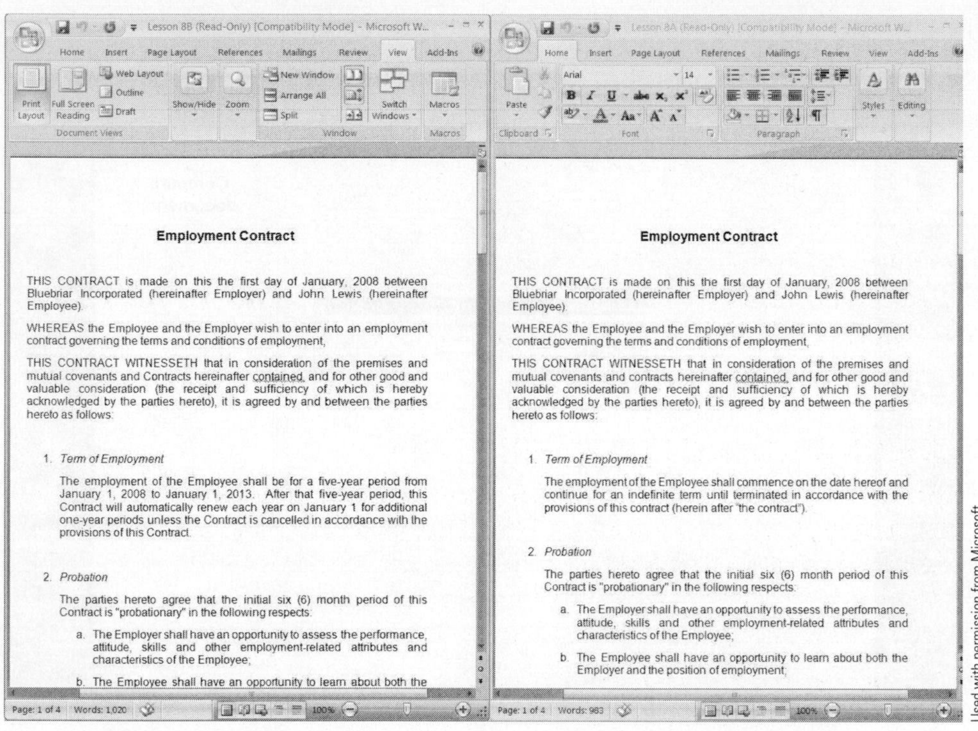

Used with permission from Microsoft.

WORD 2007 EXHIBIT 13
Comparing documents side by side

8. You will now learn how to merge the changes into one document. ***Click anywhere in Lesson 8A.doc, then click the Office button and then on Close.***
9. ***Do the same to close Lesson 8B.doc.***
10. You should now have no documents open.
11. ***From the Review ribbon tab, click Compare in the Compare group. Then, click "Compare. . ."***
12. The "Compare Documents" window should now be displayed (see Word 2007 Exhibit 14). ***Under Original document, click the down arrow; use the Browse. . . feature to find Lesson 8A.doc, then click it*** (see Word 2007 Exhibit 14).
13. ***Next, under Revised document, click the down arrow; use the Browse feature to find "Lesson 8B.doc" and then click it*** (see Word 2007 Exhibit 14).
14. Next to "Label changes with," type **John Lewis' Attorney** and then ***click OK in the "Compare Documents" window.***
15. Notice that a new document has been created that merges the documents (see Word 2007 Exhibit 15). Scroll through the new document and review all of the changes.
16. The Compare and Merge Document feature is extremely helpful when you are comparing multiple versions of the same file. By right-clicking on any of the additions or deletions, you can accept or reject the change. This is called Track Changes, and you will learn how to do this in more detail in Lesson 9.
17. To print the document, ***click the Quick Print icon on the Quick Access toolbar,*** or ***click the Office button, click Print, then click OK.***

WORD 2007 EXHIBIT 14
Comparing documents—Legal blackline settings

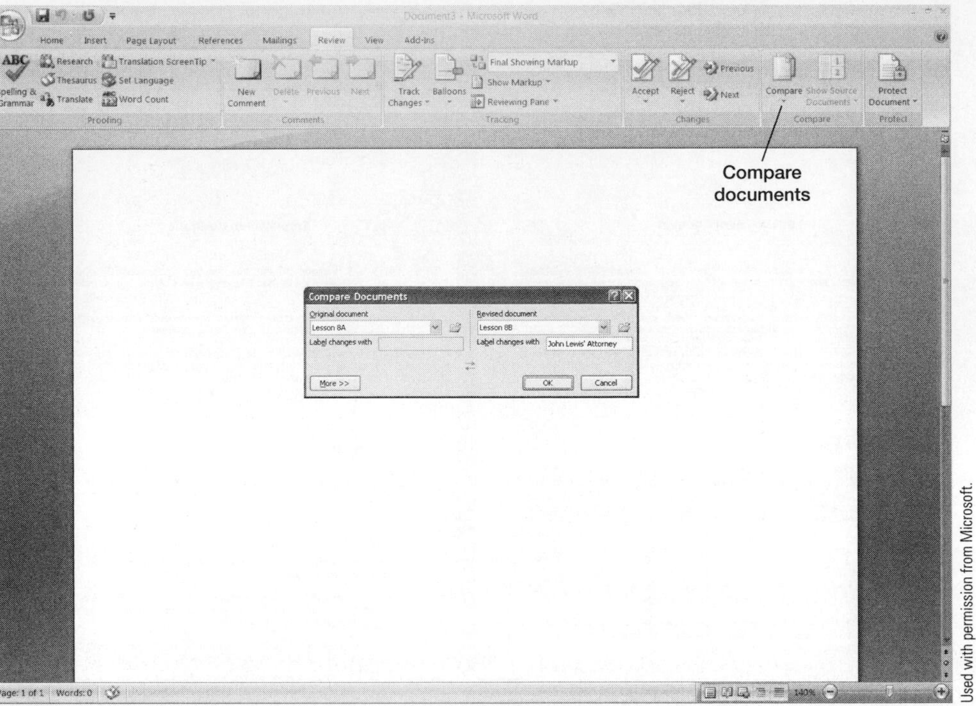

WORD 2007 EXHIBIT 15
Completed blackline document

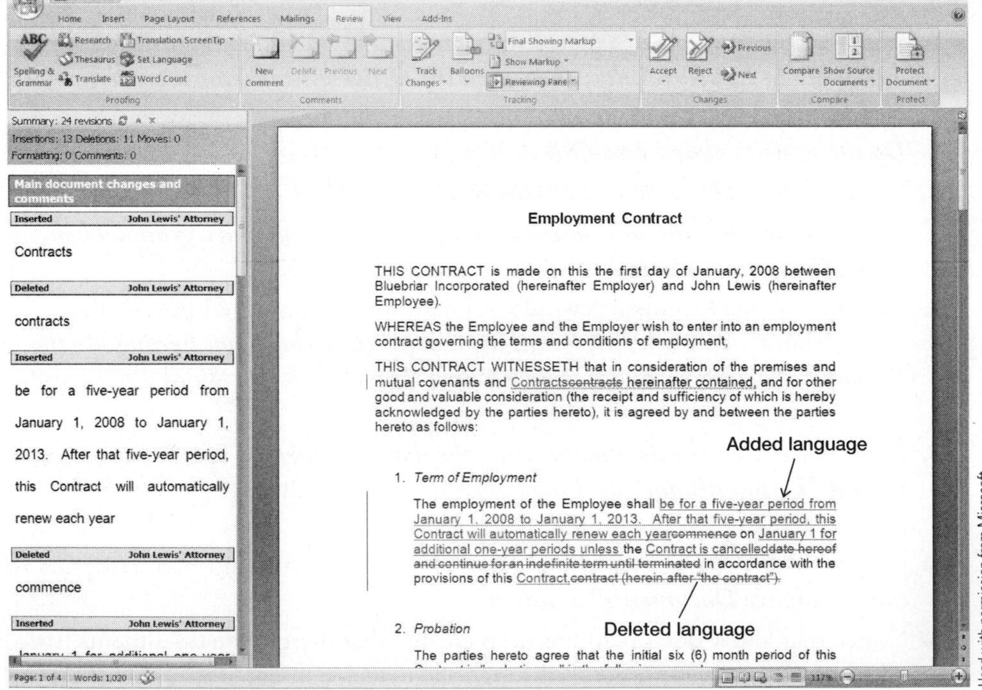

18. To save the document, ***click the Office button, point to Save As, and then click Word 97-2003 Document. Under Save in, select the drive or folder*** in which you would like to save the document. Next to File name:, type **Done—Word 2007 Lesson 8 Merged Document** and then ***click Save*** to save the document.
19. ***Click the Office button and then on Close*** to close the document, or ***click the Office button and then on Exit Word*** to exit the program.

This concludes Lesson 8.

LESSON 9: USING TRACK CHANGES

In this lesson, you will learn how to use the Track Changes feature by editing a will, and then accepting and/or rejecting the changes.

1. Open Windows. ***Double-click the Microsoft Office Word 2007 icon on the desktop*** to open Word 2007 for Windows. Alternatively, ***click the Start button, point the cursor to Programs or All Programs, then click the Microsoft Word 2007 icon.*** (You can also ***point to Microsoft Office and then click Microsoft Office Word 2007.***) You should now be in a new, clean, blank document. If you are not in a blank document, ***click the Office button, click New, then double-click Blank document.***
2. The first thing you will do is open the "Lesson 9" file from the Premium Website. On the Premium Website, click the Data Files: Word Processing tab, then under Word 2007, click the "Lesson 9" file.
3. The text "LAST WILL AND TESTAMENT" should now be displayed on your screen (see Word 2007 Exhibit 16). Notice in Word 2007 Exhibit 16 that several revisions have been made to this document. Your client, William Porter, has asked you to use the Track Changes feature to show your supervising attorney the changes he would like to make. Mr. Porter is rather leery of the legal process and wants to make sure your supervising attorney approves of the changes.
4. ***From the Review ribbon tab, click Track Changes from the Tracking group. Click Track Changes from the drop-down menu*** to turn on Track Changes.
5. Make the changes shown in Word 2007 Exhibit 16. Everything that should be added is in red and underlined, and everything that should be deleted is in red and has a line through it.

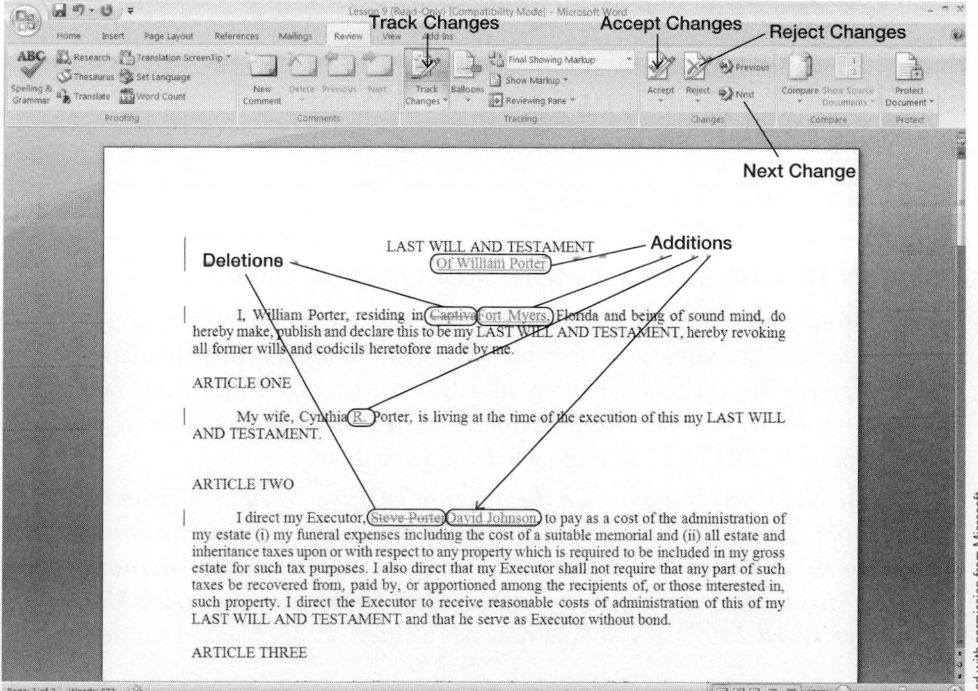

WORD 2007 EXHIBIT 16
Using Track Changes

6. Assume now that you have shown the changes to your supervising attorney. ***From the Review ribbon tab, click Track Changes, then click Track Changes on the drop-down menu*** to turn off Track Changes (see Word 2007 Exhibit 16). This allows you to make changes to the document without having them show up as revisions.
7. ***Point and right-click anywhere on the text, "Of William Porter," which you added just under "LAST WILL AND TESTAMENT."*** Notice that a menu is displayed that allows you to accept or reject the insertion, among other actions. ***Click Accept Change.*** The revision has now been accepted.
8. ***From the Review ribbon tab, click Next in the Changes group***. This should take you to the next change. ***From the Review ribbon tab, click Accept in the Changes group, then click Accept and Move to Next to accept the change.*** Notice that one of the options is "Accept All Changes in Document." This is a quick way to accept all changes in a document without going through each one of them. However, do not select it; we do not want to accept all the changes in this document.
9. Use the Next feature to continue to go to each change and accept the revisions. The only revision you will *not* accept is changing the executor from Steve Porter to David Johnson; reject this change. Assume that the supervising attorney has learned that Mr. Johnson is terminally ill and most likely will not be able to serve as executor, so the client has decided to keep Steve Porter as the executor.
10. To print the document, ***click the Quick Print icon on the Quick Access toolbar,*** or ***click the Office button, click Print, then click OK.***
11. To save the document, ***click the Office button, then point to Save As, then click Word 97-2003 Document. Under Save in, select the drive or folder*** in which you would like to save the document. Next to File name:, type **Done—Word 2007 Lesson 9 Document** ***and then click Save*** to save the document.
12. ***Click the Office button and then on Close*** to close the document, or ***click the Office button and then on Exit Word*** to exit the program.

This concludes Lesson 9.

ADVANCED LESSONS

LESSON 10: CREATING A MAIL MERGE DOCUMENT

In this lesson, you will create a merge document for an open house that you will send to three clients (see Word 2007 Exhibit 17). First, you will create the data file that will be merged into the letter. Then, you will create the letter itself, and finally, you will merge the two together. Keep in mind that if you make a mistake at any time, you may press **[CTRL]+[Z]** to undo what you have done.

1. Open Windows. ***Double-click the Microsoft Office Word 2007 icon on the desktop*** to open Word 2007 for Windows. Alternatively, ***click the Start button, point the cursor to Programs or All Programs, then click the Microsoft Word 2007 icon.*** (You may also ***point to Microsoft Office and then click Microsoft Office Word 2007.***) You should now be in a new, clean, blank document. If

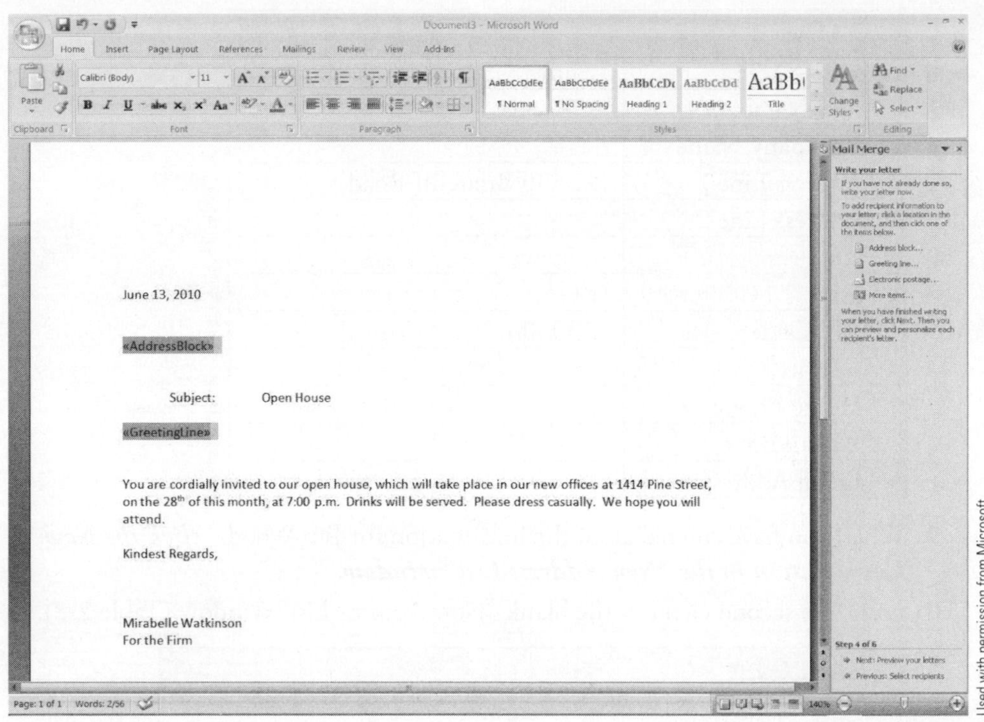

Used with permission from Microsoft.

WORD 2007 EXHIBIT 17
Mail merge letter

you are not in a blank document, ***click the Office button, click New, then double-click Blank document.***

2. ***From the Mailings ribbon tab, click Start Mail Merge from the Start Mail Merge group. From the drop-down menu, select Step by Step Mail Merge Wizard. . . .*** The Mail Merge task pane is now shown to the right of your document.
3. The bottom of the Mail Merge task pane shows that you are on Step 1 of 6. You are asked to **"Select document type."** You are typing a letter, so the default selection, "Letters," is fine. To continue to the next step, ***click Next: Starting document at the bottom of the Mail Merge task pane under Step 1 of 6.***
4. The bottom of the Mail Merge task pane shows that you are on Step 2 of 6. You are asked to **"Select starting document."** You will be using the current document to type your letter, so the default selection, "Use the current document," is fine. To continue to the next step, ***click Next: Select recipients at the bottom of the Mail Merge task pane under Step 2 of 6.***
5. The bottom of the Mail Merge task pane shows that you are on Step 3 of 6. You are asked to **"Select recipients."** You will be typing a new list, so ***click Type a new list.***
6. ***Under the "Type a new list" section of the Mail Merge task pane, click Create. . . .***
7. The "New Address List" window is now displayed. You will now fill in the names of the three clients to whom you want to send your open-house letter.
8. Type the following (Table 2-7). (*Note:* You can use the **[TAB]** key to move between the fields, or you can use the mouse.) Only complete the fields below; skip the fields in the "New Address List" window that we will not be using.

TABLE 2-7	
First Name	Jim
Last Name	Woods
Company Name	
Address Line 1	2300 Briarcliff Road
Address Line 2	
City	Atlanta
State	GA
ZIP Code	30306
Country	
Home Phone	
Work Phone	
Email Address	

9. When you have entered all of the information for Jim Woods, ***click the New Entry button in the "New Address List" window.***
10. Enter the second client in the blank "New Address List" window (Table 2-8).

TABLE 2-8	
First Name	Jennifer
Last Name	John
Company Name	
Address Line 1	3414 Peachtree Road
Address Line 2	
City	Atlanta
State	GA
ZIP Code	30314
Country	
Home Phone	
Work Phone	
Email Address	

11. When you have entered all of the information for Jennifer John, ***click the New Entry button in the "New Address List" window.***
12. Enter the third client in the blank "New Address List" window (Table 2-9).

TABLE 2-9	
First Name	Jonathan
Last Name	Phillips
Company Name	
Address Line 1	675 Clifton Road
Address Line 2	
City	Atlanta
State	GA
ZIP Code	30030
Country	
Home Phone	
Work Phone	
Email Address	

13. **When you have entered all of the information for Jonathan Phillips, *click OK in the "New Address List" window.***
14. The "Save Address List" window is now displayed. You need to save the address list so that it can later be merged with the open-house letter. In the "Save Address List" window, next to File name:, type **Open House List** and then ***click Save in the "Save Address List" window*** to save the file to the default directory.
15. The "Mail Merge Recipients" window is now displayed (see Word 2007 Exhibit 18). ***Click the Last Name field in the "Mail Merge Recipients" window*** to sort the list by last name (see Word 2007 Exhibit 18). Notice that the order of the list is now sorted by last name.
16. ***Click OK in the "Mail Merge Recipients" window.*** You are now back at a blank document with the Mail Merge task pane open to the right. The bottom of the Mail Merge task pane indicates that you are still at Step 3 of 6. ***Click Next: Write your letter at the bottom of the Mail Merge task pane under Step 3 of 6*** to continue to the next step.
17. The bottom of the Mail Merge task pane indicates that you are on Step 4 of 6. In the Mail Merge task pane, **"Write your letter"** is displayed. You are now ready to write the letter. ***On the Home ribbon tab, click the Paragraph Group dialog launcher. In the "Paragraph" window in the Indents and Spacing tab, click the down arrow below Line spacing and select Single.*** Make sure the Before and After spacing are both 0 point. Then, ***click OK.***
18. Press the **[ENTER]** key four times.
19. Type the current date and press the **[ENTER]** key three times.
20. ***Click Address block. . . in the Mail Merge task pane under "Write your letter."***
21. The "Insert Address Block" window is now displayed. You will now customize how the address block will appear in the letters.

HANDS-ON EXERCISES

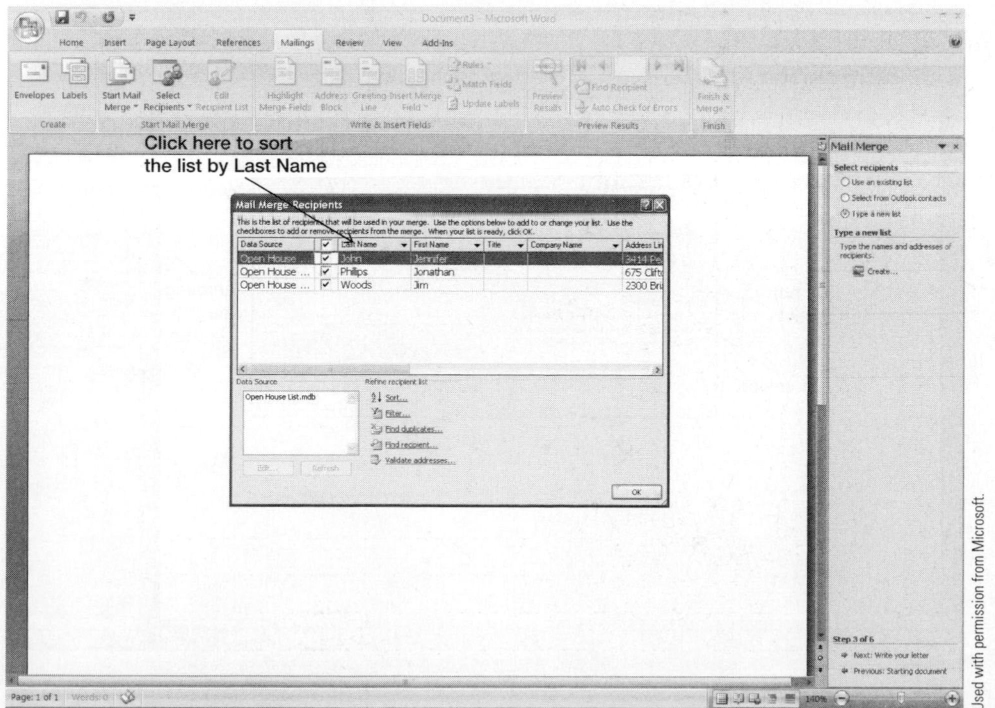

WORD 2007 EXHIBIT 18
Entering mail merge recipients

22. ***In the "Insert Address Block" window, under Insert recipient's name in this format:, click the second entry, "Joshua Randall Jr." Click "Insert company name" to deselect it,*** because we did not include company names in our data list (see Word 2007 Exhibit 19).
23. ***Under Insert postal address:, click "Never include the country/region in the address"*** (see Word 2007 Exhibit 19).
24. ***Click OK in the "Insert Address Block" window.***
25. The words **"<<AddressBlock>>"** are now displayed in your document.
26. Press the **[ENTER]** key three times.
27. Press the **[TAB]** key twice and then type **Subject:**.
28. Press the **[TAB]** key once and then type **Open House.**
29. Press the **[ENTER]** key twice.
30. ***In the Mail Merge task pane, under Write your letter, click Greeting line...*** (see Word 2007 Exhibit 19).
31. The "Insert Greeting Line" window is now displayed. You will now customize how the greeting or salutation will appear in the letter. In the "Insert Greeting Line" window, ***click the down arrow next to "Mr. Randall" and then scroll down and click "Josh." Click OK in the "Insert Greeting Line" window.***
32. The words **"<<GreetingLine>>"** are now displayed in your document.
33. Press the **[ENTER]** key three times.
34. Type **You are cordially invited to our open house, which will take place in our new offices at 1414 Pine Street, on the 28th of this month, at 7:00 p.m. Drinks will be served. Please dress casually. We hope you will attend.**
35. Press the **[ENTER]** key twice.
36. Type **Kindest Regards,**.
37. Press the **[ENTER]** key four times.

WORD 2007 EXHIBIT 19
Insert address block

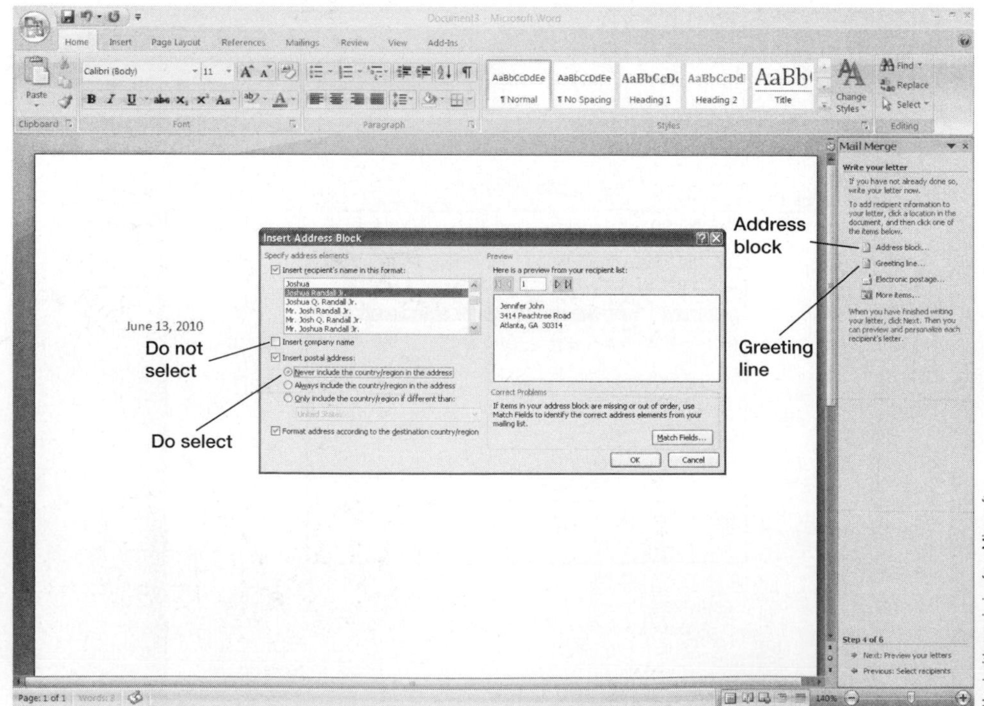

38. Type **Mirabelle Watkinson**.
39. Press the **[ENTER]** key once and type **For the Firm**.
40. You are now done typing the letter. Your letter should look similar to Word 2007 Exhibit 17. The only thing left to do is merge the recipient list with the form.
41. Under "Step 4 of 6" at the bottom of the Mail Merge task pane, ***click Next: Preview your letters*** to continue to the next step.
42. Your first letter is now displayed. ***In the Mail Merge task pane, under Preview your letters, click the button showing two arrows pointing to the right to see the rest of your letters.***
43. To continue to the next step, ***click Next: Complete the merge at the bottom of the Mail Merge task pane under Step 5 of 6.***
44. The Mail Merge task pane now will display **"Complete the merge."** ***Click Print in the Mail Merge task pane under Merge, then click OK. At the "Merge to Printer" window, click OK*** to print your letters.
45. ***Click Edit individual letters... in the Mail Merge task pane under Merge.*** In the "Merge to New Document" window, ***click OK.*** Word has now opened a new document with all of the letters in it. (*Note:* At this point, you can edit and personalize each letter if you so desire.)
46. To save the document, ***click the Office button, point to Save As, then click Word 97-2003 Document. Under Save in, select the drive or folder*** in which you would like to save the document. Then, next to File name:, type **Open House Letters** and then ***click Save*** to save the document.
47. ***Click the Office button and then on Close*** to close the personalized letters.
48. You should be back at the mail merge letter. ***Click the Office button and point to Save As. Click Word 97-2003 Document. Under Save in, select the drive or folder*** in which you would like to save the document. Next to File name:, type **Open House Mail Merge** and then ***click Save*** to save the document.
49. ***Click the Office button and then on Close*** to close the document, or ***click the Office button and then on Exit Word*** to exit the program.

This concludes Lesson 10.

LESSON 11: CREATING A TABLE OF AUTHORITIES

In this lesson, you will prepare a table of authorities for a reply brief (see Word 2007 Exhibit 22). You will learn how to find cases, mark cases, and then automatically generate a table of authorities.

1. Open Windows. ***Double-click the Microsoft Office Word 2007 icon on the desktop*** to open Word 2007 for Windows. Alternatively, ***click the Start button, point the cursor to Programs or All Programs, then click the Microsoft Word 2007 icon.*** (You may also ***point to Microsoft Office and then click Microsoft Office Word 2007.***) You should now be in a new, clean, blank document. If you are not in a blank document, ***click the Office button, click New, then double-click Blank document.***
2. The first thing you will do is open the "Lesson 11" file from the Premium Website. On the Premium Website, click the Data Files: word Processing tab, then under Word 2007, click the "Lesson 11" file.

3. The text ***"In the Supreme Court of the United States–Ted Sutton, Petitioner, v. State of Alaska, Respondent"*** should now be displayed on your screen.
4. In this exercise you will build the case section of the table of authorities for this reply brief. There are five cases to be included and they are all shown in bold so that you can easily identify them. Your first task will be to mark each of the cases so that Word knows they are to be included; you will then execute the command for Word to build the table.
5. If you are not at the beginning of the document, press **[CTRL]+[HOME]** to go to the beginning.
6. You will now mark the cases. ***From the References ribbon tab, click Mark Citation from the Table of Authorities group.***
7. The "Mark Citation" window should now be displayed (see Word 2007 Exhibit 20). Notice next to Category: that "Cases" is displayed. This indicates that you will be marking case citations. ***Click the down arrow next to Cases*** to see that you can also mark citations to be included for statutes, rules, treatises, regulations, and other sources.
8. ***Click Cases again,*** because you will now start marking cases to be included in the table of authorities.
9. ***In the "Mark Citation" window, click Next Citation.*** Word looks for terms such as "vs" or "v." when finding citations. The cursor should now be on the "v." in *Ted Sutton, Petitioner, v. State of Alaska.* Because this is the caption of the current case, we do not want to mark it for inclusion in the table. *Note:* If the "Mark Citation" window gets in the way and prevents you from seeing the brief, ***put the cursor on the blue title bar of the "Mark Citation" window and drag it out of your way.***
10. ***Click Next Citation in the "Mark Citation" window.*** Again, this is the caption of the current case, *Ted Sutton, Petitioner, v. State of Alaska,* so we do not want to mark it.

WORD 2007 EXHIBIT 20
Marking a citation for inclusion in a table of authorities

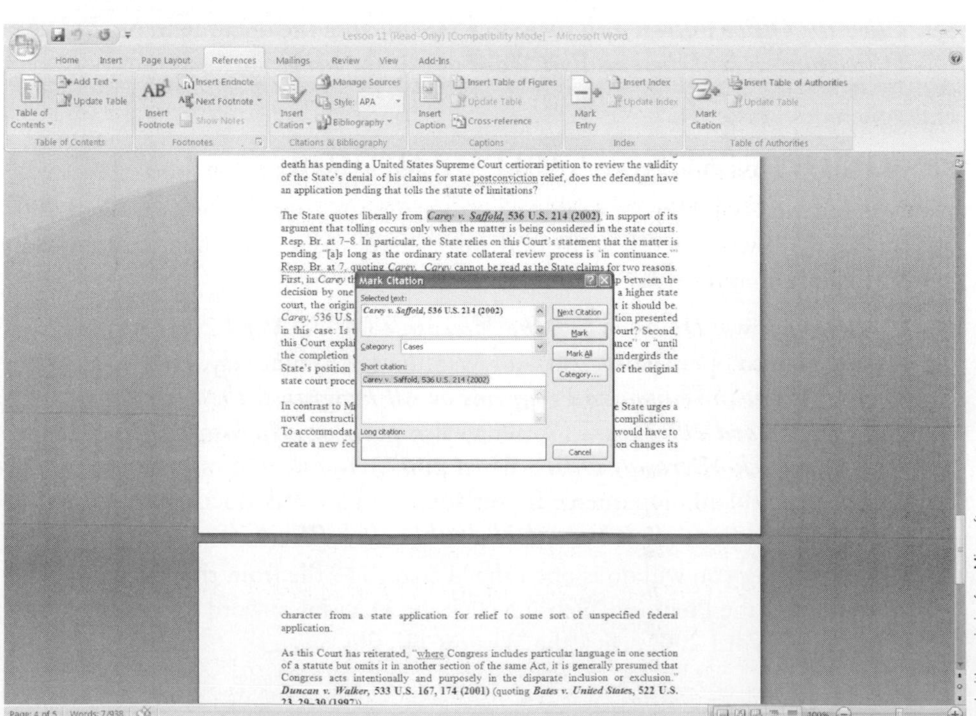

11. ***Click again on Next Citation in the "Mark Citation" window.*** Word has now found the case *Carey v. Saffold.* We want to mark this case so that it is included in the table of authorities.
12. ***Click once on the*** **Carey v. Saffold** ***case.***
13. ***Drag the pointer to highlight Carey v. Saffold, 536 U.S. 214 (2002), then click in the white box under Selected text: in the "Mark Citation" window.*** The case is automatically copied there (see Word 2007 Exhibit 20).
14. ***Click Mark in the "Mark Citation" window.*** *Note:* When you mark a citation, Word changes your view to the Show/Hide paragraph view. It shows you that you have embedded table-of-authorities formatting codes in the document. To switch out of Show/Hide view, ***from the Home ribbon tab, click the Show/Hide icon in the Paragraph group.*** (It looks like a paragraph sign.)
15. ***Click Next Citation in the "Mark Citation" window.***
16. ***Click once on the*** **Duncan v. Walker** ***case.***
17. ***Drag the mouse to highlight*** **Duncan v. Walker, 533 U.S. 167, 174 (2001)** and then ***click in the white box under Selected text: in the "Mark Citation" window.*** The case is automatically copied there.
18. ***Click Mark in the "Mark Citation" window.*** Notice that, under Short citation: in the "Mark Citation" window, the *Carey* and *Duncan* cases are listed. Again, if at any time the "Mark Citation" window prevents you from seeing the case you need to highlight, just ***click the blue bar at top of the "Mark Citation" window and drag to the left or right*** to move the window out of your way.
19. To switch out of Show/Hide view, ***from the Home ribbon tab, click the Show/Hide icon in the Paragraph group.***
20. ***Click Next Citation in the "Mark Citation" window.***
21. ***Click once on the*** **Bates v. United States** ***case.***
22. ***Drag the pointer to highlight*** **Bates v. United States, 522 U.S. 23, 29–30 (1997)** ***and then click in the white box under Selected text: in the "Mark Citation" window.*** The case is automatically copied there.
23. ***Click Mark in the "Mark Citation" window.***
24. ***Click Next Citation in the "Mark Citation" window.***
25. ***Click once on the*** **Abela v. Martin** ***case.***
26. ***Drag the pointer to highlight*** **Abela v. Martin, 348 F.3d 164 (6th Cir. 2003)** ***and then click in the white box under Selected text: in the "Mark Citation" window.*** The case is automatically copied there.
27. ***Click Mark in the "Mark Citation" window.***
28. ***Click Next Citation in the "Mark Citation" window.***
29. ***Click once on the*** **Coates v. Byrd** ***case.***
30. ***Drag the pointer to highlight*** **Coates v. Byrd, 211 F.3d 1225, 1227 (11th Cir. 2000)** ***and then click in the white box under Selected text: in the "Mark Citation" window.*** The case is automatically copied there.
31. ***Click Mark in the "Mark Citation" window.***
32. ***Click Close in the "Mark Citation" window*** to close it.
33. ***Click the Show/Hide paragraph icon on the Home ribbon tab*** to make the paragraph marks disappear.
34. Using the cursor keys or the scroll bar, ***place the cursor on page 3 of the document two lines under the title "TABLE OF AUTHORITIES"*** (see Word 2007 Exhibit 21). You are now ready to generate the table.

35. ***From the References ribbon tab, click the Insert Table of Authorities icon in the Table of Authorities group*** (see Word 2007 Exhibit 21).
36. ***The "Table of Authorities" window should now be displayed*** (see Word 2007 Exhibit 21). ***Click Cases under Category and then click OK.***
37. Notice that the table of authorities has been prepared and completed, and that the cases and the page numbers where they appear in the document have been included (see Word 2007 Exhibit 22).

WORD 2007 EXHIBIT 21
Inserting a table of authorities

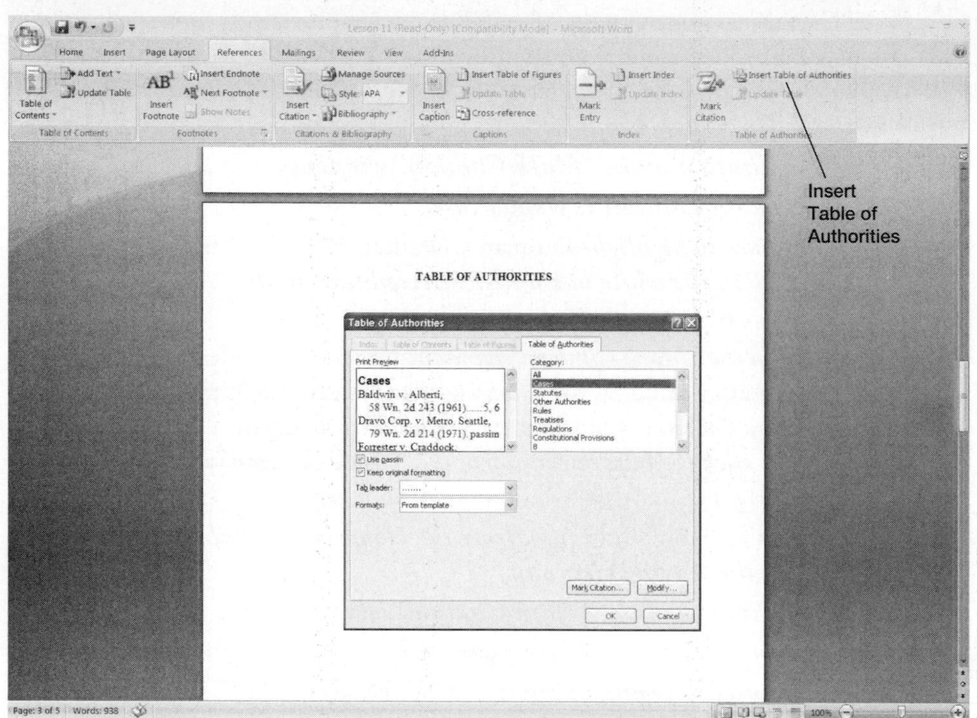

WORD 2007 EXHIBIT 22
Completed table of authorities

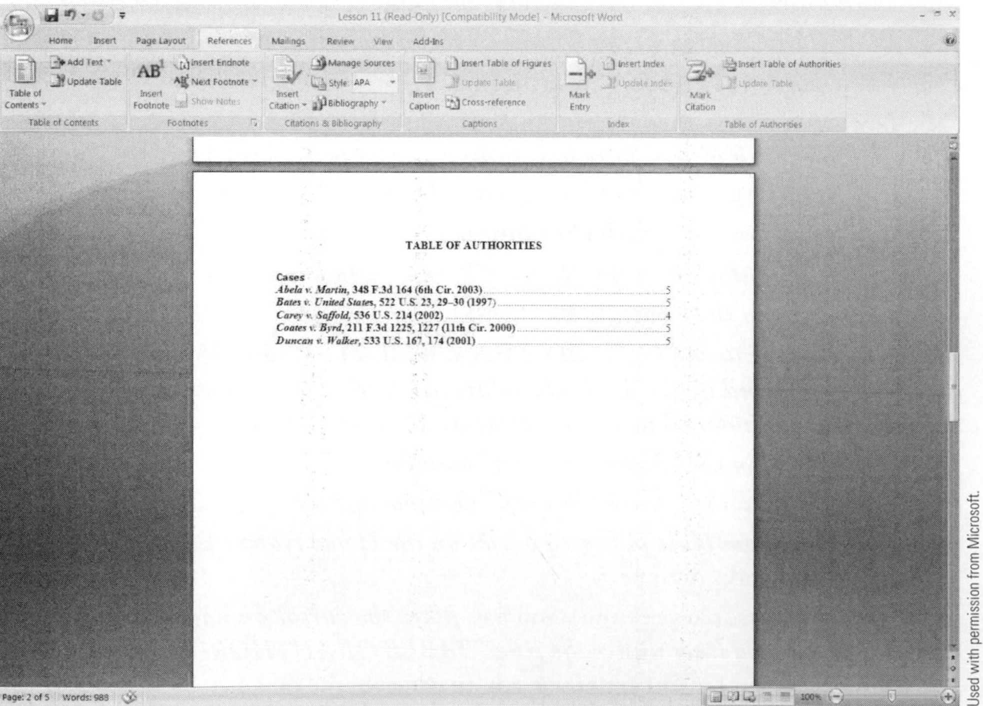

38. To print the document, ***click the Quick Print icon on the Quick Access toolbar,*** or ***click the Office button, click Print, then click OK.***
39. To save the document, ***click the Office button and point to Save As, then click Word 97-2003 Document. Under Save in, select the drive or folder*** in which you would like to save the document. Next to File name:, type **Done—Word 2007 Lesson 11 Document** and ***click Save*** to save the document.
40. ***Click the Office button and then on Close*** to close the document, or ***click the Office button and then on Exit Word*** to exit the program.

This concludes Lesson 11.

LESSON 12: CREATING A MACRO

In this lesson you will prepare a macro that will automatically type the signature block for a pleading (see Word 2007 Exhibit 23). You will then execute the macro to make sure that it works properly.

1. Open Windows. ***Double-click the Microsoft Office Word 2007 icon on the desktop*** to open Word 2007 for Windows. Alternatively, ***click the Start button, point to Programs or All Programs, then click the Microsoft Word 2007 icon.*** (You can also ***point to Microsoft Office and then click Microsoft Office Word 2007.***) You should now be in a new, clean, blank document. If you are not in a blank document, ***click the Office button, click New, then double-click Blank document.***
2. The first thing you need to do to create a new macro is to name the macro and then turn on the Record function. ***From the View ribbon tab, click the down arrow under Macros in the Macros group*** (see Word 2007 Exhibit 23).
3. ***Click Record Macro . . . on the drop-down menu.***
4. The "Record Macro" window should now be displayed (see Word 2007 Exhibit 23). In the "Record Macro" window, under Macro name:, type **Pleadingsignblock** ***and then click OK*** (see Word 2007 Exhibit 23).
5. Notice that your cursor looks like a cassette tape. The cassette-tape cursor indicates that Word is now recording all of your keystrokes and commands.
6. Type the information in Word 2007 Exhibit 23. When you have completed typing the information, ***from the View ribbon tab, click the down arrow under Macros in the Macros group*** (see Word 2007 Exhibit 23).
7. ***Click Stop Recording on the drop-down menu.***
8. You will now test your macro to see if it works properly. ***Click the Office button and then on Close*** to close the document. At the prompt "Do you want to save the changes to document?," ***click No.***
9. To open a blank document, ***click the Office button, click New, then double-click Blank document.***
10. To run the macro, ***from the View ribbon tab, click the down arrow under Macros in the Macros group*** (see Word 2007 Exhibit 23).
11. ***Click View Macros.***
12. ***In the "Macros" window, click*** **Pleadingsignblock** ***and then click Run.*** Your pleading signature block should now be in your document.
13. To print the document, ***click the Quick Print icon on the Quick Access toolbar,*** or ***click the Office button, click Print, then click OK.***
14. To save the document, ***click the Office button, point to Save As, then click Word 97-2003 Document. Under Save in, select the drive or folder*** in which you

WORD 2007 EXHIBIT 23
Creating a pleading signature block macro

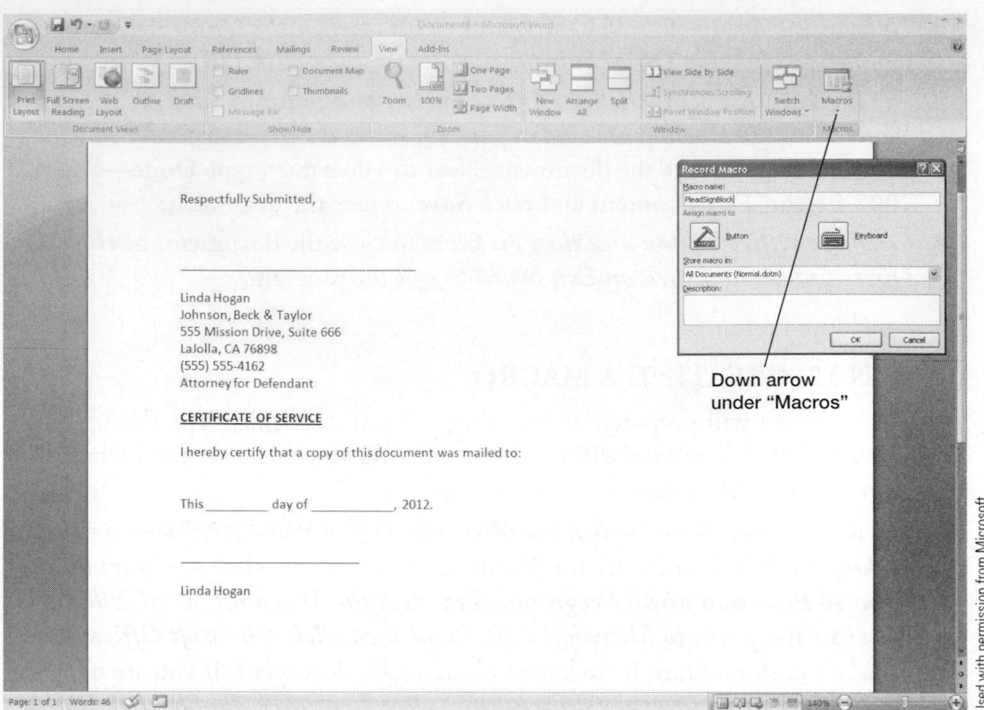

would like to save the document. Then, next to File name:, type **Done—Word 2007 Lesson 12 Document** ***and click Save*** to save the document.

15. ***Click the Office button and then on Close*** to close the document, or ***click the Office button and then on Exit Word*** to exit the program.

This concludes Lesson 12.

LESSON 13: DRAFTING A WILL

Using the websites at the end of Chapter 2 in the main text, or using a form book from a law library, draft a simple will that would be valid in your state. You will be drafting the will for Thomas Mansell, who is a widower. The will should be dated July 1 of the current year. Mr. Mansell requests the following:

- That his just debts and funeral expenses be paid.
- That his lifelong friend, Elizabeth Smith, receive $50,000 in cash.
- That his local YMCA receive his 100 shares of stock in Google.
- That all of his remaining property (real or personal) descend to his daughter Sharon Mansell.
- That in the event Mr. Mansell and his daughter die simultaneously, for all of his property to descend to Sharon's son Michael Mansell.
- That Elizabeth Smith be appointed the executor of the will; if Ms. Smith predeceases Mr. Mansell, that Mr. Stephen Dear be appointed executor.

Mr. Mansell has also requested that his will be double-spaced and have one-inch margins. He would like the will to look good and be valid in his state.

- Three witnesses will watch the signing of the will: Shelley Stewart, Dennis Gordon, and Gary Fox.
- You will notarize the will.

Print out a hard copy of the will and email it to your instructor.

This concludes the lessons in the Word 2007 Hands-On Exercises.

HANDS-ON EXERCISES

HOTDOCS 11

HANDS-ON EXERCISES

I. INTRODUCTION—READ THIS!

HotDocs lets you transform any PDF or word-processor file into an interactive template by marking changeable text with "HotDocs variables." Then the next time you want to generate a completed form or text document, you can assemble it from the template you've created.

II. INSTALLATION INSTRUCTIONS

Below are step-by-step instructions for installing HotDocs on your computer. Note that installing this software requires you to restart your system when it is completed.

1. Log in to your CengageBrain.com account.
2. Under "My Courses & Materials," find the Premium Website for Using Computers in the Law Office, 7th edition.
3. ***Click Open to go to the Premium Website.***
4. ***Locate Book Resources in the left navigation menu.***
5. ***Click the link for HotDocs 11.***
6. A screen requesting your contact information and a "Download Code" should now be displayed. You will need to supply the following download code: **k3gh87ht**
7. ***Enter the information necessary to complete the form, including the Download Code, and click Submit.***
8. You will receive an email response from HotDocs Corporation that will include a link for downloading the HotDocs 11 software. ***Click the HotDocs 11 Educational Download link in the email.*** A web page will open that includes links for both the 32-bit and 64-bit versions of HotDocs.
9. ***Double-click the appropriate file to install HotDocs.*** If you are unsure which version of Windows you have, you can check by ***right-clicking My Computer, then selecting Properties.*** Under System, you can view the system type. In Windows 7, either **"32-bit operating system"** or **"64-bit operating system"** will be displayed. In Windows XP, if you don't see **"x64 Edition"** listed, you're running the 32-bit version of Windows XP. If **"x64 Edition"** is listed, you're running the 64-bit version of Windows XP. If you are still not sure which version to install, choose the 32-bit version, as that is the more common version. If you choose the incorrect version and the program does not load, you can always try the other version.

10. A screen similar to HotDocs Installation Exhibit 1 should now be displayed. ***Click Run.***

HOTDOCS INSTALLATION EXHIBIT 1

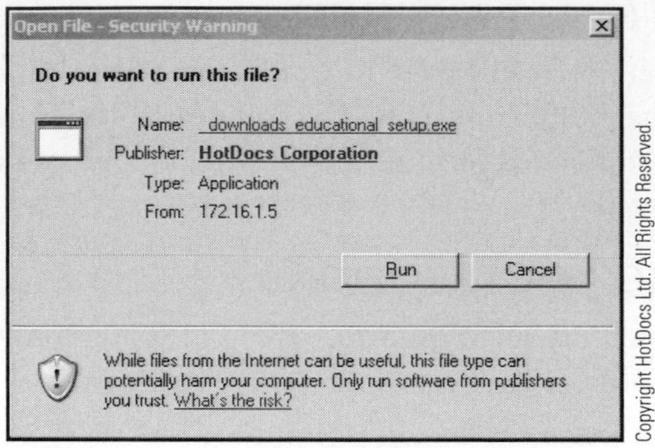

11. In the "HotDocs Developer 11 Setup" window, ***click Next.***
12. In the "Software License Agreement" window, ***click the button next to "I accept the terms in the license agreement" and click Next.*** (See HotDocs Installation Exhibit 2.)

HOTDOCS INSTALLATION EXHIBIT 2

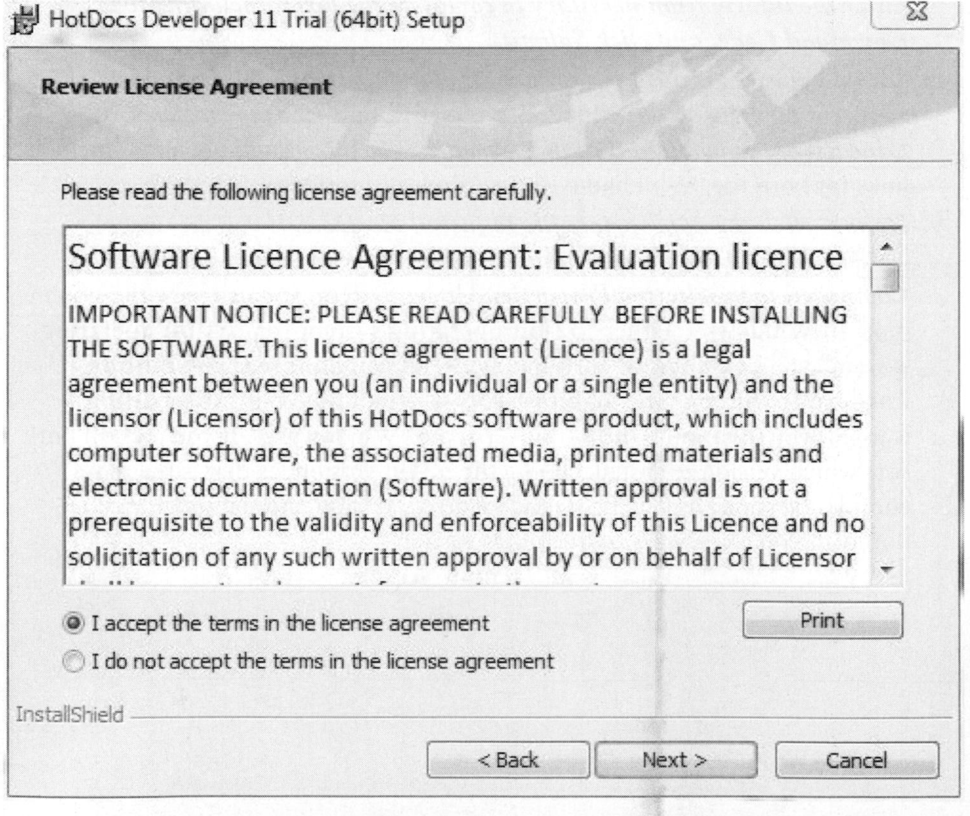

13. The screen in HotDocs Installation Exhibit 3 should now be displayed. ***Click Next*** to install the software in the default directory.

HOTDOCS INSTALLATION EXHIBIT 3

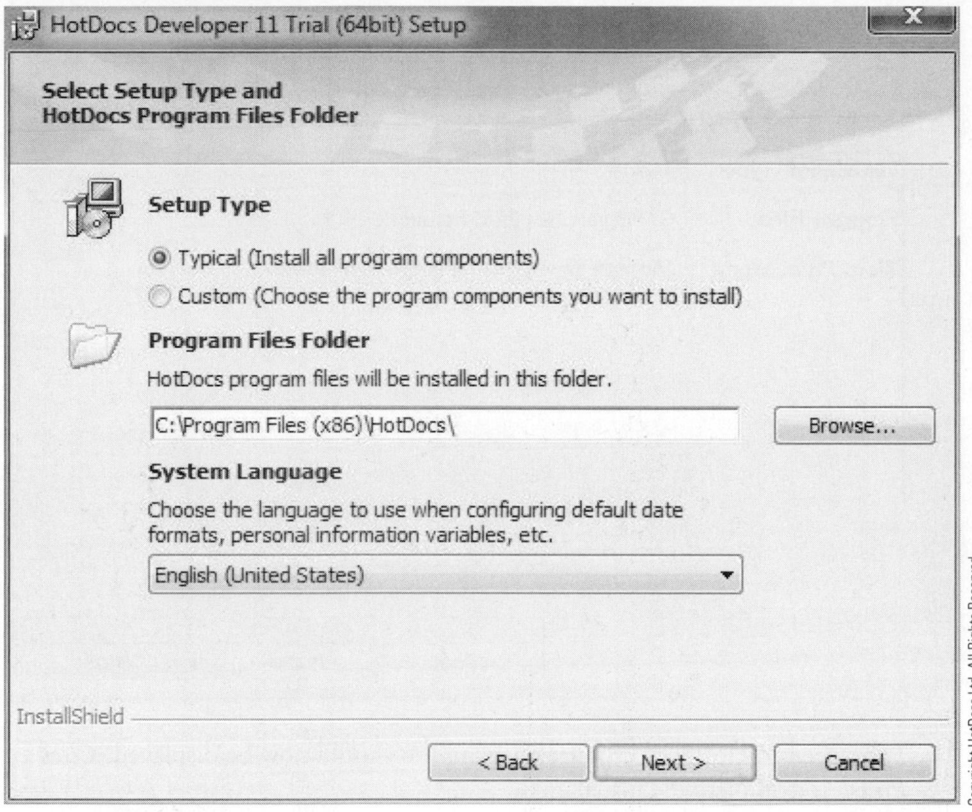

14. Choose the word-processing programs you would like to use with HotDocs and ***click Next.*** (See HotDocs Installation Exhibit 4.)

HOTDOCS INSTALLATION EXHIBIT 4

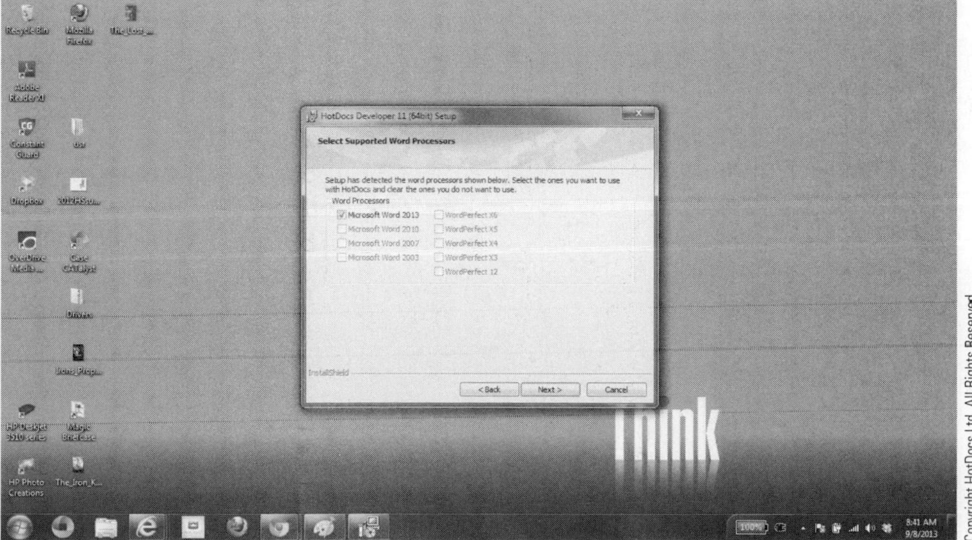

15. The screen in HotDocs Installation Exhibit 5 should now be displayed. Confirm the settings listed and ***click Install.***

HANDS-ON EXERCISES

HOTDOCS INSTALLATION EXHIBIT 5

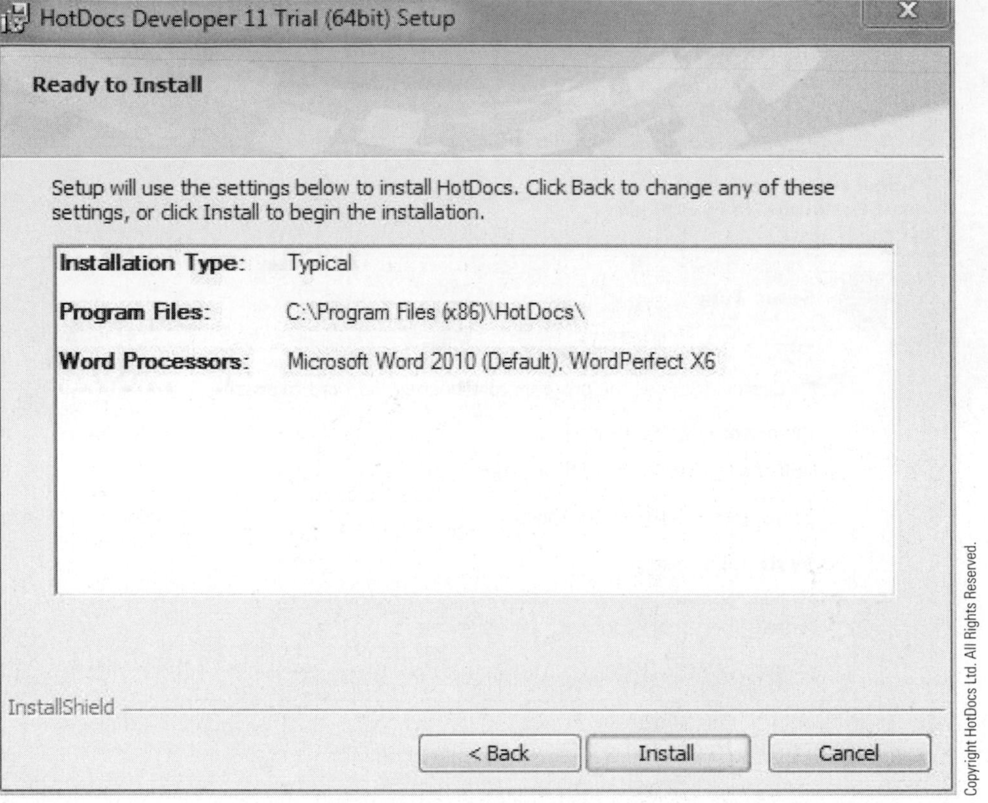

16. The screen in HotDocs Installation Exhibit 6 should now be displayed. ***Click Finish*** to complete the installation.

HOTDOCS INSTALLATION EXHIBIT 6

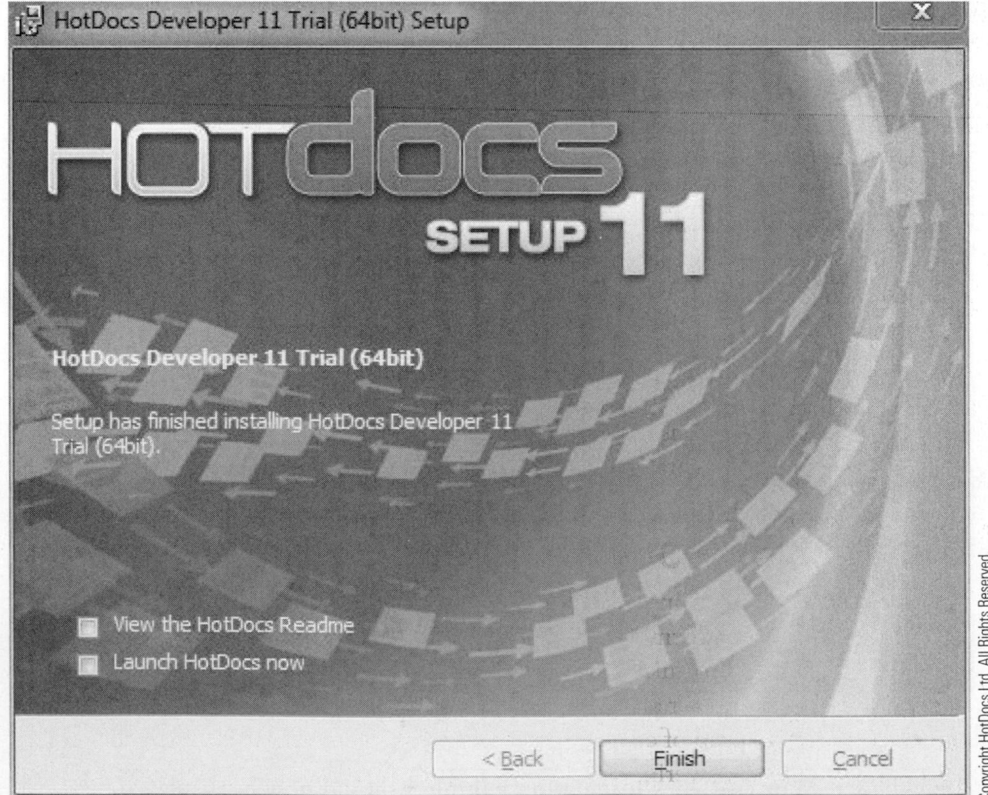

17. HotDocs has now been installed.

III. INSTALLATION TECHNICAL SUPPORT

If you have problems installing this software, please contact Cengage Learning first at http://cengage.com/support. If Cengage Learning is unable to resolve your installation question, you will need to contact HotDocs Ltd. at http://www.hotdocs.com/support.

Number	Lesson Title	Concepts Covered
BASIC LESSONS		
Lesson 1	Creating a Document from a Text Template	Template libraries; assembling a document from an existing template, editing a document, saving, and printing
Lesson 2	Creating a Template Library	Creating a new template library, adding templates to a library
INTERMEDIATE LESSONS		
Lesson 3	Creating a New Text Template	, , Finding a document to convert to a template, creating interview questions
Lesson 4	Creating a New Text Template (replacing numbers with variables)	Replacing numbers with variables, create a variable for monthly salary, and create a computation variable to calculate annual salary
ADVANCED LESSONS		
Lesson 5	Creating a New Text Template (replacing pronouns with variables)	Replacing pronouns with variables
Lesson 6	Creating a New Text Template (creating new dialogs)	Creating new dialogs (groups of related interview questions)

GETTING STARTED

Introduction

Throughout these lessons and exercises, information you need to type into the program will be designated in several different ways:

- Keys to be pressed on the keyboard are designated in brackets, in all caps, and in bold (e.g., press the **[ENTER]** key). A key combination, where two or more keys are pressed at once, is designated with a plus sign between the key names (e.g., **[CTRL]+[BACKSPACE]**). You should not type the plus sign.
- Movements with the mouse pointer are designated in bold and italics (e.g., ***point to File on the menu bar and click***).
- Words or letters that should be typed are designated in bold (e.g., type **Training Program**).
- Information that is or should be displayed on your computer screen is shown in bold, with quotation marks (e.g., **"Press ENTER to continue."**).

OVERVIEW OF HOTDOCS 11

Below are some tips on using HotDocs 11 that will help you complete these exercises:

HotDocs can transform any document into an interactive template that can be changed and adapted to suit the requirements of different cases. This allows you to create a single template for a particular use (e.g., a contract, divorce pleading, articles of incorporation) instead of creating new documents from scratch for each client. This is accomplished by answering a series of questions. In these exercises, you will first complete a prepared text template to assemble a new document. You will then create a new template and assemble a new document from that newly formed text template.

The diagram below shows the HotDocs process, from template development to document assembly:

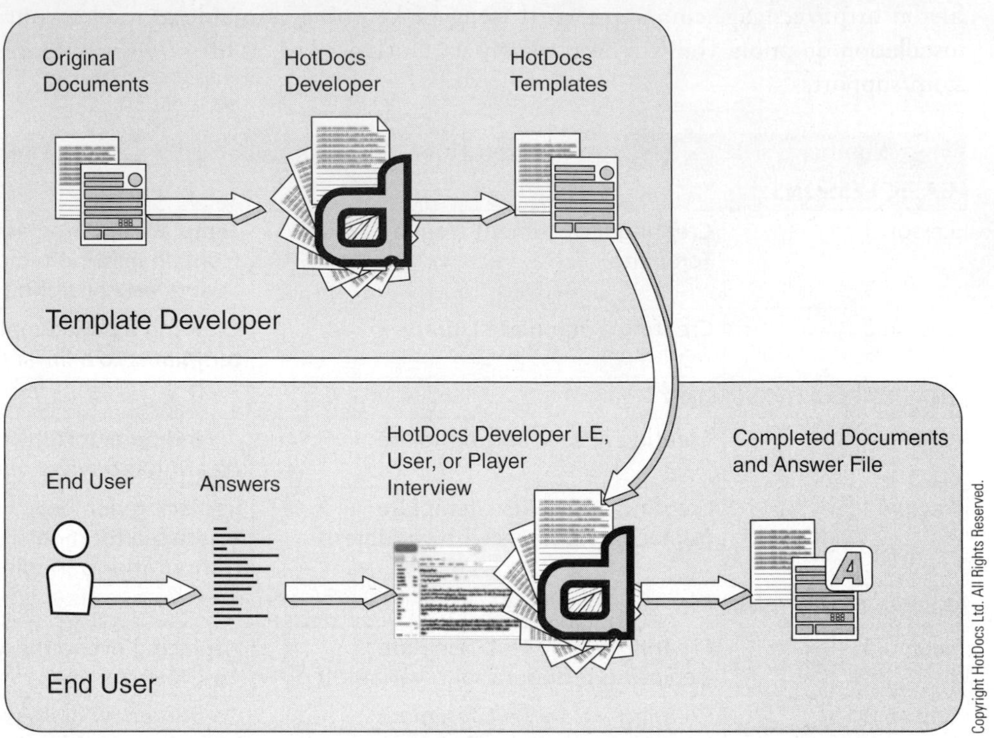

BASIC LESSON

LESSON 1: CREATING A DOCUMENT FROM A TEXT TEMPLATE

This lesson shows you how to assemble a document from a text template. It assumes that you already have a viable text template designed for use with the HotDocs software. (In later lessons, you will see how to create a new text template from scratch and then assemble a new document using that text template.)

1. Open Windows. ***Click the Start button, point the cursor to Programs or All Programs, then click HotDocs 11, then click HotDocs Developer.*** The Tutorial Templates library will appear on your screen (see HotDocs Exhibit 1).

HOTDOCS EXHIBIT 1

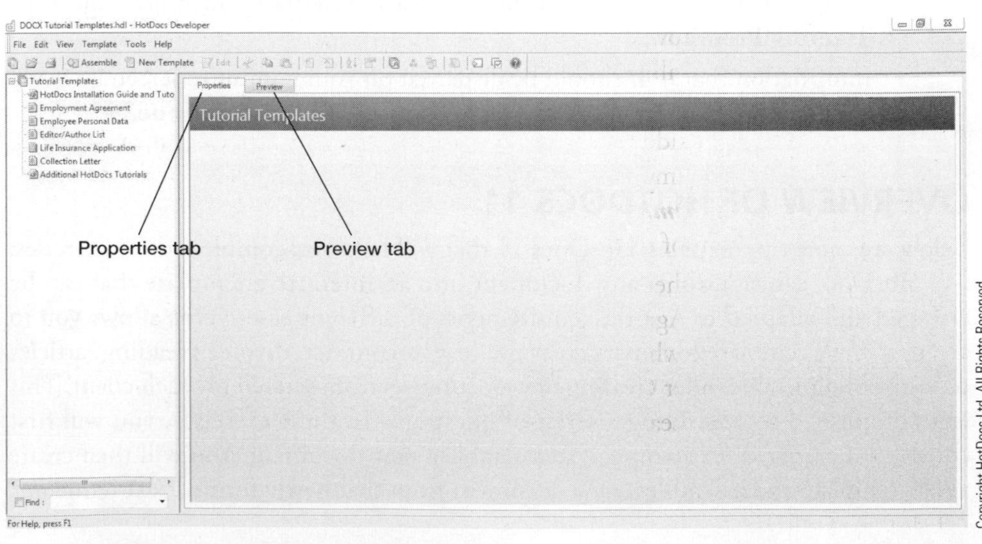

2. In this lesson, you will create an employment agreement using a text template created with HotDocs 11 software. This employment agreement was installed on your computer with the HotDocs 11 software; it is intended as a demonstration template and should not be used for any other purpose.
3. The HotDocs 11 window has two panes. The pane on the left lists the templates contained within the library. Right now, the library contains only the demonstration templates provided with the software. The pane on the right has two tabs; one shows the properties of the selected template and the other shows a preview of the document being assembled.
4. To open the Employment Agreement text template, ***click Employment Agreement File from the list called Tutorial Templates.*** Click the Preview tab to see the complete template (see HotDocs Exhibit 2).
5. To begin assembling the employment agreement, ***click the Assemble icon on the HotDocs toolbar*** (it looks like a green arrow). Two new windows open. The larger of the two is the Interview. The smaller of the two is called Answer File. As this file does not yet contain any information, the Answer File dialog box shows a New Answer File. ***Click OK.***

HOTDOCS EXHIBIT 2

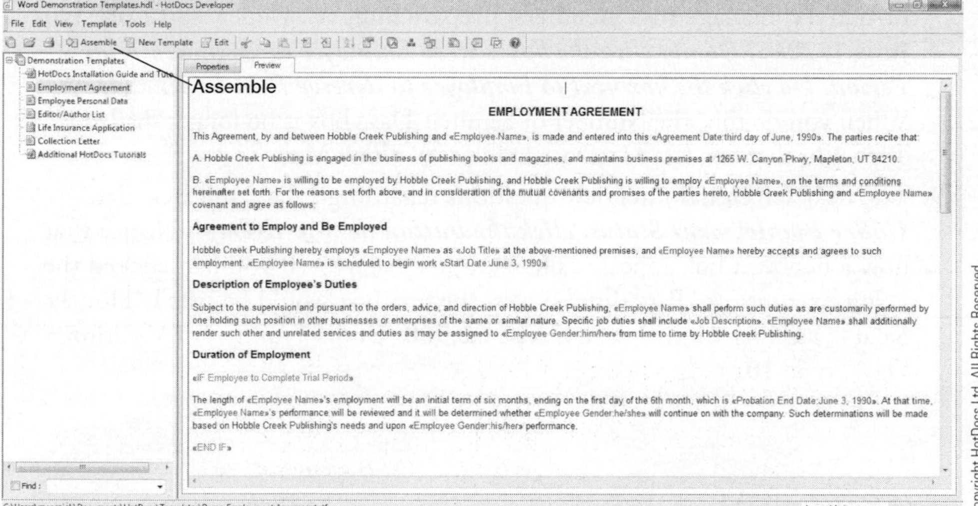

6. The larger window now shows the first of the Interview Questions; the answers you supply will populate the fields of the Employment Agreement text template. Notice that on the left side of the window is a list of the interview topics. On the right side are interview questions called Employee Information. For the Employee Name, type **Abigail Shannon**. For Employee Gender, ***click the button next to Female*** (see HotDocs Exhibit 3). ***Click Next*** (one blue arrow at the bottom of the window).
7. The next screen has the interview questions regarding the Agreement Information. Under Agreement Date, type **April 29, 2015** ***and click the ENTER key.*** Notice when you do this, the Agreement Date becomes "29 Apr 2015". Under Company Representative, ***click the button for Stephanie Hanson.*** Leave the Signature Date blank. ***Click Next.***

HOTDOCS EXHIBIT 3

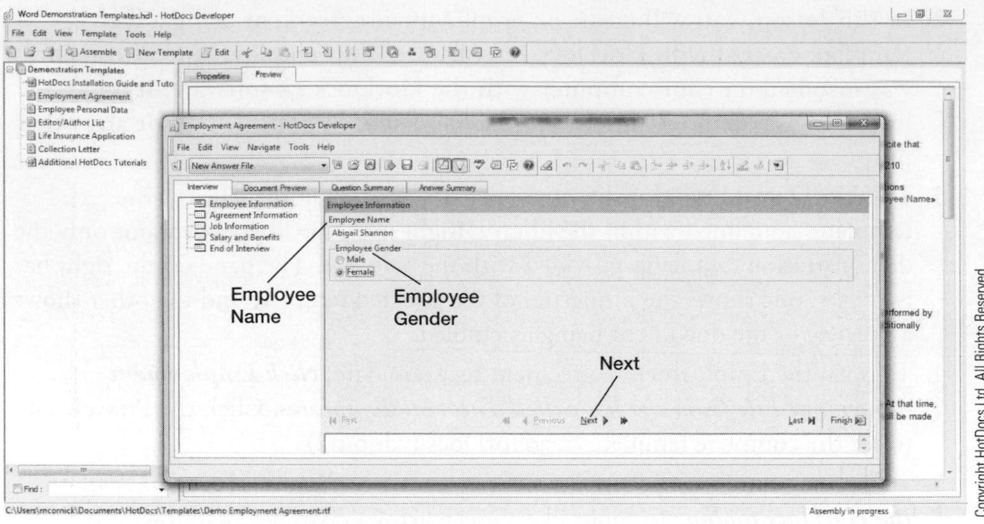

8. The next screen has the interview questions regarding the Job Information. Under Job Title, type **Creative Director**. Under Complete the following sentence: Job duties shall include, type **Oversee advertising and marketing initiatives; manage staff members; prepare budgets.** Under Start Date, type **June 1, 2015.** ***Do not click the box next to Employee to Complete Trial Period. Do click the box next to Employee to Receive Paid Seminar Days.*** When you do this, the Number of Seminar Days box is no longer shaded. Type **2** in that box (see HotDocs Exhibit 4). ***Click Next.***
9. The next screen has interview questions regarding Salary and Benefits. ***Under Employment Status, click the button next to Exempt.*** Notice that now a new text box appears called "Annual Salary." (If you had clicked the "Non-exempt" or "Part-time" boxes, the text box would be titled "Hourly Salary.") Under Annual Salary, type **62,500**. Under Number of Vacation Days, type **10**.

HOTDOCS EXHIBIT 4

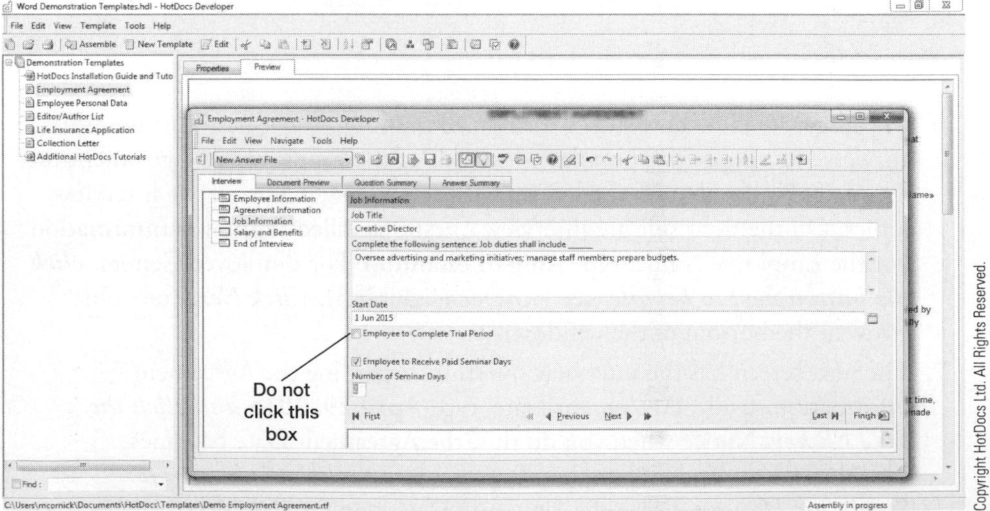

10. Notice that there are four tabs: Interview, the window you have been viewing; Document Preview, which provides a preview of the assembled document at any point during the assembly process; Question Summary, which lists the specific questions contained within the interview; and Answer Summary, which lists the answers you provided to the specific questions.
11. You can edit any of the answers by viewing the Document Preview tab. When you edit an answer, HotDocs automatically edits all questions affected by that answer. ***Click the Document Preview tab. Point the cursor to any reference to Abigail Shannon*** (highlighted in blue). ***Right-click the mouse and click Edit Answer.*** This will open a dialog box called Employee Information (see HotDocs Exhibit 5). Type the initial **E.** to make the name "Abigail E. Shannon." ***Click Next at the bottom of the dialog box.*** Notice that every reference to the employee now reads "Abigail E. Shannon."
12. ***Click the Interview tab again. Click Next.*** The next screen is End of Interview. If you failed to answer any questions, you would be prompted to click a button that would take you back to missed question(s). Because we answered all of the questions, we are given the option of sending the assembled document to Microsoft Word. ***Click the first option*** (it looks like a blue arrow), ***then click the box next to Close this window. Click Finish.***
13. Two new windows will open. One is a small dialog box asking if you want to save the answers to this template. It is not necessary to save these answers, so ***click Don't Save.*** You are then asked if you want to save a copy of the assembled document. ***You may click Don't Save.*** The second window is a Word copy of the assembled employment agreement. At this point, the employment agreement document is no longer associated with HotDocs. It is an independent Word document that can be edited, saved, and printed as a Word document (see HotDocs Exhibit 6).
14. On the Employment Agreement Word file, ***click File, then Save As.*** Next to File name, type **Shannon Agreement**. ***Click Save*** to save the document. ***Then click the X at the top right corner of the screen*** to close the file.

HOTDOCS EXHIBIT 5

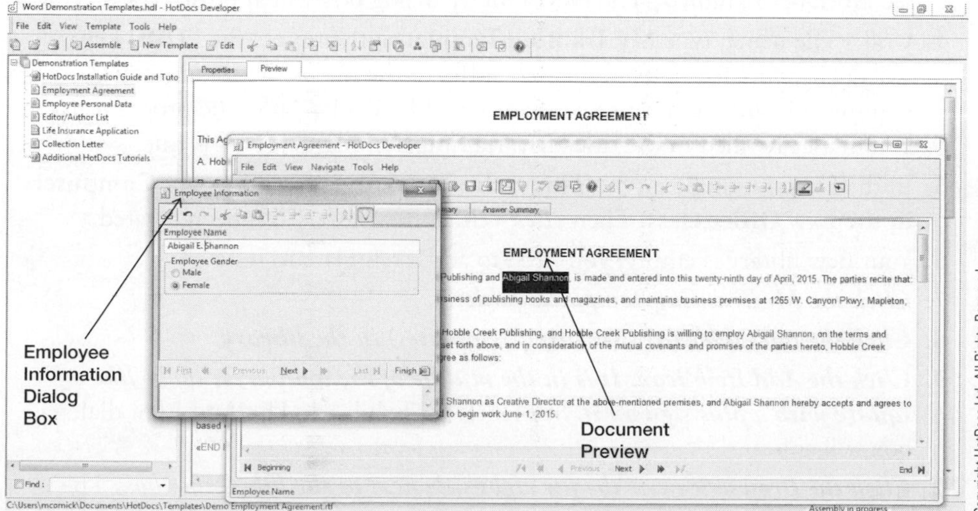

HOTDOCS EXHIBIT 6

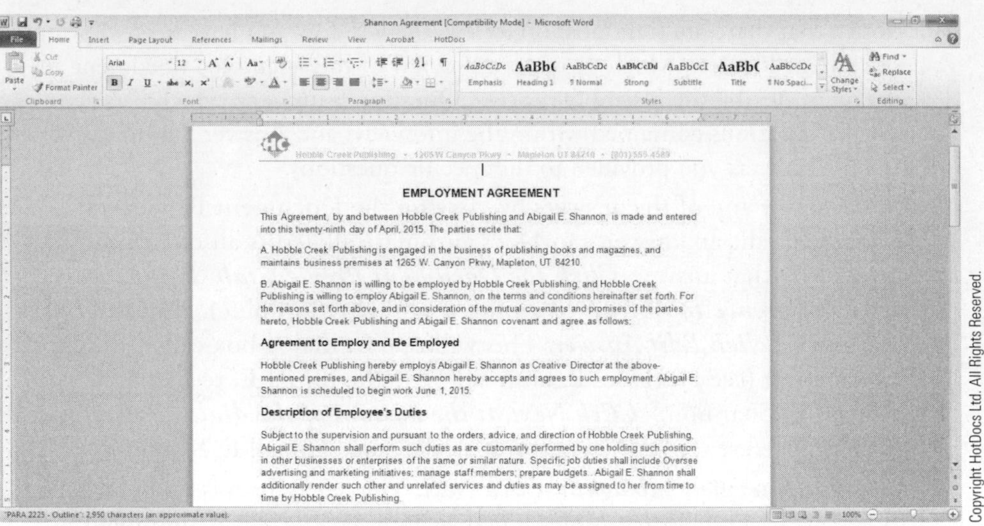

This concludes Lesson 1.

LESSON 2: CREATING A TEMPLATE LIBRARY

This lesson shows you how to create a new template library. It assumes that you already have a viable text template designed for use with the HotDocs software. (In later lessons, you will see how to create a new text template from scratch and then assemble a new document using that text template.)

1. Open Windows. ***Click the Start button, point the cursor to Programs or All Programs, then click HotDocs 11, then click HotDocs Developer.*** The Tutorial Templates library will appear on your screen (see HotDocs Exhibit 1).
2. In this lesson, you will create a new template library with HotDocs 11 software. A template library is essentially just a collection of related files (templates) used to create customized documents. Files included within a template library are really shortcuts to the actual files residing on your computer's hard drive. The Tutorial Templates library is built into the software; we will now create our own Template library. Template libraries use the .hdl file name extension.
3. ***Click the New Library icon.*** It is the first icon on the left side of the screen; see HotDocs Exhibit 1. The New Library dialog box will appear.
4. Under File name, type **My Training Templates**, then press the **[TAB]** key twice. HotDocs has entered the .hdl suffix to the file name; the program requires this suffix to properly identify the file. Under Title, the program has automatically filled in the title "My Training Templates." This is fine.
5. In the Description box, type **This is the template I created in my Computers in the Law Office class.** Then ***click OK.*** A new library has been created.
6. Your new library is empty; you need to add a template to it.
7. ***Click the My Training Templates folder.***
8. ***Click the top folder (My Training Templates) in the library.***
9. ***Click the Add Item icon. It is in the middle of the toolbar; it looks like a square with a plus sign on it.*** See HotDocs Exhibit 1. The Add Item dialog box will appear.
10. ***Click the Browse icon at the far right side next to the File name box.*** The Add Item File Name dialog box will appear.

11. ***Scroll down and select Personal Data.docx and click OK.*** (Be sure to select the Word file and not the Rich Text file also named Personal Data.)
12. The Add Item dialog box now appears again.
13. ***Click OK.*** The new file has been added to the library.

This concludes Lesson 2.

INTERMEDIATE LESSONS

LESSON 3: CREATING A NEW TEXT TEMPLATE (REPLACING TEXT WITH VARIABLES)

This lesson will show you how to create a new text template and replace text with variables for an Employment Agreement using the HotDocs 11 software. This lesson assumes that you have completed the prior lessons and that you are familiar with HotDocs 11.

1. Start Windows. ***Click the Start button, point the cursor to Programs or All Programs, then click HotDocs 11, then click HotDocs Developer.*** The Training Templates library will appear on your screen.
2. ***Go to the Premium Website. Click the Data Files: HotDocs tab to locate and download the file labeled Employee Agreement to your computer.***
3. ***In the My Training Templates library, click the My Training Templates folder.***
4. ***Click the New Template icon*** (it looks like a rectangle with a star in the upper left corner). The New Template dialog box will open. ***Next to Type, select Word DOCX Template (.docx);*** this is the appropriate choice for Word users.
5. In the File name box, type **Employment Agreement (leave two spaces between the words Employment and Agreement),** then press the **[TAB]** key twice. Notice that HotDocs has added the suffix .docx to the file name. ***Click the text box under Title*** and you will see that HotDocs has suggested the title "Employment Agreement." This is fine. Under Description, type **This is the template I created for my Computers in the Law Office class.** (See HotDocs Exhibit 7.)
6. Under Initial contents, ***click the last button, called Other file, then click the Browse button to the right of the text box.***

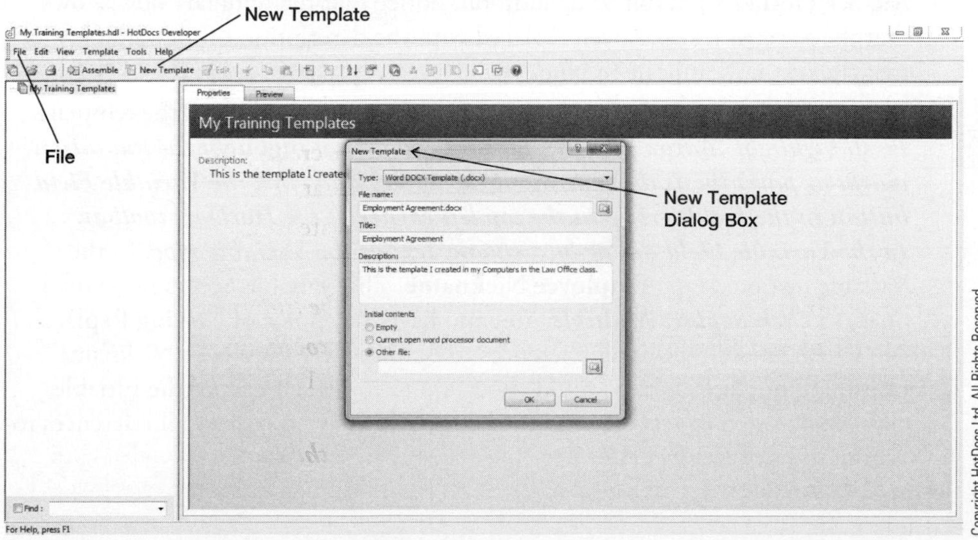

HOTDOCS EXHIBIT 7

7. This opens the New Template Initial Contents dialog box, which will enable you to choose the text file you will convert to a text template. ***Select Employment Agreement.docx.***
8. ***Click OK.*** This creates the new template file and adds it to your library. It also opens the template as a Word document—but notice that a new HotDocs toolbar has been added (see HotDocs Exhibit 8). You will now begin selecting the text fields in this document that are to serve as variables.
9. The first variable we will create is the name of the employee. ***Highlight the text*** **"Aaron Jameson"** ***at the top of the page, and then click the Variable Field button in the Fields group on the HotDocs toolbar.*** It is the first icon on the left side of the toolbar and looks like this: <<>>. The Variable Field dialog box will open.
10. ***From the Variable type list, select Text.*** In the Variable text box, type **Employee Name**. This variable occurs several times in the document, so ***click***

HOTDOCS EXHIBIT 8

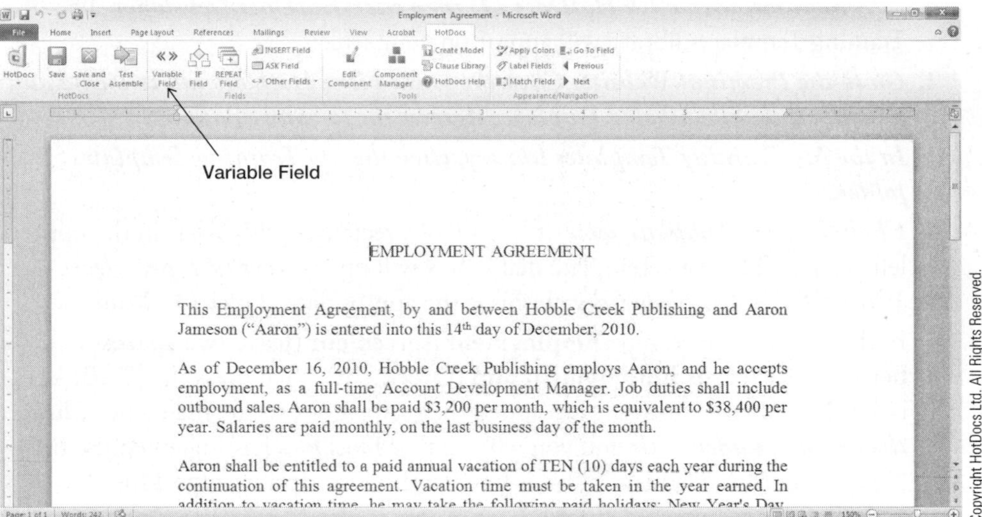

Replace Multiple. The Find and Replace dialog box will appear. ***Click Replace All.*** See HotDocs Exhibit 9. In addition, notice that the template now shows that the selected text has been replaced with the description of the variable and that the text now appears in blue.

11. You need to follow similar steps to replace other text variables in the template. ***First, highlight "Aaron" (be careful that you do not highlight the quotation marks or parenthesis that surround the name) and click the Variable Field button in the Fields group at the top left corner of the HotDocs toolbar.*** ***In the Variable Field dialog box, choose Text as the Variable type.*** In the Variable text box, type **Employee Nickname**. This variable occurs more than once, so ***click Replace Multiple***. You also have the choice of clicking Replace All, which would replace all references to Aaron with "Employee Nickname"; or using Find Next, which would allow you to review all uses of the variable and decide when to replace it one at a time. We want to replace all references to Aaron, so ***click Replace All.***

HOTDOCS EXHIBIT 9

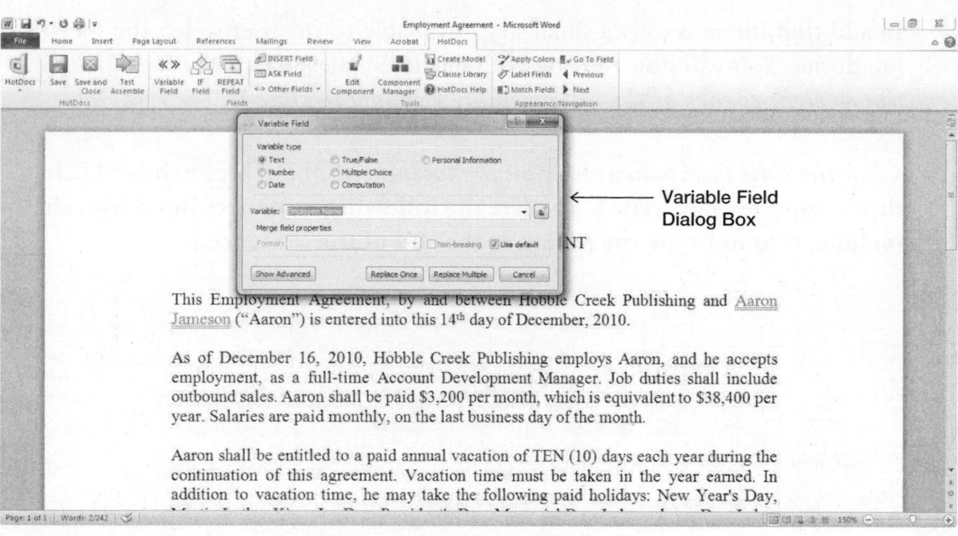

12. Next you will replace the job title. ***Highlight* "Account Development Manager" *and click the Variable Field button at the top left corner of the HotDocs toolbar. In the Variable Field dialog box, choose Text as the Variable type.*** In the Variable text box, type **Job Title.** This variable occurs just once, so ***click Replace Once.***
13. The next portion of text to be replaced with a variable is different from the ones we have seen so far. The list of job duties is just that: a list. There may be any number of items included in this list. ***Highlight the text "outbound sales". (Do not highlight the period.) Click the Variable Field button in the Fields group at the top left corner of the HotDocs toolbar.***
14. ***In the Variable Field dialog box, choose Text as the Variable type.*** In the Variable text box, type **Job Duties**. Before you replace the text with this variable, it is possible to test the variable to see how it will look in the interview. To do this, within the Variable Field dialog box, click the Edit icon. It is on the right side of the Variable: text box. See HotDocs Exhibit 10. The Text Variable Editor will appear.
15. ***Click Test.*** A test assembly window appears with the question and answer field appearing as it will to the user. Notice that the prompt for the user is the title we have given this variable ("Job Duties"). This is not a very helpful prompt.

HOTDOCS EXHIBIT 10

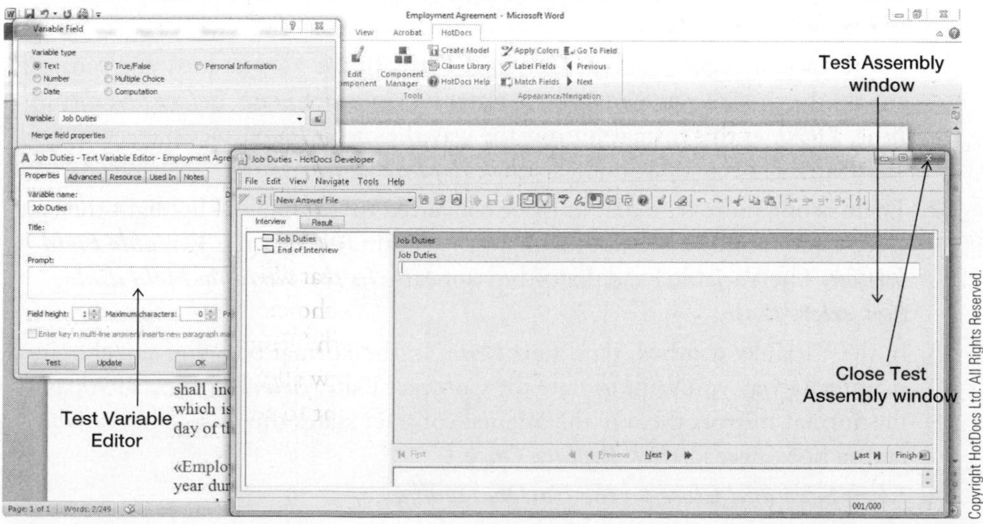

In addition, there is only a small space available to the user to list the specific job duties. You will now remedy both of these issues. ***Click the red X in the upper right corner of the test assembly window to close it.*** See HotDocs Exhibit 10.

16. ***Click the Edit Component icon on the toolbar.*** See HotDocs Exhibit 11. In the Prompt: textbox, **type Complete the following sentence: Job duties shall include. (Do not type the period at the end of the sentence.)**

HOTDOCS EXHIBIT 11

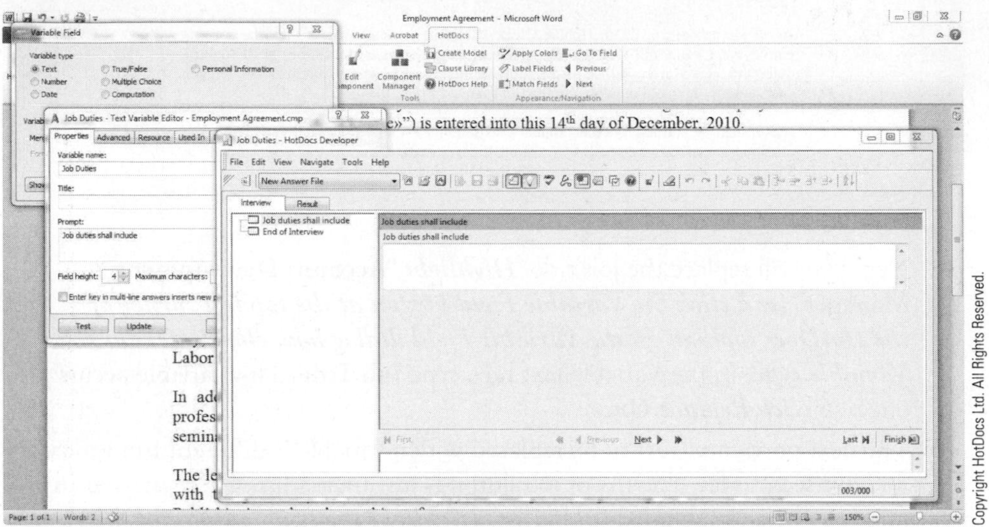

17. ***In the Field height box, click the up arrow until the number 4 appears***. This will make the answer field four lines high.
18. ***Click Update*** to view the revised test assembly window. See HotDocs Exhibit 11. ***Click the red X in the upper right corner of the test assembly dialog box to close it.***
19. ***Click OK in the Text Variable Editor***. This variable occurs just once, so ***click Replace Once*** in the Variable Field dialog box.
20. The next variable you will create is the date variable. ***Highlight the text "14th day of December, 2010" (do not highlight the period). Click the Variable Field button.*** The Variable Field dialog box appears. ***In the Variable Field dialog box, select Date.***
21. In the Variable: text box, type **Contract Date.** In the Format box, you can choose the precise way you want to state the Contract Date. ***Select 3rd day of June, 1990,*** as this format mirrors the way the original contract states this date. This variable occurs just once, so ***click Replace Once***.
22. There is one more date that must be converted to a variable. Highlight the text December 16, 2010 (do not highlight the comma). Click the ***Variable Field button.*** The Variable Field dialog box appears. ***In the Variable Field dialog box, select Date.***
23. In the Variable: text box, type **Start Date.** In the Format box, you can choose the precise way you want to state the Contract Date. ***Select June 3, 1990,*** as this format mirrors the way the original contract states this date. This variable occurs just once, so ***click Replace Once***.
24. ***Click Save and Close on the HotDocs toolbar***.

This concludes Lesson 3.

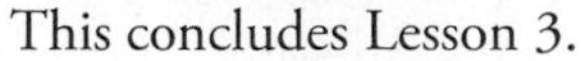

LESSON 4: CREATING A NEW TEXT TEMPLATE (REPLACING NUMBERS WITH VARIABLES)

This lesson will show you how to create a new text template and replace numbers with variables for an Employment Agreement using the HotDocs 11 software. You will also learn how to test a newly-created template. This lesson assumes that you have completed the prior lessons and that you are familiar with HotDocs 11.

1. Start Windows. ***Click the Start button, point the cursor to Programs or All Programs, then click HotDocs 11, then click HotDocs Developer.*** The Training Templates library will appear on your screen.
2. ***Click Employment Agreement and then click Edit on the HotDocs toolbar.*** The Employment Agreement will open as a Word document.
3. Numbers appear several times and in different formats throughout the Employment Agreement. The first one we will convert to a variable is the number of days of paid annual vacation as noted in the third paragraph of the Employment Agreement. ***Highlight the text TEN and click the Variable Field button in the Fields group at the top left corner of the HotDocs toolbar.***
4. ***In the Variable Field dialog box, choose Number as the Variable type.*** In the Variable: text box, type **Number of Days of Paid Annual Vacation.** Notice that in the format box, the suggested format is presented as NINE (meaning spelling the number out using all upper-case letters). This is the correct format. This variable appears just once, so ***click Replace Once.***
5. It is common in contracts for numbers to be presented as text as well as numbers, and that is the case with this variable. ***Highlight the number 10 (do not highlight the parenthesis) and click the Variable Field button in the Fields group at the top left corner of the HotDocs toolbar.*** The Variable Field dialog box will appear.
6. ***In the Variable Field dialog box, choose Number as the Variable type.*** This is a continuation of the same variable we just created above, so instead of creating a new variable, we will use the same one (Number of Days of Paid Annual Vacation). ***Click the down arrow at the end of the Variable: text box and select Number of Days of Paid Annual Vacation. If the Use default box is checked, click it to remove the check mark.***
7. In the format box, select the format 09 (meaning using digits to present the number). This variable appears just once, so ***click Replace Once.***
8. The next variable we will create is the number of seminar days in the fourth paragraph of the Employment Agreement. ***Highlight the text 3 and click the Variable Field button in the Fields group at the top left corner of the HotDocs toolbar. In the Variable Field dialog box, choose Number as the Variable type.*** In the Variable text box, type **Number of Seminar Days.**
9. ***If the Use default box is checked, click it to remove the check mark.*** In the format box, select the format 09 (meaning using digits to present the number). This variable appears just once, so ***click Replace Once.***
10. The last number variable to be created is the employee's salary. Notice that the salary is presented as both a monthly and an annual salary. Instead of creating two independent variables, we will create a variable for the monthly salary and then use that variable as part of a computation variable to calculate the annual salary.
11. ***Highlight the number 3,200 in the second paragraph (do not highlight the dollar sign) and click the Variable Field button in the Fields group at the top left corner of the HotDocs toolbar.*** The Variable Field dialog box appears. In the Variable Field dialog box, ***select Number as the Variable type and enter Salary Monthly in the Variable: textbox Click the Edit Component icon.*** See HotDocs Exhibit 12. The Number Variable Editor dialog box appears.

HOTDOCS EXHIBIT 12

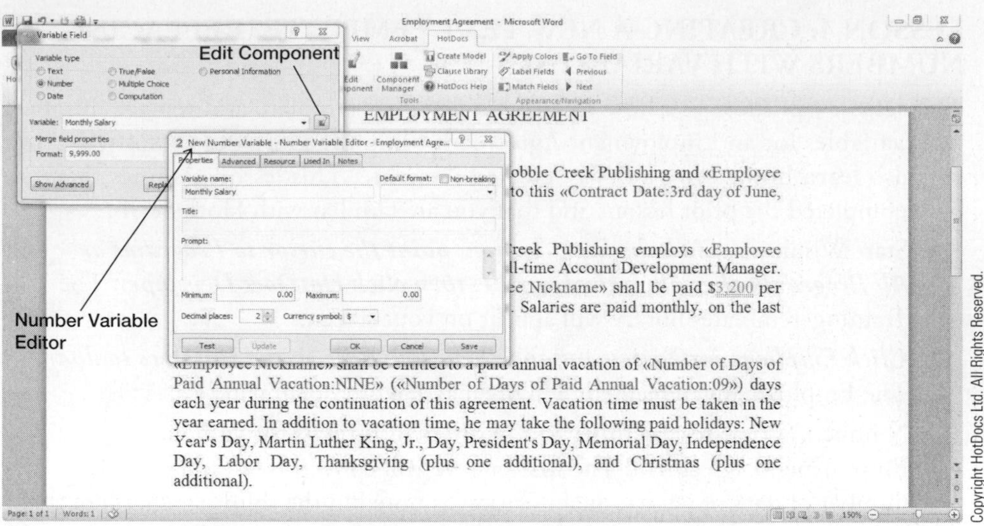

12. In the Number Variable Editor dialog box, ***click the up arrow next to Decimal places until the number 2 appears. Click the Currency symbol drop-down button and select $.*** See HotDocs Exhibit 12.
13. Click OK in the Number Variable Editor dialog box. This variable appears just once, so **click Replace Once.**
14. ***Highlight the number 38,400 (do not highlight the dollar sign) and click the Variable Field button in the Fields group at the top left corner of the HotDocs toolbar.*** The Variable Field dialog box appears. In the Variable Field dialog box, ***select Computation as the Variable type and enter Salary Annual in the Variable: textbox. Click the Edit Component icon.*** The Computation Editor appears.
15. In the Computation Editor is a large empty box called the Script box. This is where you can build an arithmetic statement to compute the annual salary. At the lower end of the Computation Editor are components that can be used in creating this arithmetic statement. See HotDocs Exhibit 13. We will do this by taking the Salary Monthly and multiply it by 12 to get the Salary Annual.

HOTDOCS EXHIBIT 13

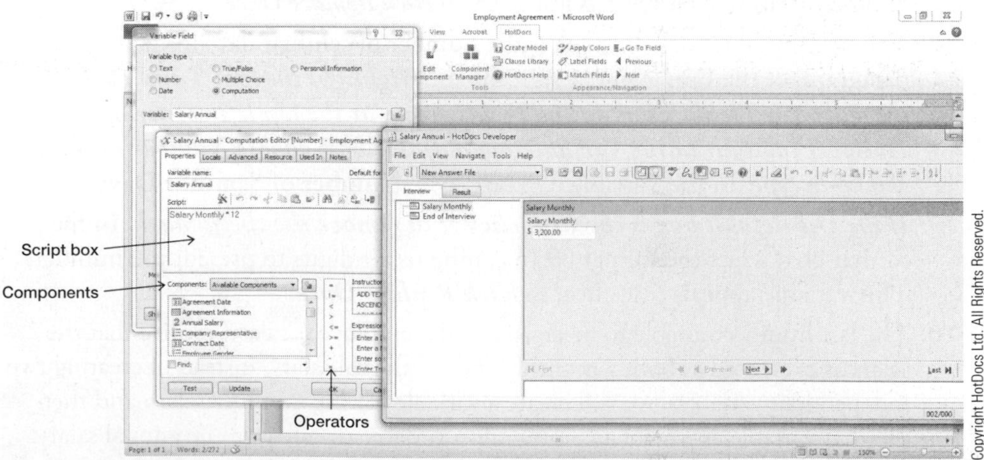

16. From the Components list, ***select Salary Monthly and drag and drop it in the Script box.*** See HotDocs Exhibit 13. ***Press the spacebar one time then drag and drop the asterisk (which is used as a multiplication symbol), from the list of Operators*** (see HotDocs Exhibit 13) ***into the Script box after Salary Monthly.***

Press the spacebar one time and type 12. See HotDocs Exhibit 13. That completed the computation for Salary Annual (Salary Monthly * 12).

17. You can test the computation by ***clicking Test.*** The test assembly window appears. See HotDocs Exhibit 13. Under Salary Monthly, enter 3,200.00, then ***click Result*** (see HotDocs Exhibit 13). The result should be 38,400. ***Click the red X in the upper right corner of the test assembly window to close it. If asked if you want to save your answer, click Don't Save.***
18. ***In the Computation Editor, click OK.*** This variable appears just once, so ***click Replace Once in the Variable Field dialog box.***
19. ***Click Save and Close on the HotDocs toolbar.***

This concludes Lesson 4.

ADVANCED LESSONS

LESSON 5: CREATING A NEW TEXT TEMPLATE (REPLACING PRONOUNS WITH VARIABLES)

This lesson will show you how to create a new text template and replace pronouns using Multiple Choice variables for an Employment Agreement using the HotDocs 11 software. This lesson assumes that you have completed the prior lessons and that you are familiar with HotDocs 11.

1. Start Windows. ***Click the Start button, point the cursor to Programs or All Programs, then click HotDocs 11, then click HotDocs Developer.*** The Training Templates library will appear on your screen.
2. ***Click Employment Agreement and then click Edit on the HotDocs toolbar.*** The Employment Agreement will open as a Word document.
3. ***Highlight the text he in the second line of the second paragraph of the Employment Agreement and click the Variable Field button in the Fields group at the top left corner of the HotDocs toolbar.*** The Variable Field dialog box appears. In the Variable Field dialog box, ***select Multiple Choice as the Variable type and enter Employee Gender in the Variable: textbox.***
4. ***Click the Edit Component icon.*** The Multiple Choice Variable Editor appears. Type **Male** in first row of the Option column and type **Female** in the second row of the Option column. See HotDocs Exhibit 14. ***Click OK in the Multiple Choice Variable Editor*** to return to the Variable Field dialog box.

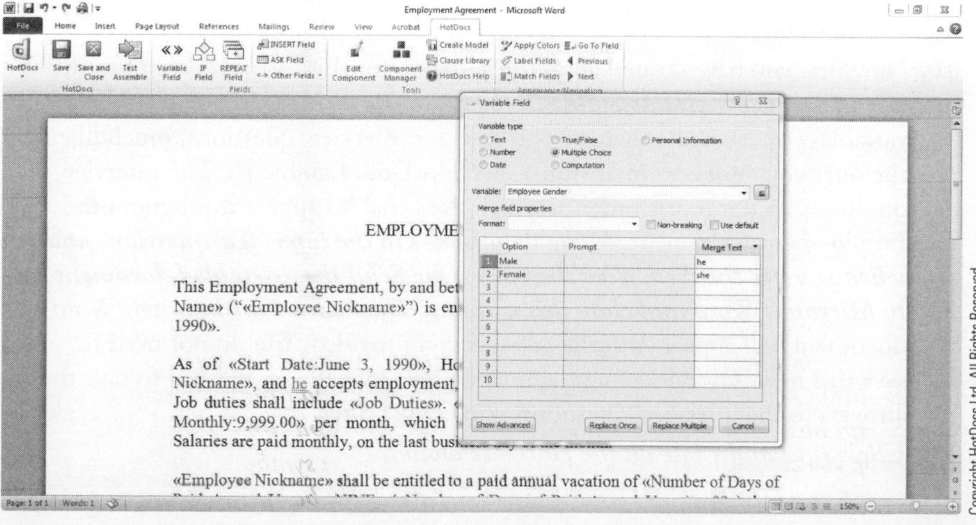

HOTDOCS EXHIBIT 14

5. If the Use default box is checked, ***click it to remove the check. Click the Merge Text column heading*** and a drop-down menu of pronouns appears. See HotDocs Exhibit 14 ***Select he/she.***
6. The pronoun "he" appears several times throughout the Employment Agreement, so ***click Replace Multiple***. The Find and Replace dialog box appears. To be sure that we replace only the word "he" and not other words containing the letters "he" within them, ***click the checkbox next to Find whole words only. Click Replace All.*** See HotDocs Exhibit 15.

HOTDOCS EXHIBIT 15

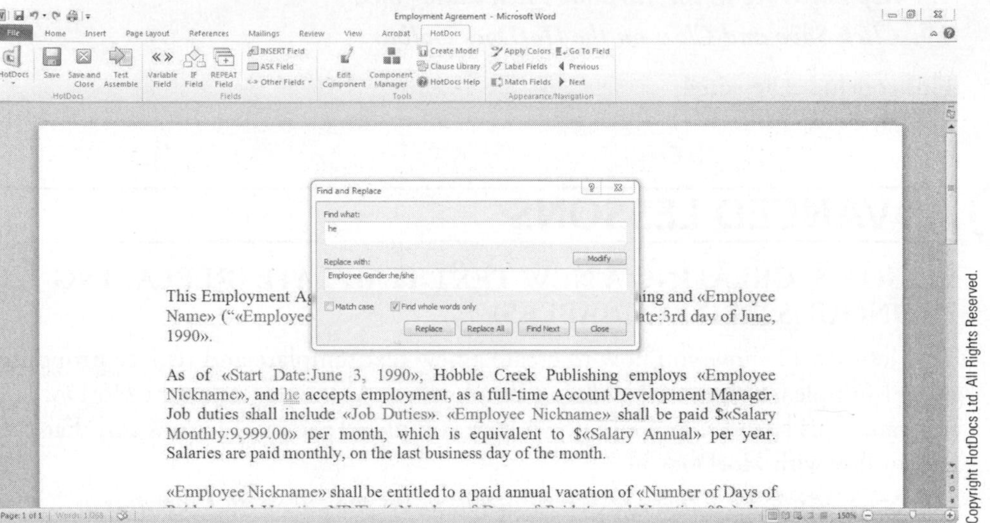

7. The next-to-last paragraph uses the pronoun "his". You can use the same Multiple Choice variable you just created, but assign different text to it. In other words, you can use the same Employee Gender variable for he, his, him, etc., but with different options assigned to different pronouns. ***Highlight the text he in the second line of the second paragraph of the Employment Agreement and click the Variable Field button at the top left corner of the HotDocs toolbar.*** The Variable Field dialog box appears. In the Variable Field dialog box, ***select Multiple Choice as the Variable type and click the drop-down menu next in the Variable: textbox. Select Employee Gender.***
8. If the Use default box is checked, ***click it to remove the check. Click the Merge Text column heading*** and a drop-down menu of pronouns appears. See HotDocs Exhibit 14. ***Select his/her.***
9. The pronoun "his" appears just once in the Employment Agreement, so ***click Replace Once.***
10. Now that you have created all of the variables for this form, you can test the document. ***Click Test Assemble in the HotDocs toolbar.*** Notice that the variables you created now form the basis for interview questions, much like the ones you answered in Lesson 1. See HotDocs Exhibit 16. The interview questions appear in the order in which the variables appear throughout the Employment Agreement. ***Make up answers to the interview questions and when you are finished, click the option for Send the assembled document to Microsoft Word and close this window. Then click Finish.*** A new Word document will appear with the answers you provided. You do not need to save this new Word document and when asked whether you want to save the answers to the interview questions, ***click Don't Save.***
11. ***Click Save and Close on the HotDocs toolbar***.

This concludes Lesson 5.

HOTDOCS EXHIBIT 16

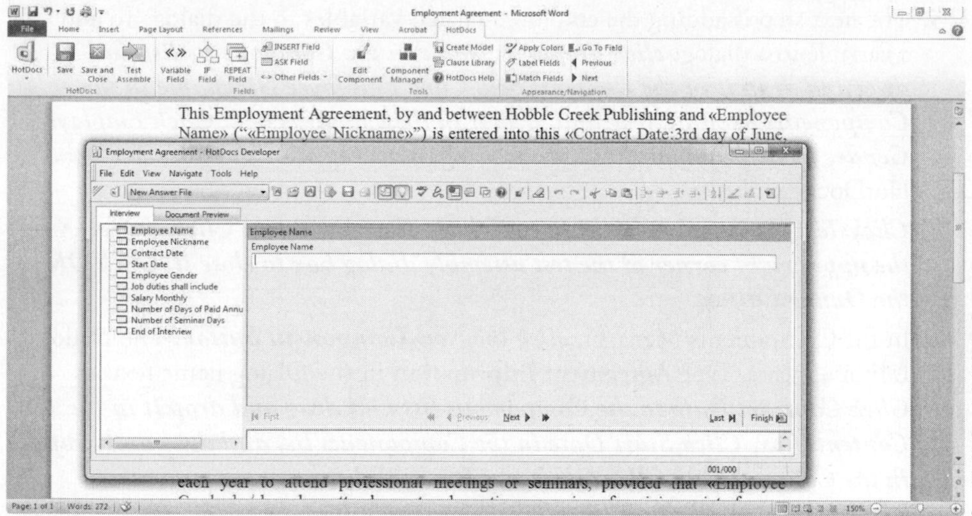

LESSON 6: CREATING A NEW TEXT TEMPLATE (CREATING NEW DIALOGS)

This lesson will show you how to create a new text template and create new custom dialogs that combine and organize the individual interview questions. Dialogs are simply groups of related interview questions presented to the user as a single group, rather than a series of separate questions. You will also test the revised Employment Agreement to see how the dialogs change and improve the user experience. This lesson assumes that you have completed the prior lessons and that you are familiar with HotDocs 11.

1. Start Windows. ***Click the Start button, point the cursor to Programs or All Programs, then click HotDocs 11, then click HotDocs Developer.*** The Training Templates library will appear on your screen.
2. ***Click Employment Agreement and then click Edit on the HotDocs toolbar.*** The Employment Agreement will open as a Word document.
3. To create a new custom dialog, ***click the Component Manager on the HotDocs toolbar.*** The Component Manager appears. The **Component Manager** lists all of the components associated with the template (you can see all of the components you created in earlier lessons, in addition to some others that were already associated with this file).
4. ***Click the Components drop-down button and select Dialogs from the list. Click the New Component button.*** The Dialog Editor appears. Type **Employee Information** in the Dialog name textbox. See HotDocs Exhibit 17.

HOTDOCS EXHIBIT 17

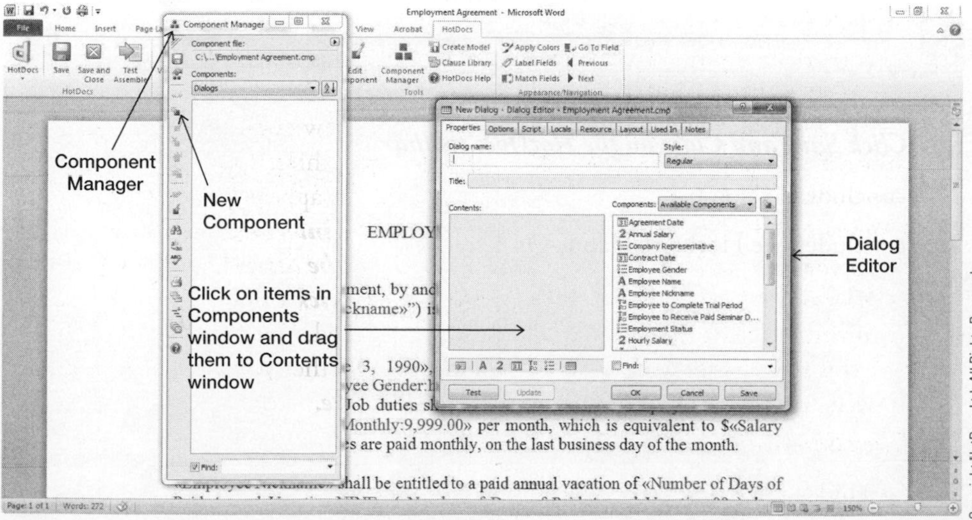

5. The next step is adding the employee-related variables to the dialog. To add a variable to a dialog, ***click Employee Name in the Components list and drag and drop it in the Contents box. Click Employee Nickname in the Components list and drag and drop it in the Contents box. Click Employee Gender in the Components list and drag and drop it in the Contents box.*** See HotDocs Exhibit 17.
6. ***Click Test to see what the dialog will look like to the user. Click the red X in the upper right corner of the test assembly dialog box to close it. Click OK in the Dialog Editor.***
7. In the Components Manager, ***click the New Component button.*** The Dialog Editor appears. Type **Agreement Information** in the Dialog name textbox. ***Click Contract Date in the Components list and drag and drop it in the Contents box. Click Start Date in the Components list and drag and drop it in the Contents box. Click OK in the Dialog Editor.***
8. In the Components Manager, ***click the New Component button.*** The Dialog Editor appears. Type **Salary and Benefits** in the Dialog name textbox. ***Click Salary Monthly in the Components list and drag and drop it in the Contents box. Click Number of Days of Paid Annual Vacation in the Components list and drag and drop it in the Contents box. Click Number of Seminar Days in the Components list and drag and drop it in the Contents box. Click OK in the Dialog Editor.***
9. ***Click the red X in the upper right corner of the Component Manager to close it.***
10. ***Click Test Assemble in the HotDocs toolbar.*** Notice that there are fewer items listed than when you tested the document in Lesson 5. See HotDocs Exhibit 18.

HOTDOCS EXHIBIT 18

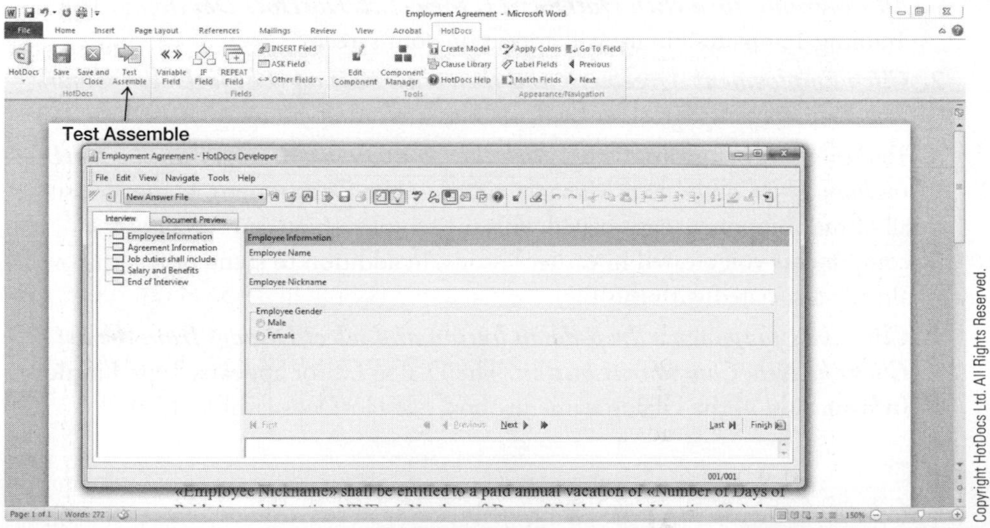

11. ***Click Save and Close on the HotDocs toolbar.***

This concludes Lesson 6.

This concludes the HotDocs Hands-On Exercises.

CHAPTER 3

Spreadsheet Software

CHAPTER OBJECTIVES

After completing this chapter, you should be able to do the following:

1. Explain what a spreadsheet is.
2. Describe how rows and columns make up the structure of a spreadsheet.
3. Explain what text, values, and formulas are.
4. Describe the types of graphs commonly found in spreadsheet programs.
5. Explain how copying formulas can simplify the use of a spreadsheet.
6. List and describe the ways in which paralegals can use spreadsheets.

INTRODUCTION

Spreadsheet software calculates and manipulates numbers using labels, values, and formulas. Legal organizations use spreadsheets to create department and firm budgets; to calculate child support and alimony payments in domestic relations cases; to prepare amortization schedules, Truth-in-Lending statements, and loan calculations in real estate matters; and to estimate taxes and help prepare tax returns for tax matters. These are just a few of the many uses of spreadsheets for law offices of all types. Spreadsheet software can automate all of these tasks.

spreadsheet software
Programs that calculate and manipulate numbers using labels, values, and formulas.

As word processors manipulate words, spreadsheets manipulate numbers. Instead of performing word processing, spreadsheets perform number processing. This chapter describes what a spreadsheet is and discusses "what if" analysis, the structure of spreadsheet programs, the fundamentals of spreadsheets, how to plan or create a spreadsheet, and how spreadsheets are used in the legal environment.

WHAT IS A SPREADSHEET?

A **spreadsheet** is a computerized version of an accountant's worksheet or ledger page. Spreadsheet software is used to create a spreadsheet, sometimes called a *worksheet*. In the past, accounting professionals primarily used ledger pages, also sometimes called *worksheets*, to track financial information. They would enter financial transactions across the rows and down the columns of the ledger paper. Each column was then added up using a calculator or an adding machine. This process was cumbersome and time-consuming if changes were needed or if errors were found.

spreadsheet
A computerized version of an accountant's worksheet or ledger page.

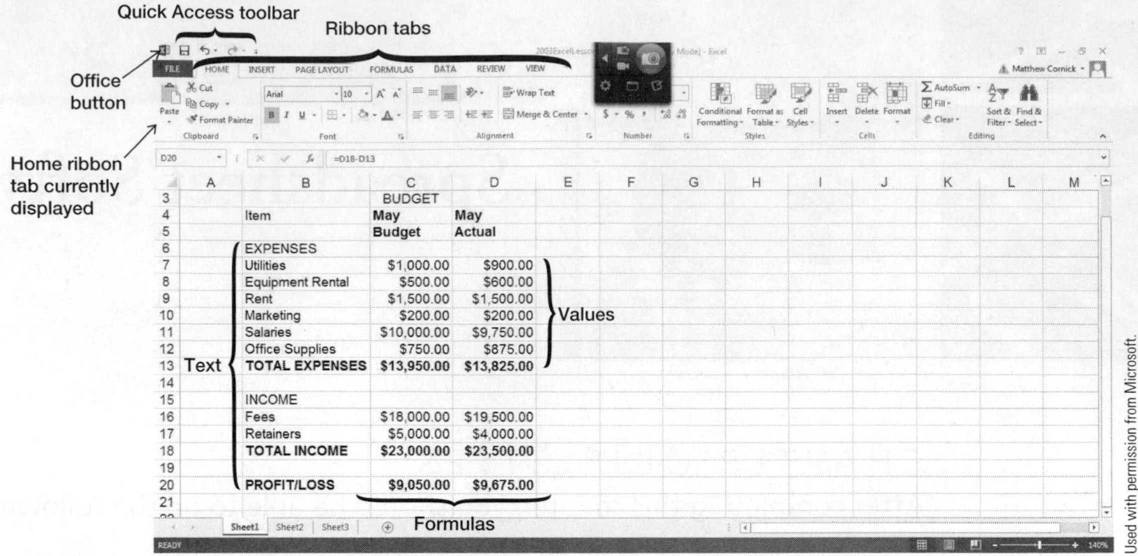

EXHIBIT 3–1
A simple spreadsheet using Microsoft Excel 2007

Spreadsheets, in contrast, are flexible and easy to use. Exhibit 3–1 is a simple spreadsheet showing a small law firm's budgeted and actual expenses for a month. This example introduces basic spreadsheet concepts. More sophisticated and more useful spreadsheets for the legal environment are introduced later in this chapter.

Spreadsheet programs were among the first general business application programs designed to run on personal computers. Spreadsheets are easier to use than manual worksheets, because the data in a spreadsheet can easily be edited and changed. In addition, spreadsheets can calculate totals and perform other mathematical functions automatically. When data are changed in a spreadsheet, the resulting totals are automatically recalculated to reflect the changes made. (Note that data is often a plural word, as shown here.) Spreadsheets have greatly altered the way businesses and legal organizations track and keep numerical data. Reports and computations that once took hours or days now take minutes.

Law firms also enjoy the benefits of spreadsheets. Numerical data are critical in almost all areas of the law. Remember, if it involves money, it involves numbers. For example, many complaints and cases include claims for damages; that is, the people filing the suits often ask for money or some type of monetary relief. Damages calculations can be complex and are often well-suited to spreadsheets; spreadsheets are used extensively in bankruptcy law, tax law, estate law, real estate law, and other areas. Law firms also use spreadsheets administratively to track income and expenses, create budgets, produce financial and accounting records, produce statistical reports about the business, and so on.

Spreadsheet software is easy and flexible to use because it

1. allows all entries to be edited, moved, or copied to other places in the spreadsheet.
2. makes it easy to insert additional columns and rows, even after the spreadsheet has been created.

3. multiplies, divides, adds, and subtracts one entry or many entries.
4. performs complex calculations (e.g., statistical functions, such as standard deviations, averages, and square roots; and financial calculations, such as present value, future value, and internal rate of return).
5. automatically recalculates totals and other calculations when information in a column or a row changes.
6. allows numerical information to be presented in several kinds of graphs and charts.
7. allows information to be saved and retrieved for future use.
8. allows information to be sorted or organized automatically.
9. allows the information in the spreadsheet to be printed.

Microsoft Excel is the spreadsheet program overwhelmingly used by most legal organizations. Versions of Excel that are widely used in the legal environment include Excel 2013, Excel 2010, and Excel 2007.

"WHAT IF" ANALYSIS

Spreadsheets can also be used for "what if" analysis. **"What if" analysis** refers to the ability to build a spreadsheet and then to change it to reflect alternative planning assumptions or scenarios. As mentioned before, when numerical data are entered into a spreadsheet and later changed, the totals are automatically recalculated. Thus, it is possible to evaluate the effects of a change simply by changing a number. This allows users to hypothesize and evaluate the effects of potential changes easily. For example, in Exhibit 3–1, if the small law firm wanted to evaluate what would happen if rent doubled for the two-month period shown, it could simply change the "4500" rent figure to "9000" and the spreadsheet would automatically recalculate the total. Most businesses are in a state of change at all times, so this feature allows users to prepare for unexpected events.

"what if" analysis
A feature of spreadsheets that allows the user to build a spreadsheet and then change the data to reflect alternative planning assumptions or scenarios.

SPREADSHEET STRUCTURE AND ORGANIZATION

An electronic spreadsheet has many of the same components as its paper ancestor, such as rows and columns. However, it also has many features unique to the electronic format, such as formulas that automatically compute and display the desired information.

Rows and Columns

Like an accountant's worksheet, a spreadsheet has rows and columns. A **row** is an area that extends across a page horizontally, and a **column** is an area that extends down a page vertically. For example, in Exhibit 3–2, rows are designated by a number (row 1, row 2, etc.), and columns are designated by a capital letter (column A, column B, etc.). Although only 21 rows and 10 columns are shown on the screen in Exhibit 3–2, the spreadsheet actually extends all the way down several thousand rows and all the way across several hundred columns. The exact length of a spreadsheet depends on the spreadsheet program. When the columns go past column Z, the column letters double up (column AA, column AB, etc.).

row
An area that extends across a page horizontally.

column
An area that extends down a page vertically.

EXHIBIT 3–2
A simple spreadsheet using Microsoft Excel 2010

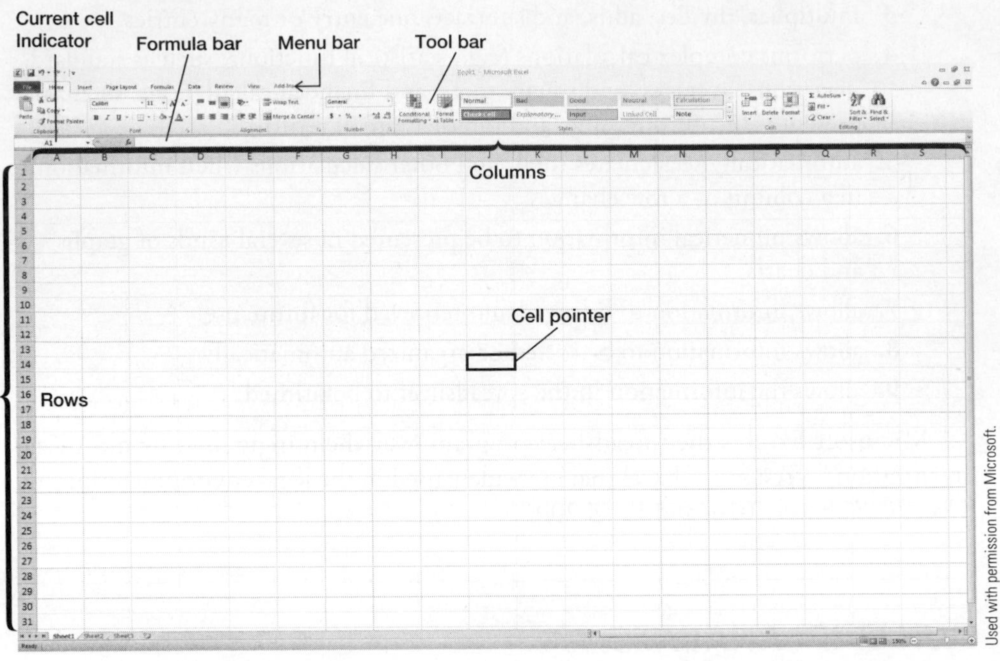

Cells and Cell Addresses

A **cell** is an intersection between a row and a column (see Exhibit 3–2). Every cell has a **cell address**. A cell address is the row and column location of a cell. The cell address is usually represented by the letter of the column and then the number of the row, such as cell A1 in Exhibit 3–2. Every cell in a spreadsheet has a cell address. Cells hold information such as values (numbers), formulas (mathematical calculations), and text.

cell
An intersection between a row and a column in a spreadsheet.

cell address
The row and column location of a cell, usually expressed with column identifier first and row identifier second.

The Elements of a Spreadsheet

Most spreadsheet programs have a user interface similar to the one in Exhibit 3–2. After a user loads a spreadsheet program, a blank spreadsheet is displayed. Exhibit 3–2 shows the various elements of a spreadsheet.

Cell Pointer All spreadsheets have a **cell pointer**, or cursor, that indicates which cell is currently selected. The cell pointer is moved by using the arrow or direction keys and can also be moved up and down pages or screens by using the [PAGE UP], [PAGE DOWN], and other keys, depending on the spreadsheet. Most spreadsheet programs also allow the cell pointer to be moved with a mouse. Finally, the cell pointer can be moved using the GO TO command. The GO TO command instructs the spreadsheet to "go to" a certain cell address. In Microsoft Excel 2013 and 2010, the [F5] key is the GO TO command.

cell pointer
The cursor in a spreadsheet program.

Current Cell Indicator and Formula Bar The current cell indicator, sometimes called the *name box*, shows the address of the cell pointer (see Exhibit 3–2). The formula bar, which is just to the right of the current cell indicator, shows the contents of the current cell. Notice in Exhibit 3–2 that the current cell indicator shows "A1" and that there is nothing in the formula bar, because cell A1 is empty. When the cell pointer is on a cell containing text, a value, or a formula, the information in the cell will be shown in the formula bar. The text, value, or formula can be edited by placing the cursor in the formula bar. When the cell pointer is moved, the current cell indicator automatically displays the current cell address.

Data Input Area Data are entered into a spreadsheet in the data input area, which is made up of cells.

Status Bar The status bar signifies the current status of the spreadsheet. For example, in Exhibit 3–2, the spreadsheet is in the ready mode, which means that it is ready to accept instructions from a user.

Menus, Toolbars, and Ribbons

Excel (see Exhibit 3–1) uses a changing ribbon as the interface with the user instead of menus. In Exhibit 3–1 the Home ribbon tab is shown. Available ribbons include: Home, Insert, Page Layout, Formulas, Data, Review, and View. The tools on the ribbon change depending on what tab is selected. Excel also has a small Quick Access toolbar that is customizable by the user (see Exhibit 3–1). Excel 2007 uses the Office button and Excel 2010 and 2013 use the File tab to access common tasks such as Open, Save, Save As, New, and Close.

Horizontal and Vertical Scroll Bars To bring other parts of the spreadsheet into view, use the horizontal and vertical scroll bars.

Worksheets Most spreadsheet programs allow multiple worksheets in one spreadsheet file. Notice in Exhibit 3–2 that three sheets are available (Sheet 1, Sheet 2, and Sheet 3). Many users find it convenient to have separate worksheets in one file. For example, if your law office had three locations, you could have one spreadsheet file called "budget" with a separate worksheet for each location. The worksheets (Sheet 1, Sheet 2, etc.) can be renamed however you wish, such as Location 1, 2, and 3.

Spreadsheets with WYSIWYG

Most spreadsheets offer a WYSIWYG ("what you see is what you get"; pronounced "wizzy-wig") screen. Exhibits 3–1 and 3–2 are examples of Windows spreadsheet programs with WYSIWYG. The WYSIWYG format allows users to add different fonts or type styles to the spreadsheets and enables application of boxes and other formatting options that can make a spreadsheet easier to read. In addition, all of the formatting appears on the screen exactly as it will print out.

SPREADSHEET FUNDAMENTALS

In this section, you will learn about spreadsheet menus and about inputting text, values, and formulas. Exhibits 3–3, 3–3A, and 3–3B show quick reference guides for Excel 2007, and Excel 2010 and Excel 2013.

Data Input

Data are usually entered into a spreadsheet using a keyboard. Data can be entered more easily and faster if the keyboard has a separate numeric keypad in addition to the direction and cursor keys. This allows you to move the cell pointer with the cursor keys and to enter values and formulas using the numeric keypad.

Three types of data can be entered into a spreadsheet: text, values, and formulas.

text
Descriptive data, such as headings and titles, used for reference purposes in a spreadsheet.

Text Descriptive data, called **text**, are entered into a cell. This type of data cannot be used in making calculations. It includes headings, titles, and so forth. For example,

Excel 2007 Quick Reference Guide

HOME RIBBON

NAVIGATION

Up One Screen	[Page Up]	To Cell A1	[Ctrl]+[Home]
Down One Screen	[Page Down]	To Last Cell with Data	[Ctrl]+[End]
Beginning of a Row	[Home]	Go To	[F5]
Cell Below Current Cell	[Enter]		

KEYBOARD SHORTCUTS

Copy Text	[Ctrl]+[C]	Undo a Command	[Ctrl]+[Z]
Paste Text	[Ctrl]+[V]	Redo/Repeat	[Ctrl]+[Y]
Cut Text	[Ctrl]+[X]	Print a Workbook	[Ctrl]+[P]
Bold Text	[Ctrl]+[B]	Save a Workbook	[Ctrl]+[S]
Underline Text	[Ctrl]+[U]	Open a Workbook	[Ctrl]+[O]
Italics Text	[Ctrl]+[I]	Find/Replace	[Ctrl]+[F]
Edit a Cell	[F2]	Absolute Cell Reference	[F4]

EXCEL FEATURES	COMMAND STRUCTURE
Absolute Cell Reference	(=B10*a1); $ signs represent an absolute cell reference, the F4 key will insert the $ signs in a formula.
Adjusting Column Width or Row Height	Drag the right border of the column header or the bottom border of the row header. Double-click to Auto Fit the column/row. Or **Home>Cells>Format>Cell Size**
Autofill	Point to the fill handle of the bottom corner of the cell(s), then drag to the destination cells(s).
Chart	**Insert>Charts>**
Clear Cell Contents	DEL key or **Home>Editing** group>**Clear, Clear Contents**
Clear Format	**Home>Editing>Clear>Clear Formats**
Delete Row/Column	**Home>Cells>Delete**
Edit a Cell	Select the cell and click the Formula bar to edit the contents or press F2
Find and Replace	**Home>Editing>Find & Select>Find or Replace**
Fit to One Page	**Page Layout>Scale to Fit Dialog Box Launcher>Fit To**
Format Cells	**Home>Font>Font Dialog Box Launcher>** or Right-click **Format Cells**
Formula	Select the cell where you want the formula, press = (equal), enter the formula, and press [ENTER] when done (e.g., =a1+a2; =a1*10). Excel performs operations in this order: ( ), :, %, ^, * and /, + and -.
Freeze Pane	**View>Window>Freeze Panes**
Functions	Click **Insert Function** icon next to the Formula Bar; or **Formulas>Function Library>Insert function**
Hide/Unhide a Column	Right-click **Column Header>Hide**; right-click **Header>Unhide;** or **View>Window>Hide**
Insert Row/Column	**Home>Cells>insert**
Macro	**View>Macros>Macros**
Page Breaks for Printing	**Page Layout>Page Setup>Breaks** or **View>Workbook Views> Page Break Preview;** Drag page break indicator line to where you want the page break to occur.
Password Protect	**Office button, Save>Tools>General Options>Password to Open**
Total a Cell Range	Click the cell where you want the total inserted, click the Autosum icon (**Home**, **Editing**, **Sum** icon), verify the range, and press [ENTER].
Worksheet Tab Name	Click Sheet1 name and type over it to rename
Wrap Text	**Format>Cells>Alignment>Wrap Text**

EXHIBIT 3–3
Excel 2007 Quick Reference Guide

Excel 2010 Quick Reference Guide

HOME RIBBON

File tab
Quick Access toolbar
Fill color
Font
Font color
Font orientation
Wrap Center
Ribbon tabs
Number format
Insert cells
Delete cells
AutoSum
Sort & Filter
Help
Cut
Paste
Copy
Format Painter
Bold
Italic
Underline
Borders
Left
Center
Right
Merge & Center
Decrease decimal
Increase decimal
Format Rows/Columns
Fill
Clear
Find & Select

NAVIGATION

Up One Screen	[Page Up]	To Cell A1	[Ctrl]+[Home]
Down One Screen	[Page Down]	To Last Cell with Data	[Ctrl]+[End]
Beginning of a Row	[Home]	Go To	[F5]
Cell Below Current Cell	[Enter]		

KEYBOARD SHORTCUTS

Copy Text	[Ctrl]+[C]	Undo a Command	[Ctrl]+[Z]
Paste Text	[Ctrl]+[V]	Redo/Repeat	[Ctrl]+[Y]
Cut Text	[Ctrl]+[X]	Print a Workbook	[Ctrl]+[P]
Bold Text	[Ctrl]+[B]	Save a Workbook	[Ctrl]+[S]
Underline Text	[Ctrl]+[U]	Open a Workbook	[Ctrl]+[O]
Italics Text	[Ctrl]+[I]	Find/Replace	[Ctrl]+[F]
Edit a Cell	[F2]	Absolute Cell Reference	[F4]

EXCEL FEATURES	COMMAND STRUCTURE
Absolute Cell Reference	(=B10*a1); $ signs represent an absolute cell reference, the F4 key will insert the $ signs in a formula.
Adjusting Column Width or Row Height	Drag the right border of the column header or the bottom border of the row header. Double-click to Auto Fit the column/row. Or **Home>Cells>Format>Cell Size**
Autofill	Point to the fill handle of the bottom corner of the cell(s), then drag to the destination cells(s).
Chart	**Insert>Charts>**
Clear Cell Contents	DEL key or **Home>Editing** group>**Clear, Clear Contents**
Clear Format	**Home>Editing>Clear>Clear Formats**
Delete Row/Column	**Home>Cells>Delete**
Edit a Cell	Select the cell and click the Formula bar to edit the contents or press [F2]
Find and Replace	**Home>Editing>Find & Select>Find or Replace**
Fit to One Page	**Page Layout>Scale to Fit Dialog Box Launcher>Fit To**
Format Cells	**Home>Font>Font Dialog Box Launcher>** or Right-click **Format Cells**
Formula	Select the cell where you want the formula, press = (equal), enter the formula, and press [ENTER] when done (e.g., =a1+a2; =a1*10). Excel performs operations in this order: ( ), :, %, ^, * and /, + and -.
Freeze Pane	**View>Window>Freeze Panes**
Functions	Click **Insert Function** icon next to the Formula Bar; or **Formulas>Function Library>Insert function**
Hide/Unhide a Column	Right-click **Column Header>Hide**; right-click **Header>Unhide;** or **View>Window>Hide**
Insert Row/Column	**Home>Cells>insert**
Macro	**View>Macros>Macros**
Page Breaks for Printing	**Page Layout>Page Setup>Breaks** or **View>Workbook Views> Page Break Preview;** Drag page break indicator line to where you want the page break to occur.
Password Protect	**File tab, Save>Tools>General Options>Password to Open**
Total a Cell Range	Click the cell where you want the total inserted, click the Autosum icon (**Home, Editing, Sum** icon), verify the range, and press [ENTER].
Worksheet Tab Name	Click Sheet1 name and type over it to rename
Wrap Text	**Format>Cells>Alignment>Wrap Text**

EXHIBIT 3–3A

Excel 2010 Quick Reference Guide

Excel 2013 Quick Reference Guide

HOME RIBBON

Quick Access toolbar, File tab, Cut, Paste, Copy, Format Painter, Bold, Italic, Underline, Font, Fill color, Font color, Borders, Left, Center, Right, Font orientation, Wrap Center, Merge & Center, Ribbon tabs, Number format, Increase decimal, Decrease decimal, Insert cells, Delete cells, Format Rows/Columns, AutoSum, Fill, Clear, Sort & Filter, Help, Find & Select

NAVIGATION

Up One Screen	[Page Up]	To Cell A1	[Ctrl]+[Home]
Down One Screen	[Page Down]	To Last Cell with Data	[Ctrl]+[End]
Beginning of a Row	[Home]	Go To	[F5]
Cell Below Current Cell	[Enter]		

KEYBOARD SHORTCUTS

Copy Text	[Ctrl]+[C]	Undo a Command	[Ctrl]+[Z]
Paste Text	[Ctrl]+[V]	Redo/Repeat	[Ctrl]+[Y]
Cut Text	[Ctrl]+[X]	Print a Workbook	[Ctrl]+[P]
Bold Text	[Ctrl]+[B]	Save a Workbook	[Ctrl]+[S]
Underline Text	[Ctrl]+[U]	Open a Workbook	[Ctrl]+[O]
Italics Text	[Ctrl]+[I]	Find/Replace	[Ctrl]+[F]
Edit a Cell	[F2]	Absolute Cell Reference	[F4]

EXCEL FEATURES	COMMAND STRUCTURE
Absolute Cell Reference	(=B10*a1); $ signs represent an absolute cell reference, the F4 key will insert the $ signs in a formula.
Adjusting Column Width or Row Height	Drag the right border of the column header or the bottom border of the row header. Double-click to Auto Fit the column/row. Or **Home>Cells>Format>Cell Size**
Autofill	Point to the fill handle of the bottom corner of the cell(s), then drag to the destination cells(s).
Chart	**Insert>Charts>**
Clear Cell Contents	DEL key or **Home>Editing** group>**Clear, Clear Contents**
Clear Format	**Home>Editing>Clear>Clear Formats**
Delete Row/Column	**Home>Cells>Delete**
Edit a Cell	Select the cell and click the Formula bar to edit the contents or press [F2]
Find and Replace	**Home>Editing>Find & Select>Find or Replace**
Fit to One Page	**Page Layout>Scale to Fit Dialog Box Launcher>Fit To**
Format Cells	**Home>Font>Font Dialog Box Launcher>** or Right-click **Format Cells**
Formula	Select the cell where you want the formula, press = (equal), enter the formula, and press [ENTER] when done (e.g., =a1+a2; =a1*10). Excel performs operations in this order: ( ), :, %, ^, * and /, + and -.
Freeze Pane	**View>Window>Freeze Panes**
Functions	Click **Insert Function** icon next to the Formula Bar; or **Formulas>Function Library>Insert function**
Hide/Unhide a Column	Right-click **Column Header>Hide**; right-click **Header>Unhide;** or **View>Window>Hide**
Insert Row/Column	**Home>Cells>insert**
Macro	**View>Macros>Macros**
Page Breaks for Printing	**Page Layout>Page Setup>Breaks** or **View>Workbook Views> Page Break Preview;** Drag page break indicator line to where you want the page break to occur.
Password Protect	**File tab, Protect workbook>Encript with Password**
Total a Cell Range	Click the cell where you want the total inserted, click the Autosum icon (**Home**, **Editing**, **Sum** icon), verify the range, and press [ENTER].
Worksheet Tab Name	Click Sheet1 name and type over it to rename
Wrap Text	**Home>Alignment>Wrap Text**

EXHIBIT 3–3B

Excel 2013 Quick Reference Guide

in Exhibit 3–1, the title "BUDGETED LAW OFFICE EXPENSES APRIL - MAY"; the column headings "Expense Item," "April," and "May"; and the row headings "Rent," "Salaries," "Insurance," "Utilities," and "TOTALS" are all text.

Text is usually entered as a series of words and/or abbreviations, but numbers can also be included, although no calculations can be performed on a number entered as text. For example, instead of writing out May for the column heading in Exhibit 3–1, the number 5 could be substituted, showing that May is the fifth month of the year. The numbers could be entered as text because no calculations will be performed using these cells, which are intended only as column headings.

When a character or letter is typed into a cell, most spreadsheets assume that it is a text entry. Likewise, when a number is typed into a cell, most spreadsheets assume that it is a value or number entry on which calculations can be performed.

The procedure for entering text into a cell is simple. Move the cell pointer to the cell where the text should be placed, then begin typing the text. As the text is being typed, the characters are displayed in the formula bar and in the cell. After you have typed the characters, press the [ENTER] key to enter the text into the cell. Most spreadsheets also allow you to enter data into a cell by pressing either the [ENTER] key or any of the four arrow or direction keys.

Text can be edited later by using the Edit command. The Edit command varies among different spreadsheet programs, but it generally allows a user to correct or change the contents of the cell. The Edit command in Microsoft Excel is [F2]. You can also double-click on a cell to edit it.

Another way to change the contents of an existing cell is to point to the cell to be changed, type new content, and enter the new text into the cell. This deletes the existing content and inserts the new content in the same cell. This procedure can be used for changing text, values, or formulas.

Values Numbers that are entered into a cell and that can be used in making calculations are **values**. In Exhibit 3–1, the amount listed for each expense item is a value. Values can be entered as either positive or negative numbers. Negative values are usually represented with parentheses around them or a negative sign before them. For example, if you wanted to enter negative 20,000, the spreadsheet would show either (20,000) or <–>20,000.

values
Numbers that are entered into a spreadsheet program for the purpose of making calculations.

Entering a value in a spreadsheet is similar to entering text. First, point to the cell where the value should be placed, then type the value. As the value is being typed, the characters are usually displayed in the formula bar and in the cell. After you have typed the value, press the [ENTER] key or a cursor key on the keyboard to enter the label into the cell. In Exhibit 3–1, notice that no commas or dollar signs are shown. A separate command is used to enter formatting codes. This is covered later in this chapter.

Formulas Calculations using the values in other cells are performed with **formulas**. For example, in Exhibit 3–4, the entry in cell D14 is a formula (=D10+D11+D12+D13) that adds the values of cells D10, D11, D12, and D13. Because the formula is placed in cell D14, the total is also placed there. The real power of a spreadsheet program is that formulas automatically recalculate totals if a cell value is changed. Thus, if any of the values in D10, D11, D12, or D13 were later changed, the program would automatically recalculate the total in D14.

formulas
Expressions used in spreadsheet programs to automatically perform calculations on other values.

Formulas can be entered using arithmetic operators or function commands or both.

EXHIBIT 3–4
Entering arithmetic operator formula

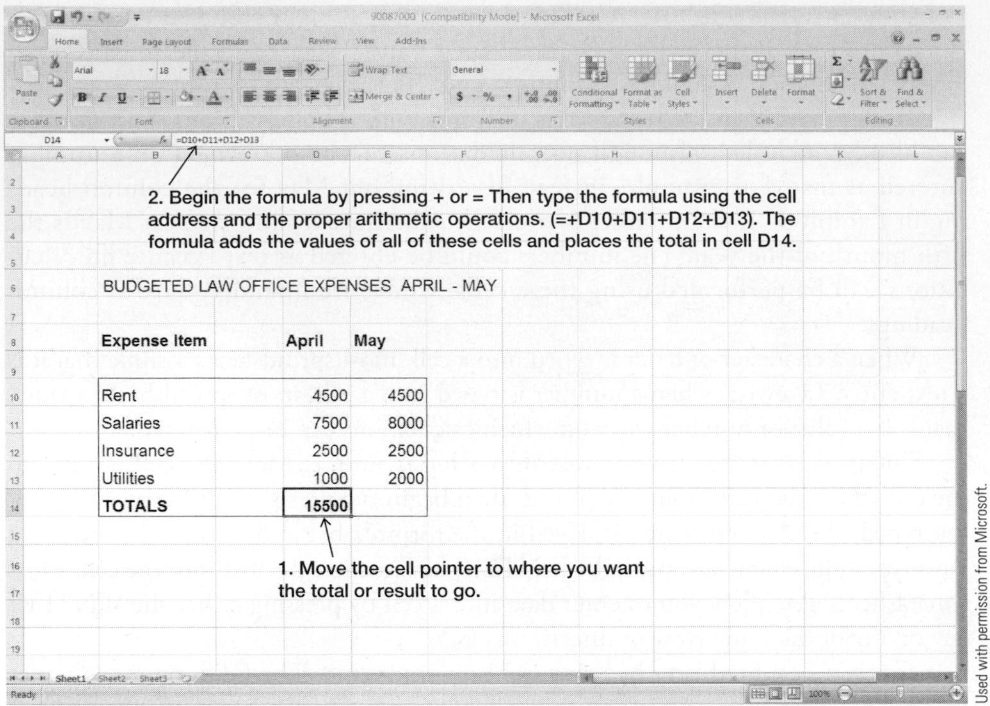

2. Begin the formula by pressing + or = Then type the formula using the cell address and the proper arithmetic operations. (=+D10+D11+D12+D13). The formula adds the values of all of these cells and places the total in cell D14.
BUDGETED LAW OFFICE EXPENSES APRIL - MAY
Expense Item April May
Rent 4500 4500
Salaries 7500 8000
Insurance 2500 2500
Utilities 1000 2000
TOTALS 15500
1. Move the cell pointer to where you want the total or result to go.

EXHIBIT 3–5
Arithmetic operators

Arithmetic Operator	Name	Formula Example
+	Addition	= C10 + C11 or = 100 + 10
–	Subtraction	= C10 – C11 or = 10 – 10
*	Multiplication	= C10 * C11 or = 100 * 10
/	Division	= C10 / C11 or = 100 / 10

arithmetic operators
Symbols that tell a spreadsheet how to compute values. Examples include addition signs, subtraction signs, and multiplication signs.

Entering Formulas Using Arithmetic Operators One way to enter formulas is to use arithmetic operators and list each cell to be computed separately (see Exhibit 3–4). **Arithmetic operators** tell a spreadsheet how to compute values (see Exhibit 3–5). With this method, you point to the cell where the total should be placed. You then begin by typing an = (equal sign) or a + (plus sign). These tell the spreadsheet that a formula will be entered. When you have typed the formula, press the [ENTER] key or a cursor key to enter it.

In Exhibit 3–4, the formula in cell D14 uses the addition arithmetic operator (+) to tell the spreadsheet program to add the values in cells D10 through D13. This is an example of using an arithmetic operator. Spreadsheets also have arithmetic operators to subtract, multiply, and divide the contents of cells. For example, in Exhibit 3–4, if instead of adding cell D12 you wanted to subtract it, the formula would read =D10+D11–D12+D13, and the total would read 10500.

In most spreadsheets, you have the option of either typing the cell addresses of the cells to be included in the formula (e.g., typing =D10+D11+D12+D13 in Exhibit 3–4) or using the cursor keys to point to the cells to be included in the formula. The second option could be accomplished by simply pointing to the D10 cell, adding an arithmetic operator (+ in this case), and then pointing to the next cell reference to be included in the formula (D11 in this case) until the formula is complete. Spreadsheet novices usually find the pointing method of entering formulas easier.

Arithmetic operators can also be used to add, subtract, multiply, and divide numbers in addition to cells. For example, in addition to a formula using an arithmetic operator to add, subtract, multiply, and divide the values entered into cells (=D10+D11), arithmetic operators can also be used in a formula to add, subtract, multiply, and divide numbers themselves (=100+10). See Exhibit 3–5.

Entering Formulas Using Function Commands Another way to enter formulas is by using function commands. A **function command** is a predefined or preprogrammed calculation that a spreadsheet can perform.

Function commands are designated by an = (equal sign) followed by the function name. For example, in Exhibit 3–6, the SUM function is used to add cells D10, D11, D12, and D13. Notice that the formula in Exhibit 3–6 reads =SUM(D10:D13). This means "add the contents of cells D10 through D13." This process of dealing with a group of cells is called entering a range (a range is a group of cells). One powerful feature that spreadsheets offer is the ability to work with a group or range of cells at one time.

function command
A predefined calculation used in a spreadsheet program to speed up the process of entering complex formulas.

Many different function commands are available in most spreadsheet programs. Some of the function commands represent long, complex formulas and make them easy to use. Both the arithmetic operators and the function commands yield the same results (compare the totals in Exhibits 3–4 and 3–6). However, for a long formula such as one that adds 100 cells together, to use the arithmetic operator method, you would have to type addition signs between all 100 cell addresses. The function commands make calculating large ranges of cells easy. For example, Exhibit 3–7 shows the Insert Function dialog box. Some of the more common functions are:

- MAX, which computes the largest value within a range of values
- AVERAGE, which computes the average of a range of values
- SUM, which adds numbers in a range and computes the total
- COUNT, which counts the number of cells that contain numbers within a range

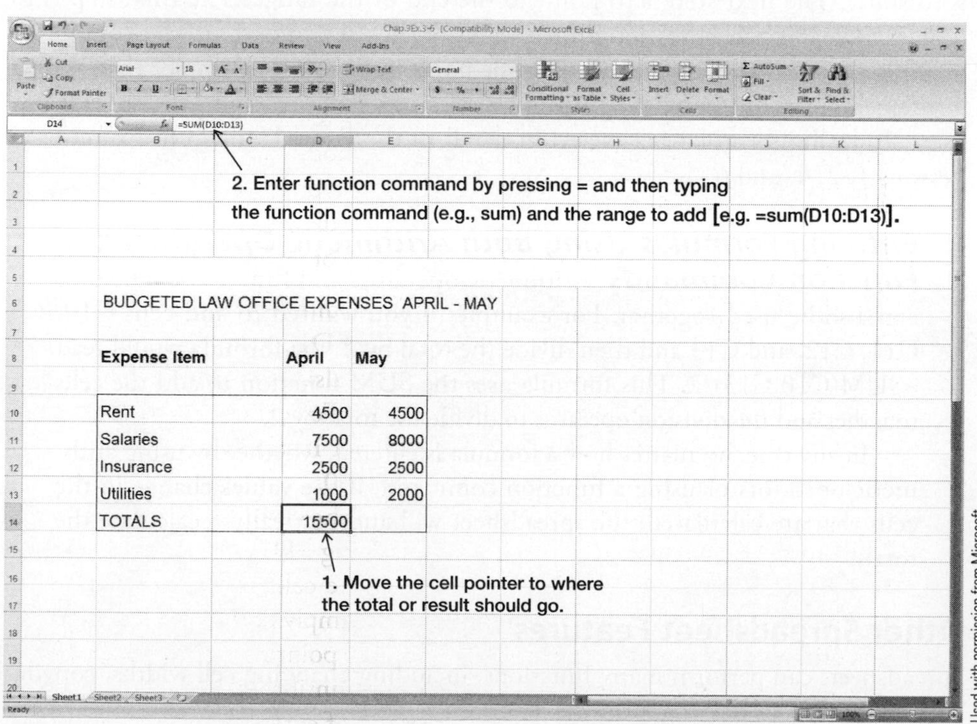

EXHIBIT 3–6
Entering formulas with function command

EXHIBIT 3–7
Commonly used function commands in Excel

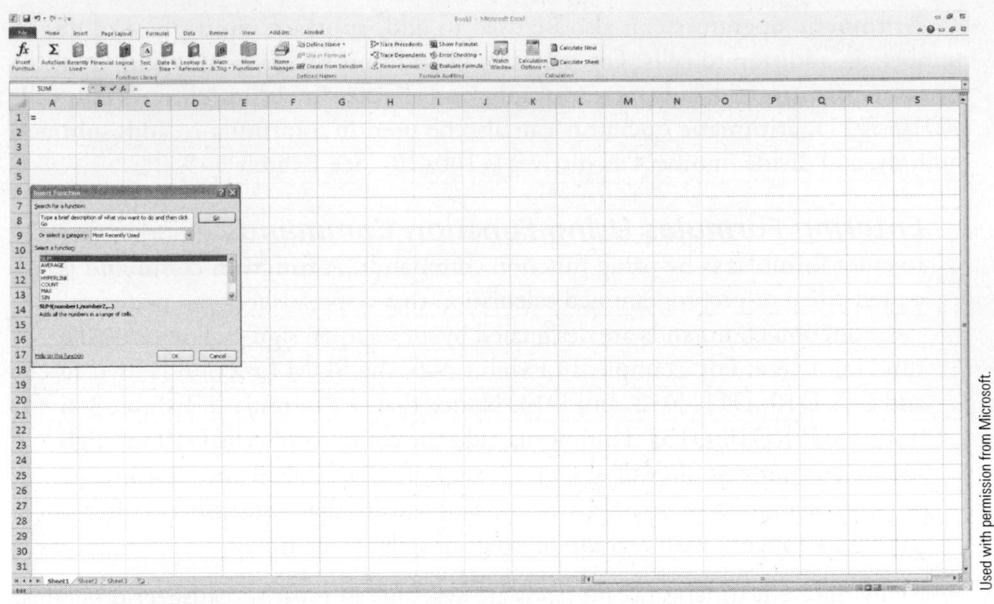

Function commands are entered in nearly the same way as arithmetic operator formulas. Point to the cell where the total should be placed. Next, enter the = sign, followed by the name of the function command and an opening parenthesis. Then, enter the beginning cell address of the range, followed by a colon (:) and the ending cell address of the range. Finally, close the parentheses and press the [ENTER] key to enter the formula into the cell.

A function formula may also be entered using the pointing method. The first step is to go to the cell where the total is to be placed. The next step is to enter the = sign, followed by an opening parenthesis: for example, =SUM(. The next step is to point to the beginning of the range that is to be included and type a colon (:). The colon anchors the range (i.e., it tells the spreadsheet program where the range is to start). The next step is to point to the end of the range. The final step is to type the closing parenthesis and hit the [ENTER] key to execute the command: for instance, =SUM(C10:C13). Using the pointing method is simpler than typing in the cell range for many people and is especially easy for beginning spreadsheet users. Entering formulas is covered in detail in the Excel Hands-On Exercises at Lessons 1, 2, 4, and 6.

Entering Formulas Using Both Arithmetic Operators and Function Commands Arithmetic operators and function commands can also be used together. For example, if you wanted to add cells C10, C11, C12, and C13 and then divide the total by 2, the formula would read =SUM(C10:C13)/2. This formula uses the SUM function to add the cells together and the division operator to divide the total by 2.

In any case, no matter how a formula is entered, whether by using arithmetic operators or using a function command, if the values change in the cells that are calculated, the spreadsheet will automatically recalculate the totals.

Other Spreadsheet Features

Spreadsheets can perform many functions, including changing cell widths, copying data and formulas, moving formulas, and sorting data.

cell width
The number of characters that can be viewed in any given cell in a spreadsheet program.

Changing Cell Width Every cell has a cell width, sometimes called a column width. The **cell width** refers to the number of characters that can be viewed in a cell. Cells in most spreadsheet programs have a starting value of nine; that is, a cell can display nine characters or numbers. But, of course, the cell width can be adjusted to display more characters or numbers.

Many times you will need to change a cell width to hold either large values (e.g., $200,000,000) or long labels. If a cell width is not large enough to hold the desired value, the cell will be filled with asterisks (*) until you enlarge it. Cell widths can also be shortened if needed. Making cells smaller allows more information to be seen on a page or computer screen at a time. The cell width is easily changed by pointing to the column to be changed and then executing the Column Width command, entering the number of characters the column should hold, and then pressing [ENTER] or clicking on OK.

Another way to change the column width is to use the pointing method. Point to the right border of the heading of the column to be changed. The pointer changes to a double arrow. Drag it to the right to expand the column or to the left to make the column smaller. When the mouse button is released, the column width is automatically changed. Lesson 1 in the Hands-On Exercises covers changing column width in detail.

Copying Data Spreadsheets have a Copy command that copies information from one part of a spreadsheet to another part or from one spreadsheet to another, while leaving the original intact (see Exhibit 3–8). Point to the cell to be copied and then click Edit > Copy. Then move the cell pointer to the location where the information is to be copied and press [ENTER]. Another way to do this is to place the mouse over the information to be copied, right-click, and click Copy. Then move the pointer to the new location and press [ENTER]. An even more convenient way

Step 1
Put cell pointer on formula to copy command

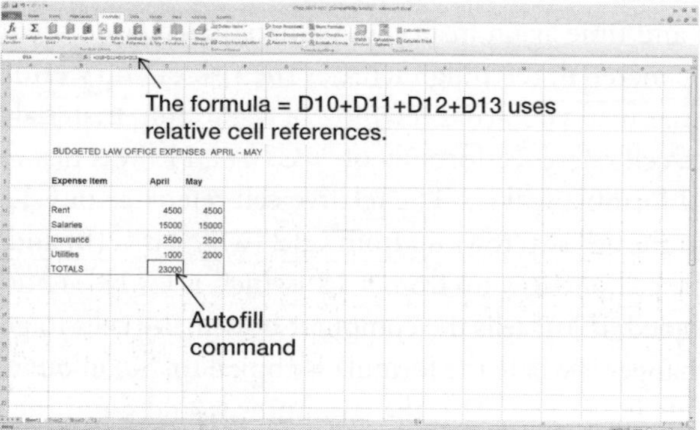

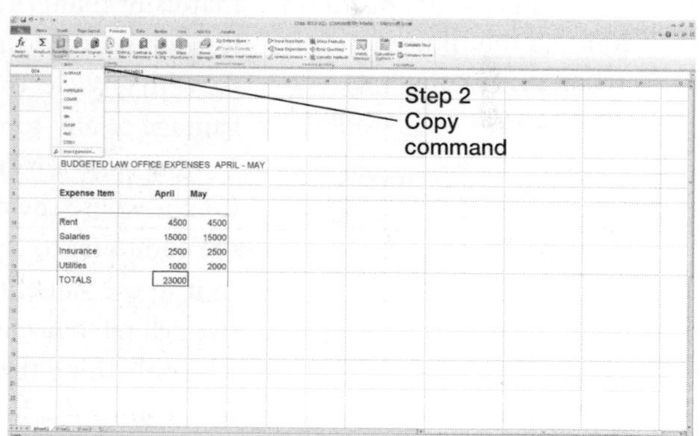

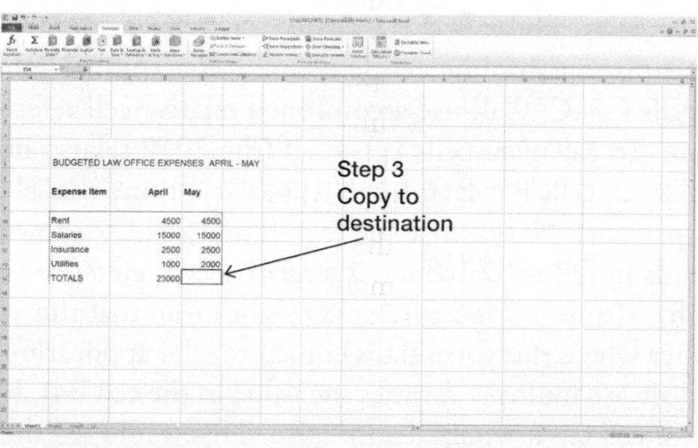

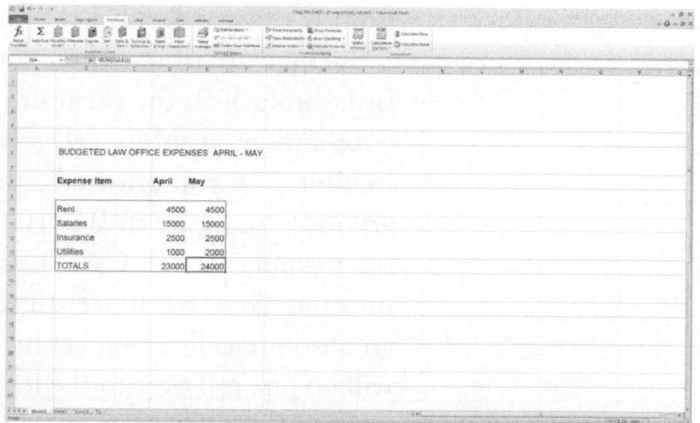

The formula automatically changes when the Copy command is used, because it contains relative cell references

Step 4
Execute

EXHIBIT 3–8
Copying formulas-relative cell references

to copy information (as long as the cells are adjacent to one another) is to use the AutoFill command. Notice in the fourth screen in Exhibit 3–8 that the pointer is on cell E14. Notice that there is a small box in the lower right corner of the pointer. To copy data, put the pointer on the cell you want to copy, position the pointer over the "AutoFill" box, drag it to the adjacent cells where the information is to be copied, and release the mouse button. The information is automatically copied. The AutoFill command also works with ranges of cells.

Copying Formulas Copying formulas is a great time-saver. The process for copying formulas is exactly the same as for copying data generally, but it is important that you understand *how* formulas are copied.

Exhibit 3–8 shows an example of copying a formula from D14 to E14. Notice that the utilities expense has increased to 2,000 for the month of May (from 1,000 in April), thus making 24,000 the correct total for May expenses. Also note that even though the formula was copied from D14 to E14, the correct total of 24,000 is shown in E14.

Most new users assume that if the formula in D14, which is =D10+D11+D12+D13, is copied to E14, the formula in cell E14 will read "=D10+D11+D12+D13" and will put the wrong total of 23,000 in the cell. This would happen if a formula used absolute cell references. An **absolute cell reference** is a cell address that does not change when it is copied to a new location. Absolute references can be placed in a formula in most spreadsheets using the dollar sign (e.g., $D$9+$D$10+$D$11+$D$12). This would give the result most people expect.

absolute cell reference
A cell address in a spreadsheet program formula that does not change when it is copied to a new location.

relative cell reference
A cell address in a spreadsheet program formula that automatically changes to reflect its new location when it is copied.

However, most spreadsheets assume that users want relative cell references. A **relative cell reference** is a cell address that automatically changes to reflect its new location when it is copied. For example, look again at Exhibit 3–8. The formula in D14 is a relative cell reference. So, when it is copied to E14, the spreadsheet automatically changes it to read "=E10+E11+E12+E13." Thus, once a formula is entered, it can be copied time and time again instead of being entered from scratch each time. As with any electronic material, retyping increases the risk of entry errors, so take advantage of any tools that help you avoid retyping or reentering materials.

Suppose a relative cell reference/formula of "=C10+C11" was placed in cell C12. C12 is where the total formula will go. The relative cell reference in C12 actually tells the computer to "go to the cell two rows up from C12 [which is C10] and add the value in it to the value in the cell one row up from C12 [which is C11]." Thus, when a relative cell reference is copied, it just tells the computer how many cells to go up and over. The only thing that changes is where the formula is copied to. So, in our example, if the user copied the formula in C12 to D12, the computer would go to the cell two rows up from D12 (which is D10) and add the value in it to the value in the cell one row up from D12 (which is D11). The formula in Exhibit 3–8 is a relative cell reference.

There are times when you must use an absolute cell reference (see Exhibit 3–9). In Exhibit 3–9, the formulas in cells C7–C10 all use a combined relative cell reference and an absolute cell reference. To calculate cells C7–C10 (the 2012 salary) in Exhibit 3–9, you must take the salary in cells B7–B10 (the 2011 salary) times the salary increase figure in B4 (103.75 percent). Notice in Exhibit 3–9 that cell D7 shows the formula for cell C7. The formula in D7 is B7 (which is a relative cell reference—meaning go one cell over to the left) * (times) $B$4 (the dollar signs mean that this is an absolute cell reference; no matter where this formula is copied to, the application will go one cell over to the left and always multiply it times the value in the cell B4). If a relative cell reference were used for cell C7 it would read B7*B4. This would tell the application to take the cell one row over to the left times the cell three rows up and one column over. This would work fine for cell C7, but if cell C7 were copied to cell

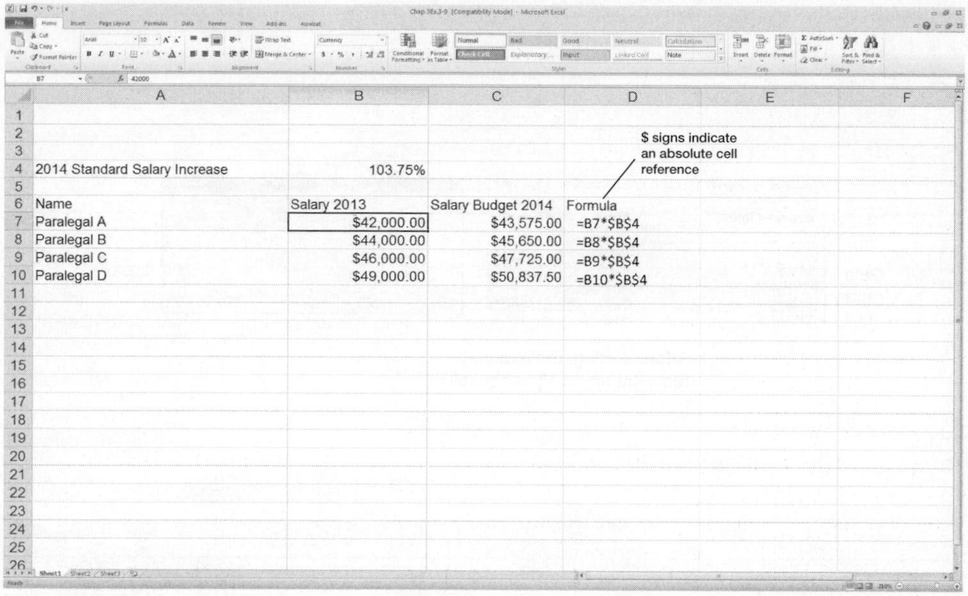

EXHIBIT 3–9
Absolute cell references

	A	B	C	D
4	2014 Standard Salary Increase	103.75%		$ signs indicate an absolute cell reference
6	Name	Salary 2013	Salary Budget 2014	Formula
7	Paralegal A	$42,000.00	$43,575.00	=B7*$B$4
8	Paralegal B	$44,000.00	$45,650.00	=B8*$B$4
9	Paralegal C	$46,000.00	$47,725.00	=B9*$B$4
10	Paralegal D	$49,000.00	$50,837.50	=B10*$B$4

C8 (or C9 or C10), the formula would not work anymore. This is because in cell C8 the computer would take the cell one row over to the left (which is B8—that is correct) times the cell three rows up and one column over (which is cell B5). Notice that nothing is entered in cell B5; it is blank. The computer would enter $44,000 ($44,000 * 0 = $0). By the time the formula got to cell C10, the results would be very bad. The formula would take cell B10 (one cell over to the left), $49,000 (which is correct) times cell B7 (three rows up and one column over), $42,000. The result would be $2,058,000 instead of the correct answer of $50,837.50. Thus, the only way for the second part of the formula to work is to always (absolutely) reference cell B4.

Copying formulas with relative cell references is covered in detail in Lesson 1 of the Hands-On Exercises. Copying formulas with absolute cell references is covered in Lesson 4.

Moving Data Moving data is similar to copying data. First, point to the cell to be moved, select Edit, then select Cut. Then point to the location where the information is to be moved and press [ENTER]. Another way to do this is to point to the cell to be moved, right-click, and then select Cut. You would then move the pointer to the new location and press [ENTER].

Inserting Rows and Columns It is sometimes necessary to go back and insert additional rows and columns into a spreadsheet. If, for example, you want to insert an expense item (such as an equipment expense item) in Exhibit 3–6, you can do this easily. To insert a row or a column, move the cell pointer to where the new row or column should be inserted. Then execute the Insert Row or Insert Column command. One new row or column is inserted. To insert more than one row or column, drag the pointer down or over the number of rows or columns you want to add, right-click, and select Insert. Use extreme caution when inserting rows and columns after formulas have been created, because it is possible that the existing formulas will not include the new row or column.

Sorting Data *Sorting* is the process of placing things in a particular order. Spreadsheets, like databases, can sort information. They can sort either values or text in ascending or descending order. In Exhibit 3–10, before sorting, the expense items are

EXHIBIT 3–10
Sorting data

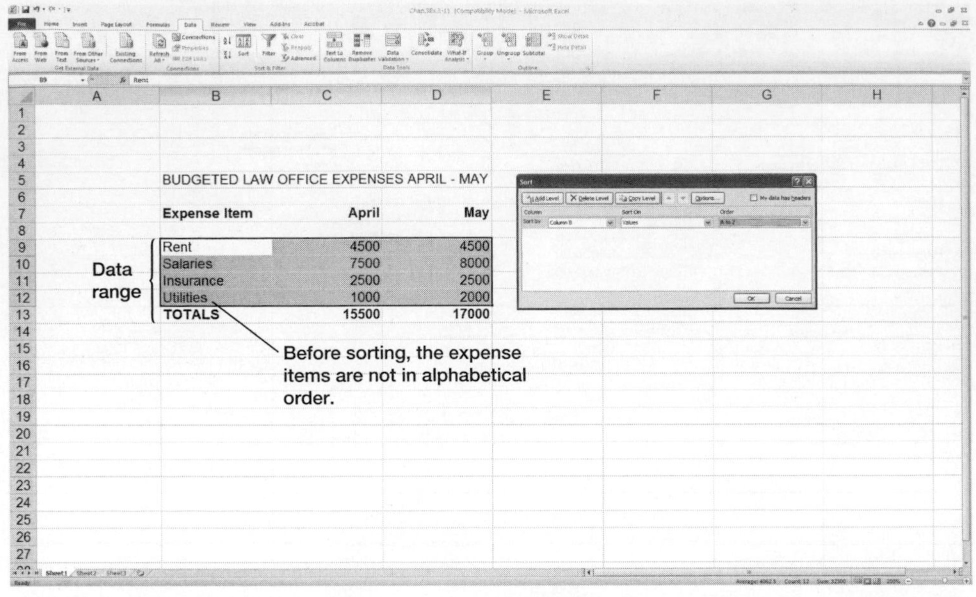

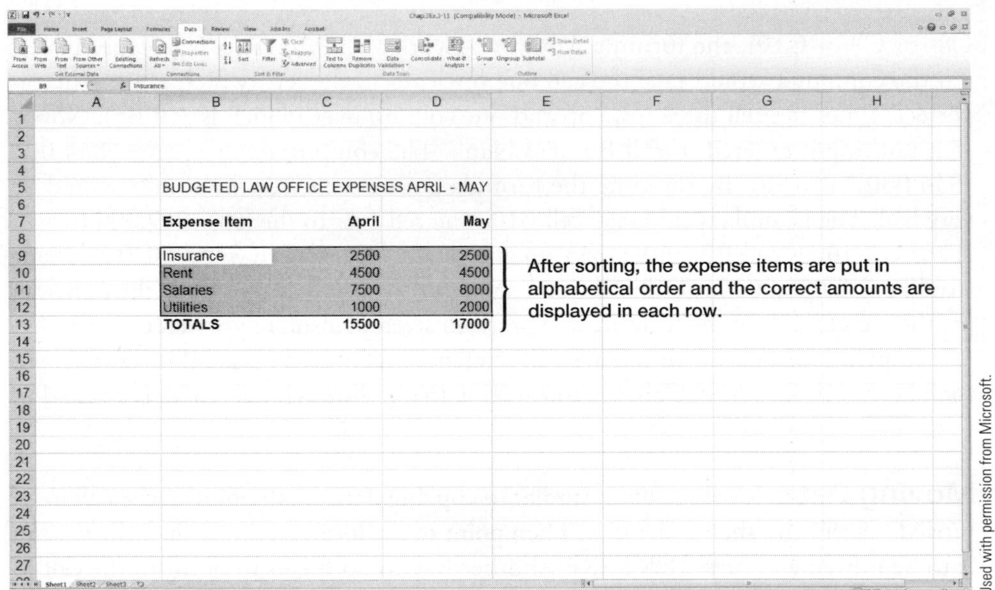

not in alphabetical order. To sort data, mark the data range of the information to be sorted, execute the Sort command (in Excel you would point to Data and click Sort), and then indicate which column to sort the data on and whether the information is to be sorted in ascending or descending order. In Exhibit 3–10, the data range must include not only the Expense Item column, but also the May and June columns. If the May and June columns were not included in the data range, the spreadsheet would put the expense items in alphabetical order, but would not move the corresponding dollar amounts. In Exhibit 3–10, with the data range properly selected, you would execute the Sort command, instruct the computer to sort the data by Column B, which is the Expense Item, in ascending order, and then select OK. The spreadsheet responds by placing the expense items and corresponding dollar amounts in alphabetical order.

Formatting Cells Most spreadsheet programs allow users to indicate which format or type of values has been entered. For example, in Exhibit 3–10, the values in the spreadsheet should be represented in dollars.

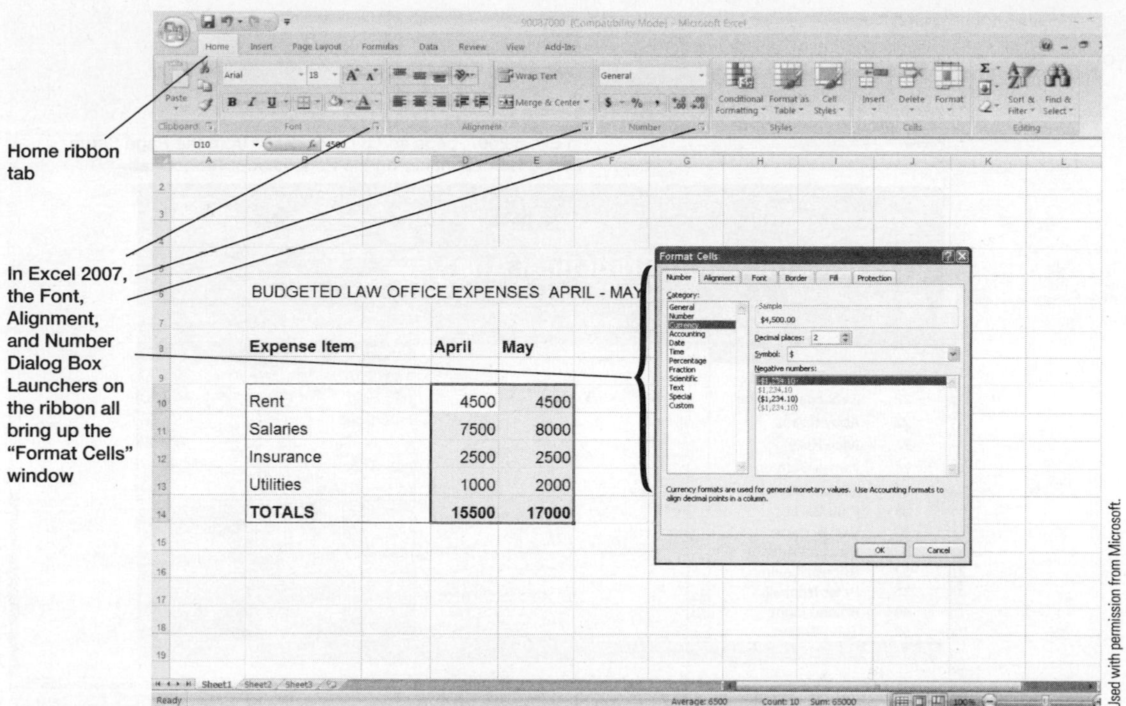

EXHIBIT 3–11
Formatting cells

To change the format of the content of the cells to dollars, drag the pointer over the cells to be changed and execute the Format Cells command. In Exhibit 3–11, notice that when the Format Cells command is initiated, you may select Currency and the desired number of decimal places. After you select OK, the cell values are automatically changed to dollar signs.

Also, notice in Exhibit 3–11 that numbers can be formatted as percentages and other expressions. Most spreadsheets can change the format of cells in many ways, such as alignment, fonts and type sizes, borders, and patterns or backgrounds. Formatting cells is covered in detail in the Hands-On Exercises.

Saving and Retrieving Files Spreadsheets can be saved and retrieved for later use, just as word-processing files and database files can. When working with any program, users should save their work often!

Printing Reports All spreadsheet programs allow the spreadsheets to be printed. Printing large spreadsheets with many columns used to be difficult, because only a limited number of columns could be printed on a page. It often meant taping pages together. Now, however, most spreadsheets and printers allow pages to print in a condensed or compressed mode as well. This means that the data are printed smaller than normal, and it allows more information to be printed on a page. In Exhibit 3–12, notice that one of the options is the Fit to: command. This option allows a print selection to be compressed into a certain number of pages, including into a single page.

Most spreadsheets allow users to change margins, add headers or footers, indicate whether the page should be printed in portrait or landscape mode, and so on. **Portrait** refers to printing down the length of the page, whereas **landscape** refers to printing across the width of the page (see Exhibit 3–12).

portrait
A method of printing that arranges data down the length of a page.

landscape
A method of printing that arranges data across the width of a page.

Using Macros As we learned in Chapter 2, a macro is a previously saved group of commands or keystrokes that allows you to save commands or procedures so that

EXHIBIT 3–12
Page setup print options in Excel

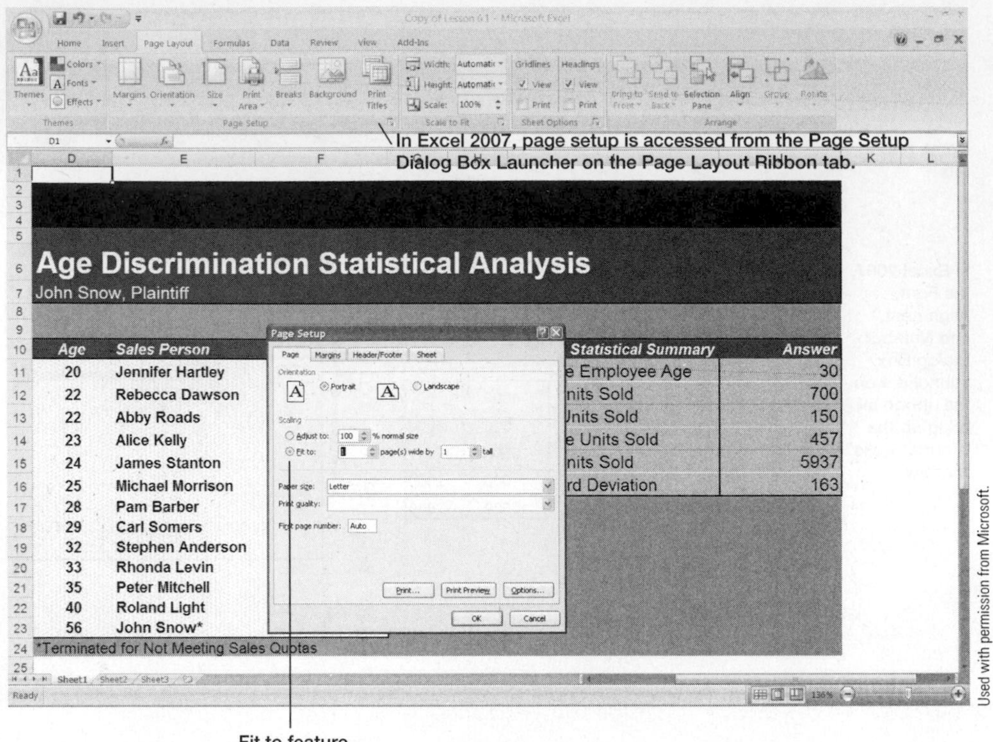

they can be used again and again. For example, if you routinely print a spreadsheet each month a certain way, you could write a macro that would automatically save the keystrokes and commands you used to produce that result. This way, you could print the spreadsheet properly by running the macro, instead of reentering all the commands every time you wanted to print it out.

Charting and Graphing The ability to visualize numerical information in a spreadsheet is beneficial. Most spreadsheet programs have graphing and charting capabilities built into them. After a graph (or chart—we will use the terms *graph* and *chart* interchangeably) has been set up, a link is created between the numerical information in the spreadsheet and the graph (see Exhibit 3–13). When the values in the spreadsheet are changed, the graph automatically reflects those changes.

Most spreadsheet programs have a chart wizard feature that takes the user through a step-by-step process and gives the user many options on how to set up a chart. Creating a chart in an Excel spreadsheet is easy. First, drag the pointer over the data that you want charted (see Exhibit 3–13) and then click on the Chart Wizard.

Many types of graphs and charts are available. The major types of graphs and charts are bar graphs, line graphs, pie charts, and stacked bar graphs. Most spreadsheets support these types of graphs. Graphs are often used in trials to convey complicated numerical data in an easy-to-understand manner. Lesson 2 in the Hands-On Exercises covers creation of a chart.

bar/column graph
A graph consisting of a sequence of bars that illustrate numerical values.

Bar/Column Graph A **bar/column graph** consists of a sequence of bars that illustrate numerical values. Bar or column graphs are common and can be either horizontal or vertical. Vertical column graphs have columns that go straight up the page (see Exhibit 3–13), and horizontal bar graphs have bars that go across the page. These graphs are best used for comparing values at a specific point in time. For example, the bar graph in Exhibit 3–13 compares the office expenses for the months of April and May.

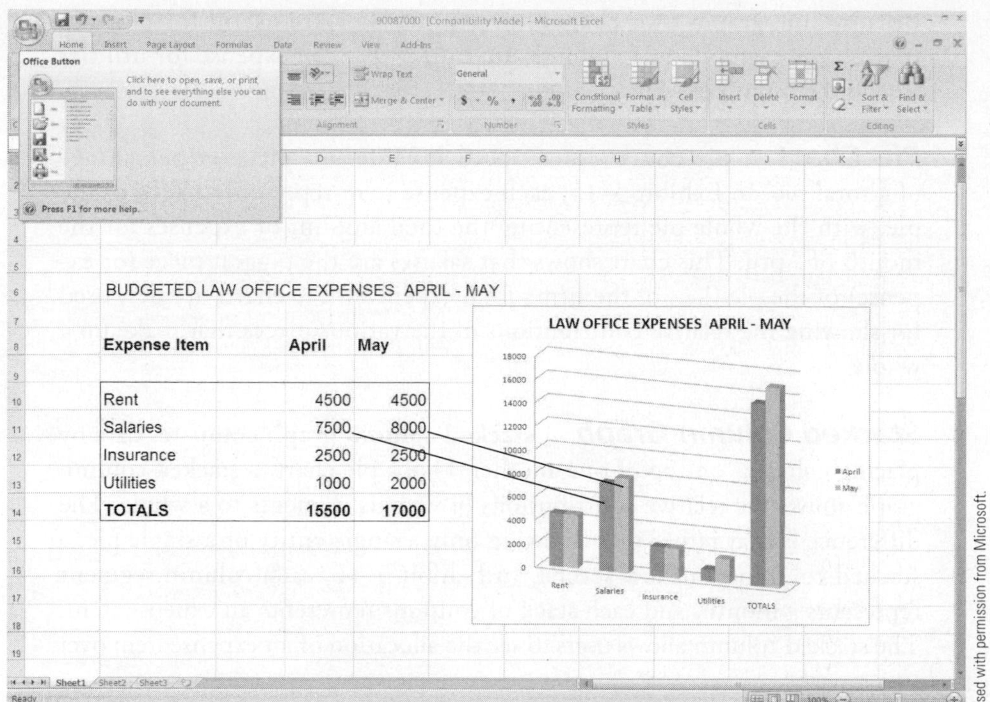

EXHIBIT 3–13
Linking the values in a spreadsheet with a graph

Bar/column graphs have many uses in legal organizations. A bar graph might be used in a personal injury case to illustrate the large earning potential of a person before an accident and her reduced earning potential after the accident. A bar graph might also be used in a breach of contract case to show the profits a business was making before the breach of contract compared with the reduced profits it made after the breach.

Line Graph A **line graph** plots the course of a value over time. In the line graph in Exhibit 3–14, each line represents a month's worth of expenses.

line graph
A graph that plots numerical values as a time line.

BUDGETED LAW OFFICE EXPENSES APRIL - MAY

Expense Item	April	May
Rent	4500	4500
Salaries	7500	8000
Insurance	2500	2500
Utilities	1000	2000
TOTALS	**15500**	**17000**

LAW OFFICE EXPENSES APRIL - MAY

EXHIBIT 3–14
Line graph

Because line graphs plot changes over time, they are useful for plotting trends. For example, in Exhibit 3–14, notice that the expense for utilities rose in the month of May.

pie chart
A chart that represents each value as a piece or percentage of a whole (a total "pie").

Pie Chart A **pie chart** represents each value as a piece or percentage of a total pie. In Exhibit 3–15, each expense item represents a slice of the pie, with the whole pie representing the total amount of expenses for the month of April. This chart shows that salaries are the biggest piece (or expense) of the pie (i.e., of the firm's total expenses). Pie charts are best used for showing the relative contributions of the various pieces that make up a whole.

stacked column graph
A graph that depicts values as separate sections in a single or stacked column.

Stacked Column Graph A **stacked column graph** compares data by placing columns on top of one another. Like a pie chart, a stacked column graph shows the relative contributions of various elements to a whole. The difference is that rather than showing only a single entity or a single pie, a stacked column can show several. In Exhibit 3–16, each column segment represents a month, and each stack of columns represents an expense item. The stacked column allows users to see the allocation of an expense item over two months.

SPREADSHEET PLANNING

Planning is critical to developing a spreadsheet that accomplishes its intended purpose. Most spreadsheets are more complex than the law-office expense spreadsheet used as an example in this chapter. Most people find it helpful to draft a model of a spreadsheet on paper before actually beginning to enter it in the computer. Some of the most complex aspects of creating a spreadsheet concern the use of formulas. Entering formulas can get complicated quickly, especially when a spreadsheet requires a lot of formulas. Take your time and plan the formulas out carefully.

This section discusses a few rules to keep in mind when planning and using a spreadsheet.

EXHIBIT 3–15
Pie chart graph

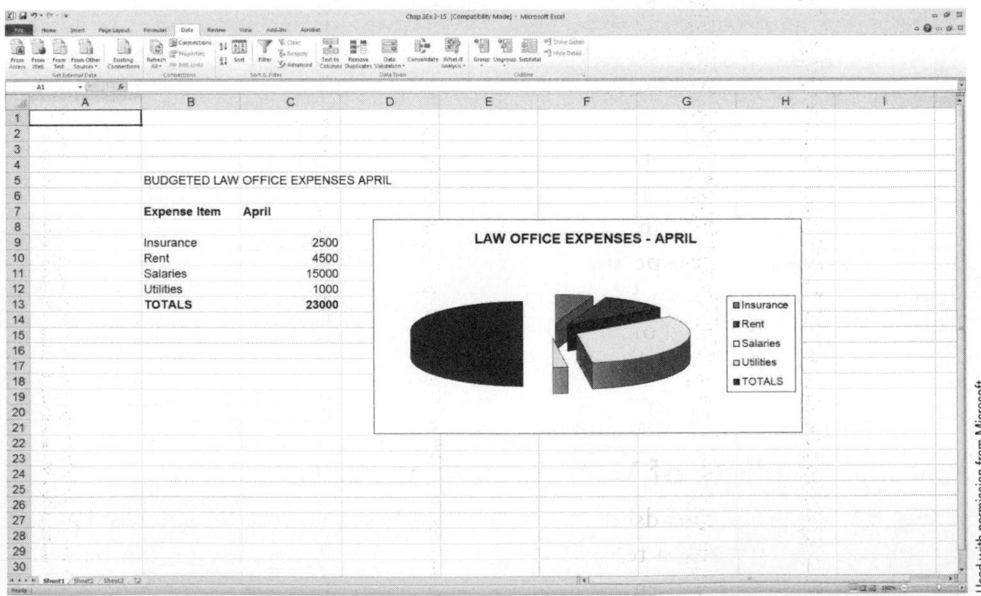

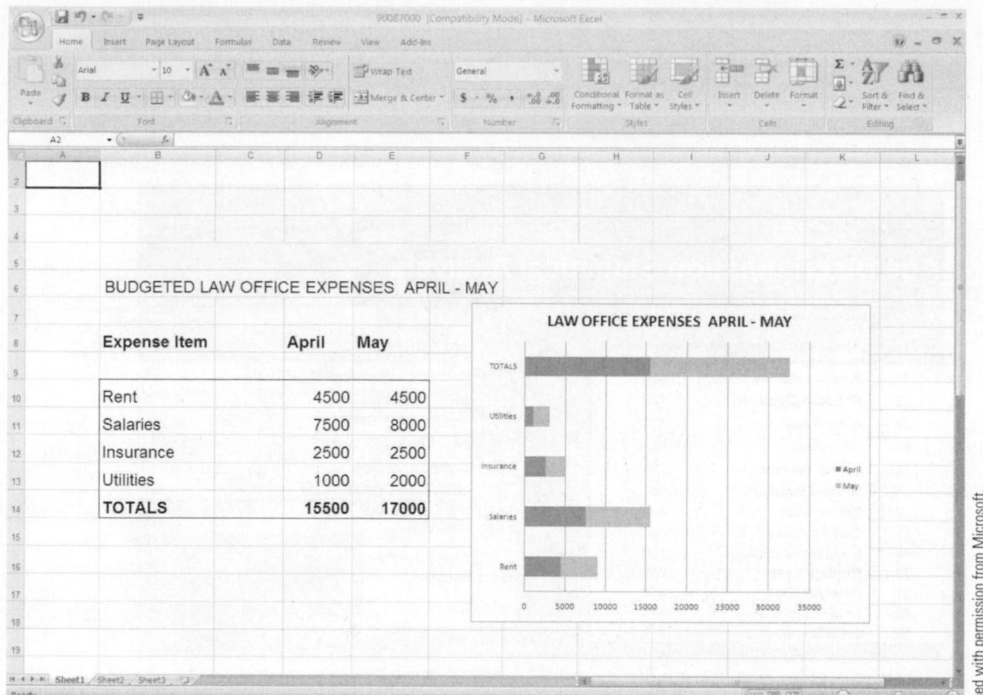

EXHIBIT 3–16
Stacked column graph

Keep Your Spreadsheet Simple

Keep your spreadsheet as simple as possible. Complex spreadsheets are more likely to have errors. In addition, other people may have to use the spreadsheet, and a simple design will keep you from having to spend hours training them to do so. It is also common for even the person who designed a spreadsheet to forget certain aspects of the spreadsheet if she has not worked with it for some time. Finally, use easy-to-understand headings and titles. Say what you mean, and mean what you say. It is confusing to read titles that do not make sense to everyone involved.

Always Document Your Spreadsheet

Always document your spreadsheet well, making notes and narrative statements right in the spreadsheet itself. Always include a section called "Notes" in your spreadsheet. It is common to make assumptions when designing a spreadsheet (such as when entering formulas) and then later forget why or how you made them. Another technique is to add a comment directly to a cell. In Excel and other spreadsheets, you can add explanatory text to a cell itself. The Comment tool is a great way to add specific information about a cell, including any assumptions or justifications you have made regarding the value or formula entered. Users can show or hide comments as they wish, depending on their needs at the time (see Exhibit 3–17). Creating a comment is covered in Lesson 7 of the Hands-On Exercises.

Make a Template of Your Spreadsheet

A template is a blank spreadsheet that has had labels and formulas entered, but has no values filled in. Once a template is made and saved, copies of it can be made and given to other users; then the only thing they will have to do is enter the values.

EXHIBIT 3–17
Adding a comment to a cell in Excel

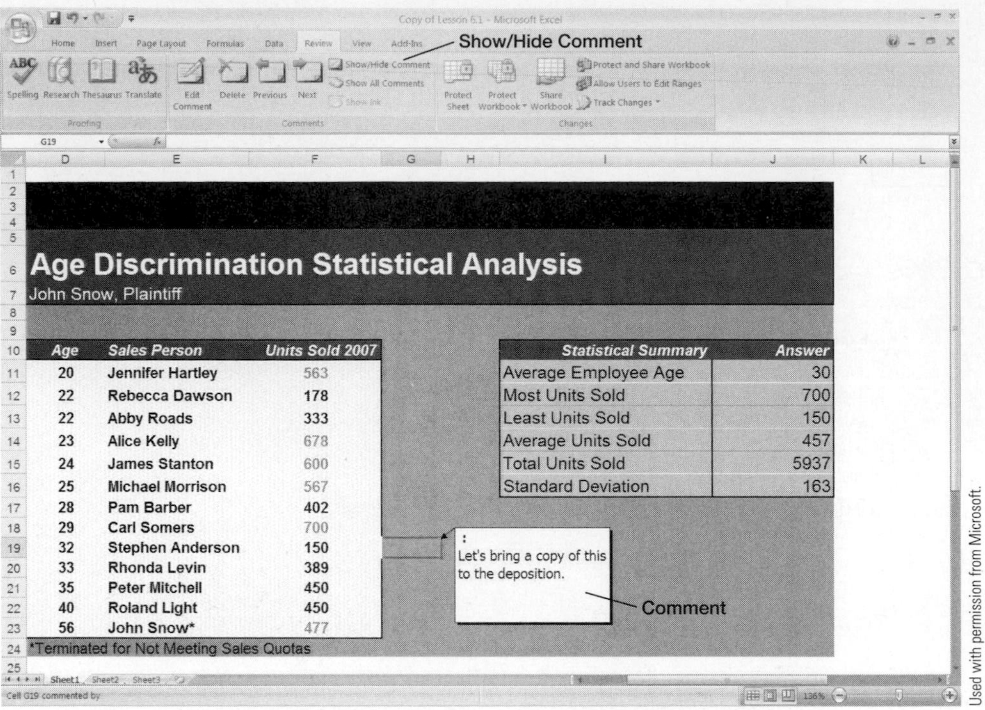

Some software companies also sell a variety of predefined templates. A template saves a user from having to rebuild the same spreadsheet over and over. Users can also access free templates online from software providers and other sources.

Leave Room in the Upper Left Corner

Do not start your spreadsheet in the far corner of the spreadsheet (e.g., at cell A1); always leave yourself some room to include additional labels and notes. Start your spreadsheet no closer to the upper left corner than cell C4. This gives you room to add notes, dates, and so forth later on.

Use Cell Widths Wisely

Cell widths should be used wisely. Some people make all their columns 20 characters wide; the problem with this is that they can then see and print only four columns at a time, which makes a spreadsheet difficult to work with. It is better to use narrow columns, which maximize the amount of information you can see and allow the spreadsheet to be printed on one page. For long labels, keep the column width the same size, but wrap the text down to the next line, using the wrap text feature found in most spreadsheets.

Be Careful Inserting Rows and Columns

If you must insert additional rows and columns after a spreadsheet has been designed and entered into the computer, be sure that the formulas you have already entered are adjusted to take the new additions into account. A celebrated lawsuit was filed against Lotus Development Corporation over this problem. A construction firm designed a spreadsheet to allow it to bid on jobs. Staff would enter job costs into the spreadsheet, and the spreadsheet would calculate what the bid on a job should be. Unfortunately, at some point, the spreadsheet user inserted additional rows, and the old formulas did not pick up, or add, the job costs in the new rows. Subsequently, the construction firm bid several hundred thousand dollars too low on a job. The firm sued Lotus, but Lotus won the suit because the user had used the program improperly. Be sure to go back and double-check your formulas!

Rigorously Test Your Spreadsheet

Rigorously test your spreadsheet to make sure it is functioning as intended. It is easy to make a mistake entering a formula, but it is often difficult to recognize and find mistakes. Always enter test data in the spreadsheet, and use a calculator to spot-check that the formulas have been entered properly and are making the calculations correctly. Most spreadsheets have an option that allows you to see the formulas entered instead of the calculations. This is a nice feature when you are checking the logic and formulas of your spreadsheet.

Audit Formulas

To access the Audit Formulas feature, point to the Formulas ribbon tab, then click on Show Formulas in the Formula Auditing group.

Occasionally Read the Spreadsheet Documentation

Most spreadsheet users employ only a fraction of the commands, operators, and function commands that are available in most spreadsheets. Although the commands covered in this book will get you started with spreadsheets, you will find that as you grow more proficient, many sophisticated features will help you solve tough problems. Take the time occasionally to read the Help features and other documentation for your spreadsheet program to learn more about its capacities and functionalities.

SPREADSHEETS IN THE LEGAL ENVIRONMENT

Numerical data are important in the outcome of many types of cases. Remember, if it involves money, it involves numbers. In some lawsuits, parties hire statisticians to research a matter in hopes that the final statistics or numerical data will support their case. Spreadsheets can be used to analyze statistical findings, look for trends, and so forth. Spreadsheet programs, like word processors and database management systems, are extremely flexible, so it is easy to use them to accomplish all types of tasks. Some common applications of spreadsheets in law offices include:

- Tax planning and tax returns
- Estate planning
- Calculations for bankruptcy actions
- Child support calculations
- Alimony payments
- Divorce asset distributions
- Truth-in-Lending statements for real estate transactions
- Amortization schedules
- Loan/payment calculations
- Calculations for collection actions regarding principal and interest due
- Present value and future value calculations regarding damages
- Lost wages and benefits calculations for worker's compensation claims

- Back wages and benefits regarding employment/discrimination actions
- Budgeting
- Accounting-related calculations

Damages Calculations

In many cases, the plaintiff (the person bringing the lawsuit) alleges that he is entitled to money damages—that is, that he should be compensated for whatever injury was sustained. The amount of damages a person should receive is always in dispute. A spreadsheet allows the law-office personnel to test different options or assumptions.

A Simple Damages Calculation Exhibit 3–18 is an example of an easy damages projection. Assume that you represent the plaintiff, John Jones, in an automobile accident case and you must prepare an exhibit for the jury to show the amount of damages the plaintiff is seeking. This spreadsheet simply lists the damage items, the amounts asked for, and a total (i.e., a formula using the SUM function).

A More Complex Damages Calculation (Net Present Value) Spreadsheets can handle complex damages calculations as well, as shown in Exhibit 3–19.

Assume that your firm represents Wendy Jones, who suffered a severe injury on the job and is bringing a worker's compensation claim. Jones is 59 years old and was going to retire at age 65. Assume that because she is now totally disabled, she is entitled to six years of income from her employer. She was making $35,000 a year before she was injured, and on average, she has received increases of about 2 percent every year. Therefore, in the first year following the accident, assume that Jones would have received $35,000, and in every year after that, she would have received a 2 percent increase. Exhibit 3–19 automatically calculates what her gross earnings would have been until retirement, for a total loss of wages of $220,784.23.

Unfortunately, Jones is not entitled to a lump-sum payment of $220,784.23. This is because Jones could take the lump-sum payment, invest it at 6 or 7 or 8 percent, and by the end of the six years have considerably more than she would have earned at her job. Thus, the future payments must be reduced to their present, or current, value.

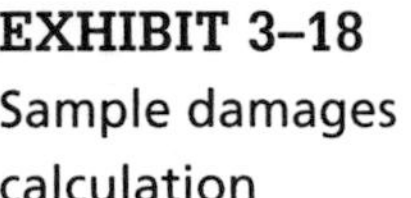

EXHIBIT 3–18
Sample damages calculation

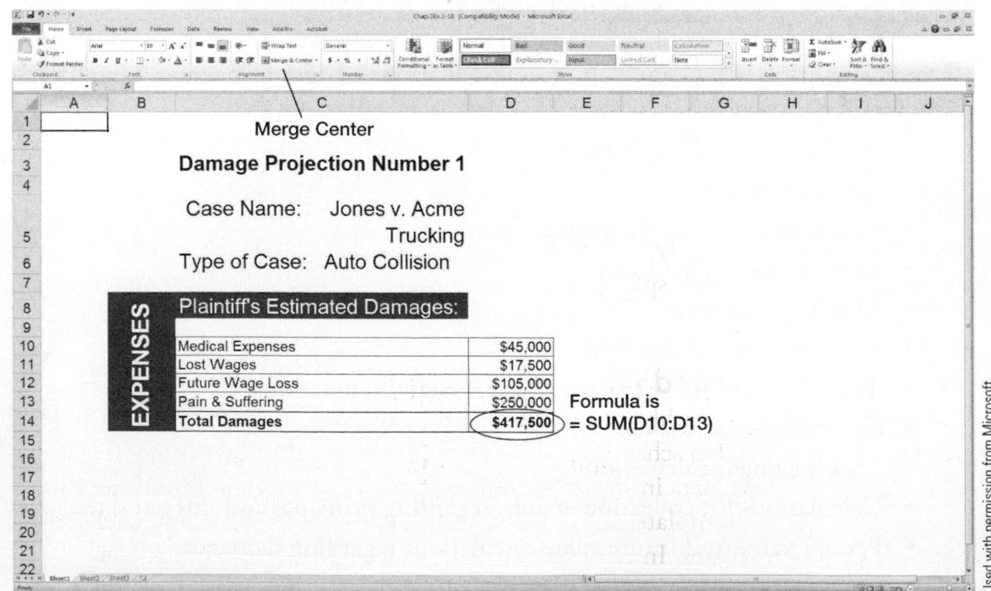

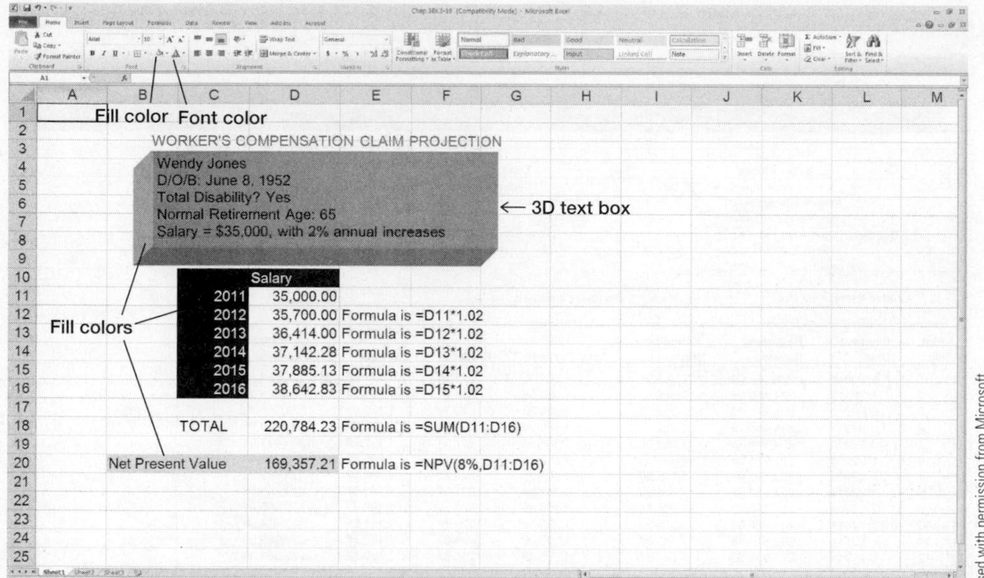

EXHIBIT 3–19
Complex damages calculation

Nearly all spreadsheets have a present value function that accomplishes this task easily. The spreadsheet in Exhibit 3–19 calculates that Jones should be awarded a lump-sum payment of $169,357.21 for future payments worth $220,784.23.

This type of calculation (reducing a payment schedule to a present value) is also useful when considering different settlement offers or options. Notice in Exhibit 3–19 that a number of graphic elements have been added to the spreadsheet. The spreadsheet includes a number of different fill (background) colors and textures, font sizes, styles, and colors. The spreadsheet also includes a text box that has been formatted in three dimensions (3-D). These are all standard features in Excel and other spreadsheets. Notice in Exhibit 3–18 that an oval has been added to the spreadsheet around the total and that the word “Expenses” appears vertically in the spreadsheet. All of these graphical features are extremely easy to use and can give spreadsheets added visual impact.

Legal Organization Budgeting

Many legal organizations prepare a yearly budget to track expenses and income. The budget is used as a planning tool and as a means of spotting potential problems.

Real Estate Law

Spreadsheets are particularly helpful for legal organizations that practice in the real estate field. An example of spreadsheet use in this field is to create an amortization schedule.

Monthly Payment and Amortization Schedules Spreadsheets can automatically calculate the monthly payment on a loan and produce an amortization schedule. The loan amortization schedule in Exhibit 3–20 is a template that comes free with Excel. Simply fill in the data in the Loan Information section and the spreadsheet does the rest. To access the template in Excel 2007, click on the Office button, click New, then click under Templates. In Excel 2010, click on the File tab, then click New, then click under Templates.

EXHIBIT 3–20
Loan amortization schedule

Ready to use Excel template

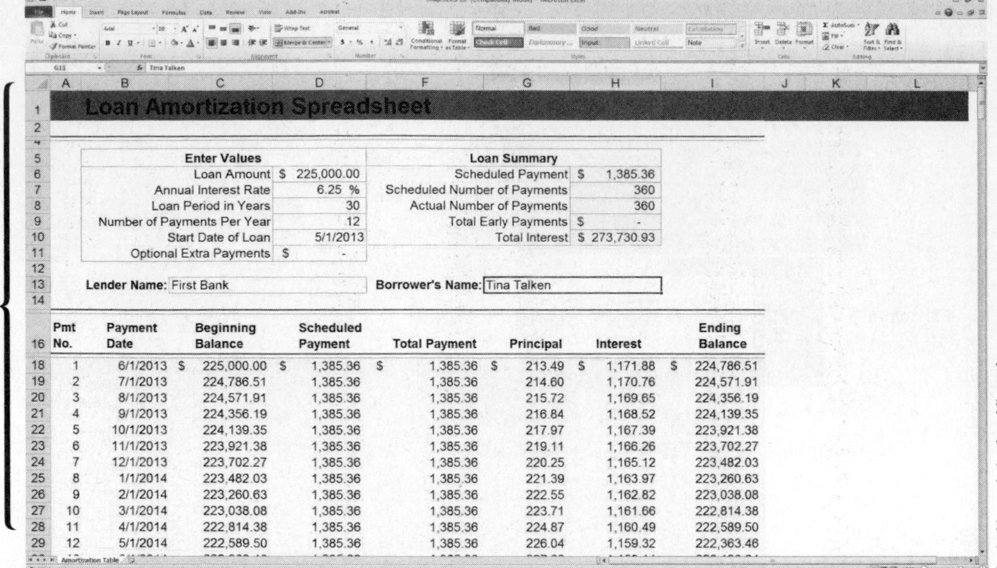

Loan Amortization Spreadsheet

Enter Values	
Loan Amount	$ 225,000.00
Annual Interest Rate	6.25 %
Loan Period in Years	30
Number of Payments Per Year	12
Start Date of Loan	5/1/2013
Optional Extra Payments	$ -

Loan Summary	
Scheduled Payment	$ 1,385.36
Scheduled Number of Payments	360
Actual Number of Payments	360
Total Early Payments	$ -
Total Interest	$ 273,730.93

Lender Name: First Bank **Borrower's Name:** Tina Talken

Pmt No.	Payment Date	Beginning Balance	Scheduled Payment	Total Payment	Principal	Interest	Ending Balance
1	6/1/2013	$ 225,000.00	$ 1,385.36	$ 1,385.36	$ 213.49	$ 1,171.88	$ 224,786.51
2	7/1/2013	224,786.51	1,385.36	1,385.36	214.60	1,170.76	224,571.91
3	8/1/2013	224,571.91	1,385.36	1,385.36	215.72	1,169.65	224,356.19
4	9/1/2013	224,356.19	1,385.36	1,385.36	216.84	1,168.52	224,139.35
5	10/1/2013	224,139.35	1,385.36	1,385.36	217.97	1,167.39	223,921.38
6	11/1/2013	223,921.38	1,385.36	1,385.36	219.11	1,166.26	223,702.27
7	12/1/2013	223,702.27	1,385.36	1,385.36	220.25	1,165.12	223,482.03
8	1/1/2014	223,482.03	1,385.36	1,385.36	221.39	1,163.97	223,260.63
9	2/1/2014	223,260.63	1,385.36	1,385.36	222.55	1,162.82	223,038.08
10	3/1/2014	223,038.08	1,385.36	1,385.36	223.71	1,161.66	222,814.38
11	4/1/2014	222,814.38	1,385.36	1,385.36	224.87	1,160.49	222,589.50
12	5/1/2014	222,589.50	1,385.36	1,385.36	226.04	1,159.32	222,363.46

Family Law Cases

Spreadsheets are commonly used to help divide assets in a divorce. When a marriage is dissolved, it is the duty of the court to try to fairly distribute or divide the assets the parties have amassed during the marriage so that neither party gets more than her or his fair share. Spreadsheets are also used to calculate a party's child support obligations. A spreadsheet enables the user to lay out different division-of-asset scenarios or options for consideration. Spreadsheets can also produce lists of assets, family budgets, balance sheets, and income comparisons (such as between husband and wife). These documents are routinely prepared in many divorce cases.

Statistical Analysis

Spreadsheets can also be used to analyze statistics. Most spreadsheets have statistical functions that can help a user analyze a group of values. Suppose your firm represents the plaintiff John Snow, a salesman, in an age-discrimination suit against his former employer. The defendant company states that Snow was terminated because he did not sell enough units of its product. Snow must convince a judge that he was really terminated because the company wanted a younger workforce.

Exhibit 3–21 shows the names and ages of the company's salespersons and the units of product they sold. Looking at the statistical analysis part of the exhibit, notice that the average age of salespersons is 30 (far below Snow's age of 56—it appears that the company may be trying to hire young salespersons). This was arrived at by using the average function (AVG), which automatically totals the values in a range and divides by the number of values.

Now, look at the Most Units Sold cell. The spreadsheet automatically placed the highest value here, using the MAX function. Notice also that the minimum number of units was placed in the Least Units Sold cell, using the MIN function. Also, look at the Average Units Sold cell, which was calculated automatically using the AVG function. (Snow was 20 units above the average units sold—it certainly seems he can make a strong argument for his case.)

Finally, the standard deviation of the values (i.e., the standard deviation from the average of each value) is high, showing that the data vary widely. The formula for calculating standard deviations is not simple, but a spreadsheet user can find it

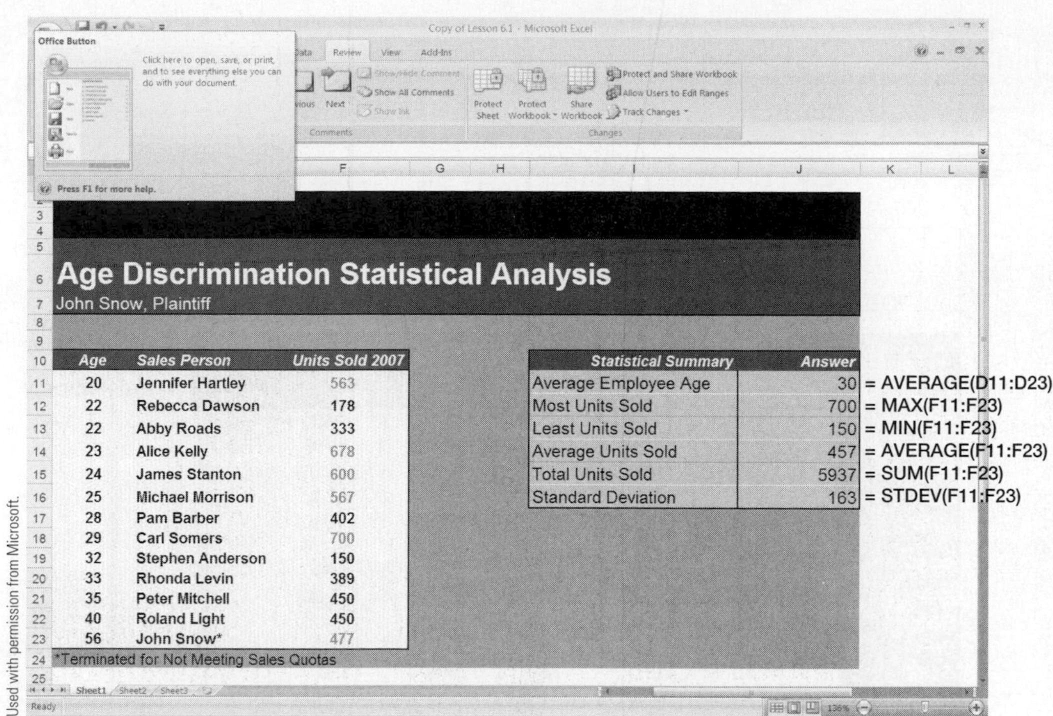

Age Discrimination Statistical Analysis

John Snow, Plaintiff

Age	Sales Person	Units Sold 2007
20	Jennifer Hartley	563
22	Rebecca Dawson	178
22	Abby Roads	333
23	Alice Kelly	678
24	James Stanton	600
25	Michael Morrison	567
28	Pam Barber	402
29	Carl Somers	700
32	Stephen Anderson	150
33	Rhonda Levin	389
35	Peter Mitchell	450
40	Roland Light	450
56	John Snow*	477

*Terminated for Not Meeting Sales Quotas

Statistical Summary	Answer	
Average Employee Age	30	= AVERAGE(D11:D23)
Most Units Sold	700	= MAX(F11:F23)
Least Units Sold	150	= MIN(F11:F23)
Average Units Sold	457	= AVERAGE(F11:F23)
Total Units Sold	5937	= SUM(F11:F23)
Standard Deviation	163	= STDEV(F11:F23)

EXHIBIT 3–21
Using statistical functions in spreadsheets

by issuing a function command and marking the range. This is an example of how spreadsheets can turn hard tasks into easy ones.

Importing Spreadsheets into Other Programs

Sometimes it is necessary to include numerical information in a word-processing document. For example, you might want to incorporate part of a spreadsheet or a graph into a brief or pleading. In most cases, it is simple to paste a spreadsheet or graph into a word-processing document.

Tracking Investments for Trusts and Estates

Sometimes attorneys or law firms act as trustees or fiduciaries for trusts and estates. Part of this responsibility often involves investing money on behalf of a trust or an estate. Such fiduciaries have a duty not to waste or neglect the trust or estate and to make reasonable investments.

Exhibit 3–22 is an example of a spreadsheet that tracks the progress of stock market investments. By tracking the current prices of the stocks, the firm can get an idea of how the investments are doing and whether it should sell them and buy something else. Notice the use of formulas in Exhibit 3–22. The market value formulas take the number of shares purchased times the current price of the stock. The dollar gain formulas subtract the total purchase price (the number of shares times the purchase price) from the market value. Finally, the percentage gain formulas arrive at results by dividing the dollar gain by the total purchase price.

ETHICAL CONSIDERATIONS

The primary ethical considerations regarding spreadsheets are accuracy and competence.

It is absolutely critical that the spreadsheets the paralegal produces be 100 percent accurate and well tested. If formulas do not correctly manipulate all the data they are supposed to, if formulas have wrong numbers in them, if data are not updated, or if

EXHIBIT 3–22
Using a spreadsheet to track investments for an estate

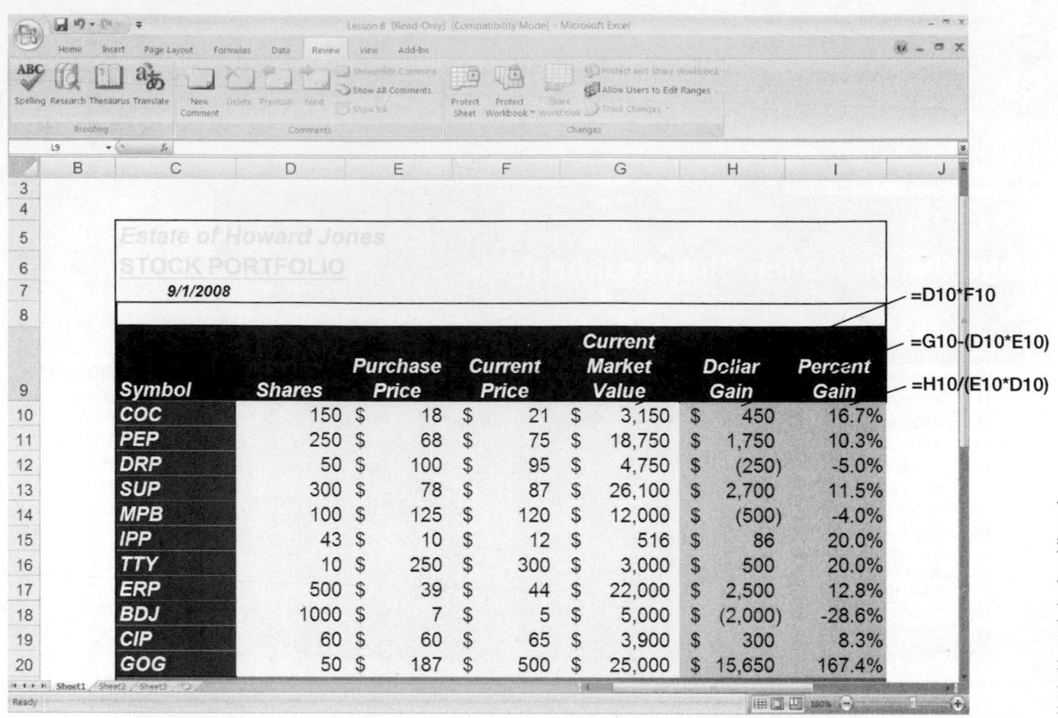

Symbol	Shares	Purchase Price	Current Price	Current Market Value	Dollar Gain	Percent Gain
COC	150	$ 18	$ 21	$ 3,150	$ 450	16.7%
PEP	250	$ 68	$ 75	$ 18,750	$ 1,750	10.3%
DRP	50	$ 100	$ 95	$ 4,750	$ (250)	-5.0%
SUP	300	$ 78	$ 87	$ 26,100	$ 2,700	11.5%
MPB	100	$ 125	$ 120	$ 12,000	$ (500)	-4.0%
IPP	43	$ 10	$ 12	$ 516	$ 86	20.0%
TTY	10	$ 250	$ 300	$ 3,000	$ 500	20.0%
ERP	500	$ 39	$ 44	$ 22,000	$ 2,500	12.8%
BDJ	1000	$ 7	$ 5	$ 5,000	$ (2,000)	-28.6%
CIP	60	$ 60	$ 65	$ 3,900	$ 300	8.3%
GOG	50	$ 187	$ 500	$ 25,000	$ 15,650	167.4%

there are any other errors in the spreadsheet, disaster will occur. Unfortunately, often when paralegals work with spreadsheets they are not just working with raw numbers, mathematics, and research—they are working with spreadsheets that relate to actual money and financial projections that have a dollar impact. Thus, errors in a spreadsheet typically have a negative financial impact as well.

These issues are not as much ethical matters (although this is a problem) as they are a malpractice risk. Most spreadsheet users fail to understand the likelihood of spreadsheet errors or the absolute importance of careful quality control of every spreadsheet, no matter how small.

How prevalent are errors in spreadsheets? A number of studies have shown that spreadsheet errors are relatively high. Cell error rates are typically around 5 percent. Thus, for every 20 cells you create, on average, you will have one error. As the total number of cells in a spreadsheet rises, so does the propensity for errors. One auditing firm found that 90 percent of all spreadsheets they reviewed that had 150 or more cells had one or more errors. In many cases the errors were serious. Every study that has been conducted on spreadsheet errors has found them at rates that would be unacceptable in most organizations.

So, what can paralegals do to minimize the potential for errors? They can:

- Double-check all numbers that are entered into a spreadsheet for accuracy.
- Triple-check every single formula in a spreadsheet, including using the Formula Auditing mode to print out all formulas.
- Make comments in specific cells regarding assumptions.
- Create a notes section at the bottom or top of the spreadsheet containing assumptions or other data the reader should be aware of.
- Be extremely careful when adding rows or columns to a spreadsheet in which formulas already exist. Double-check each inserted row or column to make sure it appears in the applicable formulas.
- Have someone else carefully review each spreadsheet, including formulas.

- Before using a new function, completely understand exactly what it does and ensure that it is working 100 percent correctly.
- Use a calculator to spot-check spreadsheets to make sure the formulas are accurate.
- Use the Protect feature to protect cells, particularly formulas, from being changed accidentally (see the following subsections).

If working with a spreadsheet is outside of your knowledge base or comfort zone, ask your supervising attorney to get an expert, such as an accountant or financial analyst, to prepare and/or review the calculations. In the end, it is far cheaper to do this than to discover an error later.

Password Protection

Passwords are an easy way to increase the security of your documents. Password-protecting spreadsheets is easy to do and should always be done if the spreadsheet is going outside of the firm. In Excel 2007, the command sequence is Office button > Save > Tools > General Options > Password to Open. In Excel 2010, the command sequence is File tab > Save > Tools > General Options > Password to Open.

Protecting Cells and Spreadsheets

Protection is a useful security tool for spreadsheet use. When multiple people work with a spreadsheet, it is common for formulas and other data to be accidentally deleted or changed by users. If a formula, for example, is deleted and the recipient tries to correct the problem by writing a new formula, but makes an error, a large problem has been created that could go a long time without being noticed. One way to solve this problem is to use the Protect Cells feature found in most spreadsheets.

In Excel, for example, to protect all or part of a spreadsheet, you must turn on the protection feature. Protection can be turned on from the Review ribbon tab by checking Protect Sheet in the Changes group. *Note:* Cells can be protected against accidental deletion simply by turning on the Protect command (which a user can turn off at a later time) or can be password-protected, in which case protection cannot be turned off unless the user has the password. For example, suppose the creator of a spreadsheet wants to protect certain formulas in an Excel spreadsheet from being accidentally typed over. The spreadsheet creator does not want users to have to type a password if they want to edit the spreadsheet; the creator just wants to protect the formulas from accidental deletion. The spreadsheet creator would use Protect Sheet and leave the password blank. The creator would mark all of the cells that were not locked, using the command right-click, Format Cells > Protection. If a user then wanted to change a formula, he or she could not; instead, the user would get an error message stating that the cell is protected. However, all that user would have to do would be to click Tools > Protection > Unprotect Sheet to turn off the protection feature. The user would then be able to edit the formula. If the spreadsheet creator did not want the user to be able to do this, the creator could use the password feature to lock the spreadsheet cells he or she wanted to keep from being edited.

SUMMARY

Spreadsheet software calculates and manipulates data using labels and formulas. Spreadsheets use rows and columns, which look similar to those on an accountant's paper worksheet. A row is an area that extends across a page horizontally; a column is an area that extends down a page vertically. A cell is an intersection between a row and a column. The cursor, or cell pointer, in a spreadsheet indicates what cell is currently selected.

Three types of data can be entered into a spreadsheet: text, values, and formulas. Text is descriptive data, such as headings and titles, that are entered into a cell; text cannot be used in making calculations. Values are numbers that are entered into a cell and can be used in making calculations. Formulas perform calculations using the values in other cells. Arithmetic operations and function commands are used in constructing formulas; they instruct a spreadsheet how to make the desired calculations.

Copying data places information from one part of a spreadsheet into another part while leaving the original intact. When copying formulas, an absolute cell reference does not change to reflect the new location of the cell pointer. A relative cell reference will automatically change to reflect the new location of the cell pointer.

Most spreadsheets provide a variety of graphing capabilities. A bar graph consists of a sequence of bars that illustrate numerical values. A line graph plots the course of a value over time. A pie chart represents each value as a piece or percentage of a total "pie." A stacked bar graph compares data by placing bars on top of one another.

Paralegals can use spreadsheets to perform and track a huge variety of information, including damages calculations, budget plans and problems, and tax plans and tax return calculations.

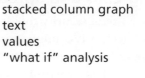

KEY TERMS

absolute cell reference
arithmetic operators
bar/column graph
cell
cell address
cell pointer
cell width
column
formulas
function command
landscape
line graph
pie chart
portrait
relative cell reference
row
spreadsheet
spreadsheet software
stacked column graph
text
values
"what if" analysis

INTERNET SITES

Internet sites for this chapter include:

ORGANIZATION	PRODUCT/SERVICE	INTERNET ADDRESS
Microsoft	Microsoft Excel spreadsheet program	www.microsoft.com
Microsoft	Home page for Microsoft, containing a wealth of information, tips, and tricks	www.microsoft.com/excel
Corel Corporation	Quattro Pro spreadsheet	www.corel.com
About.com	General site about spreadsheets, with information and tips	www.spreadsheets.about.com

TEST YOUR KNOWLEDGE

1. An area on a spreadsheet that extends vertically up and down the page is called a __________.
2. An area on a spreadsheet that extends horizontally across a page is called a __________.
3. True or False: An intersection between a row and a column in a spreadsheet is called a *location.*
4. Descriptive data entered in a spreadsheet, such as titles and headings, are called __________.
5. Numbers entered in a spreadsheet are called __________.
6. Expressions used in a spreadsheet program to automatically perform calculations are called __________.

7. True or False: The plus sign, minus sign, multiplication sign, and division sign are examples of function commands.
8. Write two formulas for adding the following cells: A1, A2, and A3.
9. "=SUM," "AVERAGE," and "MAX" are examples of what kind of formulas?
10. Name two kinds of cell references.
11. Name three things that should be kept in mind when planning a spreadsheet.
12. True or False: It is difficult to make errors in spreadsheets because the built-in templates, formulas, and function commands are automatic.
13. One way to keep formulas and cells from being accidentally deleted is to use which command?

ON THE WEB EXERCISES

1. Using the "Internet Sites" listed in this chapter and a general Internet search engine (such as www.google.com or www.yahoo.com), research the issue of errors in spreadsheets. Write a two-page paper on your findings.
2. Go to www.microsoft.com/excel and, under the "Templates" section, view 10 of the many ready-to-use templates for Excel.
3. Research legal-related Excel templates, including tax, real estate, child support, financial planning, estate planning, and related subjects. Write a two-page paper summarizing the types of free and fee-based sites and templates you found.

QUESTIONS AND EXERCISES

1. Using a spreadsheet, track the daily price of any four stocks in which you have an interest for one week. Show the daily beginning stock price, ending stock price, and difference. Calculate the stock's total per-share movement for the week and calculate the stock's average price per share for the week.
2. Using a spreadsheet program, prepare an expense budget for a mythical start-up law firm for one year. Assume that the law firm will have four attorneys (two of whom are partners and two of whom are associates), two paralegals, and two secretaries. Be sure to include leased space, office equipment (computers, copiers, printers, phones, etc.), office supplies, utilities, and miscellaneous expenses.
3. Using a spreadsheet program, summarize the amount of time you spend attending class and studying for your classes for a week. Assume that you will be paid for the time spent studying or attending classes, but that you must present a detailed bill of your activities. The bill must be professional in appearance and be accurately calculated. Assume that you will be paid $60 an hour.
4. Using a spreadsheet program, enter the names, complete addresses, and telephone numbers of 20 relatives and/or friends. The list must be professional in appearance and sorted alphabetically by last name.
5. You have requested a new computer from your law firm in next year's budget. Your managing attorney has asked you to provide a detailed, itemized list of the equipment and the price for each component of the system. Your managing attorney is very frugal, so include a one-page memorandum (with the itemized listing) summarizing why the system you have selected is appropriate.

ETHICS QUESTION

You work in a state that requires use of a spreadsheet in the calculation of child support payments. The attorney you work for does not know how to use a spreadsheet. If the attorney is to take on the representation of a parent in a contested divorce case, what ethical issue(s) may arise?

HANDS-ON EXERCISES

FEATURED SOFTWARE
Microsoft Excel 2013
Microsoft Excel 2010
Microsoft Excel 2007

SPREADSHEET SOFTWARE HANDS-ON EXERCISES

READ THIS FIRST!

1. Microsoft Excel 2013
2. Microsoft Excel 2010
3. Microsoft Excel 2007

I. DETERMINING WHICH TUTORIAL TO COMPLETE

To use the Spreadsheet Hands-On Exercises, you must already own or have access to Microsoft Excel 2013, Excel 2010, or Excel 2007. If you have one of these programs but do not know which version you are using, it is easy to find out. For Excel 2007, click the Office button, and click Excel Options > Resources; it will tell you what version you are using. For Excel 2010, click the File tab, and click Excel Options > Help; it will tell you what version you are using. For Excel 2013, click the File tab, then click Account. You must know the version of the program you are using and select the correct tutorial version or the tutorials will not work correctly.

II. USING THE SPREADSHEET HANDS-ON EXERCISES

The Spreadsheet Hands-On Exercises in this section are easy to use and contain step-by-step instructions. They start with basic spreadsheet skills and proceed to intermediate and advanced levels. If you already have a good working knowledge of Excel, you may be able to proceed directly to the intermediate and advanced exercises. To truly be ready for using spreadsheets in the legal environment, you must be able to accomplish the tasks and exercises in the advanced exercises.

III. ACCESSING THE DATA FILES THAT COME WITH THE TEXT

Some of the intermediate and advanced Excel Hands-On Exercises use documents on the Premium Website. To access them, go to your CengageBrain account and click on the link for Premium Website for Cornick's *Using Computers in the Law Office*, 7th edition. A new window will open. Under Book Level Resources, click on Data Files: Excel tab, then under Excel 2013, click the link to the desired lesson. When prompted, click Open.

HANDS-ON EXERCISES

MICROSOFT EXCEL 2013 FOR WINDOWS

Number	Lesson Title	Concepts Covered
BASIC LESSONS		
Lesson 1	Building a Budget Spreadsheet—Part 1	[CTRL]+[HOME] command, moving the pointer, entering text and values, adjusting the width of columns, changing the format of a group of cells to currency, using bold, centering text, entering formulas, using the AutoFill/Copy command to copy formulas, and printing and saving a spreadsheet
Lesson 2	Building a Budget Spreadsheet—Part 2	Opening a file, inserting rows, changing the format of cells to percent, building more formulas, creating a bar chart with the Chart Wizard, printing a selection, and fitting/compressing data to one printed page
Lesson 3	Building a Damage Projection Spreadsheet	Changing font size, font color, and fill color; using the AutoSum feature; using the wrap text feature; creating borders; and setting decimal points when formatting numbers
INTERMEDIATE LESSONS		
Lesson 4	Child Support Payment Spreadsheet	Creating a white background, creating formulas that multiply cells, creating formulas that use absolute cell references, and using the AutoFormat feature
Lesson 5	Loan Amortization Template	Using a template, protecting cells, freezing panes, splitting a screen, hiding columns, and using Format Painter
Lesson 6	Statistical Functions	Using functions including average, maximum, minimum, and standard deviation; sorting data; checking for metadata; using the format clear command; using conditional formatting; and inserting a picture
ADVANCED LESSONS		
Lesson 7	Tools and Techniques 1—Marketing Budget	Creating and manipulating a text box, advanced shading techniques, working with a 3-D style text box, creating vertical and diagonal text, creating a cell comment, and using lines and borders
Lesson 8	Tools and Techniques 2—Stock Portfolio	Using the Merge and Center tool, using the Formula Auditing feature, using the oval tool, and password-protecting a file

GETTING STARTED

Overview

Microsoft Excel 2013 is a powerful spreadsheet program that allows you to create formulas, "what if" scenarios, graphs, and much more.

Introduction

Throughout these lessons and exercises, information you need to operate the program will be designated in several different ways:

- Keys to be pressed on the keyboard are designated in brackets, in all caps, and in bold (e.g., press the **[ENTER]** key).
- Movements with the mouse pointer are designated in bold and italics (e.g., ***point to File and click***).

- Words or letters that should be typed are designated in bold (e.g., type **Training Program**).
- Information that is or should be displayed on your computer screen is shown in bold, with quotation marks (e.g., **"Press ENTER to continue."**).
- Specific menu items and commands are designated with an initial capital letter (e.g., click Open).

OVERVIEW OF EXCEL 2013

I. Worksheet

A. *Entering Commands: The Ribbon*—The primary way of entering commands in Excel 2013 is through the ribbon. The ribbon is a set of commands or tools that change depending on which ribbon is selected (see Excel 2013 Exhibit 1). There are seven ribbon tabs: Home, Insert, Page Layout, Formulas, Data, Review, and View (see Excel 2013 Exhibit 1). Each tab has groups of commands. For example, on the Home tab, the Font group contains a group of commands that govern font choice, font size, bold, italics, underlining, and other attributes (see Excel 2013 Exhibit 1).

EXCEL 2013 EXHIBIT 1
Excel 2013 interface

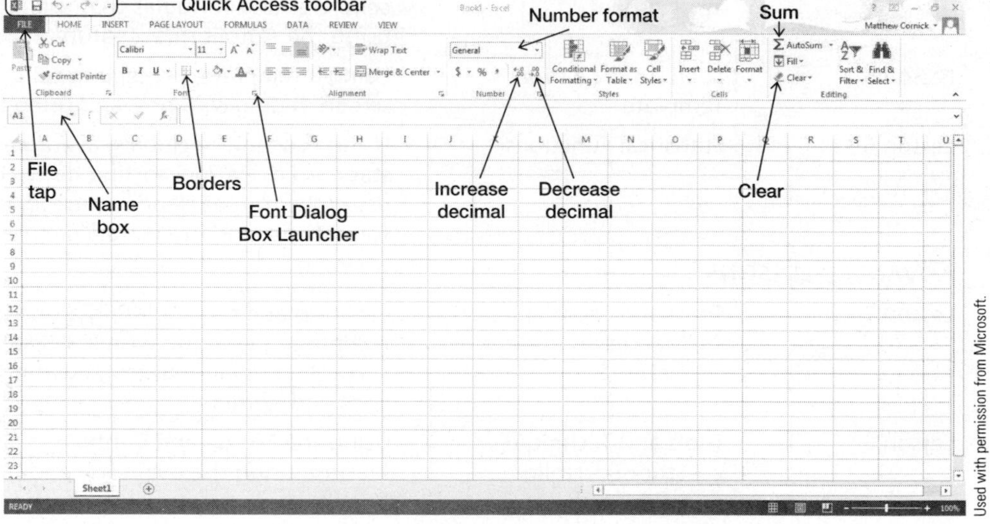

Used with permission from Microsoft.

B. *File tab*—The File tab (see Excel 2013 Exhibit 1) is where a user accesses commands such as New, Open, Save, and Print. The File tab replaces the Office button used in Excel 2007.

C. *Entering Data*—To enter data, type the text or number in a cell, and press the **[ENTER]** key or one of the arrow (cursor) keys.

D. *Ranges*—A *range* is a group of contiguous cells. Cell ranges can be created by ***clicking and dragging the pointer*** or holding down the **[SHIFT]** key and using the arrow (cursor) keys.

E. *Format*—Cells can be formatted, including changing the font style, font size, shading, border, cell type (currency, percentage, etc.), alignment, and other attributes by ***clicking the Home ribbon tab, and then clicking one of the dialog box launchers in the Font group, Alignment group, or Number group.*** Each of these dialog box launchers brings up the same "Format Cells" window. You can also enter a number of formatting options directly from the Home tab.

F. *Editing a Cell*—You can edit a cell by ***clicking in the cell and then clicking in the formula bar.*** The formula bar is directly under the ribbon and just to the right of the fx sign (see Excel 2013 Exhibit 1). The formula bar shows the current contents of the selected cell, and it allows you to edit the cell contents. You can also edit the contents of a cell by ***clicking in the cell*** and then pressing the **[F2]** key.

G. *Column Width/Row Height*—You can change the width of a column by ***clicking the line to the right of the column heading.*** (This is the line that separates two columns. When you point to a line, the cursor changes to double-headed vertical arrows.) ***Next, drag the pointer to the right or to the left to increase or decrease the column width, respectively.*** Similarly, you can change the height of a row ***clicking and dragging the horizontal line separating two rows.*** You can also change the width of a column or height of a row by ***clicking somewhere in the column you want to change, clicking the Home tab, and then clicking Format in the Cells group.***

H. *Insert*—You can insert one row or column by ***clicking the Home tab, then clicking the down arrow below the Insert icon in the Cells group, and clicking either Insert Sheet Rows or Insert Sheet Columns.*** You can also insert a number of rows or columns by ***dragging the pointer over the number of rows or columns you want to add, clicking the Home tab, clicking the down arrow below the Insert icon in the Cells group, and then clicking either Insert Sheet Rows or Insert Sheet Columns.*** Finally, you can ***right-click and select Insert from the menu.***

I. *Erase/Delete*—You can erase data by ***dragging the pointer over the area*** and then pressing the **[DEL]** key. You can also erase data by ***dragging the pointer over the area, clicking the Home ribbon tab, clicking the down arrow next to the Clear icon in the Editing group, and then clicking Clear All.*** You can delete whole columns or rows by ***pointing and clicking in a column or row, then clicking on the Home ribbon tab, clicking on the down arrow next to Delete in the Cells group, and then clicking either Delete Sheet Rows or Delete Sheet Columns.*** You can also delete whole columns or rows by ***pointing in the column or row and then right-clicking and selecting Delete.***

J. *Quit*—To quit Excel, ***click on the File tab and then click Close.***

K. *Copy*—To copy data to adjacent columns or rows, ***click in the cell you wish to copy and then select the AutoFill command,*** which is accessed from the small black box at the bottom right corner of the selected cell. Then, ***drag the pointer to where the data should be placed.*** You can also copy data by ***clicking in the cell, right-clicking, clicking Copy, clicking in the location where the information should be copied,*** and pressing the **[ENTER]** key. Finally, data can be copied by ***clicking and dragging to highlight the information to be copied, clicking the Home tab, and then clicking Copy in the Clipboard group.*** Then go to the location where the information should be copied, ***click the Home tab, and click Paste in the Clipboard group.***

L. *Move*—Move data by ***clicking in the cell, right-clicking, selecting Cut, clicking in the location where the information should be inserted,*** and pressing the **[ENTER]** key. Data can also be moved by ***highlighting the information to be copied, clicking the Home tab, and then clicking Cut in the Clipboard group.*** Then go to the location where the information should be moved, ***click the Home tab, and click Paste in the Clipboard group.***

M. *Saving and Opening Files*—Save a file by ***clicking the File tab, then clicking Save or Save As,*** and typing the file name. You can also save a file by ***clicking***

the Save icon (it looks like a floppy disk) on the Quick Access toolbar (see Excel 2013 Exhibit 1). Open a file that was previously saved by ***clicking the File tab, clicking Open,*** and typing (or clicking) the name of the file to be opened.

N. *Print*—To print a file, ***click the File tab, then click Print, and then click Print.***

II. Numbers and Formulas

A. *Numbers*—To enter a number in a cell, ***click in the cell,*** type the number, and press the **[ENTER]** key or an arrow (cursor) key.

B. *Adding Cells (Addition)*—You can add the contents of two or more cells by three different methods:

1. To add the contents of a range of two or more cells:

a. ***Click in the cell where the total should be placed.***

b. ***Click the Home tab, then click the Sum icon in the Editing group*** (see Excel 2013 Exhibit 2). The Sum icon looks like the Greek letter "E." *Note:* To see the name of an icon, point to the icon for a second and the name of the icon will be displayed.

EXCEL 2013 EXHIBIT 2
Budgeting spreadsheet

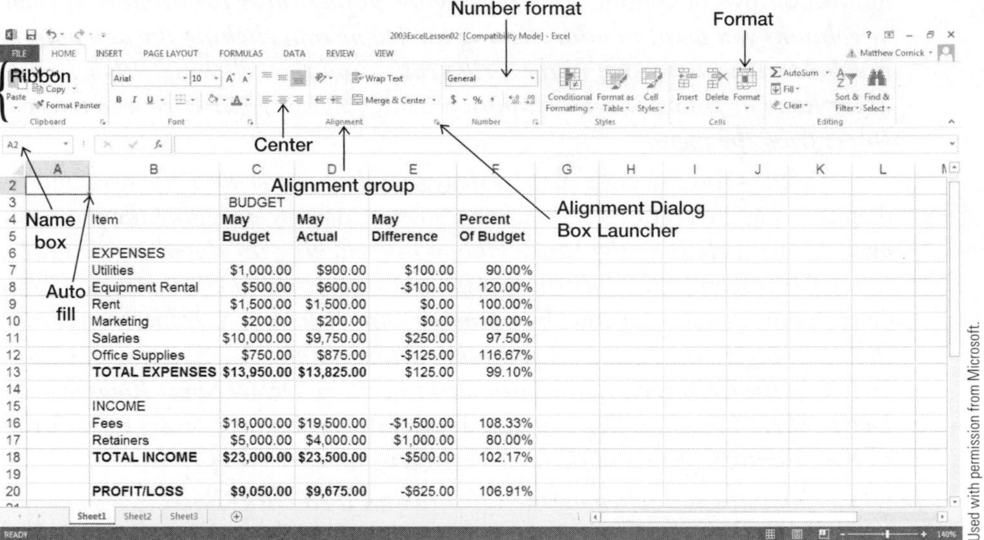

		BUDGET			
Item	May Budget	May Actual	May Difference	Percent Of Budget
EXPENSES				
Utilities	$1,000.00	$900.00	$100.00	90.00%
Equipment Rental	$500.00	$600.00	-$100.00	120.00%
Rent	$1,500.00	$1,500.00	$0.00	100.00%
Marketing	$200.00	$200.00	$0.00	100.00%
Salaries	$10,000.00	$9,750.00	$250.00	97.50%
Office Supplies	$750.00	$875.00	-$125.00	116.67%
TOTAL EXPENSES	$13,950.00	$13,825.00	$125.00	99.10%
INCOME				
Fees	$18,000.00	$19,500.00	-$1,500.00	108.33%
Retainers	$5,000.00	$4,000.00	$1,000.00	80.00%
TOTAL INCOME	$23,000.00	$23,500.00	-$500.00	102.17%
PROFIT/LOSS	$9,050.00	$9,675.00	-$625.00	106.91%

c. Excel guesses which cells you want to add. Press **[ENTER]** if the correct range is automatically selected, or select the correct range by highlighting it (i.e., ***clicking and dragging until the range of cells to be added is selected***). Then, press the **[ENTER]** key.

2. To add the contents of two cells, which need not comprise a range:

a. ***Click in the cell where the total should be placed.***

b. ***Press*** = (the equals sign).

c. Type the address of the first cell to be added (e.g., B4), or ***click in that cell.***

d. ***Press*** + (the plus sign).

e. Enter the address of the second cell to be added (or ***click in it***).

f. ***Press*** the **[ENTER]** key. (For example, to add the values of cells C4 and C5, you would type **=C4+C5**.)

3. To add the contents of a range of two or more cells:

a. ***Click in the cell where the total should be placed.***

b. Type **=SUM(**.

c. Enter the address of the first cell to be added (or ***click in it***).
d. Press **:** (a colon).
e. Enter the address of the second cell to be added (or ***click in it***).
f. Press **)** (a closing parenthesis).
g. Press the **[ENTER]** key. (For example, to add the values of C4 and C5, the formula would read **"=SUM(C4:C5)."**)

C. *Subtracting Cells*—To subtract the contents of one or more cells from those of another:

1. ***Click in the cell where the result should be placed.***
2. Press **=**.
3. Enter the first cell address (or ***click in it***).
4. Press **–** (the minus sign).
5. Enter the second cell address (or ***click in it***).
6. Press the **[ENTER]** key. (For example, to subtract the value of C4 from the value of C5, you would type **=C5–C4**.)

D. *Multiplying Cells*—To multiply the contents of two (or more) cells:

1. ***Click in the cell where the result should be placed.***
2. Press **=**.
3. Enter the first cell address (or ***click in it***).
4. Press * (**[SHIFT]**+**[8]**).
5. Enter the second cell address (or ***click in it***).
6. Press the **[ENTER]** key. (For example, to multiply the value in C4 times the value in C5, you would type **=C5*C4**.)

E. *Dividing Cells*—To divide the contents of two (or more) cells:

1. ***Click in the cell where the result should be placed.***
2. Press **=**.
3. Enter the first cell address (or ***click in it***).
4. Press **/** (the forward slash).
5. Enter the second cell address (or ***click in it***).
6. Press the **[ENTER]** key. (For example, to divide the value in C4 by the value in C5, you would type **=C4/C5**.)

BASIC LESSONS

LESSON 1: BUILDING A BUDGET SPREADSHEET—PART 1

This lesson shows you how to build the spreadsheet in Excel 2013 Exhibit 3. It explains how to use the [CTRL]+[HOME] command; move the cell pointer; enter text, values, and formulas; adjust the width of columns; change the format of cells to currency; use the bold feature; use the AutoFill and Copy features to copy formulas; and print and save a spreadsheet. Keep in mind that if at any time you make a mistake in this lesson, you may press **[CTRL]+[Z]** to undo what you have done.

1. Open Windows. When it has loaded, ***double-click the Microsoft Office Excel 2013 icon on the desktop*** to open the program. Alternatively, ***click the Start button, point to Programs or All Programs, point to Microsoft Office, and***

HANDS-ON EXERCISES

EXCEL 2013 EXHIBIT 3
Expanded budget spreadsheet

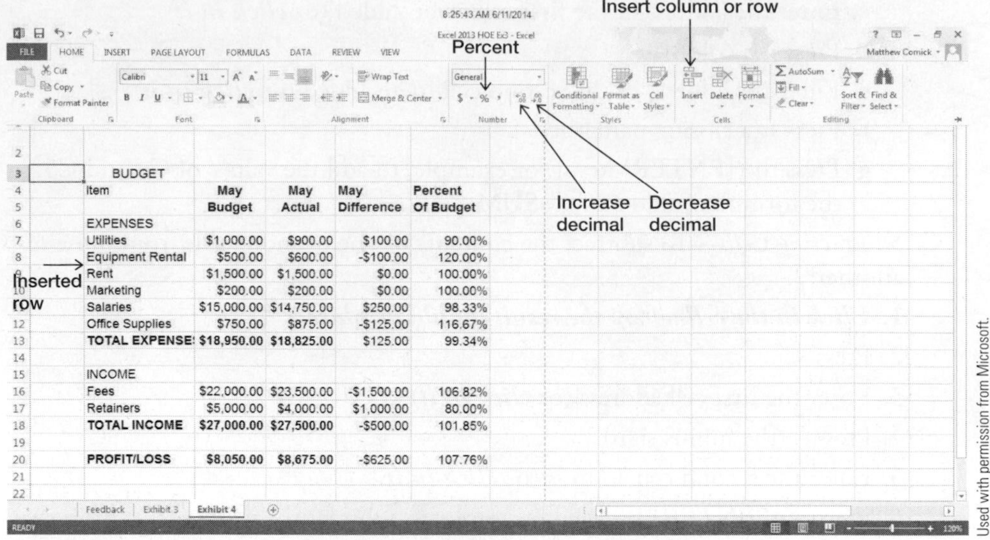

then click Microsoft Excel 2013. You should be in a clean, blank workbook. If you are not in a blank workbook, ***click the File tab*** (see Excel 2013 Exhibit 1), ***click on New, and then click Blank Workbook.***

2. Notice that the pointer is at cell A1, and the indicator that displays the address of the current cell (called the "name" box in Excel) says **A1**. The "name" box is just under the ribbon and all the way to the left (see Excel 2013 Exhibit 1). Also, notice that you can move the pointer around the spreadsheet using the cursor keys. Go back to cell A1 by pressing the **[CTRL]+[HOME]** keys.
3. Go to cell C3 by ***clicking in cell C3*** or by pressing the **[RIGHT ARROW]** twice, and then pressing the **[DOWN ARROW]** twice.
4. You will now enter the title of the spreadsheet in cell C3. Type **BUDGET** and then press the **[ENTER]** key.
5. Notice that the pointer is now at cell C4.
6. Press the **[UP ARROW]** to go back to cell C3. Notice that BUDGET is left-aligned. To center BUDGET in the cell, ***from the Home tab, click the Center icon in the Alignment group.*** It is the icon with several lines on it that appear centered (see Excel 2013 Exhibit 3). *Note:* If you hover the mouse over an icon on the ribbon for a second, the name of the icon will be displayed. Alternatively, ***from the Home tab, click the Alignment Group Dialog Box Launcher. Next, on the Alignment tab, under the Horizontal field, click the down arrow and select Center. Click OK.***
7. You should now be ready to enter the budget information. First, move the cell pointer to where the data should go, then type the data, and finally enter the data by pressing the **[ENTER]** key or one of the arrow (cursor) keys. Type the remaining row labels as follows:

   Item in B4.
   EXPENSES in B6.
   Utilities in B7.
   Equipment Rental in B8.
   Rent in B9.
   Marketing in B10.

Salaries in B11.
Office Supplies in B12.
TOTAL EXPENSES in B13.
INCOME in B15.
Fees in B16.
Retainers in B17.
TOTAL INCOME in B18.
PROFIT/LOSS in B20.

8. Notice that in column B, some of the data entries (such as "TOTAL EXPENSES" and "Equipment Rental") actually extend into column C. To correct this, you must increase the width of column B. ***Put the mouse pointer in the cell lettered B at the top of the screen. Move the pointer to the right edge of the cell.*** The pointer should then change to a double-headed vertical arrow and the column width will be displayed in a small box. ***Drag the pointer to the right until the column width is 18.00.*** Alternatively, you can change the cell width by ***placing the cell pointer anywhere in column B; then, from the Home tab, click Format in the Cells group, click Column Width…,*** type **18,** and ***click OK.***
9. Notice that all of the data entries now fit in the columns. Enter the following:
   May in C4.
   Budget in C5.
   May in D4.
   Actual in D5.
10. ***Click in cell C4 and drag the pointer over to cell D5*** (so that the whole cell range is highlighted); ***then, from the Home tab, click the Bold icon in the Font group, and click the Center icon in the Alignment group.***
11. You are now ready to enter values into your spreadsheet.
12. ***Move the pointer to cell C7.*** Type **1000.** Do not type a dollar sign or comma; these will be added later. Press the **[ENTER]** key to enter the value.
13. Enter the following:
    500 in C8.
    1500 in C9.
    200 in C10.
    15000 in C11.
    750 in C12.
    22000 in C16.
    5000 in C17.
    900 in D7.
    600 in D8.
    1500 in D9.
    200 in D10.
    14750 in D11.
    875 in D12.
    23500 in D16.
    4000 in D17.

HANDS-ON EXERCISES

14. The values you entered do not have dollar signs or the commas appropriate to a currency format. You will now learn how to format a range of cells for a particular format (such as the Currency format).
15. ***Click in cell C7 and drag the pointer over to cell D20. From the Home tab, click the down arrow next to the "Number Format" box in the Number group, which should say General. Then, click Currency.*** Notice that dollar signs have been added to all of the values. ***Click in any cell to deselect the cell range.***
16. ***Click in cell B13 and drag the pointer over to cell D13; then, from the Home tab, click the Bold icon in the Font group.*** This will make the TOTAL EXPENSES row appear in bold.
17. ***Click in cell B18 and drag the pointer over to cell D18; then, from the Home tab, click the Bold icon in the Font group.*** This will make the TOTAL INCOME row appear in bold.
18. ***Click in cell B20 and drag the pointer over to cell D20; then, from the Home ribbon tab, click on the Bold icon in the Font group.*** This will make the PROFIT/LOSS row appear in bold.
19. Your spreadsheet is nearly complete; all you need to add are the six formulas.
20. ***Click in cell C13.***
21. Type =**SUM(** and press **[UP ARROW]** until the cell pointer is at cell C7. Press **.** (a period) to anchor the range.
22. Press the **[DOWN ARROW]** five times, then press **)** (a closing parenthesis), and then press the **[ENTER]** key.
23. Go back to cell C13 and look at the formula in the formula bar. The formula should read **"=SUM(C7:C12)."** The total displayed in the cell should read **"$19,700.00."** Note that you also could have typed the formula **=C7+C8+C9+C10+C11+C12.**
24. Enter the following formulas:
    =SUM(D7:D12) in D13.
    =SUM(C16:C17) in C18.
    =SUM(D16:D17) in D18.
25. You now need to enter formulas for the PROFIT/LOSS columns. Enter the following formula in C20:
    =C18−C13 (the total should read $8,050.00)
26. ***Go to cell C20 and click the AutoFill command*** (it is the small square at the bottom right of the cell—see Excel 2013 Exhibit 3). ***Drag it one column to the right and release the mouse button.*** Notice that the formula has been copied. The total should be $8,675.00. Alternatively, ***go to cell C20, right-click, click Copy, then move the pointer to cell D20*** and press the **[ENTER]** key.
27. The spreadsheet is now complete. To print the spreadsheet, ***click the File tab, then click Print, and then click Print.***
28. You will need to save the spreadsheet, because you will use it in Lesson 2. To save the spreadsheet, ***click the File tab and then click Save.*** You may save the file to your computer, to Microsoft SkyDrive or both. ***Under Save in:, select the drive or folder*** in which you would like to save the document. Next to File Name, type **Budget1** and ***click Save.***
29. To quit Excel, ***click the File tab and then click on Close.***

This concludes Lesson 1.

LESSON 2: BUILDING A BUDGET SPREADSHEET—PART 2

This lesson assumes that you have completed Lesson 1, have saved the spreadsheet created in that lesson, and are generally familiar with the concepts covered in that lesson. Lesson 2 gives you experience in opening a file, inserting a row, formatting numbers as percentages, building additional formulas, creating a bar chart, printing selections, and fitting and compressing data onto one printed page. If you did not exit Excel after Lesson 1, skip steps 1 and 2, and go directly to step 3.

1. Open Windows. ***Double-click on the Microsoft Office Excel 2013 icon on the desktop*** to open the program. Alternatively, ***click the Start button, point to Programs or All Programs, point to Microsoft Office, and then click Microsoft Excel 2013.*** You should now be in a clean, blank workbook.
2. To retrieve the spreadsheet from Lesson 1, ***click on the File tab and then click Open. Next, click the name of your file*** (e.g., **Budget 1**). ***If you do not see it, look under Recent Workbooks to*** find the file. When you have found it, ***click on Open.***
3. You will be entering the information shown in Excel 2013 Exhibit 3. Notice in Excel 2013 Exhibit 3 that a line for Travel appears in row 9. You will insert this row first.
4. ***Click in cell B9. From the Home tab, click the down arrow below Insert in the Cells group. On the Insert menu, click Insert Sheet Rows.*** A new row has been added. You could also have ***right-clicked and selected Insert*** to open a dialog box with the option to insert another row.
5. Enter the following:
   Travel in B9.
   750 in C9.
   650 in D9.
6. Notice that when the new values for Travel were entered, all of the formulas were updated. Because you inserted the additional rows in the middle of the column, the formulas recognized the new numbers and automatically recalculated to reflect them. Be extremely careful when inserting new rows and columns into spreadsheets that have existing formulas. In some cases, the new number will not be reflected in the totals, such as when rows or columns are inserted at the beginning or end of the range that a formula calculates. It is always prudent to go back to each existing formula, examine the formula range, and make sure the new values are included in the formula range.
7. Change the column width of column E to 12 by ***clicking the column heading*** (the letter E) at the top of the screen. ***Move the pointer to the right edge of the column.*** The pointer should change to a double-headed vertical arrow. ***Drag the pointer to the right until the column width is 12.*** Alternatively, you can change the cell width by ***placing the cell pointer anywhere in column E and, from the Home tab, clicking Format in the Cells Group, and selecting Column Width….*** Then type **12** and ***click OK.***
8. Enter the following:
   May in E4.
   Difference in E5.
   Percent in F4.
   Of Budget in F5.

9. ***Click in cell E4 and drag the pointer over to cell F5*** so that the additional column headings are highlighted. ***Right-click.*** Notice that in addition to a menu, the Mini toolbar appears. It has a number of formatting options on it, including Font, Font size, Bold, and others. ***Click the Bold icon on the Mini toolbar. Point and click the Center icon on the Mini toolbar.***
10. ***Click in cell E14 and drag the pointer over to cell F14. Then, right-click and click on the Bold icon on the Mini toolbar.***
11. ***Click in cell E19 and drag the pointer over to cell F19. Then, right-click and click on Bold icon on the Mini toolbar.***
12. ***Click in cell E21 and drag the pointer over to cell F21. Then, right-click and click on Bold icon on the Mini toolbar.***
13. You are now ready to change the cell formatting for column E to Currency and column F to Percent. ***Click in cell E7 and drag the pointer down to cell E21. Right-click and select Format Cells. From the Number tab in the "Format Cells" window, click Currency and then OK. Click in any cell to get rid of the cell range.***
14. ***Click in cell F7 and drag the pointer down to cell F21. From the Home tab, click the Percent (%) icon in the Number group*** (see Excel 2013 Exhibit 3). ***Then, from the Home tab, click the Increase Decimal icon twice.***
15. ***Click in any cell to get rid of the cell range.***
16. All that is left to do is to enter the formulas for the two new columns. The entries in the May Difference column subtract the actual amount from the budgeted amount for each expense item. A positive amount in this column means that the office was under budget on that item. A negative balance means that the office was over budget on that line item. The Percent Of Budget column divides that actual amount by the budgeted amount. This shows the percentage of the budgeted money that was actually spent for each item.
17. You will first build one formula in the May Difference column, and then copy it. ***Click in cell E7***, type **=C7–D7**, and press the **[ENTER]** key.
18. Using the AutoFill command or the Copy command, copy this formula down through cell E14. (To copy, ***right-click and then click Copy; highlight the area where the information should go; then right-click and select Paste.*** Alternatively, you can use the Copy and Paste icons in the Clipboard group on the Home tab.)
19. ***Click in cell E17***, type **=D17–C17**, and press the **[ENTER]** key.
20. Using the AutoFill command, copy this formula down through cell E21. Delete the formula in cell E20 by ***clicking in cell E20*** and pressing the **[DEL]** key.
21. You will now build on the formula in the Percent Of Budget column and copy it. ***Click in cell F7***, type **=D7/C7**, and press the **[ENTER]** key.
22. Using the AutoFill command, copy this formula down through cell F21. Delete the formula in cells F15, F16, and F20 by ***clicking in the cell*** and then pressing the **[DEL]** key.
23. The spreadsheet has now been built. We will now build a bar chart that shows our budgeted expenses compared to our actual expenses (see Excel 2013 Exhibit 4).
24. ***Click in cell B7 and then drag the pointer down and over to cell D14.***
25. ***At the lower right corner of the highlighted data, you should see the Quick Analysis icon. Click the Quick Analysis icon, then click CHARTS, then click***

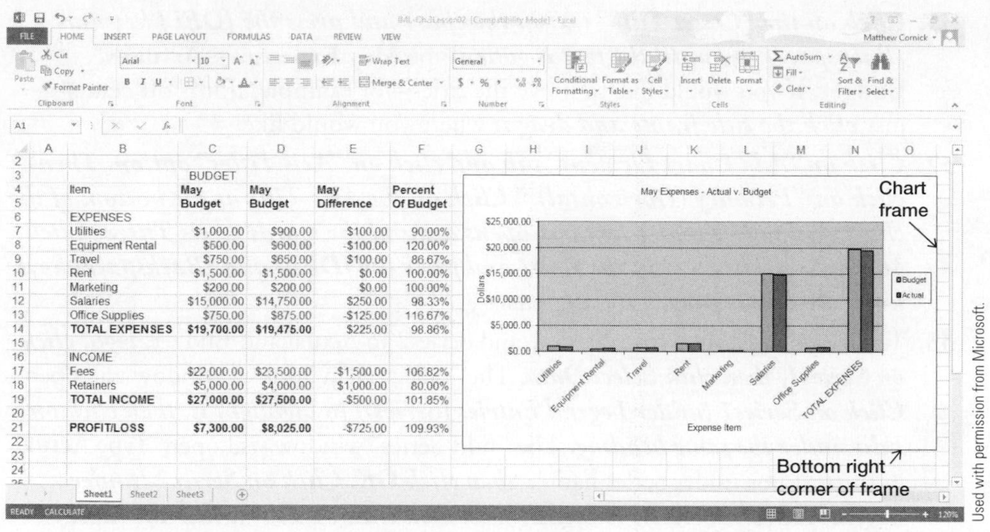

Used with permission from Microsoft.

EXCEL 2013 EXHIBIT 4
Completed column grid

More Charts. See Excel 2013 Exhibit 5. The Insert Chart box will open. ***Click All Charts in the Insert Chart box. Click Column on the left side of the Insert Chart box, then click the fourth option from the left, 3-D Clustered Column. Click OK.***

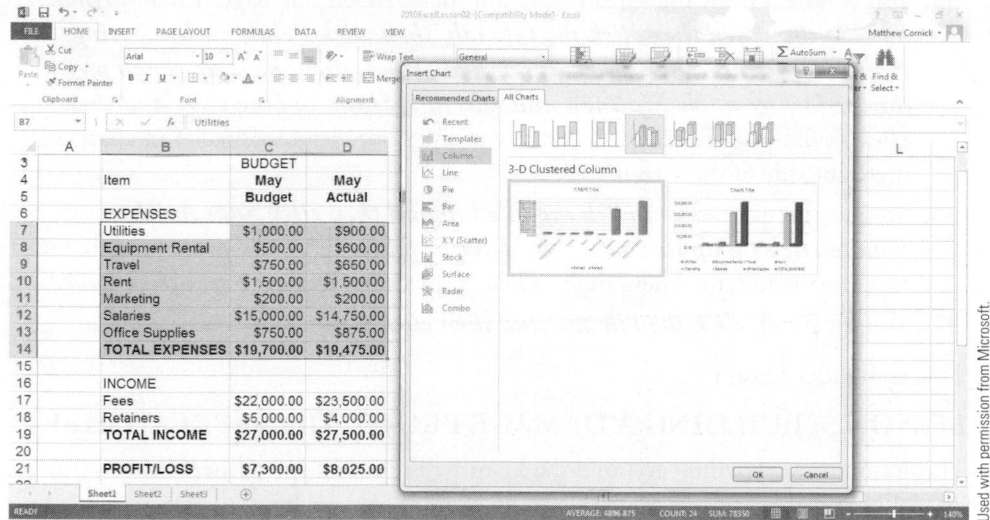

Used with permission from Microsoft.

EXCEL 2013 EXHIBIT 5
Creating a column chart

26. Notice that a draft bar chart has been created. ***Move your mouse anywhere in the chart frame*** (see Excel 2013 Exhibit 4), ***and your pointer will turn to a four-headed arrow. Drag the chart across the spreadsheet so the upper left corner of the chart is near cell H4.***
27. ***Using the horizontal scroll bar*** (see Excel 2013 Exhibit 4), ***scroll to the right*** so the chart is completely in your screen, if necessary.
28. ***Move your cursor so it is on the bottom right corner of the chart frame. Your cursor should change to a two-headed arrow that is diagonal. Drag the chart so that the bottom right corner ends near cell P26*** (see Excel 2013 Exhibit 4).
29. Notice that new options have been added to the ribbon (Chart Tools Design and Format). ***Click the Design ribbon tab under Chart Tools.***
30. ***Click Chart Title in the chart and notice that a text box opens around the words "Chart Title."***

31. ***Click on the "Chart Title" text in the chart and press the [DEL] key and [Backspace] key until the text is gone.*** Type **May Expenses—Actual v. Budget**. If you would like to move the title—for example, if it is off center—just ***click the title frame and drag it*** where you would like.
32. ***Click on "Add Chart Element" tab and click on "Axis Titles" option. Then click on "Primary (Horizontal)." Click on the Axis Title at the bottom of the chart and notice that a text box opens around the words "Axis Title." Click on the Axis Title text in the chart and press the [DEL] and [Backspace] keys until the text is gone.*** Type **Expenses**.
33. To change the legend from Series1 and Series2 to Actual and Budget, ***right click on Series1, then click Select Data.*** The "Select Data Source" window will open. ***Click on Series1 (under Legend Entries (Series)) to highlight it, then click on Edit under the same heading.*** The "Edit Series" window will open. Type **Actual** in the text box under Series name:, ***then click OK. Click on Series2 (under Legend Entries (Series)) to highlight it, then click on Edit under the same heading.*** The "Edit Series" window will open. Type **Budget** in the text box under Series name:, ***then click OK.*** Then, ***click OK in the Select Data Source window.***
34. To print the chart, ***click the File tab, then click Print; under Settings, make sure Print Selected Chart is selected and then click Print.*** You should see a preview of the printed chart on the right side of the screen.
35. You will next print the spreadsheet and the chart on one page. ***Click anywhere outside the chart, then click the File tab, then click Print; under Settings, make sure Print Active Sheets is selected. Then, click the drop-down menu for the last item (No Scaling), and select Fit Sheet on One Page and then click Print.*** You should see a preview of the printed spreadsheet and chart on the right side of the screen.
36. To save the spreadsheet, ***click the File tab and then click Save As, then double-click Computer, select the drive or folder*** in which you would like to save the document. Then, next to File Name, type **Budget2** and ***click Save.***
37. To quit Excel, ***click the File tab and then click Close.***

This concludes Lesson 2.

LESSON 3: BUILDING A DAMAGE PROJECTION SPREADSHEET

This lesson shows you how to build the Damage Projection spreadsheet shown in Excel 2013 Exhibit 6. It explains how to increase the size of type, how to wrap text in a cell,

EXCEL 2013 EXHIBIT 6
Damages projection spreadsheet

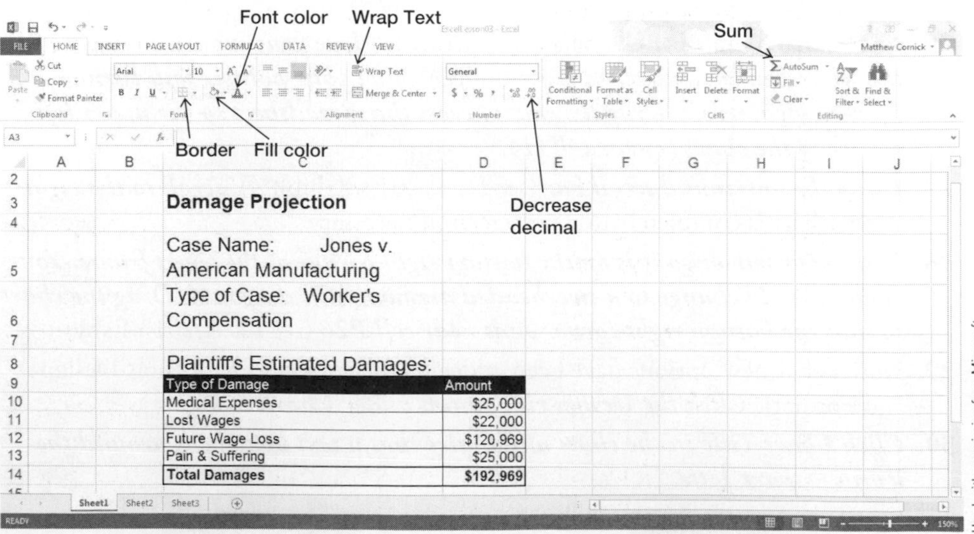

how to use the border features, how to use the font and fill color features, how to use the AutoSum feature, and how to change the decimal places for a number. This lesson assumes you have successfully completed Lessons 1 and 2. Keep in mind that if at any time you make a mistake in this lesson, you may press **[CTRL]+[Z]** to undo what you have done.

1. Open Windows. When it has loaded, ***double-click the Microsoft Office Excel 2013 icon on the desktop*** to open the program. Alternatively, ***click on the Start button, point to Programs or All Programs, point to Microsoft Office, and then click Microsoft Excel 2013.*** You should now be in a clean, blank workbook. If you are not in a blank workbook, ***click the File tab*** (see Excel 2013 Exhibit 1), ***then click New, and then double-click Blank Workbook.***
2. To start building the spreadsheet in Excel 2013 Exhibit 6, begin by ***increasing size of column C to a width of 37 (Home tab > Cells group > Format > Column Width).***
3. In cell C3, type **Damages Projection.** With the pointer on C3, highlight the text and then ***click the Bold icon from Font group on the Home tab. Change the size to 14 point by clicking the Font Size box in the Font group on the Home tab;*** then type **14.**
4. Type the text shown in cell C5 (see Excel 2013 Exhibit 6). ***On the Home tab, click the Font Size box in the Font group and change the type to 14 point.*** Notice that the text goes into the next cell. To wrap part of the text down to the next line within the current cell (see Excel Exhibit 6), ***from the Home tab, click the Wrap Text icon in the Alignment group*** (see Excel 2013 Exhibit 6). The text has now been wrapped down to the next line within the cell C5.
5. Type the text shown in cell C6, make the text 14 point, and wrap the text down so it does not go into cell D6.
6. Type the text shown in cell C8 and make the text 14 point.
7. Type the text and values shown in cells C9 to D13.
8. Type the text shown in cell C14.
9. To enter the formula in cell D14, ***click cell D14.*** Then, ***from the Editing group on the Home tab, click the AutoSum icon.*** Notice that Sum assumed you wanted to add the values in D10 to D13. You could adjust the range by pressing **[SHIFT]+[ARROW]** keys, but the range should be fine as is (i.e., D10 to D13). Press the **[ENTER]** key to enter the formula.
10. ***Click in cell C9, drag the mouse pointer to cell D14, and change the font size to 14 point.***
11. ***Click in cell C9 and drag the pointer to cell D9. Right-click. On the Mini toolbar, click the down arrow next to the Fill Color icon*** (the paint bucket) ***and select the black square.*** (You also could have clicked the Fill Color icon in the Font group on the Home tab.) The cells are all black; now you just need to change the font color to white to see the text.
12. With cells C9 and D9 still highlighted, ***on the Home tab click the down arrow next to the Font Color icon in the Font group, and click on the white square.***
13. ***Click in cell C10 and drag the pointer to cell D14. From the Font group on the Home tab, click on the down arrow next to the Borders icon.*** (It is typically just to the left of the Fill Color icon.) ***Click All Borders*** (it looks like a windowpane). Notice that there is now a border around every square that was highlighted.
14. ***Click in cell C14 and drag the pointer to cell D14. From the Font group on the Home tab, click the down arrow next to the Border icon again. Then click on the Thick Box border*** (it looks like a heavy black window frame). Move the pointer and notice that there is now a heavy black border around cells C14 and D14.

15. ***Click in cell D10 and drag the pointer to cell D14. From the Number group or the Home tab, click the dollar sign*** ($). Notice that two decimal places are shown (e.g., $25,000.00). It is not necessary to show two decimal places in our projection, so we will change it to zero decimal places. ***From the Number group on the Home tab, click the Decrease Decimal icon twice.*** Notice that whole dollars are now shown.
16. To print the spreadsheet, ***click on the File tab, then click Print, and then click Print.***
17. To save the spreadsheet, ***click on the File tab and then click Save As, then double-click Computer, select the drive or folder*** in which you would like to save the document. Then, next to File Name, type ***Damages Projection*** and ***click Save.***
18. To quit Excel, ***click on the File tab and then click Close.***

This concludes Lesson 3.

INTERMEDIATE LESSONS

LESSON 4: CHILD SUPPORT PAYMENT SPREADSHEET

This lesson shows you how to build the Child Support Payment spreadsheet in Excel 2013 Exhibit 7. It explains how to create a white background, create formulas to multiply cells and formulas that use an absolute cell reference, and use the Auto-Format feature. This lesson assumes that you have successfully completed Lessons 1 through 3. Keep in mind that if at any time you make a mistake in this lesson, you may press **[CTRL]+[Z]** to undo what you have done.

1. Open Windows. When it has loaded, ***double-click the Microsoft Office Excel 2013 icon on the desktop*** to open the program. Alternatively, ***click the Start button, point to Programs or All Programs, point to Microsoft Office, and then click Microsoft Excel 2013.*** You should now be in a clean, blank workbook. If you are not in a blank workbook, ***click on the File tab*** (see Excel 2013 Exhibit 1), ***then click New, and then double-click on Blank Workbook.***
2. When you start to build the spreadsheet in Excel 2013 Exhibit 7, notice that the background is completely white. A completely white background gives you a crisp, clean canvas on which to work and to which you can add colors and graphics.

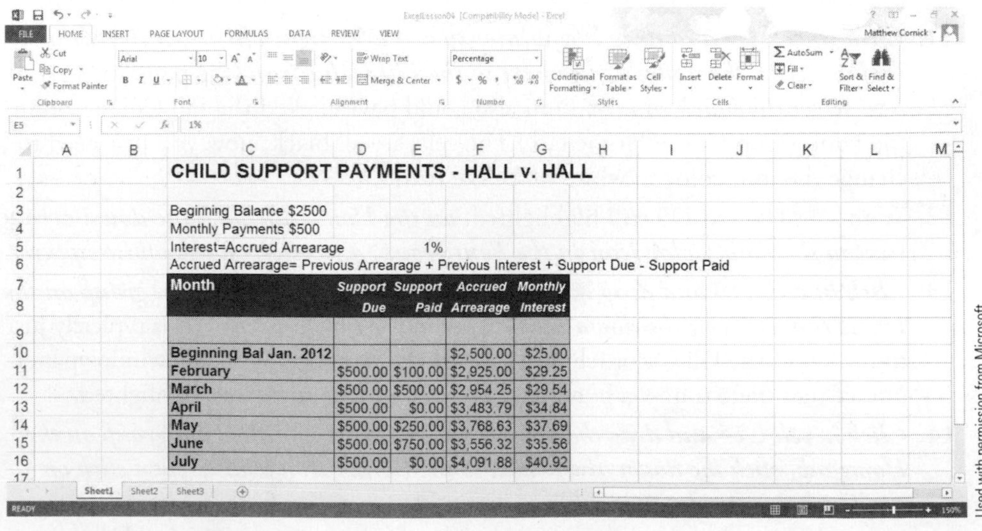

EXCEL 2013 EXHIBIT 7
Child support payment spreadsheet

3. Press **[CTRL]+[A].** The whole spreadsheet is now selected. ***From the Font group on the Home tab, click the down arrow next to the Fill Color icon, and then click the white square*** (it is all the way in the upper right corner). ***Click in any cell*** to make the highlighting disappear. Notice that the background of the spreadsheet is completely white.
4. Enter the text shown in cell C1; change the font to Bold and the font size to 14 point.
5. Increase the width of column C to 20.
6. Enter the text shown in cells C3 to C6.
7. In cell E5, type **.01** and press the **[ENTER]** key. Change the number format to Percent (zero decimal places).
8. Enter the text shown in cell C7 and in the cell range from D7 to G8. ***Click on C7 and click on bold icon from Font group in Home tab. Click on D7 and drag the pointer to G8, click on Italic icon from font group in Home tab.***
9. Enter the text shown in the cell range from C10 to C16.
10. Enter the numbers (values) shown in cells in D11 to E16.
11. In cell F10, type **2500.**
12. In cell G10, press the = key. ***Click in cell F10,*** then press **[SHIFT]+[8]** (an asterisk will appear), then ***click in cell E5*** and press the **[F4]** key once. The formula **"=F10*$E$5"** should be on the screen; press the **[ENTER]** key. The formula multiplies the accrued arrearage (how much the individual is behind on payments) times the interest rate (which is 1 percent). The reason you pressed **[F4]** is that the formula had to be an absolute cell reference; pressing **[F4]** simply put the dollar signs ($) into the formula for you. The dollar signs tell Excel that this is an absolute cell reference, rather than a relative cell reference. In this manner, when you copy the formula to other cells (see below), the accrued arrearage will always be multiplied by the value in E5. Said another way, the second half of this formula (**$E$5**) will not change when the formula is copied to other cells.
13. If you want to find out for yourself why the formula **=F10*E5** will not work once it is copied from cell G10 (where it will work fine), type **=F10*E5** in cell G10, and then copy the formula to cells G11 to G16. Once you have seen the effect of this, delete the changes you made and change the formula in cell G10 to **=F10*$E$5.**
14. To copy the formula from G10 to cells G11 to G16, ***click in cell G10, click the AutoFill handle*** (the little black box at the lower right corner of the cell), ***and drag the mouse pointer down to cell G16.***
15. In cell F11, type **=F10+G10+D11–E11**. The formula adds the accrued amount in the previous month to the previous month's interest and the current support due, and then subtracts the current amount paid.
16. To copy the formula from F11 to cells F12 to F16, ***click in cell F11, click the AutoFill handle, and drag the pointer down to cell F16.***
17. ***Click in cell D10 and drag the pointer to cell G16. Right-click; then click Format Cells. Click the Number tab, click Currency, and then click OK.***
18. Notice that the spreadsheet is very plain. We will use the Cell Styles feature to give the spreadsheet some color. ***Click in cell C7 and drag the pointer to cell G8. From the Styles Group on the Home tab, click the down arrow next to Cell Styles. Click Accent4*** (it is solid yellow with white letters).
19. ***Click in cell C9 and drag the pointer to cell G16. From the Styles group on the Home tab, click the down arrow next to Cell Styles. Click***

20%—Accent1. (It is light blue with black letters.) ***Click in any cell to make the highlighting disappear.***

20. To add borders to the spreadsheet, ***click in cell C9 and drag the mouse pointer to cell G16. Then, from the Font group on the Home tab, click the down arrow next to the Borders icon. Next, click the All Borders icon*** (it looks like a windowpane).
21. ***Click in cell E5. From the Font group on the Home tab, click the down arrow next to Borders. Then, click Thick Box border.*** Press the **[ENTER]** key. The spreadsheet is now complete and should look like Excel 2013 Exhibit 7.
22. To print the spreadsheet, ***click the File tab, then click Print, and then click Print.***
23. To save the spreadsheet, ***click the File tab and then click Save, then double-click Computer, select the drive or folder*** in which you would like to save the document. Then, next to File Name, type **Child Support Payments** and ***click Save.***
24. To quit Excel, ***click the File tab and then click Close.***

This concludes Lesson 4.

LESSON 5: LOAN AMORTIZATION TEMPLATE

This lesson shows you how to open a loan amortization template and fill it in (see Excel 2013 Exhibit 8). Templates are a great way to simplify complicated spreadsheets. You will also learn how to protect cells, freeze panes, split a screen, hide a column, and use the Format Painter tool. This lesson assumes that you have successfully completed Lessons 1 through 4. Keep in mind that if at any time you make a mistake in this lesson, you may press **[CTRL]+[Z]** to undo what you have done.

1. Open Windows. When it has loaded, ***double-click the Microsoft Office Excel 2013 icon on the desktop*** to open the program. Alternatively, ***click the Start button, point to Programs or All Programs, point to Microsoft Office, and then click Microsoft Excel 2013.*** You should now be in a clean, blank workbook.
2. The first thing you will do to complete the template in Excel 2013 Exhibit 8 is to open the "Lesson 5" file from the Premium Website. Go to your CengageBrain account and ***click on the link for Premium Website*** for Cornick's *Using Computers in the Law Office*, 7th edition. A new window will open. ***Under Book Level Resources, click the Data Files: Excel tab, then under Excel 2013, click on the "Lesson 5" file, click the link to Lesson 5.*** When prompted, ***click Open.*** If you get a Security Warning, ***click Enable Editing to continue.***

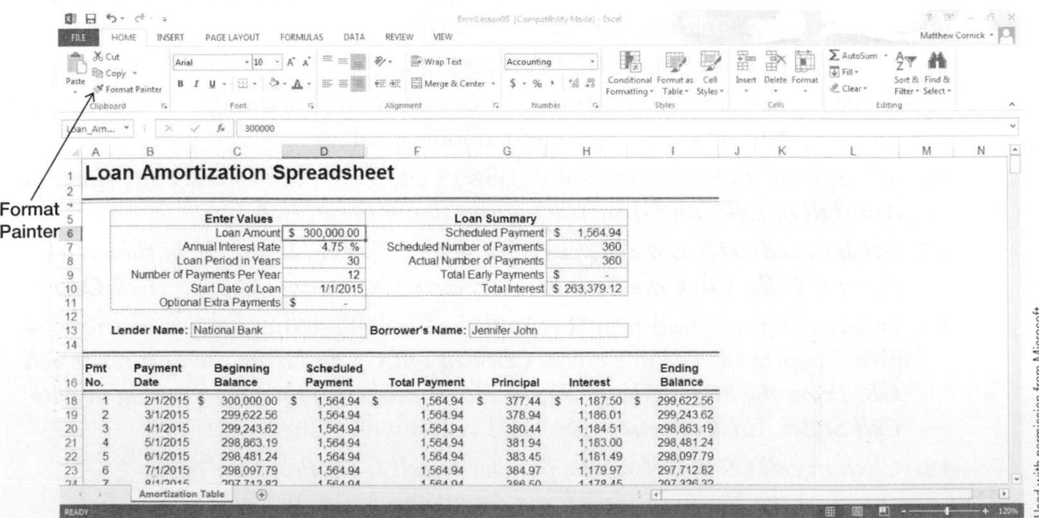

Pmt No.	Payment Date	Beginning Balance	Scheduled Payment	Total Payment	Principal	Interest	Ending Balance
1	2/1/2015	$ 300,000.00	$ 1,564.94	$ 1,564.94	$ 377.44	$ 1,187.50	$ 299,622.56
2	3/1/2015	299,622.56	1,564.94	1,564.94	378.94	1,186.01	299,243.62
3	4/1/2015	299,243.62	1,564.94	1,564.94	380.44	1,184.51	298,863.19
4	5/1/2015	298,863.19	1,564.94	1,564.94	381.94	1,183.00	298,481.24
5	6/1/2015	298,481.24	1,564.94	1,564.94	383.45	1,181.49	298,097.79
6	7/1/2015	298,097.79	1,564.94	1,564.94	384.97	1,179.97	297,712.82

EXCEL 2013 EXHIBIT 8
Loan amortization template

3. You should now have the Loan Amortization Spreadsheet shown in Excel 2013 Exhibit 8 opened, except that your spreadsheet has no data yet.
4. Enter the following information:
   Cell D6: **300000**
   Cell D7: **4.75**
   Cell D8: **30**
   Cell D9: **12**
   Cell D10: **1/1/2015**
   Cell D11: **0** (When you click in Cell D11, a note will appear regarding extra payments; just type **0** (a zero) and press the **[ENTER]** key and the note will disappear.)
   Cell C13: **National Bank**
   Cell G13: **Jennifer John**
5. Notice that your spreadsheet now appears nearly identical to Excel 2013 Exhibit 8.
6. Notice that in your spreadsheet, just about everything below row 16 is a formula. If a user accidentally deletes one of these formulas, the whole spreadsheet could be affected. You will now turn on the Protection feature and lock some of the cells so they cannot be accidentally deleted.
7. ***Right-click in cell D6. Then click Format Cells… . Click the Protection tab in the "Format Cells" window.*** Notice that there is no check mark next to Locked. Cells D6 to D13 and cell G13 are unlocked even when the Protection feature is turned on. When the Protection feature is off, you can change the lock/unlock format of cells by using the ***right-click, Format Cells… > Protection*** command sequence. Interestingly, when a new blank spreadsheet is opened in Excel, all cells default to "Locked," but this has no effect because the Protection feature is always turned off in a blank workbook.
8. ***Click Cancel in the "Format Cells" window*** to close the window.
9. Let's open a new spreadsheet so you can see that all cells in Excel start out with the format locked. ***Click the File tab, then click New, and then double-click Blank Workbook.***
10. You should now have a new blank spreadsheet displayed. ***Right-click in any cell and then click Format Cells… . Next, click the Protection tab.*** Notice that the cell is locked. However, the cell is not truly locked until you turn on the Protection feature.
11. ***Click Cancel in the "Format Cells" window in the new spreadsheet. Click the File tab and then click Close*** to close the file. You should now be back at your Amortization spreadsheet.
12. To turn on the Protection feature, ***on the Review tab, click Protect Sheet in the Changes group.***
13. The "Protect Sheet" window should now be displayed (see Excel 2013 Exhibit 9). Make sure that the first two selections under Allow all users of this worksheet to: are selected (e.g., Select locked cells and Select Unlocked Cells). Notice that you could enter a password in the white box under Password to unprotect sheet. This would completely lock the spreadsheet (so only unlocked cells could be modified) to users who do not know the password. In this case this is not necessary; it is fine for someone to intentionally change the values at the top of the spreadsheet—we are just using this feature to prevent someone from accidentally changing the formulas below row 16.

EXCEL 2013 EXHIBIT 9

Protecting cells

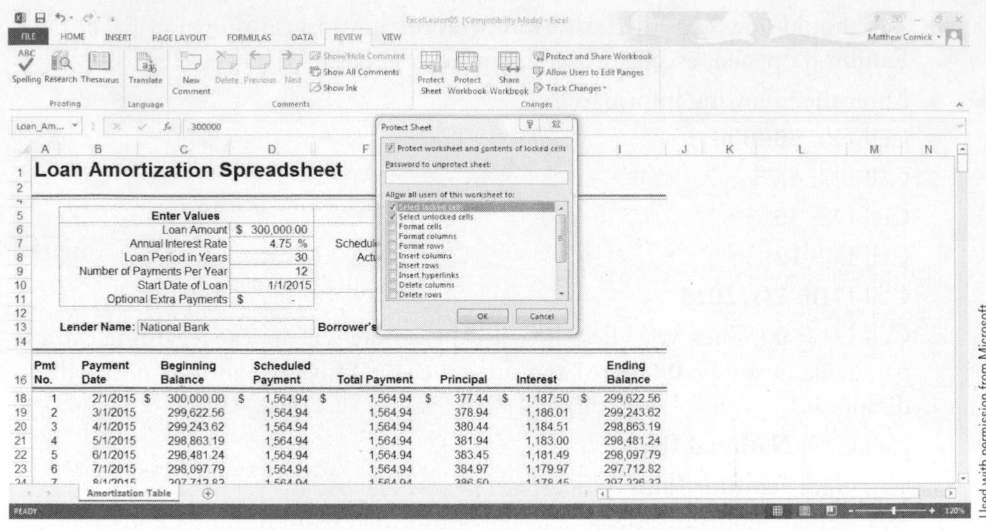

14. After the first two items are check-marked under Allow all users of this worksheet to:, ***click OK.***
15. ***Click in any cell other than D6 to D13 or cell G13*** and try to type something in the cell. You should get an error message that says **"The cell or chart you're trying to change is on a protected sheet. To make changes, click Unprotect Sheet in the review tab (you might need a password)."** ***Click OK*** to close the error window.
16. The whole spreadsheet is now locked, except for cells D6 to D13 and cell G13, because these were not formatted as locked in the template.
17. Now you will turn off the Protection feature because you are still building the spreadsheet. ***On the Review tab, click Unprotect Sheet in the Changes group.***
18. You will now use the Format Painter tool to copy the formatting from one set of cells to another set of cells. Notice that cells F13 and G13 do not look like cells B13 and C13. You will copy the format from cells B13 and C13 to cells F13 and G13.
19. ***Point in cell B13 and drag the pointer to cell C13. Next, on the Home tab, click the Format Painter icon in the Clipboard group.*** (It looks like a paintbrush.) Your pointer now should have a paintbrush icon on it.
20. ***Click in cell F13, drag the pointer to cell H13, and then let go of the mouse button. Click anywhere to see the cell.*** Notice that the formatting has now been copied.
21. Column E in the amortization schedule of the spreadsheet is the "Extra Payment" column. Assume for the purposes of this exercise that you will not have any extra payments and that you do not need this column, but you want to leave the column there in case you need it at a later date. For now, you can hide column E until you need it later.
22. ***Right-click on the "E" in the E column heading*** (see Excel 2013 Exhibit 9). ***From the drop-down menu, click Hide.***
23. ***Click in any cell.*** The vertical line will disappear. Notice that column E is no longer displayed. The column heading goes from D to F.
24. We will now Unhide column E. ***Point on the D column heading and drag the pointer to the F column heading so that both columns are highlighted. Right-click, then click Unhide on the drop-down menu.*** Notice that column E reappears.
25. ***Click in any cell to make the highlighting disappear.***

26. ***Click in cell D18.*** Use the **[DOWN ARROW]** key to go to cell D50. Notice that column titles, such as "Pmt No.," and "Payment Date," are no longer visible, so it is difficult to know what the numbers mean.
27. Press **[CTRL]+[HOME]** to go to the top of the spreadsheet.
28. ***Click cell A18.*** You will now use the Split Screen command to see the column titles.
29. ***On the View tab, click Split in the Window group.***
30. Use the **[DOWN ARROW]** key to go to cell A50. Notice that because you split the screen at row 18, you can still see column titles. Next, use the **[UP ARROW]** key to go to cell A1. You should now see the top portion of your spreadsheet in both the top and bottom screens.
31. ***On the View tab, click Split again in the Window group.*** The bottom screen is now gone.
32. The Freeze Panes feature is another way to show the column headings when you scroll down a document. The Freeze Panes feature is a convenient way to see both column and row titles at the same time. ***Click in cell B18.***
33. ***On the View tab, click Freeze Panes in the Window group and then click the first option, Freeze Panes.***
34. Use the **[DOWN ARROW]** key to go to cell B50. Notice that because you froze the screen at cell B18, you can still see column titles. Next, use the **[RIGHT ARROW]** key to go to cell R50. You should still see the "Pmt No." column, including the payment numbers.
35. Press **[CTRL]+[HOME]** to go to the beginning of the spreadsheet.
36. ***On the View tab, click Freeze Panes in the Window group and then click the first option, Unfreeze Panes.***
37. To print the spreadsheet, ***click the File tab, then click Print, and then click Print.***
38. To save the spreadsheet, ***click the File tab and then click Save As, then double-click Computer, select the drive or folder*** in which you would like to save the document. Next to File Name, type **Excel Lesson 5 Spreadsheet DONE** and ***click Save.***
39. Templates are a great way to utilize the power of Excel. There are many free templates available on the Internet. Microsoft alone offers more than 100 Excel templates on its website. To access them, ***click the File tab, then New.*** They are listed to the left under Office.com Templates.
40. To quit Excel, ***click the File tab and then click Close.***

This concludes Lesson 5.

LESSON 6: STATISTICAL FUNCTIONS

This lesson demonstrates how to use and enter statistical formulas such as average, maximum, minimum, and standard deviation. It also shows how to sort data, check for metadata in spreadsheets, use the Format Clear command, use conditional formatting, and insert a clip-art file. When the spreadsheet is complete, it will look like Excel 2013 Exhibit 10. Keep in mind that if at any time you make a mistake in this lesson, you may press **[CTRL]+[Z]** to undo what you have done.

1. Open Windows. When it has loaded, ***double-click the Microsoft Office Excel 2013 icon on the desktop*** to open the program. Alternatively, ***click the Start button, point to Programs or All Programs, point to Microsoft Office, and then click Microsoft Excel 2013.*** You should now be in a clean, blank workbook. If you are not in a blank workbook, ***click the File tab*** (see Excel 2013 Exhibit 1), ***then click New, and then double-click on Blank Workbook.***

EXCEL 2013 EXHIBIT 10
Statistical spreadsheet

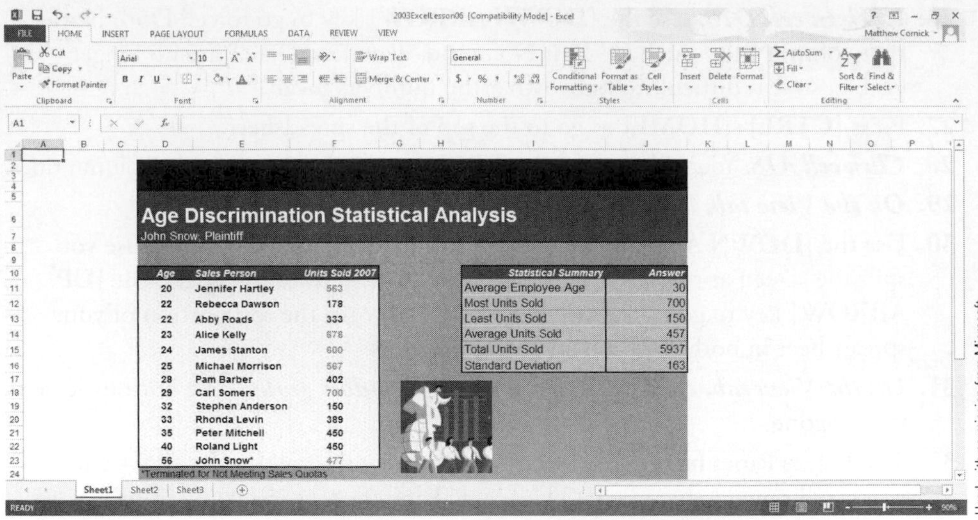

2. The first thing you will do to complete the template shown in Excel 2013 Exhibit 10 is to open the "Lesson 6" file from the Premium Website. Go to your CengageBrain account and ***click on the link for Premium Website*** for Cornick's *Using Computers in the Law Office*, 7th edition. A new window will open. ***Under Book Level Resources, click on the Data Files: Excel tab, then under Excel 2013, click on the "Lesson 6" file.*** When prompted, ***click Open.*** If you get a Security Warning, ***click Enable Editing to continue.***
3. You should now see the Age Discrimination Statistical Analysis spreadsheet shown in Excel 2013 Exhibit 10, except your spreadsheet has no formulas in the statistical summary section, the data have not yet been sorted, and there is no clip art yet.
4. You will now enter the formulas in the Statistical Summary section of the spreadsheet. The first formula will calculate the average age of employees of the company. ***Click in cell J11.*** Type the following formula: **=AVERAGE(D11:D23)** and then press the **[ENTER]** key. The result should be 30.
5. The next formula will calculate the most units sold. ***Click in cell J12.*** Type the following formula: **=MAX(F11:F23)** and then press the **[ENTER]** key. The result should be 700.
6. The next formula will calculate the least units sold. ***Click in cell J13.*** Type the following formula: **=MIN(F11:F23)** and then press the **[ENTER]** key. The result should be 150.
7. The next formula will calculate the average units sold. ***Click in cell J14.*** Type the following formula: **=AVERAGE(F11:F23)** and then press the **[ENTER]** key. The result should be 457.
8. The next formula will calculate the total units sold. ***Click in cell J15.*** Type the following formula: **=SUM(F11:F23)** and then press the **[ENTER]** key. The result should be 5937.
9. The last formula will calculate the standard deviation for units sold. The standard deviation is a measure of how widely values are dispersed from the average value (the arithmetic mean). Large standard deviations show that the numbers vary widely from the average. ***On the Formulas tab, click Insert Function in the Function Library group. Next to Or select a category, click the down arrow and select Statistical. Then, scroll down the list and click***

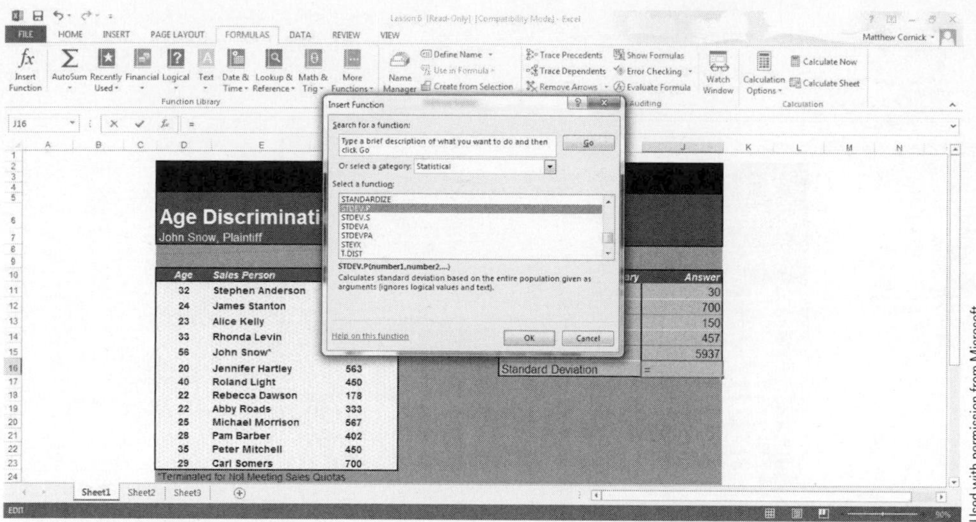

Used with permission from Microsoft.

EXCEL 2013 EXHIBIT 11
Entering a standard deviation formula using the insert function command

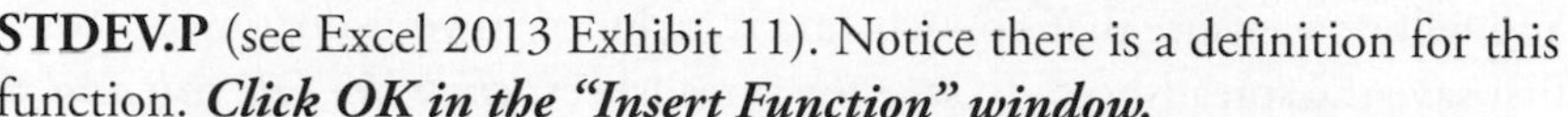

STDEV.P (see Excel 2013 Exhibit 11). Notice there is a definition for this function. ***Click OK in the "Insert Function" window.***

10. The "Function Arguments" window should now be displayed (see Excel 2013 Exhibit 12). In the "Function Arguments" window, next to Number 1, press **[DEL]** until the box is blank; type **F11:F23** and then ***click OK***. The result should be 163.

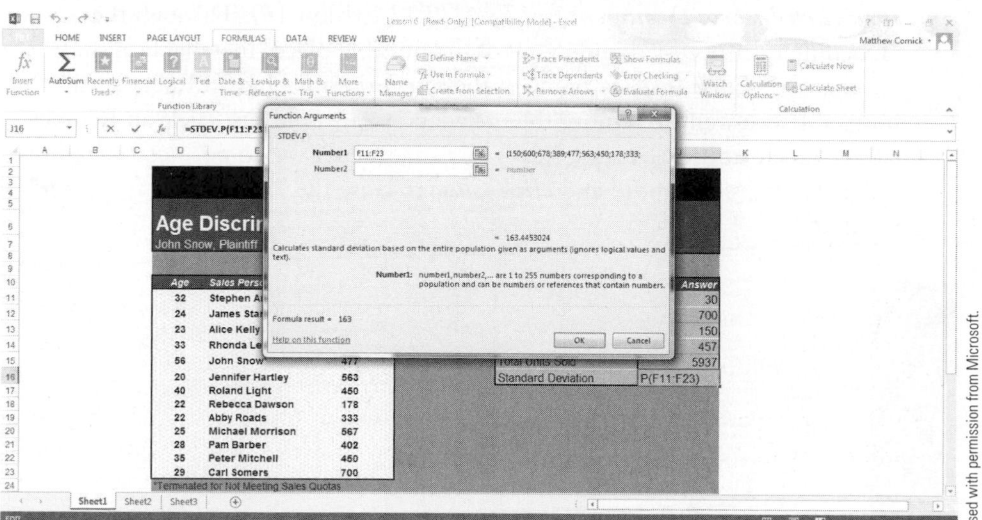

Used with permission from Microsoft.

EXCEL 2013 EXHIBIT 12
Entering a standard deviation formula using the functions argument window

11. You will now sort the data based on the age of the employees. ***Click in D11 and then drag the pointer down to F23. From the Data tab, click Sort in the Sort and Filter group.***
12. The "Sort" window should now be displayed (see Excel 2013 Exhibit 13). *Note:* Even though you just want to sort by age, you must select the full data range that includes all of the information, or the age data will be sorted but the other columns and rows will stay where they are. The data will therefore be mismatched (each age will not be matched with the correct person and number of units sold).
13. ***In the "Sort" window, click the down arrow next to Sort by, then click Age*** (see Excel 2013 Exhibit 13). Notice that under Order, the default of Smallest to Largest is selected; this is fine, so ***click OK in the "Sort" window.*** The data should now be sorted according to the age of the individual, with John Snow appearing last in the spreadsheet.

EXCEL 2013 EXHIBIT 13
Sorting data

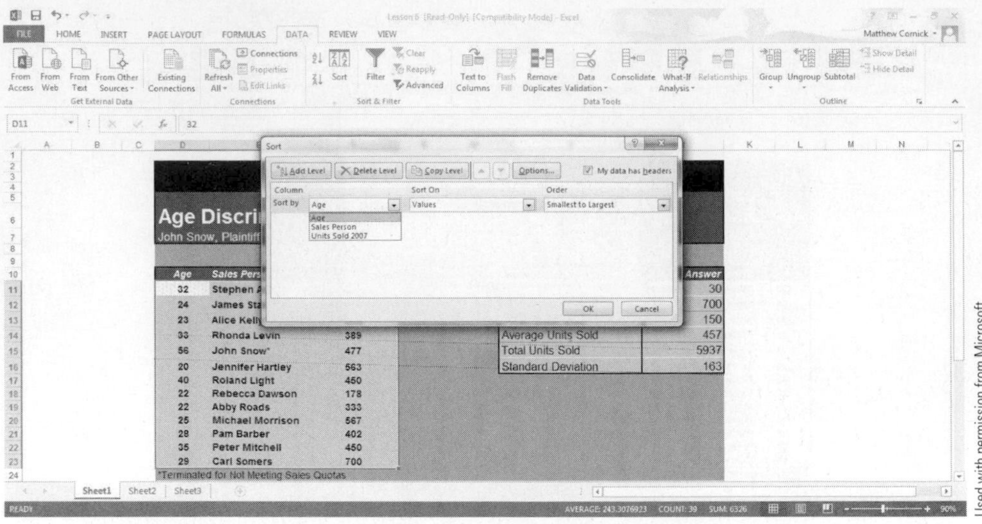

Used with permission from Microsoft.

14. You will now ensure that no metadata is included in your document. You must first save the spreadsheet. To save the spreadsheet, ***click the File tab and then click Save As, double-click Computer, select the drive or folder*** in which you would like to save the document. Next to File Name, type **Excel Lesson 6 Spreadsheet DONE** and ***click Save.***
15. Excel 2013 has a special feature called Inspect Document that can extract all metadata from your spreadsheet. ***Click the File tab; click Check for Issues, then click Inspect Document*** (see Excel 2013 Exhibit 14). Through the "Document Inspector" window, all of the possible places metadata can hide are checked. ***Click Inspect.*** Some of the categories may have a Remove All button. If you want to remove the metadata, you would just click on Remove All for each category. Because this is just an exercise, we do not need to remove the metadata, so go ahead and ***click Close*** to close the "Document Inspector" window.

EXCEL 2013 EXHIBIT 14
Removing metadata

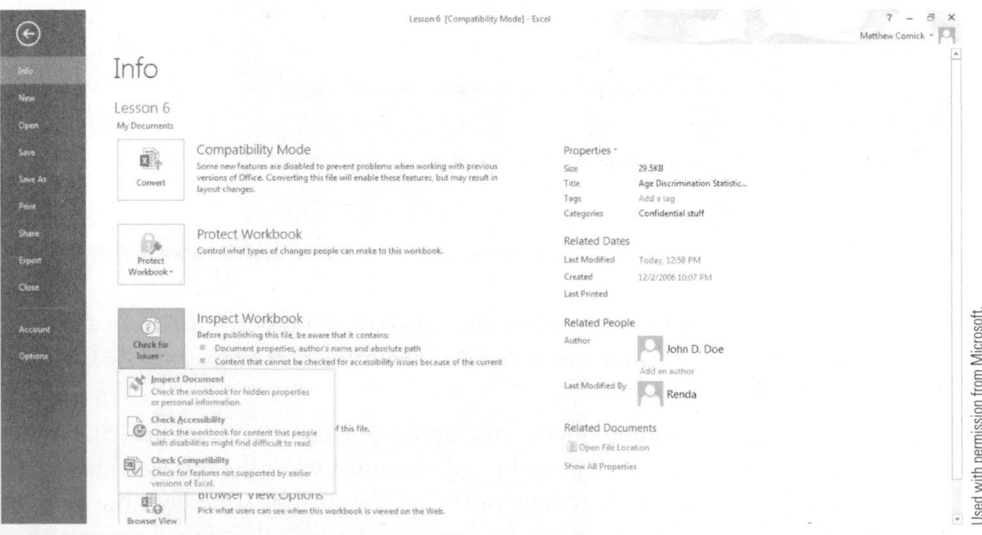

Used with permission from Microsoft.

16. Sometimes it is helpful to clear a cell or cells of all formatting information at one time. Notice that cell D6, the one titled "Age Discrimination Statistical Analysis," is elaborately formatted, including 24-point font, white letters, red background, and bold text. You will now quickly remove all of the formatting. ***Click in cell D6. Then, on the Home tab, click the down arrow next to***

HANDS-ON EXERCISES

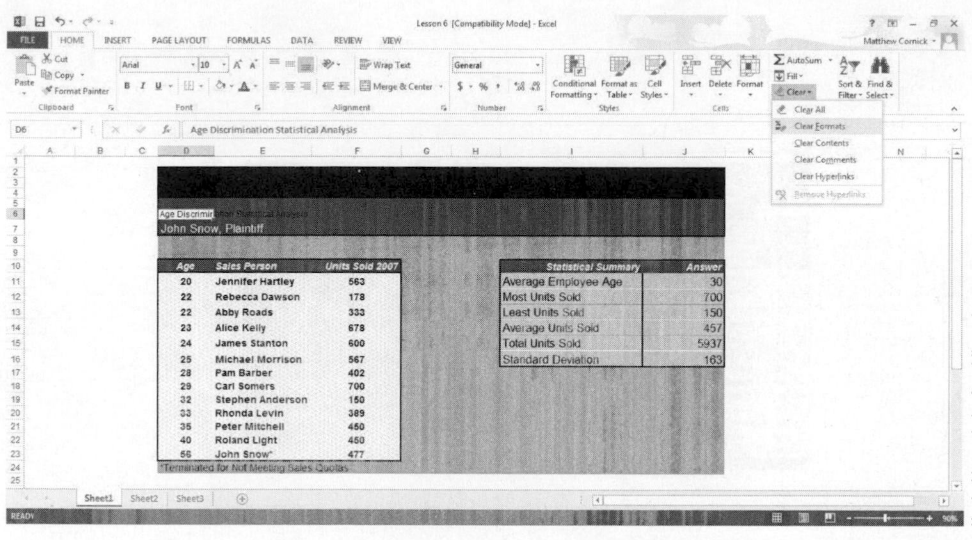

EXCEL 2013 EXHIBIT 15
Clear command

the Clear icon in the Editing group (it looks like an eraser—see Excel 2013 Exhibit 15). ***Click Clear Formats.*** All of the formatting should be gone. Notice in Excel 2013 Exhibit 15 that one of the options when using the Clear command is Clear All. Clicking Clear All will not only clear the formatting, but will also clear the contents of the selected cell(s).

17. Press **[CTRL]+[Z]** (invoking the Undo feature) to restore the original formatting to the cell.
18. Sometimes, particularly in large spreadsheets, it is helpful to have the formatting of a cell change if certain conditions are present. For example, in an actual-versus-budget report, if an item goes over budget by more than 10 percent it might be helpful for that to be bolded so it catches the reader's attention. To accomplish this, you will now learn how to use the Conditional Formatting feature of Excel.
19. Notice that the average sales for the sales team in your spreadsheet is 457. It might be helpful to highlight any salesperson who was over the average. ***Click in F11 and then drag the pointer to F23. From the Home tab, click Conditional Formatting in the Styles group*** (see Excel 2013 Exhibit 16).
20. ***Now, point to the first option, Highlight Cells Rules, and then click the first option again, which is Greater Than*** (see Excel 2013 Exhibit 16).

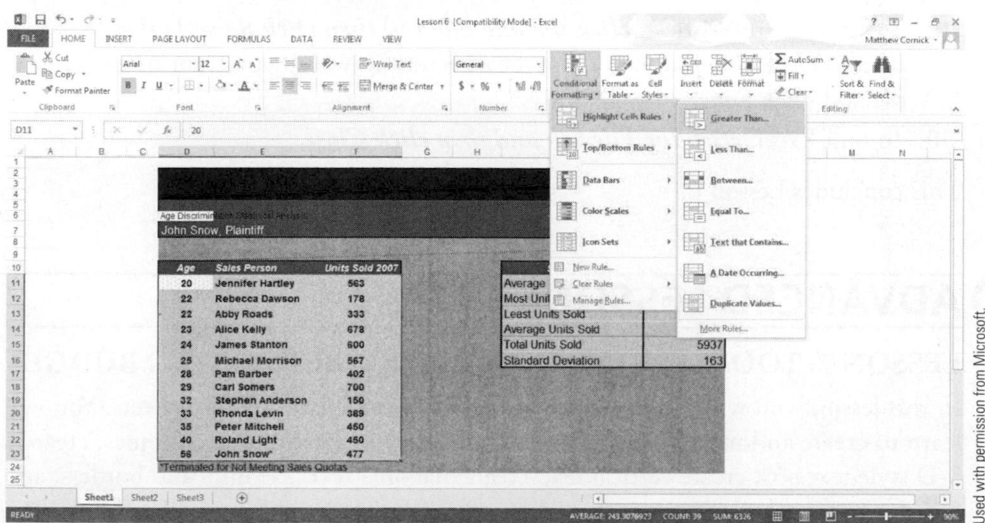

EXCEL 2013 EXHIBIT 16
Creating conditional formatting

EXCEL 2013 EXHIBIT 17
Creating a "Greater Than" conditional formatting

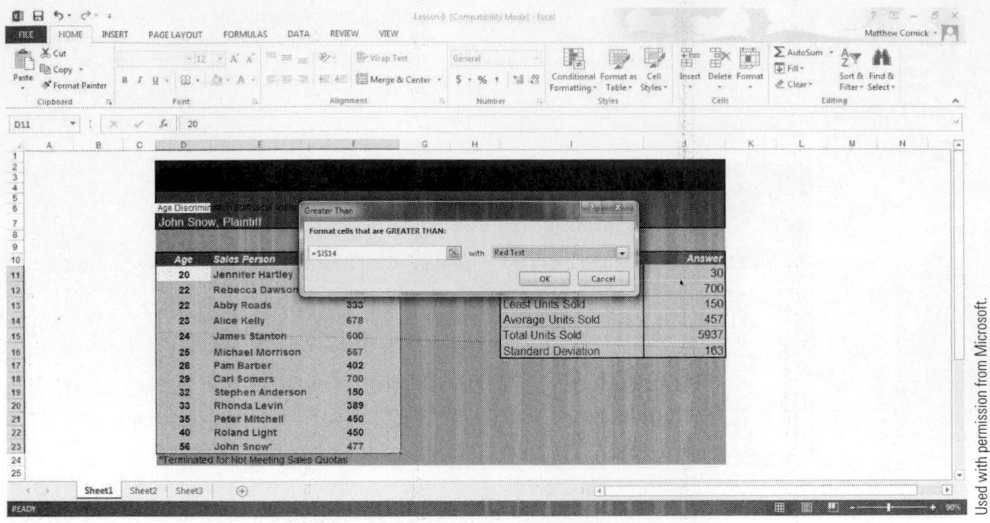

Used with permission from Microsoft.

21. The "Greater Than" window should now be displayed (see Excel 2013 Exhibit 17). Press the **[DEL]** key to remove the value under Format Cells that are GREATER THAN:.
22. ***Click cell J14 on the spreadsheet.*** Notice that cell J14 has been entered under Format Cells that are GREATER THAN:. Dollar signs have been added to the cell reference because this is an absolute cell reference.
23. ***Click the down arrow next to Light Red Fill with Dark Red Text and select Red Text.*** Cells over the average will be shown in red text. ***Click OK in the "Greater Than" window.***
24. You will now add clip art to your spreadsheet (assuming that clip art was included when Excel 2013 was installed). ***Click in cell I18. Then, from the Insert tab, click Online Pictures in the Illustrations group.***
25. The Insert Pictures task pane will appear. Next to Office.com: type **Money** and then ***click the Enter key.***
26. ***Click on any illustration you like***. The clip art used in Exhibit 10 is just an example. The clip art has now been added to your spreadsheet. ***Position the clip art where you want it by clicking and dragging it into position.***
27. ***Click the "X" in the Clip Art task pane*** to close the task pane.
28. To print the spreadsheet, ***click the File tab, then click Print, and then click Print.***
29. To save the spreadsheet, ***click the File tab and then click Save As then double-click Computer.*** Choose the directory in which you want to save the file and ***click Save.***
30. To quit Excel, ***click the File tab and then click Close.***

This concludes Lesson 6.

ADVANCED LESSONS

LESSON 7: TOOLS AND TECHNIQUES 1—MARKETING BUDGET

In this lesson, you will learn how to create visual impact with spreadsheets. You will learn to create and manipulate a text box, use advanced shading techniques, create a 3-D style text box, create vertical text, create diagonal text, use lines and borders, and create a comment. When the spreadsheet is complete, it will look like Excel 2013

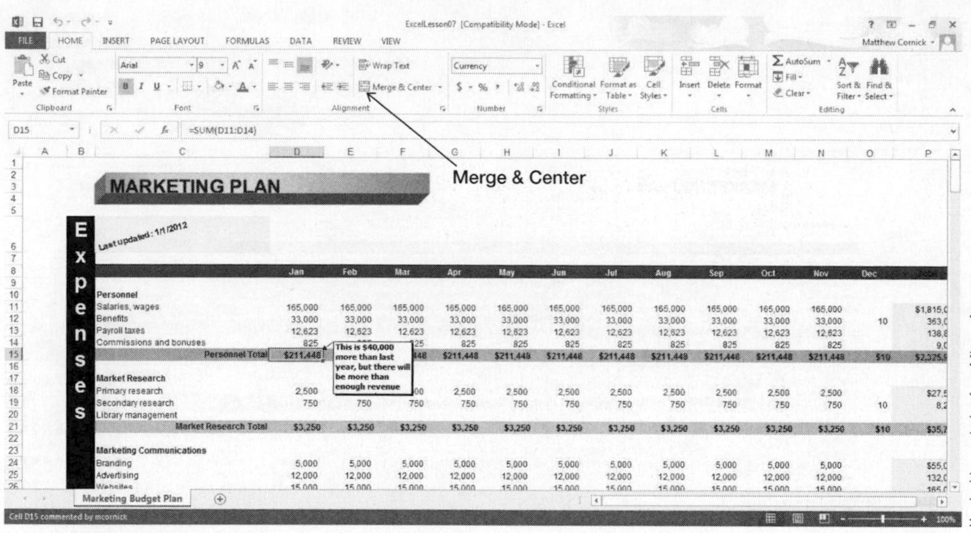

EXCEL 2013 EXHIBIT 18
Creating visual impact in spreadsheets

Exhibit 18. Keep in mind that if at any time you make a mistake in this lesson, you may press **[CTRL]+[Z]** to undo what you have done.

1. Open Windows. When it has loaded, ***double-click the Microsoft Office Excel 2013 icon on the desktop*** to open the program. Alternatively, ***click the Start button, point to Programs or All Programs, point to Microsoft Office, and then click Microsoft Excel 2013.*** You should now be in a clean, blank workbook.
2. The first thing you will do to complete the spreadsheet in Excel 2013 Exhibit 18 is to open the "Lesson 7" file from the Premium Website. Go to your CengageBrain account and ***click on the link for Premium Website*** for Cornick's *Using Computers in the Law Office*, 7th edition. A new window will open. ***Under Book Level Resources, click on the Data Files: Excel tab, then under Excel 2013, click on the "Lesson 7" file.*** When prompted, ***click Open.*** If you get a Security Warning, ***click Enable Editing*** to continue.
3. You should now have the Marketing Plan spreadsheet in Excel 2013 Exhibit 18 opened, except the spreadsheet is missing some of the formatting that gives it visual impact. You will add the formatting to the spreadsheet to make it more visually compelling.
4. You will first add the text box that holds the title "Marketing Plan," as shown in Excel 2013 Exhibit 18. ***From the Insert tab, click Text Box in the Text group.*** Notice that your mouse pointer just turned into an upside down letter "T."
5. ***Point to cell C2 and drag the pointer to about cell F4***. An outline of a box should now be shown from C2 to F4. This is a *text box.*
6. ***Click inside the text box. Click the Bold icon and change the font size to 20.***
7. Type **MARKETING PLAN.**
8. ***Right-click on the outline of the text box you just created. In the drop-down menu, click Format Shape.*** The "Format Shape" window should now be displayed on the right side of the screen. See Excel 2013 Exhibit 19.
9. ***In the Format Shape window, click Fill and notice that Solid fill is currently selected. Click Gradient fill.***
10. ***Click the down arrow next to Colors***. This will open a box with many colors; ***click Grey-25%, Background 2.***
11. ***Staying in the Format Shape window, point to the down arrow next to Type: and click Linear.***

EXCEL 2013 EXHIBIT 19
Formatting a shape

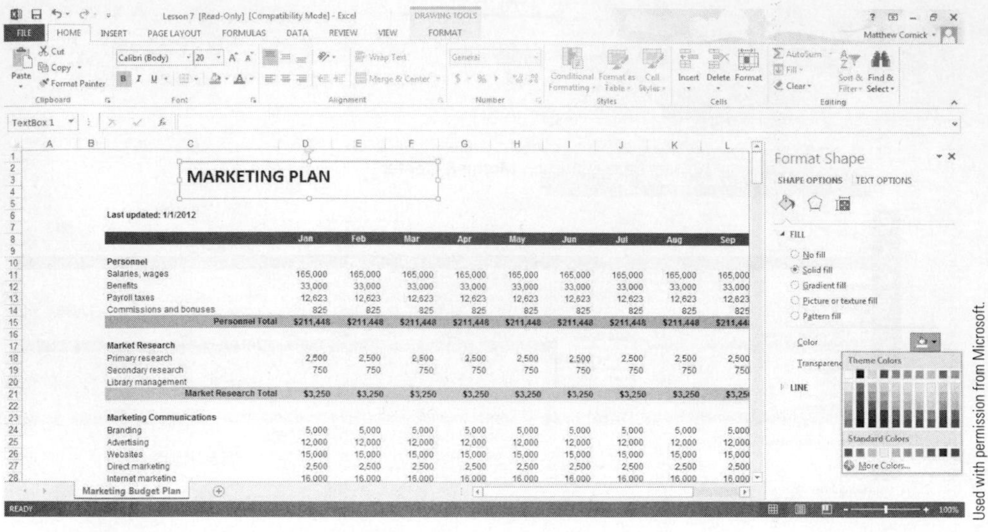

12. ***Still in the "Format Shape" window, click the second icon, Effects, then click 3-D Format.*** You will now add a 3-D style to the text box. ***Under Top Bevel, point to the down arrow and click the first selection under Bevel, which is Circle*** (see Excel 2013 Exhibit 20).

EXCEL 2013 EXHIBIT 20
Adding 3-D effect to a text box

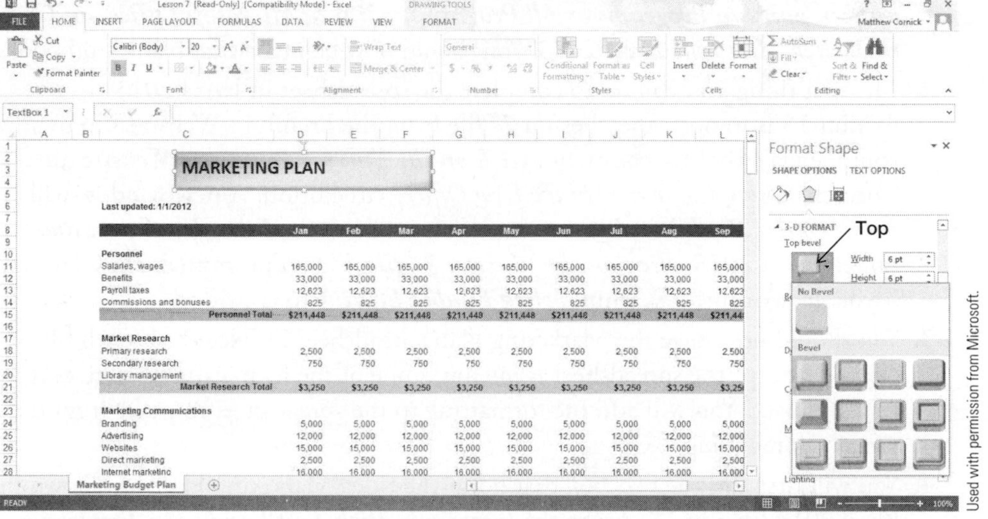

13. ***Click the small x in the upper right corner of the Format Shape window to close the Format Shape window. Click in any other cell so you can see the effect.***
14. You will now create the vertical text in Column B that says "Expenses," as shown in Excel 2013 Exhibit 18. Notice that this is actually one long cell. The first thing you will do is to merge cells B6 through B53 into one cell; you will then add the text and format it to be vertical.
15. ***Click in cell B6, drag the pointer down to cell B53, and then let go of the mouse button.***
16. ***From the Home tab, click the Merge and Center icon in the Alignment group.*** Notice that the selected cells have now been merged into one cell from B6 to B53.
17. With the cursor still in cell B6, ***change the Font Size to 22 and click the Bold icon.*** Type **Expenses** and press the **[ENTER]** key. The text is shown at the bottom of the cell; you will now correct this.

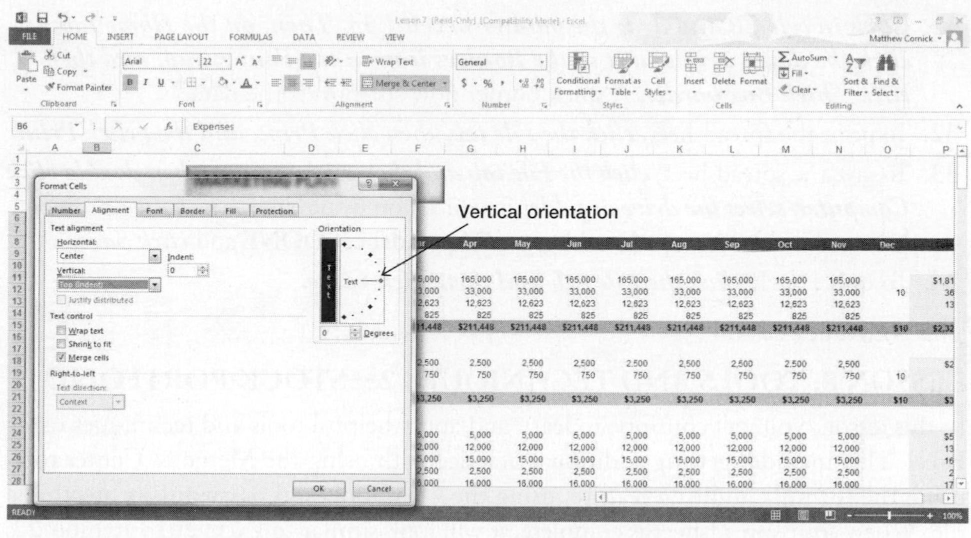

EXCEL 2013 EXHIBIT 21
Creating vertical text

18. ***Right-click anywhere in cell B6; then click Format Cells… .*** The "Format Cells" window should now be displayed. ***Click the Alignment tab*** (see Excel 2013 Exhibit 21).
19. ***In the "Format Cells" window, under Orientation, click the box that shows the word*** **Text** ***displayed vertically*** (see Excel 2013 Exhibit 21).
20. ***In the "Format Cells" window, under Vertical, click the down arrow and select Top (Indent).***
21. ***Click OK in the "Format Cells" window.*** The word "Expenses" should now be displayed vertically down the cell.
22. ***With the pointer still in cell B6, on the Home tab, click the down arrow next to the Fill Color icon*** (a paint bucket) ***in the Font group and then select Black.***
23. ***On the Home tab, click the down arrow next to the Font Color icon and select Yellow.***
24. You will next make the text in cell C6 appear diagonally. ***Right-click in cell C6; then click Format Cells… .*** The "Format Cells" window should now be displayed and the Alignment tab should be selected.
25. ***In the "Format Cells" window, under Orientation, click the up arrow next to Degrees until it reads*** **"15 degrees."**
26. ***In the "Format Cells" window, click the Fill tab. Click the yellow square; then click OK.***
27. ***Click in any cell to make the highlighting disappear.*** The words "Last updated 1/1/2012" should now be displayed diagonally in black letters with a yellow background.
28. You will now add the Comment shown in Excel 2013 Exhibit 18. ***Right-click in cell D15. On the drop-down menu, click Insert Comment.*** Type **This is $40,000 more than last year, but there will be more than enough revenue to cover this.** ***Click in any cell to exit the Comment box.***
29. ***Hover your cursor over cell D15*** so you can see the comment.
30. You will now add borders to the spreadsheet. ***Point to cell C53 and drag the pointer to cell P53. Then, on the Home tab, click the down arrow next to the Borders icon in the Font group and click All Borders.*** The "Totals" row should now have borders around each cell.

31. ***Click in cell C8 and drag the pointer to cell P53. Then, on the Home tab, click the down arrow next to the Borders icon in the Font group, and then click Thick Box border.*** A thick border now surrounds the data.
32. To print the spreadsheet, ***click the File tab, then click Print, and then click Print.***
33. To save the spreadsheet, ***click the File tab and then click Save As, then double-click Computer, select the drive or folder*** in which you would like to save the document. Next to File Name:, type **Excel Lesson 7 Spreadsheet DONE** and ***click Save.***
34. To quit Excel, ***click the File tab and then click Close.***

This concludes Lesson 7.

LESSON 8: TOOLS AND TECHNIQUES 2—STOCK PORTFOLIO

In this lesson, you will continue to learn and apply helpful tools and techniques using Excel. This includes getting additional practice with using the Merge & Center tool, using the formula auditing feature, using the Oval tool, and password- protecting a file. When your spreadsheet is complete, it will look similar to Excel 2013 Exhibit 22. Some of these tools have been covered in previous lessons, and this lesson will help cement your ability to use them effectively. This tutorial assumes that you have completed Lessons 1 through 7, and that you are quite familiar with Excel.

1. Open Windows. When it has loaded, ***double-click the Microsoft Office Excel 2013 icon on the desktop*** to open the program. Alternatively, ***click the Start button, point to Programs or All Programs, point on Microsoft Office, and then click Microsoft Excel 2013.*** You should now be in a clean, blank workbook. If you are not in a blank workbook, ***click the File tab*** (see Excel 2013 Exhibit 1), ***then click New, and then double-click Blank Workbook.***
2. The first thing you will do to complete the spreadsheet in Excel 2013 Exhibit 22 is to open the "Lesson 8" file from the Premium Website. Go to your CengageBrain account and ***click on the link for Premium Website*** for Cornick's *Using Computers in the Law Office*, 7th edition. A new window will open. ***Under Book Level Resources, click on the Data Files: Excel tab, then under Excel 2013, click on the "Lesson 8" file.*** When prompted, ***click Open.*** If you get a Security Warning, ***click Enable Editing to continue.***
3. You should now have the stock portfolio spreadsheet shown in Excel 2013 Exhibit 22 opened, except the spreadsheet will be missing two rows of data and some of the formatting. You will add the rows and formatting to the spreadsheet.

EXCEL 2013 EXHIBIT 22
Stock portfolio

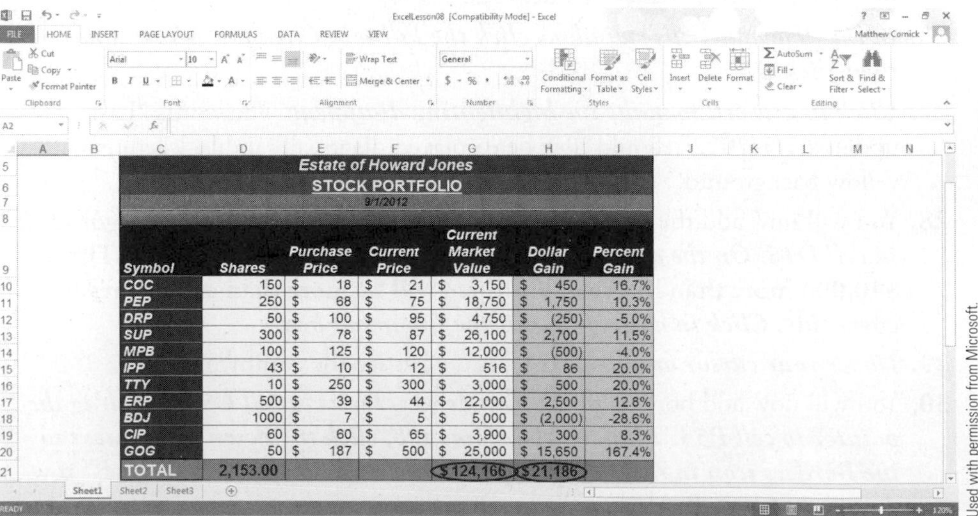

Estate of Howard Jones
STOCK PORTFOLIO
9/1/2012

Symbol	Shares	Purchase Price	Current Price	Current Market Value	Dollar Gain	Percent Gain
COC	150	$ 18	$ 21	$ 3,150	$ 450	16.7%
PEP	250	$ 68	$ 75	$ 18,750	$ 1,750	10.3%
DRP	50	$ 100	$ 95	$ 4,750	$ (250)	-5.0%
SUP	300	$ 78	$ 87	$ 26,100	$ 2,700	11.5%
MPB	100	$ 125	$ 120	$ 12,000	$ (500)	-4.0%
IPP	43	$ 10	$ 12	$ 516	$ 86	20.0%
TTY	10	$ 250	$ 300	$ 3,000	$ 500	20.0%
ERP	500	$ 39	$ 44	$ 22,000	$ 2,500	12.8%
BDJ	1000	$ 7	$ 5	$ 5,000	$ (2,000)	-28.6%
CIP	60	$ 60	$ 65	$ 3,900	$ 300	8.3%
GOG	50	$ 187	$ 500	$ 25,000	$ 15,650	167.4%
TOTAL	2,153.00			$ 124,166	$ 21,186	

4. ***Use the Merge and Center icon on the Home tab in the Alignment group to merge cells C5 to I5.***
5. ***Use the Merge and Center icon on the toolbar to merge cells C6 to I6.***
6. ***Use the Merge and Center icon to merge cells C7 to I7.***
7. Make sure the titles are aligned as shown in Excel 2013 Exhibit 22 ***(use the Left and Center Align icons on the Home tab in the Alignment group).***
8. ***Use the Fill Color icon on the Home tab, in the Font group, to make the fill color for cell C5 dark blue*** (or any color you choose).
9. ***Use the Fill Color icon to make the fill color for cell C6 purple*** (any light purple is fine).
10. ***Use the Fill Color icon to make the fill color for cell C7 gray*** (any light gray is fine).
11. The cell range from C8 to I8 is a text graphic box (similar to a text box, except that it is just more difficult to see). ***Right-click the box and select Format Shape. Click Fill, then click Gradient fill; next to Color, click on the first one of the Standard Colors, Dark Red*** (just hover your cursor over a color and the name will be displayed). ***Under Direction, click the first option, Linear Diagonal; then click Close to close the "Format Shape" window.***
12. ***Use the Borders icon on the Home tab, in the Font group, to give cells D10 to I21 a border of All Borders.***
13. ***From the Insert tab, click Shapes in the Illustrations group. Under Basic Shapes, click the Oval tool*** (it should be the second shape). ***Start in the upper left corner of cell G21 and drag the pointer to the lower right corner of G21 to make an oval around the total.*** *Note:* You can slightly move the oval by using the cursor keys on the keyboard to nudge it into place so it is centered in the cell.
14. The color of the oval must now be corrected. Notice that the ribbon has changed: the Drawing Tools Format ribbon is now displayed. ***Click the down arrow next to Shape Fill in the Shape Styles group of the Drawing Tools Format tab. Then, click No Fill.*** The oval is now surrounding the number, but the line color of the oval must be changed.
15. ***Right-click the oval and select Format Shape. In Format Shape window, click Line, then click Color. Then, click the down arrow next to Color, click Black, Text 1 and click Close in the "Format Shape" window.*** Make an oval in cell H21 identical to that in cell G21 using the same process.
16. You will now use the Formula Auditing mode to see the formulas that are in the spreadsheet and to ensure they are accurate.
17. ***On the Formulas tab, click Show Formulas in the Formula Auditing group.*** Scroll over to the right and look at all of the cells in your spreadsheet. Notice that instead of seeing the result of the formulas, you see the formulas themselves. This is a great tool for checking the accuracy of your spreadsheets. Look at your formulas and make sure they are correct. When you are sure your formulas are accurate, ***turn off the Formula Auditing mode by clicking on Show Formulas again.***
18. You will now learn how to password-protect your spreadsheet files. ***Click the File tab and then click Save As, then double-click Computer. In the "Save As" window, click Tools*** (it is in the lower portion of the window) and then ***click General Options...*** . Under File Sharing and next to Password to open, type **A** and ***click OK.*** At the "Confirm Password" window, type **A**, and

HANDS-ON EXERCISES

then ***click OK.*** At the "Save As" window, ***click Save*** to save the file to My Documents (or the folder of your choice—you must remember where you save it). You will then get a prompt that asks you whether you want to increase the security of the document by conversion to Office Open XML Format. Because this is just an exercise, ***click No.***

19. If you get a compatibility prompt, just ***click Continue.***
20. ***Click the File tab and then click Close to close the file.***
21. ***Now, click the File tab, and under Recent Workbooks click on the file you just saved.***
22. The "Password" window should now be displayed. Type **A** in the "Password" window. (The password is case sensitive, so if you typed a capital A when you created the password, you must type a capital A to open the document.) ***Click OK.*** The file should now be displayed.
23. You can turn off a password in the same way. ***Click the File tab, and then Save As. In the "Save As" window, click Tools and then click on General Options… .*** Under File Sharing and next to Password to open, use the **[DEL]** key to remove the asterisk. ***Then, click OK and click Save.*** At the **"Do you want to replace the existing file?"** prompt, ***click Yes.***
24. If you get a compatibility prompt, just ***click Continue.***
25. Close the file and then reopen it, and you will see that you no longer need a password to open it.
26. To print the spreadsheet, ***click the File tab, then click Print, and then click Print.***
27. To quit Excel, ***click the File tab and then click Close.***

This concludes the Excel 2013 Hands-On Exercises.

HANDS-ON EXERCISES

MICROSOFT EXCEL 2010 FOR WINDOWS

Number	Lesson Title	Concepts Covered
BASIC LESSONS		
Lesson 1	Building a Budget Spreadsheet—Part 1	[CTRL]+[HOME] command, moving the pointer, entering text and values, adjusting the width of columns, changing the format of a group of cells to currency, using bold, centering text, entering formulas, using the AutoFill/Copy command to copy formulas, and printing and saving a spreadsheet
Lesson 2	Building a Budget Spreadsheet—Part 2	Opening a file, inserting rows, changing the format of cells to percent, building more formulas, creating a bar chart with the Chart Wizard, printing a selection, and fitting/compressing data to one printed page
Lesson 3	Building a Damage Projection Spreadsheet	Changing font size, font color, and fill color; using the AutoSum feature; using the wrap text feature; creating borders; and setting decimal points when formatting numbers
INTERMEDIATE LESSONS		
Lesson 4	Child Support Payment Spreadsheet	Creating a white background, creating formulas that multiply cells, creating formulas that use absolute cell references, and using the AutoFormat feature
Lesson 5	Loan Amortization Template	Using a template, protecting cells, freezing panes, splitting a screen, hiding columns, and using Format Painter
Lesson 6	Statistical Functions	Using functions including average, maximum, minimum, and standard deviation; sorting data; checking for metadata; using the format clear command; using conditional formatting; and inserting a picture
ADVANCED LESSONS		
Lesson 7	Tools and Techniques 1—Marketing Budget	Creating and manipulating a text box, advanced shading techniques, working with a 3-D style text box, creating vertical and diagonal text, creating a cell comment, and using lines and borders
Lesson 8	Tools and Techniques 2—Stock Portfolio	Using the Merge and Center tool, using the Formula Auditing feature, using the oval tool, and password-protecting a file

GETTING STARTED

Overview

Microsoft Excel 2010 is a powerful spreadsheet program that allows you to create formulas, "what if" scenarios, graphs, and much more.

Introduction

Throughout these lessons and exercises, information you need to operate the program will be designated in several different ways:

- Keys to be pressed on the keyboard are designated in brackets, in all caps, and in bold (e.g., press the **[ENTER]** key).
- Movements with the mouse pointer are designated in bold and italics (e.g., ***point to File and click***).

- Words or letters that should be typed are designated in bold (e.g., type **Training Program**).
- Information that is or should be displayed on your computer screen is shown in bold, with quotation marks (e.g., **"Press ENTER to continue."**).
- Specific menu items and commands are designated with an initial capital letter (e.g., click Open).

OVERVIEW OF EXCEL 2010

I. Worksheet

A. *Entering Commands: The Ribbon*—The primary way of entering commands in Excel 2010 is through the ribbon. The ribbon is a set of commands or tools that change depending on which ribbon is selected (see Excel 2010 Exhibit 1). There are seven ribbon tabs: Home, Insert, Page Layout, Formulas, Data, Review, and View (see Excel 2010 Exhibit 1). Each tab has groups of commands. For example, on the Home tab, the Font group contains a group of commands that govern font choice, font size, bold, italics, underlining, and other attributes (see Excel 2010 Exhibit 1).

EXCEL 2010 EXHIBIT 1
Excel 2010 interface

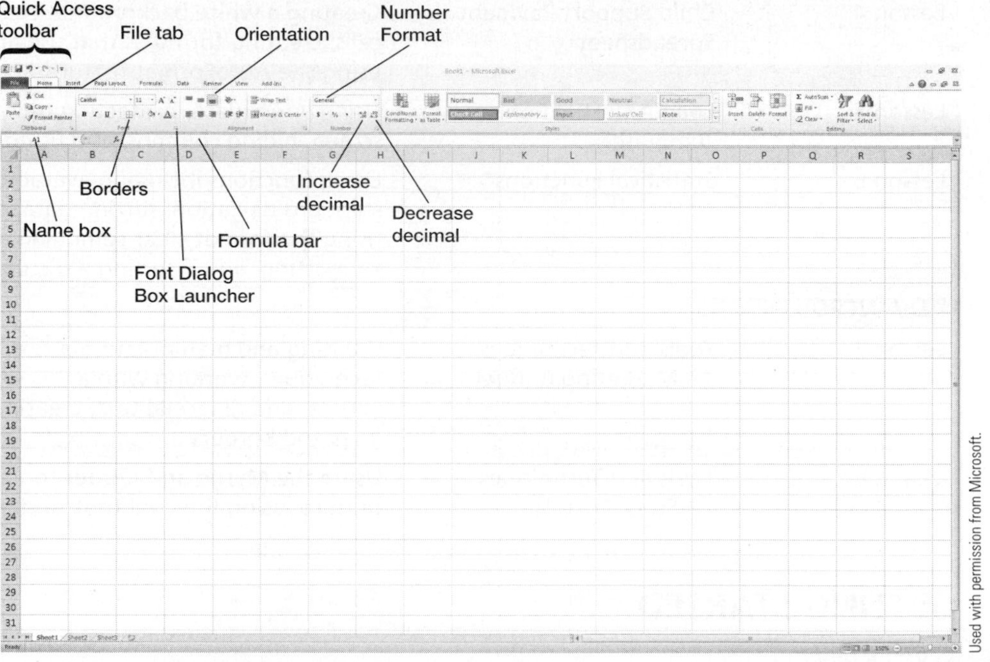

B. *File tab*—The File tab (see Excel 2010 Exhibit 1) is where a user accesses commands such as New, Open, Save, and Print. The File tab replaces the Office button used in Excel 2007.

C. *Entering Data*—To enter data, type the text or number in a cell, and press the **[ENTER]** key or one of the arrow (cursor) keys.

D. *Ranges*—A *range* is a group of contiguous cells. Cell ranges can be created by ***clicking and dragging the pointer*** or holding down the **[SHIFT]** key and using the arrow (cursor) keys.

E. *Format*—Cells can be formatted, including changing the font style, font size, shading, border, cell type (currency, percentage, etc.), alignment, and other attributes by ***clicking the Home ribbon tab, and then clicking one of the dialog box launchers in the Font group, Alignment group, or Number group.***

Each of these dialog box launchers brings up the same "Format Cells" window. You can also enter a number of formatting options directly from the Home tab.

F. *Editing a Cell*—You can edit a cell by ***clicking in the cell and then clicking in the formula bar.*** The formula bar is directly under the ribbon and just to the right of the fx sign (see Excel 2010 Exhibit 1). The formula bar shows the current contents of the selected cell, and it allows you to edit the cell contents. You can also edit the contents of a cell by ***clicking in the cell*** and then pressing the **[F2]** key.

G. *Column Width/Row Height*—You can change the width of a column by ***clicking the line to the right of the column heading***. (This is the line that separates two columns. When you point to a line, the cursor changes to double-headed vertical arrows.) ***Next, drag the pointer to the right or to the left to increase or decrease the column width, respectively.*** Similarly, you can change the height of a row ***clicking and dragging the horizontal line separating two rows***. You can also change the width of a column or height of a row by ***clicking somewhere in the column you want to change, clicking the Home tab, and then clicking Format in the Cells group.***

H. *Insert*—You can insert one row or column by ***clicking the Home tab, then clicking the down arrow below the Insert icon in the Cells group, and clicking either Insert Sheet Rows or Insert Sheet Columns.*** You can also insert a number of rows or columns by ***dragging the pointer over the number of rows or columns you want to add, clicking the Home tab, clicking the down arrow below the Insert icon in the Cells group, and then clicking either Insert Sheet Rows or Insert Sheet Columns.*** Finally, you can ***right-click and select Insert from the menu.***

I. *Erase/Delete*—You can erase data by ***dragging the pointer over the area*** and then pressing the **[DEL]** key. You can also erase data by ***dragging the pointer over the area, clicking the Home ribbon tab, clicking the down arrow next to the Clear icon in the Editing group, and then clicking Clear All.*** You can delete whole columns or rows by ***pointing and clicking in a column or row, then clicking on the Home ribbon tab, clicking on the down arrow next to Delete in the Cells group, and then clicking either Delete Sheet Rows or Delete Sheet Columns.*** You can also delete whole columns or rows by ***pointing in the column or row and then right-clicking and selecting Delete.***

J. *Quit*—To quit Excel, ***click on the File tab and then click Exit.***

K. *Copy*—To copy data to adjacent columns or rows, ***click in the cell you wish to copy and then select the AutoFill command,*** which is accessed from the small black box at the bottom right corner of the selected cell. Then, ***drag the pointer to where the data should be placed.*** You can also copy data by ***clicking in the cell, right-clicking, clicking Copy, clicking in the location where the information should be copied,*** and pressing the **[ENTER]** key. Finally, data can be copied by ***clicking and dragging to highlight the information to be copied, clicking the Home tab, and then clicking Copy in the Clipboard group.***

L. *Move*—Move data by ***clicking in the cell, right-clicking, selecting Cut, clicking in the location where the information should be inserted,*** and pressing the **[ENTER]** key. Data can also be moved by ***highlighting the information to be copied, clicking the Home tab, and then clicking Cut in the Clipboard group.*** Then go to the location where the information should be moved, ***click the Home tab, and click Paste in the Clipboard group.***

M. *Saving and Opening Files*—Save a file by ***clicking the File tab, then clicking Save or Save As,*** and typing the file name. You can also save a file by ***clicking the Save icon*** (it looks like a floppy disk) on the Quick Access toolbar (see Excel 2010 Exhibit 1). Open a file that was previously saved by ***clicking the File tab, clicking Open,*** and typing (or clicking) the name of the file to be opened.

N. *Print*—To print a file, ***click the File tab, then click Print, and then click Print.***

II. Numbers and Formulas

A. *Numbers*—To enter a number in a cell, ***click in the cell,*** type the number, and press the **[ENTER]** key or an arrow (cursor) key.

B. *Adding Cells (Addition)*—You can add the contents of two or more cells by three different methods:

1. To add the contents of a range of two or more cells:

a. ***Click in the cell where the total should be placed.***

b. ***Click the Home tab, then click the Sum icon in the Editing group*** (see Excel 2010 Exhibit 2). The Sum icon looks like a Greek letter "E." *Note:* To see the name of an icon, point to the icon for a second and the name of the icon will be displayed.

EXCEL 2010 EXHIBIT 2
Budgeting spreadsheet

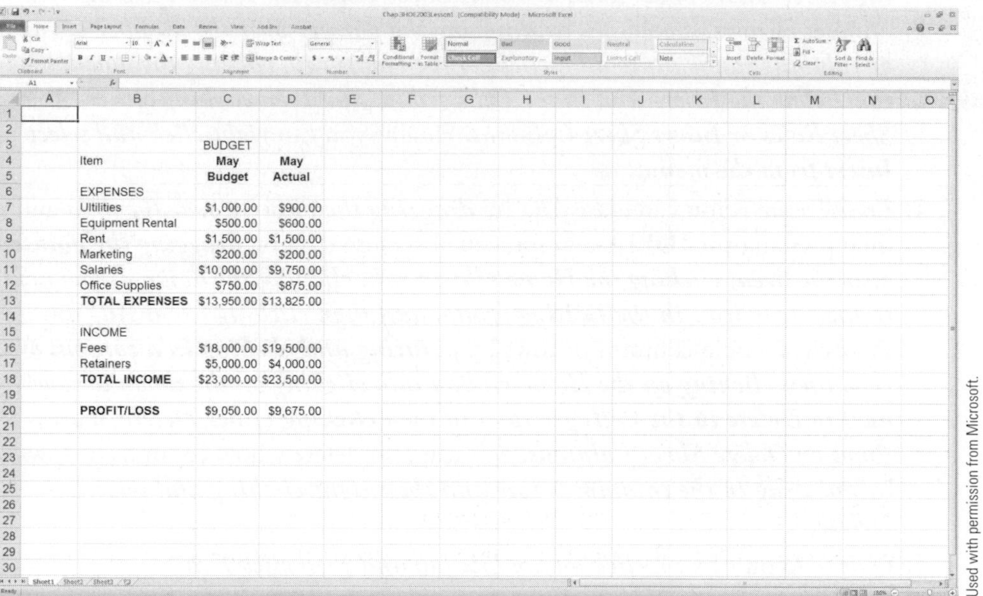

c. Excel guesses which cells you want to add. Press **[ENTER]** if the correct range is automatically selected, or select the correct range by highlighting it (i.e., ***clicking and dragging until the range of cells to be added is selected***). Then, press the **[ENTER]** key.

2. To add the contents of two cells, which need not comprise a range:

a. ***Click in the cell where the total should be placed.***

b. Press = (the equals sign).

c. Type the address of the first cell to be added (e.g., B4), or ***click in that cell.***

d. Press + (the plus sign).

e. Enter the address of the second cell to be added (or ***click in it***).

f. Press the **[ENTER]** key. (For example, to add the values of cells C4 and C5, you would type = **C4+C5**.)

3. To add the contents of a range of two or more cells:
    a. ***Click in the cell where the total should be placed.***
    b. Type **=SUM(**.
    c. Enter the address of the first cell to be added (or ***click in it***).
    d. Press **:** (a colon).
    e. Enter the address of the second cell to be added (or ***click in it***).
    f. Press **)** (a closing parenthesis).
    g. Press the **[ENTER]** key. (For example, to add the values of C4 and C5, the formula would read "**=SUM(C4:C5).**"

C. *Subtracting Cells*—To subtract the contents of one or more cells from those of another:
1. ***Click in the cell where the result should be placed.***
2. Press =.
3. Enter the first cell address (or ***click in it***).
4. Press − (the minus sign).
5. Enter the second cell address (or ***click in it***).
6. Press the **[ENTER]** key. (For example, to subtract the value of C4 from the value of C5, you would type **=C5–C4.**)

D. *Multiplying Cells*—To multiply the contents of two (or more) cells:
1. ***Click in the cell where the result should be placed.***
2. Press =.
3. Enter the first cell address (or ***click in it***).
4. Press * (**[SHIFT]+[8]**).
5. Enter the second cell address (or ***click in it***).
6. Press the **[ENTER]** key. (For example, to multiply the value in C4 times the value in C5, you would type **=C5*C4.**)

E. *Dividing Cells*—To divide the contents of two (or more) cells:
1. ***Click in the cell where the result should be placed.***
2. Press =.
3. Enter the first cell address (or ***click in it***).
4. Press **/** (the forward slash).
5. Enter the second cell address (or ***click in it***).
6. Press the **[ENTER]** key. (For example, to divide the value in C4 by the value in C5, you would type **=C4/C5.**)

BASIC LESSONS

LESSON 1: BUILDING A BUDGET SPREADSHEET—PART 1

This lesson shows you how to build the spreadsheet in Excel 2010 Exhibit 3. It explains how to use the **[CTRL]+[HOME]** command; move the cell pointer; enter text, values, and formulas; adjust the width of columns; change the format of cells to currency; use the bold feature; use the AutoFill and Copy features to copy formulas; and print and save a spreadsheet. Keep in mind that if at any time you make a mistake in this lesson, you may press **[CTRL]+[Z]** to undo what you have done.

1. Open Windows. When it has loaded, ***double-click the Microsoft Office Excel 2010 icon on the desktop*** to open the program. Alternatively, ***click the Start button, point to Programs or All Programs, point to Microsoft Office, and then click Microsoft Excel 2010.*** You should be in a clean, blank workbook.

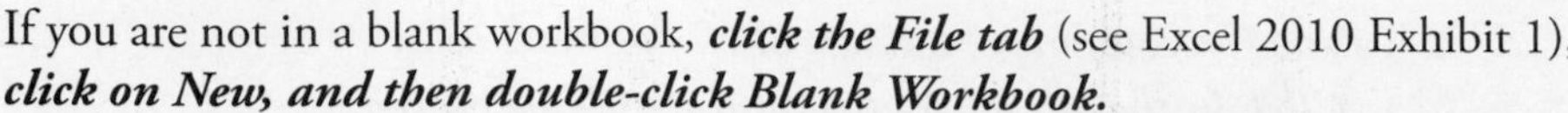

If you are not in a blank workbook, ***click the File tab*** (see Excel 2010 Exhibit 1), ***click on New, and then double-click Blank Workbook.***

2. Notice that the pointer is at cell A1, and the indicator that displays the address of the current cell (called the "name" box in Excel) says **A1**. The "name" box is just under the ribbon and all the way to the left (see Excel 2010 Exhibit 1). Also, notice that you can move the pointer around the spreadsheet using the cursor keys. Go back to cell A1 by pressing the **[CTRL]+[HOME]** keys.
3. Go to cell C3 by ***clicking in cell C3*** or by pressing the **[RIGHT ARROW]** twice, and then pressing the **[DOWN ARROW]** twice.
4. You will now enter the title of the spreadsheet in cell C3. Type **BUDGET** and then press the **[ENTER]** key.
5. Notice that the pointer is now at cell C4.
6. Press the **[UP ARROW]** to go back to cell C3. Notice that BUDGET is left-aligned. To center BUDGET in the cell, ***from the Home tab, click the Center icon in the Alignment group.*** It is the icon with several lines on it that appear centered (see Excel 2010 Exhibit 3). *Note:* If you hover the mouse over an icon on the ribbon for a second, the name of the icon will be displayed. Alternatively, ***from the Home tab, click the Alignment Group Dialog Box Launcher. Next, on the Alignment tab, under the Horizontal field, click the down arrow and select Center. Click OK.***

HANDS-ON EXERCISES

EXCEL 2010 EXHIBIT 3
Expanded budget spreadsheet

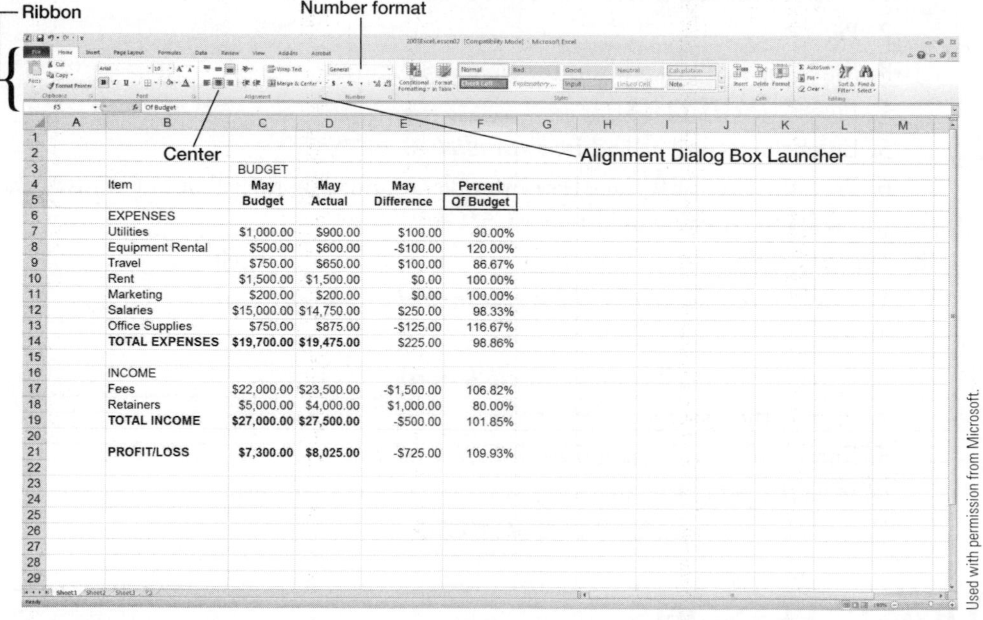

	B	C	D	E	F
3		BUDGET			
4	Item	May	May	May	Percent
5		Budget	Actual	Difference	Of Budget
6	EXPENSES				
7	Utilities	$1,000.00	$900.00	$100.00	90.00%
8	Equipment Rental	$500.00	$600.00	-$100.00	120.00%
9	Travel	$750.00	$650.00	$100.00	86.67%
10	Rent	$1,500.00	$1,500.00	$0.00	100.00%
11	Marketing	$200.00	$200.00	$0.00	100.00%
12	Salaries	$15,000.00	$14,750.00	$250.00	98.33%
13	Office Supplies	$750.00	$875.00	-$125.00	116.67%
14	TOTAL EXPENSES	$19,700.00	$19,475.00	$225.00	98.86%
16	INCOME				
17	Fees	$22,000.00	$23,500.00	-$1,500.00	106.82%
18	Retainers	$5,000.00	$4,000.00	$1,000.00	80.00%
19	TOTAL INCOME	$27,000.00	$27,500.00	-$500.00	101.85%
21	PROFIT/LOSS	$7,300.00	$8,025.00	-$725.00	109.93%

7. You should now be ready to enter the budget information. First, move the cell pointer to where the data should go, then type the data, and finally enter the data by pressing the **[ENTER]** key or one of the arrow (cursor) keys. Type the remaining row labels as follows:
Item in B4.
EXPENSES in B6.
Utilities in B7.
Equipment Rental in B8.
Travel in B9.
Rent in B10.
Marketing in B11.
Salaries in B12.

Office Supplies in B13.
TOTAL EXPENSES in B14.
INCOME in B16.
Fees in B17.
Retainers in B18.
TOTAL INCOME in B19.
PROFIT/LOSS in B21.

8. Notice that in column B, some of the data entries (such as "TOTAL EXPENSES" and "Equipment Rental") actually extend into column C. To correct this, you must increase the width of column B. ***Put the mouse pointer in the cell lettered B at the top of the screen. Move the pointer to the right edge of the cell.*** The pointer should then change to a double-headed vertical arrow and the column width will be displayed in a small box. ***Drag the pointer to the right until the column width is 18.00.*** Alternatively, you can change the cell width by ***placing the cell pointer anywhere in column B; then, from the Home tab, click Format in the Cells group, click Column Width…*** , type **18,** and ***click OK.***
9. Notice that all of the data entries now fit in the columns. Enter the following:
   May in C4.
   Budget in C5.
   May in D4.
   Actual in D5.
10. ***Click in cell C4 and drag the pointer over to cell D5*** (so that the whole cell range is highlighted)***; then, from the Home tab, click the Bold icon in the Font group, and click the Center icon in the Alignment group.***
11. You are now ready to enter values into your spreadsheet.
12. ***Move the pointer to cell C7.*** Type **1000.** Do not type a dollar sign or comma; these will be added later. Press the **[ENTER]** key to enter the value.
13. Enter the following:
   500 in C8.
   750 in C9.
   1500 in C10.
   200 in C11.
   15000 in C12.
   750 in C13.
   22000 in C17.
   5000 in C18.
   900 in D7.
   600 in D8.
   650 in D9.
   1500 in D10.
   200 in D11.
   14750 in D12.
   875 in D13.
   23500 in D17.
   4000 in D18.
14. The values you entered do not have dollar signs or the commas appropriate to a currency format. You will now learn how to format a range of cells for a particular format (such as the Currency format).
15. ***Click in cell C7 and drag the pointer over to cell D21. From the Home tab, click the down arrow next to the "Number Format" box, which should say***

HANDS-ON EXERCISES

"General" Then, click Currency. Then click OK. Notice that dollar signs have been added to all of the values. ***Click in any cell to deselect the cell range.***

16. ***Click in cell B14 and drag the pointer over to cell D14; then, from the Home tab, click the Bold icon in the Font group.*** This will make the TOTAL EXPENSES row appear in bold.
17. ***Click in cell B19 and drag the pointer over to cell D19; then, from the Home tab, click the Bold icon in the Font group.*** This will make the TOTAL INCOME row appear in bold.
18. ***Click in cell B21 and drag the pointer over to cell D21; then, from the Home ribbon tab, click on the Bold icon in the Font group.*** This will make the PROFIT/LOSS row appear in bold.
19. Your spreadsheet is nearly complete; all you need to add are the formulas.
20. ***Click in cell C14.***
21. Type **=SUM(** and press **[UP ARROW]** seven times until the cell pointer is at cell C7. Press **.** (a period) to anchor the range.
22. Press the **[DOWN ARROW]** six times, then press) (a closing parenthesis), and then press the **[ENTER]** key.
23. Go back to cell C14 and look at the formula in the formula bar. The formula should read "=SUM(C7:C13)." The total displayed in the cell should read "$19,700.00." Note that you also could have typed the formula **=C7+C8+C9+C10+C11+C12+C13.**
24. Enter the following formulas:
    =SUM(D7:D13) in D14.
    =SUM(C17:C18) in C19.
    =SUM(D17:D18) in D19.
25. You now need to enter formulas for the PROFIT/LOSS columns. Enter the following formula in C21:
    =C19–C14 (the total should read $7,300.00)
26. ***Go to cell C21 and click the AutoFill command*** (it is the small black square at the bottom right of the cell—see Excel 2010 Exhibit 2). ***Drag it one column to the right and release the mouse button.*** Notice that the formula has been copied. The total should be $8,025.00. Alternatively, ***go to cell C21, right-click, click Copy, then move the pointer to cell D21*** and press the **[ENTER]** key.
27. The spreadsheet is now complete. To print the spreadsheet, ***click the File tab, then click Print, and then click Print.***
28. You will need to save the spreadsheet, because you will use it in Lesson 2. To save the spreadsheet, ***click the File tab and then click Save. Under Save in:, select the drive or folder*** in which you would like to save the document. Next to File Name, type **Budget1** and ***click Save.***
29. To quit Excel, ***click the File tab and then click on Exit.***

This concludes Lesson 1.

HANDS-ON EXERCISES

LESSON 2: BUILDING A BUDGET SPREADSHEET—PART 2

This lesson assumes that you have completed Lesson 1, have saved the spreadsheet created in that lesson, and are generally familiar with the concepts covered in that lesson. Lesson 2 gives you experience in opening a file, inserting a row, formatting numbers as percentages, building additional formulas, creating a bar chart, printing selections, and fitting and compressing data onto one printed page. If you did not exit Excel after Lesson 1, skip steps 1 and 2, and go directly to step 3.

1. Open Windows. ***Double-click on the Microsoft Office Excel 2010 icon on the desktop*** to open the program. Alternatively, ***click the Start button, point to Programs or All Programs, point to Microsoft Office, and then click Microsoft Excel 2010.*** You should now be in a clean, blank workbook.
2. To retrieve the spreadsheet from Lesson 1, ***click on the File tab and then click Open. Next, click the name of your file*** (e.g., **Budget 1**). ***If you do not see it, click through the options under Look in:*** to find the file. When you have found it, ***click on Open.***
3. You will be entering the information shown in Excel 2010 Exhibit 4. Notice in Excel 2010 Exhibit 4 that a line for insurance appears in row 9. You will insert this row first.
4. ***Click in cell B9. From the Home tab, click the down arrow below Insert in the Cells group. On the Insert menu, click Insert Sheet Rows.*** A new row has been added. You could also have ***right-clicked and selected Insert*** to open a dialog box with the option to insert another row.
5. Enter the following:
   Insurance in B9.
   500 in C9.
   450 in D9.
6. Notice that when the new values for insurance were entered, all of the formulas were updated. Because you inserted the additional rows in the middle of the column, the formulas recognized the new numbers and automatically recalculated to reflect them. Be extremely careful when inserting new rows and columns into spreadsheets that have existing formulas. In some cases, the new number will not be reflected in the totals, such as when rows or columns are inserted at the beginning or end of the range that a formula calculates. It is always prudent to go back to each existing formula, examine the formula range, and make sure the new values are included in the formula range.
7. Change the column width of column E to 12 by ***clicking the column heading*** (the letter E) at the top of the screen. ***Move the pointer to the right edge of the column.*** The pointer should change to a double-headed vertical arrow. ***Drag the pointer to the right until the column width is 12.*** Alternatively, you can change the cell width by ***placing the cell pointer anywhere in column E and, from the Home tab, clicking Format in the Cells Group, and selecting Column Width… .*** Then type **12** and ***click OK.***
8. Enter the following:
   May in E4.
   Difference in E5.
   Percent in F4.
   Of Budget in F5.
9. ***Click in cell E4 and drag the pointer over to cell F5*** so that the additional column headings are highlighted. ***Right-click.*** Notice that in addition to a menu, the Mini toolbar appears. It has a number of formatting options on it, including Font, Font size, Bold, and others. ***Click the Bold icon on the Mini toolbar. Point and click the Center icon on the Mini toolbar.***
10. ***Click in cell E15 and drag the pointer over to cell F15. Then, right-click and click on the Bold icon on the Mini toolbar.***
11. ***Click in cell E20 and drag the pointer over to cell F20. Then, right-click and click on Bold icon on the Mini toolbar.***
12. ***Click in cell E22 and drag the pointer over to cell F22. Then, right-click and click on Bold icon on the Mini toolbar.***

13. You are now ready to change the cell formatting for column E to Currency and column F to Percent. ***Click in cell E7 and drag the pointer down to cell E22. Right-click and select Format Cells. From the Number tab in the "Format Cells" window, click Currency and then OK. Click in any cell to get rid of the cell range.***
14. ***Click in cell F7 and drag the pointer down to cell F22. From the Home tab, click the Percent (%) icon in the Number group*** (see Excel 2010 Exhibit 3). ***Then, from the Home tab, click the Increase Decimal icon twice.***
15. ***Click in any cell to get rid of the cell range.***
16. All that is left to do is to enter the formulas for the two new columns. The entries in the May Difference column subtract the actual amount from the budgeted amount for each expense item. A positive amount in this column means that the office was under budget on that item. A negative balance means that the office was over budget on that line item. The Percent Of Budget column divides that actual amount by the budgeted amount. This shows the percentage of the budgeted money that was actually spent for each item.
17. You will first build one formula in the May Difference column, and then copy it. ***Click in cell E7***, type **=C7–D7**, and press the **[ENTER]** key.
18. Using the AutoFill command or the Copy command, copy this formula down through cell E15. (To copy, ***right-click and then click Copy; highlight the area where the information should go; then right-click and select Paste and click the icon on the right, Match Destination Formatting.*** Alternatively, you can use the Copy and Paste icons in the Clipboard group on the Home tab.)
19. ***Click in cell E18***, type **=D18–C18**, and press the **[ENTER]** key.
20. Using the AutoFill command, copy this formula down through cell E22. Delete the formula in cell E21 by ***clicking in cell E21*** and pressing the **[DEL]** key.
21. You will now build on the formula in the Percent Of Budget column and copy it. ***Click in cell F7***, type **=D7/C7**, and press the **[ENTER]** key.
22. Using the AutoFill command, copy this formula down through cell F22. Delete the formula in cells F16, F17, and F21 by ***clicking in the cell*** and then pressing the **[DEL]** key.
23. The spreadsheet has now been built. We will now build a bar chart that shows our budgeted expenses compared to our actual expenses (see Excel 2010 Exhibit 4).

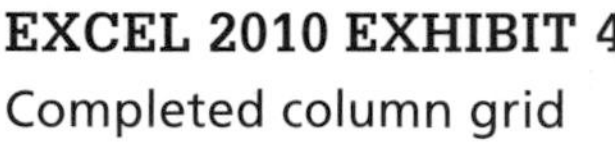

EXCEL 2010 EXHIBIT 4
Completed column grid

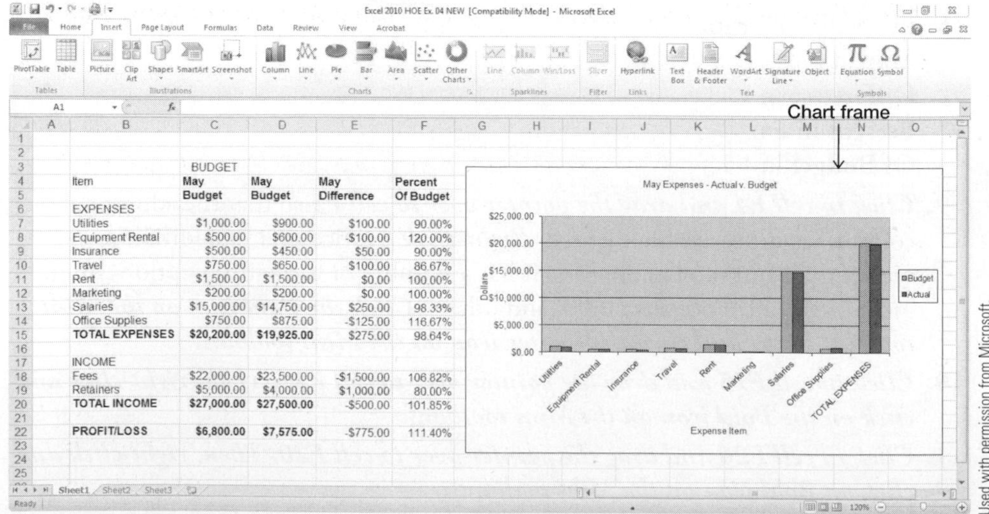

24. ***Click in cell B7 and then drag the pointer down and over to cell D15.***

25. ***From the Insert tab, click Column from the Charts group. Under 3-D Column, click the first option, 3-D Clustered Column*** (see Excel 2010 Exhibit 5).

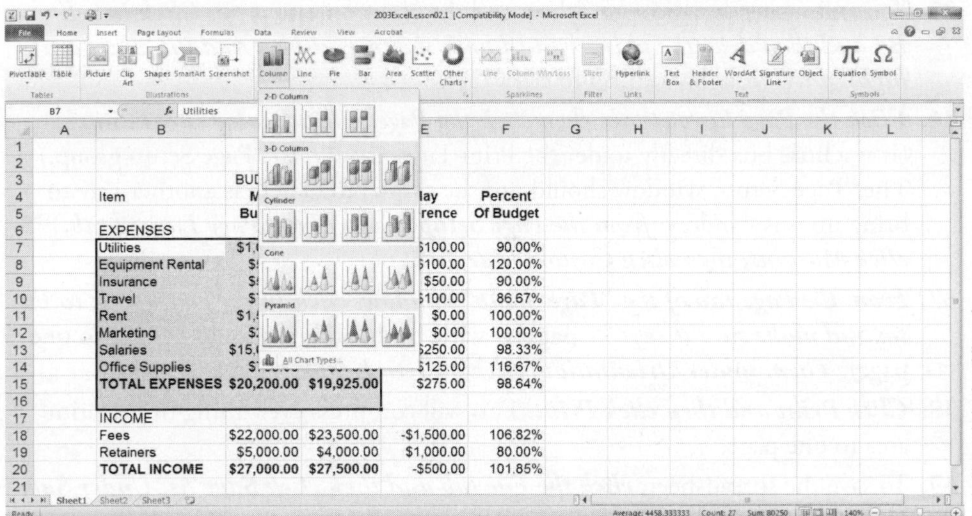

EXCEL 2010 EXHIBIT 5
Creating a column chart

26. Notice that a draft bar chart has been created. ***Click anywhere in the chart frame*** (see Excel 2010 Exhibit 4), ***and your pointer will turn to a four-headed arrow. Drag the chart across the spreadsheet so the upper left corner of the chart is near cell H4.***

27. ***Using the horizontal scroll bar*** (see Excel 2010 Exhibit 4), ***scroll to the right*** so the chart is completely in your screen.

28. ***Click the bottom right corner of the chart frame. Your cursor should change to a two-headed arrow that is diagonal. Drag the chart so that the bottom right corner ends near cell P26*** (see Excel 2010 Exhibit 4).

29. Notice that new options have been added to the ribbon (Chart Tools Design, Layout and Format). ***Click the Layout ribbon tab under Chart Tools.***

30. ***Click Chart Title in the Labels Group, and then select Above Chart.*** Notice that a title has been added, Chart Title.

31. ***Click on the "Chart Title" text in the bar chart*** and press the **[DEL]** key until the text is gone. Type **May Expenses—Actual v. Budget**. If you would like to move the title—for example, if it is off center—just ***click the title frame and drag it*** where you would like.

32. ***From the Layout tab (under Chart Tools), click Axis Titles in the Labels Group. Click Primary Vertical Axis Title and then select Vertical Title.*** Notice that a vertical axis title of "Axis Title" has been added. ***Click Axis Title*** and use the **[DEL]** key until the text is gone. Type **Expenses**.

33. To change the legend from Series1 and Series2 to Actual and Budget, ***right click on Series1, then click Select Data.*** The "Select Data Source" window will open. ***Click on Series1 (under Legend Entries (Series)) to highlight it, then click on Edit under the same heading.*** The "Edit Series" window will open. Type **Actual** in the text box under Series name:, ***then click OK.***

Click on Series2 (under Legend Entries (Series)) to highlight it, then click on Edit under the same heading. The “Edit Series” window will open. Type **Budget** in the text box under Series name:, ***then click OK.***

34. To print the chart, ***drag the pointer from cell G3 to cell Q27. Then click the File tab and click Print; under Print what, click Selection and then click Print.***
35. You will next print the spreadsheet and the chart on one page. ***Click in cell B3 and then drag the pointer until both the spreadsheet and the chart are highlighted*** (roughly cell B3 to cell Q27).
36. ***Click the Page Layout tab, then click the Page Setup Dialog Box Launcher.*** (It is a little box directly under the Print Titles icon in the Page Setup group.) The “Page Setup” window should now be displayed. There is another way to bring up this window: ***from the Page Setup group of the Page Layout tab, click Margins, then click Custom Margins.***
37. ***From the Page tab of the “Page Setup” window, click in the circle next to Fit to: and make sure it says “1 page(s) wide by 1 tall”*** (it should default to one page). ***Then, under Orientation, click on Landscape.***
38. ***Click Print and then click Print.*** This will compress everything in the print area to one page.
39. To save the spreadsheet, ***click the File tab and then click Save As. Under Save in:, select the drive or folder*** in which you would like to save the document. Then, next to File Name, type **Budget2** and ***click Save.***
40. To quit Excel, ***click the File tab and then click Exit.***

This concludes Lesson 2.

LESSON 3: BUILDING A DAMAGE PROJECTION SPREADSHEET

This lesson shows you how to build the Damage Projection spreadsheet shown in Excel 2010 Exhibit 6. It explains how to increase the size of type, how to wrap text in a cell, how to use the border features, how to use the font and fill color features, how to use the Auto-Sum feature, and how to change the decimal places for a number. This lesson assumes you have successfully completed Lessons 1 and 2. Keep in mind that if at any time you make a mistake in this lesson, you may press **[CTRL]+[Z]** to undo what you have done.

EXCEL 2010 EXHIBIT 6
Damages projection spreadsheet

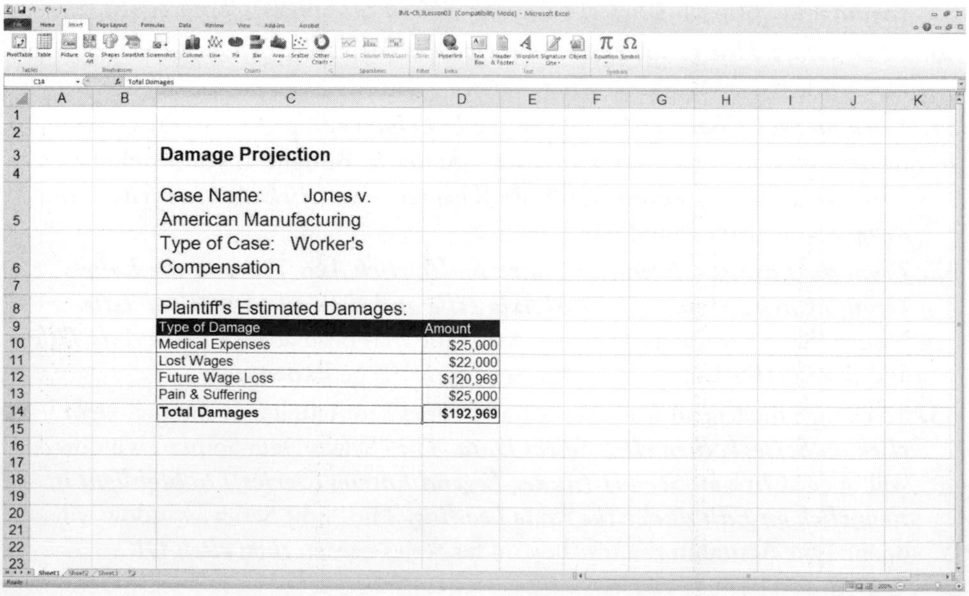

Damage Projection

Case Name: Jones v. American Manufacturing

Type of Case: Worker's Compensation

Plaintiff's Estimated Damages:

Type of Damage	Amount
Medical Expenses	$25,000
Lost Wages	$22,000
Future Wage Loss	$120,969
Pain & Suffering	$25,000
Total Damages	**$192,969**

1. Open Windows. When it has loaded, ***double-click the Microsoft Office Excel 2010 icon on the desktop*** to open the program. Alternatively, ***click on the Start button, point to Programs or All Programs, point to Microsoft Office, and then click Microsoft Excel 2010.*** You should now be in a clean, blank workbook. If you are not in a blank workbook, ***click the File tab*** (see Excel 2010 Exhibit 1), ***then click New, and then double-click Blank Workbook.***
2. To start building the spreadsheet in Excel 2010 Exhibit 6, begin by ***increasing size of column C to a width of 37 (Home tab > Cells group > Format > Column Width).***
3. In cell C3, type **Damages Projection.** With the pointer on C3 select the cell C3 and then, ***click the Bold icon from Font group on the Home tab. Change the size to 14 point by clicking the Font Size box in the Font group on the Home tab;*** then type **14.**
4. Type the text shown in cell C5 (see Excel 2010 Exhibit 6). ***On the Home tab, click the Font Size box in the Font group and change the type to 14 point.*** Notice that the text goes into the next cell. To wrap part of the text down to the next line within the current cell (see Excel Exhibit 6), ***from the Home tab, click the Wrap Text icon in the Alignment group*** (see Excel 2010 Exhibit 6). The text has now been wrapped down to the next line within the cell C5.
5. Type the text shown in cell C6, make the text 14 point, and wrap the text down so it does not go into cell D6.
6. Type the text shown in cell C8 and make the text 14 point.
7. Type the text and values shown in cells C9 to D13.
8. Type the text shown in cell C14.
9. To enter the formula in cell D14, ***click cell D14.*** Then, ***from the Editing group on the Home tab, click the Sum icon***. Notice that Sum assumed you wanted to add the values in D10 to D13. You could adjust the range by pressing **[SHIFT]+[ARROW]** keys, but the range should be fine as is (i.e., D10 to D13). Press the **[ENTER]** key to enter the formula.
10. ***Click in cell C9, drag the mouse pointer to cell D14, and change the font size to 14 point.***
11. ***Click in cell C9 and drag the pointer to cell D9. Right-click. On the Mini toolbar, click the down arrow next to the Fill Color icon*** (the paint bucket) ***and select the black square.*** (You also could have clicked the Fill Color icon in the Font group on the Home tab.) The cells are all black; now you just need to change the font color to white to see the text.
12. With cells C9 and D9 still highlighted, ***on the Home tab click the down arrow next to the Font Color icon in the Font group, and click on the white square.***
13. ***Click in cell C10 and drag the pointer to cell D14. From the Font group on the Home tab, click on the down arrow next to the Border icon.*** (It is typically just to the left of the Fill Color icon.) ***Click All Borders*** (it looks like a windowpane). Notice that there is now a border around every square that was highlighted.
14. ***Click in cell C14 and drag the pointer to cell D14. From the Font group on the Home tab, click the down arrow next to the Border icon again. Then click on the Thick Box border*** (it looks like a heavy black window frame). Move the pointer and notice that there is now a heavy black border around cells C14 and D14.
15. ***Click in cell D10 and drag the pointer to cell D14. From the Number group or the Home tab, click the dollar sign*** ($). Notice that two decimal places are shown (e.g., $25,000.00). It is not necessary to show two decimal places in

HANDS-ON EXERCISES

our projection, so we will change it to zero decimal places. ***From the Number group on the Home tab, click the Decrease Decimal icon twice.*** Notice that whole dollars are now shown.

16. To print the spreadsheet, ***click on the File tab, then click Print, and then click Print.***
17. To save the spreadsheet, ***click on the File tab and then click Save. Under Save in:, select the drive or folder*** in which you would like to save the document. Then, next to File Name, type ***Damages Projection*** and ***click Save.***
18. To quit Excel, ***click on the File tab and then click Exit.***

This concludes Lesson 3.

INTERMEDIATE LESSONS

LESSON 4: CHILD SUPPORT PAYMENT SPREADSHEET

This lesson shows you how to build the child support payment spreadsheet in Excel 2010 Exhibit 7. It explains how to create a white background, create formulas to multiply cells and formulas that use an absolute cell reference, and use the Auto-Format feature. This lesson assumes that you have successfully completed Lessons 1 through 3. Keep in mind that if at any time you make a mistake in this lesson, you may press **[CTRL]+[Z]** to undo what you have done.

EXCEL 2010 EXHIBIT 7
Child support payment spreadsheet

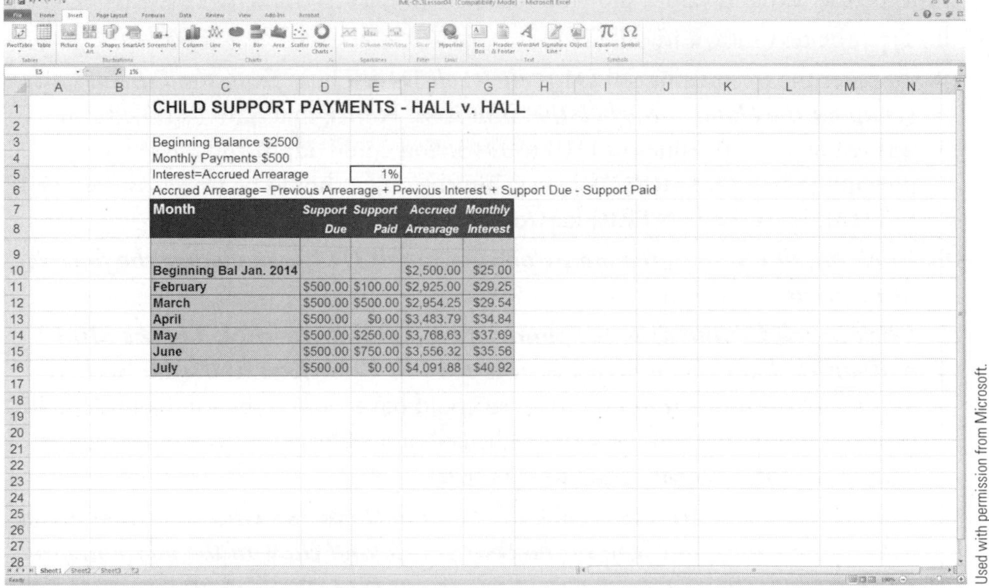

CHILD SUPPORT PAYMENTS - HALL v. HALL

Beginning Balance $2500
Monthly Payments $500
Interest=Accrued Arrearage 1%
Accrued Arrearage= Previous Arrearage + Previous Interest + Support Due - Support Paid

Month	Support Due	Support Paid	Accrued Arrearage	Monthly Interest
Beginning Bal Jan. 2014			$2,500.00	$25.00
February	$500.00	$100.00	$2,925.00	$29.25
March	$500.00	$500.00	$2,954.25	$29.54
April	$500.00	$0.00	$3,483.79	$34.84
May	$500.00	$250.00	$3,768.63	$37.69
June	$500.00	$750.00	$3,556.32	$35.56
July	$500.00	$0.00	$4,091.88	$40.92

1. Open Windows. When it has loaded, ***double-click the Microsoft Office Excel 2010 icon on the desktop*** to open the program. Alternatively, ***click the Start button, point to Programs or All Programs, point to Microsoft Office, and then click Microsoft Excel 2010.*** You should now be in a clean, blank workbook. If you are not in a blank workbook, ***click on the File tab*** (see Excel 2010 Exhibit 1), ***then click New, and then double-click on Blank Workbook.***
2. When you start to build the spreadsheet in Excel 2010 Exhibit 7, notice that the background is completely white. A completely white background gives you a crisp, clean canvas on which to work and to which you can add colors and graphics.

3. Press **[CTRL]+[A]**. The whole spreadsheet is now selected. ***From the Font group on the Home tab, click the down arrow next to the Fill Color icon, and then click the white square*** (it is all the way in the upper right corner). ***Click in any cell*** to make the highlighting disappear. Notice that the background of the spreadsheet is completely white.
4. Enter the text shown in cell C1; change the font to Bold and the font size to 14 point.
5. Increase the width of column C to 20.
6. Enter the text shown in cells C3 to C6.
7. In cell E5, type **.01** and press the **[ENTER]** key. Change the number format to Percent (zero decimal places).
8. Enter the text shown in cell C7 and in the cell range from D7 to G8. ***Click on C7 and click on Bold icon from Font group in Home tab. Click on D7 and drag the pointer to G8, click on Italic icon from font group in Home tab.***
9. Enter the text shown in the cell range from C10 to C16.
10. Enter the numbers (values) shown in cells in D11 to E16.
11. In cell F10, type **2500.**
12. In cell G10, press the = key. ***Click in cell F10***, then press **[SHIFT]+[8]** (an asterisk will appear), then ***click in cell E5*** and press the **[F4]** key once. The formula **=F10*$E$5** should be on the screen; press the **[ENTER]** key. The formula multiplies the accrued arrearage (how much the individual is behind on payments) times the interest rate (which is 1 percent). The reason you pressed **[F4]** is that the formula had to be an absolute cell reference; pressing **[F4]** simply put the dollar signs ($) into the formula for you. The dollar signs tell Excel that this is an absolute cell reference, rather than a relative cell reference. In this manner, when you copy the formula to other cells (see below), the accrued arrearage will always be multiplied by the value in E5. Said another way, the second half of this formula (**$E$5**) will not change when the formula is copied to other cells.
13. If you want to find out for yourself why the formula **=F10*E5** will not work once it is copied from cell G10 (where it will work fine), type **=F10*E5** in cell G10, and then copy the formula to cells G11 to G16. Once you have seen the effect of this, delete the changes you made and change the formula in cell G10 to **=F10*$E$5.**
14. To copy the formula from G10 to cells G11 to G16, ***click in cell G10, click the AutoFill handle*** (the little black box at the lower right corner of the cell), ***and drag the mouse pointer down to cell G16.***
15. In cell F11, type **=F10+G10+D11–E11**. The formula adds the accrued amount in the previous month to the previous month's interest and the current support due, and then subtracts the current amount paid.
16. To copy the formula from F11 to cells F12 to F16, ***click in cell F11, click the AutoFill handle, and drag the pointer down to cell F16.***
17. ***Click in cell D10 and drag the pointer to cell G16. Right-click; then click Format Cells. Click the Number tab, click Currency, and then click OK.***
18. Notice that the spreadsheet is very plain. We will use the Cell Styles feature to give the spreadsheet some color. ***Click in cell C7 and drag the pointer to cell G8. From the Styles Group on the Home tab, click the down arrow next to Cell Styles. Click Accent4*** (it is solid purple with white letters).
19. ***Click in cell C9 and drag the pointer to cell G16. From the Styles group on the Home tab, click the down arrow next to Cell Styles. Click***

20%—Accent1. (It is light blue with black letters.) ***Click in any cell to make the highlighting disappear.***

20. To add borders to the spreadsheet, ***click in cell C9 and drag the mouse pointer to cell G16. Then, from the Font group on the Home tab, click the down arrow next to the Border icon. Next, click the All Borders icon*** (it looks like a windowpane).
21. ***Click in cell E5. From the Font group on the Home tab, click the down arrow next to Borders. Then, click Thick Box border.*** Press the **[ENTER]** key. The spreadsheet is now complete and should look like Excel 2010 Exhibit 7.
22. To print the spreadsheet, ***click the File tab, then click Print, and then click Print.***
23. To save the spreadsheet, ***click the File tab and then click Save. Under Save in:, select the drive or folder*** in which you would like to save the document. Then, next to File Name, type **Child Support Payments** and ***click Save.***
24. To quit Excel, ***click the File tab and then click Exit.***

This concludes Lesson 4.

LESSON 5: LOAN AMORTIZATION TEMPLATE

This lesson shows you how to open a loan amortization template and fill it in (see Excel 2010 Exhibit 8). Templates are a great way to simplify complicated spreadsheets. You will also learn how to protect cells, freeze panes, split a screen, hide a column, and use the Format Painter tool. This lesson assumes that you have successfully completed Lessons 1 through 4. Keep in mind that if at any time you make a mistake in this lesson, you may press **[CTRL]+[Z]** to undo what you have done.

EXCEL 2010 EXHIBIT 8
Loan amortization template

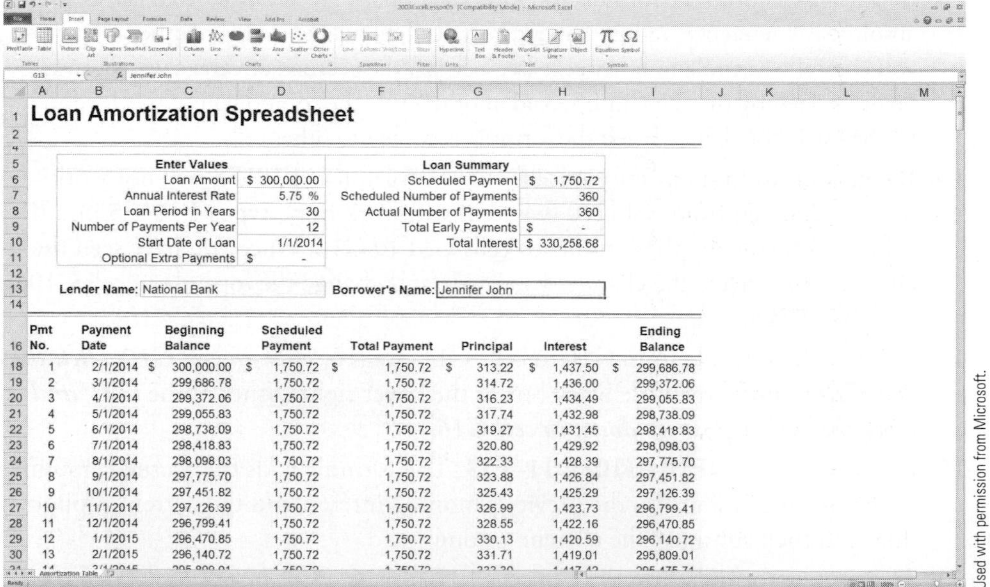

1. Open Windows. When it has loaded, ***double-click the Microsoft Office Excel 2010 icon on the desktop*** to open the program. Alternatively, ***click the Start button, point to Programs or All Programs, point to Microsoft Office, and then click Microsoft Excel 2010.*** You should now be in a clean, blank workbook.
2. The first thing you will do to complete the template in Excel 2010 Exhibit 8 is to open the "Lesson 5" file from the Premium Website. Go to your

CengageBrain account and ***click on the link for Premium Website*** for Cornick's *Using Computers in the Law Office,* 7th edition. A new window will open. ***Under Book Level Resources, click on the Data Files: Excel tab, then under Excel 2010, click on the "Lesson 5" file.*** When prompted, ***click Open.***

3. You should now have the Loan Amortization spreadsheet shown in Excel 2010 Exhibit 8 opened, except that your spreadsheet has no data yet.
4. Enter the following information:
   Cell D6: **300000**
   Cell D7: **5.75**
   Cell D8: **30**
   Cell D9: **12**
   Cell D10: **1/1/2014**
   Cell D11: **0** (When you click in Cell D11, a note will appear regarding extra payments; just type **0** (a zero) and press the **[ENTER]** key and the note will disappear.)
   Cell C13: **National Bank**
   Cell G13: **Jennifer John**
5. Notice that your spreadsheet now appears nearly identical to Excel 2010 Exhibit 8.
6. Notice that in your spreadsheet, just about everything below row 16 is a formula. If a user accidentally deletes one of these formulas, the whole spreadsheet could be affected. You will now turn on the Protection feature and lock some of the cells so they cannot be accidentally deleted.
7. ***Right-click in cell D6. Then click Format Cells... . Click the Protection tab in the "Format Cells" window.*** Notice that there is no green check mark next to Locked. Cells D6 to D13 and cell G13 are unlocked even when the Protection feature is turned on. When the Protection feature is off, you can change the lock/unlock format of cells by using the ***right-click, Format Cells... > Protection*** command sequence. Interestingly, when a new blank spreadsheet is opened in Excel, all cells default to "Locked," but this has no effect because the Protection feature is always turned off in a blank workbook.
8. ***Click Cancel in the "Format Cells" window*** to close the window.
9. Let's open a new spreadsheet so you can see that all cells in Excel start out with the format locked. ***Click the File tab, then click New, and then double-click Blank Workbook.***
10. You should now have a new blank spreadsheet displayed. ***Right-click in any cell and then click Format Cells... . Next, click the Protection tab.*** Notice that the cell is locked. However, the cell is not truly locked until you turn on the Protection feature.
11. ***Click Cancel in the "Format Cells" window in the new spreadsheet. Click the File tab and then click Close*** to close the file. You should now be back at your Amortization spreadsheet.
12. To turn on the Protection feature, ***on the Review tab, click Protect Sheet in the Changes group.***
13. The "Protect Sheet" window should now be displayed (see Excel 2010 Exhibit 9). Make sure that the first two selections under Allow all users of this worksheet to: are selected (e.g., Select locked cells and Select Unlocked Cells).

Notice that you could enter a password in the white box under Password to unprotect sheet. This would completely lock the spreadsheet (so only unlocked cells could be modified) to users who did not know the password. In this case this is not necessary; it is fine for someone to intentionally change the values at the top of the spreadsheet—we are just using this feature to prevent someone from accidentally changing the formulas below row 16.

EXCEL 2010 EXHIBIT 9

Protecting cells

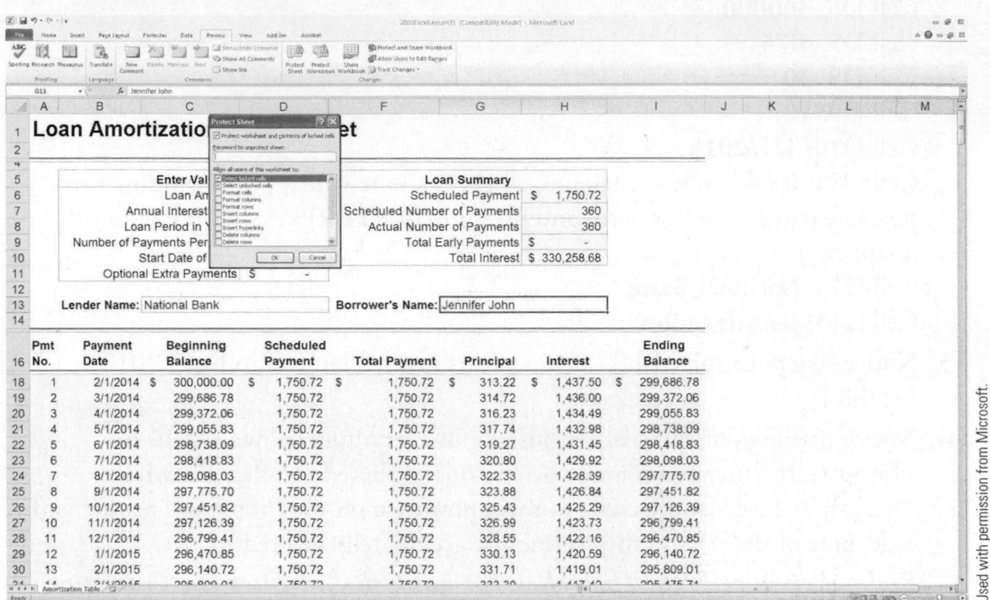

Used with permission from Microsoft.

14. After the first two items are check-marked under Allow all users of this worksheet to:, ***click OK.***
15. ***Click in any cell other than D6 to D13 or cell G13*** and try to type something in the cell. You should get an error message that says **"The cell [or chart] you are trying to change is protected and therefore read-only."** ***Click OK*** to close the error window.
16. The whole spreadsheet is now locked, except for cells D6 to D13 and cell G13, because these were not formatted as locked in the template.
17. Now you will turn off the Protection feature because you are still building the spreadsheet. ***On the Review tab, click Unprotect Sheet in the Changes group.***
18. You will now use the Format Painter tool to copy the formatting from one set of cells to another set of cells. Notice that cells F13 and G13 do not look like cells B13 and C13. You will copy the format from cells B13 and C13 to cells F13 and G13.
19. ***Point in cell B13 and drag the pointer to cell C13. Next, on the Home tab, click the Format Painter icon in the Clipboard group.*** (It looks like a paintbrush.) Your pointer now should have a paintbrush icon on it.
20. ***Click in cell F13, drag the pointer to cell H13, and then let go of the mouse button. Click anywhere to see the cell.*** Notice that the formatting has now been copied.

21. Column E in the amortization schedule of the spreadsheet is the "Extra Payment" column. Assume for the purposes of this exercise that you will not have any extra payments and that you do not need this column, but you want to leave the column there in case you need it at a later date. For now, you can hide column E until you need it later.
22. ***Right-click on the "E" in the E column heading*** (see Excel 2010 Exhibit 9). ***From the drop-down menu, click Hide.***
23. ***Click in any cell.*** The vertical line will disappear. Notice that column E is no longer displayed. The column heading goes from D to F.
24. We will now Unhide column E. ***Point on the D column heading and drag the pointer to the F column heading so that both columns are highlighted. Right-click, then click Unhide on the drop-down menu.*** Notice that column E reappears.
25. ***Click in any cell to make the highlighting disappear.***
26. ***Click in cell D18.*** Use the **[DOWN ARROW]** key to go to cell D60. Notice that the some column titles, such as "Pmt No.," and "Payment Date," are no longer visible, so it is difficult to know what the numbers mean.
27. Press **[CTRL]+[HOME]** to go to the top of the spreadsheet.
28. ***Click cell A18.*** You will now use the Split Screen command to see the column titles.
29. ***On the View tab, click Split in the Window group.***
30. Use the **[DOWN ARROW]** key to go to cell A50. Notice that because you split the screen at row 18, you can still see column titles. Next, use the **[UP ARROW]** key to go to cell A1. You should now see the top portion of your spreadsheet in both the top and bottom screens.
31. ***On the View tab, click Split again in the Window group.*** The bottom screen is now gone.
32. The Freeze Panes feature is another way to show the column headings when you scroll down a document. The Freeze Panes feature is a convenient way to see both column and row titles at the same time. ***Click in cell B18.***
33. ***On the View tab, click Freeze Panes in the Window group and then click the first option, Freeze Panes.***
34. Use the **[DOWN ARROW]** key to go to cell B50. Notice that because you froze the screen at cell B18, you can still see column titles. Next, use the **[RIGHT ARROW]** key to go to cell R50. You should still see the "Pmt No." column, including the payment numbers.
35. Press **[CTRL]+[HOME]** to go to the beginning of the spreadsheet.
36. ***On the View tab, click Freeze Panes in the Window group and then click the first option, Unfreeze Panes.***
37. To print the spreadsheet, ***click the File tab, then click Print, and then click Print.***
38. To save the spreadsheet, ***click the File tab and then click Save As. Under Save in:, select the drive or folder*** in which you would like to save the document. Next to File Name, type **Excel Lesson 5 Spreadsheet DONE** and ***click Save.***
39. Templates are a great way to utilize the power of Excel. There are many free templates available on the Internet. Microsoft alone offers more than 100 Excel templates on its website. To access them, ***click the File tab, then New.*** They are listed to the left under Office.com Templates.

40. To quit Excel, ***click the File tab and then click Exit.***

This concludes Lesson 5.

LESSON 6: STATISTICAL FUNCTIONS

This lesson demonstrates how to use and enter statistical formulas such as average, maximum, minimum, and standard deviation. It also shows how to sort data, check for metadata in spreadsheets, use the Format Clear command, use conditional formatting, and insert a clip-art file. When the spreadsheet is complete, it will look like Excel 2010 Exhibit 10. Keep in mind that if at any time you make a mistake in this lesson, you may press **[CTRL]+[Z]** to undo what you have done.

EXCEL 2010 EXHIBIT 10

Statistical spreadsheet

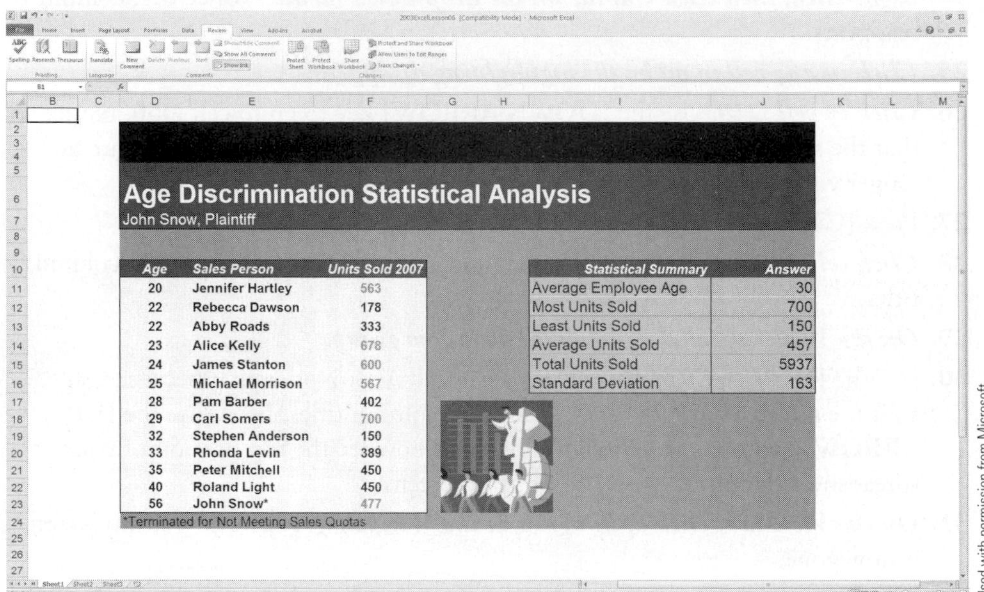

1. Open Windows. When it has loaded, ***double-click the Microsoft Office Excel 2010 icon on the desktop*** to open the program. Alternatively, ***click the Start button, point to Programs or All Programs, point to Microsoft Office, and then click Microsoft Excel 2010.*** You should now be in a clean, blank workbook. If you are not in a blank workbook, ***click the File tab*** (see Excel 2010 Exhibit 1), ***then click New, and then double-click on Blank Workbook.***
2. The first thing you will do to complete the template shown in Excel 2010 Exhibit 10 is to open the "Lesson 6" file from the Premium Website. Go to your CengageBrain account and ***click on the link for Premium Website*** for Cornick's *Using Computers in the Law Office,* 7th edition. A new window will open. ***Under Book Level Resources, click on the Data Files: Excel tab, then under Excel 2010, click on the "Lesson 6" file.*** When prompted, ***click Open.***
3. You should now see the Age Discrimination Statistical Analysis spreadsheet shown in Excel 2010 Exhibit 10, except your spreadsheet has no formulas in the statistical summary section, the data have not yet been sorted, and there is no clip art yet.
4. You will now enter the formulas in the Statistical Summary section of the spreadsheet. The first formula will calculate the average age of

employees of the company. ***Click in cell J11.*** Type the following formula: **=AVERAGE(D11:D23)** and then press the **[ENTER]** key. The result should be 30. *Note:* Another way to enter the average function is to ***go to the Formulas tab and click Insert Function in the Function Library group; next to Or select a category, click the down arrow, then click Statistical, average, and OK.***

5. The next formula will calculate the most units sold. ***Click in cell J12.*** Type the following formula: **=MAX(F11:F23)** and then press the **[ENTER]** key. The result should be 700.
6. The next formula will calculate the least units sold. ***Click in cell J13.*** Type the following formula: **=MIN(F11:F23)** and then press the **[ENTER]** key. The result should be 150.
7. The next formula will calculate the average units sold. ***Click in cell J14.*** Type the following formula: **=AVERAGE(F11:F23)** and then press the **[ENTER]** key. The result should be 457.
8. The next formula will calculate the total units sold. ***Click in cell J15.*** Type the following formula: **=SUM(F11:F23)** and then press the **[ENTER]** key. The result should be 5937.
9. The last formula will calculate the standard deviation for units sold. The standard deviation is a measure of how widely values are dispersed from the average value (the arithmetic mean). Large standard deviations show that the numbers vary widely from the average. ***On the Formulas tab, click Insert Function in the Function Library group. Next to Or select a category, click the down arrow and select Statistical. Then, scroll down the list and click*** **STDEV.P** (see Excel 2010 Exhibit 11). Notice there is a definition for this function. ***Click OK in the "Insert Function" window.***

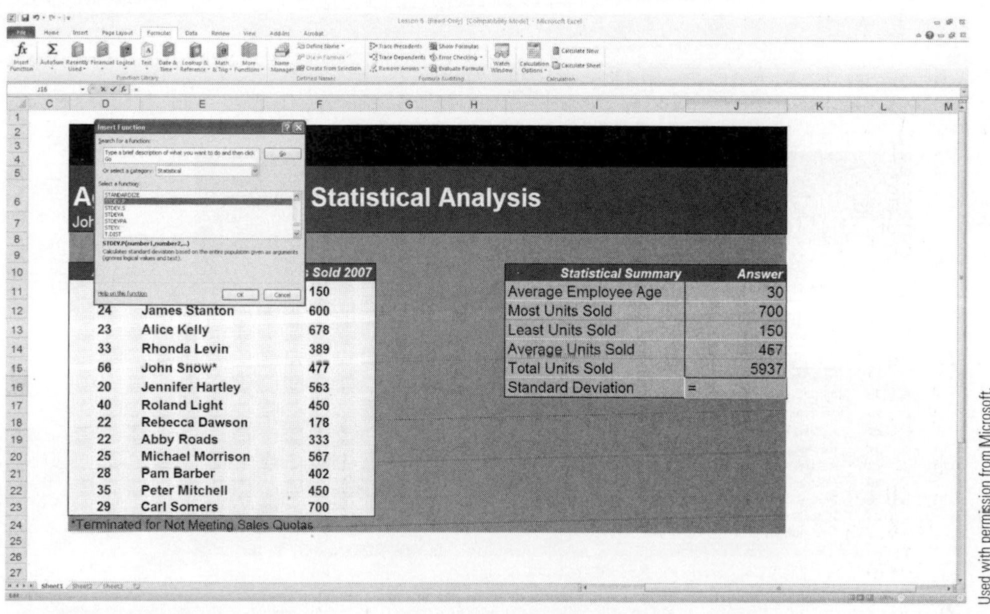

EXCEL 2010 EXHIBIT 11
Entering a standard deviation formula using the insert function command

10. The "Function Arguments" window should now be displayed (see Excel 2010 Exhibit 12). In the "Function Arguments" window, next to Number 1, press **[DEL]** until the box is blank; type **F11:F23** and then ***click OK.*** The result should be 163.

EXCEL 2010 EXHIBIT 12
Entering a standard deviation formula using the functions argument window

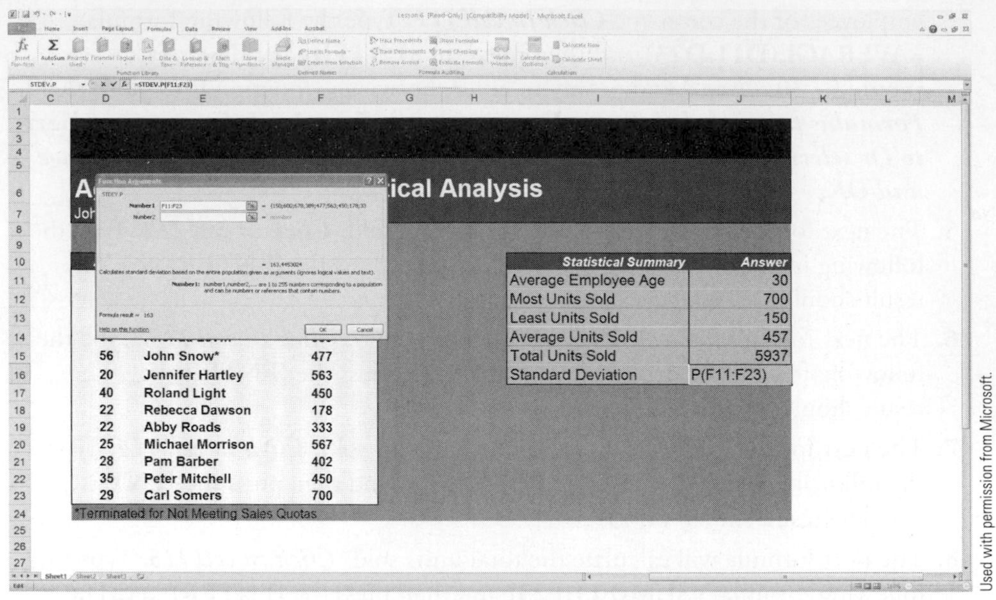

11. You will now sort the data based on the age of the employees. ***Click in D11 and then drag the pointer down to F23. From the Data tab, click Sort in the Sort and Filter group.***
12. The "Sort" window should now be displayed (see Excel 2010 Exhibit 13). *Note:* Even though you just want to sort by age, you must select the full data range that includes all of the information, or the age data will be sorted but the other columns and rows will stay where they are. The data will therefore be mismatched (each age will not be matched with the correct person and number of units sold).

EXCEL 2010 EXHIBIT 13
Sorting data

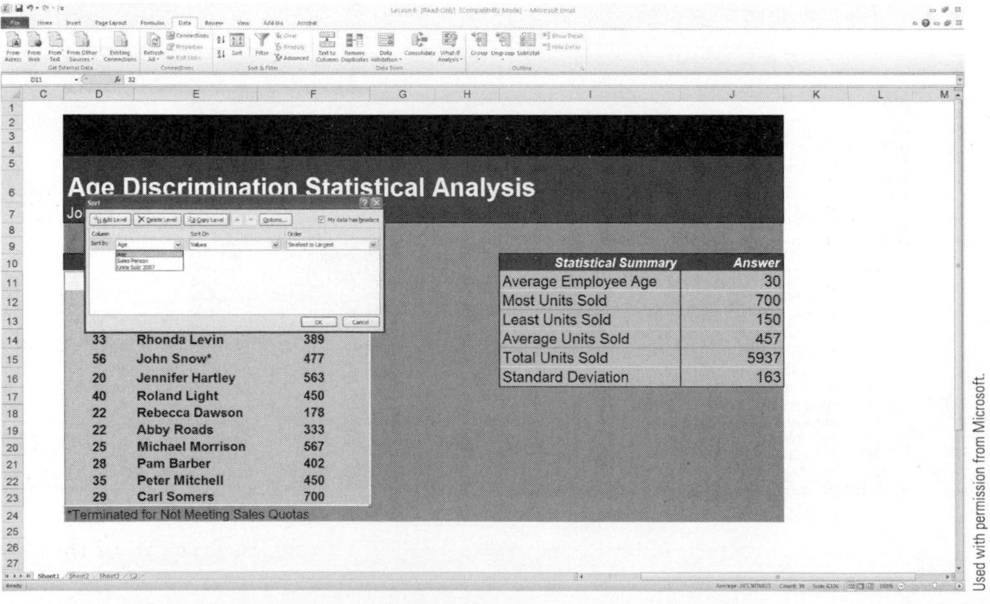

13. ***In the "Sort" window, click the down arrow next to Sort by, then click Age*** (see Excel 2010 Exhibit 13). Notice that under Order, the default of Smallest to Largest is selected; this is fine, so ***click OK in the "Sort" window.*** The data

should now be sorted according to the age of the individual, with John Snow appearing last in the spreadsheet.

14. You will now ensure that no metadata is included in your document. You must first save the spreadsheet. To save the spreadsheet, ***click the File tab and then click Save As. Under Save in:, select the drive or folder*** in which you would like to save the document. Next to File Name, type **Excel Lesson 6 Spreadsheet DONE** and ***click Save.***
15. Excel 2010 has a special feature called Inspect Document that can extract all metadata from your spreadsheet. ***Click the File tab; next to Prepare for Sharing, click Check for Issues, then click Inspect Document*** (see Excel 2010 Exhibit 14). Through the "Document Inspector" window, all of the possible places metadata can hide are checked. ***Click Inspect.*** Some of the categories may have a Remove All button. If you wanted to remove the metadata, you would just click on Remove All for each category. Because this is just an exercise, we do not need to remove the metadata, so go ahead and ***click Close*** to close the "Document Inspector" window.

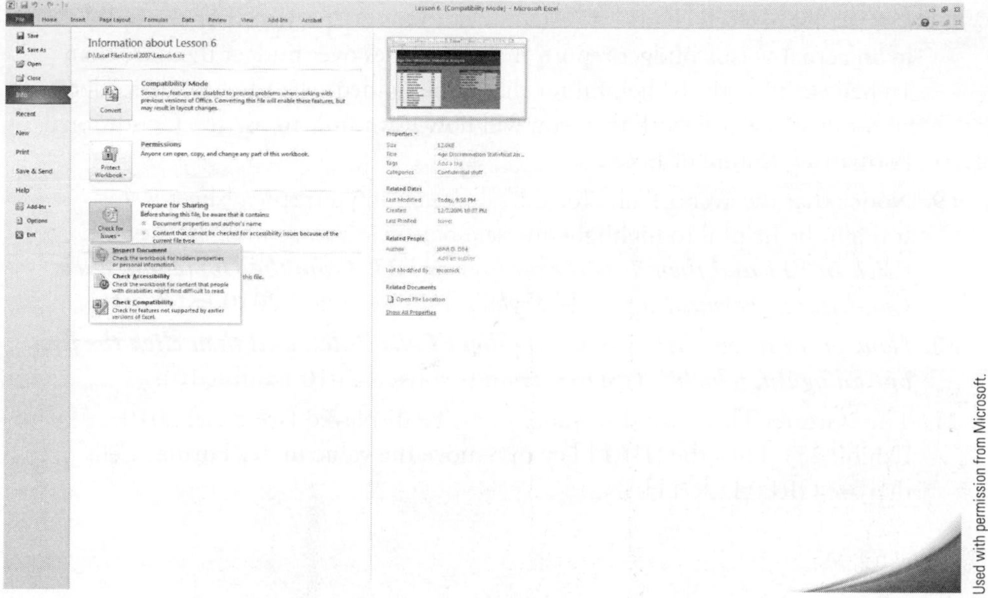

EXCEL 2010 EXHIBIT 14
Removing metadata

16. Sometimes it is helpful to clear a cell or cells of all formatting information at one time. Notice that cell D6, the one titled "Age Discrimination Statistical Analysis," is elaborately formatted, including 24-point font, white letters, red background, and bold text. You will now quickly remove all of the formatting. ***Click in cell D6. Then, on the Home tab, click the down arrow next to the Clear icon in the Editing group*** (it looks like an eraser—see Excel 2010 Exhibit 15). ***Click Clear Formats.*** All of the formatting should be gone. Notice in Excel 2010 Exhibit 15 that one of the options when using the Clear command is Clear All. Clicking Clear All will not only clear the formatting, but will also clear the contents of the selected cell(s).
17. Press **[CTRL]+[Z]** (invoking the Undo feature) to restore the original formatting to the cell.

EXCEL 2010 EXHIBIT 15
Clear command

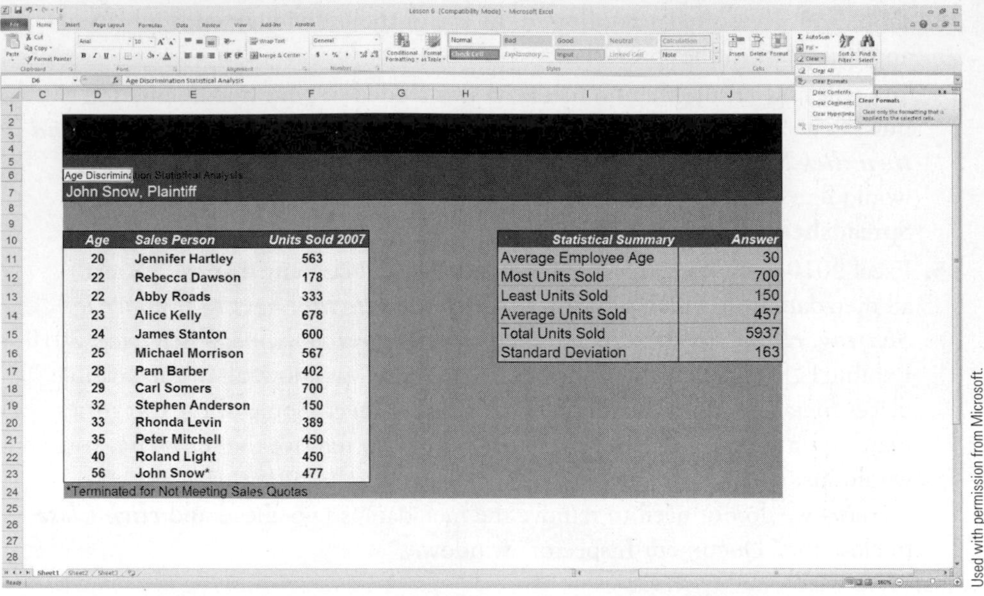

18. Sometimes, particularly in large spreadsheets, it is helpful to have the formatting of a cell change if certain conditions are present. For example, in an actual-versus-budget report, if an item goes over budget by more than 10 percent it might be helpful for that to be bolded so it catches the reader's attention. To accomplish this, you will now learn how to use the Conditional Formatting feature of Excel.
19. Notice that the average sales for the sales team in your spreadsheet is 457. It might be helpful to highlight any salesperson who was over the average. ***Click in F11 and then drag the pointer to F23. From the Home tab, click Conditional Formatting in the Styles group*** (see Excel 2010 Exhibit 16).
20. ***Now, point to the first option, Highlight Cells Rules, and then click the first option again, which is Greater Than*** (see Excel 2010 Exhibit 16).
21. The "Greater Than" window should now be displayed (see Excel 2010 Exhibit 17). Press the **[DEL]** key to remove the value under Format Cells that are GREATER THAN:.

EXCEL 2010 EXHIBIT 16
Creating conditional formatting

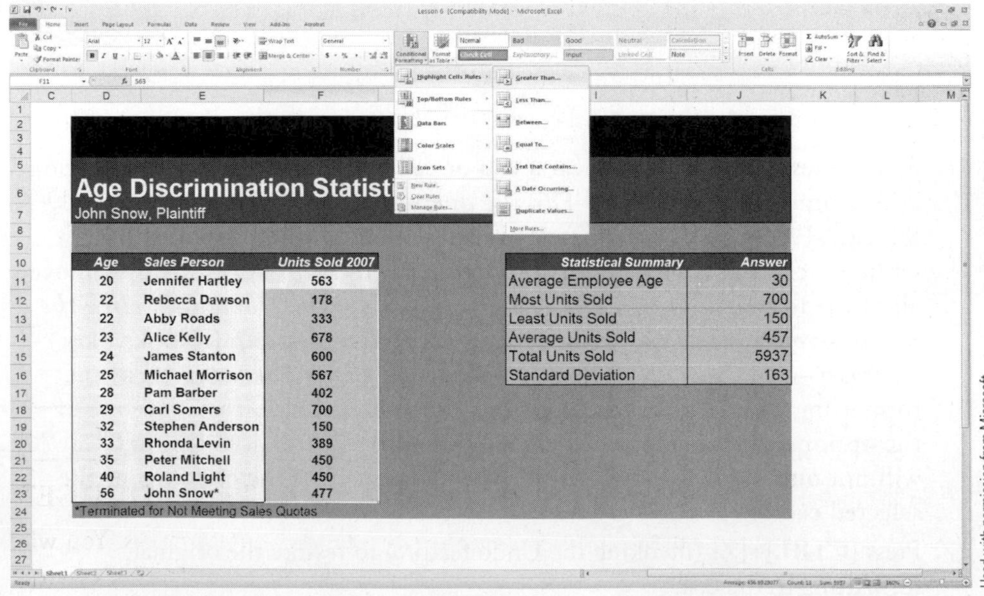

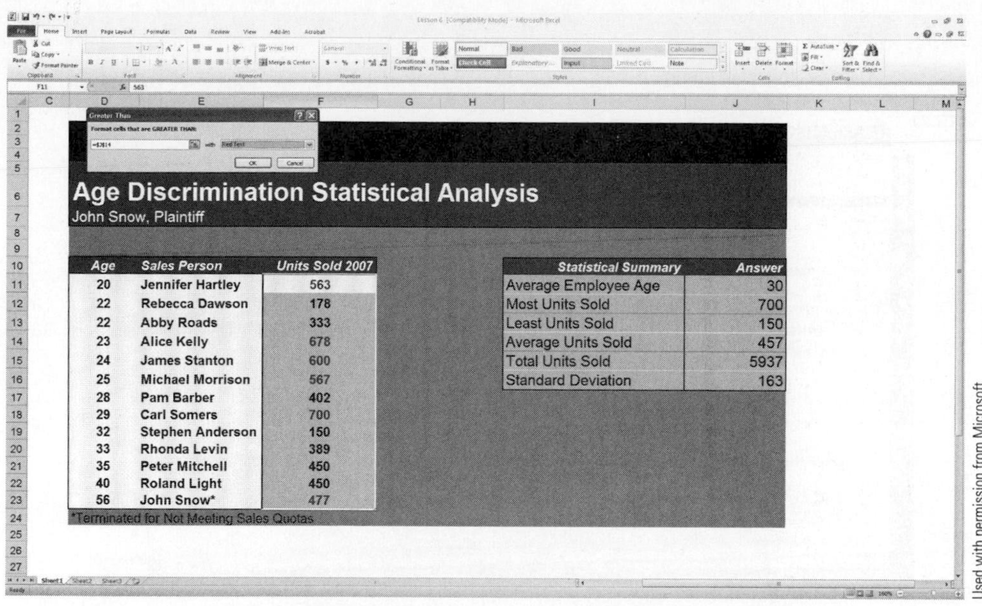

EXCEL 2010 EXHIBIT 17
Creating a "Greater Than" conditional formatting

22. ***Click cell J14 on the spreadsheet.*** Notice that cell J14 has been entered under Format Cells that are GREATER THAN:. Dollar signs have been added to the cell reference because this is an absolute cell reference.
23. ***Click the down arrow next to Light Red Fill with Dark Red Text and select Red Text.*** Cells over the average will be shown in red text. ***Click OK in the "Greater Than" window.***
24. You will now add clip art to your spreadsheet (assuming that clip art was included when Excel 2010 was installed). ***Click in cell I18. Then, from the Insert tab, click Clip Art in the Illustrations group.***
25. The Clip Art task pane will appear to the right of the screen. Under Search For: type **Money** and then ***click Go.*** You may get a message that asks if you want to include clip art from Microsoft Office Online; ***click No.***
26. ***Click on the clip art in Excel 2010 Exhibit 10*** (a blue bar chart with people in it and a person climbing a dollar sign). The clip art has now been added to your spreadsheet. ***Position the clip art where you want it by clicking and dragging it into position.***
27. ***Click the "X" in the Clip Art task pane*** to close the task pane.
28. To print the spreadsheet, ***click the File tab, then click Print, and then click Print.***
29. To save the spreadsheet, ***click the File tab and then click Save As.*** Choose the directory in which you want to save the file and ***click Save.***
30. To quit Excel, ***click the File tab and then click Exit.***

This concludes Lesson 6.

ADVANCED LESSONS

LESSON 7: TOOLS AND TECHNIQUES 1—MARKETING BUDGET

In this lesson, you will learn how to create visual impact with spreadsheets. You will learn to create and manipulate a text box, use advanced shading techniques, create a

EXCEL 2010 EXHIBIT 18
Creating visual impact in spreadsheets

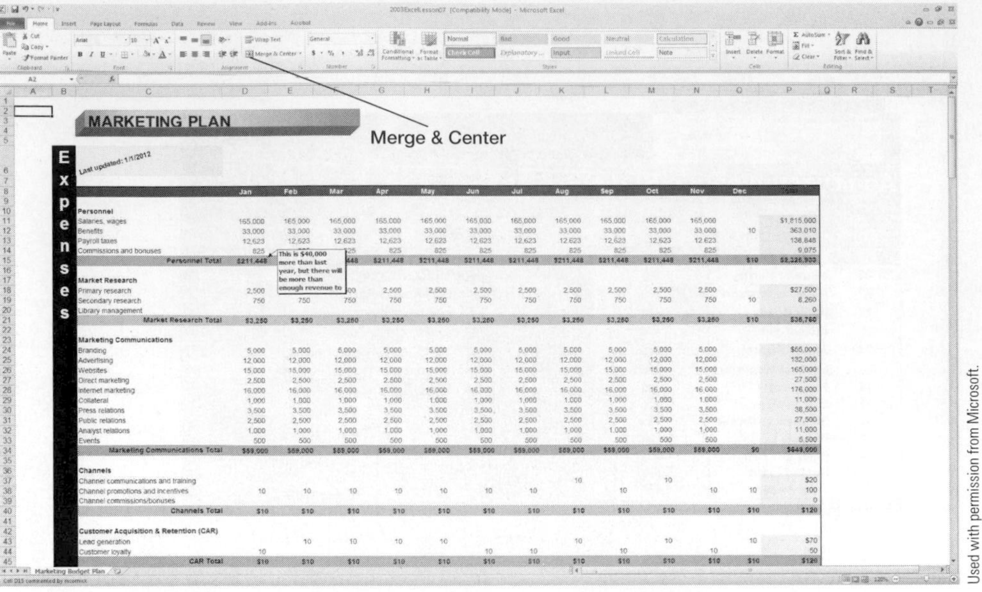

3-D style text box, create vertical text, create diagonal text, use lines and borders, and create a comment. When the spreadsheet is complete, it will look like Excel 2010 Exhibit 18. Keep in mind that if at any time you make a mistake in this lesson, you may press **[CTRL]+[Z]** to undo what you have done.

1. Open Windows. When it has loaded, ***double-click the Microsoft Office Excel 2010 icon on the desktop*** to open the program. Alternatively, ***click the Start button, point to Programs or All Programs, point to Microsoft Office, and then click Microsoft Excel 2010.*** You should now be in a clean, blank workbook.
2. The first thing you will do to complete the spreadsheet in Excel 2010 Exhibit 18 is to open the "Lesson 7" file from the Premium Website. Go to your CengageBrain account and ***click on the link for Premium Website*** for Cornick's *Using Computers in the Law Office,* 7th edition. A new window will open. ***Under Book Level Resources, click on the Data Files: Excel tab, then under Excel 2010, click on the "Lesson 7" file.*** When prompted, ***click Open.***
3. You should now have the Marketing Plan spreadsheet in Excel 2010 Exhibit 18 opened, except the spreadsheet is missing some of the formatting that gives it visual impact. You will add the formatting to the spreadsheet to make it more visually compelling.
4. You will first add the text box that holds the title "Marketing Plan," as shown in Excel 2010 Exhibit 18. ***From the Insert tab, click Text Box in the Text group.*** Notice that your mouse pointer just turned into an upside down letter "T."
5. ***Point to cell C2 and drag the pointer to about cell F4.*** An outline of a box should now be shown from C2 to F4. This is a *text box.*
6. ***Click inside the text box. Click the Bold icon and change the font size to 20.***
7. Type **MARKETING PLAN.**

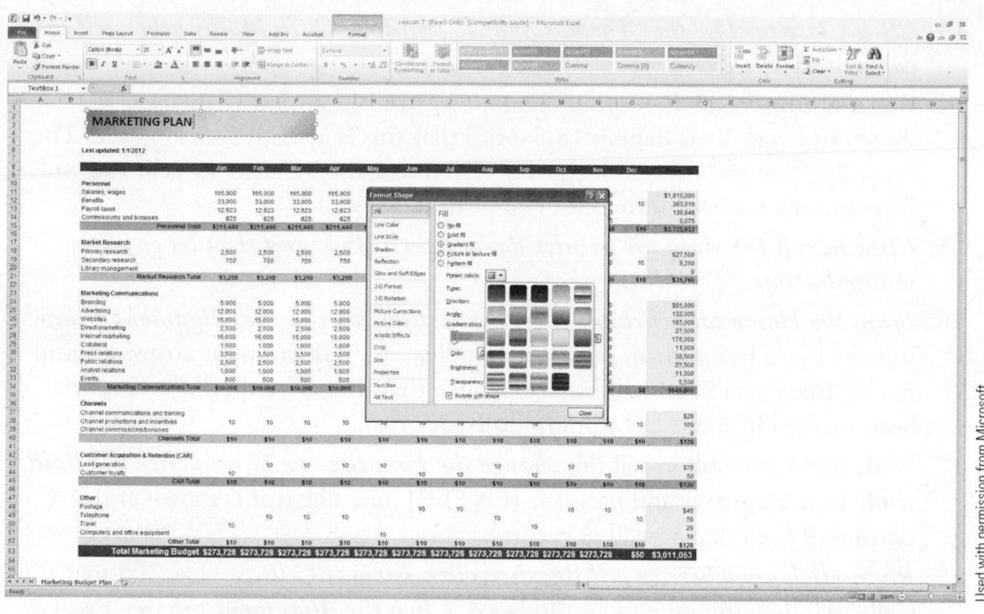

EXCEL 2010 EXHIBIT 19
Formatting a shape

8. ***Right-click on the outline of the text box you just created. In the drop-down menu, click Format Shape.*** The "Format Shape" window should now be displayed (see Excel 2010 Exhibit 19).
9. ***In the "Format Shape" window, notice that Fill is currently selected. Click Gradient fill.***
10. ***Click the down arrow next to Preset Colors.*** This will open a box with many colors; ***click Fog.***
11. ***Staying in the "Format Shape" window, point to the down arrow next to Type: and click Linear.***
12. ***Still in the "Format Shape" window, click 3-D Format on the left side of the window.*** You will now add a 3-D style to the text box. When the 3-D style choices appear, under Bevel and next to Top, ***point to the down arrow and click the first selection under Bevel, which is Circle*** (see Excel 2010 Exhibit 20).

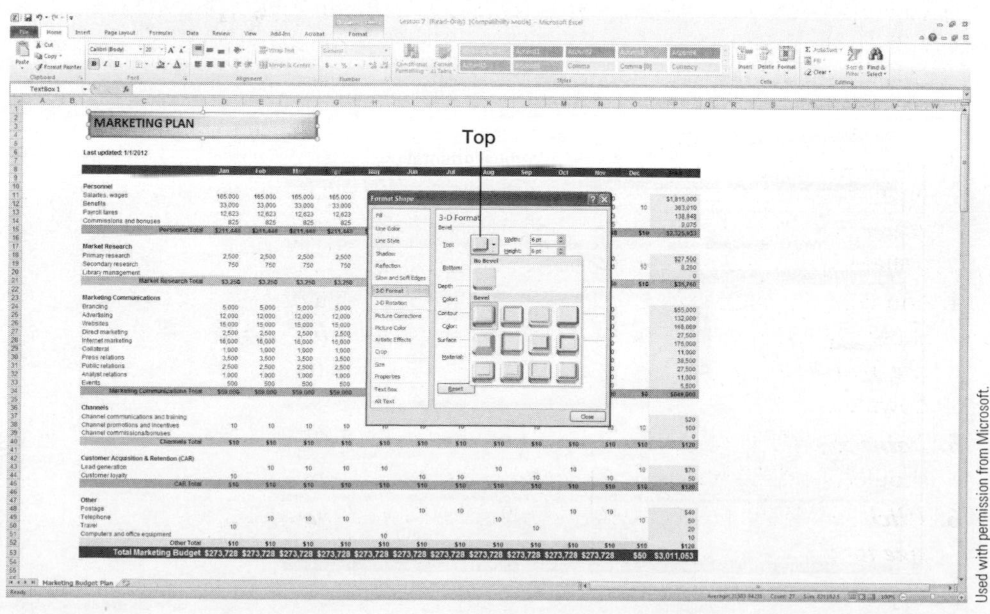

EXCEL 2010 EXHIBIT 20
Adding 3-D effect to a text box

13. ***Click Close to close the "Format Shape" window. Click in any other cell so you can see the effect.***
14. You will now create the vertical text in Column B that says "Expenses," as shown in Excel 2010 Exhibit 18. Notice that this is actually one long cell. The first thing you will do is to merge cells B6 through B53 into one cell; you will then add the text and format it to be vertical.
15. ***Click in cell B6, drag the pointer down to cell B53, and then let go of the mouse button.***
16. ***From the Home tab, click the Merge & Center icon in the Alignment group.*** It looks like a box with an "a" in the middle, with left and right arrows around the "a" (see Excel 2010 Exhibit 18). Notice that the selected cells have now been merged into one cell from B6 to B53.
17. With the cursor still in cell B6, ***change the Font Size to 22 and click the Bold icon.*** Type **Expenses** and press the **[ENTER]** key. The text is shown at the bottom of the cell; you will now correct this.
18. ***Right-click anywhere in cell B6; then click Format Cells… .*** The "Format Cells" window should now be displayed. ***Click the Alignment tab*** (see Excel 2010 Exhibit 21).
19. ***In the "Format Cells" window, under Orientation, click the box that shows the word*** **Text** ***displayed vertically*** (see Excel 2010 Exhibit 21).
20. ***In the "Format Cells" window, under Vertical, click the down arrow and select Top (Indent).***
21. ***Click OK in the "Format Cells" window.*** The word "Expenses" should now be displayed vertically down the cell.
22. ***With the pointer still in cell B6, on the Home tab, click the down arrow next to the Fill Color icon*** (a paint bucket) ***in the Font group and then select Black.***
23. ***On the Home tab, click the down arrow next to the Font Color icon and select Yellow.***
24. You will next make the text in cell C6 appear diagonally. ***Right-click in cell C6; then click Format Cells… .*** The "Format Cells" window should now be displayed and the Alignment tab should be selected.

EXCEL 2010 EXHIBIT 21
Creating vertical text

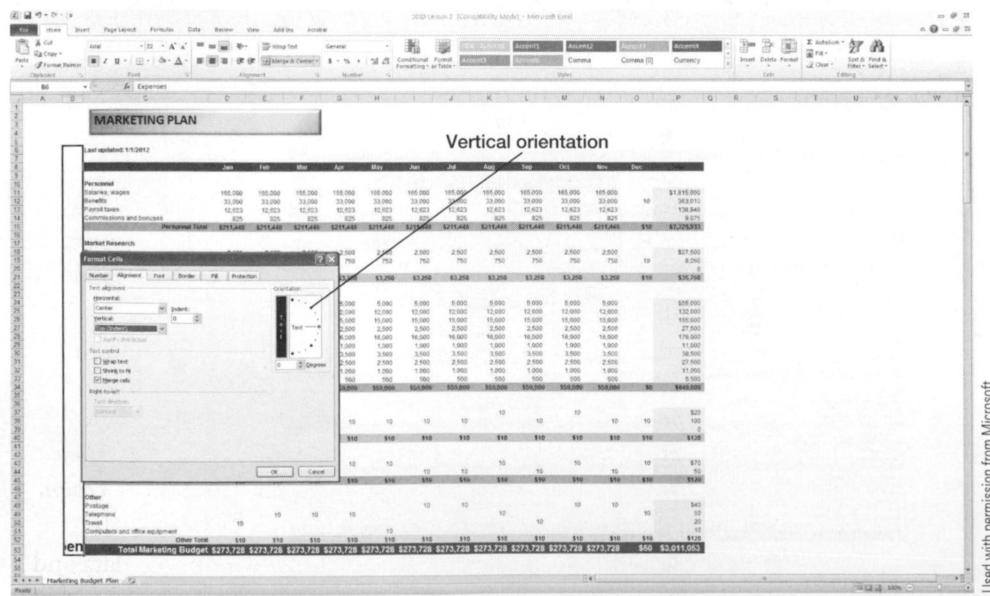

25. ***In the "Format Cells" window, under Orientation, click the up arrow next to Degrees until it reads* "15 degrees."**
26. ***In the "Format Cells" window, click the Fill tab. Click the yellow square; then click OK.***
27. ***Click in any cell to make the highlighting disappear.*** The words "Last updated 1/1/2012" should now be displayed diagonally in black letters with a yellow background.
28. You will now add the Comment shown in Excel 2010 Exhibit 18. ***Right-click in cell D15. On the drop-down menu, click Insert Comment.*** Type **This is $40,000 more than last year, but there will be more than enough revenue to cover this.** ***Click in any cell to exit the Comment box.***
29. ***Hover your cursor over cell D15*** so you can see the comment.
30. You will now add borders to the spreadsheet. ***Point to cell C53 and drag the pointer to cell P53. Then, on the Home tab, click the down arrow next to the Borders icon in the Font group and click All Borders.*** The "Totals" row should now have borders around each cell.
31. ***Click in cell C8 and drag the pointer to cell P53. Then, on the Home tab, click the down arrow next to the Borders icon in the Font group, and then click Thick Box border.*** A thick border now surrounds the data.
32. To print the spreadsheet, ***click the File tab, then click Print, and then click Print.***
33. To save the spreadsheet, ***click the File tab and then click Save As. Under Save in:, select the drive or folder*** in which you would like to save the document. Next to File Name:, type **Excel Lesson 7 Spreadsheet DONE** and ***click Save.***
34. To quit Excel, ***click the File tab and then click Exit.***

This concludes Lesson 7.

LESSON 8: TOOLS AND TECHNIQUES 2—STOCK PORTFOLIO

In this lesson, you will continue to learn and apply helpful tools and techniques using Excel. This includes getting additional practice with using the Merge & Center tool, using the formula auditing feature, using the Oval tool, and password-protecting a file. When your spreadsheet is complete, it will look similar to Excel 2010 Exhibit 22. Some of these tools have been covered in previous lessons, and this lesson will help cement your ability to use them effectively. This tutorial assumes that you have completed Lessons 1 through 7, and that you are quite familiar with Excel.

1. Open Windows. When it has loaded, ***double-click the Microsoft Office Excel 2010 icon on the desktop*** to open the program. Alternatively, ***click the Start button, point to Programs or All Programs, point on Microsoft Office, and then click Microsoft Excel 2010.*** You should now be in a clean, blank workbook. If you are not in a blank workbook, ***click the File tab*** (see Excel 2010 Exhibit 1), ***then click New, and then double-click Blank Workbook.***
2. The first thing you will do to complete the spreadsheet in Excel 2010 Exhibit 22 is to open the "Lesson 8" file from the Premium Website. Go to your CengageBrain account and ***click on the link for Premium Website*** for Cornick's *Using Computers in the Law Office,* 7th edition. A new window will open. ***Under Book Level Resources, click on the Data Files: Excel tab, then under Excel 2010, click on the "Lesson 8" file.*** When prompted, ***click Open.***
3. You should now have the Stock Portfolio spreadsheet shown in Excel 2010 Exhibit 22 opened, except the spreadsheet will be missing two rows of data and some of the formatting. You will add the rows and formatting to the spreadsheet.

EXCEL 2010 EXHIBIT 22
Stock portfolio

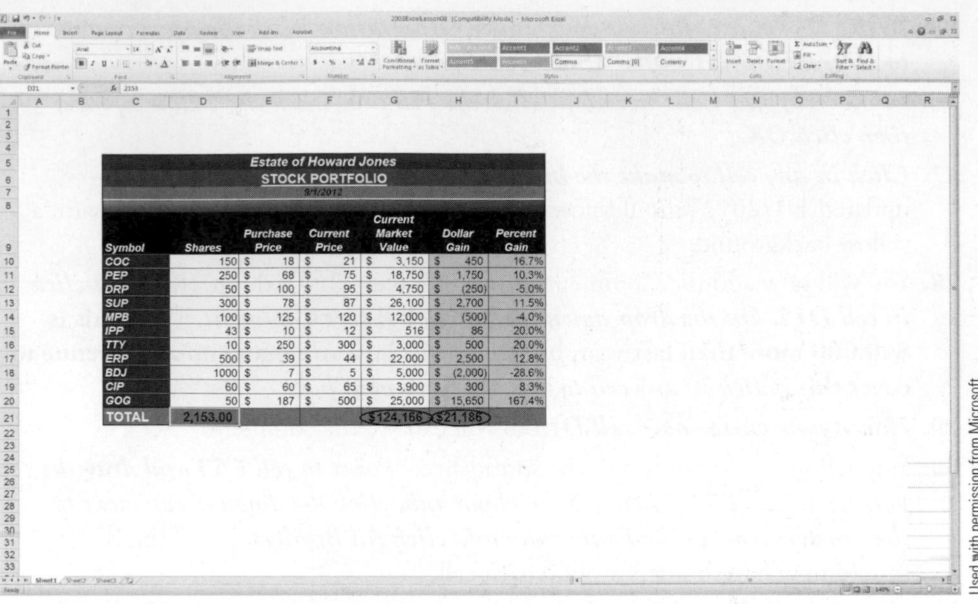

Estate of Howard Jones
STOCK PORTFOLIO
9/1/2012

Symbol	Shares	Purchase Price	Current Price	Current Market Value	Dollar Gain	Percent Gain
COC	150	$ 18	$ 21	$ 3,150	$ 450	16.7%
PEP	250	$ 68	$ 75	$ 18,750	$ 1,750	10.3%
DRP	50	$ 100	$ 95	$ 4,750	$ (250)	-5.0%
SUP	300	$ 78	$ 87	$ 26,100	$ 2,700	11.5%
MPB	100	$ 125	$ 120	$ 12,000	$ (500)	-4.0%
IPP	43	$ 10	$ 12	$ 516	$ 86	20.0%
TTY	10	$ 250	$ 300	$ 3,000	$ 500	20.0%
ERP	500	$ 39	$ 44	$ 22,000	$ 2,500	12.8%
BDJ	1000	$ 7	$ 5	$ 5,000	$ (2,000)	-28.6%
CIP	60	$ 60	$ 65	$ 3,900	$ 300	8.3%
GOG	50	$ 187	$ 500	$ 25,000	$ 15,650	167.4%
TOTAL	2,153.00			$124,166	$21,186	

4. ***Use the Merge and Center icon on the Home tab in the Alignment group to merge cells C5 to I5.***
5. ***Use the Merge and Center icon on the toolbar to merge cells C6 to I6.***
6. ***Use the Merge and Center icon to merge cells C7 to I7.***
7. Make sure the titles are aligned as shown in Excel 2010 Exhibit 22 ***(use the Left and Center Align icons on the Home tab in the Alignment group).***
8. ***Use the Fill Color icon on the Home tab, in the Font group, to make the fill color for cell C5 dark blue*** (or any color you choose).
9. ***Use the Fill Color icon to make the fill color for cell C6 purple*** (any light purple is fine).
10. ***Use the Fill Color icon to make the fill color for cell C7 gray*** (any light gray is fine).
11. The cell range from C8 to I8 is a text graphic box (similar to a text box, except that it is just more difficult to see). ***Right-click the box and select Format Shape. Then, in the Fill section, click Gradient fill; next to Preset Color, click on the first one, Early Sunset*** (just hover your cursor over a color and the name will be displayed). ***Under Direction, click the first option, Linear Diagonal; then click Close to close the "Format Shape" window.***
12. ***Use the Borders icon on the Home tab, in the Font group, to give cells D10 to I21 a border of All Borders.***
13. ***From the Insert tab, click Shapes in the Illustrations group. Under Basic Shapes, click the Oval tool*** (it should be the second shape). ***Start in the upper left corner of cell G21 and drag the pointer to the lower right corner of G21 to make an oval around the total.*** *Note:* You can slightly move the oval by using the cursor keys on the keyboard to nudge it into place so it is centered in the cell.
14. The color of the oval must now be corrected. Notice that the ribbon has changed: the Drawing Tools Format ribbon is now displayed. ***Click the down arrow next to Shape Fill in the Shape Styles group of the Drawing Tools Format tab. Then, click No Fill.*** The oval is now surrounding the number, but the line color of the oval must be changed.

15. ***Right-click the oval and select Format Shape. On the left side of the "Format Shape" window, click Line Color. Then, click the down arrow next to Color, click Black, and click Close in the "Format Shape" window.*** Make an oval in cell H21 identical to that in cell G21 using the same process.
16. You will now use the Formula Auditing mode to see the formulas that are in the spreadsheet and to ensure they are accurate.
17. ***On the Formulas tab, click Show Formulas in the Formula Auditing group.*** Scroll over to the right and look at all of the cells in your spreadsheet. Notice that instead of seeing the result of the formulas, you see the formulas themselves. This is a great tool for checking the accuracy of your spreadsheets. Look at your formulas and make sure they are correct. When you are sure your formulas are accurate, ***turn off the Formula Auditing mode by clicking on Show Formulas again.***
18. You will now learn how to password-protect your spreadsheet files. ***Click the File tab and then click Save As. In the "Save As" window, click Tools*** (it is in the lower portion of the window) and then ***click General Options…*** . Under File Sharing and next to Password to open, type **A** and ***click OK.*** At the "Confirm Password" window, type **A**, and then ***click OK.*** At the "Save As" window, ***click Save*** to save the file to My Documents (or the folder of your choice—you must remember where you save it). You will then get a prompt that asks you whether you want to increase the security of the document by conversion to Office Open XML Format. Because this is just an exercise, ***click No.***
19. If you get a compatibility prompt, just ***click Continue.***
20. ***Click the File tab and then click Close to close the file.***
21. ***Now, click the File tab, and under Recent Documents click on the file you just saved.***
22. The "Password" window should now be displayed. Type **A** in the "Password" window. (The password is case sensitive, so if you typed a capital A when you created the password, you must type a capital A to open the document.) ***Click OK.*** The file should now be displayed.
23. You can turn off a password in the same way. ***Click the File tab, and then Save As. In the "Save As" window, click Tools and then click on General Options…*** . Under File Sharing and next to Password to open, use the **[DEL]** key to remove the asterisk. ***Then, click OK and click Save.*** At the **"Do you want to replace the existing file?"** prompt, ***click Yes.***
24. If you get a compatibility prompt, just ***click Continue.***
25. Close the file and then reopen it, and you will see that you no longer need a password to open it.
26. To print the spreadsheet, ***click the File tab, then click Print, and then click Print.***
27. To quit Excel, ***click the File tab and then click Exit.***

This concludes the Excel 2010 Hands-On Exercises.

HANDS-ON EXERCISES

MICROSOFT EXCEL 2007 FOR WINDOWS

Number	Lesson Title	Concepts Covered
BASIC LESSONS		
Lesson 1	Building a Budget Spreadsheet—Part 1	[CTRL]+[HOME] command, moving the pointer, entering text and values, adjusting the width of columns, changing the format of a group of cells to currency, using bold, centering text, entering formulas, using the AutoFill/Copy command to copy formulas, printing and saving a spreadsheet
Lesson 2	Building a Budget Spreadsheet—Part 2	Opening a file, inserting rows, changing the format of cells to percent, building more formulas, creating a bar chart with the Chart Wizard, printing a selection, fitting/compressing data to one printed page
Lesson 3	Building a Damage Projection Spreadsheet	Changing font size, font color, using the AutoSum feature, using the wrap text feature, creating borders, setting decimal points when formatting numbers
INTERMEDIATE LESSONS		
Lesson 4	Child Support Payment Spreadsheet	Creating a white background, creating formulas that multiply cells, creating formulas that use absolute cell references, using the AutoFormat feature
Lesson 5	Loan Amortization Template	Using a template, protecting cells, freezing panes, splitting a screen, hiding columns, using Format Painter
Lesson 6	Statistical Functions	Using functions including average, maximum, minimum, and standard deviation; sorting data; checking for metadata; using the Format Clear command; using conditional formatting; inserting a picture
ADVANCED LESSONS		
Lesson 7	Tools and Techniques 1—Marketing Budget	Creating and manipulating a text box, advanced shading techniques, working with a 3-D style text box, creating vertical and diagonal text, creating a cell comment, using lines and borders
Lesson 8	Tools and Techniques 2—Stock Portfolio	Using the Merge and Center tool, using the Formula Auditing feature, using the oval tool, password-protecting a file

GETTING STARTED

Overview

Microsoft Excel 2007 is a powerful spreadsheet program that allows you to create formulas, "what if" scenarios, graphs, and much more.

Introduction

Throughout these lessons and exercises, information you need to operate the program will be designated in several different ways:

- Keys to be pressed on the keyboard are designated in brackets, in all caps, and in bold (e.g., press the **[ENTER]** key).
- Movements with the mouse pointer are designated in bold and italics (e.g., ***point to File and click***).
- Words or letters that should be typed are designated in bold (e.g., type **Training Program**).
- Information that is or should be displayed on your computer screen is shown in bold, with quotation marks (e.g., "**Press ENTER to continue.**").
- Specific menu items and commands are designated with an initial capital letter (e.g., click Open).

OVERVIEW OF EXCEL 2007

I. Worksheet

A. *Entering Commands: The Ribbon*—The primary way of entering commands in Excel 2007 is through the ribbon. The ribbon is a set of commands or tools that change depending on which ribbon is selected (see Excel 2007 Exhibit 1). There are seven ribbon tabs: Home, Insert, Page Layout, Formulas, Data, Review, and View (see Excel 2007 Exhibit 1). Each tab has groups of commands. For example, on the Home tab, the Font group contains a group of commands

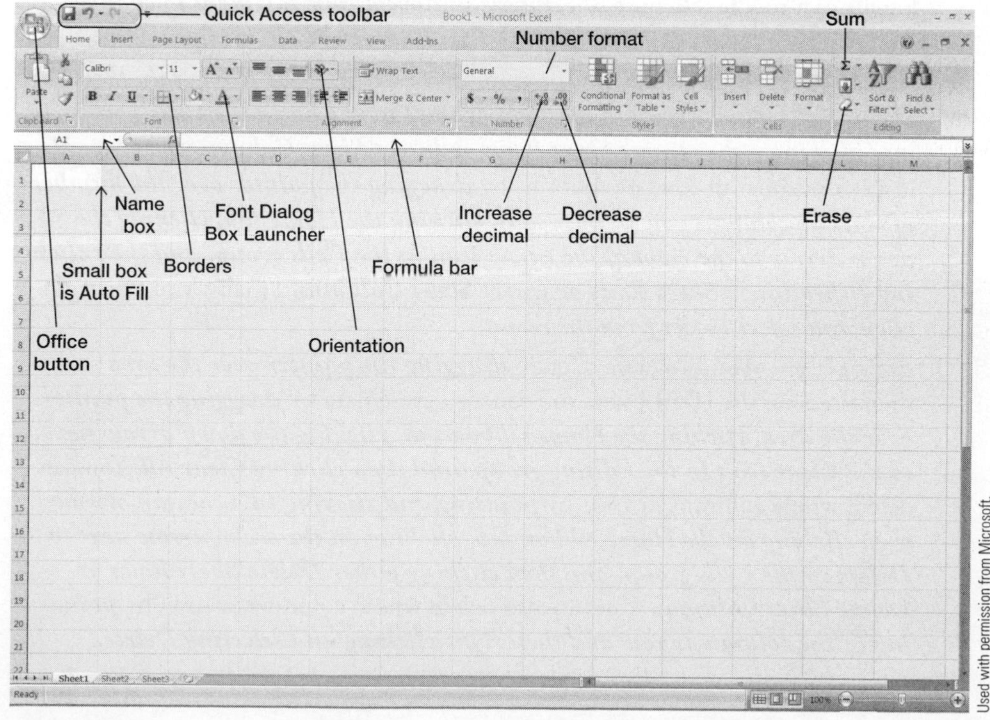

EXCEL 2007 EXHIBIT 1
Excel 2007 interface

HANDS-ON EXERCISES

that relate to font choice, font size, bold, italics, underlining, and other attributes (see Excel 2007 Exhibit 1).

B. *Office Button*—The Office button (see Excel 2007 Exhibit 1) is where a user accesses commands such as New, Open, Save, and Print. The Office button replaces the File menu that was used in previous versions of Excel.

C. *Entering Data*—To enter data, type the text or number in a cell, then press the **[ENTER]** key or one of the arrow (cursor) keys.

D. *Ranges*—A *range* is a group of contiguous cells. Cell ranges can be created by ***clicking and dragging the pointer*** or holding the **[SHIFT]** key down and using the arrow (cursor) keys.

E. *Format*—Cells can be formatted, including changing the font style, font size, shading, border, cell type (currency, percentage, etc.), alignment, and other attributes. To do this, ***click the Home ribbon tab, then click the Dialog Box Launcher in the Font group, Alignment group, or Number group.*** Each of these dialog box launchers brings up the same "Format Cells" window, with a different tab in view. You can also enter a number of formatting options directly from the Home tab.

F. *Editing a Cell*—You can edit a cell by ***clicking in the cell and then clicking in the formula bar.*** The formula bar is directly under the ribbon and just to the right of the **fx** sign (see Excel 2007 Exhibit 1). The formula bar shows the current contents of the selected cell, and it allows you to edit the cell contents. You can also edit the contents of a cell by ***clicking in the cell*** and then pressing the **[F2]** key.

G. *Column Width/Row Height*—You can change the width of a column by ***clicking the line to the right of the column heading, seen right below the formula bar***. (This is the line that separates two columns. When you point to a line, the cursor changes to a double-headed vertical arrow.) ***Drag the pointer to the right or left to increase or decrease the column width, respectively.*** Similarly, you can change the height of a row by ***clicking and dragging the horizontal line separating two rows***. You can also change the width of a column or height of a row by ***clicking somewhere in the column you want to change, clicking the Home tab, then clicking Format in the Cells group.***

H. *Insert*—You can insert one row or column by ***clicking the Home tab, then clicking the down arrow to the right of the Insert icon in the Cells group, and clicking either Insert Sheet Rows or Insert Sheet Columns.*** You can also insert a number of rows or columns by ***dragging the pointer over the number of rows or columns you want to add, clicking the Home tab, clicking the down arrow to the right of the Insert icon in the Cells group, and then clicking either Insert Sheet Rows or Insert Sheet Columns.*** Finally, you can ***right-click and select Insert from the menu.***

I. *Erase/Delete*—You can erase data by ***dragging the pointer over the area*** and then pressing the **[DEL]** key. You can also erase data by ***dragging the pointer over the area, clicking the Home ribbon tab, clicking the down arrow next to the Clear icon in the Editing group, and then clicking Clear All.*** You can delete whole columns or rows by ***pointing and clicking in a column or row, then clicking on the Home ribbon tab, clicking on the down arrow next to Delete in the Cells group, and then clicking either Delete Sheet Rows or Delete Sheet Columns.*** You can also delete whole columns or rows by ***pointing in the column or row and then right-clicking and selecting Delete.***

J. *Quit*—To quit Excel, ***click on the Office button and then click Exit Excel.***

K. *Copy*—To copy data to adjacent columns or rows, ***click in the cell you wish to copy and then select the AutoFill command,*** which is accessed from the small black box at the bottom right corner of the selected cell. ***Drag the pointer to where the data should be placed.*** You can also copy data by ***clicking in the cell, right-clicking, clicking Copy, clicking in the location where the information should be copied,*** and pressing the **[ENTER]** key. Finally, data can be copied by ***clicking and dragging to highlight the information to be copied, clicking the Home tab, then clicking the Copy icon in the Clipboard group.***

L. *Move*—Move data by ***clicking in the cell, right-clicking, selecting Cut, clicking in the location where the information should be inserted,*** and pressing the **[ENTER]** key. Data can also be moved by ***highlighting the information to be copied, clicking the Home tab, then clicking the Cut icon in the Clipboard group.*** Then go to the location where the information should be moved, ***click the Home tab, then click the Paste icon in the Clipboard group.***

M. *Saving and Opening Files*—Save a file by ***clicking the Office button, then clicking Save or Save As,*** and typing the file name. You can also save a file by ***clicking the Save icon*** (it looks like a floppy disk) on the Quick Access toolbar (see Excel 2007 Exhibit 1). Open a file that was previously saved by ***clicking the Office button, clicking Open,*** and typing (or clicking) the name of the file to be opened.

N. *Print*—You can print a file by ***clicking the Office button, then Print, then OK.***

II. Numbers and Formulas

A. *Numbers*—To enter a number in a cell, click in the cell, type the number, and press the **[ENTER]** key or an arrow (cursor) key.

B. *Adding Cells (Addition)*—You can add the contents of two or more cells by three different methods:

1. To add the contents of a range of two or more cells:

- **a.** ***Click in the cell where the total should be placed.***
- **b.** ***Click the Home tab, then click the Sum icon in the Editing group*** (see Excel 2007 Exhibit 2). The Sum icon looks like a Greek letter "E." *Note:* To see the name of an icon, point to the icon for a second and the name of the icon will be displayed.
- **c.** Excel guesses which cells you want to add. Press **[ENTER]** if the correct range has been automatically selected, or select the correct range by highlighting it (i.e., ***click and drag until the range of cells to be added is selected***). Then press **[ENTER]**.

2. To add the contents of two cells, which need not comprise a range:

- **a.** ***Click in the cell where the total should be placed.***
- **b.** Press = (the equals sign).
- **c.** Type the address of the first cell to be added (e.g., B4); alternatively, ***click in that cell.***
- **d.** Press + (the plus sign).
- **e.** Enter the address of the second cell to be added (or ***click in that cell***).
- **f.** Press the **[ENTER]** key. (For example, to add the values of cells C4 and C5, you would type **=C4+C5**.)

EXCEL 2007 EXHIBIT 2
Budgeting spreadsheet

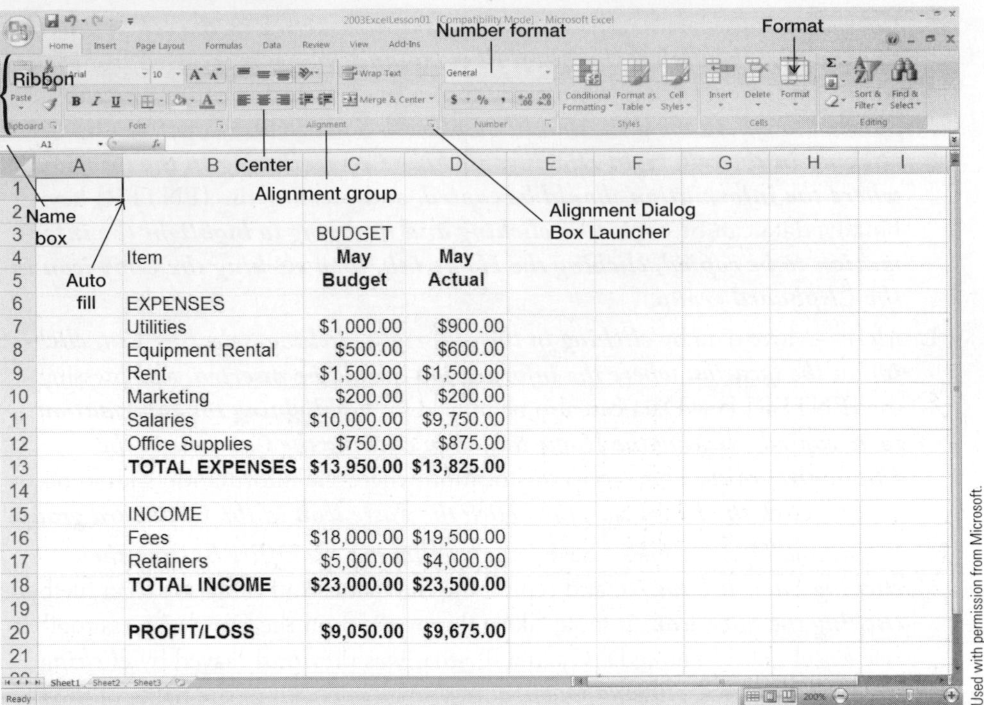

3. To add the contents of a range of two or more cells:
   a. ***Click in the cell where the total should be placed.***
   b. Type =**SUM(**.
   c. Enter the address of the first cell to be added (or ***click in that cell***).
   d. Type **:** (a colon).
   e. Enter the address of the second cell to be added (or ***click in it***).
   f. Type **)** (a closing parenthesis).
   g. Press the **[ENTER]** key. (For example, to add the values of C4 and C5, the formula would read "**=SUM(C4:C5).**"

C. *Subtracting Cells*—To subtract the contents of one or more cells from those of another:
1. ***Click in the cell where the result should be placed.***
2. Press **=.**
3. Enter the first cell address (or ***click in it***).
4. Press – (a minus sign).
5. Enter the second cell address (or ***click in it***).
6. Press the **[ENTER]** key. (For example, to subtract the value of C4 from the value of C5, you would type **=C5–C4**.)

D. *Multiplying Cells*—To multiply the contents of two (or more) cells:
1. ***Click in the cell where the result should be placed.***
2. Press =.
3. Enter the first cell address (or ***click in it***).
4. Press * (**[SHIFT]**+**[8]**).
5. Enter the second cell address (or ***click in it***).
6. Press the **[ENTER]** key. (For example, to multiply the value in C4 times the value in C5, you would type **=C5*C4**.)

E. *Dividing Cells*—To divide the contents of two (or more) cells:
   1. ***Click in the cell where the result should be placed.***
   2. Press =.
   3. Enter the first cell address (or ***click in it***).
   4. Press **/** (the forward slash).
   5. Enter the second cell address (or ***click in it***).
   6. Press the **[ENTER]** key. (For example, to divide the value in C4 by the value in C5, you would type **=C4/C5**.)

BASIC LESSONS

LESSON 1: BUILDING A BUDGET SPREADSHEET—PART 1

This lesson shows you how to build the spreadsheet in Excel 2007 Exhibit 2. It explains how to use the [CTRL]+[HOME] command; move the cell pointer; enter text, values, and formulas; adjust the width of columns; change the format of cells to currency; use the bold feature, use the AutoFill and Copy features to copy formulas; and print and save a spreadsheet. Keep in mind that if you make a mistake at any time in this lesson, you may press **[CTRL]+[Z]** to undo what you have done.

1. Open Windows. After it has loaded, ***double-click the Microsoft Office Excel 2007 icon on the desktop*** to open the program. Alternatively, ***click the Start button, point to Programs or All Programs, point to Microsoft Office, then click Microsoft Office Excel 2007.*** You should be in a new, clean, blank workbook. If you are not in a blank workbook, ***click the Office button*** (see Excel 2007 Exhibit 1), ***click on New, then double-click Blank Workbook.***
2. Notice that the pointer is at cell A1, and the indicator that displays the address of the current cell (called the "name" box in Excel) says A1. The "name" box is just under the ribbon and all the way to the left (see Excel 2007 Exhibit 2). Also, notice that you can move the pointer around the spreadsheet using the cursor keys. Go back to cell A1 by pressing the **[CTRL]+[HOME]** keys.
3. Go to cell C3 by ***clicking in cell C3*** or by pressing the **[RIGHT ARROW]** key twice, then pressing the **[DOWN ARROW]** key twice.
4. You will now enter the title of the spreadsheet in cell C3. Type **BUDGET** and then press the **[ENTER]** key.
5. Notice that the pointer is now at cell C4.
6. Press the **[UP ARROW]** key to go back to cell C3. Notice that BUDGET is left-aligned. To center BUDGET in the cell, ***from the Home tab, click the Center icon in the Alignment group.*** It is the icon with several lines on it that appear centered (see Excel 2007 Exhibit 3). *Note:* If you hover the mouse over an icon on the ribbon for a second, the name of the icon will be displayed. Alternatively, ***from the Home tab, click the Alignment Group Dialog Box Launcher. On the Alignment tab, under the Horizontal field, click the down arrow and select Center. Click OK.***
7. You should now be ready to enter the budget information. First, move the cell pointer to where the data should go, then type the data, and finally enter the data by pressing the **[ENTER]** key or one of the arrow (cursor) keys. Type the remaining row labels as follows:
   Item in B4.
   EXPENSES in B6.

HANDS-ON EXERCISES

EXCEL 2007 EXHIBIT 3
Expanded budget spreadsheet

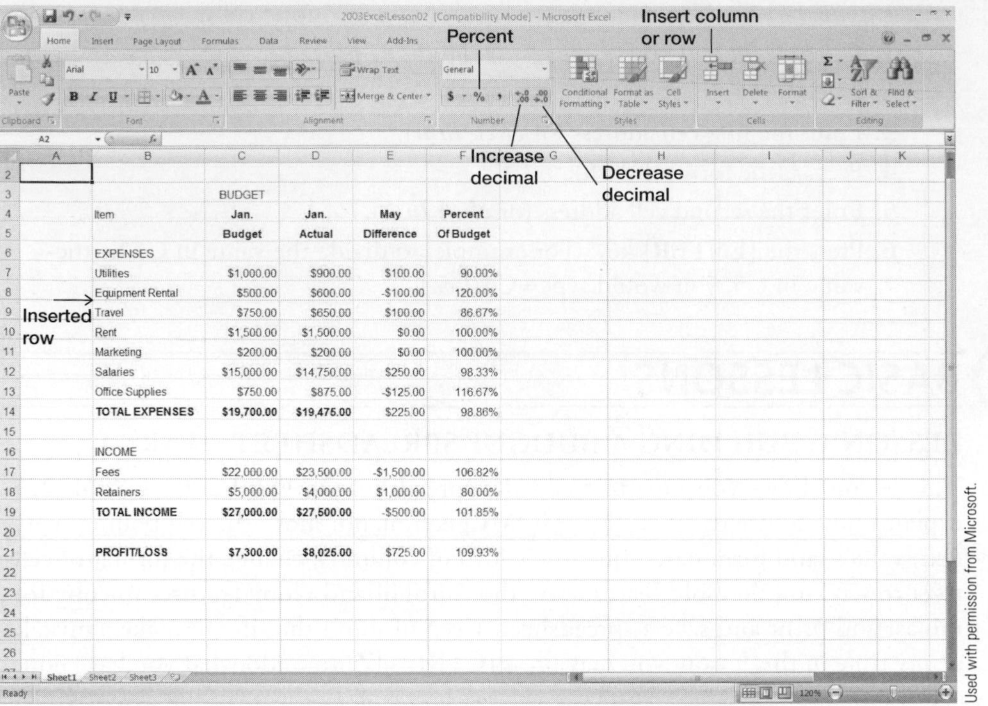

Utilities in B7.
Equipment Rental in B8.
Rent in B9.
Marketing in B10.
Salaries in B11.
Office Supplies in B12.
TOTAL EXPENSES in B13.
INCOME in B15.
Fees in B16.
Retainers in B17.
TOTAL INCOME in B18.
PROFIT/LOSS in B20.

8. Notice in column B that some of the data entries (such as "EXPENSES" and "Equipment Rental") actually extend into column C. To correct this, you must increase the width of column B. ***Put the mouse pointer in the cell lettered B at the top of the screen. Move the pointer to the right edge of the cell.*** The pointer should then change to a double-headed vertical arrow and the column width will be displayed in a small box. ***Drag the pointer to the right until the column width is 18.00***. Alternatively, you can change the cell width by ***placing the cell pointer anywhere in column B. Then, from the Home tab, click Format in the Cells group, then click Column Width...***, type **18**, and ***click OK.***
9. Notice that all of the data entries now fit in the columns. Enter the following:
   Jan in C4.
   Budget in C5.
   Jan in D4.
   Actual in D5.

10. ***Click in cell C4 and drag the pointer over to cell D5*** (so that the whole cell range is highlighted)***; then, from the Home tab, click the Center icon in the Alignment group.***
11. You are now ready to enter values into your spreadsheet.
12. ***Move the pointer to cell C7.*** Type **1000.** Do not type a dollar sign or comma; these will be added later. Press the **[ENTER]** key to enter the value.
13. Enter the following:
    500 in C8.
    1500 in C9.
    200 in C10.
    10000 in C11.
    750 in C12.
    18000 in C16.
    5000 in C17.
    900 in D7.
    600 in D8.
    1500 in D9.
    200 in D10.
    9750 in D11.
    875 in D12.
    19500 in D16.
    4000 in D17.
14. The values you entered do not have dollar signs or the commas appropriate to a currency format. You will now learn how to format a range of cells for a particular format (such as the Currency format).
15. ***Click in cell C7 and drag the pointer over to cell D20. From the Home tab, click the down arrow next to the "Number Format" box, which should say "General." Click Currency. Then click OK.*** Notice that dollar signs have been added to all of the values. ***Click in any cell to deselect the cell range.***
16. ***Click in cell B13 and drag the pointer over to cell D13. Then, from the Home tab, click the Bold icon in the Font group.*** This will make the TOTAL EXPENSES row appear in bold.
17. ***Click in cell B18 and drag the pointer over to cell D18. Then, from the Home tab, click the Bold icon in the Font group.*** This will make the TOTAL INCOME row appear in bold.
18. ***Click in cell B20 and drag the pointer over to cell D20. Then, from the Home tab, click on the Bold icon in the Font group.*** This will make the PROFIT/LOSS row appear in bold.
19. Your spreadsheet is nearly complete; all you need to add are the six formulas.
20. ***Click in cell C13.***
21. Type **=SUM(** and press the **[UP ARROW]** key six times until the cell pointer is at cell C7. Press **.** (a period) to anchor the range.
22. Press the **[DOWN ARROW]** key five times, then press **)** (a closing parenthesis). Press the **[ENTER]** key.
23. Go back to cell C13 and look at the formula in the formula bar. The formula should read **"=SUM(C7:C12)."** The total displayed in the cell should read "$13,950.00." Note that you also could have typed the formula **=C7+C8+C9+C10+C11+C12.**

HANDS-ON EXERCISES

24. Enter the following formulas:
    =SUM(D7:D12) in D13.
    =SUM(C16:C17) in C18.
    =SUM(D16:D17) in D18.
25. You now need to enter formulas for the PROFIT/LOSS columns. In C20, enter **=C18–C13** (the total should read $9,050.00).
26. ***Go to cell C20 and click the AutoFill command*** (it is the small black square at the bottom right of the cell). ***Drag it one column to the right and release the mouse button.*** Notice that the formula has been copied. The total should be $9,675.00. Alternatively, ***go to cell C20, right-click, click Copy, move the pointer to cell D20,*** and press the **[ENTER]** key.
27. The spreadsheet is now complete. To print the spreadsheet, ***click the Office button, then click Print, then click OK.***
28. You will need to save the spreadsheet, because you will use it in Lesson 2. To save the spreadsheet, ***click the Office button and then click Save. Under Save in:, select the drive or folder*** in which you would like to save the document. Next to File name:, type **Budget1** and ***click Save.***
29. To exit Excel, ***click the Office button and then click on Exit Excel.***

This concludes Lesson 1.

LESSON 2: BUILDING A BUDGET SPREADSHEET—PART 2

This lesson assumes that you have completed Lesson 1, have saved the spreadsheet from that lesson, and are generally familiar with the concepts covered in that lesson. Lesson 2 gives you experience in opening a file, inserting a row, formatting numbers as percentages, building additional formulas, creating a bar chart, printing selections, and fitting and compressing data onto one printed page. If you did not exit Excel after Lesson 1, skip Steps 1 and 2 in this lesson and go directly to Step 3.

1. Open Windows. ***Double-click on the Microsoft Office Excel 2007 icon on the desktop*** to open the program. Alternatively, ***click the Start button, point to Programs or All Programs, point to Microsoft Office, then click Microsoft Office Excel 2007.*** You should now be in a new, clean, blank workbook.
2. To retrieve the spreadsheet from Lesson 1, ***click on the Office button and then click Open. Next, click the name of your file*** (e.g., **Budget 1**). If you do not see it, ***click through the options under Look in: to find the file.*** When you have found it, ***click on Open.***
3. You will be entering the information shown in Excel 2007 Exhibit 3. Notice in Excel 2007 Exhibit 3 that a line for travel appears in row 9. You will insert this row first.
4. ***Click in cell B9. From the Home tab, click the down arrow below Insert in the Cells group. On the Insert menu, click Insert Sheet Rows.*** A new row is added. You could also ***right-click and select Insert*** to open a dialog box with the option to insert another row.
5. Enter the following:
   Travel in B9.
   750 in C9.
   650 in D9.

6. Notice that when the new values for travel were entered, all of the formulas were updated. Because you inserted the additional row in the middle of the column, the formulas recognized the new numbers and automatically recalculated to reflect them. Be extremely careful when inserting new rows and columns into spreadsheets that have existing formulas. In some cases, the new number will not be reflected in the totals, such as when rows or columns are inserted at the beginning or end of the range that a formula calculates. It is always prudent to go back to each existing formula, examine the formula range, and make sure the new values are included in the formula range.
7. Change the column width of column E to 12 by ***clicking the column heading*** (the letter E) at the top of the screen. ***Move the pointer to the right edge of the column.*** The pointer should change to a double-headed vertical arrow. ***Drag the pointer to the right until the column width is 12.*** Alternatively, you can change the cell width by ***placing the cell pointer anywhere in column E and, from the Home tab, clicking Format in the Cells Group and selecting Column Width… ;*** then type **12** and ***click OK.***
8. Enter the following:
   May in E4.
   Difference in E5.
   Percent in F4.
   Of Budget in F5.
9. ***Click in cell E4 and drag the pointer over to cell F5*** so that the additional column headings are highlighted. ***Right-click. Notice that in addition to a menu, the Mini toolbar appears.*** It has a number of formatting options on it, including Font, Font size, Bold, and others. ***Click the Bold icon on the Mini toolbar. Point and click the Center icon on the Mini toolbar.***
10. ***Click in cell E14 and drag the pointer over to cell F14. Right-click and then click on the Bold icon on the Mini toolbar.***
11. ***Click in cell E19 and drag the pointer over to cell F19. Right-click and then select the Bold icon on the Mini toolbar.***
12. ***Click in cell E21 and drag the pointer over to cell F21. Right-click and then select the Bold icon on the Mini toolbar.***
13. You are now ready to change the cell formatting for column E to Currency and column F to Percent. ***Click in cell E7 and drag the pointer down to cell E21. Right-click and select Format Cells. From the Number tab in the "Format Cells" window, click Currency and then OK. Click in any cell to get rid of the cell range.***
14. ***Click in cell F7 and drag the pointer down to cell F21. From the Home tab, click the Percent Style (%) icon in the Number group*** (see Excel 2007 Exhibit 3). ***Then, from the Home tab, click the Increase Decimal icon twice in the Number group.***
15. ***Click in any cell to get rid of the cell range.***
16. All that is left to do is enter the formulas for the two new columns. The entries in the May Difference column subtract the actual amount from the budgeted amount for each expense item. A positive amount in this column means that the office was under budget on that line item. A negative balance means that the office was over budget on that line item. The Percent Of Budget column divides that actual amount by the budgeted amount. This shows the percentage of the budgeted money that was actually spent for each item.
17. You will first build one formula in the May Difference column, and then copy it. ***Click in cell E7,*** type **=C7–D7**, and press the **[ENTER]** key.

EXCEL 2007 EXHIBIT 4
Completed column grid

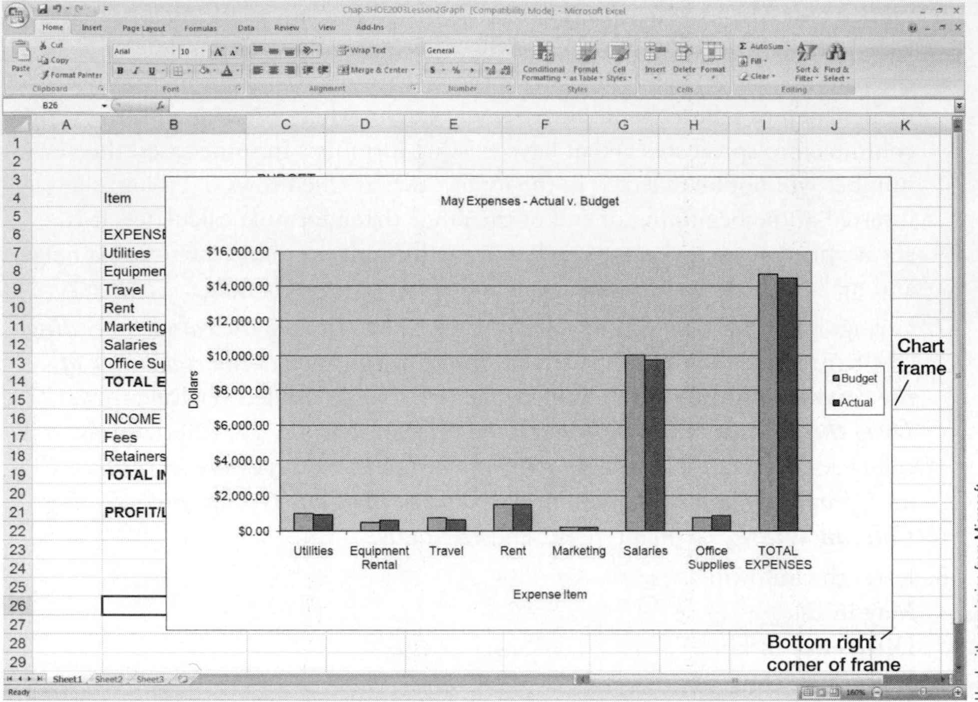

18. Using the AutoFill command or the Copy command, copy this formula down through cell E14. (To copy, ***right-click and then click Copy; highlight the area where the information should go; then right-click and select Paste.*** Alternatively, you can use the Copy and Paste icons in the Clipboard group on the Home tab.)
19. ***Click in cell E17,*** type **=C17–D17**, and press the **[ENTER]** key.
20. Using the AutoFill command, copy this formula down through cell E21. Delete the formula in cell E20 by ***clicking in cell E20*** and pressing the **[DEL]** key.
21. You will now build on the formula in the Percent Of Budget column and copy it. ***Click in cell F7,*** type **=D7/C7**, and press the **[ENTER]** key.
22. Using the AutoFill command, copy this formula down through cell F21. Delete the formula in cells F15, F16, and F20 by ***clicking in the cell*** and then pressing the **[DEL]** key.
23. The spreadsheet has now been built. You will now build a column chart that shows budgeted expenses compared to actual expenses (see Excel 2007 Exhibit 4).
24. ***Click in cell B7, then drag the pointer down and over to cell D14.***
25. ***From the Insert tab, click Column from the Charts group. Under 3-D Column, click the first option, 3-D Clustered Column*** (see Excel 2007 Exhibit 5).
26. Notice that a draft column chart has been created. ***Click anywhere in the chart frame*** (see Excel 2007 Exhibit 4). Your pointer will turn to a four-headed arrow. ***Drag the chart across the spreadsheet so the upper left corner of the chart is near cell B4.***
27. ***Using the horizontal scroll bar*** (see Excel 2007 Exhibit 4), ***scroll to the right*** so the chart is completely in your screen.
28. ***Click the bottom right corner of the chart frame.*** Your cursor should change to a two-headed arrow that is diagonal. ***Drag the chart so that the bottom right corner ends near cell H22*** (see Excel 2007 Exhibit 4).

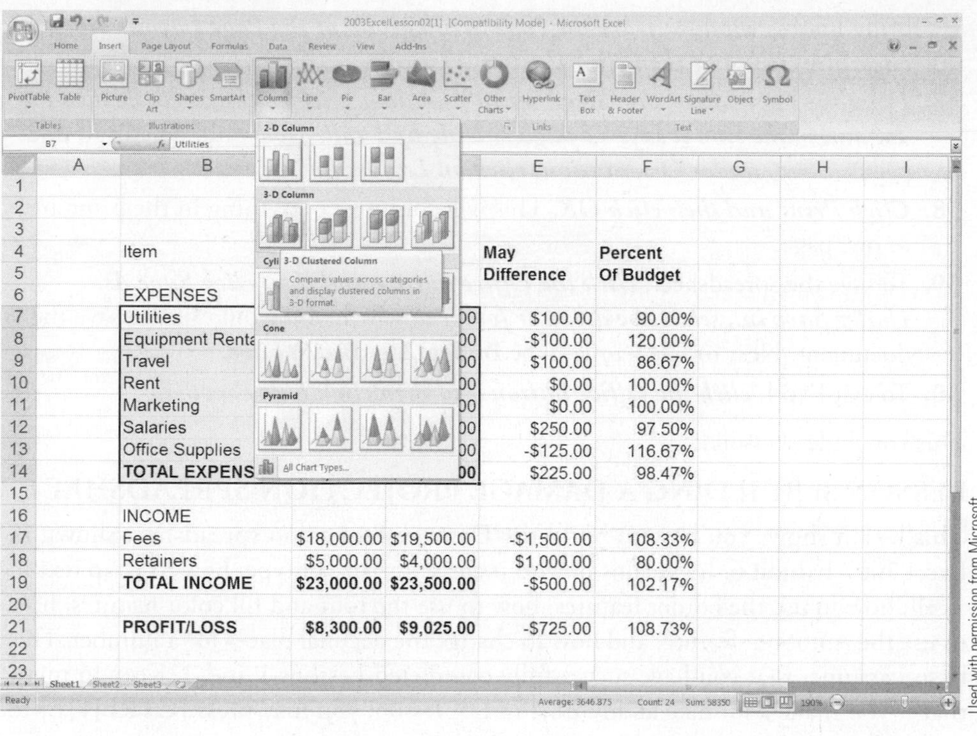

EXCEL 2007 EXHIBIT 5
Creating a column chart

29. Notice that new options have been added to the ribbon (e.g., Chart Tools Design, Layout, and Format). ***Click the Layout ribbon tab under Chart Tools.***
30. ***Click Chart Title in the Labels group, then select Above Chart.*** Notice that a title has been added, "Chart Title."
31. ***Point and click on the "Chart Title" text in the bar chart*** and press the **[DEL]** key until the text is gone. Type **May Expenses—Actual v. Budget**. If you would like to move the title—for example, if it is off-center—***just click the title frame and drag it where you would like.***
32. ***From the Layout tab (under Chart Tools), click Axis Titles in the Labels group. Click Primary Horizontal Axis Title and then select Title Below Axis.*** Notice that a horizontal axis title of "Axis Title" has been added. ***Click Axis Title*** and use the **[DEL]** key until the text is gone. Type **Expenses**.
33. To change the legend from Series1 and Series2 to Actual and Budget, ***right-click on Series1, then click Select Data.*** The "Select Data Source" window will open. ***Click on Series1 (under Legend Entries (Series)) to highlight it, then click on Edit under the same heading.*** The "Edit Series" window will open. Type **Actual** in the text box under Series name:, ***then click OK. Click on Series2 (under Legend Entries (Series)) to highlight it, then click on Edit under the same heading.*** The "Edit Series" window will open. Type **Budget** in the text box under Series name:, ***then click OK. Click OK in the "Select Data Source" window.***
34. To print the chart, ***drag the pointer from cell G3 to cell Q27. Click the Office button and click Print; then, under Print what, click Selection and then click OK.***
35. You will next print the spreadsheet and the chart on one page. ***Click in cell B3 and drag the pointer until both the spreadsheet and the chart are highlighted*** (roughly cell B3 to cell Q27).
36. ***Click the Page Layout tab, then click the Page Setup Dialog Box Launcher.*** (It is a little box directly under the Print Titles icon in the Page Setup group). The "Page Setup" window should now be displayed. There is another way to

bring up this window: ***from the Page Setup group of the Page Layout tab, click Margins, and then click Custom Margins.***

37. ***From the Page tab of the "Page Setup" window, click in the circle next to Fit To: and make sure it says "1 page(s) wide by 1 tall"*** (it should default to one page). ***Then, under Orientation, click on Landscape.***
38. ***Click Print and then click OK.*** This will compress everything in the print area to one page.
39. To save the spreadsheet, ***click the Office button and then click Save As. Under Save in:, select the drive or folder*** in which you would like to save the document. Next to File name:, type **Budget2** and ***click Save.***
40. To exit Excel, ***click the Office button and then click Exit Excel.***

This concludes Lesson 2.

LESSON 3: BUILDING A DAMAGE PROJECTION SPREADSHEET

This lesson shows you how to build the Damage Projection spreadsheet shown in Excel 2007 Exhibit 6. It explains how to increase the size of type, how to wrap text in a cell, how to use the border features, how to use the font and fill color features, how to use the AutoSum feature, and how to change the decimal places for a number. This lesson assumes that you have successfully completed Lessons 1 and 2. Keep in mind that if you make a mistake at any time in this lesson, you may press **[CTRL]+[Z]** to undo what you have done.

EXCEL 2007 EXHIBIT 6
Damages projection spreadsheet

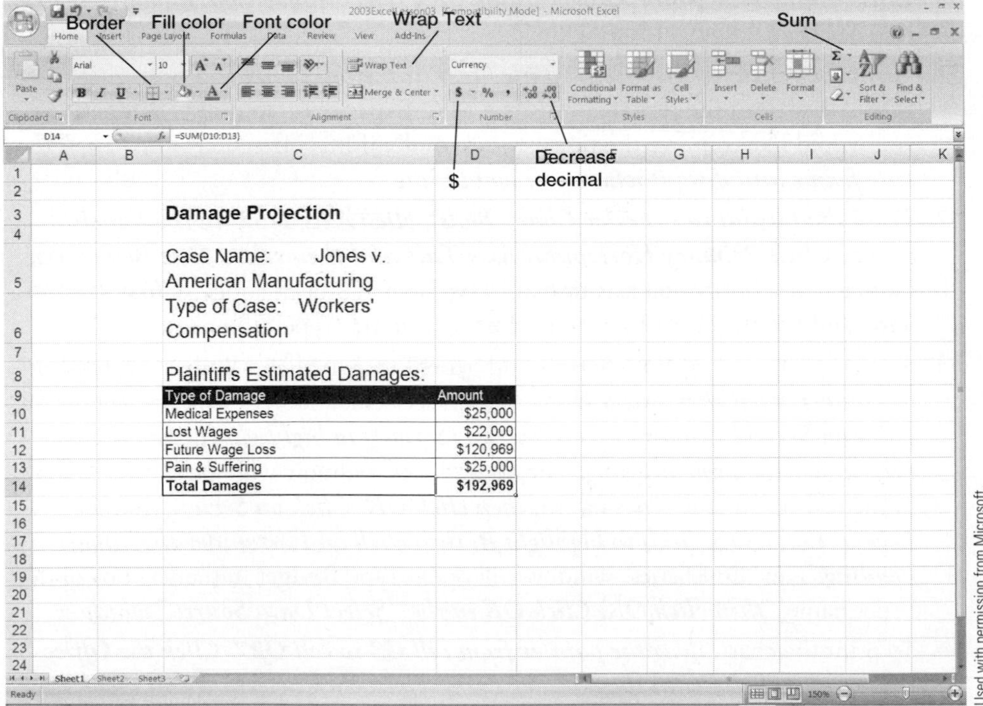

1. Open Windows. ***Double-click the Microsoft Office Excel 2007 icon on the desktop*** to open the program. Alternatively, ***click on the Start button, point to Programs or All Programs, point to Microsoft Office, then click Microsoft Office Excel 2007.*** You should now be in a new, clean, blank workbook. If you are not in a blank workbook, ***click the Office button*** (see Excel 2007 Exhibit 1), ***then click New and double-click Blank Workbook.***

2. To start building the spreadsheet in Excel 2007 Exhibit 6, begin by increasing the size of column C to a width of 37 ***(Home tab > Cells group > Format > Column Width).***
3. In cell C3, type **Damage Projection.** With the pointer on C3, ***click the Bold icon from the Font group on the Home tab.*** Change the size to 14 point by ***clicking the Font Size box in the Font group on the Home tab*** and typing **14**.
4. Type the text shown in cell C5 (see Excel 2007 Exhibit 6). Select the text in cell C5 and then ***Click the Font Size box in the Font group on the Home tab and change the type to 14 point.*** Notice that the text goes into the next cell. To wrap part of the text down to the next line within the current cell (see Excel Exhibit 6), ***from the Home tab, click the Wrap Text icon in the Alignment group*** (see Excel 2007 Exhibit 6). The text now wraps down to the next line within cell C5.
5. Type the text shown in cell C6, make the text 14 point, and wrap the text down so it does not go into cell D6.
6. Type the text shown in cell C8 and make the text 14 point.
7. Type the text and values shown in cells C9 to D13.
8. Type the text shown in cell C14.
9. To enter the formula in cell D14, ***click cell D14.*** Then, ***from the Editing group on the Home tab, click the Sum icon*** (see Excel 2007 Exhibit 6). Notice that when you clicked Sum, Excel assumed that you wanted to add the values in D10 to D13. You could adjust the range by pressing the **[SHIFT]+[ARROW]** keys, but the range should be fine as is (i.e., D10 to D13). Press the **[ENTER]** key to enter the formula.
10. ***Click in cell C9, drag the mouse pointer to cell D14,*** and change the font size to 14 point.
11. ***Click in cell C9 and drag the mouse pointer to cell D9. Right-click. On the Mini toolbar, click the down arrow next to the Fill Color icon (the paint bucket) and select the black square.*** (You could also click the Fill Color icon in the Font group on the Home tab.) The cells are all black; now you just need to change the font color to white to see the text.
12. With cells C9 and D9 still highlighted, ***on the Home tab, click the down arrow next to the Font Color icon in the Font group, and click on the white square.***
13. ***Click in cell C10 and drag the mouse pointer to cell D14. From the Font group on the Home tab, click on the down arrow next to the Border icon.*** (It is typically just to the left of the Fill Color icon—see Excel 2007 Exhibit 6). Then, ***click All Borders*** (it looks like a windowpane). Notice that there is now a border around every square that was highlighted.
14. ***Click in cell C14 and drag the mouse pointer to cell D14. From the Font group on the Home tab, click the down arrow next to the Border icon again.*** Then ***click on the Thick Box Border*** (it looks like a heavy black window frame). Move the pointer and notice that there is now a heavy black border around cells C14 and D14. ***From the Font group on the Home tab, click on the Bold icon again.***
15. ***Click in cell D10 and drag the pointer to cell D14. From the Number group on the Home tab, click the dollar sign ($).*** Notice that two decimal places are shown (e.g., 25,000.00). It is not necessary to show two decimal places in this projection, so you will now change it to zero decimal places. ***From the Number group on the Home tab, click the Decrease Decimal icon twice.*** Notice that whole dollars are now shown.
16. To print the spreadsheet, ***click the Office button, click Print and then click OK.***

17. To save the spreadsheet, ***click on the Office button and then click Save. Under Save in:, select the drive or folder*** in which you would like to save the document. Next to File name:, type **Damage Projection** and ***click Save.***
18. To exit Excel, ***click the Office button and then click Exit Excel.***

This concludes Lesson 3.

INTERMEDIATE LESSONS

LESSON 4: CHILD SUPPORT PAYMENT SPREADSHEET

This lesson shows you how to build the Child Support Payment spreadsheet in Excel 2007 Exhibit 7. It explains how to create a white background, how to create formulas to multiply cells and formulas that use an absolute cell reference, and how to use the AutoFormat feature. This lesson assumes that you have successfully completed Lessons 1 through 3. Keep in mind that if you make a mistake at any time in this lesson, you may press **[CTRL]+[Z]** to undo what you have done.

EXCEL 2007 EXHIBIT 7
Child support payment spreadsheet

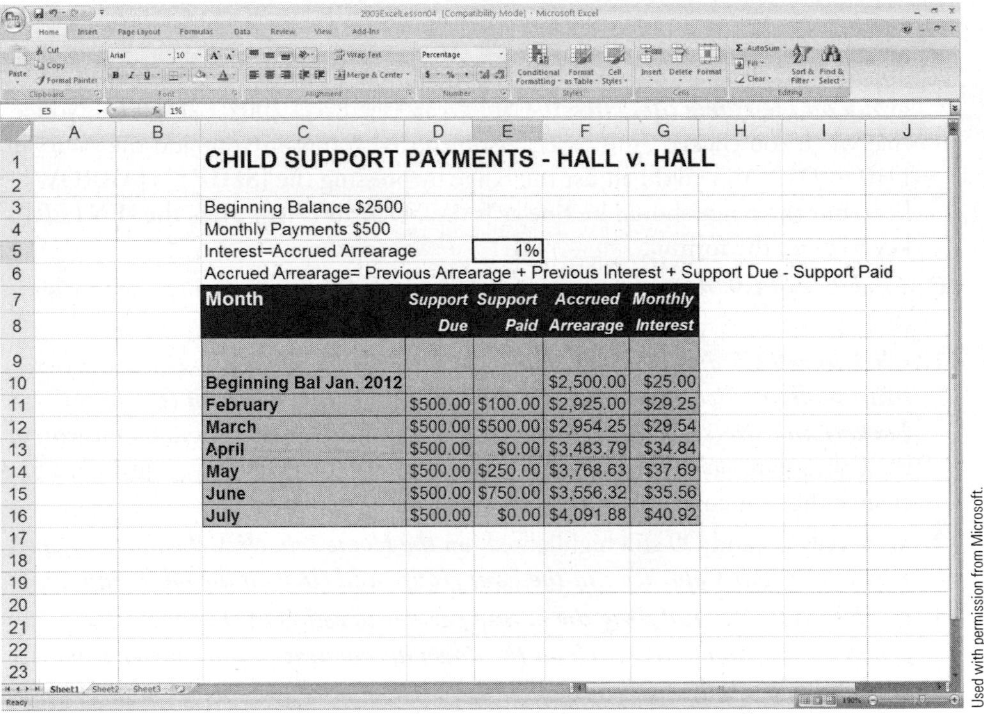

1. Open Windows. ***Double-click the Microsoft Office Excel 2007 icon on the desktop*** to open the program. Alternatively, ***click the Start button, point to Programs or All Programs, point to Microsoft Office, and then click Microsoft Office Excel 2007.*** You should now be in a new, clean, blank workbook. If you are not in a blank workbook, ***point and click the Office button*** (see Excel 2007 Exhibit 1), ***then click New, then double-click on Blank Workbook.***
2. When you start to build the spreadsheet in Excel 2007 Exhibit 7, notice that the background is completely white. A completely white background gives you a crisp, clean canvas on which to work and to which you can add colors and graphics.
3. Press **[CTRL]+[A]**. The whole spreadsheet is now selected. ***From the Font group on the Home tab, click the down arrow next to the Fill Color icon, then click the white square*** (it is all the way in the upper right corner). ***Click***

in any cell to make the highlighting disappear. Notice that the background of the spreadsheet is completely white.

4. Enter the text shown in cell C1, then change the font to Bold and the font size to 14 point.
5. Increase the width of column C to 20.
6. Enter the text shown in cells C3 to C6.
7. In cell E5, type **.01** and press **[ENTER].** Change the number format to Percent (zero decimal places).
8. Enter the text shown in cells C7 and in the cell range from D7 to G8. ***Click on C7 and click on the Bold icon from the Font group in the Home tab. Click on D7 and drag the pointer to G8, then click on the Italic icon from the Font group in the Home tab.***
9. Enter the text shown in the cell range from C10 to C16.
10. Enter the numbers (values) shown in cells in D11 to E16.
11. In cell F10, type **2500.**
12. In cell G10, type = (an equals sign), ***click in cell F10,*** then press **[SHIFT]+[8]** (an asterisk will appear). ***Click in cell E5*** and press the **[F4]** key once. The formula **=F10*$E$5** should be on the screen; press the **[ENTER]** key. This formula multiplies the accrued arrearage (how much the individual is behind on payments) times the interest rate (which is 1 percent). The reason you pressed **[F4]** is that the formula had to be an absolute cell reference; pressing **[F4]** simply put the dollar signs ($) into the formula for you. The dollar signs tell Excel that this is an absolute cell reference rather than a relative cell reference. Hence, when you copy the formula to other cells (see following steps), the accrued arrearage will always be multiplied by the value in E5. Said another way, the second half of this formula ($E$5) will not change when the formula is copied to other cells.
13. If you want to find out for yourself why the formula **=F10*E5** will not work once it is copied from cell G10 (where it will work fine), type **=F10*E5** in cell G10 and then copy the formula to cells G11 to G16. Once you have seen the effect of this, delete the changes you made and change the formula in cell G10 to **=F10*$E$5.**
14. To copy the formula from G10 to cells G11 to G16, ***click in cell G10, click the AutoFill handle*** (the little black box at the lower right corner of the cell) ***and drag the mouse pointer down to cell G16.***
15. In cell F11, type **=F10+G10+D11–E11**. Press the **[ENTER]** key. This formula adds the accrued amount in the previous month with the previous month's interest and the current support due, and then subtracts the current amount paid.
16. To copy the formula from F11 to cells F12 to F16, ***click in cell F11, click the AutoFill handle, and drag the mouse pointer down to cell F16.***
17. ***Click in cell D10 and drag the mouse pointer to cell G16. Right-click, then click Format Cells. Click the Number tab, click Currency, then click OK.***
18. Notice that the spreadsheet is very plain. We will use the Cell Styles feature to give the spreadsheet some color. ***Click in cell C7 and drag the mouse pointer to cell G8. From the Styles Group on the Home tab, click the down arrow next to Cell Styles. Click Accent4*** (it is solid purple with white letters).
19. ***Click in cell C9 and drag the mouse pointer to cell G16. From the Styles group on the Home tab, click the down arrow next to Cell Styles. Click 20%—Accent1.*** (It is light blue with black letters.) ***Click in any cell to make the highlighting disappear.***
20. To add borders to the spreadsheet, ***click in cell C9 and drag the mouse pointer to cell G16. From the Font group on the Home tab, click the down arrow***

next to the Border icon. Next, click the All Borders icon (it looks like a windowpane).

21. ***Click in cell E5. From the Font group on the Home tab, click the down arrow next to Borders. Click Thick Box Border.*** Press the **[ENTER]** key. The spreadsheet is now complete and should look like Excel 2007 Exhibit 7.
22. To print the spreadsheet, ***click the Office button, click Print, then click OK.***
23. To save the spreadsheet, ***click the Office button and then click Save. Under Save in:, select the drive or folder*** in which you would like to save the document. Next to File name:, type **Child Support Payments** and ***click Save.***
24. To exit Excel, ***click on the Office button and then click Exit Excel.***

This concludes Lesson 4.

LESSON 5: LOAN AMORTIZATION TEMPLATE

This lesson shows you how to open a Loan Amortization template and fill it in (see Excel 2007 Exhibit 8). Templates are a great way to simplify complicated spreadsheets. You will also learn how to protect cells, freeze panes, split a screen, hide a column, and use the Format Painter tool. This lesson assumes that you have successfully completed Lessons 1 through 4. Keep in mind that if you make a mistake at any time in this lesson, you may press **[CTRL]+[Z]** to undo what you have done.

EXCEL 2007 EXHIBIT 8
Loan amortization template

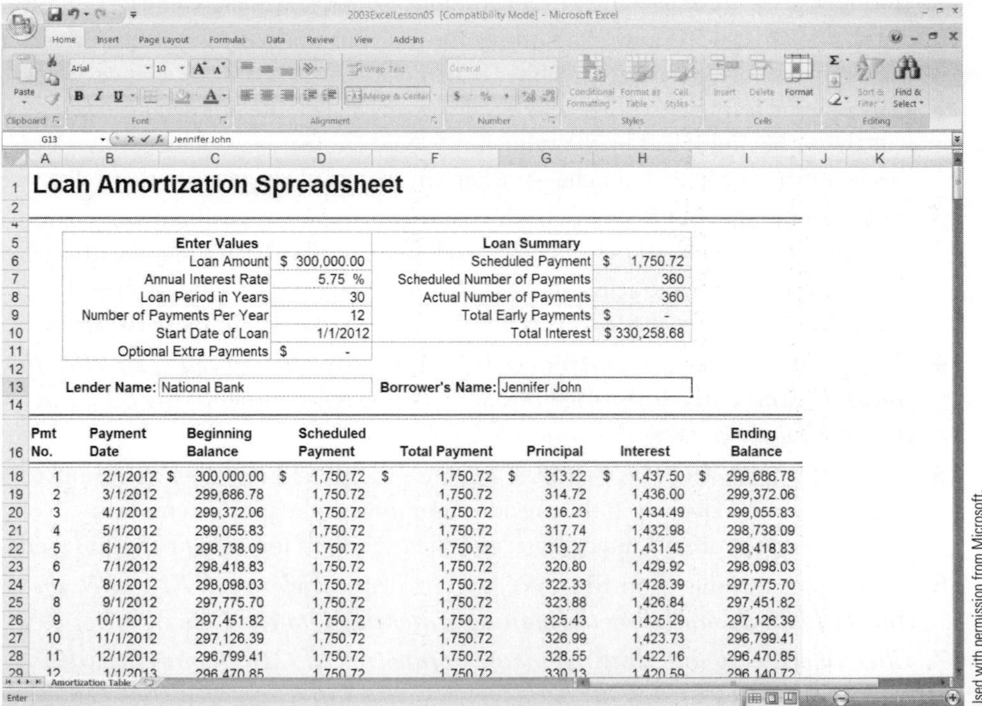

Loan Amortization Spreadsheet

Enter Values		Loan Summary	
Loan Amount	$ 300,000.00	Scheduled Payment	$ 1,750.72
Annual Interest Rate	5.75 %	Scheduled Number of Payments	360
Loan Period in Years	30	Actual Number of Payments	360
Number of Payments Per Year	12	Total Early Payments	$ -
Start Date of Loan	1/1/2012	Total Interest	$ 330,258.68
Optional Extra Payments	$ -		

Lender Name: National Bank **Borrower's Name:** Jennifer John

Pmt No.	Payment Date	Beginning Balance	Scheduled Payment	Total Payment	Principal	Interest	Ending Balance
1	2/1/2012	$ 300,000.00	$ 1,750.72	$ 1,750.72	$ 313.22	$ 1,437.50	$ 299,686.78
2	3/1/2012	299,686.78	1,750.72	1,750.72	314.72	1,436.00	299,372.06
3	4/1/2012	299,372.06	1,750.72	1,750.72	316.23	1,434.49	299,055.83
4	5/1/2012	299,055.83	1,750.72	1,750.72	317.74	1,432.98	298,738.09
5	6/1/2012	298,738.09	1,750.72	1,750.72	319.27	1,431.45	298,418.83
6	7/1/2012	298,418.83	1,750.72	1,750.72	320.80	1,429.92	298,098.03
7	8/1/2012	298,098.03	1,750.72	1,750.72	322.33	1,428.39	297,775.70
8	9/1/2012	297,775.70	1,750.72	1,750.72	323.88	1,426.84	297,451.82
9	10/1/2012	297,451.82	1,750.72	1,750.72	325.43	1,425.29	297,126.39
10	11/1/2012	297,126.39	1,750.72	1,750.72	326.99	1,423.73	296,799.41
11	12/1/2012	296,799.41	1,750.72	1,750.72	328.55	1,422.16	296,470.85
12	1/1/2013	296,470.85	1,750.72	1,750.72	330.13	1,420.59	296,140.72

1. Open Windows. ***Double-click the Microsoft Office Excel 2007 icon on the desktop*** to open the program. Alternatively, ***click the Start button, point to Programs or All Programs, point to Microsoft Office, then click Microsoft Office Excel 2007.*** You should now be in a new, clean, blank workbook.
2. The first thing you will do to complete the template in Excel 2007 Exhibit 8 is open the "Lesson 5" file from the Premium Website. Go to your CengageBrain account and click on the link for Premium Website for Cornick's *Using Computers in the Law Office*, 7th edition. A new window will open.

Under Book Level Resources, click on the Data Files: Excel tab, then under Excel 2007, click on the "Lesson 5" file.

3. You should now have the Loan Amortization spreadsheet shown in Excel 2007 Exhibit 8 open. However, your spreadsheet has no data yet.
4. Enter the following information:
Cell D6: **300000**
Cell D7: **5.75**
Cell D8: **30**
Cell D9: **12**
Cell D10: **1/1/2012**
Cell D11: **0**

(When you click in Cell D11, a note will appear regarding extra payments; just type a zero and press **[ENTER]** and the note will disappear.)

Cell C13: **National Bank**
Cell G13: **Jennifer John**

5. Notice that your spreadsheet now appears nearly identical to Excel 2007 Exhibit 8.
6. Notice in your spreadsheet that just about everything below row 16 is a formula. If a user accidentally deletes one of these formulas, the whole spreadsheet could be affected. You will now turn on the Protection feature and lock some of the cells so they cannot be accidentally deleted.
7. ***Right-click in cell D6. Then click Format Cells … . Click the Protection tab in the "Format Cells" window.*** Notice that there is no green check mark next to Locked. Cells D6 to D13 and cell G13 are unlocked even when the Protection feature is turned on. When the Protection feature is off, you can change the lock/unlock format of cells by using the ***right-click, Format Cells > Protection*** command sequence. Interestingly, when a new blank spreadsheet is open in Excel, all cells default to Locked, but this has no effect because the Protection feature is always turned off in a blank workbook.
8. ***Click Cancel in the "Format Cells" window to close the window.***
9. Let's open a new spreadsheet so you can see that all cells in Excel start out with the format locked. ***Click the Office button, then click New, then double-click Blank Workbook.***
10. You should now have a new, blank spreadsheet displayed. ***Right-click in any cell and then click Format Cells… . Click the Protection tab.*** Notice that the cell is locked. However, the cell is not truly locked until you turn on the Protection feature.
11. ***Click Cancel in the "Format Cells" window in the new spreadsheet. Click the Office button and then click Close*** to close the file. You should now be back at your Loan Amortization spreadsheet.
12. To turn on the Protection feature, ***on the Review tab, click Protect Sheet in the Changes group.***
13. The "Protect Sheet" window should now be displayed (see Excel 2007 Exhibit 9). Make sure that the first two selections under Allow all users of this worksheet to: are selected (e.g., Select locked cells and Select unlocked cells). Notice that you could enter a password in the white box under Password to unprotect the sheet. This would completely lock the spreadsheet (so that only unlocked cells could be modified) to users who did not know the password. In this instance, this is not necessary; it is fine for someone to intentionally change the values at the top of the spreadsheet. We are

EXCEL 2007 EXHIBIT 9
Protecting cells

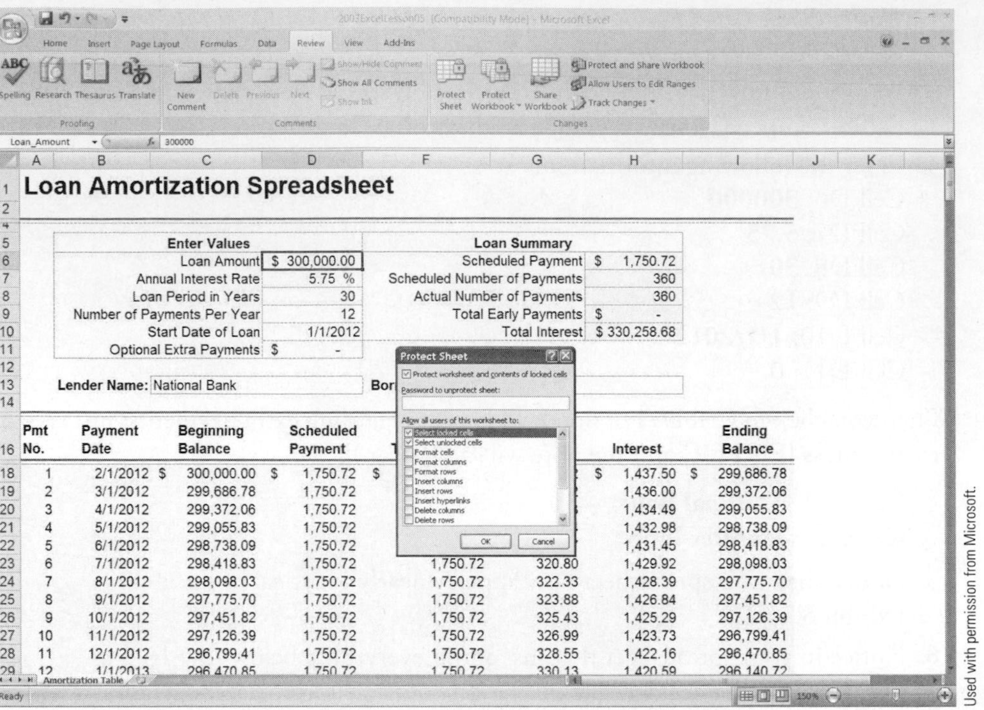

Used with permission from Microsoft.

just using this feature to prevent someone from accidentally changing the formulas below row 16.

14. After the first two items are check-marked under Allow all users of this worksheet to:, ***click OK.***
15. ***Now click in any cell other than D6 to D13 or cell G13 and try to type something in the cell.*** You should get an error message that says **"The cell or chart that you are trying to change is protected and therefore read-only."** ***Click OK*** to close the error window.
16. The whole spreadsheet is now locked, except for cells D6 to D13 and cell G13, because these were not formatted as locked in the template.
17. Now you will turn off the Protection feature because you are still building the spreadsheet. ***On the Review tab, click Unprotect Sheet in the Changes group.***
18. You will now use the Format Painter tool to copy the formatting from one set of cells to another set of cells. Notice that cells F13 and G13 do not look like cells B13 and C13. You will copy the format from cells B13 and C13 to cells F13 and G13.
19. ***Point in cell B13 and drag the mouse pointer to cell C13. On the Home tab, click the Format Painter icon in the Clipboard group.*** (It looks like a paintbrush.) Your pointer now should have a paintbrush icon on it.
20. ***Click in cell F13, drag the mouse to cell H13, and then let go of the mouse button. Click anywhere to see the cell.*** Notice that the formatting has now been copied.
21. Column E in the amortization schedule of the spreadsheet is the "Extra Payment" column. Assume for the purposes of this exercise that you will not have any extra payments and that you do not need this column, but you want to leave the column there in case you need it at a later date. For now, you can hide column E (and unhide it if you need it later).

22. ***Point and right-click on the "E" in the E column heading. From the drop-down menu, click Hide.***
23. ***Click in any cell.*** The vertical line will disappear. Notice that column E is no longer displayed. The column headings go from D to F.
24. We will now unhide column E. ***Point on the D column heading and drag the mouse to the F column heading so that both columns are highlighted. Right-click, then click Unhide on the drop-down menu.*** Notice that column E reappears.
25. ***Click in any cell to make the highlighting disappear.***
26. ***Click in cell D18.*** Use the **[DOWN ARROW]** key to go to cell D60. Notice that some column titles, such as "Pmt No.," and "Payment Date," are no longer visible, so it is difficult to know what the numbers mean.
27. Press **[CTRL]+[HOME]** to go to the top of the spreadsheet.
28. ***Click cell A18.*** You will now use the Split Screen command to see the column titles.
29. ***On the View tab, click Split in the Window group.***
30. Use the **[DOWN ARROW]** cursor key on the keyboard to go to cell A50. Notice that because you split the screen at row 18, you can still see column titles. Next, use the **[UP ARROW]** cursor key on the keyboard to go to cell A1. You should now see the top portion of your spreadsheet in both the top and bottom screens.
31. ***On the View tab, click Split again in the Window group.*** The bottom screen is now gone.
32. The Freeze Panes feature is another way to show the column headings when you scroll down a document. The Freeze Panes feature is a convenient way to see both column and row titles at the same time. ***Click in cell B18.***
33. ***On the View tab, click Freeze Panes in the Window group and then click the first option, Freeze Panes.***
34. Use the **[DOWN ARROW]** key to go to cell B50. Notice that because you froze the screen at cell B18, you can still see column titles. Next, use the **[RIGHT ARROW]** key to go to cell R50. You should still see the "Pmt No." column, including the payment numbers.
35. Press **[CTRL]+[HOME]** to go to the beginning of the spreadsheet.
36. ***On the View tab, click Freeze Panes in the Window group and then click the first option, Unfreeze Panes.***
37. To print the spreadsheet, ***click the Office button, click Print, then click OK.***
38. To save the spreadsheet, ***click the Office button and then click Save As. Under Save in: select the drive or folder in which you would like to save the document.*** Next to File name:, type **Excel Lesson 5 Spreadsheet DONE** and ***click Save.***
39. Templates are a great way to utilize the power of Excel. Many free templates are available on the Internet. Microsoft alone offers more than 100 Excel templates on its website. To access them, ***click the Office button, then New.*** They are listed to the left under Microsoft Office Online.
40. To exit Excel, ***click on the Office button and then click Exit Excel.***

This concludes Lesson 5.

HANDS-ON EXERCISES

LESSON 6: STATISTICAL FUNCTIONS

This lesson demonstrates how to use and enter statistical formulas such as average, maximum, minimum, and standard deviation. It also shows how to sort data, check for metadata in spreadsheets, how to use the Format Clear command, how to use conditional formatting, and how to insert a clip-art file. When the spreadsheet is complete, it will look like Excel 2007 Exhibit 10. Keep in mind that if you make a mistake at any time in this lesson, you may press **[CTRL]+[Z]** to undo what you have done.

EXCEL 2007 EXHIBIT 10
Statistical spreadsheet

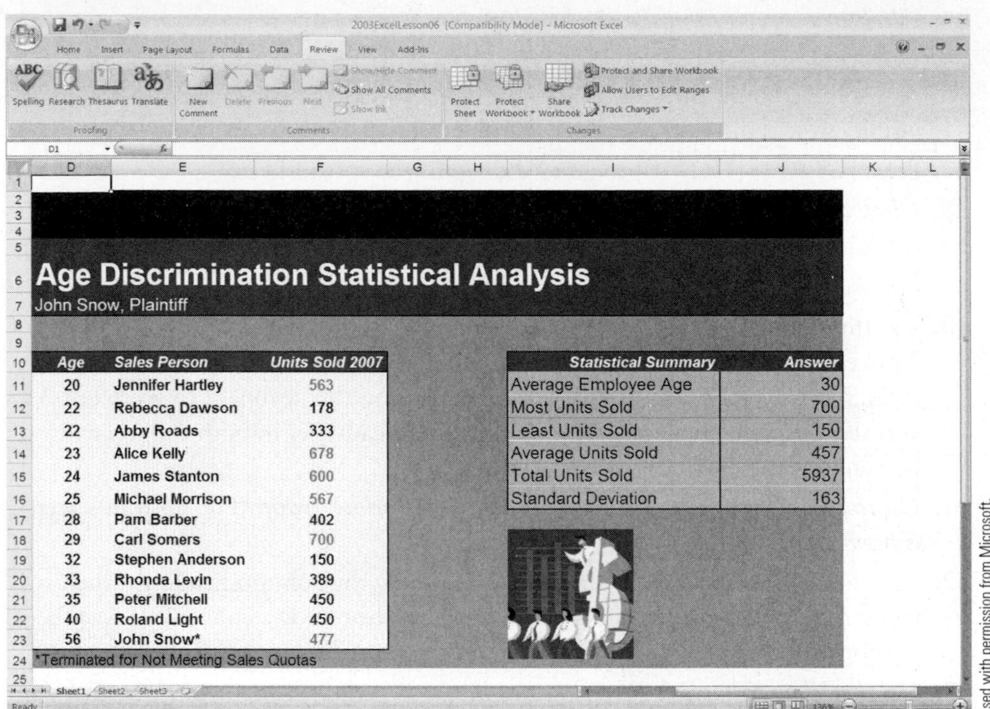

1. Open Windows. ***Double-click the Microsoft Office Excel 2007 icon on the desktop*** to open the program. Alternatively, ***click the Start button, point to Programs or All Programs, point to Microsoft Office, then click Microsoft Office Excel 2007.*** You should now be in a new, clean, blank workbook. If you are not in a blank workbook, ***click the Office button*** (see Excel 2007 Exhibit 1), ***then click New, then double-click on Blank Workbook.***
2. The first thing you will do to complete the template shown in Excel 2007 Exhibit 10 is open the "Lesson 6" file from the Premium Website. Go to your CengageBrain account and click on the link for Premium Website for Cornick's *Using Computers in the Law Office*, 7th edition. A new window will open. ***Under Book Level Resources, click on the Data Files: Excel tab, then under Excel 2007, click on the "Lesson 6" file.***
3. You should now see the Age Discrimination Statistical Analysis spreadsheet shown in Excel 2007 Exhibit 10; however, your spreadsheet has no formulas in the statistical summary section, the data have not yet been sorted, and there is no clip art yet.
4. You will now enter the formulas in the statistical summary section of the spreadsheet. The first formula will calculate the average age of employees of the company. ***Click in cell J11.*** Type the following formula: **=AVERAGE(D11:D23)** and then press the **[ENTER]** key. The result

should be 30. *Note:* Here is another way to enter the average function: ***on the Formulas tab, click Insert Function in the Function Library group; next to Or select a category, click the down arrow, then click Statistical > AVERAGE > OK.***

5. The next formula calculates the most units sold. ***Click in cell J12.*** Type the following formula: **=MAX(F11:F23)** and then press the **[ENTER]** key. The result should be 700.
6. The next formula calculates the least units sold. ***Click in cell J13.*** Type the following formula: **=MIN(F11:F23)** and then press the **[ENTER]** key. The result should be 150.
7. The next formula calculates the average units sold. ***Click in cell J14.*** Type the following formula: **=AVERAGE(F11:F23)** and then press the **[ENTER]** key. The result should be 457.
8. The next formula calculates the total units sold. ***Click in cell J15.*** Type the following formula: **=SUM(F11:F23)** and then press the **[ENTER]** key. The result should be 5937.
9. The last formula calculates the standard deviation for units sold. *Standard deviation* is a measure of how widely values are dispersed from the average value (the arithmetic mean). Large standard deviations show that the numbers vary widely from the average. ***On the Formulas tab, click Insert Function in the Function Library group. Next to Or select a category, click the down arrow and select Statistical. Scroll down the list and click*** **STDEVP** (see Excel 2007 Exhibit 11). Notice that there is a definition for this function. ***Click OK in the "Insert Function" window.***
10. The "Function Arguments" window should now be displayed. In the "Function Arguments" window, next to Number 1, press **[DEL]** until the box is blank. Type **F11:F23,** then ***click OK*** (see Excel 2007 Exhibit 12). The result should be 163.

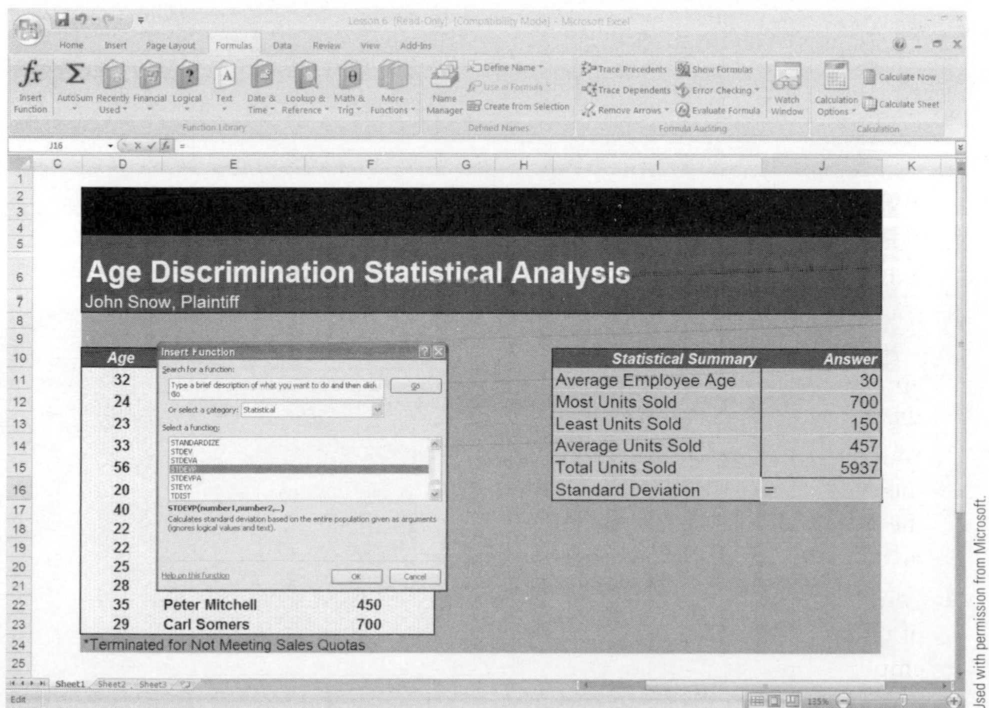

EXCEL 2007 EXHIBIT 11
Entering a standard deviation formula using the insert function command

EXCEL 2007 EXHIBIT 12
Entering a standard deviation formula using the functions argument window

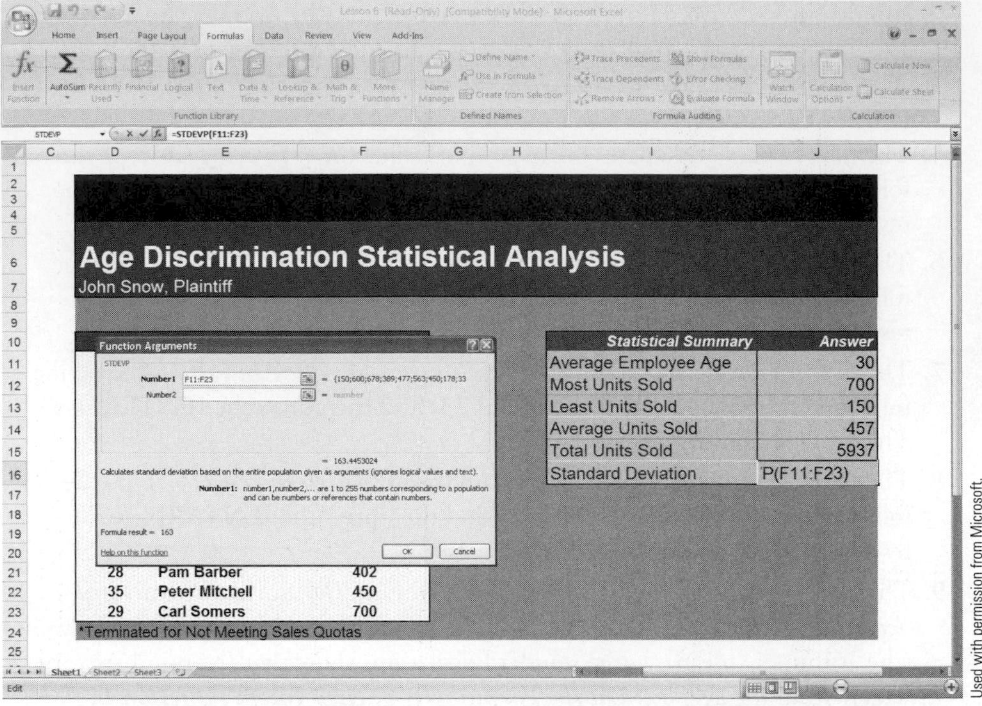

11. You will now sort the data based on the age of the employees. ***Click in D11 and then drag the mouse down to F23. From the Data tab, click Sort in the Sort & Filter group.***
12. The "Sort" window should now be displayed (see Excel 2007 Exhibit 13). *Note:* Even though you just want to sort by age, you must select the full data range that includes all of the information, or the age data will be sorted but the other columns and rows will stay where they are. The data will therefore be mismatched (each age will not be matched with the correct person and number of units sold).

EXCEL 2007 EXHIBIT 13
Sorting data

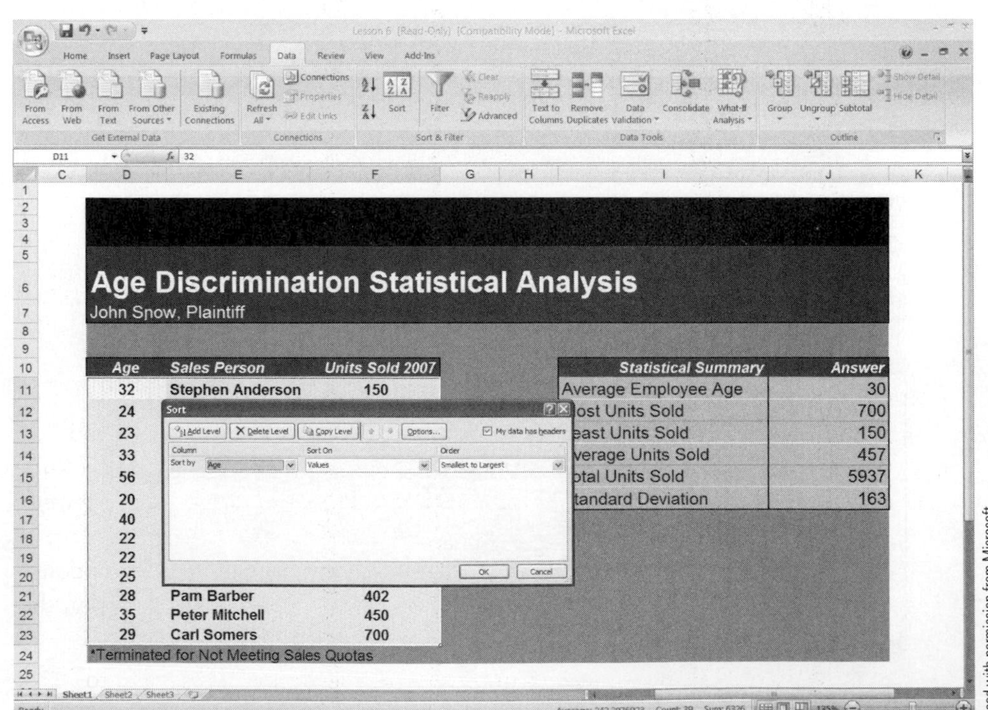

13. ***In the "Sort" window, click the down arrow next to Sort by, then click Age*** (see Excel 2007 Exhibit 13). Notice that under Order, the default of Smallest to Largest is selected; this is fine, so ***click OK in the "Sort" window.*** The data should now be sorted according to the age of the individual, with John Snow appearing last in the spreadsheet.
14. You will now ensure that no metadata is included in your document. You must first save the spreadsheet. To save the spreadsheet, ***click the Office button and then click Save As. Under Save in:, select the drive or folder*** in which you would like to save the document. Next to File name:, type **Excel Lesson 6 Spreadsheet DONE** and ***click Save.***
15. Excel 2007 has a special feature called Inspect Document that can extract all metadata from your spreadsheet. ***Click the Office button, click Prepare, then click Inspect Document*** (see Excel 2007 Exhibit 14). Through the "Document Inspector" window, all of the possible places metadata can hide are checked. ***Click Inspect.*** Some of the categories may have a Remove All button. If you wanted to remove the metadata, you would just click on Remove All for each category. Because this is just an exercise, we do not need to remove the metadata, so go ahead and ***click Close*** to close the "Document Inspector" window.

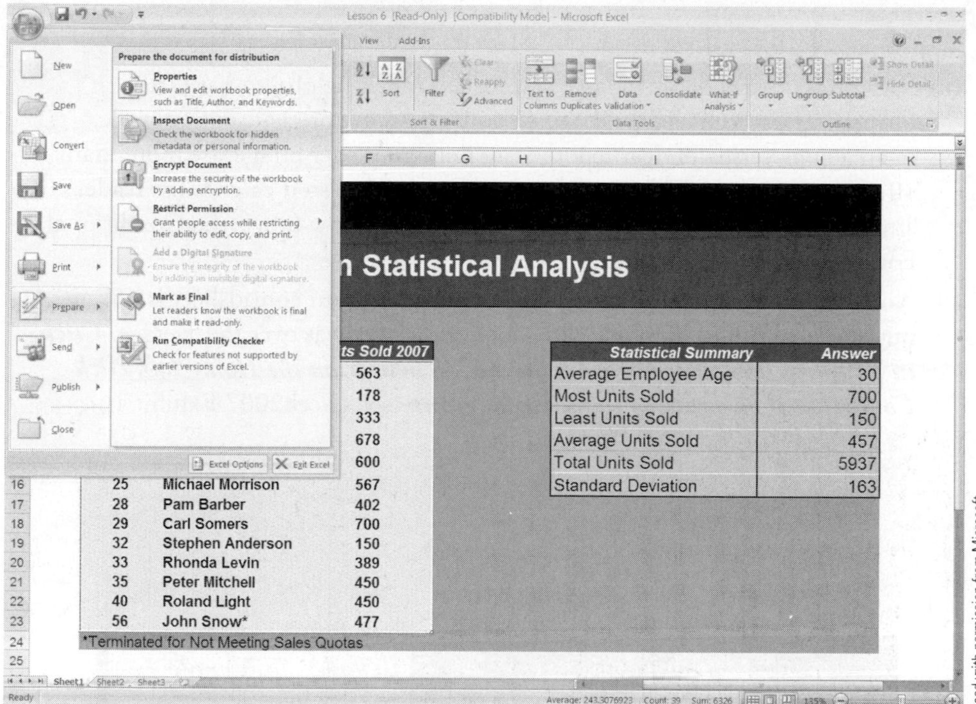

EXCEL 2007 EXHIBIT 14
Removing metadata

16. Sometimes it is helpful to clear a cell or cells of all formatting information at one time. Notice that cell D6, the one titled "Age Discrimination Statistical Analysis," is elaborately formatted, including 24-point font, white letters, red background, and bold text. You will now quickly remove all of that formatting. ***Click in cell D6. Then, on the Home tab, click the down arrow next to the Clear icon in the Editing group*** (it looks like an eraser—see Excel 2007 Exhibit 15). ***Click Clear Formats.*** All of the formatting should disappear. Notice in Excel 2007 Exhibit 15 that one of the options when using the Clear commands is Clear All. Clicking Clear All will not only clear the formatting, but will also clear the contents of the selected cell(s).
17. Press **[CTRL]**+**[Z]** (the Undo feature) to restore the original formatting to the cell.

EXCEL 2007 EXHIBIT 15
Clear command

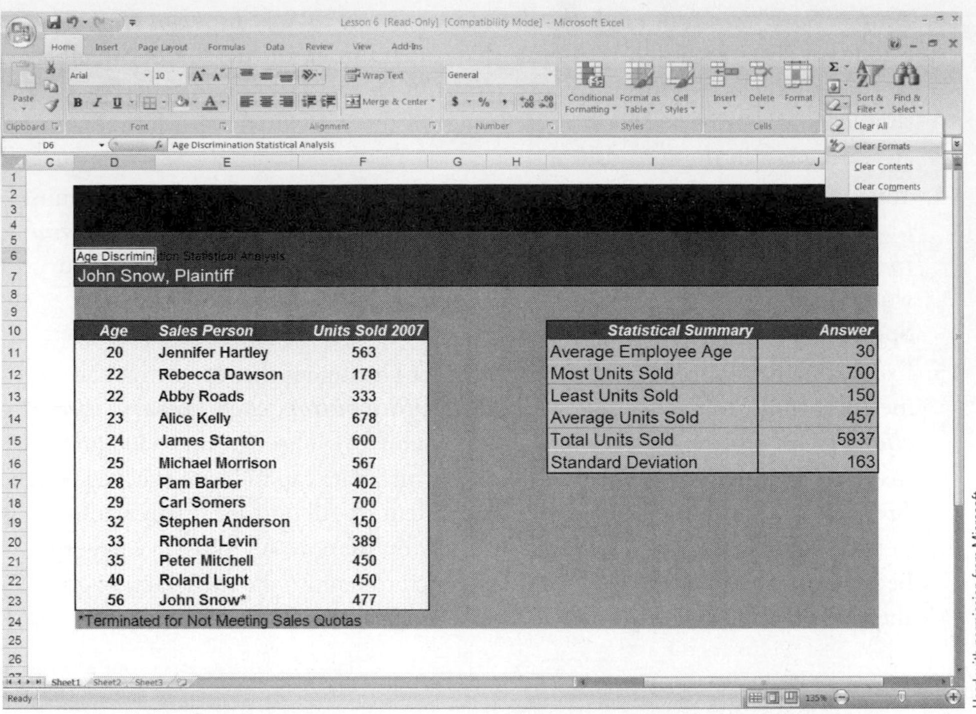

18. Sometimes, particularly in large spreadsheets, it is helpful to have the formatting of a cell change if certain conditions are present. For example, in an actual-versus-budget report, if an item goes over budget by more than 10 percent it might be helpful for that to be bolded so it catches the reader's attention. To accomplish this, you will now learn how to use the Conditional Formatting feature of Excel.

19. Notice that the average sales for the sales team in your spreadsheet is 457. It might be helpful to highlight any salesperson who was over the average. ***Click in F11 and then drag the mouse to F23. Then, from the Home tab, click Conditional Formatting in the Styles group*** (see Excel 2007 Exhibit 16).

EXCEL 2007 EXHIBIT 16
Creating conditional formatting

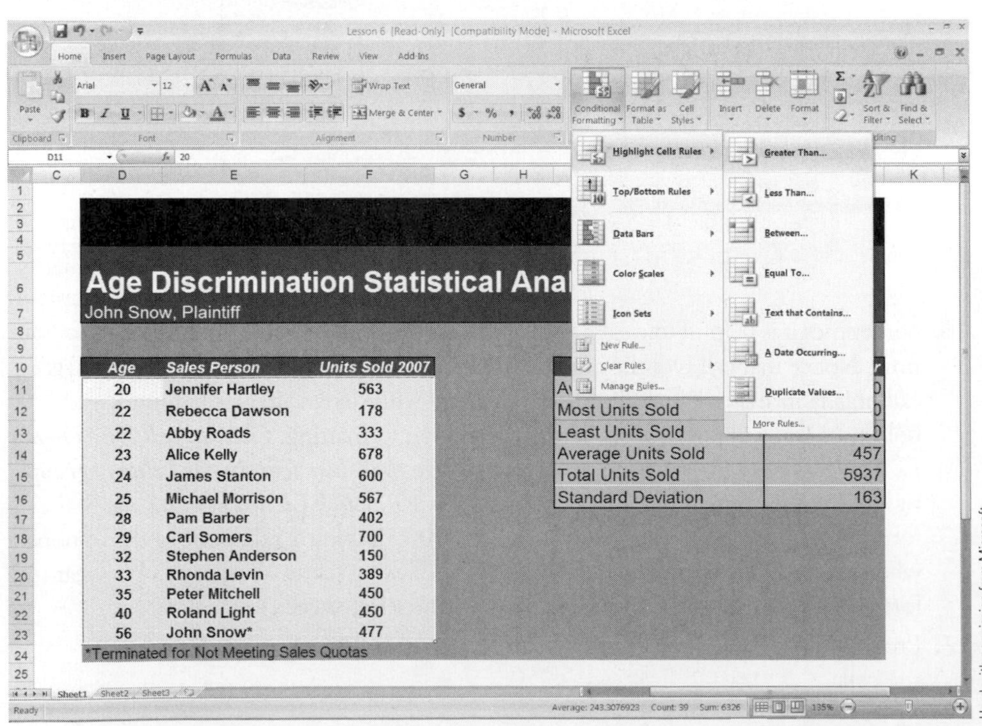

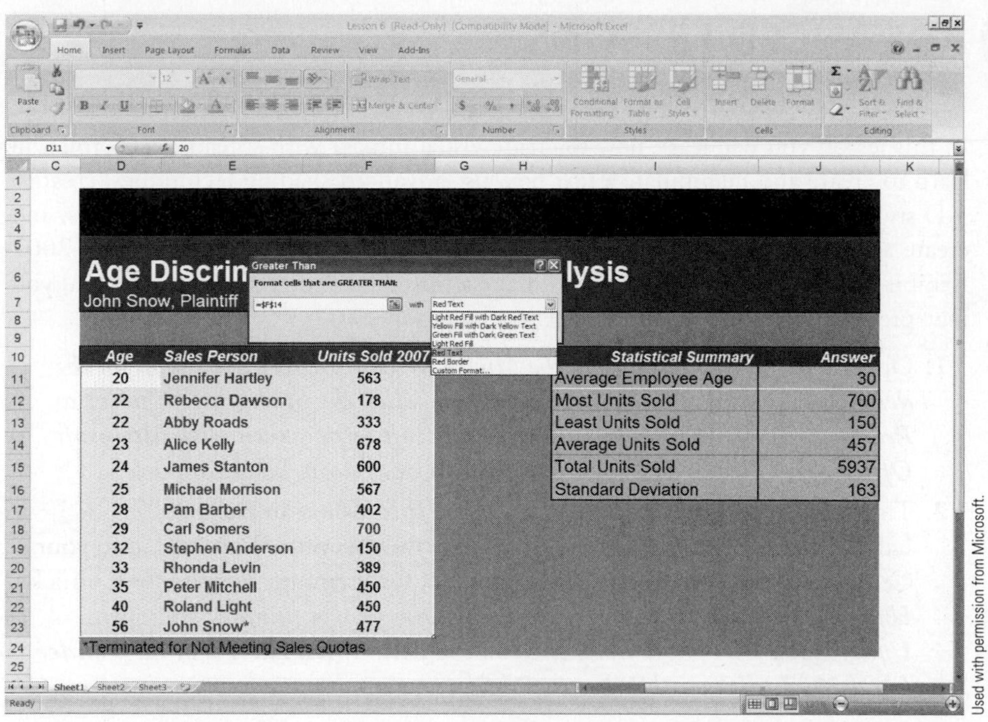

EXCEL 2007 EXHIBIT 17
Creating a "Greater Than" conditional formatting

20. ***Point to the first option, Highlight Cells Rules, and then click the first option again, which is Greater Than...*** (see Excel 2007 Exhibit 16).
21. The "Greater Than" window should now be displayed (see Excel 2007 Exhibit 17). Press the **[DEL]** key to remove the value under Format cells that are GREATER THAN:.
22. ***Click cell J14.*** Notice that cell J14 has been entered under Format cells that are GREATER THAN:. Dollar signs have been added to the cell reference because this is an absolute cell reference.
23. ***Click the down arrow next to Light Red Fill with Dark Red Text and select Red Text.*** Cells over the average will be shown in red text. ***Click OK in the "Greater Than" window.***
24. You will now add clip art to your spreadsheet (we are assuming that clip art was included when Excel 2007 was installed). ***Click in cell I18. From the Insert tab, click Clip Art in the Illustrations group.***
25. The Clip Art task pane will appear to the right of the screen. Under Search for, type **Money** and then ***click Go.*** You may get a message that asks if you want to include clip art from Microsoft Office Online; ***click No.***
26. ***Click on the clip art in Excel 2007 Exhibit 10*** (a blue bar chart with people in it and a person climbing a dollar sign). The clip art has now been added to your spreadsheet. ***Position the clip art where you want it by clicking and dragging it into position.***
27. ***Click the X in the Clip Art task pane*** to close the task pane.
28. To print the spreadsheet, ***click the Office button, click Print, then click OK.***
29. To save the spreadsheet, ***click the Office button and then click Save As.*** Choose the directory in which you want to save the file and ***click Save.***
30. To exit Excel, ***click the Office button and then click Exit Excel.***

This concludes Lesson 6.

ADVANCED LESSONS

LESSON 7: TOOLS AND TECHNIQUES 1—MARKETING BUDGET

In this lesson you will learn how to create visual impact with spreadsheets. You will learn to create and manipulate a text box, use advanced shading techniques, create a 3-D style text box, create vertical text, create diagonal text, use lines and borders, and create a comment. When the spreadsheet is complete, it will look like Excel 2007 Exhibit 18. Keep in mind that if you make a mistake at any time in this lesson, you may press **[CTRL]+[Z]** to undo what you have done.

1. Open Windows. ***Double-click the Microsoft Office Excel 2007 icon on the desktop*** to open the program. Alternatively, ***click the Start button, point to Programs or All Programs, point to Microsoft Office, then click Microsoft Office Excel 2007.*** You should now be in a new, clean, blank workbook.
2. The first thing you will do to complete the spreadsheet in Excel 2007 Exhibit 18 is open the "Lesson 7" file from the Premium Website. Go to your CengageBrain account and click on the link for Premium Website for Cornick's *Using Computers in the Law Office,* 7th edition. A new window will open. ***Under Book Level Resources, click on the Data Files: Excel tab, then under Excel 2007, click on the "Lesson 7" file.***

EXCEL 2007 EXHIBIT 18
Creating visual impact in spreadsheets

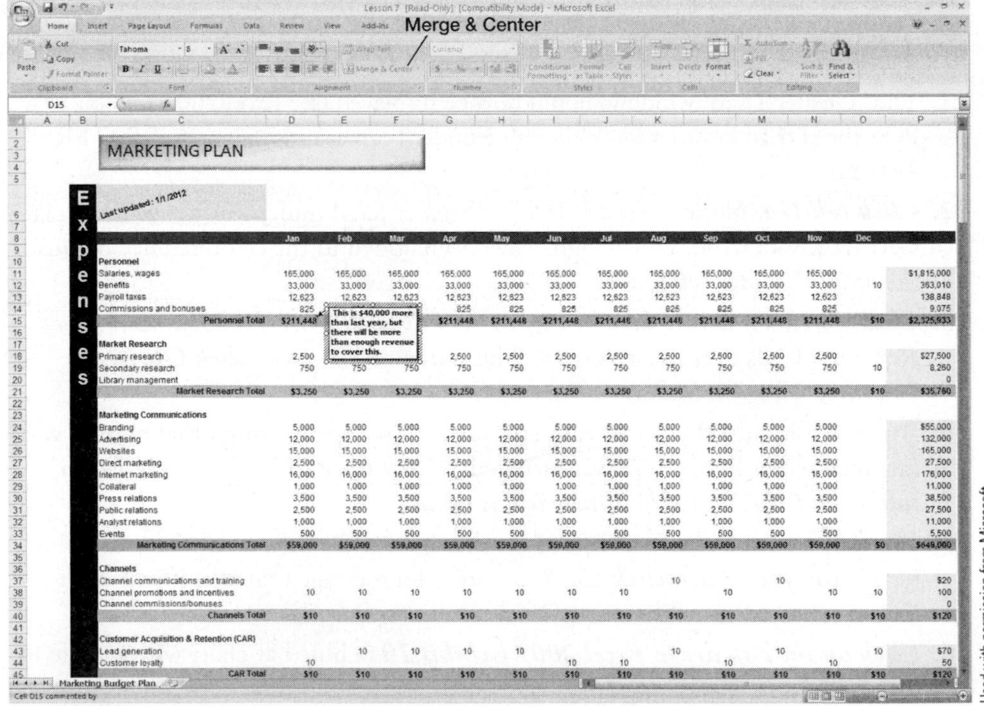

Used with permission from Microsoft.

3. You should now have the Marketing Plan spreadsheet in Excel 2007 Exhibit 18 open, except that your spreadsheet is missing some of the formatting that gives it visual impact. You will add the formatting to the spreadsheet to make it more visually compelling.
4. You will first add the text box that holds the title "Marketing Plan," as shown in Excel 2007 Exhibit 18. ***From the Insert tab, click Text Box in the Text group.*** Notice that your mouse pointer just turned into an upside-down letter "T."

5. ***Point to cell C2 and drag the mouse to about cell F4.*** An outline of a box should now be shown from C2 to F4. This is a *text box.*
6. ***Click inside the text box. Click the Bold icon and change the font size to 20.***
7. Type **MARKETING PLAN.**
8. ***Right-click on the outline of the text box you just created. In the drop-down menu, click Format Shape.*** The "Format Shape" window should now be displayed (see Excel 2007 Exhibit 19).

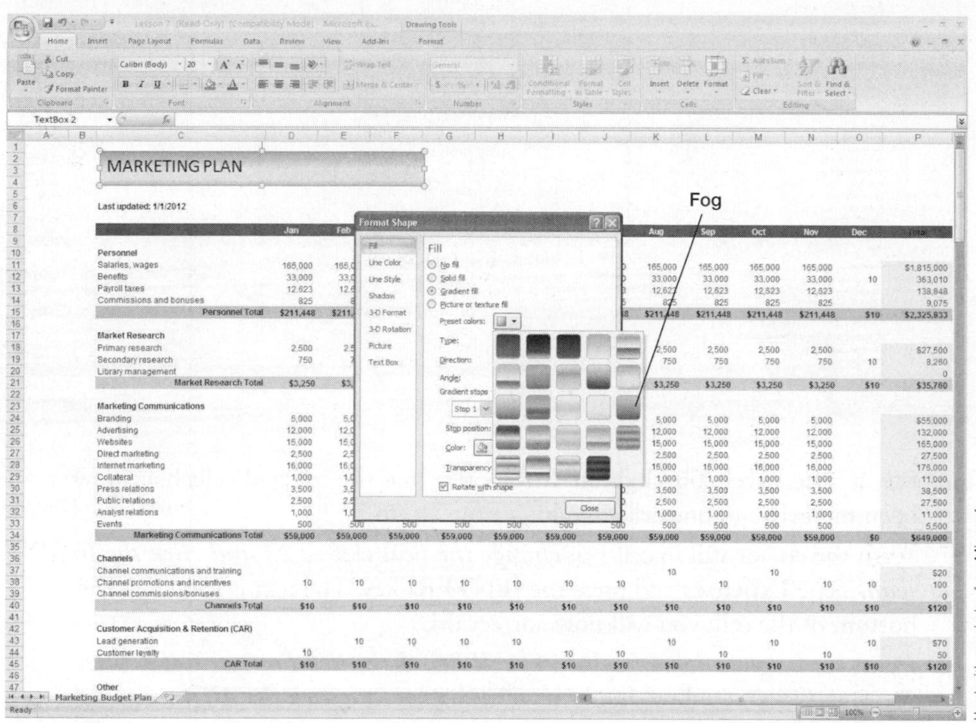

EXCEL 2007 EXHIBIT 19
Formatting a shape

9. ***In the "Format Shape" window, notice that Fill is currently selected. Click Gradient fill.***
10. ***Click the down arrow next to Preset colors:.*** This will open a box with many colors; ***click Fog.***
11. ***Staying in the "Format Shape" window, point to the down arrow next to Direction and click the first option, which is Linear Diagonal.***
12. ***Still in the "Format Shape" window, click 3-D Format on the left side of the window.*** You will now add a 3-D style to the text box. When the 3-D style choices appear, under Bevel and next to Top, ***point to the down arrow and click the first selection under Bevel, which is Circle*** (see Excel 2007 Exhibit 20).
13. ***Click Close to close the "Format Shape" window. Click in any other cell so you can see the effect.***
14. You will now create the vertical text in Column B that says "Expenses," as shown in Excel 2007 Exhibit 18. Notice that this is actually one long cell. The first thing you will do is merge cells B6 through B53 into one cell; you will then add the text and format it to be vertical.
15. ***Click in cell B6, drag the mouse down to cell B53, and then let go of the mouse button.***
16. ***From the Home tab, click the Merge & Center icon in the Alignment group.*** It looks like a box with an "a" in the middle, with left and right arrows around

EXCEL 2007 EXHIBIT 20

Adding 3-D effect to a text box

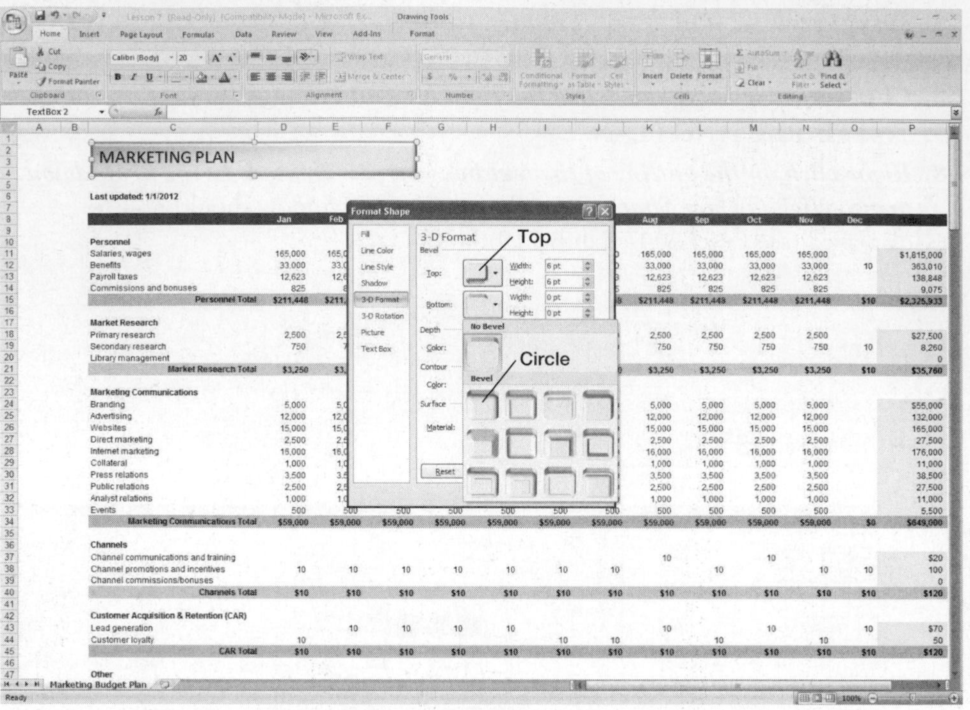

the "a" (see Excel 2007 Exhibit 18). Notice that the selected cells have now been merged into one cell stretching from B6 to B53.

17. With the cursor still in cell B6, ***change the font size to 22 and click the Bold icon.*** Type **Expenses** and press the **[ENTER]** key. The text is shown at the bottom of the cell; you will now correct this.
18. ***Point and right-click anywhere in cell B6, then click Format Cells.*** The "Format Cells" window should now be displayed. ***Click the Alignment tab*** (see Excel 2007 Exhibit 21).

EXCEL 2007 EXHIBIT 21

Creating vertical text

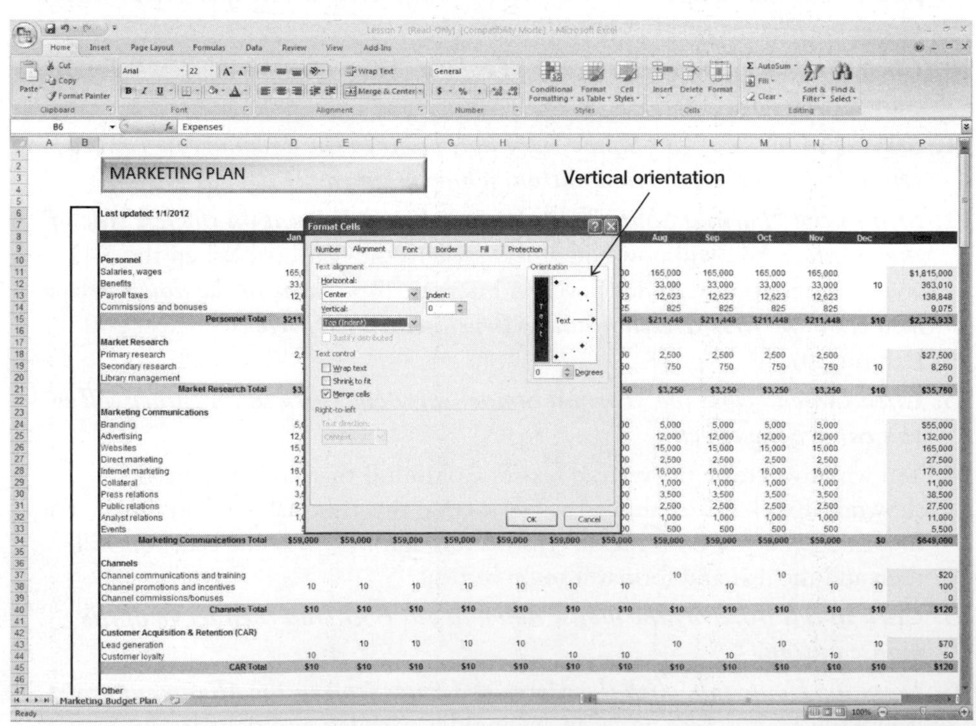

19. ***In the "Format Cells" window under Orientation, click the box that shows the word Text displayed vertically*** (see Excel 2007 Exhibit 21).
20. ***In the "Format Cells" window under Vertical, click the down arrow and select Top (Indent).***
21. ***Click OK in the "Format Cells" window.*** The word "Expenses" should now be displayed vertically down the cell.
22. ***With the pointer still in cell B6, on the Home tab, click the down arrow next to the Fill Color (a paint bucket) icon in the Font group and then select Black.***
23. ***On the Home tab, click the down arrow next to the Font Color icon in the Font group and select Yellow.***
24. You will next make the text in cell C6 appear diagonally. ***Right-click in cell C6, then click Format Cells.*** The "Format Cells" window should now be displayed and the Alignment tab should be selected.
25. ***In the "Format Cells" window under Orientation, click the up arrow next to Degrees until it reads 15.***
26. ***In the "Format Cells" window, click the Fill tab. Click the yellow square, then click OK.***
27. ***Click in any cell to make the highlighting disappear.*** The words "Last updated: 1/1/2012" should now be displayed diagonally in black letters on a yellow background.
28. You will now add the comment shown in Excel 2007 Exhibit 18. ***Right-click in cell D15. On the drop-down menu, click Insert Comment.*** Press **[BACKSPACE]** twice to delete the colon, and then type **This is $40,000 more than last year, but there will be more than enough revenue to cover this.** ***Click in any cell to exit the "Comment" box.***
29. ***Hover your mouse over cell D15*** so you can see the comment.
30. You will now add borders to the spreadsheet. ***Point to cell C53 and drag the mouse to cell P53. On the Home tab, click the down arrow next to the Borders icon in the Font group and click All Borders.*** The "Totals" row should now have borders around each cell.
31. ***Click in cell C8 and drag the mouse to cell P53. On the Home tab, click the down arrow next to the Borders icon in the Font group, then click Thick Box Border.*** A thick border now surrounds the data.
32. To print the spreadsheet, ***click the Office button, click Print, then click OK.***
33. To save the spreadsheet, ***click the Office button and then click Save As. Under Save in: select the drive or folder*** in which you would like to save the document. Next to File name:, type **Excel Lesson 7 Spreadsheet DONE** and ***click Save.***
34. To exit Excel, ***click the Office button and then click Exit Excel.***

This concludes Lesson 7.

LESSON 8: TOOLS AND TECHNIQUES 2—STOCK PORTFOLIO

In this lesson, you will continue to learn and apply helpful tools and techniques using Excel. This includes getting additional practice with using the Merge & Center tool, using the formula auditing feature, using the Oval tool, and password-protecting a file. When your spreadsheet is complete, it will look similar to Excel 2007 Exhibit 22. Some of these tools have been covered in previous lessons, and this lesson will help reinforce your ability to use them effectively. This tutorial assumes that you have completed Lessons 1 through 7, and that you are quite familiar with Excel.

EXCEL 2007 EXHIBIT 22
Stock portfolio spreadsheet

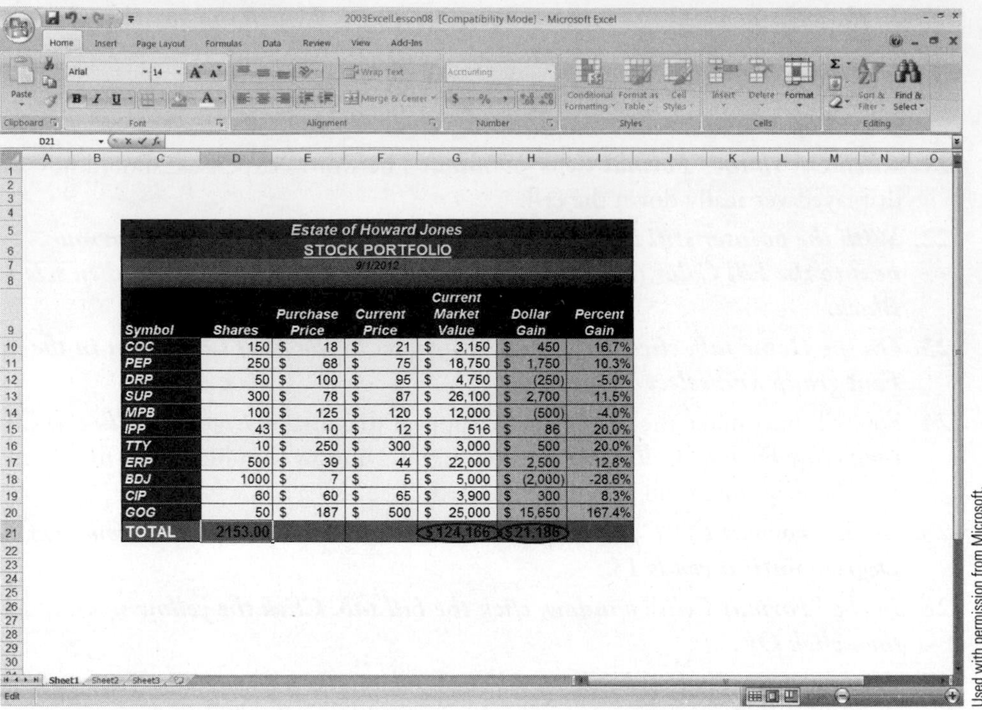

Estate of Howard Jones
STOCK PORTFOLIO
9/1/2012

Symbol	Shares	Purchase Price	Current Price	Current Market Value	Dollar Gain	Percent Gain
COC	150	$ 18	$ 21	$ 3,150	$ 450	16.7%
PEP	250	$ 68	$ 75	$ 18,750	$ 1,750	10.3%
DRP	50	$ 100	$ 95	$ 4,750	$ (250)	-5.0%
SUP	300	$ 78	$ 87	$ 26,100	$ 2,700	11.5%
MPB	100	$ 125	$ 120	$ 12,000	$ (500)	-4.0%
IPP	43	$ 10	$ 12	$ 516	$ 86	20.0%
TTY	10	$ 250	$ 300	$ 3,000	$ 500	20.0%
ERP	500	$ 39	$ 44	$ 22,000	$ 2,500	12.8%
BDJ	1000	$ 7	$ 5	$ 5,000	$ (2,000)	-28.6%
CIP	60	$ 60	$ 65	$ 3,900	$ 300	8.3%
GOG	50	$ 187	$ 500	$ 25,000	$ 15,650	167.4%
TOTAL	2153.00			$124,166	$21,186	

1. Open Windows. ***Double-click the Microsoft Office Excel 2007 icon on the desktop*** to open the program. Alternatively, ***click the Start button, point to Programs or All Programs, point on Microsoft Office, then click Microsoft Office Excel 2007.*** You should now be in a new, clean, blank workbook. If you are not in a blank workbook, ***click the Office button*** (see Excel 2007 Exhibit 1), ***then click New, then double-click Blank Workbook.***
2. The first thing you will do to complete the spreadsheet in Excel 2007 Exhibit 22 is open the "Lesson 8" file from the Premium Website. Go to your CengageBrain account and click on the link for Premium Website for Cornick's *Using Computers in the Law Office,* 7th edition. A new window will open. ***Under Book Level Resources, click on the Data Files: Excel tab, then under Excel 2007, click on the "Lesson 8" file.***
3. You should now have the Stock Portfolio spreadsheet shown in Excel 2007 Exhibit 22 open, except that your spreadsheet will be missing two rows of data and some of the formatting. You will add the rows and formatting to the spreadsheet.
4. ***On the Home tab, use the Merge & Center icon in the Alignment group to merge cells C5 to I5.***
5. ***Use the Merge & Center icon to merge cells C6 to I6.***
6. ***Use the Merge & Center icon to merge cells C7 to I7.***
7. Make sure the titles are aligned as shown in Excel 2007 Exhibit 22 ***(on the Home tab, use the Left and Center Align icons in the Alignment group).***
8. ***On the Home tab, use the Fill Color icon in the Font group to make the fill color for cell C5 dark blue*** (or any color you choose).
9. ***Use the Fill Color icon to make the fill color for cell C6 purple*** (any light purple is fine).

HANDS-ON EXERCISES

10. ***Use the Fill Color icon to make the fill color for cell C7 gray*** (any light gray is fine).
11. The cell range from C8 to I8 is a text graphic box (similar to a text box—it is just more difficult to see). ***Right-click the box and select Format Shape. Then, in the Fill section, click Gradient fill. Next to Preset Colors, click on the first one, Early Sunset*** (just hover your cursor over a color and the name will be displayed). ***Under Direction, click the first option, Linear Diagonal, then click Close to close the "Format Shape" window.***
12. ***On the Home tab, use the Borders icon in the Font group to give cells D10 to I21 a border of All Borders.***
13. ***From the Insert tab, click Shapes in the Illustrations group. Under Basic Shapes, click the Oval tool*** (it should be the second shape). ***Start in the upper left corner of cell G21 and drag the mouse to the lower right corner of G21 to make an oval around the total.*** *Note:* You can slightly move the oval by using the cursor keys on the keyboard to nudge it into place so it is centered in the cell.
14. The color of the oval must now be corrected. Notice that the ribbon has changed and that the Drawing Tools Format ribbon is now displayed. ***Click the down arrow next to Shape Fill in the Shape Styles group of the Drawing Tools Format tab. Click No Fill.*** The oval now surrounds the number, but the line color of the oval must be changed.
15. ***Right-click the oval and select Format Shape. On the left side of the "Format Shape" window, click Line Color. Click the down arrow next to Color, click Black, then click Close in the "Format Shape" window. Make an oval in cell H21 identical to that in cell G21, using the same process.***
16. You will now use the Formula Auditing mode to inspect the formulas in the spreadsheet and ensure that they are accurate.
17. ***On the Formulas tab, click Show Formulas in the Formula Auditing group.*** Scroll over to the right and look at all of the cells in your spreadsheet. Notice that instead of seeing the result of the formulas, you see the formulas themselves. This is a great tool for checking the accuracy of your spreadsheets. Look at your formulas and make sure they are correct. When you are sure your formulas are accurate, ***turn off the Formula Auditing mode by clicking on Show Formulas again.***
18. You will now learn how to password-protect your spreadsheet files. ***Click the Office button and then click Save As. In the "Save As" window, click Tools*** (it is in the lower portion of the window), ***then click General Options.*** Under File sharing and next to Password to open, type **A.** ***Click OK.*** At the "Confirm Password" window, type **A**, then ***click OK.*** At the "Save As" window, ***click Save*** to save the file to My Documents (or the folder of your choice—you must remember where you save it). You will then get a prompt that asks whether you want to increase the security of the document by conversion to Office Open XML Format. Because this is just an exercise, ***click No.***
19. If you get a compatibility prompt, just ***click Continue.***
20. ***Click the Office button, then click Close*** to close the file.
21. ***Now, click the Office button, and under Recent Documents click on the file you just saved.***

22. The "Password" window should now be displayed. Type **A** in the "Password" window. (The password is case-sensitive, so if you typed a capital A when you created the password, you must type a capital A to open the document.) ***Click OK.*** The file should now be displayed.
23. You can turn off a password in the same way. ***Click the Office button and then Save As. In the "Save As" window, click Tools, then click on General Options.*** Under File sharing and next to Password to open, use the **[DEL]** key to remove the asterisk. ***Click OK and then click Save.*** At the **"Do you want to replace the existing file?"** prompt, ***point and click Yes.***
24. If you get a compatibility prompt, just ***click Continue.***
25. Close the file and then reopen it, and you will see that you no longer need a password to open it.
26. To print the spreadsheet, ***click the Office button, click Print, then click OK.***
27. To exit Excel, ***click the Office button and then click Exit Excel.***

This concludes the Excel 2007 Hands-On Exercises.

CHAPTER 4

Legal Timekeeping and Billing Software

CHAPTER OBJECTIVES

After completing this chapter, you should be able to do the following:

1. Explain what timekeeping and billing are.
2. Explain the computerized timekeeping and billing process.
3. Describe the different types of legal fee agreements.
4. Identify why accurate billings are important to law firms.
5. List the basic features and functions of timekeeping and billing programs.
6. Describe how timeslips are entered into a timekeeping and billing system.
7. Explain how management reports generated from a timekeeping and billing system can help a firm.
8. Explain what electronic billing is.
9. Describe the factors for determining whether a fee is reasonable.

INTRODUCTION

A lawyer's time is the only thing he or she has to sell. Therefore, it is important to keep accurate records of how that time is spent. In the legal environment, the process of tracking time for the purpose of billing clients is called **timekeeping**. In addition to being paid for their time, attorneys must also be reimbursed for the expenses that they incur on each case (such as for postage, copies, court filing fees, expert witness costs, and so forth).

timekeeping
Tracking time for the purpose of billing clients.

In the legal environment, the process of issuing bills to collect monies for legal services performed and for expenses incurred is called **billing**. This chapter introduces the principles of legal timekeeping and billing, compares manual and computerized billing systems, describes the computerized timekeeping and billing process, introduces the kinds of fee agreements attorneys and clients enter into, describes what a good billing system is intended to accomplish, shows how computerized timekeeping and billing software can improve efficiency and accuracy in this process, and discusses ethical issues related to timekeeping and billing.

billing
The process of issuing invoices (bills) to collect monies for legal services performed and for expenses incurred.

INTRODUCTION TO TIMEKEEPING AND BILLING

Law firms, like all businesses, must generate income. As with other businesses, the running of law firms has a management side. One important management duty that law offices perform is to track the time and expenses of their staff and then generate accurate billings for clients so that law-office staff can be paid. Attorneys spend their time advising clients, talking to witnesses, drafting documents, taking depositions, appearing in court, and undertaking other activities on behalf of their clients. All these activities must be tracked so that clients can be accurately billed for the work the attorneys do. In addition, the expenses attorneys incur on behalf of their clients must be tracked so that the attorneys can be reimbursed. Expenses incurred on behalf of clients include the cost of making photocopies of documents for a client's file, the cost of mailing letters and other documents, travel expenses incurred while working on a client's case, court filing fees, deposition transcription costs, and much more.

If time and expenses were not tracked, law firms could not generate bills, get paid, or adequately run the business. Although timekeeping and billing are not glamorous, they are necessary to the survival of nearly all law firms. Firms that do not put a priority on billing clients, on a regular and accurate basis, will most likely not be around long. It is simply bad business practice to work 70 hours a week, bill for 50 hours, and be paid for 30 hours.

The timekeeping and billing problem becomes even worse when large law firms have to track the time and expenses of hundreds of attorneys and hundreds of paralegals. A good timekeeping and billing system is an absolute necessity.

Why Do Paralegals Need to Know Timekeeping and Billing?

Paralegals need to know about timekeeping and billing for several reasons. In many private law practices, paralegals are required to track their time so it can be charged to the case(s) they are working on. Many law practices that use this system require paralegals to bill a minimum number of hours each year. It is important to remember that private law firms are fundamentally businesses—and like any other business, they need to make money, operate at a profit, and earn money for their owners. Therefore, the billing of time to a firm's clients is crucial to its operations and success as a business. It is not uncommon for a firm to require each paralegal to bill between 26 and 35 hours a week (1,352 and 1,820 hours annually). Paralegals may be terminated from their jobs if they fail to bill the required number of hours. Thus, it is necessary for paralegals to understand how timekeeping and billing work.

In addition, paralegals are sometimes put in charge of the timekeeping and billing system, including managing the timekeeping process and generating bills. This usually occurs in smaller law offices. In those situations, it is important for the paralegals not only to know the process, but also to know how to actually run and operate the system.

MANUAL VERSUS COMPUTERIZED BILLING SYSTEMS

Before legal billing software came along, bills were generated manually, using typewriters or word processors. The manual method was cumbersome and slow, commonly issued bills that contained mathematical errors, and often produced billings that were outdated or inaccurate. This was especially true of large firms with hundreds of clients.

Long ago, it was common for law firms to send out bills only when they needed to pay their own bills (rent, staff salaries, etc.). Attorneys often sat down with a client's file months after work had been performed and tried to remember what they did on the case and how much time it took to do it. Of course, these billings were very inaccurate; it is extremely hard to remember this type of information after the fact, even by the end of a day, let alone after weeks or months. In addition, with manual methods, the billing process took hours or days to complete, especially if a large number of bills were being done.

The more traditional way of handling manual billing is to send out bills based on timeslips that each attorney or paralegal fills out every day. A **timeslip** is a piece of paper or a computer entry that legal professionals use to record information about the legal services they provide to each client. Most timeslips contain information such as the name of the case worked on, the date a service was provided, a description of the service, and so on (see Exhibit 4–1). In addition to tracking time, all law firms

timeslip
A slip of paper or computer record that records information about the legal services legal professionals provide to each client.

		Time Conversion	
PC—Phone Conference	R—Review		
LR—Legal Research	OC—Office Conference	6 Minutes 0.1 Hour	36 Minutes 0.6 Hour
L—Letter	T—Travel	12 Minutes 0.2 Hour	42 Minutes 0.7 Hour
	CT—Court Hearing	15 Minutes 0.25 Hour	45 Minutes 0.75 Hour
		18 Minutes 0.3 Hour	48 Minutes 0.8 Hour
		24 Minutes 0.4 Hour	54 Minutes 0.9 Hour
		30 Minutes 0.5 Hour	60 Minutes 1.0 Hour

Date	Client/Case	File No.	Services Performed	Attorney	Time Hours & Tenths	
5-7	Smith v. United Sales	118294	Summarized 6 depositions; Client; Δ (Defendant) Helen; Δ Barney, Δ Rose; Witness Forrest & Johnson	BJP	6.	5
5-8	Marcel v. True Oil	118003	PC w/Client Re: Settlement offer; Discussions w/Attorney; Memo to file Re: offer	BJP		3
5-8	Johnson v. State	118118	PC w/Client's Mother, PC w/Client; LR Re: Bail; Memo to file; R correspondence	BJP		75
5-8	Potential claim of Watkins v. Leslie Grocery	Not Assigned Yet	OC w/Client; (New client); Reviewed facts; Received medical records Re; accident; Conf. w/atty	BJP	1.	50
5-8	Smith v. United Sales	118294	Computerized searches on depositions for attorney	BJP		75
5-8	Jay Tiller Bankruptcy	118319	PC w/Creditor, Bank One; Memo to file; Client; LJ to Client	BJP		3
5-8	Potential Claim of Watkins v. Leslie Grocery	—	LR Slip & Fall cases generally; Standard of care	BJP	1.	00
5-8	Marcel v. True Oil	118003	Conf. w/atty, & Client Re: Settlement; Drafted & prepared LJ to Δs Re: Settlement offer	BJP	1.	10
5-8	Jay Tiller Bankruptcy	118319	Drafted Bankruptcy petition; OC w/Client; List of Debts; Fin. Stmt; Conf. w/atty	BJP	1.	00
5-8	Smith v. United Sales	118294	Drafted and prepared depo notice to Witness Spring	BJP		25
5-9	Seeley Real Estate Matter	118300	Ran amortization schedule to attach to 'Contract for Deed'	BJP		25

EXHIBIT 4–1
Typical manual timeslip/time record form

EXHIBIT 4–2
Expense slip

Johnson, Beck & Taylor
Expense Slip

Expense Type & Code

1 Photocopies	4 Filing Fees	7 Facsimile	10 Travel
2 Postage	5 Witness Fees	8 Lodging	11 Overnight Delivery
3 Long Distance	6 Westlaw/Lexis	9 Meals	12 Other ________

Date 4-5-08	Case Name: Smith v. United		File No. 118294
Expense Code: 1	Quantity 20 pages	Amount File rate	(Billable) Nonbillable
Expense Code: 2	Quantity 4 packages	Amount $4.66	(Billable) Nonbillable
Expense Code:	Quantity sent	Amount	Billable Nonbillable

Name of Person Making Expense Slip: JBP

Description of Expense(s) Incurred:
Copies and postage re: Motion to compel 4/5

expense slip
A record of each expense item a firm incurs on behalf of the client.

must also track expenses. An **expense slip** is a record of each expense item a firm incurs on behalf of a client (see Exhibit 4–2). Some common expenses include:

- copying costs
- court reporter fees
- electronic legal research (Westlaw/Lexis)
- expert witness fees
- filing fees
- overnight delivery charges
- postage
- travel expenses
- witness/subpoena fees

When a member of a firm incurs an expense for a client, such as by making copies of documents, using postage to send out material, or making a long-distance telephone call, an expense slip is filled out. Then, usually on a monthly basis, manual billings are sent out, based on the timeslips and expense slips that have been collected. Although billings based on timeslips are more accurate than those based on memory, the billing process itself is still quite tedious and slow when done manually.

Computerized billing systems solve many of these problems. Exactly how much time a computerized time and billing program saves over a manual system is somewhat debatable, but a study by one attorney found that manual billing systems can take up to three times longer than computerized methods to produce bills every billing cycle (i.e., every time billings are sent, whether it be biweekly, monthly, or according to some other schedule).

timekeeper
Anyone who bills for time, including partners, associates, and paralegals.

Generally, timekeepers still must record what they do with their time on a timeslip, whether the billing system is manual or computerized. A **timekeeper** is anyone who bills out his or her time; this includes partners, associates, and paralegals. Usually, the information from paper timeslips is entered into the legal billing software on a daily basis. However, the common practice today is for attorneys and paralegals to enter their time directly into the computerized timekeeping and billing system without using a separate timeslip at all. It is common for firms using computerized billing systems to produce monthly or even weekly bills, according to the wishes of the client.

In addition to alleviating cash-flow problems, most legal billing software produces reports that management can use to help operate the law-firm business (this is covered in more detail later in the chapter). Computerized timekeeping and billing systems also produce billings that are more accurate than those produced by manual methods, because all mathematical computations are performed automatically by the computer.

THE COMPUTERIZED TIMEKEEPING AND BILLING PROCESS

Timekeeping and billing software packages differ greatly from one another. However, the computerized timekeeping and billing process for most billing packages is as shown in Exhibit 4–3.

1. The Client and the Attorney Reach Agreement on Legal Fees

An attorney can bill for services in many different ways. At the outset of most cases, the client and the attorney reach an agreement regarding how much the attorney will charge for her or his services. Preferably, the agreement is in writing in the form of a

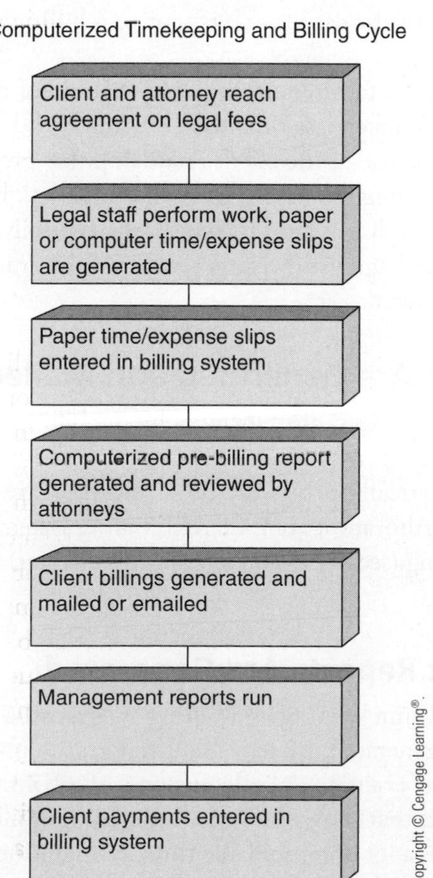

EXHIBIT 4–3
Computerized timekeeping and billing cycle

contract. After the legal fee has been agreed on, the new matter is set up in the computerized billing package by entering the client's name and address, the type of case it is, the type of legal fee that has been agreed on, and any other relevant information the law office has identified for inclusion.

2. Legal Staff Perform Services and Prepare Timeslips

When attorneys or paralegals perform work on a legal matter for a client, they fill out a timeslip to track the exact services (either using a manual timeslip form or entering the information directly into the computer). Many timekeeping and billing programs also support data entry from a tablet computer or smartphone. Expense slips are also generated this way.

3. Timeslips and Expense Slips Are Entered into the Billing System

If manual timeslips are used, the information they contain must be entered into the billing system. Usually the information is typed into the computer in roughly the same format as it appears on the timeslip. It is essential that the information be accurately entered into the computer. In addition, expense slips are entered into the computer to track the expenses the firm has incurred on behalf of a client.

4. A Pre-Billing Report Is Generated and Reviewed

pre-billing report
A rough draft compilation of billings.

After legal services have been performed and recorded in the time and billing software, the next step is for a **pre-billing report** to be generated. This is done before the final client bills are produced. A pre-billing report is a rough draft of the billings that eventually will be sent to clients (see Exhibit 4–4). The pre-billing report is given to the attorney in charge of the case for review or to a billing committee to make sure the billings are accurate.

Attorneys may choose to discount bills for a variety of reasons, including thinking the task should have taken less time than it actually did. Discounts are also given for good customers, because of the client's hardship, for professional courtesy or for friends, or because the billing looks unreasonable. This can, however, be very frustrating to a paralegal who has his or her time cut back. Typically, only the amount that is actually billed is counted against the target or minimum number of billable hours a paralegal is expected to work.

5. Client Billings Are Generated and Mailed or Emailed

Formal client billings (invoices) are generated by the billing system (see Exhibit 4–5). Most timekeeping and billing programs can produce many different billing formats. The computer automatically prints the bills, and they are subsequently mailed or emailed to the clients. Also, most computerized billing systems can now produce some form of electronic billing (see discussion later in this chapter) or can produce PDF files to be emailed.

6. Management Reports Are Generated

In most computerized timekeeping and billing programs, a wide variety of management reports may be generated. Management reports are not used for billing clients; rather, they are used to evaluate the effectiveness of a firm. For example, most programs generate a report that shows how much time is nonbillable (i.e., not chargeable to clients). If a firm has a lot of nonbillable time, it might indicate that the firm is not productive and is losing valuable time from its timekeepers.

EXHIBIT 4–4
Pre-billing report

JOHNSON, BECK & TAYLOR

8/01	Pre-billing Report	Page 1

Refrigeration, Inc.	Corporate Matters
Miscellaneous Corporate Matters	Monthly
Case Number: Refrig-002	Trust Balance: $2,825
P.O. Box 10083	Case Rate: $125
500 East Fifth Street	Case Attorney: MJB
Los Angeles, CA 90014	
Phone: (213) 555-9342	

Previous Bill Owed $470.20

—Legal Fees—

Date	Atty	Description	Time	Amount
7/6	MJB	Telephone conference with Stevenson re: June minutes	.50 hr	$62.50
7/7	MJB	Preparation of June minutes; prepared for review at next meeting of the board of directors	~~1.50~~ 1.00 hr	~~$187.50~~ $125.00 MJB
7/9	MJB	Conference with Stevenson at home	.25 hr	none
		Total Legal Fees	~~**2.25**~~ 1.75 **hr**	~~**$250.00**~~ $187.50 MJB

—Costs Advanced—

Date	Atty	Description	Quantity	Amount
7/7	MJB	Photocopy documents; June 2005 minutes (for board meeting)	$.25 ea 100 items	$25.00
		Total Costs Advanced		**$25.00**

Continued on Page Two

Management reports can also be used to make management decisions, such as that particular types of cases are no longer profitable, the firm needs to raise hourly rates, or other such finance-related decisions.

7. Client Payments Are Entered into the Billing System

Finally, payments made as a result of billings must be recorded or entered into the billing system, giving clients proper credit for the payments they have made.

The Billing Cycle

The timekeeping and billing process is a recurring cycle. Once bills are produced and payments are made for a period, the process starts over if more work is performed on a case. The timeslips for the new period are entered, bills are generated, and so forth. Once a year or so, old timeslips should be purged or deleted from the computer. Without the outdated information, the computer can operate faster.

In essence, manual systems go through the same process or cycle as do computerized systems, except that the pre-billing reports, final billings, and payments are all generated and recorded by hand. However, most manual systems do not have the capability to produce management reports.

EXHIBIT 4–5
Final client billing

JOHNSON, BECK & TAYLOR
555 Flowers Street, Suite 200
Los Angeles, California 90038
(213) 555-2342

Mary Smith
Refrigeration, Inc.
P.O. Box 10083
500 East Fifth Street
Los Angeles, CA 90014

Billing Date: 8/02

Acct. Number: 4345AS3234
Previous Bal. in Trust
$2,825.00

RE: Refrigeration Miscellaneous Corporate Matters

DATE	PROFESSIONAL SERVICES	INDIV.	TIME	
7/6	Telephone conference with Stevenson re: June minutes	MJB	.50	$62.50
7/7	Preparation of June minutes: prepared for review at next meeting of the board of directors	MJB	1.00	$125.00
7/9	Conference with Stevenson at home	MJB	.25	$-0-
TOTAL FOR THE ABOVE SERVICES			**1.75**	**$187.50**

DATE	EXPENSES	
7/7	Photocopy documents; June minutes (for board meeting)	$25.00
TOTAL FOR ABOVE EXPENSES		**$25.00**
TOTAL BILLING		**$212.50**
CURRENT BALANCE IN TRUST		**$2,612.50**

KINDS OF LEGAL FEE AGREEMENTS

All bills are, of course, based on the fees the law firm charges. Legal fees can be charged and structured in many different ways. The kind of legal fee depends on the type of case or client matter, the specific circumstances of each particular client, and the law practice's preference for certain types of fee arrangements. Fee agreements may specify hourly rates, contingency fees, flat fees, or retainer fees.

Regardless of the type of agreement, a fee agreement should also specify what legal procedures, if any, the attorney is *not* obligated to provide to the client. For example, in Exhibit 4–6, paragraph 3 specifically excludes representation on appeal from this fee agreement. Another example of legal services commonly excluded is collection activities to collect the money awarded by the court or in a settlement. Of course, these activities may always be the subject of another (separate) fee agreement. If there is ambiguity in a fee agreement, the client will generally get the benefit of the doubt: courts will assume that the legal professional drafted the fee agreement and included all the rights and privileges desired.

Hourly Rate Fees

hourly rate fee
A fee for legal services that is billed to the client by the hour at an agreed upon rate.

Hourly rate agreements are the most common. An **hourly rate fee** is a fee for legal services that is billed to the client by the hour at an agreed-upon rate. For example, suppose a client hires an attorney to draft a business contract. The client agrees to pay $250 for every hour the attorney spends drafting the contract and advising the client. If the attorney spent four hours working on the contract, the client would owe the attorney $1,000 ($250 times 4 hours equals $1,000).

Hourly Rate Contract for Legal Services

This contract for legal services is entered into by and between H. Thomas Weber (hereinafter "Client") and Johnson, Beck & Taylor (hereinafter "Attorneys") on this ____ day of December, 201__. The following terms and conditions constitute the entirety of the agreement between Attorneys and Client and said agreement supersedes and is wholly separate and apart from any previous written or oral agreements.

1. Client hereby agrees to employ Attorneys and Attorneys hereby agree to represent Client in connection with a contract dispute in Jefferson County District Court of Client's claim against Westbridge Manufacturing.
2. Client agrees to pay a retainer fee of $5,000.00, which will be held in Attorney's trust account until earned.
3. Client agrees to pay associate attorneys at $250.00 per hour, partners at $350.00 per hour, paralegals at $100.00 per hour and senior paralegals at $115.00 per hour for legal services rendered regarding the matter in paragraph (1). Attorneys are not hereby obligated to take an appeal from any judgment at the trial court level; if an occasion for an appeal arises, Attorneys and Client hereby expressly agree that employment for such an appeal must be arranged by a separate contract between Attorneys and Client.
4. Client agrees to reimburse Attorneys for all expenses incurred in connection with said matter, and Client agrees to advance all expenses requested by Attorneys during the duration of this contract. Client understands that he is ultimately responsible for the payment of all expenses incurred in connection with this matter.
5. Client understands that Attorneys will bill Client periodically (usually on a monthly or quarterly basis, depending on how quickly the case moves through the system) for copying costs at the rate of $.25 per copy, postage and handling costs, long-distance telephone costs, travel costs, and other costs, and that Client is obligated to make payments upon said billing for said fees and expenses described at paragraphs (2), (3) and (4) above, or otherwise satisfy said fees and expenses. Attorneys will also bill Client for all deposition costs incurred and Client is solely responsible for said deposition costs and Client will be required to advance the sum of **$10,000.00** (or more as necessary) for trial costs (including subpoenas, travel costs, and preparation costs) once the case is set for trial.
6. Client understands and agrees that this litigation may take two to five years or longer to complete and that he will make himself available for Attorneys to confer with and generally to assist Attorneys in said matter. Client agrees he will not discuss the matter of his litigation with any unauthorized person at any time or in any way. Client understands and agrees that Attorneys may withdraw from representation of Client upon proper notice. Client further understands that he can apply for judicial review and approval of this fee agreement if he so desires.
7. Client agrees that associate counsel may be employed at the discretion of Attorneys and that any attorney so employed may be designated to appear on Client's behalf and undertake Client's representation in this matter and such representation shall be upon the same terms as set out herein. **Client understands that Attorneys cannot and do not guarantee any particular or certain relief and expressly state that they cannot promise or guarantee Client will receive any money damages or money settlement.**

The undersigned hereby voluntarily executes this agreement with a full understanding of same and without coercion or duress. All agreements contained herein are severable and in the event any of them shall be deemed to be invalid by any competent court, this contract shall be interpreted as if such invalid agreements or covenants were not contained herein. Client acknowledges receiving a fully executed copy of this contract.

Date ________ ______________________________

Date ________ Johnson, Beck & Taylor

NOTE: THIS IS ONLY AN EXAMPLE AND IS NOT INTENDED TO BE A FORM. CHECK WITH YOUR STATE BAR FOR A PROPER FORM.

Hourly rate language

EXHIBIT 4–6

Attorney/paralegal hourly rate contract

Hourly rate agreements can be complicated. Law offices have several specific types of hourly rate contracts, including:

- attorney or paralegal hourly rate
- client hourly rate
- blended hourly rate fee
- activity hourly rate

Some law practices use a combination of these as the basis of client billings.

attorney or paralegal hourly rate
A fee based on the attorney's or paralegal's level of expertise and experience in a particular area.

Attorney or Paralegal Hourly Rate The attorney's or paralegal's level of expertise and experience in a particular area determines the **attorney or paralegal hourly rate**. Exhibit 4–6 is an example of this type of contract. If a partner worked on a case, his or her hourly rate charge might be considerably more than an associate's or paralegal's hourly rate charge. Partners typically can bill from $300 to $600 or more an hour, compared with associates, who might bill $200 to $350 an hour. Paralegals typically charge from $65 to $135 (or more) per hour. The difference in price is based on the expertise and experience of the individual working on the case, her or his job title, and locally acceptable rates. In this type of fee agreement, it is possible for a client to be billed at several different rates in a given period if several attorneys or paralegals work on a matter, as they may all charge different rates.

client hourly rate
A fee based on a single hourly charge for the client, regardless of which attorney works on the case and what she or he does on the case.

Client Hourly Rate The **client hourly rate** method is based on only one hourly charge for the client, regardless of which attorney works on the case and what is done on the case. For example, if an insurance company hired a law practice to represent it, the insurance company and the law practice might negotiate a client rate of $200 per hour for attorneys and $85 an hour for paralegals. This means that no matter which attorney or paralegal works on the case, whether the attorney or paralegal has 1 year's or 20 years' experience, and regardless of what the attorney or paralegal does (e.g., making routine phone calls or appearing in court), the insurance company will be charged $200 an hour for attorney time or $85 an hour for paralegal time.

blended hourly rate fee
A single hourly rate that is set by taking into account the mix of attorneys working on the matter.

Blended Hourly Rate Fee An hourly rate that is set taking into account the blend or mix of law office staff working on a matter is a **blended hourly rate fee**. The "mix" includes the associates, partners, and sometimes paralegals working on the matter. Some states allow the "blend" to include only associates and partners, whereas other states allow paralegals to be included. The advantage to this is that billing is simpler, because there is one rate for all paralegal and attorney time spent on the case. The bill is easier for the law office to produce and easier for the client to read. Some states allow paralegals to have their own "blend," which results in one rate for all paralegals (whether experienced or inexperienced, senior or junior, etc.) who work on the matter.

activity hourly rate
A fee based on hourly rates that vary depending on the type of service or activity performed and the degree of difficulty of the activity.

Activity Hourly Rate An **activity hourly rate** is based on the different hourly rates attaching to the type of service or activity actually performed. For example, offices using this approach might bill legal staff time to clients as follows:

Court appearances	$350 per hour
Legal research by attorneys	$225 per hour
Drafting by attorneys	$175 per hour
Telephone calls by attorneys	$150 per hour
Legal research by paralegals	$ 80 per hour
Drafting by paralegals	$ 70 per hour

This sliding-scale hourly fee is based on the difficulty of an activity.

Contingency Fees

contingency fee
A fee collected if the attorney successfully represents the client; typically a percentage of the total recovery.

A **contingency fee** agreement entitles the attorney to a certain percentage of the total amount of money awarded to the client. If no money is recovered, the attorney collects no legal fees, but is still entitled to be reimbursed for all expenses incurred (see Exhibit 4–7). Contingency fees are typically used by law firms that represent plaintiffs in personal injury, worker's compensation, civil rights, medical malpractice, and other types of cases in which monetary damages may be awarded. The individual

Contingency Fee Contract for Legal Services

Date:
Name: D.O.B.
Address: Phone:

1. I hereby employ **Johnson, Beck & Taylor** (hereinafter "attorneys") to perform legal services in connection with the following matter as described below:
   Personal injury claims arising out of an automobile accident which occurred January 12, 2012, on Interstate I-70.
2. I agree to pay a nonrefundable retainer fee of $2,500; plus,
3. I agree attorneys will receive 20% of any recovery, if prior to filing suit;
   I agree attorneys will receive 25% of any recovery, if prior to pretrial conference;
   I agree attorneys will receive 33% of any recovery, if after first trial begins;
   I agree attorneys will receive 33% of any recovery, if after appeal or second trial begins.
   Attorneys are not hereby obligated to take an appeal from any judgment at the trial court level; if an occasion for an appeal arises, attorneys and client hereby expressly agree that employment for such an appeal will be arranged by a separate contract between these parties. Further, I agree that attorneys will be entitled to the applicable above-mentioned percentage of recovery minus whatever a court may award, if I am a prevailing party and the court awards fees following my request therefore.
4. As to the expenses of litigation: I agree to reimburse attorneys for all expenses incurred in connection with said matter, and any expenses not fully paid as incurred may be deducted from my portion of any recovery. I agree to advance any and all expenses requested by attorneys during the duration of this contract. I agree to make an advance of expenses upon execution of this contract in the amount of $1500.00. I understand that these litigation expenses do not pertain to the retainer fee or percentage of any recovery, and I am ultimately responsible for the payment of all litigation expenses.
5. I understand that attorneys will bill client periodically, and that client is obligated to make payments upon said billing for said fees and expenses described at paragraphs (2), and (4), or otherwise satisfy said fees and expenses.
6. I understand and agree that this litigation may take 2 to 5 years, or longer to complete, and that I will make myself available to attorneys to confer with, and generally to assist attorneys in said matter. I will not discuss the matter of my litigation with any unauthorized person at any time in any way. I understand and agree that attorneys may withdraw from representation of client at any time upon proper notice.
7. I agree that associate counsel may be employed at the discretion of Johnson, Beck & Taylor, and that any attorney so employed may be designated to appear on my behalf and undertake my representation in this matter and such representation shall be upon the same terms as set out herein. Attorneys have **not** guaranteed, nor can they guarantee, any particular or certain relief.
   The undersigned herewith executes this agreement with a full understanding of same, without coercion or duress, and understands the same to be the only agreement between the parties with regard to the above matter, and that if any other terms are to be added to this contract, the same will not be binding, unless and until they are reduced to writing and signed by all parties to this contract. I acknowledge receiving a fully executed copy of this contract. Further, the undersigned Client understands that said Client is entitled to apply for judicial review and approval of this fee agreement, if Client so desires.

Date

Date Johnson, Beck & Taylor

NOTE: THIS IS ONLY AN EXAMPLE AND IS NOT INTENDED TO BE A FORM. CHECK WITH YOUR STATE BAR FOR A PROPER FORM.

Contingency fee language

EXHIBIT 4–7
Contingency fee contract

who would like to bring the lawsuit usually has little or no money to pay legal fees up front. Contingency fees typically range from 20 percent to 50 percent.

Contingency fee agreements must be in writing. Exhibit 4–7 shows a sample contingency fee contract. Some states put a cap (a maximum percentage) on what an attorney can collect for claims in areas such as worker's compensation and medical malpractice. For example, some states prohibit attorneys from receiving more than a 25 percent contingency fee in a worker's compensation case.

By their nature, contingency fees are risky because if no money is recovered, the attorney receives no fee. However, even if no money is recovered, the client must still pay legal expenses such as filing fees and photocopying. Contingency fees and hourly fees also may be used together. When clients agree to this arrangement, some offices reduce their hourly fee and/or lessen the percentage of the contingency portion of the fee.

Flat Fees

flat fee
A fee for specific legal services that is billed as a fixed amount.

A **flat fee** (sometimes called a *fixed fee*) is a fee for specific legal services that is billed as a specific dollar amount. Some offices have a set fee for handling certain types of matters, such as preparing a will or handling an uncontested divorce, a name change, or a bankruptcy. For example, suppose a client agreed to pay an attorney a flat fee of $500 to prepare a will. No matter how many hours the attorney spends preparing the will, the fee is still $500. Flat fee agreements are usually used when a legal matter is simple, straightforward, and involves few risks.

Retainer Fees

The word *retainer* has several meanings in the legal environment. Generally, retainer fees are monies paid by the client at the beginning of a case or matter. However, there are many types of retainers. When an attorney or paralegal uses the term *retainer*, it could mean a retainer for general representation, a case retainer, a pure retainer, or a cash advance. In addition, all retainer fees are either earned or unearned.

earned retainer
The money the law office or attorney has earned and is entitled to deposit in the office's or attorney's own bank account.

operating account
Bank account used by a law firm for the deposit of earned fees and payment of law-firm expenses.

unearned retainer
Money that is paid up front by the client as an advance against the attorney's future fees and expenses. Until the money is actually earned by the attorney or law office, it actually belongs to the client.

trust or escrow account
A bank account, separate and apart from a law office's or attorney's operating bank account, where unearned client funds are deposited.

Earned versus Unearned Retainers

There is a *very* important difference between an earned retainer and an unearned retainer. An **earned retainer** means that the law office or attorney has done work to earn the money and is entitled to deposit the money in the office's or attorney's **operating account**. Firms use monies from the operating account to pay the attorney's or law office's operating expenses, such as salaries and rent.

An **unearned retainer** is money that is paid up front by the client as an advance against the attorney's future fees and expenses; it is a kind of down payment. Until the money is actually earned by the attorney or law office, it belongs to the client. According to ethical rules, unearned retainers may *not* be deposited in the attorney's or law office's normal operating (checking) account. Unearned retainers must be deposited into a separate trust account and can be transferred into the firm's operating account only as they are earned.

A **trust or escrow account** is a separate bank account, apart from a law office's or attorney's operating account, where unearned client funds are deposited. As an attorney or law office begins to earn money by providing legal services to the client, the attorney can bill the client and move the earned portion from the trust account to his or her own law office operating account.

The written contract should set out whether the retainer is earned or unearned. However, in some instances the contract may be vague on this point. Typically, when a contract refers to a nonrefundable retainer, this means an earned retainer.

Additionally, in many contracts, flat-fee rates, as discussed earlier, are said to be nonrefundable and thus are treated as earned. However, some state ethical rules regulate this area heavily: Some hold that all flat fees are a retainer, so they are considered unearned and must be placed in trust until they are "earned out." Hence, whether a retainer is earned or unearned will depend on your state's ethical rules and on the written contract.

Where Does the Interest Go? All bank accounts earn interest, even if the interest is not paid to the account holder. The money in a trust account belongs to the client, but the account is in the name of the law firm. So, who gets the interest? The law firm cannot keep interest earned on client funds. It might seem that the easy answer is to pay the interest to the client, especially if the amount held in trust is large enough or is held in the trust account long enough. However, that is not usually either possible or feasible.

The problem is twofold: First, the amount of interest that any individual client might earn is typically very small. (Remember that, in most instances, a single trust account contains funds belonging to many clients.) Second, it costs money to calculate and remit the exact amount of interest that might be owed to each client. For example, it might cost a firm $20 to send a client a check for less than $1.00. So, who gets the interest?

The answer is IOLTA, which stands for "Interest on Law Office Trust Accounts." Banks participating in the IOLTA program take the interest earned by trust accounts and pay that money to the state IOLTA program. The money is then used to fund or support legal aid or indigent defense programs in the state.

Cash Advance Retainer One type of retainer is a **cash advance**: this money is unearned and is an advance against the attorney's future fees and expenses. Until the attorney does the work to earn the money, it actually belongs to the client. The cash advance is a typical type of unearned retainer.

cash advance
Unearned monies that are paid before services are rendered, to cover the attorney's future fees and expenses.

For example, suppose a client wishes to hire an attorney to litigate a contract dispute. The attorney agrees to represent the client only if the client agrees to pay $200 per hour with a $10,000 cash advance against fees and expenses. The attorney must deposit the $10,000 in a trust account. If the attorney deposits the cash advance in her own account (whether it is the firm's account or the attorney's own personal account), the attorney has violated several ethical rules. As the attorney works on the case and bills the client for fees and expenses, the attorney will write checks out of the trust account for the amounts of those billings. The attorney must tell the client that money is being withdrawn and keep an accurate balance of how much the client has left in trust. So, if after a month the attorney has billed the client for $500, the attorney would write a check for $500 from the trust account, deposit the $500 in the attorney's or the firm's own bank account, and inform the client that the remaining retainer (trust balance) is $9,500. If the case ended at this point, the client would be entitled to a refund of the $9,500 remaining in trust.

Retainer for General Representation Another type of retainer is a **retainer for general representation**. This type of retainer is typically used when a client such as a corporation requires continuing legal services throughout the year. The client pays a specific amount, typically up front or on a prearranged schedule, to receive these ongoing services. For example, suppose a small school board would like to be able to contact an attorney at any time with general legal questions. The attorney and the school board could enter into this type of agreement for a fee of $7,500 every 6 months. The school board could contact the attorney at any time and ask general questions, but the attorney would never receive more (or less) than $7,500 for the six-month period regardless of how often they did so.

retainer for general representation
A retainer is typically used when a client such as a corporation or school board requires continuing legal services throughout the year.

Retainers for general representation allow the client to negotiate and anticipate what the fee will be for the year. This type of agreement usually covers only general legal advice, and does not include matters such as litigation. Depending on the specific arrangements between the client and the attorney, and on the specific state's rules of ethics, many retainers for general representation are viewed as being earned, since the client can call at any time and get legal advice. Retainers for general representation resemble a flat-fee agreement. The difference is that in a flat-fee agreement, the attorney or law office is contracting to do a specific thing for a client, such as prepare a will or file a bankruptcy. In the case of a retainer for general representation, the attorney is agreeing to make himself available to the client for all nonlitigation needs.

case retainer
A fee that is billed at the beginning of a matter, is not refundable to the client, and is usually paid at the beginning of the case as an incentive for the office to take the case.

Case Retainer Another type of retainer is a **case retainer**, which is a fee that is billed at the beginning of a matter, is not refundable to the client, and is usually paid to the office at the beginning of the case as an incentive for the office to take the case. For example, a client comes to an attorney with a criminal matter. The attorney agrees to take the case only if the client agrees to pay a case retainer of $1,000 up front plus $200 an hour for every hour worked on the case. The $1,000 is paid to the attorney as an incentive to take the case and thus is earned. The $200 per hour is a client hourly rate charge. Because the case retainer is earned, the attorney can immediately deposit it in the office's own bank account.

Another example of use of a case retainer is a case involving a contingency fee. Suppose a client comes to an attorney asking her to file an employment discrimination case. The attorney agrees to accept the case only if the client agrees to a 30 percent contingency fee and a nonrefundable or case retainer of $1,000. Again, the earned retainer is an incentive for the attorney to take the case and can be deposited in the attorney's or the office's own bank account.

pure retainer
A fee that obligates the office to be available to represent the client throughout the agreed-upon time period.

Pure Retainer A rather rare type of retainer is a **pure retainer**. A pure retainer obligates the law office to be available to represent the client throughout the time period agreed upon. The part that distinguishes a pure retainer from a retainer for general representation is that the office typically must agree not to represent any of the client's competitors and not to undertake any type of representation adverse to the client. Some clients, typically major corporations, think that listing the name of a prestigious law firm as counsel has a business value that they are willing to pay for.

Retainers for general representation, case retainers, and pure retainers are usually earned retainers, and a cash advance is an unearned retainer. However, *the language of the contract determines whether amounts paid to attorneys up front are earned or unearned.* The earned/unearned distinction is extremely important and is yet another reason all fee agreements should be in writing.

Value Billing

Recently, much has been written in the legal press about why private law practices should stop billing by the hour and use a different billing method. The reasons for the change from hourly billing include:

- The client never knows during any stage of the work how much the total legal fee will be.
- Clients sometimes avoid calling (or otherwise communicating with) paralegals and attorneys because they know they will be charged for the time, even if it is a simple phone call.
- Clients have trouble seeing the relationship between what is performed by the paralegal or attorney and the enormous fees that can be incurred.
- Hourly billing encourages lawyers and paralegals to be inefficient (i.e., the longer it takes to perform a job, the more revenue they earn).
- Many law offices force attorneys and paralegals to bill a quota number of hours a year, which puts a tremendous amount of pressure on the individual paralegal and attorney.

Value billing has been proposed as an alternative to the traditional system. The **value billing** concept uses a type of fee agreement that is based not on the time required to perform the work, but on the basis of the perceived value of the services to the client. Value billing typically requires that the attorney and client reach a consensus on the amount of fees to be charged. Because of increased competition in the legal environment and because of the power of the client as a buyer of legal services, clients are demanding that they have a say in how much they are going to pay for legal services, what type(s) of service will be provided, and what quality of legal services they will get for that price.

value billing
A type of fee agreement that is based not on the time required to perform the work, but on the basis of the perceived value of the services to the client.

LEGAL EXPENSES

Under most ethical canons, attorneys must charge for the expenses they incur on behalf of a client. Expenses include the costs of photocopies, postage for mailing letters and documents regarding a case, filing fees, and so forth. Legal expenses for cases that are litigated or filed in court can sometimes be very high. They include court reporter fees (fees charged by a court reporter to transcribe hearings, oral statements, trial testimony, etc.) and expert witness fees (fees charged, usually by the hour, by subject matter experts to give testimony), just to name two.

TIMEKEEPING AND BILLING FOR PARALEGALS

Many law offices are still firmly wedded to the billable hour concept, and thus set billable hour quotas that paralegals must meet. As indicated previously, an average number of billable hours for paralegals ranges from 1,400 to 1,800 hours annually. Historically, this was not the case. In the late 1950s, 1,300 billable hours was thought to be realistic. The minimum number of billable hours varies greatly depending on the location and size of the law office and on the types of cases it handles.

Recording Time

A **billable hour** consists of 60 minutes of legal services. Clients expect to receive a full 60 minutes of legal services when they are billed for one hour. Interruptions, calls home, and checking personal email are not billable. It is imperative that legal professionals take great care when billing clients for their time.

billable hour
Sixty minutes of legal services.

There are several different ways to actually record and/or track your time. One method is to bill time in tenths of an hour, with 0.5 being a half-hour and 1.0 being an hour. Every six minutes is a tenth of the hour, so you would be billing for six-minute intervals. Billing in tenths works out as follows:

0–6 minutes = 0.1 hour
7–12 minutes = 0.2 hour
13–18 minutes = 0.3 hour
19–24 minutes = 0.4 hour
25–30 minutes = 0.5 hour
31–36 minutes = 0.6 hour
37–42 minutes = 0.7 hour
43–48 minutes = 0.8 hour
49–54 minutes = 0.9 hour
55–60 minutes = 1.0 hour

As an alternative, some offices bill using a quarter of an hour as the smallest increment of time, as follows:

0–15 minutes = 0.25 hour
16–30 minutes = 0.50 hour
31–45 minutes = 0.75 hour
46–60 minutes = 1.0 hour

Although the quarterly basis is easier to use, it is not as accurate as the tenth-of-an-hour system. Suppose you took a five-minute phone call from a client and your average billing rate was $70 an hour. Using the tenth-of-an-hour system, the fee for the phone call would be $7.00 (0.1 hour times $70 equals $7.00). However, using the quarterly system, the fee for the phone call would be $17.50, since 0.25 is the least possible billable interval (0.25 times $70 equals $17.50), or more than twice as much.

It is important that you include as much detail as possible when completing your time records, that the language be clear and easily understandable, and that the time record itself be legible. Clients are usually more willing to pay a bill when they know exactly what service was performed for them. For example, compare these bill excerpts:

1. Telephone conference—0.50 hr., $35.00.
2. Telephone conference with client on Plaintiff's Request for Production of Documents regarding whether client has copies of the draft contracts at issue—0.50 hr., $35.00.

Most clients prefer the latter, as they are able to see, and hopefully remember, exactly what specific services they received. Which of these bills would *you* rather receive?

Timekeeping Practices

If the average paralegal is required to bill between 1,400 and 1,800 hours a year, it is very important that he or she take the timekeeping function extremely seriously. The following are some suggestions regarding time tracking.

- *Find out how many hours you must bill annually, monthly, and weekly up front, and track where you are in relationship to the quota.* One of the first things you should do when you start a new paralegal job is find out how many billable hours you must submit. If the office requires that you bill 1,400 hours a year, budget this on a monthly and weekly basis, and keep track of where you are so that you will not have to try to make it all up at the end of the year.
- *Find out when timesheets are due.* Find out exactly what day of the week timesheets are due, so that you can submit yours on time.
- *Keep copies of your timesheets.* Always keep a copy of your timesheet for your own file in case the original is lost or misplaced. Having a copy also allows you to go back and calculate the number of billable hours you have put in to date.
- *Record your time contemporaneously on a daily basis.* One of the biggest mistakes you can make is to not record your time as you go along during the day. If you wait until the end of the day and then try to remember all the things you did, there is absolutely no way you will be able to accurately reconstruct everything. In the end, you will be the one who suffers, doing work you did not get credit for. Keep a timesheet handy and fill it out as you go along.
- *Record your actual time spent; do not discount your time.* Do not discount your time because you think you should have been able to perform a job faster.

If it took you four hours to finish an assignment and you worked the whole four hours, there is no reason to discount the time. If the supervising attorneys think a discount is warranted, they can decide to do so, but it is not up to you to do that. However, if you made a mistake or had a problem that you do not think the client should be billed for, tell your supervising attorney, and let him or her help you make the decision.

- *Be aware if billable hours are related to bonuses or merit pay increases.* Be aware of how billable hours are used. In some law offices, billable hours are used in allocating bonuses and merit increases, and may be considered in performance evaluations, so know up front how your office uses the tally.
- *Be ethical.* Always be honest and ethical in the way you fill out your timesheets. Padding your timesheets is unethical and simply wrong. Eventually, wrongdoing regarding timekeeping, billing, or handling client funds will become apparent.
- *Be aware of things that keep you from billing time.* Be aware of distractions and things that decrease your productivity, such as:
  - People who lay their troubles at your feet or who are constantly taking your attention away from your work. An appropriate approach is to say, "I would really like to hear about it at lunch, but right now I am very busy."
  - Time wasted trying to track down other people or trying to find information you need.
  - Constant interruptions, including phone calls. If you really need to get something done, go someplace where you can get the work done and tell others to hold your calls. However, check in every once in a while to return client phone calls. Client calls should be returned as soon as possible (note also that calls with clients probably constitute billable time!).

Billing for Paralegal Time—Paralegal Profitability

Many law offices bill for paralegal time as well as for attorney time. Many clients prefer this, because the paralegal hourly rates are much lower than the attorney hourly rates. The average actual billing rate for paralegals ranges from $65 to $135 per hour.

For example, assume that an associate attorney and a paralegal can both prepare discovery documents in a case and that the task will take seven hours. If the paralegal bills at $75 an hour and the associate bills at $150 an hour, the cost to the client if the paralegal does the job is $525, whereas the cost if the associate drafts the discovery is $1,050. Thus, the client will have saved $525 simply by allowing the paralegal to do the job. The client would still have to pay for the attorney's time to review the paralegal's work, but that cost would be minimal. This strategy represents substantial savings to clients.

The question of whether law offices can bill for paralegal time was considered by the U.S. Supreme Court in *Missouri v. Jenkins,* 491 U.S. 274 (1989). In that case, the plaintiff was successful on several counts in a civil rights lawsuit and was attempting to recover attorney's fees from the defendant under a federal statute. The statutory language provided that the prevailing party could recover "reasonable attorney's fees" from the other party. The plaintiff argued for recovery for the time that paralegals spent working on the case as well as for the time that attorneys spent. The defendant argued that paralegal time was not "attorney's fees." Alternatively, the defendants argued that if they did have to pay something for paralegal time, they should have to pay only about $15 an hour, which represented the overhead costs to the office for a paralegal.

The Court noted that paralegals carry out many useful tasks under the direction of attorneys and found that "reasonable attorney's fees" refers to the reasonable fee for work produced, whether it be by attorneys or paralegals. The Court also found that under the federal statute, paralegal time should not be compensated for at the overhead cost to the office, but should be paid at the prevailing market rates in the area for paralegal time. The Court noted that the prevailing rate for paralegals in that part of the country at that time was about $40 an hour and held that the office was entitled to receive that amount for paralegal hours worked on the case. Thus, it is clear that offices can bill for paralegal time if they choose to do so. The case also reminds us that purely clerical tasks or secretarial tasks cannot be billed at the paralegal rate—or any other rate.

Although the *Missouri v. Jenkins* case was a landmark decision for paralegals, the opinion involved the interpretation of a specific statute, the Civil Rights Act. Fee questions arise in many different situations, and if another court is deciding a fee question other than in the context of the Civil Rights Act, it may reach a different decision. Since *Missouri v. Jenkins* was decided, many courts in many different jurisdictions have allowed the recovery of paralegal time at the prevailing local rate. In addition, courts have also found that billing for an attorney's time spent on a matter is not reasonable (for purposes of court awarded fees) if the tasks performed "are normally performed by paralegals." Thus, many courts have recognized the unique niche that paralegals fill in the legal field.

FUNCTIONS OF A SUCCESSFUL BILLING SYSTEM

An often forgotten requirement for any billing system is that it must please the firm's customers or clients: the quality of the billing system is determined in large part by whether the firm's clients are satisfied with the billings and whether they pay the bills that are sent to them. One of the quickest ways for a firm to lose a good client is by mishandling the client's money in some way, by overbilling the client, or by giving the client the impression that its money is being used unjustly or unfairly. In addition, mishandling a client's money is a top reason that attorneys are disciplined. A good billing system, whether or not it is computerized, must do several things, including accurately track each client's account, provide regular billings, and itemize the services performed. In short, a billing system should satisfy the law office customers so that they are willing to make timely payments.

Accurately Track How Much a Client Has Paid the Firm

A successful billing system must be able to accurately track how much clients have paid the firm, and whether the payments were made in cash, through a trust account, or otherwise. Although this may seem easy, it often is not. Consider how you feel when a creditor either loses one of your payments or misapplies it in some manner. This is especially important for a law firm because in many instances large sums of money are involved. Payments can be lost, not entered into the billing system, or applied to the wrong client's account. It is important that the firm take great care with what goes into and comes out of the billing system, and that the information be accurate.

Send Regular Billings

We all expect to receive regular billings for routine things, such as credit card balances, utility use, and so forth. This makes budgeting and financial planning much easier. Likewise, most clients like to receive timely billings, at least monthly.

Imagine the frustration of a client who receives a quarterly billing that is four or five times more expensive than expected. Regular billings will alert clients to how they are being billed and how much they need to budget for legal services. In addition, if a client sees timely bills that are higher than were planned for, he can tell the firm how to proceed so as to limit future bills before costs are incurred. This at least gives the client the option of cutting back on legal services instead of having to overspend and get angry at the firm for not communicating the charges on a timely basis.

Provide Client Billings That Are Fair and Respectful

Billings that are fair and courteous are essential to a good billing system. If a client believes that the firm is overcharging for services or that the billings are curt and unprofessional, the client may simply not pay a bill, or may delay payment. If you ever speak to a client regarding a bill, always be courteous and respectful, and try to understand the situation from the client's point of view. If a dispute arises, simply make notes on the client's side of the story, relay the information to the attorney in charge of the matter, and let the attorney resolve the situation.

Provide Client Billings That Identify What Services Have Been Provided

It is important for the client to know exactly what services she received and what the bill covers. Bills that just say "For Services Rendered" are for the most part a thing of the past. Although the format of the bill will depend on the client, it is recommended that invoices indicate exactly what service was performed, by whom, on what date, for how long, and for what charge. With an itemized record, the client can see exactly what the firm is doing and how hard the staff is working, and may thus be more willing to pay the bill.

Provide Client Billings That Are Clear

Finally, billings should be clear and free of legalese. They should be easy to read and contain the information a client wants to see. Payments on billings that are complicated and hard to understand are often held up while the client tries to decipher the bill.

COMPUTERIZED TIMEKEEPING AND BILLING: SOFTWARE

Many different billing and timekeeping programs are available. As with most software applications, competing programs offer a wide range of diverse features, structures, and prices. Some programs just do timekeeping and billing; others offer functionalities in a variety of related areas such as general ledger, accounts payable, accounts receivable, payroll, trust accounting, docket control and calendaring, and case management. Programs are available for all sizes and types of law firms. Some timekeeping and billing software packages are designed for particular sizes of law firms, usually designated as large (100 to a thousand attorneys), medium (25 to 100 attorneys), and small (1 to 25 attorneys).

This text only covers the basics of timekeeping and billing software; the manner in which any particular package handles these functions will depend on the package. In this section you will learn to understand the fundamentals of computerized timekeeping and billing: the main menu and the primary tasks that most timekeeping and billing programs perform; the client information screen and how client records are set up in timekeeping and billing programs; how time and expense slips are entered into the billing system; how client bills are produced; and what management reports most systems can run (such as case/client lists, aged accounts receivable reports, and timekeeper productivity reports). This text also touches on the nature of and systems involved in electronic billing.

Main Menu/Fundamental Tasks of Timekeeping and Billing Programs

Exhibit 4–8 shows the main menu of Tabs3, a popular timekeeping and billing program. Exhibit 4–8 is a good example of the functions found in most timekeeping and billing programs. These include entering and maintaining client accounts and preferences, entering time records, tracking attorneys' fees, entering and tracking expenses, recording client payments, managing client trust funds (some programs do this and others do not), managing and tracking client accounts, generating and managing pre-bills and final bills/statements, tracking accounts receivable, and producing management reports. Some of these tasks and activities are discussed in more detail in this chapter, but these are the general functions that most timekeeping and billing programs provide.

Entering Client-Related Information

Before timekeeping data can be entered into the computer or a bill can be generated for a client, certain information regarding the client must be entered into the

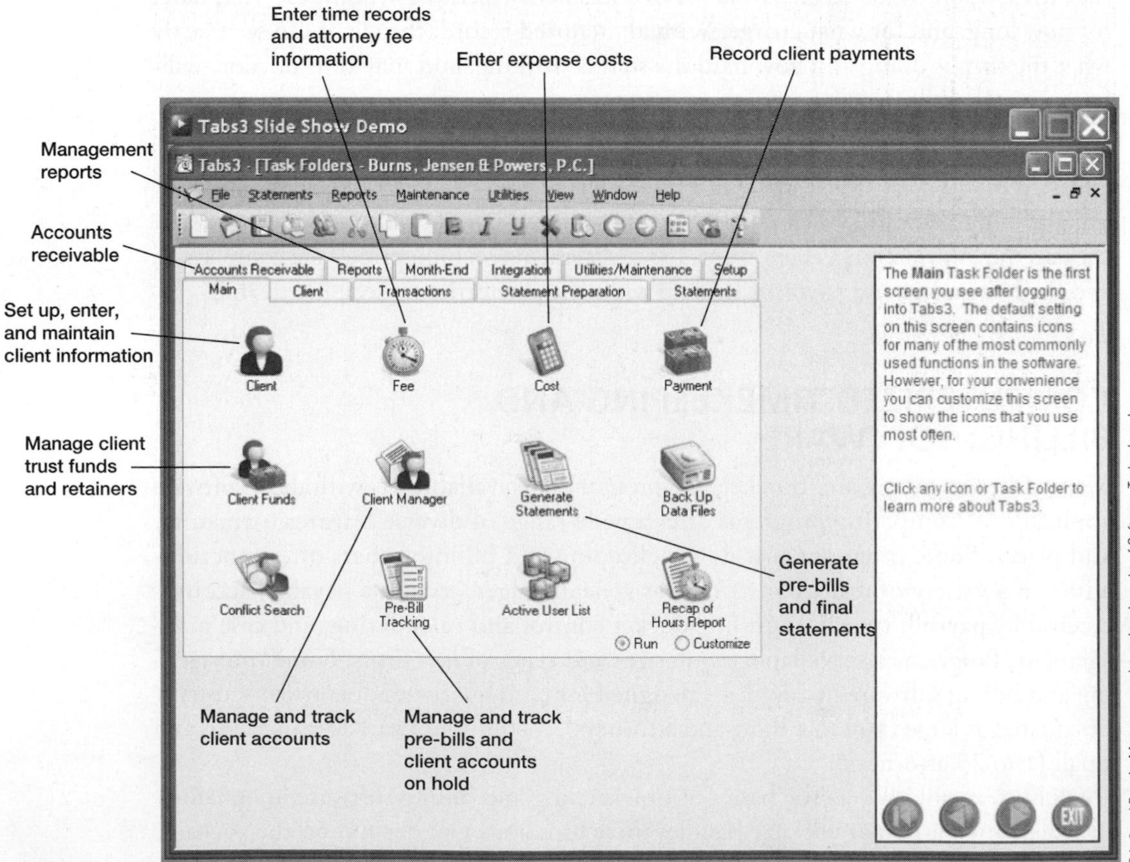

EXHIBIT 4–8
Timekeeping and billing program main menu

EXHIBIT 4–9
Client information screens

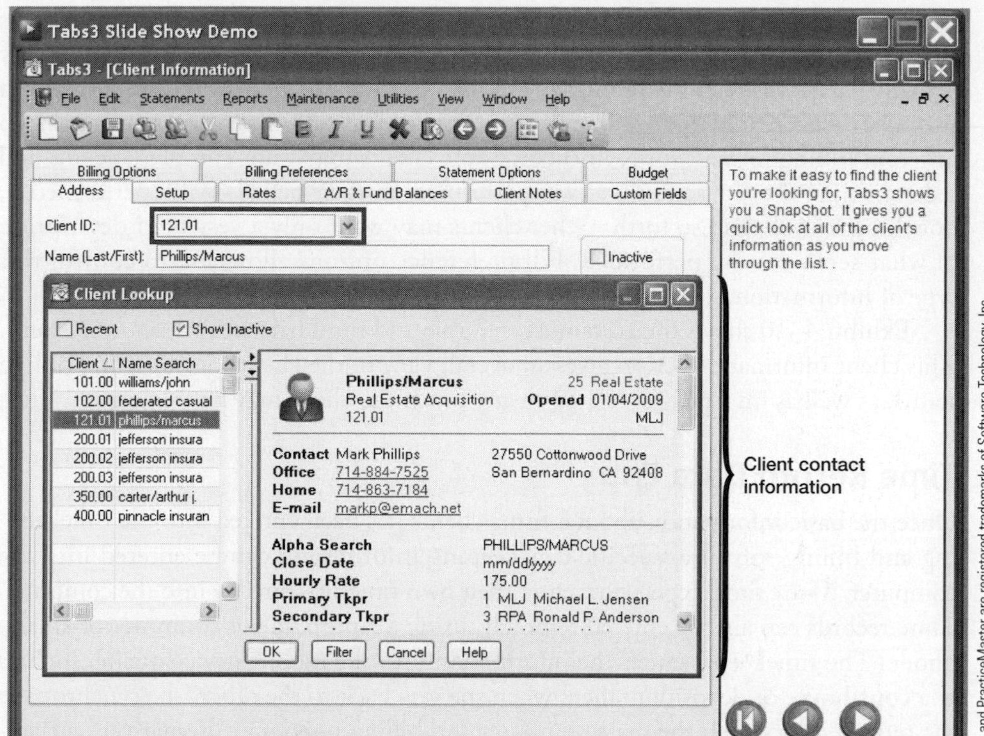

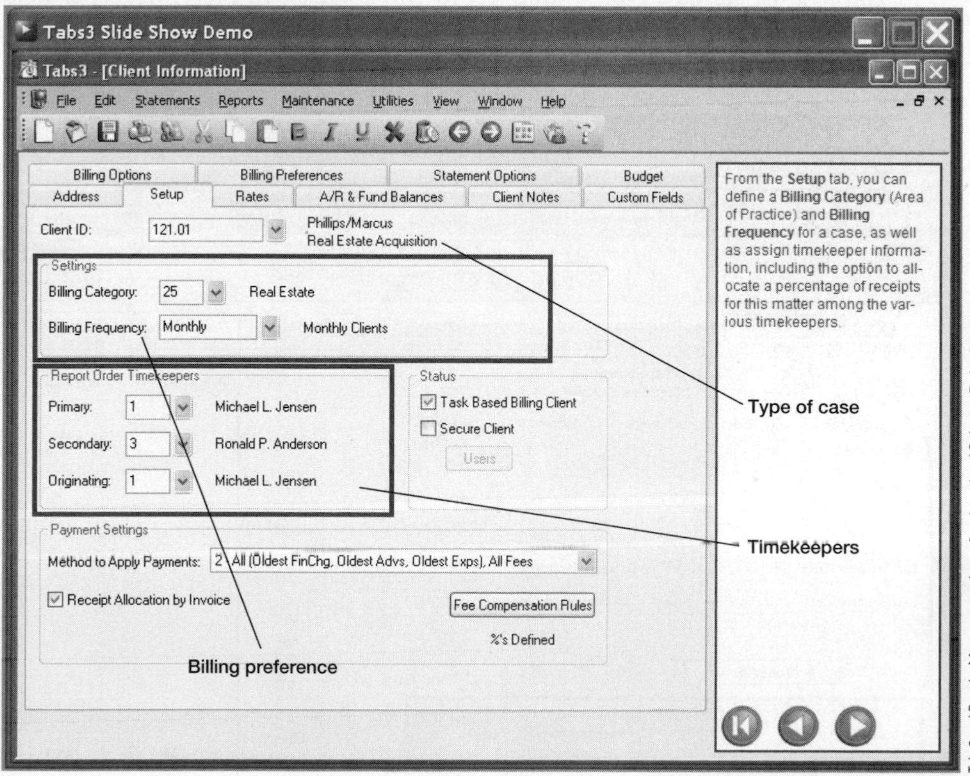

timekeeping and billing software. Exhibit 4–9 shows two client information screens in a timekeeping and billing system. Information such as a client's name and address and client identification number must be entered. Fee-related information must also be entered, such as how the case will be billed and whether the fee is an hourly rate, a flat fee, or another type of fee, and who is the primary timekeeper for the file (see Exhibit 4–9). Most legal billing programs are very flexible regarding how cases are to be billed. Notice in the second screen of Exhibit 4–9 that the billing frequency for this particular client is monthly. This can be changed depending on how often the client wants to be billed. The Billing Preferences option allows a firm to set up different billing formats for each client. Some clients may want complete details and a description of every action that was performed on their behalf—who performed it, how long it took, and so forth. Other clients may want only a very brief description of what services were performed. Bill preference options allow you to control this type of information.

Exhibit 4–10 shows the accounts receivable and fund balances screen for a client. This client information screen gives an overall view of the client's account and billing status, as well as information related to any funds the client may have in trust.

Time Record Data Entry

Once the basic information about a firm's clients has been entered into the timekeeping and billing software, specific timekeeping information can be entered into the computer. Many timekeepers now enter their own timeslips directly into the computer. Time records can also be entered remotely, using a laptop, tablet computer or smartphone. The timekeeper enters the information into the mobile device offsite, such as at a courthouse or deposition; then, when she gets back to the office, she synchronizes the mobile device with the main computer and billing program. Alternatively, a timekeeper may complete a manual timeslip and have a clerk enter it into the computer.

Exhibit 4–11 shows a typical time record entry screen. In the Timekeeper field, the timekeeper's initials (or name) are entered. (Remember, a timekeeper is anyone who bills for his or her time.) In Exhibit 4–11, the timekeeper's name is Michael

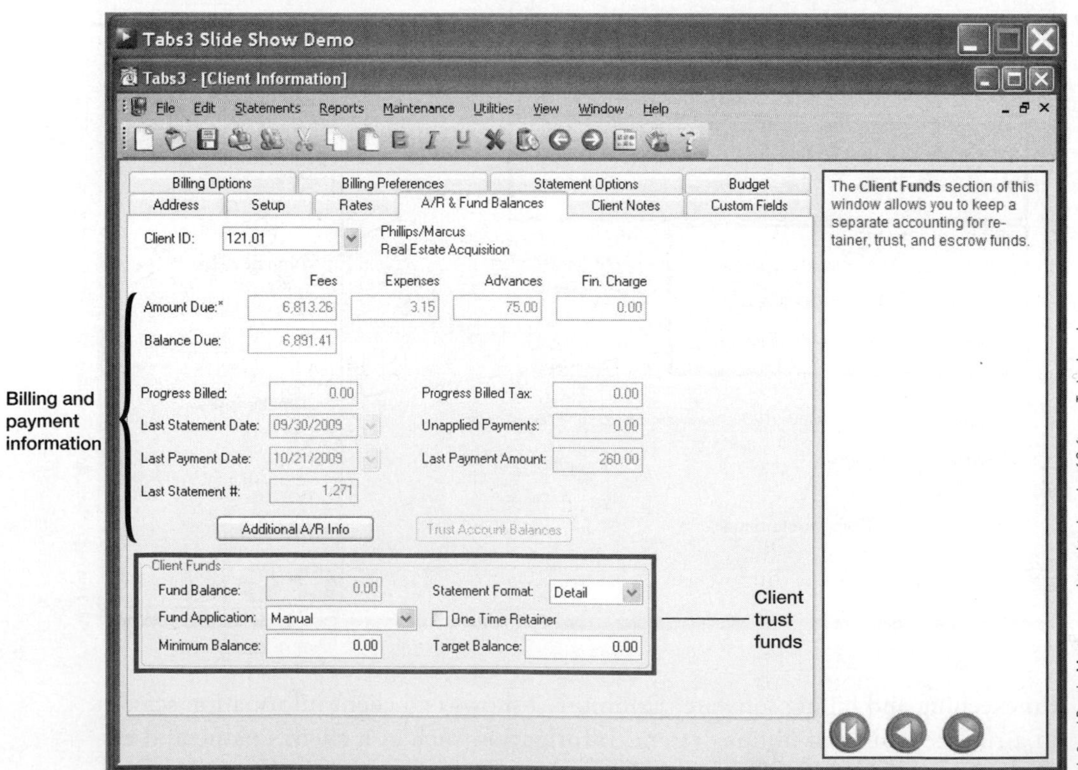

EXHIBIT 4–10
Client information—accounts receivable and fund balances screen

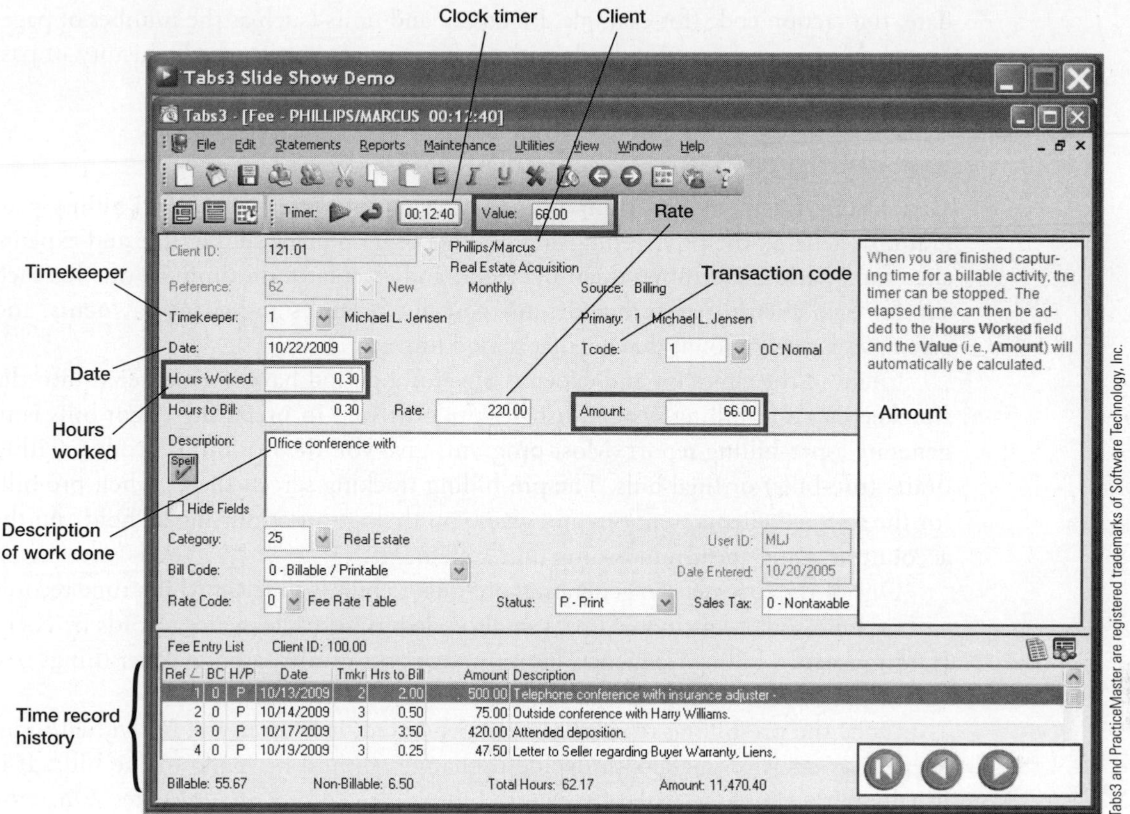

EXHIBIT 4–11
Entering a time record

Jensen. Many programs allow the user to "pop up" a list of all the possible timekeepers in a firm. Notice the clock/timer feature in Exhibit 4–11. It shows that the timekeeper has been performing a task for the client for 12 minutes and 40 seconds. Many timekeeping and billing programs allow users to interactively turn on a clock or meter as they are providing legal services to clients so that they know exactly how much time they have spent on a matter. Exhibit 4–11 also shows the current hours worked on the project (three-tenths of an hour), the rate at which the client is being billed ($220 an hour), and the current amount being charged to the client for the task. The Tcode field in Exhibit 4–11 accepts transaction codes; in this example, the code is 1, which in this system represents an office conference. Other standard transaction codes represent legal research, court appearances, depositions, drafting, and so forth.

The Client ID field indicates which client is to be billed for this time record. In Exhibit 4–11, the client is Marcus Phillips and the matter is a real estate acquisition. Most programs allow the user to select a client's account from a list of active clients. The Description field contains a listing of what services were performed. This can be detailed or brief, depending on the particular client's needs. The Date field, obviously, shows when the services were provided. The bill code in Exhibit 4–11 shows that the service is billable, as opposed to nonbillable. The time record screen in Exhibit 4–11 even shows a history of past time records that have been entered for this client.

Expense/Cost Record Data Entry

The data entry screen for entering expense or cost records is nearly the same as the time record data entry screen in most programs. It will include areas for entering a client ID, date, transaction code (for example, fax costs), and units (such as the number of pages faxed). Many programs also display an expense history, similar to the history of past time records shown at the bottom of Exhibit 4–11.

Pre-Billing and Final Statements

Generating bills is the most important aspect of any timekeeping and billing program. In general, the timekeeping and billing program takes all the time and expense slips for a period, assembles them by client, and calculates the amount due for each slip for each client. It then includes any past due balances and client payments, and calculates a total amount due for that period for each client.

Once all the timeslips and expense slips for a period have been entered into the timekeeping and billing system, usually the next step in preparing client bills is to generate a pre-billing report. Most programs give you the option to produce either drafts (pre-bills) or final bills. The pre-billing tracking screen shows when pre-bills for the selected clients were run and gives you the option of putting a "hold" on the account or going ahead and issuing final statements.

One of the first steps in generating pre-bills or bills is to select which time records and expense slips to include. Users can also select time and expense records by client ID, timekeeper, billing frequency, location, or status of files, among other things (see first screen of Exhibit 4–12).

Once the pre-billing report has been generated, it is up to the individual timekeepers or decision makers to decide if changes should be made to the bills. It is usually fairly simple to make changes in bills and to correct any mistakes. Once the information is accurate, the final step is to generate the actual client billings.

In many programs, the format of a bill is set up in the client information screen (see second screen of Exhibit 4–12). Law firms use many different formats to bill clients. For example, some bill formats contain only general information about the services provided, whereas other formats show greater detail. The look and format of billings depend on the law firm, its clients, the type of law practiced, and so forth. Thus, it is important that any timekeeping and billing package be flexible as to client billing formats and have a variety of formats easily available.

Producing detailed bills takes work. It requires timekeepers to prepare accurate, current timeslips of what work they have done. This seems easy enough, but it is not. It is sometimes difficult to convince timekeepers to write down each service they perform for each client. However, most clients strongly prefer detailed billings. So, although itemized billings are sometimes inconvenient for the timekeepers and take longer to produce, if the bill is paid in the end, the extra work has "paid off."

Management Reports

management reports
Reports used to help managers analyze whether the office is operating in an efficient, effective, and profitable manner.

Almost all timekeeping and billing software packages can produce a wide variety of management reports (see Exhibit 4–13). **Management reports** are used to help law office managers analyze whether the office is operating efficiently and effectively. Management reports can be used to track problems an office may be experiencing and to help devise ways to correct any problems. The following subsections explain some common management reports and how law office staff use them.

Case/Client List Most billing packages allow the user to produce a case or client list. An accurate list of all active cases is very important when a firm is trying to effectively manage a large caseload. Most reports list clients not only by name, but also by the appropriate account number (called the client identification number by some programs). This cross-listing is useful when trying to locate a client's identification number.

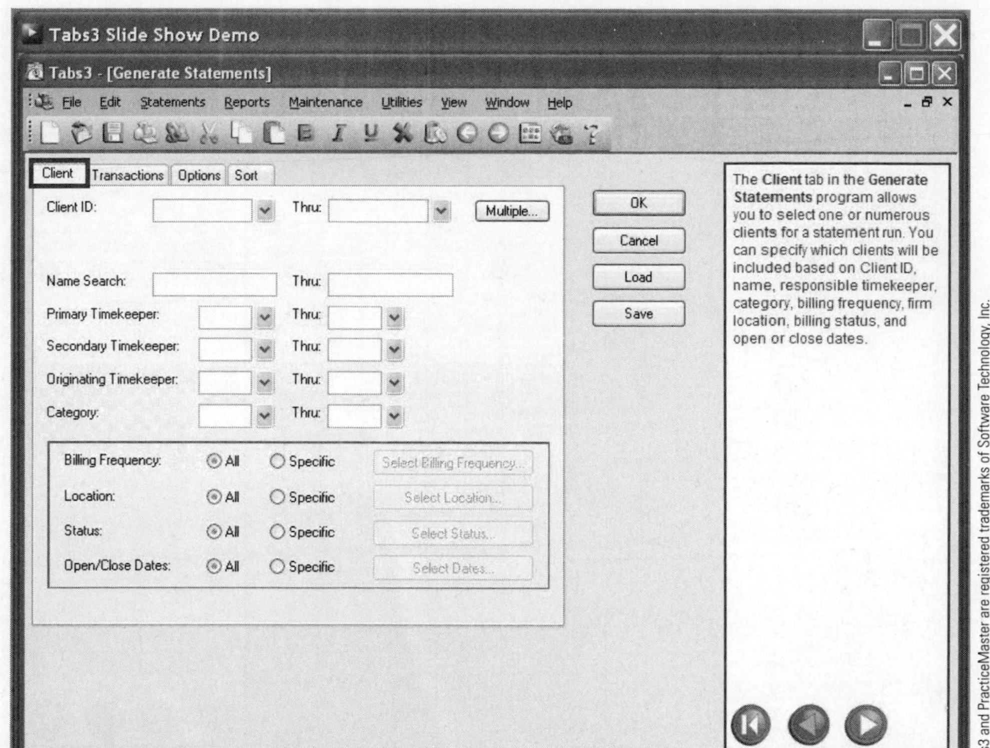

Tabs3 and PracticeMaster are registered trademarks of Software Technology, Inc.

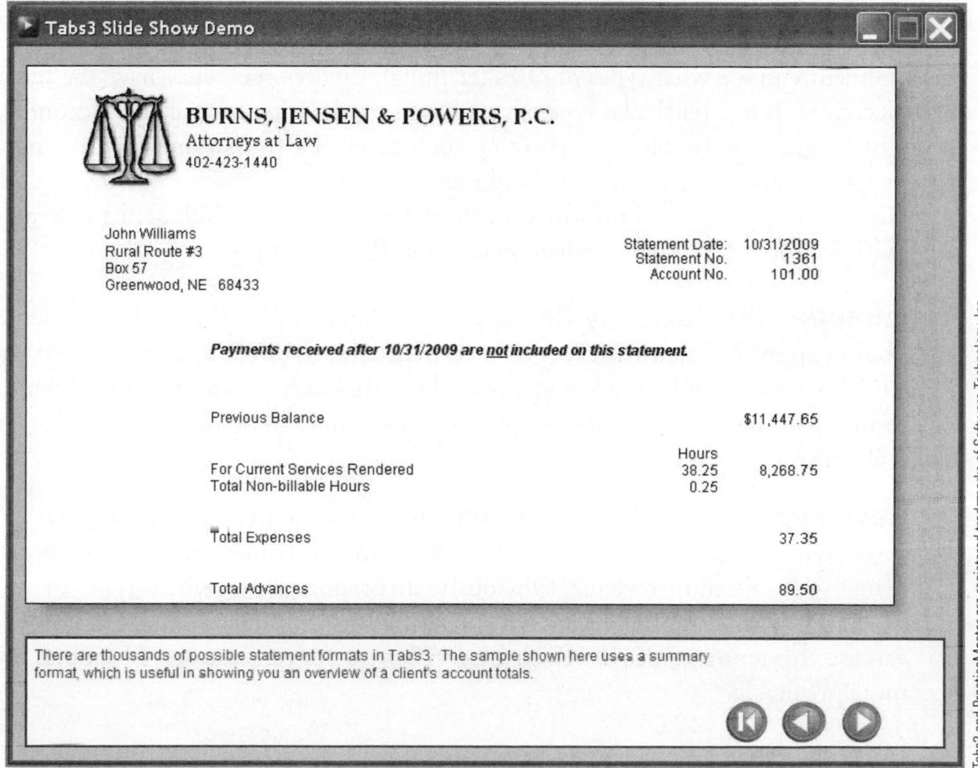

Tabs3 and PracticeMaster are registered trademarks of Software Technology, Inc.

EXHIBIT 4–12
Generating final bills

aged accounts receivable report
A report showing all cases that have outstanding balances due and how much these balances are past due.

Aged Accounts Receivable Report The **aged accounts receivable report** shows all clients that have outstanding balances owed to the office and how long these balances are past due. This report allows management to clearly see which clients are not paying and how old the balances are. This report also is helpful for identifying and following up with clients who are slow to pay their bills.

EXHIBIT 4–13
Management reports

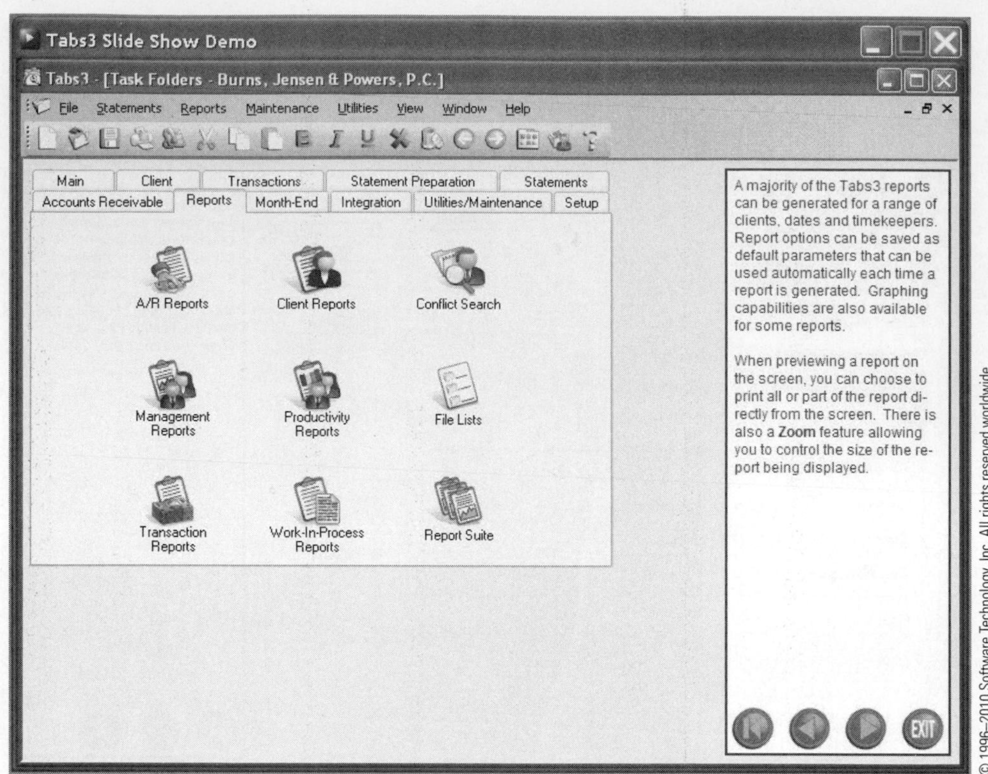

Most programs allow such a report to be run according to the type of case. Thus, management can see what types of cases (criminal, divorce, tax, etc.) have the most aged accounts. If one particular type of case has more than its share of aged accounts, it might be more profitable to stop taking such cases. So, from a management perspective, this can be a very important and useful report.

Note that aged account information should not appear on bills sent to clients. Bills with balances that are more than 30 days old should simply say "past due."

timekeeper productivity report
A report showing how much billable and nonbillable time is being spent by each timekeeper.

Timekeeper Productivity Report The amount of billable and nonbillable time being spent by each timekeeper is shown in the **timekeeper productivity report**. This report can be used to identify which timekeepers are the most diligent or productive. Most packages allow a productivity report to be run for a quarter or a whole year.

case type productivity report
A report showing which types of cases (e.g., criminal, personal injury, bankruptcy, etc.) are the most profitable.

Case Type Productivity Report The **case type productivity report** shows which types of cases (criminal, personal injury, bankruptcies, etc.) are bringing in the most revenue. Obviously, this report shows which types of cases are the most profitable and which are the least profitable. Management can use this report to decide which areas of law to concentrate on to become more profitable.

Electronic Billing

electronic billing
Client billing that uses a standard electronic format, using such means as the Internet, and conforms to standard billing codes.

When using **electronic billing**, law firms bill clients in a fashion that conforms to standard billing codes and uses a standard electronic format, using such means as the Internet. Many large clients, such as Fortune 1000 corporations and other businesses, demand that law firms bill them using electronic means. For large clients, electronic billing is a big improvement over traditional paper billing, although it introduces a certain amount of rigidity and places some administrative burden on the law firm.

Electronic billing is actually a term of art; it does not mean, for example, just sending a bill as a PDF or Microsoft Word email attachment to the client. Rather, electronic billing means sending bills that conform to the Uniform Task-Based Management System (UTBMS, a standard way of referring to timekeeper tasks) and comply with the Legal Electronic Data Exchange Standard (LEDES). LEDES is a standardized, uniform billing format in which to output billing data to clients regardless of the timekeeping and billing system that produced the bill.

Some timekeepers do not like e-billing because it mandates that they keep track of their time according to rigid, inflexible UTBMS codes. Many e-billing vendors are application service providers (ASPs), third-party vendors that set up the e-billing part of the system, receive data from law firms, and operate the software over the Internet. Clients are able to see bills (from any law firm they use) in a standard format and then customize the reports they output to meet their particular needs.

Some clients are even taking e-billing to the next level by contracting with their own ASP clearinghouses to audit bills, to ensure that the bills they receive are in strict compliance with the client's internal requirements. If the law firm's bill does not meet the client's requirements, the ASP rejects the bill and the client does not even get the electronic data. For example, if a client requires that each task be billed for separately (itemized), the client's clearinghouse would reject bills that include block entries covering three or four separate activities (e.g., "drafting letter to client; legal research for discovery motion, drafting discovery motion; telephone call with witness: 5 hours").

INTEGRATING TIMEKEEPING AND BILLING, ACCOUNTING, AND CASE MANAGEMENT

In a fully automated legal organization, the "back office" computer system will have at least three main components: (1) timekeeping and billing software, (2) accounting software, and (3) case management software. Timekeeping and billing have already been discussed in this chapter. Accounting software handles the financial side of the legal organization: receiving and applying money, making deposits, issuing checks, paying taxes, tracking aged accounts receivable, writing payroll checks, and the like. Case management software helps a legal organization provide services to clients by tracking client cases; tracking schedules, appointments, deadlines, and things to be done in cases; and tracking case-related information such as opposing parties and opposing counsel. For example, when a new client comes to a legal organization with a matter to be handled, case management software would be used to set up the new case, including client name, client address, client matter/case name, type of case, things to be done, and so forth. The same client will have to be set up in the time and billing system (to receive bills, have monies applied correctly, etc.), by entry of such data as client name, client matter, and when payments are made and recorded in the time and billing system. The legal organization's accounting software will need to know this so that deposits can be made, accounts receivable balances adjusted, and so on. The point is that all of these back-office systems have to be able to communicate with each other and share information; otherwise there will be much duplication of effort, and the possibility of error will increase greatly because of repetitive data entry.

Software manufacturers typically handle integration in one of three ways. (1) Separate software programs (from different manufacturers) exchange information among themselves (this is becoming much more common, but does not always work as promised). (2) One manufacturer makes a product that handles all of the back-office needs of the legal organization (this is also fairly common). (3) Integration is ignored and the legal organization must duplicate its efforts. It should be fairly clear that it is most efficient to design legal organization computer systems that are integrated and share information seamlessly across functions.

WHAT TO LOOK FOR IN TIMEKEEPING AND BILLING SOFTWARE

As with most software, no single timekeeping and billing program is best for all attorneys and all firms. Attorneys bill clients in very different formats and ways. The size of the firm also plays a role in choosing the right package. A timekeeping and billing package that works for a five-member law firm may not work well for a fifty-member firm.

Although paralegals do not always play a part in deciding which timekeeping and billing package to purchase, often they are consulted. (They may even be charged with the task of researching the software available and making recommendations!) When considering purchasing timekeeping and billing software, keep in mind that the billing program should do the following:

1. Be flexible, allowing the firm to charge different hourly rates, mix different fee arrangements, and so on.
2. Provide a wide variety of billing formats for different types of clients. An inflexible program that allows only one or two billing formats is usually not a good idea.
3. Be easy to use. Programs that allow users to look up information instead of memorizing keystrokes are almost always easier and more convenient to use.
4. Give the user the flexibility to bill each client whenever the user wishes, instead of having to bill all clients at one time.
5. Allow users to define a list of timekeepers and activities. Such programs are almost always easier and faster to use than programs that have predefined lists.
6. Include plenty of room for a description of the legal service provided. Some programs allow only one or two lines, which is often inadequate for recording a complicated entry.
7. Permit users to edit timeslips or expense slips instead of reentering slips that have mistakes in them.
8. Offer plenty of management reports and formats to help management operate the firm.
9. Utilize a robust security system, such as passwords, to keep unauthorized or unwanted users from accessing the system. Some programs have different levels of security; for example, a secretary might have access to the password that allows him to enter data, but not to the password to run bills or management reports. Security is an important aspect of any system.
10. Have the ability to integrate with accounting and case management software.
11. Include the ability to comply with the UTBMS and LEDES protocols.

THE ETHICS OF TIMEKEEPING AND BILLING

More ethical complaints related to timekeeping and billing are filed against attorneys and law offices than all other types of complaints combined. It is important that paralegals completely understand the ethics of timekeeping and billing. In years past, timekeeping and billing complaints were viewed simply as "misunderstandings" between the client and the law office. More recently, state bars have come to see timekeeping and billing disputes as having major ethical implications for attorneys. In fact, such disputes were often not simply misunderstandings; law offices were sometimes flagrantly violating ethical rules regarding money and financial issues.

Timekeeping and billing complaints by clients do not just lead to ethical complaints against attorneys. They may also turn into the basis for criminal fraud charges filed against attorneys and paralegals.

Confidentiality and the Cloud

Chapter 6 of this text discusses the ethical issues that can arise when confidential client information is stored online, or in other words, "in the cloud." But it is worth discussing, in the context of timekeeping and billing, the specific confidentiality issues that should be considered. In this context, a law office is like any other business in that it must take all necessary precautions to protect client financial data (credit card information, social security, birthdate, maybe even a mother's maiden name). And the specific information in the billing files may contain confidential information about the client's legal issues. And the client may have access to this information on the cloud (to make payments, review bills, etc.). If client timekeeping and billing information is to be stored in the cloud, the client should be notified of this in writing and the best practices discussed in Chapter 6 should be implemented.

Ethical Considerations Regarding Legal Fee Agreements

We should stress several important ethical considerations regarding fee agreements. The first is that *all fee agreements should be in writing*, especially when a contingency fee is involved. Second, contingency fees should not be used in criminal or domestic relations matters. Third, only a reasonable fee can be collected. Disputes regarding attorney handling of fees are taken seriously and can lead to adverse ethical findings or worse.

Fee Agreements Should Be in Writing

It is highly recommended that, as a matter of course, all fee arrangements be in writing. The days of a handshake cementing an agreement between an attorney and a client are long gone. There is no substitute for reducing all fee agreements to writing. If the firm and the client have a dispute over fees, the document will clarify the understanding between the parties.

Why is it so important for legal fee agreements to be in writing?

1. Clients file more ethical complaints against attorneys and law offices for fee disputes than for any other type of dispute or problem.
2. The client and the attorney may (will) forget what the exact fee agreement was unless it is reduced to writing.
3. In a factual dispute regarding a fee between a client and an attorney, the evidence is typically construed in the light most favorable to the client.

Contingency Fee Agreements Must Be in Writing When a contingency fee is involved, most jurisdictions state that the agreement *must* be in writing for the office to collect the fees. The primary reason that a contingency fee agreement must be in writing is that in many cases, large sums of money are recovered; the difference between 20 percent and 30 percent may be tens of thousands of dollars. Contingency agreements are risky for the attorney, and they simply must be reduced to writing so that the client and the attorney both know what the proper percentage of fees should be. It also is important that the contingency agreement state—and the client understand—that even if there is no recovery in the case, the client must still pay for expenses.

Contingency Fees Are Not Allowed in Criminal and Domestic Relations Proceedings in Some Jurisdictions Many jurisdictions prohibit contingency fees in criminal and domestic relations proceedings as a matter of public policy. For example, assume that an attorney agrees to represent a client in a criminal matter. The client agrees to pay the attorney $10,000 if the client is found not guilty, but the attorney will receive nothing if the client is found guilty. This is an unethical contingency fee agreement. It rewards the attorney not for efforts, but for results that are not entirely within the attorney's control; thus, the attorney may be tempted or pressured to engage in unethical or even criminal pursuits to ensure the desired verdict. To avoid such possibilities and protect the public interest, contingency fees in these types of cases are prohibited.

Only a "Reasonable" Fee Can Be Collected

It is important to keep in mind that no matter what the contract or legal fee agreement is with a client, attorneys and paralegals can receive only a "reasonable" fee. Unfortunately, there is no absolute standard for determining reasonableness, except that reasonableness will be determined on a case-by-case basis. However, most states have set out a number of factors to be considered in determining reasonableness:

1. The time and labor required, including the novelty and difficulty of the questions involved, and the skill required to perform the legal services.
2. The likelihood that acceptance of the legal matter will preclude the lawyer from accepting other cases.
3. The customary fee in the area for such legal services.
4. The outcome of the matter, including the amount involved.
5. Any time limitations imposed by the client or by the circumstances.
6. The type, nature, and length of the professional relationship with the client.
7. The ability of the lawyer involved, including experience, reputation, and ability.
8. Whether the type of fee was fixed or contingent.

Rules of Many State Bars Provide for Oversight/Arbitration on Fee Issues

One of the ways in which state bar associations and courts have dealt with the plethora of fee disputes is by providing for immediate and informal review and/or arbitration of fee disputes. Many state ethical rules and court rules provide that clients have the right, at any time, to request that the judge in the case or an attorney representing the state bar review the reasonableness of the attorney's fees. In many states, the attorney is required to inform the client of this right. In those states, the judge or attorney hearing the matter has the right to set the fee and determine what is reasonable under the particular facts and circumstances of the case.

Fraud and Criminal Charges

Charging an unreasonable fee is no longer simply a matter of ethics. Attorneys and paralegals have been criminally charged with fraud for intentionally recording time and sending bills for legal services that were never provided. Criminal fraud is a false representation of a present or past fact made by the defendant, upon which the victim relies, and which results in the victim suffering damages.

Criminal charges for fraud are not filed against attorneys and paralegals when there is simply a disagreement over what constitutes a reasonable fee. Criminal charges are filed when an attorney or paralegal acts intentionally to defraud clients. This usually happens when the attorney or paralegal bills for time when he or she did not really work on the case, or in instances in which the office intentionally billed a grossly overstated hourly rate far above the market rate.

Interestingly, many of the most recent criminal cases are being brought against well-respected law offices (both large and small) specializing in insurance defense and corporate work. Some insurance companies and corporations, as a matter of course when a case has been concluded, hire an audit firm or independent attorney to go back and audit the legal billings and files to be sure they were billed accurately. In some instances, these audits have concluded that intentional criminal fraud was perpetrated, and the cases were referred to prosecutors who filed criminal charges. No matter what type of firm is involved, intentionally overstating bills can lead to very big problems.

Ethical Problems

The general subject of timekeeping and billing brings up a wide variety of ethical issues and considerations, only a few of which are mentioned here. No matter what kind of timekeeping and billing system your office uses, whether it be manual or computerized, it is critically important that the underlying agreement between the law office and the client be in writing. Second, ethical rules state that only a "reasonable" fee can be collected from clients. It is very important that bills be accurately produced the first time and that no errors occur, so that only a "reasonable" fee is collected. Data entry is absolutely crucial to timekeeping and billing. If a timeslip is entered twice so that a client is billed twice for the same service, if a payment is not recorded to a client's account, or if a client is overcharged for legal services, the firm could lose that client or be faced with an ethical complaint. Thousands of ethical complaints are filed every year against attorneys regarding timekeeping and billing practices, so it is of utmost importance that this function be handled properly.

Several difficult ethical problems regarding timekeeping and billing are explored in this section, although they have no definite answers or solutions. The rule in deciding ethical questions such as these is to use your common sense and notions of fairness and honesty.

Can You Bill More than One Client for the Same Time? From time to time a paralegal or attorney has the opportunity to bill more than one client for the same time period. This is known as double billing. For instance, while you are monitoring the opposing side's inspection of your client's documents in case A, you are drafting discovery for case B. Another example: while travelling to attend an interview with a witness in case A, you work on case B.

If you were the client, would you think it is fair for the attorney to charge full price for travel time related to your case while also billing another case? Reasonable approaches are to bill only the case you are actively working on, to split the time between the cases, or to bill the case you are actively working on at the regular hourly rate and bill the case you are inactively working on at a greatly reduced rate. Be fair and honest; your clients as well as judges and others looking at your time records will respect you for it.

When Billing by the Hour, Is There an Ethical Obligation to Be Efficient? Does the firm have to have a form file, rather than researching each document anew each time? Must an office use a computer to save time? These types of ethical questions are decided on a case-by-case basis. The point is that billing by the hour rewards people for working slowly: the more slowly they work, the more they are paid.

Common sense tells you that if you were the client, you would want your legal staff to be efficient and not to "milk" you for money. The real issue is whether the attorney or paralegal acted so inefficiently and charged so much, when compared with what a similar attorney or paralegal with similar qualifications would charge in the same community, that the fee is clearly unreasonable. When judges rule on the reasonableness of fees, there is no doubt that they will consider what a reasonably efficient attorney or paralegal in the same circumstances would have charged. Use your common sense and be honest and efficient, because someone in your office might have to justify your time and charges someday.

Should You Bill for Clerical or Secretarial Duties? Law offices cannot bill clients for clerical or secretarial time or tasks. These tasks are viewed as overhead costs, a normal part of doing business. An easy, but unethical, way to bill more hours is for a paralegal to bill time to clients for clerical functions such as copying documents or filing materials. Paralegals clearly should not bill for time spent performing these types of clerical tasks. Paralegals bill time for professional services, not for clerical functions. If you are unsure about whether a task is clerical, ask your supervising attorney, or record the time initially and point it out to the supervising attorney and let him or her decide.

Should You Bill for the Mistakes of the Law Office? This is another tough problem. People make mistakes all the time. Clients generally feel that they should not have to pay for mistakes; after all, the reason they went to an attorney in the first place was to get an expert to handle their situation. This decision should be left for each law office to decide, but generally the practice of billing for mistakes is discouraged.

Must a Task Be Assigned to Less Expensive Support Staff When Possible? Common sense and efficiency will tell you that tasks should be delegated as low as possible. Clients should not have to pay for attorney time when the task could be completed by an experienced paralegal. In addition, this arrangement is more profitable for the law office, because higher-paid persons are freed to do tasks for which they can bill clients at their normal rates.

SUMMARY

In the legal environment, the process of tracking time for the purpose of billing clients is called timekeeping. The process of issuing bills for the purpose of collecting monies for legal services performed and for expenses is called billing. Timekeeping and billing software is the second most popular kind of software for law offices, right after word processing.

The computerized timekeeping and billing process or cycle includes the following steps: the client and the attorney reach an agreement with regard to how fees will be calculated; the attorney performs legal services and prepares manual or computer timeslips; paper timeslips and expense slips are entered into the timekeeping and billing software; a pre-billing report is generated; client billings are generated; management reports are generated; and client payments are entered into the computer.

Many types of fee arrangements are available, including hourly rate fees, contingency fees, flat fees, and retainers.

Every timekeeping and billing program has a screen where relevant information about each client is entered. The client information screen usually shows and receives client information such as name, address, identification number, fee arrangements, bill formatting options, and the like.

The data entry screen is where timeslips and expense slips are entered into the computer. Computerized timeslip entry screens look much like manual timeslips.

Generating accurate and timely client bills is an important function of any timekeeping and billing system. Many timekeeping and billing programs allow users to choose from among several different billing formats.

Management reports are used to help management analyze whether a law firm is operating efficiently and effectively. Many programs allow you to generate a case or client list, aged accounts receivable report, timekeeping productivity report, case type productivity report, and more.

Many ethical complaints are filed against attorneys due to timekeeping and billing issues. It is important to have written fee agreements, bill honestly and accurately, and bill only reasonable fees.

KEY TERMS

activity hourly rate
aged accounts receivable report
attorney or paralegal hourly rate
billable hour
billing
blended hourly rate fee
case retainer
case type productivity report
cash advance
client hourly rate
contingency fee
earned retainer
electronic billing
expense slip
flat fee
hourly rate fee
management reports
operating account
pre-billing report
pure retainer
retainer for general representation
timekeeper
timekeeper productivity report
timekeeping
timeslip
trust or escrow account
unearned retainer
value billing

INTERNET SITES

Internet sites for this chapter include:

ORGANIZATION	PRODUCT/SERVICE	INTERNET ADDRESS
Abacus Data Systems, Inc.	Abacus Silver, timekeeping, billing, accounting and case management software	www.abacuslaw.com
Aderant	CMS Open Billing	www.cmsopen.com
Amicus Attorney	Case management software, including timekeeping and billing	www.amicusattorney.com
Clio	Cloud based practice management. Includes timekeeping and billing	www.goclio.com
IOLTA	Information about IOLTA and IOLTA programs	www.iolta.org
Juris	Juris legal timekeeping and billing software	www.juris.com
LEDES	Legal Electronic Data Exchange Standard (LEDES)	www.ledes.org
LexisNexis	PC LAW legal timekeeping and billing software	www.pclaw.com
Micro Craft, Inc.	Verdict Time & Billing	www.micro-craft.net
Omega Legal Systems	Omega Billing & Accounting	www.omegalegal.com
Orion Law Management Systems	Timekeeping and billing software	www.Orionlaw.com
Perfect Law Software	Timekeeping and billing software and comprehensive back-office systems	www.perfectlaw.com
ProVantage Software, Inc.	Timekeeping and billing software and comprehensive back-office systems	www.provantagesoftware.com
Rainmaker Software, Inc.	Rainmaker Gold timekeeping and billing software	www.rainmakerlegal.com
Sage Software	Timeslips legal timekeeping and billing software	www.timeslips.com
Tabs3	Tabs3 legal timekeeping and billing software	www.Tabs3.com
Thomson	Elite Enterprise and Prolaw timekeeping and billing software systems	www.elite.com

TEST YOUR KNOWLEDGE

1. What is the difference between timekeeping and billing?
2. Name four types of hourly rates.
3. When a lawyer takes a percentage of the recovery in the case, it is called a __________ fee.
4. True or False: It is strongly recommended that all fee arrangements be in writing.
5. True or False: A flat-fee agreement must be in writing.
6. A retainer that can be deposited in the firm's or attorney's operating checking account is called a(n) __________ retainer.
7. True or False: An account where unearned client monies are deposited is called a trust fund.
8. A retainer for general representation is a(n) __________ retainer.
9. A case retainer is a(n) __________ retainer.
10. A cash advance retainer is a(n) __________ retainer.
11. For what activity do clients file the most ethical complaints against lawyers?
12. True or False: A contingency agreement can be used in all kinds of cases.
13. True or False: If a client signs a contract with an attorney and the fee turns out to be clearly excessive, it doesn't matter, because a contract was signed and the contract prevails.
14. Name four of the eight factors that courts use to determine if a fee is unreasonable.
15. True or False: Paralegals can bill for time spent doing photocopying and other clerical tasks.
16. Define electronic billing.
17. True or False: Integrated programs that include timekeeping and billing, accounting, and other features do not really offer the modern law office much advantage.

ON THE WEB EXERCISES

1. Using the "Internet Sites" listed in this chapter or a general Internet search engine (such as www.google.com or www.yahoo.com), research three timekeeping and billing programs. Compare the features, price, training options, and other information about the products and write a three-page paper on your findings, including which program you liked the best and why.
2. Using the "Internet Sites" listed in this chapter or a general Internet search engine (such as www.google.com or www.yahoo.com), research legal electronic billing. Write a three-page paper on the results of your research. Include what it is; how it works; what, if any, problems there are regarding implementation of electronic billing; and what benefits clients and legal organizations derive from electronic billing.
3. Using the "Internet Sites" listed in this chapter or a general Internet search engine (such as www.google.com or www.yahoo.com), find a minimum of three articles on legal timekeeping and billing. Write a one-page summary of each article.
4. Visit five state bar association websites and find three articles on either legal timekeeping, billing, or legal fees.
5. Go to the Georgia Bar Association's website at www.gabar.org and use the Search tool to find a sample contingency fee agreement. Go to several other state bar association websites and try to find another sample contingency fee or hourly rate contract agreements.
6. Visit the National Association of Legal Assistants website at www.nala.org and review the latest NALA National Utilization and Compensation Survey Report. Read and print out the section related to paralegal billing rates. If you have difficulty finding it, try using the "Search" feature on the website. If you still have trouble finding it, use www.google.com and search on the full title.
7. Go to the ABA Law Practice Management Section home page at www.americanbar.org and find two articles on timekeeping, billing, fees, and finance-related matters. Summarize the articles in a two-page paper.

QUESTIONS AND EXERCISES

1. You are a new paralegal and have worked for a medium-sized law office for three months. It has been a tremendous experience for you, as you learned how the office does business; its policies and procedures; what type of service you are expected to give to clients; where resources are; and how to use resources, such as the office's computer systems, law library, copy machines, and form files. Although it has taken time for you to learn these things, you have also been productive and have received several compliments on the quality of your work.
   One day, you read in the office's staff manual that all paralegals are required to bill 1,500 hours annually or face possible discipline. You immediately contact your supervisor and ask whether, as a new paralegal, you will be expected to bill this amount. Your supervisor responds, "Of course. You were told that when you were hired." You immediately begin gathering copies of your timesheets to compile your total. You also request that the billing department send you the total numbers of hours you have billed to date. When you get the report from billing, you panic; you have billed only 300 hours. What do you do now, and how could you have avoided this unfortunate situation?
2. On June 30, a billing goes out to Susan Simon, one of the clients whose cases you have been working on. Ms. Simon calls you a few days later and complains about the amount of time shown on the bill. She is extremely rude and discourteous. Ms. Simon flatly states that she thinks she is being overbilled. How do you handle the phone call?
3. You are interviewing a new client. The client wants to hire your office to help negotiate the purchase of a small business. The seller has proposed $20,000. The new client would be willing to pay this amount, although she thinks it is a bit high, but she does not feel comfortable negotiating with the seller and would rather have an attorney involved in the deal for her protection. However, she is suspicious of paralegals and attorneys and is especially concerned about how much it will cost to get the representation she needs. You inform the client that the attorney will be the one who actually talks to her about the fee issue, but that typically this type of case is taken on an hourly basis and that the attorney will be able to give her only a very broad estimate of what the total matter will cost. The client states that this would be unacceptable to her because she "does not have a lot of money to pay overpriced attorneys." The client also states that she would like this matter settled as soon as possible. You must prepare a memorandum to the attorney outlining the issue and possible solutions. What type of fee arrangement would you suggest to the attorney? Please keep in mind the client's anxieties and her particular needs.
4. Recently, your office has found a niche in representing spouses collecting on past-due child support. In most cases, your clients have little money to pay you with and are financially strapped, because they no longer have the income of their former spouses to support their children and have not been receiving the child support. In some cases, large amounts of money are owed, but finding the former spouses has proven difficult. Your supervising attorney decides that the best way to handle these types of cases is on a one-third contingency basis. Your supervising attorney asks for your comments. How do you respond?
5. Yesterday was a hectic day. Although you wanted to record your time earlier, you just could not get to it. Record your time now, using a spreadsheet. Build the spreadsheet so it has columns for the date, client/case name, timekeeper, services rendered, billable time, and nonbillable time. For each activity listed, decide whether it is billable or not billable. Record your time, first using tenths of hours.
   You should also fill out expense slips for items that should be charged back to clients. Build the spreadsheet to include date, client/case name, type of expense, and cost. The firm charges 25 cents each for copies and 50 cents per page to send a fax. Assume that long-distance phone calls cost 25 cents a minute. Total the cost of each expense slip. As best you can recall, this is how your day went:

8:00 a.m.–8:12 a.m.: Got a cup of coffee, talked to other law office staff members, reviewed your schedule/things-to-do sheet for the day, and reviewed the email in your inbox.

8:13 a.m.–8:25 a.m.: Talked to your supervising attorney (Lisa Mitchell) about some research she needs done on the grounds to support a motion to dismiss *Johnson v. Cuttingham Steel.* Ms. Mitchell also asked you to find a bankruptcy statute she needs for *Halvert v. Shawnee Savings & Loan.*

8:26 a.m.–8:37 a.m.: A paralegal from another office calls to remind you that the paralegal association you belong to is having a meeting at noon and that you are running the meeting.

8:38 a.m.–8:40 a.m.: One of your least favorite clients, John Hamilton, calls to ask you when he is supposed to be at your office to prepare for his deposition tomorrow. You access the weekly schedule electronically and read him the information he needs.

8:40 a.m.–8:50 a.m.: You find the information you need for the motion to dismiss in *Johnson v. Cuttingham Steel* in a motion in another case you helped to prepare last month. The research is still current, and Ms. Mitchell is pleased that you found it so fast. You note that it took you two hours to research this issue when you did it the first time. You copy the material Ms. Mitchell needs (five pages) and put it on her desk, and also send it to her electronically.

8:55 a.m.–9:30 a.m.: You speak with a witness you have been trying to contact in *Menly v. Menly.* The call is long-distance. The call lasts 15 minutes and writing the memo to the file documenting the call takes 15 minutes.

9:30 a.m.–9:54 a.m.: Ms. Mitchell asks you to contact the attorney in *Glass v. Huron* regarding a discovery question. You spend 10 minutes on hold. The call is long-distance but you get an answer to Ms. Mitchell's question.

10:00 a.m.–10:15 a.m.: Coffee break and talk with attorney about the ballgame.

10:15 a.m.–10:45 a.m.: One of the secretaries informs you that you must interview a new client, Richard Sherman. The person who was supposed to see Mr. Sherman got delayed. Mr. Sherman comes to your office regarding a simple adoption. However, in talking to Mr. Sherman you find out that he also needs someone to incorporate a small business that he is getting ready to open. You gladly tell him that your office has a department that handles this type of matter. You take down the basic information regarding both matters. You tell the client that you will prepare a memo regarding these matters to the appropriate attorney and that one of the office's attorneys will contact him within two days to further discuss the matter. You also copy 10 pages of information that Mr. Sherman brought.

10:45 a.m.–10:54 a.m.: One of the secretaries asks you to cover her phone for her while she takes a quick break. Because the secretary always helps you when you ask for it, you gladly cover the phone for a few minutes. Ms. Mitchell asks you to send a fax regarding *Stewart v. Layhorn Glass*, so you use this time to send the six-page fax.

10:55 a.m.–12:00 noon: Yesterday Ms. Mitchell asked you to organize some exhibits in *Ranking v. Siefkin.* The deadline was noon today. You finally have some free time to organize the exhibits.

12:00 noon–1:00 p.m.: Lunch.

1:00 p.m.–2:00 p.m.: You work on a pro bono criminal case for a client whom Ms. Mitchell is representing on appeal. In an effort to become familiar with the case, you read some of the transcripts from the trial.

2:00 p.m.–3:30 p.m.: Ms. Mitchell hands you a new case and says that your firm will be representing the defendant, Maude Pinchum. She asks you to read the petition and client file, analyze the case, and draft interrogatories to send to the plaintiff. You spend the rest of the day working on this case.

3:30 p.m.–3:45 p.m.: Make personal phone calls.

3:45 p.m.–5:00 p.m.: Continue working on Pinchum case.

ETHICS QUESTION

It is the first day of your new job as a paralegal. As you perform your first job assignment, you discover that it is taking longer than you think it should. You do not want your boss to think that you are incompetent or lazy, so when you submit the bill for your time, you report only half the time you actually spent on the assignment. What ethical issues, if any, are raised by this scenario?

TABS3 BILLING SOFTWARE

READ THIS FIRST!

I. INTRODUCTION–READ THIS!

The Tabs3 timekeeping and billing program demonstration version is a full working version of the program with a few limitations. The main limitation is that only a limited number of clients can be entered into the program. The demonstration version does *not* time out (quit working after a set number of days).

II. USING THE TABS3 HANDS-ON EXERCISES

The Tabs3 Hands-On Exercises are easy to use and contain step-by-step instructions. Each lesson builds on the previous exercise, so please complete the Hands-On Exercises in order. Tabs3 is a user-friendly program, so using the program should be intuitive. Tabs3 also comes with sample data, so you should be able to try many features of the program.

III. INSTALLATION INSTRUCTIONS

Below are step-by-step instructions for loading the Tabs3 timekeeping and billing demonstration version on your computer.

1. Log in to your CengageBrain.com account.
2. Under "My Courses & Materials," find the Premium Website for *Using Computers in the Law Office,* 7th edition.
3. ***Click "open" to go to the Premium Website.***
4. Locate "Book Level Resources" in the left navigation menu.
5. ***Click on the link for "Tabs3".***
6. ***On the next screen, click the link next to "To access the demo:"***
7. ***Complete the form to request a free download. When you receive the email from Tabs3, click the link as instructed to begin installation process.***

8. The screen in Tabs3 Installation Exhibit 1 should now be displayed. ***Click "Download Trial."*** If asked whether you want to run or save the file, ***click Run.***

TABS3 INSTALLATION EXHIBIT 1

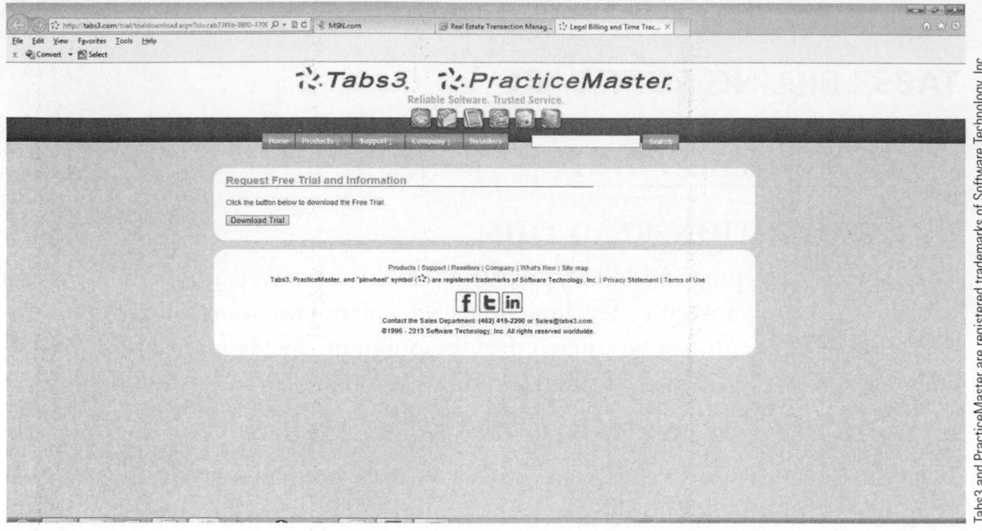

Tabs3 and PracticeMaster are registered trademarks of Software Technology, Inc.

9. The Tabs3 Trial Software Setup window should now be displayed. (See Installation Exhibit 2.) ***Click Next.***

TABS3 INSTALLATION EXHIBIT 2

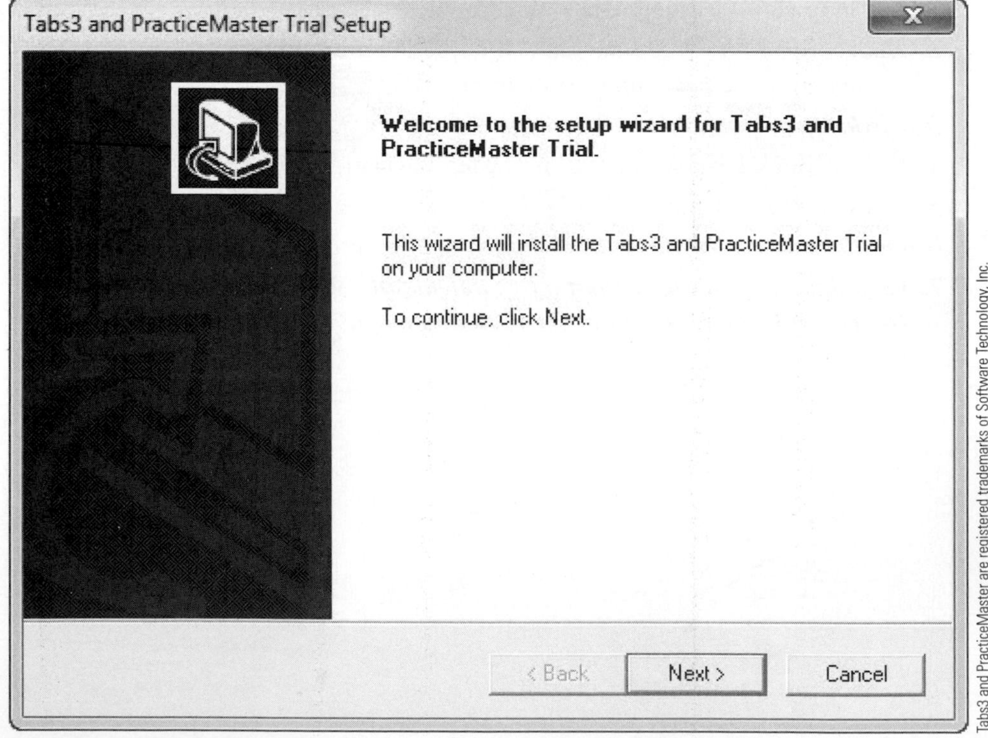

Tabs3 and PracticeMaster are registered trademarks of Software Technology, Inc.

10. Your screen will look like Tabs3 Installation Exhibit 3. Review the license agreement, and then ***click Yes.***

TABS3 INSTALLATION EXHIBIT 3

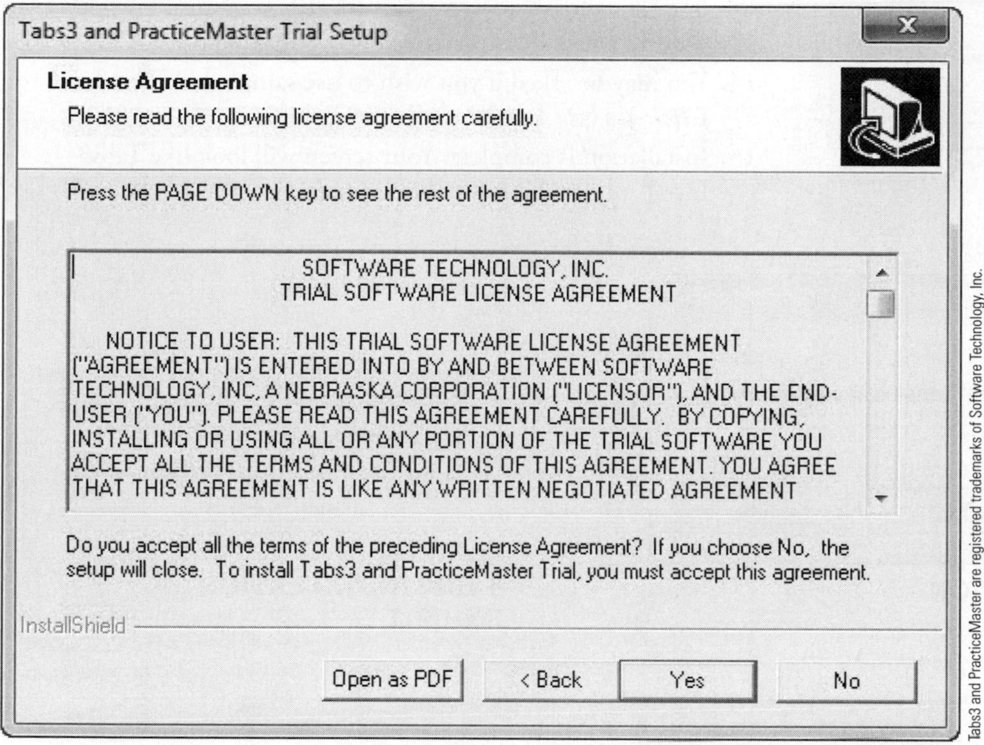

11. Your screen will look like Tabs3 Installation Exhibit 4. ***Click Next.***

TABS3 INSTALLATION EXHIBIT 4

Tabs3 and PracticeMaster Trial Setup

Choose installation location

Please enter the location to install the files. Click "Browse" to navigate to the correct folder, or click "Search" to search for the correct folder.

C:\Tabs3New

Browse...

Search...

InstallShield

< Back   Next >   Cancel

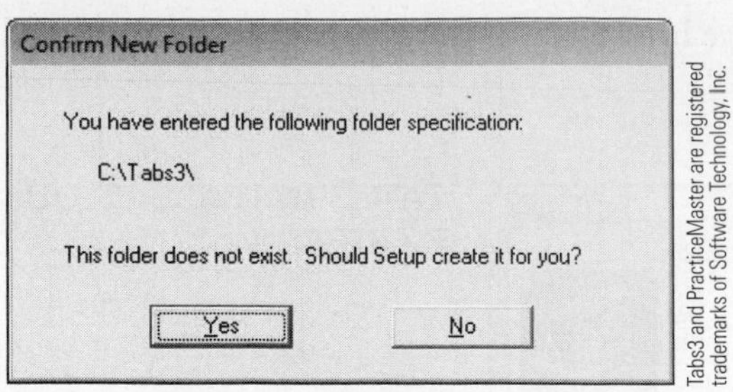

Tabs3 and PracticeMaster are registered trademarks of Software Technology, Inc.

TABS3 INSTALLATION EXHIBIT 5

12. You may be asked to confirm the creation of a new folder (see Tabs3 Installation Exhibit 5). ***Click Yes.***
13. You may be asked if you want to create icons on the desktop (see Tabs3 Installation Exhibit 6). It is your choice whether you want to create desktop icons.
14. You may be asked if you wish to use sample law firm data. ***Click Yes*** (see Tabs3 Installation Exhibit 7).
15. Installation is complete. Your screen will look like Tabs3 Installation Exhibit 8. ***Click Finish.***

Tabs3 and PracticeMaster are registered trademarks of Software Technology, Inc.

TABS3 INSTALLATION EXHIBIT 6

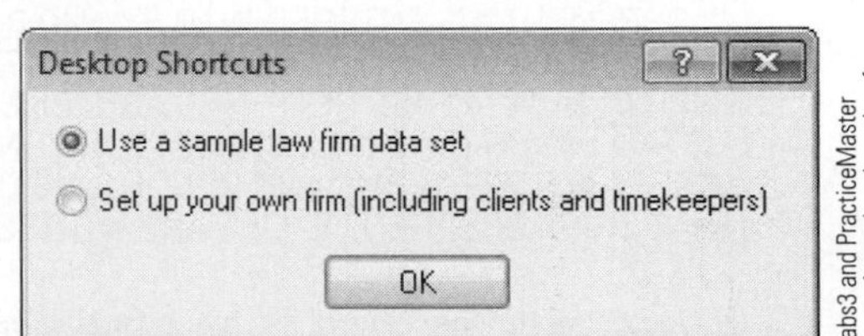

Tabs3 and PracticeMaster are registered trademarks of Software Technology, Inc.

TABS3 INSTALLATION EXHIBIT 7

TABS3 INSTALLATION EXHIBIT 8

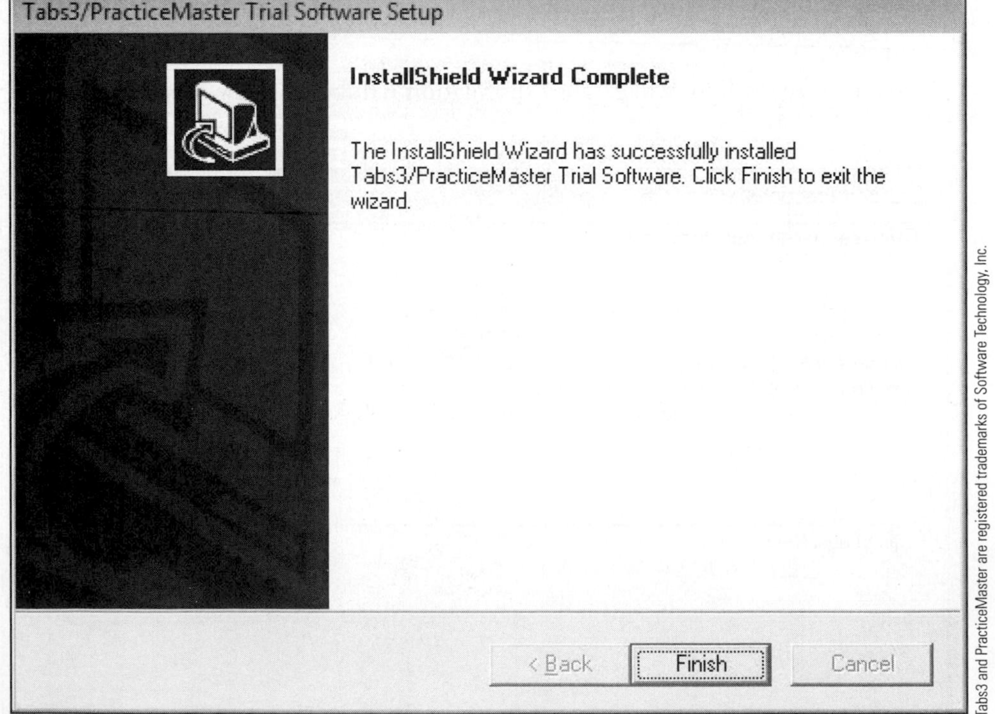

Tabs3 and PracticeMaster are registered trademarks of Software Technology, Inc.

IV. INSTALLATION TECHNICAL SUPPORT

If you have problems installing the demonstration version of Tabs3 please contact Cengage Learning Technical Support first at http://cengage.com/support. Please note that Tabs3 is a licensed product of Software Technology, Inc. If Cengage Learning Technical Support is unable to resolve your installation question, or if you have a non-installation–related question, you will need to contact Software Technology, Inc. directly at **(402) 419-2210.**

HANDS-ON EXERCISES

TABS3 BILLING SOFTWARE

Number	Lesson Title	Concepts Covered
BASIC LESSONS		
Lesson 1	Introduction to Tabs3	An introduction to the Tabs3 interface
Lesson 2	Entering a New Client	Entering a new client into Tabs3, including entering contact data, setup, rates, billing, and statement information
INTERMEDIATE LESSONS		
Lesson 3	Entering Fee/Time Records	Entering several different types of fee/time record entries
Lesson 4	Entering Cost/Expense Records and Using the Fee Timer Feature	Entering several different types of cost/expense records and learning how to use the Fee Timer feature
Lesson 5	Generating and Printing Draft and Final Statements	Generate and print draft statements and final statements; update statements
Lesson 6	Entering a Payment	Enter and apply a payment
ADVANCED LESSON		
Lesson 7	Processing and Printing Reports	Process and print a number of management, productivity, and client reports

GETTING STARTED

Introduction

Throughout these lessons and exercises, information you need to type into the software will be designated in several different ways:

- Keys to be pressed on the keyboard are designated in brackets, in all caps, and in bold (e.g., press the **[ENTER]** key).
- Movements with the cursor are designated in bold and italics (e.g., ***point to File on the menu bar and click***).
- Words or letters that should be typed are designated in bold (e.g., type **Training Program**).
- Information that is or should be displayed on your computer screen is shown in bold, with quotation marks (e.g., **"Press ENTER to continue."**).
- Specific menu items and commands are designated with an initial capital letter (e.g., click Open).

OVERVIEW OF TABS3

Tabs3 is a full-featured time, accounting, and billing system. Software Technology, Inc. also produces additional modules that integrate with the billing software, including general ledger software, accounts payable software, trust accounting software, Tabs3 and GLS Report Writers, and PracticeManager case management software. This tutorial covers only the billing software. Tabs3 Exhibit 1 shows the main Tabs3 window with task folders displayed. With Tabs3, you can enter new clients, fee/time records, expense entries, and payments; run billing/management

TABS3 EXHIBIT 1
Tabs3 window with task folders

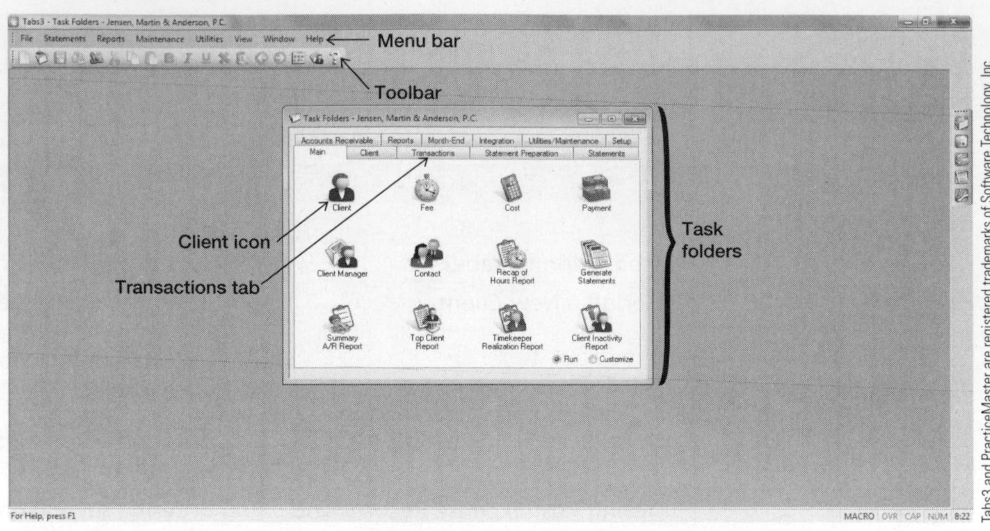

reports; and control a firm's overall billing system. Tabs3 is robust and offers many advanced billing features, and it is also easy to use. By the end of the exercises, you should have a good understanding of the basics of legal time entry and billing with Tabs3.

BASIC LESSONS

LESSON 1: INTRODUCTION TO TABS3

This lesson introduces you to Tabs3. It explains basic information about the Tabs3 interface, including an overview of clients, fees, costs, payments, generating bills and statements, and running reports.

Before you start, install the Tabs3 trial version on your computer by following the instructions entitled "Tabs3 Hands-On Exercises—Read This First!" *Note:* The Tabs3 Billing Software trial version does *not* time out (quit working after a set number of days). The main limitation of the trial version is that only 30 clients can be entered into the software.

1. Open Windows. After it has loaded, ***double-click Tabs3 with Sample Data on the desktop,*** or ***click the Start button on the Windows desktop, point to Programs or All Programs, point to the Tabs3 & PracticeMaster group, point to Trial Software with Sample Data, and then click Tabs3 with Sample Data.*** Tabs3 will then open with sample data already present in the software. *Note:* If a message about the integration between Tabs3 and PracticeMaster is displayed, you have opened the trial software without sample data. ***Click OK, and then click Close in the "Tip of the Day" window.*** Press **[CTRL]+[S]** to save customization settings, ***click the Close icon*** (the "X" in the upper right corner of the "Tip of the Day" window) to exit the software, and then try again to open the program.
2. The screen in Tabs3 Exhibit 2 should now be displayed. The Tabs3 window states that sample data is being used and that the system date in use with the sample data is set to 11/17/2014. This date will not affect any other software on your computer. ***Click OK in the "Tabs3" window.***

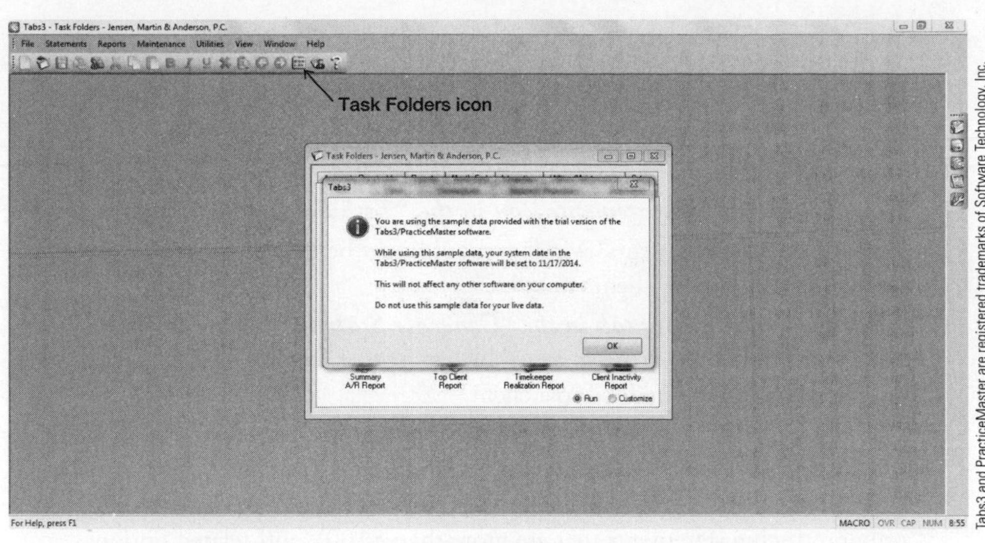

TABS3 EXHIBIT 2
Sample data/date notice

3. The "Tip of the Day" window should now be displayed. ***Click Close in the "Tip of the Day" window.*** *Note:* If you do not want to see the Tip of the Day, ***select the* "Do not show tips at startup" *box before clicking Close.***
4. The screen in Tabs3 Exhibit 1 should now be displayed. Notice the "Task Folders—Jensen, Martin & Anderson, P.C." window (hereinafter referred to as the "Task Folders" window) in the middle of the screen in Tabs3 Exhibit 1. If the Task Folders windows is set elsewhere on the screen, you may move it by ***clicking the Task Folders icon*** (see Tabs3 Exhibit 2), then ***dragging the Task Folders window to the center***. *Note:* Sample data for the fictitious law firm of Jensen, Martin & Anderson, P.C. are used throughout this tutorial.
5. Notice in Tabs3 Exhibit 1 that the Main tab in the "Task Folders" window is currently displayed (other tabs include Client, Transactions, Statements, Reports, etc.). The icons change depending on which tab is selected. We will now explore the Main tab.
6. ***Click the Client icon in the "Task Folders" window.*** (See Tabs3 Exhibit 1.)
7. A blank "Client Information" window should now be displayed. This is where you enter information about a client, such as name, contact information, billing options, setup options, statement options, and so on. In Lesson 2 you will set up a new client using this window.
8. ***Click the Close icon*** (the red square with a white "X") ***at the upper right of the "Client Information" window.*** *Note:* To have the computer display the name of an icon, just hover the cursor over the icon for a second; the name will be displayed.
9. ***Click the Fee icon in the "Task Folders" window.***
10. The "Fee Entry" window should now be displayed. This is where client time/fee entries (time records) are entered into Tabs3. In this window, the user designates the client to be billed, timekeeper, date of the record, transaction code (the activity), number of hours worked, a description of the activity, and other data. In Lesson 3, you will enter a number of fee records into Tabs3.
11. ***Click the Close icon in the upper right of the "Fee Entry" window.***
12. ***Click the Cost icon in the "Task Folders" window.***
13. The "Rapid Cost Entry" window should now be displayed. This is where client cost entries (cost records or expenses) are entered into Tabs3. These include

costs such as photocopying, courier fees, transcription fees, and travel expenses. In this window the user designates the client to be billed, the date the cost was incurred, a description of the cost, and related information. In Lesson 4, you will enter a number of cost records into Tabs3.

14. ***Click the Close icon in the upper right of the "Rapid Cost Entry" window.***
15. ***Click the Generate Statements icon in the "Task Folders" window.***
16. The "Generate Statements" window should now be displayed. This is where users designate which clients to bill.
17. ***Click the Transactions tab in the "Generate Statements" window.*** See Tabs3 Exhibit 1. This is where users control what type of fees, expenses, advances, and payments are billed/credited to a client.
18. ***Click the Options tab in the "Generate Statements" window.*** This is where users select whether to produce draft (pre-billing) statements or final statements, and assign beginning statement numbers, individual billing thresholds (e.g., only producing statements that are more than $100), and related options.
19. ***Click the Close icon at the upper right of the "Generate Statements" window.***
20. ***Click the Payment icon in the "Task Folders" window.***
21. The "Rapid Payment Entry" window should now be displayed. This is where users can enter and apply payments to client invoices and accounts.
22. ***Click the Close icon at the upper right of the "Rapid Payment Entry" window.***
23. ***Click the Client tab in the "Task Folders" window.*** Notice that the icons have now changed.
24. ***Click each of the remaining tabs in the "Task Folders" window to see all of the icons listed.***
25. ***Click back to the Main tab in the "Task Folders" window.***
26. ***Click File on the menu bar and then click Exit.***

This concludes Lesson 1.

LESSON 2: ENTERING A NEW CLIENT

In this lesson you will learn how to enter a new client into Tabs3. In doing so, you will explore the many options users have to set up a client with respect to billing and payments.

1. Open Windows. ***Double-click Tabs3 with Sample Data on the desktop,*** or ***click the Start button on the Windows desktop, point to Programs or All Programs, point to the Tabs3 & PracticeMaster group, point to Trial Software with Sample Data, and then click Tabs3 with Sample Data.*** Tabs3 will then open with sample data already present in the software.
2. The screen in Tabs3 Exhibit 2 should now be displayed. The Tabs3 window states that sample data is being used and that the system date in use with the sample data is set to 11/17/14. This date will not affect any other software on your computer. ***Click OK in the "Tabs3" window.***
3. The "Tip of the Day" window may now be displayed. ***Click Close in the "Tip of the Day" window.*** *Note:* If you do not want to see the Tip of the Day, ***select the* "Do not show tips at startup" *box before clicking close.***
4. ***Click the Client icon in the "Task Folders" window.*** The "Client Information" window should now be displayed (see Tabs3 Exhibit 3). Notice that the Address tab is selected.
5. Your cursor should be in the Client ID field. ***Click the New icon on the toolbar*** (see Tabs3 Exhibit 3). The New Client Record dialog box will open. Tabs3 automatically generates the next Client ID number, which is 851.00. ***Click OK*** in the New Client Record dialog box.

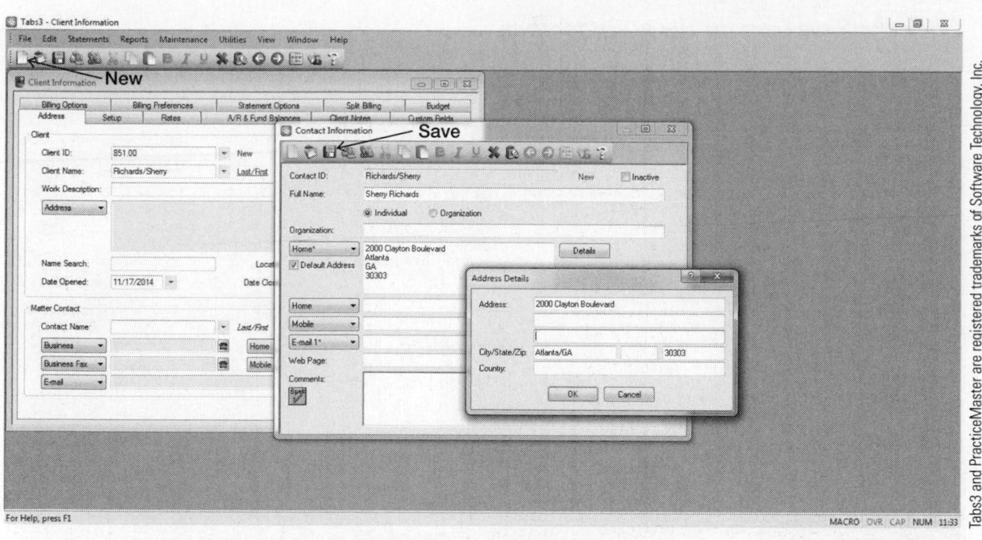

TABS3 EXHIBIT 3
Entering a new client in the Address tab of the "Client Information" window

6. Enter **Richards/Sherry** in the Client Name box in the Client Information window, then press the [TAB] key. The Contact Information dialog box will then open. **Enter the information in Table 4–1 in the Contact Information dialog box.** Note that Tabs3 requires that address information be entered in a particular order so after you enter the required information, the Address Details window may open. Enter the information as shown in Tabs3 Exhibit 3, then ***click OK.*** Note: You can press the [TAB] key to move forward through the fields, or press [SHIFT] + [TAB] to move backward through the fields. If a field is left blank in the following list, just skip that field. When you are done, ***click the Save icon*** (see Tabs3 Exhibit 3).

TABLE 4–1

FIELD	INFORMATION TO BE ENTERED
Organization	
Home	**2000 Clayton Boulevard**
	Atlanta
	GA
	30303
Home:	**888-555-3999**
Business:	**888-555-5429**
Mobile:	**888-555-5567**
Business Fax:	
E-mail 1	**srichards@aom.com**

In the "Client Information" window, enter the following information:

FIELD	INFORMATION TO BE ENTERED
Work Description:	**Richards v. EZ Pest Control**
Date Opened:	**11/17/2014**
Date Closed:	

Click the Save icon on the main toolbar.

TABS3 EXHIBIT 4
Entering a new client—setup options

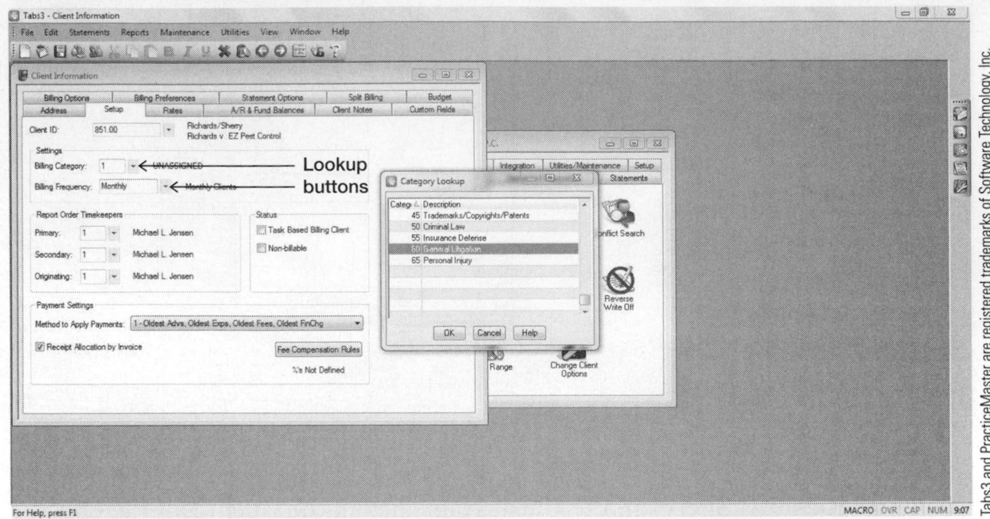

7. ***Click the Setup tab in the "Client Information" window, and then click the Lookup button.*** (It is the down arrow to the right of the Billing Category field.) The "Category Lookup" window should now be displayed (see Tabs3 Exhibit 4). ***Scroll down, click 60 General Litigation, and then click OK in the "Category Lookup" window.***
8. ***Click the Lookup button*** (down arrow) ***to the right of the Billing Frequency field.*** The "Billing Frequency Lookup" window should now be displayed. Notice that you can select Bill on Demand, Monthly, Quarterly, etc. ***Click Monthly in the "Billing Frequency Lookup" window and then click OK.***
9. ***Under Report Order Timekeepers, click the Lookup button*** (down arrow) ***next to Primary:.*** The "Timekeeper Lookup" window should now be displayed.
10. ***Double-click Kendra I. Michaels.*** The primary timekeeper is the attorney who is responsible for the case; in this example the primary timekeeper is an associate.
11. ***Under Report Order Timekeepers, click the Lookup button*** (down arrow) ***next to Secondary:.*** The "Timekeeper Lookup" window should again be displayed.
12. ***Double-click on Jennifer A. Noonan.*** The secondary timekeeper is the support staff person who is responsible for the case; in this example, the secondary timekeeper is a paralegal. (*Note:* The *originating timekeeper* is the person who brought the client to the firm. We will leave the originating timekeeper as Michael L. Jensen.)
13. ***Click the Rates tab in the "Client Information" window*** (see Tabs3 Exhibit 5). Notice that the screen has a number of options for customizing the billing rate for a client. In this example, the Billing Rate Code that will be used is "1 - Timekeeper Rate 1" (see Tabs3 Exhibit 5). This indicates that each timekeeper's Hourly Rate 1 will be used as the default billing rate.

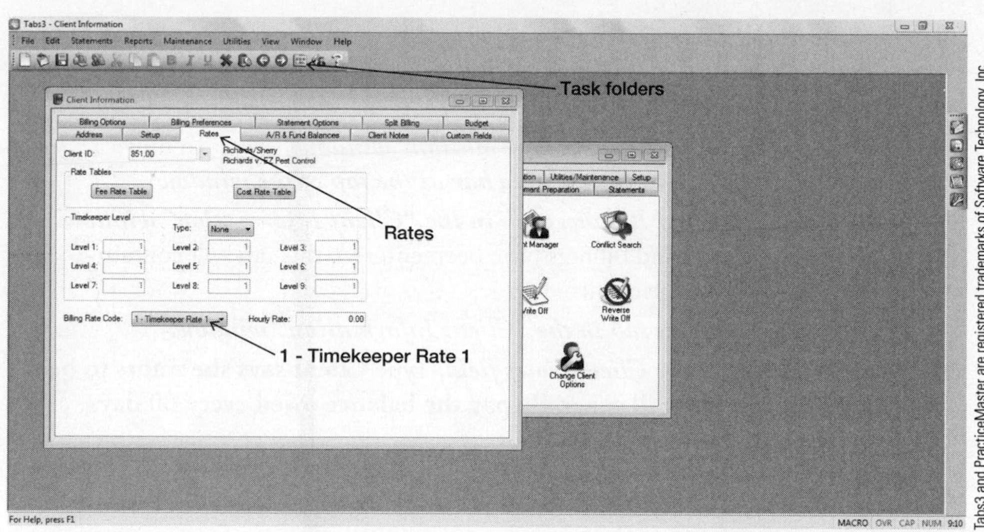

Tabs3 and PracticeMaster are registered trademarks of Software Technology, Inc.

TABS3 EXHIBIT 5
Entering a new client—rates options

14. You will now look at what the Timekeeper Rate 1 amount is for Kendra I. Michaels and Jennifer A. Noonan. ***Click the Task Folders icon on the toolbar*** (see Tabs3 Exhibit 5). The "Task Folders" window should now be displayed.
15. ***Click the Setup tab in the "Task Folders" window.***
16. ***Click Timekeeper on the Setup tab.***
17. ***In the "Miscellaneous" window, click the Lookup button next to Timekeeper:*** (see Tabs3 Exhibit 6).

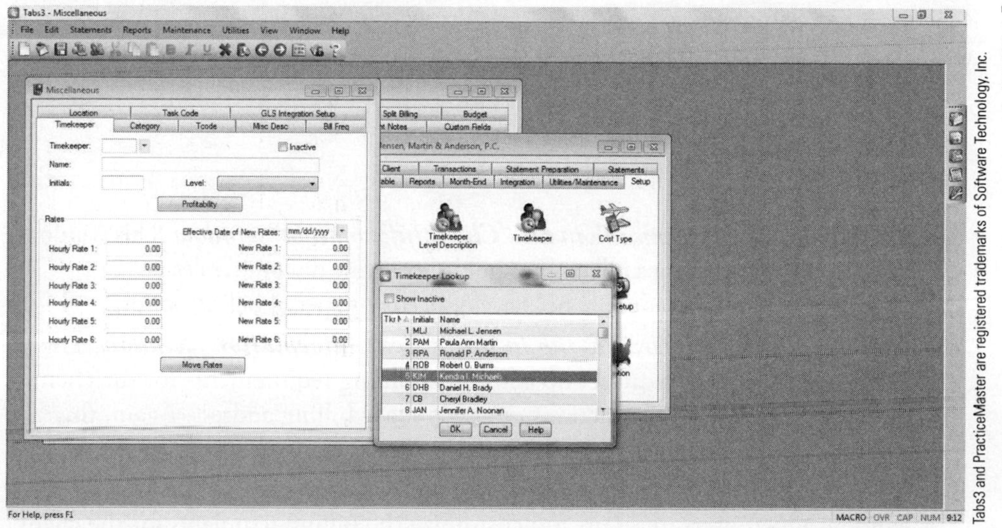

Tabs3 and PracticeMaster are registered trademarks of Software Technology, Inc.

TABS3 EXHIBIT 6
Hourly rates for Kendra I. Michaels

18. ***Double-click Kendra I. Michaels.*** Notice that the amount in her Hourly Rate 1: field is $150.00.
19. ***In the "Miscellaneous" window, click the Lookup button next to Timekeeper.***

20. ***Double-click Jennifer A. Noonan.*** Notice that the amount in her Hourly Rate 1: field as a paralegal is 100.00.
21. ***Click the Close icon at the upper right of the "Miscellaneous" window.***
22. ***Click anywhere in the "Client Information" window.*** (*Note:* To move a window, just ***click and drag the title bar at the top of the window***).
23. ***Click the A/R & Fund Balances tab in the "Client Information" window.*** Once fees, expenses, and billings have been entered, this tab will contain current balances for the client.
24. ***Click the Client Notes tab in the "Client Information" window.***
25. ***Put your cursor in the Client Notes field.*** Type **Client says she wants to be billed monthly, but will generally pay the balance owed every 60 days.** (see Tabs3 Exhibit 7).

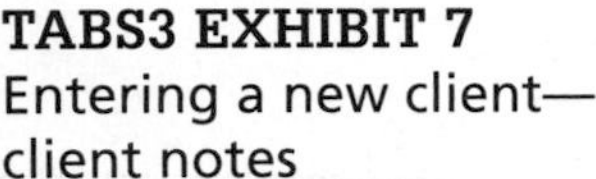

TABS3 EXHIBIT 7
Entering a new client—client notes

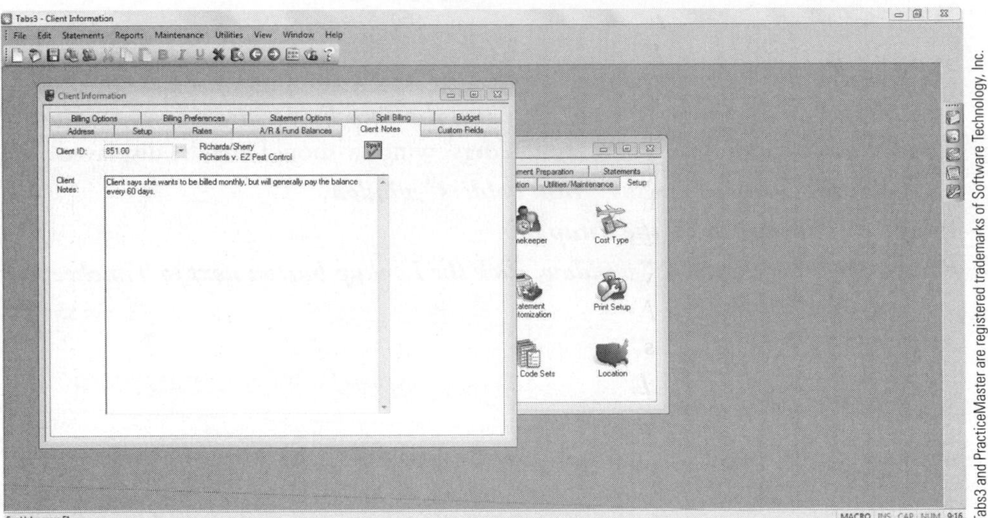

26. ***Click the Billing Options tab in the "Client Information" window.*** This window is where users can set up a billing threshold, a courtesy discount, sales tax, or a finance charge. This client does not have or need any special billing options.
27. ***Click the Billing Preferences tab in the "Client Information" window.*** This window is where users can set up additional billing requirements for the client, such as special billing instructions or a secondary billing address. Again, this client has no special needs.
28. ***Click the Statement Options tab in the "Client Information" window.*** This window allows users to set up and customize the billing templates for the client. The default options are fine for this client.
29. ***Click the Budget and Custom Fields tabs in the "Client Information" window*** to see what these tabs look like. You will not enter any information in these tabs.
30. ***Click the Save icon on the toolbar*** (it looks like a floppy disk).
31. ***Click the Close icon at the upper right of the "Client Information" window.***
32. To make sure the client has been entered into Tabs3, ***click the Main tab in the "Task Folders" window, and then click the Client icon.***

33. ***In the "Client Information" window, click the down arrow next to the Client ID: field.*** The Client Lookup screen should now be displayed.
34. ***Double-click on 851.00 richards/sherry.*** The information for *Sherry Richards* and *Richards v. EZ Pest Control* should now be displayed.
35. ***Click the Close icon at the upper right of the "Client Information" window.***
36. ***Click File on the menu bar and then click Exit.***

This concludes Lesson 2.

INTERMEDIATE LESSONS

LESSON 3: ENTERING FEE/TIME RECORDS

In this lesson, you will learn how to enter time records into Tabs3.

1. Open Windows. ***Double-click Tabs3 with Sample Data on the desktop,*** or ***click the Start button on the Windows desktop, point to Programs or All Programs, point to the Tabs3 & PracticeMaster group, point to Trial Software with Sample Data, and then click Tabs3 with Sample Data.*** Tabs3 will then open with sample data already entered into the program.
2. The screen in Tabs3 Exhibit 2 should now be displayed. The Tabs3 window states that sample data is being used and that the system date in use with the sample data is set to 11/17/2014. This date will not affect any other software on your computer. ***Click OK in the "Tabs3" window.***
3. The "Tip of the Day" window may now be displayed. ***Click Close in the "Tip of the Day" window.*** *Note:* If you do not want to see the Tip of the Day, ***select the* "Do not show tips at startup" *box before clicking close.***
4. ***Click the Fee icon in the "Task Folders" window.***
5. ***Click the Detail/Rapid icon on the toolbar in the "Fee Entry" window*** (*not* the main toolbar—see Tabs3 Exhibit 8). The Detail/Rapid icon toggles between a detail fee entry window that has several fields, and a rapid data entry window that has fewer fields. Make sure you select the Fee-Richards/Sherry window.
6. Your cursor should already be in the Client ID: field, with the last Client ID number, 851.00, listed. Press the **[TAB]** key to go to the Reference: field.
7. Press the **[TAB]** key to go to the Timekeeper: field.
8. ***Click the Lookup button next to the Timekeeper: field. Double-click on Jennifer A. Noonan.***

HANDS-ON EXERCISES

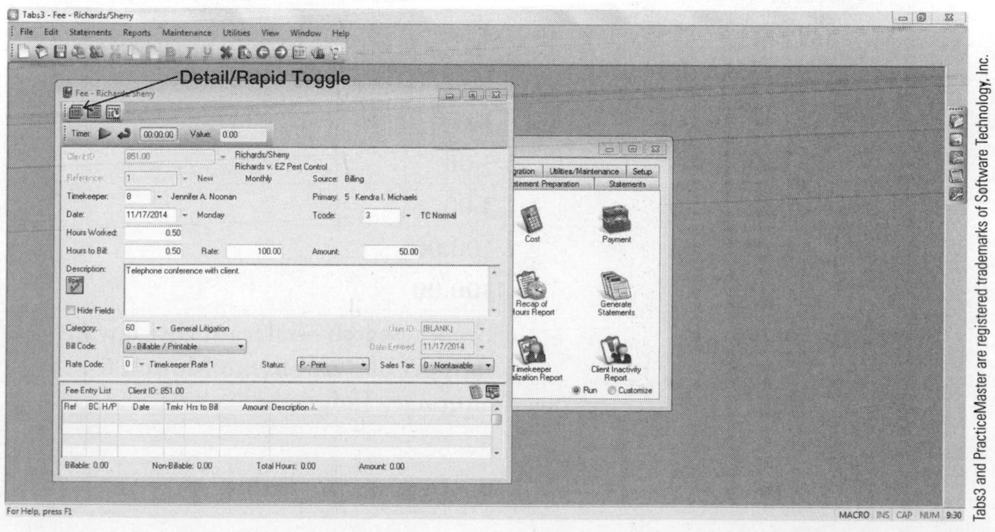

TABS3 EXHIBIT 8
Entering a fee/time record

9. At the Date: field, press the **[TAB]** key to accept the default date of 11/17/2014.
10. ***Click the Lookup button next to the Tcode: (transaction code) field.*** The "Tcode Lookup" window should now be displayed. ***Double-click on 3 TC Telephone conference with.***
11. In the Hours Worked: field, type **.50** and then press the **[TAB]** key.
12. The cursor should now be in the Amount: field with 50.00 highlighted. Press the **[TAB]** key.
13. The cursor should now be in the Description: field. At the end of **"Telephone conference with"** type **client.** and then press the **[TAB]** key.
14. ***Click the Save icon on the main toolbar.*** A blank fee/time record is now displayed.
15. Enter and save each of the following fee/time records Tables 4–2—4–5:

TABLE 4–2

FIELD	INFORMATION TO BE ENTERED
Client ID:	**851.00**
Reference:	
Timekeeper:	**5**
Date:	**11/17/2014**
Tcode:	**8**
Hours Worked:	**6.00**
Hours to Bill:	**6.00**
Rate:	**150.00**
Amount:	**900.00**
Description:	**Draft and revise Response to Motion for Summary Judgment.**
Category:	**60**
Bill Code:	**0 – Billable / Printable**

TABLE 4–3

FIELD	INFORMATION TO BE ENTERED
Client ID:	**851.00**
Reference:	
Timekeeper:	**8**
Date:	**11/17/2014**
Tcode:	**10**
Hours Worked:	**3.00**
Hours to Bill:	**3.00**
Rate:	**100.00**
Amount:	**300.00**
Description:	**Legal research—relevant case law in support of Response to Motion for Summary Judgment.**
Category:	**60**
Bill Code:	**0 – Billable / Printable**

TABLE 4–4	
FIELD	**INFORMATION TO BE ENTERED**
Client ID:	**851.00**
Reference:	
Timekeeper:	**2**
Date:	**11/18/2014**
Tcode:	**3**
Hours Worked:	**1.00**
Hours to Bill:	**1.00**
Rate:	**225.00**
Amount:	**225.00**
Description:	**Telephone conference with expert witness.**
Category:	**60**
Bill Code:	**0 – Billable / Printable**

TABLE 4–5	
FIELD	**INFORMATION TO BE ENTERED**
Client ID:	**851.00**
Reference:	
Timekeeper:	**8**
Date:	**11/18/2014**
Tcode:	**3**
Hours Worked:	**1.00**
Hours to Bill:	**1.00**
Rate:	**100.00**
Amount:	**100.00**
Description:	**Telephone conference with client regarding Response to Motion for Summary Judgment.**
Category:	**60**
Bill Code:	**0 – Billable / Printable**

16. ***Click the Save icon on the main toolbar.***
17. Notice in the bottom of the "Fee" window that you can see the prior fee/time records you have entered. ***Click the Close icon at the upper right of the "Fee" window.***
18. ***Click File on the menu bar and then click Exit.***

This concludes Lesson 3.

LESSON 4: ENTERING COST/EXPENSE RECORDS AND USING THE FEE TIMER FEATURE

In this lesson, you will learn how to enter cost/expense records into Tabs3 and how to use the Fee Timer feature.

1. Open Windows. ***Double-click Tabs3 with Sample Data on the desktop,*** or ***click the Start button on the Windows desktop, point to Programs or All Programs, point to Tabs3 & PracticeMaster group, point to Trial Software with Sample Data, and then click Tabs3 with Sample Data.*** Tabs3 will then open with sample data already present in the software.
2. The screen in Tabs3 Exhibit 2 should now be displayed. The Tabs3 window states that sample data is being used and that the system date in use with the sample data is set to 11/17/2014. This date will not affect any other software on your computer. ***Click OK in the "Tabs3" window.***
3. The "Tip of the Day" window may now be displayed. ***Click Close in the "Tip of the Day" window.*** *Note:* If you do not want to see the Tip of the Day, ***select the* "Do not show tips at startup" *box before clicking close.***
4. ***Click the Cost icon in the "Task Folders" window.***
5. The "Rapid Cost Entry" window should now be displayed (see Tabs3 Exhibit 9).

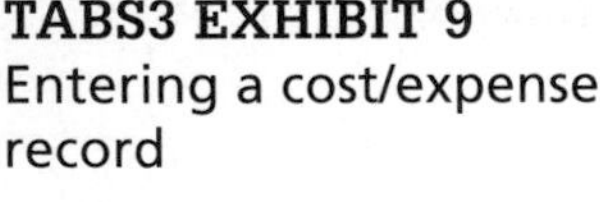

TABS3 EXHIBIT 9
Entering a cost/expense record

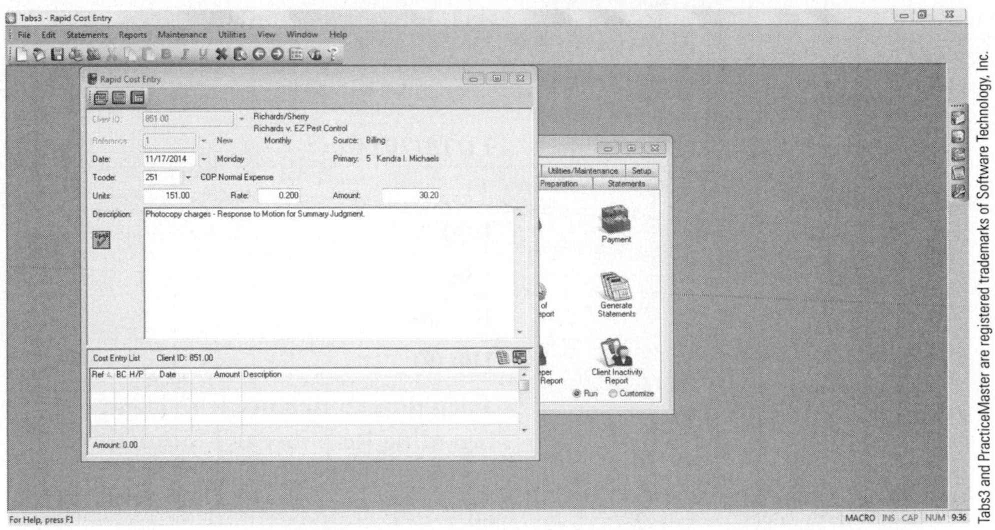

6. Your cursor should be in the Client ID: field with **851.00** filled in. Press the **[TAB]** key to accept the entry.
7. Press the **[TAB]** key again to go to the Date: field.
8. Press the **[TAB]** key to accept the default date of 11/17/2014.
9. ***Click the Lookup button next to the Tcode: field. Scroll down to and double-click on* "251 COP Photocopy charges."**
10. In the Units: field, type **151** (151 copies at the firm default rate of 20 cents a copy). Press the **[TAB]** key.
11. The calculation in the Amount: field is 30.20. Press the **[TAB]** key.

12. In the Description: field, enter **Photocopy charges—Response to Motion for Summary Judgment.**
13. ***Click the Save icon on the main toolbar.***
14. Enter and save each of the following cost/expense records (Tables 4–6—4–8):

TABLE 4–6	
FIELD	**INFORMATION TO BE ENTERED**
Client ID:	**851.00**
Reference:	
Date:	**11/17/2014**
Tcode:	**102**
Units:	**1.00**
Rate:	
Amount:	**20.00**
Description:	**Courier fee—info re: Response to Motion for Summary Judgment.**

TABLE 4–7	
FIELD	**INFORMATION TO BE ENTERED**
Client ID:	**851.00**
Reference:	
Date:	**11/17/2014**
Tcode:	**106**
Units:	**1.00**
Rate:	
Amount:	**50.00**
Description:	**Online legal research—Response to Motion for Summary Judgment.**

TABLE 4–8	
FIELD	**INFORMATION TO BE ENTERED**
Client ID:	**851.00**
Reference:	
Date:	**11/17/2014**
Tcode:	**107**
Units:	**1.00**
Rate:	
Amount:	**375.00**
Description:	**Transcription fees—defendant's deposition.**

15. ***Click the Save icon on the main toolbar.***

16. ***Click the Close icon*** (the red square with a white "X") ***at the upper right of the "Rapid Cost Entry" window.***
17. You will now learn how to use the Fee Timer feature in Tabs3. ***Click the Fee icon in the "Task Folder" window.*** The "Fee Entry" window should now be displayed.
18. ***Click the green triangle just to the right of the word* "Timer" *in the "Fee Entry" window.*** This is the Start Timer icon. Notice that the timer begins to count. The timer is now timing how long it takes you to complete a task such as making a phone call or drafting a letter.
19. Fill in the rest of the following information in the "Fee Entry" window (Table 4–9):

TABLE 4–9	
FIELD	**INFORMATION TO BE ENTERED**
Client ID:	**851.00**
Reference:	
Timekeeper:	**5**
Date:	**11/17/2014**
Tcode:	**3**
Hours Worked:	**0.00**
Hours to Bill:	**0.00**
Rate:	**150**
Amount:	**0.00**
Description:	**Telephone conference with counsel.**
Category:	**60**
Bill Code:	**0 – Billable / Printable**

20. ***Click the red square next to Timer: on the Fee Entry toolbar to stop the timer.*** (Assuming it took you less than a few minutes to enter the fee information, the value should be 15.00).
21. ***Click the Save icon on the main toolbar.***
22. A window should now be displayed asking you if you want to **"Add timer to Hours?"** ***Click Yes.***
23. ***At the window that displays* "Add to Amount?", *click Yes.*** Notice at the bottom of the screen that the entry has been added and a cost of $15.00 has been recorded.
24. ***Click the Close icon at the upper right of the "Fee" window.***
25. ***Click File on the menu bar and then click Exit.***

This concludes Lesson 4.

LESSON 5: GENERATING AND PRINTING DRAFT AND FINAL STATEMENTS

In this lesson, you will learn how to generate and print draft and final statements in Tabs3.

1. Open Windows. ***Double-click Tabs3 with Sample Data on the desktop,*** or ***click the Start button on the Windows desktop, point to Programs or All Programs, point to the Tabs3 & PracticeMaster group, point to Trial Software with Sample Data, and then click Tabs3 with Sample Data.*** Tabs3 will then open with sample data already present in the software.

2. The screen in Tabs3 Exhibit 2 should now be displayed. The Tabs3 window states that sample data is being used and that the system date in use with the sample data is set to 11/17/2014. This date will not affect any other software on your computer. ***Click OK in the "Tabs3" window.***
3. The "Tip of the Day" window may now be displayed. ***Click Close in the "Tip of the Day" window.*** *Note:* If you do not want to see the Tip of the Day, ***select the* "Do not show tips at startup" *box before clicking close.***
4. ***Click the Generate Statements icon in the "Task Folders" window.*** The Generate Statements window will open.
5. In the Client ID: field, type **851** and then press the **[TAB]** key. At the Thru: field, press the **[TAB]** key again.
6. ***Click the Options tab in the "Generate Statements" window.*** Notice that the default entry for Statement Type: is "Draft." Because you want to print a draft statement for Sherry Richards, leave it as is.
7. ***Click the Lookup button next to Statement Date: and select* November 20, 2014 *then click OK.*** (*Note:* Statements are usually done at the end of the month, but this client has asked for a special mid-month bill.)
8. ***Click OK in the "Generate Statements" window.***
9. ***In the "Generate Statements" window, click the Lookup button under Selected Printer: to select a printer, and make sure that Printer is selected under Output To.***
10. ***Click OK in the "Generate Statements" window.*** (*Note:* You can also save the statement as a PDF or text file, or print it to the DropBox for easy attachment to an email).
11. Normally, the timekeeper responsible for the case reviews and approves the draft statement. The next steps instruct you how to mark a statement as having been reviewed, how to run the statement as final, and how to update a statement.
12. ***Click the Close icon at the upper right of the "Generate Statements" window.***
13. ***Click Statements on the menu bar*** (see Tabs3 Exhibit 10).
14. ***Click Pre-Bill Tracking.*** The "Pre-Bill Tracking" window should now be displayed (see Tabs3 Exhibit 10).

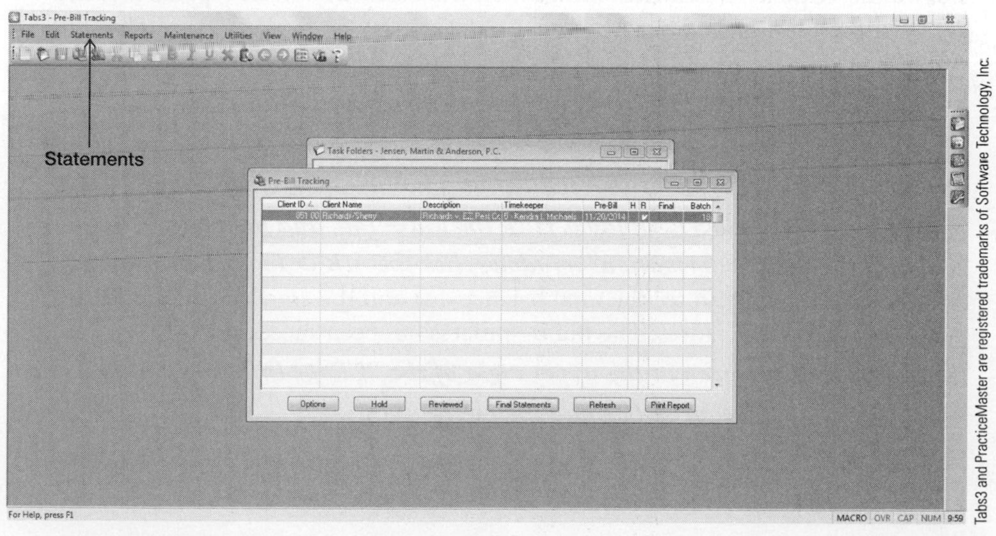

TABS3 EXHIBIT 10
Pre-billing tracking

15. ***Double-click* "851.00."** Notice that a check mark appears in the "R" column. This means that the statement has been reviewed and is ready for a final statement. If there is no check mark in the "R" column, then ***double-click in the box in the "R" column in the line for 851.00 Richards/Sherry.***
16. ***Click the Final Statements button at the bottom of the "Pre-Bill Tracking" window.***
17. The "Generate Statements" window is now displayed. ***Click the Options tab in the "Generate Statements" window.*** Change the statement date to **11/20/2014**.
18. ***Click OK in the "Generate Statements" window.***
19. ***In the "Generate Statements" window, click the Lookup button under Selected Printer: to select a printer. Then click Printer.***
20. ***Click OK in the "Generate Statements" window***. (*Note:* You can also save the statement as a PDF or text file, or print it to the DropBox for easy attachment to an email. Also, note that the DropBox is cleared each time the software is closed. Therefore, if you are waiting to print statements or other documents for class and are using the DropBox as a temporary holding area, the files must be printed or saved to another location before you close the software.)
21. ***Click the Close icon at the upper right of the "Generate Statements" window.***
22. ***Click the Close icon at the upper right of the "Pre-Bill Tracking" window.***
23. The final stage in the billing process in Tabs3 is to run the Update Statements program. In Tabs3, changes can be made to the final statements until the Update Statements program is run. The Update Statements program updates accounts receivable and billed productivity information, and moves work-in-process transactions into the archive.
24. ***Click the Statements tab (not the Statement Preparation tab) in the "Task Folders" window. Click Update Statements.***
25. A warning window will be displayed asking if you would like to back up your data first. ***Click No.*** *Note:* When using the full version of the software and running bills in an office setting, you will want to click Yes to create a backup.
26. In the "Update Statements" window, in the Client ID: field, type **851** in the first box, and press the **[TAB]** key. ***Click OK.***
27. When the "Update Statements Status" window indicates that **"Statements are now updated,"** ***click OK in the "Update Statements Status" window.***
28. ***Click the Close icon at the upper right of the "Update Statements" window.***
29. ***In the "Update Statements Verification List" window, click Cancel.***
30. ***In the "Task Folders" window, click the Main tab, and then click Client.***
31. ***In the "Client Information" window, click the A/R & Fund Balances tab.*** Notice that you can see the total balance due and the amount due for fees, expenses, and advances. The billing process has been successful.
32. ***Click the Close icon at the upper right of the "Client Information" window.***
33. ***Click File on the menu bar and then click Exit.***

This concludes Lesson 5.

LESSON 6: ENTERING A PAYMENT

In this lesson, you will learn how to enter a payment and apply it to a client's accounts receivable balance.

1. Open Windows. ***Double-click Tabs3 with Sample Data on the desktop,*** or ***click the Start button on the Windows desktop, point to Programs or All Programs, point to the Tabs3 & PracticeMaster Technology group, point to Trial Software with Sample Data, and then click Tabs3 with Sample Data.*** Tabs3 will then open with sample data already present in the software.
2. The screen in Tabs3 Exhibit 2 should now be displayed. The Tabs3 window states that sample data is being used and that the system date in use with the sample data is set to 11/17/2014. This date will not affect any other software on your computer. ***Click OK in the "Tabs3" window.***
3. The "Tip of the Day" window may now be displayed. ***Click Close in the "Tip of the Day" window.*** *Note:* If you do not want to see the Tip of the Day, ***select the* "Do not show tips at startup" *box before clicking close.***
4. ***Click the Payment in the "Task Folders" icon window.*** The "Rapid Payment Entry" window should now be displayed (see Tabs3 Exhibit 11).

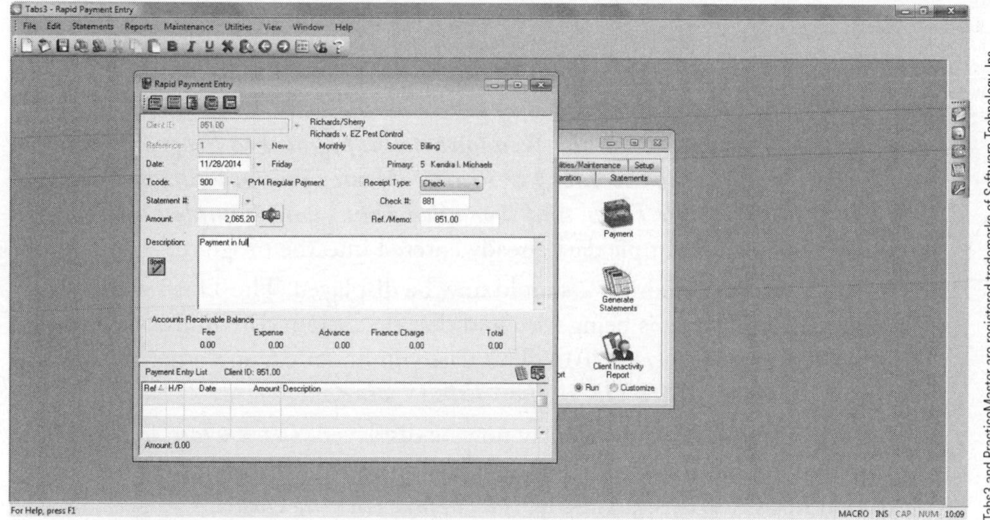

TABS3 EXHIBIT 11
Recording a payment

Tabs3 and PracticeMaster are registered trademarks of Software Technology, Inc.

5. The cursor should be in the Client ID: field with **851.00** already entered. Press the **[TAB]** key to go to the Reference: field.
6. Press the **[TAB]** key to go to the Date: field.
7. Enter **11/28/2014** in the Date: field.
8. Press the **[TAB]** key to go to the Tcode: field. A Tcode of **900** should be entered in the field.
9. Press the **[TAB]** key to go to the Statement: field.
10. Press the **[TAB]** key to go to the Amount: field. In the Amount: field, type **2065.20**
11. Press the **[TAB]** key to go to the Description: field. In the Description: field, type **Payment in full.**

12. Press the **[TAB]** key to go to the Receipt Type: field.
13. Press the **[TAB]** key to accept the default value of Check.
14. In the Check #: field, **enter 881** as the check number.
15. ***Click the Save icon on the main toolbar.***
16. ***Click the Close icon*** (the red square with a white "X") ***at the upper right of the "Rapid Payment Entry" window.***
17. ***Click the Close icon at the upper right of the "Payment Verification List" window.***
18. ***Within the Main tab of the "Task Folders" window, click Client.***
19. The number **851** should be displayed in the Client ID: field. ***Click the A/R & Fund Balances tab in the "Client Information" window.*** Notice that the Amount Due: is $0.00 and the Last Payment Amount: is $2,065.20.
20. ***Click the Close icon at the upper right of the "Client Information" window.***
21. ***Click File on the menu bar and then click Exit.***

This concludes Lesson 6.

ADVANCED LESSON

LESSON 7: PROCESSING AND PRINTING REPORTS

In this lesson, you will learn how to process and print several reports using Tabs3.

1. Open Windows. ***Double-click Tabs3 with Sample Data on the desktop,*** or ***click the Start button on the Windows desktop, point to Programs or All Programs, point to the Tabs3 & PracticeMaster group, point to Trial Software with Sample Data, and then click Tabs3 with Sample Data.*** Tabs3 will then open with sample data already entered into the program.
2. The screen in Tabs3 Exhibit 2 should now be displayed. The Tabs3 window states that sample data is being used and that the system date in use with the sample data is set to 11/17/2014. This date will not affect any other software on your computer. ***Click OK in the "Tabs3" window.***
3. The "Tip of the Day" window may now be displayed. ***Click Close in the "Tip of the Day" window.*** *Note:* If you do not want to see the Tip of the Day, ***select the* "Do not show tips at startup" *box before clicking close.***
4. ***Click the Reports tab in the "Task Folders" window.***
5. ***Click Productivity Reports.***
6. ***Click Category Productivity.***
7. The default values for the report are all fine, so ***click OK in the "Category Productivity Report" window.***
8. ***In the "Print Category Productivity Report" window, click the Lookup button under Selected Printer: to select a printer; then select Printer:.***
9. ***Click OK in the "Print Category Productivity Report" window.*** (*Note:* You can also save the statement as a PDF or text file, or print it to the DropBox for easy attachment to an email.)
10. The report breaks out hours worked, billed hours, and other information by category (case type) for the reporting period of August to November 2014.
11. ***Click the Close icon*** (the red square with a white "X") ***at the upper right of the "Category Productivity Report" window.***

12. ***Click Productivity Reports in the Reports tab of the "Task Folders" window.***
13. Print the Timekeeper Productivity report.
14. Print the Timekeeper Analysis Report.
15. Print the Client Analysis Report.
16. ***At the Reports tab of the "Task Folders" window, click Management Reports.***
17. Print the Client Realization Report.
18. Print the Timekeeper Realization Report.
19. Print the Timekeeper Profitability Report.
20. ***At the Reports tab of the "Task Folders" window, click A/R Reports.***
21. ***Print the Collections Report.***
22. ***Print the A/R by Invoice Report.***
23. ***Close all of the open windows.***
24. ***Click File on the menu bar and then click Exit.***

This concludes the Tabs3 Hands-On Exercises.

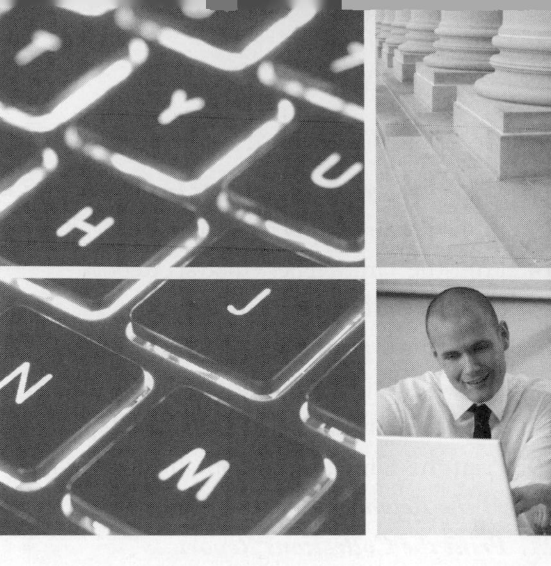

CHAPTER 5

Databases, Case Management, and Docket Control Software

CHAPTER OBJECTIVES

After completing this chapter, you should be able to do the following:

1. Define relevant terms, including database, field, record, table, and query.
2. Explain what a docket control system is.
3. Explain what case management is.
4. Describe the computerized docket cycle.
5. Describe how a computerized case management system can prevent cases from being forgotten or overlooked.
6. Discuss why docket control and case management are important to a legal organization from an ethics perspective.

INTRODUCTION

Why are case management and docket control important? This is why.

A client sued his former attorney (and the attorney's partners) for legal malpractice for failing to file a medical malpractice claim in a timely manner. Nearly two years earlier, the client had met with the Michigan attorney regarding a claim against a hospital for medical malpractice. After the initial meeting, the client made repeated telephone calls and sent letters to the attorney. However, the attorney never responded to the client's communications. Twenty months later, the attorney finally responded with the following letter.

> My sincere apologies for the delay in responding to your earlier communications; however, we have been making a thorough inquiry into the facts of your alleged complaints. We have not been able to find an expert to make the appropriate causal relationship to support our theories of possible malpractice. Accordingly, we are not going to be proceeding on your claim and will close our file.

Within two weeks, the client sought the advice of another attorney and filed a legal malpractice claim against the first attorney. A jury awarded the client $150,000 in damages against the attorney for allowing the statute of limitations on the medical malpractice claim to lapse. *Gore v. Rains & Block*, 189 Mich. App. 729, 473 N.W.2d 813 (1991).

WHAT IS A DATABASE?

All businesses, including legal organizations, must maintain and track information. Businesses routinely use database management systems to collect and analyze information. A **database management system (DBMS)** is an application software that stores, searches, sorts, and organizes data. A **database** is a collection of pieces of related data. For example, a database can be anything from a list of appointments, to a card catalog in a library, to an address book. These databases, whether or not they are on a computer, contain related information: appointments, listing of books, and addresses, respectively. They are organized by the date of the appointment; by the subject, title, and/or author of the book; and by the name of the person. A DBMS allows users to track and organize this kind of information using a computer.

database management system (DBMS)
Application software that manages a database by storing, searching, sorting, and organizing data.

database
A collection of related data items. Databases are created because the information contained in them must be accessed, organized, and used.

DBMSs are used in millions of businesses to manage and track vital information. They are powerful and flexible and can be used for thousands of different purposes. For example, a law firm might use a DBMS to track its clients' names and addresses; a manufacturer might use a DBMS to track its inventory of parts and finished products. A DBMS not only stores or holds information, but can also organize that information in a relevant manner. For example, the law firm might need an alphabetical list of its clients' names and addresses to be used for reference purposes. The manufacturer might use a DBMS to generate an inventory list of products by completion date. It is sometimes easy to think of databases simply as organized lists, catalogs, or compilations of information.

In the legal environment, organizations use databases to track many kinds of information. Legal organizations use DBMSs to track specific information about a particular case, such as the many thousands of documents in large cases. This process is called litigation support. Each document is entered into a litigation support system, which is another kind of DBMS.

A DBMS allows users to manipulate data as they wish. For example, if a legal organization wanted a list displaying only its clients' names and home phone numbers on a report (and no other information), a query report could be developed to display this information while still leaving the underlying data unchanged. Even though a vast amount of information is entered into a database, that information need not be displayed or printed out in every report. Information in a database is selected and used as needed.

Database software is flexible, powerful, and convenient to use and operate because it allows users to:

- Store and retrieve information easily
- Arrange and rearrange data over and over without affecting the data itself
- Update and change information
- Add or delete information
- Search for information
- Sort and organize information
- Print information in many different formats

Legal organizations and paralegals use databases for a wide variety of purposes in addition to litigation support. They may maintain an opposing attorney database, forms database, class action database, judges database, legal research database, conflict of interest database, factual database (for a specific case), expert witness database, library catalog database, active file database, inactive file database, licensed software database, marketing database, trial database, and many others.

Microsoft Access is a common and widely available database program, typically used for "small" databases that may contain several hundred or even several thousand records. However, for large databases that contain millions of records, Access would not be appropriate.

EXHIBIT 5–1
Client database structure

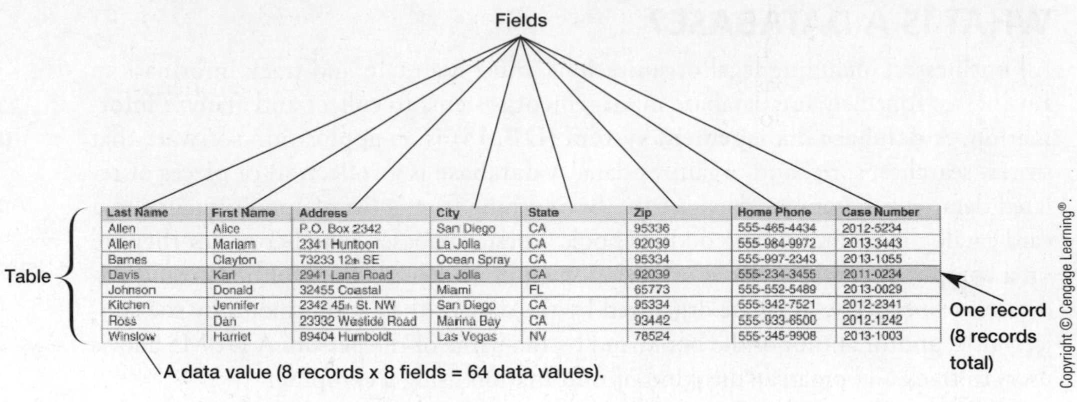

Last Name	First Name	Address	City	State	Zip	Home Phone	Case Number
Allen	Alice	P.O. Box 2342	San Diego	CA	95336	555-465-4434	2012-5234
Allen	Mariam	2341 Huntoon	La Jolla	CA	92039	555-984-9972	2013-3443
Barnes	Clayton	73233 12th SE	Ocean Spray	CA	95334	555-997-2343	2013-1055
Davis	Karl	2941 Lana Road	La Jolla	CA	92039	555-234-3455	2011-0234
Johnson	Donald	32455 Coastal	Miami	FL	65773	555-552-5489	2013-0029
Kitchen	Jennifer	2342 45th St. NW	San Diego	CA	95334	555-342-7521	2012-2341
Ross	Dan	23332 Westide Road	Marina Bay	CA	93442	555-933-8500	2012-1242
Winslow	Harriet	89404 Humboldt	Las Vegas	NV	78524	555-345-9908	2013-1003

DATABASE STRUCTURE

Databases are organized into tables, fields, records, and data values.

Table

table
A collection of related information stored in rows and columns.

A **table** is a collection of related information stored in rows and columns. A database is made up of tables that contain related information and the tools necessary to manipulate the data. The entirety of the data in Exhibit 5–1 is a table.

A table stores information about a particular topic. The table in Exhibit 5–1 stores contact information about a law office's clients. Many databases have more than one table. Having additional tables simplifies and speeds up searching or querying the database and in some ways makes the database easier to manipulate. Instead of having one file with everything dumped in it, the database creator has broken up the information into smaller subunits while still keeping the various information elements connected or related to each other.

Field

field
A column in a table that contains a category of information.

A **field** is a column in a table that contains a category of information. (It is common for DBMSs to refer to fields as columns.) For example, Exhibit 5–1 shows eight fields in the table:

1. Last Name
2. First Name
3. Address
4. City
5. State
6. Zip
7. Home Phone
8. Case Number

Fields will differ from database to database. For example, in a docket control database used to track and control a legal organization's deadlines and appointments, the fields might include date of event, event description, case name, and place of event. The client information database in Exhibit 5–1 uses other fields relevant to its purpose.

All databases must have fields where data are input and collected. Large databases commonly have hundreds of fields in which to enter information.

Record

record
A collection of fields that is treated as a unit; essentially, one row in a table.

A **record** is a collection of fields treated as a unit. It is essentially one row in a table. In Exhibit 5–1, each record has all the information for one client entry—that is, the complete set of field data for one entry. A total of eight records, or clients, are entered in Exhibit 5–1. Large databases may have millions of records. For example, litigation support databases in large class action cases involving thousands of plaintiffs can easily have millions of records.

Data Value

A **data value** is one item of information and is the smallest piece of information in a table. For example, in Exhibit 5–1, each individual piece of information is a data value (e.g., "Winslow," "Harriett," "Allen," "San Diego"). There are 64 data values in Exhibit 5–1. Multiply the number of records times the number of fields for each table to compute the total number of data values (e.g., 8 records x 8 fields = 64 data values).

data value
One item of information; the smallest piece of information in a table.

COMMON DATABASE TERMS

Most database programs use tools, sometimes called objects, that allow users to manipulate the data therein. Some common tools include forms, queries, and reports.

A **form** allows a user to view, enter, and edit data in a special (custom) format designed by the user.

form
Setup that allows a user to view, enter, and edit data in a custom format designed by the user.

A **query** extracts data from a table based on criteria specified by the user. A query allows you to search for and sort only the information you are looking for at that time. Queries create a specific view of data and allow you to answer specific questions. Once you create a query, you can save it and then use it whenever you need to. After a query has been created, you must run or execute the query to see the results.

query
Statement that extracts data from a table based on criteria designed by the user. A query allows a user to search for and sort only the information the user is looking for at that time.

A **report** prints data from a table or query in a format designed and specified by the user. Whereas forms are designed to be used on the screen, reports are designed to be printed. A report consists of information that is pulled from tables or queries, as well as information that is stored with the report design, such as labels, headings, and graphics.

report
Function that extracts and prints data from a table or query as designed by the user. Whereas forms are designed to be used on the screen, reports are designed to be printed.

CALENDARING, DOCKET CONTROL, AND CASE MANAGEMENT

The practice of law is filled with an array of appointments, deadlines, hearings, and many other commitments for every case that is handled. Considering that a single legal professional can have a caseload of between 20 and 100 cases at any one time, just staying organized and on top of all of the things that must be done is a big job. It is extremely important that these dates, deadlines, and commitments be accurately tracked and that the legal work get done accurately and on time—for ethical reasons, customer service reasons, general business/profitability reasons, and malpractice avoidance reasons. All legal organizations must track deadlines, whether they use manual systems or computers or both. Most legal organizations now use some type of computerized method to track deadlines.

This chapter discusses specific law-office database programs that assist legal professionals with computerized calendaring, docket control, and case management. Though these terms each have a fairly specific meaning, they are often (somewhat confusingly) used interchangeably.

Calendaring is a generic term used to describe the recording of appointments and other schedule items. Many personal information managers (PIMs), such as Microsoft Outlook, fall into this category. These programs can be used by any business to manage appointments and scheduling. In addition, most include a host of other general productivity tools as well.

calendaring
A generic term used to describe the function of recording appointments for any type of business; includes personal information management.

docket control
A legal-specific term that refers to entering, organizing, tracking, and controlling all the appointments, deadlines, and due dates for a legal organization.

case management
A legal term that usually encompasses functions such as docket control, deadlines, things to do, contact information by case, case notes, document assembly, document tracking by case, integrated billing, and email.

Docket control is a legal-specific term that refers to entering, organizing, and controlling the appointments and deadlines for a legal organization. Docket control is sometimes referred to as a tickler or a tickler system because it "tickles" the memory for upcoming events.

Case management (sometimes called practice management) is also a legal-specific term, but it always means more than just tracking appointments and schedules. The breadth of features in current case management programs seem to grow every day. Some of the features found in case management programs include docket control (scheduling/appointments), things to do, a contact information database (name, address, email, phone, etc.) organized by case (parties, co-counsel, opposing counsel, judges, etc.), case notes, document assembly, integrated billing, email, and more. In case management programs, all data are tied to cases. This is very helpful for legal organizations that view and organize most of their data according to what case a piece of information is tied to. This is a different approach than general calendaring/PIM applications.

As the legal software market has matured, more legal software manufacturers have entered it. In addition, nearly all of the current legal products available in this market are significantly more sophisticated and targeted at meeting the needs of attorneys, paralegals, and legal organizations. The products today do far more than just docket control. The end result is that currently, legal organizations really only use two kinds of products to handle calendaring and docket control functions:

1. Generic calendaring/personal information management programs such as Microsoft Outlook. These are found in many legal organizations because they come as a part of the Microsoft Office suite program (bundled together with word-processing, spreadsheet, and database programs) and because they typically have an email component.
2. Full case management programs that have a wide array of features for handling client cases in addition to calendaring and docket control. The advantage of case management programs to legal organizations is that information is organized by case/matter.

Most PIMs and case management programs can now synchronize with handheld computers (PDAs); this enhances the ability of attorneys and paralegals to access and control their appointments, scheduling, and things-to-do lists. Also, nearly all legal organizations operate in a computer network environment. Most PIMs and case management programs now have network-based group scheduling capabilities so that users can share information related to scheduling/case management. Throughout the rest of this chapter, we use the terms docket control or case management to describe the process of tracking appointments, deadlines, and schedules in legal organizations. This chapter presents general information about docket control in legal organizations and gives an overview of the features found in many legal case management programs.

INTRODUCTION TO DOCKET CONTROL/CASE MANAGEMENT

Docket control/case management works differently depending on the specific legal organization, the type(s) of cases handled, and the organization's or users' philosophies on how the function should be managed. In many legal organizations, each attorney and paralegal enters docket control information in a central office-wide system, but they still manage their own dockets. In others, secretaries enter and manage all dockets. Some of the events that are regularly tracked include appointments, deadlines and reminders, and hearing and court dates.

Appointments

During the course of a case or legal matter, a legal professional will have many appointments: meetings with clients and co-counsel, witness interviews, interoffice meetings, and so forth. Keeping appointments is very important. Law offices that constantly reschedule appointments with clients may find their clients going to other attorneys who provide better service.

Deadlines and Reminders

The practice of law encounters deadlines at practically every stage of a legal matter. One of the most important types of deadlines is a statute of limitations. A **statute of limitations** is a law that sets a limit on the length of time a party has to file a suit. For instance, some states impose a five-year statute of limitations on lawsuits alleging a breach of a written contract. That is, if a lawsuit is brought or filed more than five years after a contract is breached or broken, the lawsuit is barred by the statute, and the court will dismiss the action. The purpose of a statute of limitations is to force parties to bring lawsuits in a timely fashion. Otherwise a defendant might be prejudiced by loss of evidence, the inability to find witnesses, or the inability of witnesses to recall relevant information. If an attorney allows a statute of limitations to expire without filing a case, he or she will likely be liable for legal malpractice.

statute of limitations
A law that sets a limit on the length of time a party has to file a suit. If a case is filed after the statute of limitations has run (expired), the claim is barred and is dismissed as a matter of law.

Many other deadlines are set after a case has been filed. In some courts, the judge and the attorneys on both sides meet and schedule the deadlines for the case. These deadlines may look something like those in Exhibit 5–2. These deadlines must be tracked and adhered to. An attorney who does not adhere to the deadlines may cause the case to be dismissed or may be sanctioned. Courts are usually reluctant to extend deadlines once they have been set.

Because attorneys and paralegals are usually busy working on more than one case at a time, a legal organization must have a system for tracking upcoming deadlines. This is done not only by calendaring the deadline itself, but also by creating reminder notices, or ticklers, in the calendar so that a deadline does not catch a person by surprise. For example, Exhibit 5–2 shows a January 30 deadline to file a motion to dismiss; the attorney or paralegal may want to be reminded 30, 15, and 5 days before this deadline. Therefore, reminder notices would be issued on January 1, January 15, and January 25, in addition to the deadline itself being recorded on January 30. It is common for an attorney or paralegal to request more than one reminder for each deadline.

EXHIBIT 5–2
A typical case schedule

Deadline Item	Deadline Date
Motion to Dismiss must be filed by	Jan. 30
Response to Motion to Dismiss must be filed by	Mar. 1
Discovery (interrogatories, requests for production, and depositions) must be completed by	July 1
Summary Judgment motion must be filed by	July 15
Response to Summary Judgment motion must be filed by	Aug. 1
Pretrial Order must be filed by	Sept. 1
Settlement conferences must be completed by	Sept. 15
Pretrial motions must be completed and decided by	Oct. 15
Trial to start no later than	Dec. 1

Some deadlines are automatically set by the prevailing rules of procedure. Rules of procedure are court rules that specify the procedures that must be followed when litigating cases. For instance, in some courts the rules of procedure hold that when a final decision in a case is rendered, all parties have 30 days after that to file an appeal.

April 15, the date on which federal income tax returns are due, is an example of an automatic or procedural deadline that must be tracked by a law office that practice tax law. Thus, tracking of this automatic or procedural deadline should be built into the office's docket system, so that appropriate reminders are issued, returns are not filed late, and penalties are avoided.

Hearings and Court Dates

Hearings and court dates are formal proceedings before a court. It is extremely important that these dates be carefully tracked; courts have little tolerance for attorneys who fail to show up for court. In some instances, the attorney can be fined or disciplined for missing a court date.

A large case that is being litigated in court may require hundreds of entries into the docket system. Exhibit 5–3 lists some common docket entries, including both substantive items and entries related to law-office management.

EXHIBIT 5–3
Common docket control entries

Accounts receivable review due dates
Answer and other pleading due dates
Appeal filing dates
Appellate briefs and arguments
Billing due dates
Board of directors meeting dates
Commercial law action dates
Copyright, trademark, and patent renewal dates
Corporate securities filing due dates
Corporation filing due dates
Discovery due dates
Employee benefit annual filing deadlines
Expiration dates for statutes of limitations
Insurance coverage renewal dates
Judgment renewal dates
Lease renewal dates
License renewal dates
Notary certificate expiration date
Performance evaluations of staff
Probate and estate tax due dates
Probate inventory and appraisal completion dates
Property tax return due dates
Stockholder meeting dates
Tax return due dates
Trial court appearance dates
Trial court brief due dates
Unemployment tax report due dates
Will and trust review dates
Withholding tax report due dates

MANUAL DOCKET CONTROL

Attorneys have used manual docket control methods for centuries. The most popular manual docket systems use a simple calendar.

Calendar

Small law offices sometimes use a simple, one-page-a-day calendaring system. Many calendars provide space or a section dedicated to recording "things to do" or reminders, in addition to providing space to write in or schedule appointments.

Before the advent of computerized systems, deadlines and reminders (i.e., ticklers) would be entered into the calendar as cases were opened. Notices from courts, attorneys, and so forth that were received in the mail would also be entered on the calendar. In addition to the due date or appointment date, any reminders also had to be manually entered into the calendar. This process could be time-consuming. For instance, for a deadline with two reminders, the information would have to be manually entered a total of three times.

Although manual calendaring systems may work for small offices that make few entries, they do not work well for large offices that have many attorneys and many appointments and deadlines. They simply do not have enough room to enter all the appointments, unless each attorney has his or her own calendar—and this is dangerous because it does not reveal conflicts.

Many calendaring systems are decentralized. In a decentralized system, each attorney or timekeeper has her or his own calendar and staff to record appointments, things to do, reminders, and so forth. This can be problematic for the administrators of the firm; because they do not have a centralized system at their disposal, they never know where an attorney or other person should be without tracking down that person's secretary. This problem is compounded when a staff meeting for the entire office must be scheduled. Instead of going to a centralized calendar, checking what dates are available, and scheduling the meeting, the organizer must contact each attorney, compile a list of available dates for each attorney, find dates and times that are acceptable to all parties, and then notify each party of the date and time of the meeting.

Manual calendaring systems also lack the ability to track information by case. For example, if a client asked to see all the upcoming events for her case, a staff person would have to go through the calendar and manually put together a list. Depending on the case, there could be many entries. Again, this is a time-consuming and inefficient process.

Yet another problem with a manual calendaring system is that successive calendars must be purchased every year (one for 2012, one for 2013, one for 2014, etc.). It is also difficult to schedule dates far in the future—five years down the road for a statute of limitations entry, for instance—because you need the appropriate calendar.

TYPES OF COMPUTERIZED DOCKET CONTROL SYSTEMS

A legal organization can use a variety of computer programs to schedule and track events. The organization can choose a generic calendaring/personal information manager program or a case management program. Most of these programs can be purchased for stand-alone computers or for local area networks. Networked systems, whether they are generic or legal-specific, have the principal advantage of allowing individual users throughout an organization to see and have access to the calendars of other users in the office.

EXHIBIT 5–4
Calendaring/PIM program: Microsoft Outlook

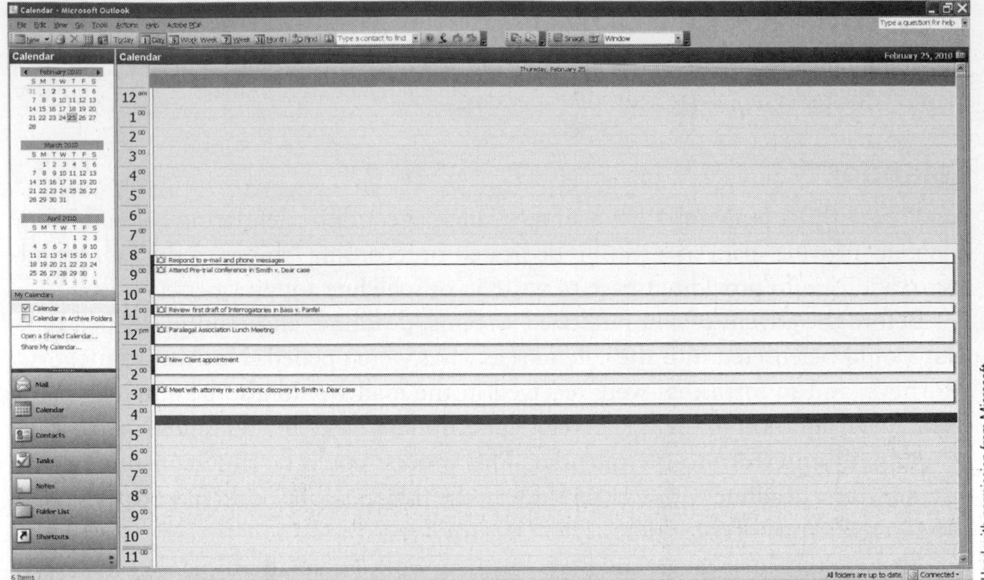

Generic Calendaring and Personal Information Manager Programs

Generic calendaring programs computerize the functions of a paper desk calendar. Because they are generic and can be used by any type of business, they lack many features that are particularly helpful to a legal organization. These types of programs are usually very inexpensive and typically manage only calendaring, things to do, contacts, and email functions.

personal information manager (PIM)
System that consolidates a number of different tasks into one computer program. Most PIMs handle or provide functions for calendaring, things to do, a contact database that tracks names and addresses of people, note-taking, email, and other tasks.

A generic **personal information manager (PIM)** program consolidates a number of different tasks into one computer program. Most PIMs include calendaring, things to do, a contact database that tracks names and addresses of people, note-taking, email, and other tasks. Exhibit 5–4 shows Microsoft Outlook, which is a PIM that often comes bundled with Microsoft's Office suite of programs.

The generic calendaring and scheduling software market has matured, and most new programs now are PIMs. PIMs are very popular and convenient to use, as they allow you to organize a number of related tasks into one easy-to-use interface. Generic PIMs, such as the one shown in Exhibit 5–4, are not specifically suited to the needs of legal professionals, but still have useful features; some legal organizations use these programs. For example, for consistency purposes a corporate law department might use a product like Microsoft Outlook, which can be implemented throughout the corporation, instead of a legal-specific program that only the legal department can use. However, as good as some PIMs are, they fundamentally lack the crucial ability to track information by case, and also lack the power, functionalities, and resources of true case management programs.

OVERVIEW OF COMPUTERIZED LEGAL CASE MANAGEMENT AND DOCKET CONTROL

The case management (sometimes called practice management) niche of the legal software market is mature and competitive, and the available programs are rich with features. Some case/practice management programs are designed for specific legal specialties, such as real estate, tax, collections, criminal defense, and so forth. Most case management programs, however, are designed for a broad spectrum of

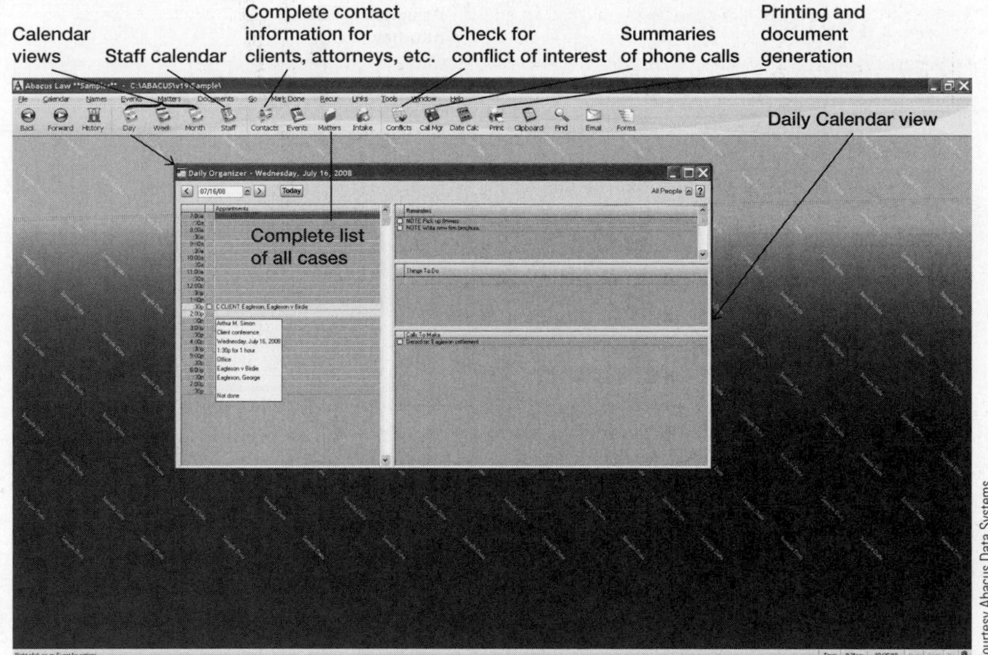

EXHIBIT 5–5
Daily calendar and menu bar/toolbar in a case management program

Courtesy Abacus Data Systems.

legal organizations, no matter what type of law they practice. Currently, the case management market is so competitive that no one product enjoys clear dominance. Further, many practicing paralegals do not use a case management program. In lieu of a case management program, many law offices use a PIM, such as Microsoft Outlook. Although this section covers the basics of case management software, the manner in which any particular package handles these tasks and functions will depend on the package.

Main Menu: Fundamental Tasks of Case Management Programs

Exhibit 5–5 shows the daily calendar and menu for AbacusLaw, a popular case management program. Exhibit 5–5 is a good example of the functions found in most case management programs, which include providing calendars in a variety of different views; capturing complete contact information for clients and others; tracking and managing events (e.g., appointments, reminders, things to do, and calls to make); recording information about matters and case files, including links to documents and case notes; checking conflicts; managing phone calls; and calculating dates, among others. Some of these tasks and activities are discussed in more detail here, but these are the general functions that most case management programs provide.

Contacts/Name Tracking

Before events such as appointments and reminders can be calendared for a case or matter in a case management system, you must first input or create basic contact information for the client. This is a good example of how a generic database function (client list) has been modified for the specific needs of legal professionals. Exhibit 5–6 shows a contact/name entry for a new client, Sherry Richards. You can enter contact information including address, phone, and email, among other items. In addition, the type or class of name entry is entered from a list; in this instance the contact is a client. Judges, vendors, colleagues, attorneys, and anyone the legal professional comes in contact with can be entered as contacts/names. Notice in Exhibit 5–6 that

EXHIBIT 5–6
Entering a new client

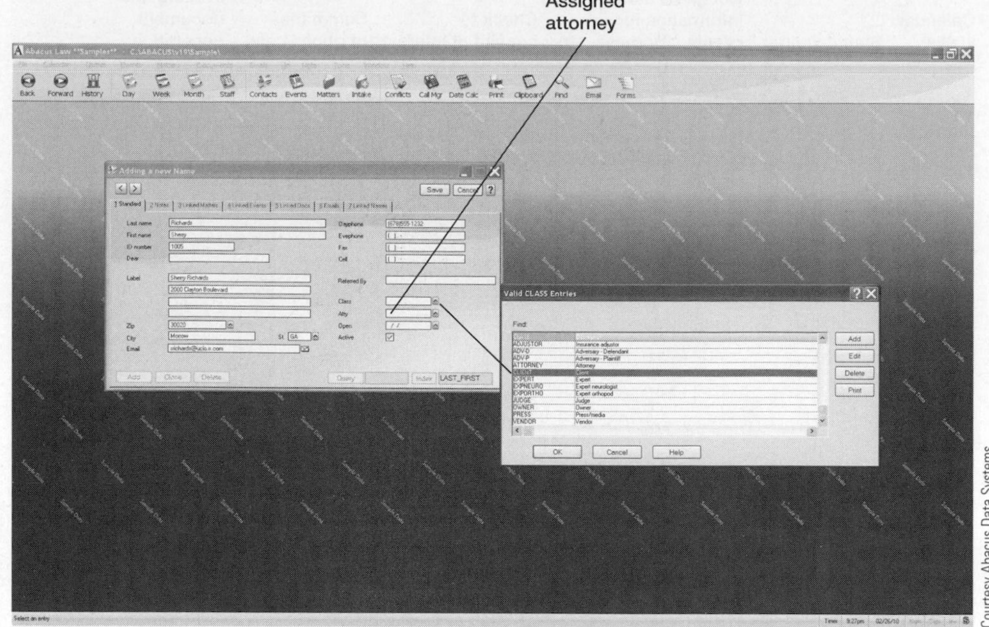

the client can be assigned to "linked matters," such as cases or legal matters; "linked events," such as calendar entries; "linked documents," such as legal documents; and "linked names," such as opposing counsel or other people associated with the client or the client's case. The ability to link contacts/names with cases and other case-related information is what separates case management systems from PIMs. Also, notice in Exhibit 5–6 that there is a space for initials to indicate which attorney has been assigned to the client. This allows the case management system to track and produce reports regarding which attorneys are assigned to which cases.

Matters/Cases

Exhibit 5–7 shows that a new matter has been created, *Richards v. EZ Pest Control*, and that the matter has been linked to Sherry Richards's contact/name record.

EXHIBIT 5–7
Creating a case/matter

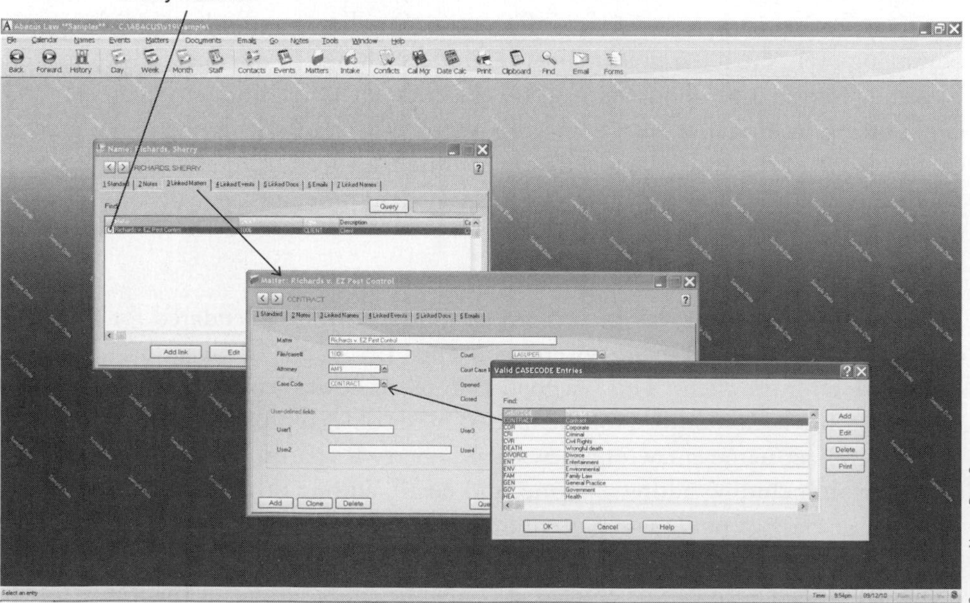

In addition, the new matter shows the attorney assigned to the case (here AMS), the case code (here a contract case), and the court, among other things. If Sherry Richards brought additional legal matters to your firm, you would simply create the new matters in the "Adding a new Matter" window and link that case to her contact/name record. You can also find the linked names for the case, all events associated with the case, and all linked documents that are related to the case. These capabilities allow you to have a tremendous amount of information at your fingertips.

Events

Once client contact and case matter information has been entered in the case management system, events can be entered and associated with the client or case. In Exhibit 5–8, an appointment has been entered and associated with Sherry Richards and with the matter *Richards v. EZ Pest Control.* The event window in Exhibit 5–8 allows the user to select who the event is for (Arthur M. Simon) and what kind of event it is (an appointment). Notice also in Exhibit 5–8 that valid "what" entries include appointments, client conferences, and many other standard event types. Events can also include reminders, things to be done, calls to be made, trials, hearings, and many other legal-related items.

In Exhibit 5–8, there are two numerals next to "Reminders": a "**1**" and a "**3**." This means that one and three days before the actual event, a notice will appear in the Reminders section of the daily calendar that this event is coming up. In Exhibit 5–8 there is also a priority field, which allows you to assign various priorities, such as "high" or "low," to events. There is also a field for Status; in this instance, an "**N**" in Exhibit 5–8 stands for "not done." This allows you to track events that did not get completed.

Users can also create recurring entries in most case management systems. A **recurring entry** is a calendar entry that happens repeatedly, typically daily, weekly, monthly, or annually. For instance, if an office has a staff meeting every Monday morning, the entry could be entered once as a weekly recurring appointment. Notice the Recur menu item on the menu bar in Exhibit 5–8. This is where a recurring entry would be designated in the case management program shown in Exhibit 5–8.

recurring entry
A calendar entry that must be done regularly or often.

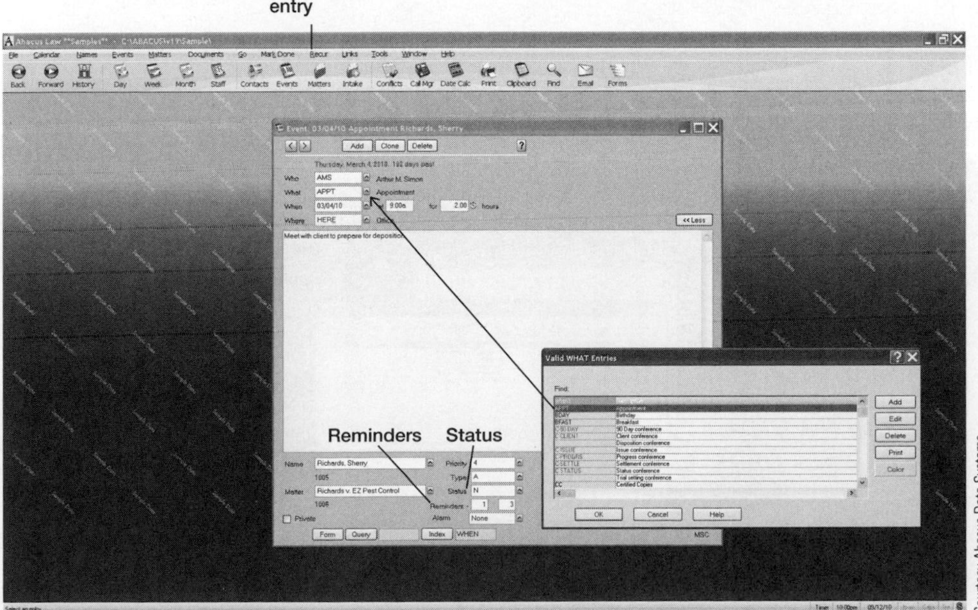

Courtesy Abacus Data Systems.

EXHIBIT 5–8
Creating a new event

EXHIBIT 5–9
List of linked events by matter/case

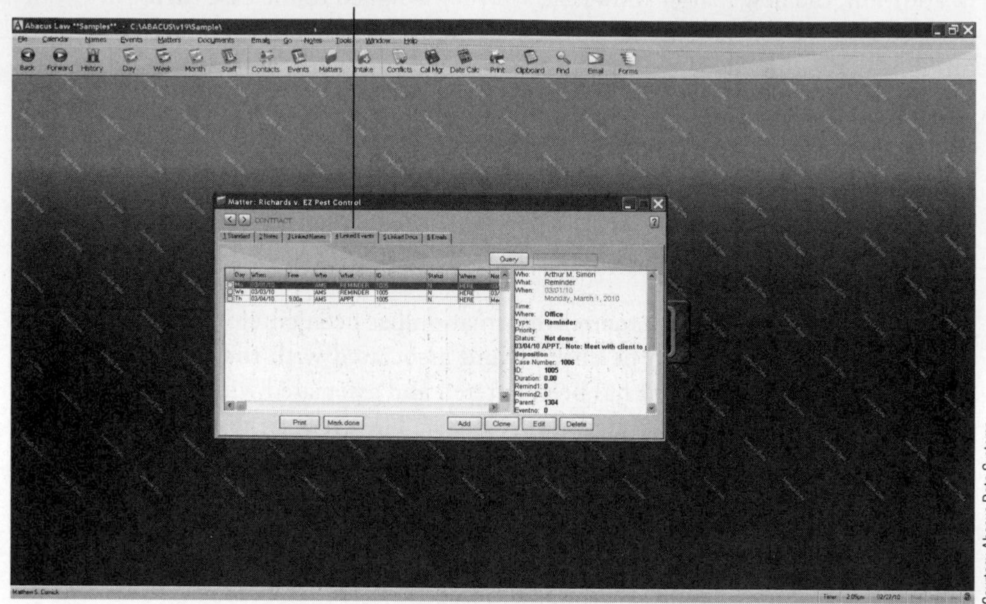

Exhibit 5–9 shows the Matter screen for *Richards v. EZ Pest Control*, except that now the Linked Events tab is selected. Notice that you get a quick snapshot of exactly what deadlines are coming up in the case. They include the two reminders and the appointment mentioned earlier. By linking events to the matter and the name/contact, you have a powerful tool with which to manage a case.

rule-based entry
A method of entering events in a case management system so that entering one event automatically triggers creation of a list of subsequent calendaring events, based on a rule that was programmed into the application.

Most case management programs allow a user to create rule-based entries. In a **rule-based entry**, one event automatically triggers the addition of a list of subsequent calendaring events based on a rule that was programmed into the application. For example, in Exhibit 5–10, a rule entitled "New case" has been created. This rule says that on the day it is executed, staff will meet with the client; that one day after the initial meeting, a conflict check entry/event will automatically be generated; and that an entry/event will be entered for a client file to be opened. Seven days after the initial meeting, the case management program will automatically create an event for a confirmation letter to the client,

EXHIBIT 5–10
Entering rule-based events

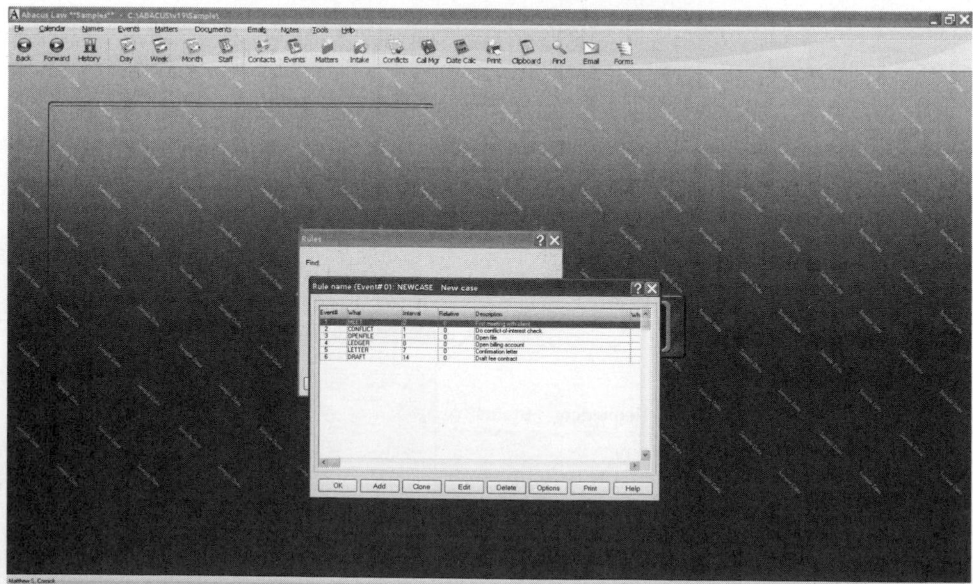

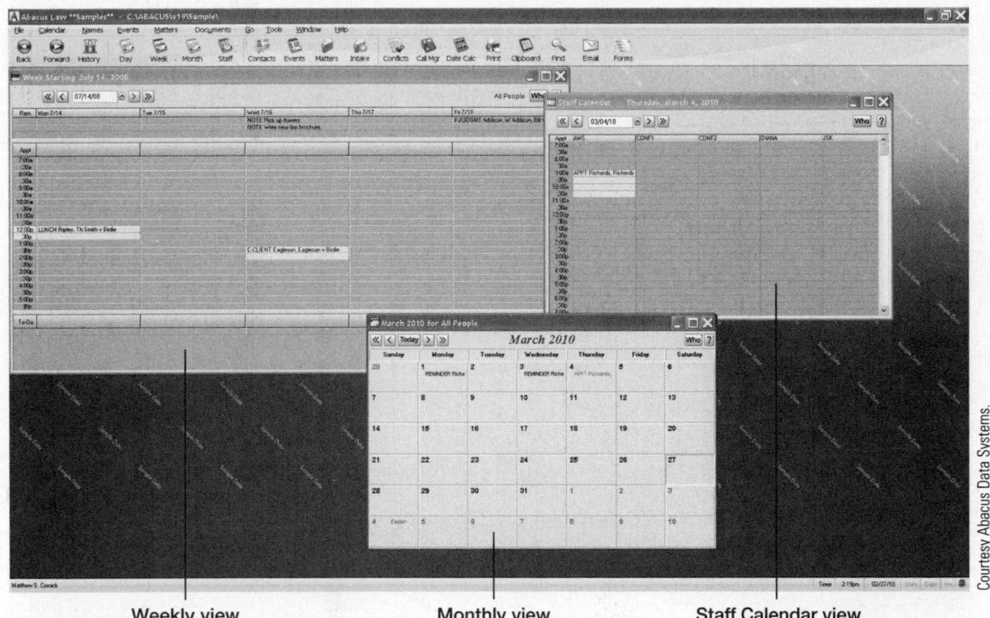

EXHIBIT 5–11
Calendar views

Courtesy Abacus Data Systems.

and fourteen days after the initial conference an entry/event will be created to draft a fee contract. All of this will take place automatically after the New case rule is executed.

Most case management programs allow you to program your own rules (as shown in Exhibit 5–10). Additionally, most case management programs have court-based rules that users can purchase. Using court-based rules that automatically generate many events is a large timesaver when a legal organization has many cases to handle.

Calendar Views

All case management programs come with a number of calendar views with which users can see their calendars. A daily calendar view is shown in Exhibit 5–4, but there are several additional views as well. Exhibit 5–11 shows a weekly view, a monthly view, and a Staff Calendar view. The Staff Calendar view shows the calendars for one day for different staff side by side.

Date Calculator

Some case management systems have a date calculator that automatically calculates the number of days between dates. For instance, suppose you receive a set of interrogatories that must be answered within 30 days. If you receive the interrogatories on January 2, 2012, when are the responses due? The "Date Calculator" window in Exhibit 5–12 shows that the responses are due on February 1, 2012. Date calculators are handy features, particularly when you need to calculate precise deadlines.

Notes/Case Diary

Most case management systems provide a place in which to maintain a case diary or notes for the file. This gives legal professionals a centralized area to place their notes, record summaries of phone calls, and share other information. The notes section allows you to create a running diary of what is happening in a case as it progresses. This is particularly helpful when multiple people are working on a case. If anyone wants an update of the case, all that person has to do is read the notes.

EXHIBIT 5–12
Date calculator

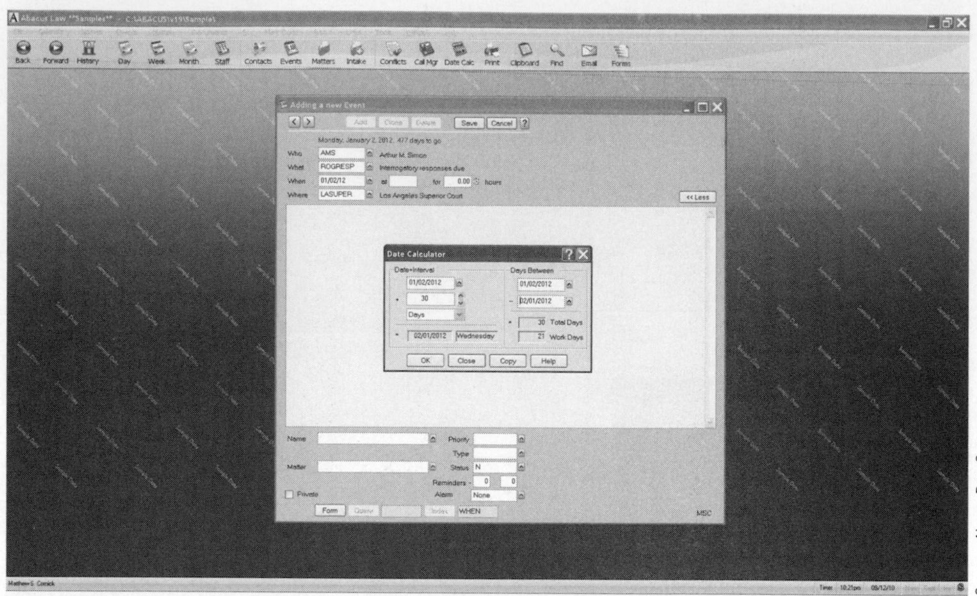

Document Assembly and Generation

Case management programs can store extensive information about a case, including items such as parties, attorneys, case-related information, and case numbers. Most case management programs can assemble this information into a merged document (see Exhibits 5–13A and 5–13B). A legal professional can therefore automatically generate standard letters, forms, pleadings, and reports either from the case management program itself or in combination with a word processor such as Word or WordPerfect. Also, in some programs, when you create a document using document generation, the case management system automatically notes this, including the date, in the case diary/notes. The ability to automatically generate standard letters and forms from a case management program is a tremendous time saver.

Synchronizing with PIMs/PDAs

Most case management systems will synchronize calendars with PIMs such as Outlook and devices such as PDAs. Thus, if a corporate law department wanted to use a

EXHIBIT 5–13A
Information setup for document generation in a case management program

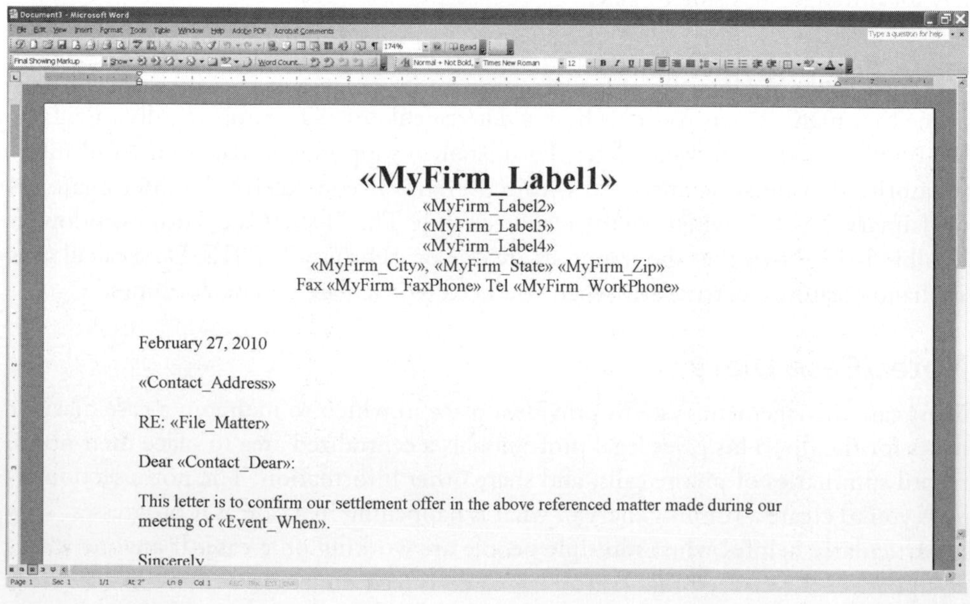

«MyFirm_Label1»
«MyFirm_Label2»
«MyFirm_Label3»
«MyFirm_Label4»
«MyFirm_City», «MyFirm_State» «MyFirm_Zip»
Fax «MyFirm_FaxPhone» Tel «MyFirm_WorkPhone»

February 27, 2010

«Contact_Address»

RE: «File_Matter»

Dear «Contact_Dear»:

This letter is to confirm our settlement offer in the above referenced matter made during our meeting of «Event_When».

Sincerely

EXHIBIT 5–13B
Case management program document assembly/generation

CASE MANAGEMENT DATABASE

Client Name:	First National Bank
Contact Person–First Name:	Sam
Contact Person–Last Name:	Johnson
Client Address:	P.O. Box 1000
Client City:	Philadelphia
Client State:	Pennsylvania
Client Zip:	98934
Client Phone:	555/233-9983
Case Number:	2012-9353
Court:	Philadelphia Superior Court—District 13, Philadelphia, Pennsylvania
Debtor Name:	Philip Jones
Debtor Address:	3242 Wilson Ave. SW
Debtor City:	Philadelphia
Debtor State:	Pennsylvania
Debtor Zip:	98984
Amount Owed to Client:	$225,234
Type of Debt:	Mortgage
Type of Asset:	House at 3242 Wilson Ave SW, Philadelphia, Pennsylvania

DOCUMENT TEMPLATE 1—Complaint

In the {Court}
{Client Name}
Plaintiff
Case No. {Case Number}
{Debtor Name}
{Debtor Address}
{Debtor City} {Debtor State} {Debtor Zip}
Defendant.
COMPLAINT
Comes now plaintiff, {Client Name}, and states that defendant, {Debtor Name}, is indebted to plaintiff in the amount of {Amount Owed to Client} on a {Type of Debt} regarding a {Type of Asset}. Attached to this complaint as Appendix "A" is a fully executed copy of the mortgage above referenced.

Merge function

MERGED DOCUMENT—Complaint

In the Philadelphia Superior Court – District 13, Philadelphia, Pennsylvania
First National Bank
Plaintiff
Case No. 2012-9353
Philip Jones
3242 Wilson Ave. SW
Philadelphia, Pennsylvania 98984
Defendant.
COMPLAINT
Comes now plaintiff, First National Bank, and states that the defendant, Philip Jones, is indebted to the plaintiff in the amount of $225,234 on a mortgage regarding a house at 3242 Wilson Ave SW, Philadelphia, Pennsylvania. Attached to this complaint as Appendix "A" is a fully executed copy of the mortgage above referenced.

case management system, but the rest of the corporation was using Outlook, the two could be set up to share and/or synchronize information so that the entries in the case management program would not have to be entered manually in Outlook.

Conflict of Interest Searches

Most case management programs allow users to do conflict of interest searches. Because the database tracks clients, parties, counsel, and an enormous amount of other case-related information, the conflict search can be very comprehensive. In Exhibit 5–14, the user executed a conflict of interest search on "Richards." The case management program returned with two possible hits, a matter/case (*Richards v. EZ Pest Control*), and a contact name-client (*Sherry Richards*).

Email Interface

Most case management programs include an email interface that allows users to send emails in conjunction with the program and to link emails with cases. This is

EXHIBIT 5–14
Conflict of interest check

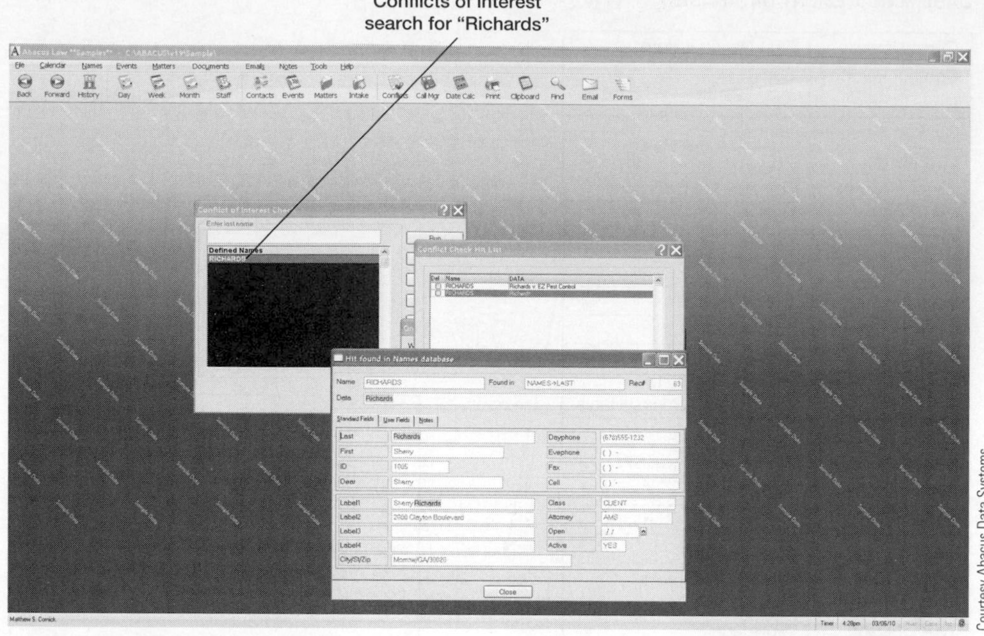

extremely important given the heavy use of emails in communicating with clients and in handling client matters.

Document Tracking

Most case management programs can now associate documents with cases. A link can be made between a document or file and a matter or contact in a case management program. This allows legal professionals to index and manage case documents directly from the case management program. Exhibit 5–15 shows that a user has linked the electronic "COMPLAINT" word-processing file with the matter and name of the client. Thus, when you pull up the matter window, you can click the Linked Documents tab and see a list of all of the electronic documents in that case.

EXHIBIT 5–15
Linking documents to matters, cases, and/or contracts

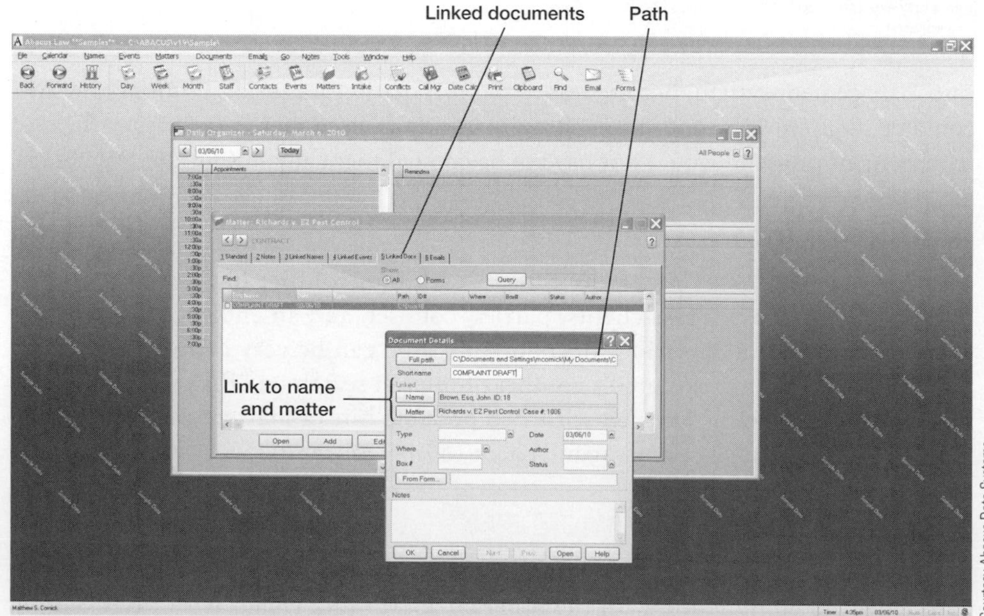

Time and Billing/Accounting Interface

Many case management programs share information with timekeeping and billing programs, and in some instances with accounting programs as well. Thus, when you create a case event (such as an appointment), you can automatically generate a time record for the event without having to retype all the information. Some case management programs have separate time and billing modules available for purchase, whereas others can interface with many popular legal time and billing programs.

Reporting

Most computerized systems allow users to generate a vast number of standard reports covering every aspect of case management. Most systems also come with a report writer feature that enables users to write customized reports and queries.

IMPLEMENTING CASE MANAGEMENT SYSTEMS—WHY THEY FAIL

Much has been written in the legal press regarding the fact that while case management programs have never been better, many legal organizations have been slow to implement them. Even when they have been purchased and implemented, it appears that many legal professionals are not using them. A commonly mentioned reason why legal professionals fail to use case management systems is a simple lack of training. This problem has two facets. First, because a case management system can be expensive, a firm may stop short of purchasing the training tools needed to train staff to use the new system. Second, overly busy legal professionals may not attend the training that is offered.

THE DOCKET CYCLE

The docket cycle refers to how information is entered into a case management program. There are three primary ways in which information can flow into and out of such a program: centralized, decentralized, and combined cycles.

Centralized Docket Control Cycle

In a centralized docket control cycle, one person typically is responsible for inputting all docket entries into the case management program. This is usually a secretary, but in some cases may be a paralegal. In this type of system, step one is for a user to manually complete a docket slip. The second step is for the secretary/keyer to enter the event into the docket control program. The third step is for reports to be generated, and the last step is for entries to be marked "done."

Decentralized Docket Control Cycle

In a decentralized docket control cycle, each user enters docket information directly into the computer, controlling his or her own docket. In this type of system, the first step is for the user to make a docket entry in the case management program. Next, the user views or prints reports as necessary; third, the user marks entries "done." The advantage of this system is that users have ultimate control over their own dockets. The disadvantage is that each user, instead of a clerk or secretary, is doing data entry.

Combined Docket Control Cycle

In a combined docket control cycle, a user can decide whether to enter information into the program or have a clerk/secretary do it. Some docket control programs allow multiple people to enter data into a user's schedule. For example, some networked docket programs allow both an attorney and her secretary to enter information into the attorney's schedule. Both have full access to the attorney's calendar.

In this type of system, the first step is for either the user or a third party to make a docket entry in the case management program. Second, either the user or the third party views or prints reports as necessary; third, either the user or the third party marks entries "done." In some ways, this is the best of both worlds: the user still has control over his calendar, but can delegate the data entry to someone else.

ETHICAL AND MALPRACTICE CONSIDERATIONS

The ramifications of missing deadlines and otherwise failing to track the progress of cases can be severe. In fact, two types of negative outcomes can result from case neglect: an ethics board proceeding against the attorney and/or a legal malpractice claim filed against the attorney or firm. An attorney who neglects a case can be disciplined by a state ethics board. Discipline in an ethics case may include reprimand, suspension, or even disbarment. In a legal malpractice case, the attorney involved is sued for damages for providing substandard legal work. These types of cases are not remote or obscure. Thousands of legal ethics and malpractice proceedings are filed throughout the country every year alleging case neglect.

Ethical Considerations

A nationwide statistical study of attorney disciplinary opinions found that the two primary reasons that clients file disciplinary proceedings against attorneys, and that courts discipline attorneys, are (1) attorneys failing to communicate with the clients and (2) attorneys neglecting or not diligently pursuing client cases. This confirms what studies have shown since the early 1980s. Both of these problems are easily preventable when attorneys and paralegals use good docket control systems and effective time management.

It is common for state rules of professional conduct to provide guidance on these issues. They typically state that attorneys should be competent in the area in which they practice and that they should be reasonably prepared to represent the client. These state rules also state that the attorney must act with reasonable diligence and promptness when representing a client. Finally, an attorney must keep the client reasonably informed about what is going on with representation of the client.

Competence and Adequate Preparation An attorney must be competent to represent the client. That is, the attorney must have a reasonable knowledge of the area of law in which the client needs representation, or, if the attorney does not know the area of law well, must put in the preparation time to become familiar enough with the case area to represent the client adequately.

The amount of preparation considered "adequate" depends on the type of legal matter the client presents. Major litigation, for example, will require far more preparation time than drafting a simple will. The point is that attorneys should not undertake to represent a client if for some reason they cannot do it with the required skill and/or cannot dedicate an appropriate amount of preparation time.

Diligence Attorneys must act with a reasonable degree of diligence in pursuing the client's case. Attorneys should carry through to conclusion all legal matters undertaken for a client unless the relationship is properly and clearly terminated. If doubt exists about whether an attorney-client relationship exists, the attorney should clarify the situation in writing.

Communication with Clients An attorney also must communicate regularly with a client. Legal professionals need to keep in reasonable contact with the client, both to explain general strategy and to keep the client reasonably informed regarding the status of the client's legal matter. "Reasonableness" always depends on the facts and circumstances of the particular case.

Clients become extremely frustrated when they pay for legal services and then the attorney refuses to take their calls, answer their letters, or otherwise communicate with them. Often, paralegals are more accessible to clients than attorneys are, so they can play an important role in communicating with clients.

Legal Malpractice Considerations

In addition to the ethical breaches involved in neglect of a client's legal matter, the client may have a legal malpractice claim against the attorney for negligence. The general theory in a **legal malpractice** claim is that the attorney breached an ordinary standard of care applicable to a reasonable attorney under those circumstances. In a legal malpractice case, both the plaintiff and the defendant must rely on attorneys who are expert witnesses to testify that the defendant either did or did not act as a reasonable attorney would have in the same situation.

legal malpractice
An attorney's breach of an ordinary standard of care that a reasonable attorney would have adhered to under the same circumstances.

A computerized case management system that is used correctly and effectively will greatly decrease an attorney's or law office's chances of being the subject of ethical complaints or malpractice suits. In fact, some malpractice insurers will refuse to write malpractice insurance for a law office that does not have an effective docket control system. However, ultimately the responsibility lies with the individuals working at the law office. Even the most technologically advanced software cannot prevent an attorney or paralegal from forgetting to enter a deadline in the case management system or putting in a wrong date when entering a docketing deadline.

SUMMARY

The practice of law involves many appointments, deadlines, hearings, and other commitments that must be carefully tracked. Docketing means entering, organizing, and controlling appointments and deadlines for a legal organization. Database programs, including case or practice management computer systems, offer legal organizations a wide variety of features for doing these tasks, including docket control, contact information, case notes, document assembly, document tracking, integrated billing, email, and conflict checking. Personal information managers such as Outlook are contact- and calendar-based programs, as opposed to case management systems, which are matter- or case-based systems.

Case management programs can link and create relationships among contact information, matters/cases, events, and documents and combine them into one integrated system. Other features include various calendar views, date calculators, notes/case diaries, synchronization with PIMs and PDAs, time and billing interfaces, and reporting capabilities.

The docket control cycle of tracking legal/case events differs depending on whether a legal organization has a centralized, decentralized, or combined procedure for entering docket entries into its docket system.

Manual docket systems are prone to mistakes, are slow and cumbersome to administer, are generally inflexible, and cannot provide the amount or quality of information that a computerized case management system can.

A legal organization can use either generic calendaring programs or true case management software for docket control. Computerized case management systems can perform functions such as maintaining perpetual calendars, making recurring entries, alerting the user to possible scheduling conflicts, providing for centralized or decentralized case management, generating past due reports, performing document assembly, and tracking case information. Most case management programs can also generate many types of reports, such as daily calendar reports for an individual or a firm, per-case docket reports, and free time reports.

Attorneys and law firms that fail to maintain an accurate docketing system may be subject to malpractice lawsuits and sanctions such as disbarment or suspension from the practice of law.

KEY TERMS

calendaring
case management
data value
database
database management system (DBMS)
docket control
field
form
legal malpractice
personal information manager (PIM)
query
record
recurring entry
report
rule-based entry
statute of limitations
table

INTERNET SITES

Internet sites for this chapter include:

ORGANIZATION	PRODUCT/SERVICE	WORLD WIDE WEB ADDRESS
Abacus Data Systems	AbacusLaw (legal PIM/case management)	www.abacuslaw.com
ADC Legal Systems	Practice management system	www.perfectpractice.com
Amicus Attorney	Amicus Attorney legal case management	www.amicusattorney.com
Bridgeway Software	Law Quest (case management for corporate law departments)	www.bridge-way.com
Chesapeake Interlink, Ltd.	Practice management system specializing in personal injury practices	www.needleslaw.com
Client Profiles	Practice management system	www.clientprofiles.com
Compulaw	Compulaw (case management)	www.compulaw.com
Corporate Legal Solutions, Inc.	Practice management system for corporate legal departments	www.caseandpoint.com
Corprasoft, Inc.	Practice management system for corporate legal departments	www.corprasoft.com
Lawex Corp.	Legal case management	www.trialworks.com
Legal Files Software	Legal Files (legal PIM/case management)	www.legalfiles.com
LegalEdge Software	Case management for criminal defense law offices, attorneys, prosecutors, and general practitioners	www.legaledge.com
LexisNexis	Time Matters (legal PIM/case management)	www.timematters.com
Orion Law Management Systems	Practice management system	www.orionlaw.com
Perfect Law Software	Practice management system	www.perfectlaw.com
RainMaker Software	Practice management system	www.rainmakerlegal.com
Software Technology	Tabs3 and PracticeMaster (legal PIM/case management)	www.tabs3.com
Solutions in Software, Inc.	Practice management system	www.casemanagerpro.com
Thomson Elite	Elite practice management system and Pro Law practice management system	www.elite.com

TEST YOUR KNOWLEDGE

1. True or False: An application program that stores and searches data is called a database.
2. A ________ is a collection of related information stored in rows and columns.
3. True or False: Calendaring and docket control are purely secretarial functions with little relationship to the practice of law.
4. ________ is a legal-specific term that always means more than just tracking appointments and schedules.
5. What is the difference between PIMs and case management programs?
6. Case management systems allow users to link or create relationships among which types of information? (name three)
7. What is a rule-based case management event entry?
8. What benefits do document assembly features offer to case management users?
9. True or False: Case management systems are universally accepted in most law offices and have a high success rate when they are implemented.
10. True or False: There is virtually no connection or relationship among ethical claims, legal malpractice, case management, and docket control.

ON THE WEB EXERCISES

1. Research and write a paper on computerized case management and docket control systems. Use one of the websites in the "Internet Sites" section of this chapter. Obtain demonstration copies of the programs if you can. Compare and contrast at least two of the different products that are available. Which one were you most impressed with, and why?
2. Visit several bar association websites (including that of the Georgia Bar Association, at www.gabar.org) and find three articles on case management, docket control, or a related subject. Write a short paper summarizing the articles you found.
3. Visit the American Bar Association Technology Resource Center at www.abanet.org, and review any materials it provides on case management software. Write a short paper summarizing the article(s) you found.
4. Using a law library, state bar journal, legal research database, or the Internet, write a paper that summarizes a minimum of three attorney discipline cases regarding failure to complete work on time. Be sure to include an analysis of the case, the court's or tribunal's findings, the ethical rules that were at issue, the rules that were violated, and what discipline was imposed.

QUESTIONS AND EXERCISES

1. A legal organization is considering moving to a computerized case management system even though its manual system has worked adequately. Give some reasons why a computerized case management system is a good idea for this organization.
2. A medium-sized law firm handles most of its cases by appointing an attorney and a paralegal for every case. How can a computerized case management system help in this situation?
3. Several of your firm's clients have complained because they never get notice of what is going on with their cases, what deadlines have been set, or even when to call after a major event has taken place in their cases. How could a case management system help?
4. Research your state bar's disciplinary proceedings regarding attorneys who have been disciplined for client neglect. Write a short paper on one of the cases.

5. Contact three legal organizations in your area, find out how they control or manage their dockets (manual or computer method), explain their procedures in detail, and then compare and contrast the three.
6. Set up and maintain a docket of class assignments for a semester using a PIM such as Outlook or a word processor. For quizzes and assignments, give yourself one three-day reminder before the assignment or quiz is due, in addition to recording the quiz or assignment itself. For exams or lengthy papers, give yourself three reminders: a ten-day reminder, a five-day reminder, and a three-day reminder, in addition to docketing the exam date or paper deadline itself.

ETHICS QUESTION

A law firm has just installed the latest and greatest case management program. The attorneys and paralegals diligently attended all of the training classes required to master the new software program. All client and case matter information was uploaded into the new program. However, when inputting data, one of the paralegals entered the wrong date for a court hearing on an opposing party's motion for summary judgment. The opposing party won its motion by default because the law firm failed to appear on behalf of its client. What ethical issues, if any, are raised by this scenario?

HANDS-ON EXERCISES

FEATURED SOFTWARE
AbacusLaw

ABACUSLAW CASE MANAGEMENT PROGRAM

I. INTRODUCTION

AbacusLaw is an integrated practice management database that manages all calendar, case, and client information. It integrates document management, document assembly, conflict of interest checks, reporting, form generation, and time, billing, and accounting. The AbacusLaw demonstration version is a full, working version of the program (with a few limitations). **The program demonstration version times out 120 days after installation. This means that the program will only work for 120 days from when you install it. So, it is highly recommended that you do not install the program on your computer until you are actually ready to go through the Hands-On Exercises and learn the program.** When you are ready to install the program, follow the instructions below.

II. USING THE ABACUSLAW HANDS-ON EXERCISES

The AbacusLaw Hands-On Exercises are easy to use and contain step-by-step instructions. Each lesson builds on the previous exercise so please complete the Hands-On Exercises in order. AbacusLaw comes with sample data so you should be able to utilize many features of the program.

III. INSTALLATION INSTRUCTIONS

1. Log in to your CengageBrain.com account.
2. Under "My Courses & Materials," find the Premium Website for *Using Computers in the Law Office*, 7th edition.
3. ***Click "Open"*** to go to the Premium Website.
4. Locate "Book Level Resources" in the left navigation menu.
5. ***Click on the link for "AbacusLaw," then click the link next to "To access the demo"***
6. Your screen may show a View File Downloads asking you if you want to run or save this file, ***Click Run.***

7. Your screen should now look like AbacusLaw Installation Exhibit 1. You do not need to enter a Customer ID or Firm Name. ***Click the first option, "At your Server, install the Abacus Programs".***

ABACUSLAW INSTALLATION EXHIBIT 1

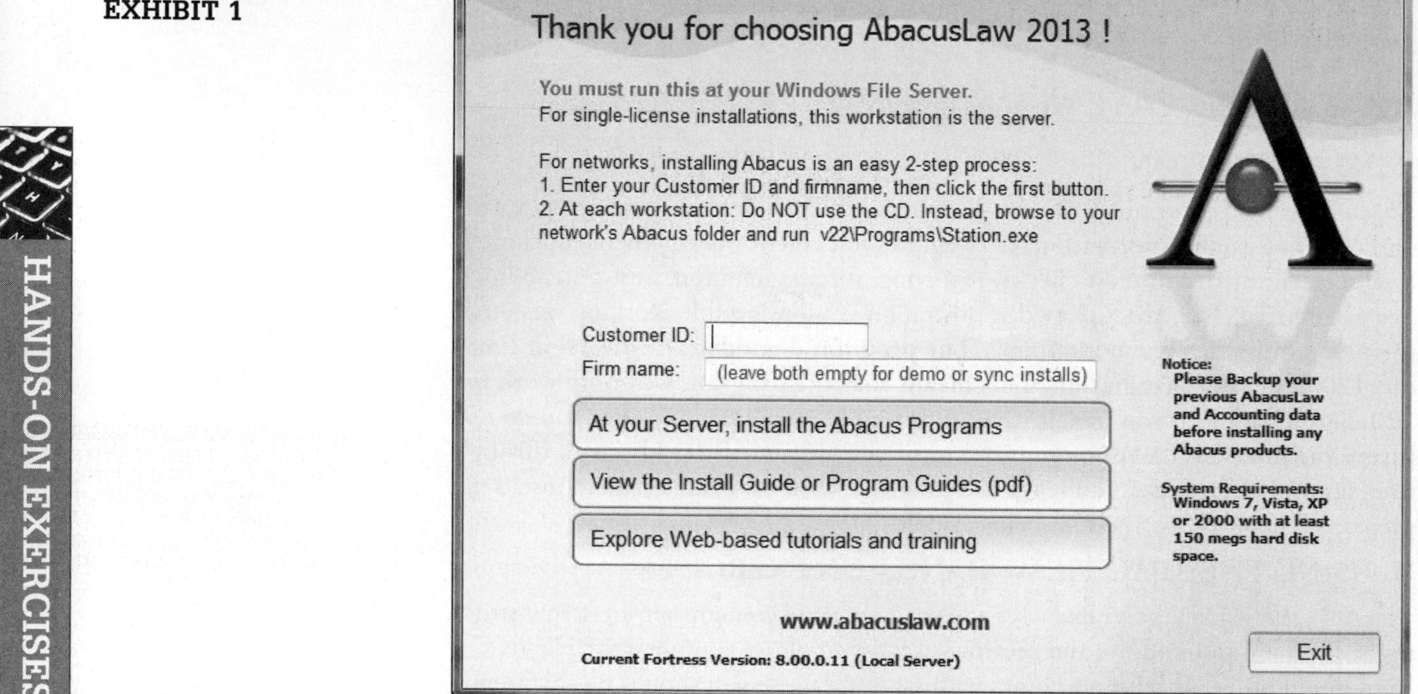

Courtesy Abacus Data Systems.

8. Your screen should now look like AbacusLaw Installation Exhibit 2. ***Click Next.***

ABACUSLAW INSTALLATION EXHIBIT 2

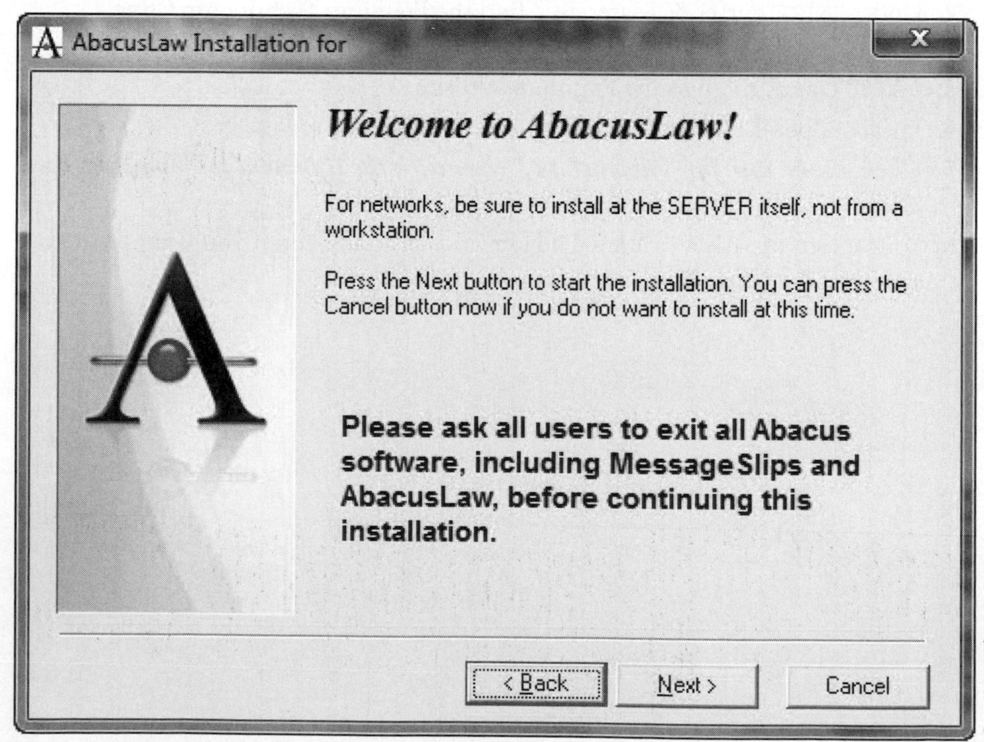

Courtesy Abacus Data Systems.

9. The Abacus License agreement window should now be displayed. (See AbacusLaw Installation Exhibit 3). ***Click Accept.***

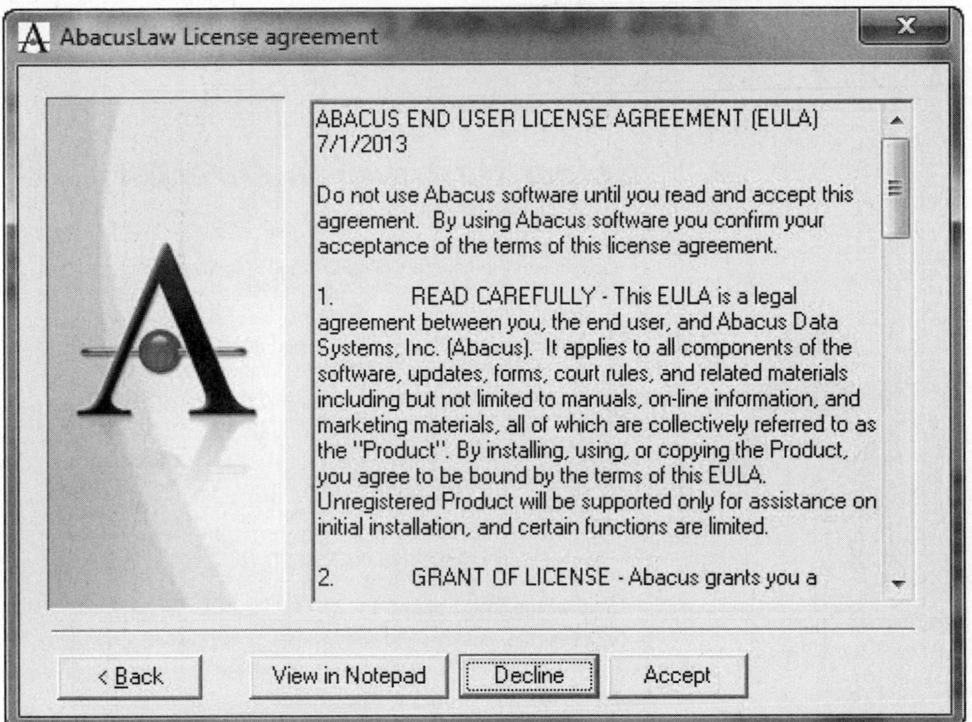

Courtesy Abacus Data Systems.

ABACUSLAW INSTALLATION EXHIBIT 3

10. The Select Components window should now be displayed (see AbacusLaw Installation Exhibit 4). ***Make sure all options other than "AbacusLaw"*** are deselected (see AbacusLaw Installation Exhibit 5). Note that if you wish to download the AbacusLaw getting Started Guide and Reference Guide, you may also select Copy Documentation to hard drive. When you are done only ***"AbacusLaw"*** should have a check mark next to it. ***Click Next.***

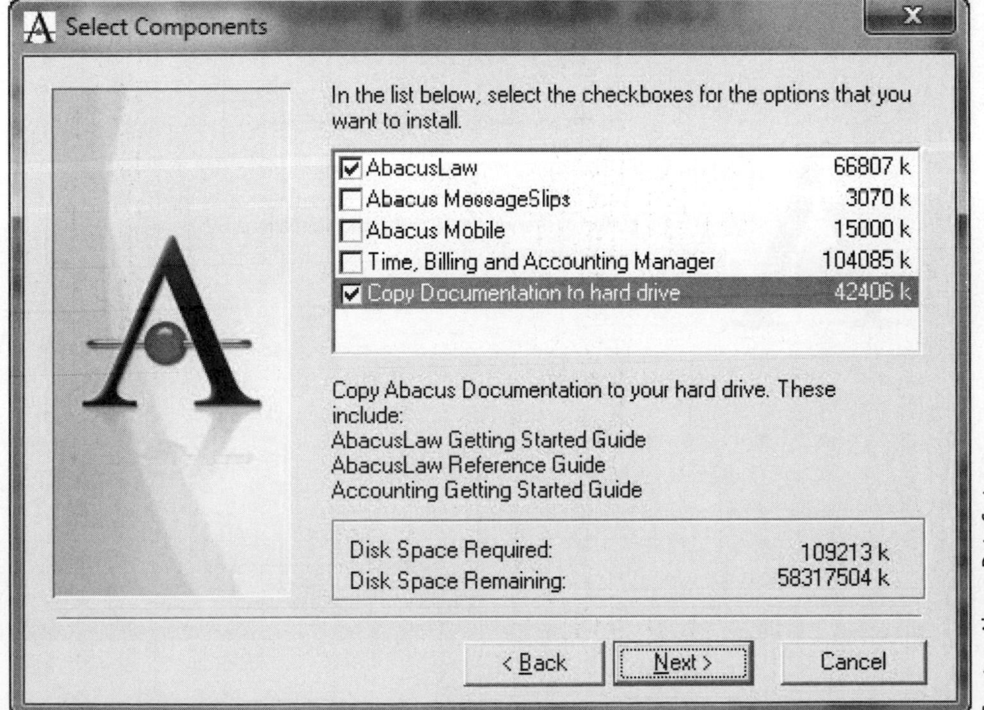

Courtesy Abacus Data Systems.

ABACUSLAW INSTALLATION EXHIBIT 4

HANDS-ON EXERCISES

11. The Select Destination Directory window should now be displayed (see AbacusLaw Installation Exhibit 5). Although you could click Browse to change where AbacusLaw will be saved on your computer, it is not recommended that you change this setting. ***Click Next.***

ABACUSLAW INSTALLATION EXHIBIT 5

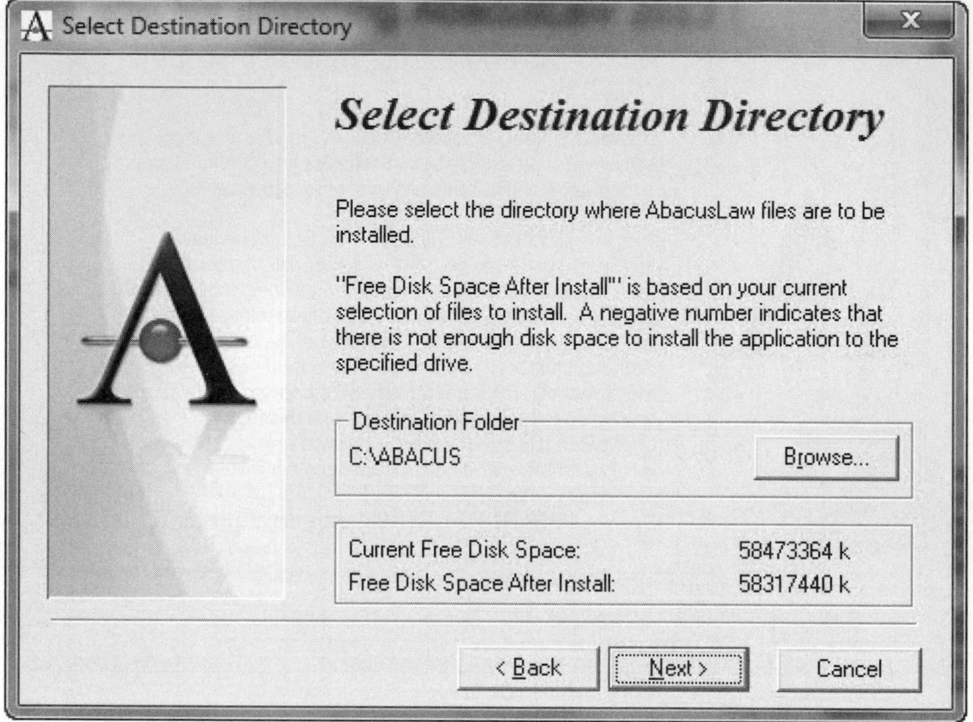

Courtesy Abacus Data Systems.

12. The Start Installation window (see AbacusLaw Installation Exhibit 6) should now be displayed and the screen should say Ready to Install. ***Click Next.***

ABACUSLAW INSTALLATION EXHIBIT 6

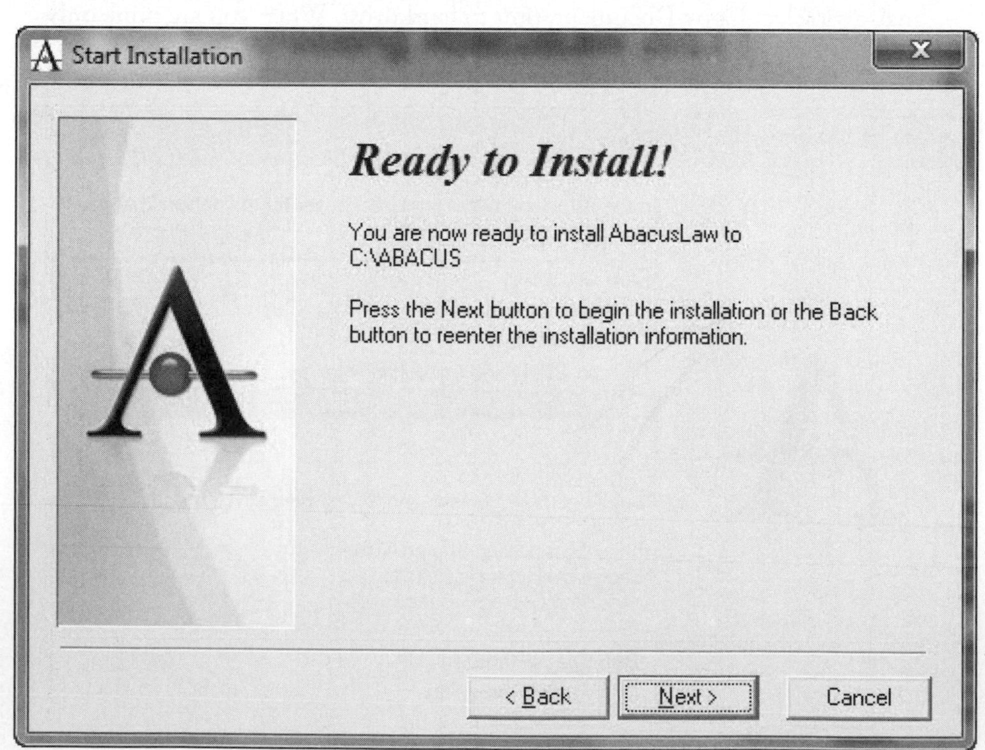

Courtesy Abacus Data Systems.

13. The Installing window should now be displayed and the program should start installing If you are asked to install the Search/Indexing Engine, ***click Yes.*** See AbacusLaw Installation Exhibit 7.

ABACUSLAW INSTALLATION EXHIBIT 7

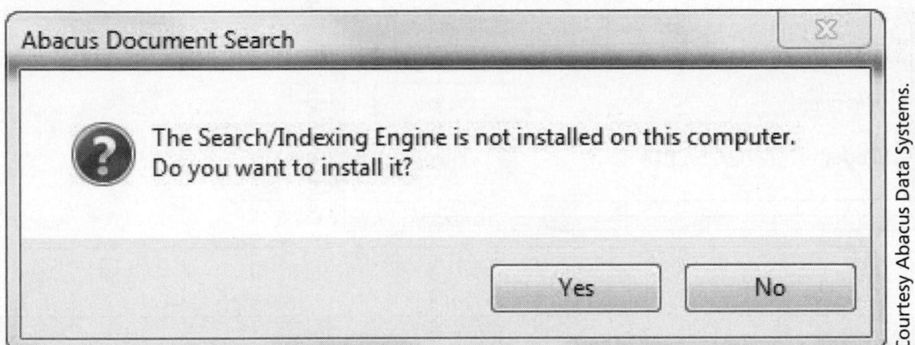

Courtesy Abacus Data Systems.

14. AbacusLaw will launch and initialize itself. You will see a screen for Document Search Setup. ***Click OK.*** See AbacusLaw Installation Exhibit 8. If you are asked to enter your initials as the User ID in the User Log on window, you should do so and then ***Click OK.*** See AbacusLaw Installation Exhibit 8. (Be sure to do this carefully as you will be asked to enter the same User ID every time you open this program.) See AbacusLaw Installation Exhibit 9. ***In the "AbacusLaw Installation Complete" window, make sure the option to Run AbacusLaw Updater is not selected and click Finish.*** See AbacusLaw Installation Exhibit 10.

ABACUSLAW INSTALLATION EXHIBIT 8

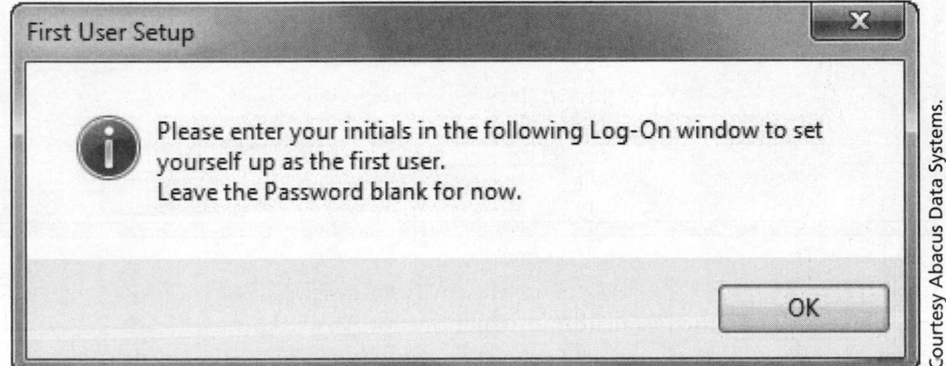

Courtesy Abacus Data Systems.

HANDS-ON EXERCISES

ABACUSLAW INSTALLATION EXHIBIT 10

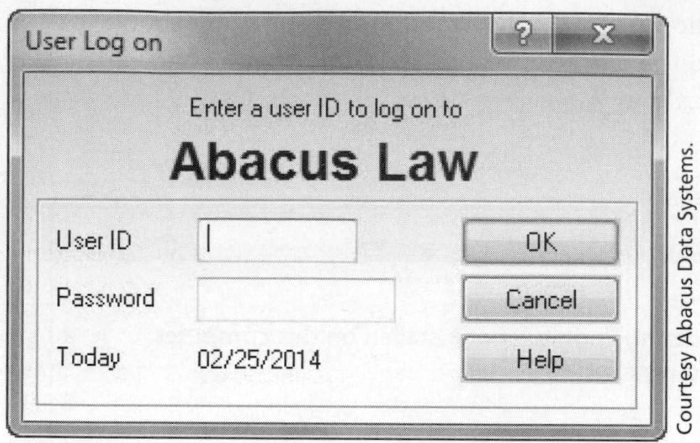

Courtesy Abacus Data Systems.

ABACUSLAW INSTALLATION EXHIBIT 9

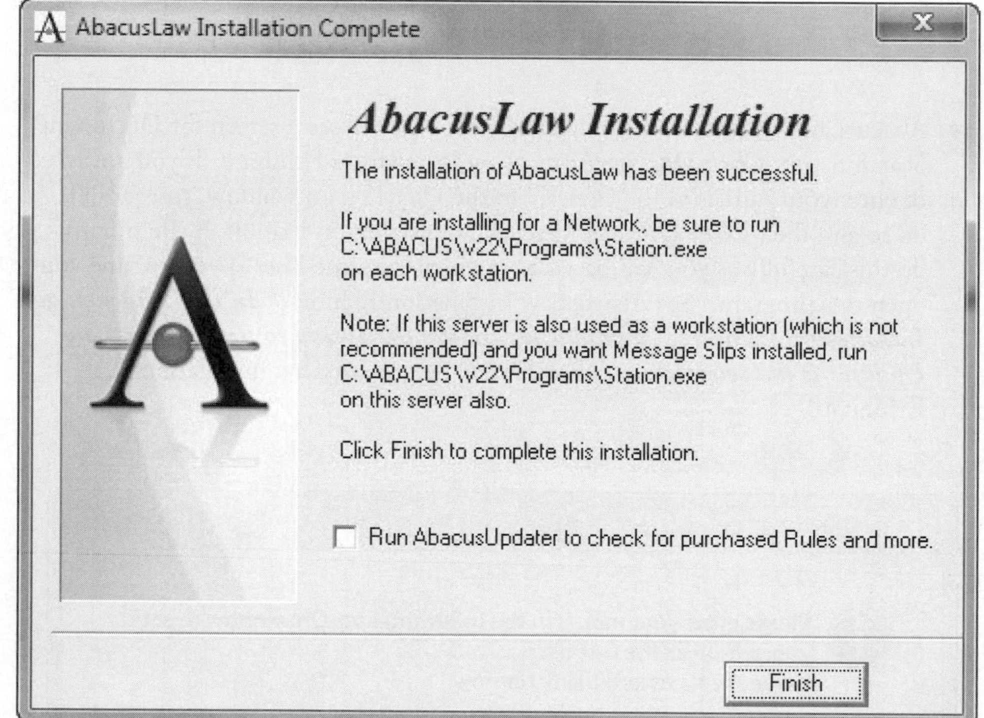

Courtesy Abacus Data Systems.

15. This concludes the installation instructions for AbacusLaw.

16. You are now ready to start the AbacusLaw Hands-On Exercises on the next page.

IV. INSTALLATION TECHNICAL SUPPORT

AbacusLaw is a licensed product of Abacus Data Systems: however, if you have problems installing the demonstration version of AbacusLaw, please contact Cengage Learning Technical Support first at http://cengage.com/support.

Number	Lesson Title	Concepts Covered
BASIC LESSONS		
Lesson 1	Introduction to AbacusLaw	Viewing and learning about the AbacusLaw interface, including an overview of calendars, events, contacts, and matters
Lesson 2	Entering New Contacts	Entering new contacts and printing a list of contacts to the screen
INTERMEDIATE LESSONS		
Lesson 3	Entering New Matters/Cases	Entering new matters/cases and associating them with clients
Lesson 4	Creating Events, Part 1	Adding a staff person who can perform events; creating events, including appointments, reminders, things to do, and calls to be made
Lesson 5	Creating Events, Part 2	Entering a recurring event; making a rule-based entry; working with the Date Calculator
Lesson 6	Creating Linked Names and Linked Notes, and Checking for Conflicts	Associating a non-client–linked name with a case; creating notes that are linked to contacts and matters; checking for conflicts of interest
ADVANCED LESSONS		
Lesson 7	Linking Documents; Using the Call Manager and the Form Generation Feature	Using the Call Manager feature; using the Form Generation feature
Lesson 8	Reports	Running a number of event and matter reports

HANDS-ON EXERCISES

GETTING STARTED

Introduction

Throughout these lessons and exercises, information you need to type into the software will be designated in several different ways:

- Keys to be pressed on the keyboard are designated in brackets, in all caps, and in bold (e.g., press the **[ENTER]** key).
- Movements with the mouse pointer are designated in bold and italics (e.g., ***point to File on the menu bar and click***).
- Words or letters that should be typed are designated in bold (e.g., type **Training Program**).
- Information that is or should be displayed on your computer screen is shown in bold, with quotation marks (e.g., **"Press ENTER to continue."**).
- Specific menu items and commands are designated with an initial capital letter (e.g., click Open).

OVERVIEW OF ABACUSLAW

AbacusLaw is a full-featured legal case management program. AbacusLaw Exhibit 1 shows the daily organizer calendar and the program's toolbar. With AbacusLaw, you can track case information; create and manage contract information for clients and others; make case notes and diaries; create calendar events that are tied (linked) to a case; and create a myriad of reminders, things-to-do, and calls-to-make entries. You can also link electronic documents to cases, create forms and routine letters using its document assembly capabilities, make recurring calendar entries, create rule-based entries, search and query the database for information, and print reports. Additional information about AbacusLaw will be provided as you complete these exercises. By the time you have finished these exercises, you should have a good understanding of the basics of legal case management and the AbacusLaw program.

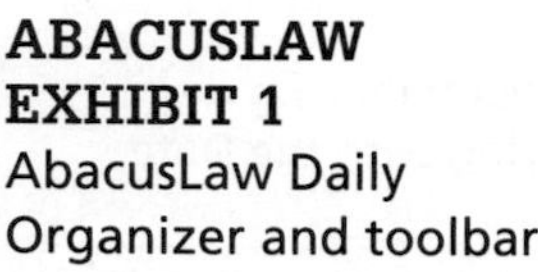

ABACUSLAW EXHIBIT 1
AbacusLaw Daily Organizer and toolbar

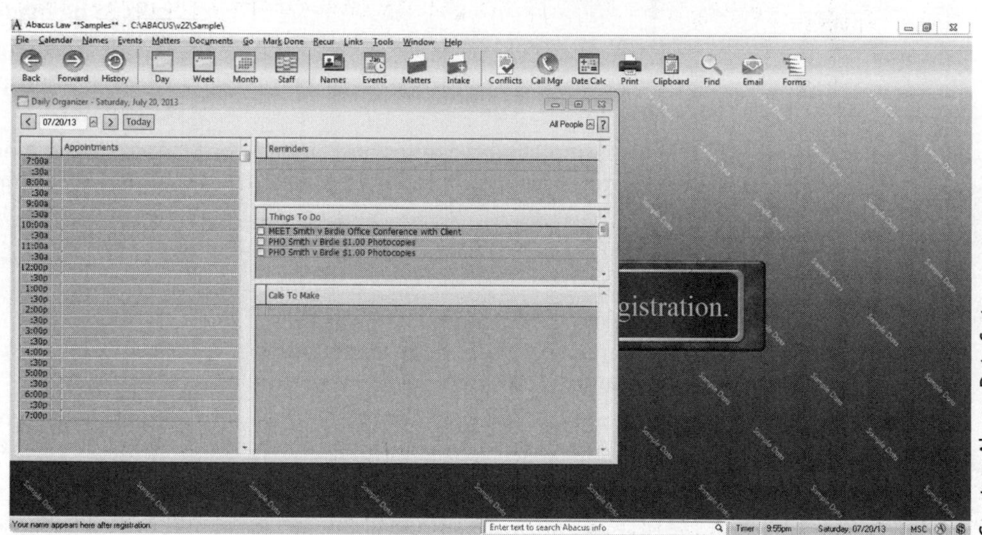

Courtesy Abacus Data Systems.

BASIC LESSONS

LESSON 1: INTRODUCTION TO ABACUSLAW

This lesson introduces you to AbacusLaw. It explains basic information about the AbacusLaw interface, including an overview of Calendars, Contacts, Matters, and Events.

Install the AbacusLaw demonstration version on your computer, following the instructions at the beginning of these exercises. Note that the AbacusLaw demonstration version will time out (cease to work) 120 days after installation. Therefore, do not install the program on your computer until you are ready to complete these Hands-On Exercises.

This version of AbacusLaw introduces a new feature: the Abacus Dashboard. The Dashboard allows a user to integrate Internet applications such as Google into Abacus. You are welcome to look at the elements of this new feature, but as it is not incorporated into any of the following exercises. When the Dashboard appears, you should press the **F3** key to hide it.

1. The first thing you will do in this lesson is populate AbacusLaw with sample data. *If you start AbacusLaw from the icon on the desktop, the sample data will not be loaded,* so please follow these directions.
2. Start Windows. ***Click the Start button on the Windows desktop, point to Programs or All Programs, point to the AbacusLaw group, then click Sample Data.*** This will load Abacus Law with some sample data. The "First User Setup" window should now be displayed. ***Click OK.***

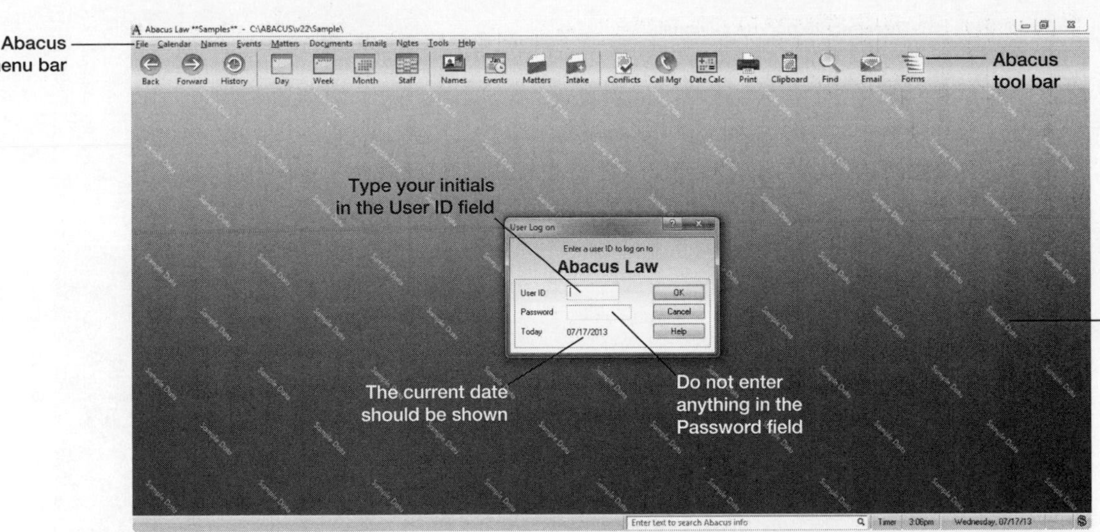

Courtesy Abacus Data Systems.

ABACUSLAW EXHIBIT 2
"User Log on" window

3. The "User Log on" window should now be displayed (see AbacusLaw Exhibit 2). If you get a message requesting you to set yourself up as the first user, ***click OK***; the AbacusLaw desktop (see AbacusLaw Exhibit 2) should say **"Sample Data."**
4. In the User ID field of the "User Log on" window, type your initials (see AbacusLaw Exhibit 2). It is important that you enter the same initials each time you load Abacus Law. Do not type anything in the Password field. ***Click OK in the "User Log on" window.*** Abacus Law will notify you that only these initials will be valid to open the demonstration version of Abacus Law.
5. The "Tip of the Day" window should now be displayed on your screen. ***Click OK in the "Tip of the Day" window.*** You should now be at the Abacus Law desktop with the name plate that reads **"Your name appears here after registration."**
6. ***Click the icon that says Day on the toolbar.*** AbacusLaw refers to this as the Daily Organizer. (To see the name of any icon, just ***hover the cursor on the icon for a second*** and its name will appear.)
7. The "Daily Organizer" window should now be displayed for the current day. The Daily Organizer is where you manage your daily calendar. The current date should be displayed at the top of the "Daily Organizer" window. ***Click the current date in the Daily Organizer,*** type **070207,** and then press the **[ENTER]** key.
8. Your screen should now look like AbacusLaw Exhibit 3, except that the "'Who' setting for Calendars" window is not yet open. The entries you see are sample data that was already loaded in the program. ***Click the less-than sign (<), which is the Previous Day icon, next to the date 07/02/07 in the "Daily Organizer" window*** (see AbacusLaw Exhibit 3). The date box should now show 07/01/07. *Note:* If the "Daily Organizer" window is too small, you can adjust its size by ***placing the cursor over the borders of the window, then clicking and dragging the window to the desired size.***
9. ***Click the greater-than sign (>), which is the Next Day icon, next to the date 07/01/07 in the "Daily Organizer" window*** (see AbacusLaw Exhibit 3). The date should once again be 07/02/07.
10. ***Click the up arrow just to the right of the date 07/02/07.*** This is the three-month pop-up calendar. By clicking on the left and right arrows in the three-month calendar, you can go backward or forward three months at a time. ***Click the Close icon*** (a square with an X in it) ***in the upper right corner of the three-month calendar window*** to close the window.

ABACUSLAW EXHIBIT 3
Daily Organizer

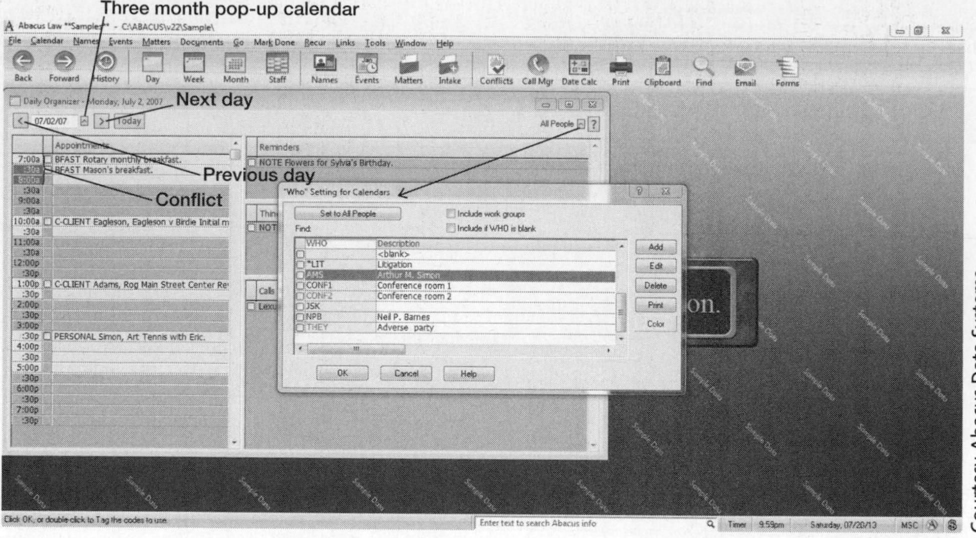

Courtesy Abacus Data Systems.

11. In the Daily Organizer, notice that the appointments at 7:30a. and 8:00a. are in red. This indicates a scheduling conflict. However, also notice the up arrow next to All People in the upper right of the "Daily Organizer" window. **"All People"** means that you are looking at the Daily Organizer for everyone in the office. Because everyone's calendar is being shown at the same time in the Daily Organizer, there may or may not be an actual scheduling conflict; one person could be going to one breakfast, and another person going to the other breakfast.
12. ***Point and click on the up arrow next to All People*** (see AbacusLaw Exhibit 5). Notice that the "'Who' Setting for Calendars" window is displayed (see AbacusLaw Exhibit 3). Notice that several people as well as several conference rooms are listed.
13. ***Click the box to the left of AMS (Arthur M. Simon) in the "'Who' Setting for Calendars" window. Click OK at the bottom of the "'Who' Setting for Calendars" window.*** The upper right of the "Daily Organizer" window now shows the name **"Arthur M. Simon,"** so you are just looking at his schedule now. Notice that one of the breakfast entries for the morning is now gone, so there is no actual scheduling conflict.
14. ***Double-click*** **NOTE Flowers for Sylvia's Birthday** ***in the Reminders section of the "Daily Organizer" window.*** The "Event" window for this note is now displayed. Notice at the bottom of the "Event" window that the field is blank next to Name and Matter. This means that the event is not related or associated with a contact name or matter. *Note:* If you do not see the Name and Matter fields, click the More button in the "Event" window.
15. Notice also that an **N** is displayed at the bottom of the window next to the Status field. ***Click the up arrow to the right of the N on the Status line.*** The "Valid STATUS Entries" window is now displayed. This is where you can indicate if the item has been completed or not. ***Click the Close icon*** (the square with an X) ***in the "Valid STATUS Entries" window.***
16. ***Click the Close icon*** (the square with an X) ***in the "Event" window.***
17. Look again at the "**Flowers for Sylvia's Birthday**" reminder and notice that to the left of it there is a an empty white box (see AbacusLaw Exhibit 3). When a user clicks the box, a check mark appears, indicating that the item has been completed. Notice that all of the event entries have the white box for indicating when an item has been completed.

18. ***Point to the 7:00a entry for* "BFAST Rotary Monthly breakfast" *and keep the cursor over that entry for a few seconds.*** Notice that a light yellow drop-down box shows additional information regarding the entry. You can point to any entry on any calendar and see the expanded information without having to open the item.
19. ***Double-click the 10:00a entry for* "C-CLIENT Eagleson, Eagleson v. Birdie Initial Meeting."** The "Event" window should now be displayed. Notice that, at the bottom of the window next to the Name field, **"Eagleson, George"** is shown (see AbacusLaw Exhibit 4). Also, notice that next to the Matter field the case of **"Eagleson v Birdie"** is shown. This indicates that this event—a client conference—is linked to "Eagleson, George" in the Contacts list, and is also linked to the matter (case) of *Eagleson v. Birdie.*

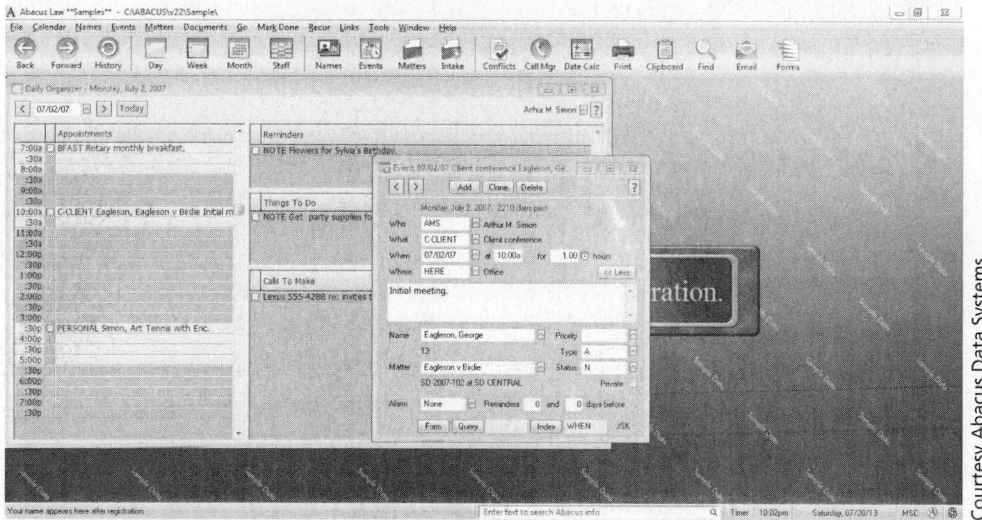

ABACUSLAW EXHIBIT 4
"Event" window for a client conference linked to a name and matter

Courtesy Abacus Data Systems.

HANDS-ON EXERCISES

20. ***Click the Close icon*** (the square with an X) ***in the "Event" window to close it.***
21. ***Click the Close icon*** (the square with an X) ***in the "Daily Organizer" window to close it.***
22. ***Click the Names icon on the toolbar.*** The "Names Browse" window should now be displayed (see AbacusLaw Exhibit 5). ***Scroll to the name "Adams, Roger".*** Notice that in the "Names Browse" window there are three columns: Name, ID, and Class. You can easily see the different types of contacts by looking at the Class field. For each name you can see the class of the entry. For example, "Adams, Roger" has been assigned the class of Client. Notice also that the contact information for each name is displayed on the right side of the "Names Browse" window when a client is selected. Remember, if a window is too small, you can adjust the size by ***placing the cursor over the borders of the window, then clicking and dragging the window to the desired size.***
23. ***Click the right arrow in the horizontal scroll bar*** (see AbacusLaw Exhibit 5) to scroll to the right and see the additional fields in the window.
24. ***Click the left arrow in the horizontal scroll bar*** to once again display the Name, ID, and Class fields.
25. ***Click the Adams, Roger name, then click the column heading Class.*** This will sort the name entries by class. Notice all of the client entries.

ABACUSLAW EXHIBIT 5
Contacts—"Names Browse" window

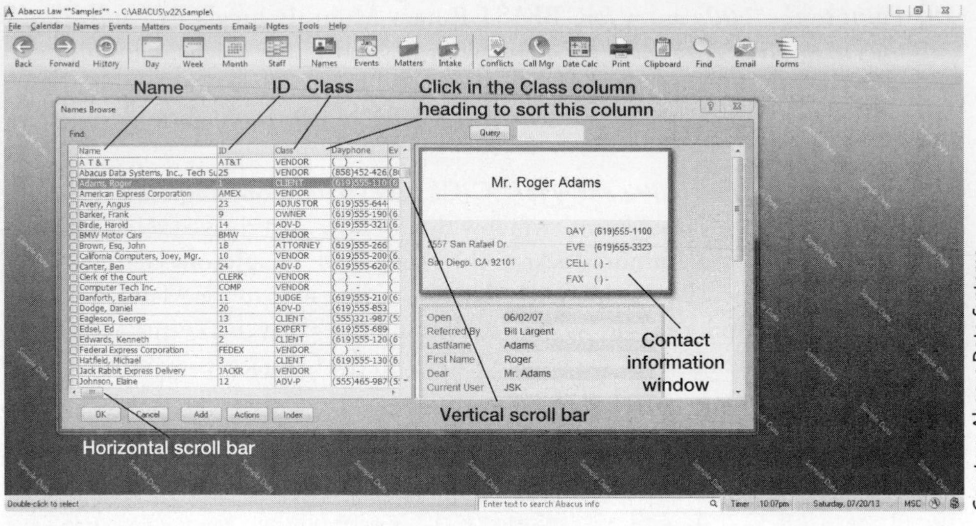

Courtesy Abacus Data Systems.

26. ***Click the Names column heading*** to display the contacts sorted by name.
27. ***Double-click on the Adams, Roger entry.***
28. The "Name: Adams, Roger" window should now be displayed (see AbacusLaw Exhibit 6).

ABACUSLAW EXHIBIT 6
"Name" window

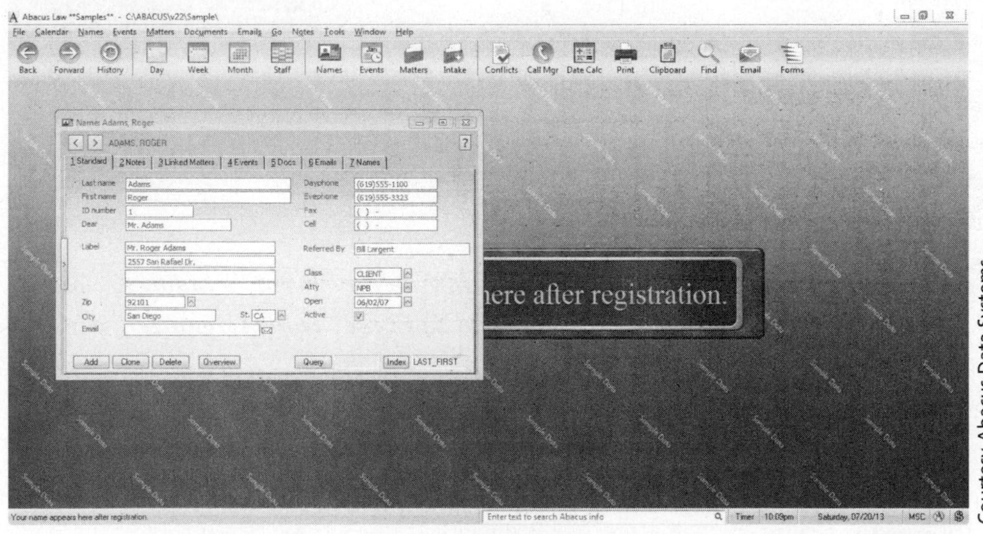

Courtesy Abacus Data Systems.

29. ***Click the Notes tab in the "Name: Adams, Roger" window.*** Notice that these include a phone entry and a background entry.
30. ***Click the Linked Matters tab in the "Name: Adams, Roger" window.*** Notice that two matters are shown, "Adams, Roger v. City of Jupite" and "Main Street Center" (a real estate matter).
31. ***Click the Events tab in the "Name: Adams, Roger" window.*** Notice that you can scroll to the right to see the other fields in the event entries.
32. ***Click the Docs tab.*** Notice that there are no linked documents listed.
33. ***Click the Emails tab.*** Notice that there are no emails listed.

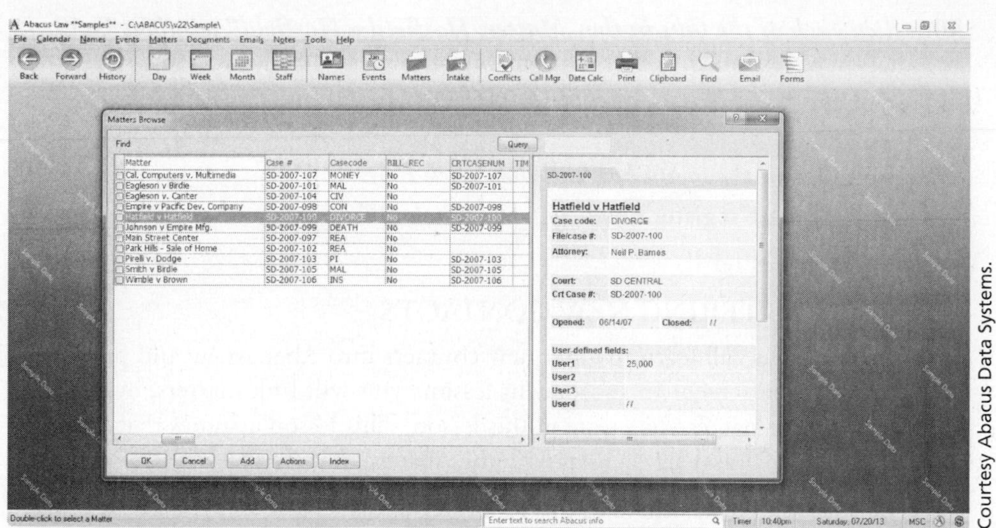

ABACUSLAW EXHIBIT 7
"Matters Browse" window

Courtesy Abacus Data Systems.

HANDS-ON EXERCISES

34. ***Click the Names tab.*** Notice that one name, **"Barker, Frank,"** is listed. Mr. Barker is the owner of the Main Street Center building that Roger Adams is purchasing.
35. ***Click the Standard tab in the "Name: Adams, Roger" window*** to return to the contact information for Roger Adams. ***Click the Overview button at the bottom of the window.*** The Overview window appears providing a chronological list of everything that has transpired for the selected name/matter, including notes, events, emails, and linked documents. ***Click the Close icon on the Overview window to close it.***
36. ***Click the Close icon in the "Name: Adams, Roger" window to close it.***
37. ***Click Matters on the toolbar.*** The "Matters Browse" window should now be displayed (see AbacusLaw Exhibit 7). ***Select the Hatfield v Hatfield case*** and notice that information about the case is shown on the right side of the "Matters Browse" window. Notice also that the third column header is **"Casecode."** This column lists the type of case for each matter.
38. ***Click the column heading Casecode.*** Press the **[HOME]** key to go to the beginning of the list. Notice that several types of cases are listed.
39. ***Double-click on the Hatfield v Hatfield matter in the "Matters Browse" window.*** The "Matter: Hatfield v Hatfield" window should now be displayed (see AbacusLaw Exhibit 8).

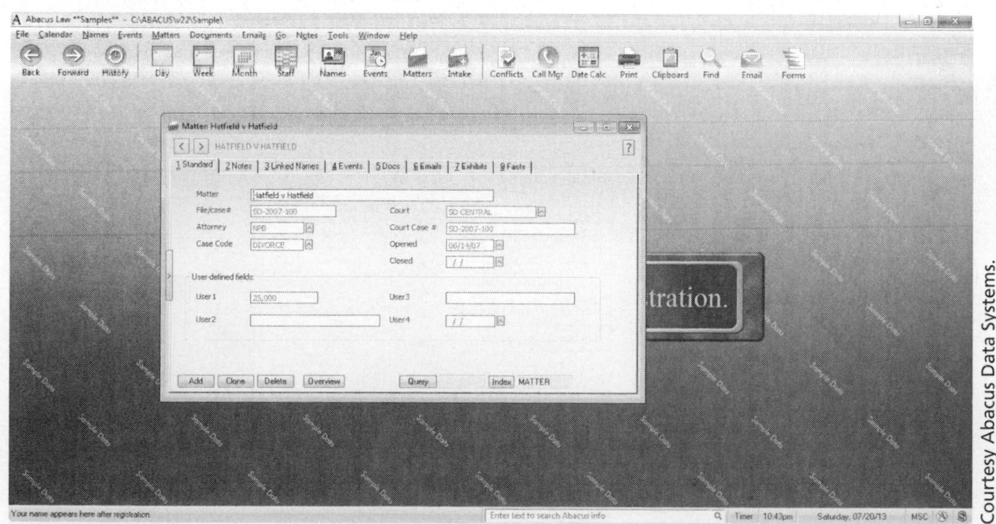

ABACUSLAW EXHIBIT 8
"Matter:" window

Courtesy Abacus Data Systems.

40. ***Click each of the tabs in the "Matter: Hatfield v Hatfield" window.*** Notice that they are similar to the tabs you accessed in the "Name" window.
41. ***Click the Close icon in the "Matter: Hatfield v Hatfield" window*** to close the window.
42. ***Click File on the menu bar and then click Exit.***
43. At the **"Please register now!"** window, ***click OK.***

This concludes Lesson 1.

LESSON 2: ENTERING NEW CONTACTS

In this lesson, you will learn to enter new contacts into AbacusLaw and print a list of contacts to the screen. In subsequent lessons you will link matters, events, and documents to the names you create in this lesson. This lesson assumes that you have completed Lesson 1 and are familiar with the AbacusLaw interface.

1. The first thing you will do in this lesson is populate AbacusLaw with sample data. *If you start AbacusLaw from the icon on the desktop, the sample data will not be loaded,* so please follow these directions.
2. Start Windows. ***Click the Start button on the Windows desktop, point to Programs or All Programs, point to the AbacusLaw group, then click Sample Data.*** This will populate Abacus Law with some sample data.
3. The "User Log on" window should now be displayed. Note that the AbacusLaw desktop should say **"Sample Data."**
4. In the User ID field of the "User Log on" window, type the same initials you entered in Lesson 1. It is important that you enter the same initials each time you start Abacus Law. Do not type anything in the Password field. ***Click OK in the "User Log on" window.***
5. The "Tip of the Day" window should now be displayed on your screen. ***Click OK in the "Tip of the Day" window.*** You should now be at the Abacus desktop with the name plate that reads **"Your name appears here after registration."**
6. ***Click Names on the toolbar.*** The "Names Browse" window will be displayed. ***Click Add.***
7. The "Adding a new Name" window should be displayed (see AbacusLaw Exhibit 9). Enter the following contact information into the "Adding a new Name" window (Table 5–1). You can use the **[TAB]** key to go the next field, or **[SHIFT]+[TAB]** to go to the previous field. You can also use the cursor to point and click in a field. In the following data list, when you come to a field that is

ABACUSLAW EXHIBIT 9
"Adding a new Name" window

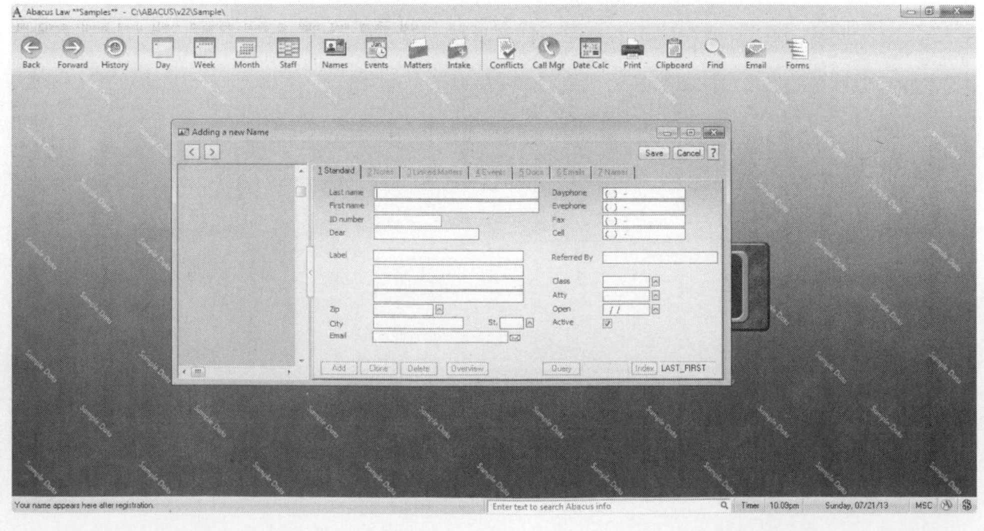

Courtesy Abacus Data Systems.

blank, just skip over it. *Note:* After you enter the Zip Code, if the "An Invalid Zip Code was Entered" window opens, ***click Add.*** The "Zip Codes" window will open. ***Enter the Zip Code, City, and State, and click OK to close the Zip Codes window,*** and then ***click OK in the "An Invalid Zip Code was Entered" window*** (Table 5–1).

TABLE 5–1

FIELD NAME	DATA TO ENTER
Last name	**Magrino**
First name	**Cathy**
ID number	**1001**
Dear	**Cathy**
Label	**Cathy Magrino**
	93 Winspear Lane
Zip	**90014**
City	**Los Angeles**
St.	**CA**
Email	**cmagrino@msc.uclo.com**
Dayphone	**323 555 2343**
Evenphone	
Fax	
Cell	
Referred By	
Class	**CLIENT**
Atty	**AMS**
Open	**06/01/15**

HANDS-ON EXERCISES

8. When you have entered all of the information (your screen should look similar to AbacusLaw Exhibit 10), ***click Save in the "Adding a new Name" window.*** Notice that on the left side of the window, there is a side panel that lets you quickly select another name record without going to another menu. ***Click the display button to show/hide the side panel.***

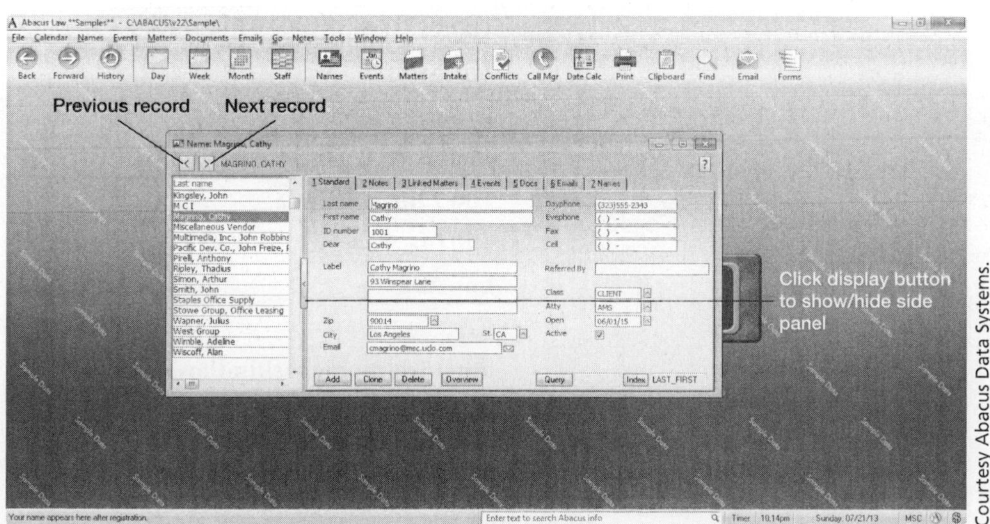

ABACUSLAW EXHIBIT 10
Completed entry—"Adding a new Name" window

Courtesy Abacus Data Systems.

9. You will now make three additional contact entries, including one additional client, one attorney, and one vendor.
10. ***In the "Name: Magrino, Cathy" window, click Add*** to add another name. Enter the data from the following list into AbacusLaw (Tables 5–2 and 5–3). *Note:* When you have completed an entry, ***click Save*** to save the record. Then, ***click Add*** to add the next record. Once the records are entered, you can use the Previous Record (<) and Next Record (>) icons (see AbacusLaw Exhibit 10) to go between records if you need to (Tables 5–2 and 5–3).

TABLE 5–2

FIELD NAME	DATA TO ENTER
Last name	**Gleason**
First name	**Colleen**
ID number	**1002**
Dear	**Colleen**
Label	**Colleen Gleason**
	300 Porter Ave
Zip	**92037**
City	**La Jolla**
St.	**CA**
Email	**cgleason@aom.com**
Dayphone	**858 555 8933**
Evenphone	
Fax	
Cell	
Referred By	
Class	**CLIENT**
Atty	**AMS**
Open	**06/01/15**
FIELD NAME	**DATA TO ENTER**
Last name	**McKie**
First name	**Dianne**
ID number	**1003**
Dear	**Ms. McKie**
Label	**Dianne McKie**
	McKie & Baskind
	100 Ellicott Circle
Zip	**90014**
City	**Los Angeles**
St.	**CA**
Email	**dmckie@mckiebaskindlaw.com**
Dayphone	**323 555 8001**
Evenphone	
Fax	

TABLE 5–3	
Cell	
Referred By	
Class	ATTORNEY
Atty	
Open	06/01/15
FIELD NAME	**DATA TO ENTER**
Last name	**Krakes**
First name	**Margaret**
ID number	**1004**
Dear	**Ms. Krakes**
Label	**Margaret Krakes**
	UB Equipment, Inc.
	18 Blue Bird Ave
Zip	**92101**
City	**San Diego**
St.	**CA**
Email	**mkrakes@ub.equip.com**
Dayphone	**858 555 0003**
Evenphone	
Fax	
Cell	
Referred By	
Class	**VENDOR**
Atty	
Open	**06/01/15**

11. Once you have saved the last record, ***click the Close icon in the "Name: Krakes, Margaret" window to close it.***
12. ***Click Names on the toolbar.*** The **"Names Browse"** window should now be displayed.
13. ***Click Query in the upper right of the "Names Browse" window. Click Quick query in the drop-down menu.***
14. ***Click in the Last name field*** and type **Gleason**, ***then click OK.***
15. The entry for **"Gleason, Colleen"** should be displayed in the **"Names Browse"** window in the right panel.
16. ***Click Query. Then, click Clear current query.*** Press the **[HOME]** key to go to the beginning of the list.
17. ***Click Actions in the "Names Browse" window. Point to Reports and click All (in query).*** The **"Names Report Control"** window should now be displayed. (***Click Output to, then click Screen, then click OK.***) You will be printing a Names report to the screen. ***Point and click on Print.*** If a printer window opens, just ***click Print.*** (*Note:* The program will not actually print the report to the printer at this time; it will only print to the screen.) The Names List report should now be displayed in the Report Viewer window. See AbacusLaw Exhibit 11.

ABACUSLAW EXHIBIT 11
Names List report

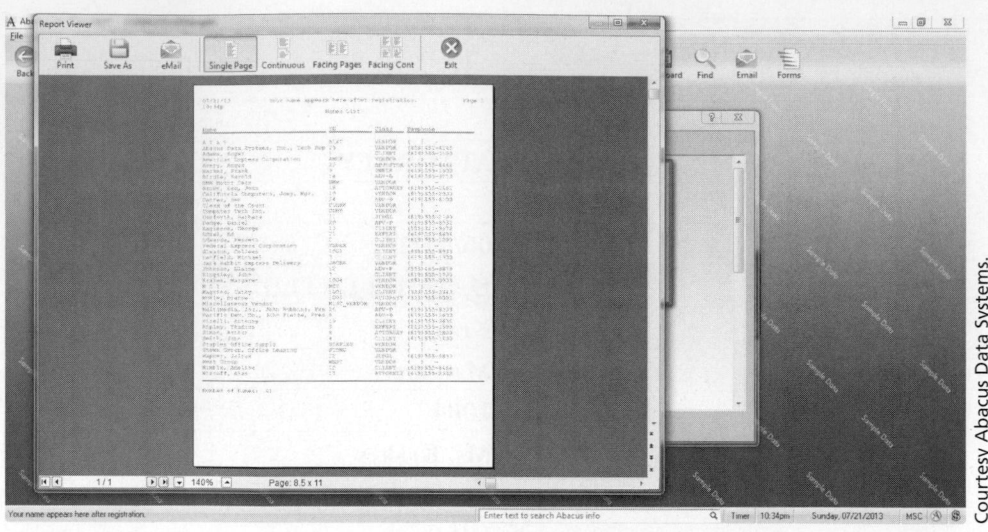

Courtesy Abacus Data Systems.

HANDS-ON EXERCISES

18. ***Click the Exit icon*** (a red X) ***on the toolbar. At the "Names Report Control" window, click Close.***
19. ***Click the Close icon*** (the square with an X) ***in the "Names Browse" window to close it.***
20. ***Click File on the menu bar and then click Exit*** (the very last entry under the Recent Files Accessed list).
21. At the **"Please register now!"** window, ***click OK.***

This concludes Lesson 2.

INTERMEDIATE LESSONS

LESSON 3: ENTERING NEW MATTERS/CASES

In this lesson, you will enter new matters and cases and associate them with existing clients. This lesson assumes that you have completed Lessons 1 and 2 and that you are familiar with the AbacusLaw interface.

1. The first thing you will do in this lesson is populate AbacusLaw with sample data. *If you start AbacusLaw from the icon on the desktop, the sample data will not be loaded,* so please follow these directions.
2. Start Windows. ***Click the Start button on the Windows desktop, point to Programs or All Programs, point to the AbacusLaw group, then click Sample Data.*** This will populate Abacus Law with some sample data.
3. The **"User Log on"** window should now be displayed. Note that the AbacusLaw desktop should say **"Sample Data."**
4. In the User ID field of the **"User Log on"** window, type the same initials you entered in Lesson 1. It is important that you enter the same initials each time you start Abacus Law. Do not type anything in the Password field. ***Click OK in the "User Log on" window.***
5. The "Tip of the Day" window should now be displayed on your screen. ***Click OK in the "Tip of the Day" window.*** You should now be at the Abacus desktop with the name plate that reads **"Your name appears here after registration."**
6. ***Click Matters on the toolbar, then click Add in the "Matters Browse" window.*** The "Adding a new Matter" window should be displayed (see AbacusLaw Exhibit 12).

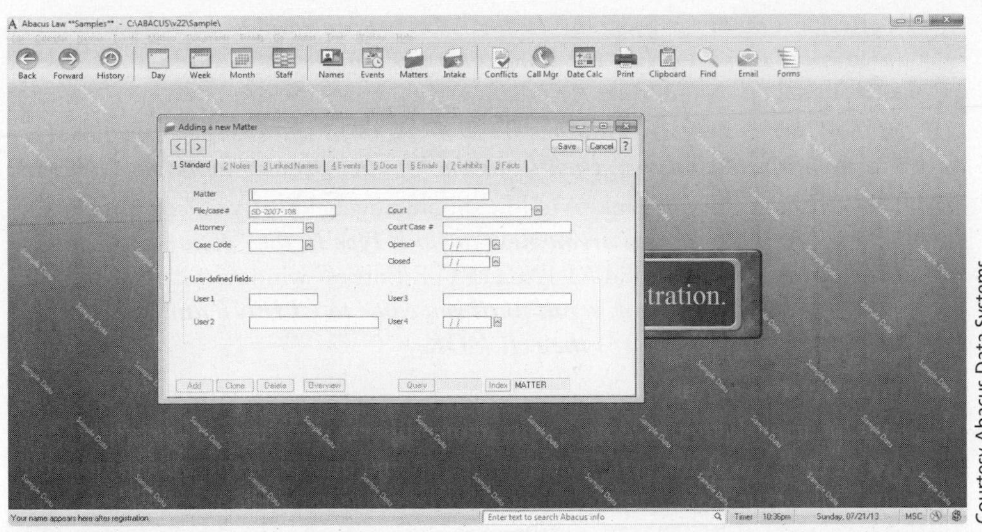

ABACUSLAW EXHIBIT 12
Adding a new matter

Courtesy Abacus Data Systems.

7. Enter the matter information from the following list in the "Adding a new Matter" window Table 5–4. You can use the **[TAB]** key to go the next field, or **[SHIFT]+[TAB]** to go to the previous field. You can also use the mouse to click in a field. In the following data list, when you come to a blank field, just skip over it. *Note:* When you get to the Court field, you will not see an existing entry for LASUPER. ***Click the up arrow next to Court field. In the "Valid Court Entries" window, click Import.*** The "Import old 'Where Codes' to Courts" window is now displayed. ***Click OK. In the "Valid WHERE Entries" window select LASUPER and click OK. Click OK in the "Valid Court Entries" window.*** *Note:* Should any other windows open, ***you can click OK*** and continue with the lesson.

TABLE 5–4

FIELD NAME	DATA TO ENTER
Matter	**Magrino v. American Insurance**
File/case#	**2015–8743**
Attorney	**AMS**
Case Code	**INS**
Court	**LASUPER**
Court Case #	
Opened	**06 01 15**
Closed	
User1	
User2	
User3	
User4	

8. When you have finished entering the information, ***click Save in the "Adding a new Matter" window.***
9. You will now create a link (or relationship) between Cathy Magrino in the Contact portion of the program and *Magrino v. American Insurance* in the

Matter portion of the program. ***In the "Matter: Magrino v. American Insurance" window, click the Linked Names tab.*** (It is the third tab.) ***Click Add link.*** The "Names Browse" window should now be displayed.

10. ***In the "Names Browse" window, scroll down until you see the entry for Magrino, Cathy and then click it. In the "Names Browse" window, click OK.***
11. The "Name-to-Matter Link" window should now be displayed (see AbacusLaw Exhibit 13). ***Click the up arrow next to Link Type in the "Name-to-Matter Link" window.*** The "Valid ATTACHTYPE Entries" window will now be displayed. ***In this window, scroll until you come to CLIENT and click it;*** (see AbacusLaw Exhibit 13) ***then click OK.***

ABACUSLAW EXHIBIT 13
Linking a name with a matter

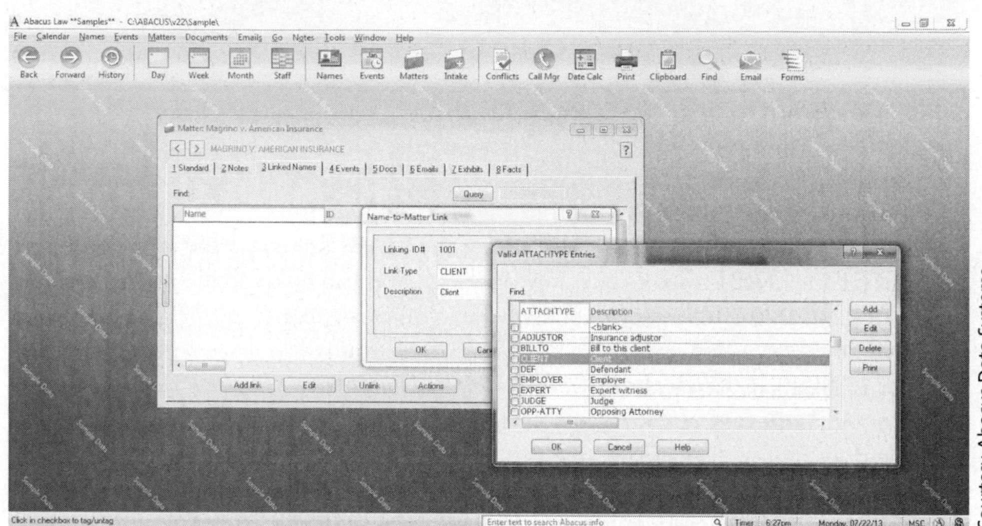

Courtesy Abacus Data Systems.

12. In the "Name-to-Matter Link" window, in the text box next to Description: after the word Client, type – **Plaintiff,** then ***click OK.*** Notice in the "Matter: Magrino v. American Insurance" window that the name "Magrino, Cathy" now shows up in the Linked Names tab.
13. ***Click the Close icon*** (the square with an X) ***in the "Matter: Magrino v. American Insurance" window to close the window.***
14. You will now check to see if the "Magrino, Cathy" entry in the Contact section of the program is linked to the matter *Magrino v. American Insurance*. ***Click Names on the toolbar, and scroll until you find "Magrino, Cathy." Check the box next to Magrino, Cathy then click OK. In the "Name: Magrino, Cathy" window, click the Linked Matters tab.*** The *Magrino v. American Insurance* matter should be shown (see AbacusLaw Exhibit 14).
15. ***Double-click Magrino v. American Insurance in the "Name: Magrino, Cathy" window.*** The "Matter: Magrino v. American Insurance" window is now displayed. The name and matter are linked.
16. ***Click the Close icon*** (the square with an X) ***in the "Matter: Magrino v. American Insurance" window to close that window.***
17. ***Click the Close icon in the "Name: Magrino, Cathy" window to close that window.***
18. You will now create one more matter and link it to another client. ***Click Matters on the toolbar, then click Add in the "Matters Browse" window.*** The "Adding a new Matter" window should be displayed.

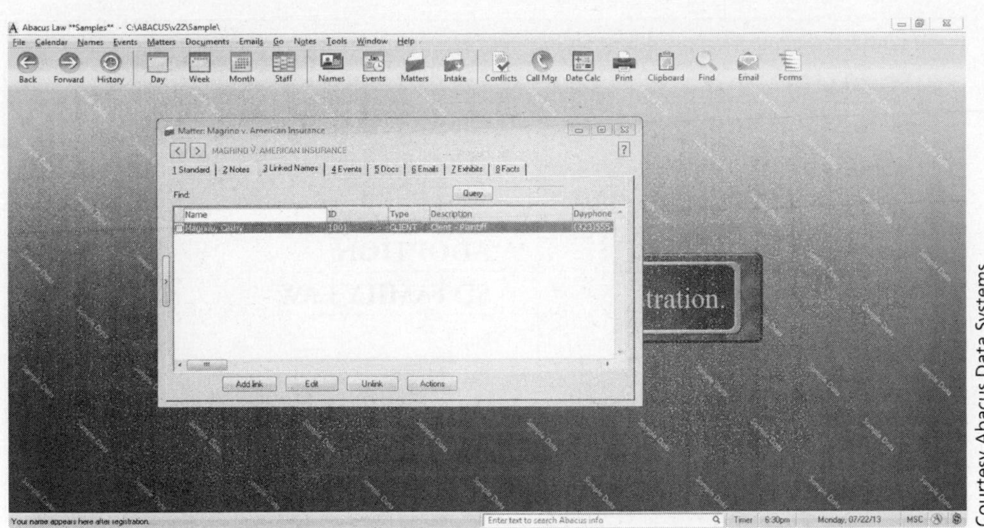

ABACUSLAW EXHIBIT 14
Contact name linked with a matter

Courtesy Abacus Data Systems.

19. Enter the matter information from the following list in the "Adding a new Matter" window (Table 5–5). *Note:* When you get to Case Code, you will not see an existing entry for Adoption, so you will need to add it. ***Click the up arrow to the right of Case Code.*** (If the Validating Listboxes window opens, ***click OK.***) ***In the "Valid CASECODE Entries" window, click Add.*** In the "New 'CASECODE' Code" window, type ***ADOPTION*** and then ***click OK.*** In the "CASECODE Code Description" window, type **Adoption in Family Court** and then ***click OK.*** Now, ***click ADOPTION in the "Valid CASECODE Entries" window, then click OK.*** A nice feature in Abacus Law is that you can create new items on the fly without having to get out of where you are and go to a special screen. You will also have to add the court. To do so, ***click the up arrow to the right of Court. In the "Valid Court Entries" window, click Populate. In the "Tag all Courts to add from the Abacus master list" window, scroll down until you see "*****SD FAMILY LAW Superior Court of California, County of San Diego,*** ***" then click the box next to the desired court and click OK.*** See AbacusLaw Exhibit 15. The "Valid Court Entries" window now lists the San Diego Family Court. ***Click to choose San Diego Family Court and click OK.***

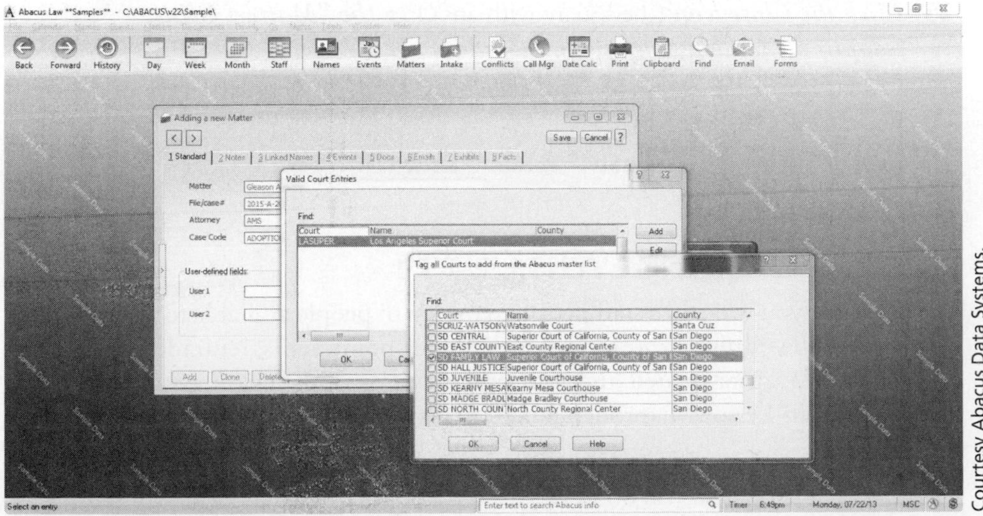

ABACUSLAW EXHIBIT 15
Selecting a jurisdiction

Courtesy Abacus Data Systems.

HANDS-ON EXERCISES

TABLE 5–5	
FIELD NAME	**DATA TO ENTER**
Matter	**Gleason Adoption**
File/case#	**2015-A-203**
Attorney	**AMS**
Case Code	**ADOPTION**
Court	**SD FAMILY LAW**
Court Case #	
Opened	**06 01 15**
Closed	
User1	
User2	
User3	
User4	

20. When you have finished entering the information, ***click Save in the "Adding a new Matter" window.***
21. You will now create a link (or relationship) between "Colleen Gleason" in the Contact portion of the program and "Gleason Adoption" in the Matter portion of the program. ***In the "Matter: Gleason Adoption" window, click the Linked Names tab. Click Add link.*** The "Names Browse" window should now be displayed.
22. ***In the "Names Browse" window, scroll down until you see the entry for Gleason, Colleen; click it. Then, in the "Names Browse" window, click OK.***
23. The "Name-to-Matter Link" window should now be displayed. ***Click the up arrow next to Link Type in the "Name-to-Matter Link" window.*** The "Valid ATTACHTYPE Entries" window will now be displayed. ***In that window, scroll until you come to CLIENT, check the box next to it and then click OK.***
24. In the "Name-to-Matter Link" window, next to Description, type – ***Petitioner*** and then ***click OK.*** Notice that in the "Matter: Gleason Adoption" window, the name "Gleason, Colleen" now shows up in the Linked Names tab.
25. ***Click the Close icon*** (the square with an X) ***in the "Matter: Gleason Adoption" window to close that window.***
26. ***Click File on the menu bar and then click Exit*** (the very last entry under the Recent Files Accessed list).
27. At the **"Please register now!"** window, ***click OK.***

This concludes Lesson 3.

LESSON 4: CREATING EVENTS, PART 1

In this lesson, you will add a staff person to the list of people available to perform work for clients. You will also create events, including appointments, reminders, and things to do, that are either related and unrelated to cases. This lesson assumes that you have completed Lessons 1 through 3, and that you are familiar with the AbacusLaw interface.

1. The first thing you will do in this lesson is populate AbacusLaw with sample data. *If you start AbacusLaw from the icon on the desktop, the sample data will not be loaded,* so please follow these directions.

2. Start Windows. ***Click the Start button on the Windows desktop, point to Programs or All Programs, point to the AbacusLaw group, then click Sample Data.*** This will populate Abacus Law with some sample data.
3. The "User Log on" window should now be displayed and the AbacusLaw desktop should say **"Sample Data."**
4. In the "User Log on" window, in the User ID field, type the same initials you entered in Lesson 1. It is important that you enter the same initials each time you start Abacus Law. Do not type anything in the Password field. ***Click OK in the "User Log on" window.***
5. The "Tip of the Day" window should now be displayed on your screen. ***Click OK in the "Tip of the Day" window.*** You should now be at the Abacus desktop with the name plate that reads **"Your name appears here after registration."**
6. The first thing you will do in this lesson is to add a paralegal staff member to AbacusLaw. ***Click File on the menu bar, then point to Setup and click Codes….*** The "Code Types" window should now be displayed (see AbacusLaw Exhibit 16).

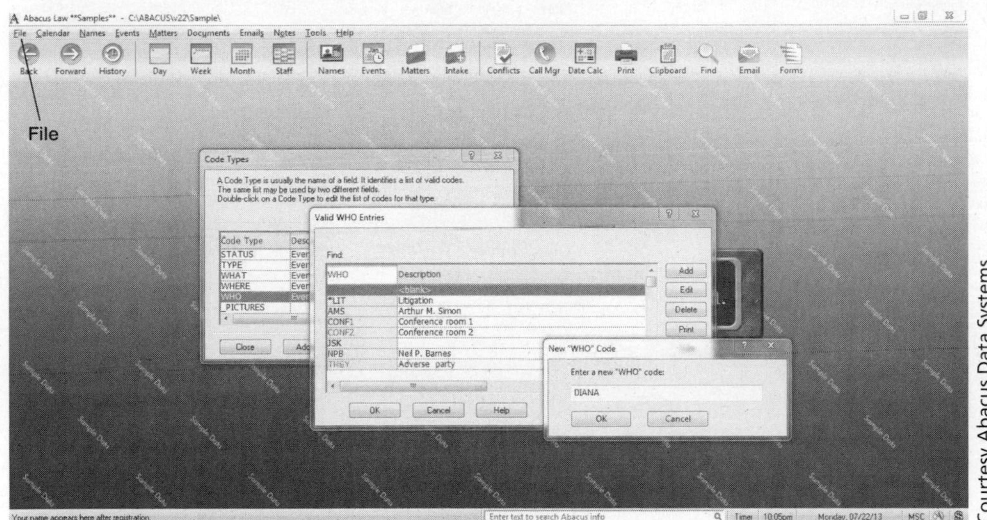

Courtesy Abacus Data Systems.

ABACUSLAW EXHIBIT 16
Entering a new staff member in the "New "WHO" Code" window

7. ***In the "Code Types" window, scroll down and click the WHO code type. Then click Edit codes*** (see AbacusLaw Exhibit 16). The "Valid WHO Entries" window should now be displayed.
8. ***Click Add.*** The "New "WHO" Code" window should now be displayed (see AbacusLaw Exhibit 16). Under Enter a new "WHO" code:, type **DIANA** and then ***click OK.***
9. The "WHO Code Description" window should now be displayed. Under Description for DIANA: type **Diana Nita, Paralegal** and then ***click OK.*** The entry should now appear in the "Valid WHO Entries" window. ***Click OK in the "Valid WHO Entries" window.***
10. ***Click Close in the "Code Types" window.***
11. You will now enter a number of appointments, reminders, things to do, and calls to be made into Diana Nita's calendar. ***Click Day on the toolbar to load the Daily Organizer.***

HANDS-ON EXERCISES

12. ***Change the date in the Daily Organizer to 06/11/15*** and then press the **[ENTER]** key.
13. ***Click the up arrow next to All People in the upper right corner of the "Daily Organizer—Thursday, June 11, 2015" window.*** The "'Who' Setting for Calendars" window should now be displayed.
14. ***Click Diana—Diana Nita, Paralegal, then click OK.*** Notice that the Daily Organizer is now set for Diana Nita, Paralegal.
15. The first event entry you will make will not be linked to a case. ***In the "Daily Organizer—Thursday, June 11, 2015" window, double-click on 12:00p.***
16. The "Adding a new Event" window should now be displayed (see AbacusLaw Exhibit 17). *Note:* The "Adding a new Event" window can either be expanded (More) or contracted (Less). In AbacusLaw Exhibit 17, the screen is contracted, so to see additional options (such as name and matter), you would just click More. The contracted screen is fine for this entry.

ABACUSLAW EXHIBIT 17
Entering a new event not associated with a matter

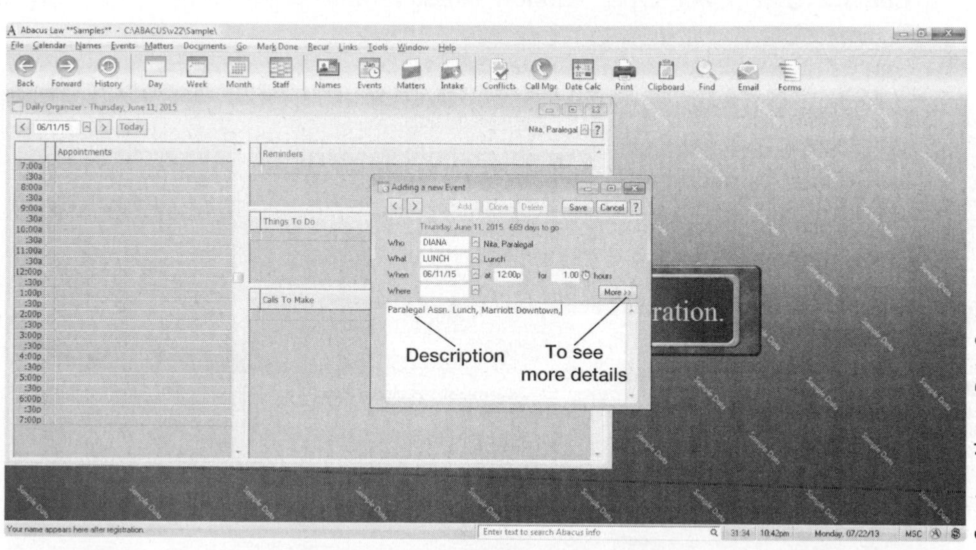

17. **"DIANA"** should already be in the Who field. ***In the What field, click the up arrow.*** The "Valid WHAT Entries" window should now be displayed. There are many entries in this screen, so type **LUNCH** to take you directly to that entry, ***click LUNCH, then click OK.***
18. The date of 06/11/15 at 12:00p should already be entered. ***Click 0.50 next to "hours" and change it to 1.00.***
19. In the Description field, type **Paralegal Assn. Lunch, Marriott Downtown.** See AbacusLaw Exhibit 17.
20. ***Click Save.*** The entry should now be made in your calendar.
21. You will now enter an event linked with a case. ***In the "Daily Organizer—Thursday, June 11, 2015" window, double-click on 1:30p.*** Because you will be linking the event to a contact and a matter, you need the expanded (More) version of the "Adding a new Event" window. If you do not see the Name and Matter fields on your screen, ***click More >> in the "Adding a new Event" window*** (see AbacusLaw Exhibit 17).

22. Enter the matter information from the following list in the "Adding a new Event" window (Table 5–6). You can use the **[TAB]** key to go the next field, or **[SHIFT]+[TAB]** to go to the previous field. You can also use the mouse to click in a field. In the following list, when you come to a blank field, just skip over it. ***When you get to the Name field, just point on the up arrow, scroll to Magrino, Cathy in the "Names Browse" window, and click OK.*** Because the "Magrino, Cathy" entry is linked to *Magrino v. American Insurance,* the case should automatically appear in the Matter field.

TABLE 5–6

FIELD NAME	DATA TO ENTER
Who	**DIANA**
What	**C-CLIENT**
When	**06/11/15 at 1:30p for 3.00 hours**
Where	**HERE**
Description (open light yellow box)	**Discuss electronic discovery production issues with client**
Name	**Magrino, Cathy**
Matter	**Magrino v. American Insurance**
Priority	
Type	**A**
Status	**N**
Reminders	**3 5**

23. When you have finished entering all of the data, ***click Save in the "Adding a new Event" window.*** The entry should now appear in your Daily Organizer.
24. You entered three-day and five-day reminders for the entry you just made. Let's see if the reminders appear correctly in the calendar. ***Click on the Previous Day icon (<) just to the left of the date in the Daily Organizer*** (see AbacusLaw Exhibit 17) ***three times so that the date 06/08/15 is shown in the Daily Organizer.*** The reminder for the client conference on 6/11/15 regarding electronic discovery should be shown in the Reminders section of the Daily Organizer.
25. ***Click the Next Day icon (>) just to the right of the date in the Daily Organizer*** (see AbacusLaw Exhibit 17) ***four times so that the date 06/12/15 is displayed in the Daily Organizer.***
26. You will now make a Things To Do entry. ***In the "Daily Organizer—Friday, June 12, 2015" window, double-click just below Things to Do.*** The "Adding a new Event" window should now be displayed. Notice that AbacusLaw entered **"NOTE"** in the What field. Also, in the When field next to the date of 06/12/15, it says **"TO-DO"** for this entry.
27. Enter the matter information from the following list in the "Adding a new Event" window (Table 5–7).

TABLE 5–7	
FIELD NAME	**DATA TO ENTER**
Who	**DIANA**
What	**NOTE**
When	**06/12/15 TO-DO**
Where	**HERE**
Description (open light yellow box)	**Send Digital Media Equipment, Inc. an electronic discovery request in Magrino case.**
Name	**Magrino, Cathy**
Matter	**Magrino v. American Insurance**
Priority	
Type	**T**
Status	**N**
Reminders	**0 0**

28. When you have finished entering all of the data, ***click Save in the "Adding a new Event" window.*** The entry should now appear in your Daily Organizer under Things To Do. *Note:* Items entered in Things to Do will perpetually stay in the Daily Organizer section of Things To Do (once the item is overdue) until the user marks it Done. Notice that in the Things To Do section of the Daily Organizer, there is a white box next to the entry you just made. You would click the box to indicate that the item had been completed. Once that box is checked, the item no longer shows up in the Things To Do section of the Daily Organizer.
29. You will now make a Calls to Make entry. ***In the "Daily Organizer—Friday, June 12, 2015" window, double-click just below Calls to Make.*** The "Adding a new Event" window should now be displayed. Notice that AbacusLaw entered **"PHONE"** in the What field. Also, in the When field next to the date of 06/12/15, it says **"TO-DO"** for this entry.
30. Enter the matter information from the following list in the "Adding a new Event" window (Table 5–8).

TABLE 5–8	
FIELD NAME	**DATA TO ENTER**
Who	**DIANA**
What	**PHONE**
When	**06/08/15 TO-DO**
Where	**HERE**
Description (open light yellow box)	**Call Colleen Gleason to see if she returned from Russia with child.**
Name	**Gleason, Colleen**
Matter	**Gleason Adoption**
Priority	
Type	**P**
Status	**N**
Reminders	**0 0**

31. When you have finished entering all of the data, ***click Save in the "Adding a new Event" window*** (Table 5–9). The entry should now appear in your Daily Organizer under Calls to Make. Notice that Abacus Law automatically entered the client's phone number in the entry. *Note:* You can also make entries in the Reminders section of the Daily Organizer by ***double-clicking just below Reminders.*** Reminders just show up on the day they are scheduled for and do not carry forward from day to day, even if they are not marked as completed.
32. Create the following events:

TABLE 5–9	
Date:	**6/12/2015 Appointment**
Who	**DIANA**
What	**DRAFT**
When	**06/12/15 at 9:00a for 3.00 hours**
Where	**HERE**
Description (open light yellow box)	**Draft discovery documents**
Name	**Magrino, Cathy**
Matter	**Magrino v. American Insurance**
Priority	**1**
Type	**A**
Status	**N**
Reminders	**1 0**
Date:	**6/09/2015 Appointment**
Who	**DIANA**
What	**APPT**
When	**06/09/15 at 9:30a for 0.50 hours**
Where	**HERE**
Description (open light yellow box)	**Call immigration agency as scheduled re: adoption papers**
Name	**Gleason, Colleen**
Matter	**Gleason Adoption**
Priority	**1**
Type	**A**
Status	**N**
Reminders	**1 3**
Date:	**6/10/2015 Appointment**
Who	**DIANA**
What	**APPT**
When	**06/10/15 at 9:00a for 2.50 hours**
Where	**HERE**
Description (open light yellow box)	**Draft amended Adoption papers**
Name	**Gleason, Colleen**

HANDS-ON EXERCISES

Matter	**Gleason Adoption**
Priority	
Type	**T**
Status	**N**
Reminders	**0 0**
Date:	**6/12/2015 Appointment**
Who	**DIANA**
What	**APPT**
When	**06/12/15 at 2:00p for 2.00 hours**
Where	**HERE**
Description (open light yellow box)	**Meet with Arthur to discuss electronic discovery issues and discovery responses**
Name	**Magrino, Cathy**
Matter	**Magrino v. American Insurance**
Priority	
Type	**T**
Status	**N**
Reminders	**1 0**

33. After you have made all of the entries, ***click Week on the toolbar.*** Your weekly calendar for the week of June 8, 2015 should look similar to AbacusLaw Exhibit 18. *Note:* The gray bars that separate the reminders, appointment, and things-to-do sections can be dragged up or down to adjust how the information appears on the screen (see AbacusLaw Exhibit 18).

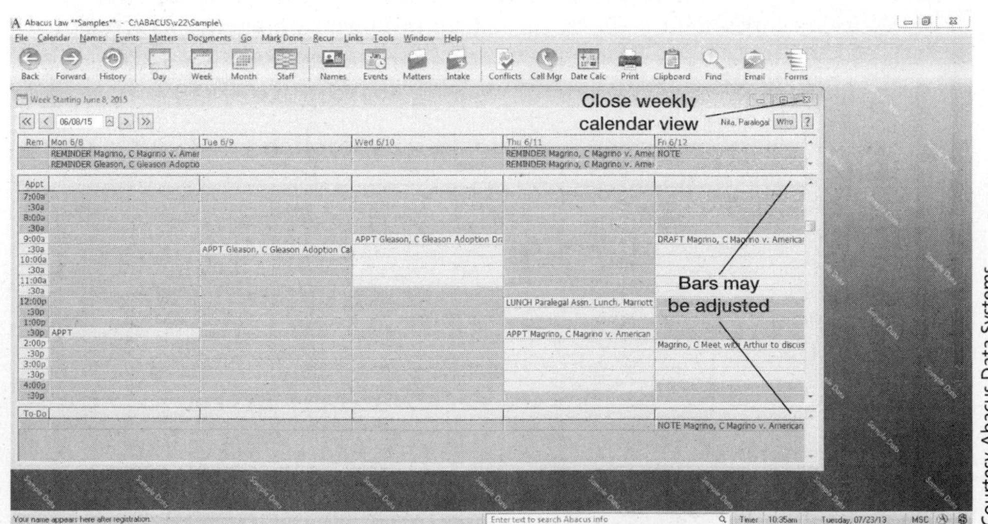

ABACUSLAW EXHIBIT 18
Weekly schedule

34. ***Click the Close (X) icon for the Weekly calendar view.***
35. ***Click the Close (X) icon for the Daily Organizer.***

36. ***Click File on the menu bar and then click Exit*** (the very last entry under the Recent Files Accessed list).
37. At the **"Please register now!"** window, ***click OK.***

This concludes Lesson 4.

LESSON 5: CREATING EVENTS, PART 2

Rule-based entries are extremely efficient and can greatly enhance data entry. In this lesson, you will create a recurring event, make a rule-based entry, and work with the Date Calculator. This lesson assumes that you have completed Lessons 1 through 4 and that you are familiar with the AbacusLaw interface.

1. The first thing you will do in this lesson is populate AbacusLaw with sample data. *If you start AbacusLaw from the icon on the desktop, the sample data will not be loaded,* so please follow these directions.
2. Start Windows. ***Click the Start button on the Windows desktop, point to Programs or All Programs, point to the AbacusLaw group, then click Sample Data.*** This will populate Abacus Law with some sample data.
3. The "User Log on" window should now be displayed. Note that the AbacusLaw desktop should say **"Sample Data."**
4. In the "User Log on" window, in the User ID field, type the same initials you entered in Lesson 1. It is important that you enter the same initials each time you start Abacus Law. Do not type anything in the Password field. ***Click OK in the "User Log on" window.***
5. The "Tip of the Day" window should now be displayed on your screen. ***Click OK in the "Tip of the Day" window.*** You should now be at the Abacus desktop with the name plate that reads **"Your name appears here after registration."**
6. You will next make a recurring entry that will occur every day. Arthur Simon has decided that he would like to have a staff meeting with Diana Nita from 8:30 a.m. to 9:00 a.m. every morning through the month of June.
7. ***Click Day on the toolbar to see the Daily Organizer. Change the date on the Daily Organizer to 06/08/2015.***
8. ***Double-click on 8:30a.*** Create the events using the data in the following list (Table 5–10). *Note:* You will need to add a new WHAT entry for the staff meeting. ***Click the up arrow to the right of the WHAT text box and in the "Valid WHAT Entries" window, click Add.*** In the "New "WHAT" Code" window, type **STAFF MT, *click OK***; then, in the "WHAT Code Description" window, type **Staff Meeting. *Click OK in the "WHAT Code Description" window.*** Finally, ***click on Staff Meeting in the "Valid WHAT Entries" window and click OK.***

TABLE 5–10	
Who	**DIANA**
What	**STAFF MT**
When	**06/08/15 at 8:30a for .50 hours**
Where	**HERE**
Description (open light yellow box)	
Name	
Matter	
Priority	
Type	**A**
Status	**N**
Reminders	**0 0**

HANDS-ON EXERCISES

9. Once you have finished creating the entry, ***click Save in the "Adding a new Event" window.***
10. In the Daily Organizer, the STAFF MT entry you just created should be selected. ***Click Recur on the menu bar*** (see AbacusLaw Exhibit 19.) The "Recur Event: STAFF MT…" window should now be displayed. ***Click Daily under Interval, change the End entry to 06/25/15, click the box to the left of Omit weekend events, then click OK.***
11. The "Select an option" window should appear and ask **"Ready to schedule up to 17 events through 06/25/15. Are you sure?"** ***Click Yes.*** The "Linked Events Browse" window is then displayed (see AbacusLaw Exhibit 20). You can see all of the entries that the program is about to make. ***Click OK.***

ABACUSLAW EXHIBIT 19
Entering a recurring event

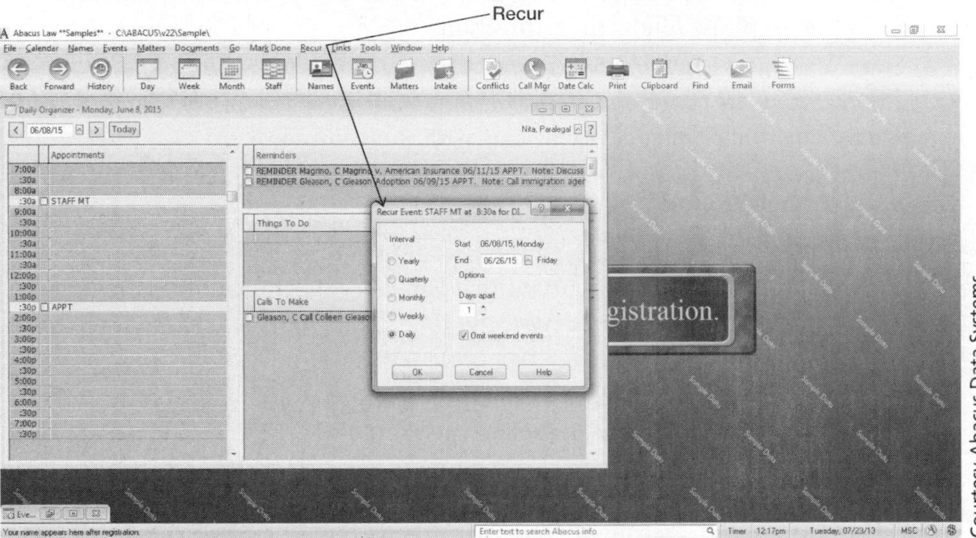

Courtesy Abacus Data Systems.

ABACUSLAW EXHIBIT 20
Recurring event—"Linked Events Browse" window

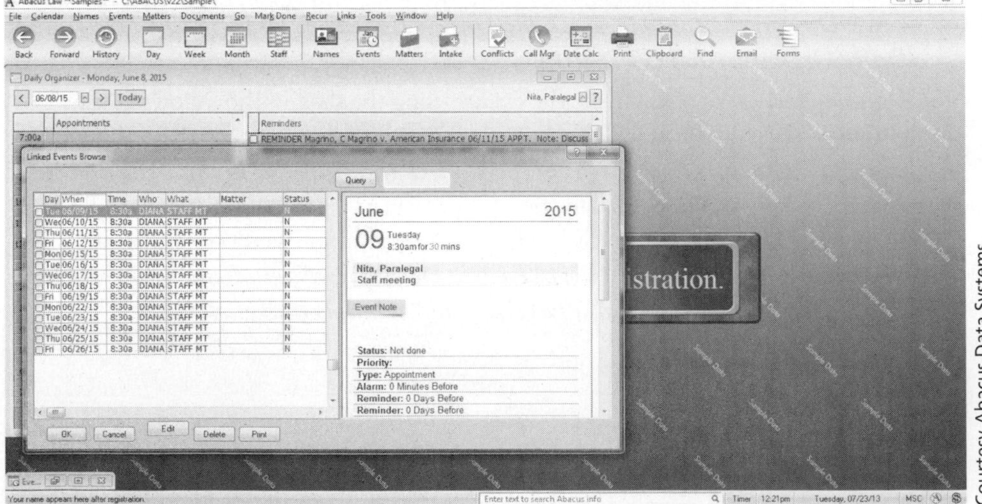
Courtesy Abacus Data Systems.

12. ***In the Daily Organizer, next to the date, click Next day > several times*** and notice that the staff meeting has been added.
13. You will next enter a new matter and learn how to make a rule-based entry for the new matter. Arthur Simon has told you that the firm will be handling a new matter for Cathy Magrino regarding the sale of a piece of property and that he would like you to schedule the normal New Matter deadlines. The initial client meeting for the matter will be on 6/10/15.

14. ***Click Matters on the toolbar, then click on Add.***
15. In the "Adding a new Matter" window, enter the data from the following list (Table 5–11).

TABLE 5–11

FIELD NAME	DATA TO ENTER
Matter	**Magrino Property Sale, 1001 Main**
File/case#	**1005**
Attorney	**AMS**
Case Code	**REA**
Court	
Opened	**06 09 15**
Closed	
User1	
User2	
User3	
User4	

16. When you are finished, ***click Save in the "Adding a new Matter" window. From the "Matter: Magrino Property Sale, 1001 Main" window, click the Linked Names tab, click Add link, click Magrino, Cathy, and click OK in the "Names Browse" window.***
17. ***In the "Name-to-Matter Link" window, click the up arrow next to Link Type. In the "Valid ATTACHTYPE Entries" window, click CLIENT and then click OK. Click OK in the "Name-to-Matter Link" window.***
18. An entry for "Magrino, Cathy" now appears in the "Matter: Magrino Property Sale, 1001 Main" window. ***Click the Close (X) icon in the "Matter: Magrino Property Sale, 1001 Main" window.***
19. You should be back at the Daily Organizer for 06/10/15. ***Right-click 1:00p. Click Add Events from a Rule.*** The "Rules" window should now be displayed (see AbacusLaw Exhibit 21).
20. ***In the "Rules" window, click NEWCASE. Then, in the "Rules" window, click Edit.***

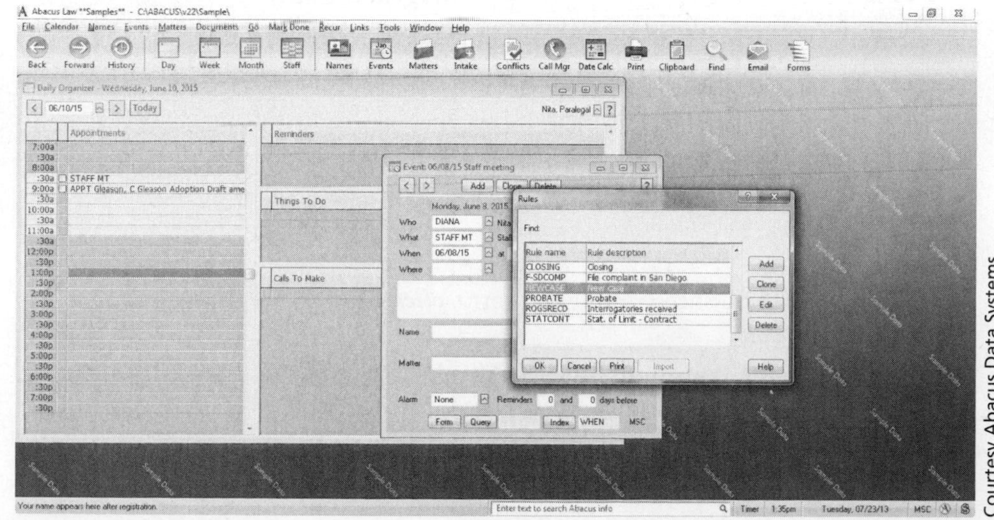

ABACUSLAW EXHIBIT 21
Making a rule-based entry

ABACUSLAW EXHIBIT 22
Rule-based entry—"Rule name" window

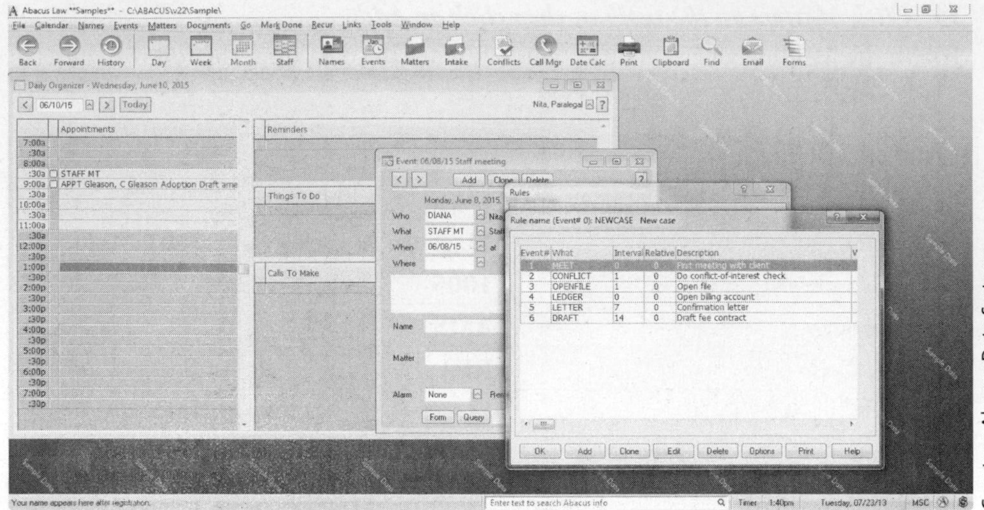

21. The "Rule name (Event #0): NEWCASE New case" window should be displayed (see AbacusLaw Exhibit 22). This screen shows the entries that will automatically be made. The Interval column refers to the number of days from the initial event (e.g., 0 days, 1 day, 1 day, 0 days, 7 days, or 14 days).
22. ***Click OK in the "Rule name (Event #0): NEWCASE New case" window.***
23. ***In the "Rules" window, click OK.*** Notice that NEWCASE has now been added to the open Event on the screen. Enter the information from the following list in the "Adding a New Event" window (Table 5–12). Note that in the Matter field you will need to ***click the up arrow next to the Matter field then click the Magrino Property Sale matter in the "Matters for Magrino, Cathy" window, then click OK.***

TABLE 5–12	
Who	**DIANA**
What	**NEWCASE**
When	**06/10/15 at 1:00p for 1.00 hours**
Where	**HERE**
Description (open light yellow box)	
Name	**Magrino, Cathy**
Matter	**Magrino Property Sale**
Priority	
Type	**A**
Status	**N**
Reminders	**0 0**

24. When you are finished creating the entry, ***click Save in the "Adding a new Event" window.***
25. The "Creating Events from Rule: NEWCASE" window is displayed. You are asked if you want the related events scheduled. ***Click Yes.***
26. The "Linked Events Browse" window should be displayed (see AbacusLaw Exhibit 23). ***Click OK in the "Linked Events Browse" window.*** Notice that

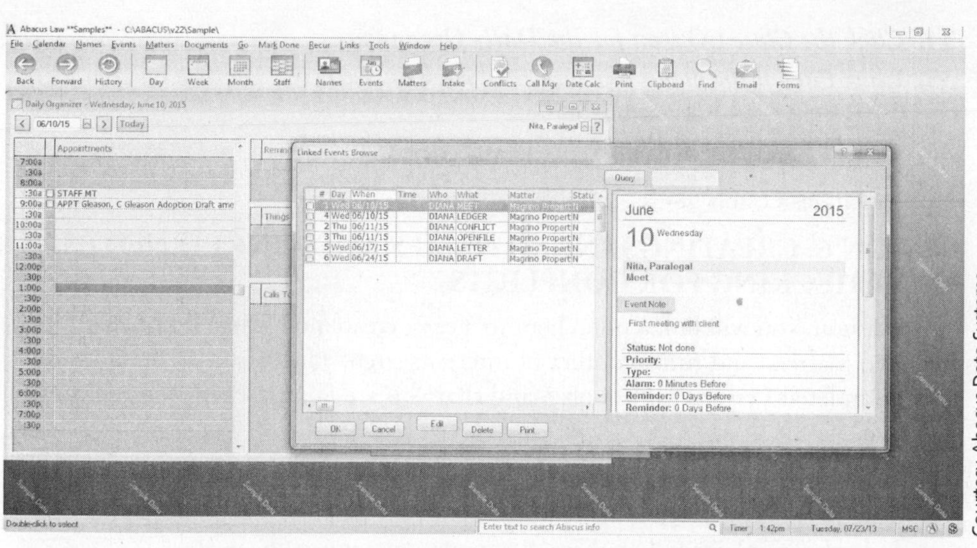

ABACUSLAW EXHIBIT 23
Rule-based entry—"Linked Events Browse" window

Courtesy Abacus Data Systems.

the initial meeting is set at 1:00 and that in the Reminders section of the Daily Organizer there are some entries regarding the new case.

27. ***Click the Next Day icon (>) in the Daily Organizer until you come to 06/17/15.*** Notice that there is a reminder to do the Confirmation Letter.
28. ***Click the Next Day icon (>) in the Daily Organizer until you come to 06/24/15.*** Notice that there is a reminder to do the fee contract.
29. In the date field in the Daily Organizer, type **06/11/15** and press the **[ENTER]** key.
30. You will now use the Date Calculator feature. On 06/11/15 the office received a motion to dismiss that must be responded to, within 20 days. Arthur Simon asks you to let him know exactly what date the response is due using the AbacusLaw Date Calculator.
31. ***Click Date Calc on the toolbar.*** The "Date Calculator" window should now be displayed (see AbacusLaw Exhibit 24).

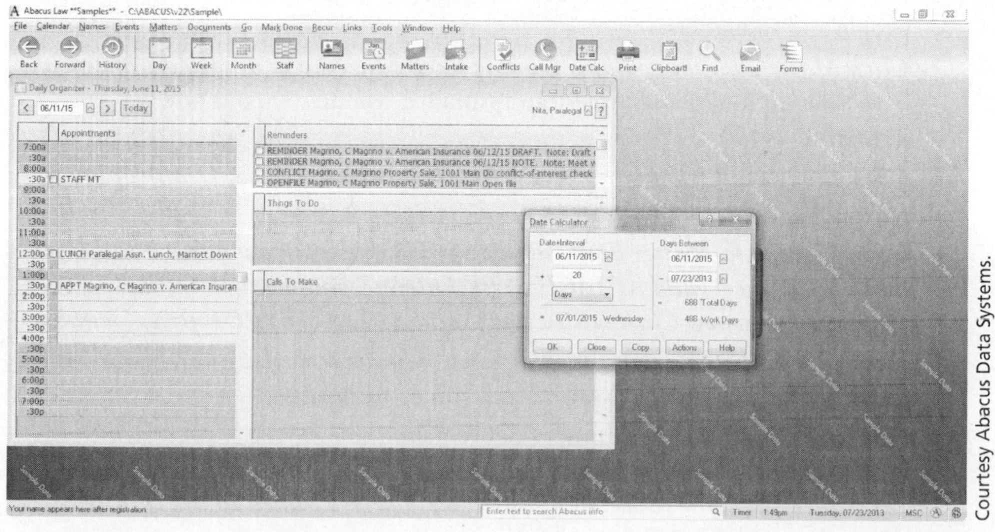

ABACUSLAW EXHIBIT 24
Date Calculator

Courtesy Abacus Data Systems.

32. Under Date+Interval, type **06/11/2015**, then enter **20** next to the plus sign (+). ***Click the down arrow next to Days and select Days.*** The Date Calculator should return a date of "07/01/2015 (Wednesday)."
33. ***Click OK to close the Date Calculator.***

34. ***Click the Close (X) icon for the Daily Organizer.***
35. ***Click File on the menu bar and then click on Exit*** (the very last entry under the Recent Files Accessed list).
36. At the **"Please register now!"** window, ***click OK.***

This concludes Lesson 5.

LESSON 6: CREATING LINKED NAMES AND LINKED NOTES, AND CHECKING FOR CONFLICTS

In this lesson, you will link a non-client to a case, create notes that are linked to contacts and matters, and run a conflict of interest search. This lesson assumes that you have completed Lessons 1 through 5 and that you are familiar with the AbacusLaw interface.

1. The first thing you will do in this lesson is populate AbacusLaw with sample data. *If you start AbacusLaw from the icon on the desktop, the sample data will not be loaded,* so please follow these directions.
2. Start Windows. ***Click the Start button on the Windows desktop, point to Programs or All Programs, point to the AbacusLaw group, and click Sample Data.*** This will populate Abacus Law with some sample data.
3. The "User Log on" window should now be displayed. Note that the AbacusLaw desktop should say **"Sample Data."**
4. In the "User Log on" window, in the User ID field, type the same initials you entered in Lesson 1. It is important that you enter the same initials each time you load Abacus Law. Do not type anything in the Password field. ***Click OK in the "User Log on" window.***
5. The "Tip of the Day" window should now be displayed on your screen. ***Click OK in the "Tip of the Day" window.*** You should now be at the Abacus desktop with the name plate that reads **"Your name appears here after registration."**
6. The first thing you will do is link an opposing attorney to a case. Just as you can link clients to matters, you can link people who are not clients to other people and to matters.
7. ***Click Matters on the toolbar. Double-click Magrino v. American Insurance.*** The "Matter: Magrino v. American Insurance" window should now be displayed.
8. ***Click the Linked Names tab. Click Add link. Click McKie, Dianne and then click OK.***
9. ***In the "Name-to-Matter Link" window, click the up arrow next to Link Type and then in the "Valid ATTACHTYPE Entries" window click OPP-ATTY-Opposing Attorney. Click OK in the "Valid ATTACHTYPE Entries" window.***
10. ***Click OK in the "Name-to-Matter Link" window.*** Notice that Dianne McKie, the defendant's attorney, has now been linked to the case.
11. You have already added a number of events to the *Magrino v. American Insurance* case. ***Click the Events tab in the "Matter: Magrino v. American Insurance" window to see all of the items that are linked to the case.*** See AbacusLaw Exhibit 25.
12. You will now create two notes that will be linked to the case.
13. ***Click the Notes tab in the "Matter: Magrino v. American Insurance" window. Click Add.***

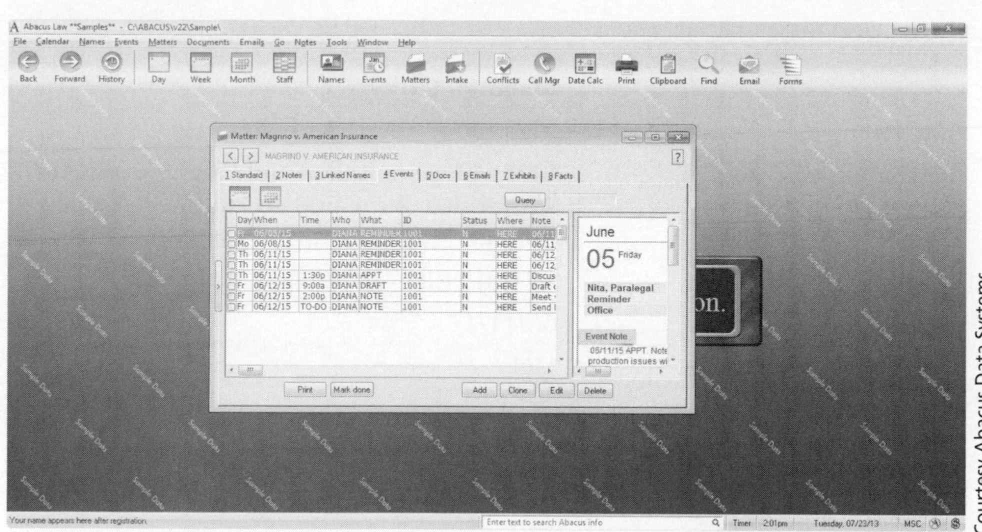

ABACUSLAW EXHIBIT 25
Listing of linked events

Courtesy Abacus Data Systems.

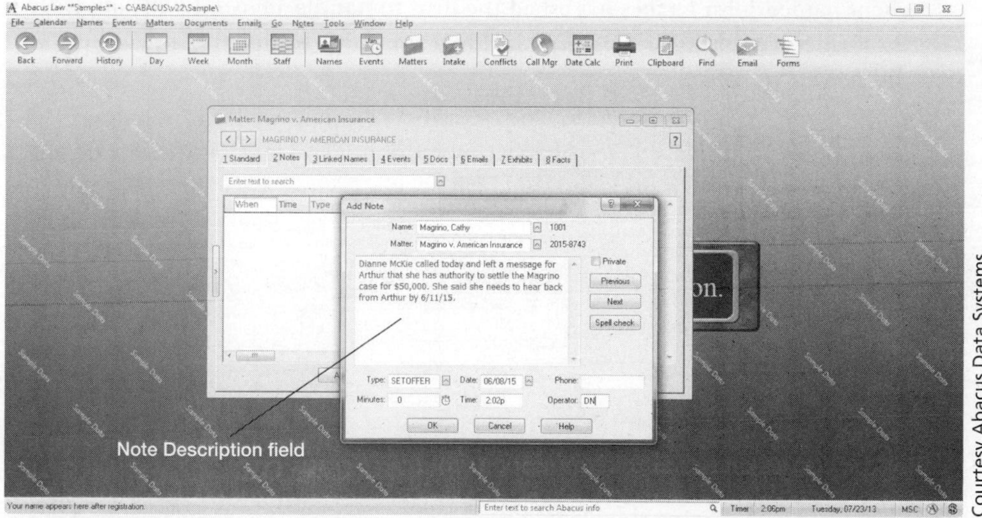

ABACUSLAW EXHIBIT 26
Adding a note

Courtesy Abacus Data Systems.

HANDS-ON EXERCISES

14. The "Add Note" window should now be displayed (see AbacusLaw Exhibit 26). Notice that **"Magrino, Cathy"** has already been entered and linked to the Name field and that **"Magrino v. American Insurance"** has already been linked as the matter concerning the note.
15. ***Click in the note description field.*** Type **Dianne McKie called today and left a message for Arthur that she has authority to settle the Magrino case for $50,000. She said she needs to hear back from Arthur by 6/11/15.** (See AbacusLaw Exhibit 26.)
16. ***Click the up arrow next to Type, click SETOFFER Settlement Offer, then click OK in the "Valid NOTETYPE Entries" window.***
17. In the Date field of the "Add Note" window, type **06/08/15.**
18. In the Operator field of the "Add Note" window, type **DN** and then ***click OK.***
19. Notice that the note has now been added.
20. ***Click Add*** to add one more note. Create the note using the data in the following list (Table 5–13).

TABLE 5–13	
Name	**Magrino, Cathy**
Matter	**Magrino v. American Insurance**
Description	**Cathy Magrino called and left a message for Arthur that she would accept the defendant's offer to settle the case for $50,000.**
Type:	**SETOFFER**
Date:	**06/11/15**
Operator:	**DN**

21. When you have finished creating the note, ***click OK in the "Add Note" window.***
22. ***Click the Close (X) icon in the "Matter: Magrino v. American Insurance" window.***
23. You will now run a conflict of interest search. Arthur Simon called and asked you to run the name of Margaret Krakes for conflicts of interest. A possible new client named John Krakes has asked the firm to handle a custody dispute with his former wife, Margaret. Arthur said that the name sounded familiar, but he did not know why.
24. ***Click Conflicts on the toolbar.*** The "Conflict of Interest Check" window should now be displayed (see AbacusLaw Exhibit 27). Under Enter last name, type **Krakes** and then press the **[ENTER]** key.

ABACUSLAW EXHIBIT 27
Running a conflict of interest search

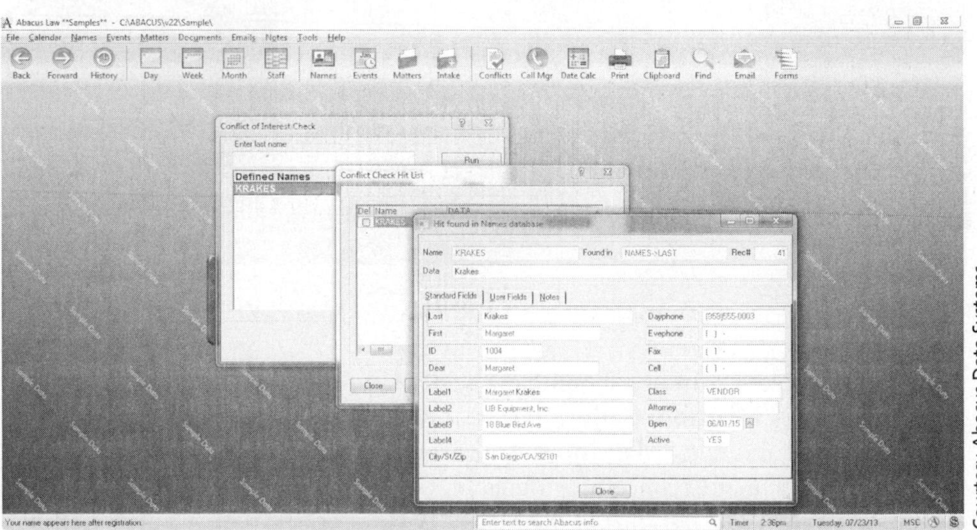

25. ***Click Run in the "Conflict of Interest Check" window*** (see AbacusLaw Exhibit 27). The "Conflict Check Hit List" window is then displayed.
26. ***Double-click KRAKES in the "Conflict Check Hit List" window.*** The "Hit found in Names database" window is then displayed (see AbacusLaw Exhibit 27). Margaret Krakes is a vendor with whom the firm works.
27. ***Click Close in the "Hit found in Names database" window and then click the Close (X) icons for the other open windows.***
28. ***Click File on the menu bar and then click Exit*** (the very last entry under the Recent Files Accessed list).
29. At the **"Please register now!"** window, ***click OK.***

This concludes Lesson 6.

ADVANCED LESSONS

LESSON 7: LINKING DOCUMENTS; USING THE CALL MANAGER AND THE FORM GENERATION FEATURE

In this lesson, you will link documents, use the Call Manager feature, use the Form Generation feature, and work with the Events Browse tool. This lesson assumes that you have completed Lessons 1 through 6 and that you are familiar with the AbacusLaw interface.

1. The first thing you will do in this lesson is populate AbacusLaw with sample data. *If you start AbacusLaw from the icon on the desktop, the sample data will not be loaded,* so please follow these directions.
2. Start Windows. ***Click the Start button on the Windows desktop, point to Programs or All Programs, point to the AbacusLaw group, then click Sample Data.*** This will populate Abacus Law with some sample data.
3. The "User Log on" window should now be displayed. Note that the AbacusLaw desktop should say **"Sample Data."**
4. In the "User Log on" window, in the User ID field, type the same initials you entered in Lesson 1. It is important that you enter the same initials each time you load Abacus Law. Do not type anything in the Password field. ***Click OK in the "User Log on" window.***
5. The "Tip of the Day" window should now be displayed on your screen. ***Click OK in the "Tip of the Day" window.*** You should now be at the Abacus desktop with the name plate that reads **"Your name appears here after registration."**
6. ***Click Matters on the toolbar.*** Press the **[HOME]** key to go the beginning of the matters in the "Matters Browse" window.
7. ***Double-click Cal. Computers v. Multimedia. In the "Matter: Cal. Computers v. Multimedia" window, click the Docs tab. Click Edit*** to see the screen that is used to add/edit a link (see AbacusLaw Exhibit 28). The process is extremely easy: The user types the path of the document, links the document to a name and/or matter, and then completes the rest of the options in the screen, if desired (see AbacusLaw Exhibit 28). ***Click the Close (X) icon in the "Document Details" window.***
8. ***Click the Close (X) icon in the "Matter: Cal. Computers v. Multimedia" window.***
9. You will now learn to use the Call Manager feature. ***Click Call Mgr on the toolbar.***
10. Enter the call in the "Call Manager" window as shown in AbacusLaw Exhibit 29. Notice that you can indicate whether the call is an incoming call or an outgoing call. You can use the Call Manager to make a record of all incoming and outgoing calls.
11. In AbacusLaw Exhibit 29, in the "Call Manager" window, notice that there is a button for an option called Bill. If AbacusLaw is set up to exchange information with a timekeeping and billing system, you can click the Bill button, the entry will be sent to timekeeping and billing, and the client will be billed for the time.

ABACUSLAW EXHIBIT 28
Adding and editing a link to a document

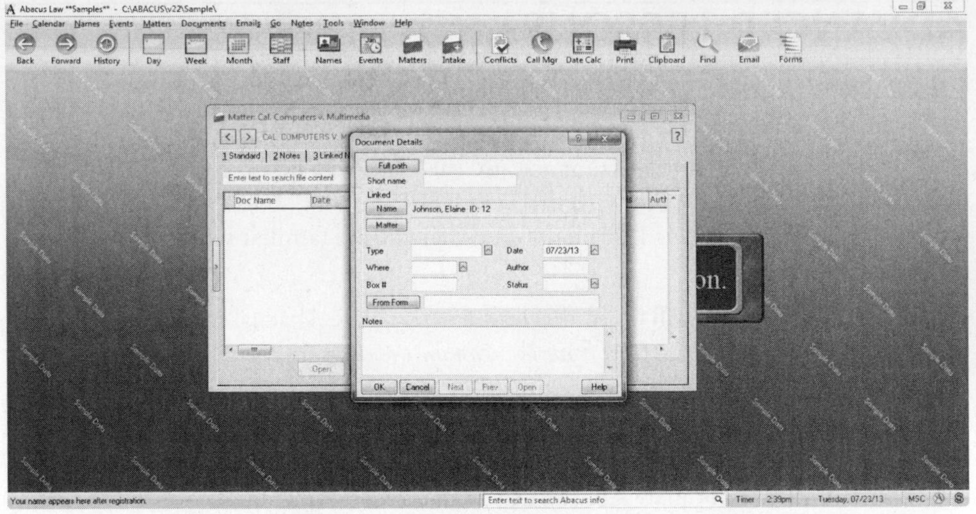

Courtesy Abacus Data Systems.

ABACUSLAW EXHIBIT 29
Entering a call in the Call Manager

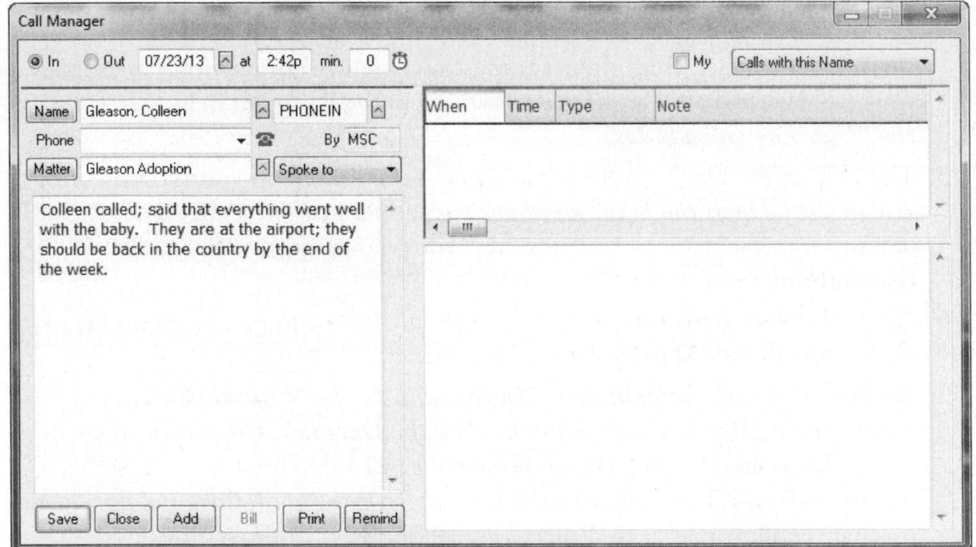

Courtesy Abacus Data Systems.

12. When you have entered the call, ***click Save and then click Close in the "Call Manager" window.***
13. You can see all calls entered in the Call Manager in either the Matters or Contacts Notes tab. ***Click Matters on the toolbar, double-click Gleason Adoption, and click the Notes tab.*** You should now see the entry for the phone call.
14. ***Click the Close (X) icon in the "Matter: Gleason Adoption" window.***
15. You will now learn how to use the Form Generation feature in AbacusLaw. (*Note:* This part of the lesson requires Microsoft Excel.) ***Click Names on the toolbar, then scroll to and double-click on Magrino, Cathy.*** The "Name: Magrino, Cathy" window should now be displayed.
16. ***Click the Events tab, then click the 06/11/15 1:30 p entry.*** The data from this entry will be referenced in the form you will generate.
17. ***Click Print on the toolbar, click Form generation, then click MS Excel.***

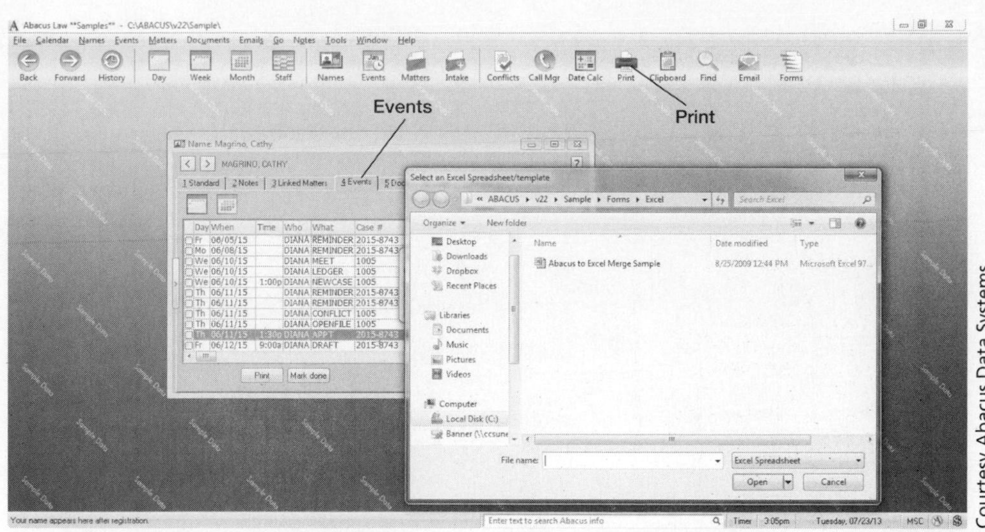

ABACUSLAW EXHIBIT 30A
Selecting a template to run with the Form Generation feature

Courtesy Abacus Data Systems.

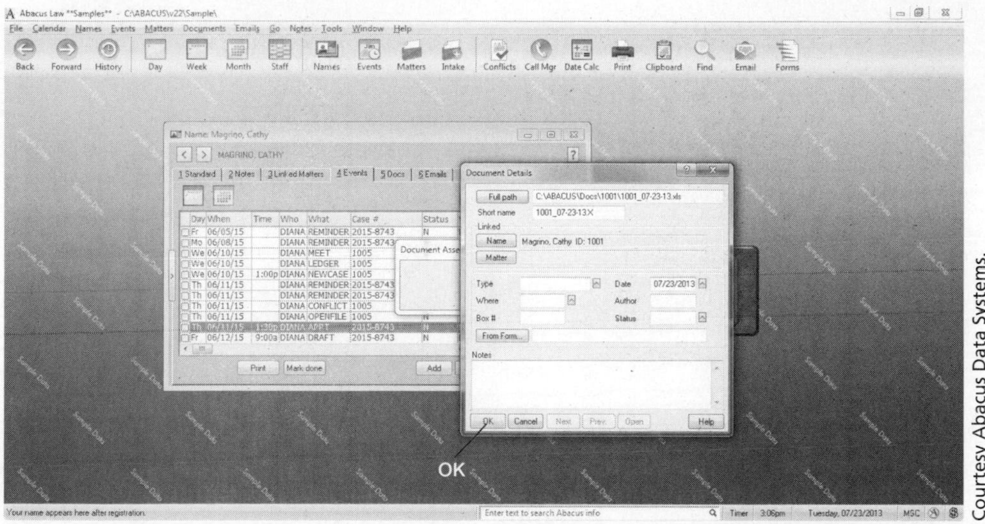

ABACUSLAW EXHIBIT 30B
Selecting a template to run with the Form Generation feature

Courtesy Abacus Data Systems.

18. The "Select an Excel Spreadsheet/template" window should now be displayed (see AbacusLaw Exhibit 30A). ***Double-click the file called Abacus to Excel Merge Sample*** (see AbacusLaw Exhibit 30A). The "Document Details" window will open; ***click OK*** (see AbacusLaw Exhibit 30B).
19. You should now be in Microsoft Excel with the template filled in (see AbacusLaw Exhibit 31). Notice that Abacus Law automatically inserted the client's address, case name, and date of the event in the form. ***Close the file in Excel.***
20. ***Click once more on the "AbacusLaw" window if it is not already shown. Close the "Name: Magrino, Cathy" window.***
21. ***Click Events on the toolbar.*** The "Events Browse" window shows you all of the events that have been entered into AbacusLaw (see AbacusLaw Exhibit 32). The default setting sorts events on the When (date) field. You can also sort the events by the What field by clicking in the What column heading. You can also use the Query feature to select fewer than all events. The "Events Browse" window allows you to manage all events in a quick and easy interface. ***Click the Close (X) icon in the "Events Browse" window.***

ABACUSLAW EXHIBIT 31
Document generation—Completed form and template

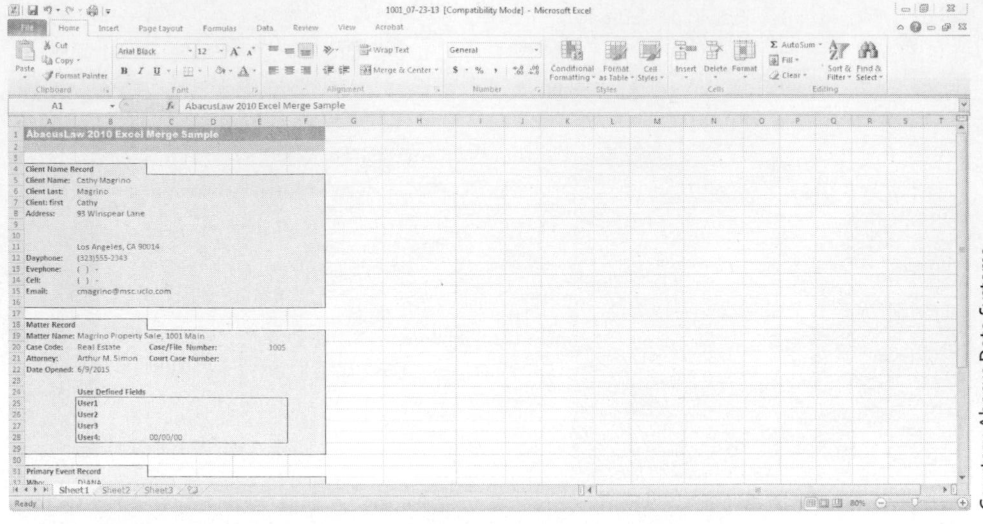

Courtesy Abacus Data Systems.

ABACUSLAW EXHIBIT 32
"Events Browse" window

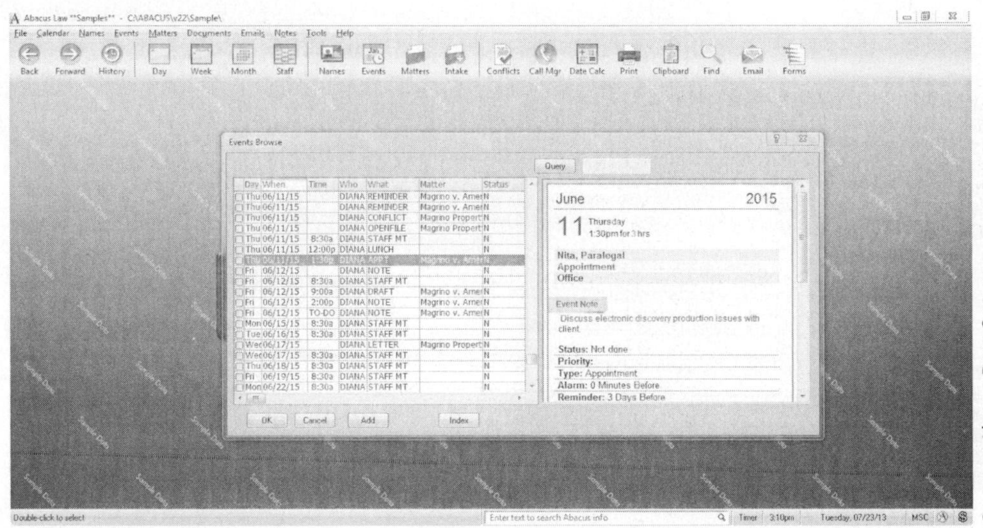

Courtesy Abacus Data Systems.

22. ***Click File on the menu bar and then click Exit*** (the very last entry on the Recent Files Accessed list).
23. At the **"Please register now!"** window, ***click OK.***

This concludes Lesson 7.

LESSON 8: REPORTS

In this lesson, you will run a number of reports in AbacusLaw. This lesson assumes that you have completed Lessons 1 through 7 and that you are familiar with the AbacusLaw interface.

1. The first thing you will do in this lesson is populate AbacusLaw with sample data. *If you start AbacusLaw from the icon on the desktop, the sample data will not be loaded,* so please follow these directions.
2. Start Windows. ***Click the Start button on the Windows desktop, point the cursor to Programs or All Programs, point to the AbacusLaw group, then click Sample Data.*** This will populate Abacus Law with some sample data.
3. The "User Log on" window should now be displayed. Note that the AbacusLaw desktop should say **"Sample Data."**

4. In the "User Log on" window, in the User ID field, type the same initials you entered in Lesson 1. It is important that you enter the same initials each time you load Abacus Law. Do not type anything in the Password field. ***Click OK in the "User Log on" window.***
5. The "Tip of the Day" window should now be displayed on your screen. ***Click OK in the "Tip of the Day" window.*** You should now be at the Abacus desktop with the name plate that reads **"Your name appears here after registration."**
6. AbacusLaw comes with more than 100 standard reports. You will run just a few of them. ***Click File on the menu bar, point to Reports, then click All reports.***
7. ***In the "Report List:" window, click OK.*** The "Report Control" window should now be displayed. This report will run a matters or case list for the whole office. The default setting will print the reports to the screen. If you wanted to change that, you would click Output to and select a printer, but **"Screen"** is fine for this exercise.
8. ***Click Print in the "Report Control" window.*** A listing of all of the clients and names linked to the cases should be displayed (see AbacusLaw Exhibit 33). To scroll through this list, ***click Continuous*** at the top of the Report Control window and use the scroll bar on the right side of the window.
9. ***Click the red X (Exit) on the toolbar in the "Report Viewer" window.***
10. The "Report Control" window is again displayed. This time you will run a report just of the cases on which Arthur Simon is the lead attorney.
11. ***In the "Report Control" window, click Query, then click Quick query.*** The "Quick Query for EVENTS" window is displayed.
12. ***Click the up arrow key next to Who and double-click AMS Arthur M. Simon. Click OK in the "Quick Query for EVENTS" window.***
13. ***In the "Report Control" window, click Print.*** Scroll through the document and look at only the matters that Arthur Simon is managing. When you are done viewing the report, ***click the red X (Exit) on the toolbar in the "Report Viewer" window.***

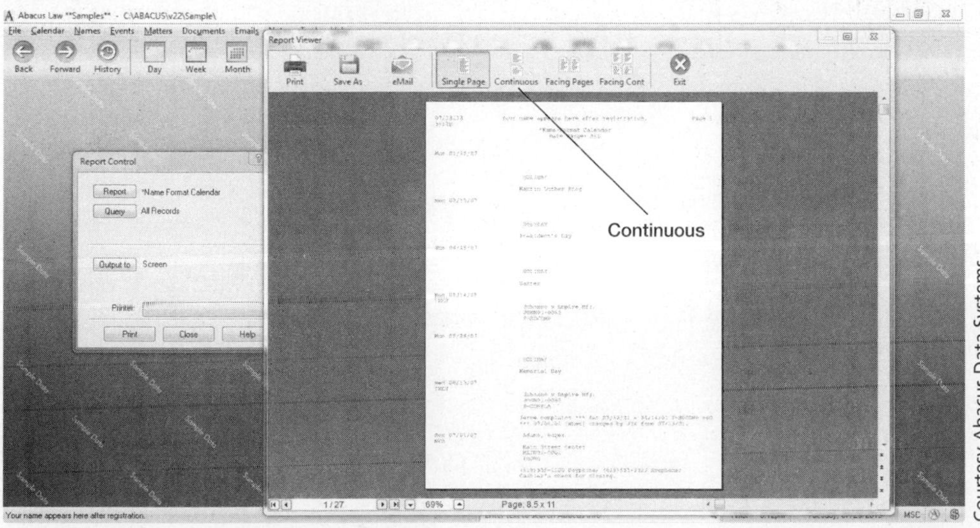

ABACUSLAW EXHIBIT 33
Report Viewer

Courtesy Abacus Data Systems.

14. The "Report Control" window should again be displayed. ***Click Query and then click Clear current query.***
15. The "Report Control" window should again be displayed. ***Click Report and then click Matter Format Calendar.*** This will produce a list of calendar events for cases. Because this list could be long, you will just run this report for the *Magrino v. American Insurance* case.

16. ***Click OK in the "Report List:" window. In the "Report Control" window, click Query and then click Quick query.*** The "Quick Query for EVENTS" window should be displayed.
17. ***Click the up arrow key next to Matter and double-click Magrino v. American Insurance. Click OK in the "Quick Query for EVENTS" window.***
18. ***In the "Report Control" window, click Print.*** Scroll through the document and look at all of the events for the *Magrino v. American Insurance* case.
19. When you are done viewing the report, ***click the red X (Exit) on the toolbar in the "Report Viewer" window.***
20. The "Report Control" window is again displayed. ***Click Query and then click Clear current query.***
21. The "Report Control" window should again be displayed. ***Click Close in the "Report Control" window.***
22. You will now print a report for a date range. ***Click File on the menu bar, point to Reports, then click Events (Calendars).*** In the "Events Report Control" window, under All, type **06/08/2015 - 06/12/2015** and then ***click Print.***
23. When you are done viewing the report, ***point and click on the red X (Exit) on the toolbar in the "Report Viewer" window.***
24. ***Click Close in the "Events Report Control" window.***
25. ***Click File in the menu bar and then click Exit*** (the very last entry on the Recent Files Accessed list).
26. At the **"Please register now!"** window, ***click OK.***

This concludes the AbacusLaw Hands-On Exercises.

CHAPTER 6

The Cloud and Social Media

CHAPTER OBJECTIVES

After completing this chapter, you should be able to do the following:

1. Understand how legal professionals use the cloud.
2. Understand the ethical issues posed by the use of the cloud by legal professionals.
3. What is social media and how it has impacted the practice of law.
4. Understand the legal ethical issues raised by the use of social media.

INTRODUCTION

Perhaps the most notable development over the last 10 years has been the development of, and acceptance of, the cloud and social media. People stream movies, listen to music, share photographs and videos, shop, and converse via social media. And social media is just one example of the "cloud"—the ability to use one computer to access information stored on other computers. Smartphones, tablet computers, and Wi-Fi have given the general public the ability to access the Internet, and therefore a virtually limitless source of information, from almost anywhere. This provides the legal profession with a wealth of information and headaches that were unknown just a few years earlier. As noted in the previous chapter, electronic discovery has changed the nature of litigation. As you will see in this chapter, discovery is not the only aspect of the legal profession that has been affected by the proliferation of the cloud in general and social media in particular. Finally, both the cloud and social media raise an array of ethical issues—diligence, competence, confidentiality, just to name a few.

WHAT IS THE "CLOUD"?

In recent years, we have all heard a lot about the cloud. People use the cloud to store photographs and music files and to access email accounts. In reality, the cloud has been around ever since the inception of the Internet and the World Wide Web. The National Institute of Standards and Technology, NIST, (www.nist.gov) defines cloud computing as "a model for enabling convenient, on-demand network access to a shared pool of configurable computing resources (e.g., networks, servers, storage, applications, and services) that can be rapidly provisioned and released with minimal management effort or service provider interaction." The "**cloud**" is nothing more than a system of interconnected computers—it is using one computer to access data that

Cloud
refers to the ability to access information residing on remote computers

resides on another computer. When you download something, you take something from the cloud. So when you load a software application on your computer (or update an application), you are using the cloud. When you download a song from iTunes, when you buy a book (or e-book) from Amazon.com, you are using the cloud. When you use your CengageBrain account to access one of the software applications that come with this text, you are using the cloud. So, downloading data FROM the cloud is not new.

What is new, is now people are uploading data TO the cloud—using the cloud as a storage facility for electronic data. The cloud offers people the opportunity to access their data anywhere and anytime (as long as there is an Internet connection). For legal professionals, this takes the concept of the paperless office to a new level. The computer made it paperless—the cloud means you don't even need a physical office. Law firms are starting to migrate much of the traditional law office paperwork to the cloud—client files, billing information, correspondence are now as likely to be found in the cloud as in a filing cabinet. Many law office software applications are now available in a form known as **Software as a Service (SaaS)**. Westlaw is a familiar example of SaaS—when you use Westlaw, you don't download the program on your computer; you access the information that resides on the computers at Westlaw. Similarly, law firms may now access document assembly, litigation support, billing and timekeeping applications (just to name a few) as SaaS. So, instead of buying a CD or software download, installing the software on the computer, updating the software as needed, and hoping the program does not crash, now a user can simply subscribe to a program, log on, and start working. Another example of the use of the cloud is Clio, which offers its users document management, time tracking, billing, and scheduling. See Exhibit 6–1.

Software as a Service (SaaS) software applications that are hosted in the cloud instead of on the user's computer.

NIST lists five essential characteristics of cloud computing:

- On-demand self-service—users can access the cloud and get the desired services when they are needed.
- Broad network access—users can access the cloud anywhere they can access the Internet.
- Resource pooling—the ability of a cloud to serve multiple customers using a multi-tenant model with different physical and virtual resources dynamically assigned and reassigned according to demand. In other words, the service provider can take advantage of the economies of scale available to large companies and assign their assets (bandwidth, storage, and memory capacity) as dictated by the needs of their customers.

EXHIBIT 6–1
Example of cloud-based law office technology

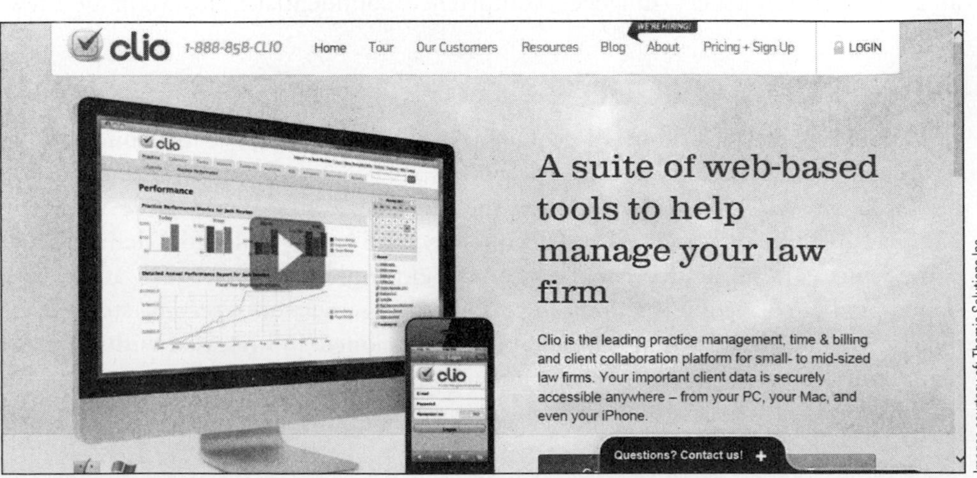

Images courtesy of: Themis Solutions Inc.

- Rapid elasticity—the service accessed by the user can be increased or decreased as needed.
- Measured Service—the user can keep track of the costs associated with the service as they accrue (a common example would be a person with a smartphone who can keep track of the minutes, text, and data used within a billing period).

While there is only one Internet, there are different ways a cloud can exist within the Internet. The most common is the public cloud—one that is owned by an entity that sells its services on the cloud to the general public (e.g., Westlaw and web-based email). A private cloud is a cloud owned and operated by one entity for their exclusive use (law firms do not typically set up a private cloud). A partner cloud is a cloud with services available to a limited number of partners.

But as with any change, while there are many advantages, there are also numerous challenges.

Advantages of Using the Cloud

Advantages of the cloud include:

- Information in the cloud is available anywhere you can access the Internet. More and more attorneys are carrying tablet computers and/or smartphones. These devices, using either a cellular phone service or **Wi-Fi** allow users to access the Internet and thus provide almost universal access to the files and applications residing in the cloud.
- Legal professionals have the ability to get precisely the degree and level of service needed at that time. This is known as rapid elasticity—the service grows and shrinks to meet your immediate needs.
- Much like a cell phone service, users can see how much they have used the service and how much it costs at any time. This helps law firms budget appropriately.
- SaaS can be more cost-effective. Installing and running complex software applications require a great deal of computing power; SaaS requires only the ability to access the Internet. Instead of requiring powerful servers, a law firm may use the software while it resides on the application provider's servers. This means that a law firm may be able to minimize, or even eliminate, its reliance on an IT staff. SaaS users do not have to purchase and install new versions of the application.
- Security provided by vendors. End users of software (you and me) are not always the most knowledgeable parties in the ways of computer security. But the lifeblood of any SaaS provider is security. The details of cloud security are discussed further below.

Wi-Fi
a system that provides wireless access to the Internet.

Ethical Issues

Foremost among the challenges associated with moving legal documents and systems to the cloud are the ethical challenges, and in particular, the ethical obligation to maintain the confidences and secrets of a client. For example, New York State Rule of Professional Conduct 1.6(c) states that

> "[a] lawyer shall exercise reasonable care to prevent the lawyer's employees, associates, **and others whose services are utilized by the lawyer** from disclosing or using confidential information of a client". (Emphasis added.)

Other states have a similar, if not identical, rule. This ethical dilemma may best be recognized in the form of an analogy. If a law firm were to store some of its confidential client paperwork in a storage facility, that law firm would be responsible for ensuring that the storage facility could provide a safe and secure environment for the paperwork containing the confidential information. The law firm has the obligation to maintain client confidences, whether it keeps physical possession of the paperwork or delegates that responsibility to a third party. By the same token, if a law firm stores some of its confidential client electronic data with a cloud provider, that law firm would still be responsible for ensuring that the cloud provider could provide a safe and secure environment for the confidential ESI.

This poses several problems for the legal professional. First, while most attorneys might feel comfortable comparing the merits of various physical storage facilities, those same attorneys may not be as qualified to make the same comparisons among cloud providers. Further complicating this issue is that technology moves at a much faster pace than legal ethics. Many states do not provide any guidance to its legal community, whether in the form of case law or a state bar ethics opinion. Those states that have issued opinions have all (to date) determined that legal professionals are required to exercise "reasonable care." The devil is in the details and some states provide more details than others.

One of the most cited and well thought-out opinions is *North Carolina Proposed 2011 Ethics Opinion 6*. It addresses the question of what specific actions should legal professionals take prior to using SaaS in the law office. The opinion states that reasonable care must be taken to protect against (1) the risk of the unauthorized disclosure of confidential information and, (2) the loss of the client's property. It states that a law firm may use a software as a service (SaaS) if

> "steps are taken to minimize the risk of inadvertent or unauthorized disclosure of confidential client information and to protect client property, including the information in a client's file, from risk of loss."

It also states that

> "a lawyer must be able to fulfill the fiduciary obligations to protect confidential client information and property from risk of disclosure and loss. The lawyer must protect against security weaknesses unique to the internet, particularly "end-user" vulnerabilities found in the lawyer's own law office. The lawyer must also engage in periodic education about ever-changing security risks presented by the internet."

Interestingly, this ethics opinion

> "does not require that a lawyer use only infallibly secure methods of communication. Rather, the lawyer must use reasonable care to select a mode of communication that, in light of the circumstances, will best protect confidential client information and the lawyer must advise effected parties if there is reason to believe that the chosen communications technology presents an unreasonable risk to confidentiality."

This North Carolina ethics opinion also provides recommendations as to the best practices to ensure data security:

- Inclusion in the SaaS vendor's Terms of Service or Service Level Agreement, or in a separate agreement between the SaaS vendor and the lawyer or law firm, of an agreement on how the vendor will handle confidential client information in keeping with the lawyer's professional responsibilities.
- If the lawyer terminates use of the SaaS product, the SaaS vendor goes out of business, or the service otherwise has a break in continuity, the law firm

will have a method for retrieving the data, the data will be available in a non-proprietary format that the law firm can access, or the firm will have access to the vendor's software or source code. The SaaS vendor is contractually required to return or destroy the hosted data promptly at the request of the law firm.

- Careful review of the terms of the law firm's user or license agreement with the SaaS vendor including the security policy.
- Evaluation of the SaaS vendor's (or any third party data hosting company's) measures for safeguarding the security and confidentiality of stored data including, but not limited to, firewalls, encryption techniques, socket security features, and intrusion-detection systems.
- Evaluation of the extent to which the SaaS vendor backs up hosted data.

Another oft-cited ethics opinion is *Iowa State Bar Association Ethics Opinion 11-01 (Use of Software as a Service—Cloud Computing)*. This opinion offers a list of questions that users of cloud computing should consider. For example,

> Access: Will I have unrestricted access to the stored data? Have I stored the data elsewhere so that if access to my data is denied I can acquire the data via another source?
>
> Legal Issues: Have I performed "due diligence" regarding the company that will be storing my data? Are they a solid company with a good operating record and is their service recommended by others in the field? What country and state are they located and do business in? Does their end user's licensing agreement (EULA) contain legal restrictions regarding their responsibility or liability, choice of law or forum, or limitation on damages? Likewise does their EULA grant them proprietary or user rights over my data?
>
> Financial Obligation: What is the cost of the service, how is it paid and what happens in the event of non-payment? In the event of a financial default will I lose access to the data, does it become the property of the SaaS company or is the data destroyed?

Some other notable state ethics opinions include:

New Jersey Advisory Committee on Professional Ethics Opinion 701 also requires lawyers to use "reasonable care" in ensuring that third parties, such as cloud providers, maintain the confidentiality of client data. This opinion found that reasonable care means when entrusting client data to a third party,

> "it must be under a circumstance in which the outside party is aware of the lawyer's obligation of confidentiality, and is itself obligated, whether by contract, professional standards, or otherwise, to assist in preserving it."

The opinion also noted the futility of mandating specific procedures to prevent disclosure of confidential information; as the technology changes so rapidly, such procedures would be all but obsolete within a short time of their enactment.

Alabama State Bar Opinion 2010–02 states that

> "[t]he duty of reasonable care requires the lawyer to become knowledgeable about how the provider will handle the storage and security of the data being stored and to reasonably ensure that the provider will abide by a confidentiality agreement in handling the data. Additionally, because technology is constantly evolving, the lawyer will have a continuing duty to stay abreast of appropriate security safeguards that should be employed by the lawyer and the third-party provider. If there is a breach of confidentiality, the focus of any inquiry will be whether the lawyer acted reasonably in selecting the method of storage and/or the third party provider."

VIRTUAL LAW OFFICES

Today, practically every law firm has a website and communicates via email. Many law firms advertise their services on the Internet. But, they still have a traditional "bricks and mortar" location. A **virtual law office** is a law office that exists without a permanent physical location. Instead it exists solely on the Internet. These Virtual Law Firms may maintain a limited physical presence to meet certain legal requirements (e.g., an address for service of legal documents) or to allow for meetings with clients, but for all practical purposes, these firms exist in the cloud.

While the majority of states permit Virtual Law Firms to operate within their state, they have not yet received universal approval. A few states, for example, New Jersey, prohibit Virtual Law Firms.

SOCIAL MEDIA

Social Media—What is it?

Social media is the process and the result of users collaboratively creating their own online community. You see this when you log onto Facebook; your home page will be different than mine. It is the unique product of what you and your friends have posted. You see this when you look up a restaurant on Yelp or Urbanspoon; the ratings will change as more people post their reviews. You can even see this when you use a search engine such as Google. If you were to type in "At" in the Search box, Google will make suggestions for completing the query based on other queries beginning with "At." (For example, Google might suggest "AT&T" or Atlanta"). When you buy a book on Amazon.com or a song from iTunes, you may be directed to other products based on what other customers have purchased. So if you believe you are not involved in social media because you do not use Facebook or Twitter, you are wrong: If you are on the Internet, you are using social media.

Social media takes many forms:

- Social networking sites allow users to exchange information about themselves and their interests. Currently, the most popular example of social networking is Facebook. In addition, there is MySpace, which was the most popular social networking site until the rise of Facebook and LinkedIn, which provides social networking for professionals. There are social networking sites for almost every group of persons imaginable, such as ravelry.com (a knit and crochet online community), cafemom.com (an online resource for moms) and, FilmBuffet.com (an online community for movie lovers).
- Blogs are websites where users can post text, images, videos, links, quotes, and audio, for example, Tumblr, Blogspot, and Wordpress. Twitter, which limits posts to 140 characters, is a form of micro-blogging.
- Wikis are websites developed together by a community of users which allow any user to add and edit content. The most famous wiki is the online encyclopedia, Wikipedia.
- Online advocacy and fundraising sites such as Causes.com and Kickstarter.com.
- Document management sites such as Google Drive, Microsoft OneDrive, and Dropbox.
- Reviews and recommendations of restaurants, shopping, and services, such as Yelp, Urbanspoon, AngiesList, and TripAdvisor.
- Photography and art sharing sites such as Flickr.com and Picasa.com. Instagram is both a photography and video sharing site and a social media site as users are

encouraged to comment and "like" the photographs and videos posted there. Snapchat is a photo sharing site that allows the party sending the photograph to determine how long the recipient will be able to view the photograph; typically, the photograph is viewable for only a few seconds before it disappears.

- Video sharing sites such as YouTube and Vimeo.
- Gaming and virtual worlds such as Second Life, The Sims Online, and World of Warcraft.

Ethical Implications of Social Media

State rules of ethics generally require that attorneys (and those who assist them, i.e., paralegals) act in a competent manner. For example, Illinois Rules of Professional Conduct 1.1 states that "[a] lawyer shall provide competent representation to a client. Competent representation requires the legal knowledge, skill, thoroughness and preparation reasonably necessary for the representation." This has been interpreted to mean that legal professionals need to maintain competence in all areas relevant to the practice of law, including technology. Similarly, Rule 1.3 of the Illinois Rules of Professional Conduct states that "[a] lawyer shall act with reasonable diligence and promptness in representing a client." (Most states have a similar rule.)

Imagine that while meeting with a client, you learn that the client has posted an incriminating photograph on Facebook. What is the ethical response? Should the client be counseled to remove the photograph to prevent any further harm? Both case law and ethical rules say "no"; the photograph is evidence and removing the evidence from Facebook would be unethical behavior. For example, Georgia Rules of Professional Conduct 3.4 states that

> "[a] lawyer shall not: (a) unlawfully obstruct another party's access to evidence or unlawfully alter, destroy or conceal a document or other material having potential evidentiary value. A lawyer shall not counsel or assist another person to do any such act."

This was the issue in *Allied Holdings v. Lester,* discussed on page 455.

Be Careful What You Blog (or Tweet)

The rules of professional responsibility require that all information relating to the representation of a client be kept confidential. That prohibition is not able to prevent all breaches of confidentiality, as noted in the case of a former state assistant public defender. She was charged with violating numerous ethical rules because she posted confidential client information on her blog. The confidential information included client first names, nicknames, or jail identification numbers, as well as details of her clients' cases, personal lives, and drug use.

Law firms also use social media in the same way other businesses do—as an advertising tool designed to attract new clients and new business. This too, can pose ethical problems for legal professionals. One such problem is the use of testimonials. Social media allows customers of a business to post their opinions of that business on various sites. However, the rules of legal ethics in many states do not permit the use of testimonials. The issue arises not when a client posts a compliment about a lawyer or a law firm on a third party website (assuming it was not at the behest of the lawyer or law firm), as the legal professional is unable to prevent such posts; but rather, when the testimonial appears on the lawyer or law firm's own website. In addition, there is a specific issue with the popular website, LinkedIn. LinkedIn is a social media site for professionals who wish to connect with other professionals, typically for business purposes. LinkedIn allows users to indicate their areas of specialization. However, the rules of legal ethics in many states do not permit attorneys to claim to be a "specialist" in any specific area of the law, or only permit it when the attorney has obtained some professional credentials that support the claim of being a "specialist." Law firms and legal professionals should take care to check the rules of professional responsibility in their jurisdictions before venturing out onto the Internet.

Another ethical issue arises when a client contacts the law firm through the website seeking legal advice or representation. The question of when an attorney/client relationship begins is not always clear. Unsolicited requests for assistance or representation do not typically create any ethical issues for lawyers. However, when a website specifically invites users to contact the law firm to allow the firm to evaluate a user's case, then it is possible for a reasonable user to assume that, at least until told otherwise, they have a lawyer working for them. Legal professionals are advised to require potential clients to use a "click-through" feature if they want to initiate contact with the law firm. A click-through requires a user to acknowledge the terms and conditions of using a website; the user clicks a box that includes a statement that the user understands that no attorney/client relationship is created by the user's inquiry to the law firm. Typically, the user is unable to send their message to the law firm without first clicking that box. Look at the websites of the attorneys that advertise heavily in your community. You will probably see that they require users to use just such a device.

Social Media Discovery

The good news for attorneys is that social media is often a goldmine of relevant information. The bad news is that it can be difficult to find social media evidence. Much social media is not as "social" as the name would imply. Access to social media may be limited to specific people and items that were previously available may be removed at any time. So if a party in litigation wants to acquire social media evidence, from whom should it be sought?

Stored Communications Act (SCA)
federal statute prohibiting most Internet service providers from releasing an individual's information to a third-party.

Can a third party service provider be compelled to produce social media evidence? The **Stored Communications Act** (SCA) (18 § U.S.C. 2701-11) creates Fourth Amendment like privacy protection for email and other digital communications stored on the Internet. This law, which was enacted as part of the Electronic Communications Privacy Act in 1986 (long before the Internet became an integral part of our lives), forbids an Internet service provider from releasing an individual's information to third-parties, even in response to a civil subpoena. Typically, a search warrant is required to obtain this information and even then, the Stored Communications Act can make this problematic. The Stored Communications Act considers two types of service providers: electronic communication services (ECS) and remote computing services (RCS). An ECS is defined as "any service which provides to users thereof the ability to send or receive wire or electronic communications" and it states that an ECS provider may not "knowingly divulge to any person or entity the contents of a communication while in electronic storage by that service." Examples of ECS are services that transmit email and text messages. An RCS is defined as those who provide to the public "computer storage and processing services by means of electronic communications systems" and it states that an RCS may not "knowingly divulge to any person or entity the contents of any communication which is carried or maintained on that service." Examples of an RCS are services that provide cloud services. Most ECS providers are also RCS providers (i.e., Google provides email services, but also stores emails). On the other hand, a service such as Dropbox (cloud storage) is only an RCS.

The leading case in this area to date is *Crispin v. Christian Audigier, Inc.*, 717 F. Supp. 2d 965 (C.D. Cal. 2010), which held that Facebook would have to respond to a civil subpoena IF the information sought was already available to the general public. The Court distinguished between private messages and posts that were visible only to "friends" (protected by the SCA and therefore not subject to a discovery request made to Facebook) and posts that were visible to anyone, regardless of whether they are a "friend" (not protected by the SCA and therefore subject to a discovery request made to Facebook).

So if the social media entity is not going to provide the social media evidence, can it be obtained directly from the party or witness who created it? The general consensus among the courts appears to be yes, IF the requesting party can demonstrate that the social media account is likely to contain relevant evidence. In other words, a court is not going to allow a party to go on a "fishing expedition" to look through a party's Facebook site with just the hope of finding relevant evidence. Rather, the better practice would be to show the court an incriminating photograph or statement found on the social media site to bolster the claim that additional evidence would also likely reside there. In *Zimmerman v. Weis Markets Inc.*, (Court of Common Pleas, Northumberland County, PA), the Court compelled an "injured" plaintiff to provide his Facebook and MySpace passwords to the defendant to permit the defendant to see if there was any evidence that plaintiff was not injured as badly as was claimed. And perhaps it would make sense for attorneys to routinely advise clients to ensure that their social media privacy settings are set to limit access to information on their pages.

Social media evidence presents a unique problem when a party tries to admit it into evidence—how to authenticate it? Tangible evidence is typically authenticated by presenting it to a witness with personal evidence of its authenticity. But social media is not tangible and it is not static—it is dynamic, always changing. Clearly, the best practice is to have the witness/creator of the social media testify to its authenticity. But what happens when you want to use social media evidence against the other party? The other party may deny writing the message or posting the photograph. Recent case law indicates that social media evidence may be admitted if it can be shown that the specific posts contain information that only the owner of that particular page could know.

Finally, there is an ethical component to social media evidence. The very nature of social media evidence makes it more susceptible to spoliation. Legal professionals have to be careful not to advise their clients to remove or alter any messages or photographs on their social media pages. In *Allied Concrete Co. v. Lester*, 736 S.E.2d 699 (Va. 2013), a wrongful death suit was filed after a woman was killed when a cement truck tipped over and crushed the vehicle she was sitting in. In the course of discovery, the defendant requested the contents of the plaintiff's Facebook account. The Facebook page then contained a photograph that showed the plaintiff holding a can of beer while wearing a t-shirt that said "I ♥ hot moms." Fearing that this photograph was not consistent with claims of being a grieving widower, the plaintiff's attorney instructed the client to delete the photograph from the Facebook account. The Facebook page was later deactivated and then reactivated. These actions were deemed to be acts of spoliation. The attorney was suspended from the practice of law for five years and ordered to pay sanctions in the amount of $542,000. The client was ordered to pay $180,000 in sanctions. The lesson here is that care must be taken not to alter a client's social media once litigation has commenced or can reasonably anticipate that litigation will commence.

GEOLOCATION

Geolocation the ability to track the precise location of a device, and by implication, its owner.

Geolocation is the ability to track the precise location of a device, and by implication, its owner. Any device that has the ability to communicate (to receive and/or send data) may be subject to geolocation. The explosion in the number and sophistication of mobile communication devices (smartphones, tablet computers, automobile GPS systems, etc.) has made this area one of the hot topics in law office technology. Chances are that right now, your location could be detected and recorded.

It is worth noting at the beginning, that different devices made by different manufacturers, using different operating systems and working on different networks all have slightly different methods of geolocation. And of course, since technology is always changing, what is true one minute may be obsolete the next. Therefore, it should be noted that this discussion is just a general overview of the principles of geolocation.

Look at a smartphone—how does it "know" where it is? First of all it is a phone. If a smartphone is "on," it has the ability to send and receive phone and text messages. To do this, the device is constantly searching for the nearest cell tower. This is sometimes referred to as "pinging." The device sends out a signal (the "ping") which is then received and returned by nearby cell towers. The phone can then determine which of the nearby cell towers offers the strongest signal. But this signal also alerts the cell tower to the presence of the mobile device within its signal range. Mobile devices have many components that have unique identifying features that can be used to determine which specific devices were within a specific cell tower's range at a specific time. Cell towers record the ID numbers of the mobile devices that "pinged" them and the time the ping was received.

The mobile device is able to determine its location based on the location of the cell towers that return its ping. Some cell towers are omnidirectional—it sends its signals out in a 360-degree range. This provides a less specific determination of the device's location as the device may be anywhere within the signal range of the cell tower. For example, see Exhibit 6–2. Some cell towers are multi-directional and send their signals out in 120-degree ranges. Even more precise geolocation is possible when the device resides within the range of multiple cell towers. The mobile device can then use a process called triangulation to determine its location. For example, see Exhibit 6–3. Service providers may maintain logs of all calls and texts sent via specific cell towers showing the tower(s) and sectors used, and possibly the distance from the tower.

In addition to cell towers, a mobile device is typically enabled with other means of communication. One such means is Wi-Fi. Wi-Fi generally refers to a local area wireless network that can send and receive high-frequency radio waves providing wireless access to the Internet. Many colleges and universities offer Wi-Fi, as do many commercial entities such as hotels and coffee shops. Many homes now have their own Wi-Fi as it is relatively easy to connect the cable bringing the Internet signal into the house to a wireless router. These Wi-Fi networks, both large and small, have been cataloged by companies such as Google and Apple. When Wi-Fi is enabled on a mobile device, it finds all available Wi-Fi networks. You have probably seen a list of available Wi-Fi networks when you turn on the Wi-Fi on a smartphone. However, as your phone recognizes the available networks, it may also send that information to a company like Google or Apple, which have created databases of Wi-Fi networks. This information (the fact that a mobile device was physically within the range of a Wi-Fi network) may be recorded and retrievable from the mobile device itself or from the Wi-Fi provider. So even if a device

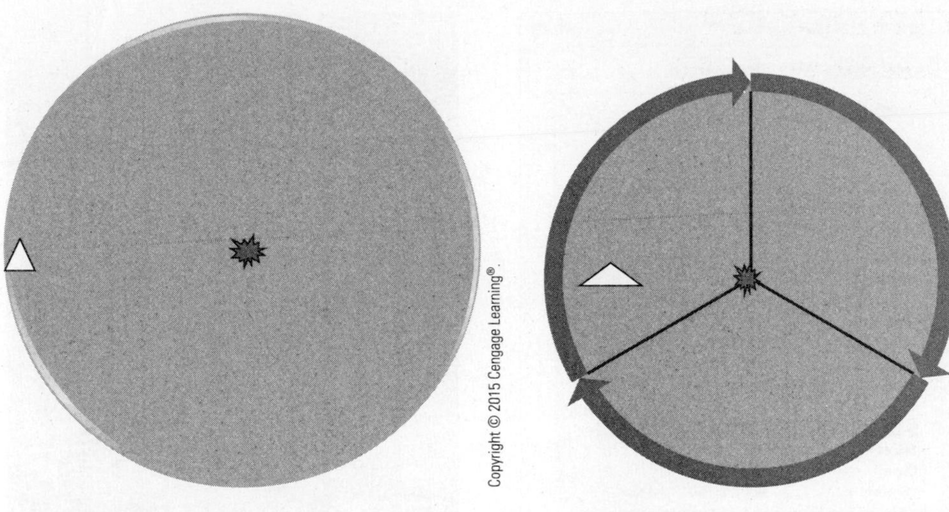

EXHIBIT 6–2
Omni-directional cell tower

EXHIBIT 6–3
Multi-directional cell tower

is not connected to a Wi-Fi network, if Wi-Fi is enabled, it may be possible to determine that the device was within the range of a specific Wi-Fi network at a specific time.

Finally, many mobile devices are equipped with GPS ("Global Positioning System"). A device with a GPS receiver has the ability to receive signals from any of the 24 satellites orbiting the globe. A GPS receiver calculates its position by precisely timing the signals sent by the GPS satellites. These satellites send messages that include the precise time the message was transmitted and the satellite's exact position at the time the message was sent. The GPS receiver then uses any messages it receives to determine the time it took for the message to reach the receiver and computes the distance to those satellites. GPS uses "line of sight" technology, meaning in order for it to work, the GPS receiver must have an unobstructed view of the GPS satellites. Obviously, if the device is indoors, that will diminish the value of the GPS system.

Geotagging

Geotagging adds geographical metadata to an e-file. For example, a photograph taken with a smartphone may add the latitude and longitude of the location where the photograph was taken. In addition, files created on a mobile device are often enabled with geotagging (e.g., posts made to Facebook, Twitter, Foursquare, etc.) And while some applications are used precisely because of its geolocation utility (e.g., Foursquare, in which the user checks in when visiting locations such as cafes and stores), users are not always aware that they may be adding geographical metadata to an electronic file. For example, users may not be aware that their Facebook posts or photographs may be traced to a specific location.

Geotagging geographical metadata embedded in an electronic file.

One common example of geotagging occurs when a person takes a photograph with a GPS-enabled device such as a smartphone. When a photograph is taken with such a device, the JPEG file created contains not only the photograph, but also metadata. JPEGs have a particular type of metadata called **Exchangeable Image File (EXIF)** data. Examples of this data include the shutter speed, the date and time the photo was taken, and the latitude and longitude. See Exhibit 6–4. When a JPEG is shared, the EXIF data is also shared. Thus, a person may unwittingly share his exact location at a precise time. This promises to be a fruitful new area for electronic discovery in coming years.

Exchangeable Image File (EXIF) metadata embedded within a JPEG file (digital photograph).

EXHIBIT 6–4
Example of digital photograph and accompanying metadata

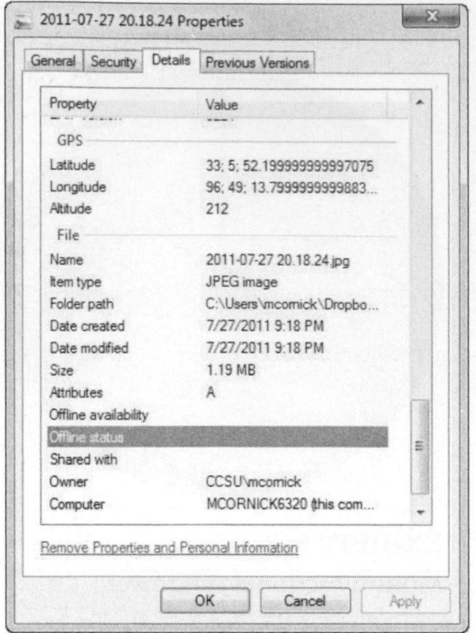

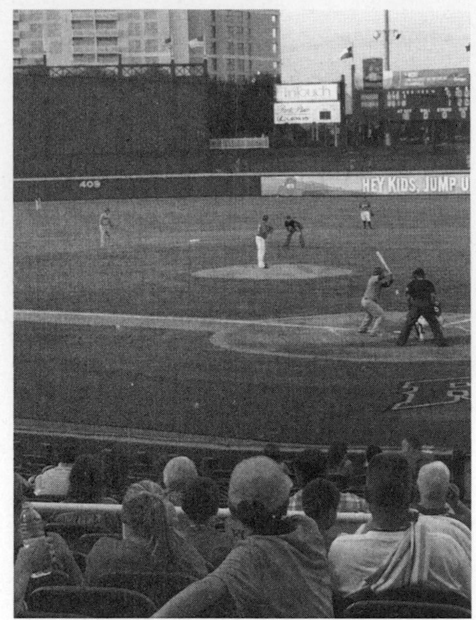

SUMMARY

The "cloud" refers to the ability of a computer to access information residing on a different computer. When you make a purchase online or log onto Facebook, you are using the cloud. One of the manifestations of the cloud in law offices in the use of Software as a Service (SaaS). However, significant ethical issues arise when legal professionals use the cloud, notably the obligation to maintain client confidentiality when entrusting client information to an online provider. Legal professionals are expected to act reasonably when using the cloud, which means that we all must be knowledgeable about how the cloud works so we can make reasonable decisions.

Social media is changing the way all of us work and live and the practice of law is not immune to these changes. When someone makes a post on a social media site, that person may not be thinking about how that post, photograph, or video might be used in future litigation. But as legal professionals, we have an ethical obligation to look for incriminating posts. The legal system is still deciding on the proper protocol for allowing one party to view the social accounts of another party in litigation. Authenticating social media, which is inherently dynamic and changing, poses a new set of issues for legal professionals. Another aspect of the increase in the use of the cloud and social media is that people carry their smartphones with them everywhere they go. These devices are constantly connected to various GPS, telephone, and Wi-Fi networks, so the location of these devices (and by implication, their owners) may be determined. Geotagging refers to the imprinting of geographical metadata within the photographs or social media posts made with a mobile device.

KEY TERMS

cloud
EXIF
geolocation
geotagging
SaaS (Software as a Service)
social media
Stored Communications Act
virtual law office
Wi-Fi

INTERNET SITES

Internet sites for this chapter include:

ORGANIZATION	PRODUCT/SERVICE	WORLD WIDE WEB ADDRESS
Clio	Online Legal Practice Management	www.clio.com
Social Intelligence	Social media background checks	www.socialintelligencehr.com
Morrison & Foerster	Socially Aware newsletter	www.mofo.com/sociallyaware
Law Technology News	Newsletter	www.law.com/jsp/lawtechnologynews/index.jsp
Technolawyer	Newsletter	technolawyer.com newsletters
X1 Discovery	Social media research	www.x1discovery.com
ABA Legal Technology Resource Center	Legal technology news and reviews	www.abanet.org/tech/trc
Brian Wassom	Blog on Social and Emerging Media	www.wassom.com
Virtual Law Practice	Resources for virtual law firms	virtuallawpractice.org
Virtual Law Partners	Virtual Law Office	vlplawgroup.com
North Carolina Bar Association	Legal Ethics opinions	www.ncbar.gov/ethics/propeth.asp

TEST YOUR KNOWLEDGE

1. T / F. The Stored Communications Act prohibits the disclosure of any information by an Internet provider.
2. According to the National Institute of Standards and Technology (NIST), there are five essential characteristics of cloud computing. What are they?
3. T / F. An example of Software as a Service is an electronic legal research provider such as Lexis.
4. T / F. Generally, an Internet service provider such as Facebook has to turn over any relevant information posted on its website in response to a valid discovery request.
5. T / F. Since social media is inherently fleeting and subject to change, social media evidence need not be preserved to avoid spoliation.
6. T/F. Geolocation does not work if a mobile device is used indoors.
7. T/F. Geolocation does not work if a mobile device is turned off.
8. T/F. The ethical obligation to be diligent and competent requires knowledge of social media.

ON THE WEB EXERCISES

1. Take a photograph with a smartphone or other GPS-enabled device. Transfer the photograph file to a computer and then find the latitude and longitude for that photograph. You can usually find this information under the Properties tab. Then type the latitude and longitude into Google Maps or other Internet map application. See how close the information within the file comes to the actual location where the photograph was taken.
2. Research the case of John McAfee. Mr. McAfee, who founded the computer antivirus company, McAfee Corporation, was the subject of a police search when a photograph of him was posted on an Internet site. The photograph still had the EXIF data, including the latitude and longitude of his location. This information led to his capture by the police.
3. Using the rules of professional responsibility (legal ethics) in your jurisdiction, find out if it is ethically permissible for attorneys to claim to be a specialist on sites such as LinkedIn. In addition, what, if any, ethical prohibitions exist against the use of client testimonials in your jurisdiction?
4. Google yourself. Be sure to search Images as well. What happens when you put quotation marks around your name? Do the search results improve? Are you surprised at what you find or what you did not find? Are there many other people with the same name as you?
5. Look at the websites of three local law firms that advertise on television. Do any of these websites invite potential clients to contact the firm to discuss a legal matter? Do these websites have a click-through requirement that must be used prior to contacting the law firm? What other resources are made available to the public (frequently asked questions, links to local courthouses, etc.)?
6. If you have any social media accounts (e.g., Facebook, Twitter, Tumblr, etc.), review your privacy settings. How public are your posts, tweets, and photos?
7. Search the Internet for corporate social media policies. What do corporations allow their employees to post on both business and personal social media sites?

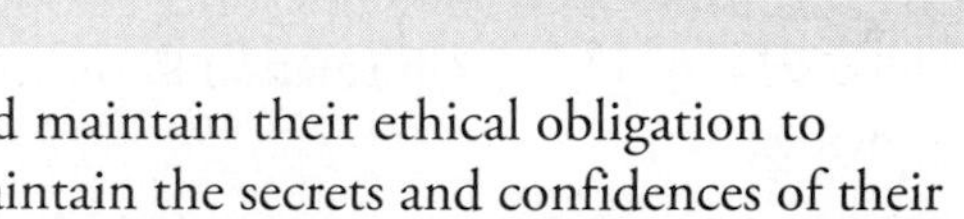

QUESTIONS AND EXERCISES

1. Interview a local attorney or paralegal regarding how they use the cloud in their practice. More specifically, ask about how they decided to use the specific services providers they use.
2. You are a paralegal working for a mid-size firm in your city. You are asked to research various cloud service providers and determine whether your firm could use their services and maintain their ethical obligation to maintain the secrets and confidences of their clients. Write a two-page paper summarizing your findings.
3. Contact local law firms to see if they have a social media policy for their employees and/or clients. What similarities, if any, exist among these different social media policies?

ETHICS QUESTION

A law firm is worried about the negative ramifications of embarrassing social media posts and photographs. The law firm wants to be proactive so it sends an email to everyone on its mailing list (current clients, former clients, expert witnesses, employees of the law firm, etc.) warning them of the consequences of inappropriate social media. The email describes various examples of inappropriate social media and suggests that offending material be removed. What are the ethical implications of this email? If you believe this action is unethical in some manner, how could the law firm achieve its goal without committing the ethical lapses you describe?

HANDS-ON EXERCISES

FEATURED SOFTWARE
Clio Hands-on Exercises

CLIO

I. INTRODUCTION–READ THIS

Clio is a web-based legal practice management system. Clio helps users stay on top of tasks, important deadlines, contacts, and conflict checks. The Clio demonstration version is a full working version of the program. The program demonstration version expires 365 days after you create your account. This means that the program will only work for 365 days once you begin using it. So, it is highly recommended that you do not activate your account until you are actually ready to go through the Hands-On Exercises and learn the program.

When you are ready to activate your account, follow the instructions in section III.

II. USING THE CLIO HANDS-ON EXERCISES

The Clio Hands-On Exercises are easy to use and contain step-by-step instructions. Each lesson builds on the previous exercise, so please complete the Hands-On Exercises in the correct order. There are files containing sample data that you will load into Clio, so you should be able to utilize many features of the program.

HANDS-ON EXERCISES

CLIO

Number	Lesson Title	Concepts Covered
BASIC LESSONS		
Lesson 1	Overview of Clio Platform	Create a Clio account; view the basic functions of Clio
Lesson 2	Set up Law Firm Profile	Set up firm profile, establish billing rate, create an Activity Description, set up bank accounts, and establish the matter numbering protocol
INTERMEDIATE LESSON		
Lesson 3	Real Estate Matter	Create a new contact (client), open a file for the new client, create a new matter, enter a flat fee time entry, take a retainer from the client, and apply the retainer to an invoice
ADVANCED LESSONS		
Lesson 4	Civil Litigation Matter	Identify relationships, add a document, log a phone call, add a time entry, add an expense entry and create a bill for a client in a litigation matter
Lesson 5	Corporate Matter	Identify relationships, add a document, log a phone call, add a time entry, add an expense entry, and create a bill for a client in a corporate matter

GETTING STARTED

Introduction

Throughout these lessons and exercises, information you need to type into the software will be designated in several different ways:

- Keys to be pressed on the keyboard are designated in brackets, in all caps, and in bold (e.g., press the **[ENTER]** key).

- Movements with the mouse pointer are designated in bold and italics (e.g., ***point to File on the menu bar and click***).
- Words or letters that should be typed are designated in bold (e.g., type **Training Program**).
- Information that is or should be displayed on your computer screen is shown in bold, with quotation marks (e.g., **"Press ENTER to continue."**).
- Specific menu items and commands are designated with an initial capital letter (e.g., ***click Open***).

III. Installation Instructions

Installation

Unlike other applications within this text, Clio is not a program that you download and install onto your computer. Instead, it is a website where you will be asked to open a free account and act as a paralegal in a hypothetical law firm. Your instructor will act as your supervising attorney in the law firm. In Lesson 1, you will create your Clio account. There are two files (one with "contacts" and one with "matters") that you will need to download and load into Clio—you can access these files through the Premium Website associated with this text.

IV. Installation Technical Support

If you have problems creating a Clio account, you will need to contact Clio directly at caap@clio.com.

Clio maintains a thorough and robust library of articles and webinars on a variety of topics that you might find helpful. You can access these at https://support.goclio.com/home.

IMPORTANT NOTICE—Since Clio is not an application that you download onto your computer, but rather is a website that you log onto, it is likely that there will be some changes in its appearance or functionality. Please check the Premium Website for updates.

BASIC LESSONS

LESSON 1: OVERVIEW OF CLIO PLATFORM

In this lesson, you will become familiar with the Clio platform and its essential functions.

1. ***Open your Internet browser and log in to your CengageBrain.com account.***
2. Under "My Courses & Materials," find the Premium Website for *Using Computers in the Law Office, 7th edition.*
3. ***Click "Open"*** to go to the Premium Website.
4. Locate "Book Level Resources" in the left navigation menu.
5. ***Click on the link for "Clio."***
6. ***Click the link next to "To access the demo:"***
7. At the Welcome Cengage Learning Users screen, ***click Get Started.*** On the next screen, enter the required information, then ***click Start Trial.***
8. You will receive an email from Clio with a link to activate your account. ***Click the link and follow the on-screen instructions to complete the registration process.***
9. Once you have completed the registration process, you may access your Clio account by **typing app.goclio.com** and press the **[ENTER] key**. ***On the next screen, enter the email address and password you provided Clio and click SIGN IN. If you check the box next to KEEP ME SIGNED IN, you will be able to skip this step in the future.***

10. Right now, there is no data in your Clio account. There are two files on the Premium Website that you will now import into Clio that will provide you with some data to work with. ***Navigate to your CengageBrain account and locate on the Premium Website the data file with Contacts named democontacts (1).csv and the data file with Matters named demomatters_output.csv. You first need to import these files to your computer. To do so, right-click on the link for democontacts(1).csv and, select Save Target As and using the default settings, save it to your computer. Then, right-click on the link for demomatters_output.csv, select Save Target As and using the default settings, save the file to your computer.***
11. To input the Contacts file, type https://app.goclio.com/imports in your Internet browser and press the **[ENTER] key.** ***Click Add and choose "Contacts from Outlook CSV." Select and upload the file named democontacts (1).csv. Click Upload.***
12. To input the Matters file, **type** https://app.goclio.com/imports **in your Internet browser and press the [ENTER] key. Select "Matters from CSV" and select the file named** ***demomatters_output.csv. Click Upload.***
13. **Click PRACTICE.** Your screen should now look like Clio Exhibit 1. (Note that you may see a Welcome message on these pages; you can click "Hide this message" if you do not wish to see them.) There are eleven tabs available in Clio; you are now in the Practice tab. You will now explore the other ten tabs. ***Click Calendar***. You many need to scroll down to see the entire page. You can change the view to see your Agenda, or Day, Week, Month, or Year views. You can view your personal calendar, the firm calendar or both.

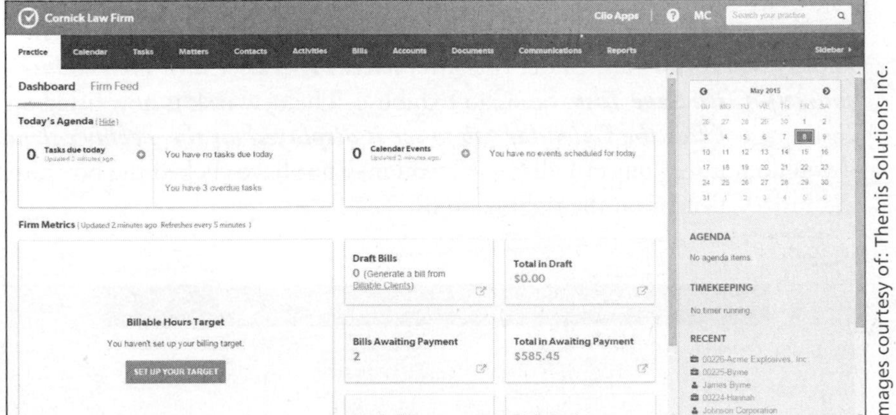

Images courtesy of: Themis Solutions Inc.

CLIO EXHIBIT 1
Clio PRACTICE tab

14. To create a calendar entry, while in the Week view, ***select the Wednesday of that week and double-click on the 10:00 am time slot***. The Create Calendar Entry window will open. See Clio Exhibit 2. Under Summary, type **Clio Training**. Under

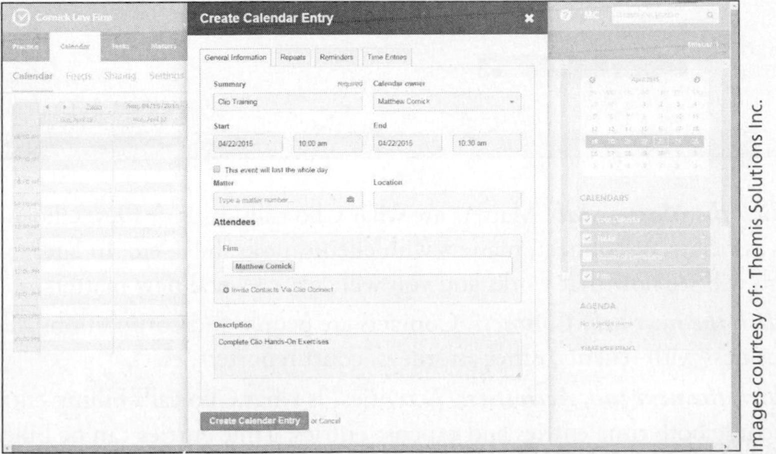

Images courtesy of: Themis Solutions Inc.

CLIO EXHIBIT 2
Create Calendar Entry

HANDS-ON EXERCISES

Start, type **10:00 AM**; under End, type **11:00 AM**. See Clio Exhibit 2. Under Description, type **Complete Clio Hands-On Exercises**. ***Click Create Calendar Entry.***

15. Your calendar should now look like Clio Exhibit 3. ***Place your cursor over the new calendar entry*** to see the description.

CLIO EXHIBIT 3
Calendar

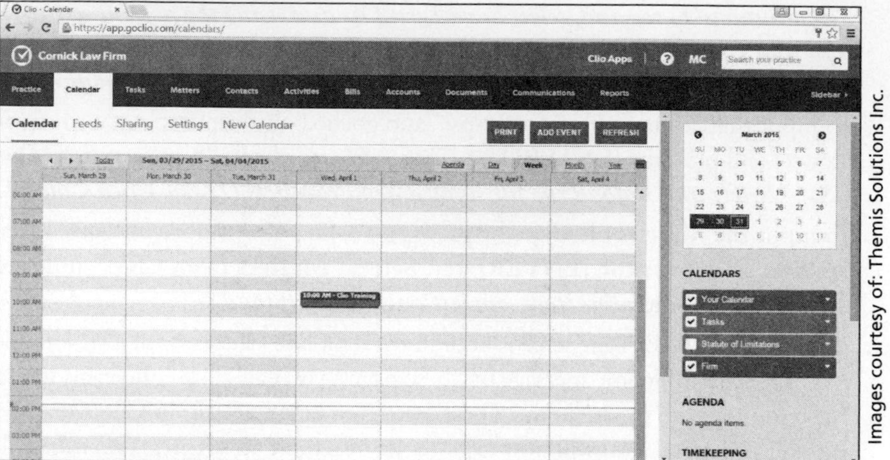

Images courtesy of: Themis Solutions Inc.

16. ***Click the next tab, Tasks.*** This is where specific tasks can be assigned to specific individuals or groups. To create a new Task, ***click Add.*** See Clio Exhibit 4. Under Task Name, type **Clio Training**. Under Description, type **Watch Clio training videos**. Under Due at, ***select the Thursday of that week.*** Under Priority, ***select Normal.*** Under Assignee, ***select Firm User and then choose yourself. Click Save Task.*** See Clio Exhibit 4. The new task is now listed on the Tasks page. ***Click the Calendar tab to see it displayed on the weekly calendar.*** If you do not see your task displayed, you may not have clicked the box next to the Tasks Calendar on the right hand list.

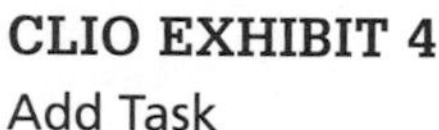

CLIO EXHIBIT 4
Add Task

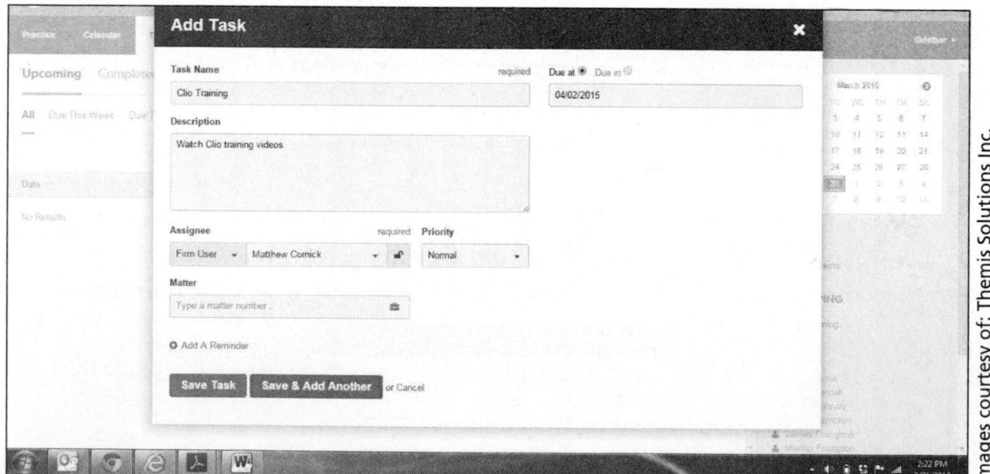

Images courtesy of: Themis Solutions Inc.

17. ***Click the Matters tab.*** Matters are what Clio calls cases or files. Clio allows you to associate, or connect, matters with clients, tasks, bills, etc. In later exercises you will see how that works and you will create several new matters.
18. ***Click the next tab, Contacts.*** Contacts are people and corporations that you do business with (clients, other attorneys, court reporters, etc.).
19. ***Click the next tab, Activities.*** "Activities" is what Clio calls billing entries. These include both time entries and expense entries. Time entries can be billed as a

flat rate or at an hourly rate. In later exercises you will create several new billing activities.

20. ***Click the next tab, Bills.*** Here, you can create a new bill, review a client's billing history, and create bill themes (designs) among other bill-related issues. In later exercises you will create several new bills.
21. ***Click the next tab, Accounts.*** Here you can view and manage the various bank accounts of a law firm.
22. ***Click the next tab, Documents.*** Here you can view and manage the documents maintained in Clio.
23. ***Click the next tab, Communications.*** Here you can view and manage communications through Clio.
24. ***Click the next tab, Reports.*** Here you can create reports on a variety of topics (billing, client, matter, productivity, and revenue).
25. To end this Clio session, ***click the drop down menu by your initials at the top of the screen. Click sign out and then close your Internet browser.***

This concludes Lesson 1 of the Clio Hands-On Exercises.

LESSON 2: SET UP LAW FIRM PROFILE

In this lesson, you set up your hypothetical law firm and establish the firm profile, establish billing rate, create an Activity Description, set up bank accounts and establish the matter numbering protocol.

1. Start your Internet browser. Type www.clio.com in the Internet browser and press the **[ENTER] key.**
2. On the Clio Home page, ***click SIGN IN. On the next screen, enter the email address and password you provided Clio and click SIGN IN. If you check the box next to KEEP ME SIGNED IN, you will be able to skip this step in the future.***
3. Before you can enter new clients, contacts, and matters in Clio, you need to set up your hypothetical law firm in Clio. The first thing you will do is set up the account information for your hypothetical law firm. ***Click on your initials at the top of the screen, then click Settings.*** Your screen should look like Clio Exhibit 5. ***Click Account and Payment Info.*** The name of your hypothetical law firm will be your last name, for example, the Cornick Law Firm. ***Under Account Info, enter the name, address, and contact information of your firm.*** (You may enter your address and actual contact information or you may make up the address and contact information.) ***Under Date& Time Format, select the option that most closely resembles 12/31/2015. Under Time format, select 11:59 PM. Click Save New Information.***

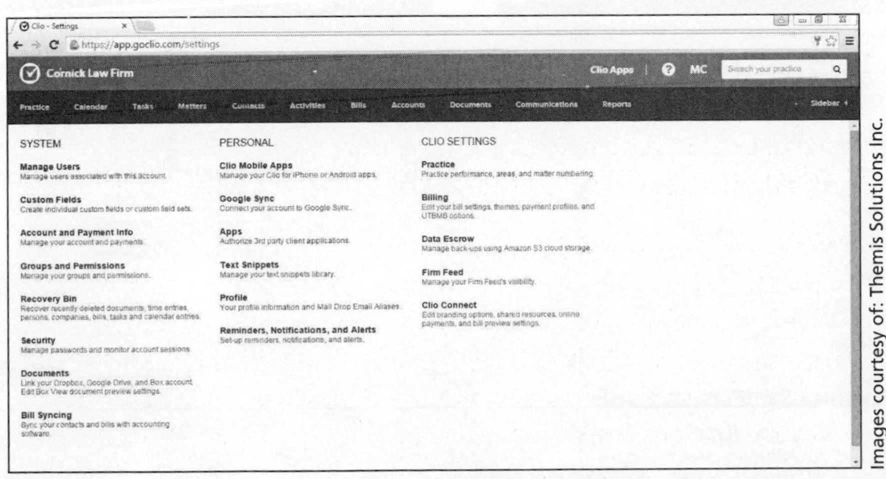

Images courtesy of: Themis Solutions Inc.

CLIO EXHIBIT 5
Settings

4. Next, you will establish your billing rates. Clio allows users to create a "User Rate." A User Rate is the default rate for Clio to use when it is not overridden by a Matter/Client/Custom rate. To see this, ***click your initials at the top of the screen, then click Settings***. From the Settings screen, ***click Profile. On the next screen, under "Your Information," scroll down to Billing Rate and enter 125 next to $/Hr. Click Save New Information.***
5. Next, you will create an Activity Description. These are used to ensure a consistent description of commonly used time entries across a law firm. It can also be used as a shortcut—you can save text in the Activity Description and when you enter in a time entry, it will populate this text for you. Activity Descriptions can be shared across a law firm so that everyone in the firm can use them. ***Click the Activities tab, then click Activity Descriptions, then click Add.*** See Clio Exhibit 6. Under Name, type **Real Estate Closing**. Under Billing Method, ***select Flat Rate***. This opens a text box called Rate; type **$500.00** in the text box. ***Click Save***. This flat rate fee will override the $125.00 hour fee established as the default rate.

CLIO EXHIBIT 6

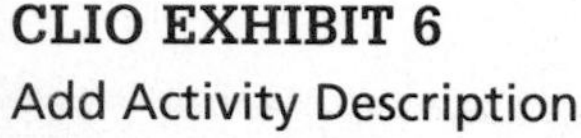

Add Activity Description

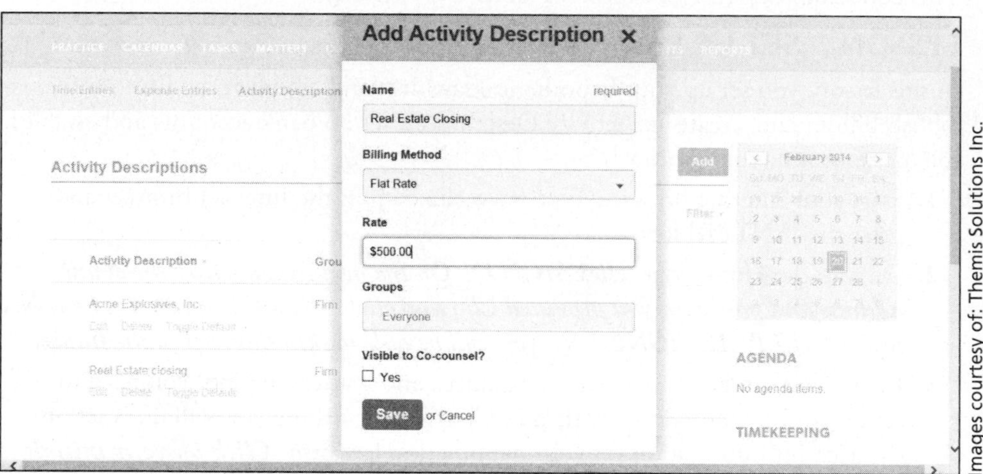

Images courtesy of: Themis Solutions Inc.

6. ***Click the Accounts tab, then click New***. See Clio Exhibit 7. You will set up two accounts—the first will be a Trust account (one that contains only attorney money) and the second will be an Operating account (one that contains only client money).

CLIO EXHIBIT 7

Create New Bank Account

Images courtesy of: Themis Solutions Inc.

7. ***Under Account type, select Trust Account.*** Under Account name, type **IOLTA** (this stands for Interest on Law Office Trust Account, commonly used for Trust accounts). See Clio Exhibit 7. It is not necessary, nor is it required, to complete the remainder of this form (although you are welcome to do so). However, you should leave the Balance at 0.0. ***Click Create New Bank Account.*** The screen will refresh (showing the new IOLTA account) so additional accounts may be created.
8. Now you will create an Operating account. ***Click New***, then under Account type, ***select Operating Account.*** Under Account name, type **Law Firm Account**. It is not necessary, nor is it required, to complete the remainder of this form (although you are welcome to do so). However, you should leave the Balance at 0.0. ***Click the box next to Default Account.*** (The default account will show up first on the Transactions tab of Matters and Clients.) ***Click Create New Bank Account.***
9. Now, you will create the matter-numbering protocol for your hypothetical law firm. ***Click your initials at the top of the screen.*** Then, ***click Settings, then click Practice.*** On the Practice screen, ***click Matter Numbering.*** See Clio Exhibit 8. ***Under Select template: click the drop-down menu arrow and click on each of the available options.*** As you do, notice how the sample matter number (00025-Newton) changes. We want to use the default option (matter number—client summary name), so ***select Standard. Under Customize with additional fields: click the drop-down menu arrow and click on each of the available options.*** These are the optional fields you could add to the matter-numbering protocol. We want to use the default option, so ***select Client Number. Click Update Settings.***

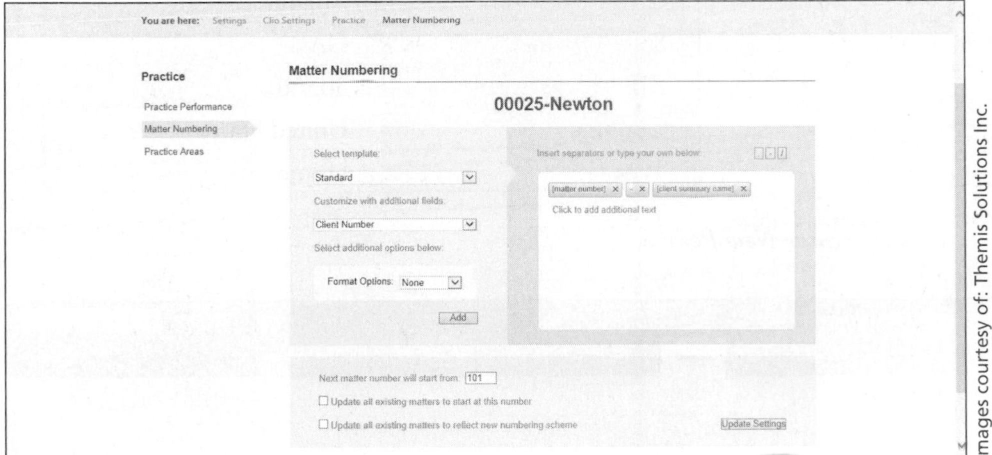

CLIO EXHIBIT 8
Matter Numbering

Images courtesy of: Themis Solutions Inc.

10. To end this Clio session, ***click on your initials at the top of the screen, click Sign Out, and then close your Internet browser.***

You are now ready to enter some new contacts and new matters.

This conclusion Lesson 2 of the Clio Hands-On Exercises.

INTERMEDIATE LESSON

LESSON 3: REAL ESTATE MATTER

In this lesson, you will create a new contact (client), open a file for the new client, create a new matter, enter a flat fee time entry, take a retainer from the client, and apply the retainer to an invoice.

HANDS-ON EXERCISES

1. **Start your Internet browser. Type www.clio.com in the Internet browser and press the [ENTER] key.**
2. **On the Clio Home page, *click SIGN IN. On the next screen, enter the email address and password you provided Clio and click SIGN IN. If you check the box next to KEEP ME SIGNED IN, you will be able to skip this step in the future.***
3. In this lesson, your law firm will do a real estate closing for a new client. The first thing to do is to create a new contact card (in this case, the contact is the new client). To create a new client card, ***click the Contacts tab, then click New Person***. See Clio Exhibit 9. ***Enter the following information in the Add New Person form.***

Prefix	Ms.
First name	Penny
Last name	Hannah

Email — penny@domain.com (make sure this is the Home email and click the button to make this the primary email address)

Phone Number — (404) 555-1982 (make sure this is the Home phone number and click the button to make this the primary phone number)

Address

Street	5 Mercer Court
City	Atlanta
State/Province	GA
ZIP	30306
Country	United States
Type	Home

Click Save New Person.

CLIO EXHIBIT 9
Add New Person

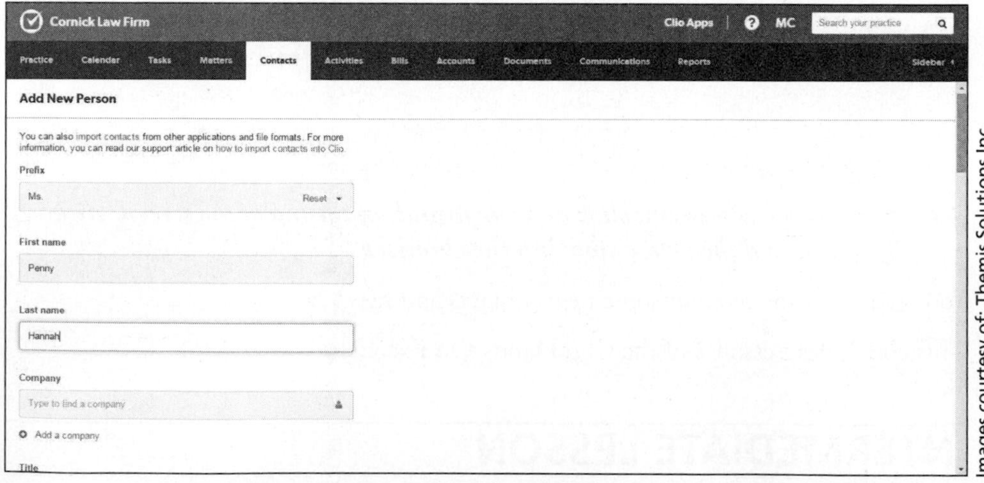

4. Now you will create a new matter card. To create a new matter card, ***click Matters, then click New***. See Clio Exhibit 10. ***Enter the following information in the Create New Matter form.***

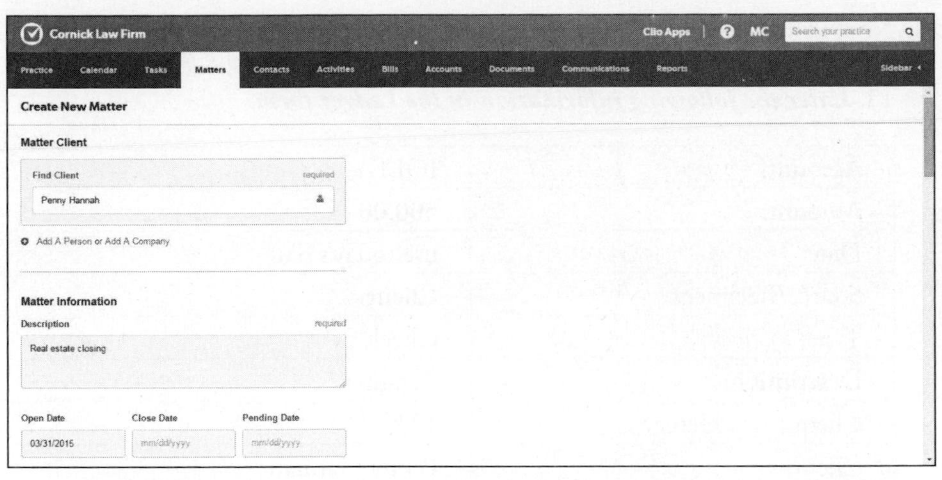

CLIO EXHIBIT 10
Create New Matter

Images courtesy of: Themis Solutions Inc.

Matter Client

Find Client	Penny Hannah (notice that as you type her name, Clio will suggest it)

Matter Information

Description	Real estate closing
Open Date	Use today's date (will be shown by default)
Status	Open
Practice Area	Conveyance (Sale)
Responsible Attorney	Use your name

Matter Permissions

	Select Everyone

Matter Billing

	Check the box so this item is billable
	Click the button next to Flat Rate, then in the text box below, select Real Estate Closing. Clio will then fill in the Rate box with the $500 fee you established in the prior lesson

Click Save New Matter. Your screen should now look like Clio Exhibit 11.

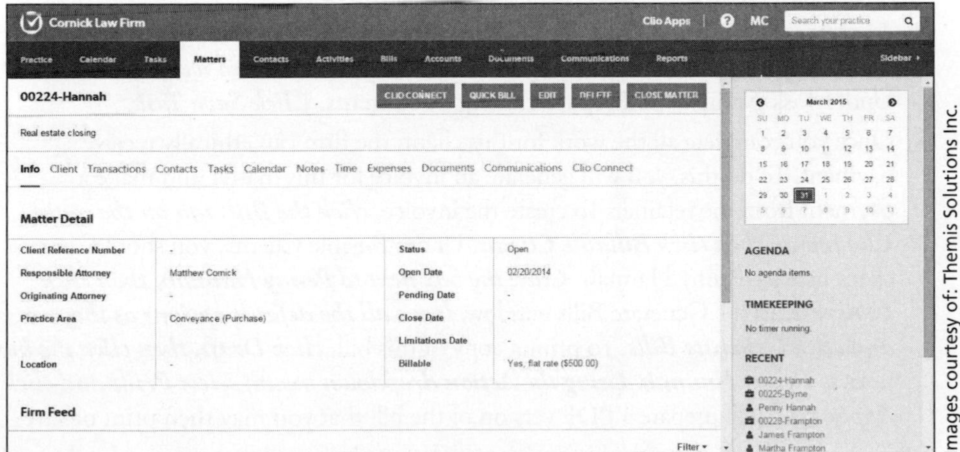

CLIO EXHIBIT 11
New Matter

Images courtesy of: Themis Solutions Inc.

HANDS-ON EXERCISES

5. Now we will assume that the client has paid a $500 retainer for this matter. To record this retainer, ***click Transactions, then click ADD***. See Clio Exhibit 12. ***Enter the following information in the Ledger form.***

Account:	IOLTA
Amount:	500.00
Date:	use today's date
Source/Recipient	Client
Type:	Check
Description:	Retainer
Cheque or Reference:	1234
Client:	Penny Hannah
Matter:	00224-Hannah

Click Record Transaction.

CLIO EXHIBIT 12
New Transaction

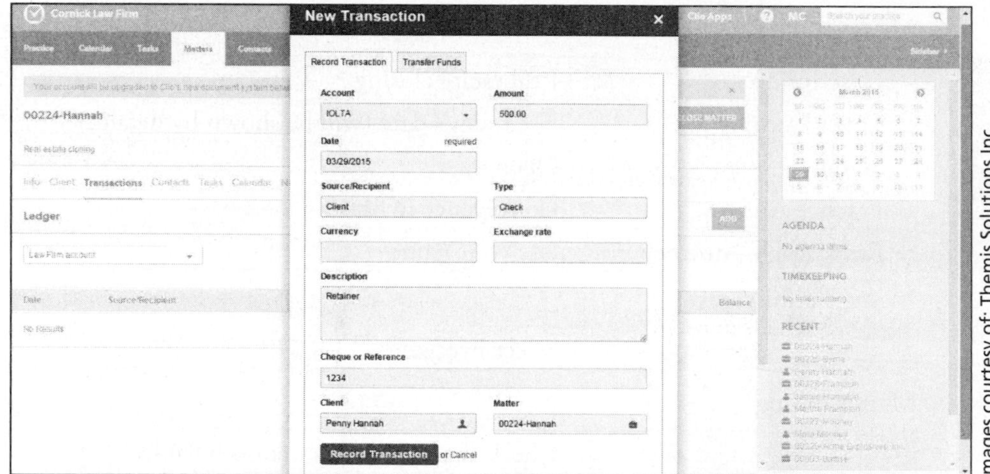

Images courtesy of: Themis Solutions Inc.

6. You will now add a calendar entry and create a task associated with this matter. To create an associated calendar entry, ***click Calendar*** on the menu bar at the top of the Hannah matter page, then ***click ADD. Schedule the meeting for a day next week, beginning at 10:00 AM and ending at 11:00 AM***. Under Summary, type **Client Meeting**. Under Description, type **Discuss real estate issues with client**. ***Click Create Calendar Entry.***
7. To create an associated task, ***click Tasks*** on the menu bar at the top of the Hannah matter page, then ***click ADD***. ***Schedule the task for a day two weeks from now.*** Under Task Name, type **Prepare closing documents**. ***Click Save Task.***
8. Once you complete all the work for this client, the firm can ethically receive payment. To do this, you will generate an invoice for this matter and make a payment from the retainer. To create the invoice, ***click the Bills tab on the main Clio menu, then click Billable Clients***. Under Billable Clients, you should see one client listed—Penny Hannah. ***Click the box next to Penny Hannah, then click Generate.*** In the Generate Bills window, ***leave all the default options as they are and click Generate Bills***. To print a copy of this bill, ***click Draft, then click the box next to Penny Hannah. Using the Action dropdown menu, select Print and click Apply***. Clio will prepare a PDF version of the bill that you may then print or save.
9. To credit the client with the retainer paid, you first need to approve the draft of Penny Hannah's bill. To do this, on the Bills page, under Drafts, ***click the box***

next to Penny Hannah. Using the Action dropdown menu, ***select Approve, then click Apply***. Next, on the Bills page, under Awaiting Payment, ***click the box next to Penny Hannah, then click Receive Payment***. See Clio Exhibit 13. In the New window, ***click Receive Payment***.

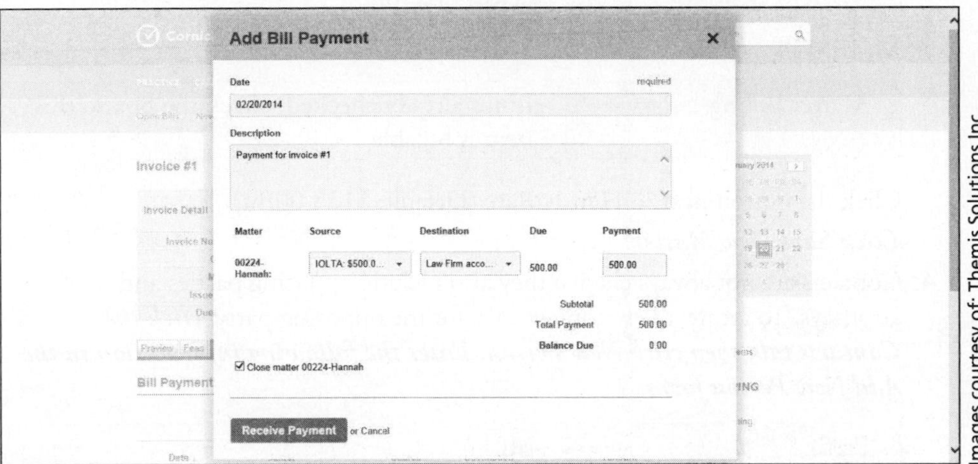

CLIO EXHIBIT 13
Add Bill Payment

Images courtesy of: Themis Solutions Inc.

10. ***To end this Clio session, click on your initials at the top of the screen, click Sign Out, and then close your Internet browser.***

This concludes Lesson 3 of the Clio Hands-On Exercises.

ADVANCED LESSONS

LESSON 4: CIVIL LITIGATION MATTER

In this lesson, you will identify relationships, add a document, log a phone call, add a time entry, add an expense entry, and create a bill for a client in a litigation matter.

1. **Start your Internet browser. Type www.clio.com in the Internet browser and press the [ENTER] key.**
2. **On the Clio Home page, *click SIGN IN. On the next screen, enter the email address and password you provided Clio and click SIGN IN. If you check the box next to KEEP ME SIGNED IN, you will be able to skip this step in the future.***
3. In this lesson, your hypothetical law firm will work on a litigation case. The plaintiff will be James Byrne, an existing client of your law firm (his contact information was included in the data files you imported to Clio). To create a new matter for an existing client, ***click the Matters tab, then click New. Enter the following information in the Create New Matter form.***

   Matter Client

Find Client	James Byrne (notice that as you type his name, Clio will suggest it)

   Matter Information

Description	Contract dispute
Open Date	Use today's date
Status	Open
Practice Area	Civil Litigation
Responsible Attorney	Use your name

HANDS-ON EXERCISES

Statute of Limitations

Due Date	Select the date one year from today

Matter Permissions

Matter Permissions	Select Everyone

Matter Billing

Matter Billing	If not already checked, check the box so this item is billable

Click the button next to Hourly Rate (Default: $125.00/hr)

Click Save New Matter.

4. Contacts are not always clients; they also include opposing parties and their attorneys. To create a new contact card for the opposing party, ***click the Contacts tab, then click New Person. Enter the following information in the Add New Person form.***

Prefix	Mr.
First name	Carl
Last name	McKay

Email carlmckay@domain.com (make sure this is the Home email and click the button to make this the primary email address)

Phone Number (404) 555-2010 (make sure this is the Home phone number and click the button to make this the primary phone number)

Address

Street	400 Johnson Road
City	Atlanta
State/Province	GA
ZIP	30307
Country	United States
Type	Home

Click Save New Person.

5. To create a new contact card for the opposing counsel, ***click the Contacts tab, then click New Person. Enter the following information in the Add New Person form.***

Prefix	Mr.
First name	Hamilton
Last name	Burgar
Title	Attorney

Email hburgar@hburgarlaw.com (make sure this is the Work email and click the button to make this the primary email address)

Phone Number (404) 555-6789 (make sure this is the Work phone number and click the button to make this the primary phone number)

Address

Street	100 Peachtree Street
City	Atlanta
State/Province	GA
ZIP	30303
Country	United States
Type	Work

Click Save New Person.

6. It is now necessary to establish the proper relationship among the newly created contacts and the newly created matter. To establish the relationship, you must first open the Byrne matter card. In the search box at the top right corner of the Clio screen, type **Byrne**, ***then select the Byrne Contract Dispute matter. Scroll to the top of the Byrne matter card and click the Contacts tab, then click Add.*** See Clio Exhibit 14. Type **Carl McKay** in the Contact field, then type **Opposing Party** in the Relationship field. ***Click Save.*** To add the relationship, ***click Add.*** Type **Hamilton Burgar** in the Contact field, then type **Opposing Counsel** in the Relationship field. ***Click Save.***

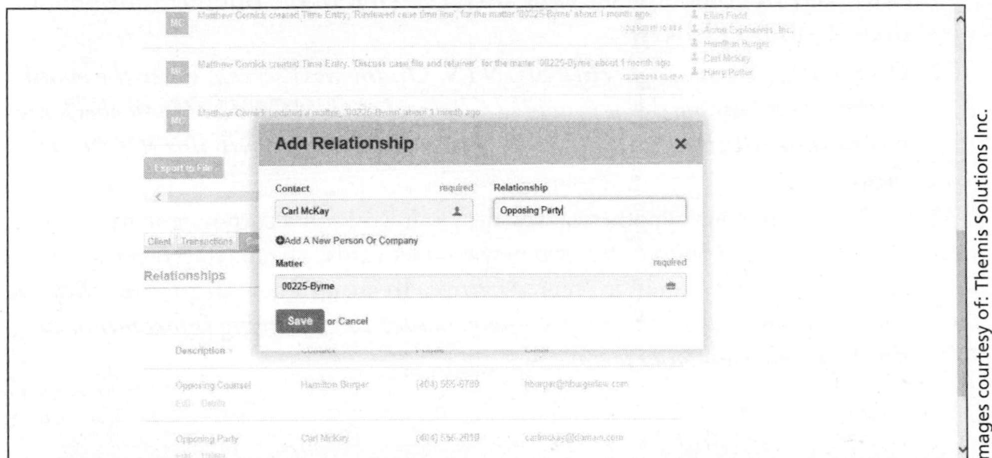

CLIO EXHIBIT 14
Add Relationship - Person

7. It is possible to add documents, such as Word files, to a matter within Clio. To do so, ***click the Documents tab at the top of the Byrne matter page, then click New, then File upload.*** From the list of documents, ***select the Lesson 1 document you prepared in the Word Hands-On Exercises and click Open to select the document.*** The document has been added to the Byrne case matter.
8. When a client is billed at an hourly rate, it is especially important to record all time spent on behalf of that client. You will now make two time entries. To do so, ***click the Time tab at the top of the Byrne matter page, then click Add.*** Under Description: ***select (no description).*** Under Duration, type **45 minutes**; Under Note, type **Discussed case file and retainer.** ***Click Save Time Entry.*** Notice that a time entry appears that charges the client $93.75. Clio calculated the precise amount of the billing for this time entry. Now, you will enter another time entry. ***Click Add.*** Under Description: ***select (no description).*** Under Duration, type **1 hour**; under Note, type **Reviewed case time line.** ***Click Save Time Entry.*** Notice that a time entry appears that charges the client $125.00.

9. Clients are billed for expenses (money paid to third parties), as well as legal fees. To do so, ***click the Expenses tab at the top of the Byrne matter page, then click Add***. Under Amount: type **$12.50**; under Note: type **Photocopies**.***Click Save.***
10. Finally, you will prepare a bill for this matter. ***Click the Bills tab on the main Clio menu, then click Billable Clients***. Under Billable Clients, you should see one client listed James Byrne. ***Click the box next to James Byrne, then click Generate***. In the Generate Bills window, ***leave all the default options as they are and click Generate Bills***. To print a copy of this bill, ***click the box next to James Bryne.*** Using the Action dropdown menu, ***select Print, then click Apply***. Clio will prepare a PDF version of the bill that you may then print or save.
11. ***To end this Clio session, click on your initials at the top of the screen, click Sign Out, and then close your Internet browser***.

This concludes Lesson 4 of the Clio Hands-On Exercises.

LESSON 5: CORPORATE MATTER

In this lesson, you will identify relationships, add a document, log a phone call, add a time entry, add an expense entry, and create a bill for a client in a corporate matter.

1. **Start your Internet browser. Type www.clio.com in the Internet browser and press the [ENTER] key.**
2. **On the Clio Home page, *click SIGN IN. On the next screen, enter the email address and password you provided Clio and click SIGN IN. If you check the box next to KEEP ME SIGNED IN, you will be able to skip this step in the future.***
3. In this lesson, your hypothetical law firm will work on a corporate matter. This will first require you to create two new contact cards; one for the corporation and one for the corporation's representative. To create a new client card, ***click the Contacts tab, then click New Company. Enter the following information in the Add New Company form***.

Company Details

Name	Acme Explosives, Inc.
Email	info@acmeexplosives.com (make sure this is the Work email and click the button to make this the primary email address)
Phone Number	(770) 555-2665 (make sure this is the Work phone number and click the button to make this the primary phone number)
Website	acmeexplosives.com

Address

Street	225 Coyote Circle
City	Alpharetta
State/Province	GA
ZIP	30312
Country	United States
Type	Work

Billing Rates

Click the + sign to create a custom rate. Then assign yourself the rate of $300.00/hr.

Click Save New Company.

4. Now you will create the contact card for the corporate representative. To create a new contact card for the corporation's representative, ***click the Contacts tab and select New Person. Enter the following information in the Add New Person form.***

Prefix	Ms.
First name	Ellen
Last name	Fudd
Company	Acme Explosives, Inc.
Title	General Counsel

Email	efudd@acmeexplosives.com (make sure this is the Work email and click the button to make this the primary email address)
Phone Number	(770) 555-2666 (make sure this is the Work phone number and click the button to make this the primary phone number)
Website	acmeexplosives.com

Address

Street	225 Coyote Circle
City	Alpharetta
State/Province	GA
ZIP	30312
Country	United States
Type	Work

Click Save New Person.

5. Now you need to create a new matter card for this case. To create a new matter, ***click the Matters tab, then click New. Enter the following information in the Create New Matter form.***

Matter Client

Client	Acme Explosives, Inc. (notice that as you type this name, Clio will suggest it)

Matter Information

Description	Business Merger
Open Date	Use the date of one week ago today
Status	Open
Practice Area	Corporate
Responsible Attorney	Use your name

HANDS-ON EXERCISES

Matter Permissions

	Select Everyone

Matter Billing

	Check the box so this item is billable
	Click the button next to Hourly Rate
	(Default: $125.00/hr)

Click Save New Matter.

6. Now you need to create a relationship between Acme Explosives, Inc. and the company it wants to merge with. To do so, you must first create a Contact for them. ***Click Contacts on the main Clio menu, then click New Company. Enter the following information in the Add New Company form.***

Company Details

Company Name	Johnson Corporation
Email primary	info@johnsoncorp.com
Phone Number primary	(770) 555-1234

Address

Street	16 Parkside Lane
City	Chapin
State	New York
ZIP/Postal Code	11803
Type	Work

Then Click Save New Company.

Click Contacts on the tab at the top of the Acme Explosives, Inc. matter page, then click Add. See Clio Exhibit 15. ***Click + Add A New Company*** and enter the following information: In the Contact field, type **Johnson Corporation.** In the Relationship field, type **Merger Partner.** ***Click Save***. See Clio Exhibit 15.

CLIO EXHIBIT 15
Add Relationship – Company

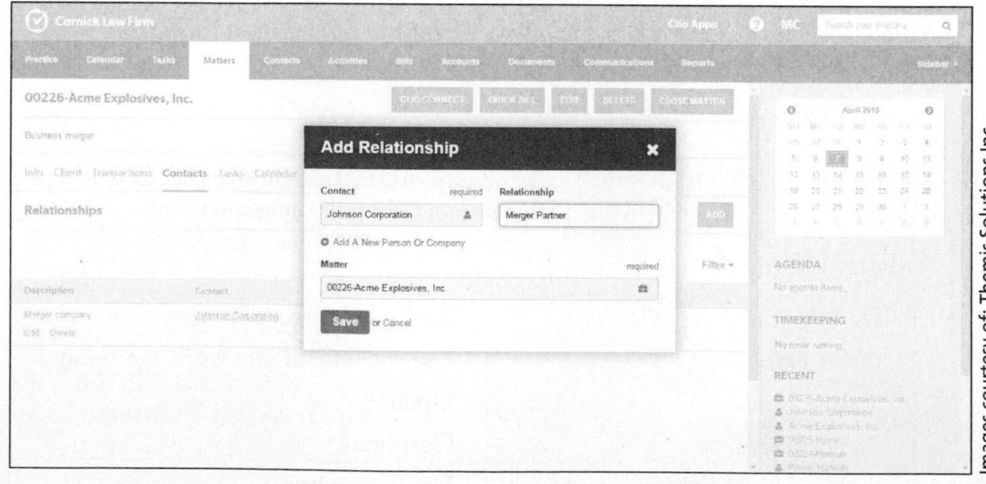

7. ***Create a Word document titled Articles of Merger between Acme Explosives, Inc. and Johnson Corporation*** (the document can be left blank) ***and save it to your computer***. In Clio, ***click the Documents tab at the top of the Acme Explosives, Inc. matter page, then click New. Click File upload and select Articles of Merger between Acme Explosives, Inc. and Johnson Corporation and click Open***. Once the document is uploaded, your screen should look like Clio Exhibit 16. You should now be able to see the document in Clio; see Clio Exhibit 16. Clio has a feature called Clio Connect—this permits Clio (including invited Contacts) to communicate over the secure Clio platform. If you wanted to share this document with the representative of Acme Explosives, Inc. you could do so securely through Clio Connect. To do so, ***scroll down to the Articles of Merger and click Share.*** Then type **Ellen Fudd** in the Share Document with Clio Connect open text field. As you type the name, it will appear in a drop-down menu. ***Select Ellen Fudd*** and ***under Delivery method, click the button next to Clio Connect, then click Share***. (You may receive an error message as the email address is not a valid one.)

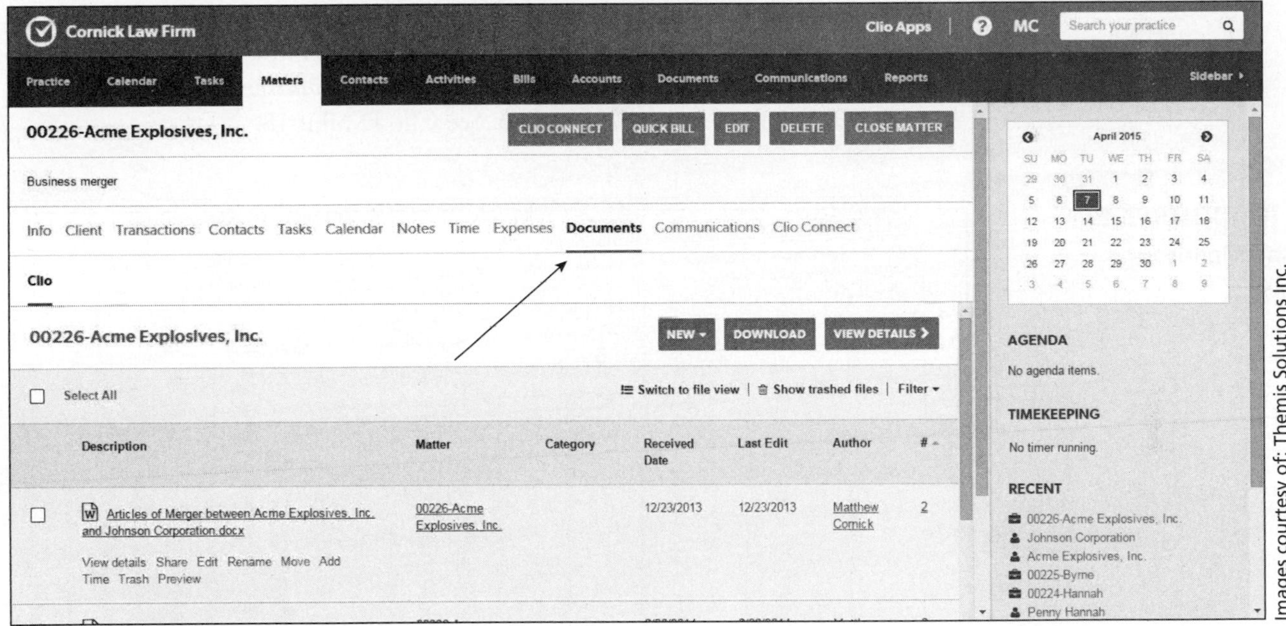

Images courtesy of: Themis Solutions Inc.

CLIO EXHIBIT 16
Documents Uploaded

8. This client is billed at $300.00/hour, so that will require that an Activity Description be created for this client (this will be used to override the default billing rate). ***Click the Activities tab on the main Clio menu, then click Activity Descriptions, then click Add***. Under Add Activity Description, in the Name field type, **Acme Explosives, Inc**. Next to Billing Method, ***select Custom Rate***, then type **$300.00**, then ***click Save***.
9. Click the Calendar tab on the main Clio menu, ***move your cursor to today's date and double-click on the 10:00 am time slot***. The Create Calendar Entry window will open. Under Summary, type **Acme Explosives, Inc. Training**. Under When, if necessary, type **10:00 AM to 11:00 AM**. Under Matter, type **Acme Explosives** (Clio will automatically suggest Acme

Explosives, Inc. - Business Merger; select that matter.) Under Description, type **Review Special Resolution of Shareholders**. ***Click Create Calendar Entry***. Then to create a time entry for this activity, ***double-click on the newly created activity on the Calendar***. The Edit Calendar Entry window will open. ***Click on the Time Entries tab, click on +Add A Time Entry. Click Create Time Entry.*** **Then** ***Click Update Calendar Entry***. The calendar entry has been billed to the client.

10. In Clio, you can send an email from your own email account and simultaneously file it with its associated matter in Clio. To do this, Clio assigns each matter a unique email address that you can use (as a bcc) to automatically save emails in Clio. ***Open the Acme Explosives, Inc. matter card, then click on the Communications tab at the top of the page. Click the link that reads "Email communications to this matter"*** The Email Maildrop window will open containing a unique matter specific email address. See Clio Exhibit 17. ***Click the Copy to clipboard icon, then open your personal email***. In the To: box, type efudd@acmeexplosives.com and ***paste the matter specific email address in the bcc box***. In the Subject line, type Merger. For the text of the email, type **Please call me to discuss the merger**. Send the email. ***Close the Email Maildrop window***. In about 15 minutes, ***check the Communications tab of the Acme Explosives, Inc. matter*** and you should see that the email has arrived in Clio. See Clio Exhibit 18.

CLIO EXHIBIT 17
Email Maildrop

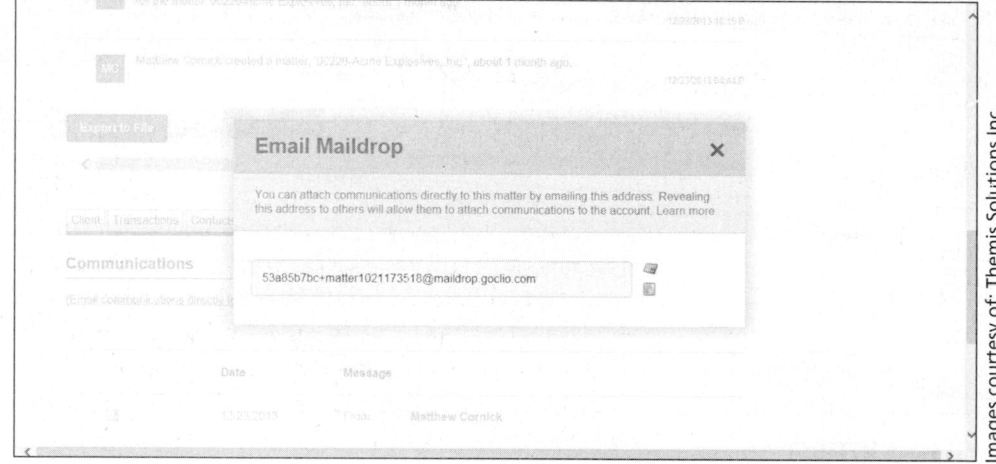

Images courtesy of: Themis Solutions Inc.

CLIO EXHIBIT 18
New Message

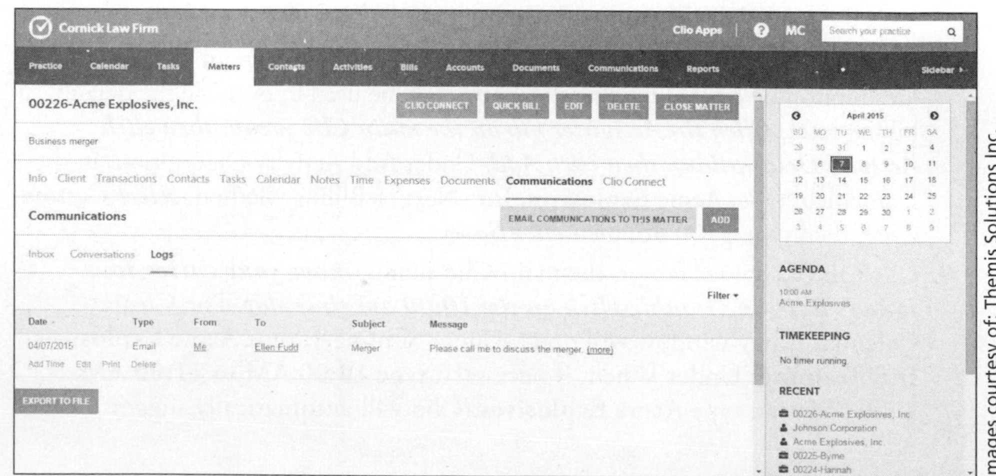

Images courtesy of: Themis Solutions Inc.

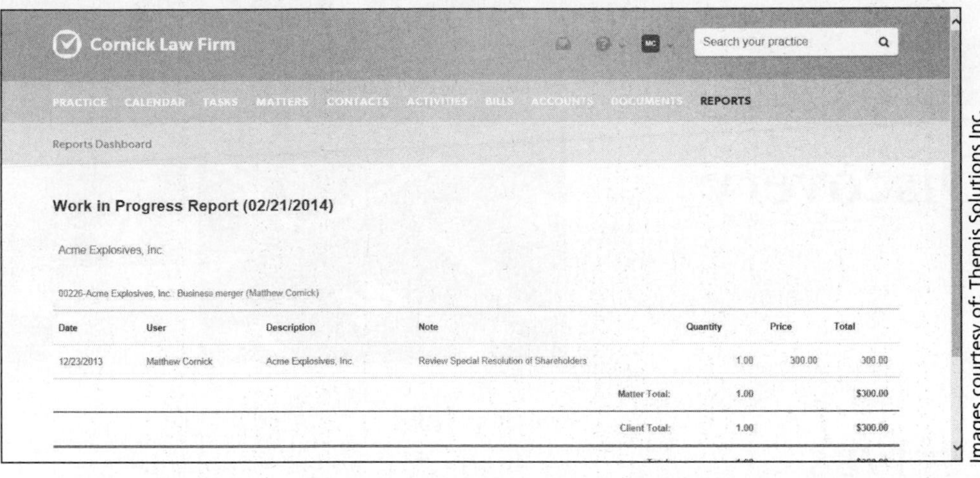

Images courtesy of: Themis Solutions Inc.

CLIO EXHIBIT 19
Work in Progress Report

11. You can run a report to see what will appear on a client's bill. ***Click the Reports tab on the main Clio menu, scroll down and click on Work In Progress.*** In the Work in Progress Report screen, ***click the button next to Specific Client***, then type **Acme Explosives, Inc**. then ***click Generate Report***. The report should look like Clio Exhibit 19.
12. ***To end this Clio session, click on your initials at the top of the screen, click Sign Out, and then close your Internet browser.***

This concludes Lesson 5 of the Clio Hands-On Exercises.

This concludes the Clio Hands-On Exercises.

CHAPTER 7

Electronic Discovery

CHAPTER OBJECTIVES

After completing this chapter, you should be able to do the following:

1. Explain why electronic discovery is an important aspect of litigation.
2. Identify the term that the Federal Rules of Civil Procedure use for all electronic data, and understand its scope.
3. Explain the purpose of the "meet and confer" pretrial conference that parties must have pursuant to the Federal Rules of Civil Procedure.
4. Discuss the duty of parties to preserve electronic information.
5. Understand the different steps of an electronic discovery procedure.
6. Explain what native and image formats are.

ELECTRONIC DISCOVERY OVERVIEW

electronic discovery (e-discovery) The process of producing and receiving litigation documents in electronic format.

discovery The pretrial stage of litigation where parties disclose to each other information about their case.

Electronic discovery or **e-discovery** refers to the process of producing and receiving litigation documents in electronic format. The **discovery** stage of litigation, which takes place before trial, is when parties disclose information about the case to each other. For decades, discovery has revolved around (1) taking pretrial oral testimony from parties and witnesses in the form of depositions; (2) the exchange of written requests for information and interrogatories, and the responses to these requests; (3) the exchange of statements of fact, called requests for admissions, which each party must admit or deny; and (4) the production of hard-copy documents in response to either a *subpoena duces tecum* (a command for a witness to appear at a certain time and place and bring documents or records) or a request for the production of documents. Document production is a crucial aspect of discovery because documents sometimes tell a story different from that of witnesses. Documents can establish facts and timelines, support conclusions, reveal complex ideas, and support inferences that are vital to any litigation.

For decades, documents have been produced in hard-copy format. In complex litigation, each party would send a request for the production of documents; in response, the other party would copy the documents (sometimes hundreds or even thousands of boxes) and give the copies to the requesting party. The requesting party would then have to sort through the boxes by hand, gleaning information slowly to learn what it could about each document and the relevance of that document to the case issues.

The use of computers in all sizes of businesses and in every aspect of life has fundamentally altered how information is exchanged. Today, most "documents" are created in an electronic format (on a computer). Recent studies have shown that more than 95 percent of all documents are now electronic. Web pages, databases, emails, word-processing files, spreadsheets, accounting information, billings, payroll, corporate records, and other documents are all stored electronically. North Americans alone send approximately 4 trillion emails each day. Practically every document produced in most organizations, large or small, is created or transmitted in an electronic format.

Many courts have held that the production of hard-copy documents when electronic versions are available is unacceptable. These courts have been on the forefront of mandating the production of electronic documents. The federal courts, for example, have adopted rules regarding the discovery of electronic documents. However, electronic documents are not tangible, unlike hard-copy documents, which can be read by anyone, which have physical dimensions, and which can be observed and examined. Electronic documents thus present many more complexities and problems than hard-copy materials when it comes to producing them in litigation.

Electronic information is said to be distributed, meaning that it is not held in just one place. Electronic information in large organizations can be dispersed among hundreds of servers; thousands of desktop computers; thousands of laptops; and hundreds or thousands of smartphones, thumb drives, CD-ROMs, DVDs, and even home computers when employees have taken documents home to work on them. Controlling, discovering, and copying information in a distributed electronic environment is not easy. Also, many companies outsource goods, services, information, administration, operations, production, technology, and other functions. Controlling and discovering information in an outsourced environment is not easy, either.

Electronic documents exist in countless formats, a fact that increases the complexity of producing and reading those documents. Some documents are in standard formats, but many others come from completely proprietary systems owned, licensed, and controlled by vendors. Computer systems themselves come from a large variety of manufacturers, and many of these systems are not necessarily standard. Just accessing data from all of these computer systems and file formats is a daunting task. Computers run a variety of operating systems; come in different sizes; and have various memory, components, and other hardware and software that further increase the complexity of producing electronic documents in litigation.

It is easy to destroy a paper document; it is difficult to destroy an electronic document. As we will see, a single document can exist in many different electronic files—and "delete" does not really mean delete. It is difficult to alter a paper document; it is easy to alter an electronic document. Furthermore, every time you look at an electronic file (even if you do not make any changes to it), you may well change the document's metadata (which is considered an integral part of the document itself). People understand what a paper document is. Very few people (and even fewer lawyers) have any understanding of what an electronic document really is. That is the essence of the problem presented by electronically stored information.

All of these issues, and many more, make the exchange of electronic data inherently complex. Why is this an important issue for paralegals? Because paralegals have historically been the legal professionals with "boots on the ground" handling, tracking, and managing document production. In many legal organizations, paralegals are the ones working with clients and vendors regarding electronic document requests.

More than ever before, paralegals must have outstanding technological skills to be effective.

Chapter 8 discusses litigation support software, which is closely associated with electronic discovery. However, although electronic discovery and litigation support are pieces of the same puzzle and are closely aligned, they are different. Electronic discovery is the process of receiving or providing electronic information during the discovery process. In contrast, litigation support software organizes, stores, retrieves, and summarizes the information acquired through discovery for use in litigation.

THE FEDERAL RULES OF CIVIL PROCEDURE AND ELECTRONICALLY STORED INFORMATION

The Federal Rules of Civil Procedure (FRCP) were amended in December 2006 specifically to address the issue of electronic discovery. Some state courts have followed the lead of the federal courts and adopted similar rules. It is certain that additional states will do so in the next few years. The FRCP now refer to any electronic data as **electronically stored information (ESI)**. FRCP 34(a) states that ESI includes "writings, drawings, graphs, charts, photographs, sound recordings, images, and other data compilations stored in any medium from which information can be obtained or translated." ESI is a term of art, and it is used broadly by the FRCP so that any new form of electronic information will be covered by the rules.

electronically stored information (ESI)
The term used by the Federal Rules of Civil Procedure to refer to all electronic data, including writings, drawings, graphs, charts, photographs, sound recordings, images, and other data compilations stored in any medium from which information can be obtained or translated.

> The wide variety of computer systems currently in use, and the rapidity of technological change, counsel against a limiting or precise definition of electronically stored information. Rule 34(a)(1) is expansive and includes any type of information that is stored electronically. A common example often sought in discovery is electronic communications, such as email. The rule covers—either as documents or as electronically stored information—information "stored in any medium," to encompass future developments in computer technology. Rule 34(a)(1) is intended to be broad enough to cover all current types of computer-based information, and flexible enough to encompass future changes and developments. References elsewhere in the rules to "electronically stored information" should be understood to invoke this expansive approach. (FRCP, Rule 34, Comment from 2006 Amendment.)

Mandatory Meet and Confer Sessions

FRCP 26(f) clearly states that as soon as practicable, attorneys for the parties must meet and confer to discuss issues related to ESI, including the preservation of discoverable information and any issues relating to disclosure or discovery of ESI, such as the format(s) in which ESI should be produced.

The rules create an expectation that the attorneys involved will work collaboratively regarding the exchange of ESI, that games of "hide the ball" should not take place, and that any matters related to the production of ESI will be openly discussed early in the case. The Judicial Conference Rules Advisory Committee noted that "the parties' discussion should pay particular attention to the balance between the competing needs to preserve relevant evidence and to continue routine operations critical to ongoing activities." Another goal of the meet and confer session is for the parties to understand the volume of the materials to be reviewed, sampled, and possibly produced. Businesses, particularly large ones, have an enormous volume of data (terabytes of information representing tens of millions of pages of hard-copy data), and the parties need to come to terms with what is discoverable (i.e., what is and is not subject to the rules of formal discovery).

The Challenges of Electronically Stored Information

An electronic document differs from a paper document in many ways. The existence (or nonexistence) and replication of ESI are two of the most important.

There's So Much of It The staggering amount of ESI is compounded by the fact that ESI can replicate itself without the user realizing it. For example, if I hand you a printed document, only one copy of the document exists unless you or I consciously create one or more copies. ESI seems to have a mind of its own. For example, when I send you an email, there is a copy on your computer. And a copy on my computer. And one on your server. And one on my server. And whenever one of our systems makes a backup copy of the electronic data, there's another copy. If you forwarded the email to someone, or if I had sent the email to five people, then even more copies of the email would have been created. And what if my original email evokes a response? The response email may contain the original email within it. That creates even more copies.

In addition, whenever you create a Word document or Excel spreadsheet, as you are working on the document, your computer is making "temporary" backup copies of the data. These copies are deleted when you save the document, but (as we shall see) "delete" does not always mean delete. Along the same lines, whenever you print a document or a screen off the Internet or a photo from a flash drive, the computer creates a copy of the image (called a spool file) and prints the spool file. The spool file is then deleted . . . or is it? A computer may retain copies of images it has printed even if those images were never saved on the computer.

Where does ESI come from? Nowadays, it can come from almost anywhere. It can be gleaned from:

- Computers (home and office; desktop, laptop and tablet)
- Network drives and servers
- Electronic storage devices (CDs, DVDs, flash drives, backup tapes, external hard drives)
- Smartphones, BlackBerries, iPods, iPads, MP3 players
- Cell phones
- Instant messages (IMs)
- Voice mail
- Web history

Also consider that relevant information may be available from sources such as:

- Records from a credit card company, providing details of a consumer's purchase
- A hotel or office building, providing information regarding the use of a hotel room key or pass card
- An automobile computer, providing details of the use of a car at a particular time (speed, brake usage)
- Global positioning system (GPS) devices in automobiles and cell phones, which may be able to pinpoint a person's location at a particular time

A printed document has no secrets: What you see is what there is. In contrast, an electronic document has so much more than just its apparent content; it has metadata. Metadata is information about the document, such as the precise time the document was created, accessed, modified, and copied. However, every time you open a document—just open it—you may permanently change the metadata. That's because by opening the document (or, in some programs, just copying a file without opening the file), you change the date the file was last accessed. If opposing counsel requests the production of ESI and you copy the electronic files in an attempt to comply with the request, you may thereby permanently change the metadata. That can lead to sanctions; this is an example of spoliation.

You Can't Get Rid of ESI When You Want To As most folks now know, just hitting "delete" does not mean that a file is actually gone. When you delete a file, all you have done is made the disk space occupied by that file available to be written over. Depending on the computer's storage capacity, the size of the deleted file, and the amount of new data being put on the hard drive, it can be a long time before a "deleted" file is actually written over. Even then, computer forensic professionals may be able to recover the deleted information. In addition, sometimes only part of a deleted file is written over; the remaining disk space is called slack. So, even when a deleted file is partially written over, some of it may be relatively accessible. In addition, because there may be so many copies of an electronic file, unless you destroy all of the copies, the ESI will still exist.

Notwithstanding the foregoing, ESI is often destroyed at the most inconvenient times. Sometimes this spoliation is not intentional. Most businesses have a regular schedule, whereby old computer backup tapes are written over after a specific amount of time. Big problems can arise even when a party in litigation institutes a **litigation hold**: instructions designed to prevent the destruction of evidence, including ESI and its metadata, pending litigation. Numerous court decisions have held that litigants may be subject to sanctions if evidence is subsequently destroyed, even if steps were taken to prevent the destruction. According to the premiere e-discovery case, *Zubulake v. UBS Warburg*, once a party is aware that litigation is likely, that party has an affirmative obligation to prevent the destruction of all relevant evidence, including metadata. Exhibit 7–2 shows a sample litigation hold letter.

litigation hold
An order suspending destruction or disposal of all relevant hard-copy and electronically stored information, instituted when a party reasonably anticipates litigation.

Duty to Exchange and Preserve Electronically Stored Information

The FRCP, in no uncertain terms, specifically require that the parties preserve and exchange ESI. No longer can there be any argument that electronic data are not discoverable under the FRCP because they are somehow not "documents." FRCP 26(a)(1)(B) provides that "without awaiting a discovery request," a party *must* provide to the other party "a copy of, or a description by category and location of, all documents, electronically stored information, and tangible things" that are in that party's possession or control. The FRCP therefore make it mandatory for the parties to disclose the existence and location of ESI even before they receive discovery requests. In addition, FRCP 34(a) specifically requires that the producing party allow the requesting party to copy, test, and sample discoverable information, including ESI. This is particularly important when large amounts of data might have to be produced. This allows the requesting party to look at and inspect data, including the format of the data, before they are actually produced. **Sampling data** also refers to the process of testing a database to see if it contains information relevant to the subject matter of the case. The FRCP contemplate a very open environment regarding the preservation and exchange of ESI. An important thing to note, in FRCP 34(b)(iii), is that a producing party has to produce information in only one form; hence, if a producing party produces ESI, it need not also produce hard copies.

sampling data
The process of testing data to determine if they are appropriate for production.

In addition, as soon as a potential party reasonably anticipates litigation, it becomes obligated to preserve electronic data. Most businesses routinely discard, erase, or write over their electronic records. Upon the reasonable anticipation of litigation, parties must stop their normal practice of document destruction and put a litigation hold in place. A litigation hold for ESI would include stopping all destruction of data possibly relevant to the subject matter of the litigation, no matter what its form; the hold extends to emails, voicemails, calendars, information in handheld devices, word-processing files, spreadsheets, databases, hard-disk drives, and all other forms of ESI. Failure to institute or comply with a litigation hold may lead to claims that the ESI was subjected to spoliation. **Spoliation** refers to the destruction or alteration of relevant documents or other evidence in litigation.

spoliation
The destruction of relevant documents (or other materials) in litigation.

In one case, an organization terminated an employee for viewing sexually explicit material on the Internet. The employee sued, alleging racial discrimination and claiming that someone had either stolen his password and used his computer to view the material, or that a previous user of the hard drive had viewed the material. The employee argued that the hard drive would prove his innocence. Unfortunately, the organization's IT staff wiped the drive clean, reformatted it, and reissued it to another employee. The court stopped short of actually fining the organization, but in its ruling it strongly reprimanded the organization for destroying the central piece of evidence in the case.

The seminal case in this area is *Zubulake v. UBS Warburg* (actually, a series of cases decided in the U.S. District Court for the Southern District of New York). The genesis of these cases is a claim of employment discrimination. In the ensuing litigation, the female employee requested that the corporation produce hundreds of emails, which she argued would bolster her claim of discrimination. The corporation reported that the emails were no longer available, having been deleted from the corporation's computers. The court ruled that the defendant had a duty to maintain the emails and a duty not to delete the emails. Further, that duty was triggered by the corporation's knowledge that an employee was complaining about sexual harassment and that it was likely litigation would result.

The Electronic Format of ESI

The electronic format in which ESI is produced is extremely important. FRCP 34(b) allows the requesting party, at least initially, to specify the form in which the ESI is to be produced. The producing party can object to the form requested, but must specifically state the reason for the objection and what format it proposes to use for the ESI. FRCP 34(b)(i) requires that a party producing ESI shall produce it as it is kept in the usual course of business, and goes on to say, in 34(b)(ii), that if the requesting party does not specify a format, the responding party is required to produce the ESI in the format in which it is ordinarily maintained or in reasonably usable format (see FRCP 34(b)). For example, suppose a Microsoft Word 2010 file is subject to production in discovery. In Microsoft Word 2010, the native format of a Word file is ".docx." That is, Microsoft Word 2010 files all have the file extension ".docx" (e.g., "letter.docx"). Would it be acceptable for the producer to produce the ".docx" file in a PDF format instead of its native ".docx" format? If the request for production did not state a format, then the production in PDF—a reasonably usable format—would most likely be allowed. Native format (discussed later in this chapter) generally refers to the file structure/program in which a piece of information was originally created. If the requesting party had wanted a Microsoft Word 2010 file to be produced as a ".docx" file, the request should have been specifically stated.

accessible data
Data that have not been deleted and can be accessed without the use of special tools and/or software.

No Duty to Produce Inaccessible Data If There Is Undue Burden or Undue Cost

inaccessible data
Data that can be accessed only with the use of special tools and/or software.

The FRCP create two classes of ESI: **accessible data** and **inaccessible data**. FRCP 26(b)(2)(B) says that ESI need not be produced if the source is not reasonably accessible because of undue burden or undue cost. If the producing party uses this rule to avoid discovery, it must be ready to give specific factual reasons to back up its claims of inaccessibility. In addition, some courts have allowed the requesting party's expert to examine the system in question to determine whether the ESI is in fact inaccessible. ESI that might fall into this category includes electronic data that have been erased, fragmented, or stored on out-of-date storage systems that are no longer supported by the organization. In any case, the producing party may still be required to produce the ESI if the requesting party can show that the information is important, relevant, and unavailable from any other source.

Claims of Privilege Can Be Asserted after Inadvertent Production

Information obtained within the context of a privileged communication (such as between attorney and client, doctor and patient, or between spouses) is generally outside the scope of discovery. FRCP 26(b)(5)(B) provides a process for a producing party to recover information that was inadvertently produced when it was in fact privileged. This is sometimes referred to as the **clawback** provision. When producing parties are requested to produce millions of pages of ESI, it is probable (perhaps highly likely) that from time to time privileged information will be inadvertently produced. If this happens, the rule states that the party receiving the information "must promptly return, sequester or destroy the specified information and any copies it has and may not use or disclose the information until the claim is resolved." The receiving party may also bring the matter to the court to decide if the ESI is in fact privileged.

clawback
The ability to have privileged material that has been produced inadvertently returned with no waiver of privilege.

Safe Harbor Regarding Electronic Information Lost through Routine, Good-Faith Operation of an Electronic Information System

According to the FRCP, parties that act in good faith but inadvertently destroy ESI during routine operation of their information systems are not subject to sanctions. This **safe harbor** provision covers inadvertent routine deletion of information such as emails to create additional space, or the regularly scheduled recycling of backup tapes. Rule 37(f) of the FRCP states that "a court may not impose sanctions under these rules on a party for failing to provide electronically stored information lost as a result of the routine, good-faith operation of an electronic information system." This rule assumes, however, that the party in question has acted in good faith, including discussing the issue of preservation of ESI with the other party, putting a litigation hold in place, and making some effort to not intentionally destroy ESI.

safe harbor
A provision of the FRCP providing that parties who act in good faith but inadvertently destroy ESI as a routine part of their information systems handling are not subject to sanctions for that destruction.

PRODUCING AND RECEIVING ESI

When it comes to ESI, legal professionals must be prepared both to request ESI from other parties and to assist the client in producing the client's own ESI for other parties. Reduced to its essence, e-discovery is not significantly different from traditional discovery. Parties must be sure to preserve and assemble the requested material; the material must be reviewed and culled to remove privileged, irrelevant, or redundant material; and it must be produced to the requesting party. Still, the devil is in the details, and there are details aplenty in e-discovery. Let's look at how e-discovery differs from traditional discovery.

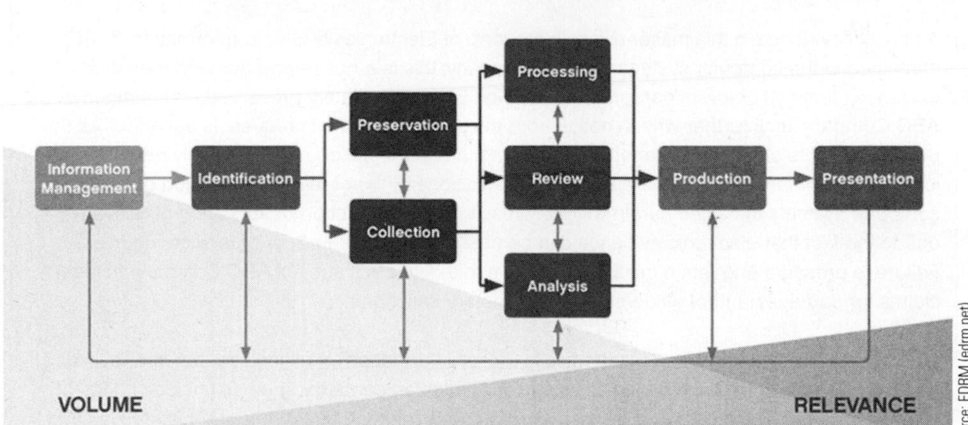

EXHIBIT 7–1
Electronic Discovery Reference Model

Exhibit 7–1 shows the Electronic Discovery Reference Model (courtesy of edrm .net), which describes the following stages of e-discovery:

Information management—Getting your electronic house in order to mitigate risk and expenses should e-discovery become an issue, from initial creation of electronically stored information through its final disposition.

Identification—Locating potential sources of ESI and determining its scope, breadth, and depth.

Preservation—Ensuring that ESI is protected against inappropriate alteration or destruction.

Collection—Gathering ESI for further use in the e-discovery process (processing, review, etc.).

Processing—Reducing the volume of ESI and converting it, if necessary, to forms more suitable for review and analysis.

Review—Evaluating ESI for relevance and privilege.

Analysis—Evaluating ESI for content and context, including key patterns, topics, people, and discussion.

Production—Delivering ESI to others in appropriate forms and using appropriate delivery mechanisms.

Presentation—Displaying ESI before audiences (at depositions, hearings, trials, etc.), especially in native and near-native forms, to elicit further information, validate existing facts or positions, or persuade an audience.

Clients Must Preserve ESI: Preservation Letter to Client

Early in the process (even before an actual case is filed), attorneys and paralegals must inform clients that they must not destroy ESI. This includes not deleting emails, reformatting hard drives, destroying backup tapes, or otherwise erasing data that might be discoverable in litigation. Legal staff should also document the instructions and process in a preservation letter to the client, so it can be proven at a later time, should the issue arise, that there was no intentional destruction of ESI.

Sending a Preservation Letter to the Opposing Party

If the opposing party has ESI, it is recommended that a preservation letter be sent as soon as possible, even before litigation is commenced, to the party or its counsel

EXHIBIT 7–2
Litigation hold letter

Dear Sir or Madam:

As critical evidence in this matter exists in the form of Electronically Stored Information ("ESI") contained in the computer systems of ABC Company, this is a notice and demand that such evidence identified below in paragraphs 2 through 5 be immediately preserved and retained by ABC Company until further written notice from the undersigned. This request is essential, as the printed contents of text and images contained in a computer file do not completely reflect all information contained within the electronic file. Additionally, the continued operation of the computer systems identified herein will likely result in the destruction or spoliation of relevant ESI due to the fact that electronic evidence can be easily altered, deleted, or otherwise modified. Failure to preserve and retain the ESI outlined in this notice will subject ABC Company to legal claims for damages and/or evidentiary and monetary sanctions.

1. For purposes of this notice, "Electronically Stored Information" shall include, but not be limited to, all text files, spreadsheets, email files and information concerning email (including logs of email history and usage, header information and any "deleted" files), Internet history files and preferences, graphical image files (including .JPG, .GIF, .BMP, and TIFF files), databases, calendar and scheduling information, computer system activity logs, and all file fragments and backup files containing ESI.

2. Please preserve and retain all ESI generated or received by [insert appropriate date].

3. Please preserve and retain all ESI containing any information about [insert appropriate date].

4. Unless and until all potentially relevant ESI has been preserved, ABC Company must refrain from operating (or removing or altering fixed or external drives and media attached thereto) stand-alone personal computers, network workstations, notebook and/or laptop computers used by [insert names of appropriate persons].

5. ABC Company must retain and preserve all backup tapes or other storage media, whether on-line or off-line, and refrain from overwriting or deleting information contained thereon, which may contain ESI identified in paragraphs 2 through 4.

stating that ESI should not be destroyed (see Exhibit 7–2). It is recommended that this letter be as specific as possible, because normal business operations must still continue, and an overly broad letter will make compliance difficult and burdensome. A specific preservation letter puts the other parties on notice regarding what type of information they should be preserving. A specific request issued early in the matter makes it difficult for the other side to argue that ESI was accidentally deleted. If specific hard drives are at issue in a case, the preservation letter should also state that new software, encryption, defragmenting, data compression, and other processes that change the file structure of the hard disk should not be implemented until a copy of the hard drive is secured.

Items to Be Negotiated between the Attorneys/Parties at the Meet and Confer Session

During the meet and confer session, the parties should negotiate agreements concerning the following items:

- Exchange of basic system data
- Exchange of listing of electronic collections of data
- Exchange of information related to backup and archival data and its preservation, including standard dates, times, and reuse of storage devices
- Discussion of how the principal actors store data (laptop, smartphone, voicemail, email, calendar, word-processing, etc.)

- Agreement to a common document production format, including methods of dealing with native-format documents
- Whether metadata is being produced in whatever file formats are agreed to
- Any privilege related to ESI
- Disclosure of databases
- Any inaccessible data

Catalog All Client ESI

Before the meet and confer session takes place, the attorney and/or paralegal should meet with the client to specifically catalog and understand all sources of the client's ESI. The catalog is crucial in preparing for the meet and confer session, because the legal representatives must document exactly what the client has. In addition, it is important to document this process, because if opposing counsel later makes spoliation accusations, the attorneys will have documentation to support the claim that reasonable measures were taken to prevent loss of or damage to ESI. Exhibit 7–3 contains a sample checklist that can be used with clients to catalog their systems and ESI issues. Exhibit 7–3 can also be used as a tool when requesting ESI from the opposing party.

Assisting Clients in Producing ESI

Attorneys and paralegals should begin thinking about helping a client to produce ESI as soon as the client walks in the door. There are three primary ways for clients to produce ESI. The first is to hire a professional third-party vendor to go on site and assist the client's information technology (IT) staff in collecting the ESI. This has the advantage of involving a third party; if the opposing party claims that not all of the data were produced, the vendor can speak to the authenticity and completeness of the review. This is the easiest method for the law firm, but the most expensive one for the client. The second way is for the client to gather all the data and send them to the law firm. The success of this option depends on the expertise of the client's information technology staff. Also, it still leaves the client open to claims from the opposing side that not all of the information was produced. A third option is for the ESI to be remotely collected by a third-party vendor.

Each of these options has advantages and disadvantages. The decision should be made on a case-by-case basis depending on the unique circumstances in each instance.

Document Formats

Electronic documents can be saved in thousands of formats and structures. **Native format** refers to an associated file structure as defined by the original creating application. As noted earlier in this chapter, the native format for a Microsoft Word 2010 document is ".docx." Native formats cause problems because often the native format requires use of the original application to view or search a document. (For example, a copy of Microsoft Word 2010 may be needed to read and access a ".docx" file.) However, some large third-party vendors have developed proprietary software solutions that allow users to see ESI in native format without using or even having the original program.

Many electronic documents can be converted to vendor-neutral file structures such as PDF (Portable Document Format) or **TIFF (Tagged Image File Format)**. These are sometimes called **image format** or static-format file structures because the image of the document is displayed as it would have been in the original application, although the viewer need not have or use the original application to do so.

native format
A file structure as defined by the original application in which the file was created.

image format
A file structure that shows an image of a document as if it were being viewed in the original application, without the need to use or even have the original application.

TIFF (Tagged Image File Format)
A vendor-neutral file structure that produces image format documents.

EXHIBIT 7–3
Checklist of items to review for ESI

Item	Date Range (x/xx/xx to xx/xx/xx)	Program Created In	Format of Data	Physical Location of Data	Estimated File Size/Volume
Email files and attachments					
Calendar files					
Contact/task list files					
Word-processing files					
Spreadsheet files					
Database files					
Graphic/sound files					
Accounting/billing/budgeting files					
Sales files					
Marketing files					
Internal/operations report files					
Payroll files					
PDF files					
Presentation files					
Files stored in file management systems					
Voicemail (and voicemail files in email)					
Network logs, audit trails, and monitoring software					
Data that are hosted by application service providers					
Internet-related files					
Intranet/Extranet					
Backup/archive data					
Smartphones					
Telephone logs					
Laptops					
Servers					
Portable storage devices (thumb drives, CD-ROMS, DVDs, portable hard drives, memory sticks, etc.)					
Disaster recovery storage and storage in other sites					
Home computers					
Cloud storage					

Listing of basic information system data, including

- Network type/configuration/structure
- Operating system
- Class/type of computers used
- All application programs (custom and off-the-shelf)
- Backup/archival systems and backup protocols
- Name of the system administrator
- Encryption systems (ask for keys)
- Email client/server
- Janitorial (email deletion) programs

A downside of some image formats, such as TIFF, is that the metadata associated with the file is no longer present. In addition, some litigants have purposefully converted documents from a native format that the requesting party could process (such as Microsoft Word) to an image format, to remove the metadata and make it more expensive and difficult for the requesting party to work with the document. The PDF image format can associate metadata, so it offers an advantage over TIFF.

The term **legacy data** refers to information on obsolete computer media (anyone remember floppy disks?) or created using obsolete programs. Imagine finding some old disks that may or may not contain relevant information. What if reading the disks requires a computer program that is no longer on the market? These are problems we did not have when information existed only on paper. Law firms have to depend on the expertise of computer professionals to obtain and work with legacy data.

legacy data
Data created with obsolete computer media and programs.

Metadata

Metadata is information stored electronically in files that may identify the origin, date, author, usage, comments, or other information about that file. Parties are generally entitled to the production of the metadata accompanying ESI. Parties often use metadata to prove their theory of a case. In one case, for example, a woman brought a class action against an employer, arguing that age was a determining factor in the employer's decision to lay off workers. The employee requested that the spreadsheets that had been used to analyze layoff options be produced in the native format, so the hidden formulas could be analyzed. The employer provided the spreadsheets with the cells locked so that the formulas and other metadata could not be viewed. The court ruled that the employer had to produce the documents in their native format, which included being able to access the metadata.

There are two different types of metadata: system metadata and application metadata. System metadata is information the computer operating system creates and uses to track the location of the data on the hard drive. Some examples include the file name; dates of creation, modification, printing, and so forth; and size of the file. To see this yourself, open a Microsoft Word file and then click on "Properties." You will see something similar to Exhibit 7–4; the first screen is an example of system metadata.

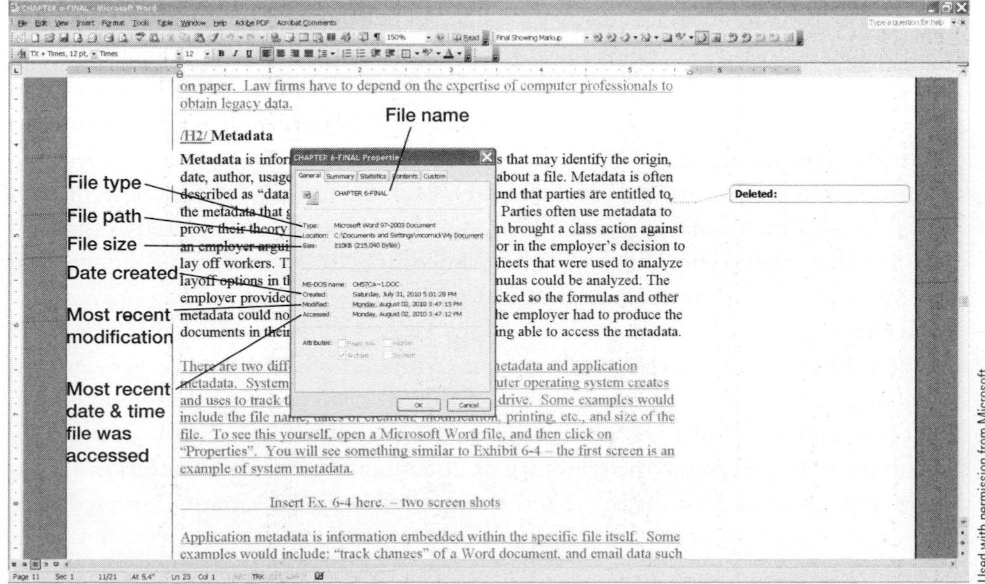

EXHIBIT 7–4A
System metadata

EXHIBIT 7–4B
Application metadata

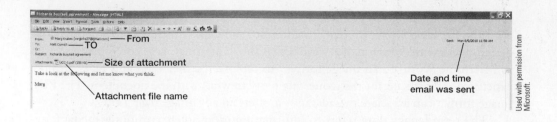

Application metadata is information embedded within the specific file itself. Some examples include Track Changes information in a Word document and email data such as "From:," "To:," "Cc:," and the like. This metadata moves with a document when it is copied. The specific examples of application metadata will change depending on the specific computer application. The second screen in Exhibit 7–4 shows a typical email; some of the application metadata have been called out.

Predictive Coding

As noted earlier, one of the problems created by the vast amount of ESI created and maintained by parties in litigation is the need to sort through all of these data in order to properly respond to a discovery request. Paper documents can be reviewed individually; ESI is far too voluminous for that. Legal professionals need some method of culling the ESI to a manageable level. The traditional method has been to search the data using specific keywords, for example, terms such as *negligence* or *breach* or names such as "John Smith" or "ABC Corporation." Courts regularly accept this practice as an effective method of locating potentially relevant documents in a cost-efficient manner. And for most of us, keyword search seems almost instinctive at this point as searching for keywords is the method we are most familiar with, due to our experiences using basic search engines such as Google and Westlaw. But there are problems with keyword search. First, it does not take into account words that are misspelled or synonyms. For example, a search for "accommodate" would not yield any documents containing "accomodate" (a commonly misspelled word). A search for "vehicle" would not return items with "car" or "truck." Searching for names is especially problematic. If you wanted to search for "Matthew S. Cornick," you might also need to search for "Matthew Cornick," "Matt Cornick," Mathew (with one "t") Cornick, and MCornick (as it might appear in an email address). And this does not even include the variations caused by typographical errors. Searching for a more common name (Jones, Smith, Peterson, etc.) has its own issues as there are likely numerous persons with a more common name (i.e., Thomas Smith) in a large corporation. Second, there may be terms that are known only to certain people within an organization (e.g., nicknames, buzzwords, and codenames) that would not be included in a keyword search because the people doing the search are not aware that the term even exists. Unlike a traditional keyword search, predictive coding uses a variety of factors including document type, language, party, time frame, individual name, conceptual meaning, and other elements to find similar relevant documents.

predictive coding
Computer software applications that use sophisticated algorithms to enable the computer to determine the relevance of documents, based on interaction with a person with knowledge of the case.

Technology creates problems; technology creates solutions. Recently, the most heralded solution is **predictive coding** (sometimes referred to as *technology assisted review* or *TAR*). There are many definitions of predictive coding, but a good one to use here is "computer software applications that use sophisticated algorithms to enable the computer to determine the relevance of documents, based on interaction with a person with knowledge of the case." You have probably used a variation on predictive coding without knowing it. If you have purchased a book or song online, the online seller may have suggested other books or songs to you. These suggestions are based on your choices, as well as the selections of other customers who have purchased the same book or song as you. Another excellent, albeit rudimentary, example of predictive coding can be found in the electronic and Internet game of "20Q"—an updated version of "20 Questions." In 20Q, a player thinks of a specific thing and the computer asks a series of "yes" or "no" questions in an effort to identify the thing the player has chosen.

The computer uses this information to eliminate items that are not relevant to the search and to eventually zero in on the correct item. Similarly, in predictive coding the computer selects a small, but representative, sample of the data to be reviewed. Those documents are presented to a small team of subject-matter experts (typically, attorneys with detailed knowledge of the case). The subject-matter experts decide whether each specific document in the sample set is relevant, privileged, or confidential. Based on the responses received, the computer "learns" what kinds of terms, speech patterns, dates, names, etc., are common to relevant documents. Then another batch of documents is reviewed by the computer, which looks for those specific characteristics in the batch of documents. The subject-matter experts then review the findings of the computer to see if it correctly identified all of the relevant documents. The subject-matter experts make any necessary corrections, and the predictive coding software further refines its search criteria. This is an iterative process, meaning that it has to be repeated many times before it has been fine-tuned sufficiently to ensure a reasonable degree of accuracy. Each successive sample batch of data may contain 100 or so individual documents, and the process may require 20–30 batches of sample data for the computer to isolate the specific words, terms, names, and dates, etc., that it will use when searching the entire database. Thus, predictive coding is a hybrid of sorts; it relies on an initial manual review of documents and uses the responses to create a computer algorithm to determine (or "predict") whether the remaining documents are relevant to the discovery requests, protected by privilege, or otherwise confidential.

Typically, this process works best with a small group of subject-matter experts, that is, three to five. This group is large enough to ensure a thorough understanding of all facets of the case, but small enough to maintain consistency throughout the review process. Predictive coding works by reviewing the text within a document, so documents that are not primarily text (photographs, spreadsheets, etc.) will have to be reviewed by other means.

Predictive coding is gaining acceptance as a valid, less expensive, and more efficient method of reviewing vast amounts of data. Studies have shown that manual review of every document for relevance is subject to human error and inconsistency and that computer-aided review, such as predictive coding, can dramatically reduce the error rate. After all, computers do not get tired or bored the way human reviewers might. In addition, a document review conducted via predictive coding can cost less money and be completed sooner than a traditional review based on keyword search. The seminal case in this area is *Da Silva Moore v. Publicis Groupe,* 287 F.R.D. 182 (S.D. N.Y. 2012), in which there were over 3,000,000 documents that had to be reviewed and predictive coding was found to be superior to the available alternative means of document review. The Court also found that predictive coding was cost effective and complied with discovery rule's doctrine of proportionality (the notion that the cost of discovery should not outweigh the benefits derived from conducting the discovery). Since that time, the use of predictive coding has been upheld in a number of cases in both federal and state courts.

Using In-House Staff or Hiring Third-Party Vendors

When a party is producing documents pursuant to a production request, it is necessary to decide whether the party wants its own information technology department to prepare the ESI or whether a third-party vendor will be hired to coordinate the production. A number of factors must be weighed in this decision. Three key factors include the amount of data to be produced, the amount of time the party has to produce them, and the complexity of transferring the data itself. Exhibit 7–5 shows a process that a client and legal team might follow to produce documents in a case.

In a Fortune 500 business merger, the U.S. Department of Justice requested a large amount of documents in a number of categories in conjunction with the merger. The organizations and their attorneys decided that the document production was too large for the organizations' own IT departments to handle. Instead, they issued a request for proposals and hired a third-party vendor. The vendor assisted the businesses in producing more than 30 million pages of documents in less than 60 days. To make matters worse, the Department of Justice required some files to be in their native format, whereas other files were to be produced as TIFF files. The vendor had special proprietary software that allowed the attorneys to review the ESI in a single database/platform while still being able to deliver the documents to the Department of Justice in multiple formats and meet its deadlines and requirements.

EXHIBIT 7–5
Steps in e-discovery production process

No.	E-Discovery Production Steps
1.	Legal team issues letter to client advising them to preserve data related to litigation.
2.	Legal team meets with client to discuss strategies and problems related to ESI early on in case, including cataloging the ESI and discussing any special problems (unique or uncommon file formats, location of files/access, dates of files that may be requested, and any problems such as backup issues, etc.).
3.	If litigation is imminent, client and legal team decide whether production will be handled by a third-party vendor or the client's internal information technology (IT) team.
4.	If a third party will be used, a request for proposal may be issued, bids received, and a vendor selected.
5.	Parties to the lawsuit have a meet and confer conference to disclose ESI information and try to reach an understanding/resolution on ESI issues, including format of requested ESI.
6.	Document request is received. Legal team analyzes the request and decides if a protective order should be sought.
7.	Legal team meets with client and third-party vendor/client's IT team regarding production strategy, timelines, and any problems.
8.	Third-party vendor/client's IT team harvests ESI, processes the data into a common file format, and creates a database.
9.	Legal team reviews the ESI gathered. Sufficient time is allowed so that relevance and privilege issues are considered. If a third-party vendor is used, it is usually done at their site or remotely using the Internet and proprietary custom software. Such review includes the ability to search the database.
10.	ESI is produced and delivered to the opposing party.

In another large case regarding potential fraud and conspiracy allegations arising out of a complex multiparty transaction, a law firm representing the plaintiff reviewed more than 30 gigabytes of restored email from the defendants. The attorneys hired a consulting firm to assist them in reviewing the production. Using specialized software, the attorneys and consultants narrowed the millions of documents to a little more than 10,000 documents and created a database to store, search, and retrieve them. In the end, the review was a success and led to a stronger case. The strategy allowed them to focus on 10,000-plus documents rather than millions. They were able to find what they needed without wading through every single document, which would have taken more than a year. Because of the third party's capabilities, they accomplished the review of the records in a few months.

It is thus obvious that third-party vendors specializing in e-discovery can help in both producing and receiving documents. The downside of third-party vendors is the cost. Large third-party vendors can charge between $300 and $500 an hour—and this is just the cost of the professionals who consult and work with the data. There may also be conversion costs and other expenses related to working with the data, and these charges can run into the tens of thousands of dollars, depending on the needs of the attorneys and clients. Nevertheless, the cost is well worth it if the ESI is usable, meets the needs of the attorneys and users, and prevents the client from being sanctioned by a court for failure to comply with ESI rules.

What Services Do Third-Party Vendors Provide and How Do They Work?

Whether a client must produce or receive ESI, third-party vendors can be helpful. Exhibit 7–6 shows a list of services that most high-quality e-discovery vendors can provide.

This is a developing market; as legal organizations become more involved in ESI, the use of e-discovery vendors will rise. The following is a more detailed explanation of the services that third-party vendors may provide.

Harvesting Data

As mentioned previously, third-party vendors can assist clients in **harvesting data**, that is, collecting from the client's information systems the data that must be produced. Depending on the size of the production, the age of the data (e.g., if the required ESI includes legacy data), its location, the amount of data, and its native format, data harvesting can be either routine or extremely complex. Because most production requests are time sensitive, it is important to have a plan for how the data will be harvested in advance of the actual production request and to know in what format the data will have to be processed.

harvesting data
The process of collecting ESI from the client's information systems.

De-duplication

De-duplication or **de-duping** is the process of marking or deleting records that are duplicates. For example, think of the number of duplicate records that are generated when a group of people exchange a series of emails. De-duping reduces the dataset, which makes searching the data more efficient. It is also less expensive to produce and process the data, because de-duping can significantly cut down on the amount of data to produce.

de-duplication (de-duping)
The process of marking or deleting records that are duplicates.

Data Filtering

Data filtering is the process of searching and culling the data to find relevant information and reduce the overall size of the dataset. Many third-party

data filtering
The process of searching and culling the data to find relevant information and reduce the overall size of the dataset.

EXHIBIT 7–6
High-quality third-party e-discovery vendor services

- Analyze IT infrastructure and make recommendations on producing/receiving ESI
- Authenticate and provide testimony regarding ESI, including providing workflow certification affidavits regarding software processes, accuracy test results, and anything that shows the validity of the processing, searching, and filtering methods
- Ability to harvest, restore, and read a large variety of standard and unique file formats, databases, and structures, including the ability to restore backups and harvest restored data
- Harvest, de-dupe, and filter dataset as needed
- Process and produce data set in an electronically searchable format
- Present data in an easy-to-use viewable interface, no matter the format of the original data, and include options such as Bates numbering, redaction, document tagging, and notes
- Preserve metadata
- Integrate paper documents and ESI into one database
- Provide data recovery and forensic services
- Deliver native format and image files to opposing party

vendors claim that by using advanced filtering software, they can reduce the size of a dataset by 75 percent. When millions of documents are at issue, the ability to reduce the dataset by 75 percent—to even several hundred thousand relevant documents—can represent an enormous savings in both time and money. Producers of documents can use filtering to help narrow the universe of potentially relevant and responsive documents so that document production requests can be met in a timely, cost-effective, and efficient manner. Requesting parties can also use filtering when they receive a large amount of data and need to reduce that dataset to a more manageable size.

Processing Data If third-party vendors are producing the ESI, they can harvest it and then produce it on CDs, DVDs, hard disks, or whatever media and in whatever formats have been agreed to. If they have been hired to receive data that have been produced, some vendors can convert the data to a common file format and create a unified database, which can then be filtered and viewed.

Viewing Data Whether a vendor is producing documents for the client to review before the documents are sent to the requesting party or is filtering data that have been produced by the other party, the vendor may provide the client with proprietary viewing software. This allows the attorney, paralegal, or client to view documents in one central window no matter what format the files are in. The viewing software provided by many vendors allows the user to see, magnify, print, add Bates numbers, redact information, add bookmarks/tags/notes, and in some cases view the metadata associated with the ESI.

Computer Forensics

Computer forensics is used to recover, authenticate, or analyze electronic data. Computer forensics can be used in a number of ways, including instances in which it is suspected that electronic data have been deleted or modified, or when advanced computer expertise is necessary concerning extremely complex computer issues. Using advanced computer forensic techniques, experts can in some cases reconstruct or recover previously deleted or destroyed information. Computer forensics is sometimes used in lawsuits to recover data that have been destroyed or to prove that electronic data were intentionally deleted or destroyed.

Deleted data are data that at one time were active on a computer, but have since been deleted. "Deleted" data may stay on storage media, either completely or partially, until they are overwritten. As an analogy, consider a traditional blackboard. Imagine that a teacher has written some information on the blackboard and also wrote "Do Not Erase" on it. Now imagine that the teacher has erased the "Do Not Erase" note. The information will continue to remain on the blackboard until someone actually erases it. Computers work in a similar fashion. When you "delete" something, you have essentially removed the "Do Not Erase" sign from that portion of the computer's memory, but the data will remain fully intact and available (to IT professionals who know how to find it) until new data are written over it.

deleted data
Data that at one time were active on a computer, but which have since been deleted.

Even after data have been overwritten, some information may still remain, such as directory entries. **Soft deletions** refers to information that has been deleted and is not available to the user, but which nonetheless has not been overwritten. Soft deletions can often be fully restored with complete integrity.

soft deletions
Information that has been deleted and is not available to the user, but which nonetheless has not been overwritten; can often be fully restored, with complete integrity, by forensic experts.

Chain of Custody

When dealing with ESI, as with any evidence, it is important that the chain of custody be preserved. One must be able to systematically trace ESI back to anyone who has had access to it. Only through an intact chain of custody can one prove that such access was never improper and that the ESI was never contaminated from the time it left the hands of the opposing party to its introduction in court. It is imperative to be able to prove that no information was added, deleted, or altered. Experts can make a forensic copy of the data with matching marks to prove that the copy is complete. Exhibit 7–7 shows a sample chain of custody log. Unless a proper chain of custody and authentication is established, ESI data will never be admitted as evidence in a case.

Overreliance on Third-Party Vendors

Legal professionals must be careful when delegating work, including ESI-related work, to third-party vendors. They must ensure that they closely watch and scrutinize the vendors and the vendors' work. In several high-profile cases, attorneys who delegated too much of the responsibility for ESI-related matters to vendors were reprimanded by judges and sued by clients for malpractice when the third-party vendor's or expert's advice was wrong.

ETHICAL CONSIDERATIONS

Perhaps we will not all become experts in the area of ESI or e-discovery, but we all need to know the basics so we can properly inform and protect our clients. Regardless of the precise language of a state's rules of professional responsibility, legal professionals have an ongoing responsibility to act in the best interests of their clients, to act zealously for their clients, and to act competently for their clients. In light of those duties, legal professionals may have an affirmative obligation to ensure that clients are aware of the dangers and opportunities that ESI presents. For example:

- Clients should be advised to prepare a document retention plan and to implement the plan immediately once the reasonable threat of litigation appears.
- Clients should be advised not to destroy (or attempt to destroy) ESI when there is a reasonable potential for litigation.

EXHIBIT 7–7
Chain of custody log

CHAIN OF CUSTODY LOG

Specific Description of Item	*Lomax 40 Gb. Hard Drive*
Evidence ID #	*1001*
Evidence Serial Number	*2934809234*
Evidence Custodian	*Steven Keys, IT Director, Chase Limited Co.*
Case/Matter	*Chase Limited v. Wax, Layman Mortgage Bankers*
Case No.	*2011-23434*

Name of Person Receiving Evidence	Date	Time	Place of Collection or Receipt	Purpose of Transfer	Signature of Person Receiving Item
Lisa Jenkins, Alpha Data Collection & Forensic Scientists, Inc.	*1/3/12*	*9:50 a.m.*	*Chase Limited Co, Exec. Headquarters, 64 Wall St. NY, NY*	*Copy and Review of Hard Drive to Determine if Confidential Trademark Secrets Were Released*	*Lisa Jenkins*
Steven Keys, IT Director, Chase Limited Co.	*1/17/12*	*4:00 p.m.*	*Chase Limited Co, Exec. Headquarters, 64 Wall St. NY, NY*	*Return of Hard Drive - Hard Drive Appears in Same Condition as it Left*	*Steven Keys*

- Clients should be advised to create and enforce a policy regarding the use of email, computers, and other sources of ESI, to limit the creation of information that may be discovered and used in later litigation.
- Clients should be told that they need to learn about their own computer systems, so that they can discuss these issues with the "techies."

Law offices will also need to be able to handle and discuss issues relating to computers and ESI competently. This means that either attorneys are going to have learn all this stuff or they will have to hire someone who understands the legal process and ESI. Sounds like a job for a paralegal!

SUMMARY

Electronic discovery refers to the process of producing and receiving litigation documents in electronic format. The Federal Rules of Civil Procedure refer to any electronic data as electronically stored information. In the FRCP, ESI includes "writings, drawings, graphs, charts, photographs, sound recordings, images and other data compilations stored in any medium from which information can be obtained or translated."

The FRCP have many provisions regarding ESI, including the duty of the parties to meet and confer early in the case to discuss ESI. Each side also has a duty to preserve evidence in a case, which may mean having the client put a litigation hold in place, and to willingly and cooperatively exchange ESI. The FRCP provide that data that are inaccessible may or may not have to be produced, depending on the circumstances. Even after a document has been produced, if it is privileged, the receiving party may be required to return or otherwise destroy the document and may not disclose or use it. The FRCP also have a safe harbor provision stating that if a party acts in good faith but inadvertently destroys ESI as part of routine operation of its information system, a court may not sanction the party.

Documents may be produced in native format, the file structure defined by and associated with the original creating application. Some ESI may be produced in image or static formats, which yield an image of the document as it would appear in the original application without any need for the original application. Metadata is information that is stored electronically in files that may identify the origin, date, author, usage, comments, or other information about a file. Parties are generally entitled to the metadata that accompanies ESI.

Third-party vendors may be used when producing or receiving litigation documents. Third-party vendors may provide a number of services, including harvesting data, which is the process of collecting ESI from the client's information system; and filtering data, which is the process of searching and culling data to find relevant information and reduce the overall size of the dataset.

KEY TERMS

accessible data
clawback
data filtering
de-duplication (de-duping)
deleted data
discovery
electronic discovery (e-discovery)
electronically stored information (ESI)
harvesting data
image format
inaccessible data
legacy data
litigation hold
native format
predictive coding
safe harbor
sampling data
soft deletions
spoliation
TIFF (Tagged Image File Format)

INTERNET SITES

ORGANIZATION	PRODUCT/SERVICE	WORLD WIDE WEB ADDRESS
Alpha Systems	Electronic discovery services	www.alpha-sys.com
Altep, Inc.	Electronic discovery services	www.altep.com
Attenex Corp.	Electronic discovery services	www.attenex.com
Capital Legal Solutions	Electronic discovery services	www.capitallegals.com
CaseCentral	Electronic discovery services	www.casecentral.com
Cricket Technologies	Electronic discovery services	www.crickettechnologies.com
DocuLex, Inc.	Electronic discovery services	www.doculex.com
Electronic Discovery Reference Model	Resource for e-discovery	www.edrm.net
Electronic Evidence Discovery Inc.	Electronic discovery services	www.eedinc.com
Equivio	Predictive Coding	www.equivio.com
Fios Inc.	Electronic discovery services	www.fiosinc.com
Forensics Consulting Solutions	Electronic discovery services	www.forensicsconsulting.com
Guidance Software, Inc.	Electronic discovery services	www.guidancesoftware.com
IE Discovery Inc.	Electronic discovery services	www.iediscovery.com
kCura	Predictive Coding (Relativity software)	www.kcura.com
Kroll OnTrack	Electronic discovery services	www.krollontrack.com
LexisNexis	Electronic discovery services	www.applieddiscovery.com
OrcaTec	Predictive Coding	www.orcatec.com
Planet Data Solutions	Electronic discovery services	www.planetds.com
Recommind	Predictive Coding	www.recommind.com
Sedona Conference	Resource for e-discovery	www.sedonaconference.com
Xact	Electronic discovery services	www.xactids.com

TEST YOUR KNOWLEDGE

1. Define the term *electronic discovery*.
2. By what name do the Federal Rules of Civil Procedure refer to electronic data?
3. True or False: Under the FRCP, parties are required to disclose information about ESI even before they receive a discovery request.
4. What is a litigation hold?
5. True or False: Under the FRCP, if a party produces a document in ESI format, it still may have to produce a hard copy of the document.
6. What does the "clawback" provision in the FRCP entail?
7. According to the FRCP, when might a party be required to produce inaccessible data?
8. What is the safe harbor provision of the FRCP?
9. Destruction of relevant documents in litigation is called __________.
10. True or False: Data harvesting is searching and culling data.

ON THE WEB EXERCISES

1. Go to three of the e-discovery websites in the "Internet Sites" section of this chapter and compare and contrast the services of the vendors. Which one were you most impressed with, and why? Write a one-page summary regarding your research.
2. Using a general search engine such as www.google.com or www.yahoo.com, find the Federal Rules of Civil Procedure as amended in 2006 and read Rules 26 and 34. Summarize what you find regarding ESI in a two-page paper.
3. Using a general search engine such as www.google.com or www.yahoo.com, find three articles on e-discovery. Write a short paper summarizing the articles you found.
4. Using a general search engine such as www.google.com or www.yahoo.com, or a legal search engine such as www.findlaw.com, find one case related to e-discovery, either cited in an article or reproduced in full. Write a one-page summary of the case.
5. Using a general search engine such as www.google.com or www.yahoo.com, find a sample of a request for proposals that a law firm might send to e-discovery vendors for document production services related to a large case.
6. Using a general search engine such as www.google.com or www.yahoo.com, find a draft preservation letter for a client and an opposing party.
7. Using either a general search engine or a law-specific site such as Westlaw or LexisNexis, research whether your state has adopted rules related to electronic discovery. If so, how are those rules similar to or different from the federal rules described in this chapter?
8. Shepardize the case of *Da Silva Moore v. Publicis Groupe*, 287 F.R.D. 182 (S.D. N.Y. 2012). Find and read an analogous case from your jurisdiction or from a nearby jurisdiction and write a two-page paper discussing whether the court permitted the use of predictive coding.

QUESTIONS AND EXERCISES

1. A legal organization is trying to decide whether to recommend to a client the use of a third-party e-discovery vendor for document production in a case. What factors should the firm consider in making this recommendation?
2. You are a new paralegal in a law firm and a client you are working with cannot understand why it should preserve unfavorable evidence. Write a one-page memo explaining how you would try to convince the client to preserve this (and similar) evidence.
3. You are a new paralegal in a law firm and you are trying to convince a client to spend $300 an hour for data-filtering services from a third-party vendor in a case in which 20,000 documents will be produced. Write a one-page summary of how you would handle the matter.

ETHICS QUESTION

A client in a divorce case comes into his attorney's office clutching a handful of papers. Excitedly, the client says, "See, I told you my wife was having an affair. And here are the emails to prove it!" The client then places the papers on the attorney's desk. What, if any, ethical issues are raised by this scenario?

FEATURED SOFTWARE
Discover FY™

DISCOVER FY™

I. INTRODUCTION–READ THIS!

Discover FY™ is an e-discovery/litigation support tool provided and supported by ILS Technologies. The ILS Technologies Discover FY™ demonstration version is a full working version of the program. This program demonstration version will not time out. However, it is still recommended that you do not install the program on your computer until you are actually ready to go through the Hands-On Exercises and learn the program. When you are ready to install the program, follow the instructions in Section III.

II. USING THE DISCOVER FY™ HANDS-ON EXERCISES

The Discover FY™ Hands-On Exercises are easy to use and contain step-by-step instructions. Each lesson builds on the previous exercise, so please complete the Hands-On Exercises in order. Discover FY™ comes with sample data, so you should be able to utilize many features of the program.

III. INSTALLATION INSTRUCTIONS

Following are step-by-step instructions for loading the ILS Technologies Discover FY™ demonstration version on your computer. Note that you will need to load two separate programs (a Microsoft program and Discover FY™).

1. Log in to your CengageBrain.com account.
2. Under **"My Courses and Materials,"** find the Premium Website for *Using Computers in the Law Office, 7th edition.*
3. ***Click Open*** to go to the Premium Website.
4. Locate **"Book-Level Resources"** in the left navigation bar.
5. ***Click the link for Discover FY™.***
6. ***Click the link for the Microsoft .NET Framework 4.*** If necessary, ***change the language to English and click Download.***
7. The "File Download—Security Warning" window will open. ***Click Run.*** An "Internet Explorer—Security Warning" window will open. ***Click Run.***
8. The "Microsoft .NET Framework 4 Setup" window will open. ***Click the box to accept the license terms and click Install.***
9. The program will load onto your computer.
10. When the installation is complete, ***click Finish; close the Microsoft Download page and return to the Premium Website and click the link for Access Discover FY™.***

11. The "File Download—Security Warning" window will open. See Discover FY™ Installation Exhibit 1. ***Click Save; then complete the following instructions to download and unzip the Discover FY™ install file.***
    a. Navigate to the folder where you saved the zip file.
    b. ***Double-click the file.*** Your default zip program (e.g., WinZip, 7-Zip, or Windows Explorer) should open, displaying the contents of the zip file. Extract the contents of the zip file.
    c. ***Double-click the file DFY_6.3.9_singleuser_demo.exe*** to begin installation.

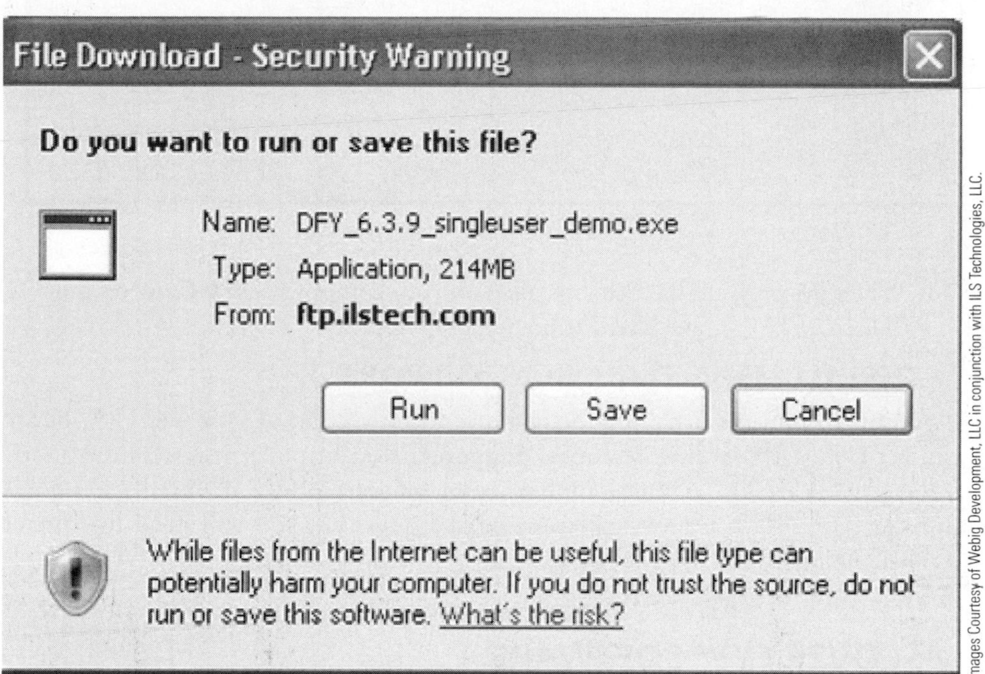

DISCOVER FY™ INSTALLATION EXHIBIT 1

12. The "Discover FY™ Single User Demo Setup: License Page" window will open. See Discover FY™ Installation Exhibit 2. ***Click I Agree.***

DISCOVER FY™ INSTALLATION EXHIBIT 2

13. The "Discover FY™ Single User Demo Setup: Installation Options" window will open. See Discover FY™ Installation Exhibit 3. ***Select the Discover FY™ Single User Demo and click Install.***

DISCOVER FY™ INSTALLATION EXHIBIT 3

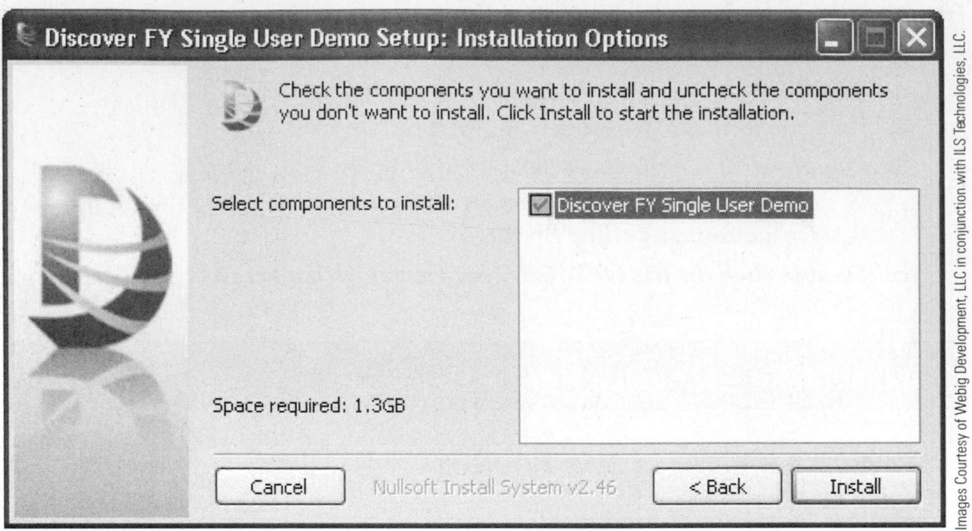

Images Courtesy of Webig Development, LLC in conjunction with ILS Technologies, LLC.

14. When the program has been installed on your computer, ***click Close*** on the "Discover FY™ Single User Demo Setup: Completed" window.

IV. INSTALLATION TECHNICAL SUPPORT

If you have problems installing the demonstration version of Discover FY™, please contact Cengage Learning Technical Support first at http://cengage.com/support. If Cengage Learning Technical Support is unable to resolve your installation question, or if you have a noninstallation-related question, you will need to contact ILS Technologies directly at (866) 359-9324.

DISCOVER FY™ SOFTWARE

Number	Lesson Title	Concepts Covered
BASIC		
Lesson 1	Introduction to Discover FY™	Explanation and introduction to the Discover FY™ interfaces
INTERMEDIATE		
Lesson 2	Processing Data	Processing new data, MD5 hash values, OCR, near duplicates
ADVANCED		
Lesson 3	Generating Productions	Searches, creating a folder, applying tags, generating a production, applying/using Bates numbers

GETTING STARTED

Introduction

Throughout these exercises, information you need to enter into the program will be designated in several different ways.

- Keys to be pressed on the keyboard are designated in brackets, in all caps, and in bold (e.g., press the **[ENTER]** key).
- Movements with the mouse pointer are designated in bold and italics (e.g., ***point to File and click***).
- Words or letters that should be typed are designated in bold (e.g., type **Training Program**).

- Information that is or should be displayed on your computer screen is shown in bold, with quotation marks (e.g., "**Press ENTER to continue**.").
- Specific menu items and commands are designated with an initial capital letter (e.g., click Open).

OVERVIEW OF DISCOVER FY™

Discover FY™ is a powerful e-discovery and litigation support tool. Discover FY™ is designed for anyone who needs to search, view, examine, or categorize volumes of electronic documents. Beyond these fundamental functions, Discover FY™ allows users to generate customized productions of subsets of documents in universally readable formats for opposing counsel, government agencies, or anyone to whom relevant documents are due. The sample data used in the demonstration program consist of real emails and documents generated by Enron Corporation.

These Hands-On Exercises are designed to introduce you to some of the practical concepts and procedures used in electronic discovery. Whether your firm uses a third-party vendor to process electronic discovery files or handles everything in-house, you will benefit from learning the terminology and theories of electronic discovery.

BASIC LESSON

LESSON 1: INTRODUCTION TO DISCOVER FY™

This lesson introduces you to the Discover FY™ litigation support program. It explains basic information about the Discover FY™ interface, including information about the Fact, Object, Issue, Question, and Research spreadsheets.

1. Start Windows. Then, ***double-click the Discover FY™ shortcut on the desktop.*** Discover FY™ will then start.
2. When you start Discover FY™, the "Login" dialog box will open and you will be asked to enter your user ID and password. Type **admin** in the User ID text box and type **password** in the Password text box. (Note: The password will appear as a series of dots. See Discover FY™ Exhibit 1.) ***Click Login.***

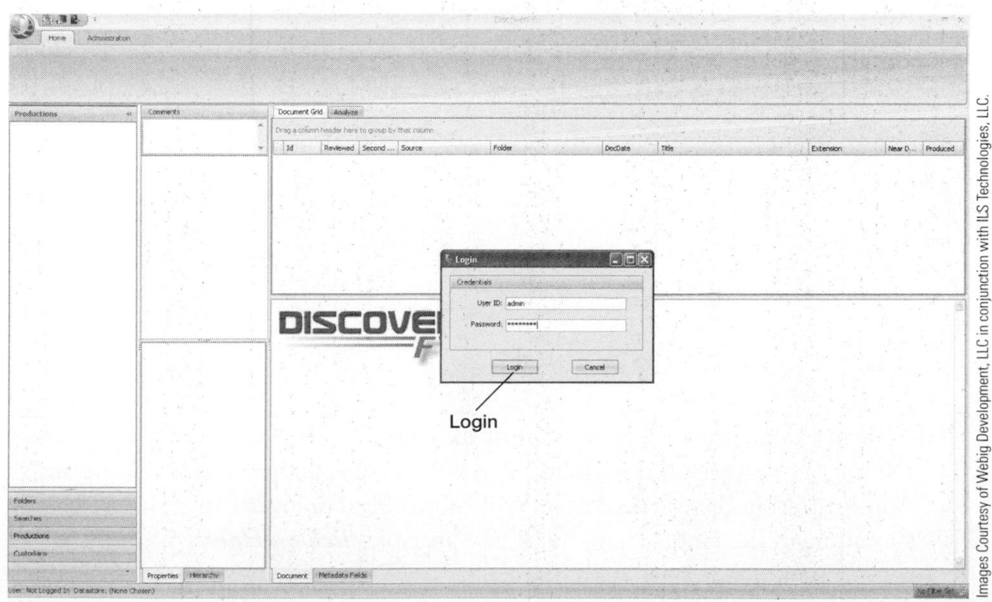

DISCOVER FY™ EXHIBIT 1

HANDS-ON EXERCISES

3. The “Choose Datastore” box will appear. We have not yet created any Datastores, so ***click DISCOVER FY™ DEMO to highlight it and click Select.*** See Discover FY™ Exhibit 2.

DISCOVER FY™ EXHIBIT 2

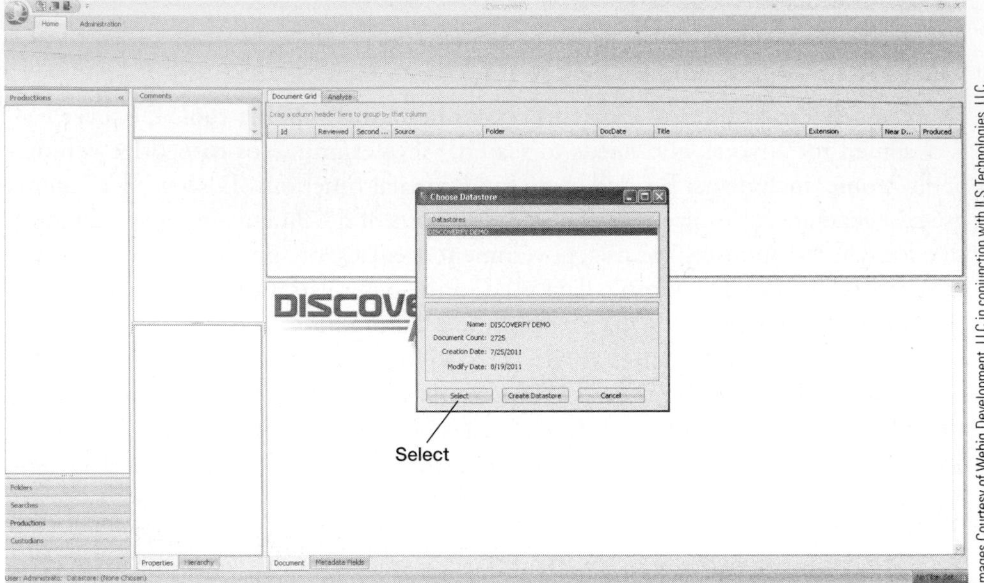

4. By default, Discover FY™ opens with the Home tab selected and the Discover FY™ window is empty because we have not yet selected any data. To access the sample data provided with the application, we need to select a Custodian. ***Click Custodians and then click the only name provided, Chris Germany.*** When you do so, the sample data will load. See Discover FY™ Exhibit 3.

DISCOVER FY™ EXHIBIT 3

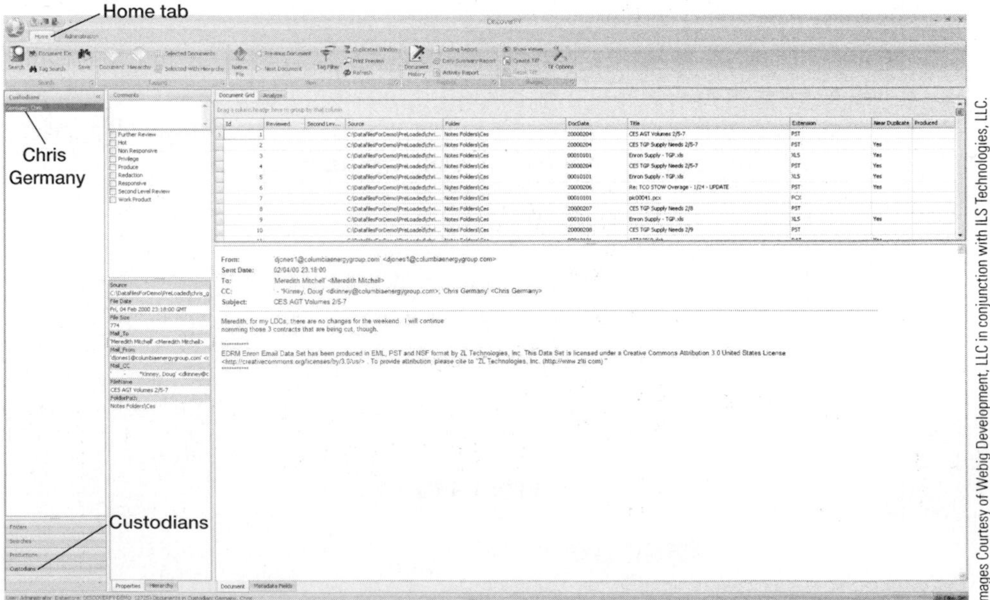

5. We will explore the various sections of the Discover FY™ screen. Running across the top of the screen is the Ribbon Bar, which consists of two tabs, Home and Administration. Home is selected by default. (See Discover FY™ Exhibit 3.) You should be in the Home View, but if you are not, ***click on Home.*** Within the

Home tab, there are five option groups: Search, Tagging, View, Reports, and Images.

6. The Search group enables you to search the datastore for specific documents. A number of search methods are available. ***Click Search*** (its icon looks like a blue square with a magnifying glass). The "Define Search" box will open. (See Discover FY™ Exhibit 4.) This enables you to search for documents by entering specific search terms within the full text of the document or by searching the metadata of the documents. You can refine your searches by using filters to search for documents of a specific custodian, documents created within a specific date range, or documents held within a specific folder. We will explore these search options in a later exercise, but now ***click Cancel*** at the bottom of the "Define Search" box.

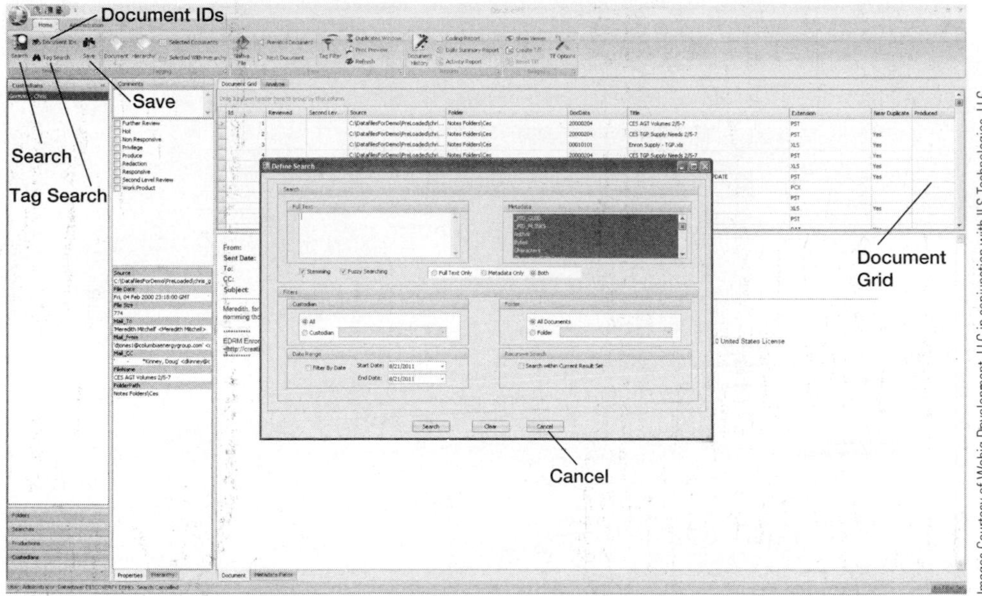

DISCOVER FY™ EXHIBIT 4

7. ***Click Document IDs*** to the right of Search. The "Search—Document ID" box opens. This allows you to search for a document by its Document ID (a specific identification number). ***Click Cancel*** in the "Search-Document ID" box.

8. ***Click Tag Search,*** which is found below the Document IDs. The "Coding Tag Search" box opens. This enables you to search for a document that has been given a specific tag, such as Privilege or Work Product. ***Click Cancel*** in the "Coding Tag Search" box,

9. ***Click Save*** (its icon looks like a pair of binocular with a green triangle on it). The "Save Search" box opens. This allows you to name and save the results of a search for later use. ***Click Cancel*** in the "Save Search" box.

10. The Tagging group allows users to apply tags to documents in the Datastore. This facilitates the process of organizing and retrieving documents. You may apply a tag to just the selected document by clicking Selected Documents. If you also wish to tag any attachments or other documents connected to the selected document, you would click Selected With Hierarchy. (Note: The term *hierarchy* refers to the attachments that may accompany an email.) We will explore tagging options in a later exercise.

11. The View group on the Home tab gives you different options for viewing documents. ***Click the third line of the Document Grid pane.*** This document

is a spreadsheet, and you can see a representation of that spreadsheet in the Document Display pane. (See Discover FY™ Exhibit 5.) ***Click Native File.*** See Discover FY™ Exhibit 5. A new window will open and display the spreadsheet as a native file; that is, it will show the spreadsheet within a spreadsheet program. If you have Microsoft Excel on your computer, Discover FY™ will open Excel to display the spreadsheet. (See Discover FY™ Exhibit 6.) This option allows you to see the formulas used in the spreadsheet and to manipulate the data, if desired. ***Close the spreadsheet.***

DISCOVER FY™ EXHIBIT 5

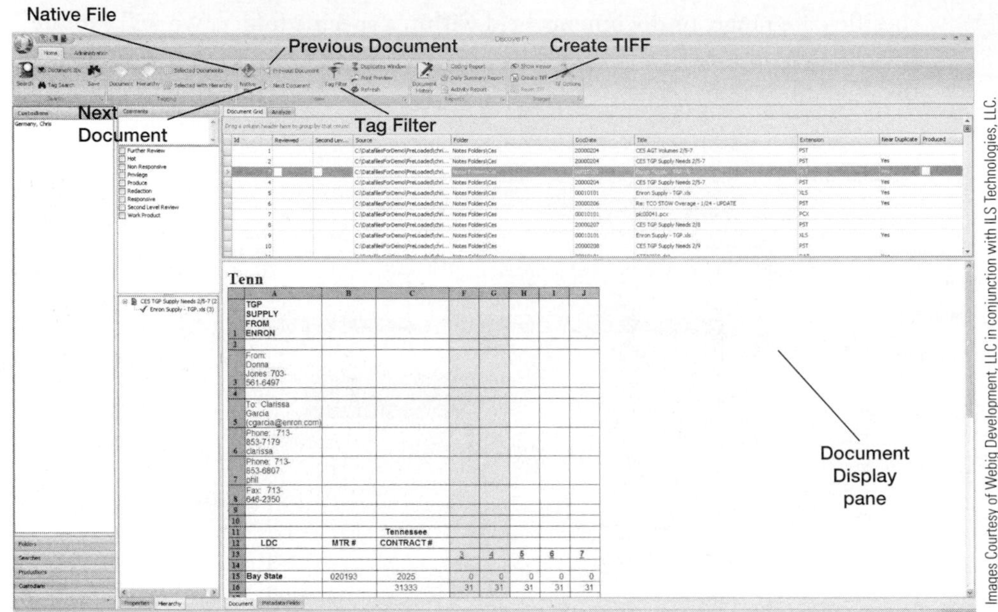

DISCOVER FY™ EXHIBIT 6

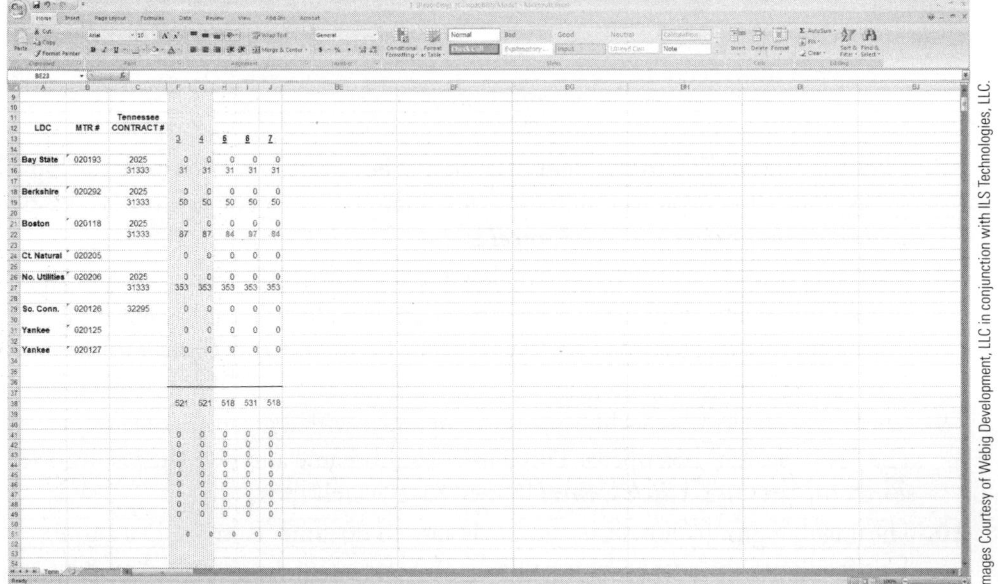

12. You can navigate between different documents listed in the Document Grid by clicking Next Document and Previous Document in the View group. The Tag Filter allows you to specify specific types of documents when executing a search.

The Duplicate Window allows you to see any documents that are duplicates of the selected document. The Print Preview lets you see what a document will look like when printed.

13. The Reports group on the Home tab gives you the ability to generate a variety of reports. The Document History report details activity related to the selected document. The Coding report shows the Document ID, Document Date, Title, and a column for each available flag for every document displayed in the Document Grid. The Daily Summary report summarizes activity during a specified time interval. The Activity report shows a selected user's coding activity within a specified time range. We will explore these various reports in a later exercise.

14. The final option group on the Home tab is the Images group. This option group allows you to create, view, and manipulate TIFF images of documents in the Datastore. A TIFF (Tagged Image File Format) is essentially a photograph of a document. It shows you what the document looks like, but, unlike with a native file, you cannot modify the document. ***Click the first line of the Document Grid and then Click Create TIFF.*** Discover FY™ will now create a TIFF of the selected document. To see the TIFF, click Show Viewer. The TIFF will appear within the Image Viewer. (See Discover FY™ Exhibit 7.)

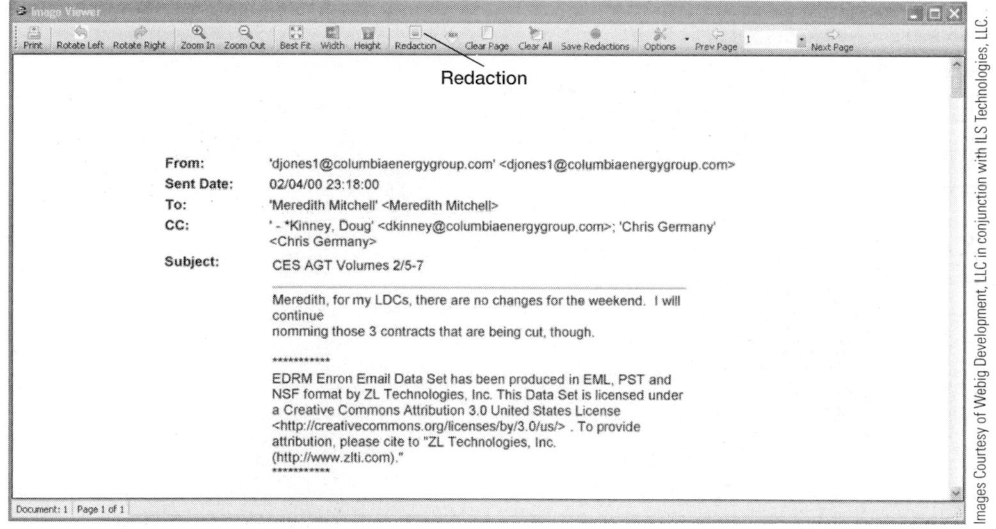

DISCOVER FY™ EXHIBIT 7

15. Within the Image Viewer, it is possible to redact a TIFF. We will now redact this TIFF.

16. To redact a TIFF, ***click Redaction Tool at the top of the Image Viewer screen. Move your cursor to the message portion of the email. Drag the cursor (+) so that the entire message portion is obscured by a black rectangle and release the cursor.*** Your screen should now look like Discover FY™ Exhibit 8. ***Click Print in the Image Viewer toolbar to print the redacted TIFF.*** If instructed to do so, turn the printed TIFF image in to your teacher. ***Click the Close button (the X in the upper right corner of the Image Viewer window) to close the Image Viewer.***

DISCOVER FY™ EXHIBIT 8

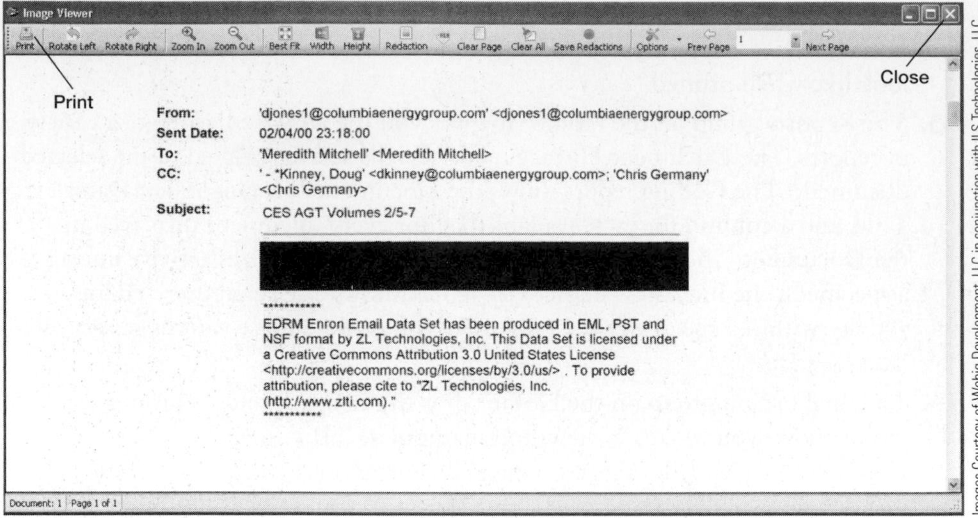

17. We will now explore the options available on the Administrator tab in the Ribbon Bar. ***Click Administration.*** There are four option groups in the Administration tab: Admin, Datastore, Processing, and Production. See Discover FY™ Exhibit 9.

DISCOVER FY™ EXHIBIT 9

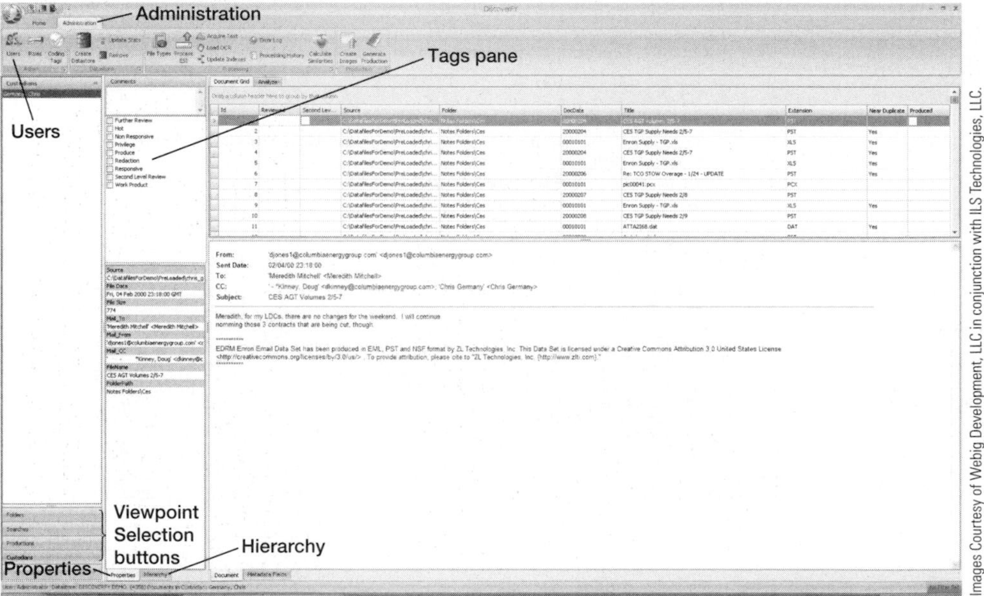

18. The Admin group provides options for managing who has access to which options available in Discover FY™. ***Click Users.*** The "User Maintenance" box will open. This gives the administrator the ability to set users' User IDs, passwords, and assigned roles. ***Click Close*** in the "User Maintenance" box.
19. The Coding Tags tool allows you to adjust the definitions of the tags that are used to code (or organize) documents.
20. The Datastore group allows you to create, delete, and update datastores.
21. The Processing group is used to work with files as part of the electronic discovery process. These features are beyond the scope of these Hands-On Exercises, which focus on the litigation support features of Discover FY™.

22. The Production group allows you to generate the documents required for production. We will explore the production utilities in a later exercise.
23. In the window under the Ribbon Bar are a number of panes. The pane on the far right side of the screen shows the current viewpoint. For example, we have been looking at the Custodians view. The Viewpoint Selection buttons at the bottom of that pane show that you have the option of Folders, Searches, Productions, as well as Custodians.
24. To the right of the Viewpoint pane is the Tags pane. By clicking on one or more of the available tags, you can apply those tags to the selected documents. The application of tags to documents makes it easier to organize and retrieve documents.
25. Under the Tags pane, there is a tabbed pane that gives you the option to see the hierarchy or properties of the selected document. For example, ***with the first document selected in the Document Grid, click the Properties tab.*** You can now see the specific properties of the selected email, such as the persons who sent and received the email, and the date, size, and file name of the selected email. ***Click the Hierarchy tab*** and you can see that this email does not have any related attachments.
26. To the right of the Tags pane is the Document Grid pane. This is where the files contained in the selected Datastore are listed. Under the Document Grid pane is the Document Display pane. This is where you can see an HTML representation of the selected document. By clicking the Metadata Fields tab at the bottom of the Document Display pane, you can view the metadata of the selected document.
27. On the far left portion of the screen, you can choose different viewpoints for the Datastore.

This concludes Lesson 1. **To close Discover FY™, *click the Close button (the X in the upper right corner of the window),*** or you may continue to Lesson 2.

HANDS-ON EXERCISES

INTERMEDIATE LESSON

LESSON 2: PROCESSING DATA

This lesson gives you the opportunity to use some of the tools available in the Processing group on the Administration tab and to process new ESI (electronically stored information) into Discover FY™. Other concepts in this lesson include MD5 hash values, optical character recognition (OCR), and near duplicates.

1. Start Windows. Then, ***double-click the Discover FY™ shortcut on the desktop, or click the Start button on the Windows desktop, point to Programs or All Programs, point to Discover FY™ folder, and then click Discover FY™.*** Discover FY™ will then start.
2. When you start Discover FY™, the "Login" box will open and you will be asked to enter your user ID and password. Type **admin** in the User ID text box and type **password** in the Password text box. (Note: The password will appear as a series of dots. See Discover FY™ Exhibit 1.) ***Click Login.***
3. The "Choose Datastore" box will appear. We have not yet created any Datastores, so ***click DISCOVER FY™ DEMO to highlight it and click Select.*** See Discover FY™ Exhibit 2.
4. By default, Discover FY™ opens with the Home tab selected and the Discover FY™ window is empty because we have not yet selected any data. To access the

sample data provided with the application, we need to select a Custodian. ***Click Custodians and then click the only name provided, Chris Germany.*** When you do so, the sample data will load. See Discover FY™ Exhibit 3.

5. We will explore the various features of the Discover FY™ window and its Ribbon Bar. (See Discover FY™ Exhibit 3.) You should be in the Home View, but for this exercise you need to be in the Administration tab, so ***click Administration***. Within the Administration tab, there are four groups: Admin, Datastore, Processing, and Production.
6. Discover FY™ allows users to enter data files into the program and process those data files so that they can be reviewed and, if appropriate, produced to comply with a discovery request. We will now process new data files. When you installed Discover FY™, you also downloaded additional data files for this purpose. You will now use the Processing group option on the Administration tab to bring your documents into Discover FY™.
7. Before you enter the new data, you can specify specific file types that should be excluded from processing. To do this, ***click File Types***. The "Exclude File Types" dialog box will open. Scroll through the list of file types to get an idea of the various file types you might encounter in a real case. If there were any files that you wanted to exclude from processing, you would select the checkbox to exclude the undesired document type to be excluded from processing. These selections apply to all Datastores processed thereafter. The selections can be changed as needed for special processing operations. ***Click Cancel.***
8. ***Click Process ESI.*** The Process Electronic Data box will open. See Discover FY Exhibit 10. The Process ESI option processes incoming data and also runs the Acquire Text, Load OCR, and Update Indexes processing modules (which can also be run separately). Several options are available in the "Process Electronic Data" dialog box. These include:

   - Remove Duplicates: This removes documents that are exact matches to other documents based upon the MD5 hash value calculated for the documents. (*MD5 hash value* refers to a code that is attached to every electronic file. It is essentially a digital fingerprint, as every electronic document/file has a unique MD5 hash value. The purpose of the MD5 hash value is to facilitate the discovery and removal of multiple copies of the same document.) If both Remove Duplicates and the Hash Per Custodian option (discussed below) are checked, duplicate removal will be within each respective custodian only. If Remove Duplicates is checked, but not Hash Per Custodian, duplicate removal will be global across the entire Datastore. Email hierarchies are never broken by the de-duplication process. If an email is not removed as a duplicate, all its attachments stay, even if one or more are exact duplicates of another document elsewhere in the Datastore.
   - Filter File Types: If checked, the file types previously selected in the Exclude File Types dialog box will be filtered out as desired. If not checked, all documents will be processed, regardless of file type.
   - Hash Per Custodian: Controls whether de-duplication occurs only within the selected Custodian or globally (see Remove Duplicates item in this list).
   - Max OCR Time (Minutes)—Sets the maximum amount of time expended by the OCR (optical character recognition) engine on any one document. (OCR is an abbreviation for *optical character recognition*. It refers to the ability of a computer program to translate handwritten or typewritten text into digital text. For example, if a handwritten letter is OCRed, the text of the handwritten letter is captured by the computer. The handwritten letter can then be searched

and archived just like a document that was originally created by a computer.) The default time allowed for OCR per document is five minutes, but it can be changed as required. Once the time allowed per document has been expended, the OCR function will stop and proceed to the next document.

- OCR All PDFs: Performs OCR on all PDFs without checking for already available extractable text. In most cases, PDFs contain extractable text. However, if you receive nonsearchable PDFs (typically, scanned images are nonsearchable), you can select OCR All PDFs to ensure that text is available for all PDFs, including those that do not contain extractable text.
- Temp Folder: The location where temporary workspace files used by Discover FY™ during processing will be stored.
- Initial Process Only: Will stop after the initial separation-of-documents step has been performed. You can select this option when you need to see quickly what the document set consists of. Initial Process Only will bring the documents into Discover FY™ and display them in the grid, but text extraction and OCR are not performed. The Acquire Text option can be run later to add the text for these documents into Discover FY™.

9. In the Input Directory / File textbox, **type C:\DFY\AdditionalTestData \chris_germany_001.pst**. In the Source textbox, type **Zip drive**. In the Custodian textbox, select **"Chris Germany."** Leave the other default settings as they are. ***Click Process***. (See Discover FY™ Exhibit 10.)

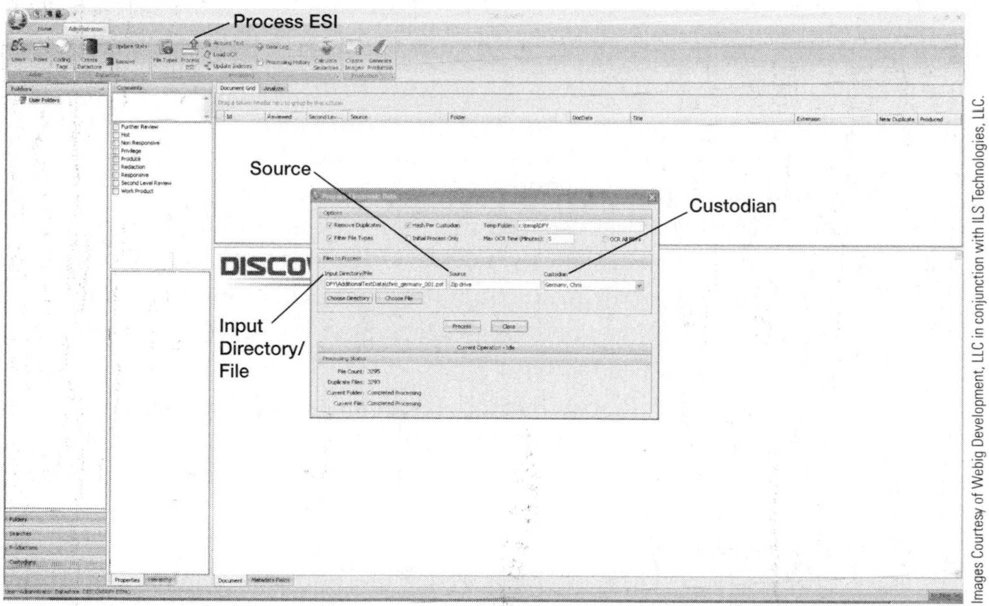

DISCOVER FY™ EXHIBIT 10

10. You can track the progress of data processing in the Processing Status pane, which displays the current status of the processing operation in its overhead status bar. Processing is not complete until **"Current Operation – Idle"** is displayed. Please note that it may take a few minutes to complete processing the data. During information processing, the smallest discrete documents are extracted from the files (e.g., emails with attachments are extracted to individual documents, zip files are extracted to individual files). The relationships of documents are tracked in an email or zip hierarchy and this information is added to the Datastore. Also, a process history log file is

generated that lists any exceptions (files that cannot be processed or other abnormal occurrences). This log file is automatically displayed in the Process History window when processing is complete. See Discover FY™ Exhibit 11. ***Click Close on the Process History window.***

DISCOVER FY™ EXHIBIT 11

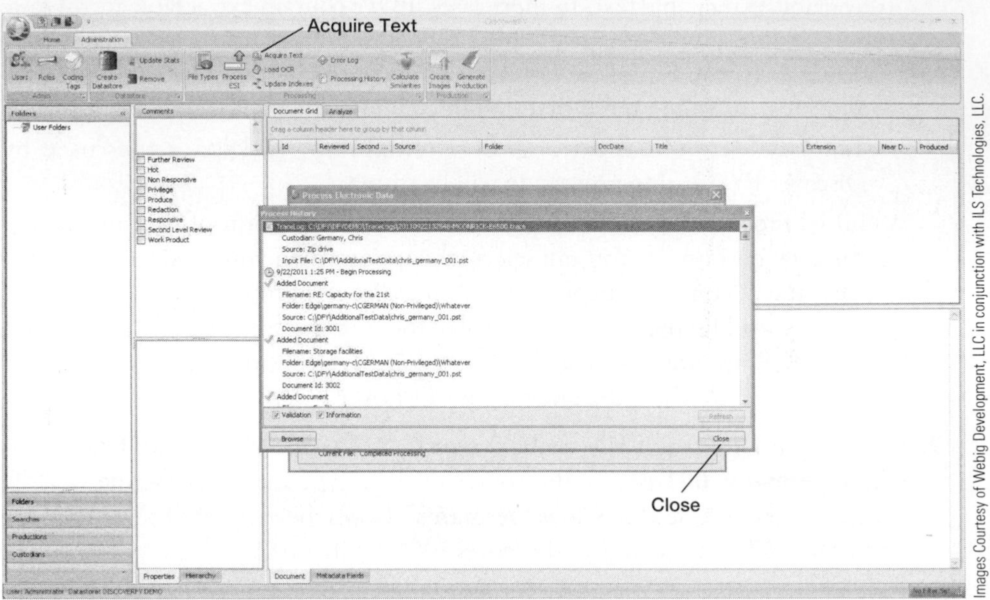

11. You can see that the additional data have been entered into Discover FY™ by looking at the Document Grid pane. ***Using the scroll bar on the right side of the Document Display pane, scroll down to Document ID 2733.*** Note that the Source for this document is **C:\DatafilesForDemo \PreLoaded\chris_germany_000.pst.** Prior to processing the additional files, this had been the last document in the Document Grid. Now look at the document below Document ID 2733. This is Document ID 3001 and under Source, it says **C:\AdditionalTestData\chris_germany_000 .pst.** This and the documents through Document ID 4633 are the new documents you processed in Step 10.

12. On the Administration Ribbon Bar, is the Acquire Text option. (See Discover FY™ Exhibit 11.) Text is typically acquired by default in the Process EFI dialog box when it is used to process data (as long as the Initial Process Only option is deselected). Because you did not select that option, the text of the processed files was acquired when you processed the data in Step 10. When it is acquired, it is rendered as an HTML document so that it can be viewed in the Document Display pane of the Discover FY™ window.

13. Many times there are documents that are nearly identical within the same Datastore. For example, the same attachment may be sent to several individuals. It would be easier if these nearly identical documents could be tagged at the same time (because they are practically identical, it is likely that they would have the same tags applied to them). To find these near duplicates, first ***click the Home View tab and then click Duplicates Window.*** The "Document Matches" dialog box will open, but will be empty. For it to display results, you need to select a document that has **"Yes"** in the Near Duplicate column of the Document Grid. ***Click the second document in the Document Grid (Document ID 2).*** In the Similar Documents pane of the Document Matches dialog box, you can now see the other documents that are near duplicates of the selected document. The degree of similarity is expressed as a percentage. See Discover FY™ Exhibit 12. ***Click Close in the Document Matches window.***

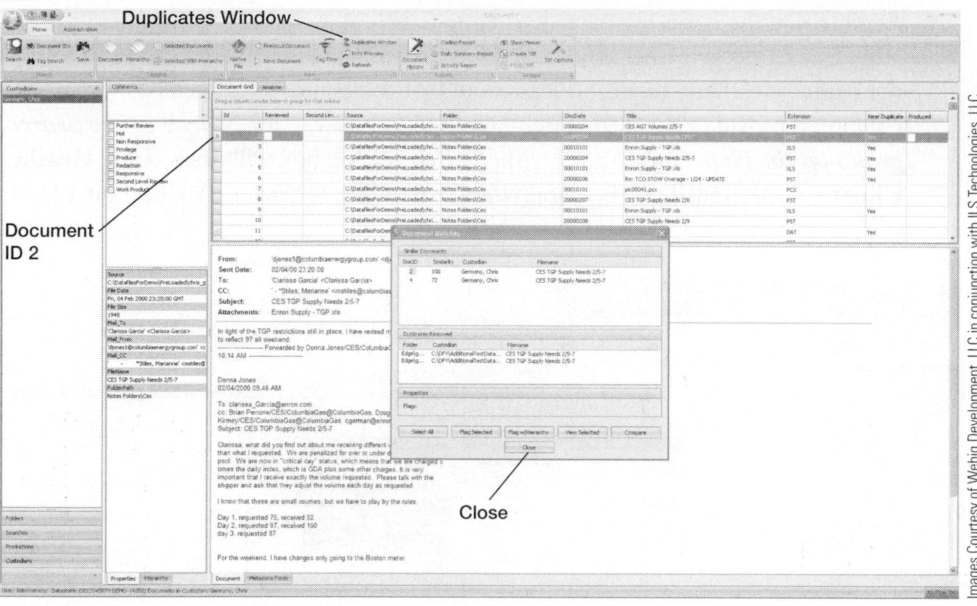

DISCOVER FY™ EXHIBIT 12

This concludes Lesson 2. To close Discover FY™, ***click the Close button (the X in the upper right corner of the window),*** or you may continue to Lesson 3.

ADVANCED LESSON

LESSON 3: GENERATING PRODUCTIONS

This lesson gives you the opportunity to create a folder, apply tags, and generate a production as you would in response to a discovery request. You will also investigate the Bates numbering feature of Discover FY™.

1. Start Windows. Then, ***double-click the Discover FY™ shortcut on the desktop, or click the Start button on the Windows desktop, point to Programs or All Programs, point to Discover FY™ folder, and then click Discover FY™.*** Discover FY™ will then start.
2. When you start Discover FY™, the "Login" box will open and you will be asked to enter your user ID and password. Type **admin** in the User ID text box and type **password** in the Password text box. (Note: The password will appear as a series of dots. See Discover FY™ Exhibit 1.) ***Click Login.*** See Discover FY™ Exhibit 1.
3. The "Choose Datastore" box will appear. We have not yet created any Datastores, so ***click DISCOVER FY™ DEMO to highlight it and click Select.*** See Discover FY™ Exhibit 2.
4. All of the sections of the Discover FY™ window are empty since we have not yet selected any date. To access the sample data provided with the application, we need to select a Custodian. ***Click Custodians and then click the only name provided, Chris Germany.*** When you do so, the sample data will load. See Discover FY™ Exhibit 3.

5. The ultimate purpose of any e-discovery software is to assist legal professionals in organizing ESI for use in litigation and to facilitate the production of relevant documents in response to a request for the production of documents. You will now search for a set of documents, place those documents in a folder, and produce the contents of that folder.
6. Assume that the opposing party has requested all documents relating to an employee named Heather Choate. First, you will search for all documents with the name "Heather Choate." (Please note that the Hands-On Exercises for Chapter 8 provide a detailed search exercise.) For now, ***click Search in the Search group on the Home tab.*** The "Define Search" dialog box will open. Type **Heather Choate** in the "Full Text" box and ***click Search***. See Discover FY™ Exhibit 13.

DISCOVER FY™ EXHIBIT 13

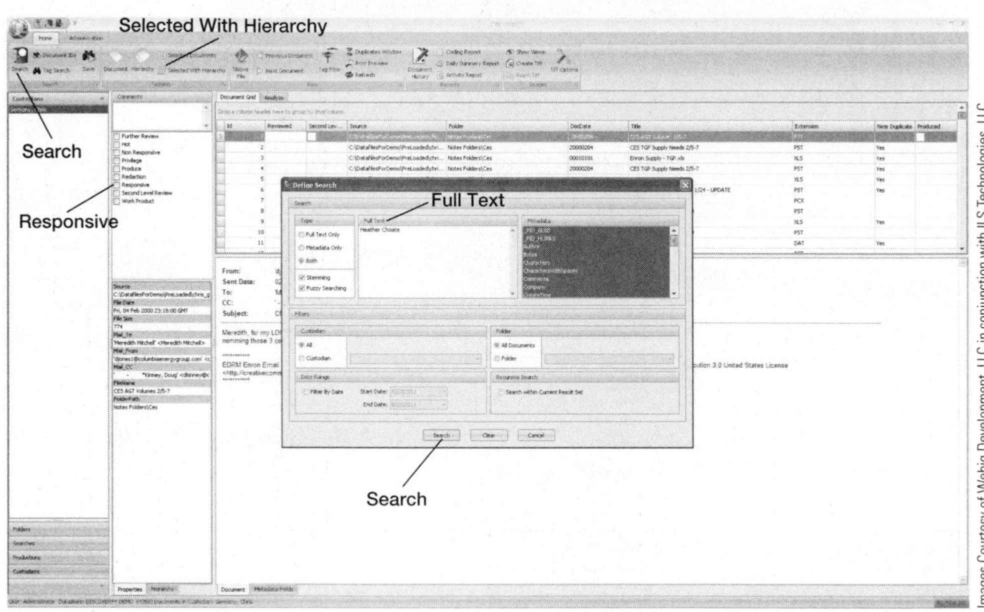

7. The documents containing the name Heather Choate will appear in the Document Grid. Notice that the search term is highlighted in the documents displayed in the Document pane beneath the Document Grid. Assume that these documents are responsive to the discovery request and that they are not privileged, so they should be included in the production of requested documents. You will now tag these documents as "Responsive" and place them in a folder so they may be found easily when they are needed.
8. To tag the selected documents, ***move the cursor into the Document Grid and click Control and the letter A at the same time*** **([CTRL]-[A]).** This will select all of the documents in the Document Grid. Then, in the Tag pane to the left of the Document Grid, ***click Responsive***. Next, in the Tagging group, ***click Selected With Hierarchy***. See Discover FY Exhibit 13. (Again, please note that a more detailed explanation of how to search for and tag documents is available in Chapter 8.) All of the documents should now have a checkmark in the Reviewed column.
9. Before the selected and tagged documents can be moved to a folder, you need to create that folder. ***Click the Folders in the Viewpoint Selection buttons found in the bottom left corner of the window.*** See Discover FY Exhibit 14. In the Folders pane, you will see a file tree heading with no folder entries. To add one, ***right-click User Folders.*** A shortcut menu will open; ***click Add Folder***. A new dialog box will open. In the Discover FY™ dialog box, type

Heather Choate, then ***click OK***. See Discover FY Exhibit 14. The new folder will now appear under User Folders.

10. To move the selected and tagged documents to the newly created folder, ***move the cursor over the Document Grid and click* [CTRL]-[A] *to select all of the documents; then move the cursor to the Heather Choate folder and release the mouse button.*** These files are now in the folder.
11. ***Right-click the newly created Heather Choate folder*** and ***click Create Production*** in the shortcut menu. The "Create Production From Folder" dialog box will open. In the Production Name text box, type **Heather Choate *and click the OK button***. Now, ***click the Productions button to change the View Selection from Folders to Productions***. You should see one item listed, Heather Choate. ***Click Heather Choate*** to highlight that folder. ***Click the Administration tab and then click Generate Production in the Production group***. The "Productions" dialog box will open. See Discover FY™ Exhibit 14.

DISCOVER FY™ EXHIBIT 14

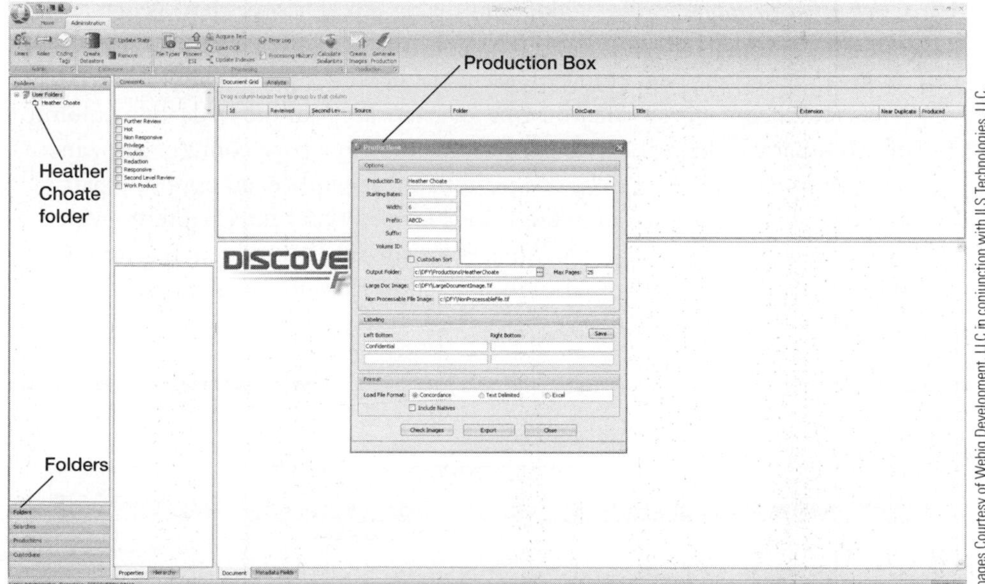

12. In the Production ID text box, click ***the drop-down menu and select* Heather Choate**. In the Starting Bates text box, type **1**. (*Bates numbers* are used to identify specific documents in discovery.) The Width text box asks how many digits the Bates number should be (e.g., 000001). Six is a fairly common width, so in the Width text box, type **6**. Bates numbers often have alphanumerical prefixes and suffixes that allow users to categorize documents and group them according to source, time period the document was created, and so on. In the Prefix text box, type **ABCD-**. Leave the suffix text box empty. (See Discover FY™ Exhibit 14.) In the Volume ID textbox, type **1**.
13. The Output Folder is where the production file will be saved on your computer. In the Output Folder text box, type **c:\DFY\Productions\HeatherChoate**. (See Discover FY™ Exhibit 14.)
14. Large Doc Image is the default placeholder image that will be generated when a document's page count exceeds the Max Pages value. Non Processable File Image is the default TIFF image file that will be placed into the production if the selected document cannot be processed for production. (See Discover FY™ Exhibit 14.) These are single-page documents that will be Bates-numbered in the production. The default settings are fine.

15. Labeling provides options for static (*static* means that the labels do not change from page to page) confidentiality legends on either the bottom left or right side of the image. The Save button allows you to save the entered information for fast and consistent use in subsequent productions. Assume that the documents being produced contain sensitive information and that we want them treated as confidential documents. Type **Confidential** in the upper textbox under Left Bottom and ***click Save.*** See Discover FY™ Exhibit 14. ***Click OK in the box that tells you that your Production Labels have been saved.***
16. The Productions dialog box also features other options. Under Format, you can specify the file format output of the production. The Concordance option is selected by default and is the most common output option. (Concordance is a litigation support software program that is used to organize electronic documents.) This output can be imported into the Concordance application. Native files can be included in the production by checking the Include Natives checkbox. (See Discover FY Exhibit 14.)
17. ***Click Check Images*** in the Productions dialog box. Discover FY™ generates a report that opens in your Web browser. It lists all the documents in the production and the page count for each. See Discover FY™ Exhibit 15. Redacted documents are identified by an asterisk "*" in the Redaction column of this report. If the report reflects documents with a page count of zero, an image of the document can be created for your law office, an opposing party, and the like. This is covered in the Hands-On Exercises for Chapter 8, which shows you how to use the Create Images feature in the Production group. ***Click the X*** in the upper right corner of this screen to close the web browser.

DISCOVER FY™ EXHIBIT 15

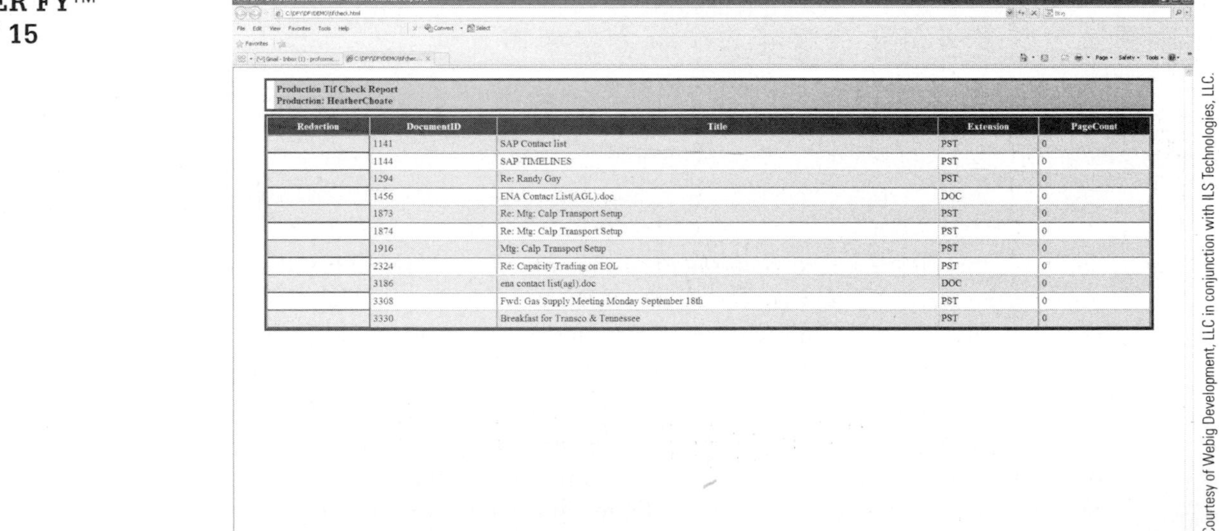

Production Tif Check Report
Production: HeatherChoate

Redaction	DocumentID	Title	Extension	PageCount
	1141	SAP Contact list	PST	0
	1144	SAP TIMELINES	PST	0
	1294	Re: Randy Gay	PST	0
	1456	ENA Contact List(AGL).doc	DOC	0
	1873	Re: Mtg: Calp Transport Setup	PST	0
	1874	Re: Mtg: Calp Transport Setup	PST	0
	1916	Mtg: Calp Transport Setup	PST	0
	2324	Re: Capacity Trading on EOL	PST	0
	3186	ena contact list(agl).doc	DOC	0
	3308	Fwd: Gas Supply Meeting Monday September 18th	PST	0
	3330	Breakfast for Transco & Tennessee	PST	0

This concludes Lesson 3 and the Chapter 7 Hands-On Exercises for Discover FY™. To close Discover FY™, ***click the Close button (the X in the upper right corner of the window).***

CHAPTER 8

Litigation Support Software

CHAPTER OBJECTIVES

After completing this chapter, you should be able to do the following:

1. Explain what litigation support is.
2. Explain why computerized litigation support methods are more successful than manual methods.
3. Explain why a legal organization might use a litigation support service provider.
4. Identify the three major types of litigation support systems.
5. Describe the litigation support process.
6. Identify and use various search methods to retrieve litigation support data.

INTRODUCTION

Litigation support software assists attorneys and paralegals in organizing, storing, retrieving, and summarizing information that is gathered for the litigation of a lawsuit. During the course of a lawsuit, large quantities of information are generated and acquired. Litigation support software helps to manage and control this information so that it is presented in a usable form to the attorney(s) working on the case. This chapter introduces the fundamentals of computerized litigation support and describes how it can be used effectively in the practice of law. This chapter covers tracking of the information and documents used in litigation, manual litigation support methods, types of computerized litigation support systems, the litigation support process, the purchase of litigation support systems, and questions and fears about using computerized litigation support.

litigation support software
Program that assists attorneys and paralegals in organizing, storing, retrieving, and summarizing the information that is gathered during the litigation of a lawsuit.

TRACKING INFORMATION AND DOCUMENTS USED IN LITIGATION

During litigation, the legal team (including attorneys, paralegals, and others) must organize, summarize, control, and understand a great deal of information so that it can be presented to a factfinder (such as a judge, jury, or administrative hearing officer) in a way that defeats the opposition's case and best promotes the client's interests. This is not an easy task, as legal issues, factual issues, and legal theories constantly change both during the course of the litigation and at trial. The more parties there are, the more complex the issues are, the more documents there are, the more attorneys/paralegals there are, and the higher the stakes, the harder it is to succeed at organizing and controlling the information.

The information and documents that must be tracked in litigation vary according to the type of case. However, the following are some of the documents most commonly tracked:

- *Litigation documents*—Documents prepared during the course of the lawsuit; they include pleadings, motions, briefs, correspondence and email between the attorneys and the court, discovery documents, deposition transcripts (including summaries), expert witness reports, and other documents filed in the case.
- *Factual documents*—Documents that arise out of the subject matter of the litigation; they might include contracts, correspondence, emails, business/financial records, photographs, diagrams, and other information concerning the parties or relevant to the lawsuit. Factual documents also include anything that might be presented as evidence in the case to prove or disprove the claim.
- *Knowledge management documents*—Documents and information that are used to help strategize, analyze, and administratively prepare the case. The focus of knowledge management is on information rather than documents. Knowledge management materials might include chronologies and timelines of the case, analyses of the issues, legal precedent, case law, management/tracking of the case docket, lists of witnesses and exhibits, internal reports or analyses of the facts of the case, and other information. In litigation, these documents, which are prepared by or for the legal professionals, are known as work product.

The following subsections explore each of these areas in more detail.

Litigation Documents

Litigation documents are prepared during the course of the lawsuit. They are extremely important, both because they are filed with a court, typically under deadlines, and because they contain the basic theories and strategies for winning the case. It is important that the legal team involved have control over these documents. Types of litigation documents include pleadings, motions, briefs, discovery documents, and miscellaneous documents.

Pleadings Formal documents filed with a court, usually stating a party's contentions regarding specific issues, are called pleadings**.** The complaint, answer, counterclaim, crossclaim, and third-party claim are types of pleadings.

Motions and Briefs During the litigation, motions and briefs are filed to argue the position a party is taking on how the case should proceed in court. These can be voluminous, especially if the issues are complex. Motions and briefs are critical to a case because they set forth the legal and factual theories of each party to the case. Some of the more important motions typically filed include motions to dismiss and motions for summary judgment; both of these motions seek to dismiss the lawsuit before it ever reaches the factfinder or the trial stage.

Discovery Documents Discovery documents include interrogatories, requests for admissions, requests for production of documents, depositions, and expert witness reports, among others.

Interrogatories Interrogatories direct a series of questions or written requests for information to an opposing party in a lawsuit. Interrogatories must be answered under oath and returned to the issuing party.

Requests for Admissions A request for admissions is a series of statements of fact directed to an opposing party in a lawsuit. The receiving party must either admit or deny each of the statements in the request for admissions.

Requests for Production of Documents A request for production of documents is a series of requests or instructions directing an opposing party in a lawsuit to produce documents and electronically stored information (ESI) that are in its possession or control so that the requesting party can examine those items. In some cases, especially those that are complex or span a number of years, anywhere from a thousand to a million documents or more may be produced. The documents that are actually produced in response to such a request are discussed in the section on factual documents.

Depositions A deposition is oral testimony that is taken before a court reporter who transcribes the testimony word for word. Depositions can be taken of parties or nonparty witnesses.

Expert Witness Reports An expert witness report is produced by an expert witness, and states the factual basis for the expert's opinion on a matter.

Miscellaneous Documents Miscellaneous documents in litigation include notes, internal memorandums, and external correspondence (both on paper and email).

Notes Written records of conversations and events are made from the first time a client steps in the door until the conclusion of a lawsuit.

Internal Memorandums Internal memorandums and emails are documents that are more formal than handwritten notes and are usually circulated only within a legal organization. They may be notes to a client's file, requests to other members of the firm to do things, or an exchange of information between individuals on a legal team.

External Correspondence Letters, email, and written communications that are exchanged between attorneys and their clients, between opposing attorneys, between attorneys and potential witnesses, and between attorneys and the court all fall into the category of external correspondence.

Factual Documents and Electronically Stored Information

Factual documents pertain to the subject matter of the litigation. Depending on the case, these can range from a couple of sheets of paper to a million or more documents. For example, suppose a jet airliner crash is being litigated. Factual documents that might be produced in the case include years of maintenance records, Federal Aviation Administration (FAA) registration and other documents, passenger lists, technical design schematics (possibly on many areas of the plane), computer models, and memorandums and email from aeronautical engineers regarding the actual manufacturing of the aircraft, among many others. Again, the kinds of documents that will be important in the case depend on the specific facts and the complexity of the case. Any information that might be presented to the factfinder as evidence to prove or disprove a claim falls into the category of factual documents.

Although many factual documents are discoverable, some are not. Some such documents might be classified as attorney work product, and as such are privileged and not discoverable.

Knowledge Management

In addition to tracking litigation documents and factual documents in a case, legal professionals must also track and organize internal organizational knowledge about a case. Knowledge management usually deals with a class of information prepared internally by legal professionals, and may cover a wide variety of miscellaneous information that can be helpful when litigating a case. Here are some examples of internal organizational knowledge:

- Chronologies or timelines of the facts of a case, which are often critical in presenting theories as to what, when, how, and why things happened in a case (for example, the timelines produced using TimeMap).
- Analyses and strategies regarding factual issues, legal issues, evidentiary issues, and other matters to be addressed at trial or at other stages of the litigation.
- Analysis of current case law and how it will affect the present case at various stages of the litigation.
- Scheduling and docket control reports, which can be important in litigation because they constitute a factual summary of the litigation process, including how and when things were accomplished in the case. This can be particularly important in large cases that are litigated over many years. In many cases, attorneys and clients strategize the timing of the litigation; this may include use of stalling/delaying techniques or attempts to "push" a case through to trial.
- Case diaries and notes made during litigation.
- Other internal reports, such as queries and searches that reveal cause and effect in evidence; reports about witnesses (such as a report listing every time a witness's name was brought up in the lawsuit); and anything else that provides information or knowledge regarding a case that is not a litigation or factual document but may nonetheless be important to the case.

WHY LITIGATION SUPPORT?

A typical case often involves hundreds of documents and extensive electronically stored information (ESI). When complex litigation is undertaken, the mountains of documents and ESI that are generated can be astounding: Some complex cases may involve a million factual documents and ESI files and several years' worth of litigation documents. Can you imagine trying to hold all of that information in your head?

The purpose of litigation support, whether through manual or computerized methods, is to organize the litigation documents, factual documents, and knowledge management in a case so that all of the information is useful to the attorney. For example, suppose that an attorney is questioning a witness in court and realizes that the witness is changing the testimony from that given in an earlier deposition. If the attorney can show this, this could impeach the witness (create doubt as to the witness's credibility). However, if the attorney is unable to find the exact place in the volumes of deposition transcripts where the witness's prior—and different—answer was given to the same question, the opportunity to impeach the witness is lost. This is how litigation support wins or loses cases.

The goal of litigation support is to make sure the second outcome of this scenario does not happen. At trial, and throughout litigation, attorneys are engaged in cross-examining hostile witnesses, preparing their own witnesses, and making objections and other legal arguments. To effectively handle a case, attorneys must be backed up by a support system that can help them quickly find the information they need.

MANUAL LITIGATION SUPPORT METHODS

One type of manual litigation support system is a simple index, produced on a word processor, that lists key issues, facts, and/or other items to remember. A printout of this index is usually kept in a notebook for use at trial. The major limitation of this manual system is that it is impossible to cover all the topics that might be brought up during the course of a trial. Also, the index must be continually updated as new issues arise.

Another type of manual litigation support system used for case organization is an index-card system, usually based on key issues. For every essential document in the case, one or more index cards are prepared. If a document is related to two different key issues, then two index cards must be prepared, summarizing the document's contents relevant to those issues. Each card is then filed behind the appropriate issue divider.

Although the index-card system is more sophisticated than the simple index listing, it also has several disadvantages:

1. This type of manual system is time-consuming and tedious to set up, as the cards must usually be prepared by hand or typed. In addition, the process is slow, because a single document might pertain to many issues, all of which must be indexed.
2. Because this type of system is tedious, it encourages entry of the fewest possible documents, instead of thoroughness and entry of all relevant (or possibly relevant) documents.
3. This type of system is useful only for simple searches.
4. Other types of indexes, such as document author and chronological indexes, usually cannot be created from an index-card system—at least not without a substantial investment of time.
5. The system is vulnerable to human error, such as misfiling of cards.
6. If cards are not put back properly, are lost, or if the system should be knocked off a desk and the cards scattered, it could be a major disaster.

Manual litigation support systems, whether they use an index-card system or other manual methods, do not suit the modern legal environment well, because they are inherently inflexible and unable to meet changing needs and circumstances. A lawsuit is a dynamic environment, where key issues can change in an instant. What was important one minute may become unimportant the next. Especially at trial, the litigation support system must be flexible and adaptable to reflect progression of the case.

OVERVIEW OF COMPUTERIZED LITIGATION SUPPORT

Computerized litigation support solves many of the problems associated with manual methods, and has many benefits in addition. Many different kinds of computerized litigation support software are available, and litigation support can be provided either in-house, by existing staff, or outsourced to a litigation support service provider.

Manual vs. Computerized Litigation Support

A comparison of the time- and cost-saving features of computerized methods over manual methods shows why computerized litigation support is popular. The productivity and cost-saving features of computerized litigation support are substantial. Computerized litigation support can also be viewed as a service to clients: simply put, legal organizations with computerized litigation support can provide better-quality representation and take less time to do it.

General Benefits of Computerized Litigation Support

General benefits of computerized litigation support include data storage, retrieval, and search capabilities; flexible organization and use of information; and the ability to analyze and share information.

Electronic Storage and Immediate Retrieval Using electronic technologies, computers can store a vast amount of data in a fraction of the space required for hard-copy documents. External hard drives and other storage media can hold millions of document images and pages of text. In addition, document images can be retrieved almost immediately and repeatedly, without the hard copy (original) of the document being lost or affected in any way.

Searches/Queries Using database technology, thousands of electronic documents can be searched in seconds, allowing immediate retrieval of the document you are looking for.

Organization/Control Electronic documents can be numbered, incorporate links to other electronic documents, be annotated with electronic notes or comments attached to them, and be organized or sorted in many different ways without affecting the documents themselves.

Analytical Reports Analytical reports can be assembled from queries and searches on documents. Information can be gathered or revealed that would never come to light using manual methods.

Flexibility Computerized litigation support is inherently flexible, in that it can be changed and adapted according to the requirements of different cases. Information can be presented in a number of different "looks" and formats, and can also be exported to many different computer programs, including word-processing, spreadsheet, presentation graphics, or trial presentation software.

Sharing of Information A huge benefit of computerized litigation support is that information can be shared with others over a local area network or the Internet, giving a variety of users access to the information 24 hours a day, 7 days a week.

Mobility Litigation support databases that include electronic images and transcripts can be downloaded to a flash drive and thus made completely transportable, unlike heavy, bulky boxes of hard-copy records.

Preservation of Information and Theories Because litigation support creates a record of factual documents, litigation documents, and case knowledge, the information can be preserved and quickly passed along to others if the attorneys or paralegals working on a case change.

Types of Computerized Litigation Support

Many computerized litigation support programs and options are currently available. The legal market for computerized litigation support programs is continually growing, offering new and exciting ways to organize, control, and present information. All of these products have their own strengths and weaknesses. A brief summary follows (in-depth coverage is included later in this chapter).

Document Abstracts Using a litigation support program or database management program, abstracts of documents can be entered into the computer. An "abstract" is basically a short summary of a single document. The fields in the database usually include document number, document type, author, date, subject, summary, and others. The abstracts can then be used to organize, track, sort, and summarize the documents in the case. In addition, the abstracts can be searched and queried.

Full-Text Retrieval In a full-text retrieval system, the entire text of a document is available for user searches and queries. Unlike a document abstract, which contains only summary information, a full-text system includes all of the text of the document; hence, searches and queries have more data to pull from. Two types of documents that full-text systems can search on include real-time transcription files and electronic discovery (ESI).

Real-Time Transcription With real-time transcription, an attorney or paralegal connects a computer to a court reporter's transcription machine and, using specialized transcription software, gets an electronic, rough-draft version of the transcript within seconds of the testimony being spoken. The transcription, which is full text, can be searched or queried using a full-text retrieval system.

Electronic Discovery Litigation support programs now support the ability to store electronic documents such as emails, word-processing files, spreadsheets, and other ESI that is produced during discovery. With a full-text retrieval system, the entire electronic discovery database may be searched and queried.

Imaging Documents can be imaged so that an electronic "photograph" of the document is maintained in the computer. The image cannot be searched (like full text), and there is no summary (as found in an abstract system), but the document can be viewed in its entirety electronically. Among other benefits, this preserves the original document and obviates the need to make numerous paper copies.

Case Management Software Case management software can be used in a litigation support capacity to electronically track and manage the scheduling and docket control of a case. In addition, you can use this software to create case diaries and notes, track legal research for the case, generate documents, and much more.

Analytical Software Analytical litigation support software can be used to create case outlines, chronologies, timelines, analyses of the issues and witnesses in a case (including reports that link documents and facts to issues or witnesses), and much more.

Trial Presentation Software Once litigation support information is in an electronic format, it can be exported to trial presentation software and presented to factfinders in a visually compelling manner. (This topic is covered in Chapter 10.)

External or Internal Litigation Support

Legal organizations have two main options when deciding how to go about providing litigation support for a case. They can either use an external litigation support service provider, or they can handle the project in-house. Alternatively, they can use a combination of both. All of these options have strengths and weaknesses.

litigation support service provider
A company that, for a fee, sets up a litigation support system and enters all documents necessary for a case.

Litigation Support Service Providers A **litigation support service provider** is a company that, for a fee, sets up a litigation support system and enters all the documents necessary to handle a case. The advantage of using a litigation support service provider is that the work is essentially done by someone else. The service provider consults with the law firm or attorney on how the system is to be set up. Once the structure of the system has been decided, the law firm delivers the documents and/or ESI to be entered to the service provider. The service provider then enters the documents into its computer or downloads/converts the ESI so that it can be used by the provider's system. When an attorney wants to search for or retrieve information, he connects to the service provider's computer, via the Internet, to access the data. Alternatively, the service provider can save the information to a DVD or flash drive. Even if the content is constantly being changed, or multiple people need access to the information, users can easily access the data using the Internet, because the data are centrally located on the service provider's computer. Some vendors offer electronic discovery services as well as litigation support services.

The main advantage of a service provider is that the labor-intensive task of data entry is performed by the service provider, not the law firm's staff. In addition, the law office does not have to hire, train, pay, manage, and then lay off extra employees. Also, because they specialize in this area, litigation support service providers can bring a great deal of experience, technological power, and knowledge to bear on the project.

The main disadvantage of using a litigation support service provider is cost: these services can be very expensive. Most service providers charge a consulting fee, a fee for entering information into the computer, a fee for each time an attorney or a firm connects to the computer, a fee for each search of information in the computer, and a storage fee. Nevertheless, using a service provider becomes economical when a case involves tens of thousands of documents.

in-house computerized litigation support system
A litigation support system set up by the firm's or attorney's own staff on their own computer(s).

In-House Computerized Litigation Support Systems An **in-house computerized litigation support system** uses a firm's or an attorney's own staff and computer to perform litigation support. Many litigation support programs are available for in-house use.

The advantage of in-house litigation support systems is that they are significantly less expensive than hiring a service provider. They also give a legal organization or attorney more control over a project. This is important, because the attorney is ultimately responsible for the litigation process and the success or failure of a lawsuit. In-house systems also enable a legal organization or attorney to use litigation support even for small cases for which it would not be cost-effective to hire a service provider.

The disadvantage of an in-house computerized litigation support system is that a significant amount of front-end work is associated with setting up and entering information into the system. The setting-up and document-entry tasks take staff away from other duties and can eat up a lot of time. However, this problem can be somewhat alleviated by hiring temporary employees to enter, or *code*, documents into the system. The problem with temporary employees is that they often have no experience in litigation support. The choice of whether to use a service provider or an in-house system will depend on the circumstances of a case.

Combination of Providers An alternative to using either in-house or third-party litigation support is to use a combination of the two. For example, a service provider might be hired to consult with a law firm regarding ESI and to assist with converting the ESI to a format compatible with the firm's own litigation support program. Given the complexity of ESI and all of the technical issues involved, this alternative sometimes serves a firm well and saves staff from having to do all the work themselves.

Litigation Support in Legal Organizations

The use of litigation support has grown in recent years as software has become easier to use and the variety of litigation support programs has risen. In many firms, paralegals use this software more than anyone else. Two of the most popular litigation support programs are Concordance and CaseMap.

TYPES OF COMPUTERIZED LITIGATION SUPPORT SYSTEMS

As indicated earlier, there are five major types or functions of litigation support software: document abstracting, full-text retrieval, imaging, case management, and analytical. Many litigation support programs can perform one or more of these functions. The lines between these different programs/functions are somewhat blurred. Exhibit 8–1 shows an overview of the programs. The following subsections describe each of the different types of litigation support programs.

Document Abstract Litigation Support Systems

A **document abstract litigation support system**, also called an indexing system, allows users to enter document abstracts or document summaries into a computer and subsequently to search and retrieve information contained in the abstract or summary. Exhibit 8–2 is an example of a document abstract. Notice in Exhibit 8–2 that abstracts of several documents are shown. The fields shown include document ID (Docid), document type, date, summary, author, and privilege. A short description of each document appears in each of these fields (according to how the user entered the information). For example, in Exhibit 8–2, document ID number EDC000001 is a spreadsheet dated 3/22/1999.

document abstract litigation support system
Software that allows users to enter document abstracts or summaries into a computer and then search and retrieve the information contained in those abstracts or summaries.

This is exactly how a document abstract database/litigation support program is designed. The system is, in essence, a database, and many legal organizations use generic database programs to create their document abstract litigation support systems. However, many prepackaged litigation support systems include an abstracting module. One main difference between a generic database program and a litigation support program with an abstract function is that the program designed specifically for litigation support will already have appropriate fields designed and set up for abstracting. For example, Exhibit 8–3 shows some standard fields for document abstracts. Users can customize the fields or the form, but it is convenient to have a predesigned form to start with.

There are two ways to construct a document abstract database: objective/bibliographical coding or subjective coding. **Objective/bibliographical coding** records only basic information about a document, including document number, document name, date, author, recipient, and so forth. Whoever is coding the document need not know anything about the case because he or she is only entering information that comes from the face of the document. The coder makes no subjective judgments about or characterizations of the document. Objective coding is fairly fast and straightforward. It might be used in very large cases in which there are hundreds of thousands of documents. Objective coding is often outsourced to a litigation support service provider, because the coders do not have to know anything about the case to input the data.

objective/bibliographical coding
System in which only basic information about documents (document number, document name, date, author, recipient, and so forth) is recorded in a document abstract database. The coder makes no subjective characterizations about the document.

Type of Program/Function	Description	Strengths	Weaknesses/Limitations
Document Abstract	A database where abstracts or summaries of documents are entered. Each document is a record and each record contains fields such as doc. number, name, date, type, author, subject, etc. The database can be set up to be either objective/biographical (with objective data only) or subjective (including notes on why the document is significant to the case)	• Provides a short summary of each document that can usually be read quickly • Excellent for drafting exhibit lists • Can produce a chronology of documents • Can produce reports based on any of the field names, documents sorted by author, subject, type, etc. • Can be linked to file with full text, images, or photos • Document reports can be sorted as needed • Documents can be searched on • Can be used to identify relationships between documents, people, etc.	• The full text of a document cannot be searched • The document must be coded and the abstract entered into the database
Full-Text Retrieval	The full text of documents is available for searches. Hard-copy documents are scanned and run through optical character recognition software or electronic files are used (such as electronic deposition transcripts or electronic discovery)	• The entire text of a document can be searched for individual words and phrases • Can be used for searching for words in depositions, trial transcripts, documents obtained from electronic discovery, and word-processing documents • Can be used to impeach witnesses when testimony does not match • Annotations and notes can be attached to an electronic document without it affecting the underlying document itself • Electronic documents can have electronic Bates numbers added	• Uniform words are not always used (Jim, James, Jimmy, Mr. Smith) • Cannot produce indexes and reports like an abstract system
Imaging	Produces a "photograph" of the document	• Produces an exact electronic duplicate of the hard copy that can be instantly viewed • Can be included in electronic presentation graphic programs • Thousands of documents can be stored on flash drives and easily transported almost anywhere	• Cannot be searched on • Cannot produce indexes and reports like an abstract system
Case Management	Organizes docket control, scheduling, case diaries, document assembly/generation, legal research, and some document tracking capabilities and makes data available over a network to the whole legal team	• Captures information such as case diaries/notes, docket control, legal research, timekeeping, phone log, etc. that is not typically maintained by other litigation support programs/functions	• Is not a substitute for abstract, full-text retrieval, or imaging
Analytical Software	Creates chronologies, timelines, and tools for analyzing, issues, facts, witnesses, and other aspects of a case	• Creates documents for analyzing important aspects of a case	• Is typically not a substitute for abstract, full-text retrieval, or imaging

EXHIBIT 8–1

Different types/functions of litigation support programs

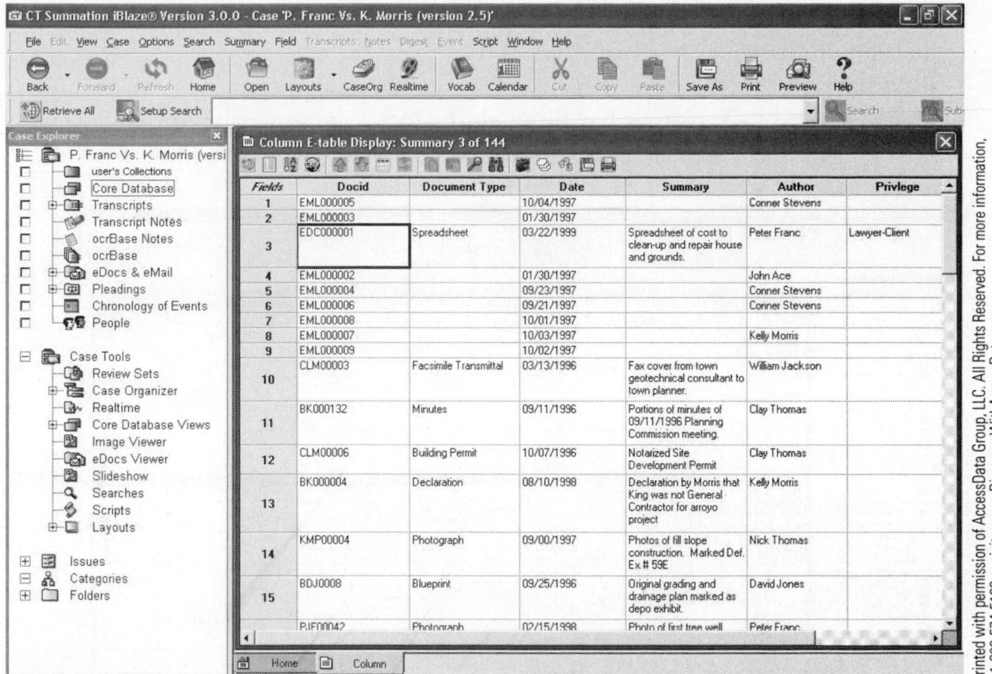

EXHIBIT 8–2
Document abstract litigation support

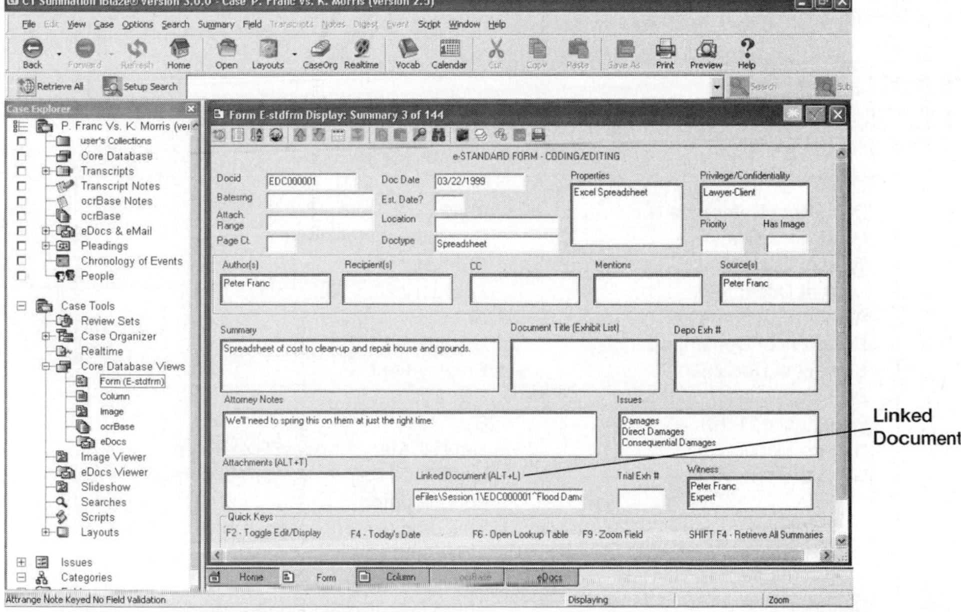

EXHIBIT 8–3
Blank document abstract form

subjective coding
Entering information in a document abstract program about what the document means, including what case issues the document is relevant to or notes about the document.

Subjective coding allows the coder to enter into the document abstract program information about what the document means, including to which case issues the document is relevant or notes about the document itself. Subjective coding takes longer than objective coding because much more thought must go into the abstracting. Exhibit 8–3 is an example of a subjective document abstract; note that "Summary," "Attorney Notes," "Issues," and other such fields are included in the design. To subjectively code documents, the coder needs to have a good understanding of the facts and legal issues involved in the case. There are pros and cons involved with both objective and subjective coding, so the particular circumstances of the case should determine which is used.

At the bottom of Exhibit 8–3, notice the field that says "Linked Document." The litigation support program in Exhibit 8–3 is able to link another file, such as an image file, an electronic discovery file, or the full text of a file, to the document abstract. Exhibit 8–4 shows an example of a linked file.

Exhibit 8–5 shows a completed record in a document abstract system. Compare Exhibits 8–5 and 8–3. Notice that although the forms are somewhat different, many of the field names are similar. The following explains the fields in Exhibit 8–5.

EXHIBIT 8–4
Linking an email or full-text document to a document abstract

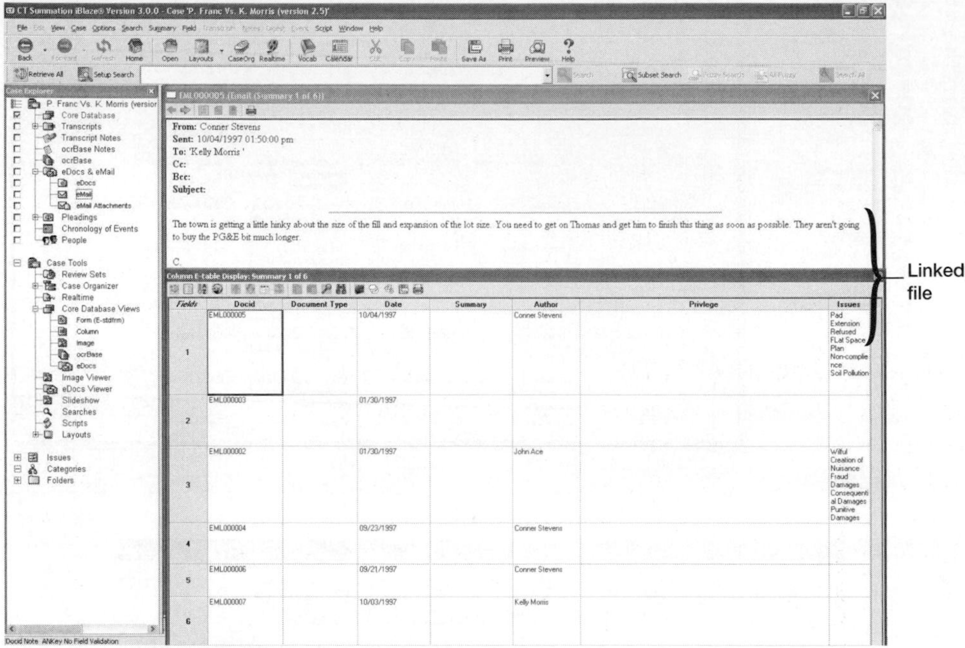

EXHIBIT 8–5
Completed record in a document abstract system

Document Reference No.:	2342
Document Title:	Employment Contract
Type of Document:	Contract
Date of Document:	February 22, 2002
Author of Document:	Jim Hill
Recipient of Document:	Mary Rhodes
Subject of Document:	Employment
Physical Location of Doc.:	Box 211
Importance (1-10):	8
Names Mentioned:	Jim Hill; Mary Rhodes; RXY Corp.
Issues:	Liquidated damages; material breach; noncompete
Description 1:	This employment contract sets out the terms and conditions of Mary Rhodes's employment.
Description 2:	There is a provision in the contract requiring each party to act in good faith to the other.
Keywords:	Employment, contract, damages, noncompete
Notes:	
Source of Document:	Plaintiff
Production History:	Plaintiff's Deposition Exhib. 1
Plaintiff's Exhibit No.:	62
Defendant's Exhibit No.:	27
Beginning Bates No.:	734
Ending Bates No.:	744
Attorney Comments:	Was signed without attorney's advice
Authenticated:	Y/N
Stipulated:	Y/N
Offered during what witness:	Jim Hill
Admitted:	Y/N
Privileged/Confidential:	NO

Document Reference Number Before document abstracts or summaries are entered into a computer, each physical document must be given a reference number or bar code. Unless each document is given a reference number and stored in order, there is an excellent chance that documents will get lost. Throughout the course of litigation, documents are moved, handled, and used so frequently that a reference number is the only way to keep a document from being misfiled (unless the legal organization uses electronic document imaging). In addition, the only link between the information contained in the litigation support system and the hard copy of a document is this number.

Document Title If the document being entered has a title, that name can be entered in the Document Title field. Coding rules (discussed later) provide guidelines so that documents are given uniform, informative titles. Also, your coding rules should include directions for how to assign titles to untitled documents like memos and letters, so that you can quickly and accurately retrieve such documents when necessary.

Type of Document The Type of Document field indicates whether a document is a letter, contract, memorandum, pleading, or other type. Again, coding rules are set so that similar documents are given the same name (sometimes referred to as vocabulary control). For instance, you would not want one letter entered into this field as a "letter" and another similar type of letter entered as "correspondence." It is important that there be strict uniformity. Many litigation support programs use drop-down menus with set options for fields like this, as limiting the available choices ensures uniformity.

Date of Document The date of a document is entered in the Date of Document field. Undated documents are also captured in this field. The date of a document is a critical feature in a litigation support system. Throughout the litigation of a case, the law office will frequently use the software's functions to provide chronologies of events and compare documents by date.

Author of Document and Recipient of Document These fields record the personal and organizational author and the recipient(s) of each document.

Subject of Document This field records what the subject or topic of a document is.

Physical Location of Document Physical location refers to the place where the actual original document is stored, whether it is in a numbered box, a file drawer, a flash drive, or some other place.

Importance This field records the relative importance of each document entered. This is usually accomplished using a numbering system or scale, such as a range between 1 and 10, with relatively unimportant documents being assigned a 1 and critical documents getting a 10. This allows users to sort documents based on their relative importance. This function is useful at trial, as it is possible to forget or overlook important documents that have not been admitted into evidence. Because the rating input into this field is subjective, it is usually decided by an attorney or a paralegal.

Names Mentioned In this field, a user enters the names of people and organizations mentioned in a document. This allows users to search for people's names and obtain a list of all documents that concern them. It is useful at trial or in preparing for the deposition of a particular witness or party. It is sometimes useful to separate these names into two fields: a Persons Mentioned field and an Organizations Mentioned field.

Issues The Issues field allows a user to note when a document concerns a key issue in a case. The user can then search the database for all documents that pertain to a specific issue. This is helpful throughout the litigation of a case, as it allows an attorney to get a handle on specific issues and determine which (and how many) documents pertain to those issues.

Description, Keywords, and Notes These fields are where a user enters notes or a summary of the documents.

Source of Document The source field allows a user to track where a document came from: whether it was produced in discovery by the opposing side, whether it was given to the attorney by her own client, and so forth. It is always important to keep the history of a document straight. This can be as simple as indicating whether the document came from plaintiff or defendant or as specific as giving a person's name as the document creator/provider.

Production History This field allows a user to track how a document has been used in litigation. For instance, if a document was used as an exhibit in a particular deposition, this fact could be tracked in the production history field.

Plaintiff's and Defendant's Exhibit Number Each party to the lawsuit prepares its own list of potential documentary exhibits and gives each document an exhibit number. The resulting lists are exchanged during discovery, allowing each party to know how the other party numbered a particular document for tracking purposes.

Bates stamp
Marks a page with a sequential number and then automatically advances to the next number.

Beginning and Ending Bates Number Every page of every document is usually given a reference number, using either a Bates stamp or a computer-generated label or number. A **Bates stamp** is a machine that marks a page with a sequential number and then automatically advances to the next number. When all the pages have been numbered, they are maintained in numerical-order files. This makes documents easier to locate. The Bates numbers (beginning and ending for each document) are then entered into the computer. Depending on the case and how the document must be tracked, a document may have either a document reference number, Bates numbers, or both. The terms "Bates stamp" and "Bates number" are often used in a legal environment even if documents were numbered by a computer and no actual Bates stamp was used.

Attorney Comments Comments are simply personal notes about the document that an attorney wants to remember. They can function merely as reminders, or they can become important work product if a different attorney takes over litigation of the case or an aspect of the case.

Authenticated A check in this field means that the document has been "authenticated" for evidence purposes. Some documents are self-authenticating, which means that by statute they are admissible into evidence without further proof (such as of origin or creator).

Stipulated Notes in this field relate to whether the parties have stipulated or agreed to the admissibility of the document.

Offered during What Witness At trial, documents are offered into evidence during witness testimony. This field records which witness was on the stand testifying when the document was offered.

Admitted This field tracks whether the judge admitted the document into evidence.

Privileged/Confidential This important field relates to whether the document is privileged or confidential and thus should not be produced in discovery. Proper notations here can save a great deal of time and trouble, as all users can immediately see whether a given document is privileged rather than relying on memory or reasoning.

Use of Document Abstract Systems Document abstracts can be helpful when attorneys are litigating cases. For example, suppose an attorney is representing Mary Rhodes in a case for breach of employment contract against her former employer. The attorney's task is to cross-examine Jim Hill, Rhodes's former supervisor, at trial. To prepare for the cross-examination, the attorney would like to see every time Hill's name was mentioned in any of the documents that the plaintiff has been able to obtain in discovery. This is a simple task using a computerized document abstract litigation support system. You simply instruct the system to search for every document abstract that mentions Hill's name. You then instruct the system to print a list of all the documents where the search term was found (see Exhibit 8–6). With this list, you can then use the document reference number to pull the original of a document for the attorney's inspection.

Document abstracts can also be used to give the attorney a chronological list of all (or a subset) of the documents by sorting on the dates of the documents. This type of list is important when the attorney is trying to put together time frames and sequences of events in cases. Document abstract systems are sometimes called document indexing systems, because the printouts they produce are nothing more than indexes (see Exhibit 8–6).

A legal professional can use document abstracts as a quick reference to refresh his or her memory about the documents involved in a case (see Exhibit 8–2). Notice in Exhibit 8–2 that a document abstract system can be used to prepare a list of exhibits for trial. Document abstract systems can also be used to search for and sort reports based on any of the field names in the database. Thus, a report could be run for all documents that were authored by "Jim Hill," or every document that concerned the issue of "liquidated damages," or every document that was produced by the plaintiff. Document abstract databases can produce an infinite number of reports, searches, and queries, depending on the user's particular needs at the time.

Disadvantages of Document Abstracts There are several disadvantages of using document abstracts. The first is that if subjective abstracting is to be used, the persons preparing the document abstracts must be trained in *exactly* what the issues of the case are. That is, nonlawyers have to make decisions about evidence and relevance, so the lawyer is in essence delegating legal judgments to nonlawyers. There is a fairly high potential for errors: for instance, irrelevant information that has no real bearing on the case may be entered in the abstracts, whereas relevant and important

SEARCH REQUEST: "Jim Hill"

Document Ref. No.	Type of Document	Recipient of Document	Date of Document
2342	Contract	Mary Rhodes	2/22/08
2346	Letter	Mary Rhodes	2/27/08
2359	Letter	John Hays	3/30/08
2365	Memo	John Hays	4/10/08
2377	Memo	John Hays	5/06/08
2390	Letter	Mary Rhodes	6/01/08
2400	Letter	Bill Green	6/30/08

EXHIBIT 8–6
Document abstract search report on the name "Jim Hill"

information might be left out. As long as experienced, highly skilled paralegals do the abstracting, there is little reason to worry, but if data entry clerks or untrained temporary staff are used, this could present a real problem.

Also, abstractors must be careful to use a controlled vocabulary so that information is entered uniformly into the abstracts. If information is not entered uniformly, searches of the document abstracts will be inconclusive. For example, if one abstractor referred to an important incident as a "collision," another abstractor referred to the same thing as an "accident," and another referred to the incident as a "wreck," anyone searching the document abstract database would encounter a significant problem, because he or she would have to do three different word searches to get all the information about the same incident.

Another disadvantage of using document abstracts is that the issues in a lawsuit change constantly. This is particularly true in complicated cases (for which full litigation support can be invaluable). When issues are added or modified, documents must be reviewed again and the abstracts updated.

Finally, the facts that the document abstract database itself does not contain the full text of documents, and that the documents have to be coded and entered into the system, may also be viewed as disadvantages.

Full-Text Retrieval Litigation Support Systems

full-text retrieval litigation support system
Software that enables a user to search (and retrieve information from) the full text of documents stored in the system.

A **full-text retrieval litigation support system** enables users to search and retrieve information contained in the full text of any documents stored in the system. Unlike document abstract systems, they are not set up like a database. They do not have fields or a file structure. In full-text retrieval systems, a whole document, not just an abstract or a summary, is entered and stored.

The full text of a document can be entered into a computer in several ways: by scanning, keyboard entry, and/or word processing; computer-aided transcription; real-time transcription; service providers; or electronic discovery.

Scanners Optical character recognition (OCR) scanners translate hard-copy documents into a computer-readable format almost instantly. Once a document is scanned into a computer, the document file is saved to a disk for later retrieval by the full-text retrieval litigation support system. OCR is not 100 percent accurate. Most OCR systems have accuracy rates of around 99 percent, so documents must be thoroughly reviewed for accuracy. (This need for checking and proofreading is a primary disadvantage of OCR systems, as these tasks take a great deal of time.)

Keyboards and Word Processing A word processor can be used to type the content of a document into a computer. Once the complete document is input into the computer, the file is then saved to a disk for later retrieval by the full-text retrieval litigation support system. Accuracy and the need for proofreading are concerns with this method as well. Also, the format and "look" of the original document are lost, as are handwritten and nontext markings.

Computer-Aided and Real-Time Transcription According to most court rules, a court reporter must record deposition testimony, court hearings, trials, and other types of formal proceedings. **Computer-aided transcription (CAT)** is a process that automatically converts a court reporter's notes into a computer-readable format. Before CAT, a court reporter, using a shorthand reporting machine to abbreviate common words and phrases by certain keystrokes, recorded the testimony as it was given. The court reporter then deciphered the notes and prepared a full transcript of the testimony, using either a typewriter or a word processor.

computer-aided transcription (CAT)
A process that automatically deciphers a court reporter's notes and converts them into a computer-readable format.

Most CAT systems automatically prepare a transcript in computer-readable format. The court reporter then makes any necessary corrections and saves the file. Because the file is saved in a machine-readable format, the court reporter can, in addition to selling attorneys hard copies of transcripts, provide transcripts in electronic format. Most full-text retrieval systems can use the electronic file of a transcript automatically. Thus, using CAT, it is easy and fairly inexpensive to get the full text of depositions and other formal documents into a full-text retrieval system.

In addition, many court reporters now have **real-time transcription** available. With this system, a cable attaches the court reporter's equipment to the attorney's computer (which has the appropriate software preloaded). As the court reporter types, the testimony appears on the attorney's computer screen within seconds. Most court reporters go back and edit the transcript documents, but it is possible for an attorney to get a rough draft of the transcript almost immediately, which can be extremely valuable at trial or deposition.

real-time transcription
System through which an attorney or paralegal connects a computer with the appropriate software to the court reporter's transcription machine, so that within seconds of the testimony being spoken, a rough-draft version of the transcript appears on the computer screen.

Service Providers Some service providers allow users to rent their trained personnel to scan data and design a full-text retrieval system.

Electronic Discovery Electronic discovery is a process during which discovery "documents" (emails, word-processing documents, spreadsheets, databases, etc.; see Chapter 7) are produced electronically. Many times attorneys want documents produced electronically because it is more difficult to destroy electronic documents. Backup tapes can be requested before documents are destroyed or possibly altered, and additional information can sometimes be learned from the metadata in electronic documents that hard-copy documents do not supply. Electronic documents can contain other documents, such as attachments, that may or may not show up on hard copies or automatically print out. Having documents produced electronically allows users to do full-text retrieval on the items produced without having to take the separate step of putting the documents through an OCR system.

Use of Full-Text Retrieval Systems Full-text retrieval systems allow users to conduct searches on the full text of a document. In the breach of employment contract example used earlier, the attorney representing Mary Rhodes has a listing of all the documents that have Jim Hill's name in them. However, the attorney would also like to see a listing of every time Hill's name is mentioned in the 15 depositions that were taken in this case. This will save the attorney from having to reread all 15 depositions and will take the attorney right to the parts relating to Hill. This cannot be done using a document abstract system, but it is quite easy using a full-text retrieval system. The user simply tells the system to search the 15 deposition files for the name *Jim Hill* or to search each file separately for the name *Jim Hill* (depending on the litigation support system). Most systems respond either by producing a list of the found occurrences (see Exhibit 8–7) that includes the deposition name and page number of each occurrence; or by displaying each

SEARCH REQUEST: "Jim Hill"

Found Occurrences: 19

Deposition Name	Deposition Page
Depo of Mary Rhodes	Page 24, 34, 56, 67, 89, 94
Depo of Bill Green	Page 11, 23, 44
Depo of John Hays	Page 10, 15, 16, 19, 20
Depo of Alice Hall	Page 15, 16, 17, 45, 46

EXHIBIT 8–7
Full-text retrieval search on the name "Jim Hill"

found occurrence on the computer screen. Some full-text systems have the capability to search across many different files at the same time.

Notice in Exhibit 8–8, just to the left of the word "Search" (just underneath the toolbar), that the user has entered the search term "drainage." Also notice, to the left of the screen under "Case Explorer," that check marks have been placed next to all of the transcripts for the case. The check marks mean that when the search on "drainage" is done, all of the transcripts will be included in the search at one time. Also notice in Exhibit 8–8 that the full text of the Conner Stevens deposition is displayed and the search term "drainage" has been highlighted.

A powerful feature found in many full-text retrieval systems allows users to add annotations (electronic sticky notes) to the file without affecting the transcript itself. Notice in Exhibit 8–8 that a line near the "drainage" hit has been highlighted and that a note has been created reminding the user to ask Stevens about other properties with drainage problems.

In addition to being able to conduct searches on the full text of a document, some full-text systems can produce a summary or digested version of a transcript or document. Full-text systems are also convenient if a document or transcript is lost, because the full text can be retrieved and printed. In addition, full-text retrieval avoids the potential of important issues or aspects of a case being missed. Finally, most full-text retrieval systems can even be used to search a firm's own word-processing documents, such as correspondence, memorandums, and other documents prepared in-house.

Disadvantages of Full-Text Retrieval Several disadvantages are associated with full-text retrieval systems. One disadvantage is that they tend to take up a large amount of hard disk space. This may strain the physical limits of storage space on a computer system, although the availability of optical storage devices and large internal and external storage devices now make this less of a problem.

Another disadvantage is the substantial amount of time and money that can be expended in entering the full text of documents. In some instances, only the most important documents are entered in full-text format, whereas in others all of the depositions, pleadings, and transcripts are in full text. This often depends on how much

EXHIBIT 8–8
Full transcript search and electronic annotation of full-text documents

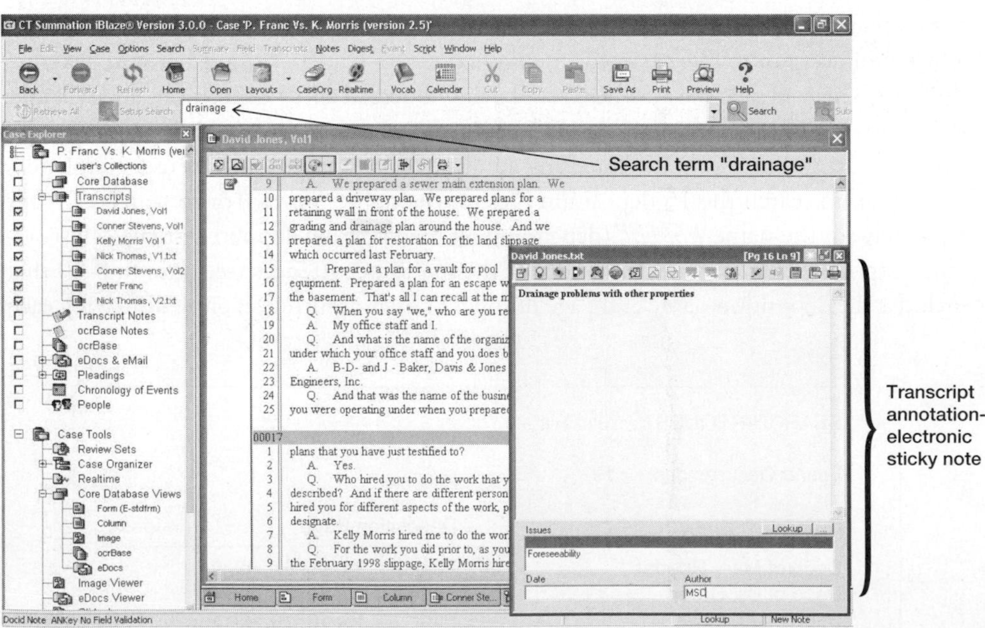

of the information can be obtained in a computer-recognized format or how much of the data can be scanned into the computer.

Yet another disadvantage is that because the vocabulary entered into the system is not controlled, it may be impossible to find all occurrences of a subject. In some cases, subjects are referred to as concepts, and it is difficult to search on concepts. For example, the person Jim Hill in the preceding example may be referred to in documents as "Mr. Jim Hill," "Mr. Hill," "Jim," "the boss," "supervisor," and so on.

A final disadvantage is that a user cannot manipulate data and report formats as with an abstract system, because a full-text system has no fields to work with. It is quite difficult even to create chronologies using such a system.

Document Imaging Litigation Support Systems

document imaging
A system in which documents are scanned into a computer and the documents' actual images (similar to photographs) are retained in the computer.

Document imaging is a litigation support method in which documents are scanned into a computer and the documents' actual images (similar to photographs) are retained in the computer, either on a hard disk, flash drive, or another device (see Exhibit 8–9). Document images offer several advantages over paper. With document imaging, paper is handled only once, when it enters the legal organization and is scanned into the computer. Thereafter, reviewing, copying, and filing can be done electronically. Unlike paper documents, imaging allows multiple people on a network to access and view the same document at the same time without moving from their computers and without requiring staff to pull the actual document. Document imaging also reduces the need for physical storage space; many file cabinets' worth of documents can be stored on one DVD. Anyone who has worked with paper documents in a legal office can testify that there is always a risk of losing files or documents, especially during pretrial preparation and at trial, because documents are constantly being used and moved by many different people. Document images solve this problem, because the document is always available for review.

A disadvantage of document imaging is that the images take up a lot of electronic storage space. Also, each document must be scanned into the computer, which requires obtaining a certain amount of computer hardware or hiring a firm to scan the

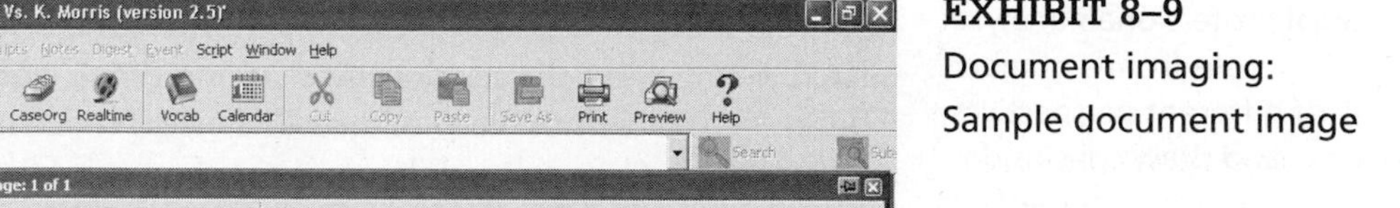

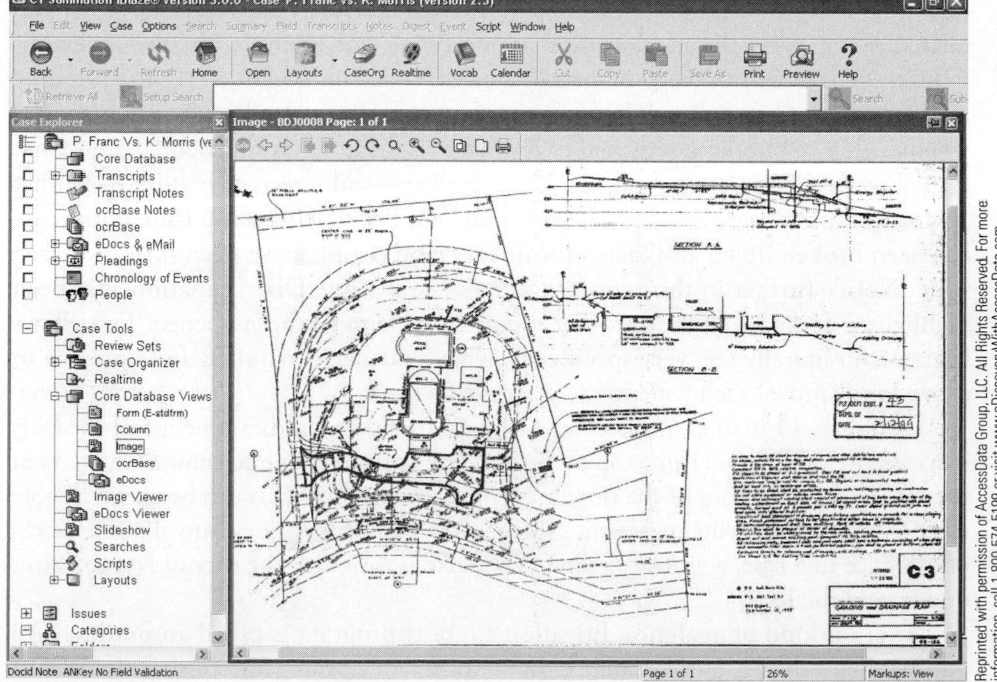

EXHIBIT 8–9
Document imaging: Sample document image

documents. There is also a risk of inaccuracy with scanned images; if the initial scan is not properly done, the image may be blurred or unreadable in part.

Document images themselves typically cannot be sorted or searched, unlike the information in a document abstract or full-text retrieval system. However, scanned images can be turned into searchable text using OCR software. Also, some systems allow scanned images to be linked to an electronic abstract of the document. Scanners, including those with OCR, are readily available and inexpensive. This is becoming a popular option in litigation support. In addition, software is available that will electronically enter Bates numbers and allow legal team members to manipulate the images.

Another useful aspect of document imaging is that electronic discovery service providers can now take just about any kind of ESI and convert it to TIFF or PDF image files and then electronically convert the information to text as well. In this way, the service provider can provide both an exact image of a document and the full text of it. Document imaging, whether it is hard copy or electronic, can be a very powerful and important tool in providing support to litigators.

Case Management

Many current case management systems now include features that are helpful to litigators, such as comprehensive docket control (including a historical representation of what has transpired in the case in the way of deadlines, appointments, hearings, etc.). In addition, case management software may allow for creation of comprehensive case diaries/notes about the case, lists of documents that have been generated in the case, records of legal research prepared for the case, timekeeping records, document tracking, and other such features. Case management systems are discussed in depth in Chapter 5.

Analytical Software

analytical litigation support programs
A type of software that helps legal professionals analyze a case from a number of different perspectives and draw conclusions about cause-and-effect relationships between facts and evidence in a case.

Analytical litigation support programs help legal professionals analyze a case from a number of different perspectives and draw conclusions about cause-and-effect relationships between facts and evidence in a case. Analytical litigation support programs help legal professionals conceptualize and think about facts, documents, people, and related matters and the relationships among them. For example, the first screen in Exhibit 8–10 is a chronology of facts in a case. Notice in Exhibit 8–10 that not only are the dates and facts listed, but a source for each fact is also listed, with a note of whether it is key to the case, whether the "fact" is disputed or undisputed, and what factual or legal issue it is linked to. Notice in the second screen of Exhibit 8–10 that an analysis of the legal issues has been conducted. Each factual/legal issue in the case has been broken down and facts, documents, and people have been linked to each issue. Notice further in this screen that the issue of "Age Discrimination" has been highlighted and a list of the facts that support the claim has been opened. This allows litigators to literally see, very specifically, what evidence is required and available to prove (or disprove) each issue.

Exhibit 8–11 is an example of an analytical tool that builds a timeline of the facts in a case. In Exhibit 8–11, the top of the timeline represents one account of the facts of the case and the bottom of the timeline represents another. This can be an invaluable tool in court when trying to present evidence to a jury. If there are many discrete pieces of evidence in a case, a visual timeline may make it easier for the trier of fact to better understand the facts.

Another kind of analytical litigation support program is called an outliner. An outliner helps the legal professional create outlines for opening and closing arguments,

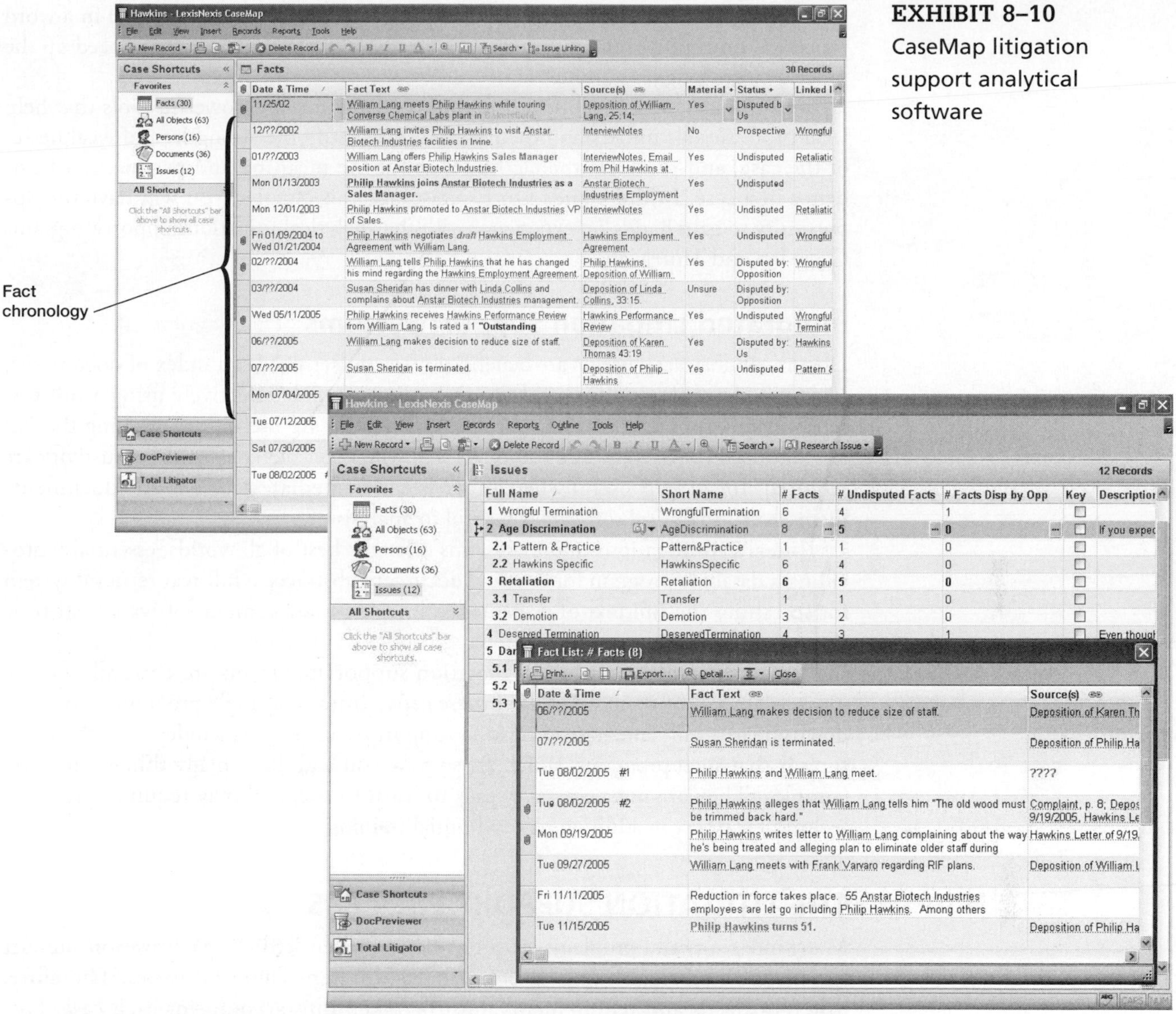

EXHIBIT 8–10
CaseMap litigation support analytical software

Fact chronology

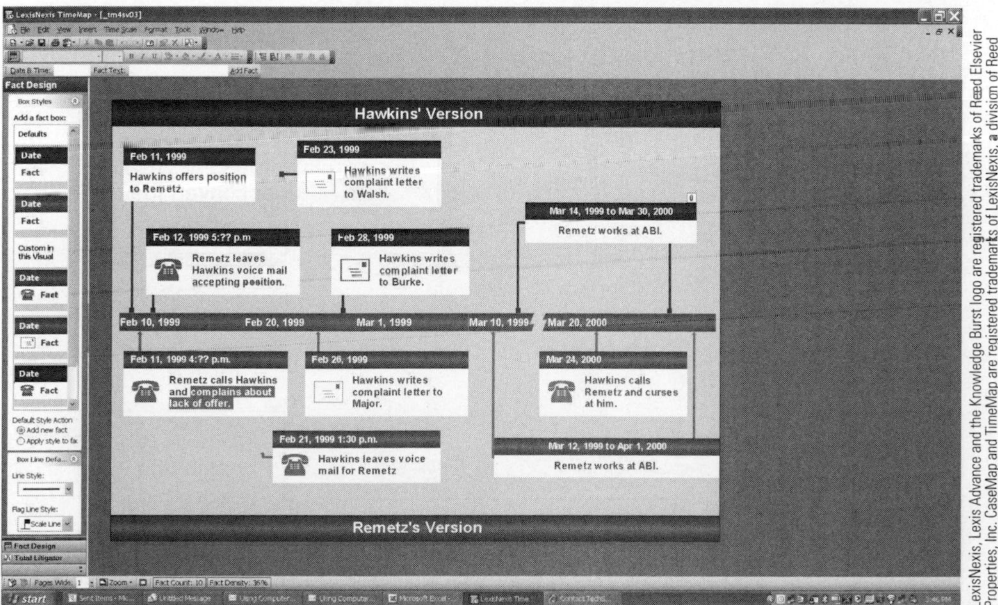

EXHIBIT 8–11
TimeMap litigation support analytical software

questioning witnesses, and other uses. Although an outline can be created in a word processor, outlining programs offer special features that can assist in and speed up the process of drafting an outline.

In summary, analytical litigation support programs are powerful tools that help legal professionals understand their own case, identify the strengths and weaknesses of the case, and persuade the factfinder about the meaning and pertinence of evidence in a case. In the Hands-On Exercises for this chapter, you will have the opportunity to gain hands-on experience with the analytical litigation support programs CaseMap and TimeMap.

Integrated Litigation Support Systems

Document abstract systems are beneficial when a user needs an index of documents, such as a chronological listing. Indexes cannot be made effectively using a full-text retrieval system. However, full-text retrieval systems are useful for searching the full text of depositions, transcripts, and so forth when completeness and exhaustivity are required. Imaging is useful when a user needs immediate access to the documents themselves. Analytical software is helpful in analysis of a case.

Integrated litigation support systems offer the best of all worlds, essentially providing a database program for entering document abstracts, a full-text retrieval system for searching the full text of documents, imaging management software, real-time transcription, and even analytical tools.

As mentioned earlier, many litigation support programs are currently on the market. Several of them offer all of these capabilities in a single program. The main downside to a fully integrated litigation support package that includes all of these features is that such programs, which are so powerful and do so many things, are fairly complex. They are not necessarily easy to learn to use, and may require significant technical support in addition to good initial training.

THE LITIGATION SUPPORT PROCESS

Many questions and problems must be resolved when setting up a litigation support system for a particular case. Every case has different facts and issues. Therefore, different needs and requirements must be taken into account for each case. Five steps should be taken when setting up a litigation support system for a particular case (see Exhibit 8–12).

EXHIBIT 8–12
Litigation support software

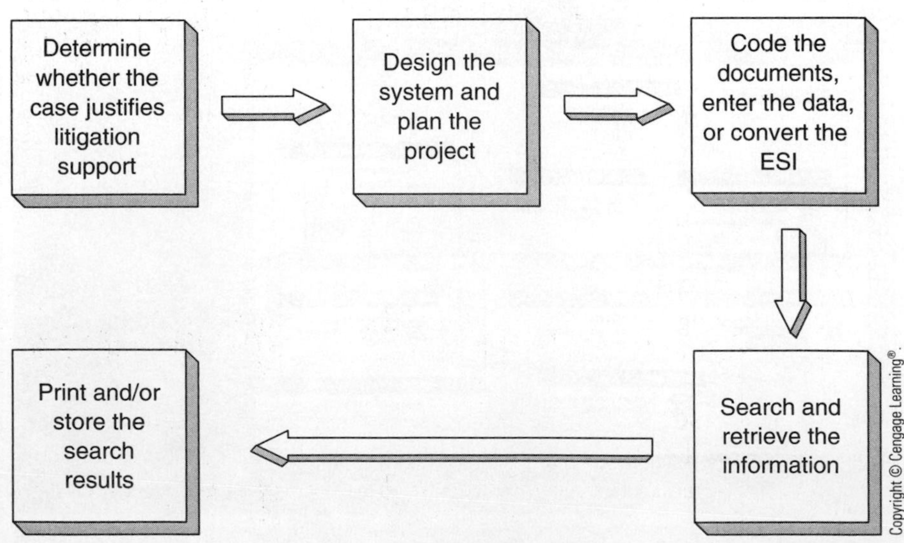

1. Determine Whether the Case Justifies Litigation Support

The first step in the litigation support process is to determine whether the case is worth the time and expense required to design and set up the system and enter the data. Before litigation support was available on personal computers, the thinking was that only large or complex cases justified the expense of litigation support. Now, however, even attorneys with routine cases are using litigation support to organize documents and evidence.

Several issues and factors must be considered when determining whether a case should be entered into a litigation support system.

How Many Parties and Witnesses Are Involved? If only a few parties and witnesses are involved, a case might not justify the expense of litigation support. If, however, numerous parties and witnesses are involved, it might be wise to use a litigation support system for optimum organization of the parties, witnesses, and documents.

How Many Issues Are Involved? If only a few issues are involved, it might not be worth the expense of litigation support. However, if a large number of issues are involved in a case, it might be prudent to use a litigation support program to keep the issues clear and separate.

How Complex or Difficult to Grasp Are the Issues? If the issues in a case are easy to understand, a litigation support system might not be required. Obviously, the converse is also true.

How Long Is the Litigation Expected to Last? Litigation that is expected to last a long time has its own inherent problems. A turnover in the attorneys and paralegals working the case is very possible. If the information they need was never entered into a database for later retrieval, or is lost, they may have to start over—this is an expensive and time-consuming proposition and may raise ethical issues in addition to the practical problems the firm faces.

How Large Are the Damages? If a case involves the possibility of large damages, it is probably worth the time and expense to use a litigation support system.

How Many Documents Have Been Produced and Must Be Tracked? If thousands of documents are to be tracked, computerized litigation support may be the only way to effectively manage the case documents. In the past, some books on litigation support suggested that a case must have 1,000 to 10,000 documents before computerized litigation support pays off. This is probably not true anymore. Whether a case can benefit from litigation support depends on many issues other than just how many documents are involved. Computerized litigation support can be used effectively in small cases as well as large ones.

Does the Client Request Automation? In some instances, a client may ask that computerized litigation support be used. Nowadays, legal organizations may have to have this capability to accommodate client needs and desires.

Is Opposing Counsel Automating? If one party to a lawsuit has litigation support, this puts all other parties at a disadvantage. Therefore, in some cases, if opposing counsel begins using computerized litigation support, your firm may be forced to do so as well.

2. Design the System and Plan the Project

Once the decision has been made to put case information into a litigation support system, the next question is how the system should be set up; that is, what type of system will be used? System design includes planning what level of detail the fields of the database will have (when using abstracts), what information will be tracked, how many fields the database will have (when using abstracts), what documents will or will not be included, what will be done with duplicates, what information will be needed during the litigation, and how the database will be used at trial.

Users must also decide whether a brief summary of a document's characteristics will be sufficient or whether the full text of each document will be needed. If the system design is poorly thought out, the litigation system will surely fail. It is important that users think the system through clearly and take all options into account when approaching system design. The responsible attorney and paralegal should help design the system, as they will most likely have the clearest understanding of the facts and issues in the case.

In some cases, a budget must be drawn up so that the firm can decide what resources can be devoted to a project. The budget will also affect the decision on whether a service provider will be used or whether the system will be developed in-house.

When developing a system design, users should consider two questions.

Which Type of System Will Be Used? In designing a litigation support system for a case, it is first necessary to decide which type of system will be used: document abstract, full-text retrieval, document imaging, or a combination. Each case is different, but many firms use a combination. For example, it might be beneficial to use a full-text system to track depositions and testimony and to use an abstract system and document imaging to track documents. It is important to determine, at the beginning of the project, what you want to get out of the litigation support system, so that the system can be designed to accomplish those goals accurately, effectively, and swiftly.

What Kinds of Information Should Be Entered? The next question concerns what kinds of information should be entered into the system. For example, when using a full-text retrieval system, the designer must determine what documents should be scanned in: do you scan all documents, or just those that are relatively important?

One way to go about answering this question is to identify all the relevant issues of fact and law in the case, the relevant parties, and the documents that will affect the factfinding. All the information concerning these questions should be tracked.

3. Code the Documents and Enter the Data, or Convert the ESI

Once the design is complete, the user should enter test data into the system to see if the design really can accomplish what it is intended to. If the design holds up, the information must then be entered into the litigation support system. *Coding* of documents refers to the process of deciding what information will be entered into the system and what form it will take.

In many instances, clerical staff enter objective data into the litigation support database (in an objective/biographical document abstract design). Because all the information must be entered into the database in the same format (so that searches retrieve all the information relevant to the request), coding rules must be developed. Coding rules limit the vocabulary that can go into a litigation support system; hence the name controlled vocabulary. It is important to understand that what you put into the system is what you get out of it. For instance, if you were entering a piece of correspondence into a document abstract litigation support database, you could enter many different abbreviations and synonyms into the Document Type field, such as *letter, lt, ltr,* and *correspondence.* The coding rules tell data entry operators exactly what vocabulary choices they have to select from (e.g., the rules might say, "The following types of documents should be entered into the Document Type field: letters, pleadings, memos, notes."). A description of exactly what is meant by each title should also be provided. The format for entering a date might be "MM, DD, YY"; the formula for entering a name in a name field might be "LAST, FIRST"; and so on. Some programs permit designers to set up fields that do not accept variants in data entry; if a term or spelling is not on the "approved" list, it cannot be input.

It is important that all information entered into the database be uniform and as objective as possible. The use of coding rules will keep clerical staff from guessing when entering information. Coding rules should be drafted for all fields in the litigation support database. Note that some firms use codes or abbreviations instead of words. For example, a firm could code a statute of limitations issue in the Subject of Document field as the number 1 instead of using the words *statute of limitations.* In addition to enhancing uniformity, this strategy helps reduce the number of data entry errors, because far less typing is involved in entering a single number.

Fields that require subjective determinations (such as the Importance field) must be entered by trained paralegals or attorneys, not clerical staff. Remember the ethical issues and possibilities for unauthorized practice of law inherent in these judgments.

Some litigation support programs allow users to set up exactly what information can and cannot be entered into the system. For example, in the Date field, the user can instruct the system to accept only dates between January 2012 and January 2013. If a clerical staff person tries to enter a date before January 2012, the program will not allow the document to be entered. In this way, data can be verified right on the spot, as it is entered.

It is sometimes hard to determine how long it will take to enter case information into a litigation support system. This will depend on what level of detail is being entered into the system, how many people are entering data, how many documents are being entered, and so on. However, once a staff member has coded documents or entered information into a computer, the next time will be considerably easier for that person. Experienced coders make a big difference in how fast data are entered into the system.

It is also important to take into account the use of ESI in the case. Using service providers or other tools, a user may be able to quickly convert ESI into formats compatible with a litigation support program. These formats will often include images and the full text of documents.

4. Search and Retrieve the Information

Using the proper search and retrieval techniques helps users obtain the information needed. An in-depth discussion of different search/retrieval techniques and strategies is presented later in this chapter.

5. Print and/or Store the Search Results

It is sometimes necessary to produce a hard copy of search results or to save the search results. The design of the litigation support system must allow this, as well as electronic transmission and access.

SEARCHING AND RETRIEVING LITIGATION SUPPORT DATA

Accurate searching and retrieval of documents are very important and take some practice at first. In some instances, you may have to make four or five changes to a search request to get a litigation support system to retrieve the information you want. Litigation support programs, whether they are document abstract or full-text retrieval systems, generally provide the same type of search features. Nevertheless, the syntax for entering the search requests varies from one program to another.

When a search request (sometimes called search criteria) is entered, a litigation support program searches through every word in the documents or abstracts associated with that case, looking for matches. If a match is found, the program will show a list of the occurrences and where they were found. In most programs, a user has the option of pulling up and viewing on the screen the text surrounding a match.

Most programs allow a user to enter several different kinds of searches, including single-word searches, wildcard searches, Boolean logic searches, and proximity searches (see Exhibit 8–13).

Single-Word Searches

single-word search
A computer search that scans a database for matches to a single word.

A **single-word search** searches a database for matches to a single word. For example, in Exhibit 8–13, the user requested that the program find any match to the single word *approve.* The system responded by retrieving a list of only the occurrences where the word *approve* was found. The potential problem with single-word searches is that derivatives or synonyms of words will not be found. For example, the single-word search for *approve* would not find derivatives or forms of the word, such as *approval,* nor will it find synonyms such as *accept, affirm,* and *ratify.*

EXHIBIT 8–13
Search types and examples

Search Type	Search Request	Words Found
Single word	approve	*approve*
Wildcard	approv*	*approve, approved, approval, approving*
Super wildcard	*approv*	*disapprove, disapproved, disapproval, disapproving, approve, approved, approval, approving*
Boolean OR	approval OR consent	*approval, consent*
Boolean AND	approval AND rate	*approval rate*
Boolean NOT	approval NOT rate	*approval but not approval rate*
Proximity—word	approval w/4 w rate	*approval* and *rate* where they are within four words of one another (the four words are retrieved each time)
Proximity—line	approval w/4 l rate	*approval* and *rate* where they are within four lines of one another (the four lines are retrieved each time)
Proximity—paragraph	approval w/4 p rate	*approval* and *rate* where they are within four paragraphs of one another (the four paragraphs are retrieved each time)
Proximity—page	approval w/4 pp rate	*approval* and *rate* where they are within four pages of one another (the four pages are retrieved each time)

Single-word searches are useful when you know exactly what you are looking for, or when the document coders used a controlled vocabulary for entering the information.

Wildcard Searches

Searching a database for derivatives of a word is called a **wildcard search**. Most litigation support programs, as well as most database programs, use an asterisk (*) to enable wildcard searches. For example, if you wanted to retrieve all the derivatives of the word *international,* you user would enter the search request as follows: "international*." The system would respond by showing all matches to the words *international, internationally,* and so forth.

wildcard search
A computer search that scans a database for derivatives of a word.

Some litigation support systems can also perform what one program calls a super wildcard search. A **super wildcard search** searches a database for derivatives of a word that vary both before and after the root word. For example, the search request "*approv*" would find all occurrences of the words *disapprove, disapproved, disapproval, disapproving, approve, approved, approval,* and *approving.*

super wildcard search
A computer search that scans a database for derivatives of a word, using variations both in front of and in back of the root word.

Wildcard searches are beneficial when you are not sure what derivatives of the word or words being searched for might appear in the documents.

Boolean Logic Searches

A **Boolean logic search** allows a search request to include or exclude words or other search criteria so that the search is either refined or broadened. Boolean searches are sometimes called logic searches or *OR, AND, NOT* searches.

Boolean logic search
A computer search that allows a search request to include or exclude words, or use other search criteria, so that the search is either refined or broadened.

OR The Boolean search operator OR is used to include synonyms of words in a search request. For example, if you wanted to search for the word *approval* and also wanted to include all synonyms of the word, so that you would not miss any occurrences of words such as *consent* and *permission,* you would enter the search request as follows: "approval OR consent OR permission." This request would find all occurrences of *any* of these three words throughout the database.

AND The Boolean search operator AND is used to include two or more words in a search request. For example, you might want to find any occurrences of the phrase *approval rate.* Using a Boolean search, the request would be as follows: "approval AND rate." This request would find all occurrences where the words *approval* and *rate* were located.

NOT The Boolean search operator NOT excludes words from a search request. For example, if you wanted to find the word *approval* but did not want to find the term *approval rate,* you would enter the search request as follows: "approval NOT rate." This search would find all the occurrences of the word *approval* in the database, but would not treat occurrences of *approval rate* as "hits."

Proximity Searches

Searching a database for words that are within a given distance from one another is called a **proximity search**. For example, you could employ a proximity search if you wanted to find the name "Cindy" within two words of the name "John." The syntax of a proximity search will depend on the program, but a typical proximity search might look like this: "Cindy w/2 John."

proximity search
A computer search that scans a database for words that are in a given proximity to one another.

Proximity searches can usually be performed based on the number of words, lines, paragraphs, or pages between two or more words. They are usually available only on full-text retrieval systems.

LITIGATION SUPPORT TIPS

There are advantages and disadvantages to using abstracts, full-text retrieval, imaging, case management, and analytical litigation support systems. To obtain the advantages of each, you really need to use all of them.

A mistake beginners sometimes make is to throw every possible document into the database. Generally, "big is bad," whether it is a big document abstract database, full-text database, or image database. The database should be only as big as you absolutely have to have to get the information you need. As much as possible, include only relevant documents. (Basically, this follows the "garbage in–garbage out" rule.) Bigger databases slow down performance.

Bigger databases also will yield more "hits" or documents than smaller ones. For example, if you search 1,500 documents and you get 40 documents back, this is manageable. You can just work your way through the 40 documents until you find what you need. However, if your database has 150,000 documents and you get 4,000 documents back, the database is basically useless. If you have a really big document collection, try to break it up into smaller document collections whenever possible. Finally, follow the rules in Exhibit 8–14.

QUESTIONS AND FEARS ABOUT COMPUTERIZED LITIGATION SUPPORT

People often share several common fears and questions about converting their manual litigation support systems to a computerized version: How long will it take to enter data? Is training hard? Can you convert a case to a computerized system in the middle of the case, or must you make that decision at the very beginning? What are the most popular programs? Can computerized litigation support be used in the courtroom?

How Long Will It Take to Enter Data?

The question of how long it takes to enter data into a litigation support system is hard to answer, because so many variables are involved. Three major variables must be considered:

1. How big is the litigation? (In other words, how many documents will have to be entered? How many witnesses are involved?) Small- to medium-sized cases with a few hundred documents and 20 to 30 witnesses can be entered in a week or two using a document abstract program, depending on some of the other variables listed here. Large cases with thousands of documents may take several months or more to complete. A lot depends on what information is to be contained in the support system and the complexity of the issues.
2. Are you using a full-text retrieval or a document abstract system? If you are using a full-text retrieval system, how will the full text be entered? If documents can be scanned into the computer or are available on disk through electronic discovery, as opposed to being typed into the computer, the process will be much faster.
3. How many people experienced with litigation support will be entering the data? Experienced people can input data much faster than people with little or no experience. In addition, many firms believe that it is smarter to have their experienced people do only the coding of the forms and to hire typists to actually enter the data into the computer. Another thing to consider is that if you begin the process of inputting data and find that you are running short of time or are shorthanded, many good litigation support service bureaus can come in and finish the inputting job for you.

How Long Will It Take to Learn a Litigation Support Program?

Generally speaking, most litigation support programs are not difficult to learn. The real trick is not learning the program itself, but learning how to set up and design the system so that you are able to retrieve the information you need when you need it. You want to be able to get at information quickly and accurately, especially when the

EXHIBIT 8–14
Litigation support tips

1. **Efficient and clean databases work best.** When you design and populate a litigation support database, keep it simple and straightforward, and enter only *relevant* information. Do not clutter your database with irrelevant information that will slow down the speed of the system or may retrieve unnecessary information during searches.
2. **Be an expert on the facts and legal issues in the case.** Before you can truly design a litigation support database that will meet your needs, you must fully understand the facts and legal issues of the case and understand the significance of the documents or information that you will be tracking.
3. **Legal documents are easier to search on than discovery documents.** You can search legal documents (depositions, pleadings, hearings, transcripts) more easily than discovery documents produced by parties.
4. **It is easier to search on documents that you produce rather than on documents the other party produces.** You can search your own documents more easily than documents you have never seen before.
5. **Searching on concepts is more difficult than searching on proper names or dates.** You can search for names and dates more easily than concepts. Concepts can be ambiguous and require you to be creative regarding what words might be used to describe them, whereas dates and names are usually straightforward and standard.
6. **Complex Boolean searches can be difficult to master.** It is sometimes difficult to construct complex Boolean searches that retrieve everything you need. It is sometimes easier to break down complex searches into smaller chunks.
7. **A quality team of legal staff who are educated on the specifics of the case and are using a well-thought-out database are more valuable than armies of untrained temporaries.** Computers cannot take the place of a good legal team. Armies of untrained office staff notwithstanding, often only an attorney or a paralegal is going to recognize the implications of a piece of evidence. Quality is more important than quantity.
8. **One piece of the pie is not enough.** Litigation support users truly need document abstract, full-text, and imaging capability for documents. The best approach is usually to standardize with one software package that can handle it all and search all of the modules at one time. Don't forget case mangement and analytical applications; they also add great value to litigation support.
9. **Don't build an inflexible litigation support database.** Design your database from the beginning for multiple purposes and multiple users. This way, if the players or the issues change, you will be prepared.
10. **Carefully number every page of every document.** Assign every document/page a Bates number, or use alternative technologies such as bar coding. To admit a document into evidence, you typically need a hard copy of the document. Thus, you must be able to lay your hands on the document. The only way this is possible is for your documents to be carefully numbered so that the needle can be found in the haystack under pressure and when it counts. If you will use imaging, you will need electronic Bates numbering as well.
11. **Make standardized rules.** Establish rules to govern the inputting of information and stick to them. Create and distribute a list of standardized rules for inputting data, and train all staff that are entering data on them. Data in the database must be consistent or problems will arise.
12. **Use the fewest amount of people possible to enter data.** The more people that are involved in entering information into the database, the more you have to train, the more you have to audit, and the harder it is to manage.
13. **Do quality audits and test as you go along.** Again, quality is more important than quantity. Don't wait until the end of the project to find out half the data was entered wrong. Do periodic quality audit checks as you go along, and test the data regularly to make sure the database is working properly. "Garbage in—garbage out" applies to databases.
14. **Input trial exhibit numbers for your opponents.** Input the opposing party's trial exhibit numbers into the database so that you will be able to quickly find your copy in the corresponding database folder when the opposing party offers the exhibit into evidence.

EXHIBIT 8–14
(continued)

15. **Don't wait until trial to enter your documents.** Enter all documents in the database as they come into the case, if possible. Preparing for trial is hard enough without trying to do a big project like creating a litigation support database at the last minute.
16. **Update the database every day at trial.** Update the database after each day of trial with all exhibits, so at the end of trial you will have an up-to-date list of what was offered and admitted.
17. **Print hard copies of documents and make backups.** Print a paper copy of anything you could not live without at trial and make *regular* backup copies of your databases. Computer systems sometimes fail and usually do so at the worst possible moment.

pressure is on and time is of the essence, such as at trial. This is something that you will quickly pick up, because you will gain experience with each new case you work on. As you become more experienced, the process will get much smoother.

Do You Have to Computerize a Case from the Beginning?

Cases can be switched over to a litigation support program even after they have started. In fact, it might be a good idea to wait a few weeks to begin designing a system until after the adversary answers some of your more important arguments. This will allow you to see where the crux of the litigation will lie. If you design a litigation support system without knowing even the basics of how an adversary will argue the case, you may not end up with a very good system; you need one that can adapt to changes required to meet the adversary's arguments.

However, it is best not to wait until a case is almost ready to go to trial, because in many instances you will not be able to get all the information you need into the system in time. Further, a litigation support system can be quite helpful in the middle of a litigation process, for tasks such as preparing to take depositions of key witnesses and framing your arguments for motions and memorandums.

Can Computerized Litigation Support Be Used in the Courtroom?

Computerized litigation support systems are welcome in most courtrooms. Laptop computers are commonplace, not only for the litigators but also for the judges, court reporters, and other judicial staff. It is not uncommon to see separate tables for computers and litigation support staff in the courtroom. This is a real benefit for litigators, because searches in the litigation support system can be performed right in the courtroom whenever information is needed.

ETHICAL CONSIDERATIONS

In many cases, litigation support means the difference between winning and losing. This is particularly true in large cases where the litigants have much at stake; in some high-stakes cases, hundreds of millions of dollars may be at issue. Whether the case is large or small, though, the law office has the ethical duty to present its client's case as well as it possibly can. This includes being competent and acting diligently. If a litigation support system is set up poorly, if the litigation support system is not used competently, or if the litigation support system fails entirely, then the client's case suffers. In addition, in most situations the client is actually paying for staff time and expenses to set up and use the litigation support system. If the litigation support system fails, then not only does the client's case suffer, but the client is also billed and pays for a service from which it did not get any benefit. Litigation support definitely carries ethical responsibilities, in that it is an extremely important aspect of any client's case and often determines whether the client wins or loses.

SUMMARY

Litigation support software is designed to assist attorneys in organizing information that has been gathered during litigation. The purpose of these programs is to help attorneys find the information they need to adequately work on and try a case.

Manual litigation support methods do not work well in the legal environment, because they are not flexible enough for the ever-changing pace of modern lawsuits. Computerized litigation support methods can adapt to this changing environment, because they allow users to search an unlimited amount of data in many ways.

Computerized litigation support can either be performed by a litigation support service provider or done in-house. Service providers offer a number of advantages, including being able to draw on their knowledge and experience, having someone other than the legal team be fully responsible for the litigation support system, being able to tie electronic discovery duties and litigation support together, and being able to handle and work with tens or even hundreds of thousands of documents, among others. However, the law office (and ultimately the client) may pay a lot for these services.

Whether litigation support is performed by a service provider or in-house, a legal organization must decide whether a document abstract or document summary system will be used and whether full-text, imaging, case management, or analytical programs, or a combination of all of them, will be used.

A document abstract litigation support system allows users to enter document abstracts summaries into a computer and subsequently to search and retrieve information contained in the abstracts or summaries. Full-text retrieval systems enable users to search and retrieve information contained in the full text of documents entered into the system. In some instances, a document abstract system will be used to track documents, and a full-text retrieval system will be used to track depositions and other types of testimony in the same case.

Document imaging allows a legal professional to see the actual image of a document, as opposed to seeing its full text or an abstract of the document. Document imaging can be accomplished by scanning hard-copy images into a computer or by converting electronic documents into an image file format such as TIFF or PDF.

Analytical litigation support software helps legal professionals view a case from a number of perspectives and helps them conceptualize and think about facts, documents, people, and the relationships among them. This type of software includes programs that create timelines or outlines of cases, as well as itemize facts, documents, issues, and people.

Some litigation support systems now offer document abstract, full-text retrieval, imaging, and analytical tools in one program. These powerful packages offer the advantages of all these types of systems, but are typically complex. No matter what type of litigation support system is used, it is necessary that users carefully plan the design of the system, taking into account what type of information is most relevant to the case and how it will be used during litigation and at trial. A litigation support system that is poorly planned will surely fail and perhaps cause the case to be lost.

KEY TERMS

analytical litigation support programs
Bates stamp
Boolean logic search
computer-aided transcription (CAT)
document abstract litigation support system
document imaging
full-text retrieval litigation support system
in-house computerized litigation support system
litigation support service provider
litigation support software
objective/bibliographical coding
proximity search
real-time transcription
single-word search
subjective coding
super wildcard search
wildcard search

INTERNET SITES

Internet sites for this chapter include:

ORGANIZATION	DESCRIPTION	WORLD WIDE WEB ADDRESS
1360 Studios, Inc.	Transcript Manager Pro transcript management	www.transcriptmanagerpro.com
Access Data Group, LLC	Summation litigation support products	www.summation.com
Anacomp	Case Logistix litigation support program	www.caselogistix.com
C2 Legal	E-discovery and litigation support services	www.c2legal.com
CaseCentral	E-discovery and litigation support services	www.casecentral.com
Cricket Technologies	E-discovery and litigation support services	www.crickettechnologies.com
DT Software Inc.	Data searching and litigation support	www.dtsearch.com
Gigatron Software	Transcription software	www.gsclion.com
I Conect Development	E-discovery and litigation support services	www.iconect.com
Kroll Ontrack	E-discovery and litigation support services	www.krollontrack.com
LexisNexis	CaseMap and TimeMap litigation support	www.casesoft.com
LexisNexis	Concordance litigation support	www.lexisnexis.com/concordance
Real Legal	Litigation support and transcript management products	www.reallegal.com
Rosen Technology Resources	E-discovery and litigation support services	www.rosentech.net
Zylab	E-discovery and litigation support products	www.zylab.com

TEST YOUR KNOWLEDGE

1. True or False: Litigation support software primarily assists legal professionals in responding to electronic discovery requests.
2. True or False: Litigation support is an easy task because, for the most part, legal issues, factual issues, and legal theories are static during the litigation of a case.
3. Distinguish between litigation documents and factual documents.
4. What is knowledge management?
5. Name three benefits of computerized litigation support.
6. Distinguish document abstracting, full-text retrieval, and imaging.
7. What advantages does use of a litigation support service provider offer?
8. Differentiate between objective and subjective coding in relation to creating document abstracts.
9. What is a controlled vocabulary, and in what litigation support system is this important?
10. What type of search uses "AND," "OR," and "NOT"?

ON THE WEB EXERCISES

1. Using the addresses listed in the "Internet Sites" section of this chapter, visit the websites of the following three vendors: Case Logistix, Summation (iBlaze), and LexisNexis (Concordance litigation support software). Write a two-page paper that summarizes the features of each product.
2. Visit the American Bar Association's website and search for articles on litigation support. Find three articles on the topic. Write a one-page summary of each article.
3. Using a general search engine such as www.google.com or www.yahoo.com, research computer-aided transcription and write a two-page article on what it is, how it works, and why it is helpful to practicing legal professionals like attorneys and paralegals.

QUESTIONS AND EXERCISES

1. As the chief litigation paralegal, you are preparing to have clerical staff enter approximately 1,000 documents into a computerized litigation support system. You are concerned that the information may not be entered uniformly, because 10 different people will be doing this data entry work. What should you do to solve the problem? Give a detailed answer.
2. An attorney in your firm is having trouble deciding whether to switch the staff from their manual litigation support system to a computerized system. Tell the attorney what you think about the situation.
3. You have been asked to give your opinion as to whether a litigation support database should be created for a particular case. The case involves approximately 200 documents, which average 150 pages each. The issues are complex, and four attorneys will need five months to try the case. Damages requested are minimal, but the public relations damage to your client could be devastating should your client lose. The opposing counsel may or may not use a litigation support database; your firm does not know. Should the case be entered into a litigation support database? Why or why not?
4. Using this chapter as a guide, and specifically the tips in Exhibit 8–14, design a litigation support system for one of the following types of lawsuits:
   - High-speed auto accident involving multiple cars, multiple witnesses, and no evidence of design defects
   - Wrongful termination claim based on age discrimination and involving multiple witnesses

- Securities fraud case in which investors claim they invested in a company that withheld information about its true financial situation
- Medical malpractice claim involving the wrongful death of a patient undergoing a medical procedure
- Product liability class action against a manufacturer alleging design defects in a tractor

Your design should consider what type of litigation support method you will use, who will enter the data and how, what type of information will be entered, when it will be entered, what issues will be disputed at trial, and other such information. Prepare a (minimum) three-page summary of your design, including specifics of how you arrived at your design.

ETHICS QUESTION

You work as a paralegal for a small law firm. Your firm does not use any of the litigation support tools discussed in this chapter. When your firm gets a new client with a very complex case, the new client agrees to pay a portion of the costs of acquiring a new litigation support software package. In return, the firm will be able to work more efficiently and produce more work per hour billed to that client. One of the attorneys suggests that the firm use the litigation support program for other clients' cases too. What, if any, ethical issues are raised by this scenario?

HANDS-ON EXERCISES

DISCOVER FY™

I. INTRODUCTION – READ THIS!

Discover FY™ is an e-discovery/litigation support tool provided and supported by ILS Technologies. The ILS Technologies Discover FY™ demonstration version is a full working version of the program. This program demonstration version will not time out. However, it is still recommended that you do not install the program on your computer until you are actually ready to go through the Hands-On Exercises and learn the program. When you are ready to install the program, follow the instructions in Section III.

II. USING THE DISCOVER FY™ HANDS-ON EXERCISES

The Discover FY™ Hands-On Exercises are easy to use and contain step-by-step instructions. Each lesson builds on the previous exercise, so please complete the Hands-On Exercises in order. Discover FY™ comes with sample data, so you should be able to utilize many features of the program.

III. INSTALLATION INSTRUCTIONS

If you installed this program for Chapter 7, you do not need to install it again.

Following are step-by-step instructions for loading the ILS Technologies Discover FY™ demonstration version on your computer. Note that you will need to load two separate programs (a Microsoft program and Discover FY™).

1. Log in to your CengageBrain.com account.
2. Under **"My Courses and Materials,"** find the Premium Website for *Using Computers in the Law Office, 7th edition.*
3. ***Click Open*** to go to the Premium Website.
4. Locate **"Book-Level Resources"** in the left navigation bar.
5. ***Click the link for Discover FY™.***
6. ***Click the link for the Microsoft .NET Framework 4.*** If necessary, ***change the language to English and click Download.***
7. The "File Download—Security Warning" window will open. ***Click Run.*** An "Internet Explorer—Security Warning" window will open. ***Click Run.***
8. The "Microsoft .NET Framework 4 Setup" window will open. ***Click the box to accept the license terms and click Install.***
9. The program will load onto your computer.
10. When the installation is complete, ***click Finish; close the Microsoft Download page and return to the Premium Website and click the link for Access Discover FY™.***

HANDS-ON EXERCISES

11. The "File Download—Security Warning" window will open. See Discover FY™ Installation Exhibit 1. ***Click Save;*** then complete the following instructions to download and unzip the Discover FY™ install file.
    a. Navigate to the folder where you saved the zip file.
    b. ***Double-click the file.*** Your default zip program (e.g., WinZip, 7-Zip, or Windows Explorer) should open, displaying the contents of the zip file. Extract the contents of the zip file.
    c. ***Double-click the file DFY_6.3.9_singleuser_demo.exe*** to begin installation.

DISCOVER FY™ INSTALLATION EXHIBIT 1

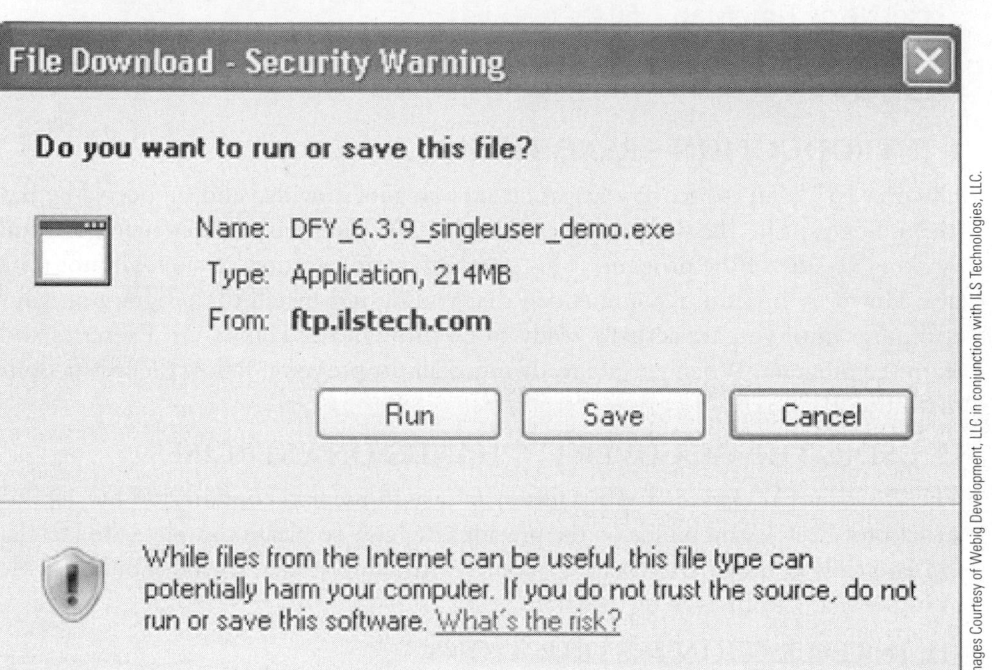

12. The "Discover FY™ Single User Demo Setup: License Page" window will open. See Discover FY™ Installation Exhibit 2. ***Click I Agree.***

DISCOVER FY™ INSTALLATION EXHIBIT 2

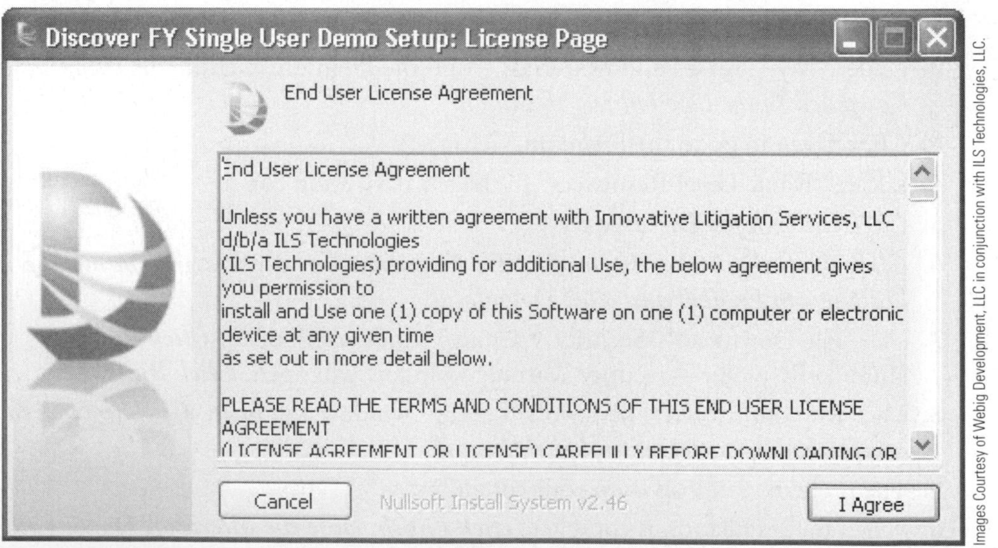

13. The "Discover FY™ Single User Demo Setup: Installation Options" window will open. See Discover FY™ Installation Exhibit 3. ***Select the Discover FY™ Single User Demo and click Install.***

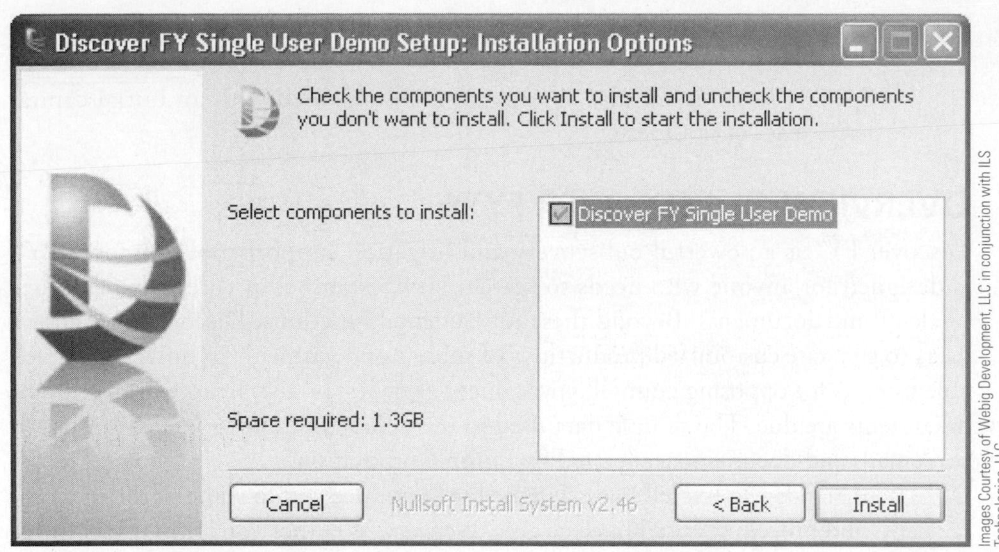

Images Courtesy of Webig Development, LLC in conjunction with ILS Technologies, LLC.

DISCOVER FY™ INSTALLATION EXHIBIT 3

14. When the program has been installed on your computer, ***click Close*** on the "Discover FY™ Single User Demo Setup: Completed" window.

IV. INSTALLATION TECHNICAL SUPPORT

If you have problems installing the demonstration version of Discover FY™, please contact Cengage Learning Technical Support first at http://cengage.com/support. If Cengage Learning Technical Support is unable to resolve your installation question, or if you have a noninstallation-related question, you will need to contact ILS Technologies directly at (866) 359-9324.

DISCOVER FY™ SOFTWARE

Number	Lesson Title	Concepts Covered
BASIC		
Lesson 1	Introduction to Discover FY™	Explanation and introduction to the Discover FY™ interfaces.
INTERMEDIATE		
Lesson 2	Searching for Documents in the Datastore	Search for documents; native format; metadata; create folders.
ADVANCED		
Lesson 3	Document Images	HTML images, native format images, Image Viewer, creating a TIFF, redacting a TIFF, clearing and saving redactions, print options.

GETTING STARTED

Introduction

Throughout these exercises, information you need to enter into the program will be designated in several different ways.

- Keys to be pressed on the keyboard are designated in brackets, in all caps, and in bold (e.g., press the **[ENTER]** key).
- Movements with the mouse pointer are designated in bold and italics (e.g., ***point to File and click***).
- Words or letters that should be typed are designated in bold (e.g., type **Training Program**).

- Information that is or should be displayed on your computer screen is shown in bold, with quotation marks (e.g., "**Press ENTER to continue.**").
- Specific menu items and commands are designated with an initial capital letter (e.g., click Open).

OVERVIEW OF DISCOVER FY™

Discover FY™ is a powerful e-discovery and litigation support tool. Discover FY™ is designed for anyone who needs to search, view, examine, or categorize volumes of electronic documents. Beyond these fundamental functions, Discover FY™ allows users to generate customized productions of subsets of documents in universally readable formats for opposing counsel, government agencies, or anyone to whom relevant documents are due. The sample data used in the demonstration program consists of real emails and documents generated by Enron Corporation.

These Hands-On Exercises are designed to introduce you to some of the practical concepts and procedures used in electronic discovery. Whether your firm uses a third-party vendor to process electronic discovery files or handles everything in-house, you will benefit from learning the terminology and theories of electronic discovery.

BASIC LESSON

If you did Hands-On Exercise 1 in Chapter 4, you may begin the Chapter 5 Hands-On Exercises with Exercise 2.

LESSON 1: INTRODUCTION TO DISCOVER FY™

This lesson introduces you to the Discover FY™ litigation support program. It explains basic information about the Discover FY™ interface, including information about the Fact, Object, Issue, Question, and Research spreadsheets.

1. Start Windows. Then, ***double-click the Discover FY™ shortcut on the desktop.*** Discover FY™ will then start.
2. When you start Discover FY™, the "Login" dialog box will open and you will be asked to enter your user ID and password. Type **admin** in the User ID text box and type **password** in the Password text box. (Note: The password will appear as a series of dots. See Discover FY™ Exhibit 1.) ***Click Login.***

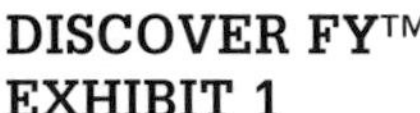

DISCOVER FY™ EXHIBIT 1

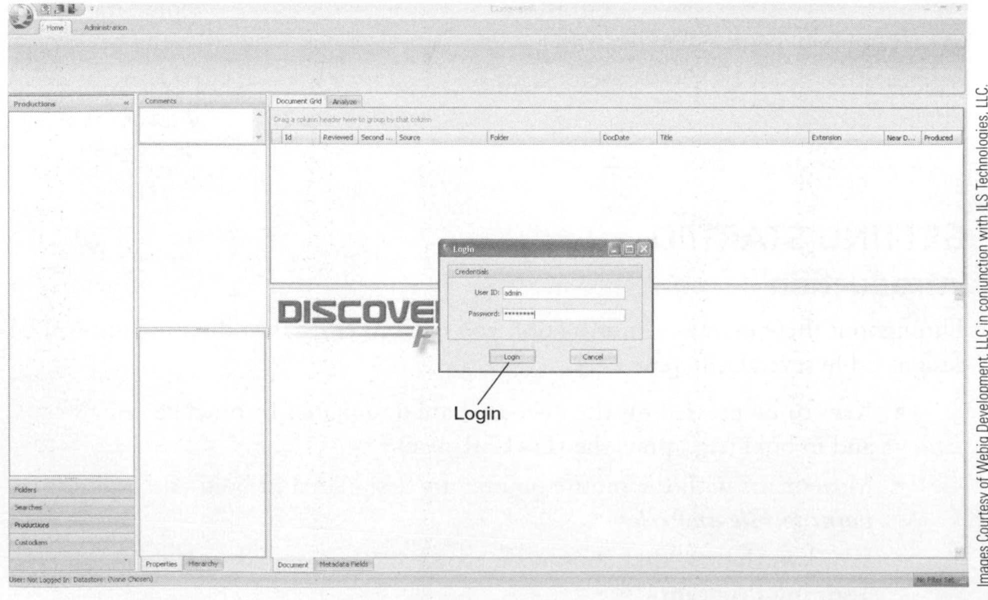

3. The "Choose Datastore" box will appear. We have not yet created any Datastores, so ***click DISCOVER FY™ DEMO to highlight it and click Select.*** See Discover FY™ Exhibit 2.

DISCOVER FY™ EXHIBIT 2

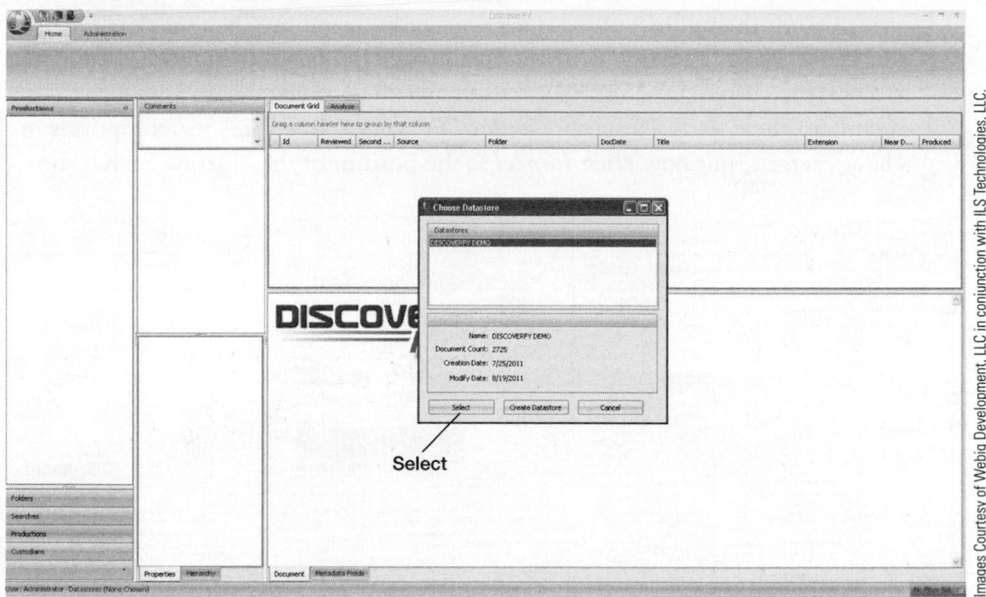

Images Courtesy of Webig Development, LLC in conjunction with ILS Technologies, LLC.

4. By default, Discover FY™ opens with the Home tab selected and the Discover FY™ window is empty because we have not yet selected any data. To access the sample data provided with the application, we need to select a Custodian. ***Click Custodians and then click the only name provided, Chris Germany.*** When you do so, the sample data will load. See Discover FY™ Exhibit 3.

DISCOVER FY™ EXHIBIT 3

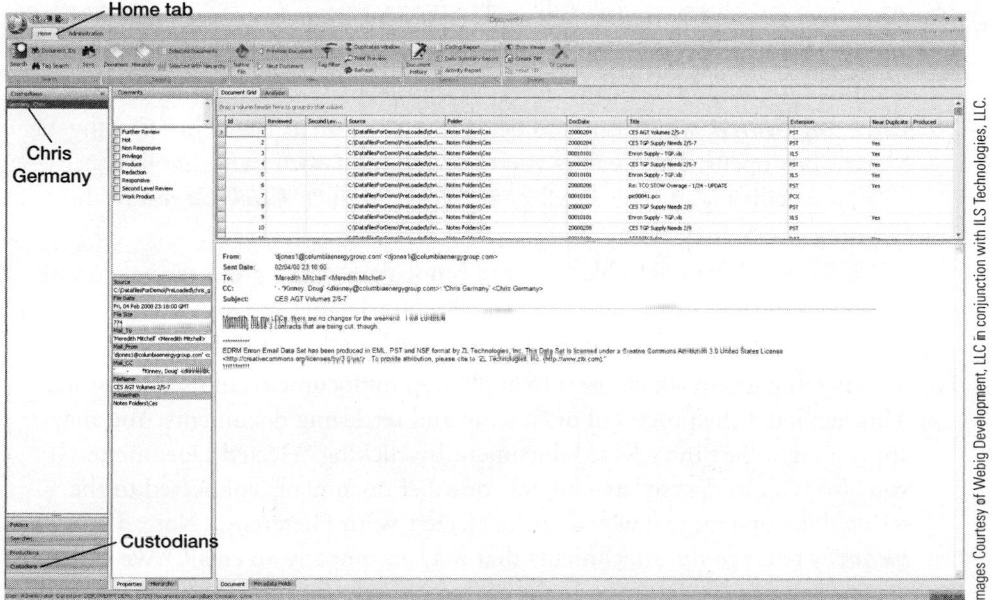

Images Courtesy of Webig Development, LLC in conjunction with ILS Technologies, LLC.

5. We will explore the various sections of the Discover FY™ screen. Running across the top of the screen is the Ribbon Bar, which consists of two tabs, Home and Administration. Home is selected by default. (See Discover FY™ Exhibit 3.) You should be in the Home View, but if you are not, ***click on Home.*** Within the Home tab, there are five option groups: Search, Tagging, View, Reports, and Images.

6. The Search group enables you to search the datastore for specific documents. A number of search methods are available. ***Click Search*** (its icon looks like a blue square with a magnifying glass). The "Define Search" box will open. (See Discover FY™ Exhibit 4.) This enables you to search for documents by entering specific search terms within the full text of the document or by searching the metadata of the documents. You can refine your searches by using filters to search for documents of a specific custodian, documents created within a specific date range, or documents held within a specific folder. We will explore these search options in a later exercise, but now ***click Cancel*** at the bottom of the "Define Search" box.

DISCOVER FY™ EXHIBIT 4

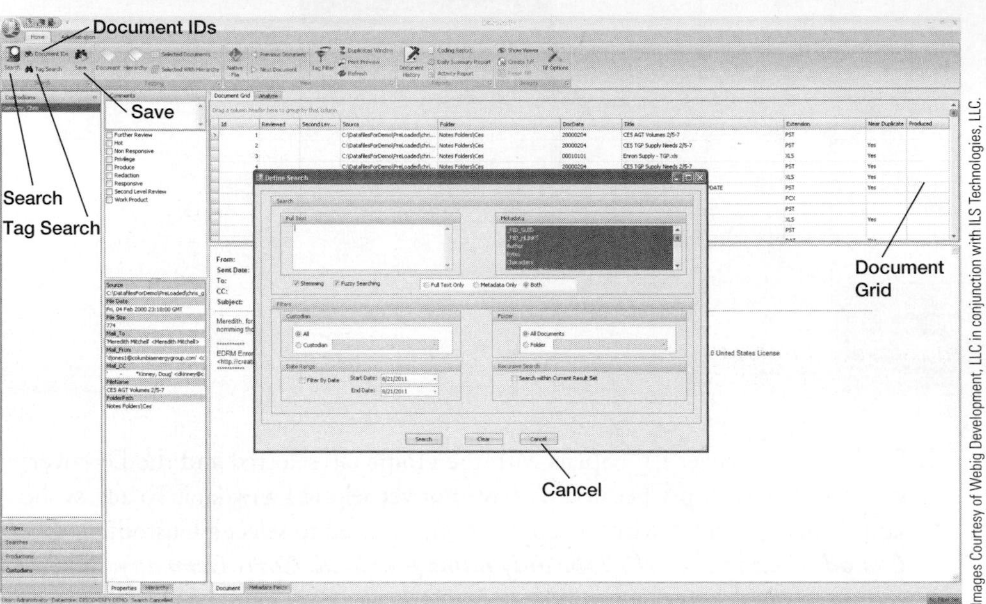

HANDS-ON EXERCISES

7. ***Click Document IDs*** to the right of Search. The "Search—Document ID" box opens. This allows you to search for a document by its Document ID (a specific identification number). ***Click Cancel*** in the "Search-Document ID" box.
8. ***Click Tag Search,*** which is found below the Document IDs. The "Coding Tag Search" box opens. This enables you to search for a document that has been given a specific tag, such as Privilege or Work Product. ***Click Cancel*** in the "Coding Tag Search" box.
9. ***Click Save*** (its icon looks like a pair of binoculars with a green triangle on it). The "Save Search" box opens. This allows you to name and save the results of a search for later use. ***Click Cancel*** in the "Save Search" box.
10. The Tagging group allows users to apply tags to documents in the Datastore. This facilitates the process of organizing and retrieving documents. You may apply a tag to just the selected document by clicking Selected Documents. If you also wish to tag any attachments or other documents connected to the selected document, you would click Selected With Hierarchy. (Note: The term *hierarchy* refers to the attachments that may accompany an email.) We will explore tagging options in a later exercise.
11. The View group on the Home tab gives you different options for viewing documents. ***Click the third line of the Document Grid pane.*** This document is a spreadsheet, and you can see a representation of that spreadsheet in the Document Display pane. (See Discover FY™ Exhibit 5.) ***Click Native File.*** See Discover FY Exhibit 5. A new window will open and display the spreadsheet as a native file; that is, it will show the spreadsheet within a spreadsheet program. If you have Microsoft

Excel on your computer, Discover FY™ will open Excel to display the spreadsheet. (See Discover FY™ Exhibit 6.) This option allows you to see the formulas used in the spreadsheet and to manipulate the data, if desired. ***Close the spreadsheet.***

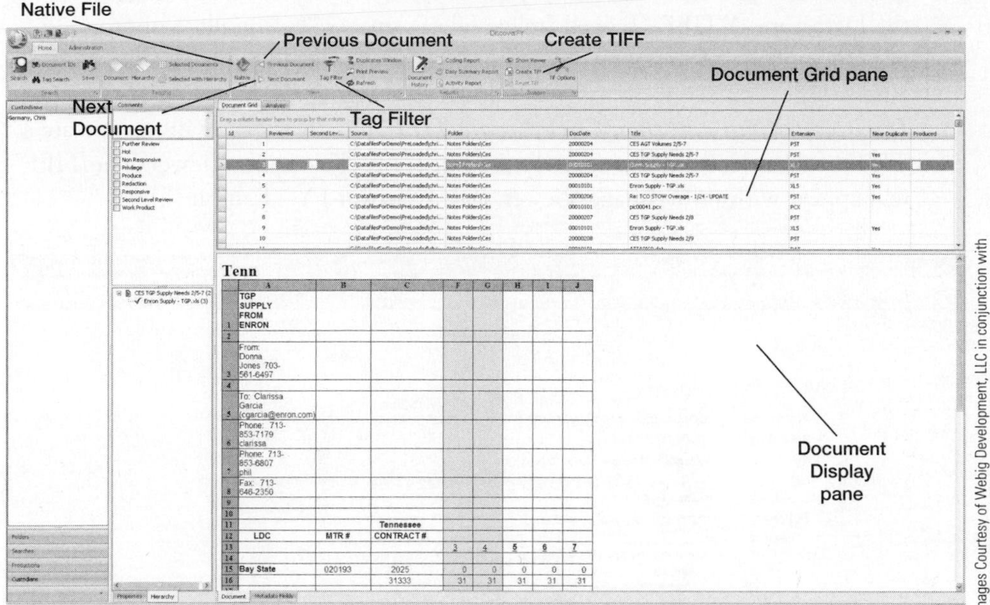

DISCOVER FY™ EXHIBIT 5

Images Courtesy of Webig Development, LLC in conjunction with ILS Technologies, LLC.

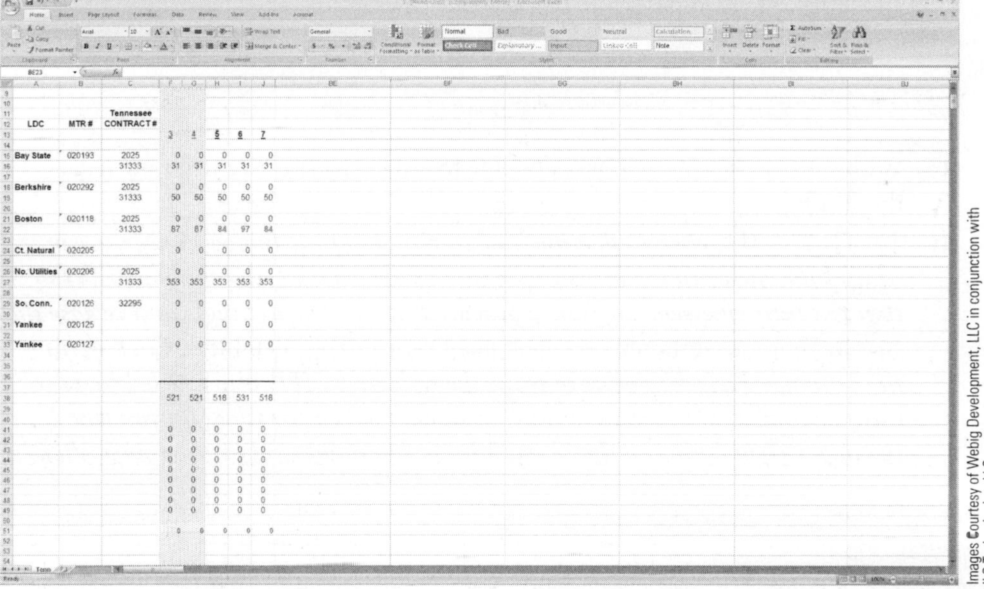

DISCOVER FY™ EXHIBIT 6

Images Courtesy of Webig Development, LLC in conjunction with ILS Technologies, LLC.

12. You can navigate between different documents listed in the Document Grid by clicking Next Document and Previous Document in the View group. The Tag Filter allows you to specify specific types of documents when executing a search. The Duplicate Window allows you to see any documents that are duplicates of the selected document. The Print Preview lets you see what a document will look like when printed.
13. The Reports group on the Home tab gives you the ability to generate a variety of reports. The Document History report details activity related to the selected document. The Coding report shows the Document ID, Document Date, Title, and a column for each available flag for every document displayed in the Document Grid. The Daily Summary report summarizes activity during a specified

time interval. The Activity Report shows a selected user's coding activity within a specified time range. We will explore these various reports in a later exercise.

14. The final option group on the Home tab is the Images group. This option group allows you to create, view, and manipulate TIFF images of documents in the Datastore. A TIFF (Tagged Image File Format) is essentially a photograph of a document. It shows you what the document looks like, but, unlike with a native file, you cannot modify the document. ***Click the first line of the Document Grid and then Click Create TIFF.*** Discover FY™ will now create a TIFF of the selected document. To see the TIFF, click Show Viewer. The TIFF will appear within the Image Viewer. (See Discover FY™ Exhibit 7.)

DISCOVER FY™ EXHIBIT 7

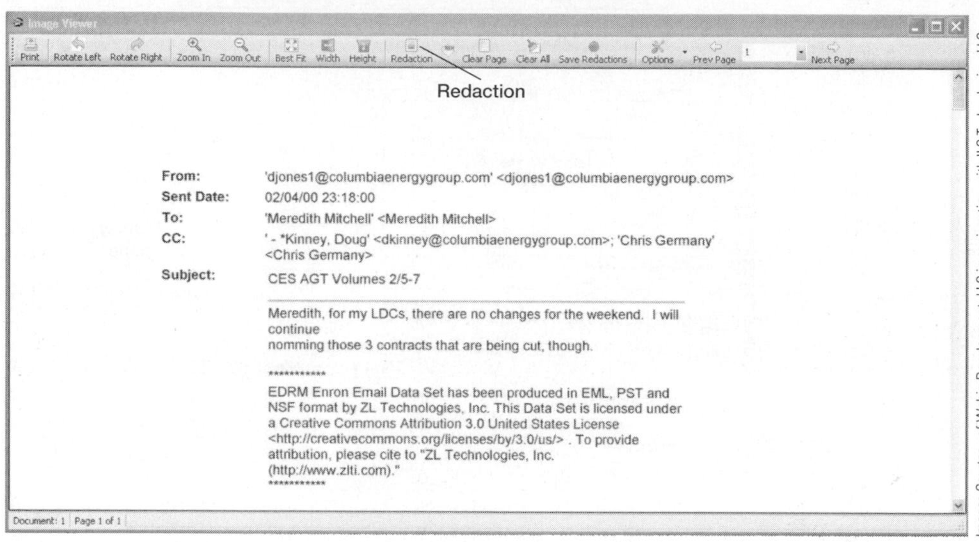

15. Within the Image Viewer, it is possible to redact a TIFF. We will now redact this TIFF.

16. To redact a TIFF, ***click Redaction Tool at the top of the Image Viewer screen. Move your cursor to the message portion of the email. Drag the cursor (+) so that the entire message portion is obscured by a black rectangle and release the cursor.*** Your screen should now look like Discover FY™ Exhibit 8. ***Click Print in the Image Viewer toolbar to print the redacted TIFF.*** If instructed to do so, turn the printed TIFF image in to your teacher. ***Click the Close button (the X in the upper right corner of the Image Viewer window) to close the Image Viewer.***

DISCOVER FY™ EXHIBIT 8

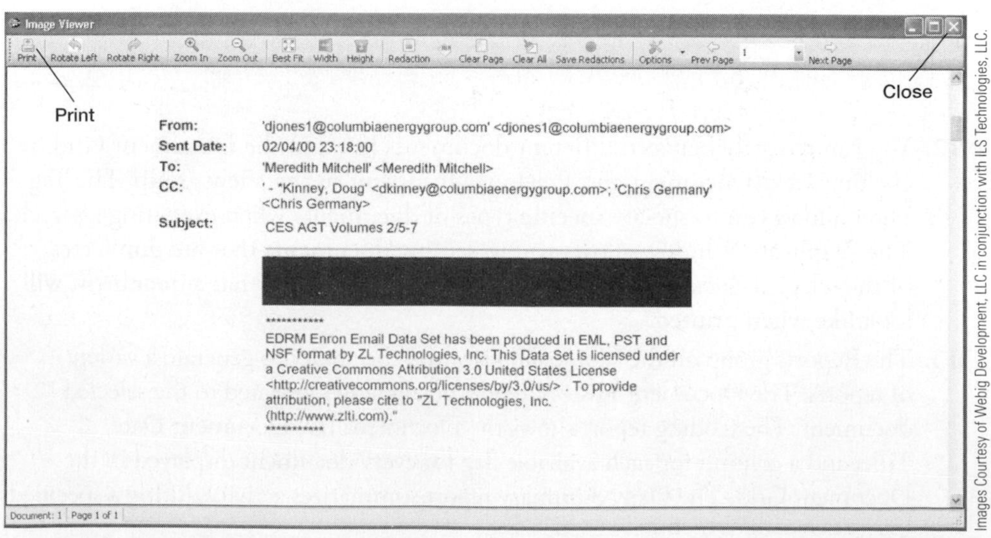

17. We will now explore the options available on the Administrator tab in the Ribbon Bar. ***Click Administration.*** There are four option groups in the Administration tab: Admin, Datastore, Processing, and Production. See Discover FY™ Exhibit 9.

DISCOVER FY™ EXHIBIT 9

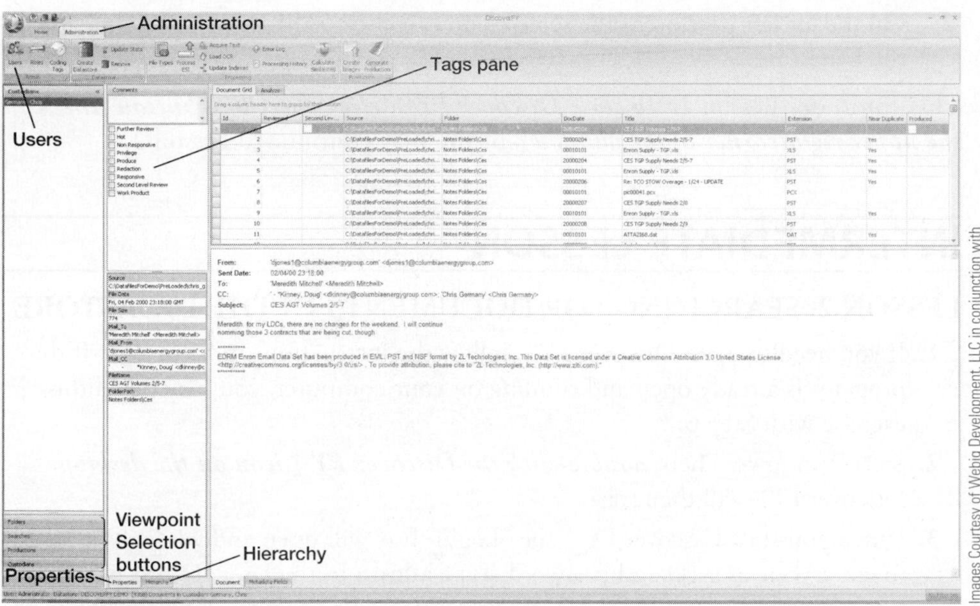

Images Courtesy of Webig Development, LLC in conjunction with ILS Technologies, LLC.

18. The Admin group provides options for managing who has access to which options available in Discover FY™. ***Click Users.*** The "User Maintenance" box will open. This gives the administrator the ability to set users' User IDs, passwords, and assigned roles. ***Click Close*** in the "User Maintenance" box.
19. The Coding Tags tool allows you to adjust the definitions of the tags that are used to code (or organize) documents.
20. The Datastore group allows you to create, delete, and update datastores.
21. The Processing group is used to work with files as part of the electronic discovery process. These features are beyond the scope of these Hands-On Exercises, which focus on the litigation support features of Discover FY™.
22. The Production group allows you to generate the documents required for production. We will explore the production utilities in a later exercise.
23. In the window under the Ribbon Bar are a number of panes. The pane on the far right side of the screen shows the current viewpoint. For example, we have been looking at the Custodians view. The Viewpoint Selection buttons at the bottom of that pane show that you have the option of Folders, Searches, Productions, as well as Custodians.
24. To the right of the Viewpoint pane is the Tags pane. By clicking on one or more of the available tags, you can apply those tags to the selected documents. The application of tags to documents makes it easier to organize and retrieve documents.
25. Under the Tags pane, there is a tabbed pane that gives you the option to see the hierarchy or properties of the selected document. For example, ***with the first document selected in the Document Grid, click the Properties tab.*** You can now see the specific properties of the selected email, such as the persons who sent and received the email, and the date, size, and file name of the selected email. ***Click the Hierarchy tab*** and you can see that this email does not have any related attachments.

26. To the right of the Tags pane is the Document Grid pane. This is where the files contained in the selected Datastore are listed. Under the Document Grid pane is the Document Display pane. This is where you can see an HTML representation of the selected document. By clicking the Metadata Fields tab at the bottom of the Document Display pane, you can view the metadata of the selected document.
27. On the far left portion of the screen, you can choose different viewpoints for the Datastore.

This concludes Lesson 1. ***To close Discover FY™, click the Close button (the X in the upper right corner of the window),*** or you may continue to Lesson 2.

INTERMEDIATE LESSON

LESSON 2: SEARCHING FOR DOCUMENTS IN THE DATASTORE

1. If you need to open Discover FY™, follow the instructions in Steps 2–5. If the program is already open and running on your computer, you may begin this exercise with Step 6.
2. Start Windows. Then, ***double-click the Discover FY™ icon on the desktop.*** Discover FY™ will then start.
3. When you start Discover FY™, the "Login" box will open and you will be asked to enter your user ID and password. Type **admin** in the User ID text box and type **password** in the Password text box. (Note: The password will appear as a series of dots. See Discover FY™ Exhibit 1.) Then ***click Login.***
4. The "Choose Datastore" box will appear. We have not yet created any Datastores, so ***click DISCOVER FY™ DEMO to highlight it and click Select.*** (See Discover FY™ Exhibit 2.)
5. All of the sections of the Discover FY™ screen are empty, because we have not yet selected any data. To access the sample data provided with the application, we need to select a Custodian. ***Click Custodians and then click the only name provided, Chris Germany.*** When you do so, the sample data will load. (See Discover FY™ Exhibit 3.)
6. Discover FY™ can be used to sort and organize files in preparation for depositions, trial, and other purposes. We will now search for specific documents, create a new folder, and place those documents in that folder.
7. Assume that your firm is about to conduct the deposition of a witness regarding business transactions between Enron and Columbia Energy Systems. Discover FY™ allows you to search for files that name Columbia Energy Systems and then to further search within those documents. To begin a search, with the Home tab selected, ***click Search*** in the upper left corner of the screen. The "Define Search" box will open. (See Discover FY™ Exhibit 10.) Type **Columbia** under Full Text. (See Discover FY™ Exhibit 10.) Notice that there are a number of boxes and buttons. You can choose to conduct a search with Stemming and Fuzzy Searching. *Stemming* enables the search engine to look for documents containing terms that use the search term as a stem; for example, using stemming with the search term "contract" can find documents with "contracts," "contracted," "contracting," and so on. *Fuzzy searches* enable the search engine to locate documents with terms that are very similar to the specified search term; it compensates for the fact that some documents may contain a misspelled version of the specified search term. It is generally a good idea to select both of these options.
8. You can limit the scope of the search to the contents of the documents or the metadata of the documents. Selecting the Full Text Only option will

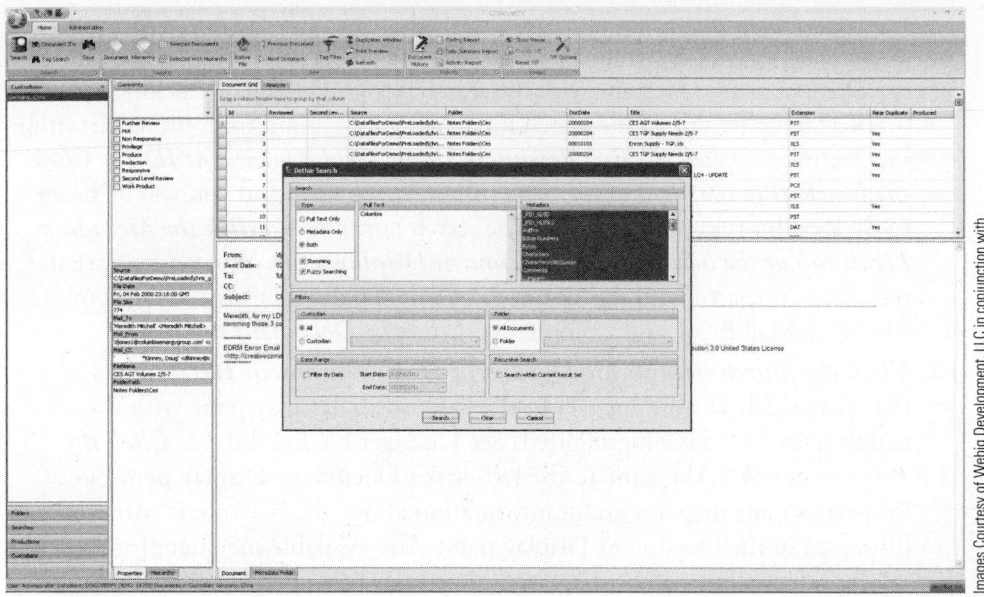

DISCOVER FY™ EXHIBIT 10

limit the search results to documents that actually contain the specified search term(s) within the document. For example, if you selected Full Text Only, your search results would be limited to those documents that contain the word *Columbia* in the text of the document; if there is an email with *Columbia* in the "To" or "From" line, that document would not be included in the search results unless the term *Columbia* also appeared in the body of the document. In contrast, by choosing Metadata Only and then selecting the desired types of metadata (they appear in the box marked "Metadata"; see Discover FY™ Exhibit 10), the search results would be limited to documents that contain the specified search term(s) in the metadata. So, if you were to select Metadata Only, your search results would not include any documents that include the term *Columbia* in the text of the document unless it also appeared in the metadata. To begin, we will not limit our search, so ***click Both and then click Search.***

9. Your screen should now look like Discover FY™ Exhibit 11. Notice that the search term (*Columbia*) is highlighted. The Document Grid pane now contains

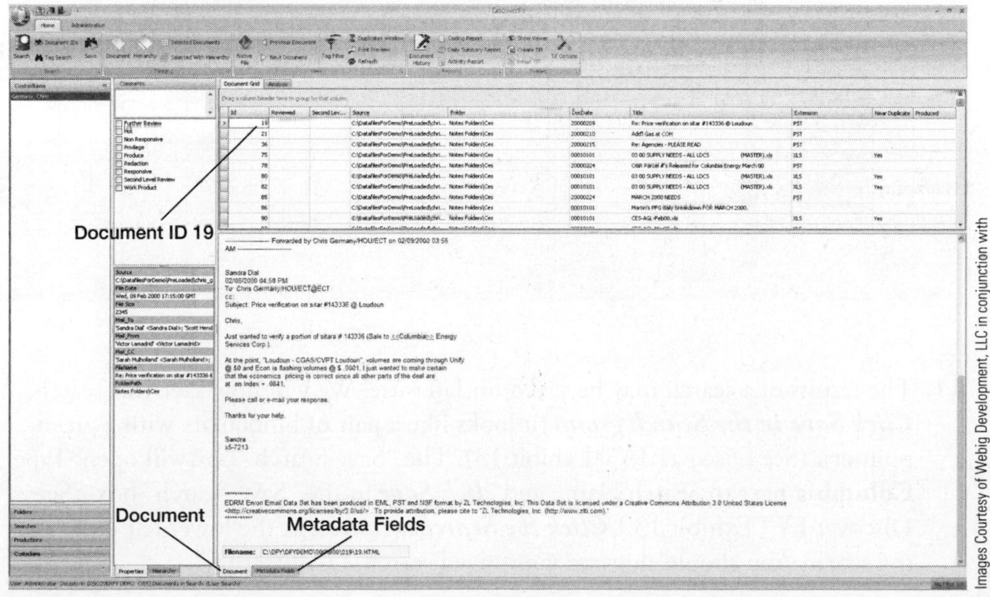

DISCOVER FY™ EXHIBIT 11

only those documents that satisfied the search query. ***Click a few different documents.*** As you do, you will notice that the document image appears in the Document Display pane with the search term highlighted. Clicking on the brackets to either side of the search hit allows you to jump from hit to hit within the document. ***Click the first document in the Grid, Document ID 19. Click the brackets to the right of the highlighted search term*** and you will be taken to the next hit (next appearance of the search term). Now, ***click the Metadata Fields tab at the bottom of the Document Display pane.*** You can now see the metadata associated with this document (Title, Folder, Mail To, Mail From, Mail CC, Mail BCC, and Comments). ***Click the Document tab again.***

10. ***Click the fourth item in the Document Grid, Document ID 75.*** Notice that a spreadsheet now appears in the Document Display pane with the search term *Columbia* highlighted. See Discover FY Exhibit 12. ***Click the Properties tab*** in the pane to the left of the Document Display pane. The Properties pane displays useful information about the document currently displayed in the Document Display pane. Any available metadata for the selected document will be displayed here. Now ***click the Hierarchy tab***. A *Hierarchy* refers to an email item and its attachment(s). The Hierarchy tab identifies the document currently shown in the Document Display pane with a red checkmark. If the document is part of an email hierarchy, all the other attachments and the email that make up the hierarchy will be displayed and can be examined by clicking on them. To see the email to which this spreadsheet is attached, ***click the line that says* "CES March Needs-Preliminary (ID 74)."** Notice that now the email appears in the Document Display pane and that the red checkmark now appears next to this document.

DISCOVER FY™ EXHIBIT 12

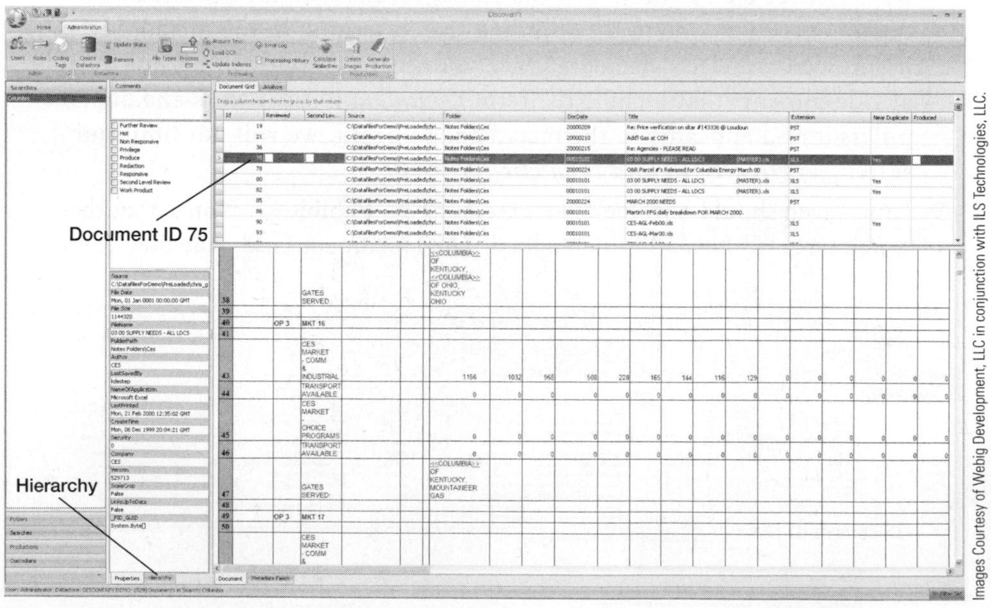

11. The results of a search may be saved for later use. We will now save this search. ***Click Save in the Search group*** (it looks like a pair of binoculars with a green pointer). (See Discover FY™ Exhibit 13). The "Save Search" box will open. Type **Columbia** next to Search Name and ***click Save*** in the "Save Search" box. (See Discover FY™ Exhibit 13.) ***Click the Searches button*** at the lower left corner of the screen. You should now see your saved search, **"Columbia."**

DISCOVER FY™ EXHIBIT 13

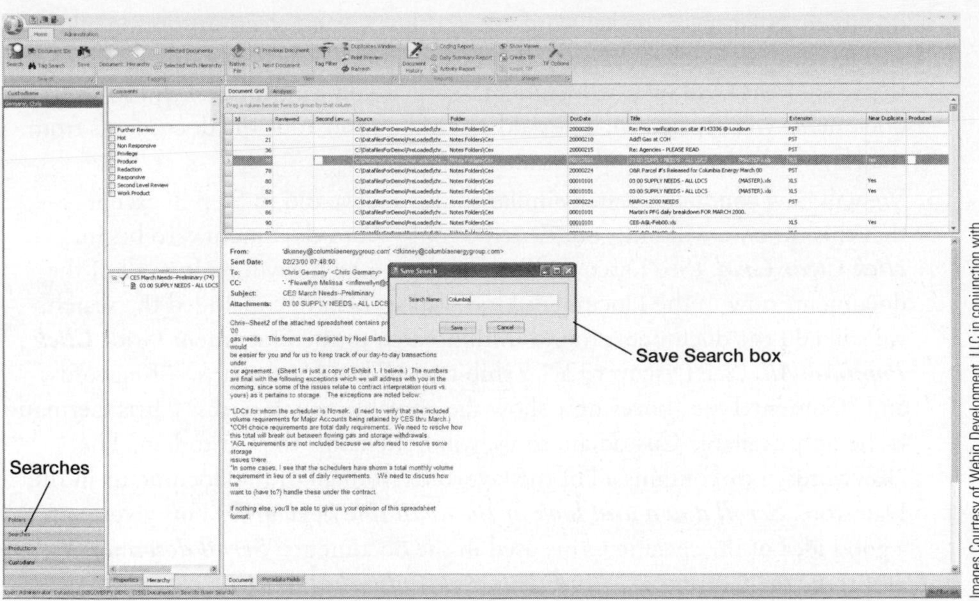

Images Courtesy of Webig Development, LLC in conjunction with ILS Technologies, LLC.

12. Another way to search for documents is to use the Analyze Tab pane next to the Document Grid pane. ***Click the Analyze Tab.*** Your screen should now look like Discover FY™ Exhibit 14. When documents are processed into Discover FY™, keywords for each document are identified. The Analyze tab gives you a quick and easy way to find documents based upon the keywords they contain. A review of the keywords list allows you to identify words or concepts contained within the document set that are of interest or importance to the review. Once keywords of interest are identified, documents containing these words can be quickly located and examined. There are a number of options within the Analyze Tab pane. Populate brings keywords into the tab for analysis. The Populate All option adds all keywords from all Custodians. The Populate from Grid option only adds keywords from documents currently displayed in the Document Grid. After keywords are added, you can click to select any combination of Custodian(s), Keyword(s), or Content Type(s) that are of interest. The Apply option applies your selections and produces a set of

DISCOVER FY™ EXHIBIT 14

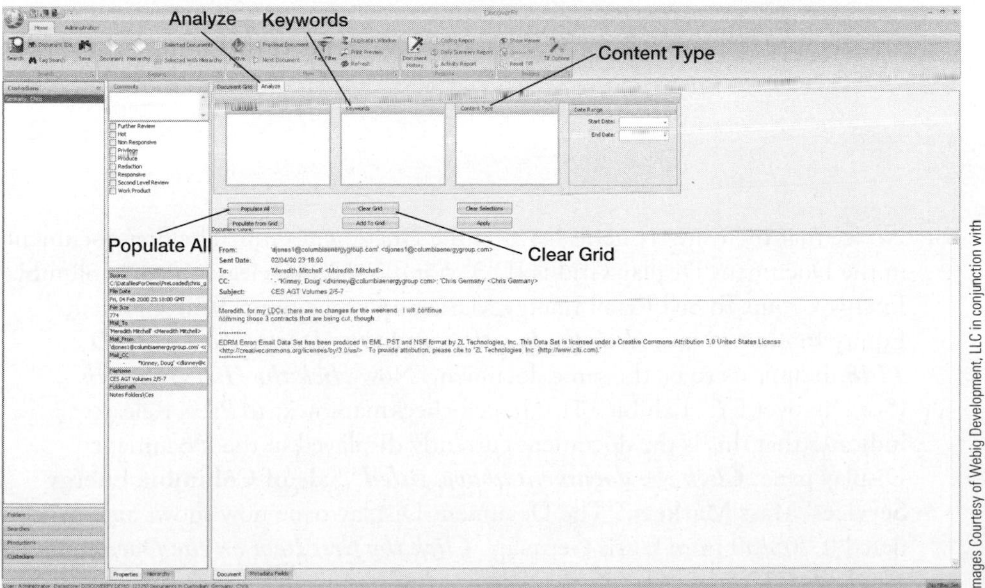

Images Courtesy of Webig Development, LLC in conjunction with ILS Technologies, LLC.

HANDS-ON EXERCISES

documents that meet the keyword criteria. The Clear Selections option allows you to clear any selected items and start over. The Clear Grid option clears the Document Grid of any documents, so that you can Add to Grid to see the documents you've selected. The Add to Grid option adds the documents from the Keyword selections to the Grid.

13. We will now conduct a search similar to the one we did in Step 8, except that this time we will limit our search to only Word documents. To begin, ***click Clear Grid.*** (See Discover FY™ Exhibit 14.) This will remove all of the documents now in the Document Grid. Once we have concluded the search, we will add the documents found in this search to the Document Grid. ***Click Populate All.*** (See Discover FY™ Exhibit 14.) The "Custodians," "Keywords," and "Content Type" boxes now show the available search terms. Chris Germany is the only available Custodian, so we will not change the Custodian. The "Keywords" box contains all of the keywords from all of the documents in the Datastore. ***Scroll down and look at the available keywords.*** This gives you a good idea of the specific terms used in the documents. ***Scroll down until you come to* "Columbia," *and then click Columbia to highlight it.*** Then, in the "Content Type" box, ***click Doc to highlight it. Click Apply, then click Add to Grid.*** A document will appear in the Document Display pane. ***Click Document Grid.*** Your screen should look like Discover FY™ Exhibit 15.

DISCOVER FY™ EXHIBIT 15

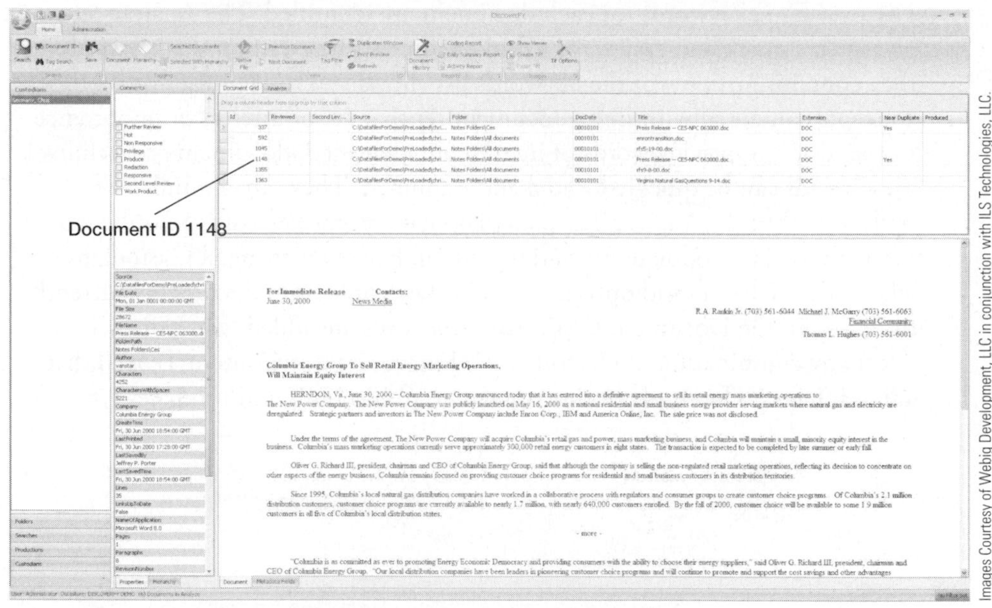

14. Notice that there are six items listed in the Document Grid. The first document in the Document Display Grid is ID 337 and is a press release titled "Columbia Energy Group To Sell Retail Energy Marketing Operations, Will Maintain Equity Interest." Now, ***click the fourth item in the Document Grid, ID 1148.*** It appears to be the same document. Now ***click the Hierarchy tab.*** (See Discover FY™ Exhibit 15). The red checkmark next to Press Release indicates that this is the document currently displayed in the Document Display pane. ***Click the document above, titled* "Sale of Columbia Energy Services' Mass Markets."** The Document Display pane now shows an email dated 07/05/00 from Chris Germany. ***Click the first item on the Document Grid, ID 337, and then, in the "Hierarchy" pane, click the document***

titled **"Sale of Columbia Energy Services' Mass Markets."** Notice that the Document Display pane now shows an email dated 07/03/00 from jporte1@columbiaenergygroup.com. Both ID 337 and 1148 (which are two different emails) were included in the search results because both contain as attachments a Word document with the specified search term within it.

15. We will now tag the documents produced by our search. *Tagging* simply refers to the process of attaching (or "tagging") a word or phrase to a document or set of documents. Among other purposes, tagging facilitates later searches and provides a degree of organization to otherwise unorganized data. Documents may be tagged individually or as a group. We will first apply a tag to a single document. Assume that the first document in the Document Grid requires further review and we want to tag it accordingly. If you click Document in the Tagging group options that will save the tag selection only to the document that is currently displayed on screen. If you click Hierarchy in the Tagging options that will save the tag selection with the document displayed on the screen, and also all other elements of an email hierarchy to which the document may belong. We want to save the tag selection to all elements of the email hierarchy, so ***with the first item (ID 337) selected in the Document Grid, click the Further Review tag in the Tag pane, and then click the Hierarchy icon.*** Notice that a green checkmark now appears under Reviewed for that item. (See Discover FY™ Exhibit 16.)

DISCOVER FY™ EXHIBIT 16

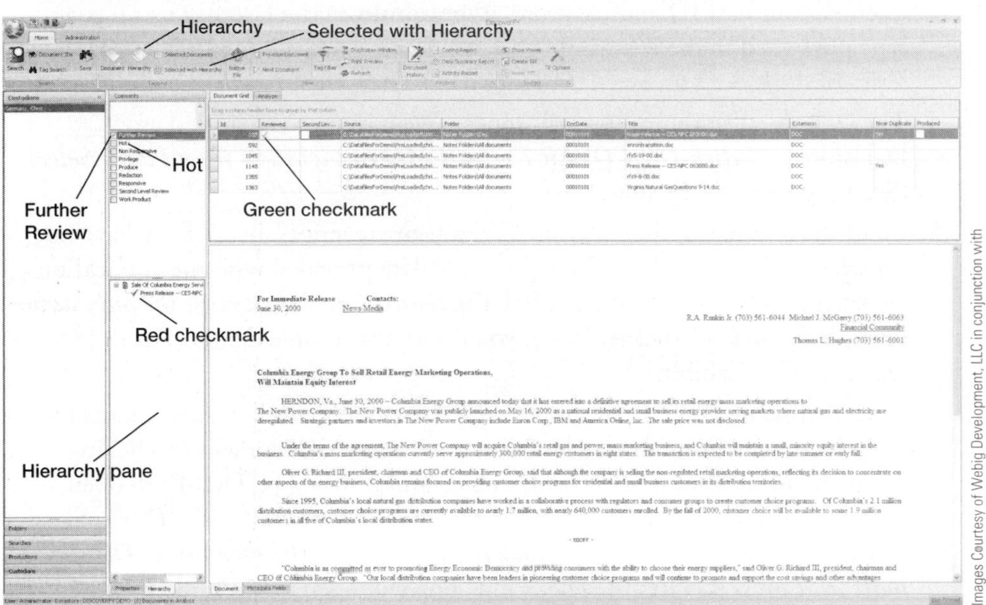

Images Courtesy of Webig Development, LLC in conjunction with ILS Technologies, LLC.

16. Now assume that the remaining documents in the Document Grid are deemed to be especially important, so we want to tag them as "Hot." To tag multiple documents simultaneously, first ***click the second item in Document Grid. Then, while holding down the Control key (Ctrl), click the other items in the Document Grid (IDs 1045, 1148, 1355, and 1363). Click the Hot tag in the Tag pane, then click Selected With Hierarchy in the Tagging options.*** (See Discover FY™ Exhibit 16.) All of the documents in the Document Grid should now have a checkmark in the Reviewed column.

This concludes Lesson 2. To close Discover FY™, ***click Close (the X in the upper right corner of the window)*** or you may continue on to Lesson 3.

ADVANCED LESSON

LESSON 3: DOCUMENT IMAGES

Discover FY™ allows three views of a document: the Document Display pane, Native View, and TIFF Viewer. The Document Display pane is an HTML representation of the document. This is the document view used most often. The text extracted from the document is displayed here and whenever possible text formatting is preserved. Native View brings up the native application used to create the document if it is installed on the local machine. Note that the native application must be installed on a computer as the default application for the specified file type in order for Native View to open. The TIFF Viewer displays TIFF images of the documents. Use the TIFF Viewer if you need to redact a document. Discover FY™ does not create TIFFs of documents up front.

You will now have the opportunity to create a TIFF that you can view in the TIFF Viewer or redact.

1. If you need to open Discover FY™, follow the instructions in Steps 2–5. If the program is already open and running on your computer, you may begin this exercise with Step 6.
2. Start Windows. Then, ***double-click the Discover FY™ icon on the desktop.*** Discover FY™ will then start.
3. When you start Discover FY™, the "Login" box will open and you will be asked to enter your user ID and password. Type **admin** in the User ID text box and type **password** in the Password text box. (Note: The password will appear as a series of dots. See Discover FY™ Exhibit 1.) Then ***click Login.***
4. The "Choose Datastore" box will appear. We have not yet created any Datastores, so ***click DISCOVER FY™ DEMO to highlight it and click Select.*** (See Discover FY™ Exhibit 2.)
5. All of the sections of the Discover FY™ screen are empty, because we have not yet selected any data. To access the sample data provided with the application, we need to select a Custodian. ***Click Custodians and then click the only name provided, Chris Germany.*** When you do so, the sample data will load. (See Discover FY™ Exhibit 3.)
6. The Document Display pane is an HTML representation of the contents of each document. You can search within the displayed document by clicking anywhere in the Document Display pane, and pressing **[CTRL-F]** to open a Find box. ***Click the fifth item on the Document Display Grid (ID No. 5) – Enron Supply - TGP.xls, then move the cursor over the Document Display pane and press* [CTRL-F].** The "Find" box will open. Type **Yankee** in the text box. Notice that as you type the search term, possible matches ("hits") are highlighted. ***Click Next to see the next hit. Click the X button to close the Find box.***
7. To view a document in its native application, users can press **CTRL-N** with that document highlighted in the Document Display Pane or click on the Native File icon on the Ribbon bar. We have already used the Native File icon, so with Document ID 5 still in the Document Display pane, ***press* [CTRL-N].** The document will open in a separate window as a Microsoft Excel spreadsheet. ***Click the spreadsheet's Close button. Click No*** if any windows open asking if you want to save any changes to the document.
8. The Show Viewer in the Images option group displays the TIFF of any document in a new window. This Image Viewer will remain open until you

HANDS-ON EXERCISES

click Show Viewer again to toggle it off. You can resize and reposition the window as needed. If the "Image Viewer" window is blank when a document is selected in the Grid, that means the document does not yet have a TIFF image. With Document ID 5 still in the Document Display pane, ***click Show Viewer.*** The "Image Viewer" window will open, but it will be blank. ***Click Show Viewer again to close the viewer. Click Create Tiff in the Images option group and then click Show Viewer.*** Your screen should now look like Discover FY™ Exhibit 17. Note that the document is rather large so it may take a few seconds to load.

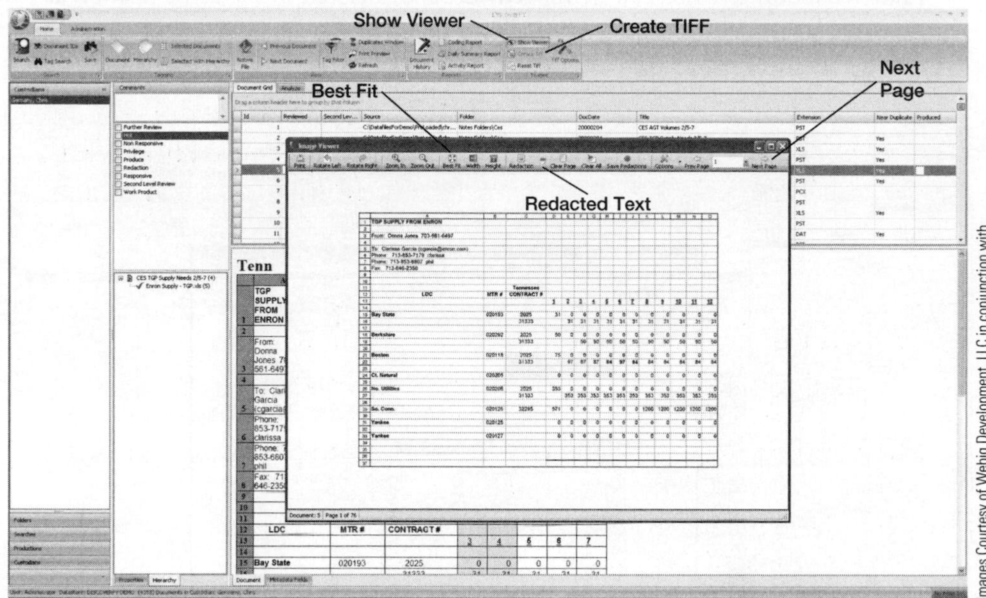

DISCOVER FY™ EXHIBIT 17

Images Courtesy of Webig Development, LLC in conjunction with ILS Technologies, LLC.

9. The content of Document ID 5 is larger than the Image Viewer can display. To see additional content, ***click Next Page*** to see page 2 of the TIFF. ***Click Prev Page*** to return to the first page of the TIFF. (See Discover FY™ Exhibit 17.) There are various page display control options. ***Click Best Fit*** (see Discover FY™ Exhibit 17). This shows the entire page of the document sized to fit the width and height of the current "Image Viewer" window. (Note: The image may already be properly sized, so you may not notice any change.) ***Click Width.*** This shows the document sized to fit the width of the current "Image Viewer" window. ***Click Height.*** This shows the document sized to fit the height of the current "Image Viewer" window.
10. It is possible to zoom in and zoom out as necessary to better view a document. ***In the Images group click the Zoom In icon twice*** to magnify the image. (See Discover FY™ Exhibit 17.) ***Click Zoom Out twice*** to return the document image to its original size.
11. It is possible to make redactions in an image in the Image Viewer. Several selections are available for creating and managing redactions. ***Click Redaction*** (see Discover FY™ Exhibit 17). Your cursor should now look like a plus sign: (+). Use the cursor to cover the information on line 3. This allows you to draw a plain black box on the document page. If necessary, you can left-click the black box to move and resize the box as needed.

12. ***Click Clear Page and if you are asked if you are sure you want to remove all redactions from this page, click Yes.*** This clears all redactions from the current page. If there were other redactions on other pages of the document, you could use the Clear All option to clear all of the redactions from the entire document.
13. Another option is to place a black box bearing the default text "Redacted" on the redacted material. ***Click Redacted Text*** (it looks like a diamond with some text on it, just to the right of Redaction). (See Discover FY™ Exhibit 17.) The Input dialog box will open. We will use the default text (REDACTED), so ***click OK.*** Your cursor should now look like a plus sign: "+." ***Use the cursor to cover the information on lines 5 through 8.*** (See Discover FY™ Exhibit 18.) The redaction text box can be moved, sized, or deleted in the same fashion as the regular redaction boxes.

DISCOVER FY™ EXHIBIT 18

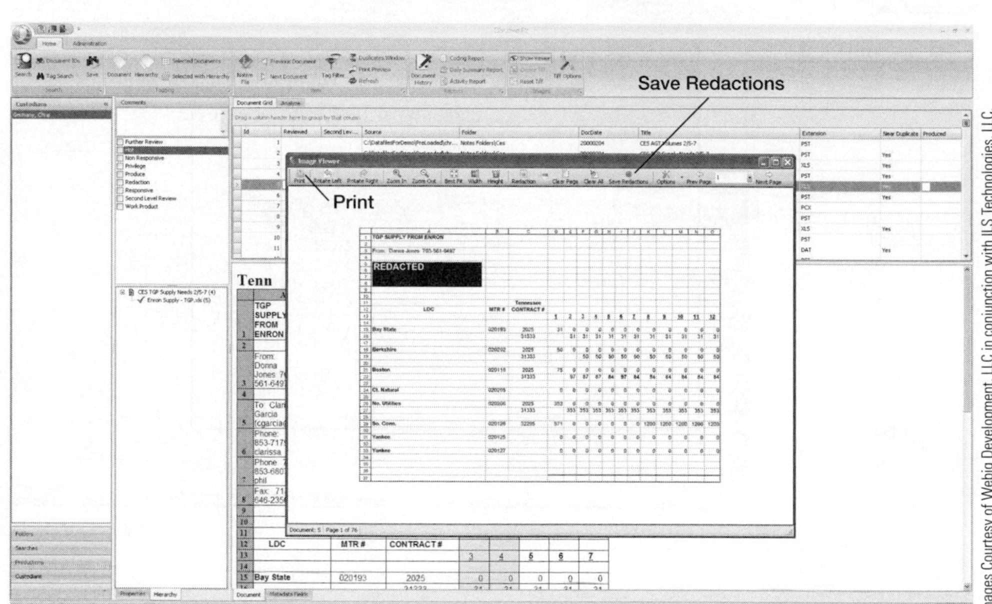

Images Courtesy of Webig Development, LLC in conjunction with ILS Technologies, LLC.

14. You can print a copy of a TIFF. ***Click Print in the Image Viewer toolbar.*** (See Discover FY™ Exhibit 18.) The "Print" window will open. This spreadsheet is a large document, so *be sure to print only the first page.* ***Select the desired printer and click Print.***
15. ***Click Save Redactions.*** This saves the redactions with the document. You will be prompted to save redactions if you move to another document without first clicking on Save.

This concludes the Discover FY™ Hands-On Exercises. To exit Discover FY™, ***click the Close button*** in the upper right corner of the screen.

HANDS-ON EXERCISES

LEXISNEXIS CASEMAP

I. INTRODUCTION – READ THIS

LexisNexis CaseMap is a litigation support analytical tool. CaseMap lets you manage, organize, and connect case facts, legal issues, and key players through in-depth research integration. The LexisNexis CaseMap demonstration version is a full working version of the program (with a few limitations). The program demonstration version times out 120 days after installation. This means that the program will only work for 120 days once you install it. So, it is highly recommended that you do not install the program on your computer until you are actually ready to go through the Hands-On Exercises and learn the program. When you are ready to install the program, follow the instructions in section III.

II. USING THE LEXISNEXIS CASEMAP HANDS-ON EXERCISES

The LexisNexis CaseMap Hands-On Exercises are easy to use and contain step-by-step instructions. Each lesson builds on the previous exercise, so please complete the Hands-On Exercises in order. CaseMap comes with sample data, so you should be able to utilize many features of the program.

III. INSTALLATION INSTRUCTIONS

The following are step-by-step instructions for loading the LexisNexis CaseMap demonstration version on to your computer.

1. Log in to your CengageBrain.com account.
2. Under *"My Courses & Materials,"* find the Premium Website for *Using Computers in the Law Office, 7th edition.*
3. ***Click Open to go to the Premium Website.***
4. Locate Book Resources in the left navigation menu.
5. ***Click on the link for CaseMap 10.***
6. You may get a File Download – Security Warning. ***Click Run.*** See CaseMap Installation Exhibit 1. The file will begin to download.

CASEMAP INSTALLATION EXHIBIT 1

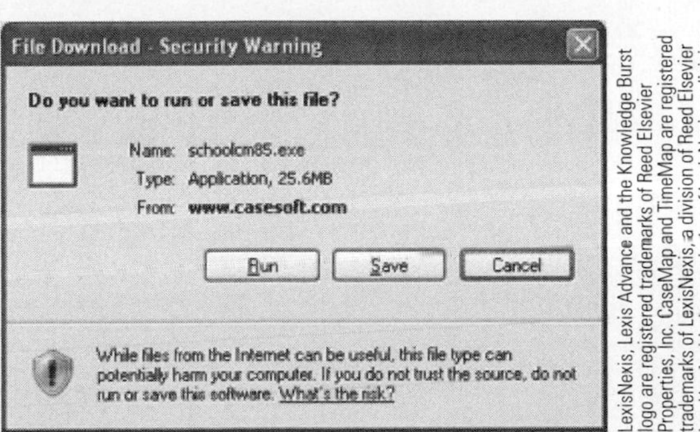

LexisNexis, Lexis Advance and the Knowledge Burst logo are registered trademarks of Reed Elsevier Properties, Inc. CaseMap and TimeMap are registered trademarks of LexisNexis, a division of Reed Elsevier Inc. Used with the permission of LexisNexis, a division of Reed Elsevier Inc.

7. You may get an Internet Explorer – Security Warning. ***Click Run.*** See CaseMap Installation Exhibit 2.

CASEMAP INSTALLATION EXHIBIT 2

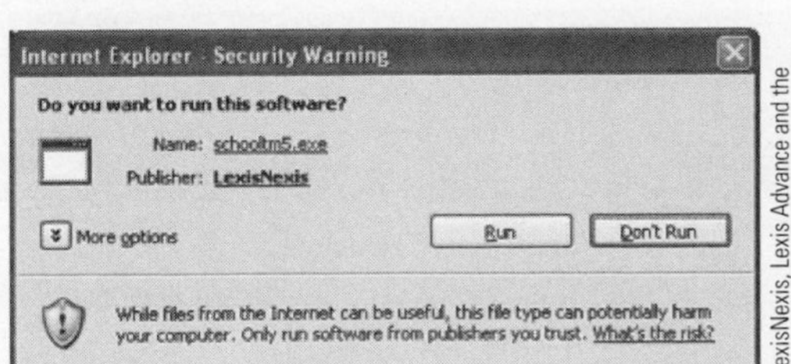

LexisNexis, Lexis Advance and the Knowledge Burst logo are registered trademarks of Reed Elsevier Properties, Inc. CaseMap and TimeMap are registered trademarks of LexisNexis, a division of Reed Elsevier Inc. Used with the permission of LexisNexis, a division of Reed Elsevier Inc.

8. Your screen will look like CaseMap Installation Exhibit 3. ***Click Next.***

CASEMAP INSTALLATION EXHIBIT 3

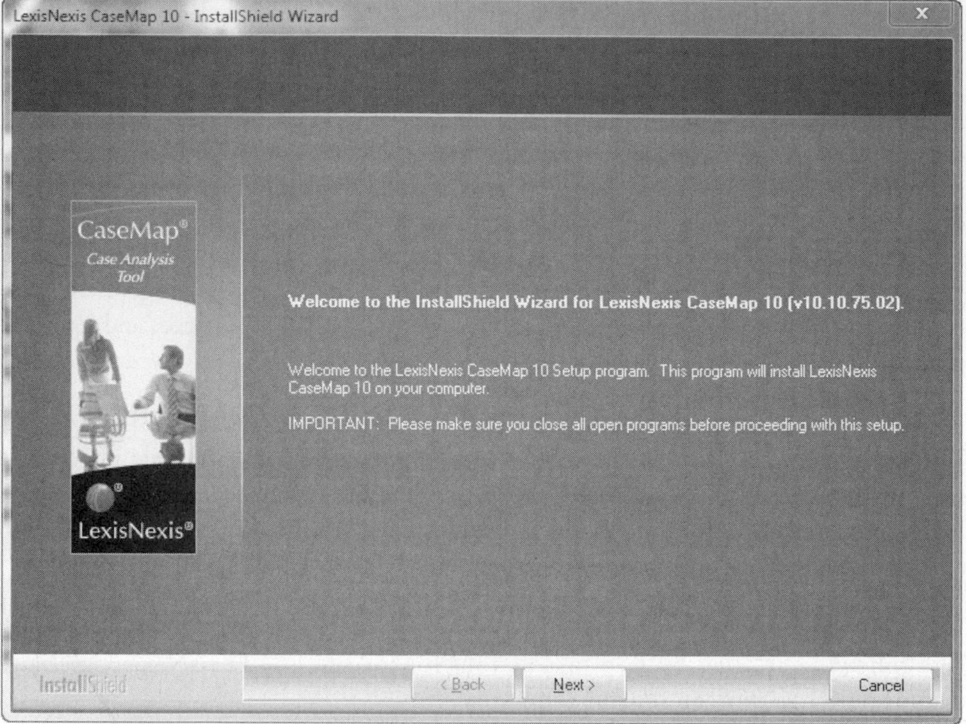

9. Your screen will look like CaseMap Installation Exhibit 4. ***Click Yes*** to agree to the License Agreement.

CASEMAP INSTALLATION EXHIBIT 4

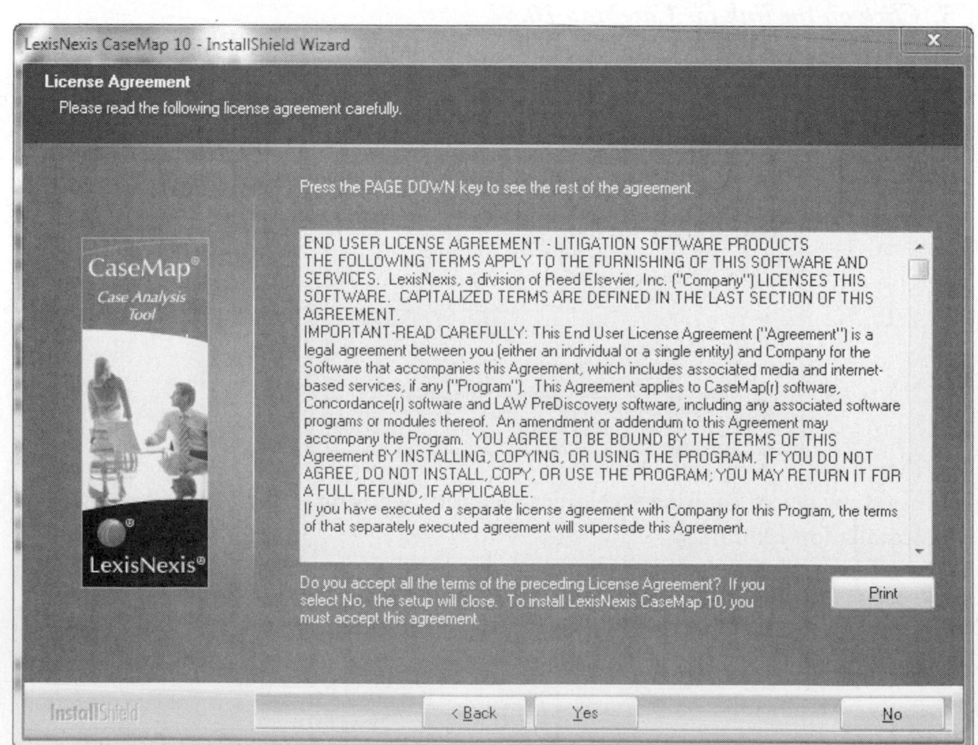

10. Your screen will look like CaseMap Installation Exhibit 5. ***Click Next.***

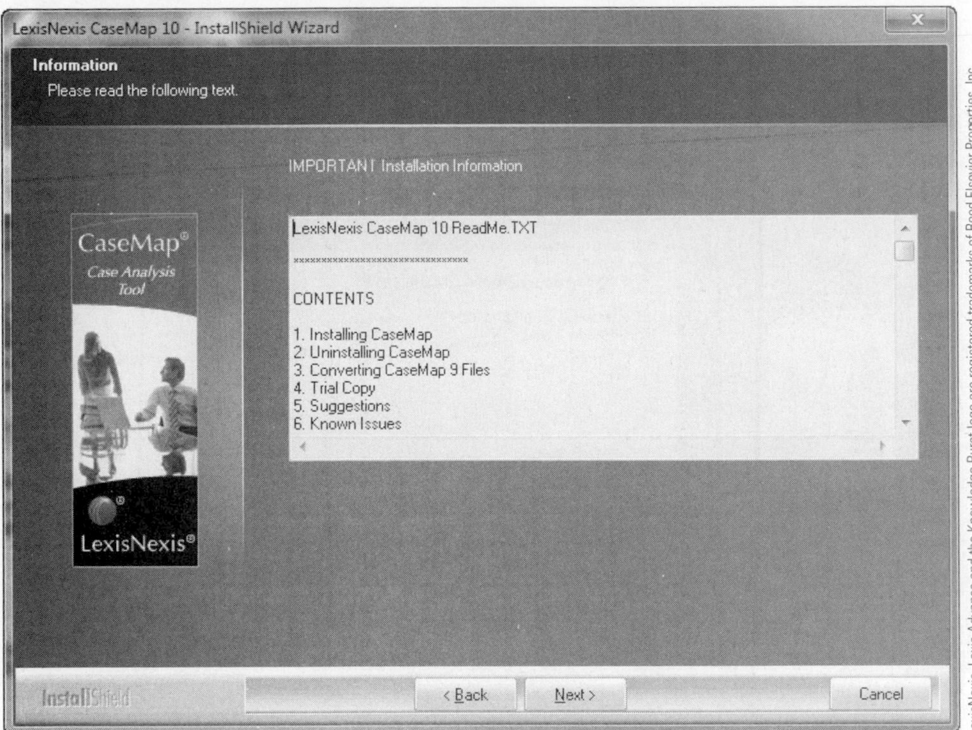

CASEMAP INSTALLATION EXHIBIT 5

11. Your screen will look like CaseMap Installation Exhibit 6. We do not need any of the CaseMap Plug-ins for Microsoft Office, so make sure both boxes are unchecked and ***click Next***.

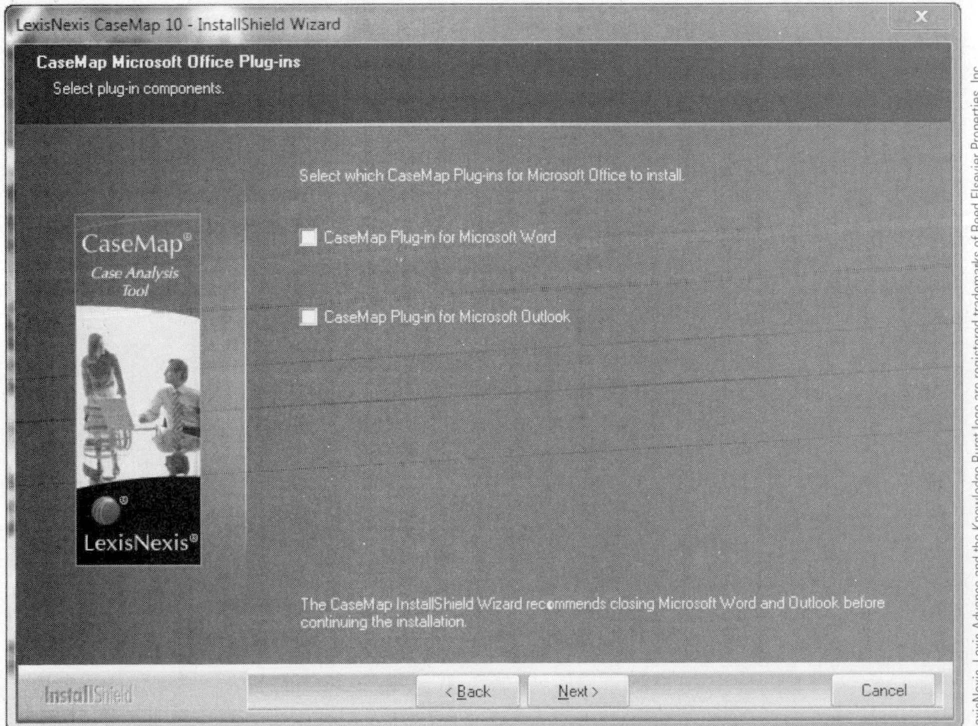

CASEMAP INSTALLATION EXHIBIT 6

12. Your screen will look like CaseMap Installation Exhibit 7. ***Click Next.***

CASEMAP INSTALLATION EXHIBIT 7

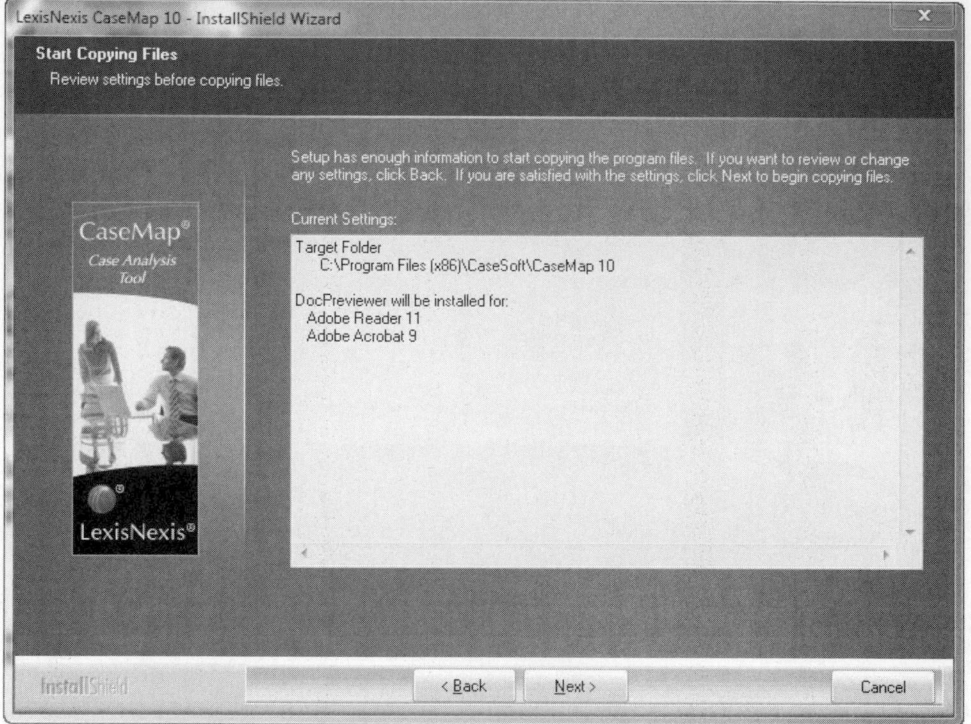

13. Your screen will like CaseMap Installation Exhibit 8. ***Click Next.*** CaseMap will be installed on your computer.

CASEMAP INSTALLATION EXHIBIT 8

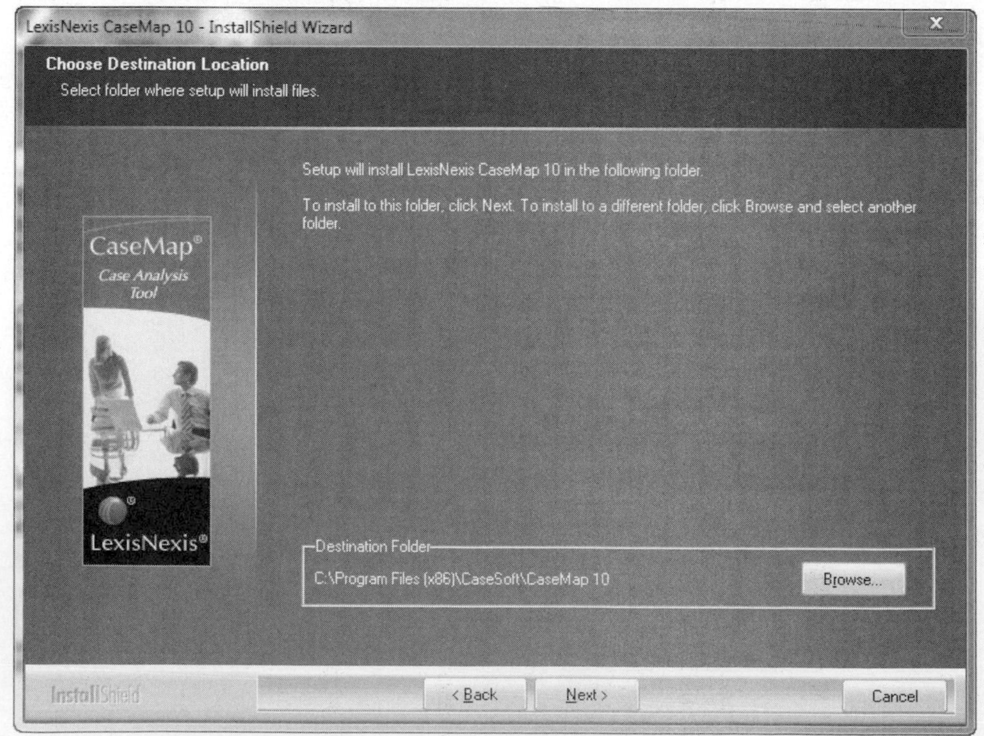

14. Your screen will look like CaseMap Installation Exhibit 9. Make sure the box next to “Yes, I want to launch LexisNexis CaseMap 10 now” is checked to open CaseMap. ***Click Finish.***

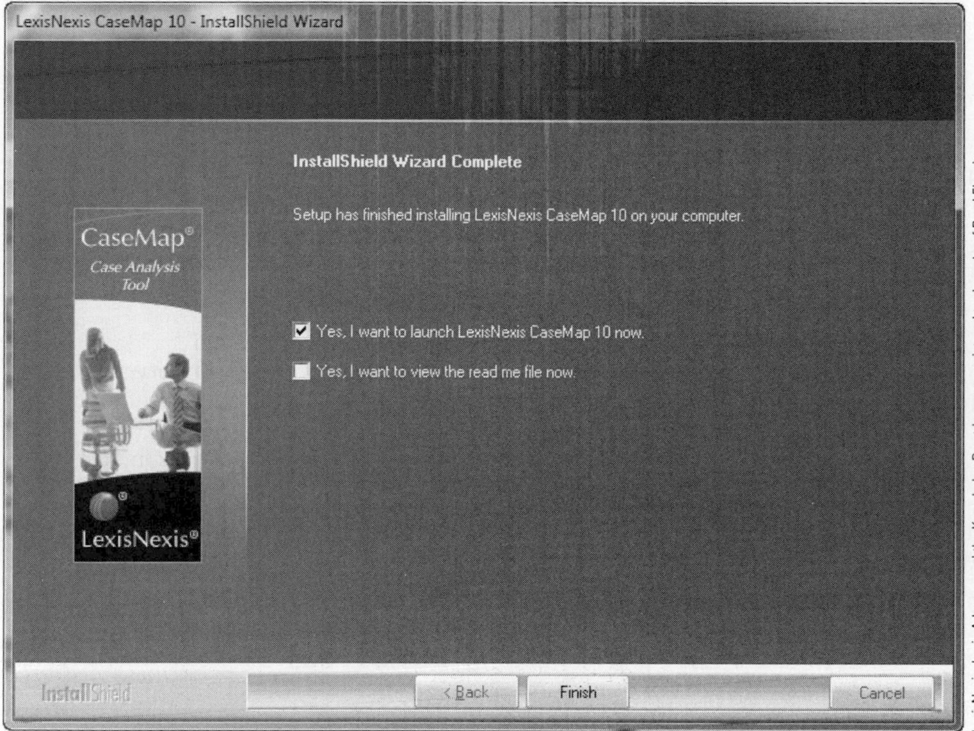

CASEMAP INSTALLATION EXHIBIT 9

15. CaseMap will open and your screen will look like CaseMap Installation Exhibit 10.

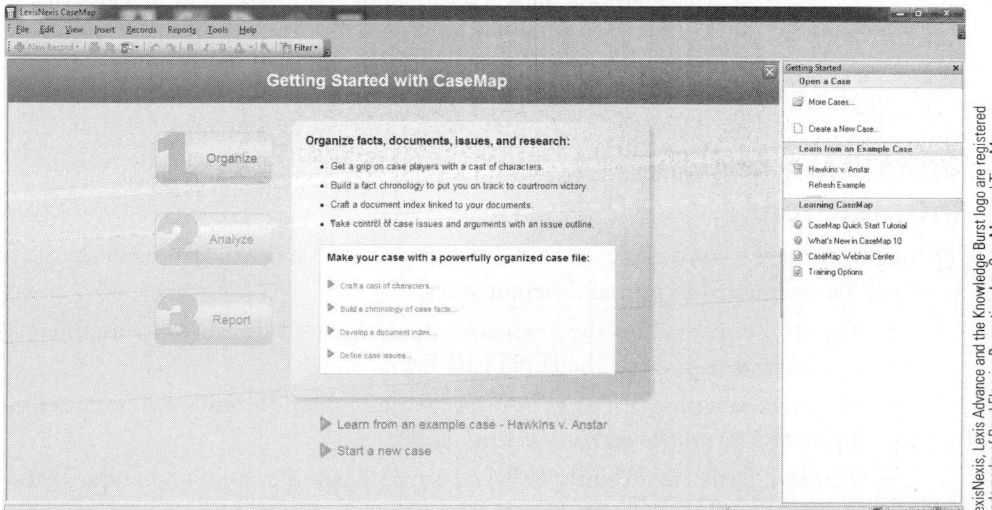

CASEMAP INSTALLATION EXHIBIT 10

IV. INSTALLATION TECHNICAL SUPPORT

If you have problems installing the demonstration version of LexisNexis CaseMap, you will need to contact LexisNexis CaseMap directly at (877) 301-0344.

Number	Lesson Title	Concepts Covered
BASIC LESSONS		
Lesson 1	Introduction to CaseMap	Explanation of and introduction to the CaseMap interface, including the Fact, Object, Issue, Question, and Research spreadsheets.
Lesson 2	Working with the Facts Spreadsheet	Introduction to entering information, fuzzy dating, date stamping, data format options, auto-sizing cell widths, correcting spelling errors, linking files, short names, sorting, linking issues (Link Assistant), Filter by Selection, Filter Tagging, and evaluating facts.
INTERMEDIATE LESSONS		
Lesson 3	Working with the Objects Spreadsheet	Entering objects, executing primary and secondary sorts, expanding and contracting column widths, the meaning of columns in the Objects spreadsheet, the different views in the Objects spreadsheet, and using the Objects spreadsheet in litigation.
Lesson 4	Working with the Issues Spreadsheet	Entering issues, promoting issues, demoting issues, and deleting issues.
Lesson 5	Working with Advanced Features	Using the Viewing CaseWide command, hiding columns, inserting columns, adjusting rows, moving columns, printing and viewing reports, adding objects on the fly, hiding shortcuts, and viewing the detail of a record.
ADVANCED LESSONS		
Lesson 6	Creating a New Case	Setting up/creating a new case in CaseMap and entering new objects, including people, organizations, and documents.
Lesson 7	Entering Issues and Facts in a New Case	Entering new issues in a case, entering new facts in a case, and copying data automatically from one cell to another.
Lesson 8	Using CaseMap for a New Case	Using CaseMap for a new case, including printing reports, viewing case data in a variety of ways, exporting to a PDF file, exporting a summary judgment report to a word processor, using the CaseWide tool, and searching/filtering data.

GETTING STARTED

Introduction

Throughout these lessons and exercises, information you need to type into the software will be designated in several different ways:

- Keys to be pressed on the keyboard are designated in brackets, in all caps, and in bold (e.g., press the **[ENTER]** key).
- Movements with the mouse pointer are designated in bold and italics (e.g., ***point to File on the menu bar and click***).
- Words or letters that should be typed are designated in bold (e.g., type **Training Program**).
- Information that is or should be displayed on your computer screen is shown in bold, with quotation marks (e.g., **"Press ENTER to continue."**).
- Specific menu items and commands are designated with an initial capital letter (e.g., ***click Open***).

OVERVIEW OF CASEMAP

CaseMap is a powerful knowledge management and litigation support tool. CaseMap helps legal professionals organize and understand facts, issues, people, documents, and other information about a case. Using CaseMap, a legal professional can prepare detailed chronologies of the facts and events in a case, a cast of characters (people) in a case, a list of important factual and legal issues in a case, a list of documents in a case, and much more. In addition, CaseMap can link all of this information together. The program is very flexible, and allows you to change views and change how information is sorted "on the fly." CaseMap also allows the legal professional to evaluate the strength of a case, to track what data/information in the case is agreed on by the parties or is disputed (and by whom), and allows the images or text of documents to be attached or linked to information stored in CaseMap.

CaseMap fills a unique niche in the litigation support market. It is not designed to be a full litigation support tool (like Summation iBlaze, which can handle millions of document abstracts, transcripts, full-text documents, etc.). Rather, it is designed to be a strategy/knowledge management tool that helps legal professionals think, prepare, and strategize about their cases. CaseMap is a database program, but looks more like a spreadsheet because it stores data in columns and rows.

The purpose of these exercises is to give you a general introduction to CaseMap and how it is used in litigation. CaseMap is a very popular litigation support program that is used extensively in all types of legal organizations throughout the country. A fully functioning demonstration version of CaseMap is used. The demonstration version of CaseMap includes a sample case, *Hawkins v. Anstar*. This hypothetical case is ready for trial and most of the information about the case has already been entered into CaseMap. In addition, this tutorial includes exercises in which you will create a new file in CaseMap for the sample case of *Richards v. EZ Pest Control.*

HANDS-ON EXERCISES

The *Philip Hawkins v. Anstar Biotech Industries* Case

An overview of the facts of the *Philip Hawkins v. Anstar Biotech Industries* case follows. Philip Hawkins (the plaintiff) was hired to be a sales manager by William Lang, the CEO of Anstar Biotech Industries (the defendant), in early 2003. In late 2003, Hawkins was promoted to vice president of sales. In May 2005, Hawkins received an outstanding performance review from Lang. In June 2005, Lang made the decision to lay off some of the company's staff. In early July 2005, Anstar's second-quarter sales were announced: Sales had dropped by 8 percent. In late July, Hawkins was demoted to the position of sales manager. Hawkins alleges that in August 2005, Lang told him that "old wood must be trimmed back hard." Hawkins claims that this was a reference to him being over the age of 40, and implied that he was "old wood" that must be "trimmed." Hawkins was transferred to another office a few weeks later. In September, Hawkins wrote Lang and complained about the way he was being treated and that the purpose of the layoffs was to eliminate older staff. In November, Anstar laid off 55 employees, including Hawkins, who turned 51 years old that month. Ten days later, Hawkins sued Anstar for age discrimination, wrongful termination, and retaliation. Anstar claims that the layoffs were due to poor sales and were completely lawful. You are acting on behalf of the law firm representing the defendant, Anstar Biotech Industries.

The *Sherry Richards v. EZ Pest Control* Case

Here are the facts of the *Richards v. EZ Pest Control* case: Sherry Richards had a contract with EZ Pest Control to conduct periodic reviews of her house several times a year and to provide preventative pest control maintenance to keep termites out.

John Lincoln of EZ Pest Control came out several times and inspected the house. Nonetheless, Sherry Richards discovered several colonies of termites in her house, and found that massive damage was being done. She called a contractor, Tim Stewart, to look at the house, and he determined that there was damage to the house and that repairs would have to be done as soon as the termites were removed. Sherry Richards is suing EZ Pest Control for breach of contract and negligence. You are acting on behalf of the law firm representing the plaintiff, Sherry Richards.

BASIC LESSONS

LESSON 1: INTRODUCTION TO CASEMAP

This lesson introduces you to the CaseMap litigation support program. It explains basic information about the CaseMap interface, including information about the Fact, Object, Issue, Question, and Research spreadsheets.

Install the CaseMap demonstration version on your computer following the instructions in section I, "Introduction—Read This," and section III, "Installation Instructions." *Note*: The CaseMap demonstration version times out (stops working) **120 days after installation.** It is highly recommended that you do not install the program on your computer until you are ready to complete these Hands-On Exercises.

1. Start Windows. After it has loaded, ***double-click the LexisNexis CaseMap 10 icon on the desktop,*** or ***click the Start button on the Windows desktop, point to Programs or All Programs, point to the LexisNexis CaseMap Suite, then click LexisNexis CaseMap 10.*** LexisNexis CaseMap 10 will then start.
2. When you start CaseMap, you will see a small window in the middle of the screen that says **"CaseMap"** and adds some information about a grace period. ***Click Continue in the "CaseMap" window.*** CaseMap will then start, with several options listed to the right of the screen.
3. Your screen should now look similar to CaseMap Exhibit 1. The Getting Started task pane should be displayed on the right side of the screen. ***Under Learn from an Example Case, click* Hawkins v. Anstar.**

CASEMAP EXHIBIT 1

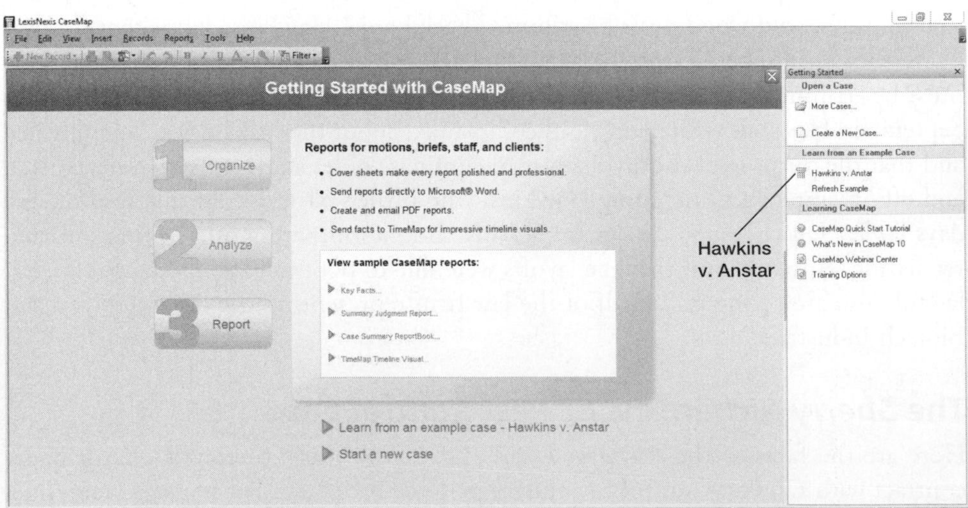

4. The "Case Log On" window should now be displayed. ***Click the down arrow icon to the right of Staff Member: Chris Attorney.*** A drop-down list should now be displayed with the name of several staff members. This is actually a very useful function in CaseMap. Using a network, many staff members can access a CaseMap case/database. In addition, because each staff member must log in with his or her own name, CaseMap can track the new information that has been entered since each staff member logged in. Using a feature called What's New, a staff member can get a summary of what new information has been entered into CaseMap since she or he last logged in.
5. ***Click Dave Paralegal, then click OK.***
6. The CaseMap Fact spreadsheet for the *Hawkins* case should now be displayed (see CaseMap Exhibit 2). CaseMap uses a series of spreadsheets to organize a case. The primary (Favorite) spreadsheets are Facts, All Objects, Persons, Documents, and Issues. CaseMap refers to these screens as spreadsheets because it uses an interface that has rows and columns, and thus looks like a spreadsheet.
7. Each of the five Favorite spreadsheets tracks different data about a case. The Fact spreadsheet allows you to build a chronology of case facts. The Fact spreadsheet contains separate facts about the *Hawkins v. Anstar Biotech Industries* case.
8. ***Click the All Objects icon to the left of the screen under the Case Shortcuts > Favorites heading.*** Your screen should now look like CaseMap Exhibit 3.
9. The Objects spreadsheet tracks a number of items, including people (this allows you to create a cast of characters in a case), documents (this allows you to create a document abstract database and document index), organizations (to track the different organizations/parties in a case), and pleadings (to track pleadings in a case), as well as other information (see CaseMap Exhibit 3). You can also attach document images to any information or record in the Objects spreadsheet. In the Objects spreadsheet, you can see all of the objects (notice in CaseMap Exhibit 3 that you can see Person, Organization, and Document), or you can select another view and see just one specific type of object, such as all Persons or all Documents.

CASEMAP EXHIBIT 2

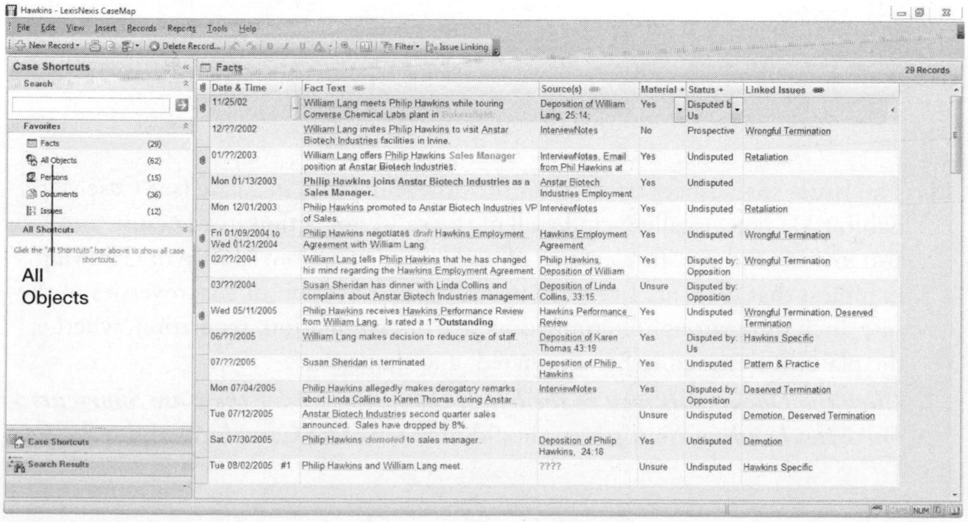

Hawkins - LexisNexis CaseMap

Facts — 29 Records

Date & Time	Fact Text	Source(s)	Material	Status	Linked Issues
11/25/02	William Lang meets Philip Hawkins while touring Converse Chemical Labs plant in Bakersfield.	Deposition of William Lang, 25:14;	Yes	Disputed by Us	
12/??/2002	William Lang invites Philip Hawkins to visit Anstar Biotech Industries facilities in Irvine.	InterviewNotes	No	Prospective	Wrongful Termination
01/??/2003	William Lang offers Philip Hawkins Sales Manager position at Anstar Biotech Industries.	InterviewNotes, Email from Phil Hawkins at	Yes	Undisputed	Retaliation
Mon 01/13/2003	**Philip Hawkins joins Anstar Biotech Industries as a Sales Manager.**	Anstar Biotech Industries Employment	Yes	Undisputed	
Mon 12/01/2003	Philip Hawkins promoted to Anstar Biotech Industries VP of Sales.	InterviewNotes	Yes	Undisputed	Retaliation
Fri 01/09/2004 to Wed 01/21/2004	Philip Hawkins negotiates *draft* Hawkins Employment Agreement with William Lang.	Hawkins Employment Agreement	Yes	Undisputed	Wrongful Termination
02/??/2004	William Lang tells Philip Hawkins that he has changed his mind regarding the Hawkins Employment Agreement.	Philip Hawkins, Deposition of William	Yes	Disputed by: Opposition	Wrongful Termination
03/??/2004	Susan Sheridan has dinner with Linda Collins and complains about Anstar Biotech Industries management.	Deposition of Linda Collins, 33:15.	Unsure	Disputed by: Opposition	
Wed 05/11/2005	Philip Hawkins receives Hawkins Performance Review from William Lang. Is rated a 1 "**Outstanding**	Hawkins Performance Review	Yes	Undisputed	Wrongful Termination, Deserved Termination
06/??/2005	William Lang makes decision to reduce size of staff.	Deposition of Karen Thomas 43:19	Yes	Disputed by: Us	Hawkins Specific
07/??/2005	Susan Sheridan is terminated.	Deposition of Philip Hawkins	Yes	Undisputed	Pattern & Practice
Mon 07/04/2005	Philip Hawkins allegedly makes derogatory remarks about Linda Collins to Karen Thomas during Anstar	InterviewNotes	Yes	Disputed by: Opposition	Deserved Termination
Tue 07/12/2005	Anstar Biotech Industries second quarter sales announced. Sales have dropped by 8%.		Unsure	Undisputed	Demotion, Deserved Termination
Sat 07/30/2005	Philip Hawkins *demoted* to sales manager.	Deposition of Philip Hawkins, 24:18	Yes	Undisputed	Demotion
Tue 08/02/2005 #1	Philip Hawkins and William Lang meet.	????	Unsure	Undisputed	Hawkins Specific

All Objects

CASEMAP EXHIBIT 3

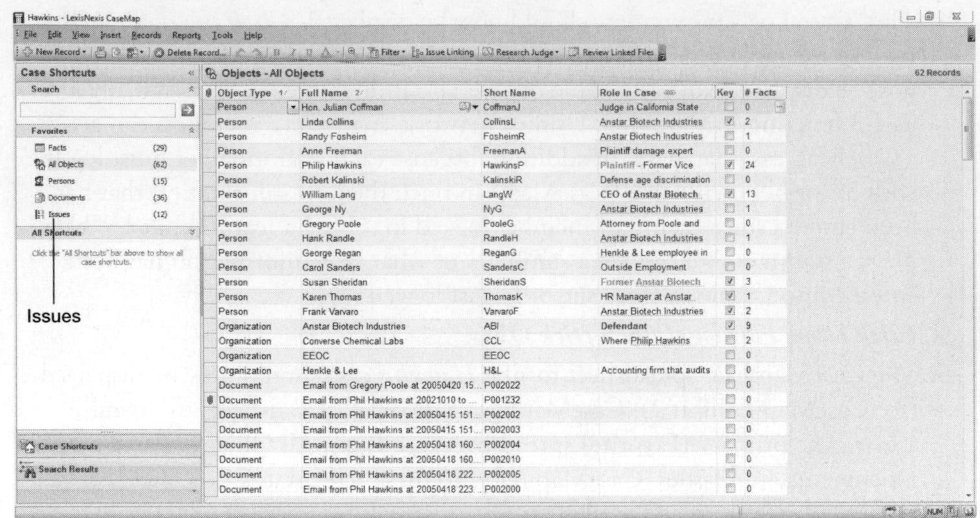

10. ***Click the Issues icon to the left of the screen under the Case Shortcuts > Favorites heading.*** Your screen should now look like CaseMap Exhibit 4.

CASEMAP EXHIBIT 4

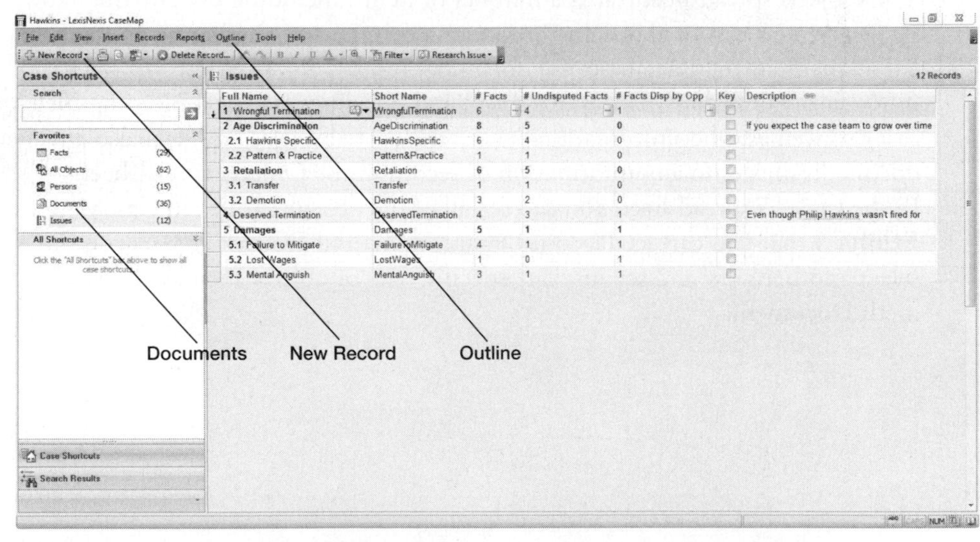

11. The Issues spreadsheet tracks all of the different issues in a case (see CaseMap Exhibit 4). This usually includes all of the causes of action in a lawsuit, and may also include the specific elements of each cause of action. Notice in CaseMap Exhibit 4 that there are five main issues/causes of action or controversies in the case, including wrongful termination, age discrimination, retaliation, whether the plaintiff deserved to be terminated, and damages.
12. ***Click the Documents icon to the left of the screen under the Case Shortcuts > Favorites heading.*** Your screen should now look like CaseMap Exhibit 5.

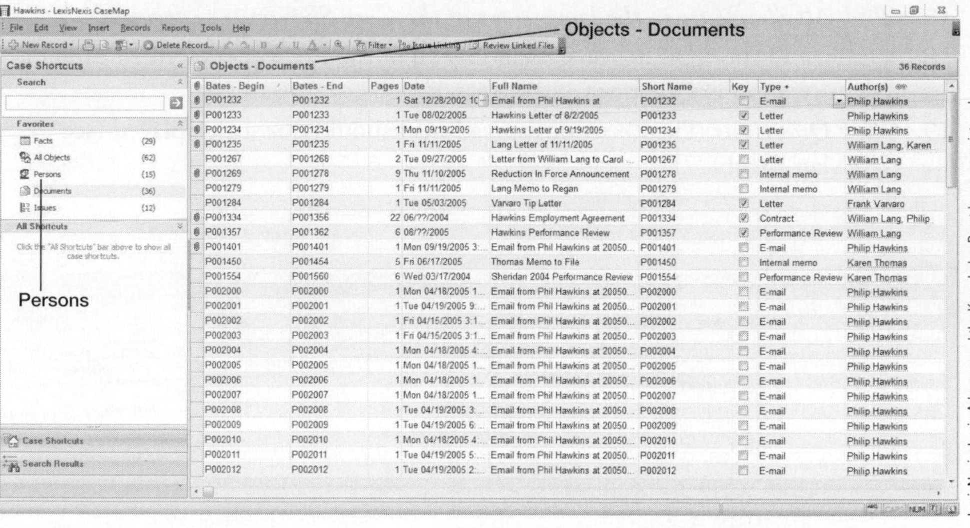

CASEMAP EXHIBIT 5

13. Notice that the heading in CaseMap Exhibit 5 says **"Objects – Documents."** These are the same documents listed previously in the All Objects spreadsheet, but in this screen the information is more complete and other objects (such as people and organizations) are not shown.
14. ***Click the Persons icon to the left of the screen under the Case Shortcuts > Favorites heading.*** Your screen should now look like CaseMap Exhibit 6.
15. The Persons spreadsheet tracks all of the different persons in a case (see CaseMap Exhibit 6). Notice that this spreadsheet includes headings for each person's full names, short names, the person's role in the case, and the type of person (fact witness, expert witness, etc.). It also links the persons to relevant facts and documents.
16. There are two other spreadsheets in CaseMap that are not listed in the Case Shortcuts Favorites.

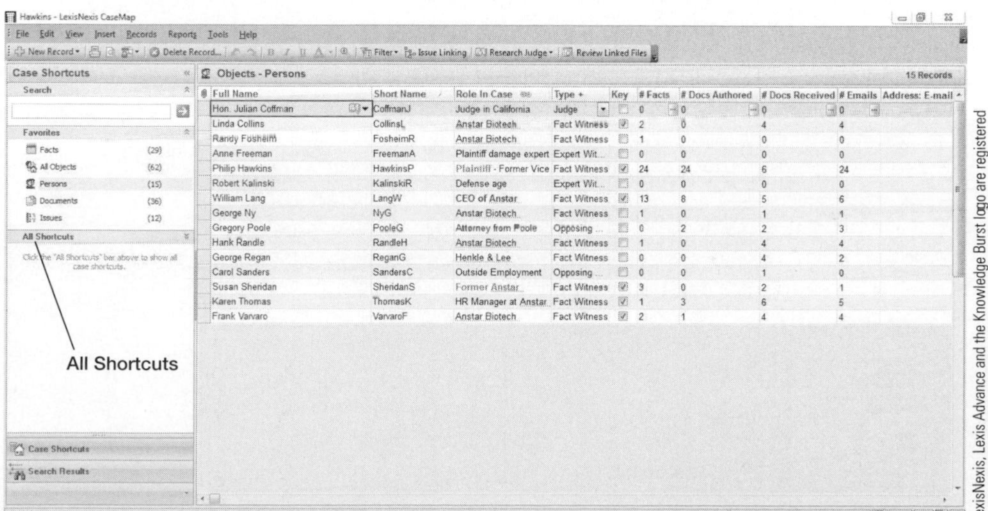

CASEMAP EXHIBIT 6

17. ***Click All Shortcuts in the lower part of the Case Shortcuts task pane.***
18. A full list of shortcuts appears, including all of the Favorites described earlier as well as two more, Questions and Research.
19. ***Click Questions.*** The Questions spreadsheet should now be displayed (see CaseMap Exhibit 7).

CASEMAP EXHIBIT 7

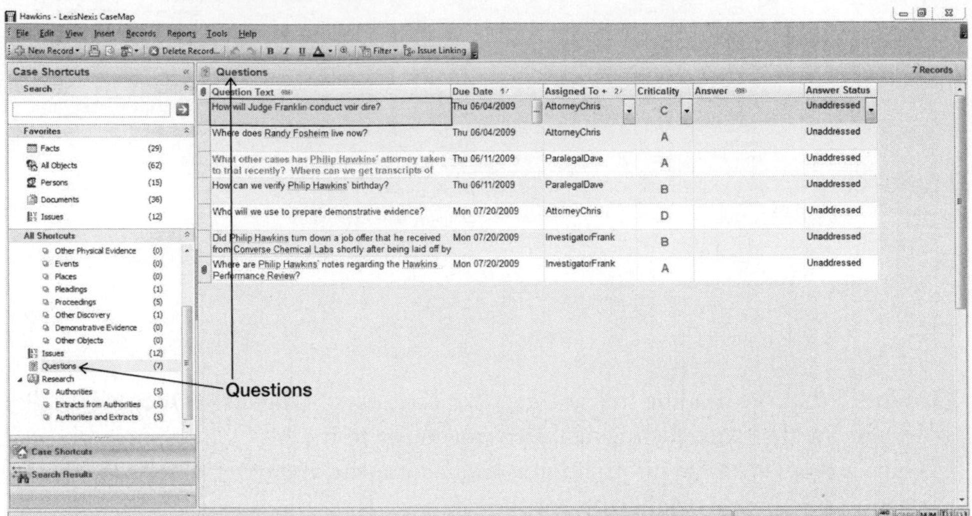

20. The Questions spreadsheet allows you to enter questions that you need to answer, gives you the opportunity to assign the responsibility for finding the answer to the question, allows you to assign a due date for completion of that task, allows you to assign the degree of criticality (importance), and provides a place to put the answer to the question (see CaseMap Exhibit 7). The Questions spreadsheet is somewhat similar to a things-to-do list, and helps to make sure that you discover everything you need to know about a case.
21. Notice that the Research icon has three subelements: Authorities, Extracts from Authorities, and Authorities and Extracts. ***Click Authorities.*** The Research – Authorities spreadsheet should now be displayed (see CaseMap Exhibit 8).

CASEMAP EXHIBIT 8

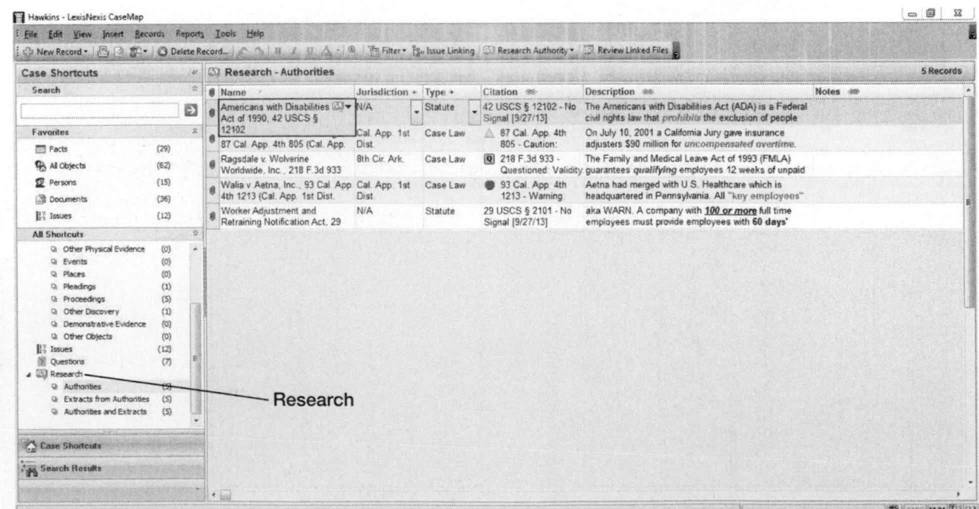

22. The Research – Authorities spreadsheet allows you to track legal citations and legal references relevant to your case. CaseMap Exhibit 8 shows the Research – Authorities spreadsheet, which lists the major statutes and cases involved in the *Hawkins* case.
23. ***Click Extracts from Authorities.***
24. ***Click in the second column of the first row.*** Your screen should now look similar to CaseMap Exhibit 9.

CASEMAP EXHIBIT 9

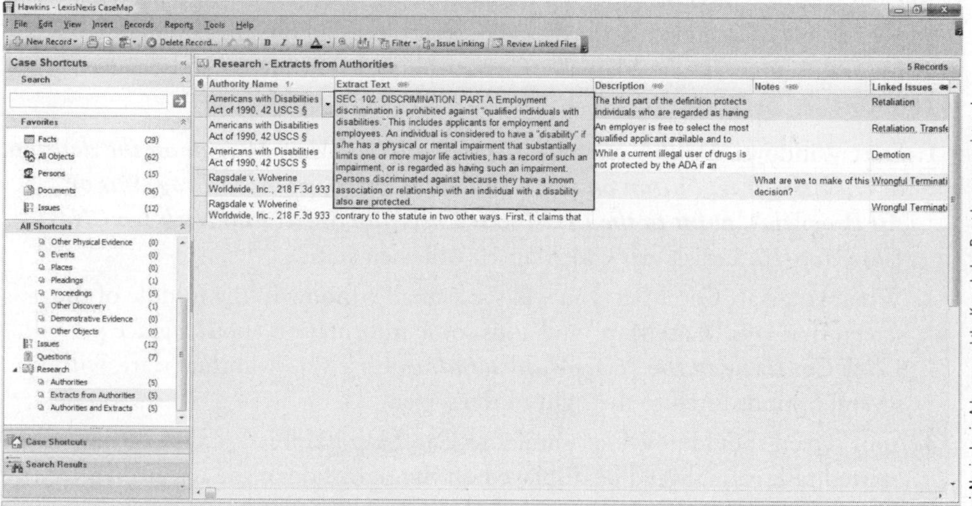

25. Notice that this is a long quote from Section 102, Part A of the Americans with Disabilities Act. The Extracts from Authorities option is where you can store long sections from authorities. It is a subelement of the Research spreadsheet that has the ability to display in-depth excerpts, quotations, and other more detailed information from other cases, statutes, and so on. You can also link the research to the specific legal issues in the Issues spreadsheet.
26. ***Click Authorities and Extracts.*** Your screen should look like CaseMap Exhibit 10. Notice that the screen now splits to show a research filter on top and the list of authorities below. The Authority Filter feature allows you to search more efficiently.

CASEMAP EXHIBIT 10

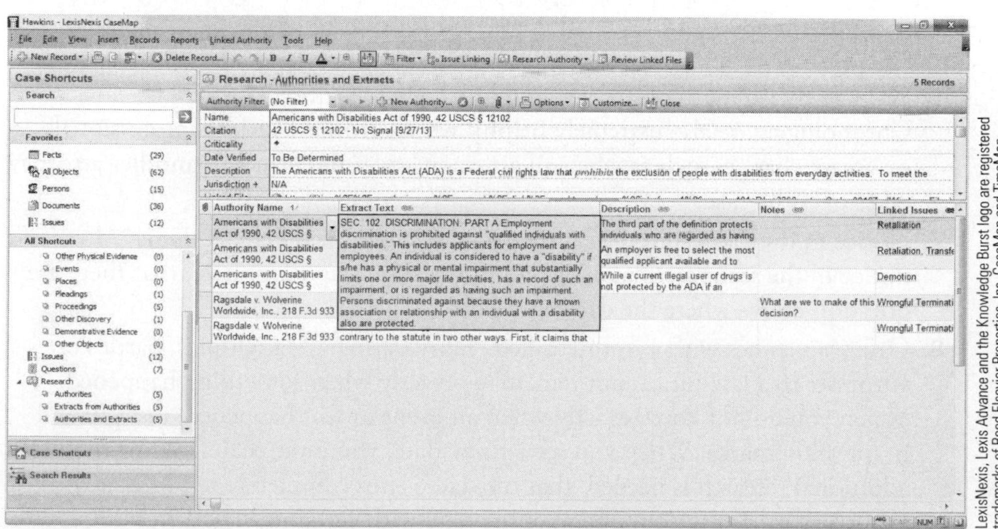

27. ***Click the Facts icon*** to go back to the Facts spreadsheet.

This concludes Lesson 1. To exit CaseMap, ***click File on the menu bar, then click Exit,*** or go to Lesson 2.

LESSON 2: WORKING WITH THE FACTS SPREADSHEET

This lesson introduces you to the CaseMap Facts spreadsheet, including how to enter information in CaseMap. This lesson also provides information about a variety of CaseMap features, including fuzzy dating, date stamping, data format options, auto-sizing cell widths, correcting spelling errors, linking files, short names, sorting, linking issues (Link Assistant), filtering by Selection, filter tagging, and evaluating facts.

If you did not exit CaseMap after Lesson 1, then skip Steps 1–5 and go directly to Step 6.

1. Start Windows. ***Double-click the LexisNexis CaseMap 10 icon on the desktop,*** or ***click the Start button on the Windows desktop, point to Programs or All Programs, point to the LexisNexis CaseMap Suite, and click LexisNexis CaseMap 10.*** LexisNexis CaseMap 10 will then start.
2. When you start CaseMap, you will see a small window in the middle of the screen that says **"CaseMap"** and adds some information about a grace period. ***Click Continue in the "CaseMap" window.*** CaseMap will then start, with several options listed to the right of the screen.
3. Your screen should now look similar to CaseMap Exhibit 1. The Getting Started task pane should be displayed on the right side of the screen. ***Under Learn from an Example Case, click*** **Hawkins v. Anstar.**
4. The "Case Log On" window should now be displayed. ***Click the down arrow icon to the right of Staff Member: Chris Attorney. Click Dave Paralegal and then click OK.***
5. CaseMap should put you back at the last spreadsheet you were using when you exited the program. Thus, the Facts spreadsheet for the *Hawkins* case should be displayed.
6. As indicated previously, the Facts spreadsheet gives you a chronology of a case. Chronologies are very useful when litigating a case. They are a great tool for refreshing the recollection of the legal professionals who are assigned to a case (particularly if it has been a while since they worked on that particular case). They are useful for sharing knowledge with everyone on the legal team, working with clients, aiding in preparation of depositions, preparing summary judgment motions, and preparing for trial. The chronologies that CaseMap can produce are particularly helpful because they also help a legal professional evaluate the strength of the case and link facts to central issues in the case. Chronologies are also extremely helpful when attorneys or legal professionals on a case change, such as when an attorney leaves the firm and another attorney takes over the case.
7. Notice in the Facts spreadsheet that the first column is Date & Time. Also, notice in the second entry, 12/??/2002 (see CaseMap Exhibit 2), that there are question marks where the day should be.
8. CaseMap comes with a feature called "fuzzy dating." Many times, parties or witnesses to a lawsuit cannot remember exactly when something happened. When you do not know exactly when an event or fact happened, just put in question marks. When you see a fuzzy date, you immediately know that additional research is needed, that the date is not completely set, or that the party or witness cannot remember the date with certainty. The 12/??/2002 date

means that the event occurred sometime during the month of December 2002. CaseMap reads the date as 12/01/02 for the purpose of sorting by date.

9. ***Click in the third record on the date 01/??/2003.*** Notice that there is a gray box to the right of the date in the Date and Time field (see CaseMap Exhibit 11). This is called the Date Stamper.
10. ***Click the gray Date Stamper box next to the date 01/??/2003 in the third record*** (see CaseMap Exhibit 11).
11. You should now see the "Date Stamper (Date & Time)" window displayed (see CaseMap Exhibit 11). Notice that a calendar is displayed. Using the Date Stamper, you can change the date interactively while you view the calendar. ***Click Cancel in the "Date Stamper" window.***
12. In the fourth record from the top in the Date & Time column, Mon 01/13/2003, notice that the day of the week, **"Mon,"** is shown. See CaseMap Exhibit 11. It is sometimes helpful to know the day of the week on which a particular event occurred. CaseMap does this automatically for you. When you enter a date (e.g., 01/13/2003), CaseMap automatically calculates and enters the day of the week for you if that is how the Date & Time column has been configured.
13. You can change how the Date & Time column is formatted. ***Click Tools on the menu bar, then click Options.*** See CaseMap Exhibit 11. The "Options" window should now be displayed. ***Click the Date tab.***
14. ***Click the down arrow just to the right of Style: MM/dd/yyyy.*** Notice that many different date formatting options are available.
15. ***Click the first style, MM/dd/yyyy.***
16. Notice under Style that there is a check mark in the box next to **"Show Day of Week."** If you did not want CaseMap to show the day of the week in the Date & Time column, you could click in that check box to turn the feature off.
17. ***Click Cancel on the Options menu.***
18. Notice in the sixth record from the top that a date range is listed (**"Fri 01/09/2004 to Wed 01/21/2004"**). See CaseMap Exhibit 11. CaseMap is very flexible and can even handle date ranges. Date ranges are sorted by the first date in the range. This is a very useful feature because witnesses often do not remember exact dates of events that happened over several days, though they may be able to narrow it down to a certain range of dates.

HANDS-ON EXERCISES

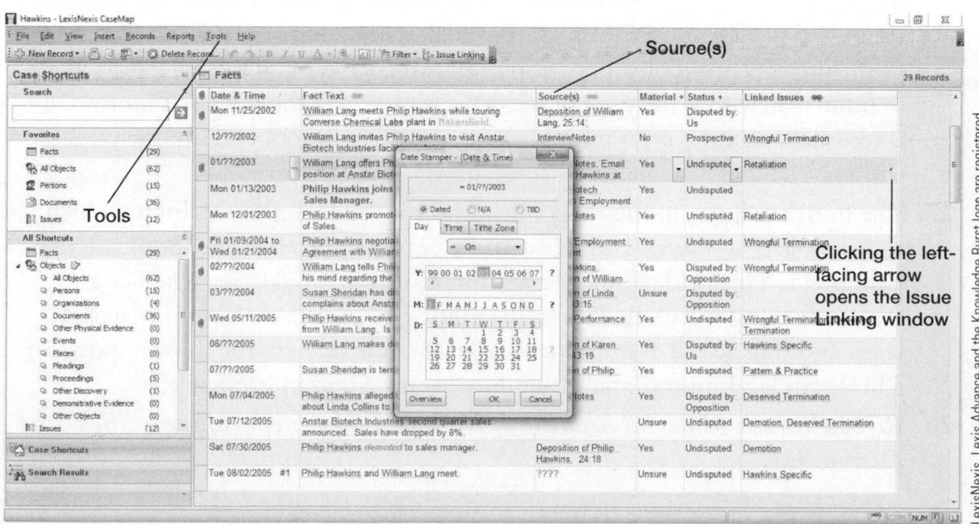

CASEMAP EXHIBIT 11

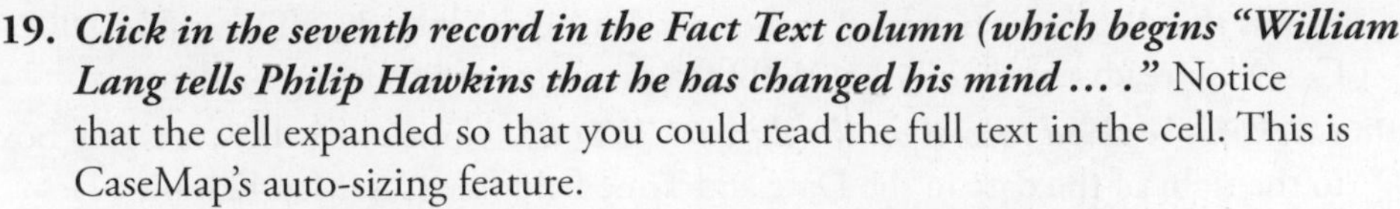

19. ***Click in the seventh record in the Fact Text column (which begins "William Lang tells Philip Hawkins that he has changed his mind . . . ."*** Notice that the cell expanded so that you could read the full text in the cell. This is CaseMap's auto-sizing feature.
20. ***Click on any other cell.*** The expanded cell will collapse back to its normal size.
21. ***Click the first record from the top*** **"William Lang meets Philip Hawkins while touring Converse Chemical Labs plant in Bakersfield."** See CaseMap Exhibit 11. Notice that there is a paper clip just to the left of the date 11/25/02. The paper clip means that there is a file linked to this fact.
22. ***Click the paper-clip icon just to the left of 11/25/02 in the first record from the top. Then click on the P001401 file (this is a PDF file).*** As long as you have Adobe Reader or some other PDF file reader, you should see an email from Philip Hawkins to William Lang.

23. ***Click the Close icon*** (a red box with a white X) ***in the "P001401" window.***
24. Notice in the first record from the top in the Fact Text column, where it says "William Lang meets Philip Hawkins . . ." that "William Lang," "Philip Hawkins," and "Converse Chemical Labs" have small dotted lines under them. The dotted lines mean that these entities are in the database. Lang and Hawkins are listed as persons and Converse Chemical Labs is listed as an organization.
25. ***Click in the first record from the top in the Fact Text column where it says*** **"William Lang meets Philip Hawkins . . . ."** Notice that once you click on the cell, it says **"LangW meets HawkinsP while touring CCL plant in Bakersfield."** LangW, Hawkins P, and CCL are short names for William Lang, Philip Hawkins, and Converse Chemical Labs. Short names are critical in a database because there are many times in a case when someone is referred to by a nickname, a first name but no last name, only by initials, and so on. If one person was referred to in all of these different ways, it would be difficult to do searches that were even close to exhaustive. The Short names feature standardizes names (short names can actually apply to any Object in CaseMap) so that all names referring to the same person are entered exactly the same.
26. Notice that the third column in the Facts spreadsheet is Source(s). See CaseMap Exhibit 11. The Sources column allows you to enter notes about where the information came from. In the first record from the top in the Sources column, it says **"Deposition of William Lang, 25:14"**; this is a reference to that deposition at page 25, line 14. This is very important because in a summary judgment motion, for example, you must include a citation for every fact submitted in the motion. Also, during trial, if a witness contradicts what he or she previously said in a deposition, the attorney can use this information to immediately find the page in the deposition where the prior testimony is recorded, read the prior testimony from the deposition, and impeach the witness.
27. The fourth column in the Facts spreadsheet is the Material + column, which classifies facts as *material*, or particularly important, to the case. See CaseMap Exhibit 11. This field allows a legal professional to quickly see whether a specific fact is particularly important to the case. You can also sort material facts, and thus see all at once the facts in the case that are the most important. This keeps legal professionals from forgetting important evidence.
28. ***Right-click the Material heading at the top of the fourth column. Click Sort Descending.***

29. Notice that all of the facts that have "Yes" in the Material + column have now been sorted and are at the top of the screen. This allows you to see all of the material facts in the case at one time. When you have hundreds of facts in a case, this feature can be very helpful.
30. To sort the facts by date (the way it was before the sort on material facts), ***right-click the word Date & Time at the top of the first column, then click Sort Ascending.*** Notice that the Fact spreadsheet is now sorted the way it was previously.
31. Look carefully at the Date & Time header. Notice that there is a small, faint outline of a triangle pointing up. Whenever you see such a triangle in a CaseMap column header, it means that column is being used to sort the spreadsheet. In addition, a triangle pointing up means that the sort is ascending (A to Z), whereas a triangle pointing down means the sort is descending (Z to A).
32. The fifth column in the Facts spreadsheet is headed Status +. See CaseMap Exhibit 11. ***Click the word Undisputed in the third record from the top*** **("01/??/2003 – William Lang offers Philip Hawkins Sales Manager position ...")** ***in the Status + column. Click the down arrow next to Undisputed.*** A list of options is now displayed.
33. The list of options allows you to identify whether the fact is undisputed, disputed by opposition, disputed by us, unsure, or prospective. A *prospective fact* is one that you would like to be true, but requires further investigation.
34. ***Click Undisputed*** to leave the status unchanged and to close the option list.
35. The sixth column in the Facts spreadsheet is the Linked Issues column. See CaseMap Exhibit 11. This is where you can connect (or link) a specific fact to an issue. This is very helpful when you are making legal arguments about specific legal causes of action or legal issues, because you can display only the facts that are related to the legal issue you are addressing.
36. ***Click the third record from the top*** **("01/??/2003 — William Lang offers Philip Hawkins Sales Manager position ...")** ***in the Linked Issues column.***
37. ***Click the left-facing arrow in the selected cell (see CaseMap Exhibit 11).*** The "Issue Linking" window opens to the right of the screen (see CaseMap Exhibit 12). To delete the current issue, click on another issue. To add another issue, click Add a new Issue at the top of the "Issue Linking" window.
38. ***Click on Retaliation*** to keep the selection. ***Click the small x at the upper right corner of the "Issues Linking" window*** to close this window.
39. Suppose, for example, that you are writing a summary judgment motion and you would like to see all of the facts regarding the issue of retaliation.
40. ***Point to the word Retaliation in the third record and right-click anywhere in that cell. Then, click the Filter by Selection icon.*** (It looks like a funnel with a lightning bolt next to it.)
41. A small LexisNexis CaseMap window should appear, stating that the issue you selected has subissues and asking whether you want to include the subissues in the search. ***Click No.*** Notice that only the facts with "retaliation" somewhere in the Linked Issues are listed.
42. To cancel the filter, ***click the Cancel icon at the top right corner of the screen.***
43. The screen should now return to what it looked like before you engaged the filter. Using the Filter by Selection tool, you can click a cell and right-click the cell and select Filter by Selection, and CaseMap will then search for the item in the cell you selected.

CASEMAP EXHIBIT 12

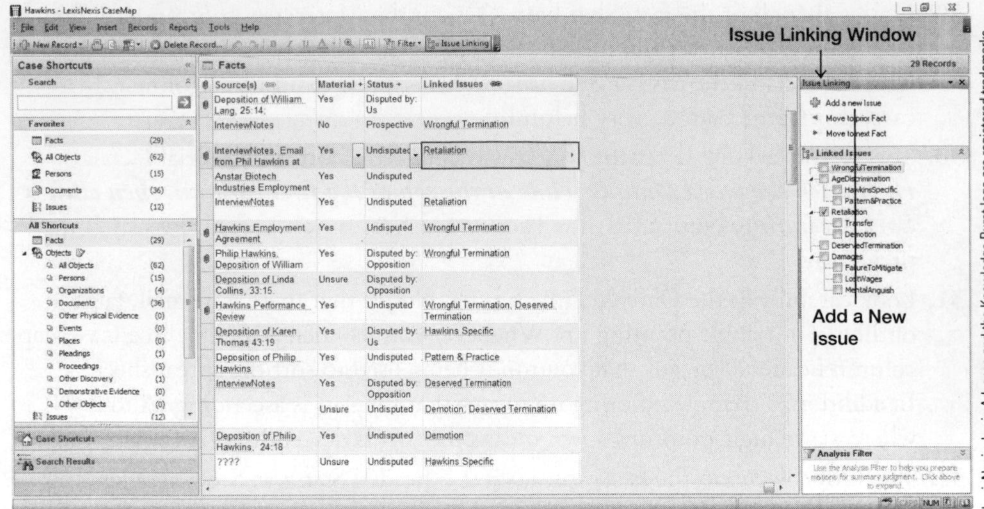

44. Now, suppose that you are writing a summary judgment motion and you want to see all of the facts in chronological order, but you would like the undisputed facts tagged or marked so you can easily identify them.
45. ***Click the word Undisputed in the third record from the top*** **("William Lang offers Philip Hawkins Sales Manager position …")** ***in the fifth column*** (Status +).
46. ***Right-click the same cell and select Tag by Selection.*** Notice in the far left column that there are now red vertical ovals ("tags") next to every cell that has Undisputed in the Status + column.
47. To cancel the tag, ***click Cancel.***
48. The tags should now have disappeared.

This concludes Lesson 2. To exit CaseMap, ***click File on the menu bar, then click Exit, then click OK*** to acknowledge the need to back up your files (if it asks), or go to Lesson 3.

INTERMEDIATE LESSONS

LESSON 3: WORKING WITH THE OBJECTS SPREADSHEET

This lesson introduces you to the CaseMap Objects spreadsheet. It covers entering objects, executing primary and secondary sorts, expanding and contracting column widths; reviews what the columns mean in the Objects spreadsheet; explains the different views in the Objects spreadsheet; and gives tips on how to use the Objects spreadsheet to its full potential.

If you did not exit CaseMap after Lesson 2, then skip Steps 1–5 and go directly to Step 6.

1. Start Windows. ***Double-click on the LexisNexis CaseMap 10 icon on the desktop,*** or ***click the Start button on the Windows desktop, point to Programs***

or All Programs, point to the LexisNexis CaseMap Suite, and point and click on LexisNexis CaseMap 10. LexisNexis CaseMap 10 will then start.

2. When you start CaseMap, you will see a small window in the middle of the screen that says **"CaseMap"** and adds some information about a grace period. ***Click Continue in the "CaseMap" window.*** CaseMap will then start, with several options listed to the right of the screen.
3. Your screen should now look similar to CaseMap Exhibit 1. The Getting Started task pane should be displayed on the right side of the screen. ***Under Learn from an Example Case, click* Hawkins v. Anstar**.
4. The "Case Log On" window should now be displayed. ***Click the down arrow icon to the right of Staff Member: Chris Attorney. Click Dave Paralegal, then click OK.***
5. CaseMap should put you back at the last spreadsheet you were using when you exited the program. Thus, the Facts spreadsheet for the *Hawkins* case should be displayed.
6. ***Click the All Objects icon on the left side of the screen under Case Shortcuts > Favorites.***
7. Notice, in the header of the Object Type column, that there is a **"1"** next to a triangle pointing up. Also notice that in the header of the Full Name column, there is a **"2"** next to a triangle pointing up. As indicated previously, the triangle shows which column is being used to sort the spreadsheet, and the direction of the triangle (pointing up) means that it is an ascending sort. The **"1"** indicates the primary sort column and the **"2"** indicates the secondary sort column. CaseMap first sorts the spreadsheet by object (not alphabetically, however; CaseMap prioritizes objects based on Persons first, then Organizations, then Documents, etc.) and then sorts the spreadsheet by the Full Name field. By right-clicking in the header of any column, you can sort a spreadsheet by that column; however, if you want to do a primary and secondary sort, you must use a menu option.
8. ***Click Records in the menu bar, click Sort, then click Advanced Sort.*** The "Advanced Sort: Object" window is now displayed. Notice that in the Sort By field it says **"Object Type."** Under that, it says **"Then By,"** and **"Full Name."** Under that, it says **"Then By"** and displays a drop-down menu with the option to choose a key or short name. Thus, using the Advanced Sort option, you can create primary, secondary, and even tertiary sorts. Notice that if you did not have a secondary sort, the Object Types would be sorted, but there would be no order beyond that.
9. ***Click Cancel in the "Advanced Sort: Objects" window.***
10. Notice the title **"Objects – All Objects"** just under the toolbar. Also, notice in the first column of the spreadsheet (Object type), that there are several different kinds of object types, including Person, Organization, Document, and others.
11. CaseMap is currently combining all of the objects into one view. This is the All Objects view. However, you can change this so that you see only Persons, or Organizations, or another object type. The reason for doing this is that additional fields are shown when you do.

12. For example, notice on your screen that no Type field is shown for the object type (e.g., whether the witness is a fact witness or an expert witness). When you view only the Persons object list, you will be able to see the Type column.
13. Toward the bottom of the Case Shortcuts window list (on the left side of the screen), notice that the topic of Objects has 12 subtopics. Notice also that next to each of the subtopics is the number of objects present in the case for that category.
14. ***Click Persons on the left side of the screen under Objects.***
15. The title directly under the menu bar should now read **"Objects – Persons"** (see CaseMap Exhibit 13). You should now see only People objects displayed on the screen. Notice that in the fourth column from the left (the "Type +" column), you can see whether the person is a fact witness or an expert witness. This column was not visible in the All Objects view. Notice that there is a column for Short Name. Also, notice the Role in Case column, where you can see a short description about the role or function of each person in the case.
16. The Objects – Persons view also has a Key column so you can identify whether a person is a key player in the case.
17. In the column called Facts, the fifth record from the top is Philip Hawkins. Notice that the Facts column tells you that he was referenced in 24 separate Fact records.
18. ***Click Documents on the left side of the screen under Objects.*** The Objects – Documents view should now be displayed (see CaseMap Exhibit 14). *Note:* You can also access the Objects – Documents view from the Case Shortcuts > Favorites list.
19. In the Objects – Documents view, the first and second columns are called **"Bates – Begin"** and **"Bates – End."** Bates numbers are important because they allow you to track and find documents numerically (assuming that every document in the case has a Bates number).
20. ***Click the second record from the top*** **("Hawkins Letter of 8/2/2005")** ***in the Type + column. Click the down arrow icon next to Letter.*** The box lists document types, including Contract, Deposition, E-mail, Internal memo, Letter, and Performance Review.

CASEMAP EXHIBIT 13

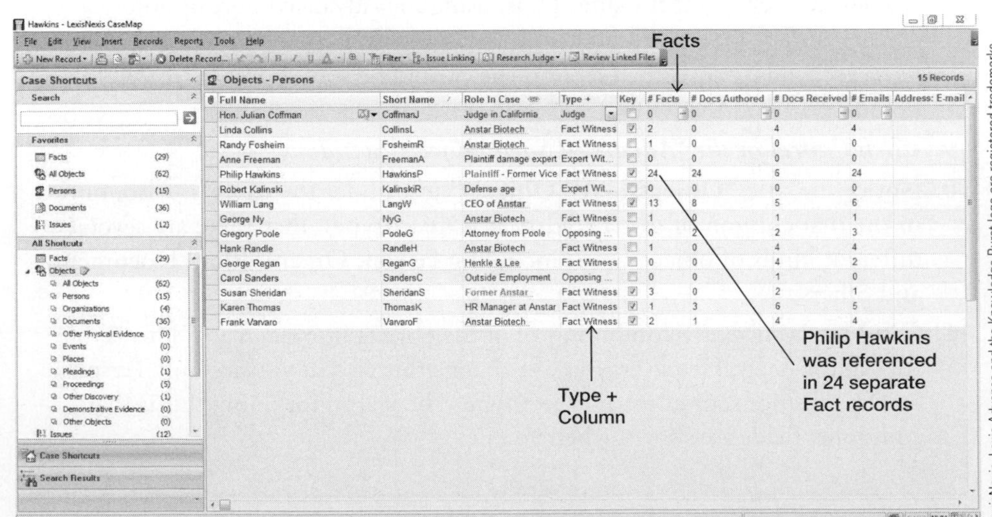

CASEMAP EXHIBIT 14

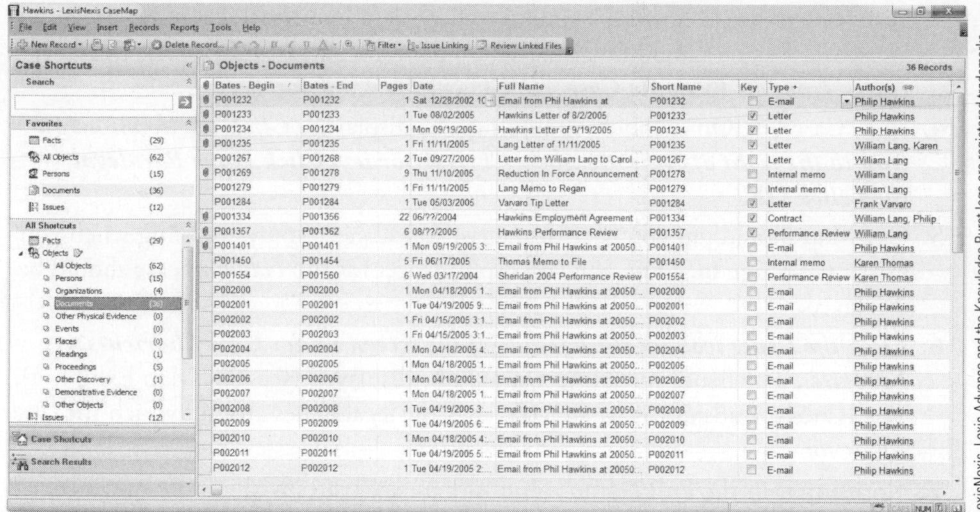

21. ***Click Letter*** to keep the current selection.
22. ***Scroll to the right using the right cursor key on the keyboard*** or ***use the horizontal scroll bar.*** There are columns for the document author(s) and recipients. Also, there is a Linked Issues column for linking the document to a specific legal issue and a Linked File column so you can see the actual image, or full text, of the document and evaluation columns.
23. ***Click Organizations on the left side of the screen under Objects.*** The Objects – Organizations view should now be displayed. The Organization columns are similar to the columns in other Object spreadsheet views.
24. ***Click the All Objects icon to the left side of the screen*** to display all of the objects again.
25. ***Click Case Shortcuts > Favorites, then click Facts*** to return to the Fact spreadsheet.

This concludes Lesson 3. To exit CaseMap, ***click File on the menu bar, then click Exit, then click OK*** to acknowledge the need to back up your files (if it asks), or go to Lesson 4.

LESSON 4: WORKING WITH THE ISSUES SPREADSHEET

This lesson introduces you to the CaseMap Issues spreadsheet, including how to enter new issues, promote and demote issues, and delete issues.

If you did not exit CaseMap after Lesson 3, then skip Steps 1–5 and go directly to Step 6.

1. Start Windows. ***Double-click the LexisNexis CaseMap 10 icon on the desktop,*** or ***click the Start button on the Windows desktop, point to Programs or All Programs, point to the LexisNexis CaseMap Suite, and click LexisNexis CaseMap 10.*** LexisNexis CaseMap 10 will then start.
2. When you start CaseMap, you will see a small window in the middle of the screen that says **"CaseMap"** and adds some information about a grace period. ***Click Continue in the "CaseMap" window.*** CaseMap will then start, with several options listed to the right of the screen.

3. Your screen should now look similar to CaseMap Exhibit 1. The Getting Started task pane should be displayed on the right side of the screen. ***Under Learn from an Example Case, click*** **Hawkins v. Anstar**.
4. The "Case Log On" window should now be displayed. ***Click the down arrow icon to the right of Staff Member: Chris Attorney. Click Dave Paralegal, then click OK.***
5. CaseMap should put you back at the last spreadsheet you were using when you exited the program. Thus, the Facts spreadsheet for the *Hawkins* case should be displayed.
6. ***Click the Issues icon on the left side of the screen under Case Shortcuts > Favorites.*** The Issues spreadsheet should be displayed (see CaseMap Exhibit 4). The Issues spreadsheet is where you enter the legal issues around which the case will revolve.
7. Notice that in the Full Name column there are issues with whole numbers (e.g., 1, 2), and then there are subissues with decimals (e.g., 2.1, 2.2,). CaseMap allows you to categorize whether an issue is a stand-alone issue, or is part of a more detailed issue.
8. ***Click the first record,*** **"1 Wrongful Termination,"** ***in the Full Name column.***
9. On the toolbar, there is an icon called New Record. See CaseMap Exhibit 4. ***Click New Record.*** From here you can select the type of item you want to enter, such as Fact, Person, and so on.
10. ***Click Issue.***
11. A blank record with the number "2" has been created. Just to the left of the "2," notice that there is a line with an up arrow, right arrow, and down arrow. ***Point to the up arrow*** and notice that it displays Move Up. ***Click the up arrow.*** The entry has now been moved up and is listed as 1.
12. Now, notice that the line next to the "1" only has a down arrow. ***Point to the down arrow*** and notice that it displays Move Down. ***Click the down arrow.*** The issue has reverted to number 2.
13. ***Point to the right arrow next to 2***, and notice that it displays **"Demote."** ***Click the right arrow next to 2.*** It now becomes 1.1. Using these arrows, you can control where each issue in the Issues list is displayed.
14. ***Click Outline on the menu bar.*** See CaseMap Exhibit 4. A list of options is displayed, including the ability to promote, demote, move up, or move down any issue in the outline hierarchy.
15. Press the **[ESC]** key to make the menu list go away.
16. With the pointer still on 1.1, type **Against Public Policy** and press the **[TAB]** key. Notice that CaseMap has entered AgainstPublicPolicy in the Short Name field. It is best to keep all Short Name entries as short as possible.
17. Press the **[DELETE]** key, type **AgPubPolicy,** and then press the **[ENTER]** key.
18. To delete the issue, ***click the Delete Record icon on the toolbar.*** (It looks like a red script X with a red left arrow next to it.)
19. ***Click Yes*** when CaseMap asks if you are sure if you want to delete this issue. The issue is now deleted.
20. ***Click Case Shortcuts > Favorites and then click Facts*** to return to the Facts spreadsheet.

This concludes Lesson 4. To exit CaseMap, ***click File on the menu bar, click Exit, then click OK*** to acknowledge the need to back up your files (if it asks), or go to Lesson 5.

LESSON 5: WORKING WITH ADVANCED FEATURES

This lesson introduces you to some advanced features in CaseMap, including using the View CaseWide command, hiding columns, inserting columns, adjusting rows, moving columns, printing and viewing reports, adding objects on the fly, hiding shortcuts, and viewing the detail of a record.

If you did not exit CaseMap after Lesson 4, then skip Steps 1–5 and go directly to Step 6.

1. Start Windows. ***Double-click the LexisNexis CaseMap 10 icon on the desktop,*** or ***click the Start button on the Windows desktop, point to Programs or All Programs, point to the LexisNexis CaseMap Suite, and click LexisNexis CaseMap 10.*** LexisNexis CaseMap 10 will then start.
2. When you start CaseMap, you will see a small window in the middle of the screen that says **"CaseMap"** and adds some information about a grace period. ***Click Run in the "CaseMap" window.*** CaseMap will then start, with several options listed to the right of the screen.
3. Your screen should now look similar to CaseMap Exhibit 1. The Getting Started task pane should be displayed on the right side of the screen. ***Under Learn from an Example Case, click* Hawkins v. Anstar.**
4. The "Case Log On" window should now be displayed. ***Click the down arrow icon to the right of Staff Member: Chris Attorney. Click Dave Paralegal, then click OK.***
5. CaseMap should put you back at the last spreadsheet you were using when you exited the program. Thus, the Facts spreadsheet for the *Hawkins* case should be displayed.
6. ***Click the View CaseWide icon on the toolbar*** (it looks like a graph; see CaseMap Exhibit 15).
7. The CaseWide view allows you to see a timeline of when the facts of the case occurred. Notice in the right corner of the graph that the "Y" is selected (see CaseMap Exhibit 15). The current graph in the CaseWide view is by year. Notice that the largest number of events occurred in 2005 (see CaseMap Exhibit 15).

HANDS-ON EXERCISES

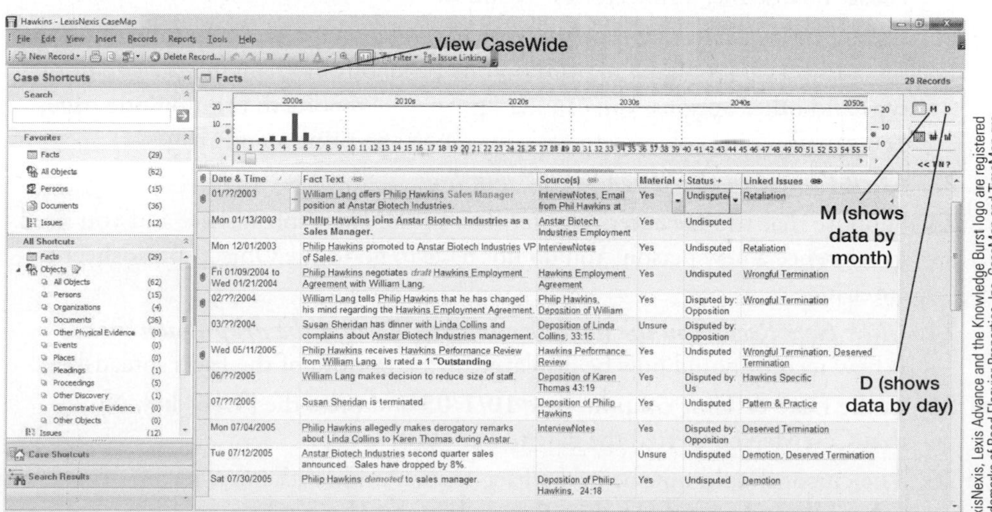

CASEMAP EXHIBIT 15

8. ***Click M to the right of the CaseWide graph.*** See CaseMap Exhibit 15. CaseMap responds by displaying the same data on a monthly basis.
9. ***Using the horizontal scroll bar under the CaseWide graph, scroll to the right.*** You can see that the largest number of events occurred in July and August 2005.
10. ***Click D to the right of the CaseWide graph.*** See CaseMap Exhibit 15. CaseMap responds by displaying the same data on a daily basis.
11. ***Use the horizontal scroll bar under the CaseWide graph to scroll to the right*** until you see some blue bars showing daily activity.
12. The CaseWide view gives you an overview of the general timing involved in a case.
13. ***Click the View CaseWide icon on the toolbar*** (it is now highlighted) to close the CaseWide view. Notice that the CaseWide icon is no longer highlighted.
14. If necessary, ***scroll to the right until you see the Linked Issues column.*** Suppose that this column is no longer important and is just taking up space in the spreadsheet view. ***Right-click the header of the Linked Issues column, then click Hide Field.***
15. Notice that the column can no longer be seen on the spreadsheet. *Note*: The data in the column/database have not been deleted; they have just been hidden and are no longer in the current view.
16. ***Right-click the header of the Status + column, then click Insert Fields.***
17. The "Selected Field(s) to Insert" window should now be displayed. Notice that a number of fields are listed, including the field that was just deleted (Linked Issues). You can use the Insert Field command to customize the views of your spreadsheets and to add other columns that include additional data. ***Scroll down and click Linked Issues, then click OK.***
18. ***Scroll to the right to see the Linked Issues column.*** If the Linked Issues column is to the left of the Status + column, ***click the Linked Issues column header and drag it to the right of the Status + column.*** The column has now been added back to the Facts spreadsheet view.
19. If necessary, ***scroll back to the left to see the first columns of the Facts spreadsheet.***
20. ***Click File and then click Print Preview*** to see how the Facts spreadsheet would look printed. ***Click Print*** if you would like to print the report, or ***click Close*** to close the "Print Preview" window.
21. ***Click File and Page Setup, then click the Report Options tab.*** Sometimes the spreadsheets are too long to print on one page, but by changing the size of the type and other options, you can manipulate the reports to print on one page. You can also hide columns to get your reports to print on one page.
22. ***Click Cancel in the "Page Setup" window.***
23. Suppose that you are entering a new fact in the Facts spreadsheet and you need to reference a new person. You do not have to go to the Object spreadsheet to enter it.
24. ***Click New Record on the toolbar and then Fact on the drop-down menu.*** A new record should now be displayed at the bottom of the Facts spreadsheet.
25. In the Date & Time column, type **10/1/05** and press the **[TAB]** key. Notice that CaseMap converted the date to Sat 10/01/2005.
26. The cursor should now be in the Fact Text column of the new record. Type **John Allen admitted HawkinsP to Laketown Hospital.**
27. ***Drag the mouse over the name*** **John Allen** ***until it is highlighted. Right-click in the highlighted area and click Add Object.*** The "Add Object" window is

HANDS-ON EXERCISES

now displayed. Everything in the "Add Object" window is correct, but if it were not, it could be edited.

28. ***Click OK in the "Add Object" window.*** The name "AllenJ" should now have a dotted line underneath it, showing that it has been listed as a Person in the Object spreadsheet, and that a Short Name has been made for the person.
29. ***Click the All Objects icon on the left side of the screen.*** Notice that John Allen has been added.
30. ***Click the Role in Case column in the row for John Allen.*** Type **Doctor for Philip Hawkins**, and then ***click any cell*** to enter the text.
31. ***Click Linda Collins in the third record from the top of the Objects – All Objects spreadsheet, in the Full Name column. Click Records on the menu bar and then click Record Detail.*** The "Object Detail" window has now been displayed. (If the window is too small, you can adjust its size by ***placing the cursor over the borders and dragging the window to the desired size.***) Notice that you can now collect and/or view a wide variety of other information about the person, including how to contact the person and other information. This is extremely helpful at trial when it is necessary to schedule witness testimony.
32. ***Click Close in the "Object Detail" window.***
33. ***Scroll down and click the document* "Hawkins Performance Review (P001357)" *in the Objects – All Objects spreadsheet.***
34. ***Click Records on the menu bar and then click Record Detail.*** Notice that the "Object Detail" window, which shows a number of additional fields about the document, is displayed. ***Scroll down in the "Object Detail" window to see all of these fields.*** Some of the additional fields include Privilege, Producing Party, Trial Ex(hibit) #, and others. *Note:* Any of these additional fields that are listed can be included in the spreadsheet view at any time by ***clicking in a header and selecting Insert Field.*** For Objects, you will need to go to the specific object spreadsheet (e.g., the Objects – Documents spreadsheet rather than the Objects – All Objects spreadsheet).
35. ***Click Close in the "Object Detail" window.***
36. ***Click Case Shortcuts > Favorites and then click on Facts*** to return to the Facts spreadsheet.

This concludes Lesson 5. To exit CaseMap, ***click File on the menu bar, click Exit, then click OK*** to acknowledge the need to back up your files (if it asks), or go to Lesson 6.

ADVANCED LESSONS

LESSON 6: CREATING A NEW CASE

This lesson introduces you to setting up (creating) a new case in CaseMap and entering new Objects, including people, organizations, and documents.

If you did not exit CaseMap after Lesson 5, then skip Steps 1–5 and go directly to Step 6.

1. Start Windows. ***Double-click the LexisNexis CaseMap 10 icon on the desktop,*** or ***click the Start button on the Windows desktop, point to Programs or All Programs, point to the LexisNexis CaseMap Suite, then click LexisNexis CaseMap 10.*** LexisNexis CaseMap 10 will then start.
2. When you start CaseMap, you will see a small window in the middle of the screen that says **"CaseMap"** and adds some information about a grace period.

Click Run in the "CaseMap" window. CaseMap will then start, with several options listed to the right of the screen.

3. Your screen should now look similar to CaseMap Exhibit 1. The Getting Started task pane should be displayed on the right side of the screen. ***Under Learn from an Example Case, click*** **Hawkins v. Anstar**.
4. The "Case Log On" window should now be displayed. ***Click the down arrow icon to the right of Staff Member: Chris Attorney. Click Dave Paralegal, then click OK.***
5. CaseMap should put you back at the last spreadsheet you were using when you exited the program. Thus, the Facts spreadsheet for the *Hawkins* case should be displayed.
6. You will now create a new case. ***Click File on the menu bar and then click New.***
7. The "New Case Wizard" window should now be displayed. ***Click Next.***
8. The "Case Setup" window should now be displayed (see CaseMap Exhibit 16).
9. In the "Case name:" box, type **Richards v. EZ Pest Control.** ***Then select your time zone as the default time zone and click Next.*** (For demonstration purposes, the example in the text will use GMT -5:00 Eastern Time.)
10. At the Select Template window, the default selection, "Use the default CaseMap template" is fine. ***Click Next.***
11. At the "Case Staff Information" window, under Enter your name: type **your name**; in the Enter your firm or organization: field, type **Johnson Beck and Taylor**; and when it asks **"Do you want to set up additional staff members for this case now?"** ***click Yes. Then click Next.***
12. At the "Manage Staff Members" window, to the right of Staff name, type **Dave Paralegal** and ***click Add; then click Next.***
13. At the "Case File" window, to the right of File name, **"Richards v. EZ Pest Control"** should already be typed in. We will use the default location for this file on the computer, so ***click Next.***
14. CaseMap will then tell you that it has enough information to create your new file and that the case is not password protected. Be sure that the box next to Launch Case Jumpstart Wizard is checked and ***click Finish.***

CASEMAP EXHIBIT 16

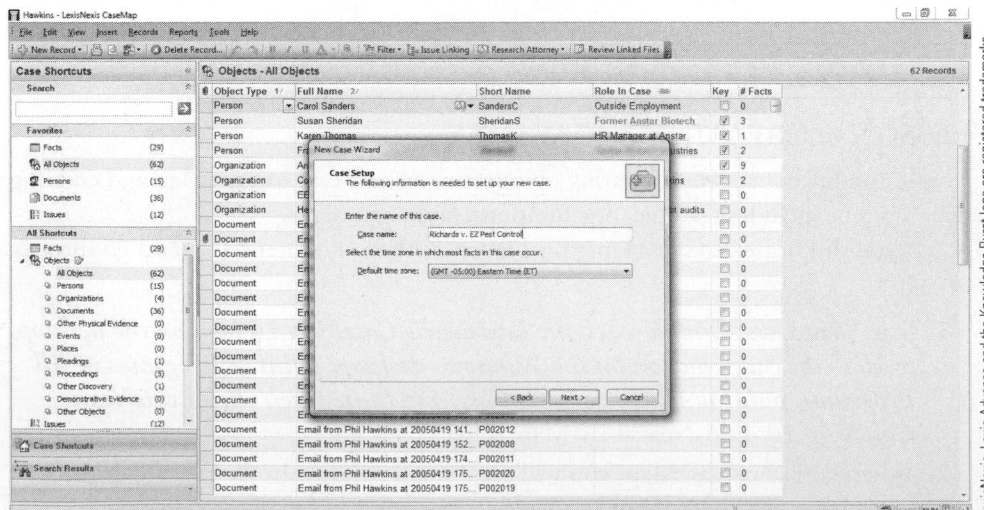

15. The "Welcome to the Case Jumpstart Wizard" window will open. This tool will help us populate the cast of characters in our case. Notice also that the wizard window is opened on top of an empty Objects – All Objects spreadsheet and that all of the numbers next to the Case Shortcuts are zero (0). ***Click Next*** (see CaseMap Exhibit 17).

CASEMAP EXHIBIT 17

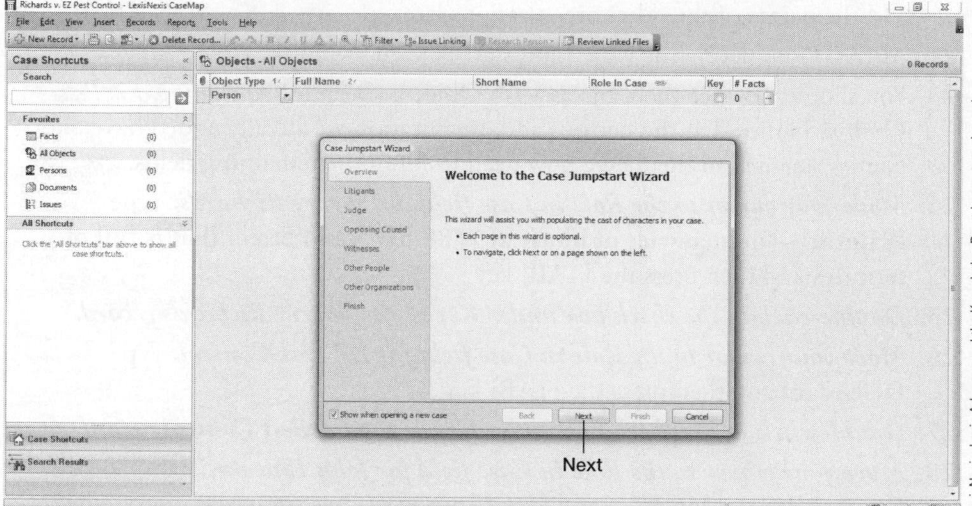

16. At the "Who are the parties in this case?" window, under Type: ***click Person*** from the drop-down list and under Party: type **Sherry Richards.** Then ***click Add Another.*** Under Type:, ***click Organization*** and under Party: type **EZ Pest Control.** Then ***click Next*** (see CaseMap Exhibit 18).

17. At the "Who is presiding over this case?" window, ***click Next.*** (The windows in this wizard are all optional and should be skipped if you do not know the names of the appropriate parties. We will assume that we do not yet know the name of the judge assigned to this case.)

CASEMAP EXHIBIT 18

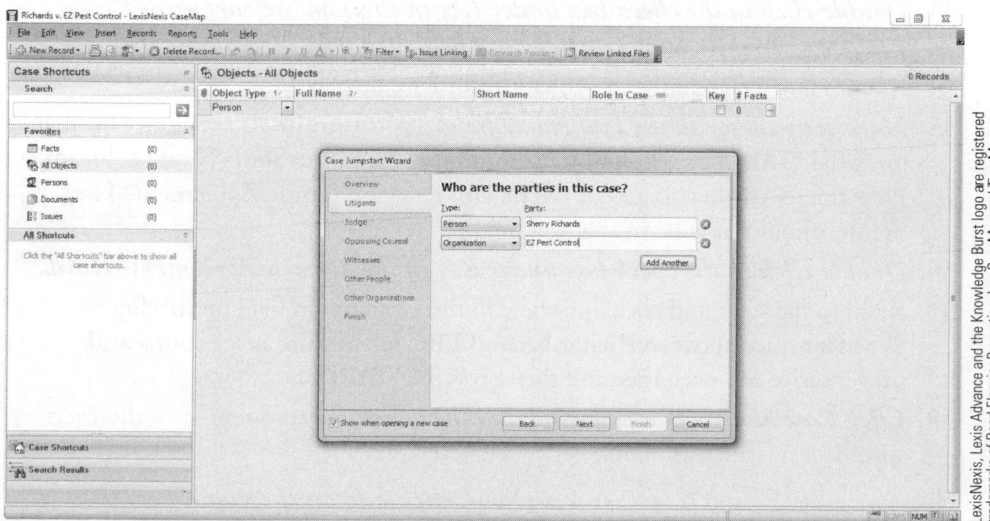

18. At the "Who are the opposing counsel?" window, under Attorney: type **Peter Gibbons** and under Firm: type **Gibbons and Kilgo**. ***Click Next.***
19. At the "Who are the witnesses in this case?" window, type **John Lincoln.** Do not check the box next to Expert. ***Click Next.***
20. At the "Who are the other people involved?" window, ***click Next.*** You could add the names of the other people later.
21. At the "What other organizations are involved?" window, ***click Next.*** You could add the names of the other organizations later.
22. At the "Completing the Case Jumpstart Wizard" window, ***click Finish.***
23. You should now see the Objects – All Objects screen for *Richards v. EZ Pest Control.* Notice that the persons and organization we already added have Short Names assigned to them. We now need to fill in the remaining fields.
24. ***Move your cursor to the Role in Case field for Sherry Richards.*** Type **Plaintiff — homeowner of house at 7788 SW 52nd Street that is full of termites** and then press the **[TAB]** key.
25. ***Double-click in the check box under Key in the Sherry Richards record.***
26. ***Move your cursor to the Role in Case field for EZ Pest Control.*** Type **Defendant** and then press the **[TAB]** key.
27. ***Double-click in the check box under Key in the EZ Pest Control record.***
28. ***Move your cursor to the Role in Case field for John Lincoln.*** Type **EZ Pest Control Branch Manager and Head Inspector; has prepared many reports to the effect that the property has no visible evidence of termites.** Leave the box under Key empty. Press the **[TAB]** key to go to the Full Name field.
29. You will now add a few new objects to this case.
30. ***Click New Record on the toolbar and then click Person.*** The Objects—Persons screen and a new blank record should be displayed.
31. ***Move your cursor to the Full Name field.*** Type **Tim Stewart** and then press the **[TAB]** key. The pointer should now be in the Short Name column. Press the **[TAB]** key to accept the default entry of StewartT. The pointer should now be in the Role in Case field.
32. Type **Contractor hired by RichardsS to repair the immense termite damage to the house; will testify about the extensive damage to the house.** Press the **[TAB]** key.
33. ***Double-click in the check box under Key in the Tim Stewart record.***
34. ***Click New Record on the toolbar and then click Document.*** The Objects – Documents screen and a new blank record are displayed.
35. ***Move your cursor to the Full Name field.*** Type **Termite Agreement** and then press the **[TAB]** key. The pointer should now be in the Short Name column. Press the **[TAB]** key to accept the default entry of TermiteAgreement. The pointer should now be in the Key field.
36. ***Double-click in the check box under Key in the Termite Agreement record.***
37. Scroll to the right and click anywhere in the Description field on this line. Type **Contract between RichardsS and EPC for termite inspections and preventative maintenance** and then press the **[TAB]** key.
38. ***Click Case Shortcuts > Favorites and then click Facts*** to return to the Facts spreadsheet, which is blank.

This concludes Lesson 6. To exit CaseMap, ***click File on the menu bar, then click Exit, then click OK*** to acknowledge the need to back up your files (if it asks), or go to Lesson 7.

LESSON 7: ENTERING ISSUES AND FACTS IN A NEW CASE

This lesson introduces you to entering issues and facts in a new case and automatically copying data from one cell to another.

If you did not exit CaseMap after Lesson 1, then skip Steps 1–5 and go directly to Step 6.

1. Start Windows. ***Double-click on the LexisNexis CaseMap 10 icon on the desktop,*** or ***click the Start button on the Windows desktop, point to Programs or All Programs, point to the LexisNexis CaseMap Suite, and click LexisNexis CaseMap 10.*** LexisNexis CaseMap 10 will then start.
2. When you start CaseMap, you will see a small window in the middle of the screen that says **"CaseMap"** and adds some information about a grace period. ***Click Continue in the "CaseMap" window.*** CaseMap will then start, with several options listed to the right of the screen.
3. Your screen should now look similar to CaseMap Exhibit 1. The Getting Started task pane should be displayed on the right side of the screen. ***Under Open a Case, click*** **Richards v. EZ Pest Control.cm10.**
4. The "Case Log On" window should now be displayed. **"Dave Paralegal"** should be the default selection, so ***click OK.***
5. CaseMap should put you back at the Facts spreadsheet.
6. ***Click the Issues icon on the left side of the screen.*** The Issues spreadsheet should now be displayed and the pointer should be in a blank record.
7. In the Full Name column, type **Breach of Contract** and then press the **[TAB]** key.
8. Press the **[TAB]** key to accept the default entry of BreachOfContract in the Short Name field. Press the **[TAB]** key until the pointer is in the Description field.
9. Type **Defendant had maintenance contract to spray the house preventively for termites for five years prior to discovery of extensive termite damage.**
10. ***Double-click in the check box under Key in the Breach of Contract record.***
11. Press the **[TAB]** key until you are in a new record. In the Full Name column, type **Negligence** and then press the **[TAB]** key.
12. Press the **[TAB]** key to accept the default entry of Negligence in the Short Name field. Press the **[TAB]** key until the pointer is in the Description field. Type **Defendant negligently failed to discover enormous termite colony that did extensive damage to the house.**
13. ***Double-click in the check box under Key in the Negligence record.***
14. ***Click Facts on the left side of the screen.*** The Facts spreadsheet should now be displayed and the cursor should be in a blank record.
15. In the Date & Time column, type **01/02/2006** and then press the **[TAB]** key to go to the Fact Text field.
16. Type **RichardsS and EPC sign TermiteAgreement** and then press the **[TAB]** key to go to the Source(s) column.
17. Type **Ter** and then press the **[ENTER]** key to accept this short name for "Termite Agreement."
18. Press the **[TAB]** key. The pointer should now be in the Material + field.
19. ***Click the down arrow in the Material + field. Click Yes,*** then press the **[TAB]** key.
20. ***Click in the Status + column in the record, click the down arrow icon, then click Undisputed.***

HANDS-ON EXERCISES

21. Press the **[TAB]** key.
22. ***Right-click in the Linked Issues column in the record, click Link Assistant, then click BreachOfContract.***
23. Press the **[TAB]** key. You should now be in a blank Fact record.
24. In the Date & Time column, type **5/15/2006** and then press the **[TAB]** key to go to the Fact Text field.
25. Type **LincolnJ completes full termite inspection of house** and then press the **[TAB]** key to go to the Source(s) column.
26. Type **Deposition of RichardsS, 32:18 and Deposition of LincolnJ, 45:9** and then press the **[TAB]** key.
27. The pointer should now be in the Material + column. ***Click the down arrow and click Yes.*** Then press the **[TAB]** key.
28. The pointer should now be in the Status + column. ***Click the down arrow icon, then click Undisputed.***
29. Press the **[TAB]** key. The pointer should now be in the Linked Issues column.
30. ***Right-click in the Linked Issues column in the record, click Link Assistant, then click BreachofContract.***
31. Type **;** (a semi-colon).
32. ***Right-click again in the Linked Issues column in the record, click Link Assistant, then click Negligence.***
33. Press the **[TAB]** key. You should now be at a blank Fact record.
34. In the Date & Time column, type **8/??/2006** and then press the **[TAB]** key to go to the Fact Text field.
35. Type **RichardsS hears noise inside walls at night; later discovered to be termites** and then press the **[TAB]** key to go to the Source(s) column.
36. Type **Deposition of RichardsS, 45:6**, and then press the **[TAB]** key.
37. ***Click the down arrow in the Material + column and click Yes.*** Then press the **[TAB]** key.
38. ***Click the down arrow in the Status + column and then click Undisputed.***
39. Press the **[TAB]** key.
40. Press the **[CTRL]+["]** (quotation mark) keys on the keyboard. **[CTRL]+["]** copies the value from the cell above. Notice that "Breach of Contract, Negligence" was copied from the cell above to the current cell. Using this command will greatly decrease data entry time if there are a number of duplicate entries; it will also lessen the possibility of making an error.
41. Press the **[TAB]** key. You should now be at a blank Fact record.
42. In the Date & Time column, type **10/15/2006** and then press the **[TAB]** key to go to the Fact Text field.
43. Type **StewartT inspects house to make a bid on repairs and finds massive termite damage**, then press the **[TAB]** key to go to the Source(s) column.
44. Type **Deposition of StewartT, 14:12**, then press the **[TAB]** key.
45. ***Click the down arrow in the Material + column and click Yes.*** Then press the **[TAB]** key.
46. ***Click the down arrow in the Status + column and then click Undisputed.***
47. Press the **[TAB]** key.
48. Press the **[CTRL]+["]** (quotation) keys on the keyboard to copy the cell above to the current cell.

49. Press the **[TAB]** key. You should now be at a blank Fact record.
50. In the Date & Time column, type **11/01/2006** and then press the **[TAB]** key to go to the Fact Text field.
51. Type **RichardsS hires another pest control service to look at the property; confirms massive termite damage** and then press the **[TAB]** key to go to the Source(s) column.
52. Type **Deposition of RichardsS, 22:7** and then press the **[TAB]** key.
53. ***Click the down arrow in the Material + column and click Yes.*** Then press the **[TAB]** key.
54. ***Click the down arrow icon in the Status + column, then click Undisputed.***
55. Press the **[TAB]** key.
56. Press the **[CTRL]+["]** (quotation) keys on the keyboard to copy the cell above to the current cell.
57. Press the **[TAB]** key. You should now be at a blank Fact record.
58. In the Date & Time column, type **07/15/2006** and then press the **[TAB]** key to go to the Fact Text field.
59. Type **LincolnJ attempts to inspect property; sees RichardsS in the house, but she will not open the door. LincolnJ is not able to inspect house.** Then press the **[TAB]** key to go to the Source(s) column.
60. Type **Deposition of LincolnJ, 52:20** and then press the **[TAB]** key.
61. ***Click the down arrow in the Material + column and click Yes.*** Then press the **[TAB]** key.
62. ***Click the down arrow in the Status + column and then click Disputed by: Us.***
63. Press the **[TAB]** key.
64. Press the **[CTRL]+["]** (quotation) keys on the keyboard to copy the cell above to the current cell.

This concludes Lesson 7. To exit CaseMap, ***click File on the menu bar, click Exit, then click OK*** to acknowledge the need to back up your files (if it asks), or go to Lesson 8.

LESSON 8: USING CASEMAP FOR A NEW CASE

This lesson introduces using CaseMap for a new case, including printing reports, viewing case data in a variety of ways, exporting to a PDF file, exporting a summary judgment report to a word processor, using the CaseWide tool, and searching/filtering data. This lesson assumes that you have completed all of the prior exercises, and that step-by-step directions are therefore not necessary.

If you did not exit CaseMap after Lesson 7, then skip Steps 1–5 and go directly to Step 6.

1. Start Windows. ***Double-click the LexisNexis CaseMap 10 icon on the desktop,*** or ***click the Start button on the Windows desktop, point to Programs or All Programs, point to the LexisNexis CaseMap Suite, and click LexisNexis CaseMap 10.*** LexisNexis CaseMap 10 will then start.
2. When you start CaseMap, you will see a small window in the middle of the screen that says **"CaseMap"** and adds some information about a grace period. ***Click Run in the "CaseMap" window.*** CaseMap will then start, with several options listed to the right of the screen.
3. Your screen should now look similar to CaseMap Exhibit 1. The Getting Started task pane should be displayed on the right side of the screen. ***Under Open a Case, click*** **Richards v. EZ Pest Control.cm10**.

4. The "Case Log On" window should now be displayed. **Dave Paralegal** should be the default selection, so ***click OK.***
5. CaseMap should put you back at the Facts spreadsheet.
6. ***Right-click in the header of the Date & Time field in the Facts spreadsheet, and sort the column in descending order.***
7. Print the Facts spreadsheet ***(click File on the menu bar, then click Print),*** or view it on the screen ***(click File on the menu bar, then click Print Preview).***
8. ***Click the record that has* "Disputed by: Us" *in the Status + column, and filter the selection by right-clicking on the entry.***
9. ***Cancel the filter using the Cancel icon on the toolbar.***
10. In the Issues spreadsheet, move the Description column to the third column by ***clicking in the column header and dragging it to the new location.***
11. Print a report that contains only Persons in the Object spreadsheet. First, ***click Persons on the left side of the screen, click File on the menu bar, then click Print.***
12. Print a report of All Objects using the Objects – All Objects spreadsheet view.
13. ***Return to the Facts spreadsheet on the left side of the screen.***
14. Using CaseMap, you can automatically print any CaseMap report to a PDF file that can then be emailed to a client. ***Click the Print to PDF icon on the toolbar*** (the fourth icon from the left). ***Click Print to PDF.***
15. At the "Save As Adobe PDF" window, ***click Save*** to save the document to the default directory with the default file name.
16. A window should now be displayed that says **"The report has been saved as an Adobe PDF file. Do you want to open it now?"** ***Click Yes.***
17. If Adobe Reader is installed on your computer, the Fact Chronology report should now be displayed.
18. ***Click the Close icon*** (a red box with a white X) ***in the "Adobe Reader" window.***
19. You will now print the Case Summary Report, which prints out each of the key spreadsheets automatically. ***Click Reports on the menu bar, then click ReportBooks, then click Case Summary and click Preview*** (see CaseMap Exhibit 19). CaseMap will then display a window stating that some spreadsheets are empty. ***Click Yes*** to indicate that you want to continue.
20. Page down through the report. When you are done, ***click Close.***

CASEMAP EXHIBIT 19

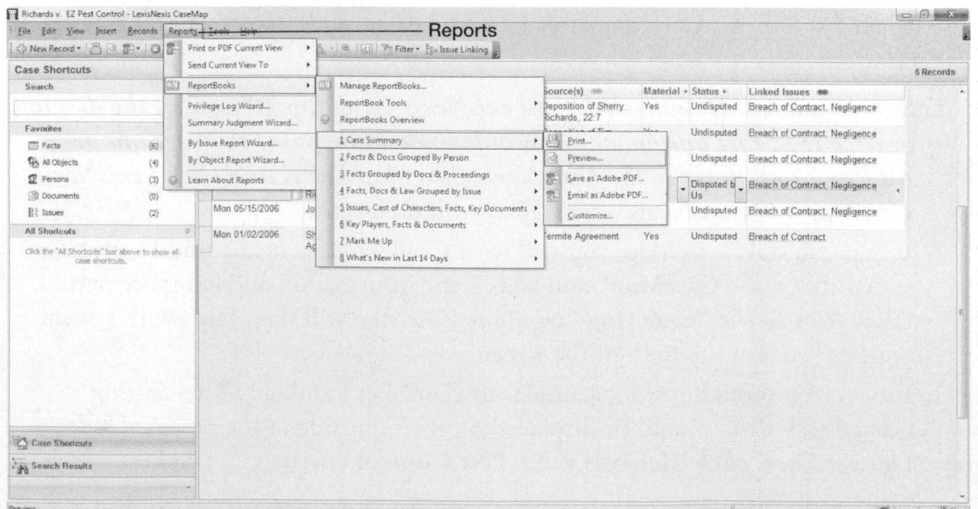

21. CaseMap has a convenient feature specifically related to summary judgment motions. CaseMap can export a word-processing file directly to Word or WordPerfect that will assist in creating a summary judgment motion or response. ***In the Facts spreadsheet, click Reports on the menu bar and then click Summary Judgment Wizard.***
22. ***In the "Welcome to the Summary Judgment Wizard" window, click Next.***
23. When the "Customize Report" window asks, **"Do you want to customize the report?"** ***click*** **"No, I want to use CaseMap's default options button"** ***and then click Next.***
24. ***In the "Report Format" window, select either Microsoft Word, Corel WordPerfect, or HTML; then click Next.***
25. ***In the "Completing the Summary Judgment Wizard" window, click Finish.***
26. Notice that a table has been created showing all of the facts that relate to each legal issue, as well as the citation for each factual reference (see CaseMap Exhibit 20).
27. After reading the document, ***click Print to print the document for your instructor and then close the word-processing file.***
28. ***Click the View CaseWide icon on the toolbar.*** (It looks like a chart.)
29. ***Click M (for Month) in the upper right of the screen.***
30. ***Click the View CaseWide icon on the toolbar again*** to make the CaseWide view disappear.
31. Suppose that you are assisting your supervising attorney in preparing for the deposition of John Lincoln and that you would like to retrieve all of the Fact records that have his name.
32. ***Right-click any occurrence of John Lincoln's name in the Facts spreadsheet.*** Notice that the first option in the menu is Selection: LincolnJ. ***Click Filter by Selection.***
33. Notice that only the records for John Lincoln are shown. ***Click Cancel on the toolbar.*** (It looks like a funnel next to a red ball.)
34. If you would like additional training on CaseMap, ***click Help on the menu bar and then click CaseMap Webinar Center***. Numerous free "webinars" (web seminars) are available on the Internet that will further assist you in learning CaseMap.
35. This concludes Lesson 8. To exit CaseMap, ***click File on the menu bar, then click Exit, then click OK*** to acknowledge the need to back up your files (if it asks).

This concludes the CaseMap exercises.

HANDS-ON EXERCISES

CASEMAP EXHIBIT 20

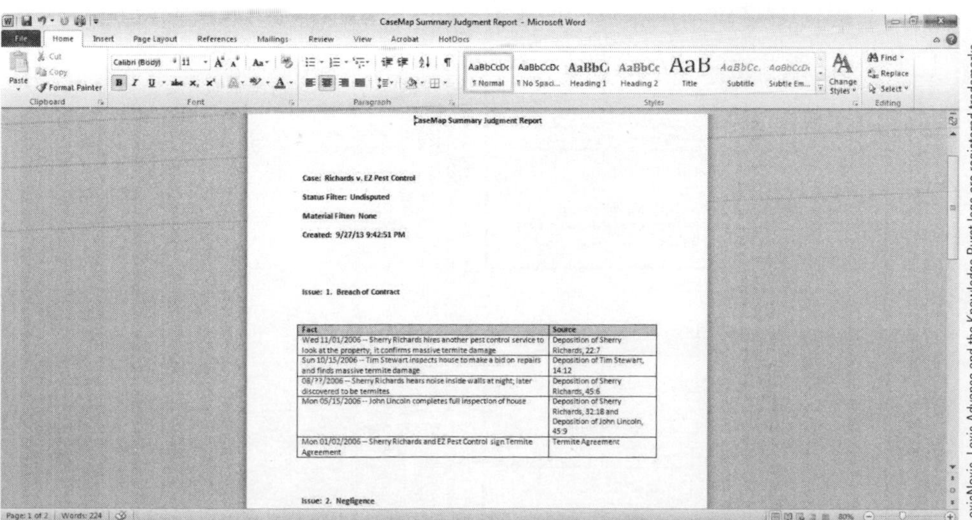

HANDS-ON EXERCISES

TIMEMAP

I. INTRODUCTION – READ THIS!

LexisNexis TimeMap is a litigation support analytical tool that creates time maps or timelines. The LexisNexis TimeMap demonstration version is a full working version of the program (with a few limitations). The program demonstration version times out 120 days after installation. This means that the program will only work for 120 days after you install it. So, it is highly recommended that you do not install the program on your computer until you are actually ready to go through the Hands-On Exercises and learn the program. When you are ready to install the program, follow the instructions in section III.

II. USING THE LEXISNEXIS TIMEMAP HANDS-ON EXERCISES

The LexisNexis TimeMap Hands-On Exercises are easy to use and contain step-by-step instructions. Each lesson builds on the previous exercise, so please complete the Hands-On Exercises in order. TimeMap comes with sample data, so you should be able to utilize many features of the program.

III. INSTALLATION INSTRUCTIONS

The following are step-by-step instructions for loading the LexisNexis TimeMap demonstration version on your computer.

1. Log in to your CengageBrain.com account.
2. Under **"My Courses & Materials,"** find the Premium Website for *Using Computers in the Law Office*, 7th edition.
3. ***Click Open to go to the Premium Website.***
4. Locate "Book Resources" in the left navigation menu.
5. ***Click on the link for TimeMap 5.***
6. You may get a File Download – Security Warning. ***Click Run.*** See TimeMap Installation Exhibit 1. You may get an Internet Explorer – Security Warning. ***Click Run.*** See TimeMap Installation Exhibit 2.

TIMEMAP INSTALLATION EXHIBIT 1

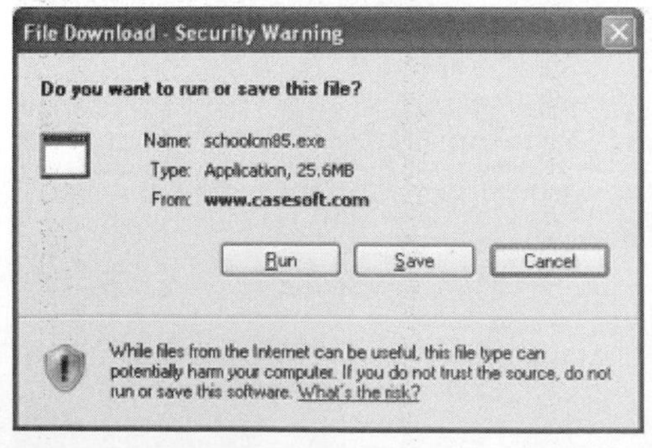

TIMEMAP INSTALLATION EXHIBIT 2

7. Your screen will look like TimeMap Installation Exhibit 3. ***Click Next.***

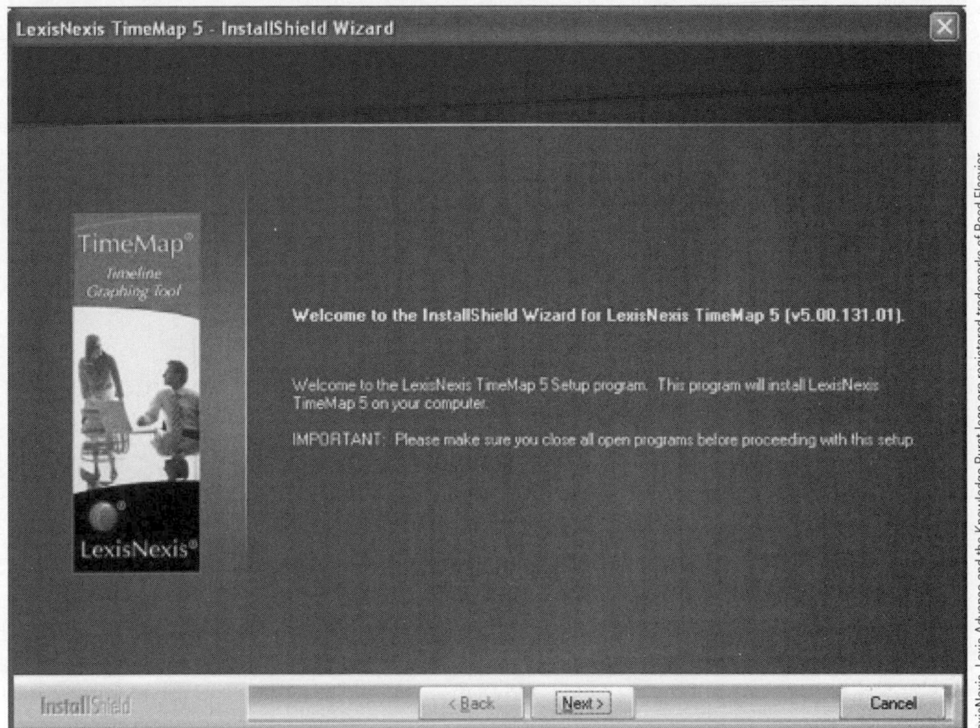

TIMEMAP INSTALLATION EXHIBIT 3

8. Your screen will look like TimeMap Installation Exhibit 4. ***Click Yes.***

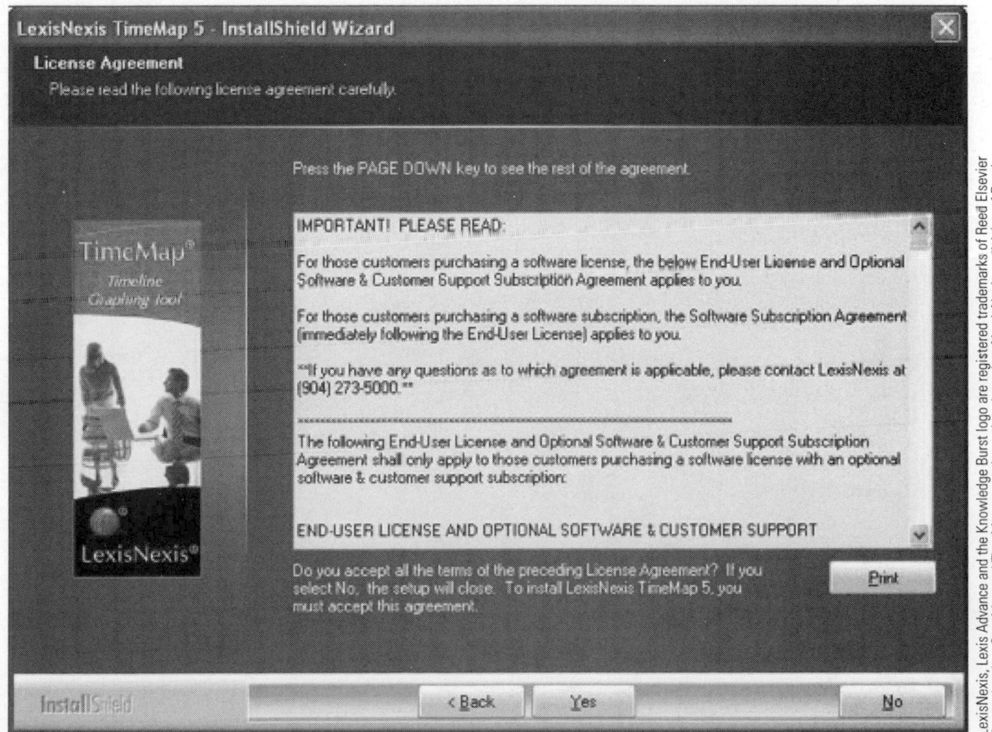

TIMEMAP INSTALLATION EXHIBIT 4

9. Your screen will look like TimeMap Installation Exhibit 5. ***Click Next.***

TIMEMAP INSTALLATION EXHIBIT 5

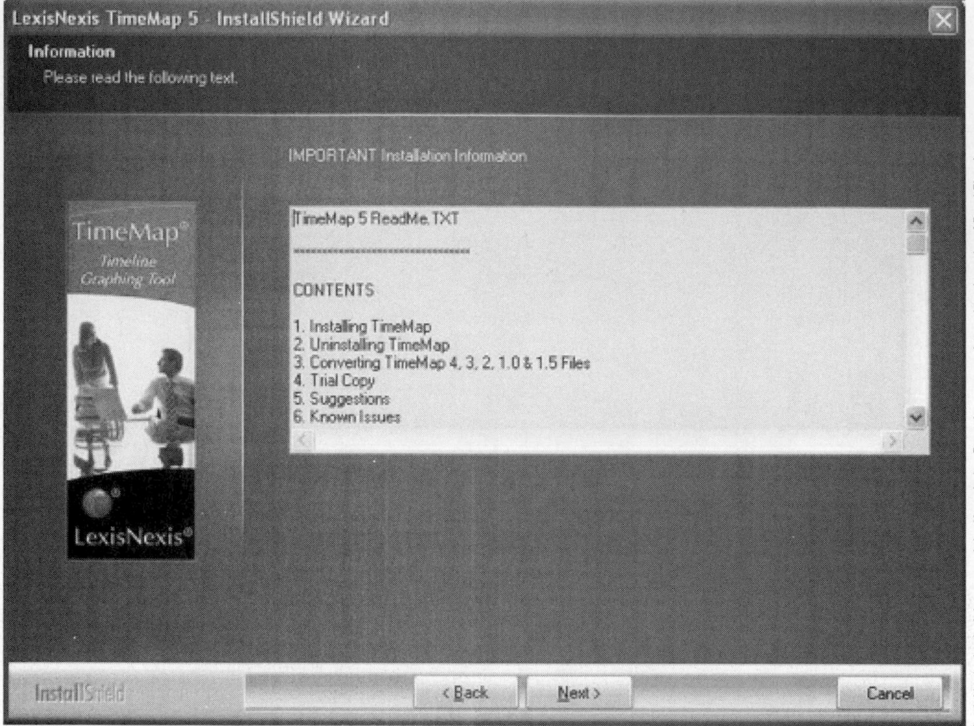

10. Your screen will look like TimeMap Installation Exhibit 6. If you wish to change the default installation location, click on Browse to navigate to the desired location. Otherwise, ***click Next.***

TIMEMAP INSTALLATION EXHIBIT 6

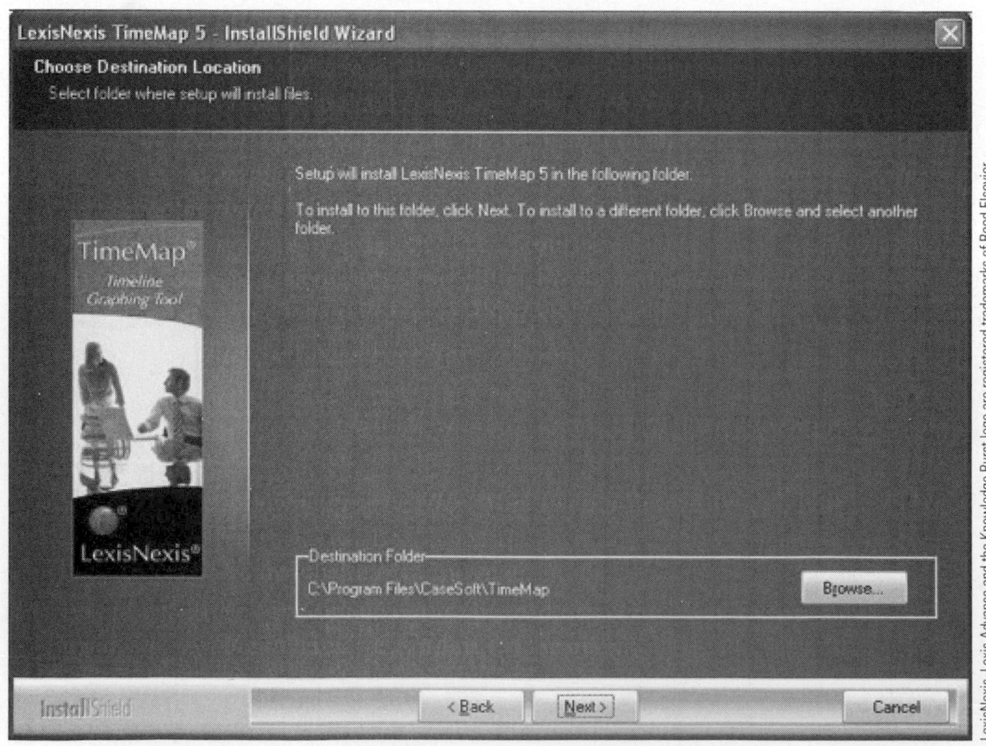

11. Your screen will look like TimeMap Installation Exhibit 7. ***Click Next.***

TIMEMAP INSTALLATION EXHIBIT 7

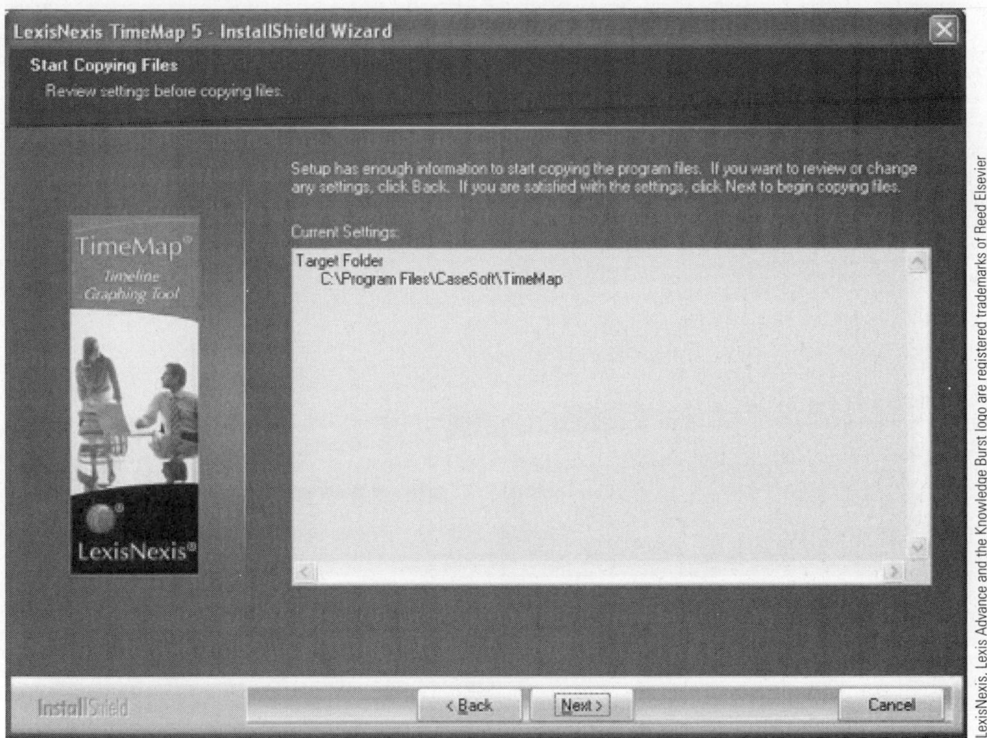

12. Your screen will look like TimeMap Installation Exhibit 8. ***Click Finish*** to finish installation and launch the program.

TIMEMAP INSTALLATION EXHIBIT 8

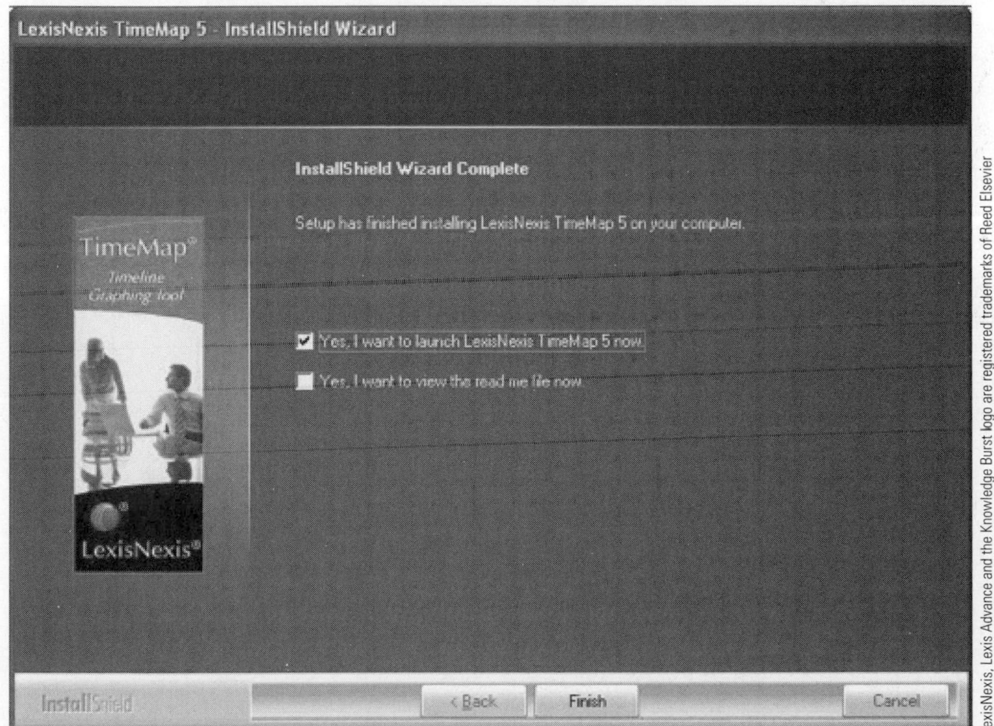

13. When you launch TimeMap you will see the screen shown in TimeMap Installation Exhibit 9. ***Click Continue.***

TIMEMAP INSTALLATION EXHIBIT 9

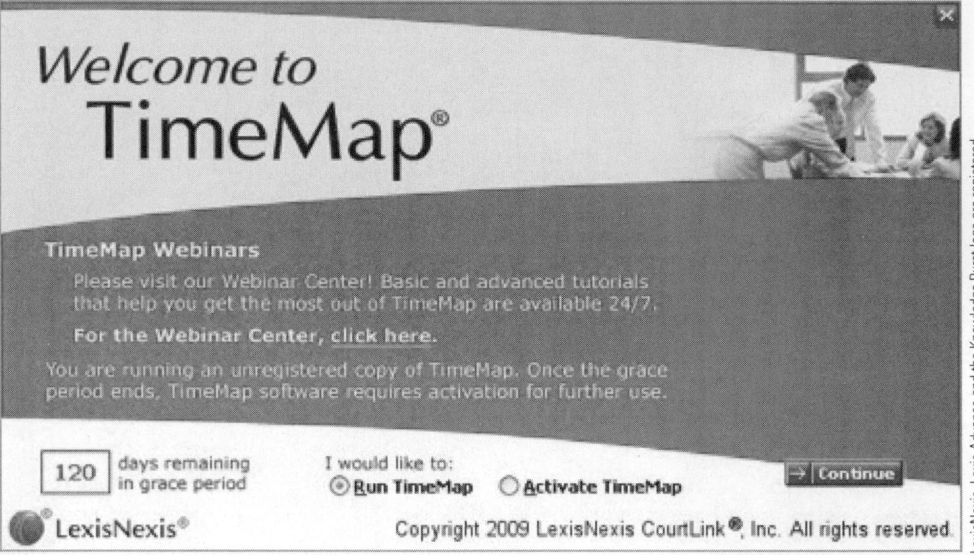

HANDS-ON EXERCISES

14. You will now see a screen like the one in TimeMap Installation Exhibit 10.

TIMEMAP INSTALLATION EXHIBIT 10

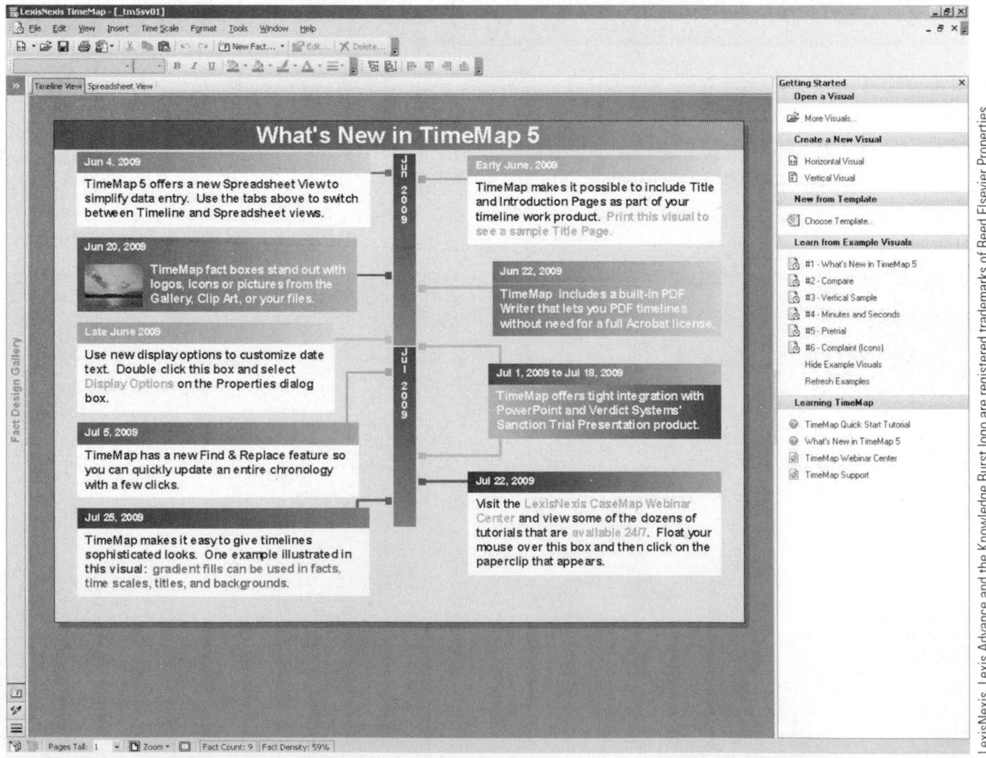

IV. INSTALLATION TECHNICAL SUPPORT

LexisNexis TimeMap is a licensed product of LexisNexis. If you have problems installing the demonstration version of LexisNexis TimeMap, you will need to contact LexisNexis TimeMap directly at (877) 301-0344.

Number	Lesson Title	Concepts Covered
BASIC LESSON		
Lesson 1	Introduction to TimeMap	Explanation of and introduction to the TimeMap interface.
INTERMEDIATE LESSON		
Lesson 2	Creating a New Timeline in TimeMap	Entering new fact boxes and customizing the chronology.
ADVANCED LESSON		
Lesson 3	Exporting CaseMap Entries to TimeMap	Exporting entries from CaseMap into TimeMap.

GETTING STARTED

Introduction

Throughout these lessons and exercises, information you need to type into the software will be designated in several different ways:

- Keys to be pressed on the keyboard are designated in brackets, in all caps, and in bold (e.g., press the **[ENTER]** key).
- Movements with the mouse pointer are designated in bold and italics (e.g., ***point to File on the menu bar and click***).
- Words or letters that should be typed are designated in bold (e.g., type **Training Program**).
- Information that is or should be displayed on your computer screen is shown in bold, with quotation marks (e.g., **"Press ENTER to continue."**).
- Specific menu items and commands are designated with an initial capital letter (e.g., click Open).

OVERVIEW OF TIMEMAP

TimeMap is a litigation support product that creates timelines or time maps. A *timeline* or *time map* is a visual representation of time, showing when events occurred and in what sequence. TimeMap computerizes this process. Timelines are extremely helpful in a litigation context because they allow a jury or other factfinder to visualize how the events in the case occurred. TimeMap is straightforward and easy to use. It can accept entries imported directly from a CaseMap chronology, so that you do not have to retype or re-enter information into the computer.

BASIC LESSON

LESSON 1: INTRODUCTION TO TIMEMAP

This lesson introduces you to the TimeMap litigation support program. It explains basic information about the TimeMap interface.

1. Start Windows. After it has loaded, ***double-click on the LexisNexis TimeMap icon on the desktop,*** or ***click the Start button on the Windows desktop, point to Programs or All Programs, point to the LexisNexis CaseMap Suite, then point and click on LexisNexis TimeMap.*** LexisNexis TimeMap will start.

2. When you start TimeMap, you may intermittently see a small window in the middle of the screen that says **"TimeMap"** and adds some information about a grace period. If this occurs, ***click Continue.***
3. Your screen should now look similar to TimeMap Exhibit 1. On the right side of the screen is the Getting Started task pane.

TIMEMAP EXHIBIT 1

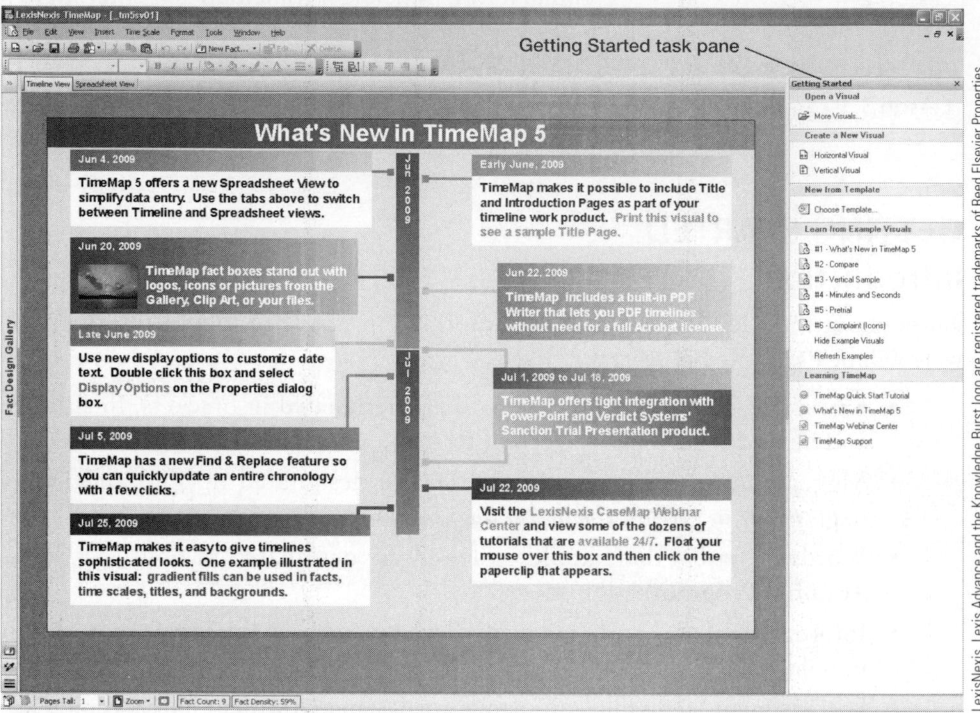

4. ***In the Getting Started task pane, under Learn from Example Visuals, click #5 – Pretrial.***
5. The Key Events Before Trial time map should now be displayed (see TimeMap Exhibit 2).

TIMEMAP EXHIBIT 2

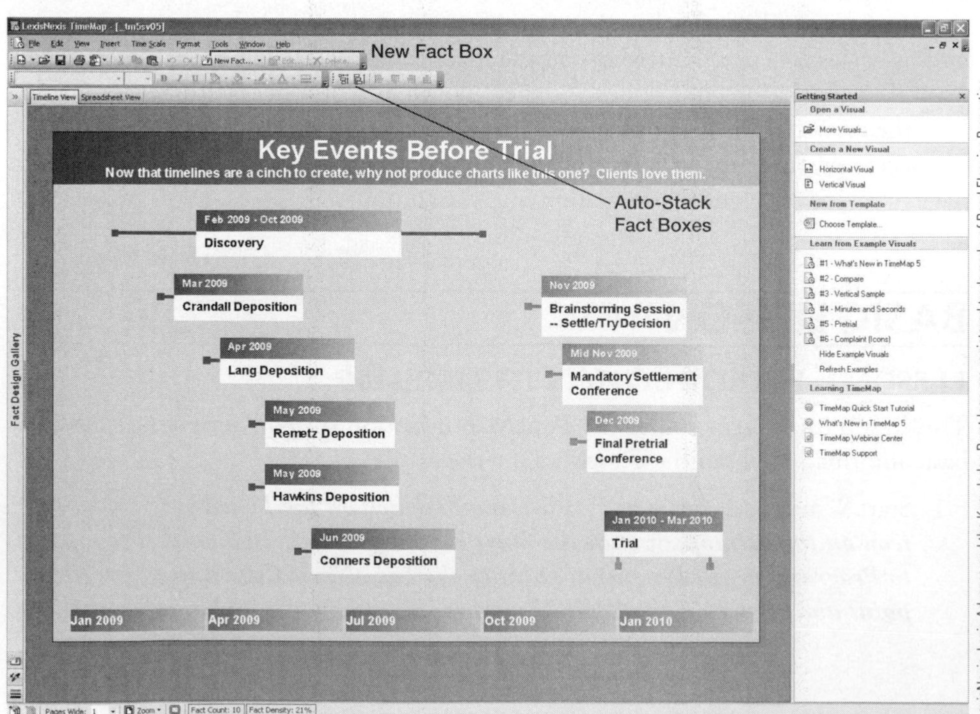

6. In TimeMap, there are three types of visual elements: Fact Boxes, Text Boxes, and the Time Scale.
7. Notice in TimeMap Exhibit 2 that 10 entries are displayed in the timeline (10 rectangular boxes that contain dates and descriptive information). These are called Fact Boxes.
8. ***Double-click the Mar 2009—Crandall Deposition Fact Box*** (it is the second Fact Box from the top on the left side of the screen).
9. Notice that a "Fact Box Properties" window is now displayed (see TimeMap Exhibit 3). ***Click the date*** and edit it so that it reads **03/15/2009.** Then change **"Crandall Deposition"** so that it reads **John Crandall Deposition**, and ***click OK in the "Fact Box Properties" window.***

TIMEMAP EXHIBIT 3

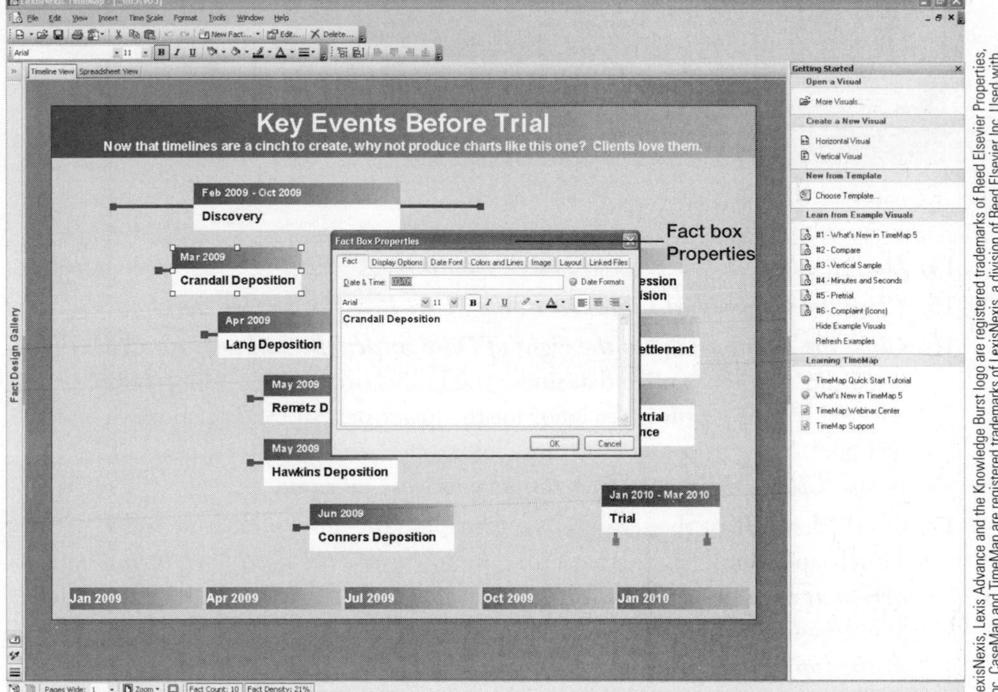

10. You will now create a new Fact Box. ***Click the New Fact Box (Ins) icon on the toolbar.*** (It looks like a yellow file folder with an "F" on it and a star in the upper left corner; see TimeMap Exhibit 2.)
11. The "New Fact Box" window is displayed. ***Click in the white box to the right of the Date & Time field,*** and type **10/01/2009.**
12. ***Click in the large white box in the "New Fact Box" window.*** Type **Client Discovery Meeting** and then ***click OK in the "New Fact Box" window.***
13. Notice that TimeMap has placed the Fact Box in the middle of the screen (see TimeMap Exhibit 4).

TIMEMAP EXHIBIT 4

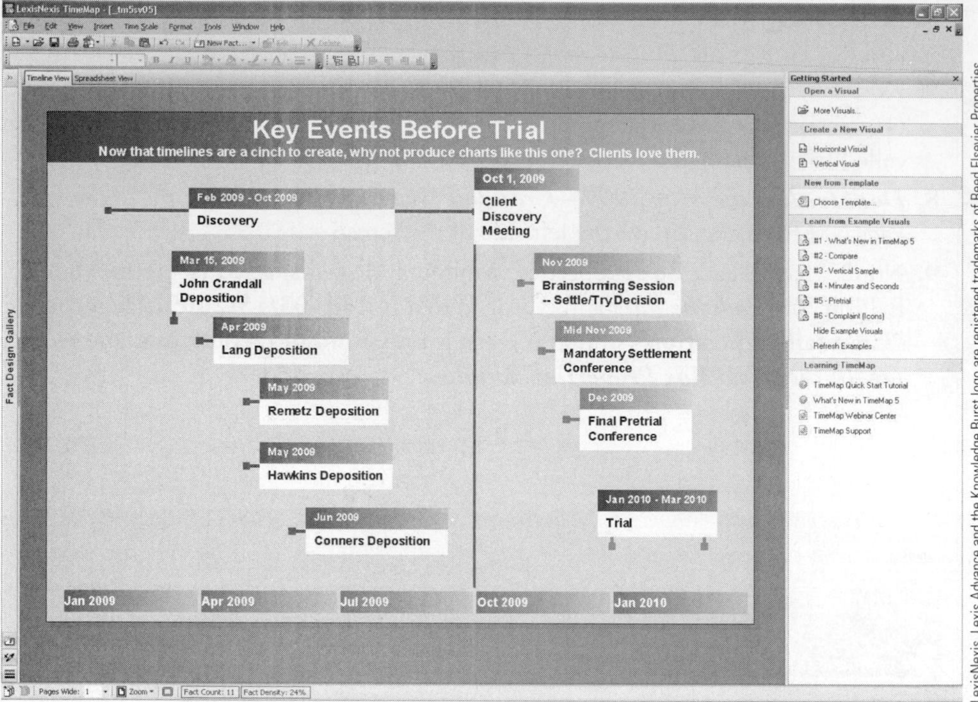

14. ***Double-click on the* "Oct 1, 2009" *Fact Box.***
15. ***Click the Colors and Lines tab in the "Fact Box Properties" window.***
16. ***Click the down arrow to the right of Date under the Fill section. Click Plum*** (medium purple). Notice that under the Fill section, next to Box, the color selected is white. This is the color for the lower part of the Fact Box where the text goes. You can control the font, color, lines, and all other aspects of Fact Boxes. ***Click OK in the "Fact Box Properties" window.***
17. On the left side of the screen is the Fact Design Gallery task pane (see TimeMap Exhibit 5). To access this window, ***click the double right-facing arrow at the top of the pane.*** And, if you have not already closed the Getting Started window on the right of the screen, do so now by ***clicking the small x at the top of that pane.*** Notice that in TimeMap Exhibit 5 there are several different box styles. For example, if you want to add a blue box, ***click the blue style fact box.*** Notice that the "New Fact Box" window is now displayed. You can now enter a new Fact Box in the blue style quickly and easily.
18. ***Click Cancel in the "New Fact Box" window.***
19. In the Fact Design Gallery task pane, notice that there is a plum style Fact Box (the one you previously created). You can now add Fact Boxes with this style by clicking on the style.
20. ***Double-click anywhere in the title* "Key Events Before Trial."** This is a Text Box. Notice that the "Text Box Properties" window is now displayed. You can create a text box anywhere in a time map.
21. Edit the Text Box Properties so that instead of saying **"Key Events Before Trial,"** it says **Key Dates—Crandall v. Conners.**
22. ***Click the Colors and Lines tab of the "Text Box Properties" window.***
23. ***Under Fill—Box, click the down arrow and select yellow.***

24. ***Click the Text tab. Drag the mouse pointer so that* "Key Dates—Crandall v. Conners" *is highlighted. Click the Font Color icon.*** (It looks like the letter "A.") It should already be black.
25. ***Click OK.*** Notice that the title of the time map has now been changed.
26. The time scale in TimeMap can be adjusted easily. ***Click Time Scale on the menu bar, then click Expand.***
27. ***Click Time Scale on the menu bar and then click Expand one more time.*** Notice that the scale has expanded and that it is now on two screens. You can make the time scale as large as you wish. This is usually done to make room for more Fact Boxes.
28. You can also compress the scale width. ***Click Time Scale on the menu bar and then click Compress. Do this a total of three times.***
29. ***Click Time Scale on the menu bar and then click Expand*** to put the scale back to where it started.
30. ***Click the* "Nov 2009 Brainstorming Session —Settle/Try Decision" *Fact Box.*** Notice that the entire box is now surrounded by small white squares. These are called *handles*. If you point to one of the handles that are in the middle, on either side, or on the bottom in the middle, the cursor will change to a double-sided arrow and you can expand or contract the box.
31. ***Point to the middle handle on the right side and then drag the mouse pointer to the left toward the center of the box about a quarter of an inch.*** Notice that the box just got smaller.
32. You can also easily delete a Fact or Text Box by ***clicking to select it*** and then pressing the **[DELETE]** key, or by ***clicking the Delete icon on the toolbar.***
33. ***Click Time Scale on the menu bar and then select Increase Pages Wide.*** TimeMap responds by expanding the time map out by a whole page. It is possible to expand the time map out over many pages.
34. ***Click Time Scale on the menu bar and then click Decrease Pages Wide*** to restore the time map to its original size.
35. ***Click the Auto-Stack fact boxes icon on the toolbar.*** (It looks like three stacked boxes with a single vertical line to the right; see TimeMap Exhibit 2.) TimeMap will condense the Fact Boxes so that they are arranged more tightly.
36. ***Drag the timeline dates at the bottom of the screen*** (the gray bar with the months on it) ***up. Drag the timeline straight up to the top of the page.*** Notice that you can change the position of the timeline by dragging it.
37. Press the **[CTRL]+[Z]** keys to undo the move. If you change something in TimeMap and then do not like how it looks, just press **[CTRL]+[Z]** (or ***click Edit > Undo)*** and TimeMap will put it back the way it was.
38. In TimeMap, you do not have to change items one at a time; you may select a number of Fact Boxes and make a change to all of them at the same time. Press the **[CTRL]+[A]** keys. Notice that all of the Fact Boxes are selected.
39. ***Double-click on any Fact Box.*** The "Fact Box Properties" window is now displayed.
40. ***Click the Date Font tab. Click Italic at the bottom of the "Fact Box Properties" window to change all of the dates to italics. Click OK.*** Notice that all of the dates have been changed to italics.
41. Press the **[CTRL]+[Z]** keys on the keyboard to undo the font change.

HANDS-ON EXERCISES

42. ***Click Tools.*** Notice that one of the options is Spelling. This allows you to run a spell check on your document. ***Click anywhere outside of the drop-down menu*** to make it disappear.
43. Notice that the primary window of TimeMap has two different views. So far, we have only used the Timeline View. Now, ***click Spreadsheet View.*** See TimeMap Exhibit 5. Now you can see the same facts listed in a spreadsheet. You can also enter new facts in this view and they will appear in the Timeline View.
44. ***Click on the line where it says "Click here to add a new fact."*** In the first column, under Date & Time, type **07/01/09.** In the second column, under Fact Text, type **Prepare Motion for Summary Judgment.**
45. ***Click on Timeline View.*** You can now see the newly added fact on the timeline.

TIMEMAP EXHIBIT 5

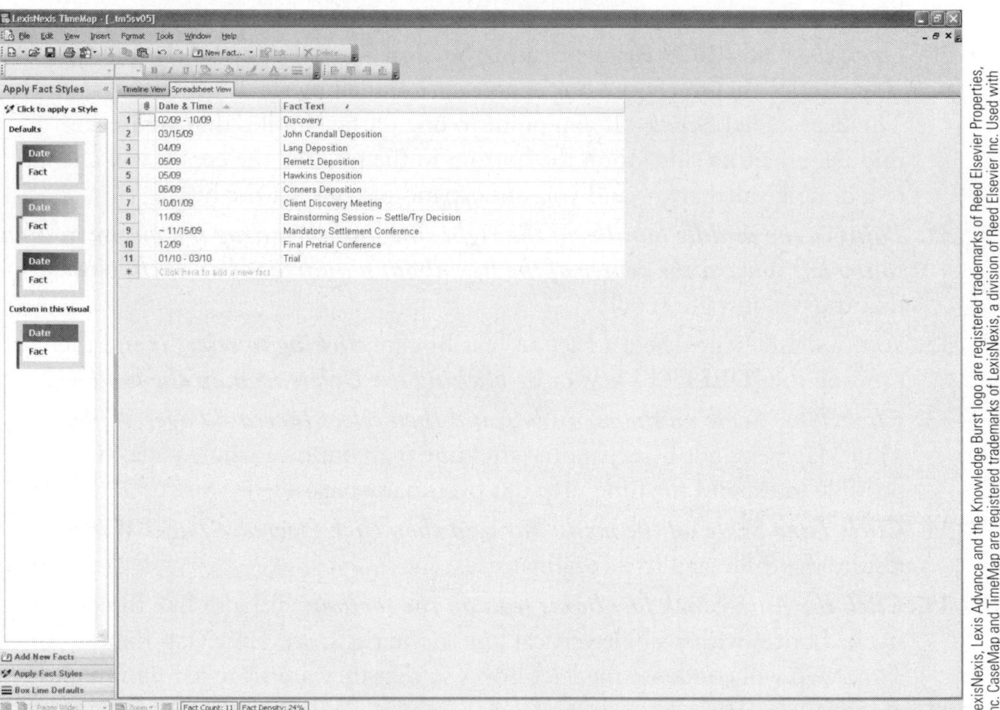

This concludes Lesson 1. ***Click File and then click Exit.*** You do not want to save your changes, so ***click No.***

INTERMEDIATE LESSVON

LESSON 2: CREATING A NEW TIMELINE IN TIMEMAP

This lesson allows you to create a completely new timeline, and assumes that you have successfully completed Lesson 1.

1. Start Windows. Then, ***double-click the LexisNexis TimeMap icon on the desktop, or click the Start button on the Windows desktop, point with the mouse to Programs or All Programs, point to the LexisNexis CaseMap Suite, and then click LexisNexis TimeMap.*** LexisNexis TimeMap will start.
2. When you start TimeMap, you may intermittently see a small window in the middle of the screen that says **"TimeMap"** and adds some information about

a grace period. If you get this message, ***click Continue in the "TimeMap" window.*** If you do not get this message, go to the next step.

3. Your screen should now look similar to TimeMap Exhibit 1. On the right side of the screen is the Getting Started task pane.
4. ***In the Getting Started task pane, under Create a New Visual, click Horizontal visual.***
5. A blank time map should be displayed.
6. ***Double-click* "Double-click to add title"** ***at the top of the page.*** Edit the text box so that it says **John R. Ewing Zoning Dispute** and then ***click OK*** to enter the title in the Text Box.
7. Using the Spreadsheet View, enter the following fact boxes:

Date & Time	*Fact Text*
01/29/12	Application for Zoning Change Filed
03/04/12	Additional Plats Filed
03/15/12	Initial Zoning Commission Hearing
03/18/12	Opposition to Zoning Change Filed by Druid Hills Homeowners Association
04/25/12	Response to Opposition to Zoning Change Filed
04/29/12	Newspaper Story on Zoning Change
05/17/12	Town Hall Meeting Druid Hills Homeowners
06/06/12	Zoning Change on County Commission Agenda
06/15/12	Zoning Commission Votes to Deny Change

See TimeMap Exhibit 6.

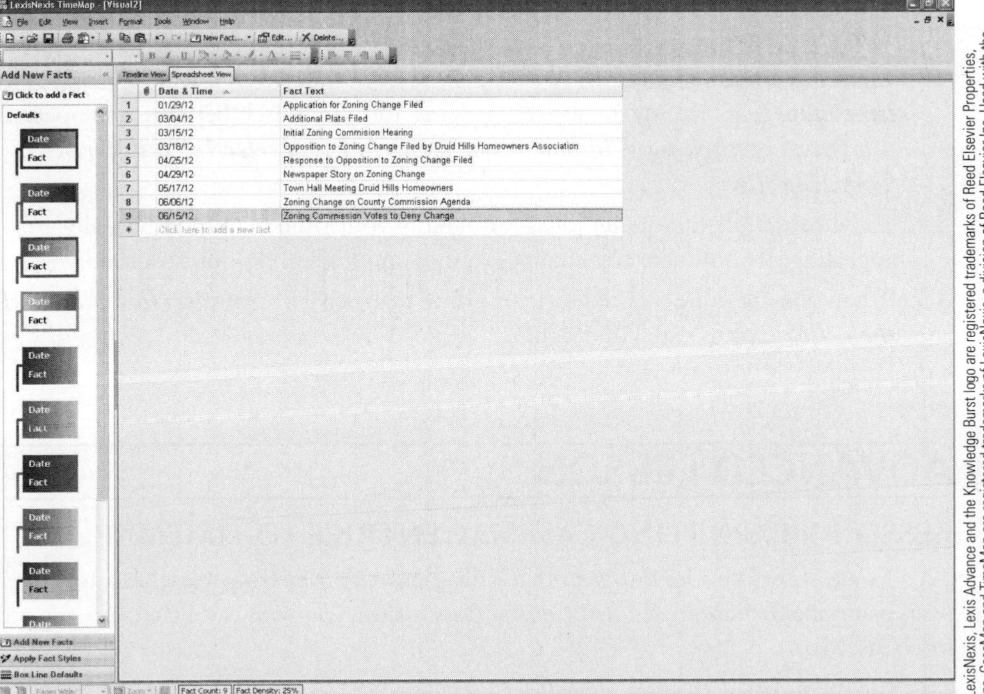

TIMEMAP EXHIBIT 6

8. ***Click Timeline View.*** Your screen should now look similar to TimeMap Exhibit 7.

TIMEMAP EXHIBIT 7

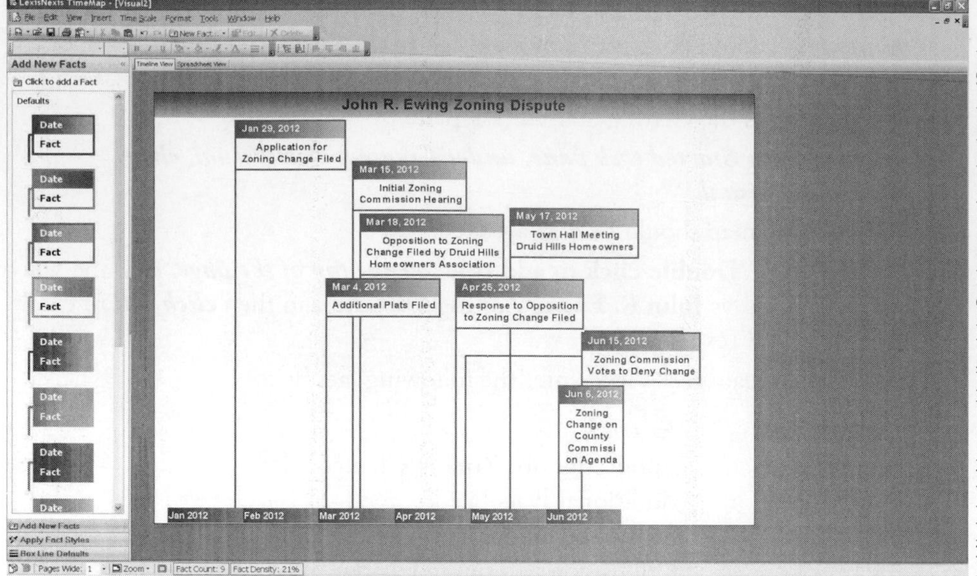

9. Press the **[CTRL]+[A]** keys on the keyboard to select all of the Fact Boxes. ***Double-click on any Fact Box*** and format the Date Font, Colors, and Lines to your liking.
10. Experiment with the features discussed in Lesson 1 to manipulate your time map, including Expand/Compress Scale Width, Increase/Decrease Pages Wide, Time Scale Break, Fit to Pages Wide, and Snap Flag Left/Right Side of Line.
11. Print your timeline by ***clicking the printer icon on the toolbar*** or by ***selecting File from the menu bar and then clicking Print.***
12. ***Click File and Save.*** Type **your name TimeMap** (e.g., Jones TimeMap), and then ***click Save.***
13. ***Click File on the menu bar, click Open, then double-click one of the example time maps*** (e.g., tm5sv01, tm5sv01). *Note*: You can switch between the open time maps by ***clicking Window on the menu bar and selecting a different TimeMap file.***
14. Use the example files to get ideas for making your time map more visually appealing. If you make any changes to the sample files, do not save them.
15. When you are done working on your time map, save it, print it, ***click File, and then click Exit*** to exit TimeMap.

This concludes Lesson 2.

ADVANCED LESSON

LESSON 3: EXPORTING CASEMAP ENTRIES TO TIMEMAP

This lesson shows you how to automatically export entries from CaseMap to TimeMap using the *Richards v. EZ Pest Control Case* (or the *Hawkins* case) that you entered into CaseMap.

1. Start Windows. ***Double-click the LexisNexis TimeMap icon on the desktop,*** or ***click the Start button on the Windows desktop, point to Programs or All Programs, point to the LexisNexis CaseMap Suite, then click LexisNexis TimeMap.*** LexisNexis TimeMap will then start.

2. When you start TimeMap, you may intermittently see a small window in the middle of the screen that says **"TimeMap"** and adds some information about a grace period. If you get this message, ***click Continue in the "TimeMap" window.*** If you do not get this message, go to the next step.
3. A blank time map should now be displayed. The right side of the screen should have the Getting Started task pane open.
4. You will now start LexisNexis CaseMap so that you can export the CaseMap entries into TimeMap. ***Click start, point to Programs or All Programs, point to the LexisNexis CaseMap Suite, then click LexisNexis CaseMap.*** When you load CaseMap, you may see a small window in the middle of the screen that says **"CaseMap"** and adds some information about a grace period. If you see this message, ***click Continue in the "CaseMap" window.*** CaseMap will then start, with several options listed on the right of the screen. If you do not see this message, go to the next step.
5. ***Under Open a Case in the Getting Started task pane,*** **Richards v. EZ Pest Control file** is not there, ***click*** **Hawkins v. Anstar** ***under Open the example case.***
6. The "Case Log On" window should now be displayed. ***Click the down arrow, click Dave Paralegal, then click OK.***
7. The CaseMap Fact spreadsheet should now be displayed. ***Click File on the menu bar, click Send To, then click LexisNexis TimeMap and click Spreadsheet.***
8. The chronology from CaseMap should now be exported into TimeMap and the Richards timeline should be displayed (see TimeMap Exhibit 8).
9. If you loaded the *Hawkins* case, you may need to select some of the longer entries and edit them down. Regardless of the case you choose, you can see how entries in CaseMap can be automatically sent to TimeMap.

TIMEMAP EXHIBIT 8

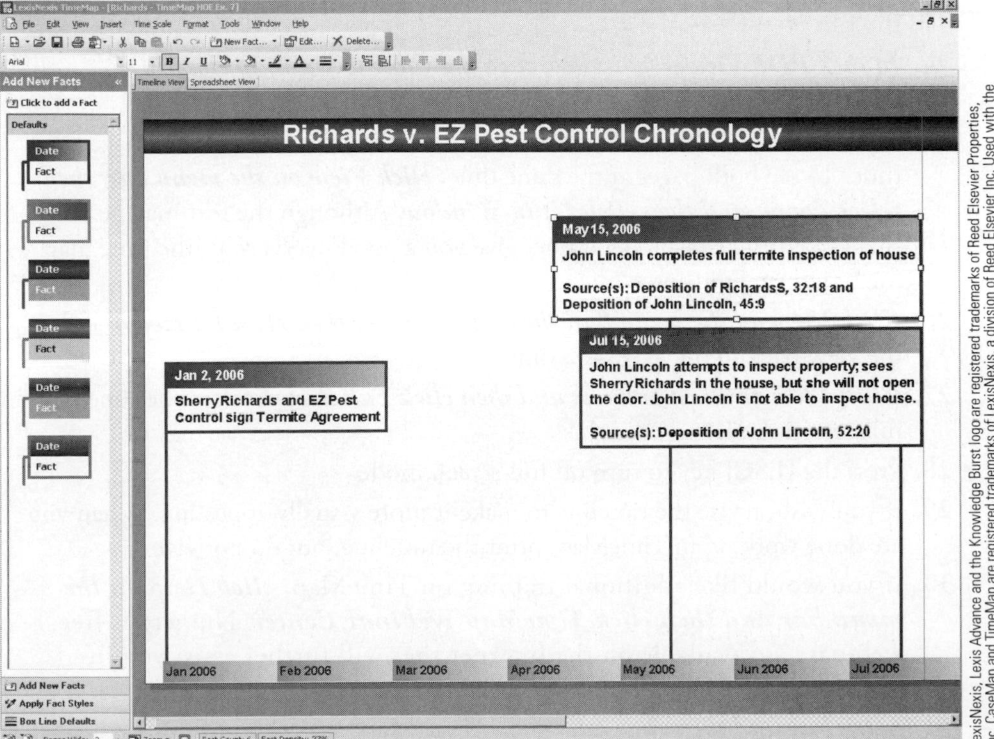

10. Note that instead of sending all entries from CaseMap to TimeMap, you can also choose to send only one entry at a time.
11. ***Click CaseMap*** at the bottom of the screen to switch to CaseMap.
12. ***Right-click any record in the Fact Text field.***
13. ***Point to Send to, then LexisNexis TimeMap, then Current Record.*** By choosing Current Record, only the specific record is sent to TimeMap, rather than the entire spreadsheet.
14. ***Click TimeMap*** at the bottom of the screen to switch to TimeMap.
15. In LexisNexis TimeMap 5, you can export time maps to other programs, such as Microsoft PowerPoint. It works best when Fact Boxes are not split across pages. If you are using the *Richards v. EZ Pest Control* case, ***drag the July 15, 2006 Fact Box to the left so that it fits on page 1 of the time map.*** Do the same thing for the Aug ??, 2006 Fact Box.
16. ***Click File on the menu bar and then point to Send to.*** Notice that one of the options is Microsoft PowerPoint.
17. If you have Microsoft PowerPoint installed on your computer, ***point to Send to Microsoft PowerPoint.***
18. ***Click One Slide per Page.***
19. Microsoft PowerPoint should now open with the time map displayed.
20. ***In the Microsoft PowerPoint window, click the Close icon*** (the X) to close Microsoft PowerPoint.
21. When a Microsoft PowerPoint dialog box opens, ***click No,*** because you do not want to save the file.
22. You can also convert time maps to PDF files. ***Click File the menu bar, point to Print to PDF, then click Print to PDF (File).***
23. ***In the Save As dialog box, click Save*** to accept the default directory and default file name. ***Click Yes*** to indicate that you would like to open the file.
24. ***In the "PDF Viewer" window, click the Close*** (X) ***icon to close PDF Viewer.***
25. The time map currently spans two pages, but you can only see one page at a time. To see both pages at the same time, ***click View on the menu bar, then select Zoom, and then click Fit in Window.*** Although the text may be too small to edit in this mode, it does give you a good overview of the time map for formatting purposes.
26. ***Click View on the menu bar, then select Zoom, then click Fit Height*** to bring the view back to one page at a time.
27. ***Click View on the menu bar and then click Full Screen*** to see the time map in full-screen mode.
28. Press the **[ESC]** key to turn off full-screen mode.
29. If you wish, revise the timeline to make it more visually appealing. When you are done working in TimeMap, print the timeline, but do not save it.
30. If you would like additional training on TimeMap, ***click Help on the menu bar and then click TimeMap Webinar Center.*** Numerous free webinars are available on the Internet that will further assist you in learning TimeMap.
31. ***Click File and then click Exit*** to exit TimeMap.

This concludes the TimeMap tutorial.

CHAPTER 9

The Internet, Computer-Assisted Legal Research, and Electronic Mail

CHAPTER OBJECTIVES

After completing this chapter, you should be able to do the following:

1. Explain the different types of services the Internet offers.
2. Discuss problems with using the Internet for research.
3. Explain what a listserv is.
4. Describe the difference between a subject-oriented search engine and a metasearch engine.
5. List resources for finding precise legal information on the Internet.
6. List resources for finding factual information on the Internet.
7. Explain why manual research and computerized research complement one another.
8. Explain what is involved in planning a search query.
9. Formulate simple search queries for Westlaw or Lexis.

INTRODUCTION TO THE INTERNET

The Internet is one of the world's largest computer networks; it is variously described as a "network of networks," "the information superhighway," or "cyberspace." It connects hundreds of millions of computers and thousands of networks around the world. Unlike Westlaw, Lexis, or other online services, no one owns the Internet as a whole or runs it. The Internet simply connects thousands of computers that use the same network protocol or language. Each network on the Internet is independently owned and operated. To access the Internet, all a user needs is a computer, communication software, communication technology such as a cable modem, and an account with an Internet access provider.

When you do **computer-assisted legal research (CALR)**, you use a computer to search for and retrieve legal information. The two best-known and most-used CALR service providers are Westlaw and Lexis.

computer-assisted legal research (CALR)
Research method in which computers are used to find and retrieve legal information.

Connecting to the Internet

To connect to the Internet, you need a computer, a modem or cable modem, a means of connecting to the Internet, Internet software, and an **Internet service provider (ISP)**. An ISP provides its users with Internet services such as the World Wide Web, email, listservs, newsgroups, and many others. Some of the largest ISPs

Internet service provider (ISP)
Supplies users with Internet services such as the World Wide Web, email, listservs, newsgroups, and others.

include Comcast and AT&T. Users now have many options for connecting to the "information superhighway," such as DSL, cable modem, T1 line, and others. These options, though more expensive than a traditional telephone line, have much larger bandwidths and thus are much faster at carrying and displaying video, sounds, and graphics. Most legal organizations now use one or more of these faster options.

World Wide Web

World Wide Web
An Internet system, navigation tool, and graphical/multimedia interface that retrieves information using links to other web pages. To access the Web, a user needs a web browser program.

The **World Wide Web** is an Internet system, navigation tool, and interface that retrieves information using Internet addresses and links to web pages. To access the Web, you need a web browser program such as Microsoft Internet Explorer, Google Chrome, or Mozilla Firefox.

The Web is a graphical and multimedia interface. Web pages can contain text, graphical images, moving pictures, animation, and sound, and often use hypermedia or hypertext links. If you are at a web page that references another website and supplies a hypermedia or hypertext link, all you have to do is click the link to be taken immediately to the new website. The millions of websites available on the Web include many law-related websites.

To find information on the Web, you often need to use a search engine. Whether you are looking for legal materials or nonlegal materials, there are tricks for how to find the desired information quickly and accurately.

Many legal organizations have their own web pages, as well as intranet and/or extranet sites. All of these are covered in detail in this chapter.

Web Browser Software

web browser
The interface or program that allows the user to see web pages.

uniform resource locator (URL)
The address of a web page.

To access the World Wide Web, you must have web browser software installed on your computer. A **web browser** is the interface or program that allows you to see web pages. Two popular web browsers are Microsoft's Internet Explorer and Mozilla Firefox. After a web browser has been properly installed, you simply load the browser software, which then connects to your ISP. Once connected to the ISP, the browser software loads your home web page.

Everything on the Web has a unique address, known as a **uniform resource locator (URL)**. When a web browser loads, it automatically defaults to the user's home URL. You can change your home URL at any time by entering the new URL in the browser, or by changing the setting in the software's "Preferences" section.

Electronic Mail

electronic mail (email)
Computerized communication function that enables users to send and receive messages almost instantly.

Electronic mail (email) enables users to send and receive messages almost instantly. Because the Internet is one of the largest networks of computers in the world, it allows hundreds of millions of users to send messages to each other, whether it is across a city or across the world. When a user obtains an Internet account, she or he is given an email address, which is what other people will use to send email to that user. Sending and receiving email is very straightforward: users send messages, receive messages, and manage their mailboxes with a mail program. Email is discussed in more detail later in this chapter.

File Transfer Protocol (FTP)

File Transfer Protocol (FTP)
A tool or standard for transferring electronic files over the Internet.

File Transfer Protocol (FTP) is a tool or standard for transferring files over the Internet. In many cases, administrators copy certain files to public directories on their FTP servers. Users can then download the files from the FTP server. There are publicly available FTP sites, allowing access to millions of files. FTP software lets you choose a computer to connect to and then enables you to upload or download files, including text, pictures, sounds, cases, and statutes. You can download files using an Internet browser or a special FTP program.

Listservs

A **listserv** (a short name that stands for "list server") is an electronic mailing list that allows people on the list to send email messages to and receive messages from everyone on the list. To join a listserv, you send an email indicating that you want to subscribe. After you have been added to the listserv, you receive copies of any emails sent to that listserv. Also, when you send an email to the listserv, everyone on the listserv gets a copy of your message.

A listserv is an easy way for people to communicate through email. There are thousands of listservs on the Internet, each dedicated to a particular topic or area of interest. You can find listserv mailing lists by searching "listserv" using a search engine (described later in this chapter).

listserv
An electronic mailing list that allows people on the list to send messages to and receive messages from everyone on the list via email.

instant messaging (IM)
Communication function that allows users to converse in real time with other users who are using the same IM program. As soon as a user connects to the Internet, the user will know which of his or her colleagues are signed on and be able to send them messages.

Instant Messaging

Instant messaging (IM) allows users to "converse" electronically, in real time, with other users. As soon as a user of an instant messaging program connects to the Internet, he or she will know exactly which colleagues are signed on to the Internet. IM software allows you to send any or all of them a message, even if they all use different ISPs.

Blogs

A **blog** (short for weblog) is a website with information contained in "posts" that are arranged in reverse chronological order. Blog postings resemble diary or journal entries, and may contain links to other websites or articles.

There are many law-related blogs on the Internet, including specialized blogs on certain types of law and even paralegal-related blogs (see paralegalgateway.typepad.com and estrinlegaled.typepad.com). Law-related blogs are sometimes called "blawgs." A good way of finding blogs on the Internet is to use Google's blog search tool, blogsearch.google.com.

blog
A website with information contained in posts (writings resembling diary or journal entries) that are arranged in reverse chronological order.

RSS

RSS is a group of formats that are used to publish and distribute news feeds, blogs, and podcasts. RSS allows users to "push" news, blog updates, and other information to RSS readers and web pages. Users can subscribe to RSS feeds and access the updated information as soon as it comes in. Free RSS reader programs are widely available on the Internet.

There are many legal-related RSS feeds, including one for recent U.S. Supreme Court opinions (www.law.cornell.edu/supct/rss/supct_recent.rss) and one for recent copyright information from the U.S. Copyright Office (see www.copyright.gov).

RSS
A group of formats that are used to publish and distribute news feeds, blogs, and podcasts.

Podcasts

A **podcast** is an audio or video recording that is posted on the Internet and is typically made available for users to download so they can listen to it on a computer or mobile computing device. Music, lectures, blogs, and other recordings can be made available as podcasts and can also be pushed to users using an RSS format. You can search for podcasts by subject matter (including legal-related podcasts) at www.allpodcasts.com and www.itunes.com.

podcast
An audio or video recording that is posted on the Internet and made available for users to download so they can listen or watch it on a computer or mobile computing device.

USE OF THE INTERNET IN LEGAL ORGANIZATIONS

Most, if not all, legal organizations are connected to the Internet and are using it in a variety of ways. Some of the most common uses include performing legal research, performing factual and business research, using email to communicate with clients and colleagues, accessing court records, filing documents electronically, marketing, taking online depositions, and conducting online learning.

Performing Legal Research on the Internet

A great deal of legal material is available on the Internet. Unfortunately, unlike Westlaw and Lexis, it is not all available in one place: it is scattered all over the Internet. The positive side of legal research on the Internet is that most of the information is free. The resources available include federal case law, federal legislative materials, government regulations, and state case law. Later in this chapter, we explore in detail the process of finding legal materials and conducting legal research on the Internet.

Performing Factual and Business Research on the Internet

You may undertake factual research to find people and information about people, find expert witnesses, find evidence useful for impeaching experts and other witnesses, gather information regarding businesses, and look for facts in newspaper articles and other sources about cases or witnesses. Later in this chapter, we discuss in more detail how to perform factual research on the Internet.

Using Email to Communicate with Clients and Colleagues

Email is a very convenient form of communication for legal professionals. It is nearly instantaneous, creates a record for both tracking and saving information, is inexpensive, is easy to use, and is convenient (unlike the telephone, you don't have to play telephone tag with busy callers). Its use is widespread, so many clients, colleagues, vendors, and others can be reached via email. Email programs even allow you to send or attach documents, such as word-processing documents, to an email message.

Email has been wholeheartedly accepted by the legal community, and is now used as much as (if not more than) the telephone for both internal communication with colleagues and external communication with clients, courts, and other legal organizations. Email is covered in depth later in this chapter.

Accessing Court Records and Filing Documents Electronically

Most courts allow legal professionals to access court records electronically, which is often more convenient (and almost always faster) than calling clerks or other staff for information or hard copies of documents. Many courts also allow documents to be filed electronically. Electronic filing offers time savings, cost savings, and convenience over filing of paper documents.

Marketing a Law Firm on the Internet

Law firms have realized that having a web page means that the firm can be marketed 24 hours a day, 7 days a week, to a potential nationwide and even worldwide audience. Law firm web pages are covered in more detail later in this chapter.

Taking Online Depositions

Attorneys can take depositions using an online deposition service. Typically, an attorney would use this kind of service to participate in an out-of-town deposition from his or her own office. The online deposition service provides live video and two-way audio on a secure Internet feed. Many such services also provide real-time transcription. The attorney is able to see and hear the witness, court reporter, and opposing counsel on his or her computer monitor and ask questions, make objections, and do nearly everything the attorney would do if he or she were at the deposition site. Some services even provide private online messaging so that information can be shared (securely and confidentially) between co-counsel.

Online Learning

The Internet is used to deliver online learning seminars and materials in a variety of areas to participants in legal organizations. Legal organizations can save thousands of dollars in travel costs when employees do their learning online; the organizations also experience productivity increases, since staff members never have to leave their desks.

This capability is very useful for fulfilling continuing education requirements, among many other learning opportunities. Legal organizations may also be able to supply (as well as receive) online learning content, such as seminars or webinars on specialized legal topics; or act as sponsor or host for an online course or seminar created and presented by a third party.

SEARCHING AND FINDING INFORMATION ON THE WORLD WIDE WEB

Searching the Web for information is one of the most common uses of the Internet for paralegals. If you do not have a URL for a desired website, or if you do not know exactly which website you want to access, you must use a search engine to try to find it. Unfortunately, it often is not easy to find the exact information you are looking for, due to the breadth and depth of information available on the Web. There are millions of different websites and more than 1 billion web pages on the Internet; therefore, you must learn how to find what you need quickly and precisely.

Search Engines

Most search engines use computerized functions or algorithms called spiders to search or "crawl" the Web to compile their databases. Once the spiders find a website, they typically index many of the words on the public pages at the site. Web page owners may also submit their URLs to search engines for crawling and eventual inclusion in the search-engine databases.

When you enter a search in a search engine, you are asking the engine to search its database; it is not actually searching the Web at that moment. In addition, no search engine covers the entire Web. Some search engines are better at finding particular kinds of information than others. Which search engine you use should depend on the particular information you are looking for. There are a number of different types and ways of classifying search engines.

individual search engine
Search engine that compiles its own searchable database.

An **individual search engine** compiles its own searchable database. One popular general individual search engine is Google (www.google.com). In addition to individual search engines that are general in nature, such as Google, there are also **specialty search engines**. A specialty search engine searches only in specific topical areas. Examples are www.searchgov.com, which searches government-related websites; and www.findlaw.com, which searches only law-related websites.

specialty search engine
Search engine that searches only in specific topical areas or sites.

metasearch engine
Search engine that does not crawl the Web or compile its own database, but instead sends the user's search request to a number of different individual search engines and then eliminates duplicates and sorts the sites retrieved.

subject directory
A site maintained by a staff of people who select sites to include in the directory.

portal
A "jumping-off" spot for many things on the Web, offering searching, hierarchical directories, news, sports, shopping, entertainment, and much more.

library gateway
A collection of databases and information sites arranged by subject.

subject-specific database
A database devoted to a single subject or area.

Another kind of search engine is a **metasearch engine**. A metasearch engine does not crawl the Web or compile its own database. Instead, it sends the user's search request to a number of different individual search engines, eliminates the duplicate hits, and sorts or ranks the sites retrieved. Metasearch engines provide a quick overview of a subject and can be used to quickly find which engines will probably yield the best results for your particular search. Popular metasearch engines include www.metacrawler.com and www.dogpile.com.

A **subject directory** is a site maintained by an organization's staff, who select sites to include in the directory database. A popular subject directory is Yahoo! (www.yahoo.com). Yahoo! editors organize directory hierarchies into subject categories; the "Web Site Directory" at www.yahoo.com is an example of this. It should be noted that the line between search engines and subject directories is becoming somewhat blurry, with each sometimes combining both types of search techniques.

Many search engines or subject directory sites, such as Yahoo!, are also portals. A **portal** is a "jumping-off" point for many things on the Web, offering searching, hierarchical directories, news, sports, shopping, entertainment, and much more. The basic portal concept is that a user will go to one place on the Web to start and then fan out to a number of other sites from that one starting point. FindLaw.com is a popular legal portal.

Another way to find information on the Web is to use a gateway site such as a **library gateway**. A library gateway is a collection of databases and information sites arranged by subject. These gateways usually support research and reference needs by pointing users to recommended, academically oriented pages on the Web. Exhibit 9–1 is an example of a library gateway.

Another way to find information on the Web is to use a **subject-specific database** that collects materials on a single subject. For example, CareerBuilder.com is a subject-specific database that is totally devoted to finding jobs. The open-position database in CareerBuilder.com usually contains hundreds of thousands of listings. There are many such subject-specific databases on the Web.

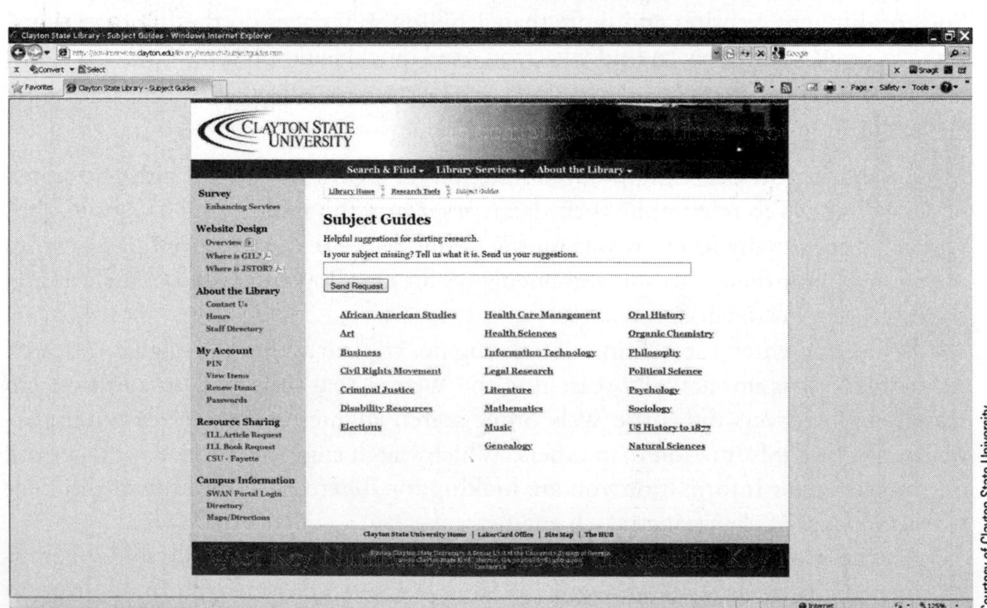

Courtesy of Clayton State University

EXHIBIT 9–1
Library gateway

The **invisible Web**, sometimes called the deep Web, refers to the fact that a large portion of the World Wide Web is not accessible to search-engine spiders. For one reason or another, search engines cannot access these sites/pages; they may be password protected, in databases, behind firewalls, or otherwise invisible or inaccessible to the search engines. It is estimated that more than 50 percent of the Web falls into this category.

invisible Web
Term for the large portion of the World Wide Web that is not accessible to search engine spiders. This includes PDF files, password-protected sites, some databases, documents behind firewalls, and other data/sites.

For example, a search engine will not find a job opening that is listed in Careerbuilder.com, because that site is a database and individual entries therein are protected. To access "invisible" websites, you must point your web browser directly to the desired site (which, of course, means that you must know its exact URL, and often that you must have permission to enter or access the site). Exhibit 9–2 shows a variety of websites for search engines, gateways, and databases on the Web.

Search Strategies

The following subsections describe a variety of general strategies for searching the Web.

EXHIBIT 9–2
Search engines, gateways, and databases of interest to paralegals

Name of Site	Web URL (Address)
General Individual/Subject Directory Search Engines	
Excite	www.excite.com
Google	www.google.com
Lycos	www.lycos.com
MSN Search	http://search.msn.com
WebCrawler	www.webcrawler.com
Yahoo	www.yahoo.com
Specialty Search Engines	
Google US Government	www.google.com
SearchGov (Government)	www.searchgov.com
SearchEdu (Education)	www.searchedu.com
SearchMil (Military)	www.searchmil.com
Metasearch Engines	
Dogpile	www.dogpile.com
Ixquick	www.ixquick.com
Kartoo	www.kartoo.com
Metacrawlor	www.metacrawler.com
Library Gateways	
Academic Information	www.academicinfo.net
Digital Librarian	www.digital-librarian.com
Infomine	http://infomine.ucr.edu
Librarians' Index to the Internet	www.lii.org
The Internet Public Library	www.ipl.org
Virtual Library	www.vlib.org
Subject-Specific Databases	
Careerbuilder.com (employment)	www.careerbuilder.com
WebMD (health/medical information)	www.webmd.com

EXHIBIT 9–3
Advanced Search options in Google

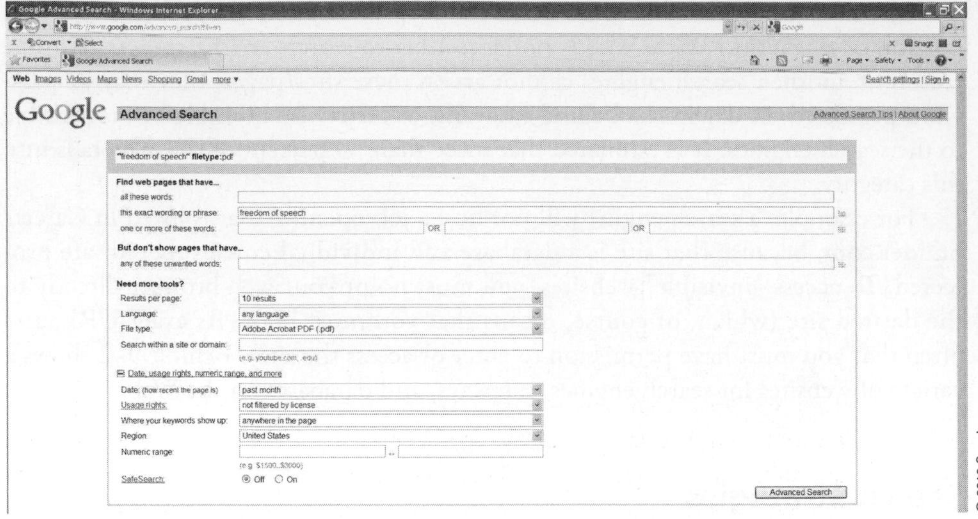

Think about Your Search Different searches require different strategies. If you are looking for general information about a topic, a subject directory search engine such as Yahoo.com or a metasearch engine such as dogpile.com are good places to start. If you are looking for a very narrow topic or specific piece of information, consider what the subject matter is and use a specialty search engine or a database to find the information. For example, if you were looking for government-related information, it would be best to start with a government search engine such as SearchGov (www.searchgov.com); if you were looking for information on a detailed medical issue, it would be best to search WebMD (www.webmd.com). The more detailed or specific the information you are looking for, the more specialized your search engine or database will most likely have to be. See Exhibit 9–2 for a listing of search engines.

Use Advanced Search Options Most search engines have an area on the title page that directs you to advanced search. Advanced search options allow you to tailor your search so that it does not return thousands of documents. For example, in Exhibit 9–3 the user has entered the exact phrase she is looking for (freedom of speech). She has also directed Google to return files in Portable Document Format (PDF) only. Note that she could have limited it to other file formats as well, such as Word, Excel, or PowerPoint. Exhibit 9–3 also shows that she limited the search to web pages that have been updated in the past month, in the hopes of getting only current articles; and that she limited the search to the title of the page, in order to get articles directly on point. Using advanced options is a great way to increase efficiency and get better search results more quickly.

Read the Help or Search Guide Files for the Search Engines You Use Different search engines may require you to use different syntax for entering searches. Always read the help file for the search engine you are currently using to make sure you are entering search commands correctly. Users all too commonly assume that the commands are the same in various search engines, only to find out later that a search was not performed properly because the syntax was incorrect for the search engine used.

Make Your Search Query Specific To return only relevant documents, make your search query specific. For example, if you are searching for documents about the United States Supreme Court Rules, do not search on the overly broad topic of "United States Supreme Court." Use modifiers, such as the following, to make your search as specific as possible.

- *Use + (plus) and – (minus) signs.* Use plus and minus signs to force inclusion or exclusion of a word in searches. For example, if the search was: *+Roosevelt –Theodore,* the search would find documents with "Roosevelt" but without the word "Theodore." If you wanted results that included Franklin Roosevelt but not Theodore Roosevelt, the query would be *+Roosevelt +Franklin –Theodore.* The plus and minus signs work in many but not all search engines; be sure to consult the help guide for each engine you want to use.
- *Search for phrases using quotation marks.* If you are looking for a specific phrase, put the phrase in quotation marks so that the search engine will retrieve only documents that have the words exactly as you typed them. For example, *"Joint tenants with rights of survivorship"* would retrieve sites and documents with exactly those words in exactly that order, but not ones where those words appear scattered throughout the document.
- *Combine plus and minus signs and phrases.* You can also combine the plus and minus signs and phrase searching in one query: for example, *"Franklin Delano Roosevelt"–"New Deal"+"World War II."* This query would yield results that had the exact phrase "Franklin Delano Roosevelt" and the phrase "World War II," but did not have the phrase "New Deal." (Again, be sure to consult the help guide for each engine you want to use to find the correct format and syntax for the search.)

Put Your Most Important Words First Usually, the best strategy is to put the most important or most specific word first in the search.

PERFORMING LEGAL RESEARCH ON THE INTERNET

You can perform legal research on the Internet, but it is not at all like researching on Westlaw or Lexis. In Westlaw and Lexis, you can look up, choose, and go to thousands of databases instantly; searches go through a uniform search engine using uniform Boolean language; and information is formatted neatly, succinctly, and uniformly. Even so, it still takes time, training, and experience to become proficient at using Westlaw or Lexis.

When performing legal research on the Internet in general (rather than through a proprietary service), you will find that little is uniform. You must search for and find information where you can, and you must learn the nuances of many different search techniques and languages. There is no one central depository of information. As with any kind of legal research, the more experience you have, the better, but it takes time, training, and experience to get good at it.

You can expect to find the following legal information on the Internet, by using the sites listed in Exhibit 9–4:

- Indexes by legal topic (tax law, intellectual property, family law, etc.)
- Government sites (extensive)
- United States Supreme Court cases (extensive)
- Federal appellate court cases (extensive)
- Federal district court cases (partial)
- Federal laws, regulations, and legislative bills (extensive—including *United States Code, Federal Register, Congressional Record, Code of Federal Regulations*)

Subject	Additional Information	Web URL (Address)
Legal Research Engine/Portal		
All Law	Legal search engine/portal	www.alllaw.com
FindLaw	Legal search engine/portal	www.findlaw.com
Internet Legal Research Group	Legal search engine	www.ilrg.com
Lawguru	Legal search engine/portal	www.lawguru.com
General Starting Points (Federal/State Case Law, Statutes, and Legal Subject Matter)		
Hieros Gamos	Large collection of links to legal resources	www.hg.org
Law Research	Large collection of links to legal resources	www.lawresearch.com
Legal Information Institute at Cornell	Large collection of links to legal resources	www.law.cornell.edu
Virtual Chase	Large collection of links to legal resources	www.virtualchase.com
WashLaw Web at Washburn University	Large collection of links to legal resources	www.washlaw.edu
Federal Government Information, Regulations, Laws, Bills, U.S. Code		
FedWorld	Government information	www.fedworld.gov
First Gov	Government search engine	www.firstgov.com
Google US Government	Government search engine	www.google.com/ig/usgov
SearchGov	Government search engine	www.searchgov.com
Code of Federal Regulations	Database for the Code of Federal Regulations	www.law.cornell.edu
GPO Access	Wide variety of federal government resources	www.gpoaccess.gov
Cornell Legal Information Institute	Wide variety of federal government resources	www.law.cornell.edu
Library of Congress	Bills, resolutions, Congressional Record	http://thomas.loc.gov
Legal Forms		
Internet Legal Resource Guide Forms	Free legal forms database	www.ilrg.com
Legal Encyclopedia and References		
Findlaw Legal Dictionary	Legal dictionary	dictionary.lp.findlaw.com
Law About (from Cornell Law School Legal Information Institute)	Legal encyclopedia	www.law.cornell.edu
Law Dictionary	Legal dictionary	http://dictionary.law.com
Legal Dictionary	Legal dictionary	www.legal-dictionary.org
Federal Courts		
Administrative Offices of the U.S. Courts	Links to all federal courts	www.uscourts.gov
Federal Courts Finder	Links to all federal courts	www.law.emory.edu
State Courts		
National Center for State Courts	Information on state (and federal) courts	www.ncsconline.org
Fee-Based Legal Research		
Casemaker.com	Online fee-based legal research	www.casemaker.us
Fastcase.com	Online fee-based legal research	www.fastcase.com
Lexis	Full online fee-based legal research	www.lexis.com
Loislaw.com	Online fee-based legal research	www.loislaw.com
Versuslaw.com	Online fee-based legal research	www.versuslaw.com
Westlaw	Full online fee-based legal research	www.westlaw.com

EXHIBIT 9–4

Legal research starting points

- Federal Rules of Civil Procedure, Federal Rules of Evidence, Federal Rules of Criminal Procedure, Federal Rules of Bankruptcy Procedure; Uniform Commercial Code
- Executive orders (extensive)
- State court cases (extensive)
- State statutes (extensive)
- Legal forms
- Legal references (extensive)

Legal Research on the Internet—An Example

If you wanted to read the U.S. Supreme Court opinion *New York Times Co. v. Sullivan,* 376 U.S. 254 (1964), on the Internet, you could take many avenues to get there. Because an historic case like this is readily available on the Internet, it would be a waste of money (unless you had a flat-rate agreement) to use Westlaw or Lexis. As indicated previously, you need to determine where your starting point will be. Although you could start at FindLaw, Lawguru, or another legal search engine, it is probable that an important case like this would be on Cornell's Legal Information Institute site (www.law.cornell.edu). Go to Cornell's site and click "Read the law," then "Supreme Court," and then "By party—historic." You will see an alphabetical list of historical decisions. Clicking "New York Times Co. v. Sullivan" will display the case on your screen.

In November 2009, the legal research landscape changed dramatically, as Google made it possible to search state and federal case law. The method of searching and the search results are strikingly similar to those you would see if you used Westlaw or Lexis. The first screen of Exhibit 9–5 shows the Google home page; from there,

EXHIBIT 9–5
Google Scholar

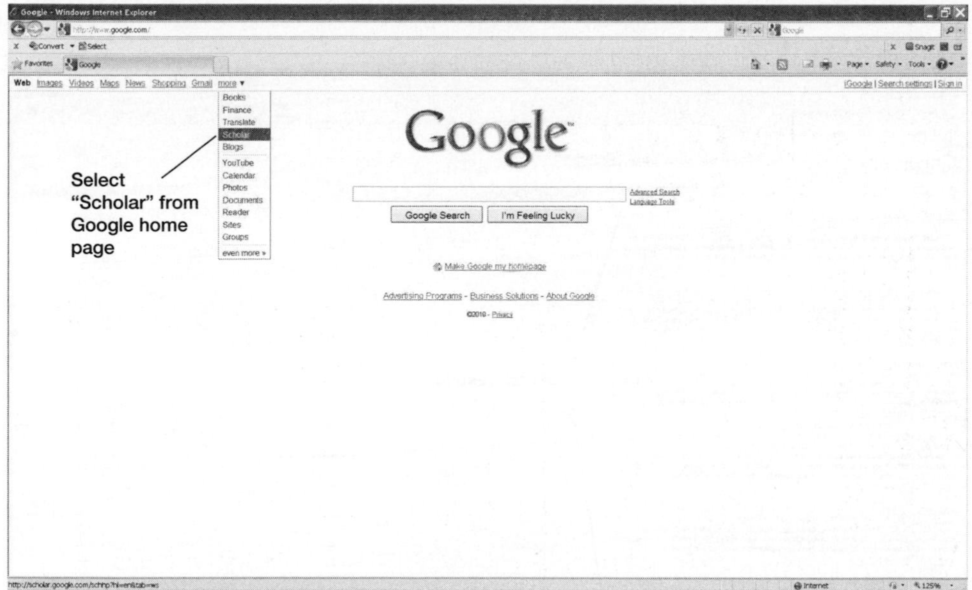

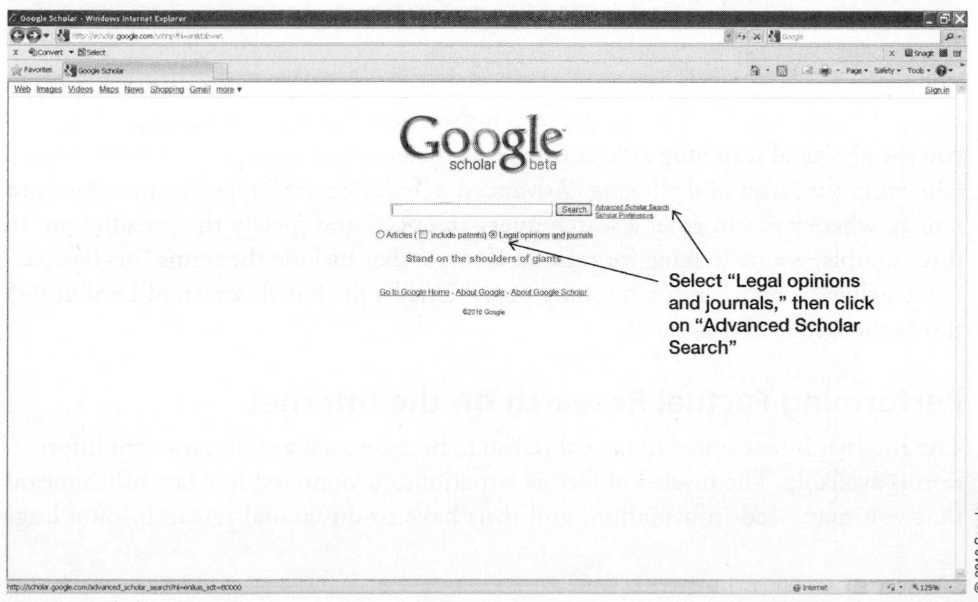

EXHIBIT 9–5
(continued)

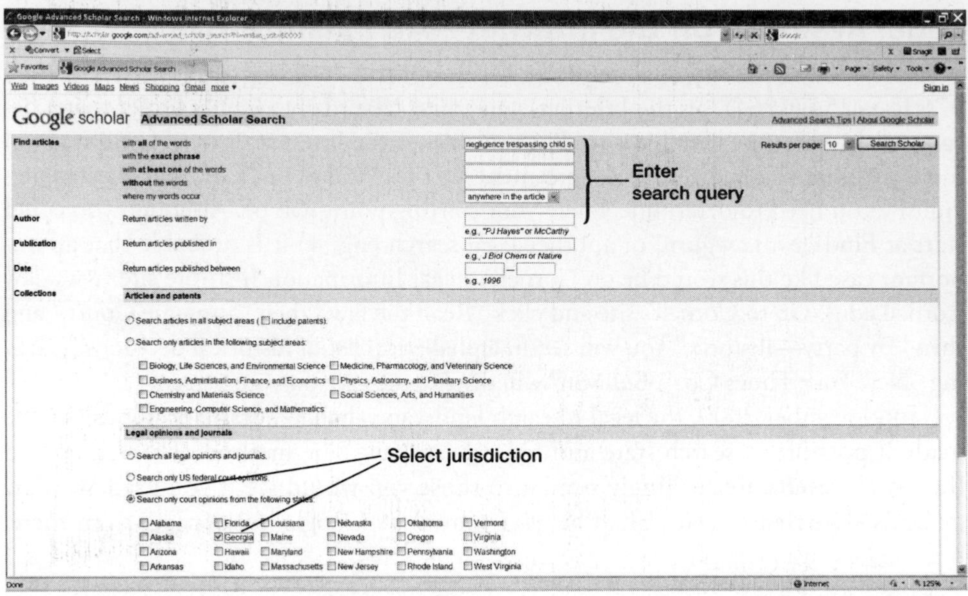

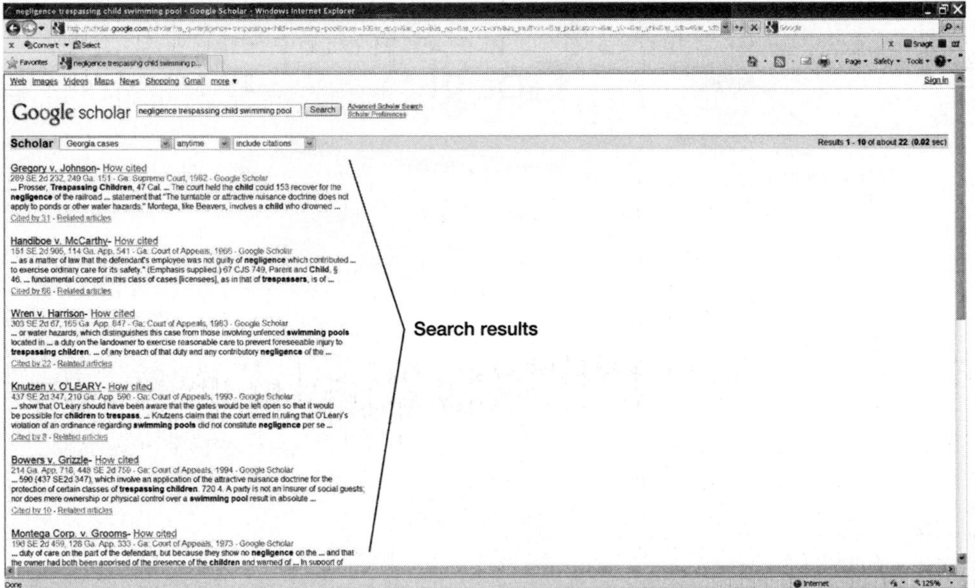

choose Google Scholar. The second screen shows the Google Scholar page that gives you the choice of searching articles (including patents) or legal opinions and journals. Choosing the latter and clicking "Advanced Scholar Search" takes you to the third screen, where you can enter a search query (request) and specify the jurisdiction. In this example, we are looking for cases in Georgia that include the terms "negligence," "trespassing," "child," and "swimming pool." Finally, the fourth screen of Exhibit 9–5 shows the results of this search.

Performing Factual Research on the Internet

The Internet is best suited to factual research, because such a wide variety of information is available. The myriad of factual situations encountered in a law office means that you may need information, and thus have to do factual research, on a huge variety of topics. Here are some examples of common situations in which a paralegal might be asked to do factual research:

- You are performing collections work and you need to do a skip-trace on a debtor who has left the area.
- Your firm has a client who was adopted, and the client wants your firm to find his birth parents.
- A crucial witness for a case you are working on has disappeared, and you need to find the witness or her relatives or neighbors so you can get a message to her.
- The attorney you are working for has to cross-examine the other party's expert witness and has asked you to find out everything you can about the expert for impeachment purposes.
- Your corporate law department needs to find reputable local counsel to litigate a breach of contract case halfway across the country.
- One of your firm's best clients is considering a merger offer from another company. You have been asked to find out as much as possible about the other company, using materials that include SEC filings, annual reports, stock prices, and any news reports on the company for the past year.
- Your firm is considering getting involved in a medical malpractice case and you need to do some general background research regarding a specific type of surgery and medical condition.
- Your client is considering purchasing a piece of real estate and you have been asked to find out as much about the property as you can.
- During litigation, the opposing party has made numerous statements to the press; you have been asked to find every such occurrence and document exactly what the person said for impeachment purposes.
- Your client was involved in an automobile collision and you have been asked to get a photograph of the intersection where it happened.

In all these situations, the Internet would be useful for finding information. Exhibit 9–6 shows listings of fact-related websites by subject. Such sites can help you find everything from an email address, to who is an inmate in a federal prison, to financial data on a publicly traded company—and much, much more.

Unfortunately, there is no standard or uniform way of entering or finding factual information on the Internet. The Internet is a virtual haystack of enormous proportions, and finding the right needle takes time and effort; the user may have to look in many, many sites to find it, or may never find it. Searching for information on the Internet is like anything else: becoming good at it takes time and experience. The more time you spend doing it, the better you will become, the more resources you will acquire, and the more tricks you will learn. The following section covers additional information regarding factual research on the Internet classified by subject.

General Information

A huge variety of general information is available on the Internet, although the quality and accuracy of this information varies enormously. General search engines are one excellent way to search for general information on the Internet. Exhibit 9–6 lists Internet sites for dictionaries, encyclopedias, maps, a Zip Code finder, thesauruses,

Name/Subject	Additional Information	URL Web (Address)
General Sites		
Dictionary	Dictionary	www.dictionary.com
Dictionary	Merriam-Webster	www.webster.com
Encyclopedia	Encyclopedia	www.reference.com
Encyclopedia	Encyclopedia Britannica	www.britannica.com
Encyclopedia	High Beam Encyclopedia	www.encyclopedia.com
General factual research site	Good starting point for any research project	www.virtualchase.com
Maps	MapQuest	www.mapquest.com
National lawyer directory	FindLaw	www.findlaw.com
National lawyer directory	Martindale-Hubbell	www.martindale.com
Google Maps	Satellite and street level images for major cities	http://maps.google.com/
Thesaurus	Thesaurus	http://thesaurus.reference.com
Zip Codes	U.S. Postal Service	www.usps.gov
Public Records (Free)		
Court cases/criminal cases (federal)	PACER (Public Access to Court Electronic Records)—Provides access to an index of filings in federal district, bankruptcy, and appellate courts	http://pacer.uspci.uscourts.gov
Criminal records	Virtual Chase.com—Excellent links to federal and state resources related to criminal records	www.virtualchase.com
Criminal records—Sex offenders	Sex offender database	www.sexoffender.com
Public record links and research strategies	Virtual Chase.com—Excellent links to public records	www.virtualchase.com
Public record portal	BRB Public Information Records—Large portal to many sites with public records	www.brbpub.com
Real estate records	NETR Online—Real estate public records	www.netronline.com
State public records	Public record information is available from individual state websites. Many, but not all, states have a standard Web address: www.state.XX.us (at XX enter the state's two-letter abbreviation). Examples: Florida = www.state.fl.us; New York = www.state.ny.us	
Vital records information	Births, marriages, deaths, divorces	www.vitalrec.com
Public Records (Fee Based)		
Public and court records	Court Records.Org—Various public information, including criminal histories, property ownership, and the like in one place	www.courtrecords.org
Public records	Accurint—Wide variety of online information	www.accurint.com
Public records	BRP—Wide variety of public information	www.brbpub.com
Public records	Courthouse Direct—Various information, including criminal histories, property ownership, and the like in one place	www.courthousedirect.com
Public records	DCS Information Systems—Wide variety of online information	www.dnis.com
Public records	KnowX—Wide variety of online information	www.knowx.com
Public records	Search Systems—Wide variety of online information	www.searchsystems.net

EXHIBIT 9–6
Factual research starting points

resources for finding attorneys, and more. One extremely helpful Internet tool for legal organizations is sites that provide free access to satellite images of a geographic area. These images are useful in a variety of contexts, including auto accidents, some criminal matters, and insurance and property casualty litigation.

Public Records

Searching for public records on the Internet is an art form. In some instances, success requires more luck than science. Generally, public records do not contain personal information such as birth date, Social Security number, or medical or financial

Finding People, Addresses, Phone Numbers, and Email Addresses		
People, addresses, phone locator	List of links for finding people	www.pipl.com
Links and articles on finding people	Finding people	www.virtualchase.com
People, addresses, phone numbers	Database America	www.databaseamerica.com
People, addresses, phone numbers, email addresses, Yellow Pages	Bigfoot	http://search.bigfoot.net
People, addresses, phone numbers, email addresses, Yellow Pages	Infospace	www.infospace.com
People, addresses, phone numbers, email addresses, Yellow Pages	Yahoo	www.people.yahoo.com
People	Classmates.com	www.classmates.com
People	Social networking site	www.facebook.com
People	Social networking site	www.myspace.com
Other Information about People		
General information about people (living and dead)	Family Finder Index—Includes information from U.S. Census, marriage, Social Security	www.familytreemaker.com
Government record search	Search of government records for finding people	www.global-locate.com
Death database	Ancestry	www.ancestry.com
Federal prison inmates	Federal Board of Prisons	www.bop.gov
Genealogy links	Genealogy-related website links	www.cyndislist.com
Military personnel	Listing of military personnel (small monthly cost)	www.militarycity.com
Physician list	American Medical Association	www.ama-assn.org
News and Directories		
News	Directory of News Links	www.newslink.org/menu.html
News	Chicago Tribune	www.chicagotribune.com
News	Los Angeles Times	www.latimes.com
News	New York Times	www.nytimes.com
News	USA Today	www.usatoday.com
News	Wall Street Journal	www.wsj.com
News	ABC News	www.abcnews.com
News	CBS News	www.cbsnews.com
News	CNN	www.cnn.com
News	Fox News	www.foxnews.com
News	NBC News	www.msnbc.com
Researching Businesses		
Business phone/address listings	Bigfoot	http://search.bigfoot.net
Yellow Page	Yellow Pages	www.bigyellow.com
Federal Securities and Exchange Commission	Electronic Data Gathering, Analysis and Retrieval (EDGAR) database	www.sec.gov/cgi-bin/srch-edgar
Federal Securities and Exchange Commission	Required public filings for public companies	www.sec.gov

EXHIBIT 9–6
(continued)

information. Nevertheless, much information is maintained in government records, which are public. Every state, every county, every city has different rules for what information is public and what is posted online, including what form it takes, what can or cannot be searched, and at what cost. There is little uniformity even in national public record searches. It pays to know a lot about the jurisdiction in which you are seeking information. This takes time.

It is also important to realize that often information published on the Internet, even when you *can* find it, is not as complete as information maintained at the source (such as a courthouse or public recorder's office). By some estimates, less than half

Annual reports for companies	Public Register's Annual Report Service	www.prars.com
Business information	Business-related information	www.hoovers.com
Business information	Business-related information	www.companiesonline.com
Complaint information	Better Business Bureau	www.bbb.org
Finding Expert Witnesses		
Expert witnesses	Expert witness directory	www.expertpages.com
Expert witnesses	Expert witness directory	www.expertwitnessnetwork.com
Expert witnesses	Expert witness directory	www.expertwitness.com
Expert witnesses	Expert witness directory	www.jurispro.com
Expert witnesses	Technical Advisory Service for Attorneys	www.tasanet.com
Expert witnesses	Washburn University School of Law	www.washlaw.edu/
Medical-Related Information		
Medical dictionary	Medical dictionary	www.medterms.com
Medical Dictionary Online	Medical dictionary	www.online-medical-dictionary.org
Medical Conditions Glossary	Medical conditions	www.medical-conditions.org
MedLinePlus Medical Dictionary	National Library of Medicine	www.nlm.nih.gov/medlineplus /mplusdictionary.html
Stedman's Electronic Medical Dictionary	Medical dictionary	www.stedmans.com

EXHIBIT 9–6
(continued)

of public records are available on the Internet, and many of those that are available are incomplete. Therefore, once you have found a helpful public record, it is recommended that you check the actual source to see if other or further information is available.

The information available in public records is vast. Public record information for a specific jurisdiction might include:

- Vital statistics (births, deaths, marriages)
- Corporate records, such as secretary of state filings and Securities and Exchange Commission filings
- Corporation commission filings
- Court records
- Criminal records
- Licenses (law, medical, nursing, public accounting, insurance, etc.)
- Sex offenders
- Adoptions
- Bankruptcies
- Campaign contributions
- Copyrights, trademarks, and patents
- Property-related information
- Judgments/liens
- Building permits and zoning
- Foreclosures
- Environmental records
- Motor vehicle records
- Driver's license records

A good place to start is with the jurisdiction and entity that keeps the information. Is the information stored by a city, county, state, or federal government? You need to know this type of information before you can do a meaningful search.

For example, suppose you wanted to know the value of a defendant's property holdings in Houston, Texas. You could start at a fee-based public records site, but a better and less expensive way would be to start with the jurisdiction in which you are interested, and determine where such information is held. This may sound easy or obvious, but it can take some time to track this down if you are not familiar with the area or entity. In Houston, and in much of the United States, property is tracked by county, not city. Trying to search for property records for the City of Houston would be futile. However, once you know that Houston is in Harris County, Texas, you could search for the county in an Internet search engine and be directed to its website. You could then find the Harris County Appraisal District website, and use their record search tool to search by the name of the defendant to find all of the defendant's property holdings (and their appraised value) in Harris County. Some U.S. counties even include pictures of the property.

The information is all right there. However, to find this kind of information, you may not be able to just "Google" it. This is how the "invisible Web" works. The more you know about what you are looking for, where it is stored, and what names or labels it goes by, the better you will be at finding the information you are looking for.

The Internet is full of websites that charge for retrieving public information. Some provide great value and access to information that would be very difficult to find on your own; others are not worth the time, money, and effort required. Again, it helps to know exactly what you are looking for. Before using a pay site, ask a lot of questions and ask for references.

Finding People and Information About Them

Obviously, there is a lot of information about people on the Internet. Sure, you can "Google" someone by putting the name in a search engine, but many times this does not work well. First of all, if you are conducting a nationwide search for a common name, you will get back thousands of hits. Even if the name is uncommon, you can still expect to get back dozens, if not hundreds, of hits. The more information you have about who you are looking for, the better. Nevertheless, when trying to locate someone, it is recommended that you start with the obvious, such as searching for the person's name in Google, Yahoo, and the other general search engines listed in Exhibit 9–2, even though doing so will most likely turn up many hits.

To reduce the number of irrelevant hits, it is recommended that you search for exact matches using quotation marks, such as "Steven Rich," or (even better) "Steven A. Rich" or "Steven A. Rich" + Buffalo. If you do not find who you are looking for, the next step is to use the resources in the "Finding People" section of Exhibit 9–6. Enter the query carefully, making sure that you have spelled the name correctly, and use many variations based on the information you have. Being creative sometimes works, particularly if you know any information about the person that can be used during the search process to narrow the results.

News

The Internet has vast numbers of news-related sites. Sometimes you may need to find background information related to business dealings or companies. News sites provide broad-based information that is sometimes invaluable (see Exhibit 9–6). Another good tool for this purpose is Google's News Alerts (www.google.com/alerts). Google News Alerts (see Exhibit 9–7) allow users to have Google automatically conduct searches and email the results to them. Notice in Exhibit 9–7 that the user has entered "interstate commerce clause" as the search term. The user can then indicate what she would like Google to search (e.g., news, blogs, the Web, newsgroups,

EXHIBIT 9–7
Google Alerts

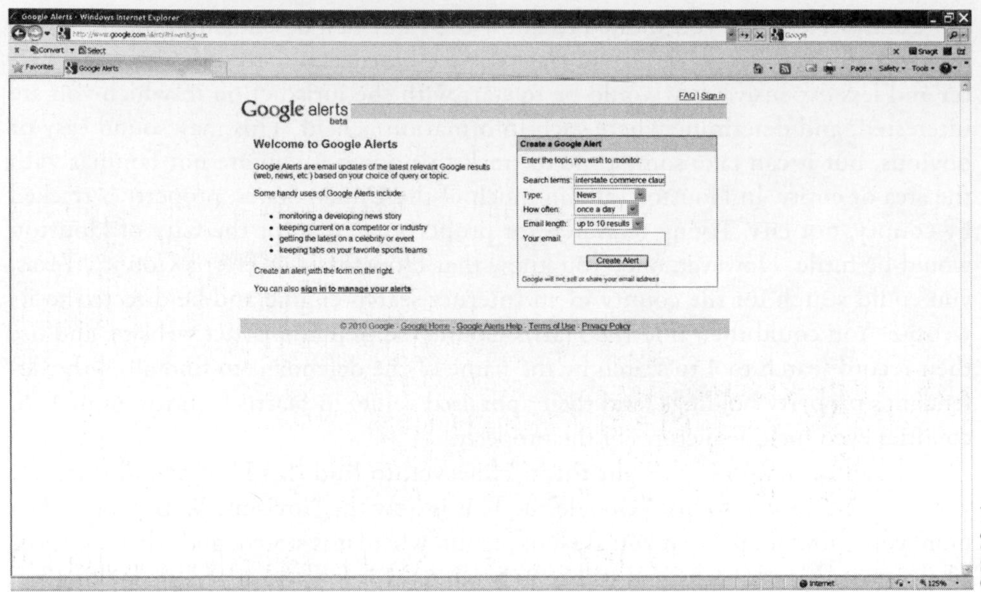

listservs) and how often. This is a convenient way to stay on top of changing events. For example, if your client was in a crash in a Toyota Corolla, you might want to stay current on information related to the vehicle, such as recalls, other crashes, and so forth. RSS feeds, covered earlier in this chapter, can also be extremely helpful in staying up-to-date on news and blogs that are relevant to a case.

Researching Businesses

The Internet is the perfect tool for researching information about companies, businesses, and organizations. Not only can you find a wealth of information using general search engines and news-related sites, but you can also find out a great deal of other information from more specialized sites. For publicly traded companies, the U.S. Securities and Exchange Commission's (SEC) Electronic Data Gathering Analysis and Retrieval (EDGAR) database (www.sec.gov) is a good place to start. The SEC requires publicly traded companies to file extensive current information, almost all of which is publicly available. Corporate websites, press releases, litigation documents, judicial decisions, public records such as state attorney general filings, and much more are readily available on the Internet as well.

Expert Witnesses

Finding lists of expert witnesses is an easy task using the Internet. There are many sites devoted to this one topic, and many general legal sites also offer numerous databases for finding an expert witness in practically any area (see Exhibit 9–6).

Medical-Related Information

Exhibit 9–6 lists a few sites for general medical information. These are often a good starting point for research into medical issues or conditions; you can follow up with searches more narrowly tailored to the issue of interest. There is a huge amount of medical- and health-related information on the Internet, but in this area you must be particularly careful about site and information authorship, sponsorship, accuracy, substantiation, and currency.

Internet Browser Tools

Internet browsers such as Microsoft Internet Explorer and Firefox have several features that are invaluable when you are conducting Internet research. The Find feature in Microsoft Internet Explorer, **[CTRL]+[F],** allows you to search for words on an open web page. It is common, when using general search engines, to click a link and be taken to pages and pages of text without being able to see where your search terms were found. Using the Find feature, you can reenter a search term and be taken directly to its location in the document.

Another helpful feature is **bookmarks** (sometimes called favorites). Bookmarks and favorites allow you to save shortcuts to particular web pages. Not only can you save shortcuts, but you can also arrange the shortcuts into groups by setting up folders such as "news websites," "legal research sites," or "public record sites." Because serious Internet users may have hundreds of bookmarks or favorites, the ability to manage them in folders is critical.

bookmark
A tool that enables a user to quickly and easily go back to a website or web page.

LEGAL ORGANIZATION INTRANETS AND EXTRANETS

An intranet is an internal network designed to provide and disseminate information to internal staff using the look and feel of the World Wide Web. Similar to how the Internet provides information to the public, an intranet provides information to a legal organization's internal users. Users access an organization's intranet by using a web browser.

Legal organizations use intranets for a variety of purposes, but their primary functions are to allow people to share internal information, improve knowledge and teamwork, and streamline internal processes. Information usually included on intranets includes human resource policies, procedural manuals, training information, forms, access to databases, articles, and links to external websites.

An extranet is a secure Web-based site that allows clients to access information about their cases and collaborate with the legal professionals who are providing services to them. An extranet employs a variety of security measures to ensure that the general public does not have access to the site, and that only clients or other authorized users can view it. Extranets can enable document exchanges; sharing of information, case strategies, calendars, and updates; forums for collaboration; and much more. Extranets are particularly helpful when a legal matter is complex, multiple parties or multiple co-counsel are involved, and sharing of information is critical to the success of the matter. An extranet allows a legal organization to distribute information to one central spot where everyone involved can access it, no matter what their geographic location, time zone, or computer platform.

ELECTRONIC MAIL

Electronic mail (email) allows users to send and receive messages via computer or PDA. When an Internet account is opened, the user is given an email address and can then send and receive messages. Hundreds of millions of people use email every day to communicate.

Email use has many advantages. First and foremost are its low cost and tremendous capabilities. With inexpensive email, messages can be sent almost instantaneously nearly anywhere in the world; word-processing, sound, and graphic files can be attached to email messages; messages can be sent, read, and replied to at the user's convenience; "telephone tag" can be made a thing of the past; messages can be sent to groups of people at the same time; users can get their messages from anywhere; and messages can be saved, tracked, and managed electronically. A common client complaint is that legal professionals are often very busy and hard to reach. Email allows legal professionals and clients to communicate with one another quickly and conveniently.

Email in the Legal Environment

Email is now a major means of communicating with clients, other attorneys, and courts, and most paralegals use email every day in their jobs. Email is being used in legal organizations for everything from routine correspondence, to billing, to newsletters, to filing court papers. Most clients now demand email access to their lawyers and paralegals. The security of email has long been a concern to legal professionals, but in recent surveys the majority of legal organizations indicate that they send confidential or privileged communications/documents to clients via email. The issue of security can be handled in a number of ways, including requiring clients to provide oral or written consent to having confidential information sent via email, adding a confidentiality statement at the end of each email message, using encryption software, or just not using email to send confidential documents.

Email Software

Sending and receiving email requires email software. Email software performs a variety of functions, including storing names and email addresses in an address book, retrieving messages, forwarding messages, storing sent messages, and attaching files to messages. Most law offices use the Microsoft Outlook program for email.

spam
Unwanted or unsolicited email messages that are sent to many recipients; the electronic equivalent of junk mail.

Spam **Spam** refers to unwanted or unsolicited email messages. It is the electronic version of junk mail. Spam has become quite common; although many laws have been passed to stop this veritable flood of unwanted messaging, it continues with almost no reduction apparent. It is now standard practice to install spam filters (programs that limit the amount of spam that gets through) on both office and personal computers.

phishing
A type of Internet fraud; "phishers" send fraudulent emails, in which they impersonate legitimate senders, in hopes of gaining personal information from responders.

Phishing **Phishing** is a type of Internet fraud. In hopes of gaining personal information from users, such as passwords, Social Security numbers, and bank account information, "phishers" send fraudulent emails in which they impersonate legitimate senders. The phishing message may ask you to confirm or reenter personal or confidential information "for security purposes," may warn you that an attempt has been made to access an account, and may even pose as a government agency alerting you to security-compromising occurrences. Many times, the phishers create exact replicas of real sites that look legitimate and authentic; however, anyone who follows links in such an email will end up at a bogus, illegitimate site where any information entered will be stolen and used fraudulently. Email and Internet users should always be suspicious of messages that ask for personal information.

Email Record Retention and Destruction

Email has become a de facto standard for client communication. This has caused a number of issues and problems that at first were not anticipated.

For example, typical email mailbox sizes can be 500 MB or more—but email boxes were never intended to be a place for storage of client information. In years gone by, legal professionals would send client correspondence via letter and keep a copy in the client's file. Now, email is so prevalent that hard-copy correspondence is the exception rather than the rule. As a way to deal with this change, many legal organizations now have record management software that paralegals and attorneys can use to store electronic case-related information in a central networked environment that allows searching and provides other capabilities. In many firms, legal professionals are now required to "file" client emails, not in the folders in their email programs, but in the folders of the firm's record management program. When an email is filed in the records management program, a record is created that both the user and others in the firm can access. In addition, once an email is in the records management program, it becomes subject to the program's retention rules, so that it is deleted and destroyed at the proper time.

This latter capability addresses another problem with email left in email folders: These messages live on forever. Record retention policies are put in place to limit the amount of information retained based on the type of information. Some legal organizations have moved to automatic deletion of emails in mailboxes (not those stored in record management programs) after a certain number of days (typically 90 or 180 days). This helps manage the amount of storage the email systems continually use, to keep the performance of the email system fast and to reduce potential liability for retaining records that are not needed but may contain information harmful to the legal organization or its clients.

Email Encryption and Digital Signatures

Because email may pass through many network servers before it reaches its destination, it is subject to being read by system administrators, hackers, and others. It is often said that email is more like a postcard than a sealed letter. Some legal organizations use encryption software to protect confidential emails sent to others. Encryption software "locks" email so that it can be opened only by the intended recipient. There are two types of encryption program designs: one is called symmetric and the other asymmetric (also called public key).

With symmetric encryption, when the sender runs the email through the encryption program, a key is created that scrambles the file. The sender then sends the encrypted email to the recipient and separately transmits the decoding key, which is typically a password or a data file. Running the same encryption program, the recipient uses the decoding key to unscramble the message. Symmetric encryption is fast but not as safe as asymmetric encryption, because someone could intercept the key and decode the messages. Because of its speed, though, symmetric encryption is commonly used for e-commerce transactions.

Asymmetric encryption (also called public-key encryption) is more complex, but it is also more secure. Two related keys are required: a public key and a private key. The user makes a public key available to anyone who might send the user encrypted information. That public key can only encode data; it cannot decode it. The private key stays safe with the user. When people wish to send the user encrypted information, they encrypt it using the user's public key (but only the user can decrypt it with the user's private key). Thus, the person sending the user a message has a digital signature file that has been encrypted with the sender's private key. When the user receives the message, the user decrypts it with the private key. Asymmetric encryption is more complex, and the process takes longer, but it is safer.

Email Etiquette and Tips

The following points of email etiquette will help you communicate your messages effectively to readers:

- Be succinct and clear; use short paragraphs.
- Spell-check and reread your emails. It is especially important that you double-check the spelling of all names within an email.
- Be careful to treat email as business correspondence. These are formal documents requiring formal language (for example, do not use the letter "u" as a substitute for the word "you"). Do not call the recipient by his or her first name unless you are sure it is appropriate to do so.

- Do not use ALL CAPS. Using all caps is equivalent to SHOUTING! Use all caps only when absolutely necessary.
- If you are unsure about a message someone has sent you, ask for clarification and do not assume that you have guessed correctly about the meaning.
- Be careful of Reply All. Sometimes users get an email with 20 other people copied on it. If the user selects Reply, only the sender of the original email will get a response, but selecting Reply All will send a reply to all 20 of the original recipients. Before you select Reply All, make sure you really want to send it to everyone on the original message.
- Check email at least daily.
- As a rule, do not use email to communicate with clients regarding sensitive information. For sensitive communications, it is probably better not to use email at all, but if you have any doubts, always ask the client first. If you do send such information via email, be aware of privacy/confidentiality issues and take appropriate security measures.
- Double-check the email address in any message to make sure you entered the correct one.
- Limit each email message to one topic. It is difficult to decide where to file multiple-topic emails, and it is sometimes difficult to follow up on them. Multiple follow-up requests or actions could be buried in one email, but they are liable to be missed by a busy client or legal professional.
- Always password-protect word-processing and other documents sent to clients. By password-protecting documents, you add some degree of security to the attachment with minimal effort.

Problems with Email

Although email is inexpensive and convenient, it is not perfect. Keep the following considerations in mind when using email:

- Do not assume that an email was read just because you sent it.
- Email relies on computer technology that occasionally fails or is delayed.
- Be careful what you say in emails, as they can be forwarded to others.
- Remember that email is not necessarily confidential. Email security can be breached in many ways, including:
  - leaving confidential emails open on your computer screen for others to read over your shoulder.
  - leaving your office for lunch or for a break while signed into your email program.
  - printing emails that others can find (such as at a network printer).
  - using a password such as "password" or names of family members that would be easy for others to guess.

INTRODUCTION TO COMPUTER-ASSISTED LEGAL RESEARCH

Computer-assisted legal research (CALR) uses online, fee-based service providers (third-party vendors) such as Westlaw and Lexis. Users subscribe to the service and are given a password with which to access it. Unlike Internet-based legal research, fee-based CALR can be expensive. CALR services have thousands and thousands of different databases, so they offer an extremely large pool of information from which to draw. After a user connects to the CALR service, the user accesses a database in which to perform legal research. The user then searches the database using key words or phrases to find the legal information he or she is looking for.

Many legal organizations use a combination of CALR, Internet-based legal research, and manual legal research, because each has its advantages and disadvantages and each may be the best, depending on the specific situation involved.

MANUAL LEGAL RESEARCH

Traditionally, legal research was accomplished using manual methods. Manual legal research is performed in a law library, using books, periodicals, indexes, and digests. Usually, the first step in researching a specific legal issue is to find the appropriate subject heading that covers that issue in a legal index or digest.

When a relevant case or statute is located in an index or digest, the researcher must locate and retrieve the bound volume containing the information so that he or she can read the entire case or statute. Cases and statutes should also be cite checked. **Cite checking** refers to the process of ensuring that a specific citation is correct (no typos), confirming that the case or statute is still valid, and that the decision has not been overturned or the statute repealed or amended.

cite checking
Doing research to verify that a case or statute is still valid and that the decision has not been overturned or the statute repealed.

Manual legal research does offer some advantages over computer-based legal research. When conducting computer-based legal research, the user becomes the "indexer," and must decide what words or phrases the author might have used to describe a situation or case the user is looking for. This is important, since the user may not be an expert (and typically is not) in that particular subject matter, so the user is searching for something that he or she may not know much about. The user is also completely dependent on the computer software to perform the search. If the user is inexperienced with the particular program or service, or makes an assumption when the computer makes a different one, cases or material can be overlooked or left out of the results. When conducting manual research, users use manual indexes that have been written by people: typically attorneys, librarians, or experts in indexing. These expert indexers can create sophisticated, conceptually focused indexes that computer searching simply cannot replicate. In addition, manual indexes include not only the exact words of the text indexed, but also synonyms, cross-references, summaries, and other analysis that can help the user find what he or she is looking for. Particularly for legal researchers who are unfamiliar with a particular area of the law, manual research provides features that give insight into doctrine, concepts, and analysis that computer-assisted legal research does not.

CALR: ONLINE LEGAL DATABASES

CALR services search the words of the cases, statutes, and documents themselves. Once connected to a legal information service, the user must select a database and then enter a search query. A **search query** instructs the information service to search a specific database for the occurrence of certain words and combinations of words. The legal information service responds by retrieving all cases or documents that match or meet the conditions of the search query. For example, a search query could be formulated to find all occurrences of the words *automobile, rollover,* and *liability* in cases for the state of California. The CALR system would then retrieve a list of cases that fulfill the search query.

search query
An instruction to an information service to search a specific database for the occurrence of certain words and combinations of words. Searches can be limited by restricting the query terms, by searching only in specific databases, and by searching only in certain parts of a document (such as the title, synopsis, headnote, etc.).

Because legal information services use the full text of a document, indexes and digests are not needed. Instead, a user simply enters common words that describe the issue, and the system retrieves all cases and documents that meet the request. Westlaw and Lexis are the exception to this general rule. Westlaw and Lexis users can either search the full text of documents (bypassing indexes or digests), or they can use headnotes (an indexing/digesting system). Because the information is stored electronically on large mainframes, the database can be searched and the documents quickly retrieved. The documents that are retrieved can be read online, sent offline to a printer, or downloaded to a user's computer and then cut and pasted into a word-processing document. **Online** means being connected to an information system and running up charges. **Offline** means not being connected to an information service and not accruing charges (except possibly a printing or downloading charge). Documents may also be sent via email or facsimile to a particular destination. Alternatively, a list of the appropriate cases or documents can be printed or downloaded so the user can go to a law library and examine the hard-copy book.

online
Connected to the Internet; in relation to fee-based CALR services, connected to the service and incurring charges.

offline
No longer connected to the Internet; in relation to fee-based CALR services, no longer connected to the information service and thus not accruing charges (except possibly for printing or downloading).

Cite checking can also be done using CALR. Many legal information systems can check the correctness of a citation and the validity of cases or statutes almost instantly.

CALR can also be more convenient than manual research. Nearly all legal information services are available 24 hours a day, unlike most law libraries. Also, the research can be done from a legal professional's own office. In addition, the information that is available online is almost always more current than information available in printed books or even supplements.

Although CALR is both fast and convenient, it is ***not*** free. Commercial legal information services charge both yearly subscription fees and fees based on the amount of time connected to their systems. Some legal information services also charge fees for every search done on their systems. Because CALR is so expensive, new or inexperienced users can run up large bills quickly. Therefore, it is particularly important that new users get good training and develop a thorough understanding of the CALR system they will be using. Legal organizations often bill this expense to their clients, either directly or by incorporating the cost of CALR into their hourly rates.

Some services, such as Westlaw and Lexis, now offer flat-rate billing options as an alternative to paying for "connect" time. For a flat monthly fee, the firm can have unlimited access to all or certain libraries or databases specified in the package. Regardless of billing method, an attorney or paralegal can access Westlaw or Lexis from anywhere.

FEE-BASED COMPUTER-ASSISTED LEGAL RESEARCH SERVICES

A number of companies currently provide CALR services to the legal community. Westlaw and Lexis are by far the largest, and offer users the most depth in terms of both legal and nonlegal electronic resources available. Other CALR providers include Loislaw (www.loislaw.com), National Law Library (www.itislaw.com), Fastcase (www.fastcase.com), and Versuslaw (www.versuslaw.com). However, Westlaw and Lexis continue to have the largest share of the market.

While users have several options for fee-based CALR, users should always plan some basic strategies before going online to do CALR, because of the cost involved. A research plan should include knowing which service to use, what database(s) to access, how to formulate queries in the language and syntax of the chosen service, and how to use related information to make search queries specific and narrow enough to yield the desired information quickly and accurately.

Know Which Databases You Want to Access

Always plan which databases you want to search. Most CALR providers have hundreds, if not thousands, of searchable databases. For instance, if you want to search for all cases on a certain topic within the state of New Mexico, you would tell the service to access the New Mexico case law database and begin the search. It is best to determine which database(s) you will need to use *before* you log on to your service provider, rather than waiting until the meter is running and costs are being incurred.

Know the Name of the Client for Which the Research Is Being Done

Find out the name of the client or case for which the search is being conducted. Your firm may charge clients for CALR expenses, so it is important to know what case the research is for.

Know the Facts and Issues of the Case

Before you undertake CALR, it is important that you have a good understanding of the facts of the case you are working on, and specifically what issue or question you need to answer by completing the research. It is remarkably easy to spend hours online, haphazardly looking through case after case and incurring costs, but not finding what you are looking for; it is important to stay focused on the goal of the research. Another reason users must have a good understanding of the factual and legal issues of the case is that often a search must be modified to be made more restrictive. (For example, you cannot skim through 800 cases returned in response to an overly broad query.) Thus, to effectively restrict a search, you must have a good understanding of the issues involved, so that you can effectively narrow the search down to only relevant information.

Know How You Want the Information Delivered

It is important to know what format the information should take when you have retrieved the cases or documents you were looking for. Westlaw and Lexis, for example, offer several different options for storing the information. You can send the information to a printer, save the document as a PDF file, have the document sent to an email address, download the information to a word-processing file, copy the information to the Clipboard, or have the document sent to a fax machine. Many users download such information to a word processor, because this gives them many options for searching and using the material. Once downloaded, users can read the information at their leisure, cut and paste the information into another document such as a brief or pleading, or print the information.

WESTLAW

This section contains general information about how to use Westlaw, its many features, how to navigate around the system, and how to use Westlaw as a research tool. Westlaw is a full-text computer-assisted legal research service provided by Thomson Reuters. According to Thomson Reuters, Westlaw is one of the largest law libraries in the world, with more than 40,000 separate databases available to its users. It contains case law from all federal and state courts, statutes from all 50 states, statutes, legislative history of acts of Congress, regulations, case dockets, public records, business and legal news, law reviews, treatises, and much more.

In February 2010, Westlaw introduced a new platform, called WestlawNext. WestlawNext has noticeably different screen views and simplified search methods (e.g., it eliminates the need to search specific databases). The rest of this section discusses both the traditional Westlaw platform and the differences between WestlawNext and "classic" Westlaw.

Accessing Westlaw

To access Westlaw via the Internet, you need a Web browser, an Internet account, and a Westlaw account. The web address for Westlaw is www.westlaw.com. To enter the Westlaw site, you enter your Westlaw user name, Westlaw password, and a Client ID. The Client ID lets users track their Westlaw usage and charge the costs back to specific clients.

Welcome to Westlaw Screen

When Westlaw is started, it typically brings up the "Welcome to Westlaw" page (see Exhibit 9–8). Current news and information about Westlaw are displayed in the main section of this screen. Note in Exhibit 9–8 that two tabs are displayed in the upper left of the screen: "Westlaw" and "Paralegal." The "Westlaw" tab is displayed in Exhibit 9–8. The tabs may be customized and are covered in more detail later in this chapter.

KeyCite is Westlaw's cite-checking feature. It allows users to determine whether cases are still good law or if they have been overturned or otherwise limited, and whether statutes are still on the books or have been repealed or amended. KeyCite also allows users to find every instance in which a case or statute has been cited or referenced by other cases. Exhibit 9–8 includes several references to KeyCite, including a KeyCite this citation: field (left center) and a link to KEYCITE (top center). KeyCite is covered in more detail later in this chapter.

EXHIBIT 9–8
Welcome to Westlaw screen

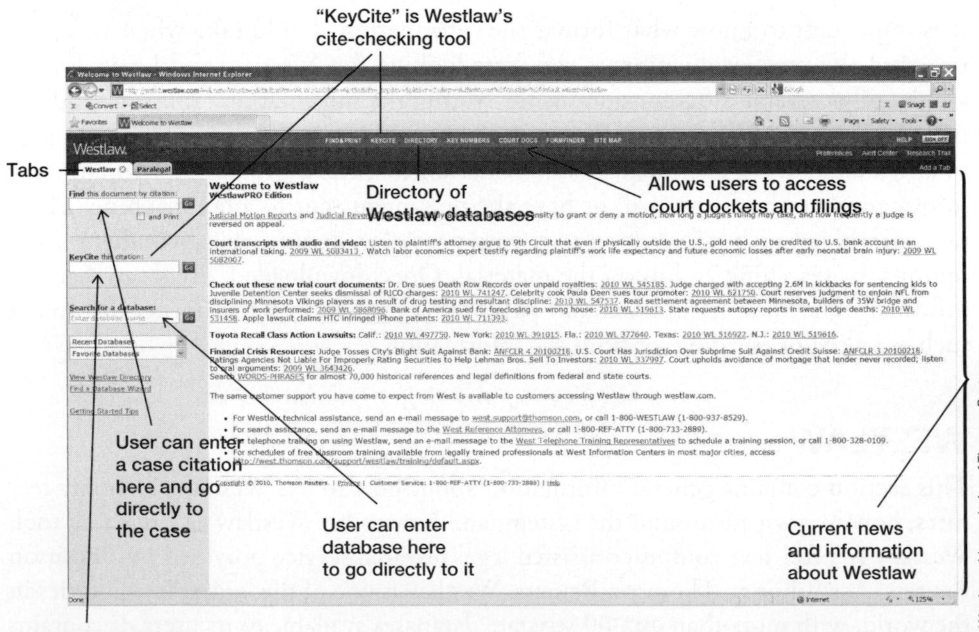
"KeyCite" is Westlaw's cite-checking tool
Tabs
Directory of Westlaw databases
Allows users to access court dockets and filings
User can enter a case citation here and go directly to the case
User can enter database here to go directly to it
Current news and information about Westlaw
User can enter case cite here to see if case is still good law

As shown in Exhibit 9–8, the Find this document by citation: feature allows you to enter a citation and then be taken directly to it. For example, if you entered "220 FRD 212" (*Note*: It is not necessary to use *Bluebook* citation style when using this feature), the case would then be automatically displayed without your having to enter a database or enter search criteria. The DIRECTORY link at the top middle of the screen displays a directory of the many Westlaw databases. (Databases are covered later in this chapter.)

The Search for a database: feature (see Exhibit 9–8 at bottom left) allows you to enter a database identifier, such as "Allcases," and then go directly to the search screen where you can enter search criteria.

In the top middle of the screen is the link to KEY NUMBERS. The West Key Number System assigns key numbers and terms to legal issues. Thus, you can conduct legal research by using a topical list of legal issues that has been compiled by Westlaw's attorney-editors. The Key Numbers feature is covered in more detail later in this chapter.

Tabs and the Paralegal Tab in Westlaw

Tabs allow a user to directly access a number of Westlaw features, including various databases. In Exhibit 9–9, notice the two tabs near the top left of the screen: "Westlaw" and "Paralegal." In Exhibit 9–9, the user clicked "Add a Tab" near the top of the screen and then selected each of these tabs. Exhibit 9–9 shows that the user can select from "General," "Business & News Information," and "Topical" tabs. Tabs can also be created for different jurisdictions (e.g., Florida). Tabs are a great way of customizing Westlaw. For example, notice in Exhibit 9–10 that the Paralegal tab is selected.

Exhibit 9–10 demonstrates that many of the tools that paralegals commonly use are now at the user's fingertips. The user can quickly access cases and statutes, public records and information about people, information about companies, court documents, forms and checklists, and other information. The Paralegal tab is a timesaving feature that Westlaw has created specifically for busy paralegals. We will use the Paralegal tab as the primary starting point in Westlaw throughout the remainder of this section.

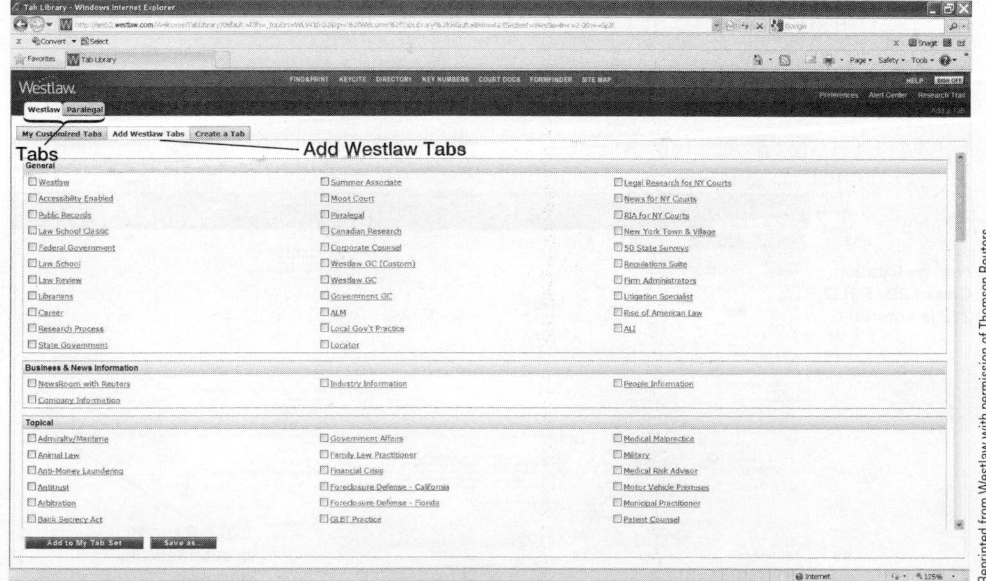

EXHIBIT 9–9
Westlaw Tabs

EXHIBIT 9–10
Paralegal Tab

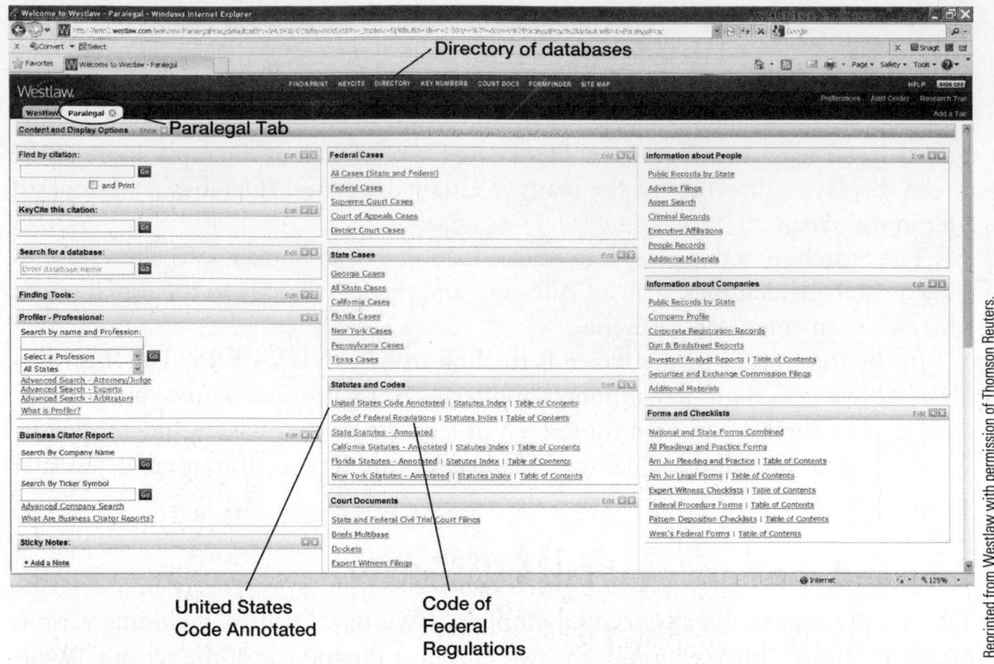

Find by Citation
A Westlaw feature that allows a user to immediately retrieve a specific case or statute by entering its citation.

Find by Citation

As mentioned earlier, the **Find by Citation** feature allows a Westlaw user to immediately retrieve a specific case or statute by entering its citation (see the first screen in Exhibit 9–11). This feature is convenient if you already have a case cite. Although it does not provide you with additional cases or documents, as it does when you execute

EXHIBIT 9–11
Find by Citation

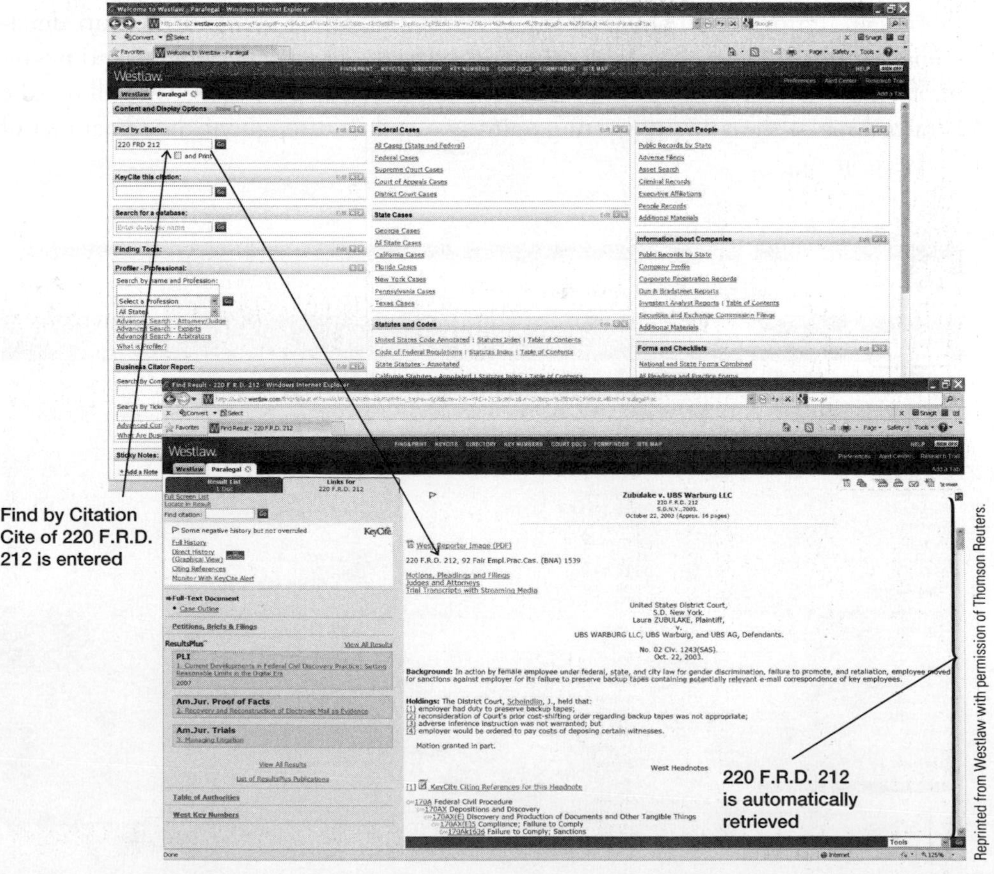

a search query, the case itself can be used as a starting point for conducting further research. The Find by Citation feature is also extremely quick because you do not have to enter a database identifier or a search query. The first screen in Exhibit 9–11 shows the citation as entered in the Find by Citation: field, and the second screen shows the case retrieved.

Find a Case by Party Name

Find a Case by Party Name (on the left side of the first screen of Exhibit 9–12) is a Westlaw feature that allows you to retrieve a case if you know the name of at least one party; you need not know the case citation or enter a search query. Notice in the first screen of Exhibit 9–12 that the user clicked Find a Case by Party Name, entered the party's name (Laura Zubulake), selected a jurisdiction (in this instance "All U.S. Federal and State Cases"), and clicked on Go. A list of possible cases was retrieved (see the second screen of Exhibit 9–12), including the actual case the user was looking for *(Zubulake v. UBS Warburg, LLC;* note that there are a number of cases with the same name). Although there are other ways to find a case by party name (discussed later in this chapter), the Find a Case by Party Name feature is convenient if you do not have a full citation for a case and do not know much about a case other than the name of one party.

Find a Case by Party Name A Westlaw feature that allows a user who knows the name of at least one party to retrieve a case without knowing the case citation or entering a search query.

Westlaw Databases

Westlaw has catalogued all of its information by subject matter and jurisdiction; Westlaw calls these divisions "databases." Westlaw offers users thousands of databases

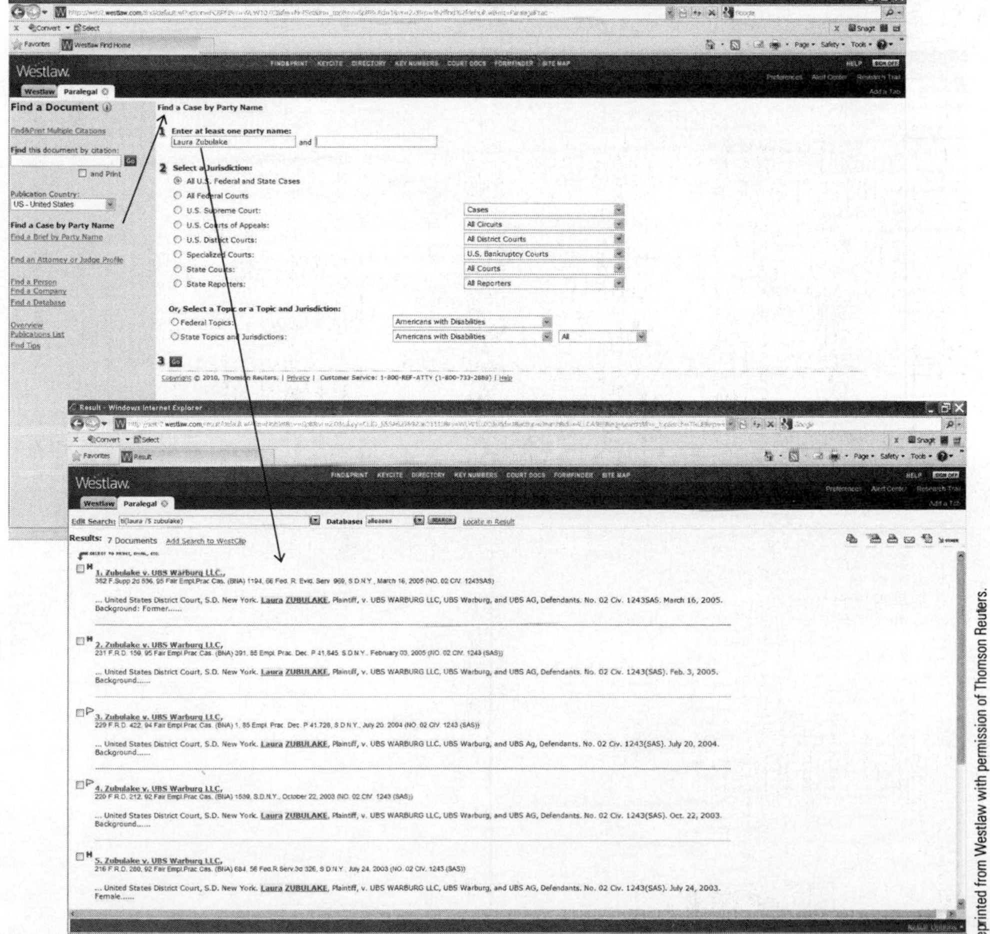

EXHIBIT 9–12
Find a Case by Party Name

to search and query. Notice that in the Paralegal tab in Exhibit 9–10, many different kinds and types of resources are available. All of these resources are databases that a user can search. For example, in Exhibit 9–10, under "Federal Cases," users can access the All Cases (State and Federal) database, which literally contains all state and federal cases. Users could also access the United States Code Annotated, the Code of Federal Regulations, public records by state, and forms. The Paralegal tab in Exhibit 9–10 shows just a few of the myriad databases available in Westlaw.

In Exhibit 9–10, notice the word "DIRECTORY" in the top middle of the screen. This is a link to the directory database shown in the first screen of Exhibit 9–13. Exhibit 9–13 shows the broad scope of databases and other information sources that are available in Westlaw. These databases include a variety of federal and state materials. The second screen in Exhibit 9–13 shows the screen for U.S. State Materials. The U.S. State Materials pages allow you to access the statutes and laws of any state, review court dockets, conduct legislative history research, and access court rules. Notice in the first screen of Exhibit 9–13 that additional databases covering international law, topical legal areas, treatises, law reviews, business news, public records, and other subjects are also available on Westlaw. (Students should note that schools often have special educational licenses; therefore, it is possible that not all Westlaw databases will be available.)

Users can also enter the name of a potential database in the Search for a database: field (see the first screen of Exhibit 9–13). For example, if you entered "New York Times" in the Search for a database: field, Westlaw would display several databases that were related to the *New York Times*. Users can also find a database using

EXHIBIT 9–13
Westlaw Directory of databases

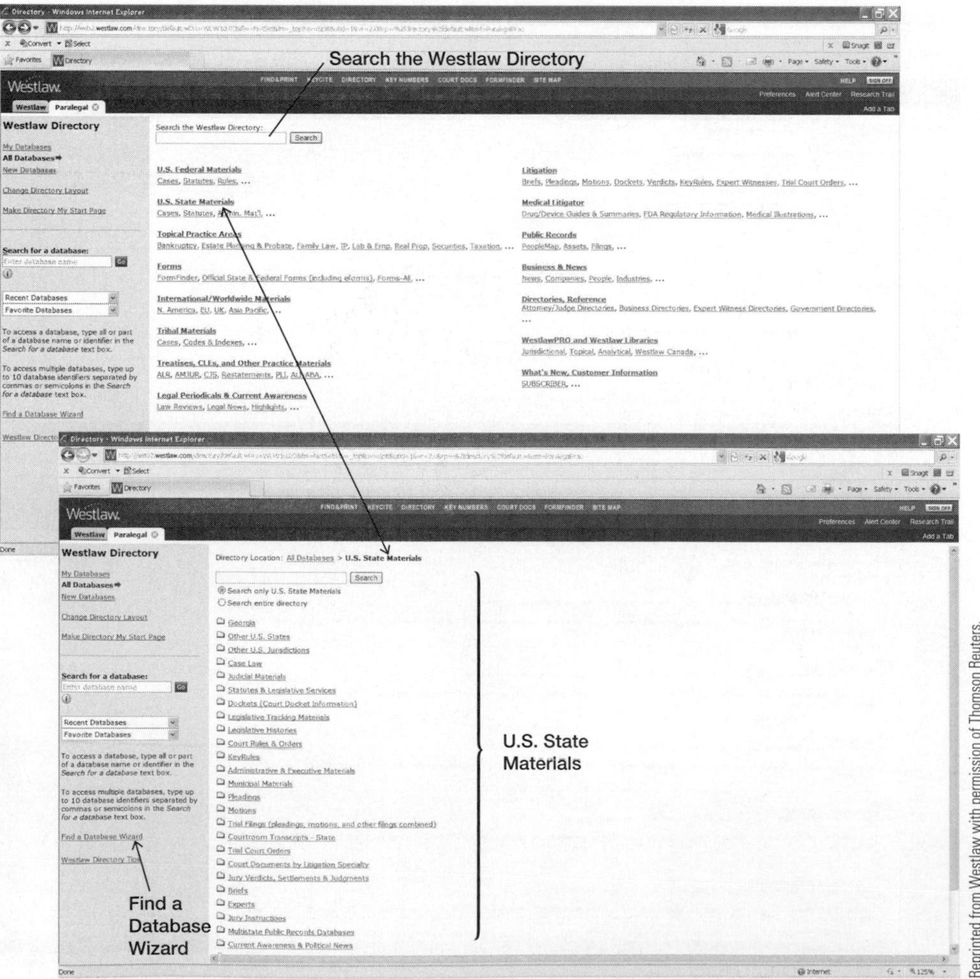

the Find a Database Wizard (see the second screen in Exhibit 9–13, bottom left). With this feature, you answer a series of questions such as "What are you trying to find?," and select a category from a multiple-choice list. Westlaw then guides you to the appropriate database.

Creating and Refining Search Queries in Westlaw

Before going online on Westlaw or any CALR system, it is helpful to plan out a query strategy in advance. This limits the time spent online, all of which incurs charges. You must decide what you want to accomplish and how to accomplish it. Formulating a good search query takes some practice and some time. Exhibit 9–14 shows an example of a query formulation for Westlaw, in the context of a search/query form.

Identify the Keywords to Be Searched and Any Synonyms Before you log in to the CALR system, always identify the keywords that describe the issue. You should also identify synonyms or alternate spellings of keywords. Computers cannot think for themselves; users must do this for them. Thus, if your search only asks for all cases that have the word *physician* in them, the system will not retrieve a relevant case that uses the word *doctor*. Failing to include an adequate number of synonyms in a query can make the query incomplete or too narrow, so relevant cases or materials will be missed.

The query in Exhibit 9–14 deals with whether a property owner may be liable in negligence for injuries sustained by a trespassing child in the property owner's swimming pool. The keywords that describe the legal issue are *negligence, trespassing, child,* and *"swimming pool."*

Identify the Type of Search to Be Performed Westlaw offers two different kinds of searching. The first kind is plain-English searching, which Westlaw calls "Natural Language." The second kind of searching, which Westlaw calls "Terms and Connectors," is a Boolean logic search method that uses operators such as *and,* to connect terms or ideas, and *or,* when two or more terms or concepts are needed to describe an idea.

EXHIBIT 9–14

Computer-assisted legal research query plan and form

COMPUTER-ASSISTED LEGAL RESEARCH QUERY FORM

Date: *June 1* **Research's Initials:** *TPB* **Client/Case:** *Jones v. Unitas*

Estimate Time on Service: *15 min.*

Service to be Used: (Westlaw) Lexis/ LoisLaw Fastcase Versus Law Internet

Database(s) to be searched:

All federal and Georgia

Type of Search: Natural Language (Terms and Connectors)

Issues/Question: *What is the liability of a property owner if a trespassing child is injured in the property owner's swimming pool?*

Search Term 1	Connector 1	Search Term 2	Connector 2	Search Term 3	Connector 3
negligence	*&*	*trespass!*	*/s*	*child*	*&*

Synonym(s)

Search Term 4	Connector 4	Search Term 5	Connector 5	Search Term 6	Connector 6
"swimming pool"	—				

Query: *negligence & trespass! /s child & "swimming pool"*

Natural Language
A query/search technique that uses plain English, without the need for complex connectors or syntax, to search for documents.

Natural Language searching in Westlaw uses plain English, without the need for complex connectors or syntax. The advantage of Natural Language is that it is easier to use; the disadvantage is that the search may not be as precise as a Terms and Connectors search. Using Natural Language, searches can be entered in the form of a sentence or question. For example, the question in the Issue/Question: field of the form in Exhibit 9–14 can be entered directly into Westlaw Natural Language (see Exhibit 9–15). In Exhibit 9–15, the user first selected the database called Georgia Cases (GA_CS) and then selected the Natural Language search tab (Exhibit 9–15, first screen). The user then entered the search query and clicked "Search Westlaw." Westlaw analyzed the statistical relevance of the terms and retrieved the documents that most closely matched the search requests (see the second screen of Exhibit 9–15). By default, a Natural Language search yields 100 results, although you can adjust the settings to allow more or fewer results. The results are presented beginning with the one that most closely matches the query terms.

Terms and Connectors
A search technique that uses Boolean logic and operators/connectors to connect query terms.

Terms and Connectors searching uses Boolean logic and operators/connectors to connect terms to describe an idea. The query at the bottom of Exhibit 9–14 shows a Terms and Connectors search in final form.

connectors
Characters that define or show a relationship between the keywords in a search query.

Once you have identified the keywords for the search, specified any synonyms, and informed the system that you will be using Terms and Connectors, you must next signify the relationships between the terms, using connectors. **Connectors** show a relationship between the keywords in a search query. For example, in Exhibit 9–14, notice the words and symbols in the "Connector" fields. These include the connector "/s," which in Westlaw means to search for two or more words within

EXHIBIT 9–15
Westlaw Natural Language search

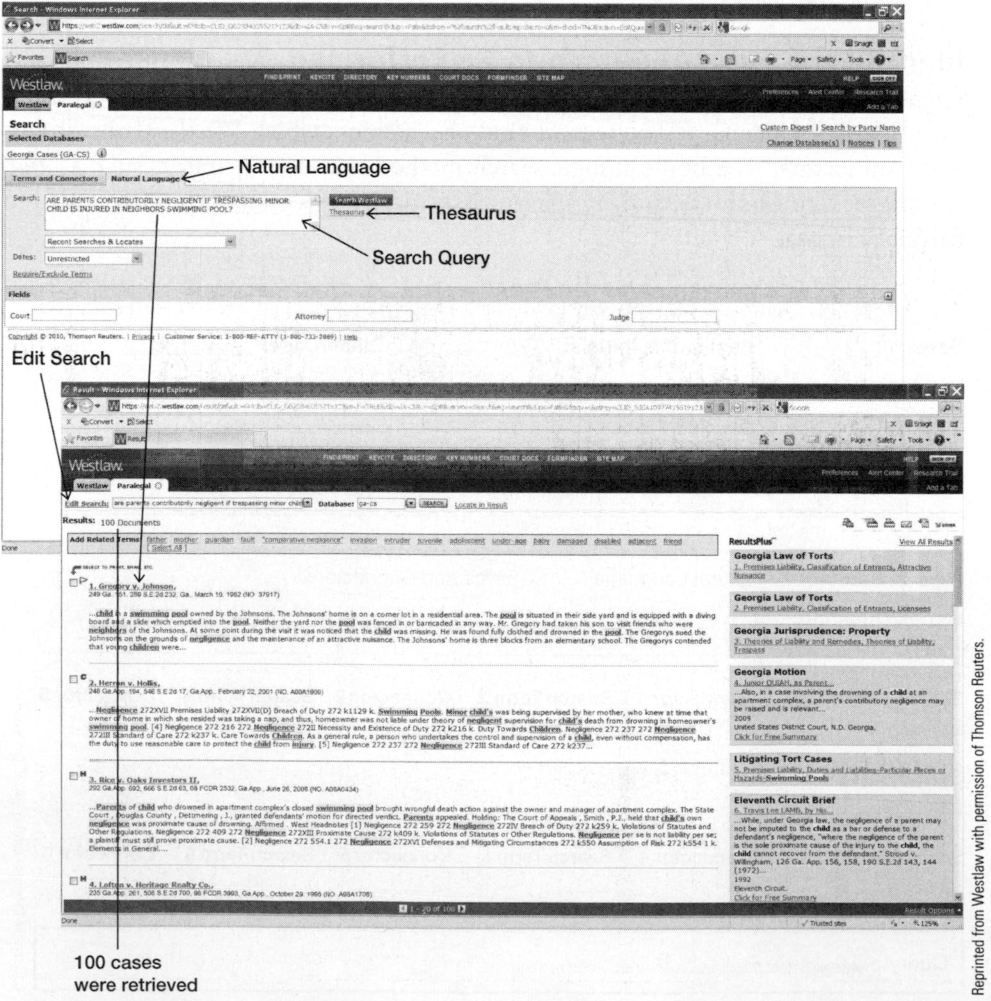

the same sentence; "/p," which in Westlaw means to search for two or more words within the same paragraph; "&," which in Westlaw means to search for two or more words within a document; and a space, which Westlaw interprets as OR and which tells Westlaw to find documents that have either one word or the other (e.g., find documents that use either the word *mortgage* OR the word *contract*). The final query in Exhibit 9–14 reads: "negligence & trespass! /s child & "swimming pool." The query tells Westlaw to search for documents in the selected databases that have the phrases "negligence" and *trespass!* (e.g., *trespasser* or *trespassing*) within the same sentence as the word "child," and which also contain the term "swimming pool" somewhere in the document.

Several different types of connectors are available in Westlaw (see Exhibit 9–16). The broader the connector, such as "OR" as opposed to "AND," the more expansive the search and the more documents will be retrieved. Conversely, the more narrow the connector, such as "/3" (within three words), the smaller the number of documents that will be retrieved. Depending on the results of a query, you can edit your query and use more expansive or more narrow connectors as necessary. Notice, in the top left of the second screen of Exhibit 9–15, that the user has an option called Edit Search.

EXHIBIT 9–16
Westlaw connectors and expanders

Connector	Definition	Search Query	Documents Found
Space bar	OR	mortgage contract	All documents that have either the word *mortgage* or the word *contract* anywhere in them
&	AND	mortgage & contract	All documents that contain both the word *mortgage* and the word *contract* anywhere in them
/p	Paragraph	mortgage /p contract	All documents that contain both the word *mortgage* and the word *contract* in the same paragraph
/s	Sentence	mortgage /s contract	All documents that contain both the word *mortgage* and the word *contract* in the same sentence
/n	Words	mortgage /3 contract	All documents that contain both the word *mortgage* and the word *contract* within three words of each other
" "	Phrase	"personal jurisdiction"	All documents where the exact phrase *"personal jurisdiction"* occurs
+s	Precedes within the same sentence	personal +s jurisdiction	All documents where *personal* precedes *jurisdiction* in the same sentence
+n	Precedes within a number of words	personal +3 jurisdiction	All documents where *personal* precedes *jurisdiction* within three words
%	BUT NOT	R.I.C.O. % "Puerto Rico"	All documents with the word *RICO* (i.e., Racketeer Influenced and Corrupt Organization Act) but not *Puerto Rico*

Expander	Definition	Search Query	Documents Found
!	Root Expander	medic!	All documents that have the words medicine, medical, medicate, or medication
*	Universal character	kn*w	All documents that have the word know or knew in them

Unlike a Natural Language search, there is no default number of results for a Terms and Connectors search; the search will list all of the relevant results. Another difference is that the results are presented in chronological order, beginning with the most recent result.

With the same search terms, it is possible to get noticeably different results, presented in a different order, depending on whether you used Natural Language or Terms and Connectors. Thus, it is advisable to use both methods when conducting a query search.

Identify Any Expanders That Might Be Necessary When writing a search query, you must also take into account variations of your chosen keywords. For example, in Exhibit 9–14, the root word *negligence* might appear in some materials in a variant form, such as *negligent*. You can include a root expander in the query so that variations of a word will not be missed when the system is searching for relevant cases. A **root expander** enables Westlaw to retrieve multiple words with the same root. The exclamation mark (!) in Exhibit 9–14 is a root expander that tells Westlaw to find all words with the root of *neglig*. Thus, the words *negligence* and *negligent* will be searched for in the database.

root expander
A character that enables a legal information system to retrieve multiple words with the same root.

Another type of expander is a **universal character**, which represents one letter or number and enables an information system to retrieve words with minor variations. The asterisk (*) is used as a universal character in Westlaw. For example, the query "kn*w" would retrieve cases containing the terms *know* and *knew*. A universal character can be placed anywhere in a word, and more than one universal character can be used in or at the end of a word (e.g., "test**" would retrieve *test*, *tests*, and *tested* but not *testify*). Exhibit 9–15 lists common Westlaw expanders.

universal character
A character that represents one letter or number; enables a legal information service to retrieve words with minor variations.

Additional Westlaw Searching Tips Exhibit 9–17 gives a number of additional search tips for using Westlaw. Another helpful feature for Westlaw query design is the Thesaurus tool. In Exhibit 9–15 (first screen), notice the word "Thesaurus" just under "Search Westlaw." Exhibit 9–18 shows the "Thesaurus" feature in Westlaw.

EXHIBIT 9–17
Westlaw search tips

Tip Number/Description	*Explanation*
1. The more terms in the query, the fewer cases retrieved	A common problem for new Westlaw users is that their searches tend to retrieve hundreds of cases, too many to look through. Adding more terms to the query limits the number of cases retrieved.
2. Use singular terms	Westlaw automatically adds plurals (e.g., *"child"* returns *"child's"* and *"children"*). If a user searches the plural (e.g., *"children"*) only the plural is searched for.
3. Use quotes cautiously	Using quotes only searches for exact phrases, so *"statute of limitations"* will not search for *limitations of action* or *limitation period.*
4. Use hyphens	When you do not know how a phrase might appear in a document, use hyphens. *Non-resident* retrieves *"non-resident," "non resident,"* and *"nonresident."*
5. Use periods in acronyms	When you do not know if an acronym might appear with periods or not, use periods. *F.B.I.* will retrieve *"F.B.I.," "FBI,"* and *"F B I."*

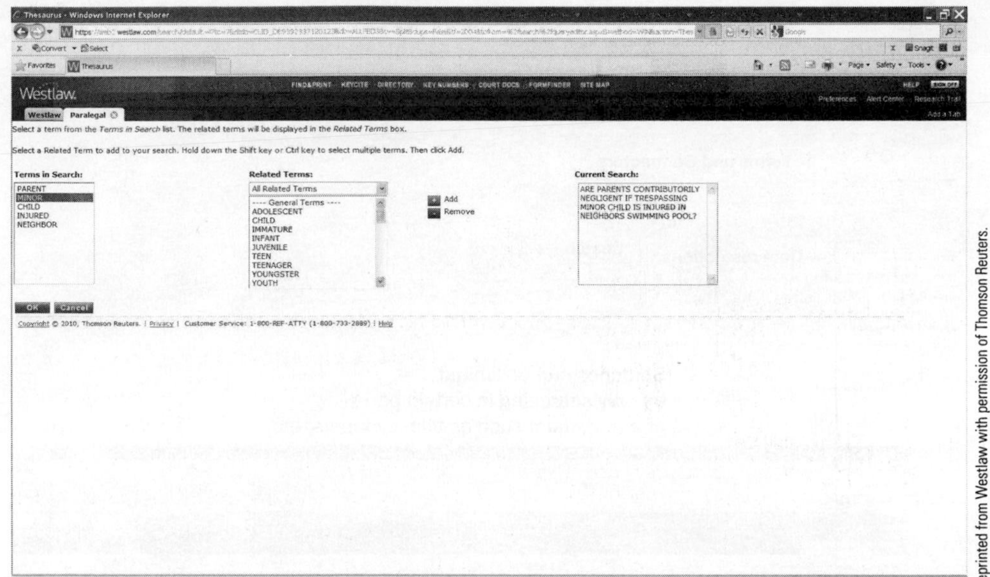

EXHIBIT 9–18
Using the Thesaurus

In Exhibit 9–18, the search word "MINOR" is highlighted, and Westlaw provides synonyms, such as "ADOLESCENT," "CHILD," and "JUVENILE." The Thesaurus tool can be very helpful when formulating search queries.

Exhibit 9–19 shows the Terms and Connectors search formulated in Exhibit 9–14 and the results of that search. Notice in the first screen of Exhibit 9–19 that one of the fields in the search screen is Dates: and that "Unrestricted" is currently shown. Users have many date options in Westlaw, including limiting searches to documents published in the past 30, 60, or 90 days; the past three years; after a user-defined date (e.g., after 1/1/2010); or before a user-defined date (e.g., before 1/1/2009).

Notice in the first screen of Exhibit 9–19 that one of the options is Fields:. Users can limit searches to certain fields or parts of a document, including the title of the case/document, the synopsis, headnotes, judge, attorneys, and so on. For example, if you wanted to search for the title of a case, you could either use the Find a Case by Party Name feature discussed previously, or select the down arrow next to Field: in the Terms and Connectors query pane and select Title. You could then enter a case name such as *Gregory & Johnson*. The completed search query would be ti(Gregory & Johnson).

Working with Retrieved Cases in Westlaw and Expanding a Search

The second screen of Exhibit 9–19 shows that 11 cases were initially retrieved. Only a brief summary of each case, showing some of the search terms found, is initially displayed. To see the full text of a case, you would click on the name of the case (in this instance, *Gregory v. Johnson*). Exhibit 9–20 (first screen) shows the first page of the *Gregory v. Johnson* case.

The Synopsis Notice in Exhibit 9–20 (first screen) that the background and holdings of the case are displayed. This is called the synopsis of the case. The synopsis of a case is written by Westlaw research attorneys to summarize and help users understand the case. This is something that many CALR services (other than Westlaw and Lexis) do not offer. By reading the synopsis, you can evaluate the case and determine whether it is on point.

Searching Terms and Moving to Additional Cases Exhibit 9–20 (first screen) shows the search terms in the synopsis as highlighted. Search terms are always

EXHIBIT 9–19
Terms and Connectors search in Westlaw

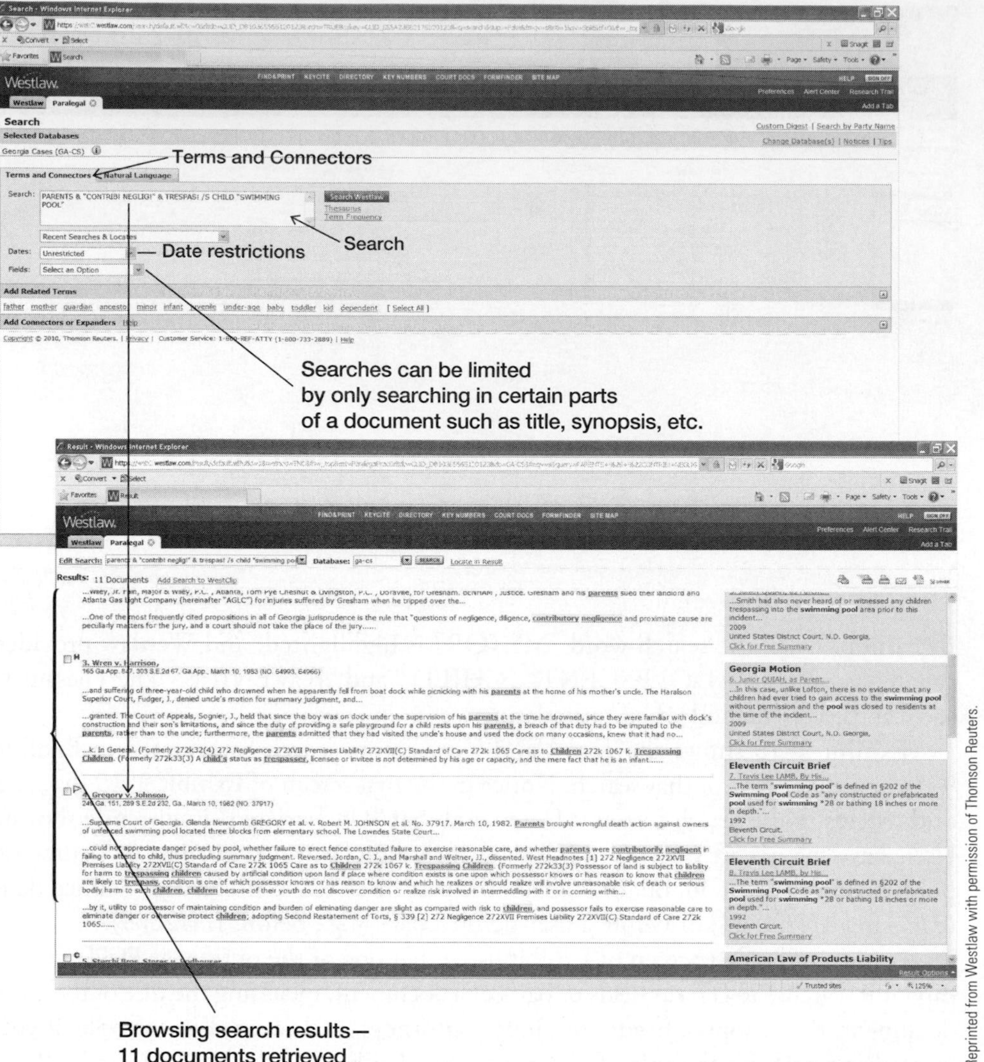

highlighted in the document so that you can clearly see the terms you are searching for. Notice in Exhibit 9–20 (at the bottom of the first screen), that the words "Doc 4 of 11" appear and there is a left arrow and a right arrow on either side. This shows that you are currently viewing the fourth case that was retrieved. To go to the next document, you would click the right arrow; to go to the previous case, you would click the left arrow. Notice also in Exhibit 9–20 (at the bottom of the first screen), that the word "Term" is shown with a left arrow and right arrow on either side. To go to your next search term, you would click the right arrow next to "Term." In this manner, you can view all of the search terms in the document to evaluate whether the document is on point or not.

If the documents are not relevant, or if too many or too few documents are identified, you should modify the query. Sometimes when cases are retrieved in Westlaw, another option appears next to "Term," called "Best." In Westlaw, "Best" means that this portion of the case has the greatest concentration of your search terms. Sometimes it is more efficient to use the "Best" option and go straight to the place in the case with the most search terms, rather than painstakingly going through the case looking at each highlighted search term.

Distribution Options After you have determined that the documents retrieved are relevant, you have several distribution options to select from (see Exhibit 9–20,

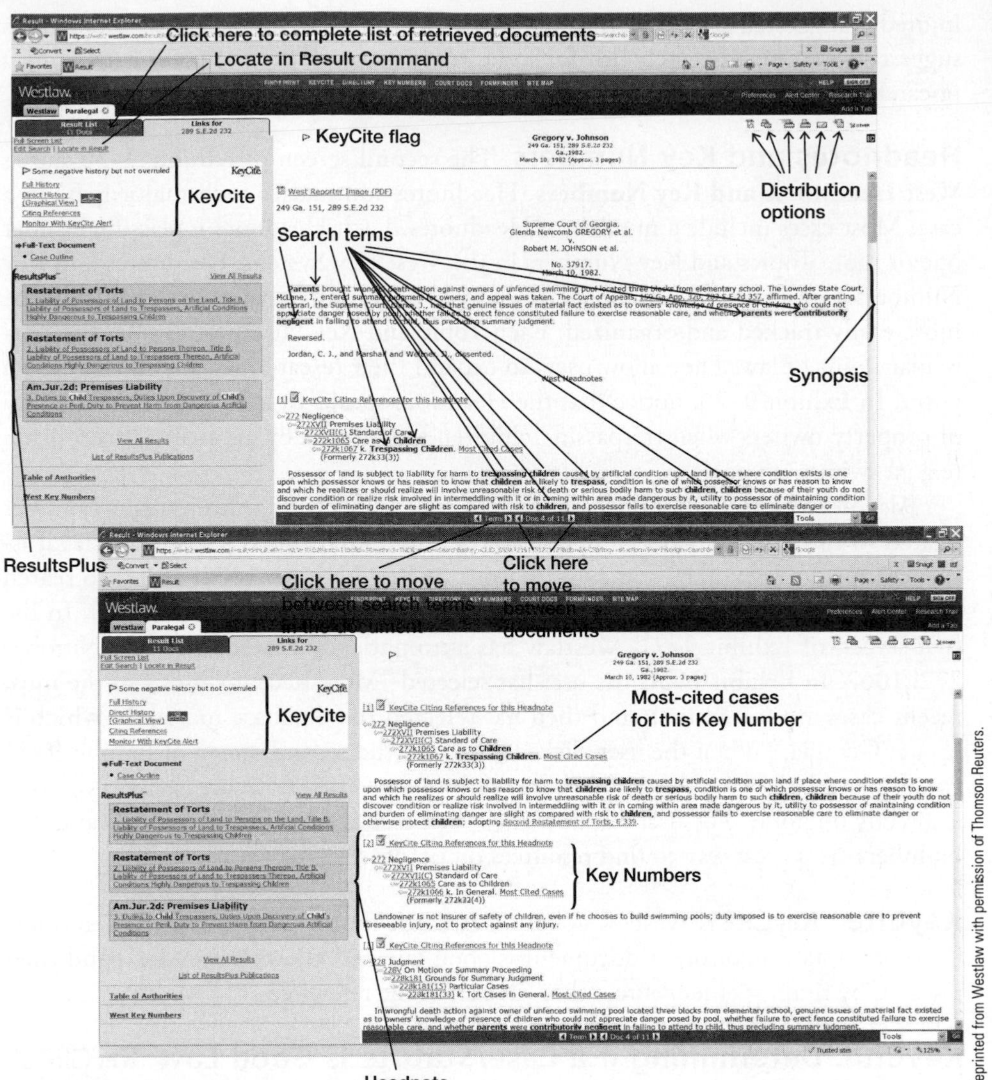

EXHIBIT 9–20
A retrieved case in Westlaw

top right of the first screen). Options include "West Reporter Image" (which creates a PDF file of the case), "Quick Print" (which quickly prints the case), "Print" (which prints the case with additional options), "email" (which emails the case to an address supplied by the user), and "Download" (which either opens the case or saves it as a word-processing document).

Locate in Result A Westlaw command that allows a user to search the retrieved documents for particular terms, whether or not those terms appeared in the user's original search.

Locate in Result Notice, in Exhibit 9–20 (top left of the first screen), the option entitled "Locate in Result." The **Locate in Result** command allows a user to search the retrieved documents for particular terms, whether or not those terms appeared in the user's original search. For instance, if the search in the example had retrieved 75 cases, you could search the retrieved cases for another term to further cull the cases retrieved. This can be particularly helpful when you retrieve more cases than you can easily skim through.

ResultsPlus A Westlaw feature that automatically includes other documents related to a user's search, such as legal texts, treatises, and law review articles; no additional search is needed to retrieve these supplementary materials.

ResultsPlus Exhibit 9–20 (lower left of the first screen) also shows a section that says "ResultsPlus." **ResultsPlus** is a Westlaw feature that automatically includes other documents, such as legal texts, treatises, law review articles, and the like, that have a high statistical likelihood of matching the concepts in a user's search (no additional search is needed to get these). In Exhibit 9–20, a section of the Restatement on Torts related to the liability of property owners when a trespassing child is injured is suggested as being a possible source of additional information. ResultsPlus suggestions can be extremely helpful and can assist you in expanding or furthering a research project.

Headnotes and Key Numbers
Westlaw feature that classifies each legal issue in a case and allows users to search and retrieve other cases with similar Headnotes and Key Numbers.

Headnotes and Key Numbers The second screen of Exhibit 9–20 shows West **Headnotes and Key Numbers**. Headnotes summarize each major issue in a case. Most cases include a number of Headnotes. Each Headnote is classified under one or more Topics and Key Numbers in the West Key System. Headnotes and Key Numbers digest the case and break down legal issues into smaller issues that can be more easily tracked and organized. Each Topic and Key Number represents a particular point of law. They allow users to expand their research while still staying on point. In Exhibit 9–20, notice that the Headnote speaks to the issue of the liability of property owners when trespassing children are injured by an artificial condition (e.g., a swimming pool).

Also in Exhibit 9–20, notice the Key Number 272k1067. This is a Key Number related to the issue at hand. Suppose, for example, that this is the specific legal issue you need to research. You could select this Key Number (272k1067) to search for other cases with the same Key Number or Headnote (see Exhibit 9–21). In the first screen of Exhibit 9–21, Westlaw has automatically entered the Key Number 272k1067. In Exhibit 9–21, the user has selected "Most Recent Cases," so the most recent cases are sorted first; and then has selected the database to search, which is "State: Georgia." When the user clicked "Search," the second screen of Exhibit 9–21 was displayed, showing the user 20 cases with the specific Headnote (272k1067) that is directly on point. The user can now click each case and read it. Headnotes and Key Numbers are a great way to find resources on point.

KeyCite
Westlaw feature that allows users to determine if a case, statute, or other document is good law and enables users to expand their research by finding other sources that have cited the reference.

KeyCite **KeyCite** is Westlaw's citation research tool. It allows users to determine if the case, statute, or other document is good law and allows users to expand their research by finding other sources that have cited the reference.

KeyCite: Determining if a Case/Statute Is Good Law KeyCite allows Westlaw users to determine whether a case has been overruled or still is good law, or if a statute has been found unconstitutional or has been repealed. In Exhibit 9–22 (first screen), the cite "249 Ga 151" has been entered in the KeyCite

EXHIBIT 9–21
Searching for similar Headnotes/Key Numbers in Westlaw

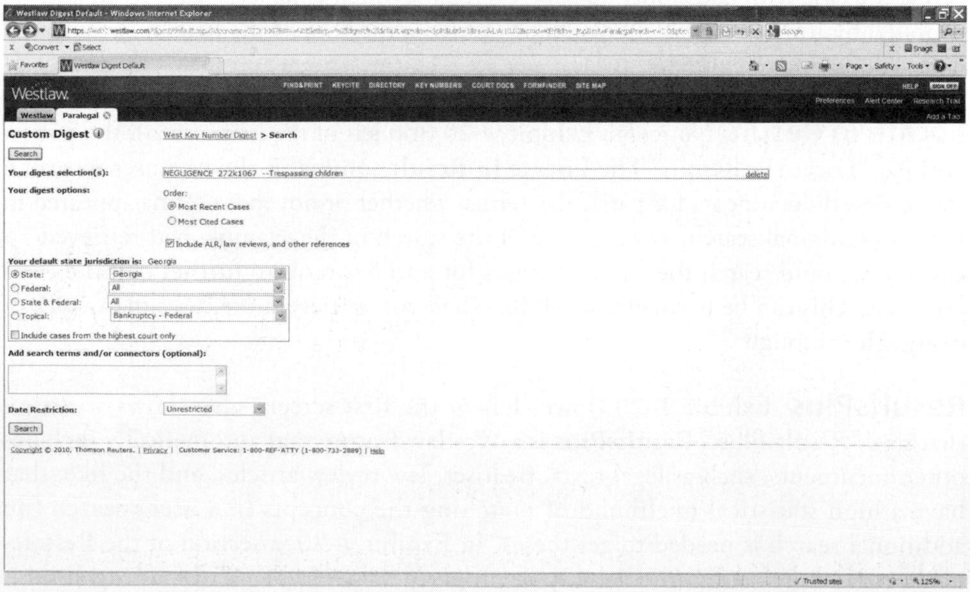

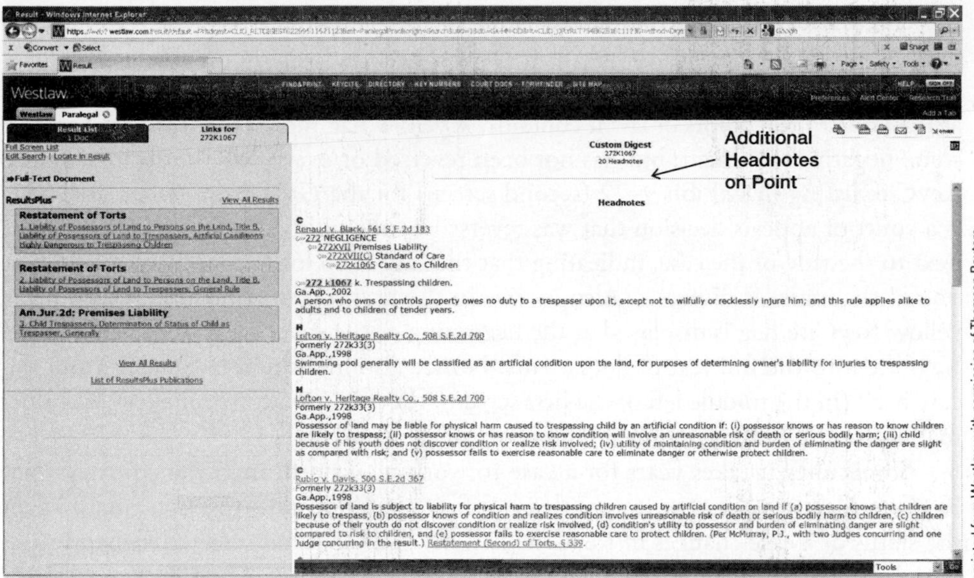

EXHIBIT 9–21
(continued)

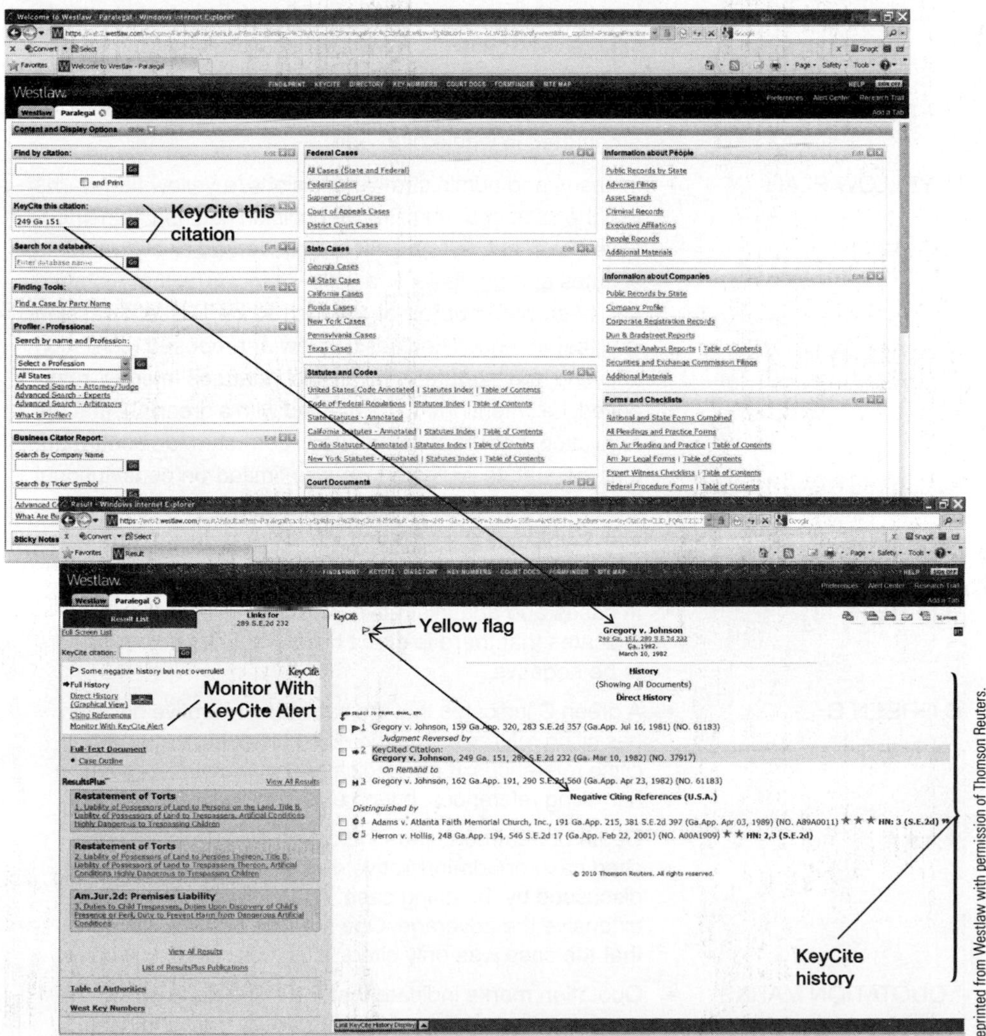

EXHIBIT 9–22
Using KeyCite

this citation: field. The second screen shows the KeyCite results as displayed. KeyCite uses a colored flag system to help you easily determine whether a case or statute is good law (see Exhibit 9–23). A red flag means that the case is no longer good law for at least one of the points of law it contains. A yellow flag means that the case had had some negative treatment, but has not been reversed or overruled. Notice that in the KeyCite listing in Exhibit 9–22 (second screen) for the *Gregory v. Johnson* case (this is a court of appeals decision that was reversed by the citing case), a red flag appears next to the title of the case, indicating that the case is no longer good law for at least one of the issues it discusses. Also, notice in the first screen of Exhibit 9–20 that a yellow KeyCite flag is displayed at the beginning of the case. Westlaw has integrated KeyCite into the full text of documents. Notice also in Exhibit 9–20 that from the case itself (in the middle left of the first screen), the user can access full KeyCite information for the case, including a full history of the case.

Sometimes it takes years for a case to work its way through the court system. KeyCite Alert is a Westlaw feature that notifies a user (typically through email) when the status of a case changes in KeyCite. Exhibit 9–22 (second screen, left-hand side) shows the Monitor With KeyCite Alert option.

EXHIBIT 9–23
KeyCite symbols

KeyCite Symbol	Explanation
▶ RED FLAG	• In cases and administrative decisions, a red flag warns that the case or administrative decision is no longer good law for at least one of the points of law it contains. In statutes and regulations, a red flag warns that the statute or regulation has been amended by a recent session law or rule, repealed, superseded, held unconstitutional, or preempted in whole or in part.
▷ YELLOW FLAG	• In cases and administrative decisions, a yellow flag warns that the case or administrative decision has had some negative treatment, but has not been reversed or overruled. In statutes and regulations, a yellow flag warns that a statute has been renumbered or transferred by a recent session law; that an uncodified session law or proposed legislation affecting the statute is available (statutes merely referenced, i.e., mentioned, are marked with a green C); that the regulation has been reinstated, corrected or confirmed; that the statute or regulation was limited on constitutional or preemption grounds or its validity was otherwise called into doubt; or that a prior version of the statute or regulation received negative treatment from a court.
H BLUE H	• In cases and administrative decisions, a blue H indicates that there is direct history but it is not known to be negative.
C GREEN C	• A green C indicates that the case/administrative decision has citing references but no direct history or negative citing references. It also indicates that a statute/regulation has citing references, but no updating documents.
★★★★	• Depth of treatment stars indicate how extensively a cited case or administrative decision has been discussed by the citing case. The more stars, the more extensive the coverage. One star, for example, means that the case was only cited.
" QUOTATION MARKS	• Quotation marks indicate that the citing case or administrative decision directly quotes the cited case.

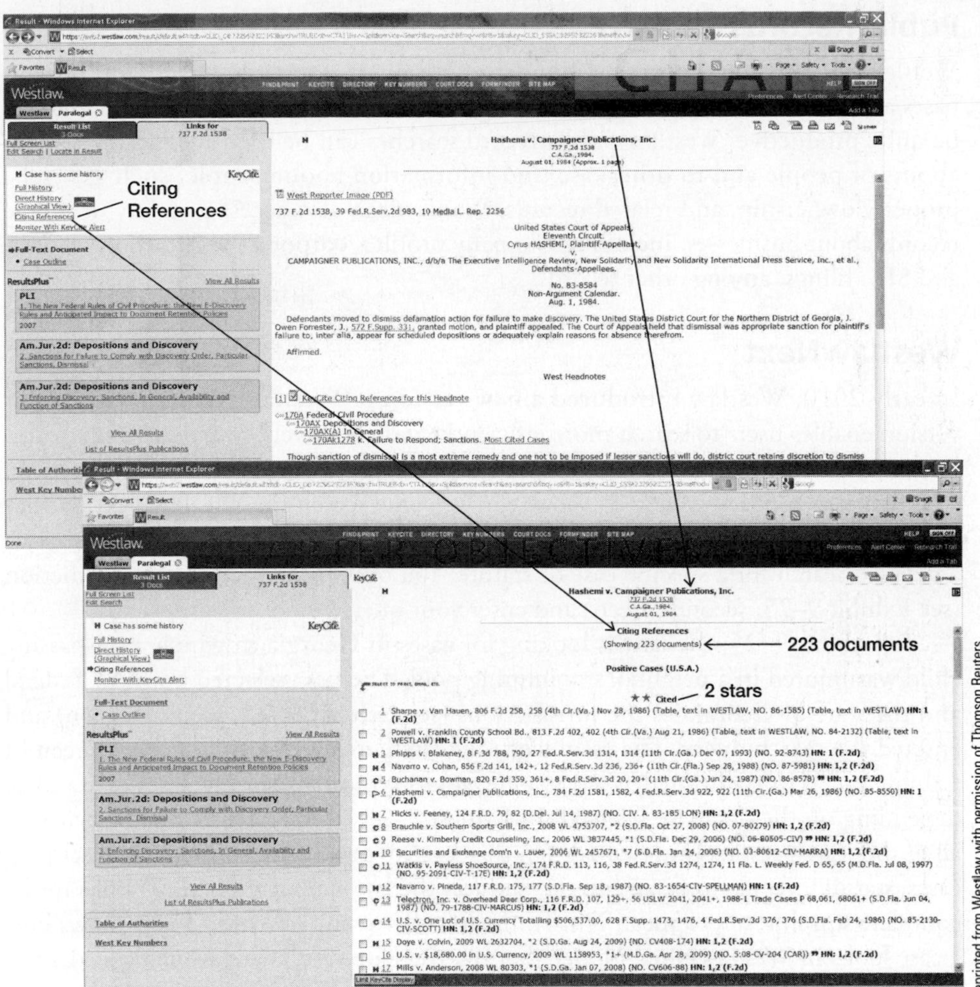

EXHIBIT 9–24
Citing references for a case in KeyCite

KeyCite: Finding Other Sources That Have Cited the Reference KeyCite allows a user to track all of the times a document has been cited by other references. Notice in Exhibit 9–24 (first screen) on the left side of the screen the words "Citing References." The second screen in Exhibit 9–24 shows the "Citing References" information in KeyCite for the case of *Hashemi v. Campaigner Publications, Inc.* Notice in the second screen of Exhibit 9–24 that the *Hashemi* case has been cited by 223 documents. Notice in Exhibit 9–24 (second screen) that over the first entry listed (*Sharpe v. Van Hauen*), there are two stars. These are depth-of-treatment stars (see Exhibit 9–23) which mean that the *Sharpe* case briefly discussed the *Hashemi* case. If the *Sharpe* case had simply cited the *Hashemi* case, the Sharpe case would have only one star. Notice also in Exhibit 9–24 that the fifth case listed (*Buchanan v. Bowman*) has quotation marks toward the end of the listing. This means that the Hashemi case was actually quoted in the *Buchanan* case.

Court Dockets/Documents

Westlaw has the capability to search many (but not all) federal and state court dockets. This is sometimes helpful if you are trying to keep track of a piece of litigation or if you are trying to find information about a person or company. The dockets retrieved usually show the type of action, case number, judge, courthouse, and the status of the case (open or closed).

Public Records Search

Westlaw allows users to search a number of state public records. Although its databases are not comprehensive or exhaustive, such searches are straightforward and can be quite productive. Westlaw public record searches can be used to find the whereabouts of people and to otherwise find information about people, such as assets, property ownership, and related records. Westlaw can also access a variety of public records about businesses, including company profiles, corporate registration records, and SEC filings, among other records.

WestlawNext

In early 2010, Westlaw introduced a new version of Westlaw, WestlawNext. This version enables users to search more efficiently and effectively. WestlawNext streamlines the research process by eliminating the traditional Westlaw tabs and databases. The first screen of Exhibit 9–25 shows the welcome screen for WestlawNext. Notice that there is only one place to enter a search query, whether it be for a cite check or a detailed search for a specific case or statute. You only have to choose a jurisdiction (see Exhibit 9–25, second screen) and enter your query.

In Exhibit 9–25, the user is looking for cases in Georgia in which a trespassing child was injured in a neighbor's swimming pool. The user selected both All Federal and the state of Georgia as the jurisdictions (see Exhibit 9–25, second screen) and entered the search query. The results of the search are shown in the third screen of Exhibit 9–25. In traditional Westlaw, one would typically see only cases or statutes, depending on the database selected. In Exhibit 9–25 (third screen), an Overview of all of the search results is presented. On this screen you can see summaries of selected cases, statutes, regulations, and so on, and (on the left side of the screen) links to the complete search results appear. Finally, the fourth screen of Exhibit 9–25 shows how a case looks in WestlawNext. Notice that the KeyCite results are available at the top of the screen and may be accessed by clicking on the desired search.

Westlaw Training

Becoming proficient at manual legal research requires one to understand the resources available and how to use them effectively. Similarly, learning to use CALR

EXHIBIT 9–25
WestlawNext

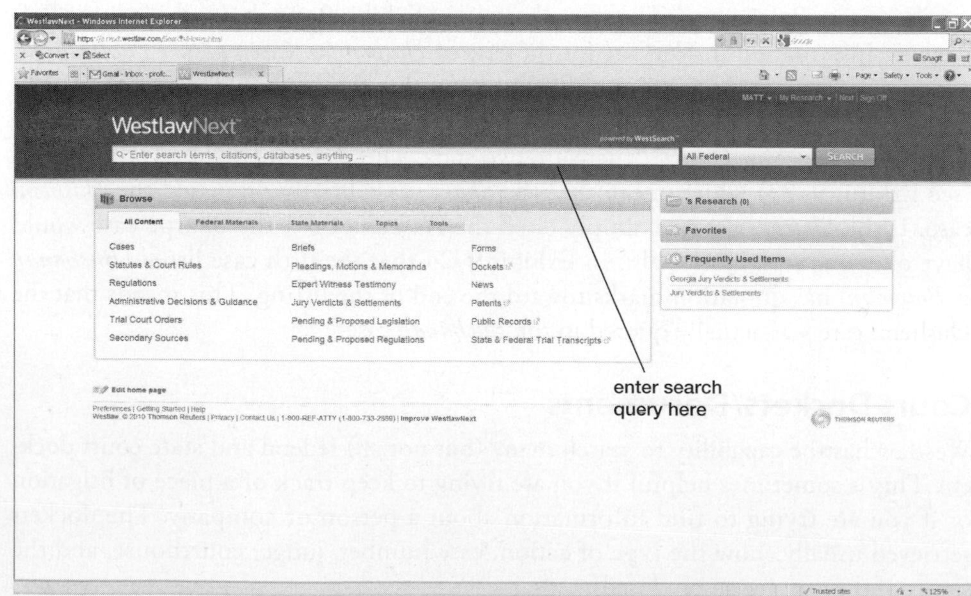

EXHIBIT 9–25
(continued)

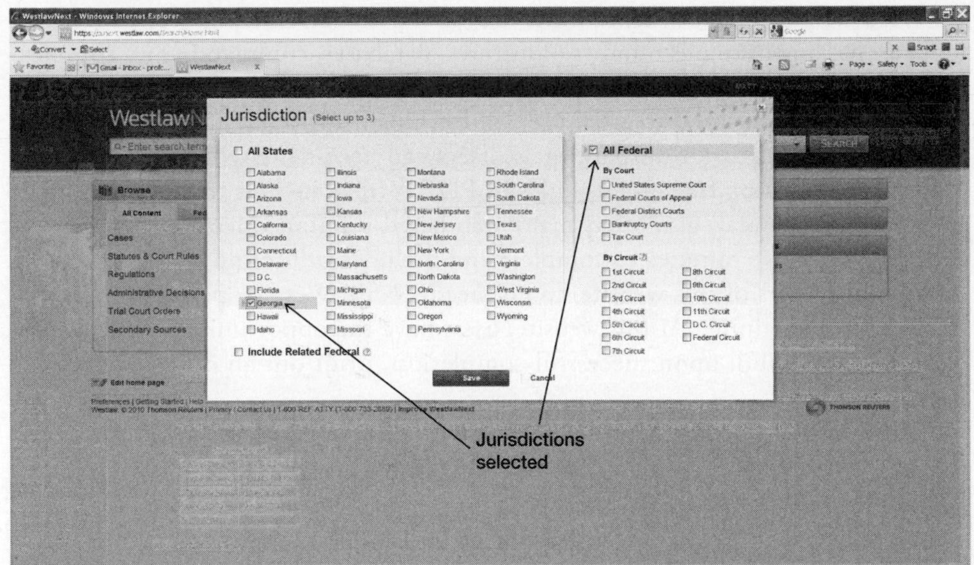

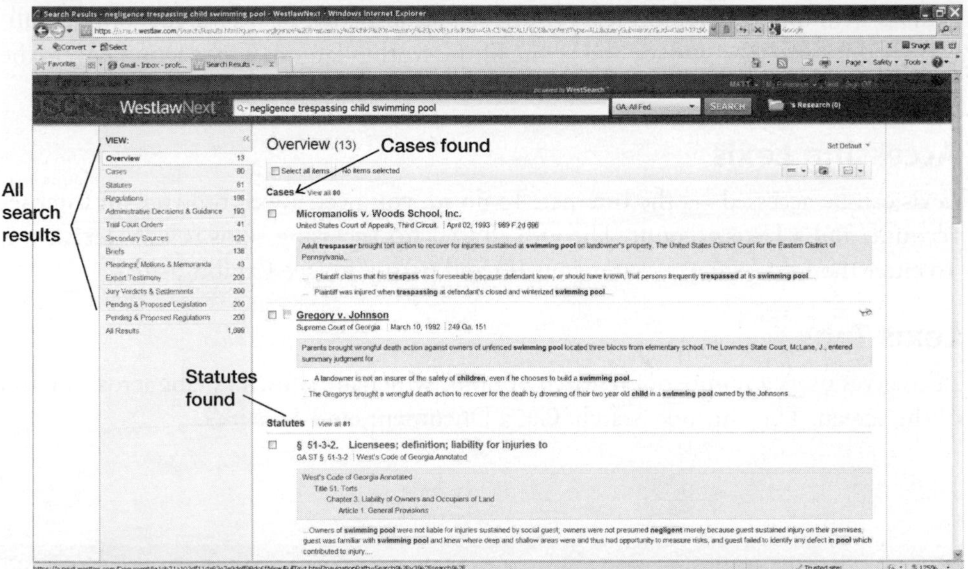

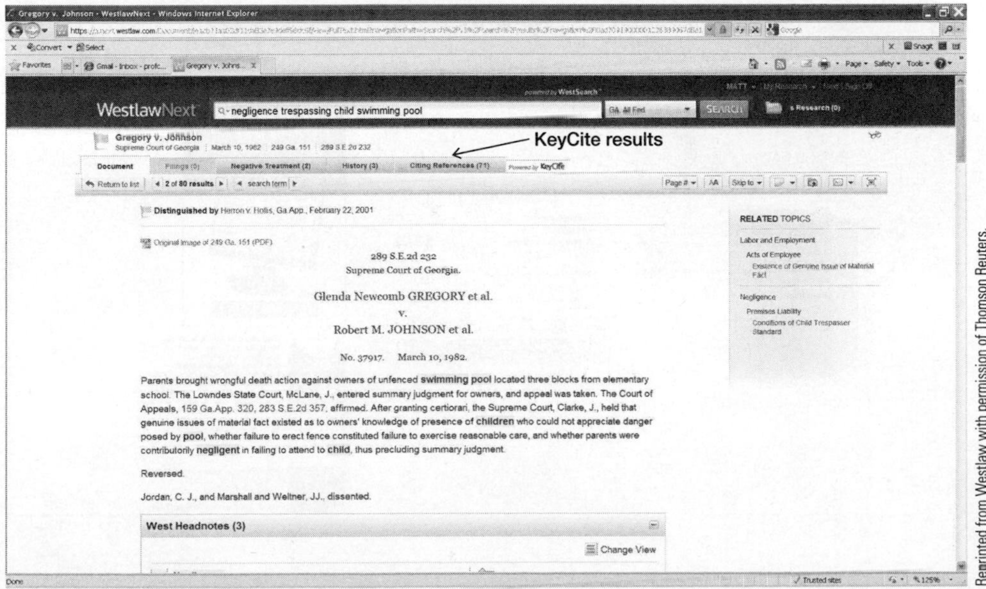

services, such as Westlaw, takes time. Westlaw is an extremely powerful research tool and has an enormous number of features, databases, commands, and complexities. To learn to use all of these vast resources takes some time. Westlaw provides a number of excellent tools to assist users in learning how to use its service. At west.thomson.com/organization/paralegals, users can access many different training programs, including free user's guides in PDF format such as the *Westlaw Guide for Paralegals*. Westlaw also offers many web-based training videos. Each one takes approximately five minutes to complete and includes full sound and step-by-step instruction. Users of this website do not need a valid Westlaw password to access the web-based training. At this website, users have the opportunity to take a short training course and, upon successful completion, print out an official certificate from Westlaw.

Many other types of training are also available. For example, Westlaw offers toll-free assistance by Westlaw research attorneys who can advise users on search strategies.

LEXIS

Lexis is a comprehensive, full-text, CALR service provider. It was the first online, full-text legal information service and is one of the world's largest. This section covers the Lexis databases, search/query structure, and other features.

Accessing Lexis

Lexis can be accessed via the Internet. To do so, you need a web browser, an Internet account, and a Lexis account. The web address for accessing Lexis is www.lexis.com. To enter the Lexis site, you enter your ID and password (see Exhibit 9–26).

Lexis Tabs

Lexis gives users a number of research options, which are shown as tabs across the top of the screen. They include Search, Get a Document, and *Shepard's*.

EXHIBIT 9–26
Lexis sign-in screen

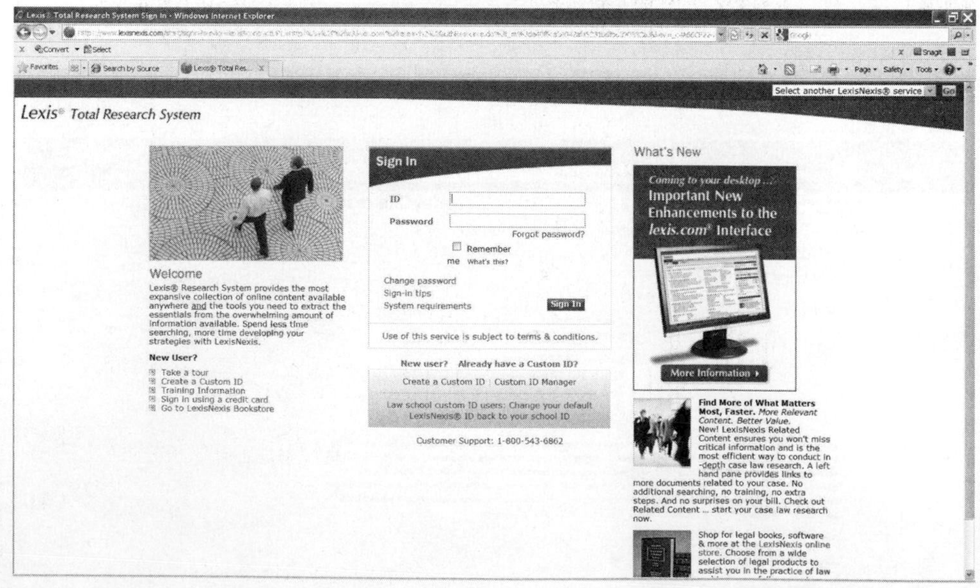

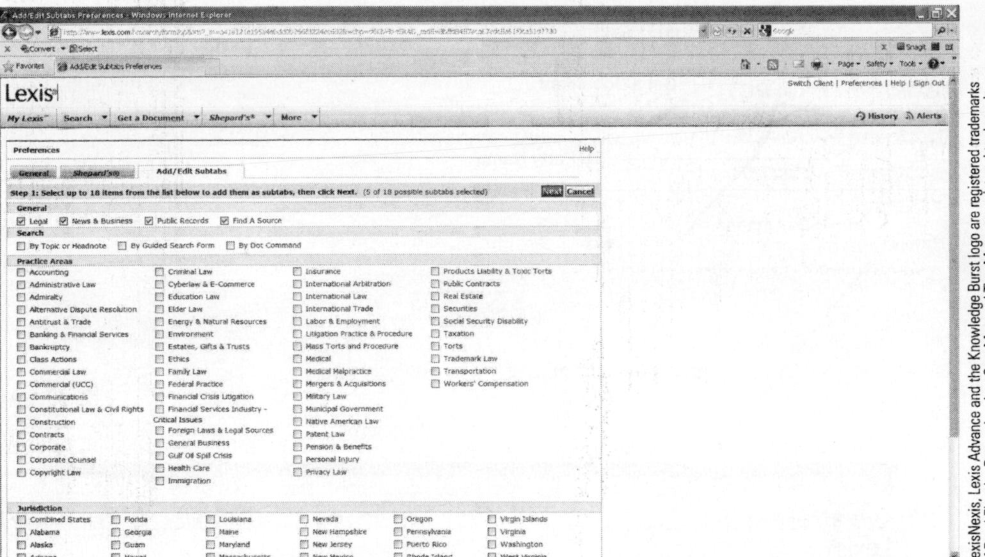

EXHIBIT 9–27
Search tab

Search Many subtabs are available under the Search tab (see Exhibit 9–27). These subtabs organize the various databases by topic. Four of the most commonly used subtabs are Legal, News & Business, Public Records, and Find A Source. The Legal subtab provides access to many of the most commonly used legal resources (see Exhibit 9-28). In addition, there are subtabs dedicated to specific legal topics and jurisdictions. The following pages present an extended discussion of how to search in Lexis.

Get a Document The Get a Document tab allows users to retrieve individual documents from Lexis quickly, by entering either the citation, the names of the parties, or the docket number. The first subtab is By Citation. The [Get a Document] By Citation subtab allows you to immediately retrieve a specific case or statute by entering its citation. In Exhibit 9–29 (first screen), the user has entered "451 F. Supp. 2d 16." Lexis- automatically retrieved the case without the user having to enter a database or search criteria (see the second screen of Exhibit 9–29). [Get a Document] By Citation is comparable to Westlaw's Find by Citation feature.

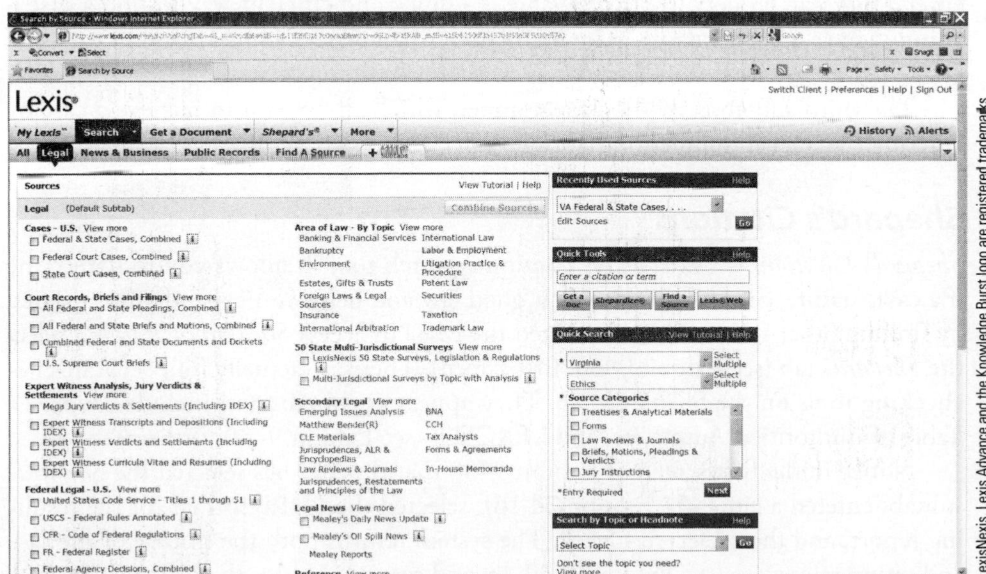

EXHIBIT 9–28
Legal sub tab

EXHIBIT 9–29
Get a Document tab

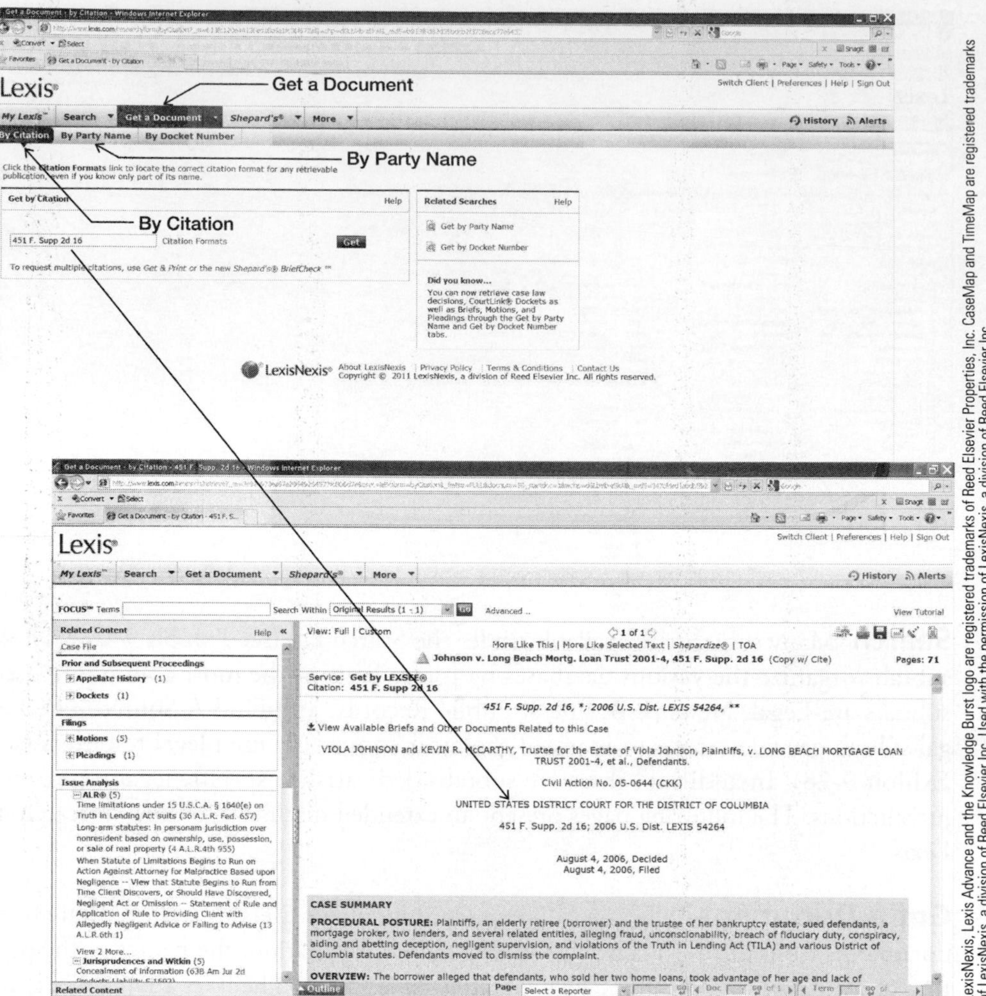

The second subtab is By Party Name. The [Get a Document] By Party Name feature allows a LexisNexis user to retrieve a document such as a case by entering the name(s) of a party or parties. You enter a party name, select the jurisdiction, and then select Search. The document is then automatically retrieved without your having to enter a full search query. By Party Name is a quick and efficient way to find a case if you just have a party's name. [Get a Document] By Party Name is similar to Westlaw's Find a Case by Party Name.

The third subtab is By Docket Number, which allows you to retrieve a case by entering the docket number of that case.

Shepard's Citations

Shepard's Citations is LexisNexis's citation research tool. It allows you to determine if a case, statute, or other document is good law and helps you expand your research by finding other sources that have cited the case. To access *Shepard's Citations,* select the *Shepard's* tab (see Exhibit 9–30, first screen). There are actually four separate cite-checking tools on the Shepard's tab. They appear as subtabs and include *Shepard's,* Table of Authorities, Auto-Cite, and LEXCITE (see Exhibit 9–30, first screen).

Notice in the first screen of Exhibit 9–30 that the user has selected the *Shepard's* subtab, entered a cite (451 F. Supp.2d 16), selected the FULL format for the resulting report, and then selected Check. The system returns both the history of the case and citing references (see Exhibit 9–30, second screen). Notice the yellow triangle at

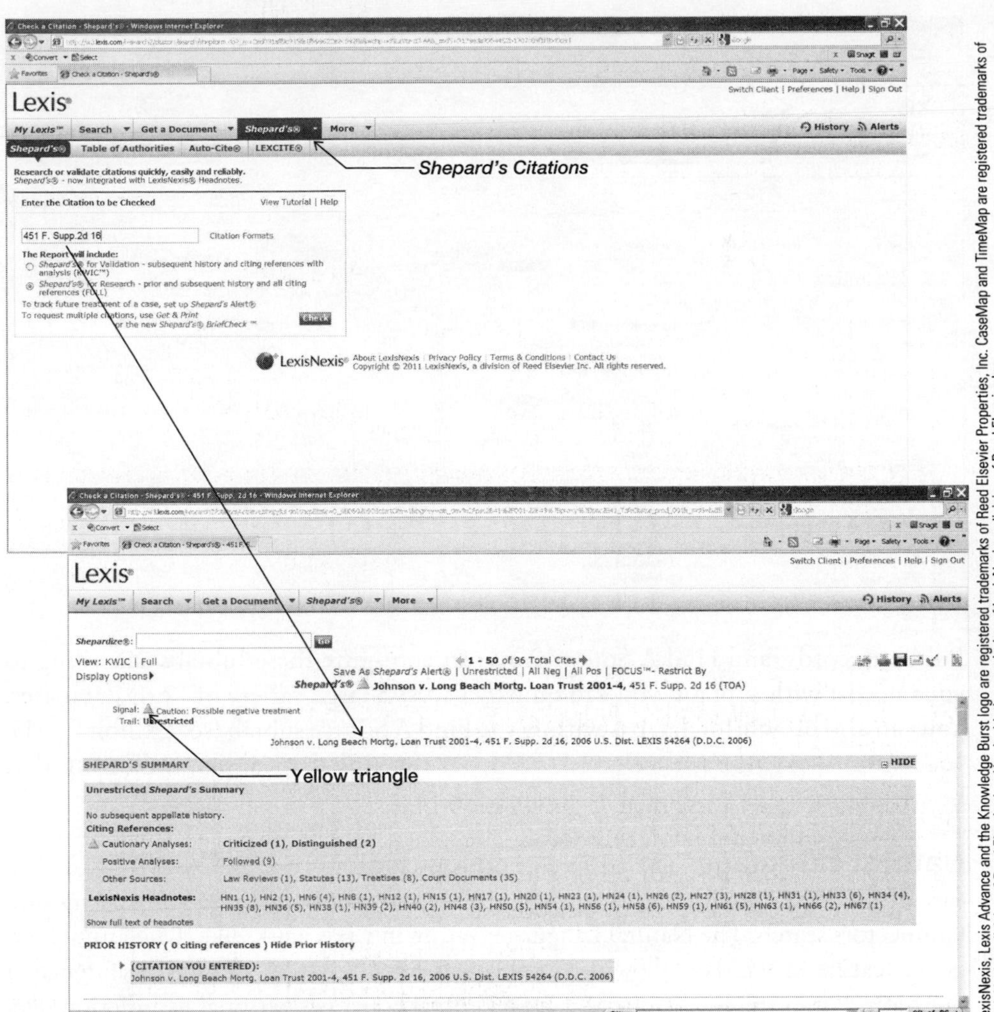

EXHIBIT 9–30
Shepard's tab

the top of the second screen in Exhibit 9–30: The yellow triangle means that the case has had some negative treatment, but has not yet been reversed or overruled. Notice that in the case itself (see Exhibit 9–34, second screen), a yellow triangle is displayed near the title of the case. *Shepard's* uses colored shapes so the user can easily determine whether a case or statute is good law (see Exhibit 9–34, second screen).

The fourth tab is called More and provides quick access to other LexisNexis products and services.

Searching in Lexis Databases

The database coverage of Lexis is extremely broad. It includes case law, statutes, news, business, medical-related information, public records, and much more. Lexis allows users to conduct research in a number of different ways.

Search Tab Notice in Exhibit 9–28 that the user is in the Search tab (near the top left of the screen). From the Legal subtab, the user can access many common databases, such as Federal & State Cases, Combined; Federal Court Cases, Combined; United States Code Service; individual state resources (not shown in Exhibit 9–28); and others. Next to the databases, there are open boxes. This is where you select which databases to search in. You can select multiples boxes/databases at one time and can search in multiple databases with one query. Notice also in Exhibit 9–28 that there are other subtabs, including News & Business,

EXHIBIT 9–31
Find A Source subtab

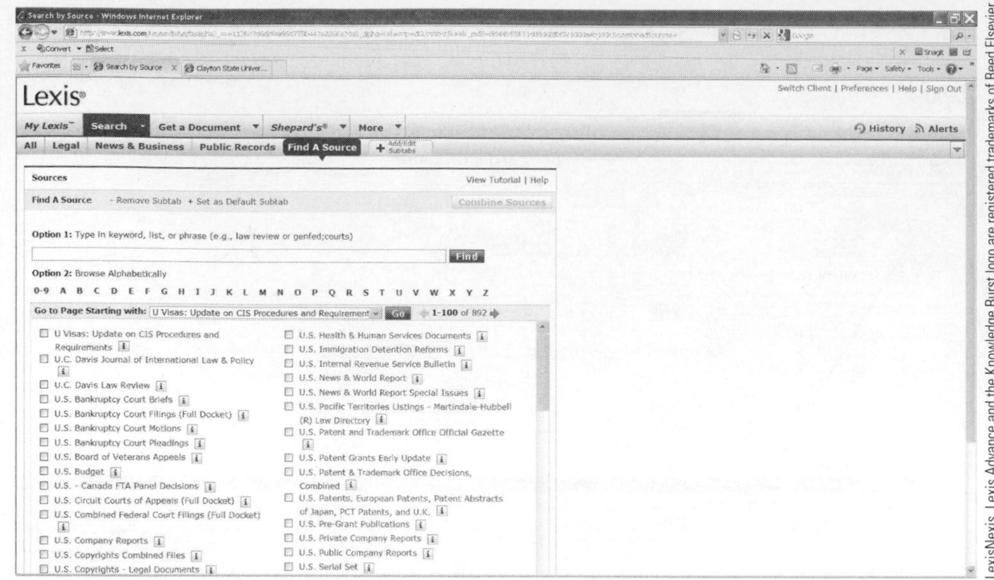

Public Records, and Find A Source. You can configure these subtabs according to your needs; with subtabs, you can quickly access a large variety of Lexis databases. You can also browse for databases using the Find A Source subtab (see Exhibit 9–31). In Exhibit 9–31, the user selected "U" from the alphabetical list, indicating that he wished to see all of the databases in Lexis that start with the letter "U."

Natural Language The advantage of using Natural Language for your search is ease of use. The disadvantage is that the search may not be as precise as a Terms and Connectors search. The Natural Language feature in Lexis works like the Natural Language feature in Westlaw, allowing searches to be entered in the form of a sentence or question. For example, the query "Can a Federal court get personal jurisdiction over a non-resident company where the only contact is assignment of a mortgage?" can be entered directly into Lexis Natural Language (see Exhibit 9–32, first screen). In this example, the user selected the "DC Federal District & State Courts, Combined" database, and then selected Natural Language in the search screen (see Exhibit 9–32, first screen). The user then entered the search query and entered some terms in the Restrict using Mandatory Terms field, including "personal jurisdiction." This means that any case retrieved must contain these terms. The user then clicked Search. Lexis analyzed the statistical relevance of the terms and retrieved the documents that most closely matched the search requests. Notice in the second screen of Exhibit 9–32 that the *Johnson v. Long Beach Mortgage* case was retrieved (first in the list).

Terms and Connectors Exhibit 9–33 shows selected connectors and expanders in Lexis. Lexis automatically searches for plurals of words and most possessive nouns. Lexis uses the exclamation mark (!) as a root expander and the asterisk (*) as a universal character, just as Westlaw does.

Lexis includes several types of connectors that for the most part are similar to those in Westlaw. Connectors in Lexis that are the same as Westlaw include OR, /p, /s, and /n. Connectors in Lexis that are similar, but not identical, to those in Westlaw are AND (which in Westlaw is represented as "&") and AND NOT (which in Westlaw is represented as %). In Lexis, some connectors can be entered in more than one way; for example, "/p" can also be entered as "w/p." The final query in Exhibit 9–34 (first screen) reads "'personal jurisdiction' /s non-resident /s compan! /p mortgage OR contract AND long-arm." The query tells Lexis to search for

EXHIBIT 9–32
Lexis Natural Language screen

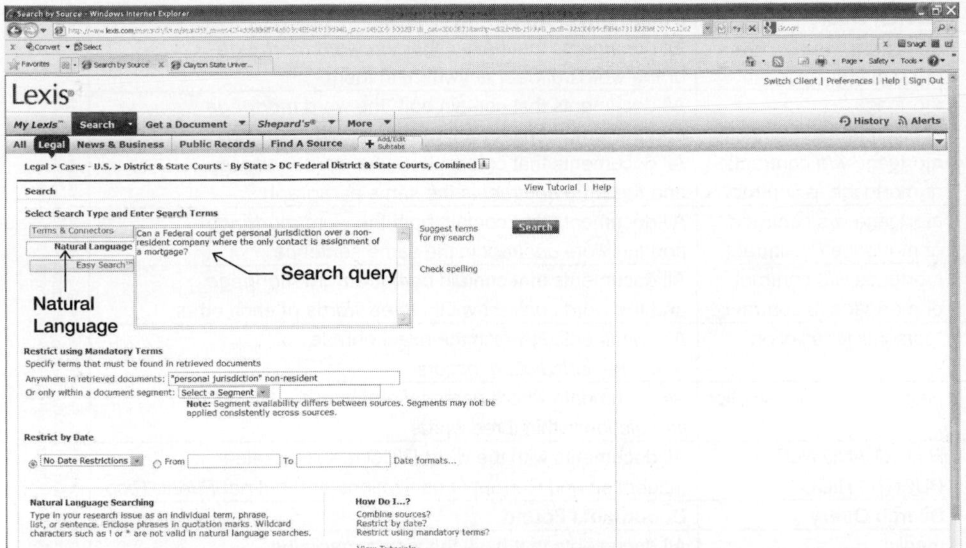

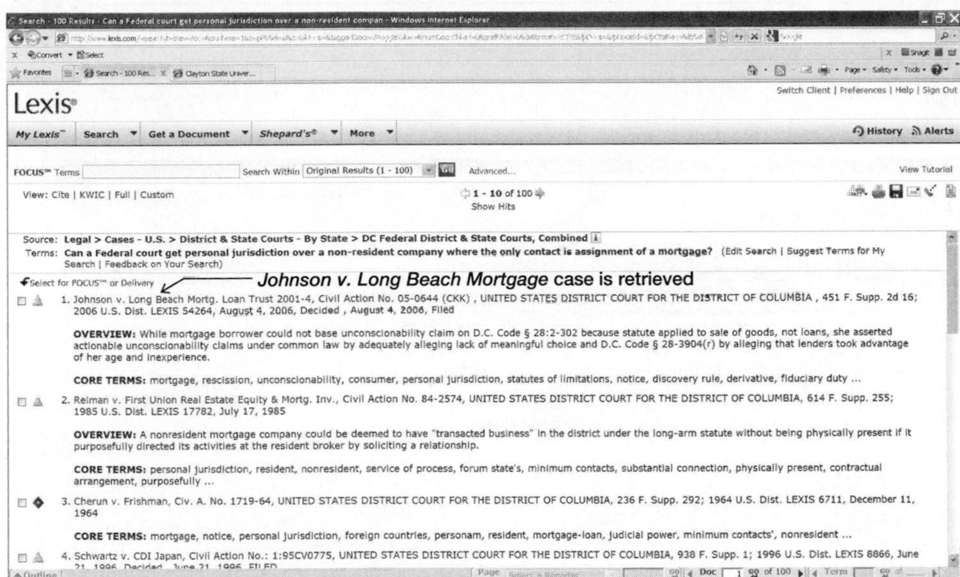

documents in the selected database (DC Federal District & State Courts, Combined) that have the phrase *personal jurisdiction* within the same sentence as the word *non-resident,* within the same sentence as compan! *(company or companies),* and within the same paragraph as mortgage or contract, and which also contain the word long-arm somewhere in the document. Notice in Exhibit 9–34 (second screen) that the Johnson v. Long Beach Mortgage case was retrieved.

Suggest Terms for My Search The Suggest Terms for My Search feature in Lexis shows synonyms for terms in the search query (see Exhibit 9-34, first screen). This is a helpful tool for refining searches. The Lexis Suggest Terms for My Search feature is similar to Westlaw's Thesaurus feature.

Working with Retrieved Cases in Lexis

Lexis gives you a number of different options for viewing and working with retrieved documents. After you have executed a search in Lexis, the system can display the retrieved documents in one of four formats. Lexis also provides features that help you work with the documents retrieved.

Connector	Definition	Search Query	Documents Found
OR	OR	mortgage OR contract	All documents that have either the word *mortgage* or the word *contract* anywhere in them
AND	AND	mortgage AND contract	All documents that contain both the word *mortgage* and the word *contract* anywhere in them
w/p or /p	Paragraph	mortgage w/p contract; or mortgage /p contract	All documents that contain both the word *mortgage* and the word *contract* in the same paragraph
w/s or /s	Sentence	mortgage w/s contract; or mortgage /s contract	All documents that contain both the word *mortgage* and the word *contract* in the same sentence
w/n or /n	Words	mortgage w/3 contract; or mortgage /3 contract	All documents that contain both the word *mortgage* and the word *contract* within three words of each other
“”	Phrase	“personal jurisdiction”	All documents in which the exact phrase “*personal jurisdiction*” occurs
Pre/n	Precedes by n words	personal Pre/3 jurisdiction	All documents where *personal* precedes *jurisdiction* within three words
AND NOT	AND NOT	R.I.C.O. AND NOT PUERTO RICO	All documents with the word *RICO* (i.e., Racketeer Influenced and Corrupt Organizations Act) but not *Puerto Rico*
Expander	**Definition**	**Search Query**	**Documents Found**
!	Root expander	medic!	All documents that have the words *medicine, medical, medicate,* or *medication*
*	Universal character	kn*w	All documents that have the word *know* or *knew* in them

EXHIBIT 9–33
Lexis connectors and expanders

EXHIBIT 9–34
Lexis Terms and Connectors search

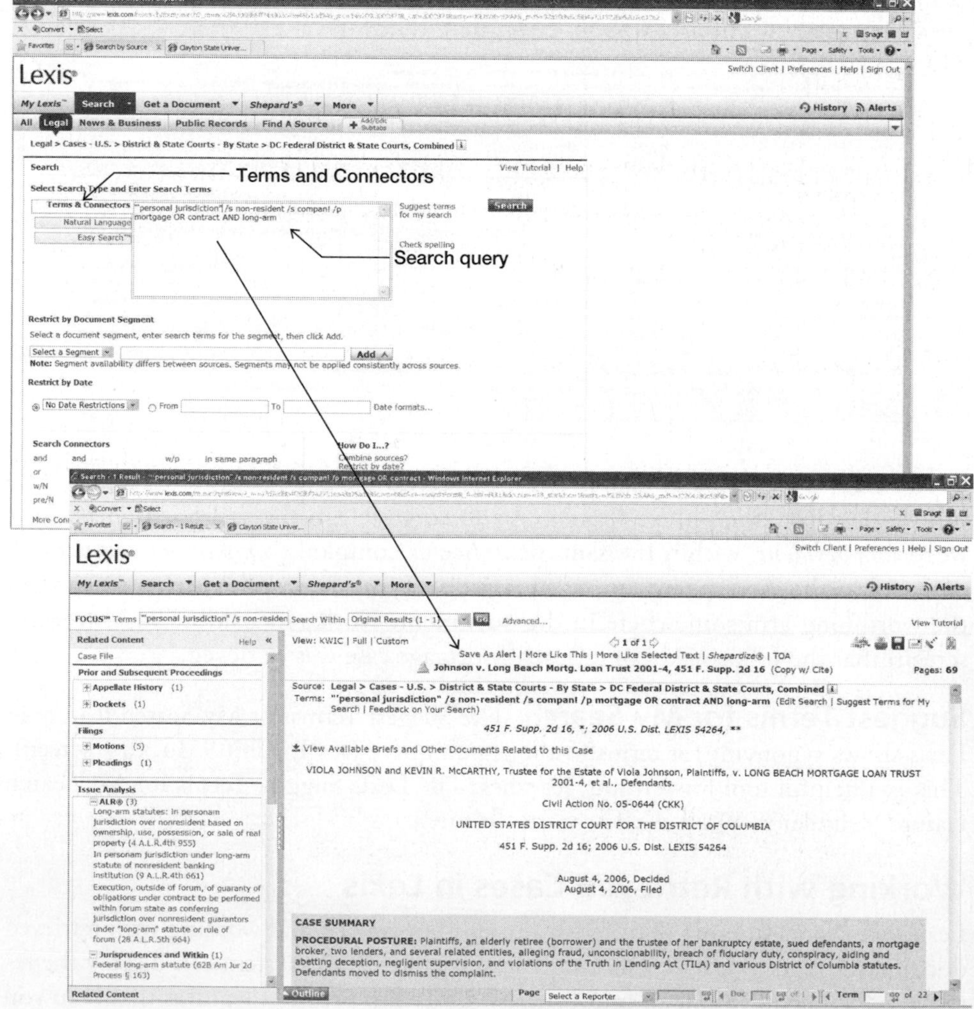

Display Formats The four main display formats available in Lexis are Cite, KWIC, Full, and Custom.

Cite The Cite format shows a bibliographic list of the citations retrieved. Cite can either display the search terms or hide the search terms (see Exhibit 9–34, second screen, where the hits are shown). In the second screen of Exhibit 9–32, to the right of the View: field, notice that Cite is selected in the upper left corner of the screen. A list of the case cites is displayed, including an overview and core terms for each. In Exhibit 9–32, second screen, the search term hits are hidden.

When you click Show Hits, the search terms as they appear in the case are included in the list (see Exhibit 9–35). You can either display or hide the hits. If you have the Show Hits option turned on, a lot of information is provided about each case, but it is difficult to quickly search through a large number of retrieved cases. If you have Hide Hits turned on (see Exhibit 9–32, second screen), you can see more cases, but with less detail. Both options are helpful, depending on what you are trying to accomplish at the time.

KWIC The KWIC option, by default, shows a 25-word window of text around your search terms. KWIC is helpful when you want to see the context in which your search terms appear, but do not want to read the full text of the case.

Full The Full view shows you the full text of the document (see Exhibit 9–34, second screen).

Custom Using the Custom view, you can configure the display format to meet your individual needs.

Case Summaries Lexis includes a Case Summary section for each case (see Exhibit 9–34, second screen). The Case Summary includes the procedural posture of the case, an overview of the case, the outcome or disposition of the case, and the "Core Terms" used in the case. The Case Summary section makes it easy to understand the context of a case and its result. Lexis's Case Summary feature is similar to Westlaw's Synopsis feature.

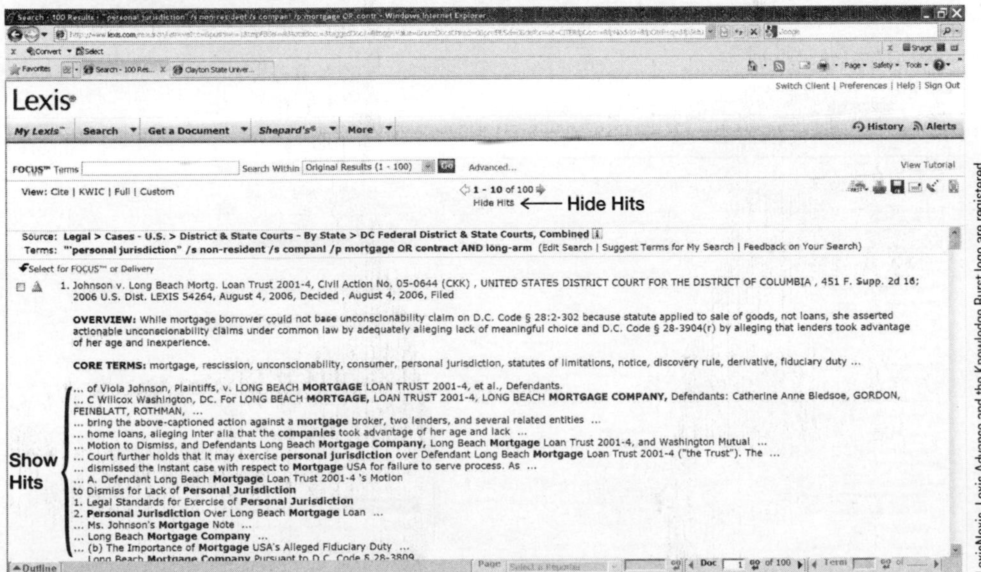

EXHIBIT 9–35
Lexis display format: Show Hits

Navigation Frame The Navigation Frame appears at the bottom of a retrieved document (see Exhibit 9–34, second screen). The Explore feature allows you to navigate within the document, moving to the top of the document, viewing the dissent, moving to the place in the document where the attorneys are listed, and so forth. The Page feature allows you to navigate to a specific hard-copy reporter page. The Doc feature takes you to the next or previous document. Alternatively, you can click in the Doc box, enter a document number, and go to the specific document. The Term feature allows you to go to the next/previous search term. Viewing the search terms is helpful when you are trying to evaluate whether a document is on point.

Headnotes

Headnotes in Lexis summarize each major issue in a case. Most cases include several Headnotes. When you find a Headnote on point, you can select the More Like This Headnote link next to that specific Headnote. In the More Like This Headnote screen that is then displayed, you can search similar Headnotes in Lexis by jurisdiction. Headnotes are a great way to expand your research while staying on point.

Public Records Searches

Using Lexis, you can access many different public records databases. Notice in Exhibit 9–36 that there is a subtab (on the Search tab) called Public Records. Exhibit 9–36 shows the databases available through the Public Records subtab.

Business Information Searches

Using Lexis, you can access a large number of news and business information sources. Notice in Exhibit 9–37 that there is a subtab called News & Business on the Search tab. Exhibit 9–37 shows the databases and topics available through the News & Business subtab.

Alerts

If you want to be sure to stay current on a specific legal issue, you can set up an alert. Alerts use searches that you have saved and run them automatically at intervals you have specified. These results can be stored for viewing online or delivered by email. This feature can be accessed by clicking the Alerts icon on the right side of the screen.

EXHIBIT 9–36
Lexis Public Records subtab

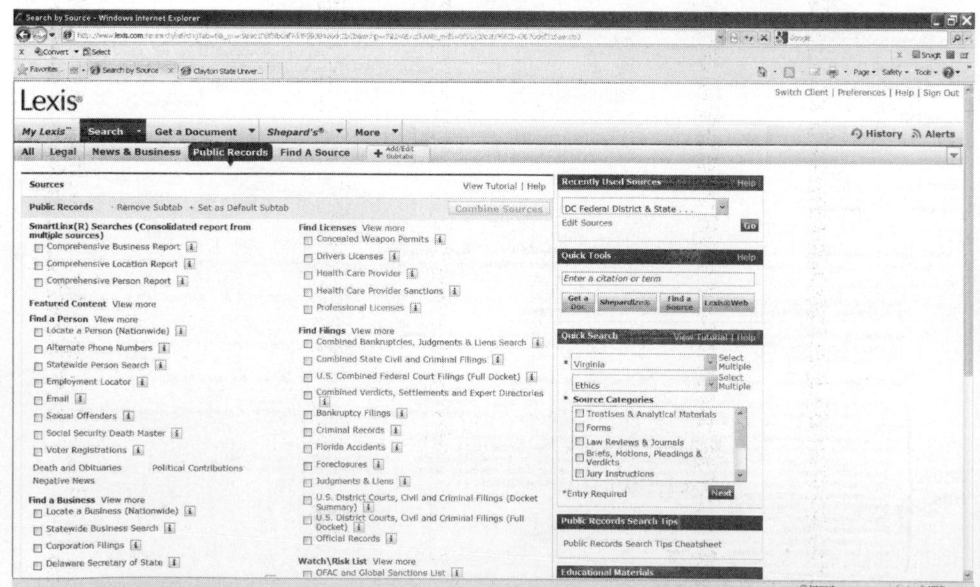

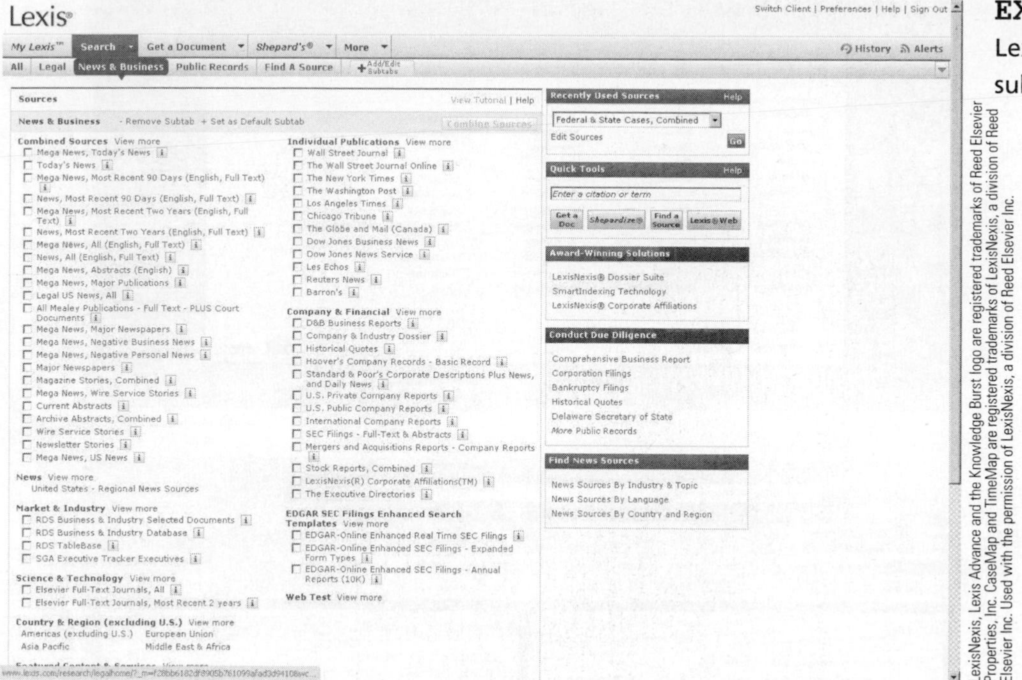

EXHIBIT 9–37
Lexis News & Business subtab

Training

Lexis offers a wide variety of training options, including e-learning modules, webinars, training guides, and seminars. See www.lexis.com. Many of the e-learning modules are available online free of charge, and you do not need a Lexis ID or password to access the e-learning modules.

LEXIS ADVANCE

Much as WestlawNext streamlines the legal research process for Westlaw users, Lexis Advance provides a similar service to users of Lexis. Lexis Advance replaces databases with content types and filters. The first screen of Exhibit 9–38 shows the welcome screen for Lexis Advance. Notice that there is only one place to enter a search query, whether it be for a cite check or a detailed search for a specific case or statute. There are several ways to filter your search results to just the specific jurisdiction and content type (case, statute, etc.) desired. You can choose a jurisdiction (see Exhibit 9–38, second screen) and enter your query. In Exhibit 9–38, the

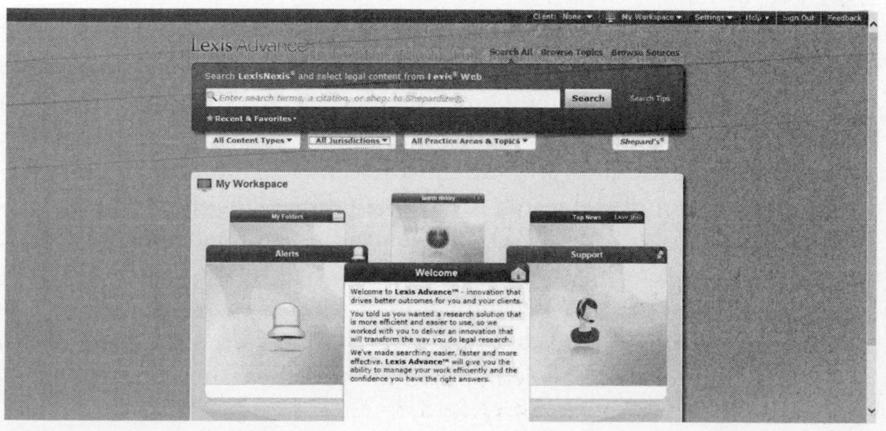

EXHIBIT 9–38
Lexis Advance screens

EXHIBIT 9–38
(Continued)

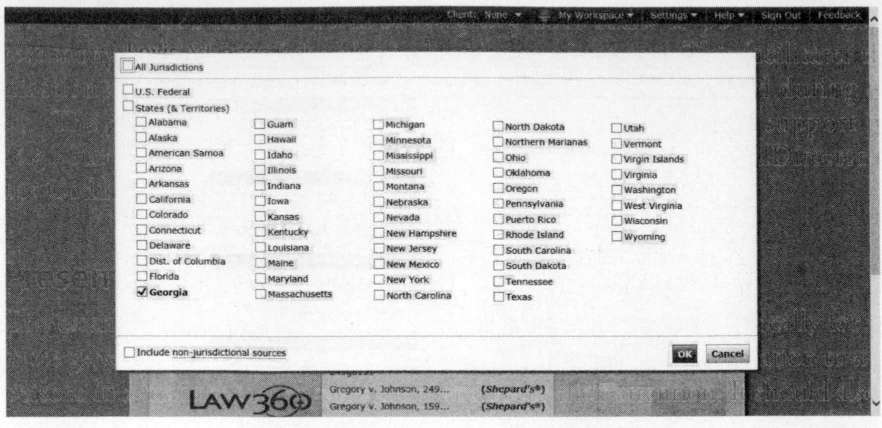

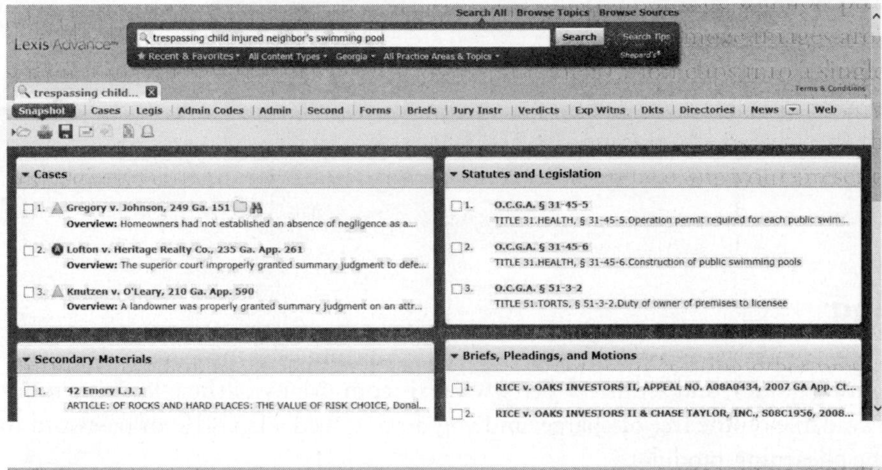

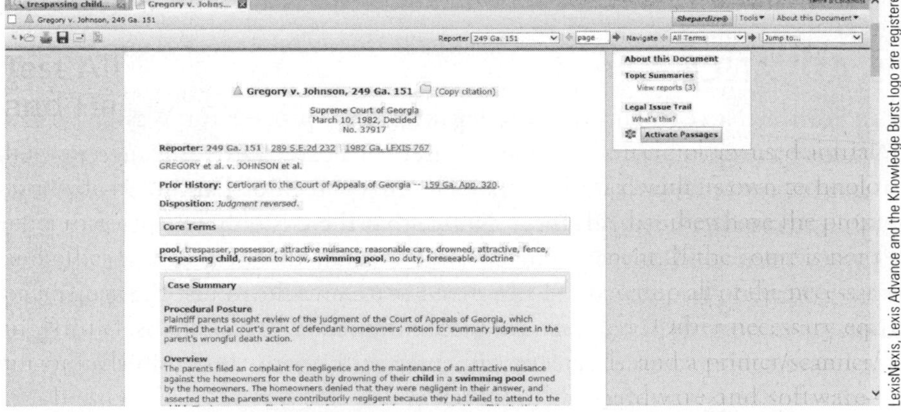

user is looking for cases in Georgia in which a trespassing child was injured while trespassing in a neighbor's swimming pool. The user selected the state of Georgia as the jurisdiction (see Exhibit 9–38, second screen) and entered the search query. The results of the search are shown in the third screen of Exhibit 9–38. Lexis Advance displays a Snapshot of the search results including all content types. Lexis would typically present only cases or statutes, depending on the database selected. In Exhibit 9–38 (third screen), the Snapshot view of all of the search results is presented. On this screen you can see summaries of selected cases, statutes, regulations, and so on, and (on the left side of the screen) links to the complete search results appear. Finally, the fourth screen of Exhibit 9–38 shows how a case looks in Lexis Advance.

OTHER CALR FEE-BASED SERVICE PROVIDERS

Other CALR service providers include Loislaw (www.loislaw.com), National Law Library (www.itislaw.com), Fastcase (www.fastcase.com), and Versuslaw (www.versuslaw.com). These service providers compete against Westlaw and Lexis on the basis of price. Their services offer less breadth of electronic information, and fewer features and functions. For some firms, this is fine. For example, if a law firm has only a few legal professionals and they practice in specific areas such as divorce, criminal, or estate law, a subscription to one of these service providers that only includes case law and statutes for the firm's state might suffice.

INCREASED PRODUCTIVITY ON CALR SYSTEMS

Every minute on an online legal database system is costly, unless the organization has negotiated a flat-rate monthly billing option. However, you can follow some general guidelines and take several precautions to increase your productivity and reduce CALR costs.

Do Not Read Cases Online

In most instances, do not stay online to read the cases you have found. If you have the book in which the case appears, simply get the cite, terminate the CALR session, and read the text of the case from the book offline.

If you do not have access to the book, print the case offline or download it. With many CALR providers, you are incurring several charges whenever you are connected, including an access service charge (if you used this method to connect to the service) and a database charge. If you read a case online, you are still incurring both types of charges.

Do Not Make Typos When Entering the Search

A typo in a search command can cost you several dollars as you wait for the CALR service to run the (inappropriate) search. Double-check your search command for typos before executing it.

Always Plan the Search

Always carefully plan out your search before going online, and always have several alternative searches ready. This can save your firm hundreds of dollars a month in online charges.

Call the CALR's Research Attorneys

If you need to do a particularly difficult search, try calling one of the research attorneys provided by many CALR systems. For Westlaw and Lexis, the call is toll-free. The research attorneys are experts at CALR and can help you prepare a successful search. They will even run a search online for you to make sure the search query is correct.

ETHICAL CONSIDERATIONS

Use of the Internet and email raise several ethical considerations. These include the reliability of Internet information that you might use to support a client's case; problems regarding marketing on the Internet, including use of unsolicited email (spam) to market a law firm; confidentiality issues surrounding use of email for correspondence with clients and others; and competence in legal research.

Reliability of Information on the Internet

As mentioned earlier in this chapter, the reliability of information on the Internet is not guaranteed. Anyone can host a website, send emails, post information on listservs and discussion groups, and generally communicate freely on the Internet with little if any oversight; therefore, users cannot assume that any information is necessarily accurate. There is a tremendous amount of information on the Internet that is opinion, hearsay, innuendo, mistaken, and flat-out untruth. As an Internet user, you should adopt a *caveat emptor* ("Let the buyer beware") philosophy. Whenever possible, you should attempt to verify information found on the Internet and develop cross-checks to make sure the information is accurate. This is particularly true when using new sites that you have never visited before. It is not unlike using *Shepard's* to check the accuracy of cases that you cite to make sure they are still valid and current law. If you cannot corroborate or verify a piece of information, or have any doubts about the source, it is probably best not to use it.

Although no ethical rule deals specifically with Internet research, attorneys do have a duty to perform work in a competent manner. Thus, when performing factual or legal research on the Internet for a client's case, legal professionals must do so in a competent and thorough manner. This, of course, includes a duty not to cite or otherwise use inaccurate information.

Marketing on the Internet

Many law firms market their services to clients using the Internet. Because of the potential for abuse, most states heavily regulate the legal ethics area of attorney advertising and marketing. According to typical ethical restrictions, lawyers cannot use false or misleading information; create unjustified expectations, such as by publishing recent jury verdicts they received; and cannot directly solicit potential clients with whom they do not or have not had a relationship (ambulance chasing).

States are currently creating new ethics rules that apply specifically to all electronic communication. These rules cover all forms of Internet marketing: law-firm web pages, use of banner ads and links, use of Internet chat rooms to solicit clients, and use of email to solicit prospective clients, among others.

Marketing on the Internet—Spam

As indicated previously, spam is unsolicited emails sent to others. In an infamous case in Tennessee, a lawyer spammed email listservs and discussion groups with a promotion for his immigration practice. His spam was reportedly received by thousands of people in many countries and resulted in many complaints to the Tennessee disciplinary authority. The attorney was charged with several ethical violations, including: (1) failing to label his email as advertising; (2) failing to submit a copy of the email to the state bar disciplinary authorities; and (3) referring to himself as an "immigration lawyer," in violation of a rule governing specialization; among other ethical breaches. The Tennessee Supreme Court suspended the attorney's license for one year as a result of the spamming.

Email Confidentiality

As discussed earlier, confidentiality is an important issue when legal professionals use email to communicate with clients. Practical considerations for using email ethically include:

- Having a policy for the legal organization regarding the use of email and how it will be used to communicate with clients.
- Consulting clients about what type of information they want communicated via email, how often the client receives or responds to email, and other information about the particulars of the client's specific email system or habits.

- Sending a test email to a client to ensure that the right email address is being used.
- Adding a confidentiality statement to all client emails. This is similar to the statements that appear on many fax cover pages, declaring that the information is intended solely for the recipient and any third party who receives it should immediately forward it or destroy it.
- Not using email at all for particularly sensitive information.

Ethical Considerations in CALR

Other ethical considerations and duties also apply to computer-assisted legal research, such as taking the time to perform competent legal research, citing quotes appropriately, and not plagiarizing.

Performing Competent Legal Research Performing competent legal research is a fundamental aspect of representing a client in a competent and ethical manner. A client comes to an attorney to be advised on both the factual and legal nature of the client's legal matter. Because the U.S. system of law is based on legal precedent, it is absolutely essential that an attorney understand the legal aspects of a client's matter. This includes performing the legal research to know how to appropriately represent and advise the client. Sometimes wading through mountains of case law, statutes, legislative history, indexes, legal encyclopedias, treatises, law review articles, regulations, court rules, and other materials to support a client's position is like finding a needle in a haystack. It takes skill, thoroughness, and exhaustive preparation to find the right information and to zealously represent the client's interests. Although a client can assist with presenting the facts of a case, the client cannot help regarding the preparation of legal arguments and authorities. This responsibility lies with the attorney and paralegal.

If attorneys fail to present competent legal arguments based on competent legal research, not only have the attorneys failed to perform their ethical duty, but they may also have committed legal malpractice. Courts have generally recognized that an attorney has a duty to perform competent legal research. For example, the court in *Gosnell v. Rentokil*, 175 F.R.D. 508, 510 n.1 (N.D. Ill. 1997), considered the question of whether an attorney had a duty to Shepardize a case (e.g., to confirm that the case the attorney was citing was still good law). In *Gosnell* the court stated:

> It is really inexcusable for any lawyer to fail, as a matter of routine, to Shepardize all cited cases (a process that has been made much simpler today than it was in the past, given the facility for doing so under Westlaw or Lexis). Shepardization would of course have revealed that the "precedent" no longer qualified as such.

Simply put, it is imperative to perform thorough legal research to adequately protect the rights and interests of your client.

Plagiarizing Plagiarizing is the act of using another person's writing or ideas and passing it off as one's own. It is important for all legal professionals to avoid plagiarizing when performing legal research and writing. This problem can be avoided easily simply by citing the authority that has been used, and making it clear where quotations begin and end.

It is dishonest to take credit for the work of another. In addition to ethical considerations, plagiarism can also be a violation of copyright and intellectual property rights. Thus, it is extremely important to appropriately cite and give credit to the author when another person's work is used.

SUMMARY

The Internet or the information superhighway connects hundreds of millions of computers and thousands of networks around the world. Services available on the Internet include email, listservs, newsgroups, instant messaging, File Transfer Protocol, World Wide Web, blogs, RSS, and podcasts.

Several different types of search engines are available on the Web, including individual search engines that compile their own searchable databases, subject-oriented search engines that organize information into topical menus of subjects, and metasearch engines that send a search to multiple search engines. The terms invisible web or deep web refer to the approximately 50 percent of the World Wide Web that lies within databases, is password protected, or is otherwise not accessible through search engines. To access those sites, the user must go to them directly.

The Internet can be used to perform legal research, but it is not at all like using Westlaw or Lexis, because the legal information there is not contained in one central depository. Legal research on the Internet is most efficient when you know exactly what you are looking for, such as a specific case or statute. The Internet is better suited to factual research than legal research. The Internet can be used for performing general research, public record searches, finding people or information about people, accessing news information, conducting business research, and finding expert witnesses, among many other things. Many legal organizations maintain web pages on the Internet. They represent a 24/7 opportunity for marketing the legal organization.

Effectively all paralegals use email on a daily basis in their jobs. Email is a de facto standard for communication throughout the legal community and between legal professionals and clients. Spam, phishing, and loss of confidentiality represent the downside of email use.

Persons doing computer-assisted legal research use computers to research and retrieve legal information. Two of the largest fee-based CALR service providers are Westlaw and Lexis. Less expensive choices, such as Loislaw and Versuslaw, are also available.

Westlaw maintains more than 40,000 databases and offers an array of features. Find by Citation is a Westlaw feature that allows a user to enter a cite and be taken directly to the cite without entering a search query or database. Westlaw's Natural Language search system uses plain English instead of complex connector strings to search for documents. Westlaw's Terms and Connectors search system uses Boolean logic and operators/connectors to combine terms into a search query. Common Westlaw connectors include /s, /p, &, and /n. Root expanders like ! enable Westlaw to retrieve words with the same root. The Locate in Result Westlaw feature allows users to search a retrieved document for particular terms, whether or not the terms appeared in the original search. Headnotes and Key Numbers in Westlaw summarize every major issue in a case and allow users to find additional cases on the same topic. KeySearch is a Westlaw tool that allows users to find documents using a topical legal index, without having to formulate a search query. KeyCite is a Westlaw citation tool that can be used to check if a case is still good law or to list all the times a source has been referred to in other documents. Westlaw also has many nonlegal databases that allow users to search public records, news, and business-related information.

Lexis is a large CALR service provider that, like Westlaw, has captured a large part of the CALR market. Lexis offers databases and features similar to those of Westlaw. Some Lexis features include Get by Citation, Get by Party Name, Natural Language, and *Shepard's Citations.* The terms and connectors used in Lexis are very similar, but not identical, to the Westlaw terms and connectors. Lexis, like Westlaw, includes value-added features, including case summaries and Headnotes.

Ethical considerations and duties apply both to law-firm use of the Internet/email and to legal research. It is important that research be conducted competently and that legal professionals avoid plagiarizing other people's work when using research results.

KEY TERMS

blog
bookmark
cite checking
computer-assisted legal research (CALR)
connectors
electronic mail (email)
File Transfer Protocol (FTP)
Find a Case by Party Name
Find by Citation
Headnotes and Key Numbers
individual search engine
instant messaging (IM)
Internet service provider (ISP)
invisible web
KeyCite
library gateway
listserv
Locate in Result
metasearch engine
Natural Language
offline
online
phishing
podcast
portal
ResultsPlus
root expander
RSS
search query
spam
specialty search engine
subject directory
subject-specific database
Terms and Connectors
uniform resource locator (URL)
universal character
web browser
World Wide Web

INTERNET SITES

Internet sites for this chapter include:

ORGANIZATION	PRODUCT/SERVICE	WORLD WIDE WEB ADDRESS
GENERAL LEGAL SITES ON THE INTERNET		
ABA Legal Technology Resource Center	In-depth information on law-related Internet, intranet, and extranet sites	www.abanet.org/tech/trc
FindLaw	Legal research portal/search engine	www.findlaw.com
Hieros Gamos	Legal research portal/search engine	www.hg.org
Internet Legal Resource Guide	Legal research portal/search engine	www.ilrg.com
Law and Politics Internet Guide	Legal research portal/search engine	www.lpig.org
Legal Information Institute at Cornell Law School	Large collection of links to law-related resources	www.law.cornell.edu
Virtual Chase	Large collection of law-related resources	www.virtualchase.com
WashLaw at Washburn University Law School	Large collection of links to law-related resources	www.washlaw.edu
COMPUTER-ASSISTED LEGAL RESEARCH INTERNET SITES		
Fastcase, Inc.	Fastcase, CALR provider	www.fastcase.com
ITIS, Inc.	National Law Library, CALR provider	www.itislaw.com

Loislaw.com, Inc.	Loislaw, CALR provider	www.loislaw.com
Reed Elsevier Inc.	Lexis, CALR provider	www.lexis.com
Thomson/West	Westlaw, CALR provider	www.westlaw.com
Thomson/West	Westlaw training	west.thomson.com/westlaw
VersusLaw, Inc.	VersusLaw, CALR provider	www.versuslaw.com

TEST YOUR KNOWLEDGE

1. To connect to the Internet, a user needs an ISP. What does ISP stand for?
2. What is another name for an electronic mailing list that allows people on the list to send email to and receive email from everyone on the list?
3. What are the differences between individual, specialty, and metasearch engines?
4. What tool can users access to better control their searches in search engines such as Google?
5. If a user wanted to search for *bikes* but not *motorcycles* in a search engine such as Google, how would the search query best be formulated?
6. True or False: The Internet is better suited to factual research than to legal research.
7. Name three categories of factual information related to a case that a paralegal might search for on the Internet.
8. A useful tool in an Internet browser that allows a user to search the contents of a web page is called ___________.
9. In Westlaw, what is the name of the plain-English search feature?
10. When using Terms and Connectors in Westlaw, a space between two search terms means what?
11. What do the /s, /p, and /n connectors signify in Westlaw?
12. What is the root expander character in Westlaw?
13. What is the universal character in Westlaw?
14. If you write a Terms and Connectors search query in Westlaw and retrieve a large number of cases, what action can you take to reduce the number of cases retrieved?
15. In Westlaw, what does the Locate in Results feature do?
16. What does Westlaw's KeyCite feature do?
17. True or False: Westlaw has Headnotes but Lexis does not.
18. What feature in Lexis allows a user to search retrieved cases for additional search terms, whether or not those terms were in the original search?
19. True or False: Westlaw's Synopsis and Lexis's Case Summary are comparable features.
20. What is the Lexis case citation tool called?
21. True or False: /p, /s, /n, and quotation marks all work the same in Westlaw and Lexis.

ON THE WEB EXERCISES

1. Using a general search engine such as Google or Yahoo!, find three law-related blogs. Write a two-page paper summarizing the content found on the three blogs.
2. Using a general search engine such as Google or Yahoo!, find one article related to accessing the "invisible" or "deep" web. Write a two-page paper summarizing the article.
3. Visit any five websites listed in Exhibit 9–4. Print out the title page of each site and write a two-page paper comparing and contrasting the five sites.
4. Using a general search engine such as Google or Yahoo!, find one article related to accessing public records on the Web. Write a two-page paper summarizing the article.

5. Visit any five websites listed in Exhibit 9–6. Print out the title page of each site and write a two-page paper comparing and contrasting the five sites.
6. Using the Google Maps feature at www.google.com, print out a satellite or street level picture of where you currently live. If it is not available, print out one of a place with which you are familiar.
7. Locate and print out the *Model Code of Ethics and Professional Responsibility* for the National Federation of Paralegal Associations.
8. Find a list of websites of local paralegal organizations that are associated with the National Association of Legal Assistants.
9. Use at least three different search engines to find the website for the Association of Trial Lawyers of America. Compare the results of each search. Which search engine did you like best, and why?
10. Find an email address for any member of Congress from your state. Write a short description of how you went about finding the email address.
11. Find a list of law-related listservs and subscribe to at least one.
12. Using the Internet, find a list of Web resources for immigration law.
13. Find regulations implementing the Family and Medical Leave Act by searching in the *Code of Federal Regulations* as published online by the U.S. government.
14. Use SEC EDGAR filings and other information to research recent developments regarding Microsoft Corporation. Use at least five different sources of information. Prepare a one-page summary of the information you gathered.
15. Go to www.west.thomson.com/support/user-guide/westlaw and review at least one Westlaw training guide. Write a two-page memo summarizing what you learned.
16. Go to www.lexis.com and take at least one free e-learning module. Write a two-page memo summarizing what you learned.
17. Visit the websites of two other CALR service providers (not Westlaw or Lexis) and compare their products and pricing, if it is available. Which of the services did you like best, and why? Write a two-page memo summarizing your research.

QUESTIONS AND EXERCISES

1. Interview an attorney, paralegal, or secretary in a legal organization regarding their use of the Internet and email. How has it changed over time?
2. As a new paralegal in a solo practitioner's office, you notice that the office has been slow to embrace technology. The office does not have a high-speed Internet connection and the attorney does not see the need to get one because the Internet is barely used in the office. The office mainly handles personal injury, divorce, and collection cases. Write a one-page memo to the attorney regarding the advantages of using the World Wide Web for this office.
3. You are a paralegal working on a personal injury case in which your firm's client had her hand cut off in an accident on the job. The defendant admits liability and is trying to settle the case for an amount that the attorney thinks is too low. The attorney asks you to formulate a search query in Westlaw or Lexis in the hope that you can determine what amount of damages juries have awarded for this type of accident or case.
4. The attorney you work for wants you to perform CALR on the following issue. The attorney is representing a client who worked for a governmental agency. The client was fired from the agency because the client was arrested for driving under the influence of alcohol while off duty. The criminal charges were dropped and the client was not formally prosecuted. The attorney asks you to formulate a search query plan, using a CALR service. What is your query?

ETHICS QUESTION

A new client has received a letter from the Internal Revenue Service informing him that unless he pays the IRS $314.23, he will be sued. The client insists that no taxes are owed and wants your firm to research the tax code, regulations, and case law to find legal authority to support his position. You estimate that it will take more than five hours to complete this research. Your firm bills $90 an hour for your services. What ethical issues, if any, are raised by this scenario?

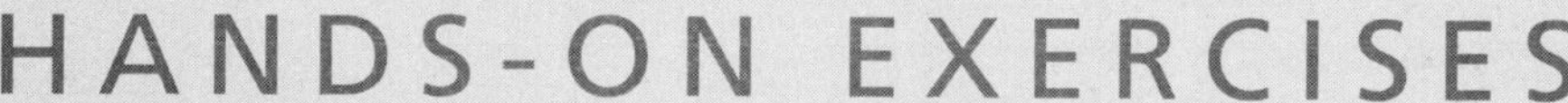

HANDS-ON EXERCISES

FEATURED SOFTWARE

LEGAL AND FACTUAL RESEARCH ON THE INTERNET

Number	Lesson Title	Concepts Covered
BASIC LESSONS		
Lesson 1	Using a Legal Search Engine, Part 1	Find practice/subject matter indexes on FindLaw.com; locate free legal forms in the Internet Legal Research Group; find free legal-related news articles in Alllaw.com
Lesson 2	Using a Legal Search Engine, Part 2	Find a legal dictionary in Lawguru.com; find a large number of law journals using the Internet Legal Research Group and Lawguru.com
INTERMEDIATE LESSONS		
Lesson 3	Conducting Legal Research on the Internet, Part 1 U.S. Supreme Court State/Federal Rules	Find United States Supreme Court cases, state court rules, and federal court rules
Lesson 4	Conducting Legal Research on the Internet, Part 2 State statutes U.S. Code Code of Federal Regulations	Do keyword searching for state statutes, in the U.S. Code, and in the *Code of Federal Regulations*
Lesson 5	Conducting Legal Research on the Internet, Part 3 Current Congressional Record State Appellate Court opinions	Perform keyword searches in and for current congressional legislation; keyword-search federal legislative history in the *Congressional Record;* keyword-search state appellate court opinions
Lesson 6	Conducting Factual Research on the Internet, Part 1 Expert witnesses Attorneys Satellite and street level images	Find expert witnesses using ExpertPages.com; find attorneys in particular specialties by city/state using Martindale.com; find satellite and street-level images using Google
Lesson 7	Conducting Factual Research on the Internet, Part 2 Federal Bureau of Prisons Inmate Locator State criminal records search	Find federal inmates using the Federal Bureau of Prisons Inmate Locator; conduct state criminal background checks
Lesson 8	Conducting Factual Research on the Internet, Part 3 Real estate/appraisal searches State vital record searches Federal statistic searches	Find county real estate appraisal records; find state vital records (birth, death, marriage, divorce); find statistics from the federal government

ADVANCED LESSONS		
Lesson 9	Conducting Factual Research on the Internet, Part 4 SEC filings (EDGAR) PDRHealth.com Prescription drug search Library Gateway—Aviation	Find Securities and Exchange Commission filings using the EDGAR database; find the side effects of a prescription drug using PDRHealth.com; find aviation-related information using a library gateway
Lesson 10	Conducting Factual Research on the Internet, Part 5 Pipl.com Salary.com	Find individuals using Pipl.com; find salary information using Salary.com

GETTING STARTED

Introduction

Throughout these lessons and exercises, information you need to type into the software will be designated in several different ways:

- Keys to be pressed on the keyboard are designated in brackets, in all caps, and in bold (e.g., press the **[ENTER]** key).
- Movements with the mouse pointer are designated in bold and italics (e.g., ***point to File on the menu bar and click***).
- Words or letters that should be typed are designated in bold (e.g., type **Training Program**).
- Information that is or should be displayed on your computer screen is shown in bold, with quotation marks (e.g., **"Press ENTER to continue."**).
- Specific menu items and commands are designated with an initial capital letter (e.g., click Open).

OVERVIEW

These Hands-On Exercises assume that you have a web browser, that you are generally familiar with it, and that you have access to the Internet. The exercises are designed to give you experience in using a number of different websites and practice at finding different kinds of information. Because the use of web browsers is straightforward and routine, only summary instructions are included in these exercises. The instructions are current as of this writing, but websites change from time to time, so it is possible that the instructions will not work on sites that have been significantly changed. If you encounter this problem, just skip that assignment and go to the next.

BASIC LESSONS

LESSON 1: USING A LEGAL SEARCH ENGINE, PART 1

Exercise 1.a. The objective of this exercise is to find a free residential lease agreement valid in the state of New York using the Internet Legal Research Group (ilrg.com).

The Internet Legal Research Group has an excellent forms archive. Many websites have legal forms for sale, but this site provides many different forms for free.

Instructions:

1. Go to http://ilrg.com.
2. ***Click ILRG Legal Forms Archive.***
3. ***Click Leases and Real Estate.***
4. ***Click Agreement to Lease (Residential Lease).***
5. ***Click New York.***
6. ***Scroll down*** to see/read the "New York Residential Lease Agreement."
7. Copy the text of the lease and paste it into a document in your word processor.
8. Print the lease agreement.

Exercise 1.b. The objective of this exercise is to find a free, law-related news site using Alllaw.com.

Instructions:

1. Go to www.alllaw.com.
2. ***Click Legal Topics.***
3. Review the available topics and ***click on a topic of interest to you.***
4. Print out the article on your selected topic.

LESSON 2: USING A LEGAL SEARCH ENGINE, PART 2

Exercise 2.a. The objective of this exercise is to find a legal term or phrase in Lawguru's legal search engine.

Instructions:

1. Go to www.lawguru.com
2. ***Click Legal Dictionary under Resources, seen at the bottom of the page.***
3. Search for "easements" and print out the definition.

Exercise 2.b. The objective of this exercise is to find access to law review articles using Internet Legal Research Group.

You can also read the full text of an article by clicking on the article title.

Instructions:

1. Go to http://ilrg.com.
2. ***Under ILRG Web Index in the Academia section, click on Law Journals.***
3. Scroll down the list of law journals and ***click on Harvard Law Review.***
4. ***Click on the link for an article of your choice;*** you can read the article or print a copy of it.

INTERMEDIATE LESSONS

LESSON 3: CONDUCTING LEGAL RESEARCH ON THE INTERNET, PART 1

Exercise 3.a. The objective of this exercise is to find the full text of the U.S. Supreme Court decision in *Faragher v. City of Boca Raton* using the Legal Information Institute at Cornell Law School.

When you know the case name, year of decision, and name of the court, it is easy to find the full text of a case on the Internet for free (especially if it is a U.S. Supreme Court case).

Instructions:

1. Go to www.law.cornell.edu.
2. Under "LEGAL RESOURCES" ***click on Supreme Court.***
3. ***Under Archive of decisions, point to By party and click 1990-present.***
4. In the next screen, next to 1997–1998, ***click 1st party.***
5. In the next screen, ***Click*** **Faragher v. City of Boca Raton.**
6. ***Place your cursor over the plus sign (+) under Supreme Court Toolbox and select Print from the drop-down menu. Print the case.***

Another method: Using a search engine such as Google.com, type **Faragher v. City of Boca Raton** in the search box. You will find numerous links to the full text of the opinion.

Exercise 3.b. The objective of this exercise is to find the Rules of Criminal Procedure for the state of Alaska using Washlaw.edu (search by keyword).

Washlaw.edu has a large index that includes references to all 50 states and many federal resources.

Instructions:

1. Go to www.washlaw.edu.
2. ***Click Alaska.***
3. ***Under Court Rules, click Rules of Court.***
4. Print the listing of the Alaska Rules of Court.
5. ***Click Criminal Procedure*** to see the Alaska Rules of Criminal Procedure.

Exercise 3.c. The objective of this exercise is to find the Federal Rules of Civil Procedure using Washlaw.edu.

Many rules for the federal courts are listed on this site.

Instructions:

1. Go to www.washlaw.edu.
2. ***Click Federal Courts.***
3. ***Under United States Supreme Court, click United States Supreme Court.***
4. On the next screen, under Research, ***click SCOTUS blog.***
5. On the SCOTUS blog site, read and print an article of interest to you.

LESSON 4: CONDUCTING LEGAL RESEARCH ON THE INTERNET, PART 2

Exercise 4.a. The objective of this exercise is to access the New Hampshire Revised Statutes, using Washlaw.edu, and find the statutes related to criminal theft.

When searching for specific state statutes, you can often enter search terms and find the relevant statutes. Although this technique works well when searching statutes, it often does not work for case law.

Instructions:

1. Go to www.washlaw.edu.
2. ***Click on New Hampshire.***
3. ***Under Statutes, click New Hampshire Revised Statutes.***
4. ***Under Full-Text Searching, click Search.***
5. Search for **Theft.**
6. ***Click Chapter 637 Theft.***
7. Print the first page of the statute.

Exercise 4.b. The objective of this exercise is to access the United States Code using the U.S. House of Representatives site (search by keyword).

The U.S. House of Representatives site is an excellent and efficient place to search the U.S. Code.

Instructions:

1. Go to http://uscode.house.gov.
2. In the Search Word(s) field, type **Racketeer-Influenced and Corrupt Organizations** (do not use quotation marks). ***Click Search.***
3. ***Click the word "Definitions" next to 18 USC 1961.*** (*Note:* There may be more than one listing; if so, choose the first one.)
4. Print the first page of the statute.

Exercise 4.c. The objective of this exercise is to access the *Code of Federal Regulations* using the Government Printing Office (GPO) website (search by keyword).

Instructions:

1. Go to www.ecfr.gov.
2. ***Click Simple Search,*** and then in the Search for: field, type **Canned fruit cocktail,** then ***click submit search.***
3. ***Click*** **Sec. 145.135 Canned fruit cocktail.** You may need to scroll down the list of results to find this.
4. Print the definition of *canned fruit cocktail.*

LESSON 5: CONDUCTING LEGAL RESEARCH ON THE INTERNET, PART 3

Exercise 5.a. The objective of this exercise is to search for a current bill in Congress using the Library of Congress's Thomas site.

Instructions:

1. Go to congress.gov.
2. In the "Search" box, select "Current Legislation" and type **Tax.** ***Click the Search icon*** (it looks like a magnifying glass). You will then see all of the bills with "Tax" in the title.
3. Print the first page.

Exercise 5.b. The objective of this exercise is to search the *Congressional Record* for legislative history using the Library of Congress's Thomas site (search by keyword).

Instructions:

1. Go to congress.gov.
2. ***Click Congressional Record on the left side of the page.***
3. In the Search text box, type **Violence Against Women Act.** ***Click the Search icon*** (it looks like a magnifying glass).
4. Scroll down and ***click REAUTHORIZATION OF THE VIOLENCE AGAINST WOMEN ACT to see Act.***
5. Print the first page.

Exercise 5.c. The objective of this exercise is to search for a case using a search query.

Google Scholar allows you to search for cases in much the same way that you would using Westlaw or Lexis. As of this writing, only cases are available, but it is likely that statutes and regulations will become available at some point in the future.

Instructions:

1. Go to www.google.com.
2. ***Click on Scholar*** (you may have to first ***click on More*** to see the link for Scholar). Alternatively, go to scholar.google.com.
3. ***Click the button for Case law.***
4. In the search box type **negligence trespassing child swimming pool.**
5. ***Click the Search icon*** (it looks like a magnifying glass). You should see a link to the case of *Gregory v. Johnson.* Note that the link may not be on the first page of search results.

LESSON 6: CONDUCTING FACTUAL RESEARCH ON THE INTERNET, PART 1

Exercise 6.a. The objective of this exercise is to find a dental expert using ExpertPages.com.

This site has a wide array of specialty areas to choose from.

Instructions:

1. Go to www.expertpages.com.
2. ***Click Medical/Surgical Specialties.***
3. ***Click on Dentistry and Oral Surgery.***
4. ***Click your state.***
5. Review the experts listed by visiting their websites.
6. Print the first page of the results.

Exercise 6.b. The objective of this exercise is to find an attorney who specializes in divorce cases using Martindale.com.

This assignment can serve two purposes: it can provide experience doing factual research on the Internet, and it can provide a list of firms to consider when you commence your job search.

Instructions:

1. Go to www.martindale.com.
2. ***Click Advanced search.***
3. ***Choose the Law Firms & Organizations tab.***
4. ***In the City field, choose your city.***
5. ***In the State field, choose your state.***
6. ***Under Practice Area,*** type **Family Law.**
7. ***Click Search.***
8. Review the list of firms by visiting their websites.
9. Print the first page of the results.

Exercise 6.c. The objective of this exercise is to find a satellite image of your home town.

The satellite map tool is a free and useful feature of Google.

Instructions:

1. Go to www.google.com.
2. ***Click Maps.*** Alternatively, you can go to maps.google.com.
3. ***Double-click on your home town.***
4. ***Continue double-clicking the map.* When street names are displayed, *click Satellite.***
5. You can use the + (plus) and – (minus) signs on the left side of the map to increase and decrease the magnification, and you can use the arrows just above the magnification tools to move the image in any direction.

Exercise 6.d. The objective of this exercise is to find a street-level image of your home town.

Instructions:

1. Go to www.google.com.
2. ***Click Maps.*** Alternatively, you can go to maps.google.com.
3. In the search box, type your address.
4. When the map appears, ***use the cursor to drag and drop the figure that looks like the silhouette of a person on your exact location.***
5. In many cases, you should now see a street-level image of your home (this is known as "Street View").
6. If you are unable to see the image, try another address.

HANDS-ON EXERCISES

LESSON 7: CONDUCTING FACTUAL RESEARCH ON THE INTERNET, PART 2

Exercise 7.a. The objective of this exercise is to perform a search for a federal inmate using the Federal Bureau of Prisons website.

Instructions:

1. Go to www.bop.gov.
2. ***Click* "Find an Inmate" under "Inmates"** option on the Menu bar.
3. In the Find By Name section, under Last Name, type **Kaczynski.**
4. Under First Name, type **Theodore.**
5. ***Under Race, click White.***
6. ***Under Sex, click Male.***
7. ***Click Search.***
8. The record for Theodore John Kaczynski (a/k/a the Unabomber) should be displayed.
9. Print the page.

Exercise 7.b. The objective of this exercise is to do a state criminal background search using VirtualChase.com.

Instructions:

1. Go to www.virtualchase.com.
2. ***Click Legal Research.***
3. ***Click State Government and Legal Resources.***
4. ***Click Georgia.***
5. ***Click the link for Georgia Inmate Query.*** You can search this database for current and past inmates.
6. ***Close the "Georgia Inmate Query" window and go back to the State Government and Legal Resources page.***
7. ***Click the link for your state*** and see if there is a link to find criminal records in your state.

LESSON 8: CONDUCTING FACTUAL RESEARCH ON THE INTERNET, PART 3

Exercise 8.a. The objective of this exercise is to find real estate records and information.

Instructions:

1. Go to www.zillow.com.
2. Type in the address of a private home (yours or someone else's).
3. You should see an estimate (Zillow refers to it as a "Zestimate") of the property's dollar value.
4. Click on the link for the address to see detailed information about the property (square footage, taxes, etc.).

Exercise 8.b. The objective of this exercise is to do a vital record search (birth, death, marriage, divorce).

Instructions:

1. Go to www.cdc.gov/nchs/nvss/state_health_departments.htm.
2. ***Click Minnesota.***
3. ***Click "Certificates & Records." Then click "death certificates" under "Death Certificates and Records."*** The screen should now display information on how to get a death certificate from the state of Minnesota.
4. Print the page.

Exercise 8.c. The objective of this exercise is to retrieve statistical records using Fedstats.gov.

Fedstats.gov gives users access to an enormous amount of data. However, finding the data you want may require time and patience. If you cannot find the data you need, a quick call to the responsible government agency can often prove helpful.

Instructions:

1. Go to www.fedstats.gov.
2. On the left side of the screen, ***click the down arrow, select South Carolina, then click Submit.***
3. Scroll down through the list and look at all of the statistical information regarding the state of South Carolina.

4. Print the list.
5. ***Click Back*** to go back to www.fedstats.gov.
6. On the right side of the screen, ***click the down arrow and select Labor, then click Submit.***
7. ***Under Bureau Of Labor Statistics, click Unemployment.***
8. Scroll down and notice that the unemployment rate for each state is listed on the right side of the screen.

ADVANCED LESSONS

LESSON 9: CONDUCTING FACTUAL RESEARCH ON THE INTERNET, PART 4

Exercise 9.a. The objective of this exercise is to find current Securities and Exchange Commission (SEC) filings for the Coca-Cola Company, using the SEC's EDGAR site.

Once you get comfortable with searching SEC filings, you will find that the EDGAR database contains a great deal of detailed information, including compensation plans, detailed financials, and other product/sales information.

Instructions:

1. Go to www.sec.gov.
2. ***Under Filings, click Company Filings Search.***
3. Under Company name, type **Coca Cola**, ***click Search.***
4. ***Click the link next to Coca Cola Co.***
5. Print the first page of the SEC filings for this company.

Exercise 9.b. The objective of this exercise is to use the Digital Librarian library gateway to find a list of the top 300 drugs used in the United States.

Library gateway sites offer users a large number of access points to relevant sites on the Web.

Instructions:

1. Go to www.pdrhealth.com.
2. In the Search box, type **Zoloft** and ***click Search.***
3. Under Search results for Zoloft, ***click the link for Zoloft.***
4. ***Scroll down the page until you find the section titled "What are the possible side effects of Zoloft?"***
5. Print that page.

LESSON 10: CONDUCTING FACTUAL RESEARCH ON THE INTERNET, PART 5

Exercise 10.a. The objective of this exercise is to find people using the Internet.

Instructions:

1. Go to www.pipl.com.
2. Type your name and state in the appropriate boxes and ***click Search.***
3. Print the results page.

HANDS-ON EXERCISES

Exercise 10.b. The objective of this exercise is to find salary data.

Instructions:

1. Go to www.salary.com.
2. Under Job Title, type **Paralegal.**
3. At Zip Code, enter your Zip Code and then ***click the Enter key.***
4. ***Click on Paralegal I*** and print the report.
5. ***Click on Paralegal II, III, and IV*** to see the full range of paralegal salaries in your area.

HANDS-ON EXERCISES

WESTLAW COMPUTER-ASSISTED LEGAL RESEARCH

Number	Lesson Title	Concepts Covered
BASIC LESSONS		
Lesson 1	Introduction to Westlaw	Signing on; introduction to the Westlaw interface; working with Westlaw tabs
Lesson 2	Find by Citation, Find by Party Name, and Exploring Retrieved Cases	Find by Citation; Find by Party Name; Star paging; Reporter Image; KeyCite overview; Case Outline; ResultsPlus
INTERMEDIATE LESSONS		
Lesson 3	Natural Language Search; Editing Searches; Changing Databases; Using the Term, Doc, and Best Features	Selecting a database; doing a Natural Language search; finding the scope of a database; editing a search; changing to a different database; using date restriction when searching; using the Require/Exclude Terms feature; using the Term, Doc, and Best features
Lesson 4	Terms and Connectors Searching	Searching using Terms and Connectors; using Thesaurus; printing a list of cases; using the Locate in Result tool
Lesson 5	KeyCite	KeyCite; depth-of-treatment stars; quotations; citing references; using the Limit KeyCite display; using the Research Trail feature
ADVANCED LESSON		
Lesson 6	KeySearch, Headnotes, and Key Numbers	Using KeySearch, Headnotes, Key Numbers, Most Recent Cases, and Most Cited Cases

HANDS-ON EXERCISES

GETTING STARTED

Introduction

Throughout these lessons and exercises, information you need to type into the software will be designated in several different ways:

- Keys to be pressed on the keyboard are designated in brackets, in all caps, and in bold (e.g., press the **[ENTER]** key).
- Movements with the mouse pointer are designated in bold and italics (e.g., ***point to File on the menu bar and click***).
- Words or letters that should be typed are designated in bold (e.g., type **Training Program**).
- Information that is or should be displayed on your computer screen is shown in bold, with quotation marks (e.g., **"Press ENTER to continue."**).
- Specific menu items and commands are designated with an initial capital letter (e.g., click Open).

BASIC LESSONS

LESSON 1: INTRODUCTION TO WESTLAW

This lesson introduces you to Westlaw. It includes instructions for signing on to Westlaw, taking a tour of Westlaw and becoming familiar with the Westlaw interface, and working with Westlaw tabs. For an overview of the features available in Westlaw, read the section on Westlaw in Chapter 9 of the text.

1. Start Windows.
2. Start your Internet browser. Type **www.westlaw.com** in the browser and press the **[ENTER]** key.
3. Your screen should look similar to Westlaw Exhibit 1. ***Click Switch to Westlaw Password Sign On.*** At the Westlaw Password field, enter your Westlaw ID and the Westlaw password supplied by your instructor. In the Client ID field, type **Hands-On Exercises** (or whatever your instructor tells you to enter; see Westlaw Exhibit 1).

WESTLAW EXHIBIT 1

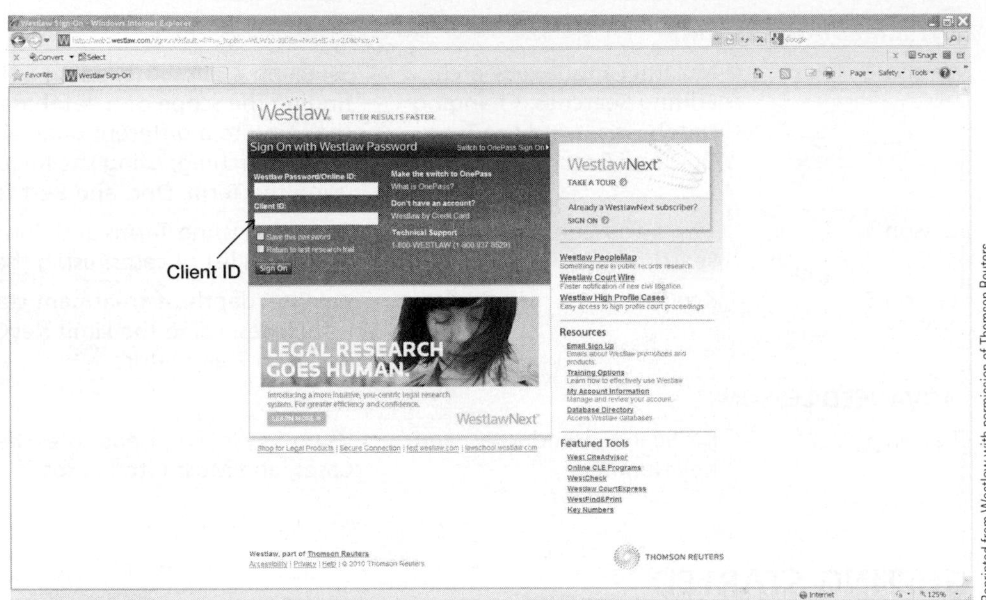

4. You will then be directed to create a Westlaw OnePass User ID and Password. From now on, you will use these credentials to log into Westlaw. If you are using your own computer, you may also want to ***click Save this Password.*** Doing so will save you the time and trouble of reentering your password every time you log on to Westlaw. You should not use this feature if you are using a public computer (e.g., a library computer).
5. ***Click Sign On*** to sign on to Westlaw. If you are asked to agree to the terms of use, ***click I Agree*** and then ***click Go.***
6. Your screen should now look similar to Westlaw Exhibit 2. This is the Welcome to Westlaw screen. *Note:* If your screen does not look like Westlaw Exhibit 2, try clicking the Westlaw tab (see Westlaw Exhibit 2) in the upper left section of the screen.
7. You will now take a brief tour of Westlaw. *Note:* In the middle of the Welcome to Westlaw screen, there may be notices or news items about new services or changes to Westlaw.
8. Notice the **Find** this document by citation: field in the upper left section of the screen (see Westlaw Exhibit 2). This is where you can enter a case or statutory citation and be taken directly to the case or statute.
9. Notice the **KeyCite** this citation: field in the middle left of the screen (see Westlaw Exhibit 2). This is where you can enter a case or statutory citation

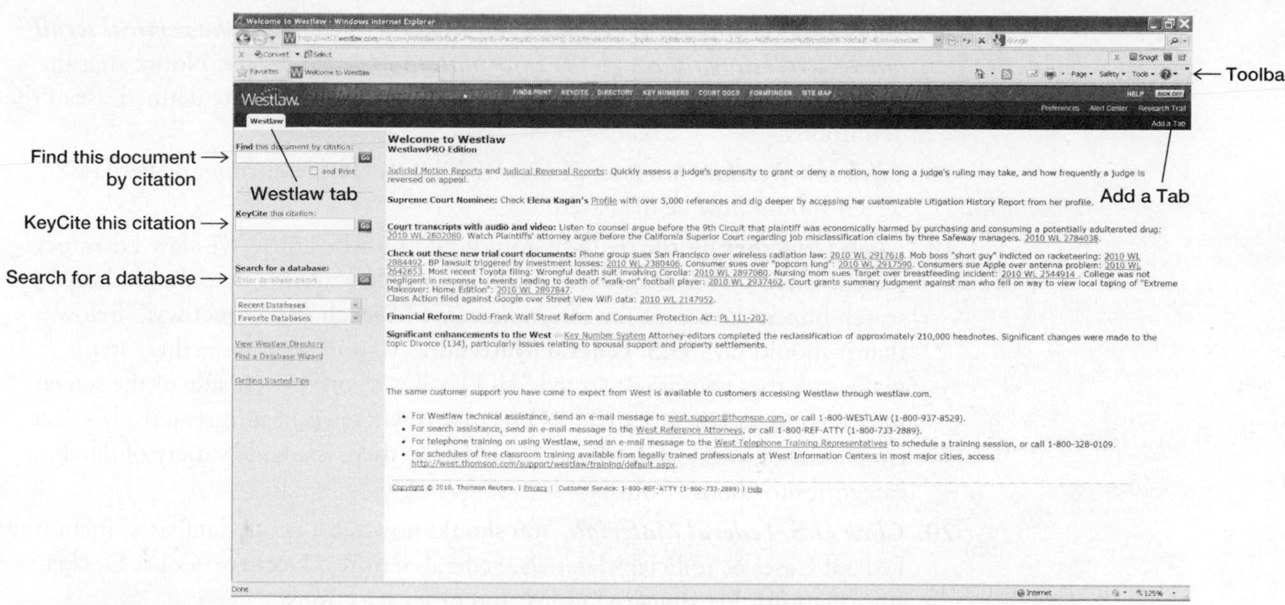

WESTLAW EXHIBIT 2

and have the history of the specified material displayed, including whether the document is still good law and other documents that cite the specified case or statute.

10. Notice the **Search for a database:** field in the lower left of the screen (see Westlaw Exhibit 2). This is where you can enter the name of a specific database and be taken to that database to search or query it.
11. Notice the words **"Recent Databases"** in the lower left of the screen, just below the **Search for a database:** field (see Westlaw Exhibit 2). ***Click the down arrow next to Recent Databases.*** You may or may not have anything listed, depending on whether you or other users have recently used Westlaw. If you recently used a database that you want to go back to, you can click here, see the database, select it from the list, and return to it immediately.
12. If a pop-up window appears, press the **[ESC]** key to make it disappear.
13. Notice the toolbar at the top of the Westlaw screen (see Westlaw Exhibit 2). This toolbar is static, meaning that it always stays the same. Hence, you can access Find&Print, KeyCite, Directory, Key Numbers, Court Docs, FormFinder, Site Map, Help, and SIGN OFF at any time.
14. ***Click Find&Print on the toolbar.*** Westlaw's Find&Print feature lets you enter multiple citations and automatically send them to a printer, download them to a word processor, such as Word or WordPerfect, email the document to whomever you choose, or fax the citation to a fax number you supply. You can also include the citation's KeyCite history or citing-references information. Find&Print can be a good tool and a tremendous timesaver if you know exactly what you want.
15. ***Click the Westlaw tab*** (see Westlaw Exhibit 2). The Welcome to Westlaw screen should now be displayed.
16. ***Click KeyCite on the toolbar.*** As discussed in the main text, KeyCite is Westlaw's citation tool; using KeyCite, you can get the history of a case, including information on whether the case has been overruled or reversed, or a list of other documents that have cited your case.

17. You should now be at the KeyCite information screen. ***Use the vertical scroll bar to scroll down through the information about KeyCite.*** Notice that the KeyCite symbols, such as the red and yellow colored flags, are defined. Read the definitions.
18. ***Click the Westlaw tab*** (see Westlaw Exhibit 2). The Welcome to Westlaw screen should now be displayed.
19. ***Click Directory on the toolbar.*** You should now be at the Westlaw Directory screen. ***Click on All Databases in the left of the screen.*** There should be a search box at the top of the screen that says **"Search the Directory."** Below that it should say **"U.S. Federal Materials."** (If you do not see these items, make sure that you have selected "All Databases" on the left side of the screen under Westlaw Directory.) The Directory is where you can interactively select from a list of Westlaw databases. Notice that there is a wide variety of database categories to choose from.
20. ***Click U.S. Federal Materials.*** You should now see a list of databases, including Federal Cases & Judicial Materials, Federal Statutes, Dockets (Court Docket Information), Pleadings, Motions, and other selections.
21. ***Click the Back button on your browser,*** or ***click Directory on the toolbar to go back to the Directory.***
22. ***Click each of the categories on the directory screen*** (U.S. State Materials, International/Worldwide Materials, Topical Practice Areas, and the other categories). Scroll down through the lists. When you are done with each category, ***click your browser's Back button*** or ***click Directory on the toolbar.***
23. ***Click the Westlaw tab.***
24. ***Click Court Docs on the toolbar.***
25. Notice that to the left of the screen it says **"Court Docs Databases."** This is where you can search for court documents. Notice also that at the left of the screen there are databases for appellate briefs, pleadings, motions, trial court orders, and other items.
26. ***Click the Westlaw tab.***
27. ***Click Site Map on the toolbar.*** The Site Map is a good place to locate a Westlaw feature if you cannot find it anywhere else. Read the selections available under each category.
28. ***Click the Westlaw tab.*** *Note:* The reason you are clicking the Westlaw tab instead of going directly to each item on the toolbar is that it is helpful to have a central starting place from which to access Westlaw tools and features, at least while you are learning Westlaw.
29. ***Click Getting Started Tips*** (on the lower left side of the screen). A "Westlaw Help Center" window should now open, offering options such as Advanced Search, FAQ (Frequently Asked Questions), and Contact Us.
30. ***Click the link for FAQ.*** Notice that there are specific help topics for printing documents, accessing databases, and many others.
31. ***Click the link for some of the FAQ.*** The specific FAQs change from time to time, so be sure to check this area often to keep up with the latest tips and tricks.
32. ***Click the Contact Us tab at the top of the "Help Center" window.*** Notice that toll-free phone numbers are available for Technical Assistance, Research Assistance, and other resources.

33. ***Click the Close icon*** (a red box with a white X) ***in the "Westlaw Help Center" window.***
34. ***Click the Westlaw tab.***
35. ***Click Add a Tab on the top far right side of the screen*** (see Westlaw Exhibit 2). ***Click Add Westlaw Tabs.***
36. ***Under the General category, click the box next to Paralegal.*** If the Paralegal box already has a check mark next to it, do not click the box.
37. Scroll down through the list, and notice that you can select from a large number of different tabs. This includes topical tabs by legal specialty, jurisdictional state choices, jurisdictional federal choices, and others.
38. ***At the bottom of the screen, click Add to My Tab Set.***
39. ***At the In Tab Display, click on Set as Default next to Paralegal.*** This selection means that from now on when you start Westlaw, the Paralegal tab will be selected.
40. ***Click the Paralegal tab.*** The Paralegal tab is a great place to start your research. Throughout the rest of these Hands-On Exercises, you will start at the Paralegal tab. On your screen there should be categories for Federal Cases, State Cases, Statutes and Codes, Court Documents, Forms and Checklists, Information about People, and Information about Companies.

HANDS-ON EXERCISES

This concludes Lesson 1 of the Westlaw Hands-On Exercises. To exit Westlaw, ***click on SIGN OFF on the toolbar,*** or stay in Westlaw and go on to Lesson 2.

LESSON 2: FIND BY CITATION, FIND BY PARTY NAME, AND EXPLORING RETRIEVED CASES

In this lesson, you will use the following features: Find by Citation, Find by Party Name, Star Paging, Reporter Image, KeyCite overview, Case Outline, and Results-Plus. If you did not exit Westlaw after completing Lesson 1, go directly to step 6 in the following instructions.

1. Start Windows.
2. Start your Internet browser. Type **www.westlaw.com** in the browser and press the **[ENTER]** key.
3. Enter your Westlaw OnePass User Name and Password.
4. In the Client ID field, type **Hands-On Exercise 2** (or whatever your instructor tells you to type).
5. ***Click Sign On*** to sign on to Westlaw. If you are asked to agree to the terms of use, ***click I Agree and then click Go.***
6. You should now be at the Paralegal tab (see Westlaw Exhibit 3). You will now learn how to retrieve a case by entering a citation, using the Find by Citation feature.
7. ***Click in the white box under Find by citation:*** Type **189 S.W.3d 777. *Click Go next to the citation you just entered.***

WESTLAW EXHIBIT 3

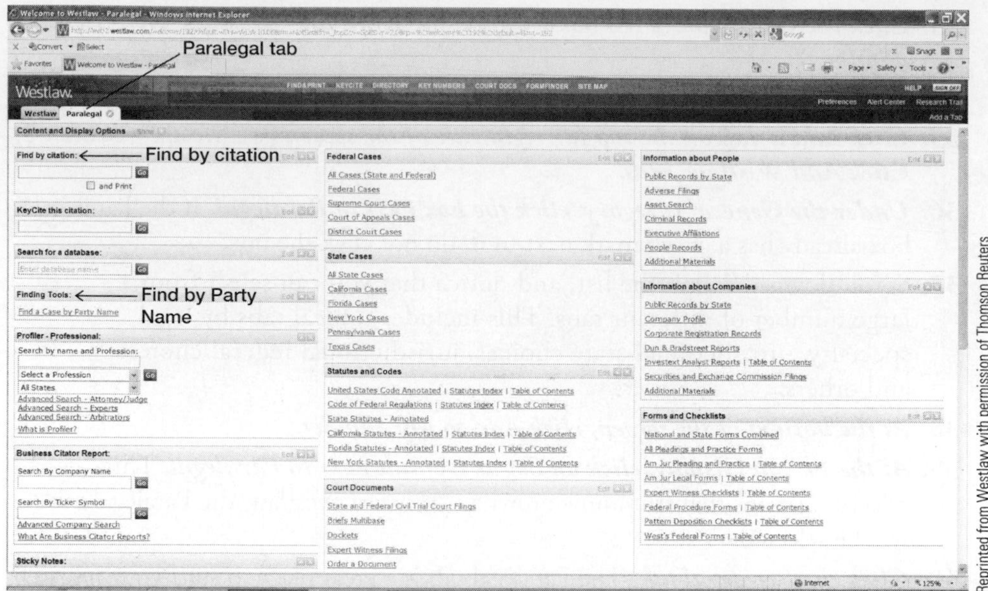

8. The case of *In re Mays-Hooper* should now be displayed (see Westlaw Exhibit 4). When you know the citation of a case, you can enter it in the Find by Citation feature, and Westlaw will immediately retrieve it without your having to indicate a database or enter a search query.

WESTLAW EXHIBIT 4

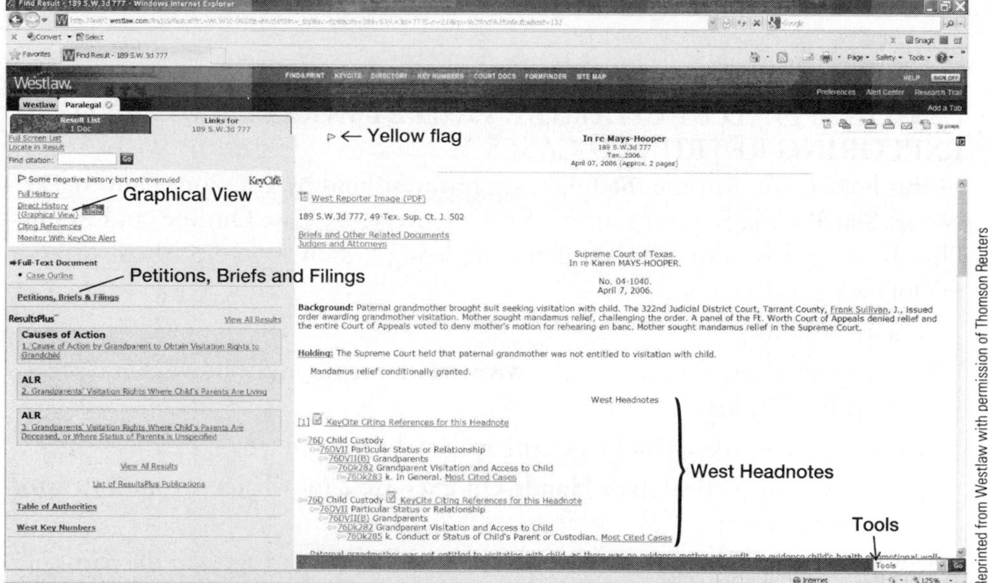

9. You will now find a case by entering the name of a party. ***Click the Paralegal tab at the upper left of the screen.*** You should now be back at the Paralegal tab screen (see Westlaw Exhibit 3).
10. On the left side of the screen is the heading **"Finding Tools:."** ***Click Find a Case by Party Name.***
11. The Find a Case by Party Name screen should now be displayed (see Westlaw Exhibit 5). Just below **"1. Enter at least one party name:,"** type **Karen Mays-Hooper** (see Westlaw Exhibit 5).
12. ***Click the radio button to the left of State Courts:*** (see Westlaw Exhibit 5). ***Click the down arrow next to All Courts and select Texas.***

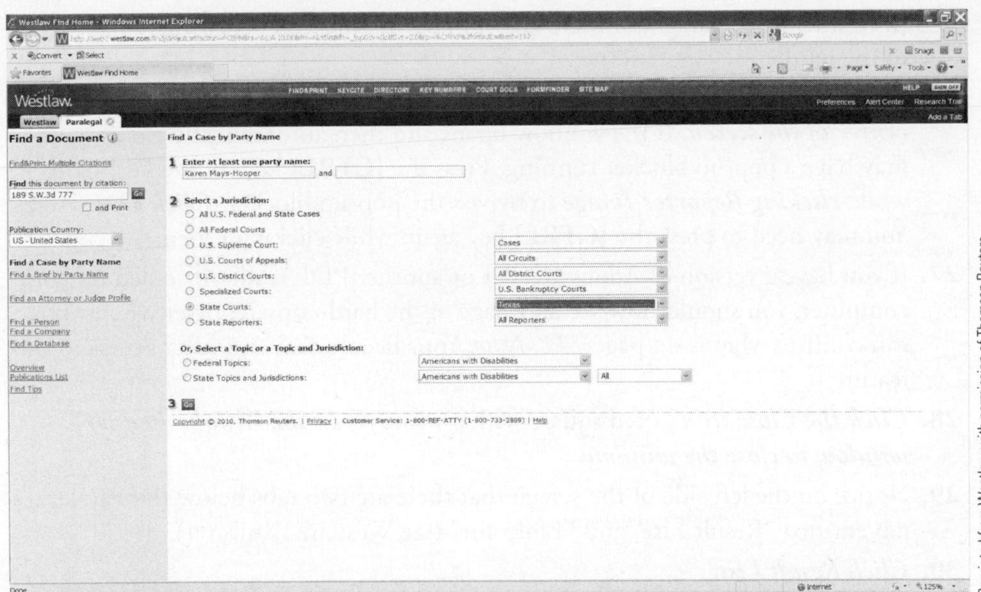

WESTLAW EXHIBIT 5

13. ***Click Go*** (see Westlaw Exhibit 5).
14. A summary of two cases, both with the title *In re Mays-Hooper*, should now be displayed. **Click In re Mays-Hooper, *189 S.W.3d 777, 49 Tex. Sup.Ct. J. 502.***
15. The *In re Mays-Hooper* case should now be displayed (see Westlaw Exhibit 4).
16. Notice in the *In re Mays-Hooper* case (see Westlaw Exhibit 4) that a Background and the Holding of the case are shown (just under the title of the case). These elements are called the *synopsis* of the case. Case synopses are written by Westlaw research attorneys. This is a value-added feature of Westlaw that many other CALR services do not offer.
17. Read the summary and holding in the *Mays-Hooper* case.
18. Notice the heading **"West Headnotes"** after the holding of the case (see Westlaw Exhibit 4), which shows the Headnotes for the case and several Topic and Key Numbers. The Headnotes and Topic Numbers/Key Numbers are also written by West research attorneys, and are a value-added feature of Westlaw that many other CALR services do not offer. These features are discussed in more detail in later exercises.
19. Skim the case by ***scrolling down through it with the vertical scroll bar.***
20. Press the **[HOME]** key on the keyboard to go back to the beginning of the case.
21. You will next learn how to use Westlaw Star Paging. Star Paging is a Westlaw feature that allows you to cite to a specific page of the hard-copy reporter. ***Click Tools in the lower right corner of the screen*** (see Westlaw Exhibit 4).
22. ***Click Go to Star Page. Click Go.***
23. At the Go to Star Page: screen, type 777. (This is the beginning page of the case.) ***Click Go.***
24. Notice that the *Mays-Hooper* case is again displayed. Look closely at the upper left of the screen and you will see "*777" in purple. This tells you that anything after "*777" is on page 777 of the hard copy. So, if you are going to cite anything on this page, you need to cite to page 777.
25. ***Scroll down through the case*** to the paragraph that starts with "The Supreme Court found the trial court's order unconstitutional . . ." and notice that on the

third line of the paragraph there is a "*778" in purple. This is where page 778 of the hard-copy report starts.

26. ***Scroll to the top of the case and click West Reporter Image (PDF) at the top center of the screen.*** If the window opens and then automatically closes, you may have a pop-up blocker running. Press the **[CTRL]** key on the keyboard while ***clicking Reporter Image*** to bypass the pop-up blocker. ***Click OK.*** (*Note:* You may need to press the **[CTRL]** key again while clicking Open.)
27. If you have a version of Adobe Reader or another PDF reader installed on your computer, you should now see an image of the hard-copy reporter where you can confirm what is on page 777. *Note:* Your license may not offer access to this feature.
28. ***Click the Close icon*** (a red square with a white X) ***in the "Adobe Reader" window to close the window.***
29. Notice on the left side of the screen that there are two tabs below the Paralegal tab entitled "Result List" and "Links for" (see Westlaw Exhibit 4).
30. ***Click Result List.***
31. On the left side of the screen, you should now see a short summary of the two cases that were retrieved. The Result List tab allows you to see a summary of the results of your query or search.
32. ***Click Links for.*** Notice that the Links for tab includes a KeyCite section (see Westlaw Exhibit 4). This is where you can find the history of the case. ***Click Graphical View in the KeyCite section on the left side of the screen*** (see Westlaw Exhibit 4).
33. Westlaw Exhibit 6 should now be displayed. This is a graphical chart that shows how the case was appealed from the Fort Worth Court of Appeals to the Texas Supreme Court.

WESTLAW EXHIBIT 6

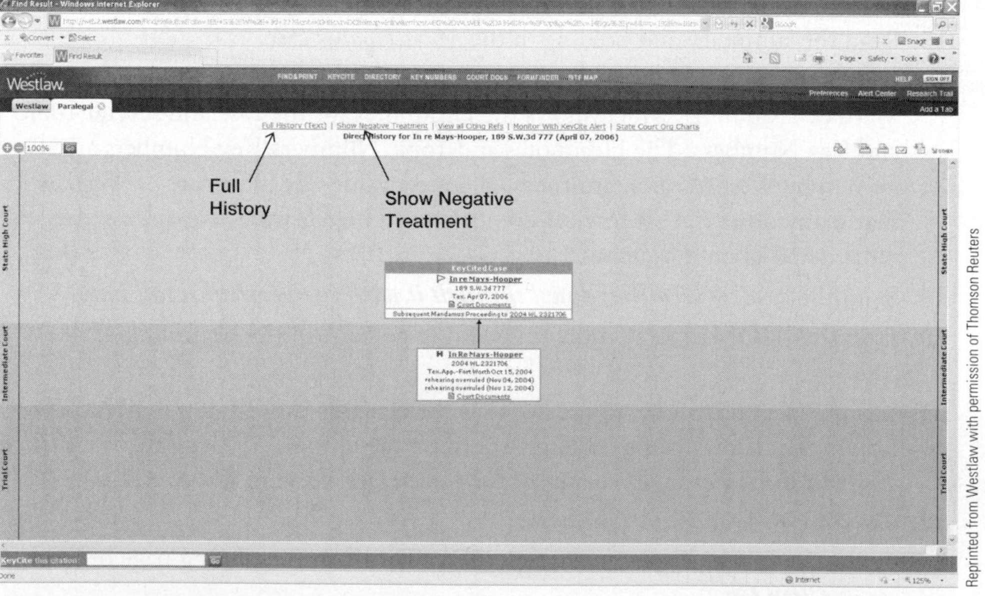

34. ***Click Full History (Text) at the top of the screen.*** You should now see a text-based history of the case.
35. ***Click Graphical View on the left side of the screen*** to go back to the graphical depiction of the history of this case.
36. ***Click Show Negative Treatment.*** (As of the date this exercise was written, there was only one example of negative history.)

37. ***Click your browser's Back button*** to go to the previous screen with the graphical depiction of the case history.
38. ***Click "In re Mays-Hooper"*** (just above the case citation) to go back to the case.
39. ***Click Citing References in the KeyCite section on the left side of the screen*** (see Westlaw Exhibit 4).
40. A screen similar to Westlaw Exhibit 7 should be displayed. (*Note:* The screen may look completely different by the time you read this.) This shows all of the times the case has been cited in other cases. Notice the yellow flag in the upper left of the screen (see Westlaw Exhibit 7). The yellow flag in KeyCite means that there is direct history, and there is negative history, but the case has not been reversed or overruled. Notice in Westlaw Exhibit 4 that the yellow flag is also shown on the first page of the case itself.

WESTLAW EXHIBIT 7

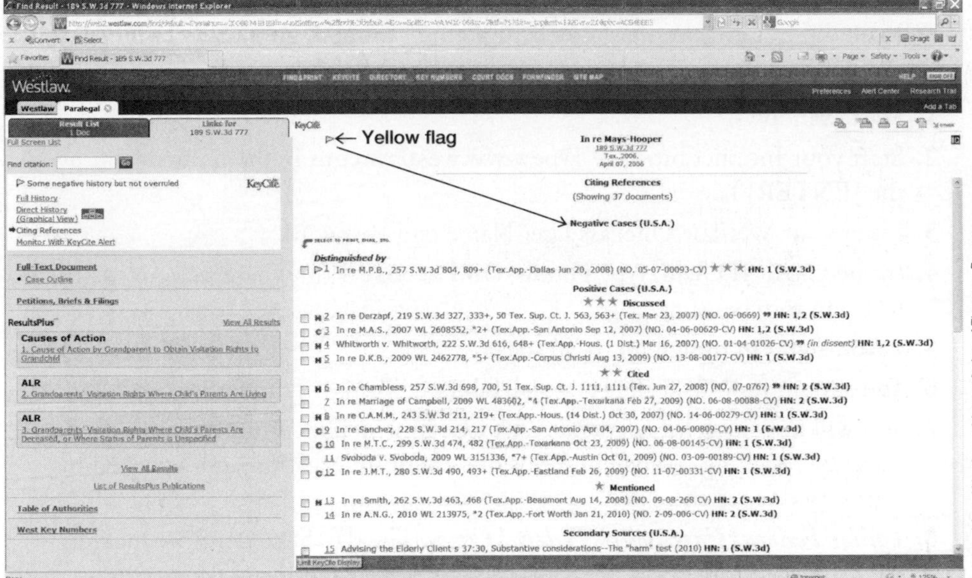

41. ***Click your browser's Back button*** to go back to the case.
42. ***Click Case Outline on the left side of the screen under Full-Text Document*** (see Westlaw Exhibit 4). You now should see the sections of the case (Synopsis, Headnote(s), and Opinion(s)). This option is particularly helpful when you are reading an extremely long case, because you can jump between the major sections of the case without having to scroll down through each page.
43. ***Click your browser's Back button*** to go back to the case.
44. ***Click Petitions, Briefs & Filings on the left side of the screen under Case Outline*** (see Westlaw Exhibit 4). Notice that a list of the Dockets is now shown. If you wanted to read the briefs of the parties, you could do so by clicking the appropriate links. Note: Your license may not offer access to this feature.
45. ***Click your browser's Back button*** to go back to the case.
46. Notice in the lower left of the screen that there is a section entitled **"ResultsPlus."** ResultsPlus is where Westlaw makes suggestions regarding other research that you might find helpful. Three options are listed in the ResultsPlus section.
47. ***Click the option under ResultsPlus that says* "ALR: 2. Grandparents' Visitation Rights Where Child's Parents Are Living."** You should now see an article from ALR regarding the issue of grandparent visitation rights.
48. ***Click your browser's Back button*** to go back to the case.

49. ***Click the Paralegal tab in the upper left of the screen.***

This concludes Lesson 2 of the Westlaw Hands-On Exercises. To exit Westlaw, ***click Sign Off on the toolbar,*** or stay in Westlaw and go to Lesson 3.

INTERMEDIATE LESSONS

LESSON 3: NATURAL LANGUAGE SEARCH; EDITING SEARCHES; CHANGING DATABASES; USING THE TERM, DOC, AND BEST FEATURES

In this lesson, you will learn how to select a database; run a Natural Language search; find the scope of a database; edit a search; change to a different database; use the date restriction feature when searching; use the Require/Exclude Terms feature; and use the Term, Doc, and Best features.

If you did not exit Westlaw after completing Lesson 2, go directly to Step 6 in the following instructions.

1. Start Windows.
2. Start your Internet browser. Type **www.westlaw.com** in the browser and press the **[ENTER]** key.
3. Enter your Westlaw OnePass User Name and Password.
4. In the Client ID field, type **Hands-On Exercise 3** (or whatever your instructor tells you to type).
5. ***Click Sign On*** to sign on to Westlaw.
6. You should now be at the Paralegal Tab (see Westlaw Exhibit 3).
7. You will now look for a federal court case in which an attorney committed fraud by retaining settlement funds of a client in litigation and breached his fiduciary duty to the client.
8. ***Under Federal Cases, click Federal Cases.*** The database identifier for this database is ALLFEDS.
9. The Search screen should now be displayed (see Westlaw Exhibit 8).

WESTLAW EXHIBIT 8

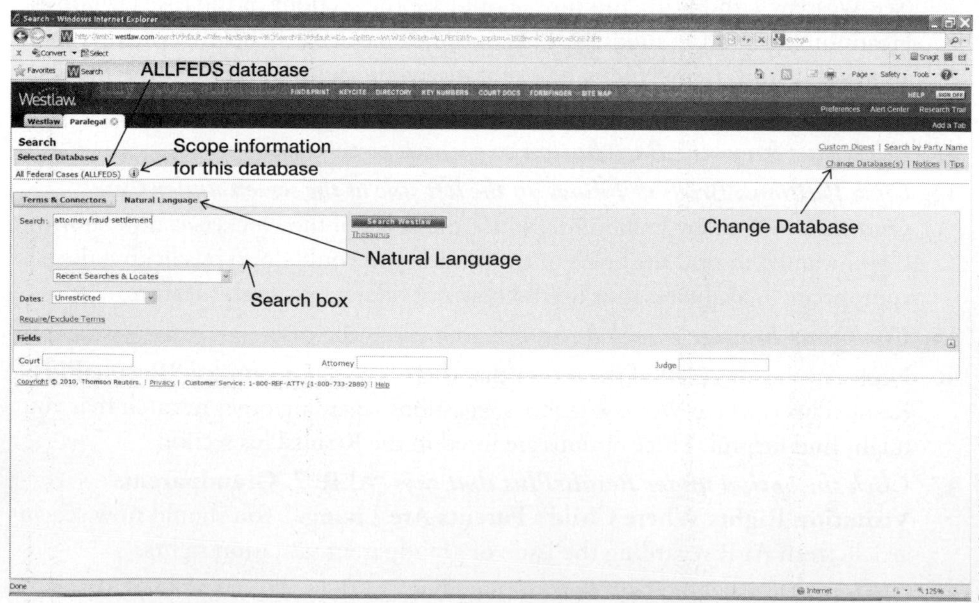

10. ***Click Natural Language*** (see Westlaw Exhibit 8). You will now enter a plain-English search into the ALLFEDS database using Westlaw's Natural Language feature.
11. In the Search box, type **attorney fraud settlement** and then ***click Search*** (see Westlaw Exhibit 8).
12. Depending on how Westlaw was set up on your computer, your search will most likely return 100 cases. This is the default setting when using Natural Language. As you scroll through the search results, notice that the cases are not in chronological order. Rather, they are presented in the order in which the search terms are used most often and in closest proximity to each other. By doing so, Westlaw is presenting the search results in order of relevance.
13. There are two main problems with the search. First, you are searching in an enormous database; second, you need to list more search terms to limit the search results to cases that are directly on point.
14. ***Click Edit Search just under the Paralegal tab in the upper left of the screen.***
15. You should now be back at the Search screen. You will now look at the scope of the ALLFEDS database to see exactly what database you are searching in.
16. ***Click the Scope Information for the database symbol,*** which looks like a round white ball with a lower-case "i" in the middle of it (see Westlaw Exhibit 8).
17. Notice the information listed about the ALLFEDS database, including the Content Highlights section, which states **"All Federal Cases has all available federal case law with coverage beginning in 1790."**
18. Scroll down to see just how large this database is. In fact, it is huge, containing tens of thousands of cases. When you search in a large database like this, you need more search terms.
19. ***Click your browser's Back button*** to go back to the Search screen.
20. It can sometimes be more efficient to search in a smaller database than in a larger one. You will now learn how to change your database.
21. ***Click Change Database(s) in the upper right of the Search screen*** (see Westlaw Exhibit 8).
22. ***Click in the white box under*** **"Add or Delete database(s):"** and press the **[DELETE]** or **[BACKSPACE]** keys until ALLFEDS has been deleted.
23. Type **DCT4** (see Westlaw Exhibit 9), ***then click Run Search.*** DCT4 is the database for U.S. District Court Cases for the Fourth Circuit. This is a much narrower database than ALLFEDS.
24. The search will once again retrieve a large number (100) of cases. Although the database is smaller, the search must still be refined and additional search terms added.
25. ***Click Edit Search in the upper left portion of the screen.***
26. In the Search box, in addition to "attorney fraud settlement," type **"legal malpractice" "fiduciary duty."** The quotes around "legal malpractice" and "fiduciary duty" force Westlaw to search for these exact phrases (see Westlaw Exhibit 10).
27. Another way to limit the number of cases retrieved is to restrict the dates of the cases retrieved. ***Click the down arrow next to*** **"Dates: Unrestricted"** ***in the Search screen.***
28. ***Click After.*** In the white box to the right of "After," type **2003** (see Westlaw Exhibit 10).
29. Still another way to limit the number of cases retrieved is to require all of the terms. ***Click Require/Exclude Terms in the Search screen*** (see Westlaw Exhibit 10).

HANDS-ON EXERCISES

WESTLAW EXHIBIT 9

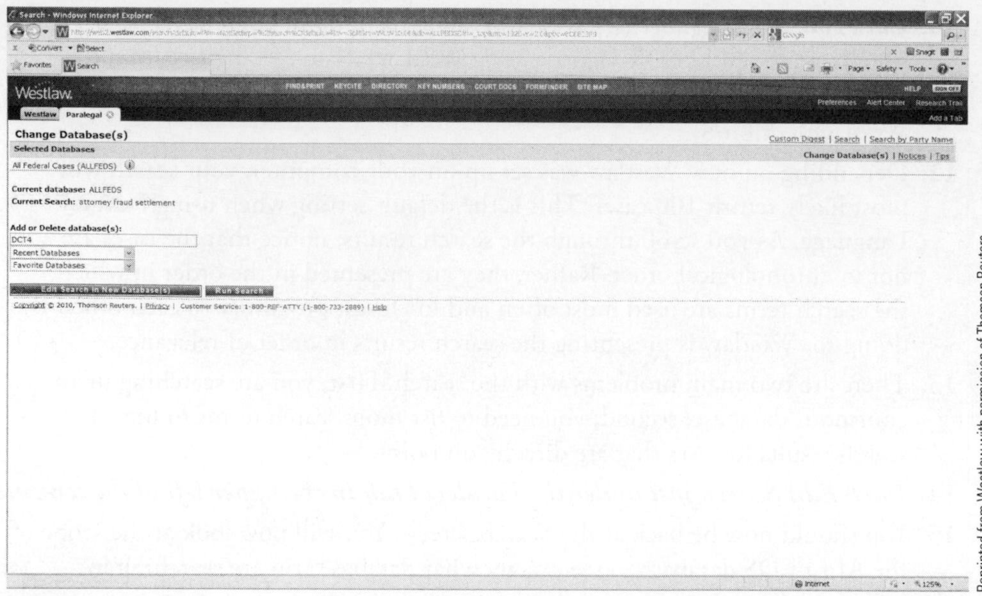

WESTLAW EXHIBIT 10

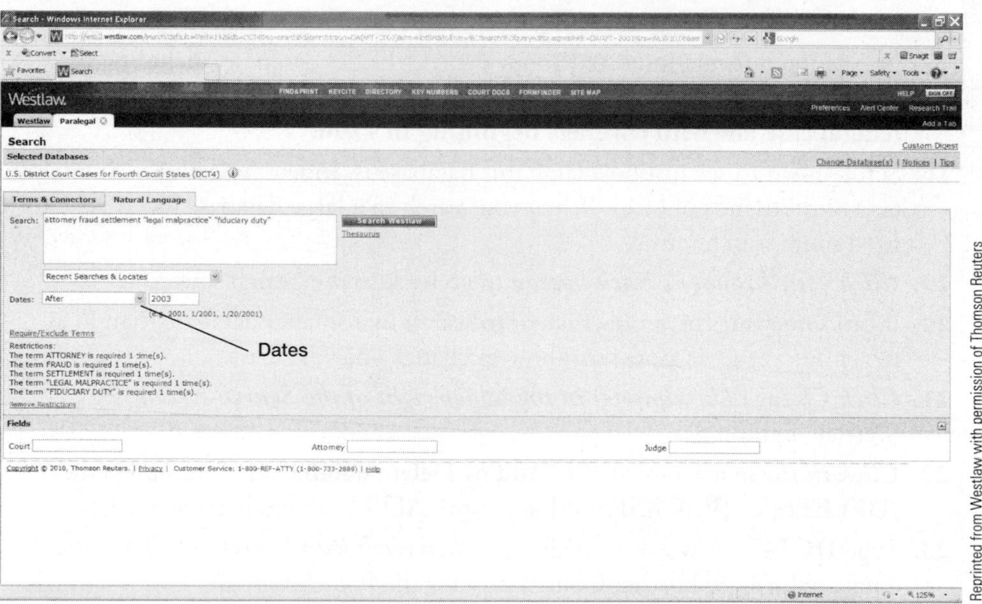

30. ***Click the boxes for each of the search terms (attorney, fraud, settlement, "legal malpractice," and "fiduciary duty"), and then click OK.*** Your screen should now look similar to Westlaw Exhibit 10.
31. ***Click Search.***
32. A much smaller number of cases should now be returned. One of the cases that should be retrieved is Hewlette v. Hovis, 318 F. Supp. 2d 332 (E.D. Va., May 19, 2004). ***Click the* Hewlette v. Hovis *case.***
33. The Hewlette v. Hovis case should now be displayed (see Westlaw Exhibit 11).
34. Notice that your search terms are highlighted in the synopsis. ***Click the right arrow to the right of Term at the bottom of the screen.*** Each time you click the right arrow next to Term, Westlaw takes you to the next page where your search terms are listed. You can also go backward in the document to look for your search terms, by clicking the left arrow next to Term.
35. ***Click the right arrow to the right of Term to continue to move through the* Hewlette *case.*** Eventually you will move to the next case.

WESTLAW EXHIBIT 11

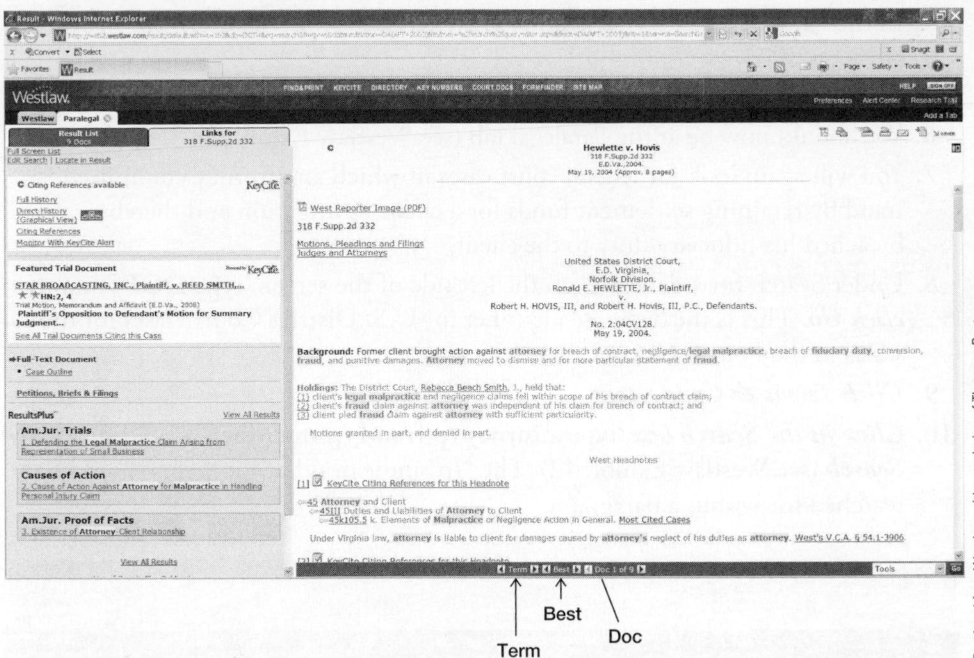

36. The Best feature allows you to go directly to what Westlaw estimates to be the most relevant part of the case in relation to your search terms. ***Click the left arrow next to Doc at the bottom of the screen*** to go back to the *Hewlette* case. The Doc arrows allow you to move forward and backward through the retrieved cases.

37. You should now be back at the beginning of the *Hewlette* case.

38. Notice that some of the text is in red. ***Scroll down through the case*** and notice that most (but not all) of the Headnotes are in red. The text in red is what Westlaw considers to the "best" part of the case (the part where the majority of your search terms are located).

39. ***Click the right arrow next to Best at the bottom of the screen.*** Westlaw should now have taken you to the best part of the next case.

40. ***Click the right arrow next to Doc at the bottom of the screen.*** You should now be at the next document of the search results. Using the left and right arrows next to Doc, you can move between the search results without returning to the list of results.

41. ***Click the Paralegal tab in the upper left of the screen.***

This concludes Lesson 3 of the Westlaw Hands-On Exercises. To exit Westlaw, ***click Sign Off on the toolbar,*** or stay in Westlaw and go to Lesson 4.

LESSON 4: TERMS AND CONNECTORS SEARCHING

In this lesson, you will learn how to search using Terms and Connectors, use the Thesaurus feature, print a list of cases, and use the Locate in Result tool. If you did not exit Westlaw after completing Lesson 3, go directly to Step 6 in the following instructions.

1. Start Windows.

2. Start your Internet browser. Type **www.westlaw.com** in the browser, and press the **[ENTER]** key.

3. Enter your Westlaw OnePass User Name and Password.

4. In the Client ID field, type **Hands-On Exercise 4** (or whatever your instructor tells you to type).
5. ***Click Sign On*** to sign on to Westlaw.
6. You should now be at the Paralegal tab (see Westlaw Exhibit 3).
7. You will again look for federal court cases in which an attorney committed fraud by retaining settlement funds for a client in litigation and thereby breached his fiduciary duty to the client.
8. Under Search for a database: on the left side of the screen, type **DCT4** and then ***click Go.*** This is the database identifier for U.S. District Court Cases for the states in the Fourth Circuit.
9. ***Click Terms & Connectors.***
10. ***Click in the Search box,*** type **attorney /p fraud /p malpractice,** and then ***click Search*** (see Westlaw Exhibit 12). The "/p" indicates that the terms should be searched for within a paragraph.

WESTLAW EXHIBIT 12

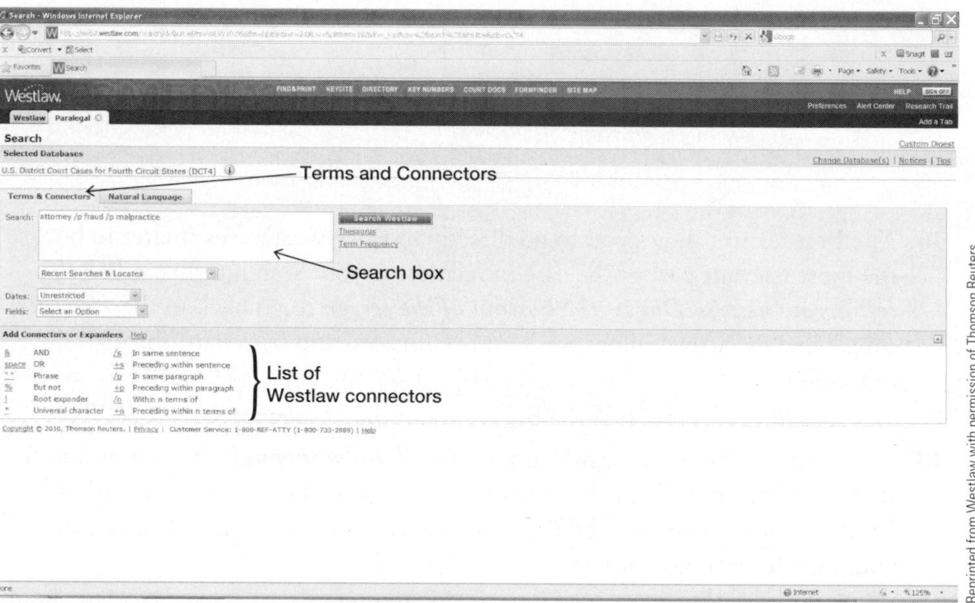

11. Westlaw should return fewer than 50 cases, but this is still quite a lot, so you should refine your search query. Note that unlike a Natural Language search, there is no preset default number of search results; also, the search results are returned in chronological order (newest to oldest). By using "/s" (search within a sentence) and "/n" (where "n" limits the search within a specific number of words), you can limit the number of cases retrieved.
12. ***Click Edit Search in the upper left of the screen just under the Paralegal tab.***
13. In the Search box, delete the current query and type **attorney /s fraud /s legal /3 malpractice /p "fiduciary duty."** Then ***click Thesaurus*** (which is just under **"Search"**). You will use the Thesaurus feature to further refine your search.
14. You should now see a screen similar to Westlaw Exhibit 13. Notice that in the first column, Terms in Search:, the search term "attorney" is highlighted, and that in the second column, Related Terms:, there are synonyms for "attorney."
15. ***In the Related Terms: column, scroll down, click "LAWYER," and then click the + (plus sign) next to Add.*** Westlaw will then add "***LAWYER***" to the current search query. There should now be a space between "attorney" and "**LAWYER.**" Westlaw interprets the space to mean OR (e.g., attorney OR lawyer).

WESTLAW EXHIBIT 13

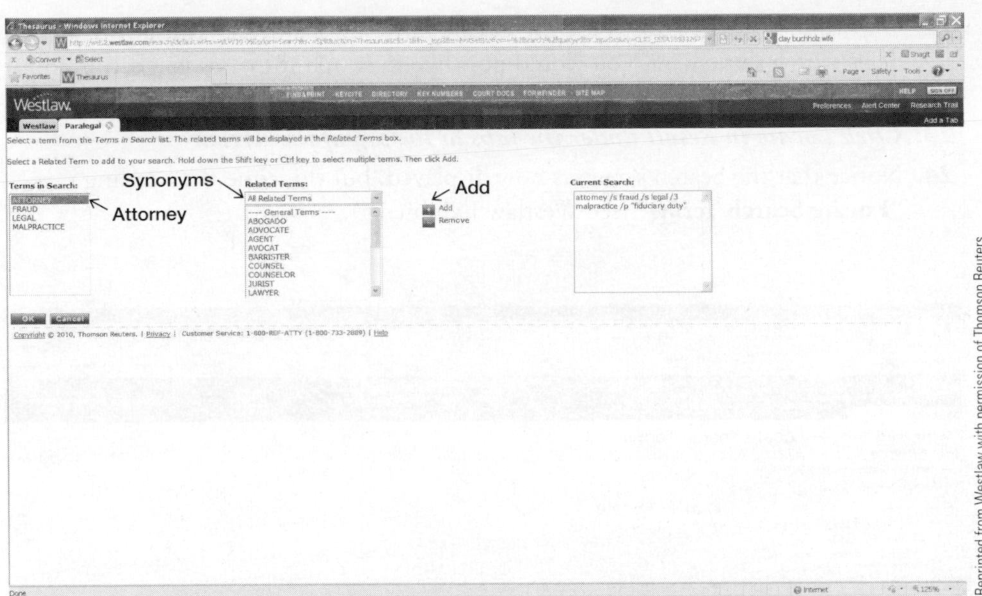

16. ***In the Terms in Search: column, click*** **"MALPRACTICE."** ***In the Related Terms: column, click*** **"NEGLIGENCE."** ***Next, click on the + (plus sign) next to Add.***
17. ***Click OK just below the Terms in Search: column.***
18. The search should now read attorney LAWYER /s fraud /s legal /3 malpractice NEGLIGENCE /p "fiduciary duty" (see Westlaw Exhibit 14).

WESTLAW EXHIBIT 14

19. ***Click Search.***
20. Westlaw should return fewer than 15 cases, and one of the cases should be the *Hewlette v. Hovis* case.
21. You will now send the results to your printer. ***Click the Quick Print icon in the upper right of the screen.*** The "Quick Print" window will then appear. After a few seconds, the "Print" window will appear. ***Select the printer you would like to print to and click Print.*** Note that, depending on your license, you may not be able to print directly from Westlaw. If you cannot print, ***click the email icon*** and email the document to yourself. You can then open the email and print the attached document.

22. You will now learn how to use the Locate in Result feature. Because your case deals with a settlement, you would now like to search the cases you retrieved for "settlement" to further weed out the cases.
23. ***Click Locate in Result under the tabs at the top of the screen.***
24. Notice that the Search screen is now displayed, but this time the heading says **"Locate Search Terms"** (see Westlaw Exhibit 15).

WESTLAW EXHIBIT 15

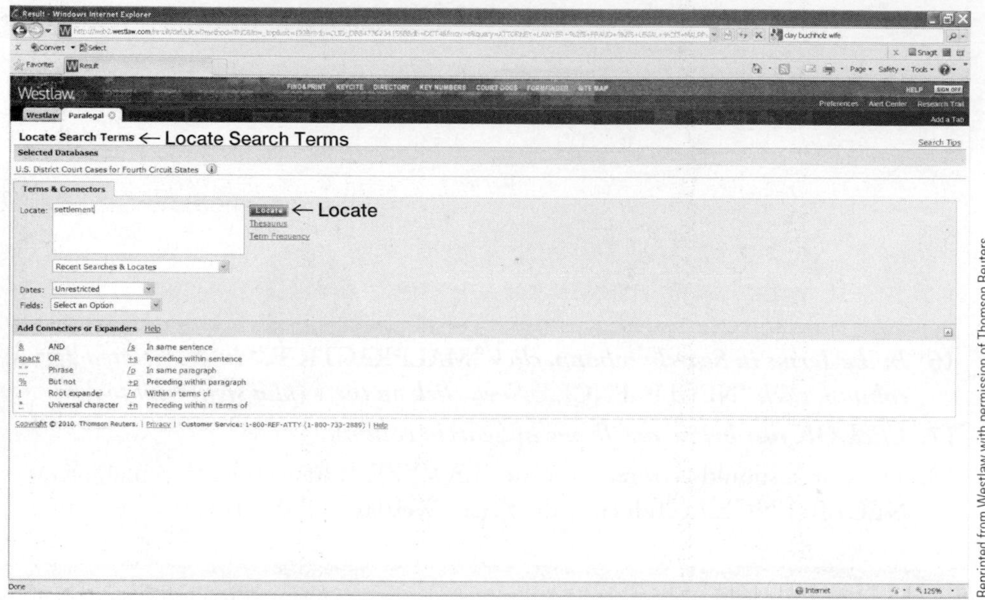

25. In the "Locate" box, type **settlement** and then ***click Locate.***
26. The number of cases should now be reduced. Notice that the word **"settlement"** is now highlighted, because it was your search term. The *Hewlette v. Hovis* case should be one of the cases that remains.
27. ***Click Cancel Locate*** to return to the original cases that were retrieved.
28. ***Click the Paralegal tab.***

This concludes Lesson 4 of the Westlaw Hands-On Exercises. To exit Westlaw, ***click on Sign Off on the toolbar,*** or stay in Westlaw and go to Lesson 5.

LESSON 5: KEYCITE

In this lesson, you will learn how to use Westlaw's research citation tool, KeyCite. You will also learn about depth-of-treatment stars, quotes, citing references, the Limit KeyCite Display tool, and the Research Trail feature. If you did not exit Westlaw after completing Lesson 4, go directly to Step 6 in the following instructions.

1. Start Windows.
2. Start your Internet browser. Type **www.westlaw.com** in the browser and press the **[ENTER]** key.
3. Enter your Westlaw OnePass User Name and Password.
4. In the Client ID field, type **Hands-On Exercise 5** (or whatever your instructor tells you to type).
5. ***Click Sign On*** to sign on to Westlaw.
6. You should now be at the Westlaw Paralegal tab (see Westlaw Exhibit 3).

7. ***Click KeyCite on the toolbar.*** You will now use KeyCite to determine if the *Hewlette v. Hovis* case, which you found in an earlier exercise, is still good law, and you will locate other cases that have cited Hewlette in hopes of expanding your research.
8. The KeyCite screen should now be displayed (see Westlaw Exhibit 16). Take a few minutes and read the narrative in the body of the KeyCite screen. The narrative describes how KeyCite works and what each of the different KeyCite symbols means.

WESTLAW EXHIBIT 16

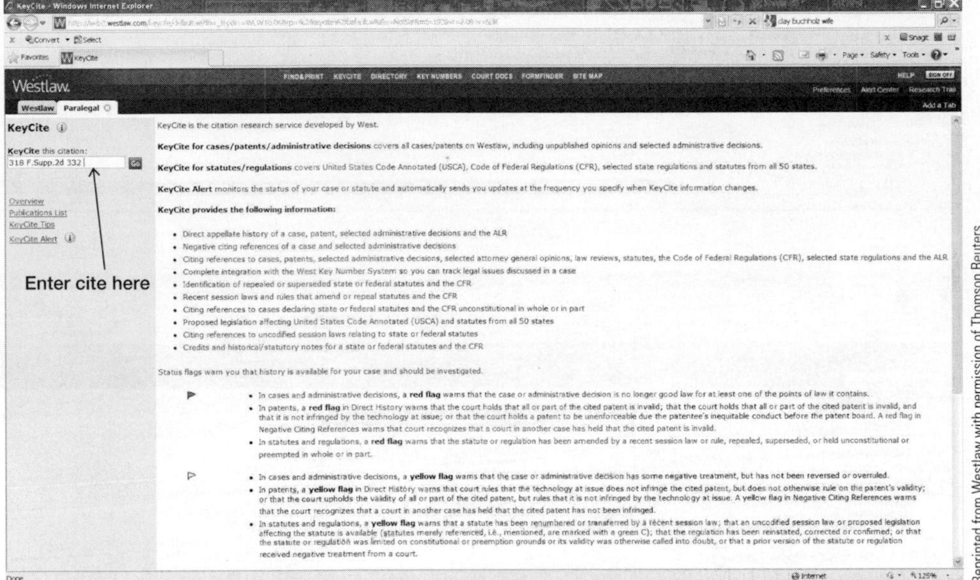

9. In the **KeyCite** this citation: field, type **318 F.Supp.2d 332** (see Westlaw Exhibit 16). This is the citation for the *Hewlette v. Hovis* case. ***Click Go.***
10. Your screen should now look similar to Westlaw Exhibit 17. Notice that a green "C" is displayed. In KeyCite, a green "C" means that the case has been cited as a reference but there is no direct history or negative citing references. This means that the *Hewlette v. Hovis* case has, to date, not been overruled or reversed, and that other cases have not negatively referred to it, and that, at least to date, the case is good law in all respects.
11. You will now use KeyCite to find other cases that have cited the *Hewlette v. Hovis* case. This may assist in expanding your research to find other cases that will support your position. However, before you do this, it would be helpful to look at the Headnotes in the *Hewlette v. Hovis* case to know which Headnote is on point for your purposes. That way, when you look at additional citing references, you can look only at the references that cite *Hewlette* for the issue you are dealing with.
12. ***Click the* "1"** (see Westlaw Exhibit 17); this is the decision itself, 318 F. Supp. 2d 332. Notice that a "Link Viewer" window opens in the middle of the screen, with the decision in it (see Westlaw Exhibit 18).
13. ***Scroll to Headnote 13*** (Federal Civil Procedure 170Ak636; see Westlaw Exhibit 18). This is the issue in the case that you are interested in. You now know that you are looking for any references to Headnote 13.

WESTLAW EXHIBIT 17

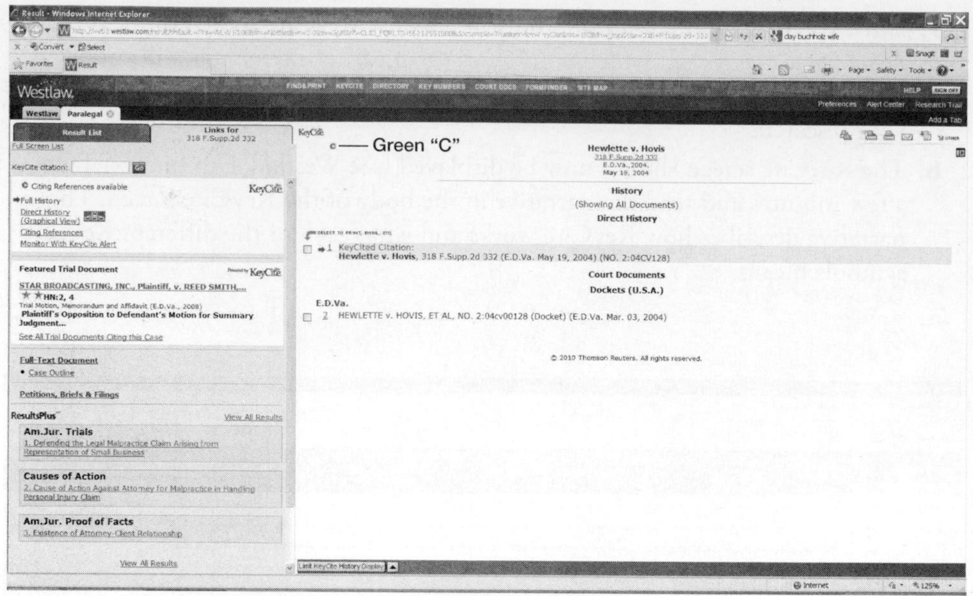

WESTLAW EXHIBIT 18

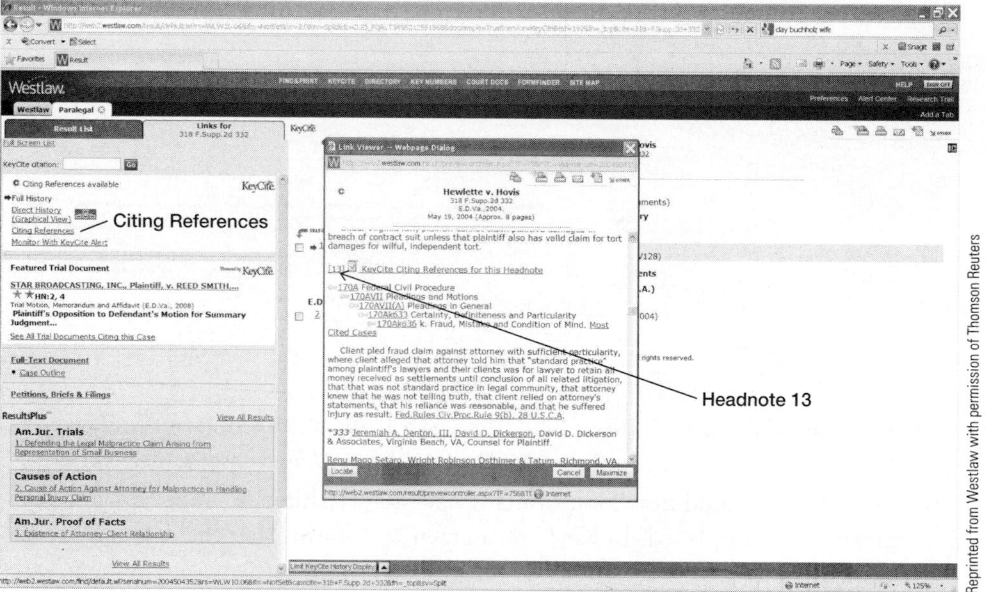

14. ***Click the Close icon*** (a red square with a white X) ***in the "Link Viewer" window.***
15. ***Click Citing References in the KeyCite section of the page*** (see Westlaw Exhibit 18).
16. Your screen should look similar to Westlaw Exhibit 19. (As of the time of this writing, there were 54 citing references; by the time you read this, there may be more, and they will be shown on your screen).
17. Notice in Westlaw Exhibit 19, just under Positive Cases (U.S.A.), that two stars are shown. These are depth-of-treatment stars. The more stars there are, the more references there are for your case. One star means that your case was merely cited with no discussion, whereas four stars means your case was considered and discussed extensively.
18. Find the seventh case listed in Westlaw Exhibit 19 (*VA Timberline, LLC v. Land Management Group, Inc.*) on your screen. Notice the purple double quotation

WESTLAW EXHIBIT 19

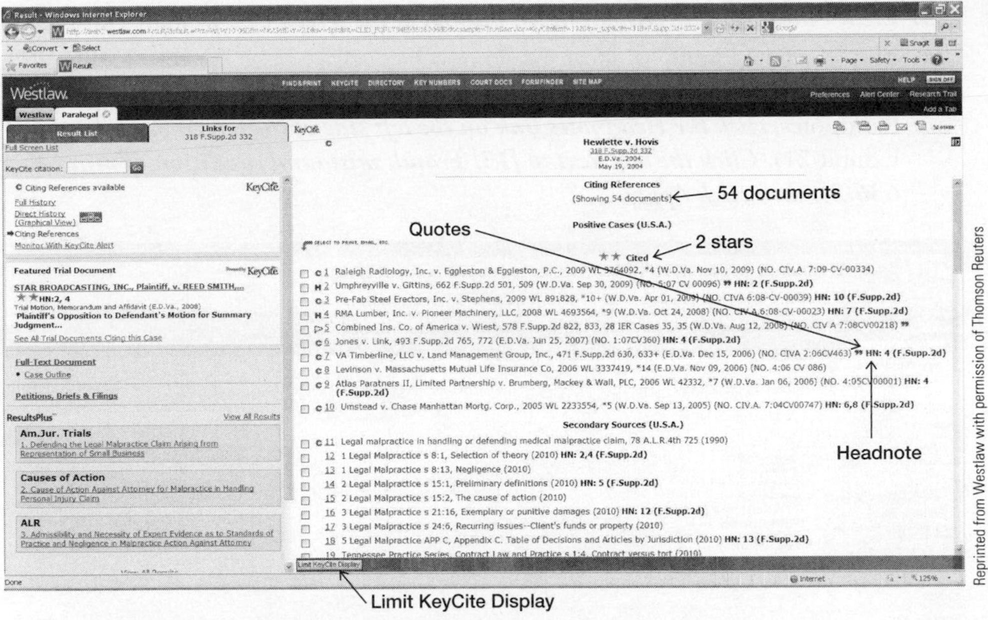

mark toward the end of the line. This means that in *VA Timberline, LLC* opinion, the court quotes from the *Hewlette v. Hovis* case related to Headnote 4.

19. ***Click the number associated with the* VA Timberline, LLC v. Land Management Group *case (9).*** A "Link Viewer" window should now be displayed that shows where the court in the *VA Timberline* case quoted the *Hewlette* case related to Headnote 4 (see Westlaw Exhibit 20).

WESTLAW EXHIBIT 20

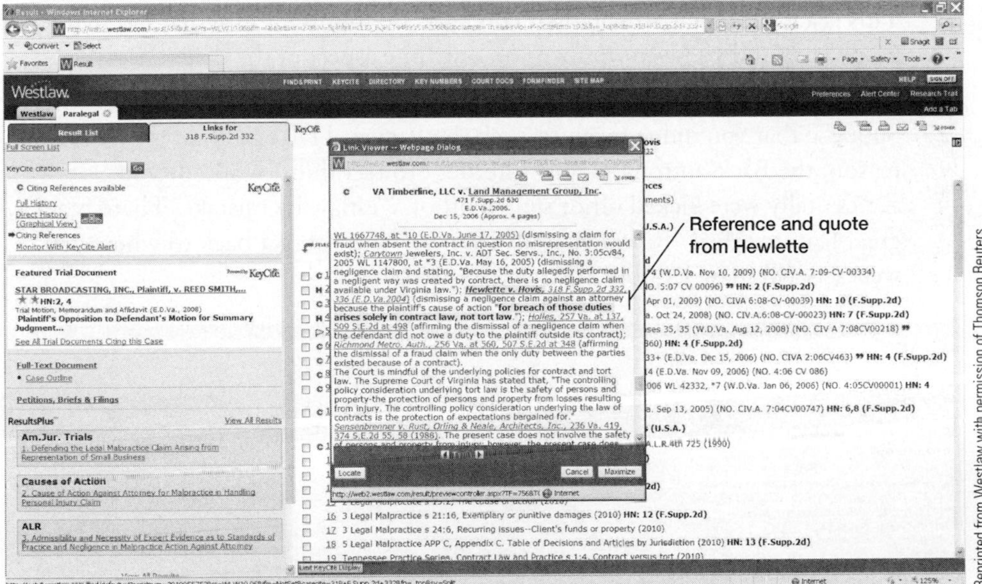

20. Notice in Westlaw Exhibit 20 that the discussion about the *Hewlette* case in the *VA Timberline* case is relatively short. That is why only two depth-of-treatment stars were shown.
21. ***Click the Close icon*** (a red square with a white X) ***in the "Link Viewer" window.***
22. You could continue to go down the list of Citing References in Westlaw Exhibit 19, reading and viewing additional cases related to your Headnote, but there is an easier way to do so if you are looking for a specific Headnote.

23. ***Click Limit KeyCite Display at the bottom of the screen*** (see Westlaw Exhibit 19).
24. The "KeyCite Limits" window should now be displayed (see Westlaw Exhibit 21). You will now tell Westlaw which cites you want to view. If you do not see a list of Headnotes, ***click the Headnotes link on the left side of the screen*** (see Westlaw Exhibit 21). ***Click the box next to [13] Fraud, mistaand condition of mind Key 636(3), then click Apply.***

WESTLAW EXHIBIT 21

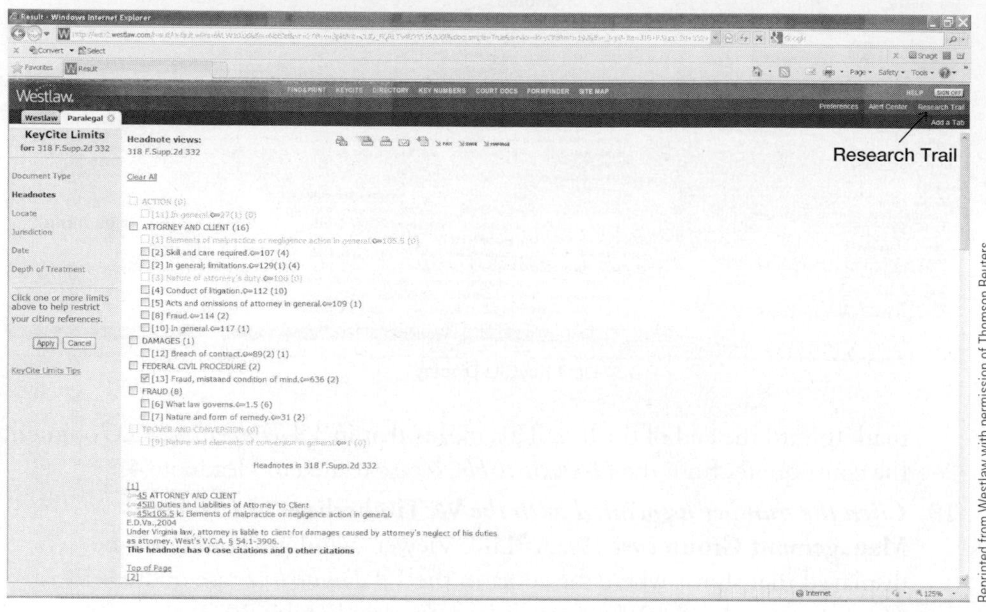

25. Westlaw will respond by only showing you the citations related to Headnote 13. This is a great tool, particularly if you have an important case that has many, many cites and you want to focus on only one aspect of the case.
26. ***Click the Paralegal tab.***
27. Suppose that you didn't mean to click the Paralegal tab and that, for whatever reason, the Back button on your Internet browser didn't work, or you accidentally were kicked off or signed off of Westlaw by mistake. There is a great feature called "Research Trail" that can help you get back to where you were (see Westlaw Exhibit 22).

WESTLAW EXHIBIT 22

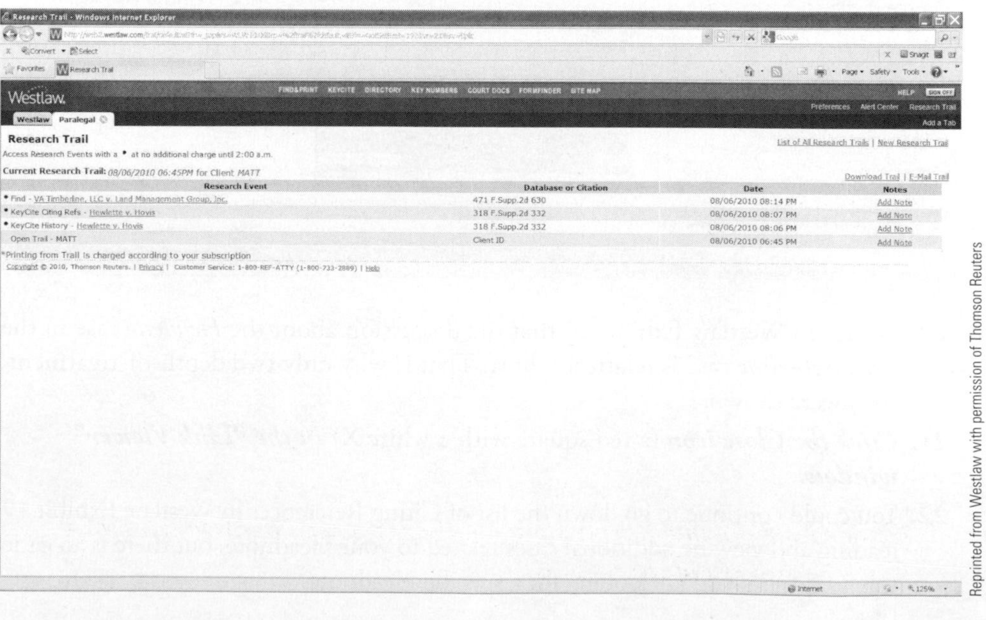

28. ***Click Research Trail in the upper right corner of the screen.*** *See Westlaw Exhibit 21.* The Research Trail feature shows you where you have been. If you wanted to go back to the *VA Timberline* case, for example, you could just click it in Research Trail.
29. ***Click the Paralegal tab.***

This concludes Lesson 5 of the Westlaw Hands-On Exercises. To exit Westlaw, ***click Sign Off on the toolbar,*** or stay in Westlaw and go to Lesson 6.

ADVANCED LESSON

LESSON 6: KEYSEARCH, HEADNOTES, AND KEY NUMBERS

In this lesson, you will learn how to use Westlaw's KeySearch tool, Headnotes and Key Numbers, and Most Recent and Most Cited Cases features. If you did not exit Westlaw after completing Lesson 5, go directly to Step 6 in the following instructions.

1. Start Windows.
2. Start your Internet browser. Type **www.westlaw.com** in the browser and press the **[ENTER]** key.
3. Enter your Westlaw OnePass User Name and Password.
4. In the Client ID field, type **Hands-On Exercise 6** (or whatever your instructor tells you to type).
5. ***Click Sign On*** to sign on to Westlaw.
6. You should now be at the Paralegal tab (see Westlaw Exhibit 3).
7. ***Click Key Numbers on the toolbar, then click KeySearch*** (see Westlaw Exhibit 23). KeySearch is a good place to begin your research because it provides you with a list of legal topics and subtopics; you do not have to know exactly what you are looking for.

HANDS-ON EXERCISES

WESTLAW EXHIBIT 23

8. ***Click Attorneys under Professional Malpractice*** (see Westlaw Exhibit 24).
9. ***Click Breach of Fiduciary Duty.***

WESTLAW EXHIBIT 24

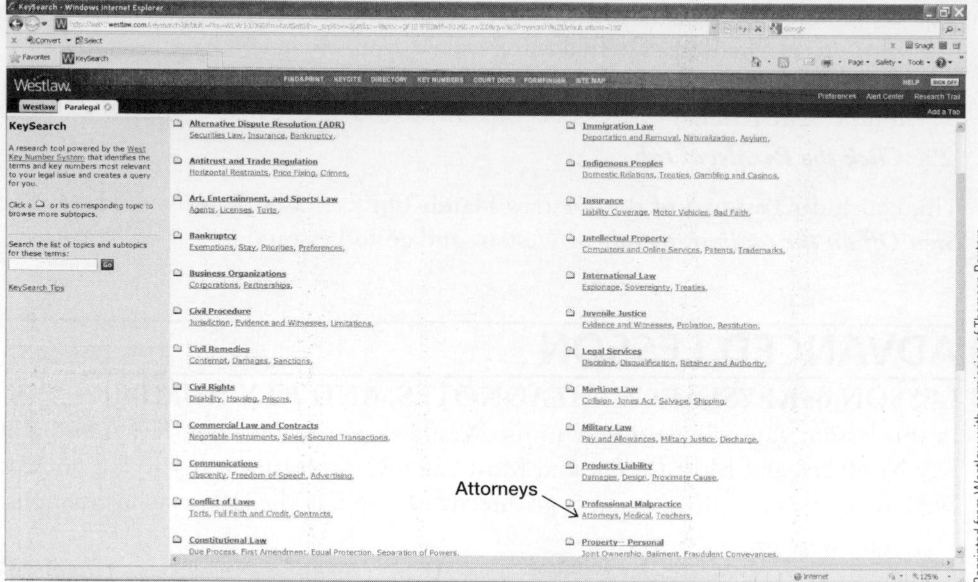

WESTLAW EXHIBIT 25

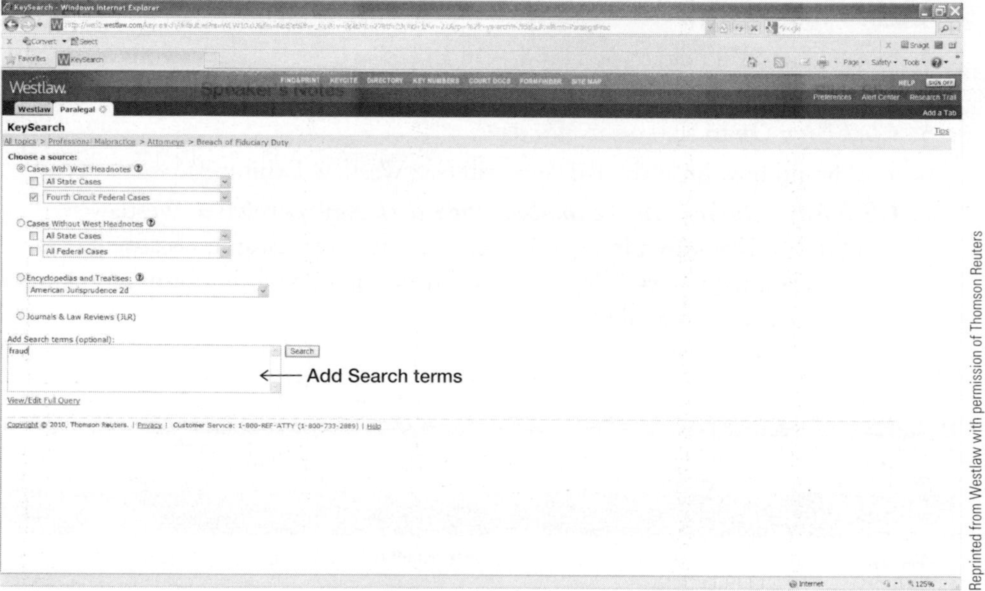

10. Your screen should now look similar to Westlaw Exhibit 25. ***Select Cases With West Headnotes, click the down arrow next to All Federal Cases, then select Fourth Circuit Federal Cases. Click in the box next to Fourth Circuit Federal Cases so that it has a check mark*** (see Westlaw Exhibit 25).
11. In the Add Search terms (optional): field, type **Fraud** and then ***click Search*** (see Westlaw Exhibit 25).
12. Your screen should now look similar to Westlaw Exhibit 26. Notice in the upper left corner of the screen the search query that KeySearch built.
13. ***Scroll down the page until you find the* Hewlette v. Hovis *case.*** In just a few seconds using KeySearch, you were able to find the case you were looking for.
14. ***Click the* Hewlette v. Hovis *case.*** You are now going to find similar cases using the Westlaw Headnote and Key Number system.
15. ***In the* Hewlette v. Hovis *case, scroll until you come to the first Headnote*** (see Westlaw Exhibit 27). Notice in Westlaw Exhibit 27 that the most specific Key

WESTLAW EXHIBIT 26

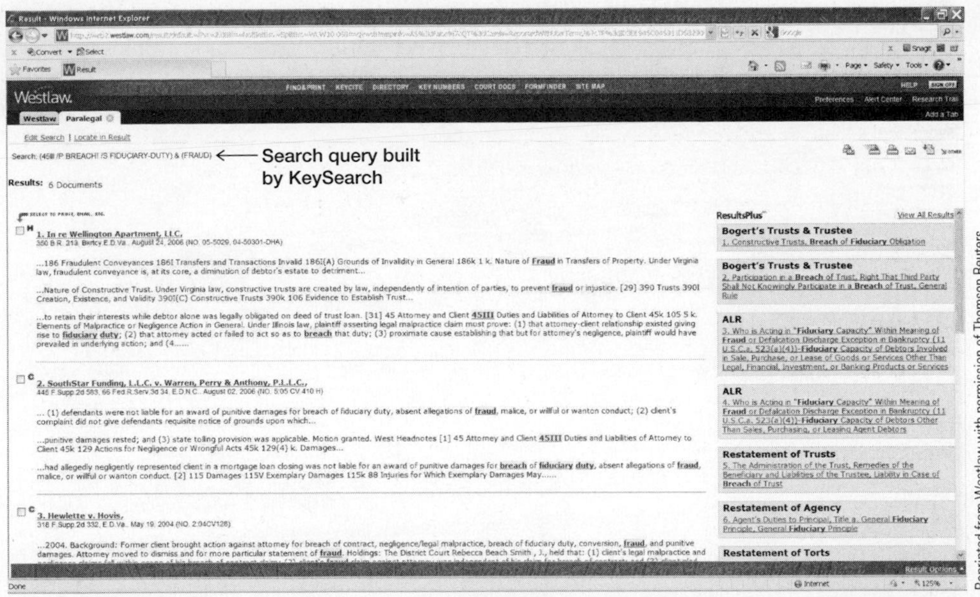

WESTLAW EXHIBIT 27

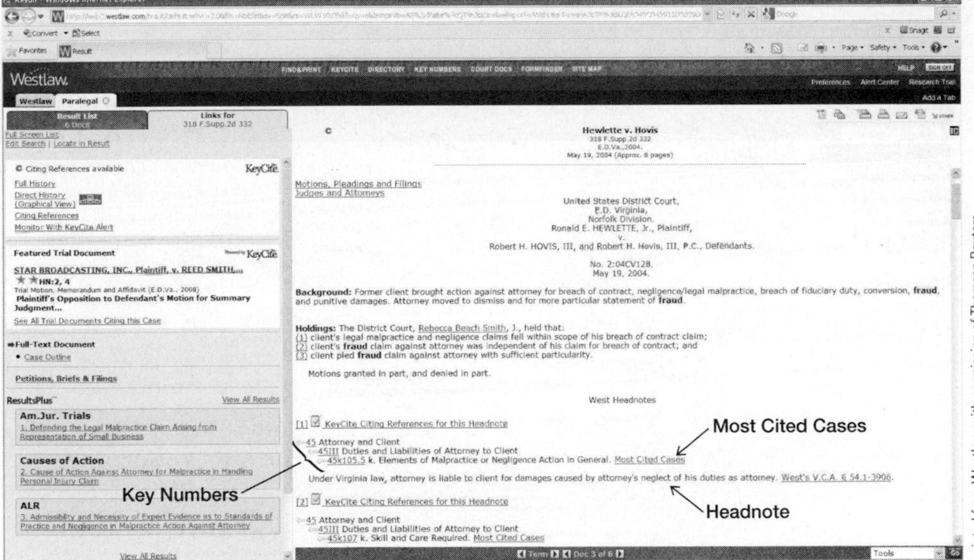

Number in Headnote 1 is 45k105.5. You are now going to search for cases that are similar to Headnote 1 using this Key Number.

16. Click Key Number 45k105.5 in Headnote 1.
17. The Custom Digest screen should now be displayed (see Westlaw Exhibit 28). Under Your digest options:, leave the order as Most Recent Cases. ***In the Your default state jurisdiction is: section, click Federal and leave All selected.***
18. ***Click Search in the bottom left of the screen.*** It may take up to a minute for Westlaw to retrieve all the cases.
19. Your screen should look similar to Westlaw Exhibit 29, but your cases will probably be different. ***Scroll down through the list*** and notice that you have quite a number of Headnotes from which to expand your research.
20. Remember that the order in which you sorted the cases and Headnotes put the most recent items first. By reading the Headnotes, you can get a good understanding of the elements of a claim for legal malpractice.

WESTLAW EXHIBIT 28

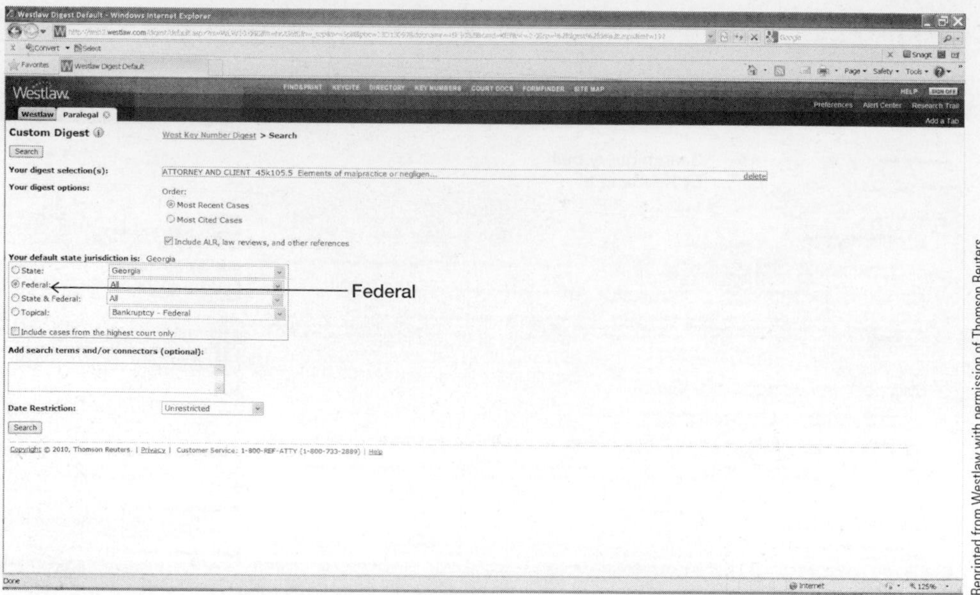

WESTLAW EXHIBIT 29

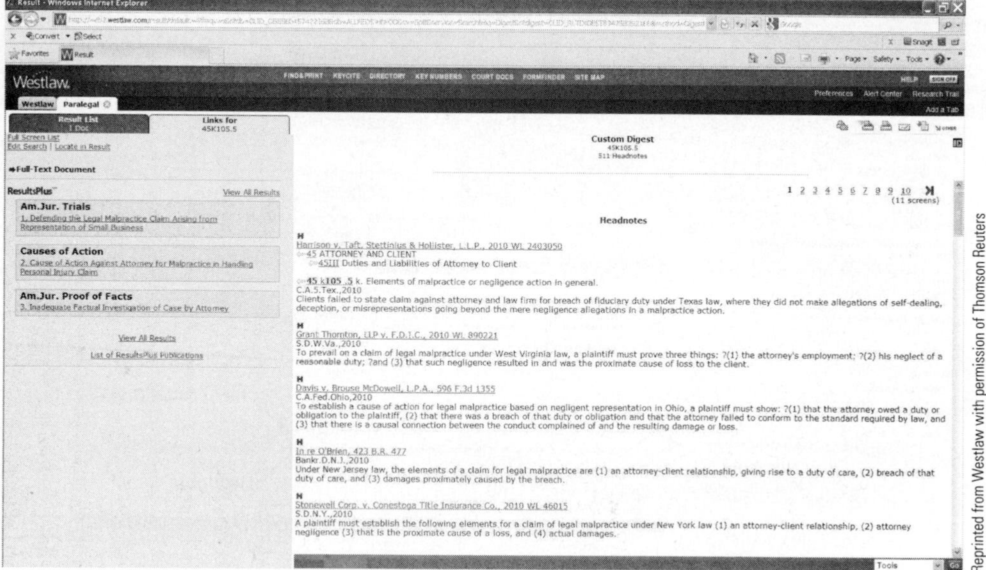

21. You will next find the cases and Headnotes that are most cited (the ones that other, similar cases tend to quote or talk about). This can give you a good idea as to which cases are the most important.

22. ***Click your browser's Back button twice.*** You should now be back at the *Hewlette v. Hovis* case (see Westlaw Exhibit 27). If not, click Research Trail in the upper right of the screen, then click on the *Hewlette v. Hovis* case.

23. ***Scroll to the first Headnote again and click Most Cited Cases at the end of Key Number 45k105.5*** (see Westlaw Exhibit 27).

24. Notice that this is the same screen as in Westlaw Exhibit 28, except that now Most Cited Cases is selected. ***Click Federal and leave All selected.***

25. ***Click Search in the lower left of the screen.***

26. Your screen should look similar to (but will probably not include the same cases as) Westlaw Exhibit 29.

27. ***Scroll down the first 10 cases or so on your list.*** Pay particular attention to the KeyCite colors of the flags. You will want to pay specific attention to red and yellow flags, which point to the negative issues in the cases, so you can evaluate how they might apply to your case. This will help you forecast what your opposing counsel may argue.
28. Once you have found a case on point, always look at the Headnote and Key Numbers, as they can provide you with a wealth of additional information.
29. ***Click the Paralegal tab.***

This concludes the Westlaw Hands-On Exercises. To exit Westlaw, ***click Sign Off on the toolbar.***

HANDS-ON EXERCISES

WESTLAWNEXT COMPUTER-ASSISTED LEGAL RESEARCH

Number	Lesson Title	Concepts Covered
BASIC LESSON		
Lesson 1	Introduction to WestlawNext	Signing on; introduction to the WestlawNext interface; finding documents by citation and by party name, and how to search using natural language and Boolean terms and connectors
INTERMEDIATE LESSON		
Lesson 2	KeyCite and Working with a Document	Using KeyCite; how to maneuver within a case, how to change the display options for a document, how to annotate a document, and the methods available to deliver a document
ADVANCED LESSON		
Lesson 3	History and Folders	Using the History tool; saving documents to a folder; creating a new folder; exporting folders

GETTING STARTED

Introduction

Throughout these lessons and exercises, information you need to type into the software will be designated in several different ways:

- Keys to be pressed on the keyboard are designated in brackets, in all caps, and in bold (e.g., press the **[ENTER]** key).
- Movements with the mouse pointer are designated in bold and italics (e.g., ***point to File on the menu bar and click***).
- Words or letters that should be typed are designated in bold (e.g., type **Training Program**).
- Information that is or should be displayed on your computer screen is shown in bold, with quotation marks (e.g., **"Press ENTER to continue."**).
- Specific menu items and commands are designated with an initial capital letter (e.g., click Open).

BASIC LESSON

LESSON 1: INTRODUCTION TO WESTLAWNEXT

This lesson introduces you to WestlawNext. It includes instructions for signing on to WestlawNext, a tour of WestlawNext, and gaining familiarity with the WestlawNext interface. You will also learn how to find a document by citation and by party name, and how to search using natural language and Boolean terms and connectors.

1. Start Windows.
2. Start your Internet browser. Type **www.next.westlaw.com** in the browser and press the [**ENTER**] key.
3. Your screen should look similar to WestlawNext Exhibit 1. Enter your WestlawNext User Name and Password. If you are using your own computer, you may also want to ***click Remember my user name and Remember my password.*** Doing so will save you the time and trouble of reentering your user name and

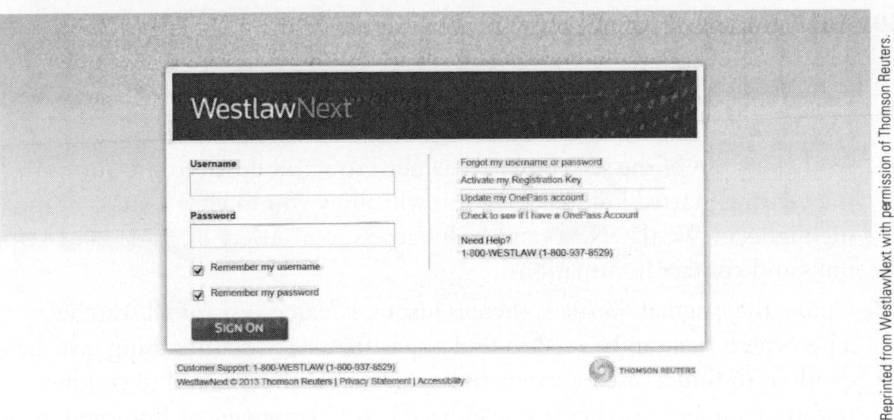

WESTLAWNEXT EXHIBIT 1

password every time you log on to WestlawNext. You should not use this feature if you are using a public computer (*e.g.*, a library computer). ***Click SIGN ON.***

4. At the next screen, you will enter a Client ID. In a law office, this is where you would assign this session of WestlawNext to a specific client and/or case file so it may be billed accordingly. For the purposes of these lessons, enter **Hands-On Exercises** (or whatever your instructor tells you to enter). You may then see a pop-up Welcome to WestlawNext window. You may want to watch the Getting Started video and download the Getting Started Guide. ***Click the box next to Don't show me this again*** if you do not see this again.
5. Your screen should now look similar to WestlawNext Exhibit 2. This is the WestlawNext Home page. You will now take a tour of the WestlawNext home page.

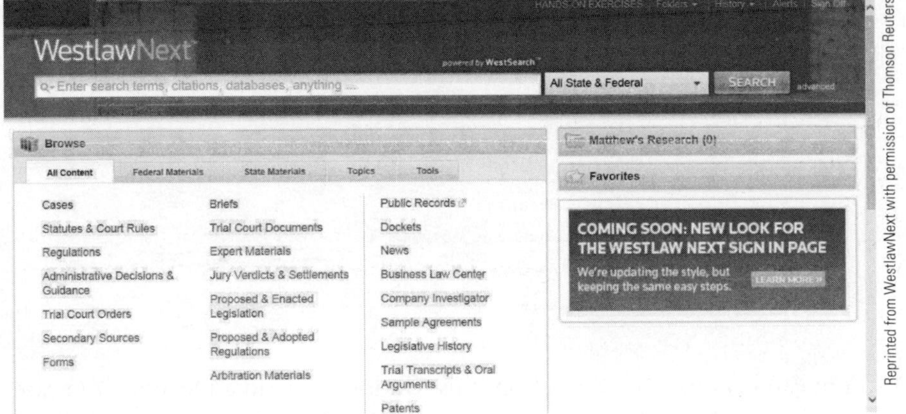

WESTLAWNEXT EXHIBIT 2

6. Notice that at the top of the screen is the Search text box. This is where you can search for a specific case or statute or conduct a complete search of a complex legal issue. See WestlawNext Exhibit 2.
7. To the right of the Search text box is the Jurisdiction selector. This gives you the option of selecting up to three jurisdictions prior to searching to limit the search to the most relevant results. See WestlawNext Exhibit 2.
8. Under the Search text box is the Browse feature where you can Browse All Content types (cases, statutes, etc.), Federal Materials, State Materials, and Practice Areas. See Westlaw Next Exhibit 2.
9. Along the right side of the screen are the Folders (virtual folders where research results can be stored) and Favorites (specific content pages designated as Favorites for easy access from the Home page). See WestlawNext Exhibit 2. Assuming you have not already done any research in this account, both of these items should be empty.

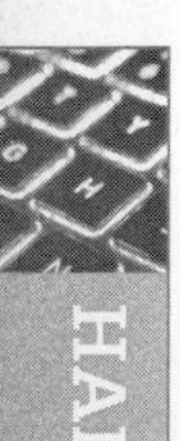

10. Along the top of the screen are Folders (access to recently used folders and a link to view and organize all folders) and History (access to recent documents and a link to access your research history for up to a year). See WestlawNext Exhibit 2.
11. At the bottom of the screen (you may need to scroll down to the bottom), there is a Getting Started link (clicking this will allow you to view a video of the highlights of WestlawNext) and Help (access to a variety of guides and helpful links and contact information).
12. Unlike the original Westlaw, there is just one Search box for all searches. This Search box can be used to find a specific case or statute using just the citation, to find a case by name, to KeyCite a document, and to conduct traditional query searches (using either Natural Language or Boolean terms and connectors).
13. To Find a Document (a statute) by Citation, Type **31 USC 5112** in the Search text box and ***click Search***. Your screen should now look like WestlawNext Exhibit 3. ***Scroll down the page and back to the top to view the entire statute.*** Notice on the right side of the screen is the Notes of Decisions (summaries of cases that have applied or interpreted this statute). ***Click Jurisdiction under Notes of Decisions***. You can now see hyperlinks to and summaries of the relevant cases. ***Click Document to return to the statute***. See WestlawNext Exhibit 3.

WESTLAWNEXT EXHIBIT 3

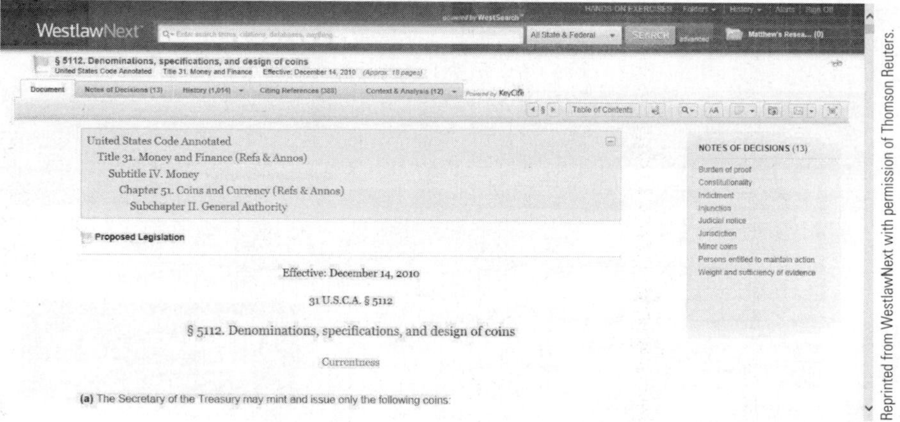

14. You can begin a new search from this window, to Find a Document (a case) by Citation in the Search text box at the top of the screen (see WestlawNext Exhibit 3), type **249 Ga. 151.** It is not necessary to select a jurisdiction and the Search text box is not case sensitive (you could have also typed 249ga151). Your screen should now look like Westlaw Exhibit 4. ***Scroll down the page and back to the top to view the entire case***. As you scroll through the case, notice the West Headnotes at the beginning of the case. In WestlawNext, it is not necessary to conduct a separate KeyCite search to determine whether the case is relevant or to see the number of Citing Decisions. At the top of the screen are the KeyCite results. See WestlawNext Exhibit 4. ***Click Negative Treatment (3)*** to see a list of the cases that have treated *Gregory v. Johnson* negatively (come to a different conclusion without overruling). ***Click Document to return to the case.*** We will review some of the specific features of a case in WestlawNext in a later lesson.
15. To Find a Document by Party Name, in the Search text box, type **Miranda v. Arizona.** You will retrieve a significant number of cases, statutes, and other

WESTLAWNEXT EXHIBIT 4

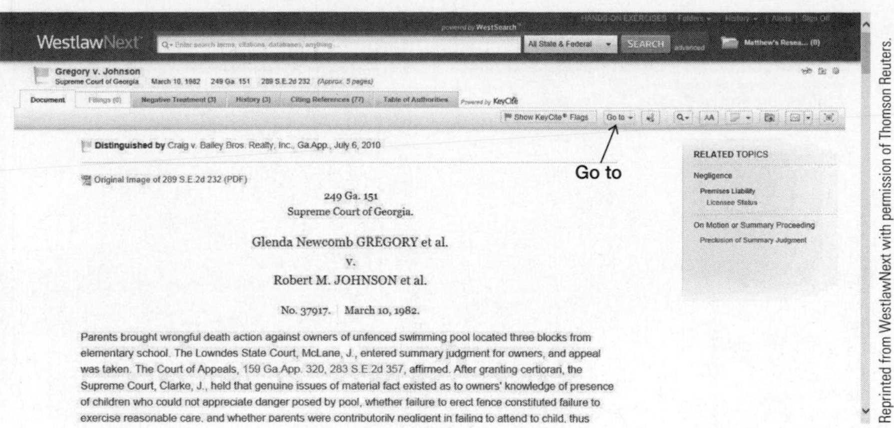

material, but whenever possible, the closest match will display at the top of the page in a blue box above your search results. Below the blue box, the search results are displayed, ranked by relevance.

16. You can KeyCite any document from the Search text box. To KeyCite in WestlawNext, enter *keycite* or *kc:* followed by a citation into the Search text box. In the Search text box, type **kc: 347 US 483.** Your screen should now look like WestlawNext Exhibit 5—the KeyCite results for *Brown v. Board of Education.* By default, WestlawNext will display the Negative Treatment. If there are no negative references, the default view will be the Citing References. We will review some of the specific features of KeyCite in a later lesson.

WESTLAWNEXT EXHIBIT 5

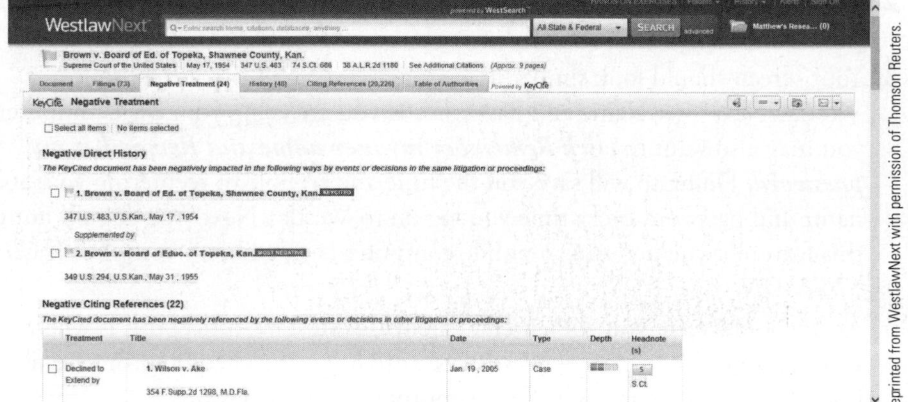

17. In WestlawNext, browsing to the content you are interested in before you search helps ensure that your results are the most relevant to your research. ***Click the WestlawNext logo at the top of the screen, then click State Materials, then from the list of states, click California, then click All California State Cases.*** Your screen should now look like WestlawNext Exhibit 6. Note that when browsing, a tab that is specific to the content you're viewing appears above the search box, automatically narrowing your search to that content. See WestlawNext Exhibit 6. The default method of search in WestlawNext is Natural Language. Type **what is the required procedure for a judicial foreclosure** and ***click Search.*** By default, WestlawNext displays the cases in order of relevance. ***Click Back to California State Cases.*** See WestlawNext Exhibit 6.

WESTLAWNEXT EXHIBIT 6

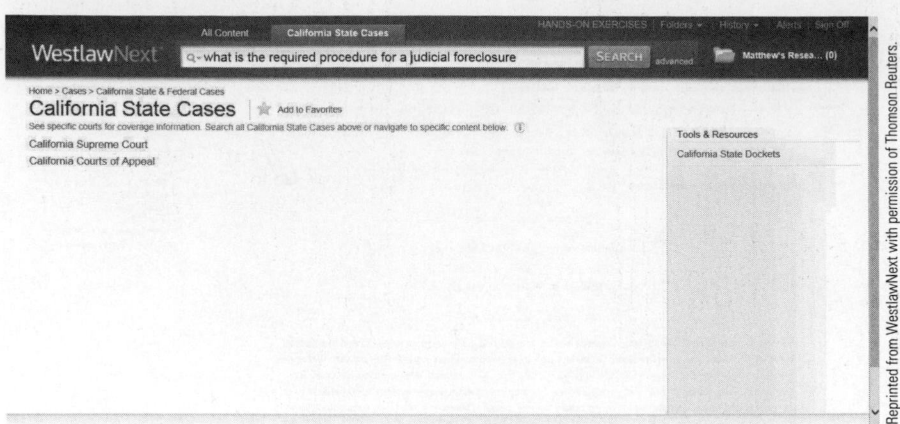

18. A Boolean search may also be conducted in WestlawNext. In the Search text box, type **required /s procedure /p "judicial foreclosure"** (include the quotation marks in the query) and ***click Search.*** The list of cases with those search terms and connectors appears.
19. ***Click Sign Off in the upper right corner to sign out of WestlawNext.***

This concludes Lesson 1 of the WestlawNext Hands-On Exercises.

LESSON 2: INTERMEDIATE LESSON

This lesson will show you how to work with KeyCite, how to maneuver within a case, how to change the display options for a document, how to annotate a document, and the methods available to deliver a document.

1. Start Windows.
2. Start your Internet browser. Type **www.next.westlaw.com** in the browser and press the **[ENTER]** key.
3. Your screen should look similar to WestlawNext Exhibit 1. Enter your WestlawNext User Name and Password. If you are using your own computer, you may also want to ***click Remember my user name and Remember my password.*** Doing so will save you the time and trouble of reentering your user name and password every time you log on to WestlawNext. You should not use this feature if you are using a public computer (*e.g.*, a library computer). ***Click SIGN ON.***
4. At the next screen, you will enter a Client ID. In a law office, this is where you would assign this session of WestlawNext to a specific client and/or case file so it may be billed accordingly. For the purposes of these lessons, enter **Hands-On Exercises** (or whatever your instructor tells you to enter). You will then see a Welcome screen which will list your recent WestlawNext History. From this screen, you can resume previous research sessions. ***Click Continue***. Your screen should now look similar to WestlawNext Exhibit 2.
5. Type **249 Ga. 151** in the Search text box and ***click Search.*** Your screen should now look like Westlaw Exhibit 4. ***Scroll down the page to the Headnotes.*** See WestlawNext Exhibit 7. From this page, it is possible to access cases available through the West Key Number system. To see the specific Key Numbers of the displayed topics, ***click a key. Click the key again to undo.*** To find additional cases from the same jurisdiction (in this case, Georgia), that discuss Care as to Children, ***click the second Headnote, Care as to Children.*** See WestlawNext Exhibit 7. You should now see a list of cases on this topic. ***Click the Back button of your Internet browser*** to return to the case.

WESTLAWNEXT EXHIBIT 7

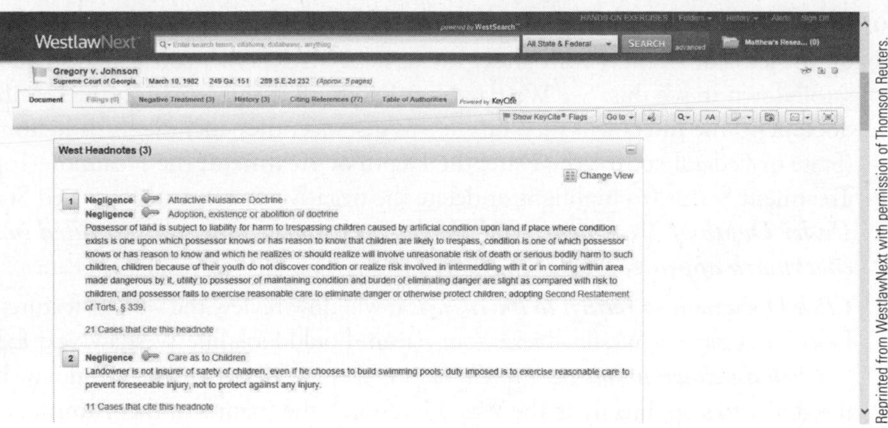

6. To see the cases that specifically cite this section of *Gregory v. Johnson*, ***click 11 Cases that cite this headnote*** (the precise number of cases is always subject to change). See WestlawNext Exhibit 7. You should see a KeyCite page listing just those cases that have specifically cited this portion of *Gregory v. Johnson*. ***Click Document to return to the case.***
7. The KeyCite results are always presented at the top of a document. For a case, they are divided into Negative Treatment, History, Citing References, and Table of Authorities (this is a listing of the cases relied upon as authority by the document you are viewing. This list can be used to quickly verify the validity of relied upon authority). ***Click Citing References, then on the left side of the screen click Cases.*** Your screen should now look like WestlawNext Exhibit 8.

WESTLAWNEXT EXHIBIT 8

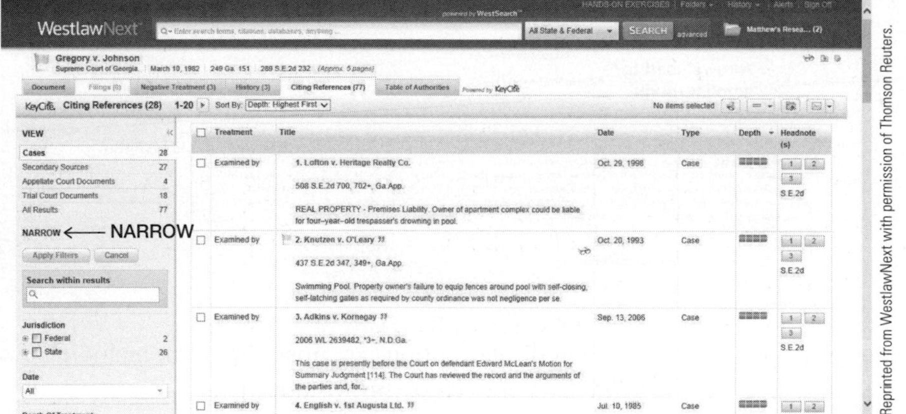

8. The quotation mark icon next to the second case listed (*Knutzen v. O'Leary*) indicates that the citing case (*Knutzen*) quotes the cited case (*Gregory*). Click the link for *Knutzen v. O'Leary*. See WestlawNext Exhibit 8. ***Scroll down through the case until you see the references to Gregory—they will be highlighted. Click Return to list at the top of the case.*** Notice that there is a small icon that looks like a pair of eyeglasses now at the left side of the reference to *Knutzen v. O'Leary*. See WestlawNext Exhibit 8. This icon indicates that you have viewed this case.
9. Under the Depth heading, you can see the depth of discussion indicators. See WestlawNext Exhibit 8. They range from four bars (fully considers the cited reference) to one bar (cites to the reference with minimal if any discussion). The specific Headnotes discussed in the citing cases are listed on the left side of the screen. See WestlawNext Exhibit 8.

10. KeyCite results can be filtered to refine the search results. You can see these on the left side of the screen under the term "NARROW"; you may have to scroll down to see this. See WestlawNext Exhibit 8. Depending on the specific document, the filters will vary, but in this instance, they include: Jurisdiction (State or Federal court); the Date; the Depth of Treatment; the Headnote Topics; Treatment Status (to highlight or delete the negative cases); and Reported Status. ***Under Depth of Treatment, click the box next to the four squares filled in so a checkmark appears, then click Apply Filters.*** The filtered results appear.
11. ***Click Document to return to the case.*** You will now review the various features of a Document page in WestlawNext. Your screen should look like WestlawNext Exhibit 4. ***Click the down arrow next to Go to.*** See WestlawNext Exhibit 4. You now have the ability to skip directly to the West Headnotes; the (names of the) Attorneys and Law Firms; the Opinion; the Parallel Citations; and Page # (number). Next to Page #, type **153**, then ***click Go.*** You should now see that portion of the case.
12. To search for a specific term within a case, ***click the down arrow next to the magnifying glass icon.*** Remember that you can see what an icon does by placing the cursor over an icon. See WestlawNext Exhibit 9. A new text box will appear in which you may search for a specific term or word within the document. In the text box, type **child**, then ***click Search.*** See WestlawNext Exhibit 9. All references to the word child or children are now highlighted. To scroll through the specific uses of the search term, click the right arrow (next use) or left arrow (prior use).

WESTLAWNEXT EXHIBIT 9

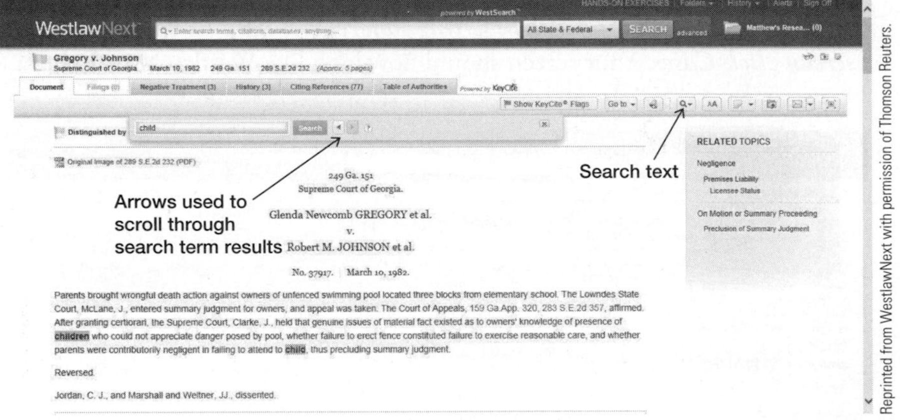

13. ***Click the AA icon.*** Various display options are now displayed, including Size, Font, and Width. ***Click Cancel*** to close this window.
14. It is possible to annotate a document in WestlawNext. Click the down arrow next to the Annotations icon. See WestlawNext Exhibit 10. The drop-down menu provides the option of adding a note or viewing the notes already added. ***Click Add Note.*** The Notes window will open. Type **Make sure the team sees this case.** ***Click Save.*** The note is now placed at the top of the case.
15. It is also possible to add a note to a particular segment of text within the case. ***Scroll down to the opinion of the case and, using the cursor, highlight a paragraph of the text.*** A new box will open. See WestlawNext Exhibit 10. The highlighted material may now be saved to a research folder to your Project Folder as a snippet. Clicking the snippet within the folder will allow you to return to that point in the document. The selected text may also be attached to a note (in a variety of colors) or highlighted (in a variety of colors). Finally, it may be copied to a Word document, such as a brief or memo, with the citation properly

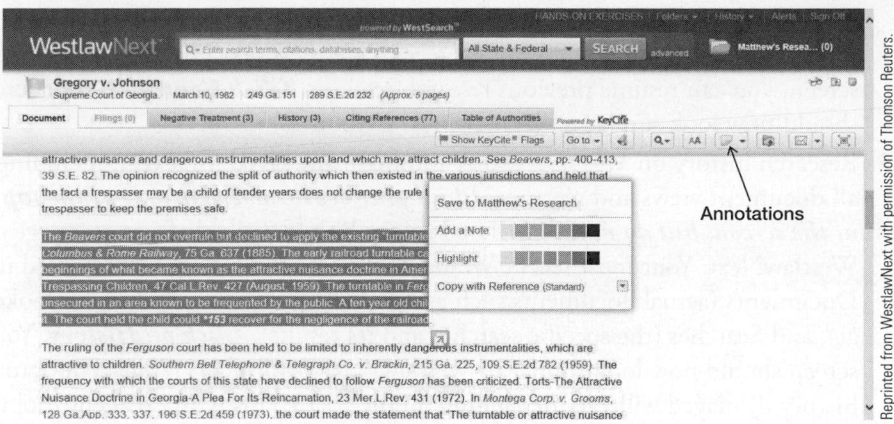

WESTLAWNEXT EXHIBIT 10

HANDS-ON EXERCISES

referenced. ***Click the down arrow next to Copy with Reference (Standard).*** WestlawNext allows you to cite a case using Bluebook (Standard) citation format, as well the ALWD format and the formats used in a variety of states. ***Click Standard. Then click Copy with Reference (Standard). Open Microsoft Word and then in a blank page, click Paste.*** You should now see the highlighted material from *Gregory v. Johnson* accompanied by a proper Bluebook citation.

16. ***Click the envelope icon on the right side of the screen.*** See WestlawNext Exhibit 4. WestlawNext provides the option to deliver a document in a variety of methods. A document can be delivered by email, it can be printed or downloaded, and it can be delivered to a Kindle e-reader. ***Click Email.*** The Email This Document window opens. ***Click the first tab, Recipients.*** Here you can enter the recipient(s) of the emailed document, add a note to the email and elect to send just the document or the document and accompanying annotations. ***Click the second tab, Layouts and Limits.*** Here you can select the layout of the document, font, color of the hyperlinks, and what to include, the headnotes, coverpage, etc. ***Click the third tab, Content to Append.*** Here you can select the specific items to append to the emailed document. ***Click Cancel.***
17. ***Click Sign Off in the upper right corner to sign out of WestlawNext.***

This concludes Lesson 2 of the WestlawNext Hands-On Exercises.

LESSON 3: ADVANCED LESSON

This lesson will show you how to work with the History tool and folders in WestlawNext.

1. Start Windows.
2. Start your Internet browser. Type **www.next.westlaw.com** in the browser and press the **[ENTER]** key.
3. Your screen should look similar to WestlawNext Exhibit 1. Enter your WestlawNext User Name and Password. If you are using your own computer, you may also want to ***click Remember my user name and Remember my password.*** Doing so will save you the time and trouble of reentering your user name and password every time you log on to WestlawNext. You should not use this feature if you are using a public computer (*e.g.*, a library computer). ***Click SIGN ON.***
4. At the next screen, you will enter a Client ID. In a law office, this is where you would assign this session of WestlawNext to a specific client and/or case file so it may be billed accordingly. For the purposes of these lessons, enter **Hands-On**

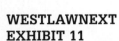

Exercises (or whatever your instructor tells you to enter). You will then see a Welcome screen which will list your recent WestlawNext History. From this screen, you can resume previous research sessions. ***Click Continue.*** Your screen should now look similar to WestlawNext Exhibit 2.

5. Research history on WestlawNext is automatically saved for a year, including all document views and searches. ***Place your cursor over History at the top of the screen, but do not click.*** The History link is available from any page on WestlawNext. Your most recent WestlawNext activity is displayed, divided into Documents (actual documents such as cases and statutes that you have looked at), and Searches (the specific searches and its results). ***Click on History.*** Your screen should now look similar to WestlawNext Exhibit 11. (*Note:* The actual history displayed will vary depending on the user.) This is an excellent tool to use when you need to pick up your research from an earlier research session.

WESTLAWNEXT EXHIBIT 11

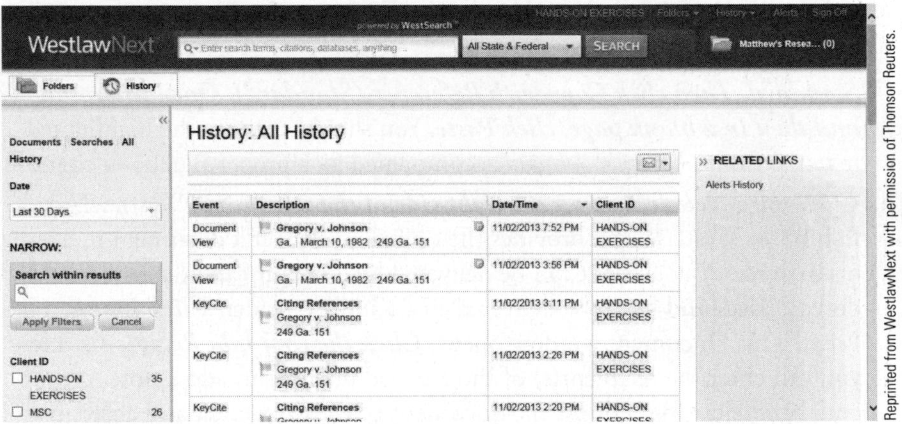

Reprinted from WestlawNext with permission of Thomson Reuters.

6. On the left side of the screen, ***click Documents.*** See WestlawNext Exhibit 11. The case of *Gregory v. Johnson* should now appear. If this case was of interest and it was found via traditional hard-copy legal research, you might make a copy of it and put it in a folder for future reference. WestlawNext allows you to perform those same tasks.
7. When you first created your WestlawNext (or Westlaw) account, WestlawNext automatically named the default folder for you. For example, the one you will see referenced in this lesson is called Matthew's Research. Yours should bear the first name you provided when the account was created. If it is not named correctly, do not worry about it—we will learn how to change the name of a folder later in this lesson.
8. To save the *Gregory v. Johnson* case to the folder, ***click the Save to Folder icon*** (it looks like a folder with a green up arrow). See WestlawNext Exhibit 12. ***In the Save 1 Item To: window, click Save*** to save this case to your folder. A message stating that Gregory v. Johnson has been saved to your folder should appear and there should be a number (1) next to your folder name at the top of the screen.
9. It is also possible to save a document that is cited within the document you are currently viewing. This is done by clicking on the cite and dragging it to the folder. ***Scroll down through the case until you find the Savannah, Fla. & W. R. Co. v. Beavers, 113 Ga. 398, 39 S.E. 82 (1901) citation*** (like most citations within a WestlawNext document, it appears as a hyperlink). ***Click on the citation and drag it up to the reference to your folder*** (where it says

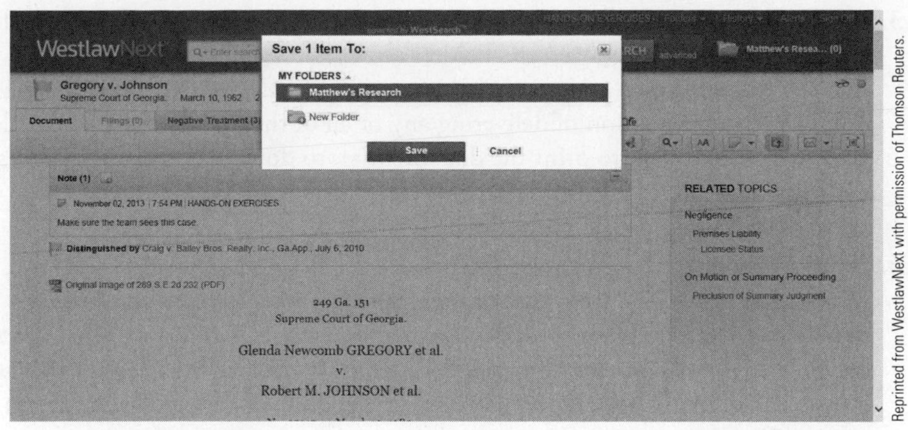

WESTLAWNEXT EXHIBIT 12

Reprinted from WestlawNext with permission of Thomson Reuters.

Matthew's Research in WestlawNext Exhibit 12). Notice that the grey arrow turns green when the citation is properly placed on the folder name. ***Release the cursor to save the cited case to the folder.*** A message stating that *Savannah, Fla. & W. R. Co. v. Beavers* has been saved to your folder will appear and now the number (2) appears next to your folder name.

10. ***Click Citing References in the KeyCite bar at the top of the case, then click Cases on the left side of the KeyCite screen.*** Your screen should look like WestlawNext Exhibit 8. You can save any or all of the cases in this list to your folder. Assume you want to save the first 20 cases that appear on this screen. ***Click the empty box at the top of the list of cases so a checkmark appears.*** Clicking here applies the checkmark to all the items on this screen, so they should all now have a checkmark. ***Click the Save to Folder icon (it looks like a folder with a green up arrow). In the Save 20 Items To: window, click Save.*** A message stating that 20 of 20 items have been saved should appear and now the number (22) appears next to your folder name.
11. ***Click Folders at the top of the screen.*** The Folders screen will appear. ***On the left side of the screen, click Options.*** See WestlawNext Exhibit 13. ***Click Rename.*** In the Rename window, type **Gregory v. Johnson.** ***Click OK. Click the WestlawNext logo to return to the Home page.*** Notice that the reference to the folder name refers to it as *Gregory v. Johnson*.
12. ***Click Folders again to return to the Folders screen.*** You will create a new folder. ***Click New on the left side of the screen.*** See WestlawNext Exhibit 13. In the New Folder window, type **New Research** and ***click OK.***

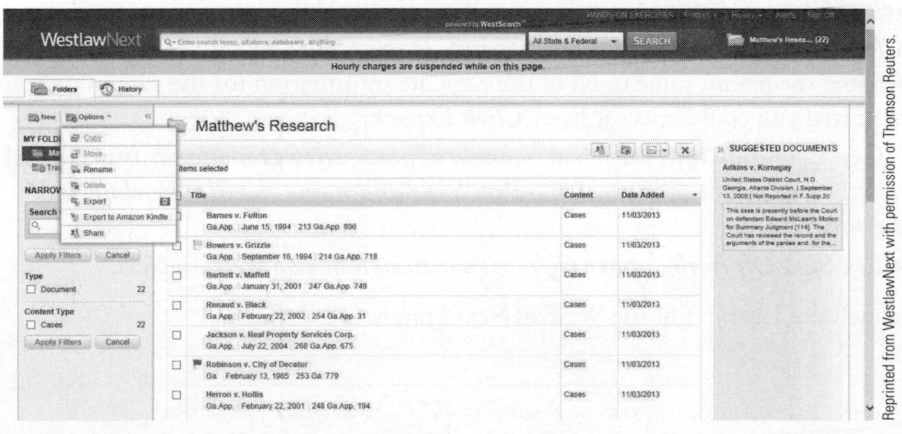

WESTLAWNEXT EXHIBIT 13

Reprinted from WestlawNext with permission of Thomson Reuters.

HANDS-ON EXERCISES

13. You now have two folders—Gregory v. Johnson and New Research (although New Research is empty). On the Folders screen, under Gregory v. Johnson, ***click the down arrow next to the envelope icon.*** See WestlawNext Exhibit 13. You now have the option of delivering any or all of the documents in this folder to someone by email, to print the document(s), to download the document(s), or to export them to a Kindle e-reader. ***Click anywhere on the screen to remove the drop-down window.***

14. It is also possible to export the contents of a folder as a zip (compressed) file. On the left side of the screen, ***click the drop-down arrow next to Options.*** See WestlawNext Exhibit 13. ***Click Export.*** The Export window opens. ***Click the box next to Gregory v. Johnson to select it.*** (You have the option to view a short video or review a PDF explaining the process of exporting files if you wish.) ***Click Next.*** A new export window opens.

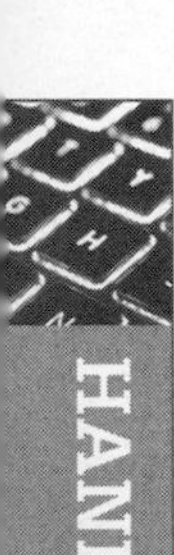

WESTLAWNEXT EXHIBIT 14

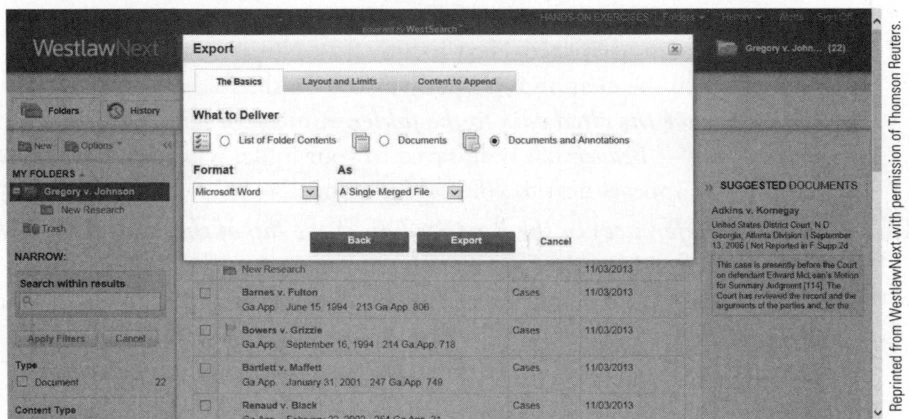

15. This new Export window has two or three tabs, depending on what is to be exported. See WestlawNext Exhibit 14. Under What to Deliver, ***click the first option List of Folder Contents.*** Notice that there are only two tabs (The Basics; Layout and Limits). ***Click the second option Documents.*** A third option (Content to Append) appears. For this exercise, ***click the third option Documents and Annotations.*** Notice that all three tabs are available. Under the first tab, make sure the file is to be delivered as a Word document and as a single file.

16. ***Click the second tab, Layout and Limits.*** Here you can select the font and the documents to include in the exported file. ***Under Page Layout, click the box next to Dual column layout for cases. Under Links, select Blue. Under Font, select Normal. Under Include, click West Headnotes.***

17. ***Click the third tab, Content to Append. Do not click any of the boxes.*** If you wanted to append some or all of the KeyCite information for the cases to be exported you could select it here. ***Click Export.***

18. When the Ready for Download window appears, ***click Download.*** When asked whether to save or open the file, ***select Save and name the file WestlawNext Lesson 3.***

19. ***Click Sign Off in the upper right corner to sign out of WestlawNext.***

This concludes Lesson 3 of the WestlawNext Hands-On Exercises.

HANDS-ON EXERCISES

LEXIS COMPUTER-ASSISTED LEGAL RESEARCH

Number	Lesson Title	Concepts Covered
BASIC LESSONS		
Lesson 1	Introduction to Lexis	Signing on; introduction to the Lexis interface; finding databases; working with Lexis tabs
Lesson 2	Get by Citation, Get by Party Name, and Exploring Retrieved Cases	Get by Citation, Get by Party Name, Cite, KWIC, Full, reporter page numbers, distribution options, and a *Shepard's* overview
INTERMEDIATE LESSONS		
Lesson 3	Natural Language Search, Editing Searches, Changing Databases, Using Doc and Term Features	Natural Language searching; editing using date restriction; requiring and excluding terms; using the Doc and Term features
Lesson 4	Terms and Connectors Search	Terms and Connectors searching; using the Suggest Terms for My Search feature; printing a list of retrieved cases
ADVANCED LESSON		
Lesson 5	*Shepard's Citations*	*Shepardizing;* Table of Authorities; Auto-Cite.

HANDS-ON EXERCISES

GETTING STARTED

Introduction

Throughout these lessons and exercises, information you need to type into the software will be designated in several different ways:

- Keys to be pressed on the keyboard are designated in brackets, in all caps, and in bold (e.g., press the **[ENTER]** key).
- Movements with the mouse pointer are designated in bold and italics (e.g., ***point to File and click***).
- Words or letters that should be typed are designated in bold (e.g., type **Training Program**).
- Information that is or should be displayed on your computer screen is shown in bold, with quotation marks (e.g., "**Press ENTER to continue**.").
- Specific menu items and commands are designated with an initial capital letter (e.g., click Open).

BASIC LESSONS

LESSON 1: INTRODUCTION TO LEXIS

This lesson introduces you to Lexis. You will learn how to sign on to Lexis, take a tour of Lexis and the Lexis interface, and learn how to find databases and work with Lexis tabs. For an overview of the features in Lexis, read the Lexis section in Chapter 9 of the text.

1. Start Windows.
2. Start your Internet browser. Type **www.lexis.com** in the browser and press the **[ENTER]** key.
3. At the ID field, type the Lexis ID supplied by your instructor.

4. At the Password field, type the Lexis password supplied by your instructor.
5. ***Click Sign In*** to sign on to Lexis.
6. Your screen should now look similar to Lexis Exhibit 1 (see Lexis Exhibit 1). If your screen does not look like Lexis Exhibit 1, ***click the Search tab.*** Lexis is highly customizable, so it is possible that your screens will look different from the screens in the exhibits.

LEXIS EXHIBIT 1

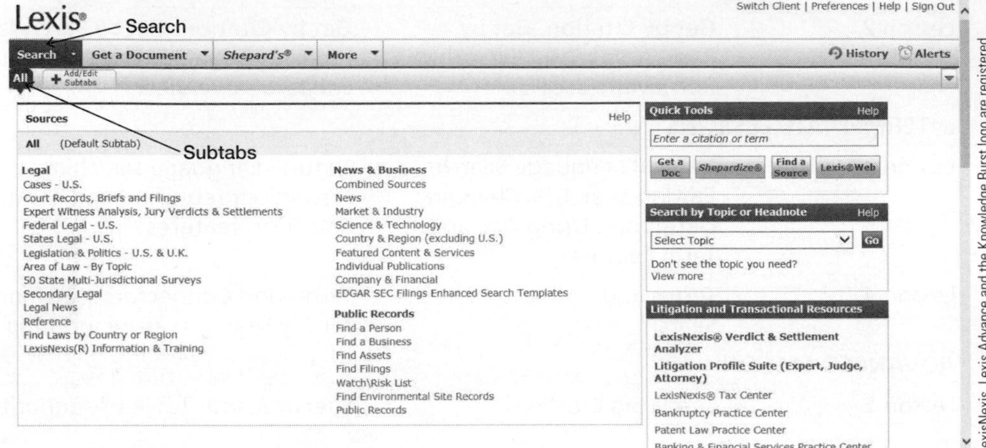

7. You will now take a brief tour of Lexis. The Search tab (first tab from the left) should be selected. (It should have a red background and **"Search"** should be in white letters; see Lexis Exhibit 1).
8. Under the **Search tab**, a number of subtabs may be displayed. You can customize the subtabs by adding your own jurisdiction or legal topics that you use a lot. (See Lexis Exhibit 1.)
9. You can customize the subtabs by adding your own jurisdiction or legal topics that you use a lot.
10. ***Click Add/Edit Subtabs,*** which is to the right of the Legal subtab (see Lexis Exhibit 2).

LEXIS EXHIBIT 2

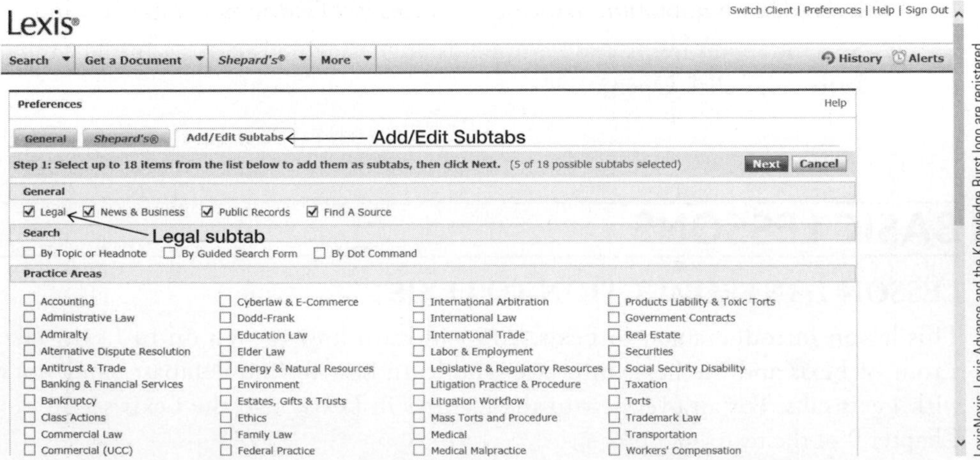

11. If you scroll down, you will see a list of legal specialty areas and a list of states. You can add subtabs by clicking a selection and then clicking Add. Most users will want to make a tab for their state.

12. Notice that at the top of the screen, under the heading "General," are four subtabs. ***Make sure that all four*** (Legal, News & Business, Public Records, and Find A Source) ***are checked; then click Next.***
13. You should now be on the Preferences screen. Under **"Your current subtabs,"** ***click Legal, then click Set as Default, then click Set.***
14. You should now be at the Legal subtab, but notice that you now have any additional subtabs you selected.
15. The Legal subtab includes sections such as "Cases – U.S." and "Federal Legal – U.S." The Legal subtab is a good place to start your legal research, because you can access many commonly used databases from this screen.
16. ***Scroll down and click States Legal – U.S. on the left side of the page.*** A list of states should now be displayed.
17. ***Click California.*** You should now see a list of databases and resources for California. If you wanted to search in one of these databases, you could click the database name and a search window would open where you could enter your search. If you wanted to search multiple databases at the same time, you could click in the check box next to each database and then select Combine sources. A search window would then open that would allow you to search multiple databases at the same time.
18. ***Click the Legal subtab*** or ***click your browser's Back button twice.*** You should be back at the Legal subtab (see Lexis Exhibit 2).
19. Notice that on the right side of the screen you can access different areas of the law by topic (e.g., "Banking & Financial Services," "Bankruptcy," and "Environment"). If you scroll down the page, you can access briefs, motions, pleadings, verdicts, other secondary legal resources, legal news, and other resources.
20. Press the **[HOME]** key to go back to the top of the page.
21. ***Click the News & Business subtab.***
22. Notice that on the left side of the screen, under Combined Sources, Lexis gives you a wide variety of general and legal news databases to search. Also notice that on the right side of the screen, under Individual Publications and Company & Financial, Lexis has a number of resources for finding company and financial information.
23. ***Click the Source Description icon for All English Language News.*** (It looks like a lower-case "i" in a square and appears at the end of each source category name.) *Note:* If you hover your cursor over an icon for a second, the name of the icon will be displayed.
24. The "Source Information" window should now be displayed. Scroll down through the list using your mouse or the cursor keys on the keyboard. Note all of the publications covered in this database.
25. ***Click the Close icon*** (a red square with a white X) ***in the "Source Information" window.***
26. You can use the Source Description icon (a lower-case "i" in a square) throughout Lexis to discover the scope of a database.
27. ***Click the Public Records subtab.*** Notice that a number of public records are available for searching in Lexis.
28. ***Click the Find A Source subtab.*** In the Find A Source subtab, you can browse an alphabetical list for a database. Alternatively, you can search for the name of a database. (See Lexis Exhibit 3.)

LEXIS EXHIBIT 3

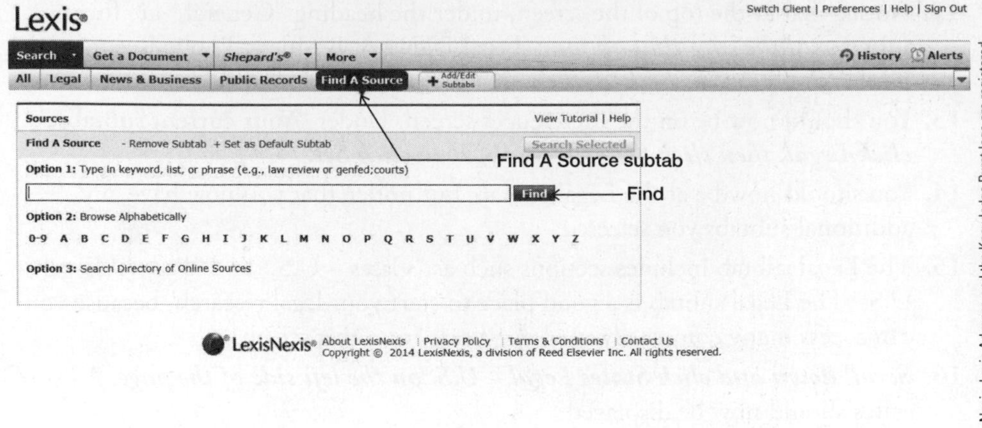

HANDS-ON EXERCISES

29. In the Find A Source Option 1: field, type **Harvard Law Review** and then ***click Find*** (see Lexis Exhibit 3). A list of resources with "Harvard" in the title, including the *Harvard Law Review,* is displayed. You can access the *Harvard Law Review* database simply by clicking it, but for this exercise it is not necessary.
30. You will now learn about the Get a Document tab. ***Click the Get a Document tab,*** which is at the top of the screen next to the Search tab. (See Lexis Exhibit 4.) Notice that there are three subtabs: By Citation, By Party Name, and By Docket Number. You could also access these resources by clicking the drop-down menu to the right of the Get a Document tab.
31. ***Click the By Citation subtab.*** Using this subtab, you can go directly to a case, statute, or other document by entering its cite.
32. ***Click the By Party Name subtab.*** Using this subtab, you can retrieve a case by entering a party name.
33. ***Click the By Docket Number subtab.*** Using this subtab, you can retrieve a case by entering its docket number.
34. You will now learn about the *Shepard's* Citations tab. ***Click the Shepard's tab.*** (See Lexis Exhibit 5.) Notice that there are four subtabs: *Shepard's*, Table of Authorities, Auto-Cite, and LEXCITE. You could also access these resources by clicking the drop-down menu to the right of the *Shepard's* tab.

LEXIS EXHIBIT 4

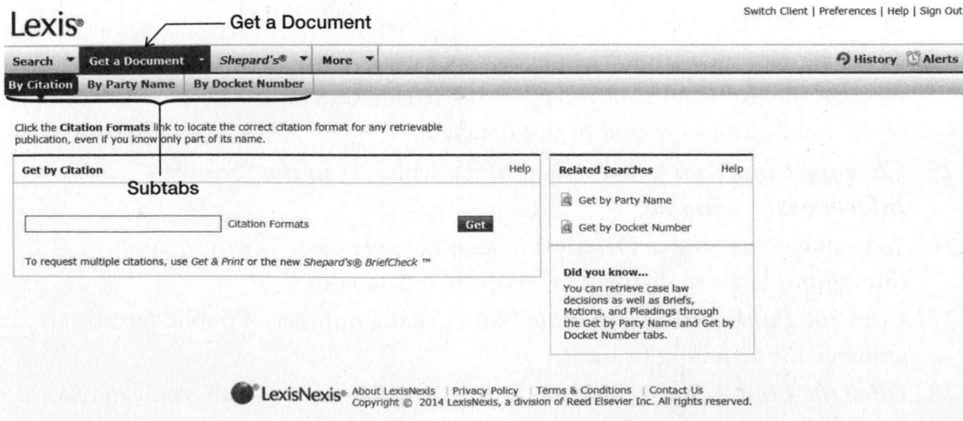

LEXIS EXHIBIT 5

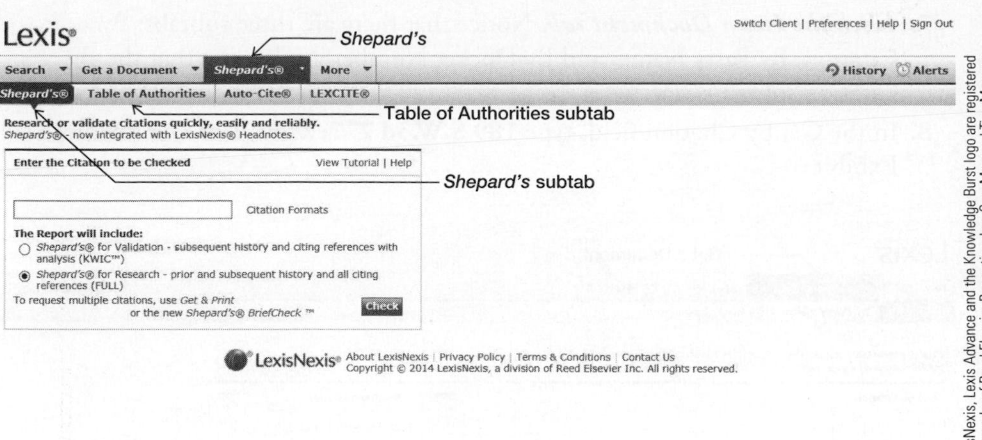

35. ***Click the Shepard's subtab*** (see Lexis Exhibit 5). This is where you can enter a cite and get a comprehensive report of the cases, statutes, secondary sources, and annotations that have cited the authority you entered.
36. ***Click the Table of Authorities subtab*** (see Lexis Exhibit 5). Table of Authorities provides an at-a-glance analysis of the cited references within your case and links to in-depth analysis.
37. ***Click the Auto-Cite subtab.*** Auto-Cite verifies the accuracy of your research and gives you a history of the opinion you are searching on, including cases that refer negatively to your case. Auto-Cite can quickly tell you whether your case or statute is still good law.
38. ***Click the LEXCITE subtab.*** LEXCITE allows you to find both reported and unreported cases.
39. ***Click on the More tab.***
40. This tab provides easy access to other Lexis products and services, such as TotalPatent, CourtLink, and Delivery Manager.

This concludes Lesson 1 of the Lexis Hands-On Exercises. To exit Lexis, ***click Sign Out on the toolbar,*** or stay in Lexis and go to Lesson 2.

LESSON 2: GET BY CITATION, GET BY PARTY NAME, AND EXPLORING RETRIEVED CASES

In this lesson you will use the Get by Citation tool, the Get by Party Name feature, Cite, KWIC, Full, reporter page numbers, and distribution options. If you did not exit Lexis after completing Lesson 1, go directly to Step 6 in the following instructions.

1. Start Windows.
2. Start your Internet browser. Type **www.lexis.com** in the browser and press the **[ENTER]** key.
3. At the ID field, type the Lexis ID supplied by your instructor.
4. At the Password field, enter the Lexis password supplied by your instructor.
5. ***Click Sign In*** to sign on to Lexis.
6. Your screen should now look similar to Lexis Exhibit 1. If your screen does not look like Lexis Exhibit 1, ***click the Search tab*** (see Lexis Exhibit 1). Lexis is highly customizable, so it is possible that your screens will look different from the screens in the exhibits.

7. ***Click the Get a Document tab.*** Notice that there are three subtabs: By Citation, By Party Name, and By Docket Number. Make sure that the By Citation subtab is selected.
8. In the Get by Citation field, type **189 S.W.3d 777*; then click Get*** (see Lexis Exhibit 6).

LEXIS EXHIBIT 6

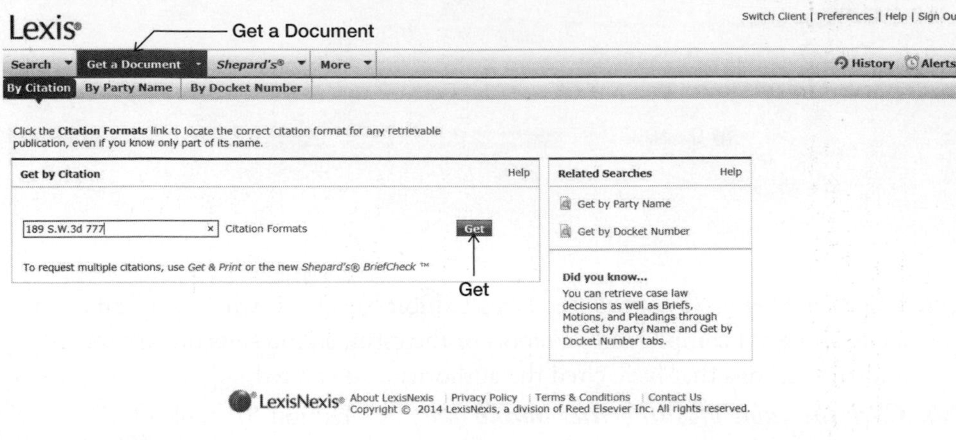

9. The case of *In re Karen Mays-Hooper* should now be displayed (see Lexis Exhibit 7). If you know the citation of a case, you can enter it in the Get by Citation feature and Lexis will immediately retrieve it without your having to indicate a database or enter a search query.
10. You will now learn how to find a case by entering the name of a party.
11. ***Click the Get a Document tab.***
12. ***Click the By Party Name subtab*** (see Lexis Exhibit 8).
13. The screen in Lexis Exhibit 8 should now be displayed.
14. In the first Party name field, type **Karen Mays-Hooper.**
15. ***Click in the circle to the left of State Courts.***
16. ***Click the down arrow next to the right of State Courts and select Texas.***
17. ***Click Search.***

LEXIS EXHIBIT 7

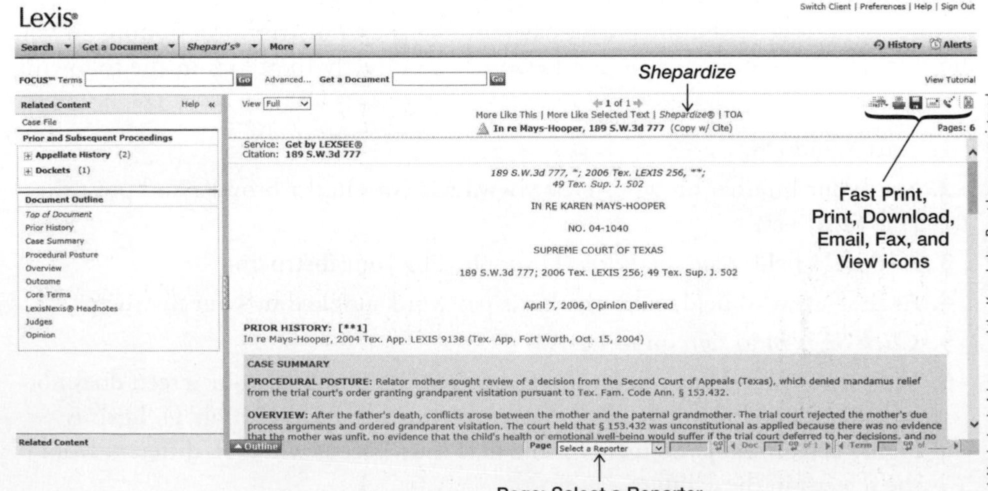

LEXIS EXHIBIT 8

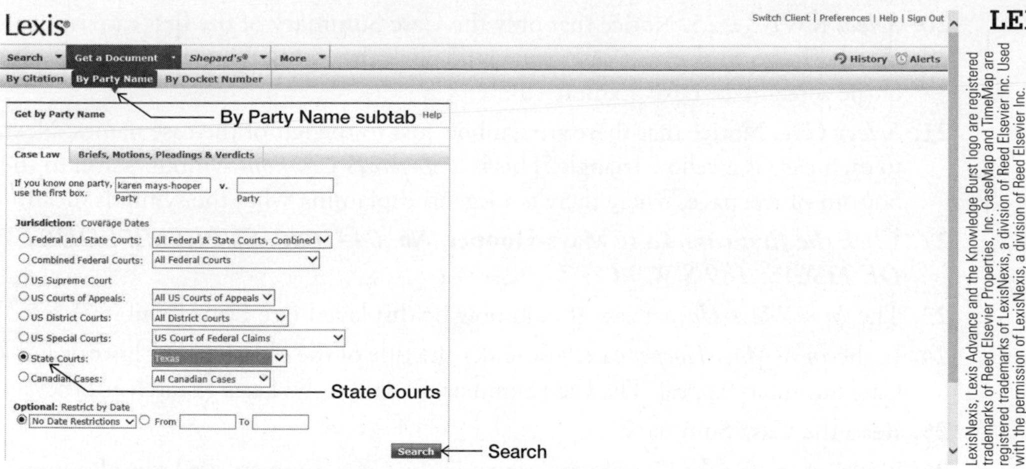

18. A summary of two cases, each with the title *In re Mays-Hooper*, should now be displayed (see Lexis Exhibit 9).

19. Notice the drop-down menu next to View: in the upper left of the screen. Cite is currently selected. Click the arrow to see the other options KWIC ± 25, Full, and Custom. These are the different options for displaying cases in Lexis.

LEXIS EXHIBIT 9

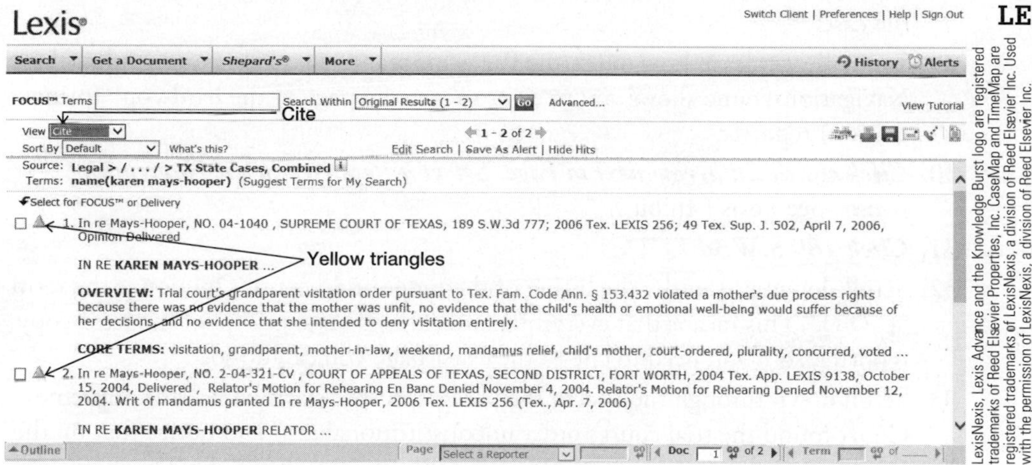

LEXIS EXHIBIT 10

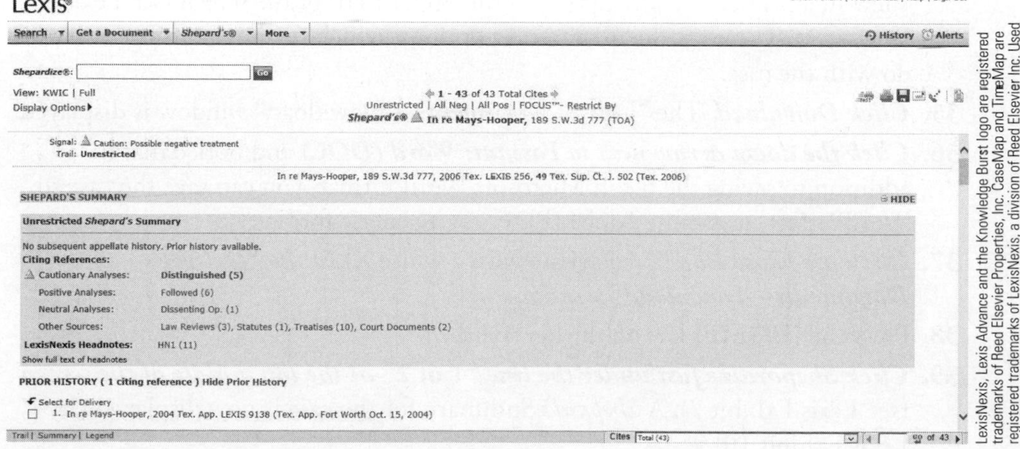

20. ***Select*** KWIC ± 25. Notice that only the Case Summary of the first case is shown. To go to the next case, you could click the right-facing arrow at the top of the screen (see Lexis Exhibit 10).
21. ***Select Cite.*** Notice that there are symbols just to the left of the case names. Next to each case is a yellow triangle. This is a *Shepard's Citations* symbol. Scroll to the bottom of the page, where there is a legend explaining what the symbols mean.
22. ***Click the first case,*** **In re Mays-Hooper,** ***No. 04–1040, SUPREME COURT OF TEXAS, 189 S.W.3d 777.***
23. The *In re Mays-Hooper* case should now be displayed (see Lexis Exhibit 7).
24. In the *In re Mays-Hooper* case, just under the title of the case, its prior history and a Case Summary appear. The Case Summary is written by Lexis research attorneys.
25. Read the Case Summary.
26. Notice that after the Core Terms section in the Case Summary are Lexis Headnotes. Headnote 1 (*HN1*) states: "So long as a parent adequately cares for his or her children (i.e., is fit), there will normally be no reason for the state to inject itself into the private realm of the family." The Headnotes, which are also written by research attorneys, are another value-added service offered by Lexis that many other CALR services do not provide. Headnotes are discussed in more detail in later exercises.
27. Skim the case by ***scrolling down through it using the vertical scroll bar.***
28. When you are finished, press the **[HOME]** key to go back to the beginning of the case.
29. You will next learn how to use the Page command. The Page command in the Navigation Frame allows you to cite to a specific page of the hard-copy (print edition) reporter.
30. ***Click the down arrow next to Page: Select a Reporter in the Navigation frame.*** See Lexis Exhibit 7.
31. ***Click 189 S.W.3d 777,*.***
32. Scroll down; just under the listing of the judge and next to Opinion is the term "[*777]." This means that everything after this is on page 777 of the hard-copy reporter, so if you need to cite to the exact page you can do so.
33. Scroll down through the case to the paragraph that starts with "The Supreme Court found the trial court's order unconstitutional . . ." and notice that on the third line of the paragraph the term "[*778]" appears in red. This is where page 778 of the hard-copy report starts.
34. Notice the icons for the options Fast Print, Print, Download, Email, Fax, and View in a printer-friendly format in the upper right of the screen (see Lexis Exhibit 7). These are the distribution options, which define the things you can do with the case.
35. ***Click Download.*** The "Deliver Documents—Download" window is displayed.
36. ***Click the down arrow next to Format: Word (DOC)*** and notice that in addition to saving the file in Microsoft Word format, you can save the case to WordPerfect, text-only, Adobe (PDF), or a generic format.
37. ***Click the Close icon*** (a red square with a white X) ***in the "Deliver Documents—Download" window.***
38. Press the **[HOME]** key on the keyboard.
39. ***Click Shepardize just under the line*** **"1 of 2"** ***at the top middle of the screen*** (see Lexis Exhibit 7). A *Shepard's* Summary for the case is now displayed (see Lexis Exhibit 10).
40. ***Click the Search tab in the upper left corner of the screen.***

This concludes Lesson 2 of the Lexis Hands-On Exercises. To exit Lexis, ***click Sign Out on the toolbar,*** or stay in Lexis and go to Lesson 3.

INTERMEDIATE LESSONS

LESSON 3: NATURAL LANGUAGE SEARCH, EDITING SEARCHES, CHANGING DATABASES, USING DOC AND TERM FEATURES

In this lesson you will learn how to select a database, run a Natural Language search, edit a search, change to a different database, use the Date Restriction feature when searching, use the Require/Exclude Terms feature, and use the Doc and Term features.

If you did not exit Lexis after completing Lesson 2, go directly to Step 6 in the following instructions.

1. Start Windows.
2. Start your Internet browser. Type **www.lexis.com** in the browser and press the **[ENTER]** key.
3. At the ID field, type the Lexis ID supplied by your instructor.
4. At the Password field, enter the Lexis password supplied by your instructor.
5. ***Click Sign In*** to sign on to Lexis.
6. Your screen should now look similar to Lexis Exhibit 1. If your screen does not look like Lexis Exhibit 1, ***click on the Search tab*** (see Lexis Exhibit 1). Lexis is highly customizable, so it is possible that your screens will look different from the screens in the exhibits.
7. You will now look for a case in federal court in which an attorney committed fraud by retaining settlement funds of a client in litigation and breached his fiduciary duty to the client.
8. ***Click Federal Court Cases, Combined;*** this is under the Cases – U.S. section (see Lexis Exhibit 2).
9. The Lexis search screen (Enter Search Terms) should now be displayed (see Lexis Exhibit 11).

LEXIS EXHIBIT 11

10. ***Click Natural Language*** (see Lexis Exhibit 11). You will now type a plain-English search request into the "Federal Court Cases, Combined" database using Lexis's Natural Language feature.

11. In the search box, type **attorney fraud settlement**; ***then click Search*** (see Lexis Exhibit 11).
12. Depending on how Lexis was set up on your computer, your search will most likely return 20 or more cases. In Lexis Exhibit 12, almost 100 cases were retrieved. This is too many cases to look through.

LEXIS EXHIBIT 12

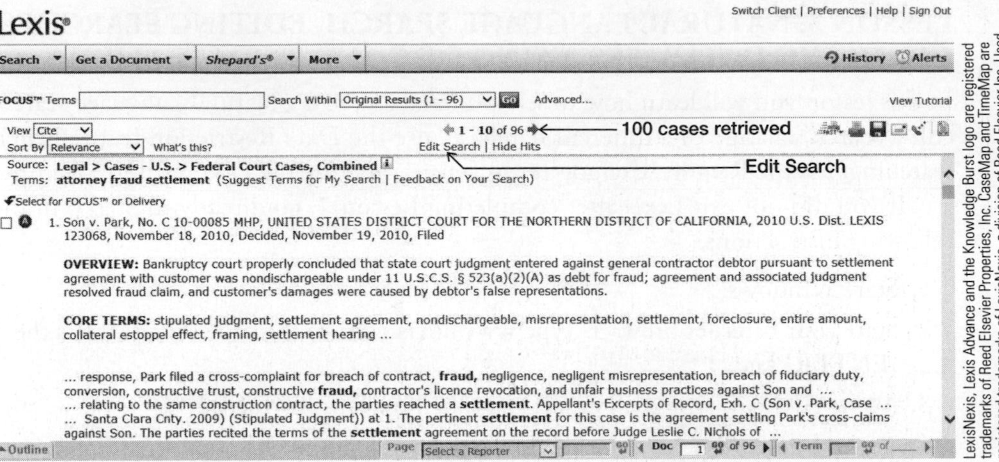

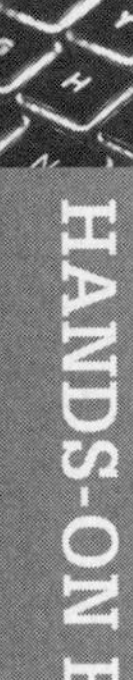

13. There are two main problems with the search as currently constructed. First, you are searching in an enormous database; second, you need to use more search terms to reduce the number of cases retrieved.
14. ***Click Edit Search,*** just above the first case that is listed (see Lexis Exhibit 12). You should be taken back to the Lexis Search screen. You will now look at the scope of the database to see exactly what database you are searching in.
15. ***Click the Source Description symbol.*** (It looks like a white square with a lower-case "i" in the middle of it and is just to the left of "Federal Court Cases, Combined," just above the Search field.)
16. Notice the information about the database that is listed, including file name, coverage, and so on.
17. Scroll down to see just how large the database is. This database happens to be extremely large, and contains tens of thousands of cases. When you search in a large database like this, you need more search terms, not fewer.
18. ***Click the Close icon*** (a red square with a white X) ***in the "Source Information" window.***
19. It can sometimes be more efficient to search in a smaller database than a larger one. You will now learn how to change your database.
20. ***Click Cases – U.S.,*** which is just to the left of Federal Court Cases, Combined.
21. ***Click All Courts – By Circuit on the right side of the screen.***
22. ***Click on 4th Circuit – Federal & State Cases, Combined.*** You will now be searching state and federal cases in the Fourth Circuit only. This is a narrower database than "All Federal Cases."
23. Even with a smaller database, this search would retrieve a large number of cases. You need to refine your search and include additional search terms.
24. In the search box, in addition to "attorney fraud settlement," type the following: **"legal malpractice" "fiduciary duty" conversion** (see Lexis Exhibit 13). The quotation marks around "legal malpractice" and "fiduciary duty" force Lexis to search for these exact phrases.

LEXIS EXHIBIT 13

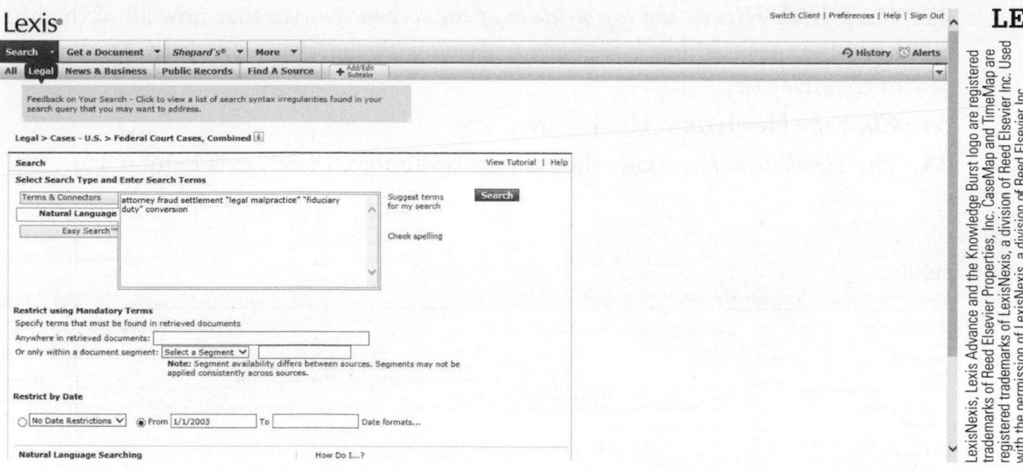

25. Another way to limit the number of cases retrieved is to restrict the dates of the cases retrieved. In the Restrict by Date section at the bottom of the screen, ***click in the From field*** and type **1/1/2003.**

26. Another way to limit the number of cases retrieved is to require some or all of the search terms to appear in the case(s). In the Restrict using Mandatory Terms section, ***click in the Anywhere in retrieved documents: field*** and type **attorney settlement "legal malpractice" "fiduciary duty."**

27. Double-check that there are no misspellings in your search query.

28. ***Click Search. Click Show Hits in the top middle of the screen.*** Your screen should now look similar to Lexis Exhibit 14.

29. Lexis should return a much smaller number of cases. One of the cases that should have been retrieved is *Hewlette v. Hovis,* 318 F. Supp. 2d 332 (E.D. Va., May 19, 2004).

30. Scroll down through the cases and notice that all of the search terms are highlighted in these cases (see Lexis Exhibit 14). If you have many cases to look through, this level of detail may or may not be helpful. Lexis refers to showing the search terms like this as showing the "hits." You will now use the Hide Hits feature to make the search terms disappear so that you see only the Overview and Core Terms sections of the cases.

31. Press the **[HOME]** key to go back to the beginning of the cases.

LEXIS EXHIBIT 14

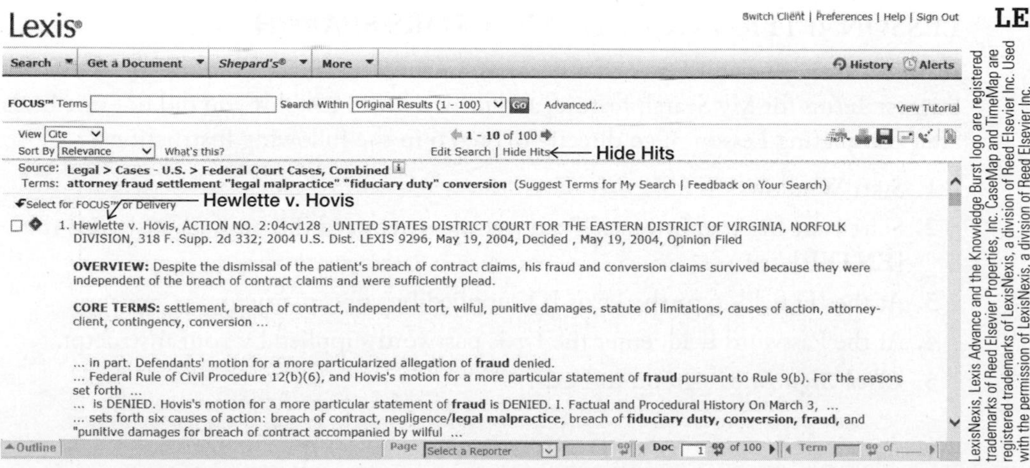

32. ***Click Hide Hits in the top middle of the screen.*** Notice that now all of the hits have disappeared; they have been replaced with the Overview and Core Terms of the first case.
33. ***Click the* Hewlette v. Hovis *case.***
34. The *Hewlette v. Hovis* case should now be displayed (see Lexis Exhibit 15).

LEXIS EXHIBIT 15

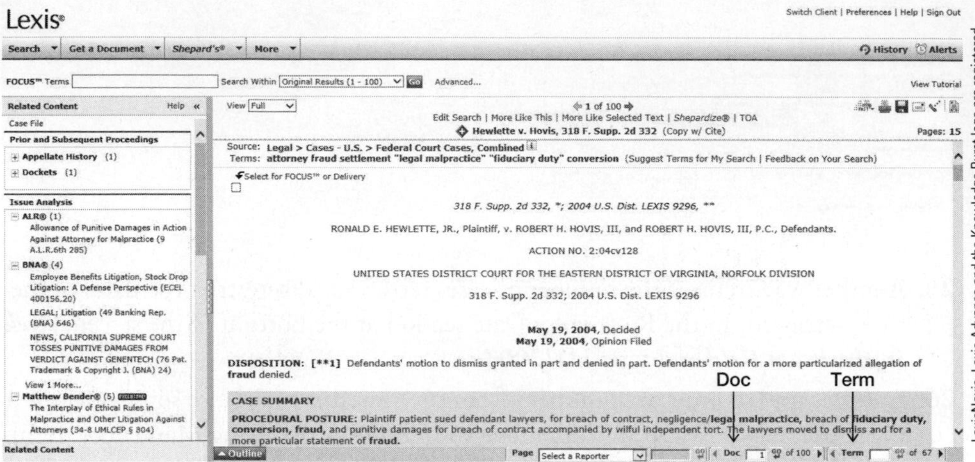

35. Scroll down and notice that the search terms are highlighted in the Case Summary.
36. At the bottom of the screen in the Navigation Frame is the Term field with two arrowheads. ***Click the right one.*** Each time you click, Lexis takes you to the next search term in your case (see Lexis Exhibit 15). You could look backward for your search terms in the document by clicking the left (previous) arrow.
37. ***Click the right arrow to the right of Term at the bottom of the screen in the Navigation Frame*** to continue to move through the *Hewlette* case.
38. ***Click the right arrow next to Doc to go to the next case.*** The Doc arrows allow you to move forward and backward through the retrieved cases.
39. ***Click the left arrow next to Doc*** to go back to the *Hewlette* case.
40. ***Click the Search tab in the upper left of the screen.***

This concludes Lesson 3 of the Lexis Hands-On Exercises. To exit Lexis, ***click Sign Out on the toolbar,*** or stay in Lexis and go to Lesson 4.

LESSON 4: TERMS AND CONNECTORS SEARCH

In this lesson you will learn how to search using Terms and Connectors, use the Suggest Terms for My Search feature, and print a list of cases. If you did not exit Lexis after completing Lesson 3, go directly to Step 6 in the following instructions.

1. Start Windows.
2. Start your Internet browser. Type **www.lexis.com** in the browser and press the **[ENTER]** key.
3. At the ID field, type the Lexis ID supplied by your instructor.
4. At the Password field, enter the Lexis password supplied by your instructor.
5. ***Click Sign In*** to sign on to Lexis.

HANDS-ON EXERCISES

6. Your screen should now look similar to Lexis Exhibit 1. If your screen does not look like Lexis Exhibit 1, ***click the Search tab*** (see Lexis Exhibit 1). Lexis is highly customizable, so it is possible that your screens will look different from the screens in the exhibits.
7. You will again look for federal court cases in which an attorney committed fraud by retaining settlement funds for a client in litigation and breached his fiduciary duty to the client. This time, however, you will search using Terms and Connectors instead of Natural Language.
8. Under Cases – U.S., click Federal Court Cases, Combined. Make sure that Terms and Connectors is selected in the Search window and type **attorney /p fraud /p malpractice.** See Lexis Exhibit 16. ***Click Search.***

LEXIS EXHIBIT 16

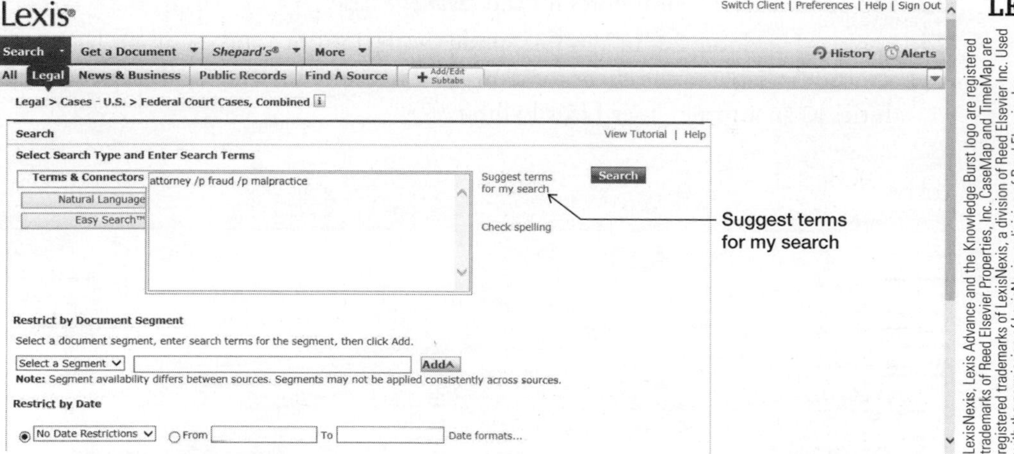

9. Lexis should return over 1400 cases. This is too many cases to look through. By using "/s" (within a sentence) and adding search terms, you can limit the number of cases retrieved.
10. ***Click Edit Search,*** just above the first case.
11. In the search box, modify the query to read **attorney OR lawyer /s fraud /p malpractice /p "fiduciary duty" /p conversion.** ***Then click Suggest terms for my search*** (just to the left of the Search button; see Lexis Exhibit 16). You will use this feature to search for synonyms to refine your search.
12. Notice that a number of synonyms are now listed under Suggested Words and Concepts for Entered Terms.
13. ***Click in the Search field and delete*** **"/p fiduciary duty."**
14. ***Click*** **"breach of fiduciary duty"** ***under Suggested Words and Concepts for Entered Terms.*** Add **/p** in front of **"breach of fiduciary duty."**
15. Your Terms and Connectors search should now read **attorney OR lawyer /s fraud /p malpractice /p conversion /p "breach of fiduciary duty"** (see Lexis Exhibit 16).
16. ***Click Search.***
17. Lexis should return about 59 cases, which is still too many. Lexis allows you to restrict the search by date, so under Restrict by Date, ***click the radio button next to From.*** In the box next to From, type **01/01/2002** and in the box next to To, type **12/31/2005,** then ***click Search.***

18. Lexis should return fewer than five cases and one of them should be *Hewlette v. Hovis.*
19. You will now send the results to your printer. ***Click the Print icon*** in the upper right corner of the screen.
20. The "Deliver Documents – Print" window should now be displayed. ***Select the printer you would like to print to, then click Print.***
21. Scroll down and ***click the*** **Hewlette v. Hovis** ***case.*** Notice that this is the same case that was retrieved using the Natural Language search in Hands-On Exercise Lesson 3.
22. Scroll down just below the Case Summary and notice the heading "LEXISNEXIS HEADNOTES." If you do not see the Headnote, ***click Show,*** just to the right of "LEXISNEXIS HEADNOTES."
23. You should see 11 Headnotes for the *Hewlette* case.
24. Look at Headnote 2 ("In Virginia, under both statutory and common law, an attorney is liable to the client for damages caused by the attorney's neglect of his duties as an attorney"; see Lexis Exhibit 17).

LEXIS EXHIBIT 17

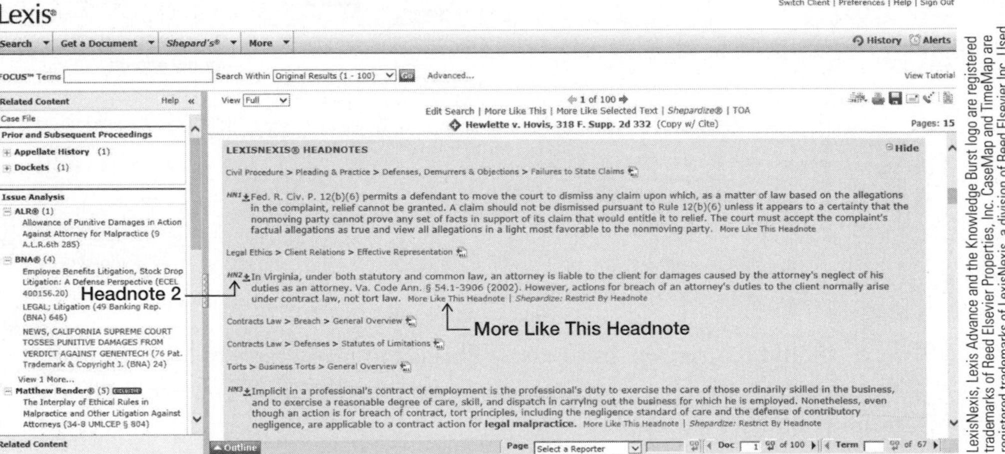

25. Suppose that this was the issue you were researching. To expand your research, you could click the More Like This Headnote option following the Headnote itself.
26. The More Like This Headnote screen is displayed.
27. ***Click the radio button next to Combined Federal Courts: All Federal Courts.***
28. ***Click Search*** at the bottom of the screen.
29. Notice that additional cases with similar Headnotes are retrieved. Headnotes are a quick and convenient way to expand your research.
30. ***Click your browser's Back button twice.*** You should now be back to the screen shown in Lexis Exhibit 17.
31. ***Click on*** **Shepardize:** ***Restrict By Headnote at the end of*** **HN2** (see Lexis Exhibit 17). This feature shows cases that have cited *Hewlette* and that have the same Headnote.

This concludes Lesson 4 of the Lexis Hands-On Exercises. To exit Lexis, ***click Sign Out on the toolbar,*** or stay in Lexis and go to Lesson 5.

ADVANCED LESSON

LESSON 5: *SHEPARD'S CITATIONS*

In this lesson, you will learn how to Shepardize a case, and use the Table of Authorities, Auto-Cite. If you did not exit Lexis after completing Lesson 4, go directly to Step 6 in the following instructions.

1. Start Windows.
2. Start your Internet browser. Type **www.lexis.com** in the browser and press the **[ENTER]** key.
3. At the ID field, type the Lexis ID supplied by your instructor.
4. At the Password field, type the Lexis password supplied by your instructor.
5. ***Click Sign In*** to sign on to Lexis.
6. Your screen should now look similar to Lexis Exhibit 1. If your screen does not look like Lexis Exhibit 1, ***click the Search tab*** (see Lexis Exhibit 1). Lexis is highly customizable, so it is possible that your screens will look different from the screens in the exhibits.
7. ***Click the Shepard's tab*** at the top of the screen.
8. ***Click the Shepard's subtab*** (see Lexis Exhibit 18). ***Click the option Shepard's for Research*** (see Lexis Exhibit 18). The *Hewlette v. Hovis* case, 318 F. Supp. 2d 332, should already be entered, but if it is not, type **318 F. Supp. 2d 332.**

LEXIS EXHIBIT 18

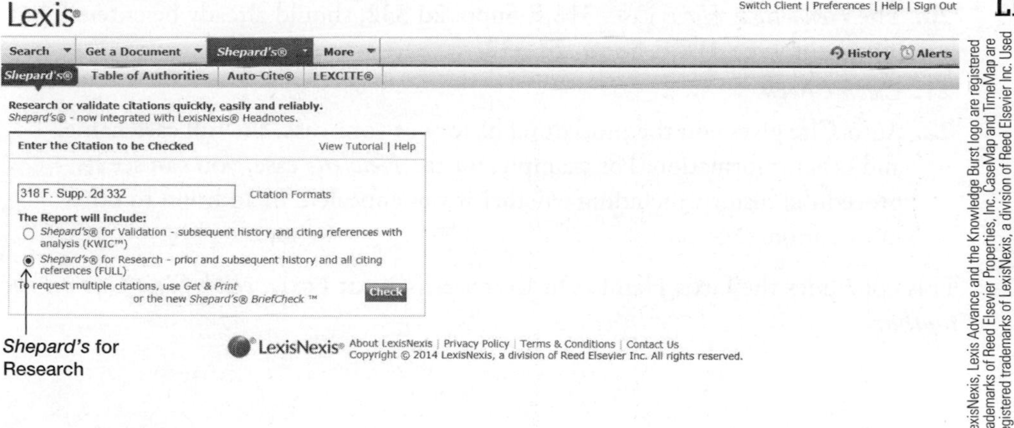

9. ***Click Check.***
10. A screen similar to Lexis Exhibit 19 should be displayed. Notice in Lexis Exhibit 19 that *Shepard's* shows the blue diamond with a white "+" (plus sign) symbol for the *Hewlette v. Hovis* case.
11. Scroll down and notice that this symbol means that the *Hewlette* case has had positive treatment.
12. Also in Lexis Exhibit 19, notice that 28 other cases have cited the *Hewlette* case.
13. ***Click the Shepard's tab*** at the top of the page.
14. ***Click the Table of Authorities subtab.***

LEXIS EXHIBIT 19

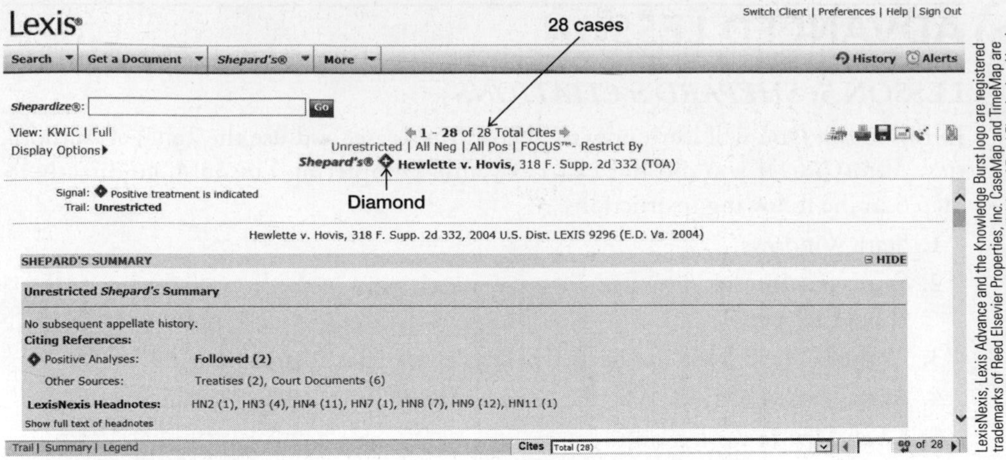

15. The *Hewlette v. Hovis* case, 318 F. Supp. 2d 332, should already be entered, but if it is not, type **318 F. Supp. 2d 332.**
16. ***Click Check.***
17. The Table of Authorities feature allows you to see a summary of all of the law cited by your case, sorted by jurisdiction.
18. ***Click your browser's Back button.***
19. ***Click the Auto-Cite subtab.***
20. The *Hewlette v. Hovis* case, 318 F. Supp. 2d 332, should already be entered, but if it is not, type **318 F. Supp. 2d 332.**
21. ***Click Check.***
22. Auto-Cite gives you the procedural history of your case, the full case name, and other information. For example, for the *Hewlette* case, you can see its procedural history, including whether it was appealed, in addition to other information.

This concludes the Lexis Hands-On Exercises. To exit Lexis, ***click Sign Out on the toolbar.***

HANDS-ON EXERCISES

LEXIS ADVANCE COMPUTER-ASSISTED LEGAL RESEARCH

Number	Lesson Title	Concepts Covered
BASIC LESSON		
Lesson 1	Introduction to LexisAdvance	Signing on; introduction to the Lexis Advance interface; conducting a basic search; filtering search results by content type, jurisdiction, and practice type and topic
INTERMEDIATE LESSON		
Lesson 2	Searching using the Browse Tools History, and Working with a Document	Browse Sources, Browse Topics, History, Maneuvering within a Document, Working with a Document
ADVANCED LESSON		
Lesson 3	Alerts and *Shepard's Citations*	Creating Alerts and Using *Shepards's Citations*

GETTING STARTED

Introduction

Throughout these lessons and exercises, information you need to type into the software will be designated in several different ways:

- Keys to be pressed on the keyboard are designated in brackets, in all caps, and in bold (e.g., press the **[ENTER]** key).
- Movements with the mouse pointer are designated in bold and italics (e.g., ***point to File and click***).
- Words or letters that should be typed are designated in bold (e.g., type **Training Program**).
- Information that is or should be displayed on your computer screen is shown in bold, with quotation marks (e.g., **"Press ENTER to continue."**).
- Specific menu items and commands are designated with an initial capital letter (e.g., click Open).

BASIC LESSON

LESSON 1: INTRODUCTION TO LEXIS ADVANCE

This lesson introduces you to LexisNexis. You will learn how to sign on to Lexis Advance, take a tour of the Lexis Advance interface, and see how some basic research tools are used within Lexis Advance.

1. Start Windows.
2. Start your Internet browser. Type **www.lexisadvance.com** in the browser and press the [ENTER] **key.**
3. At the ID field, type the Lexis Advance ID supplied by your instructor.

4. At the Password field, type the Lexis Advance password supplied by your instructor.
5. ***Click Sign In*** to sign on to Lexis Advance.
6. Your screen should now look similar to Lexis Advance Exhibit 1 (see Lexis Advance Exhibit 1).This is the Lexis Advance Home page. If at any time, you wish to return to this screen, ***click the Lexis Advance logo on any screen.***

LEXIS ADVANCE EXHIBIT 1

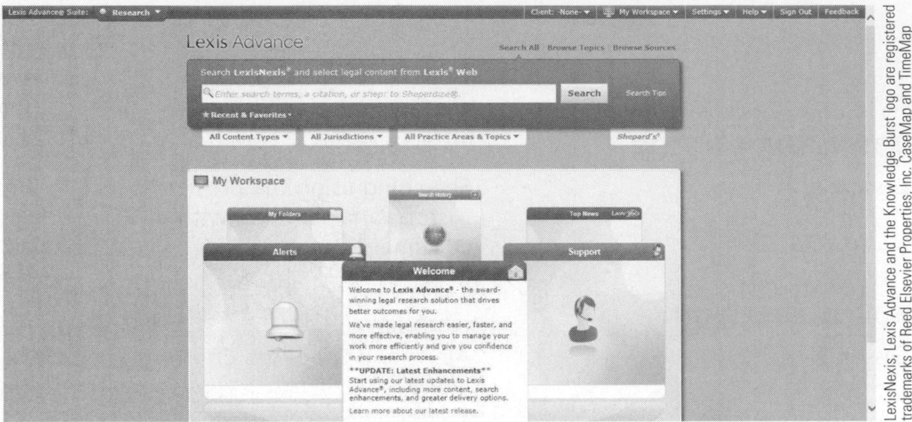

7. You will now take a brief tour of Lexis Advance. The Home page shows a series of tiles: Welcome, Support, Top News, Alerts, My Folders and Search History. ***Click the Support tile.*** The Support tile provides access to Help menus and tutorials. ***Click the Top News tile.*** The Top News tile shows you the latest law-related news. The Alerts tile will list any alerts you have created. (Alerts will be discussed in a later lesson.) The Search History will list your latest search history. (At this point, both the Alerts and Search History tiles will be empty.)
8. The text box located near the top of the screen is where you enter your search tab terms. Immediately below the Search text box are filters that you may use to narrow and refine your search. (See Lexis Advance Exhibit 1.) These filters include "All Content Types," "All Jurisdictions," and "All Practice Areas & Topics."
9. In the Search text box, type **attractive nuisance.** Notice that as you type, Lexis Advance suggests possible search terms. ***Click Search***. (See LexisNexis Exhibit 1.)
10. Your screen should now look like Lexis Advance Exhibit 2 (please note the specific cases you retrieve may vary as legal research is fluid and always subject to change). Unless you specify otherwise, Lexis Advance will retrieve items from all content types (cases, statutes, regulations, secondary sources, forms, etc.). By default, Lexis Advance displays the relevant cases first. In this example, the search retrieved over 3,000 cases (and by clicking the link for Expanded Results, produces over 70,000 cases). By default, Lexis Advance has sorted the cases by relevance. You can choose other methods of sorting the search results (Document Title, Jurisdiction, Court, and Date). ***Click the drop-down menu next to Sort by and click Date (Newest-Oldest).*** Notice how recent the first case is. It is possible that the case now listed as the first search result was decided no more than a day or two ago. Now ***click Snapshot*** (see Lexis Advance Exhibit 2). This gives you a quick look at the most relevant search results from a variety of content types. See Lexis Advance Exhibit 3. Here you can see, at a glance, relevant Cases, Statutes and Legislation, Secondary Materials, Briefs, Pleadings, and Motions, and Administrative Materials. ***Scroll down this page*** to see other Content Types such as Jury Instructions and Forms. ***Scroll back to the top of the screen and click on some of the other content types.***

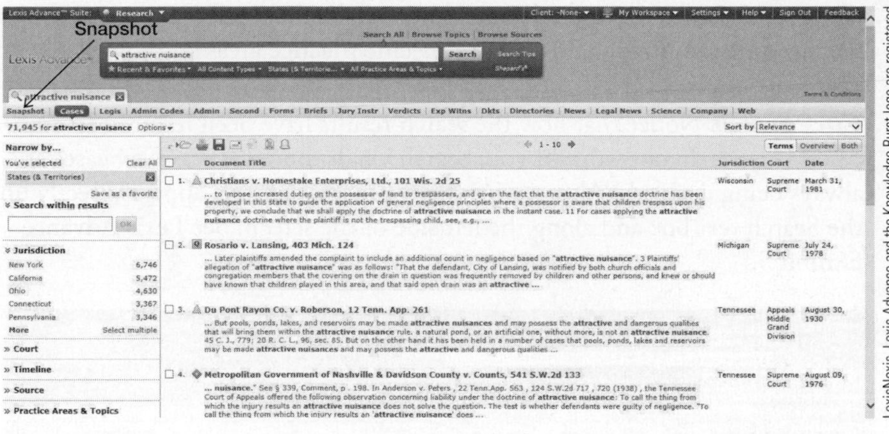

LEXIS ADVANCE EXHIBIT 2

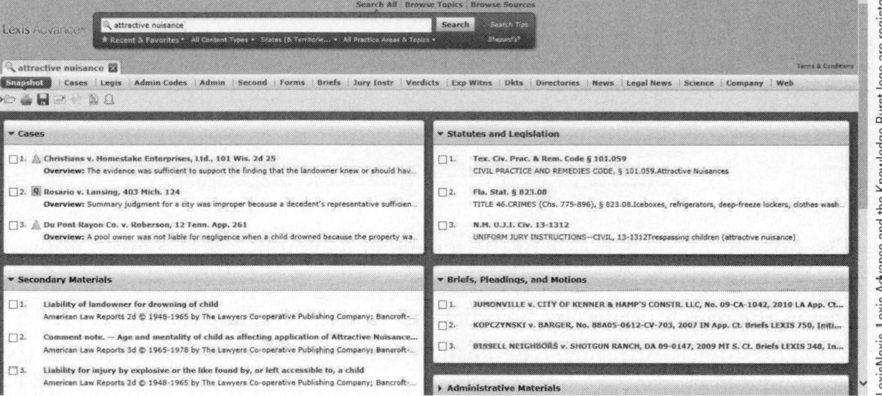

LEXIS ADVANCE EXHIBIT 3

11. ***Click Cases*** again. As noted in step 8, Lexis Advance gives you the ability to filter your results. ***Click All Content Types*** and the All Content Types dialog box will open. Here you can filter your search to include only the specific content types desired. ***Click the box next to Cases (a checkmark will appear), then click OK.***
12. ***Click All Jurisdictions*** and a dialog box will open. Here you can filter your search to include only the states or territories desired. ***Click the box next to Georgia (a checkmark will appear), then click OK.*** See Lexis Advance Exhibit 4.

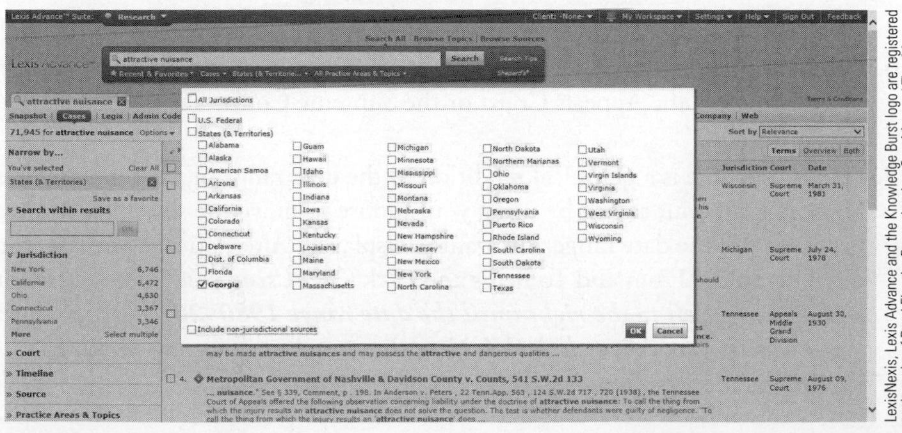

LEXIS ADVANCE EXHIBIT 4

13. ***Click All Practice Areas and Topics*** and a dialog box will open. Here you can filter your search to include only the specific practice areas and topics desired. ***Click the box next to Torts (a checkmark will appear), then click OK.***
14. ***Click Search.*** Notice that now the search results have been reduced to 842 cases. (Again, do not worry if your search yields more cases as new cases are always being decided.) Also, notice that your search filters appear directly under the Search text box and along the left side of the screen. See Lexis Advance Exhibit 5.

LEXIS ADVANCE EXHIBIT 5

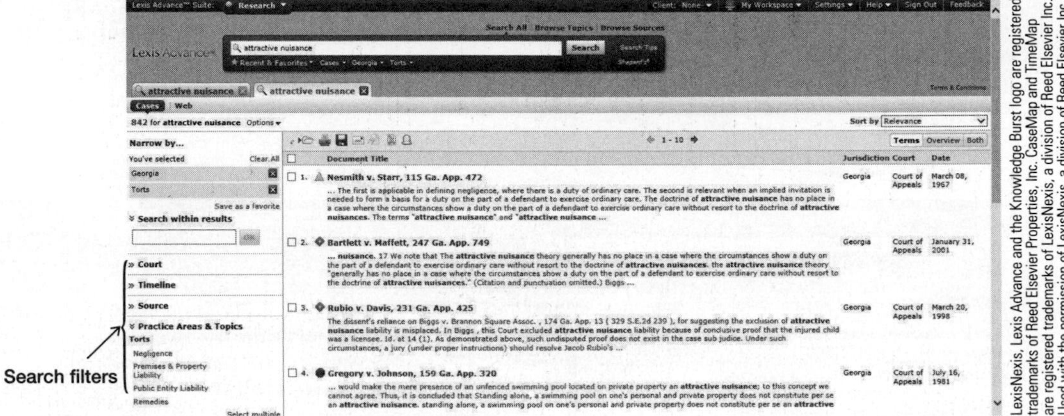
Search filters
LexisNexis, Lexis Advance and the Knowledge Burst logo are registered trademarks of Reed Elsevier Properties, Inc. CaseMap and TimeMap are registered trademarks of LexisNexis, a division of Reed Elsevier Inc. Used with the permission of LexisNexis, a division of Reed Elsevier Inc.

15. The options on the left side of the screen allow you to search within your results. You can narrow your search by searching for specific terms or phrases within the search results, by Jurisdiction, Court, Timeline, Source, Practice Area and Topics, Attorney, Law Firm, Most Cited, Keyword, and Judge. (Note that you will have to scroll down the page to see all of these options.) See Lexis Advance Exhibit 6.

LEXIS ADVANCE EXHIBIT 6

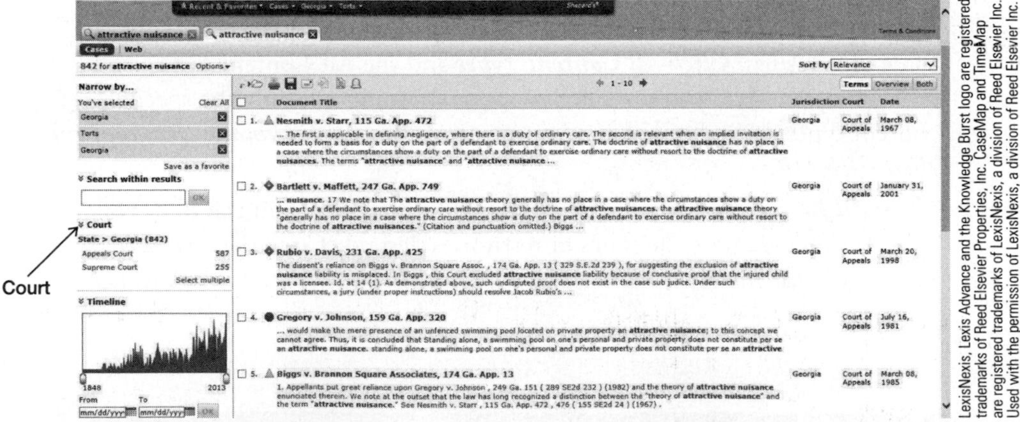
Court
LexisNexis, Lexis Advance and the Knowledge Burst logo are registered trademarks of Reed Elsevier Properties, Inc. CaseMap and TimeMap are registered trademarks of LexisNexis, a division of Reed Elsevier Inc. Used with the permission of LexisNexis, a division of Reed Elsevier Inc.

16. Click the heading Court. Notice that this gives you the opportunity to select cases from only the Appeals Court or the Supreme Court. See Lexis Advance Exhibit 6.
17. Under Timeline is a graphical rendition of the date range of the cases retrieved. You can limit your search by using your mouse to move the sliders to the left or right until the date range you want is displayed. Alternatively, you can enter the dates in the From and To fields and click OK. ***Using your mouse, move the sliders on the left to the right until the date range 1980–2013 (or the current year) is displayed, then click OK.*** Now there are just 369 cases retrieved (again, the precise number of cases you retrieve may vary).

18. Now that the search results have been filtered, there are several options for preserving the results of the search. To download the results, ***click the Save icon*** (it looks like a floppy disk). See Lexis Advance Exhibit 2. The Download window opens, providing the opportunity to save the search results as a PDF or Docx (Microsoft Word file). ***Click Cancel in the Download window.*** To email the results, ***click the email icon*** (it looks like an envelope). See Lexis Advance Exhibit 2. The Email window opens, providing the opportunity to select up to five recipients, compose the text of the email and select the format of the emailed documents (PDF or Docx). ***Click Cancel*** in the Email window. Options to print and save to a folder are also available.
19. ***Scroll down until you see the case Gregory v. Johnson, 249 Ga. 151. Click on that case.*** Your screen should now look like Lexis Advance Exhibit 7. Scroll down through the case and you will see that the search terms are in bold text. You will also see a summary of the case and headnotes describing the specific legal issues raised in the case.

LEXIS ADVANCE EXHIBIT 7

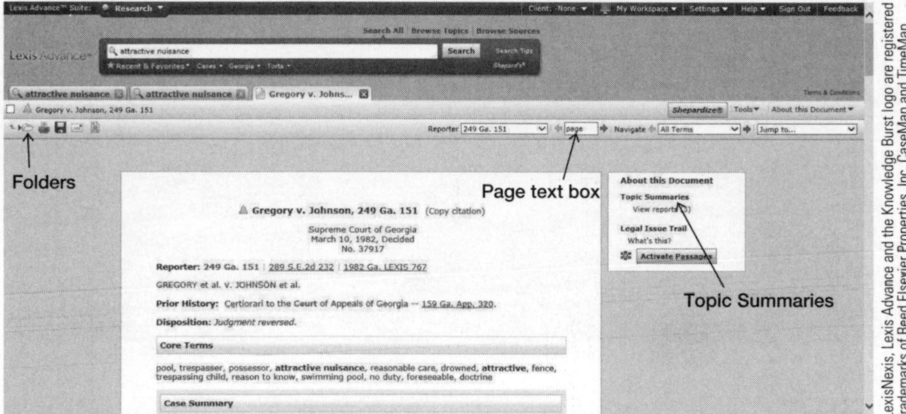

20. There are several tools available from this screen. To Shepardize this case, ***click Shepardize on the menu bar*** (see Lexis Advance Exhibit 7). (Alternatively, you could ***click the yellow triangle to the left of the case name,*** see Lexis Advance Exhibit 7.) If it is not already selected, click Citing Decisions. Your screen should now look like Lexis Advance Exhibit 8. (Remember that as the case law changes, the results will change.) You can see which cases follow or are distinguished from the Gregory case. Citing Decisions lists the cases that have cited *Gregory v. Johnson*. Appellate History lists other appellate cases directly related to this case. ***Click the small x in the Shepard's tab to close it.***

LEXIS EXHIBIT 8

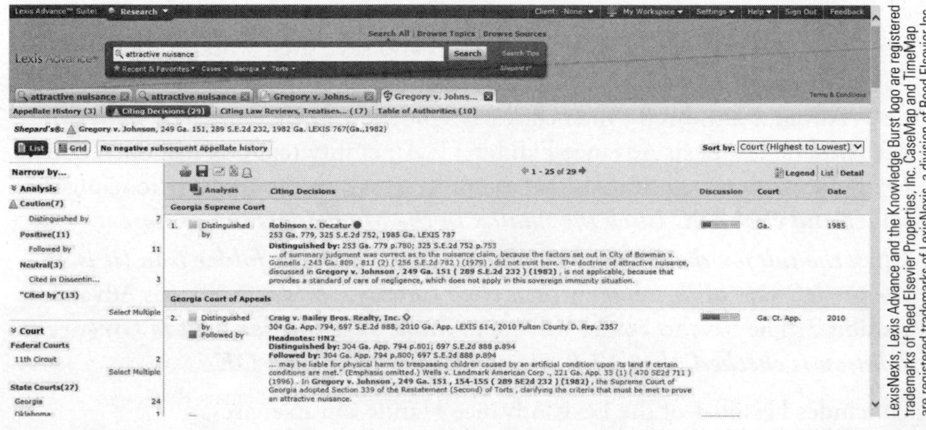

21. Your screen should again look like Lexis Advance Exhibit 7. Lexis Advance offers Topic Summaries—short articles on issues of law raised by the case. ***Click View Reports (3) under Topic Summaries.*** Your screen should now look like Lexis Advance Exhibit 9. ***Click on the first topic listed Torts > Premises and Property Liability > Trespass to Real Property.*** You can now read the Topic Summary: Trespass to Real Property if you wish. ***Click the small x in the Trespass to Real Property tab and the Topic Summaries tabs to close those tabs.***
22. You should now be back at the *Gregory v. Johnson* case. Now you will use the Legal Issue Trail tool. The Legal Issue Trail lists cases that cite to the case you are viewing as well as cases your case has cited for a specific legal issue or point of law. ***Click Activate Passages and then click in the passage highlighted in Lexis Advance Exhibit 10.*** The next screen will list the cases retrieved by *Shepard's* for that particular issue.

LEXIS ADVANCE EXHIBIT 9

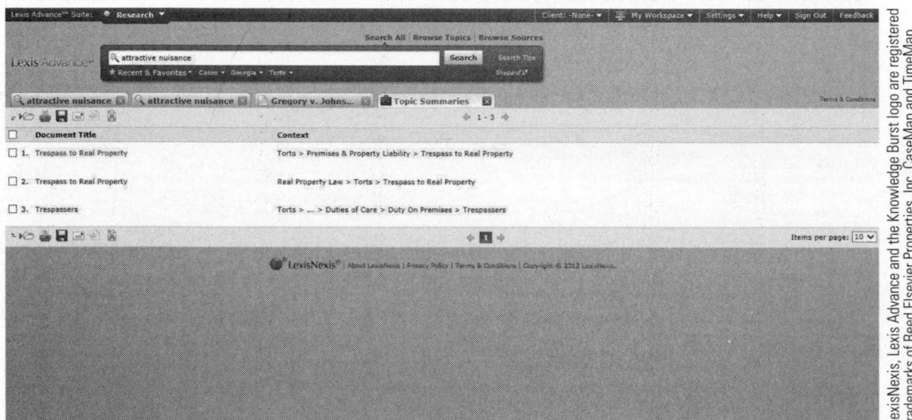

LEXIS ADVANCE EXHIBIT 10

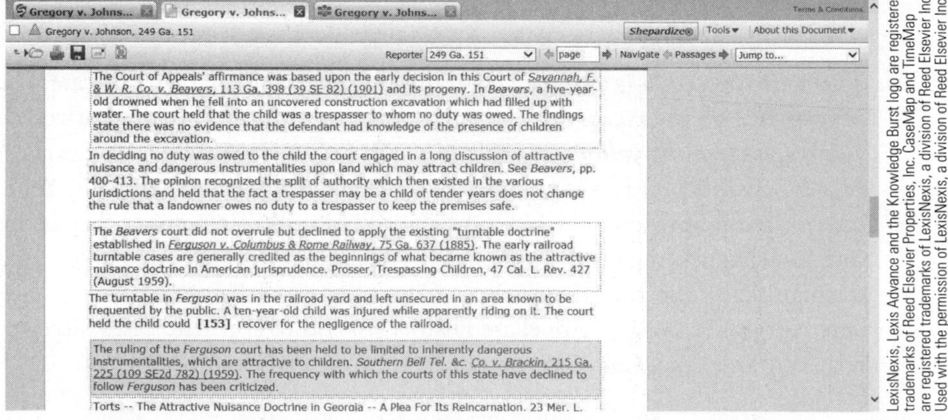

23. Lexis Advance allows users to create folders and save their work in those folders. Click the drop-down arrow next to My Workspace at the top of the screen (see Lexis Advance Exhibit 8), then click My Folders. ***Click Create new folder in My Folders.*** See Lexis Advance Exhibit 11. An empty text box will open under My Folders. Type your initials (for example, MSC) in the text box to name the folder ***and click OK. Click the small x in the My Folders tab to close it.***
24. ***Click the tab for the Gregory v. Johnson case. Click the folder icon (it is at the far left side of the screen), then click Choose a folder.*** See Lexis Advance Exhibit 7. The Save to Folder will open. ***Make sure the box next to Gregory v. Johnson is checked, then click on your folder, then click OK.***

This concludes Lesson 1 of the Lexis Advance Hands-On Exercises.

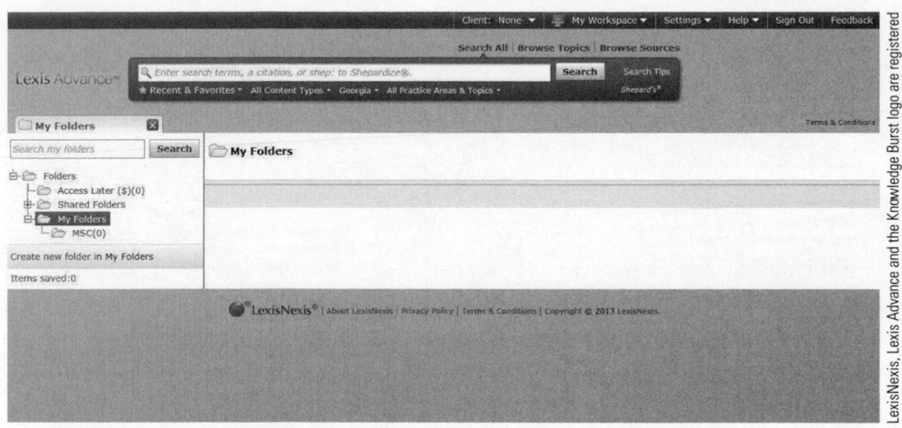

LexisNexis, Lexis Advance and the Knowledge Burst logo are registered trademarks of Reed Elsevier Properties, Inc. CaseMap and TimeMap are registered trademarks of LexisNexis, a division of Reed Elsevier Inc. Used with the permission of LexisNexis, a division of Reed Elsevier Inc.

LEXIS ADVANCE EXHIBIT 11

LESSON 2: INTERMEDIATE LESSON

In this lesson, you will learn about the Browse Sources and Browse Topics search tools; using the History tool; maneuvering within a case; and, using text from a document in Lexis Advance.

1. Start Windows.
2. Start your Internet browser. Type **www.lexisadvance.com** in the browser and press the [ENTER] key.
3. At the ID field, type the Lexis Advance ID supplied by your instructor.
4. At the Password field, type the Lexis Advance password supplied by your instructor.
5. ***Click Sign In*** to sign on to Lexis Advance.
6. Your screen should now look similar to Lexis Advance Exhibit 1 (see Lexis Advance Exhibit 1).This is the Lexis Advance Home page. If at any time, you wish to return to this screen, ***click the Lexis Advance logo on any screen.***
7. You will now learn about other search functions available on Lexis Advance. ***Click Browse Sources.*** See Lexis Advance Exhibit 12. Your screen should now look like Lexis Advance Exhibit 12. From this screen you can search through all of the sources available to you. You can use this as a filter to limit your search results to just the specific sources selected. ***Click the letter H and then scroll down and click on Harvard Law Review.*** You now have the option to View all information for this source, Add this source to your search, and Get source documents. ***Click on View all information for this source.*** A new tab opens with information about this specific source. ***Click the small x in the Harvard Law Review tab to close it.***

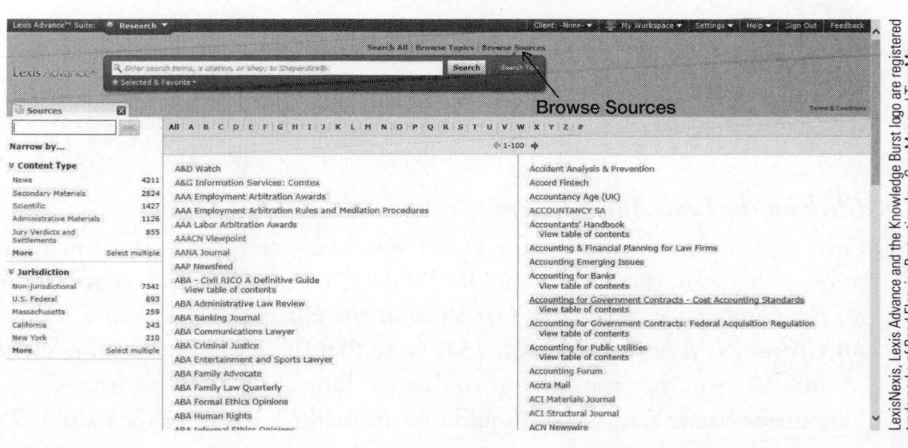

LexisNexis, Lexis Advance and the Knowledge Burst logo are registered trademarks of Reed Elsevier Properties, Inc. CaseMap and TimeMap are registered trademarks of LexisNexis, a division of Reed Elsevier Inc. Used with the permission of LexisNexis, a division of Reed Elsevier Inc.

LEXIS ADVANCE EXHIBIT 12

LEXIS ADVANCE EXHIBIT 13

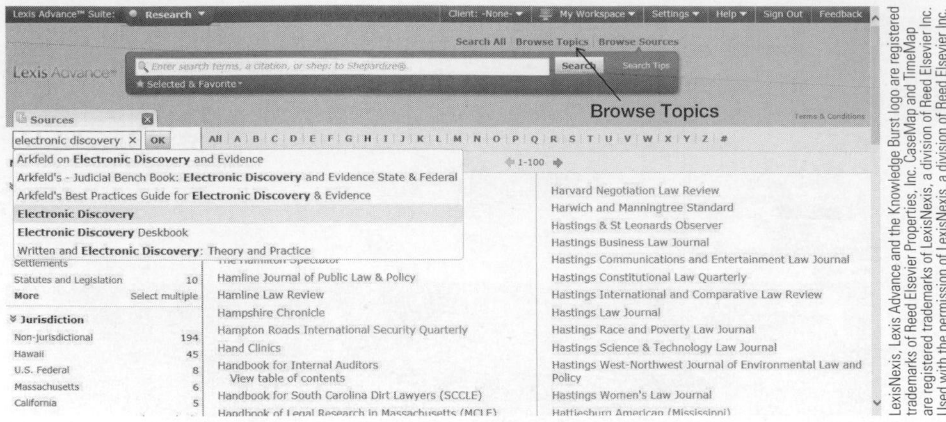

8. You can also search for a source if you do not know the name of that source. In the Search Sources text box, slowly type **electronic discovery.** Notice that as you type, various sources are suggested. From the list of suggested search topics, ***click on Electronic Discovery.*** See Lexis Advance Exhibit 13. You can now see all of the sources related to electronic discovery in Lexis Advance.
9. ***Click on the Lexis Advance logo to return to the Home page. Click Browse Topics.*** Your screen should now look like Lexis Advance Exhibit 14. You can use this as a filter to limit your search results to just the specific topics selected. ***Click Civil Procedure, then click Discovery & Disclosure.*** In the small pop-up window, you can now see how to search within this topic. You can also search for a topic that is not shown on this screen. ***Click the small x in the pop-up window to close it.*** In the Search for topics text box, slowly type **electronic discovery.** Notice that as you type, various sources are suggested. ***Click Search.*** Now you can see a list of the specific practice areas containing references to electronic discovery. The green icons next to the items denote the number of such references. By clicking on a green icon, you will be able to see the precise practice areas.

LEXIS ADVANCE EXHIBIT 14

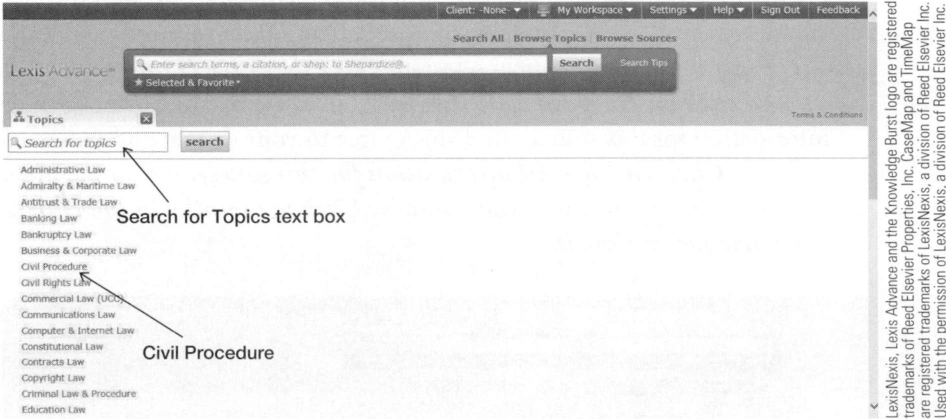

10. ***Click on the Lexis Advance logo to return to the Home page.***
11. Lexis Advance automatically stores your searches, search terms, documents and other activities in the History tool for 90 days. ***Click the Search History panel on the Home page, then click List View at the bottom of that panel. Click on Gregory v. Johnson, 249 Ga. 151.*** Note that there will be several references to this case; you may click on any of them as long as under Type, it says Document View. Your screen should now look like Lexis Advance Exhibit 7.

12. When viewing a document in Lexis Advance, you can see it in alternative formats. For example, *Gregory v. Johnson* is published in the Georgia Reports, but it is also published in the Southeastern Reporter. To see a different version (perhaps to note the page on which a particular quotation may be found), ***click the down-arrow next to Reporter***. See Lexis Advance Exhibit 7. Notice that the same case may be found at 289 S.E.2d 232 and at 1982 Ga. Lexis 767.
13. To move to another page within the case, type **153** in the page text box. See Lexis Advance Exhibit 7. You should now see the part of the case that appears on page 153.
14. To move to another section of the document, click the down-arrow next to Jump to . . . You can now select a different section of the case to view (e.g., Prior History, Disposition, Core Terms, Case Summary, Procedural Posture, Overview, Outcome, and LexisNexis Headnotes). ***Click Outcome.*** You should see the section of this document detailing the outcome of this case. If you had retrieved this case from a Lexis Advance search, you would also be able to move to the specific sections of the case where your search terms are located.
15. ***Click the Jump to... drop-down menu and select Top of Document*** to return to the beginning of this document. See Lexis Advance Exhibit 15. ***Click Tools and then select Copy Citation***. See Lexis Advance Exhibit 15. The Copy Citation to Clipboard window opens. This gives you the ability to copy the full case citation into the document you are writing. You have the options to include the parallel citations and to create a hyperlink back to the full text of the case. ***Click Close*** in the Copy Citation to Clipboard window.
16. The text of a document may be utilized in several ways. ***Select and highlight a paragraph from Gregory v. Johnson.*** Notice that the Options for Selected Text box opens. See Lexis Advance Exhibit 15. The options include copying the selected text to a clipboard, saving the selected text to a folder, searching within the selected text, creating an annotation (a note up to 4,000 characters) about the selected text, and highlighting the selected text. Click anywhere on the document to undo the highlight. Alternatively, ***click the down-arrow next to Tools*** (see Lexis Advance Exhibit 15) to access these same options. Click anywhere on the document to close that window.

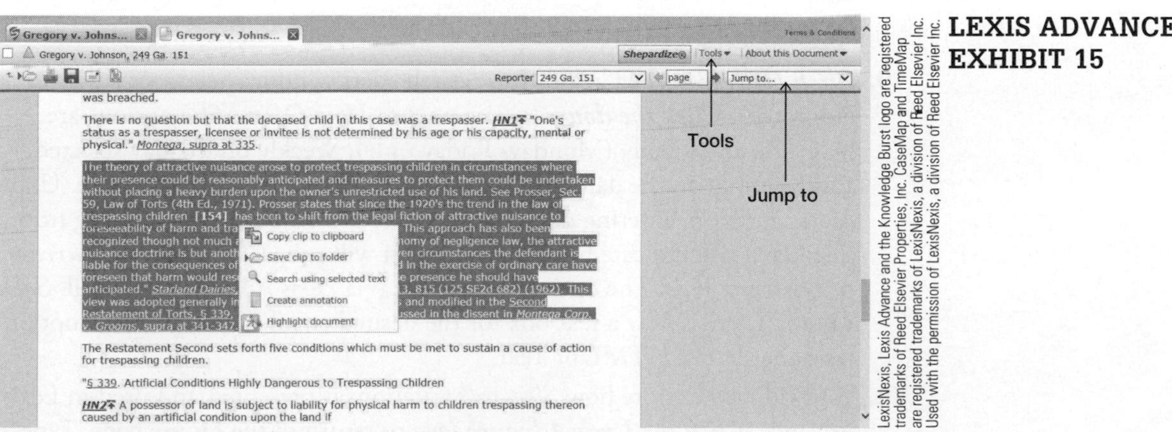

LEXIS ADVANCE EXHIBIT 15

This concludes Lesson 2 of the Lexis Advance Hands-On Exercises.

LESSON 3: ADVANCED LESSON

In this lesson, you will learn how to use Alerts and *Shepard's Citations* in Lexis Advance.

1. Start Windows.
2. Start your Internet browser. Type **www.lexisadvance.com** in the browser and press the [ENTER] key.
3. At the ID field, type the Lexis Advance ID supplied by your instructor.
4. At the Password field, type the Lexis Advance password supplied by your instructor.
5. ***Click Sign In*** to sign on to Lexis Advance.
6. Your screen should now look similar to Lexis Advance Exhibit 1 (see Lexis Advance Exhibit 1).This is the Lexis Advance Home page. If at any time, you wish to return to this screen, ***click the Lexis Advance logo on any screen.***
7. Lexis Advance offers the option of creating alerts. An alert is a search that is set to run automatically and provide notification of new search results. To set an alert, it is necessary to first conduct a search or Shepardize a citation.
8. Type attractive nuisance in the Search text box and ***click Search. Click the Alert icon (it looks like a bell).*** See Lexis Advance Exhibit 2. The Create New Search Alert window will open. See Lexis Advance Exhibit 16. The alert can retrieve all content types or just the ones specified. If Cases is not already checked, ***click the box next to Cases so it is checked.***

LEXIS ADVANCE EXHIBIT 16

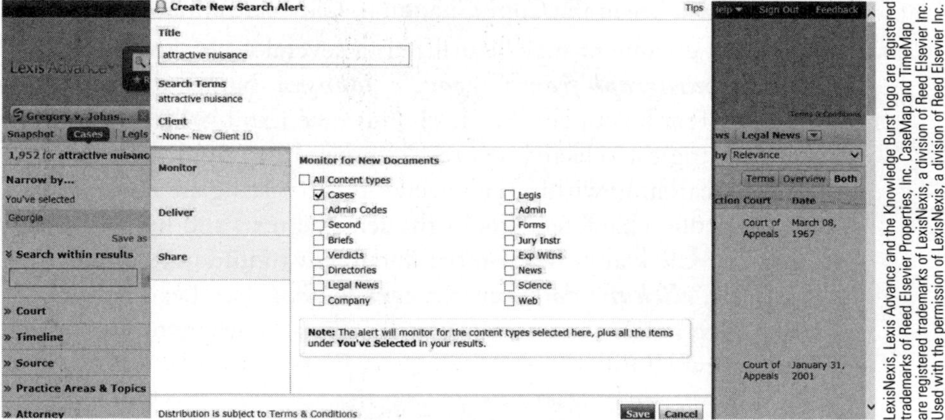

9. ***Click Deliver*** in the Create New Search Alert window. See Lexis Advance Exhibit 16. ***Click the down-arrow next to How Often.*** The options are Daily, Business Daily (Monday–Friday only), Weekly on the day selected, and Monthly on the date selected. The default option of Daily is fine. Under Alert Duration, entering dates in the From and To boxes (or selecting from the calendars) will indicate how long this alert will run. ***Click the down-arrow next to Delivery Type.*** The options are online (via Lexis Advance) or email. ***Select Email.*** There is now a text box for the desired email address and the option to send the alert as HTML or Text.
10. You will now explore how *Shepard's* Citations is presented and used in Lexis Advance. ***Click the Lexis Advance logo*** to return to the Home page. Type **249 Ga. 151** in the Search text box and ***click Search.*** Your screen should now look like Lexis Advance Exhibit 7. ***Click Shepardize.*** *Note:* Another method of

Shepardizing a case when you already know the citation would be to type **Shep: 249 Ga. 151** in the Search text box and click Search. Your screen should now look like Lexis Advance Exhibit 17. (Note that legal research is always subject to change as new cases are decided, so your screen may look a little different than the exhibit shown.)

11. *Shepard's* reports are divided into four tabs: Appellate History, Citing Decisions, Citing Law Reviews, Treatises . . . (also includes Annotated Statutes, Court Documents, Restatements and other Secondary Sources), and Table of Authorities. Notice that the number of items retrieved is indicated within each tab. See Lexis Advance Exhibit 17.

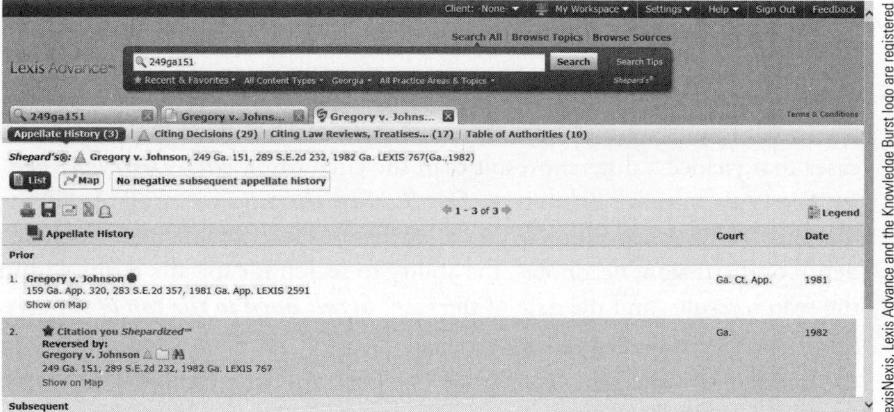

LEXIS ADVANCE EXHIBIT 17

12. If it is not already selected, ***click the Appellate History tab***. You can quickly see that this case has no negative subsequent appellate history—in other words, the case has not been reversed or overruled. See Lexis Advance Exhibit 17. However, there was a prior case that has negative history. Lexis Advance assigns color-coded indicators to cases to quickly inform the user how that case treats the case you are *Shepardizing*. The red indicator next to the first case listed is intended as a warning that this case negatively treats the *Shepardized* case. See Lexis Advance Exhibit 17.

13. In the Appellate History tab, there is an option to see the results in a list or as a graphical map. ***Click Map***. See Lexis Advance Exhibit 17. You can now see how this case went from the state intermediate court of appeals to the state high court and back to the state intermediate court of appeals.

14. ***Click the Citing Decisions tab.*** Your screen should now look like Lexis Advance Exhibit 18. There are 29 cases that have cited *Gregory v. Johnson*, 249 Ga. 151. ***Scroll down the list of cases, then return to the top of the list.*** Notice that each case has a color-coded indicator. (Red = warning; Green = positive; Yellow = Caution; Orange = questioned; Blue = Neutral). ***Click Legend.*** See Lexis Advance Exhibit 18. The Legend window has detailed explanations of all of the symbols and indicators found on this page. ***Click Close*** in the Legend window.

15. Under the Discussion heading, you can see the *Shepard's* depth of discussion indicators. See Lexis Advance Exhibit 18. They range from four bars (Analyzed – fully considers the cited reference) to one bar (Cited – cites to the reference with minimal if any discussion).

LEXIS ADVANCE EXHIBIT 18

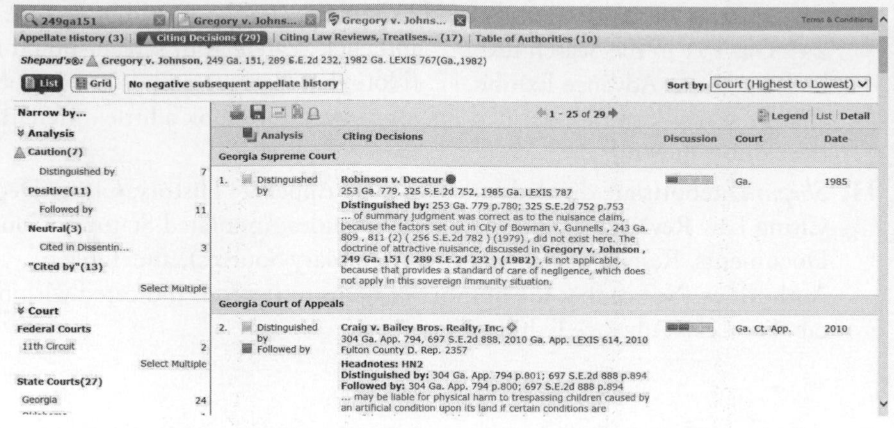

16. On the left side of the screen are a variety of filters that can be used to refine the search results. To find cases that were distinguished from the cited case (i.e., cases that yielded a different result than the cited case), ***click Distinguished by***. See Lexis Advance Exhibit 18. ***Scroll down the page*** to see all of the cases that are distinguished from *Gregory v. Johnson*. Other notable filters include the depth of discussion, headnotes, the ability to search for specific terms within the search results, and the date of the case. ***Scroll back to the top of the screen.***

17. Similar to the Map view in the Appellate History tab, there is a Grid view in the Citing Decisions tab. ***Click Grid***. See Lexis Advance Exhibit 18. The first grid displays the citing cases by court and analysis (i.e., details which cases from which court treated the cited case positively, negatively, etc.). The second grid displays the citing cases by year and analysis (i.e., details which cases from specific years treated the cited case positively, negatively, etc.).

18. ***Click the Citing Law Reviews, Treatises . . .tab***. All secondary sources that have cited *Gregory v. Johnson* are listed here. ***Scroll down*** to see the various law review and legal periodical articles, treatise excerpts, briefs, and motions. Depending on the cited case, the types of secondary material displayed will vary. ***Scroll back to the top of the screen.***

19. ***Click the Table of Authorities tab.*** The Table of Authorities tab displays the cases that the cited case cited (i.e., the cases cited within *Gregory v. Johnson*) as well as the current legal relevance and weight of those cases.

This concludes Lesson 3 of the Lexis Advance Hands-On Exercises.

CHAPTER 10

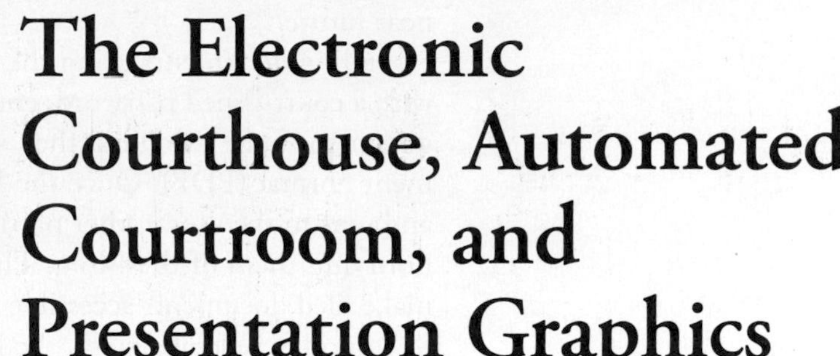

The Electronic Courthouse, Automated Courtroom, and Presentation Graphics

CHAPTER OBJECTIVES

After completing this chapter, you should be able to do the following:

1. Explain what the "electronic courthouse" is.
2. Describe how an automated courtroom works.
3. Describe what presentation software does.
4. Explain how presentation software can be used in the legal environment.

The courthouses of the past, with paper files and manual systems, have changed. Electronic courthouses, which allow electronic filing of court documents and access to court records, dockets, files, and other data via the Internet, are a reality in many jurisdictions. Courtrooms have changed as well. In many jurisdictions, automated courtrooms have evidence display systems, which include computers and monitors for the judge, attorneys, court reporter, jurors, and the public. In these automated courtrooms, presentation graphics and trial presentation software are used to present evidence to the court and jurors electronically, using computers and monitors. The presentations can include text, photographs, video, animation, sound, clip art, re-creations of scenes or actions, and much more.

THE ELECTRONIC COURTHOUSE

The notion of the local courthouse as a place to which legal professionals must mail documents, or where they must hand-file documents and access court records and court files using manual methods, is rapidly disappearing. In many jurisdictions, legal professionals can now instantly file motions, briefs, and other documents electronically, and can instantly access court dockets and court records using the Internet. With electronic filing, courts accept electronic versions of legal documents via the Internet or other electronic means instead of requiring a hard copy of the document to be physically presented.

The federal district and bankruptcy courts have been on the cutting edge of this technology for several years. As of this writing, the Case Management/Electronic Case Filing (CM/ECF) system is used in more than 98 percent of the federal courts: 93 district courts, 93 bankruptcy courts, the Court of International Trade, the Court of Federal Claims, and 10 of the United States Courts of Appeals. To date, more than 41 million cases have been put on the CM/ECF system. More than 700,000 legal professionals have filed documents using the Internet and CM/ECF. The plan is for all United States courts to convert to use of CM/ECF in the near future.

Filing documents using the system is easy. The user logs in to a court's website with a court-issued password, enters some general information about the case and the document to be filed, and then submits the document to be filed in Portable Document Format (PDF). Once the PDF file is received, a notice of receipt is generated and sent to the user. Other parties to the action then automatically receive an email notifying them of the filing. The CM/ECF system also gives courts the option to make filed documents accessible to the public over the Internet.

Another federal system, the Public Access to Court Electronic Records (PACER) program, allows the public to access court-related information (see Exhibit 10–1). PACER is an electronic public access service that allows users to obtain a variety of docket and case-related information regarding federal courts using the Internet. Links to all courts are provided from the PACER website. To access PACER, a user must register with the PACER Service Center, have an Internet connection, and log in to the system. There is also a small charge for the service. PACER allows users to request information about an individual or case, including:

- Party and participant listings, including attorneys and judges
- General case-related data, including the nature of the lawsuit, the cause(s) of action alleged, and the amount of damages requested
- A chronology of events/docket items in the case
- The case status
- Judgment(s) and appeals

Using PACER, a person can also access the United States Case/Party Index, which allows one to search for party names throughout much of the federal court system.

Although the federal court system is rapidly nearing the end of its electronic courthouse implementation project, it may take some years for all the states to catch up. Some states have completed the move to electronic systems, but many are still moving through the implementation stage. Traditional roadblocks to these types of

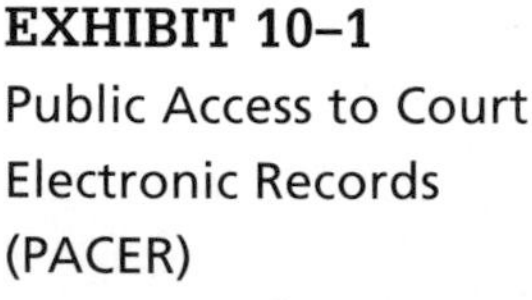

EXHIBIT 10–1
Public Access to Court Electronic Records (PACER)

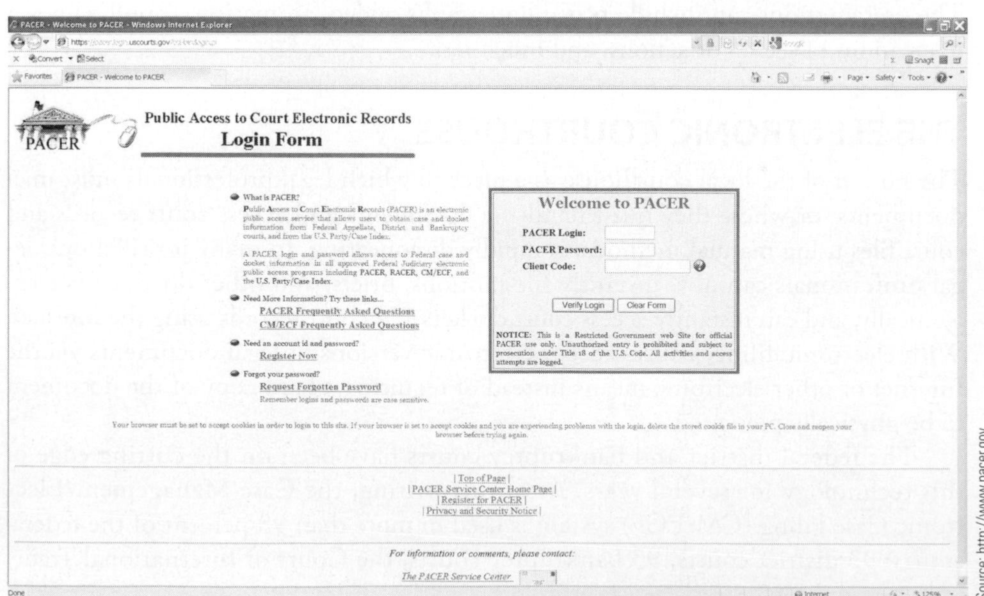

Source: http://www.pacer.gov

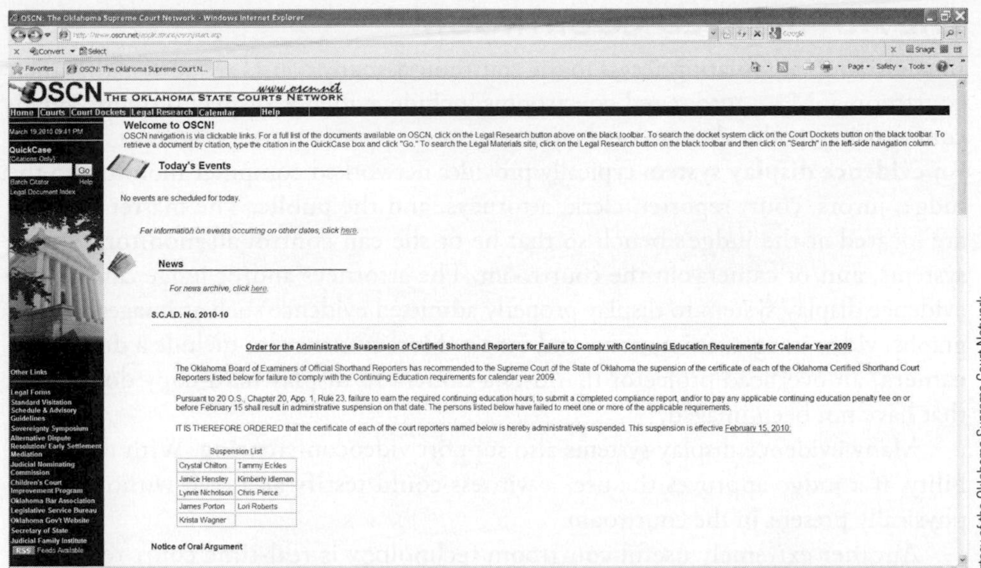

Courtesy of the Oklahoma Supreme Court Network

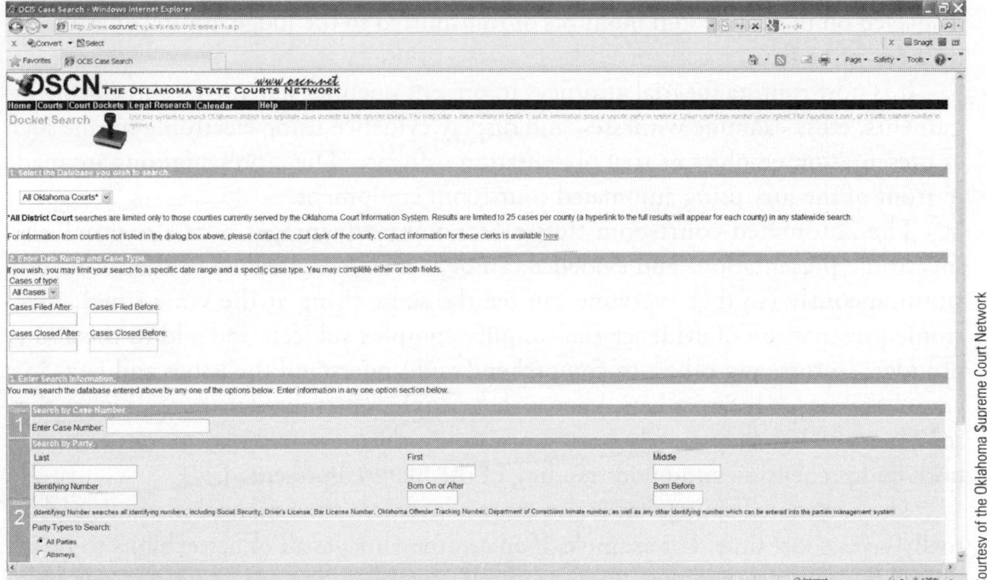

Courtesy of the Oklahoma Supreme Court Network

EXHIBIT 10–2
Internet access to the Oklahoma State Courts Network

systems include cost, standardization issues, security, and obtaining the hardware and software needed to support electronic filing. Like the federal court system, many state courts have selected PDF as their standard for filing documents electronically.

The Oklahoma State Courts Network (www.oscn.net) is a good example of state implementation of this technology. It allows users to access court dockets statewide, including the Oklahoma Supreme Court, the Court of Criminal Appeals, the Court of Civil Appeals, and 77 district courts (see Exhibit 10–2).

Electronic services such as Westlaw and LexisNexis also have access to some court dockets and can electronically track document filings in cases and access court records. Some of these services even automatically alert the legal professional (electronically) to new filings in cases, at intervals such as once or twice a week. Although a legal organization must pay the vendor for these services (as opposed to getting them free when states or courts implement the program), many legal organizations find it worth the cost.

THE AUTOMATED COURTROOM

In addition to automating access to the courthouse, many courts are automating their courtrooms. Most automated courtrooms include evidence display systems, videoconferencing, and real-time court reporting.

evidence display system
Technology that provides networked computer monitors to a judge, jury, court reporter, clerk, attorneys, and the public.

An **evidence display system** typically provides networked computer monitors to the judge, jurors, court reporter, clerk, attorneys, and the public. The master controls are located at the judge's bench so that he or she can control all monitors, sound systems, and/or cameras in the courtroom. The attorneys and/or judge can use the evidence display system to display properly admitted evidence such as images, photographs, video images, animations, and others. Most systems also include a **document camera**, an overhead projector that uses a camera to display hard-copy documents that have not been imaged.

document camera
An overhead projector that uses a camera to display hard-copy documents that have not been imaged.

Many evidence display systems also support videoconferencing. With this capability, if a judge approves the use, a witness could testify at a trial without being physically present in the courtroom.

Another extremely useful courtroom technology is real-time court reporting. With this system, a witness's testimony, as transcribed by a court reporter, becomes available within a few seconds after utterance of the testimony. The testimony can be displayed on the courtroom monitors or transmitted to the judge, jurors, or attorneys on a real-time basis.

It is now routine for trial attorneys to present opening statements and closing arguments, cross-examine witnesses, and display evidence using electronic means such as presentation graphics or trial presentation software. These presentations are made in front of the jury using automated courtroom equipment.

The automated courtroom thus offers many advantages over a manual one. Electronic presentations and evidence can be viewed by everyone in the courtroom simultaneously (so that everyone can see the same thing at the same time). Electronic presentation of evidence can simplify complex subjects and add to the ability of judges, jurors, and others to comprehend and understand the issues and facts in a case. For years, educators have known that people remember far more of what they see than of what they merely hear. Combining these two sensory modes enhances both comprehension and understanding of the material presented.

The automated courtroom is also more convenient than manual methods and actually saves court time. For example, if an attorney images all of her exhibits to be admitted for trial, they can then be electronically displayed; there is no need to rely on or shuffle through hard-copy documents, which can be lost or damaged. Computer software that automatically tracks trial exhibits, in addition to displaying them using the evidence display system, can also save time for everyone involved. In some courts, criminal defendants who are too hostile to appear in court can view the proceedings offsite via a live video/audio feed. Using presentation graphics and trial presentation programs, legal professionals are able to get the most out of automated courtroom equipment.

OVERVIEW OF PRESENTATION AND TRIAL PRESENTATION SOFTWARE

Presentation software allows users to create visually interesting electronic presentations. Many legal professionals use generic presentation graphics programs, such as Microsoft PowerPoint, to create presentations for trials, such as exhibits, graphs, and charts, as well as presentations for internal training purposes or public seminars. Using presentation software, one can combine a number of elements to create visually interesting presentations, including text, color, video, animation, clip art, graphs,

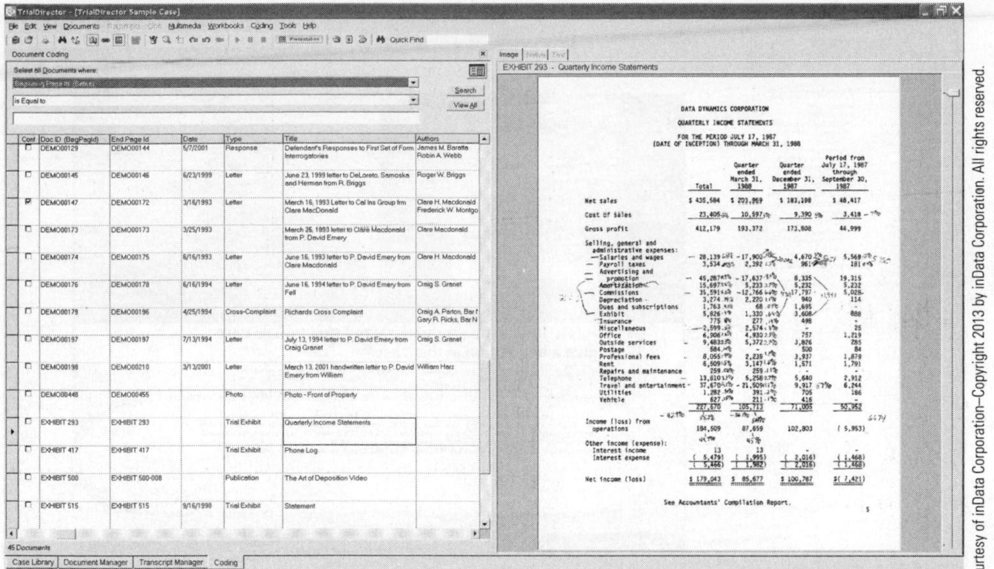

EXHIBIT 10–3
Some trial presentation programs can manage documents

charts, and sound. A user builds a presentation by organizing evidence, transcripts, images, photographs, and other materials into individual slides; the software then gives the user the options of showing all the slides at one time, or controlling the timing of presentation with a remote control. Most presentation programs can also create outlines and speaker's notes.

In addition to generic presentation programs, there are **trial presentation programs** that have been specifically designed to meet the needs of practicing attorneys, particularly those who try cases to juries and courts. TrialDirector and Sanction are examples of trial presentation programs designed specifically for the legal market.

trial presentation programs
Presentation graphics programs specifically designed to meet the needs of trial attorneys.

Trial presentation programs can do much more than just display electronic slides. Some trial presentation programs can manage documents, including maintaining document abstracts and tracking: who admitted the document (plaintiff or defendant); the Bates number of the document; the date the document was admitted into evidence; the witness who was on the stand when the document was admitted; the status of the document, including whether introduction of the document was objected to; and other information (see Exhibit 10–3). Even in relatively small cases, managing and tracking all the documents in a trial can be difficult and time-consuming. Trial presentation programs can automate that process in addition to displaying electronic documents.

Trial presentation programs can manage complex tasks, such as combining video/audio, graphs, and documents into a single slide or presenting these materials individually (see Exhibit 10–4). Trial presentation software also can synchronize the playback of video/audio with a transcript of prior testimony, so that a factfinder can not only read the words of the transcript, but can also see and hear the witness speaking the words. Trial presentation programs can also display presentations in applications such as Microsoft PowerPoint.

Notably, trial presentation programs can access data nonsequentially. PowerPoint works well when everything is linear and goes straight from beginning to end. However, most trials do not proceed this way. Attorneys need to be able to produce a particular document on a moment's notice. Trial presentation programs can access data quickly and conveniently, unlike PowerPoint. In addition, most trial presentation programs have the ability to search the trial database and access data quickly and efficiently. Generally speaking, trial presentation programs are quite powerful and are generally better suited to most trial purposes than generic presentation programs.

EXHIBIT 10–4
Trial presentation software can manage both video and documentary material

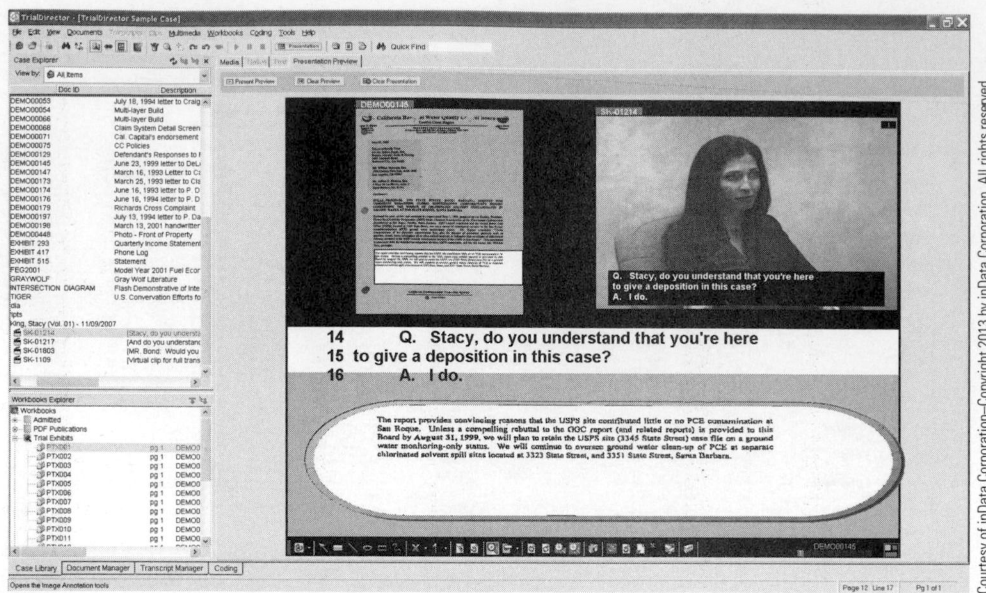

Q. Stacy, do you understand that you're here to give a deposition in this case?
A. I do.
14 Q. Stacy, do you understand that you're here
15 to give a deposition in this case?
16 A. I do.

CREATING LEGAL PRESENTATIONS WITH MICROSOFT POWERPOINT

It is quite easy to create legal presentations with general presentation software like Microsoft PowerPoint. In this chapter, we walk through the process of creating an opening statement for a case using the interface of Microsoft PowerPoint 2007.

The Screen and Views

Exhibit 10–5 shows the title page for the opening statement presentation. Notice that the ribbon bar, File tab, title bar, and Quick Access toolbar are displayed. In Exhibit 10–5, the slide counter in the lower left of the screen shows that the user is on the first of six slides. This helpful feature lets you know at all times where you are in the presentation.

EXHIBIT 10–5
PowerPoint 2007 slide

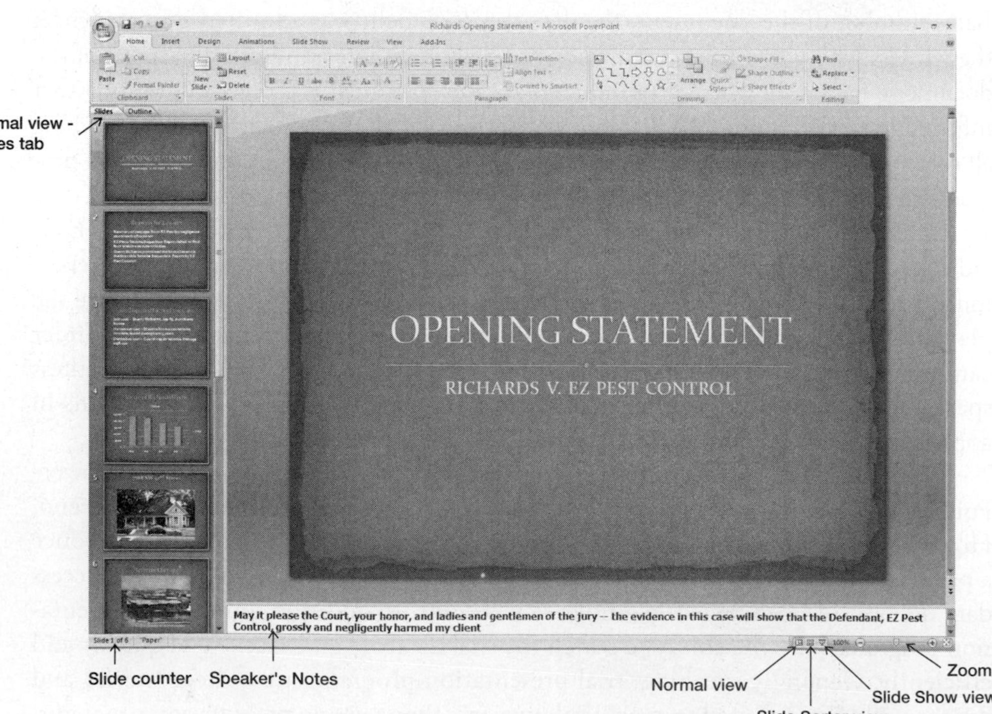

Normal view - Slides tab
OPENING STATEMENT
RICHARDS V. EZ PEST CONTROL
May it please the Court, your honor, and ladies and gentlemen of the jury -- the evidence in this case will show that the Defendant, EZ Pest Control, grossly and negligently harmed my client
Slide counter
Speaker's Notes
Normal view
Slide Sorter view
Slide Show view
Zoom

Three icons are displayed at the lower right of the screen. These three icons represent the different ways the user can view or see this presentation: Normal view, Slide Sorter view, and Slide Show view.

Normal View The Normal view for this particular program is shown in Exhibit 10–6. The **Normal view** shows the slide that is being created. On the left side of the screen is the text for all the slides in this presentation. Notice in Exhibit 10–5 that the Slides tab is selected. In Normal view, you can select either Slides or Outline display mode (see the upper left of Exhibit 10–6). Exhibit 10–6 shows the sixth slide of the presentation; this time the slide is shown in Normal view and the Outline tab in the upper left of the window is selected. The outline portion of the screen, as the name implies, shows an outline of the presentation. Notice in Exhibit 10–6 that the outline portion of the screen shows some of the same information contained in the current slide but without any graphic elements. Also, Exhibit 10–5 shows a section of the screen (under the slide) where you can enter speaker's notes about that particular slide. These can be printed out for reference purposes when you are ready to give the presentation. Speaker's notes can be created for each slide of the presentation.

Normal view
PowerPoint screen that shows the slide that is being created, an outline of the total presentation, and speaker's notes for the slide currently displayed.

Slide Sorter View The **Slide Sorter view** shows the slides in the presentation, but in a greatly reduced format. The Slide Sorter view is typically used to review and/or change the order of slides. For example, to move slide 8 in front of slide 3, you would simply click on slide 8 and drag it in front of slide 3. The program will automatically renumber the slides, but you must manually recheck and change cross-references on other slides when you do this. Slide Sorter view gives you a big picture of the presentation and allows you to easily organize or reorganize the presentation.

Slide Sorter view
PowerPoint screen that shows the slides in the presentation, but in a greatly reduced format; typically used to review and/or change the order of slides.

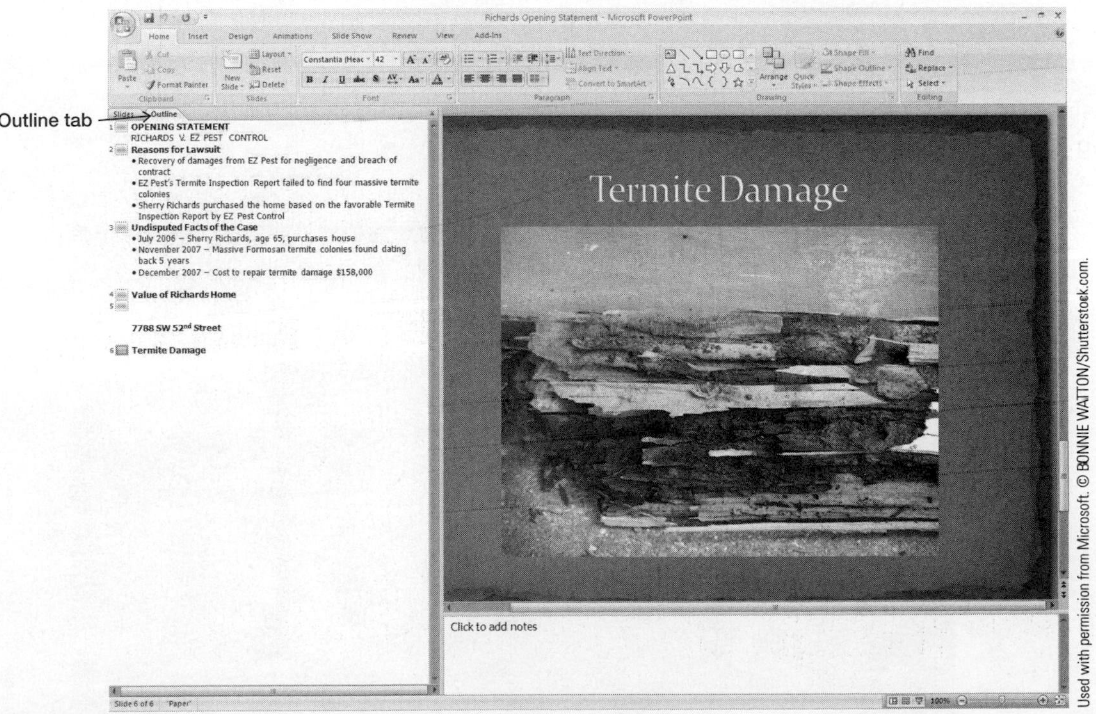

EXHIBIT 10–6
Microsoft PowerPoint Normal view—Outline display mode

Slide Show view
PowerPoint screen used during a presentation or when the user wants to preview how the audience will actually see the slide. Only the current slide is shown on the screen. The program interface, menus, outline view, and speaker's notes are not shown.

Slide Show View The **Slide Show view** is used during a presentation or when you are developing a presentation and want to learn how the audience will actually see the slide. The only thing shown on the screen is the slide itself. The program interface, outline, and speaker's notes are not shown.

Backgrounds, Adding Slides, and Formatting a Presentation

background
The design on which the other elements of the presentation (words, clip art, etc.) are placed.

The first step in creating a presentation is to select the background. The **background** is the design on which the other elements of the presentation (words, clip art, etc.) will be placed. It is similar to the canvas of a painting. PowerPoint comes with several predesigned backgrounds that you can choose from. You can also create your own backgrounds or select backgrounds from Microsoft Office Online.

The next step in creating a presentation is to add slides. PowerPoint has a New Slide command, found on the Home ribbon (see Exhibit 10–7). The New Slide command gives you a menu of different formats for creating a slide. These automatic formats make it easy to select a format and then quickly begin entering the information.

Photographs, Clip Art, and Word Art

clip art
Predrawn art.

PowerPoint allows you to include clip art, photographs, and word art in presentations. **Clip art** is predrawn art. Be careful when considering the use of clip art in trial and legal presentations; some clip art actually diminishes the professional appearance of the presentation. Make sure that what you choose is appropriate, well executed, and (most importantly) enhances the impact or comprehensibility of your presentation; never throw in images just for the sake of having a picture.

Notice that the presentation in Exhibit 10–8 includes clear, high-impact photographs. High-quality photographs can enhance the professionalism of a presentation and create strong visual impact. Word art may also be useful for highlighting

EXHIBIT 10–7
Options for adding a new slide

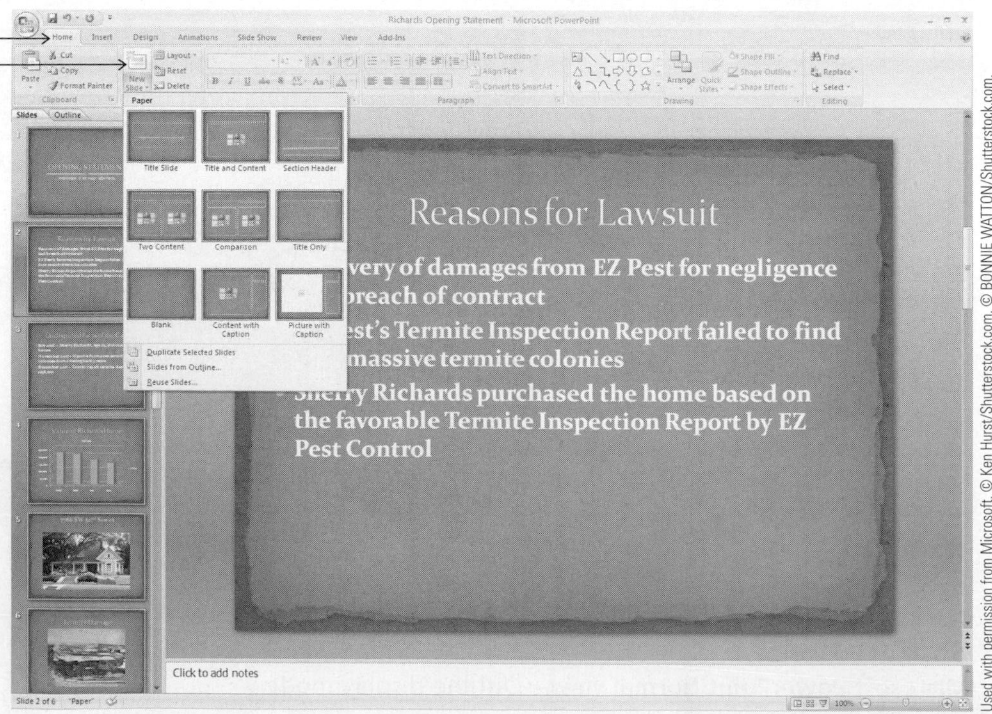

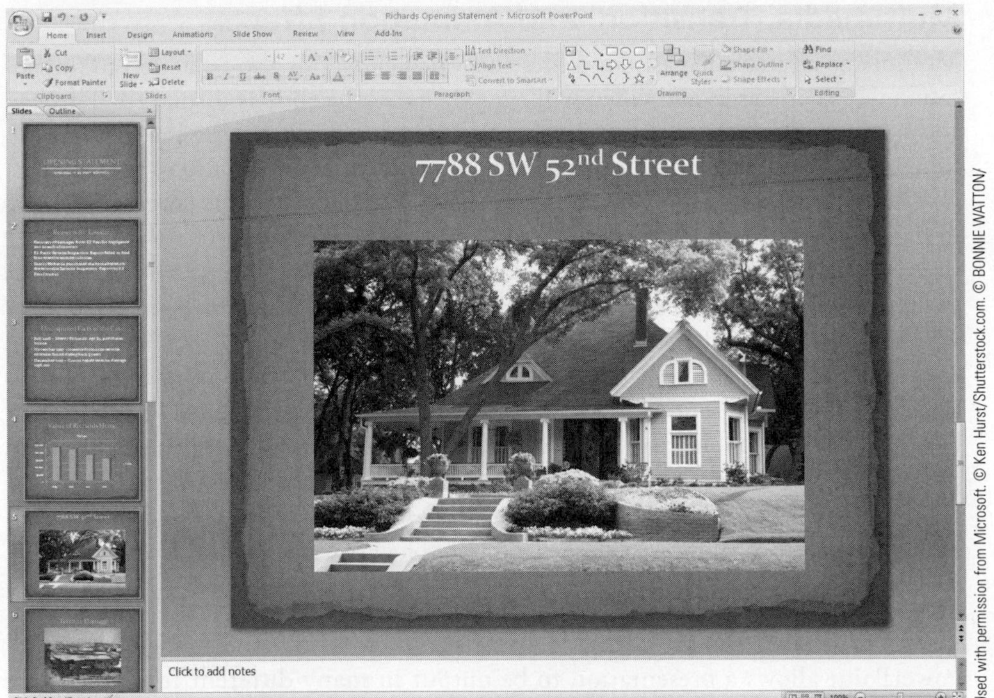

EXHIBIT 10–8
Photographs in PowerPoint

material or for creating a consistent visual theme throughout a presentation. Word art features allow you to add special formatting to text, including three-dimensional (3-D) designs.

Graphs/Charts

PowerPoint allows you to create graphs and charts, either as stand-alone elements (such as a graph for a case) or as part of a presentation. Notice in Exhibit 10–9 that the graph has the same background as the rest of the presentation and that it is in 3-D. PowerPoint provides a wide variety of graph and chart formats to choose from, including column charts, bar graphs, and pie charts.

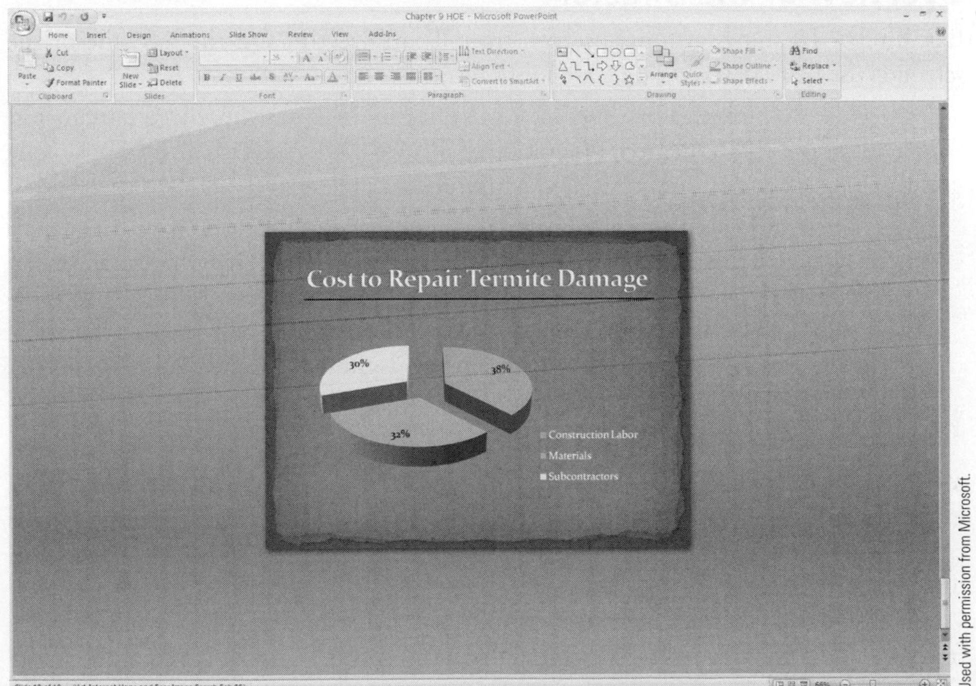

EXHIBIT 10–9
Graph in PowerPoint

Multimedia, Transition, and Animation Effects

Multimedia effects, such as sound files and video clips, can also be added to presentations, so that sound and video will run whenever the slide is displayed. This can add interest and excitement to a presentation. (It also engages more sensory modalities, so that fact-finders are more likely to comprehend and remember the material.)

slide transition
Effects that control how the program proceeds from one slide to another.

Another option is a **slide transition** effect, which controls how the program proceeds from one slide to another. For example, you could move from slide 2 to slide 3 and make slide 3 appear on the screen much like horizontal blinds being drawn, with each piece sliding onto the screen individually until the slide is complete. *Animation* refers to other effects, such as how bullet points appear on the screen. You could make bullet points and text "fly" onto the screen individually, either automatically or when the mouse button is pushed. Animation is similar to slide transitions, but it happens within a slide instead of between slides. Again, be careful in using transition and animation effects so as to not diminish the professionalism (or comprehensibility) of the presentation. Always remember that the reason for using any effect is to enhance the impact, interest, and comprehensibility of your presentation, not to show off technological capabilities.

Displaying a Presentation

PowerPoint allows a presentation to be output in many different formats. These include slide show presentations, printing the presentation in black and white or color, printing it as overhead transparency slides, or exporting it into web-based learning software. In addition, you can print the slides, an outline, speaker's notes, or a combination of these items.

CREATING PRESENTATIONS WITH TRIALDIRECTOR

Trial presentation software such as TrialDirector allows you to integrate images of physical evidence, excerpts of video depositions, and slides from PowerPoint into your presentation.

Overview of TrialDirector

Exhibit 10–10 shows a sample screen from TrialDirector. On the left side of the screen is the Case Library. The Case Library consists of:

- Case Explorer. This lists all of the items in a case in three categories: Documents (Imaged Documents, Photo Documents, and Native File Documents), Transcripts, and Multimedia.
- Workbooks Explorer. Workbooks are electronic files that you can use to organize items as needed. Three Workbooks are provided when a new case is opened (Search Results, Trial Exhibits, and Witnesses). Additional Workbooks can be created for specific purposes requiring presentation of visual information (opening argument, closing argument, examination of specific witnesses, etc.).

On the right side of the screen is the Desktop Workspace. This is where you can see the items contained in the Case Explorer and Workbooks. By clicking on a document in the Case Library, you can see it in the Desktop Workspace. Individual items can be placed in a Workbook by clicking on the item, dragging it, and dropping it in the desired Workbook.

At the bottom of the screen are the Quick Access tabs, which allow you to change from the Case Library to the Document Manager, the Transcript Manager, or the Coding database.

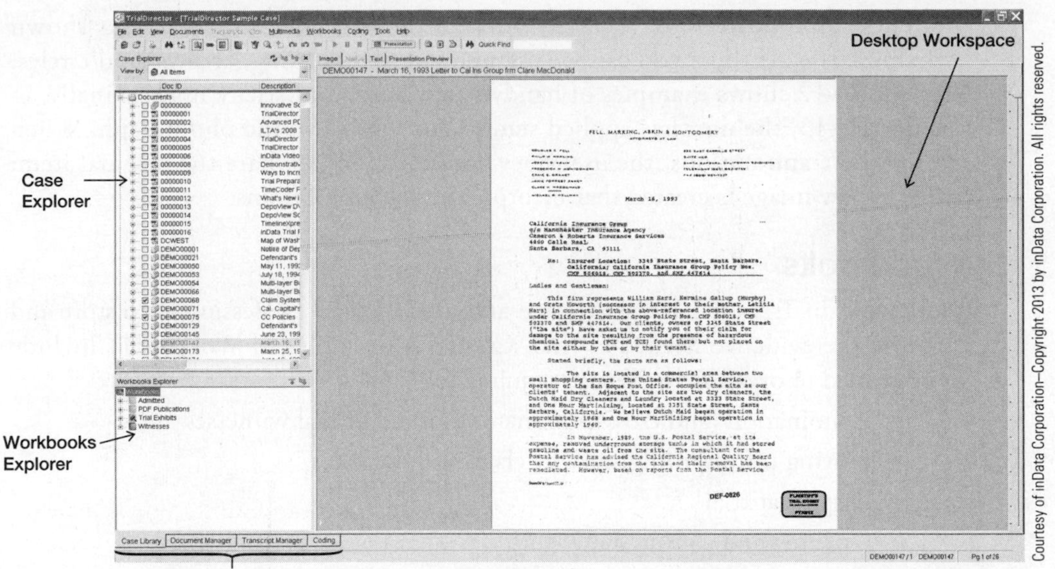

EXHIBIT 10–10
TrialDirector screen

The Document Manager organizes electronic exhibits, including scanned images, excerpts of video depositions, and presentations created in Adobe Acrobat or Microsoft PowerPoint. These documents can then be prepared for presentation at trial using annotation tools that include a highlighter, arrow, note, and stamp tools. Excerpts of video depositions (called clips) can be included, which lets you integrate key portions to be presented at trial.

The Transcript Manager allows you to show all or part of a video deposition and have the text/transcript of the deposition scrolling on the screen simultaneously.

The Coding database is a searchable repository of information about the specific items contained within the Case Library. For example, the Coding database may include the document ID, the date of the document, the author of the document, the specific issues related to the document, and so on. This information can be input directly, using TrialDirector, or it may be imported from another program (such as Summation). When you are in the Coding tab, you can choose either Column view (which displays multiple records) or Form view (which displays a single record).

Presentation mode is the tool that displays the specific item(s) for the court to see. With a video projector, you may use the Presentation mode to display images of evidence, video clips from depositions, and slides made to inform and persuade the factfinder.

Image Annotations

Images of documents and other items may be annotated (or "marked up") to emphasize specific portions for the jury or to communicate an idea to a colleague. Examples of annotations include:

- Highlighting
- Arrows pointing to specific items
- Boxes and circles
- Redactions
- Handwritten notes
- Sticky notes
- Labels
- Stamps
- Callouts

Some of these items can be assigned varying colors and widths.

These annotations are accessed through the Annotation toolbar, as shown in Exhibit 10–11; there you can see examples of highlighting, arrows, and circles. Exhibit 10–12 shows examples of handwritten notes and sticky notes. Finally, in Exhibit 10–13, the user has applied stamps and a label to the photograph. When adding these annotations, the user does not destroy or spoliate the original item; rather, a new image is created that incorporates the annotations.

Workbooks

Workbooks in TrialDirector are created and used by legal professionals to store and organize the evidence needed at trial. Common examples of Workbooks include those created to organize the images required for:

- Examination (and cross-examination) of individual witnesses
- Proving (or disputing) specific claims for damages
- Display at trial
- Opening and closing statements

EXHIBIT 10–11
Annotations on a TrialDirector slide

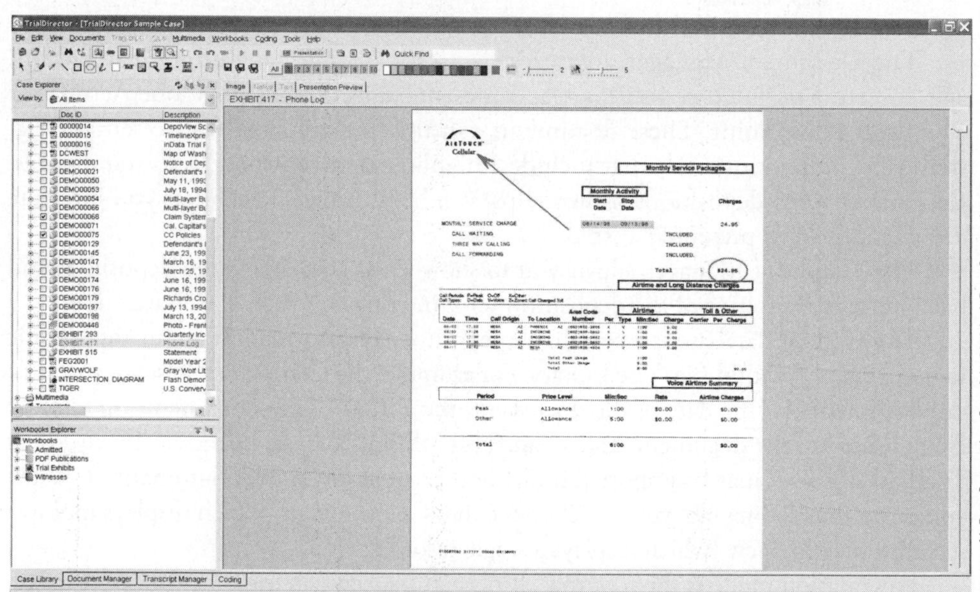

EXHIBIT 10–12
Notes on a TrialDirector slide

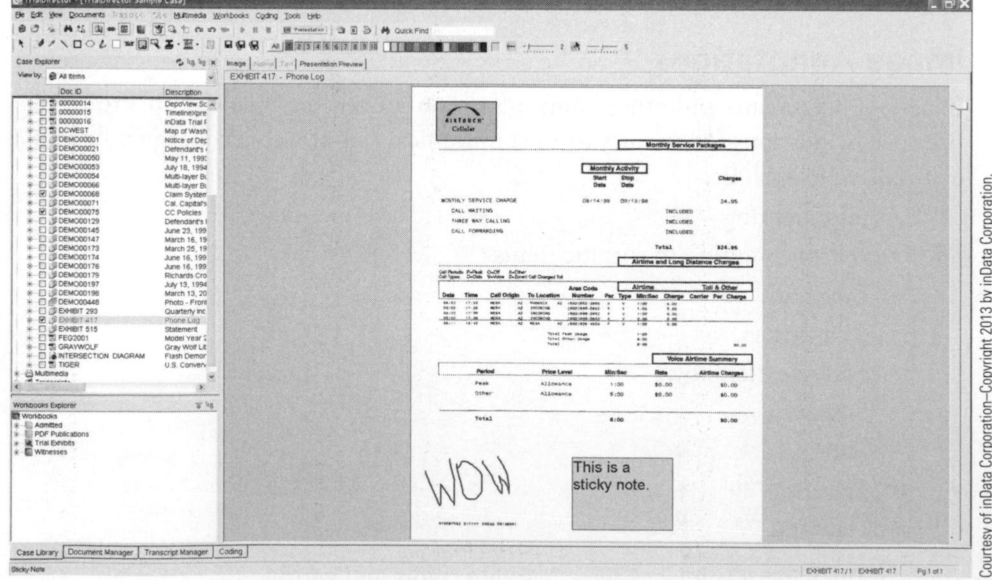

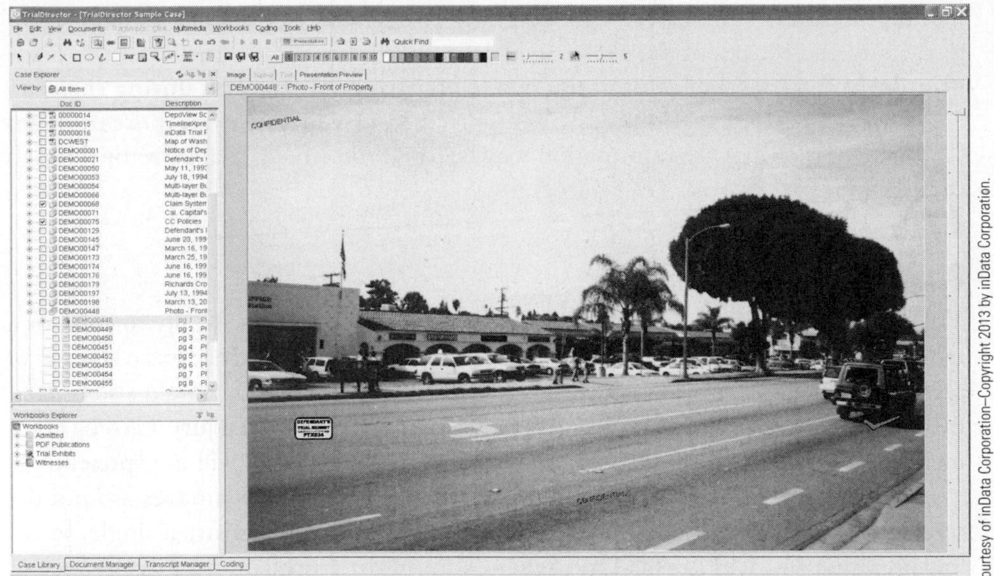

EXHIBIT 10–13
Photograph with stamps and labels in TrialDirector

The items held within the Workbooks are not removed from the Case Explorer; rather, they are newly created image files (essentially, they are copies of the documents held within the Case Explorer). Individual Workbooks are maintained and accessed through the Workbook Explorer.

Working with Depositions

Trial presentation programs typically offer the ability to store, organize, edit, and display depositions. The deposition may be displayed alone or accompanied by a scrolling transcript. In addition, it is possible to display specific images at precise times during presentation of the deposition. This allows the jurors to see and hear the witness talk about a piece of evidence while also allowing them to see an image of the actual evidence.

In addition, other types of videos may be presented to the jury, such as videos displaying the effects of a person's negligence or malpractice, damage done by a storm, or videos showing the site where the cause of action occurred (e.g., the intersection where an automobile collision occurred).

Coding

Trial presentation software gives you the opportunity to add information to individual images, which should make it easier for you to organize them prior to trial and to find them during trial.

In TrialDirector, this is accomplished by "coding" images. The Coding tab enables you to add related information to an image, such as:

- Whether an image is privileged
- Whether an image is confidential
- Page numbers
- Date
- Type of document
- Title of document
- Author(s) of document
- Recipients of document
- Source of the image

Coding may also take the form of assigning issue codes to portions of deposition testimony and images of the physical evidence of the case. This facilitates the organization and retrieval of information while preparing for trial and during the trial.

The coding information may be imported from a litigation support program (e.g., Summation), or the information may be input directly in TrialDirector through the Coding tab.

Presentation

The essence of any presentation software, be it one designed specifically for trial or a more generic one such as PowerPoint, is the ability to present information to a group of persons in a manner that engages them and keeps their attention. It should also be relatively simple to use, especially if it is to be used in court in front of a jury. Closing argument is not a good time to discover that the presentation software will not "present."

The Presentation mode in TrialDirector allows you to move images around the screen, integrating still images, video clips, and deposition clips into a single, seamless presentation. It is possible to prepare a script for a presentation in advance of trial, so that you do not have to fuss with the computer in the presence of the judge and jury. (See the following section for notes about rehearsing your presentations.)

COURTROOM PRESENTATION TIPS

In some legal organizations, the creation of presentations for trials falls to paralegals. Creating and designing trial presentations is different from creating other presentations. In addition, often a paralegal actually operates the computer and presentation/equipment during trial, to allow the attorney(s) to concentrate on litigation. This section offers a variety of tips and tricks related to preparing and showing courtroom presentations.

Test All Computer Equipment in Advance and Have Staff Support

It is impossible to overstate the importance of having the technology used at trial actually work when it is supposed to. If the courtroom is equipped with its own technology, such as a projector and screen, then users only have to ensure that they have the proper cables and other hardware to interface with the court's equipment. If the court is not properly or adequately equipped, then users will have supply and set up all of the necessary equipment, such as a portable projector, screen, and speakers. Other necessary equipment might include a laptop computer, cables, extension cords, and a printer/scanner/copier.

It is crucial that you test and retest *all* of the hardware and software—in the configuration in which you plan to use it—to make sure that it works. Leave nothing to chance and have backup equipment available if at all possible. Little things, such as testing electrical outlets, are critical; just because they are there doesn't mean they work. Never add or include new or untested equipment at the last minute; leave yourself enough time to work out any possible kinks. Thoroughly check out the courtroom in advance of the trial, if possible, so that you understand the complete layout of the room and what problems could potentially arise.

Possible complications include incompatible computer platforms, insufficient electrical connections, slow or spotty Internet or wireless connections, awkward or obstructed lines of sight for the factfinders, poor lighting, display monitors that are too small or poorly placed, and inadequate sound systems, among many, many others. The more of these obstacles you can predict and plan for (or work around), the better off your team will be.

Always Rehearse

Always rehearse, many times, before putting on a presentation to a judge or jury. This is particularly critical if a support person (such as a paralegal) will be running the hardware and/or software. It takes time to prepare trial presentations and to work out all the kinks and problems. In addition, even if the technology works, in the end it really comes down to the presenter and how well that person presents the information to the judge or jury. For the presentation to be effective, everything must work together and flow well—and that takes time and practice.

Don't Keep Judges or Juries Waiting—Bring Powerful Technology

Always make sure that the software you are using can run adequately on the computer hardware you are using. Judges and juries get extremely impatient when a user's computer constantly shows the Windows "hourglass" icon. The new class of trial presentation software, in particular, has hefty computing needs in terms of both active and storage memory. Always use a computer with more than enough horsepower to get the job done. (Of course, you will have thoroughly tested your setup and presentation(s) before you get to trial, so you should know well ahead of time if there are problems in this area.)

Always Have a Backup Plan

Always have a backup plan—*always*, every time. It is a sad fact that hard disks crash, CDs and DVDs get scratched, software freezes, computers get unplugged, cables wear out, bright lights wash out computer screens, operator errors occur, and information gets accidentally deleted. Even if a presentation is stored in the cloud where it should always be available, Internet access may be interrupted and access to the cloud may be problematic. It is critical that you always have a backup plan in case the technology fails. Something—anything—is better than nothing. A presentation that is printed out and can be copied and handed to the judge or jurors is better than no presentation at all.

Keep It Simple—Don't Overload Slides with Too Much Information

Presentations should be professional, clean, and simple. A common mistake is to put too many bullet points on a single slide. This makes the slide difficult to read. In addition, the font size of slide text should be relatively large, because some jurors may have trouble reading small fonts. Ambient lighting, such as from overhead fixtures or glare from courtroom windows, can wreak havoc with visibility, especially if the display monitors are undersized or poorly placed. Know ahead of time what you will be dealing with and prepare the presentation accordingly.

Use Color Conservatively

It is fine to include some color, but presentation designs should be conservative and professional—no loud, extravagant colors, and not too many colors. Color should be used to enhance the presentation, not distract the viewers.

Use Animation, Sound, and Clip Art Cautiously

Use animation, sound clips, and clip art cautiously in trial presentations. Because they often have a cartoonish quality, they tend to diminish the quality and professionalism of a presentation. It is easy for these elements to come off as cheap, cheesy, or just in poor taste. The acid test for any element is whether it enhances the comprehensibility, interest, and overall impact of the presentation.

Use Images, Maps, Video, and Charts/Graphs When Possible

Include graphical elements, such as images (photographs), maps, video, and charts/graphs, in a presentation whenever possible. They add excitement and diversity to text and many times make it easier for jurors to understand the concept you are trying to convey.

Video testimony is particularly important. For example, if a witness states something in open court that is different from his or her testimony given in a video deposition, the ability to play the video deposition in front of the jury and impeach the witness's current testimony is priceless.

Scan Key Documents and Use Markup Tools

Scan the key documents in a case, so that you can include them as part of a complete presentation. If documents are in electronic form, you can use presentation software to mark or highlight important passages for easy identification by the factfinder.

Include Timelines

Timelines are critical in just about every case that goes to trial. They explain what happened, in chronological order. Attorneys often present things out of sequence for specific reasons, and witnesses often jump around in their testimony or are unclear regarding dates and times. Hence, timelines are crucial for bringing everything in a case together for a jury.

Allow Extra Time to Pass Security Checkpoints

If you have ever tried to take a laptop computer onto an airplane, you may have an idea of what it will take to get through courthouse security with computers, projectors, speakers, and other equipment. Be sure to give yourself enough time to physically get the equipment into the courthouse and set up in the courtroom.

ETHICAL CONSIDERATIONS

Ethical considerations regarding trial and presentation software and graphics revolve around competency and rules of evidence. It is important, when putting together anything that will be used in a client's case, to make sure that it is well thought out and competently executed. It is certainly not unusual for a paralegal to be asked to create a chart, graph, table, exhibit, or even a full presentation for trial. It is extremely important that these be prepared with a high degree of accuracy and competency.

In addition, anything that is presented at trial or to a factfinder will be subject to the rules of evidence and could be objected to by the opposing party. Charts, graphs, and tables may be viewed as **demonstrative evidence**. Examples of demonstrative evidence include maps, diagrams, models, charts, and illustrations. The admissibility of demonstrative evidence is largely controlled by the rules of evidence and the judge sitting on the case. Arguments between attorneys regarding a piece of demonstrative evidence often concern whether it fairly and reasonably depicts the subject matter it covers. Thus, the heart of admissibility of demonstrative evidence depends on the accuracy, quality, and competency of the exhibit itself.

demonstrative evidence
All evidence other than testimony.

SUMMARY

Electronic courthouses, where legal professionals file documents electronically and have instant access to court information, are becoming a reality. Automated courtrooms with computers and monitors for all participants are also a reality.

Presentation software allows users to create visually interesting electronic presentations. Presentation graphics programs are used in legal organizations for creating internal training programs, public seminars, and presentations for clients, and developing trial presentations. Some of these programs are generic business presentation programs. A trial presentation program is specifically designed to meet the needs of practicing attorneys, particularly those who try cases to juries and courts.

Most presentation graphics programs have several views and display presentations to work with. Creating new presentations entails creating a background design; adding slides; adding and formatting text; adding photographs, clip art, and word art; adding graphs and charts; and creating multimedia effects and transition/animation effects.

Designing and presenting trial presentations to judges and juries takes a great deal of preparation and thought. Tips for doing this well include testing computer equipment in advance, always having a backup plan, and always rehearsing presentations. To create professional, effective presentations, keep slides simple and uncluttered; use color conservatively; use animation, sound, and clip art cautiously; use images, maps, video, and charts/graphs as much as possible; scan key documents; use markup tools; and include timelines.

KEY TERMS

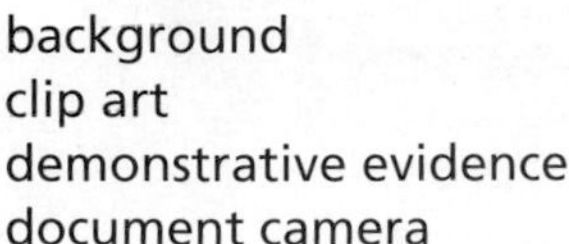

background
clip art
demonstrative evidence
document camera
evidence display system
Normal view
Slide Show view
Slide Sorter view
slide transition
trial presentation programs

INTERNET SITES

Internet sites for this chapter include:

ORGANIZATION	SOFTWARE PRODUCT	WORLD WIDE WEB ADDRESS
Adobe Acrobat	PDF file creation program	www.adobe.com
Case Management/Electronic Case Files	The federal courts' case management and electronic case files system	www.uscourts.gov
Corel Corp.	Presentations X3 presentation program	www.corel.com
Doar	Trial presentation services vendor	www.doar.com
Idea, Inc.	Trial Pro	www.trialpro.com
InData Software	TrialDirector trial presentation software	www.indatacorp.com
LexisNexis	TimeMap (timeline creation software)	www.casemap.com
Microsoft Corp.	PowerPoint presentation software	www.microsoft.com
Public Access to Court Electronic Records	PACER (electronic public access to federal court information)	pacer.psc.uscourts.gov
LexisNexis	Sanction trial presentation software	www.sanction.com

TEST YOUR KNOWLEDGE

1. True or False: Only a few courts, cases, or attorneys participate in the federal courts' Case Management/Electronic Case Filing system.
2. What standard do most courts use for submission of electronic documents?
3. What is a document camera?
4. True or False: Trial presentation programs and generic presentation programs such as Microsoft PowerPoint have the same features.
5. Why should you be careful when using clip art and sound files in trial presentations?
6. Name four things to remember when using presentation programs in the courtroom.

ON THE WEB EXERCISES

1. Use a general search engine, such as Google or Yahoo!, to find several articles regarding use of computer presentation programs in the courtroom or before a jury. Write a two-page paper summarizing your research.
2. Use the Internet sites listed in this chapter and/or a general search engine (such as Google or Yahoo!) to find two trial presentation programs. Compare the prices, features, support, and training available. Download trial versions of the programs if you can. Write a two-page memo summarizing your research and findings. Identify the program that you think is best and explain why.

QUESTIONS AND EXERCISES

1. Contact an attorney, paralegal, or court staff member in your area and interview that person regarding his or her experiences using technology in the courtroom, in electronic filing, or in accessing electronic court records. Write a two-page memo summarizing your interview.

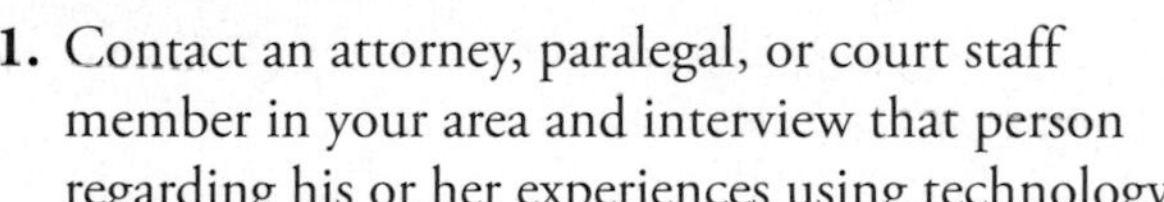

ETHICS QUESTION

You are working with trial presentation software to prepare a brief video clip of an opposing party's deposition. As you are creating the clip, you notice that if you stop the clip one second sooner, the opposing witness appears to be scowling. You would like to present the opposing witness in a less than flattering light. What ethical issues, if any, arise from this scenario?

HANDS-ON EXERCISES

FEATURED SOFTWARE
TrialDirector

TRIALDIRECTOR

I. INTRODUCTION

inData's TrialDirector is case management software that helps you manage transcripts, video depositions, and documents for trial presentations.

II. INSTALLATION INSTRUCTIONS

1. Log in to your CengageBrain.com account.
2. Under "My Courses & Materials," find the Premium Website for *Using Computers in the Law Office,* 7th edition.
3. ***Click Open to go to the Premium Website.***
4. Locate "Book Level Resources" in the left navigation menu.
5. ***Click the link for TrialDirector 6.5.***
6. ***Click the link next to To access the demo:*** and the installer will be automatically downloaded to your computer according to your browser's download settings. If asked to Open or Save the file, ***click Open.***
7. You may get a File Download–Security Warning. ***Click Run.*** The screen in TrialDirector Installation Exhibit 1 should now be displayed.
8. The screen in TrialDirector Installation Exhibit 2 should now be displayed. ***Click Next.***
9. The screen in TrialDirector Installation Exhibit 3 should now be displayed. ***Click the button next to* "I accept the terms in the license agreement"** then ***click Next.***

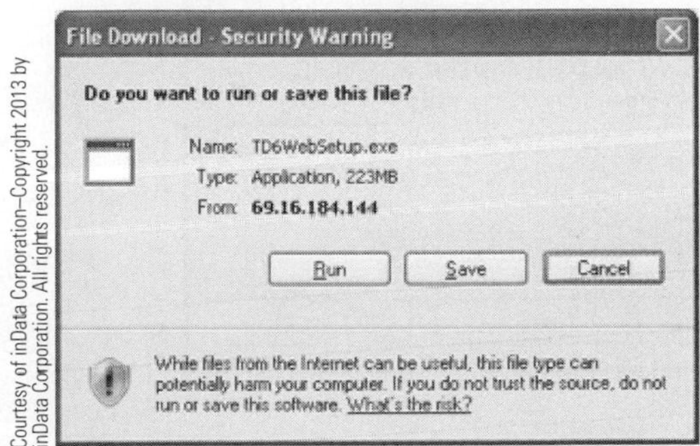

TRIALDIRECTOR INSTALLATION EXHIBIT 1

TRIALDIRECTOR INSTALLATION EXHIBIT 2

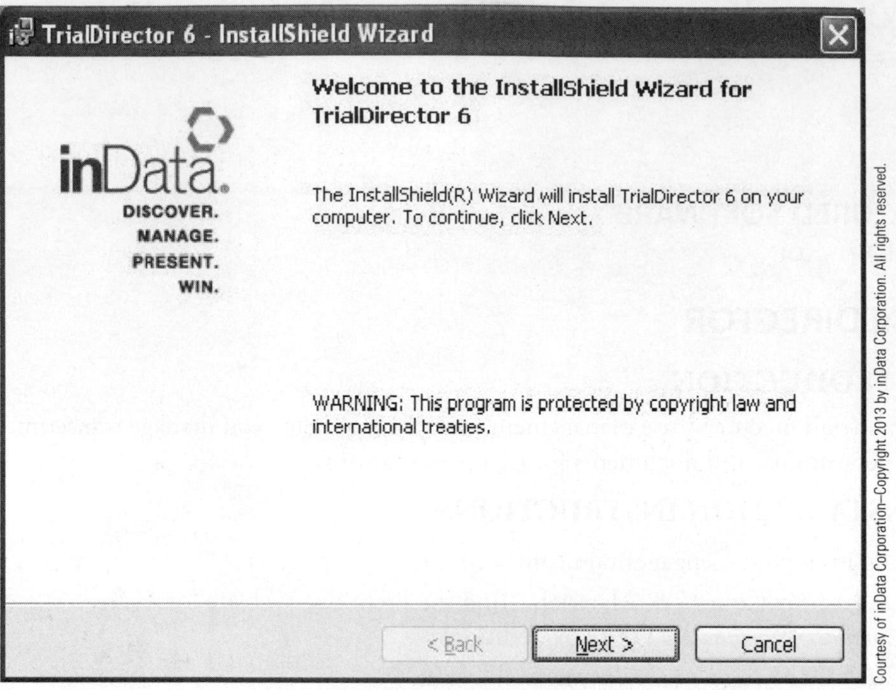

TRIALDIRECTOR INSTALLATION EXHIBIT 3

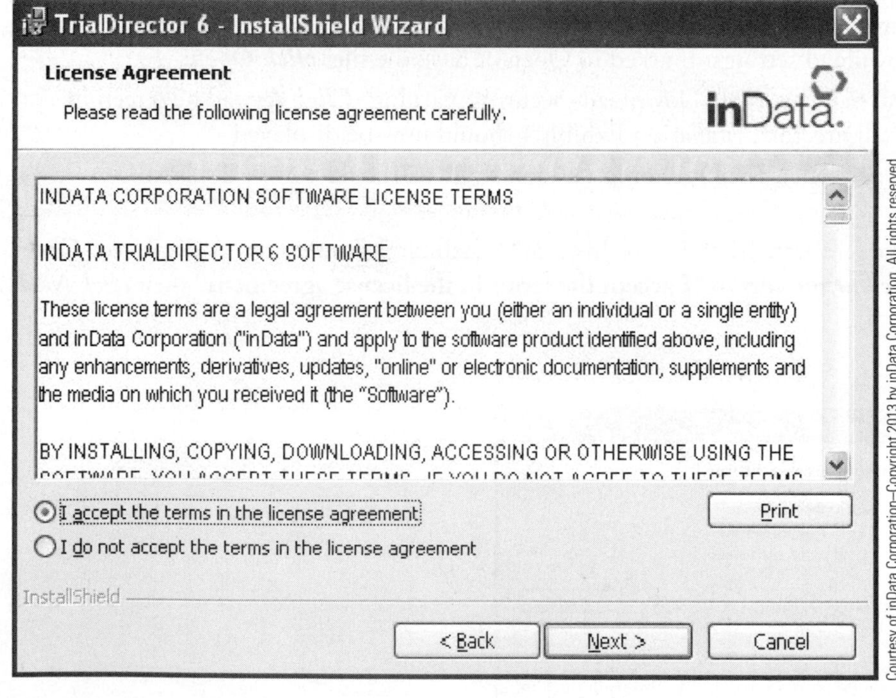

10. The screen in TrialDirector Installation Exhibit 4 should now be displayed. ***Click Install.***

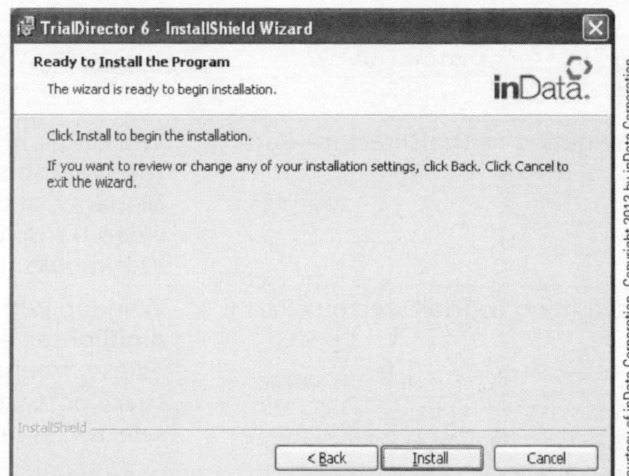

TRIALDIRECTOR INSTALLATION EXHIBIT 4

11. When the installation is finished, the screen in TrialDirector Installation Exhibit 5 should be displayed. ***Click Finish.***

TRIALDIRECTOR INSTALLATION EXHIBIT 5

12. You have now successfully installed TrialDirector 6; however, the program has no data in it for you to manipulate. So, go back to the CengageBrain Premium Website screen you used to download TrialDirector. ***Click the link to download the Sample Data, then follow the on-screen instructions.***

HANDS-ON EXERCISES

HANDS-ON EXERCISES

TRIALDIRECTOR

Number	Lesson Title	Concepts Covered
BASIC LESSONS		
Lesson 1	Navigating in TrialDirector—Part I	Working with the Case Library and the Workbooks Explorer, Document Manager, and Coding tools; playing video transcripts; creating new Workbooks
Lesson 2	Navigating in TrialDirector—Part II	Working with annotations tools: highlighter, arrow, line, rectangle, ellipse, freehand draw, redaction, text, sticky note, stamp, label, and annotation selector; saving annotations
INTERMEDIATE LESSONS		
Lesson 3	Working with the Transcript Manager	Multimedia Player; Word Index; closed captioning; creating a new video clip
Lesson 4	Creating a New Case and Issue Codes	Creating a new case; creating new issue codes; assigning issue codes to sections of a deposition
ADVANCED LESSON		
Lesson 5	Working in Presentation Mode	Opening Presentation mode; using zones; loading and moving images in Presentation mode; creating enlargements and callouts; displaying video and deposition clips

GETTING STARTED

Overview

TrialDirector is a trial presentation graphics program. It allows you to organize and manipulate items of evidence to be used in trial presentations.

Introduction to This Training Manual

Throughout this training manual, information you need to operate the program will be designated in several different ways.

- Keys to be pressed on the keyboard will be designated in brackets, in all caps, in bold and enlarged type (press the **[ENTER]** key).
- Movements with the mouse will be designated in bold and italic type (***point to File on the menu bar and click the mouse***).
- Words or letters that should be typed will be designated in bold and enlarged type (type **Training Program**).
- Information that is or should be displayed on your computer screen is shown in the following style: ***Press ENTER to continue.***

BASIC LESSONS

LESSON 1: NAVIGATING IN TRIALDIRECTOR—PART I

In this lesson, you will start TrialDirector.

1. Start Windows. Then, ***double-click the TrialDirector icon on the desktop*** to start TrialDirector. Alternatively, ***click the Start button, point to Programs or All Programs, and then click the TrialDirector icon.*** If the Trial Registration window appears, ***click Continue***. If a Product Bulletin window opens, ***click OK***.
2. ***In the "Open a Case" window, select TrialDirector 6 Sample Case, then click Open***. Your screen should look like TrialDirector Exhibit 1. TrialDirector opens in the Case Library tab.

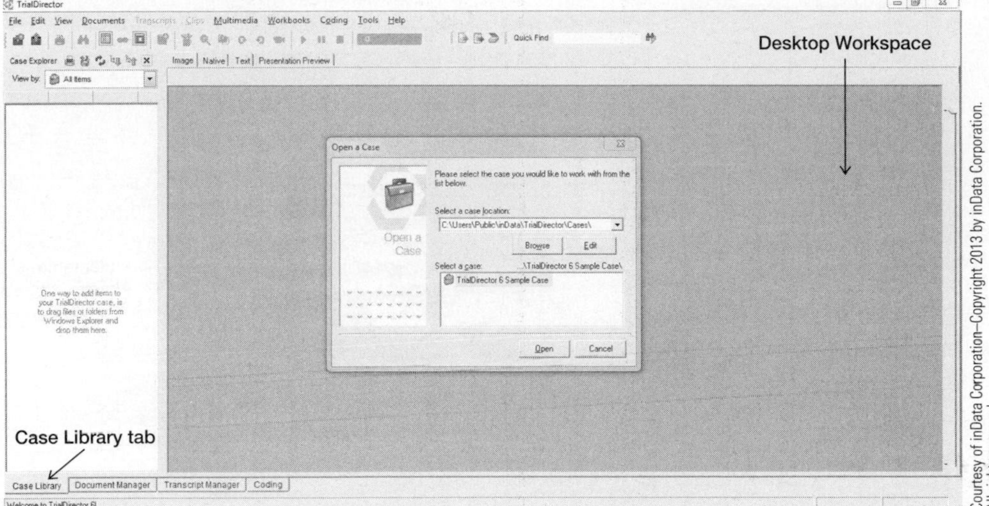

TRIALDIRECTOR EXHIBIT 1

3. The right side of the screen contains the Desktop Workspace. This is where the selected documents, transcripts, images, and so on appear. The left side of the screen contains the Case Explorer and the Workbooks Explorer. See TrialDirector Exhibit 2. The Case Explorer is the main repository of all files in TrialDirector. The default categories in the Case Explorer are Documents, Multimedia, and Transcripts. We will now look at each of these.
4. ***Click the small plus sign next to Documents to expand this category. Click DEMO00145***. On the right side of the screen (In the Desktop Workspace), you should now see the image of a letter dated June 23, 1999 (see TrialDirector Exhibit 2). Notice that the file you just selected also has a plus sign next to it. ***Click the plus sign next to DEMO00145.*** Two additional sub-files appear: DEMO00145 and DEMO00146. This allows you to see individual pages of a multi-page document.
5. ***Click the small plus sign next to Multimedia to expand this category. Click VIDEO01***. On the right side of the screen, you should now see a video screen and controls (see TrialDirector Exhibit 3). ***Click the small green arrow (fourth icon from the left) to play the video.*** You can stop it by clicking the square icon. Remember, if you position your cursor over any of the icons, you can see its function.
6. ***Click the small plus sign next to Transcripts to expand this category. Double-click King, Stacy (Vol. 01) – 11/09/2007 [MPEG-1 Video].***

HANDS-ON EXERCISES

TRIALDIRECTOR EXHIBIT 2

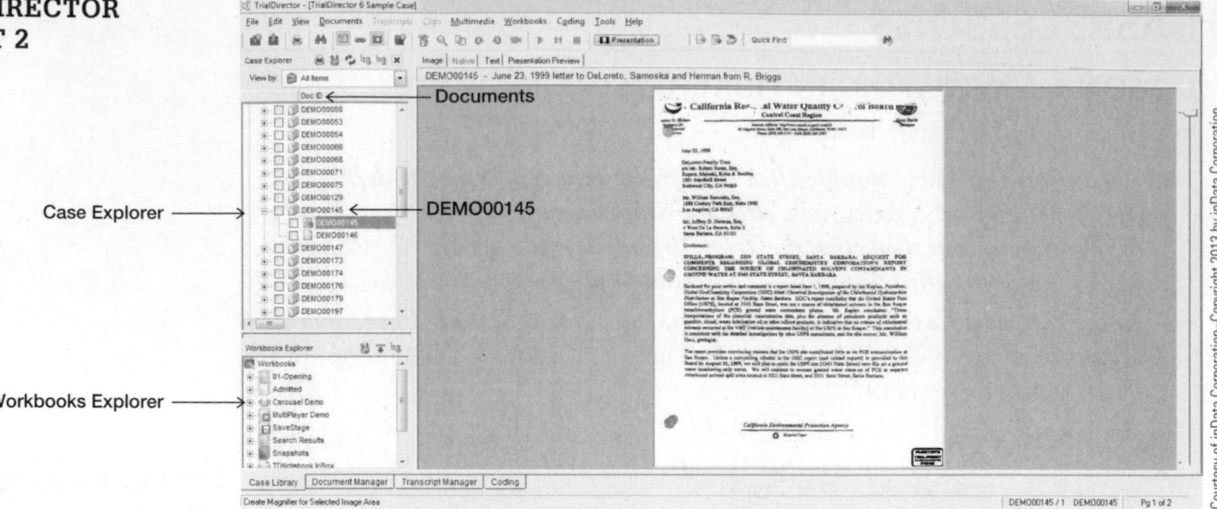

TRIALDIRECTOR EXHIBIT 3

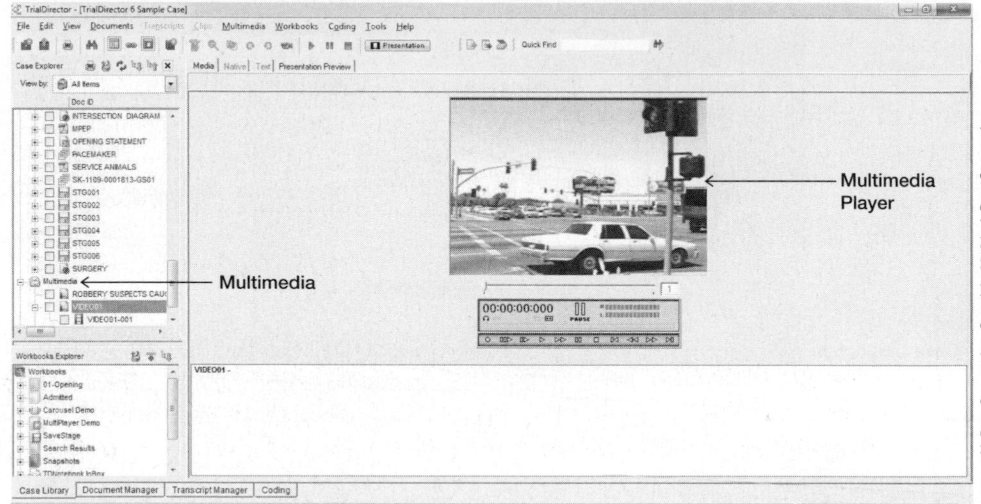

(*Note*: If you cannot read the full name of an item in the Case Explorer, you can expand it by clicking and dragging the border between the Case Explorer and the Desktop Workspace.) On the right side of the screen, you should now see the transcript of a deposition and a multimedia player and exhibit preview. Notice that a number of sub-files now appear and the Transcript Manager tab opened automatically. ***Click the small green arrow (third arrow from the left) under the video screen*** (see TrialDirector Exhibit 4). Notice that as the video plays, the transcript has a rolling scroll simultaneously highlighting the words being spoken in the video of the witness's testimony.

7. ***Double-click the sub-file Clip SK-01217 ["And do you understand that you've been…"].*** A new set of sub-files appears; these contain individual segments of the deposition. ***Double-click the sub-file Page 13:12 to 13:13.*** Notice that the video screen now plays this brief segment and that the transcript now shows the corresponding section of the deposition.
8. ***Click the plus sign next to Exhibits, and then double-click one of the sub-files EXHIBIT 417 [Phone Log].*** Notice that the phone log now appears in the Exhibit Preview screen directly under the video player. This allows the user to simultaneously display the audio/visual of the deposition, the transcript, and the exhibits as they are discussed in the deposition.

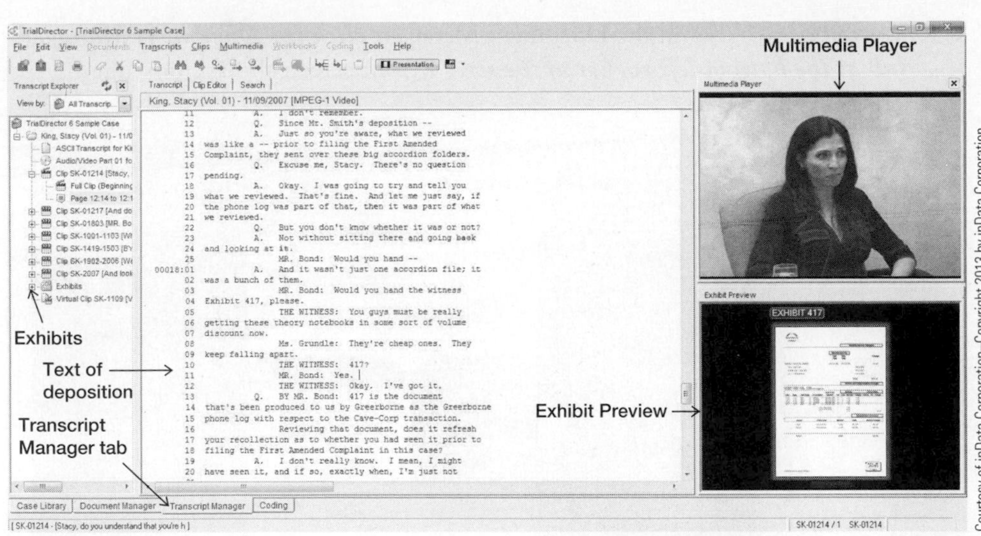

TRIALDIRECTOR EXHIBIT 4

9. ***Click the Case Library tab at the bottom left corner of the screen to return to the Case Library.*** We previously looked at the Case Explorer. We will now look at the Workbooks Explorer. Workbooks are essentially electronic files in which the user may place specific images for use at trial. Additional Workbooks may be created as needed.
10. ***Click the plus sign next to 01-Opening*** to see the exhibits that are to be used during the Opening Statement in this case. ***Then, double-click DEMO00071.*** The corresponding exhibit (a document from the California Insurance Group) appears in the Desktop Workspace.
11. We will now add another file to the 01-Opening Workbook. ***Click the plus sign next to the Exhibit DCWEST from the Documents file in the Case Explorer.*** Notice that a sub-file appears containing the one page of this document. ***Place your cursor on this sub-file, then click and drag the file down to 01-Opening Workbook.*** You will need to place the cursor directly over this file. You should now see DCWEST as a sub-file in the 01-Opening Workbook.
12. We will now create a new Workbook. To do so, ***right-click Workbooks in the Workbooks Explorer, then click Create New Workbook, then select Standard.*** Notice that a new workbook appears in the Workbook Explorer. It has the default name of New Workbook. We want this to contain our to-do list; to change the name to To Do List, type **To Do List** and press the [**ENTER**] key.
13. ***Click File, then click Exit.*** When prompted to **"Quit TrialDirector 6?,"** ***click Yes.***

This concludes Lesson 1.

LESSON 2: NAVIGATING IN TRIALDIRECTOR—PART II

In this lesson, you will work with the various annotation tools available in TrialDirector.

1. Start Windows. Then, ***double-click the TrialDirector icon on the desktop*** to start TrialDirector. Alternatively, ***click the Start button, point to Programs or All Programs, and then click the TrialDirector icon.*** If the Trial Registration window appears, ***click Continue. In the "Open a Case" window, select TrialDirector 6 Sample Case, then click Open.*** Your screen should look like TrialDirector Exhibit 1.
2. TrialDirector opens in the Case Library tab.

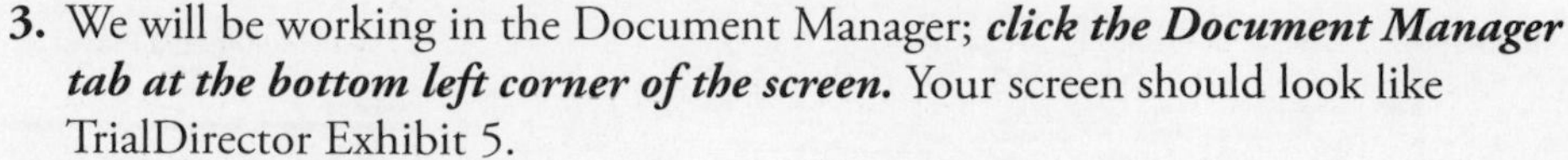

3. We will be working in the Document Manager; ***click the Document Manager tab at the bottom left corner of the screen.*** Your screen should look like TrialDirector Exhibit 5.

TRIALDIRECTOR EXHIBIT 5

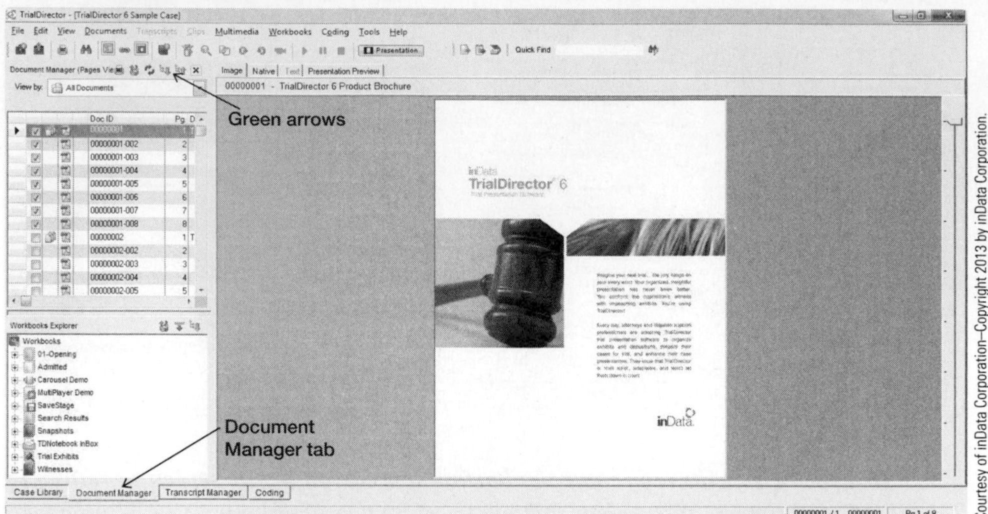

4. The grid view of documents allows you to list just the individual documents in the case or to list every page of each document. ***Click the green up arrow above the Case Explorer to show a list of just the individual documents. Click the green down arrow above the Case Explorer to show the list of every page of each document. Now, scroll down and click DEMO00001.*** A document titled Notice of Deposition of California Capital Insurance Company should appear in the Desktop Workspace.
5. ***Click the next document, DEMO00001-GS01.*** Your screen should now look like TrialDirector Exhibit 6. This is an example of how you can select a portion of a document you want to highlight for your audience and add annotations (or "markups") to it. Notice how the user has highlighted a portion of the text and has added an arrow, an ellipse, and a rectangle to draw attention to specific portions of the text. We will now explore the various annotation tools available in TrialDirector.
6. You will now mark up some documents, ***so click DEMO00003. Then, click the ninth icon on the toolbar*** (it looks like a coffee cup with some markers in it) to open the Image Annotation toolbar. The Annotation toolbar will open

TRIALDIRECTOR EXHIBIT 6

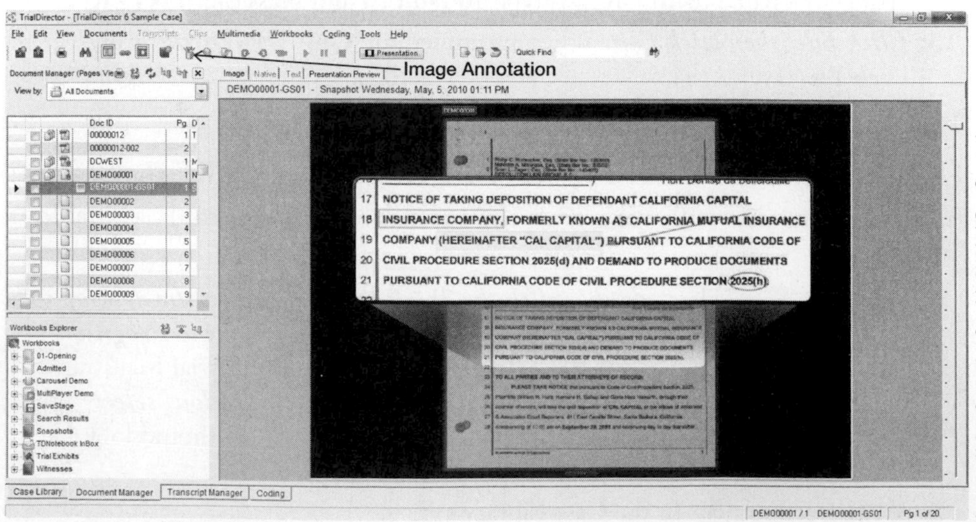

(see TrialDirector Exhibit 7). The first icon from the left is the Annotation Selector. It is used to adjust markups. We will use this tool later in this exercise.

7. The second icon from the left is the Highlighter. ***Click the Highlighter icon; the default color is yellow.*** For now, that is fine. We want to highlight paragraph 1 so ***move your cursor over paragraph 1 and then click and drag the cursor over the paragraph until the entire paragraph is highlighted yellow*** (see TrialDirector Exhibit 7). Note that if you make a mistake while annotating a document, you can remove an annotation (except redactions). ***To remove an annotation, with the same annotation tool selected, press [CTRL] while you right-click on the annotation you want to remove.***
8. On the right-hand side of the Annotation toolbar is the color selection palette. We will now highlight paragraph 2 in green (or whatever color you prefer). ***With the Highlighter tool still selected, click green on the color selection palette. Then, move your cursor over paragraph 2 and then click and drag the cursor over the paragraph until the entire paragraph is highlighted green*** (see TrialDirector Exhibit 7).
9. The third icon from the left is the Arrow tool, which can be used to point to an important point on an image. ***Click the Arrow tool icon, move the cursor next to the word "PLAINTIFFS," then click and drag the arrow*** (see TrialDirector Exhibit 7).
10. On the far right of the Annotation toolbar are tools to adjust the tool line width and the arrow pointer. ***Use your cursor to move both the tool line width and arrow pointer tools to the maximum (all the way to the right).*** You can also change the color of the arrow, so ***click the color black from the color selection palette. Then, with the Arrow tool still selected, move the cursor next to the words "ENVIRONMENTAL ACTIONS" then click and drag the arrow.*** See TrialDirector Exhibit 7.

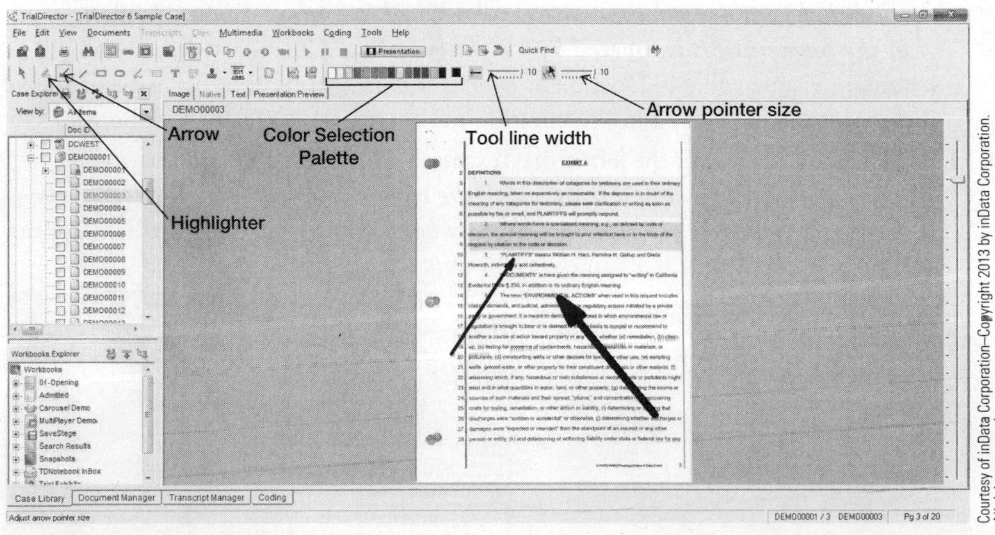

TRIALDIRECTOR EXHIBIT 7

11. We will now choose another image (DEMO00005) to markup. ***Click DEMO00005.*** Notice that when you do, a small window opens with options for saving the annotations. You can save the image with the markups or you can save a new image with the markups, leaving the original image unaltered. We will save these markups on a new image, so ***click Save as New Revision.*** Notice that a new file now appears on the grid (DEMO00003-01). ***Click DEMO00005*** and the image will appear in the Desktop Workspace.

12. The fourth icon from the left is the Line tool. This is used to underline something on an image. ***Click the Line tool icon, move the cursor under paragraph 10, then click and drag to draw a line under paragraph 10*** (see TrialDirector Exhibit 8). Notice that the Color and Width tools we used with the Arrow tool can also be used with the Line tool.
13. The fifth icon from the left is the Rectangle tool. This is used to draw a box around an important area of an image. We will draw a box around the section of the image titled I. PROCEDURES, GUIDELINES AND POLICIES INFORMATION. ***Click the Rectangle tool icon, move your cursor to the upper left corner of the desired section, then click and drag until the entire section is included within the box*** (see TrialDirector Exhibit 8). Notice that the Color and Width tools we used with the Arrow tool can also be used with the Rectangle tool.
14. The sixth icon from the left is the Ellipse tool. This is used to draw a circle or oval around an important area of an image. We will draw an ellipse around the text <u>HARZ v. ZELL ACTION</u> in paragraph 10 at the top of the image. ***Click the Ellipse tool icon and then click and drag it around the desired text until it is completely enclosed within the oval*** (see TrialDirector Exhibit 8). Notice that the Color and Width tools we used with the Arrow tool can also be used with the Ellipse tool.
15. The seventh icon from the left is the Freehand Draw tool. This is used to draw a freehand line or other mark on an image. We will use it to place your initials on the image. ***Click the Freehand Draw icon and then draw your initials at the bottom of the page*** (see TrialDirector Exhibit 8). Notice that the Color and Width tools we used with the Arrow tool can also be used with the Freehand Draw tool.
16. The eighth icon from the left is the Redaction tool. This is used to redact or cover up a section of an image. We will use it to redact the name of the Word file at the bottom right corner of the image. ***Click the Redaction tool icon and then click and drag the cursor over the Word file name seen at the bottom of the page until it is covered by a light gray box.*** The redacted material will remain visible while in Document Manager, but it would not be visible if the document were viewed in Presentation mode (see TrialDirector Exhibit 8).
17. The ninth icon from the left is the Text tool. This is used to add text to an image. ***Click the Text tool icon, move the cursor to the area to the left of the rectangle you drew earlier, then draw a box.*** This is where the text will appear.

TRIALDIRECTOR EXHIBIT 8

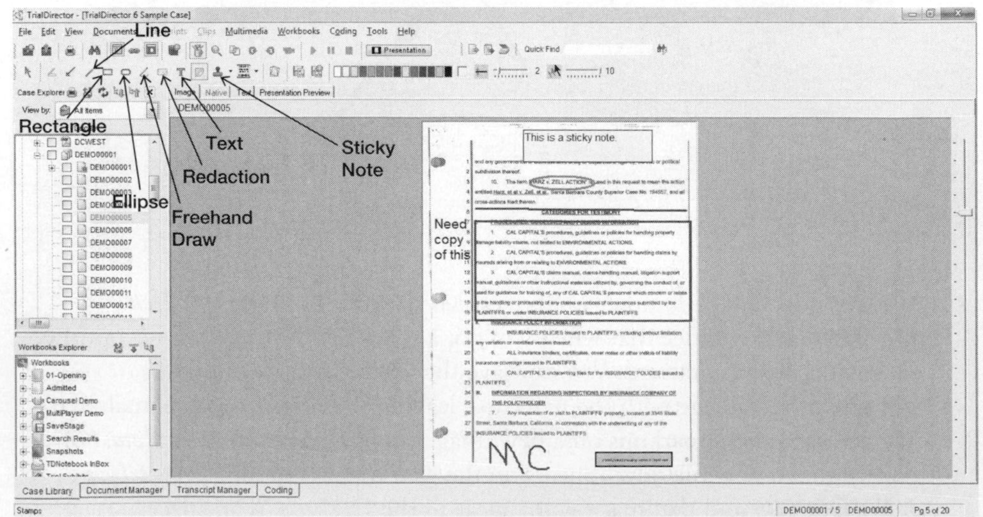

After you draw the box, type **Need copies of this**. ***Then, click somewhere outside of the text box;*** the box will disappear and only the text will remain (see TrialDirector Exhibit 8). It is possible that you may not be able to see all of your text now; you will when we change the font size later. You can also change the color of the text by selecting a color from the color selection palette.

18. The tenth icon from the left is the Sticky Note tool icon. It is used to create an electronic sticky note that looks like and acts like a real sticky note. ***Click the Sticky Note tool icon, move the cursor to the upper right corner of the image, then click and drag the cursor to draw a box similar to the one in TrialDirector Exhibit 8.*** Inside the box, type **This is a sticky note**, ***then click somewhere on the image outside of the sticky note box*** (see TrialDirector Exhibit 9).
19. The eleventh icon from the left is the Stamp tool icon. It is used to place a stamp on an image similar to the rubber stamps (and ink pads) that were used on paper documents. First, ***click the down arrow to the right of the Stamp tool icon***. A drop-down menu of the available stamps appears.
20. ***From the drop-down menu, click the Redact icon and then place your cursor over the redacted material at the bottom of the page and click one time.*** The word Redacted should now appear over that portion of the image (see TrialDirector Exhibit 9).

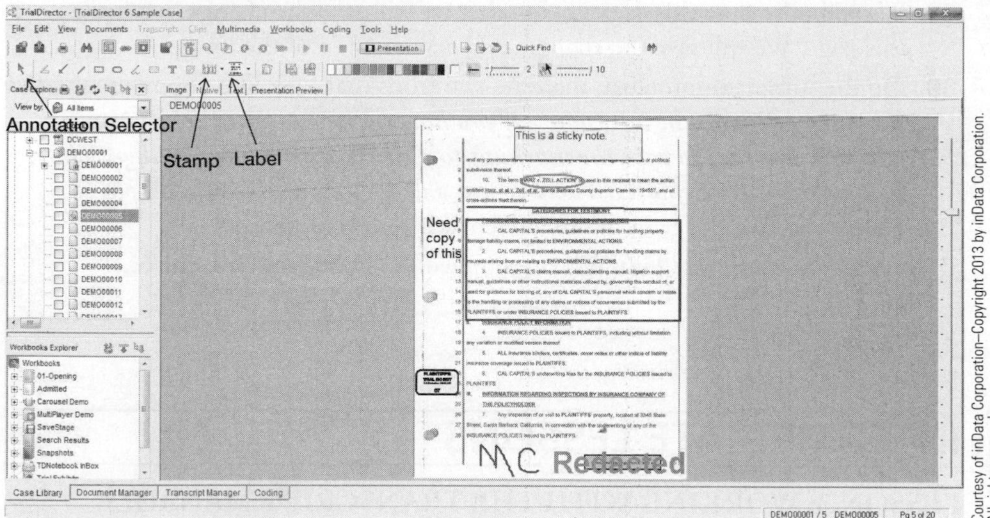

TRIALDIRECTOR EXHIBIT 9

21. The twelfth icon from the left is the Label tool icon. It is used to place an electronic label on an Image similar to the sticky labels that are applied to paper documents. ***First, click the down arrow to the right of the Label tool icon.*** A drop-down menu of the available labels appears.
22. ***From the drop-down menu, click the PLAINTIFF'S TRIAL EXHIBIT label.*** A window will open asking for the Exhibit number. Type **07**, ***then click OK. Then, move your cursor to the lower left hand corner of the image and click one time.*** The label should now appear in that spot (see TrialDirector Exhibit 9).
23. We will now go back to the first icon on the Annotation toolbar, the Annotation Selector tool. The Annotation Selector tool allows you to edit, move, resize, or delete an annotation. We will use the Annotation Selector to move the label we just made and placed at the lower left corner of the image to the upper left corner of the image.

24. ***Click one time on the Annotation Selector tool icon (the first icon on the left). Then, move your cursor over the label and click.*** Notice that the label now has a box around it with handles on the corners and sides. You can use these handles to move the label to another location on the image. ***To move the label, click the image and drag it to upper left corner of the image.***
25. The Annotation Selector tool can also be used to change the font of text within an annotation. We will change the font of the text within the sticky note at the upper right corner of the image.
26. ***With the Annotation Selector tool still selected, move your cursor over the text box and click.*** Again, notice that the text box now has a box around it with handles at the sides and corners. ***Now right-click the sticky note and a menu of options appears. Click the fifth option, Choose Font,*** and the Font dialog box opens.
27. In the Font dialog box, we will change the font to 22, ***so scroll down the size list until 22 appears. Click one time on 22 to select that size.***
28. You can also change the style of the font, add effects (strikeout and underline), and change the color of the font. ***Click the down arrow under Color and from the drop-down menu, click one time on Red. Then, click OK.*** The sticky note now has the new font and color. If you need to enlarge the sticky note so you can see all the text, you can do so by clicking on one of the handles and dragging it to the desired size.
29. We will now close this exercise, but first we will save the changes we made to this page. We will save the changes to a new revision of the image.
30. On the Annotation toolbar, there are two icons that look like floppy discs. ***Click the floppy disk on the left (note - if you hover your mouse over the icon, its title will appear) to save the markups to a new revision of the image. Then, look at the Case Explorer.*** There is now a new file DEMO0005-01. This is the new image of this document with the annotations.
31. ***Click File, then click Exit.*** When prompted to **"Quit TrialDirector 6?,"** ***click Yes.***

This concludes Lesson 2.

INTERMEDIATE LESSONS

LESSON 3: WORKING WITH THE TRANSCRIPT MANAGER

In this lesson, you will work with depositions, use the Word Index, and create a new clip.

1. Start Windows. Then, ***double-click the TrialDirector icon on the desktop*** to start TrialDirector. Alternatively, ***click the Start button, point to Programs or All Programs, and then click the TrialDirector icon.*** If the Trial Registration window appears, ***click Continue. In the "Open a Case" window, select TrialDirector 6 Sample Case, then click Open.*** Your screen should look like TrialDirector Exhibit 1.
2. TrialDirector opens in the Case Library tab.
3. We will be working with transcripts in this lesson, so ***click the Transcript Manager tab.*** Your screen should look like TrialDirector Exhibit 10. The components of the Transcript Manager include the Transcript Explorer, the Transcript Viewer, the Multimedia Player, and the Exhibit Preview.
4. ***Click the plus sign next to King, Stacy (Vol. 01)-11/09/2007- [MPEG -1 Video], then double-click the sub-file ASCII Transcript for King, Stacy (Vol. 1)-11/09/2007- [MPEG -1 Video]*** (an ASCII file is essentially just a text

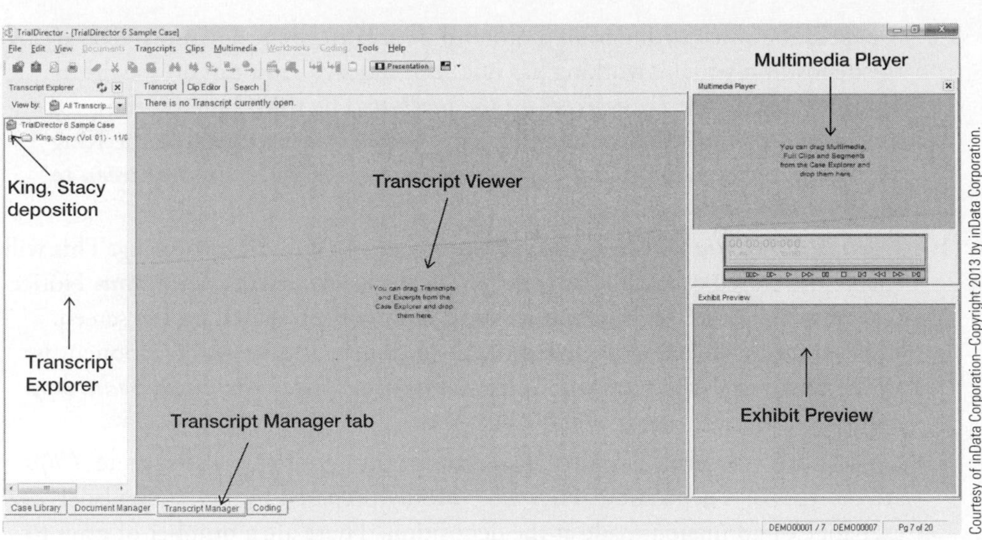

TRIALDIRECTOR EXHIBIT 10

file). Remember, if you cannot read the full file name, you can change the size of any screen component by dragging the borders to the desired location. The text of the King deposition now appears in the Transcript Viewer. ***Click the play button under the Multimedia Player*** (it is an arrow; the third icon from the left). The audio/video will begin to play in Multimedia Player. Notice that the transcript scrolls in time to the audio/video.

5. ***Click the stop button under the Multimedia Player*** (it is a square; the sixth icon from the left) to stop the audio/visual.
6. ***Click View on the toolbar and then click Word Index.*** The Word Index now appears to the left of the Transcript Viewer (see TrialDirector Exhibit 11). The Word Index is a comprehensive of every word (and non-words such as numbers) with links to their specific locations within the transcript.
7. ***Scroll down the Word Index until you see the word* "fraud." *Click the link 9:10 to the right of the word* "fraud."** Notice that the Transcript Viewer now highlights the testimony on page 9, line 10 of the deposition (see TrialDirector Exhibit 11). ***Clicking the multimedia arrow begins the Multimedia Player at that part of the deposition.***
8. ***Click the small x at the top right corner of the Word Index to close the Word Index.***

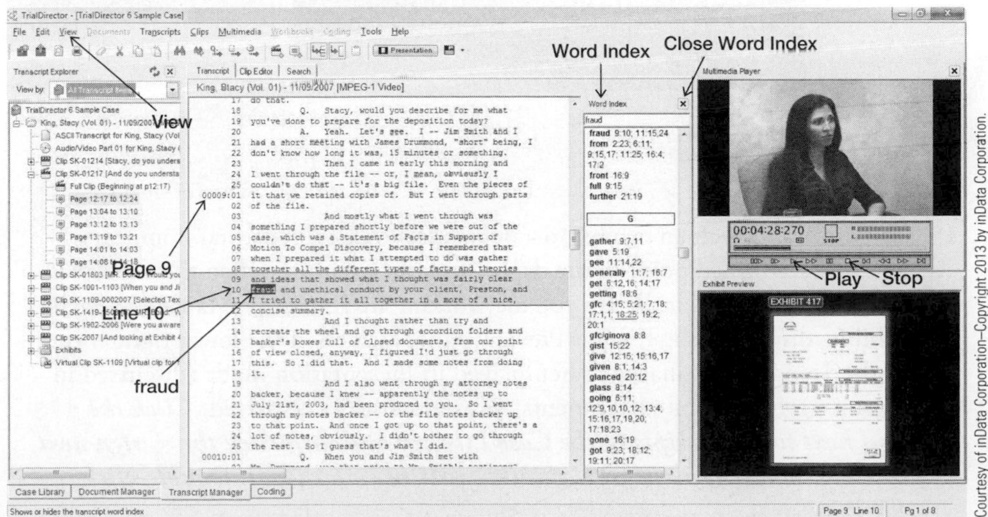

TRIALDIRECTOR EXHIBIT 11

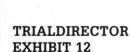

9. A deposition must be indexed in order to be able to create a Word Index. If the deposition you are working has not been indexed, you can do so within TrialDirector. ***Click Transcripts on the toolbar.*** The third item on the drop-down menu is Index Transcript. It is greyed out now because the King deposition has already been indexed. ***Click somewhere else on the screen to close the drop-down menu.***
10. ***Click Multimedia on the main menu, then click Closed Captioning.*** This will enable the closed captioning feature. ***Click the multimedia play arrow.*** Notice that now as the audio/visual plays, the testimony is presented on the screen. This can be beneficial when it is difficult to understand what the deponent is saying or can assist viewers with impaired hearing. ***Click the multimedia stop arrow*** (see TrialDirector Exhibit 11).
11. Look at the Transcript Explorer. There are a number of clips listed there. *Clips* are excerpts of a deposition. They are typically prepared to highlight a brief exchange or admission made at the deposition. There are a number of ways to create a new clip. We will use the one-step clip creation method.
12. The first step is to select the portion of the text to be included. ***Scroll through the transcript until you come to page 8, line 18. Place your cursor on that line and click and drag the cursor down to page 9, line 25*** (see TrialDirector Exhibit 12).
13. ***With your cursor on the selected text, right-click. From the menu, click Create New Clip from Selected Text*** (see TrialDirector Exhibit 11).
14. The new clip has been created and may now be found in the Transcript Explorer (see TrialDirector Exhibit 12).

HANDS-ON EXERCISES

TRIALDIRECTOR EXHIBIT 12

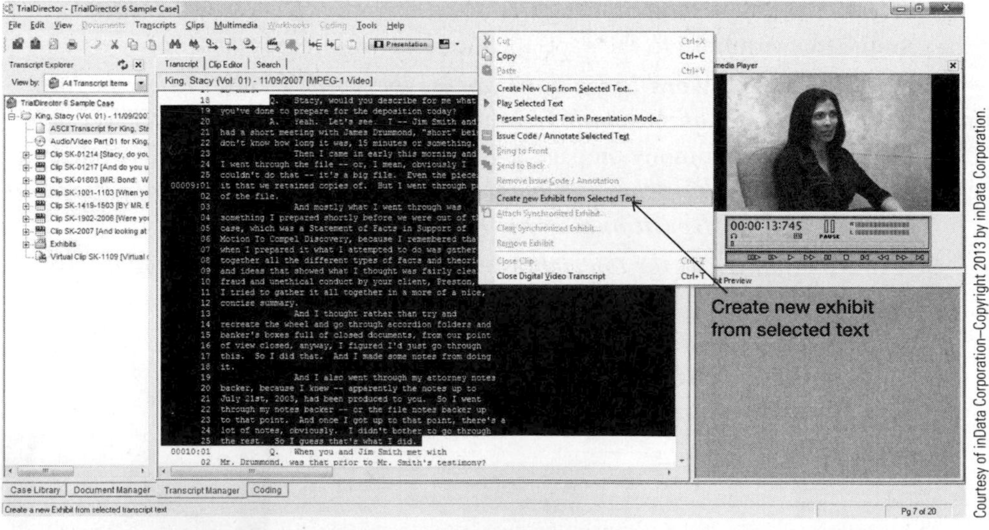

15. You can also attach an exhibit to a deposition transcript so that it appears at a predetermined point in the deposition; for example, when the witness is discussing the exhibit. When you are working in Transcript Manager, attached exhibits display in the Exhibit Preview pane, located in the lower right corner of the Transcript Manager. When played in Presentation mode (discussed in Lesson 5), the exhibit attachments are automatically displayed. ***Click the + sign next to Transcripts in the Case Library and then click the + sign next to King, Stacey (Vol. 01)-11/09/2007 [MPEG - 1 Video]. Double-click SK-2007.***

16. You should now be in the Transcript Manager tab. Notice that Exhibit 417 (a phone log) is discussed at page 20, line 7. We want that exhibit to appear at this point of the deposition, so we will attach a copy of the exhibit to this part of the transcript. First, ***click the Transcripts drop-down menu and select Display Attached Exhibits (so it has a checkmark next to it); then click the View drop-down menu, click Options, and then click both Show Attached Exhibits and Synchronize Exhibits (so they have a checkmark next to them). Click the Apply button.*** Note - if the specified options are already selected, and the Apply button is not responsive, you may need to click on them again (but be sure both options have a checkmark).

17. ***Click the Case Library and then click the + sign next to Documents. Scroll down to Exhibit 417 and click it. Click the Transcript Manager to return to the selected portion of the deposition. Place your cursor at the end of page 20, line 10.*** (Note that TrialDirector advises placing the exhibit a few lines below the specific reference to it.) ***Right-click and select Attach Synchronized Exhibit.*** The Attach Synchronized Exhibit window will open. The Exhibit description and Exhibit identifier have already been filled in, so ***click Next.*** At the next screen, ***click Attach.*** The exhibit is now attached to the deposition.

18. Now it is necessary to remove the attached exhibit after it has been discussed by the deponent. ***Place your cursor at the end of page 20, line 17. Right-click and select Clear Synchronized Exhibit and then click Clear.*** At run time the exhibit would disappear from the deposition at this point.

19. To view this clip with the exhibit attached, ***click SK-2007 and then double-click Full Clip (Beginning at p.20:7).*** You should see the clip with Exhibit 417 appearing and then disappearing. In Lesson 5, you will have the opportunity to view this in Presentation Preview.

20. ***Click File and then click Exit.*** When prompted to **"Quit TrialDirector 6?,"** ***click Yes.***

This concludes Lesson 3.

LESSON 4: CREATING A NEW CASE AND ISSUE CODES

In this lesson, you will create a new case and assign issue codes to a deposition.

1. Start Windows. Then, ***double-click the TrialDirector icon on the desktop*** to start TrialDirector. Alternatively, ***click the Start button, point to Programs or All Programs, and then click the TrialDirector icon.*** If the Trial Registration window appears, ***click Continue. In the "Open a Case" window, select TrialDirector 6 Sample Case, then click Open.*** Your screen should look like TrialDirector Exhiblt 1.
2. TrialDirector opens in the Case Library tab.
3. To create a new case in TrialDirector, there are several options. ***Click the New Case icon*** (the first icon on the left—it looks like a briefcase). The "Create a New Case" window opens and asks where the new case should be located in the computer. The default location is fine, so ***click Next.***
4. In the next window, you need to enter the name of the case. Type **Hatfield v. McCoy** in the text box under Description. The Matter Number is the internal file number assigned the case by the law firm. Type **123ABC** in the text box next to Matter number. The text box next to Notes: can be used to include the court's civil action number, the name of the judge assigned to the case, and other information. In the text box next to Notes: type **CV-JDC-120429** (see TrialDirector Exhibit 13). ***Click Next.***

HANDS-ON EXERCISES

TRIALDIRECTOR EXHIBIT 13

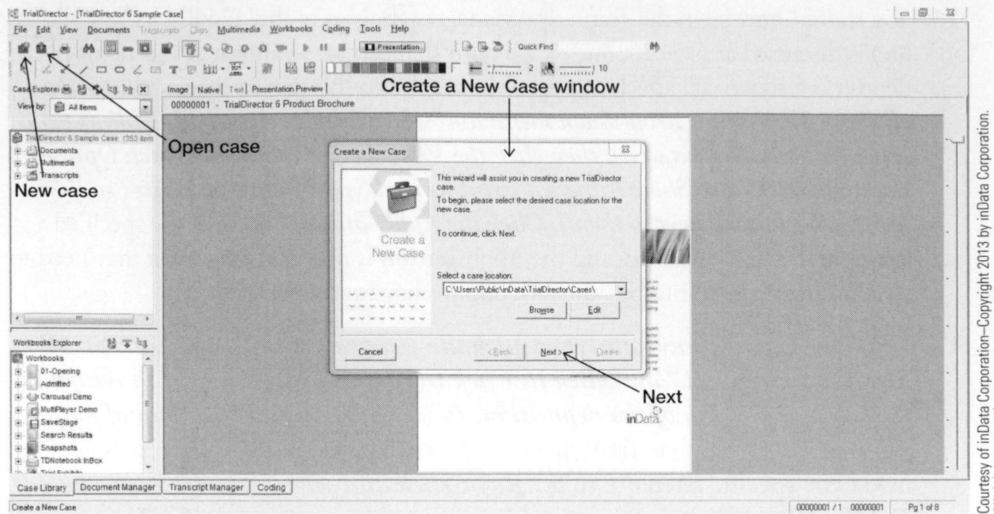

5. The next window gives the user the opportunity to enable additional layers of security by creating a password that would be required of any users seeking access to this case and enable case encryption to encrypt the case databases. We will not enable security for this case, so ***click Create***. Your screen should now look like TrialDirector Exhibit 14.

TRIALDIRECTOR EXHIBIT 14

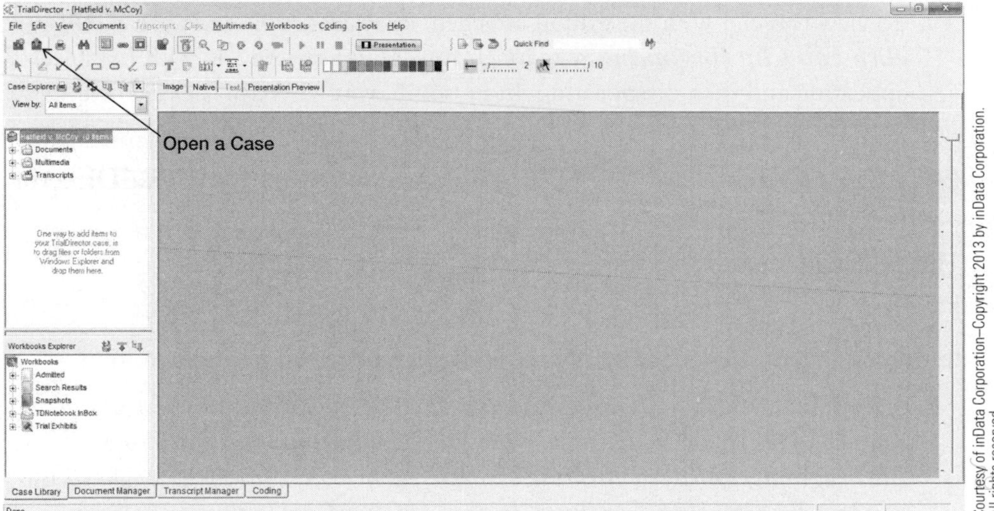

6. We will now go back to the Transcript Manager and see how issue codes are created and used to facilitate the organization and retrieval of information at trial.
7. Since our new case does not have any files in it, ***click the Open a Case icon, see TrialDirector Exhibit 14, and then select TrialDirector 6 Sample Case. Click Open. Then, click the Transcript Manager tab.***
8. TrialDirector allows the user to assign issue codes to specific images and sections of depositions. Similar to the way issue codes are used in litigation support software, they organize disparate pieces of evidence into coherent files. (*Note*: It is possible to import issue codes that have already been created in Summation at the time those files are imported.) Issue codes thus make it easier to retrieve specific pieces of evidence when they are needed. (When you are at a trial or hearing, the judge is not going to wait while you rifle through your notebooks looking for the "smoking gun.")

HANDS-ON EXERCISES

9. We will assign issue codes to portions of the deposition of Stacy King. ***In the Transcript Manager, click the plus sign to the left of King, Stacy (Vol. 01)-11/09/2007-MPEG in the Transcript Explorer. Then, double-click ASCII Transcript for King, Stacy (Vol. 1)-11/09/2007-[MPEG - 1 Video].***
10. We will create an issue code for discussions of "fraud" during the deposition. To find these portions of the deposition, we will use the Word Index feature we looked at in an earlier lesson.
11. ***Click View from the toolbar and then click Word Index.***
12. ***At the top of the Word Index is an empty text box.*** Type **fraud** in the text box, ***then click the first entry (9:10).*** Notice that the reference to "fraud" occurs toward the end of the answer to a question that appears at page 8, line 18. Generally, when making video clips or assigning an issue code, it is better practice to include more than just the specific line in which the key word is uttered. You want to provide some context for this information, so we will include the question asked of the witness and the entire answer in our issue code. Before you can begin to work with issue codes, you need to ***click Transcripts on the main toolbar and click Display Issue Codes*** (make sure there is a checkmark next to it).
13. To create an issue code, you must first select the specific portion of the text to which this code is to be assigned. ***So move your cursor to the question beginning at page 8, line 18 and then click and drag the cursor down to page 9, line 25.***
14. ***Then, with the cursor over the selected text, right-click and then click Issue Code/Annotate Selected Text. The Issue Code/Annotate Selected Text box will open. Click Manage....***
15. The Manage Issue Codes... box opens. ***Click New.*** A new issue code (F1) appears next to a yellow rectangle. The description currently reads New issue code. ***The cursor should already be at the end of this description, so click the Backspace key one time to clear the text*** and then type **Fraud** (see TrialDirector Exhibit 15). ***Click Exit to close this box.***

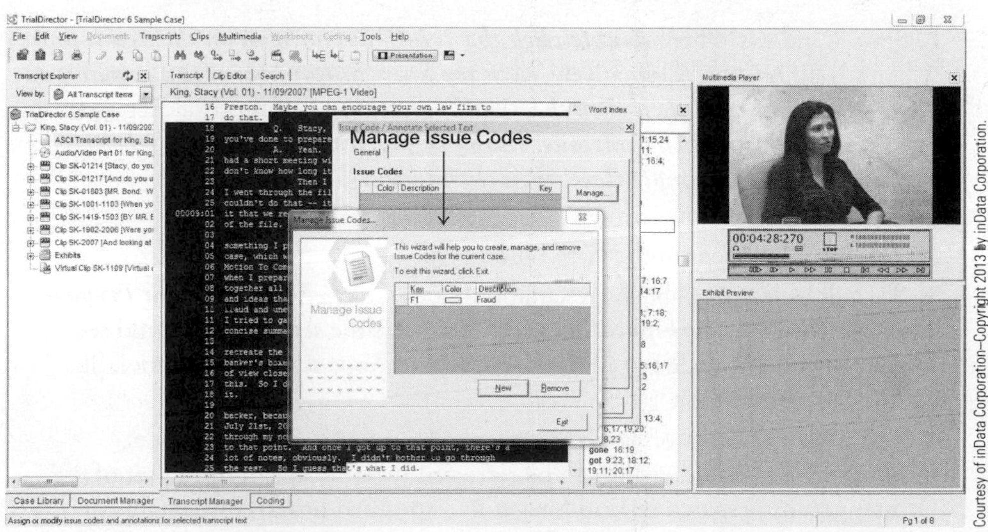

TRIALDIRECTOR EXHIBIT 15

16. You are now back in the Issue Codes/Annotate Selected Text box, but now notice that the new issue code for fraud appears. ***Click the small square at the left of the line on which Fraud appears; a checkmark should appear. Then, click Apply.*** The color of the selected text will change. ***Click Exit to close the Issue Codes/Annotate Selected text box, then click anywhere on the***

transcript. Notice that the selected text is highlighted and that a new sub-file appears in the Transcript Explorer under the file Issue Codes and Annotations, called Fraud, with a reference to the specific portion of the text we selected.

17. We will now repeat this process for the two other references to fraud. ***Click the link to the second reference to fraud at page 11, line 15***. Again we want to include the complete question and answer with the reference to fraud. ***Place your cursor at page 11, line 4 and click and drag the cursor to page 12, line 5.***
18. ***Then, with the cursor over the selected text, right-click and then click Issue Code/Annotate Selected Text. The Issue Code/Annotate Selected Text box will open.*** Notice that the issue code for fraud already exists, so ***click the small square at the left of the line on which Fraud appears; a checkmark should appear. Then, click Apply.*** The color of the selected text will change. ***Click Exit to close the Issue Codes/Annotate Selected text box, then click anywhere on the transcript.*** Notice that the selected text is now highlighted and that a new sub-file appears in the Transcript Explorer under the Issue Codes and Annotations file called Fraud with a reference to the specific portion of the text we selected.
19. ***Click the link to the third reference to fraud at page 11, line 24.*** Notice that this reference is part of the text selected for the issue code of fraud in the previous step, so no further action is required.
20. ***Click File, then click Exit.*** When prompted to **"Quit TrialDirector 6?,"** ***click Yes.***

This concludes Lesson 4.

ADVANCED LESSON

LESSON 5: WORKING IN PRESENTATION MODE

In this lesson, you will explore Presentation mode.

1. Start Windows. Then, ***double-click the TrialDirector icon on the desktop*** to start TrialDirector. Alternatively, ***click the Start button, point to Programs or All Programs, and then click the TrialDirector icon.*** If the Trial Registration window appears, ***click Continue. In the "Open a Case" window, select TrialDirector 6 Sample Case, then click Open.*** Your screen should look like TrialDirector Exhibit 1.
2. TrialDirector opens in the Case Library tab.
3. We will be learning about Presentation mode, so ***click Presentation Preview in the Desktop Workspace.*** This tool simulates the screens you would see in Presentation mode but is easier to navigate. Your screen should look like TrialDirector Exhibit 16.
4. There are a number of ways to display images in Presentation mode. For example, images made can be retrieved by creating a script (a set of instructions prepared to load images in a specified order), by using a bar code reader (each image in TrialDirector is assigned a unique bar code), or by entering the exhibit number. We will use exhibit numbers to load images into Presentation mode.
5. Before loading a document into Presentation mode, it is important to understand the concept of zones. It is possible to load images using the full screen or place two zones side by side (or one atop the other), or to place up to

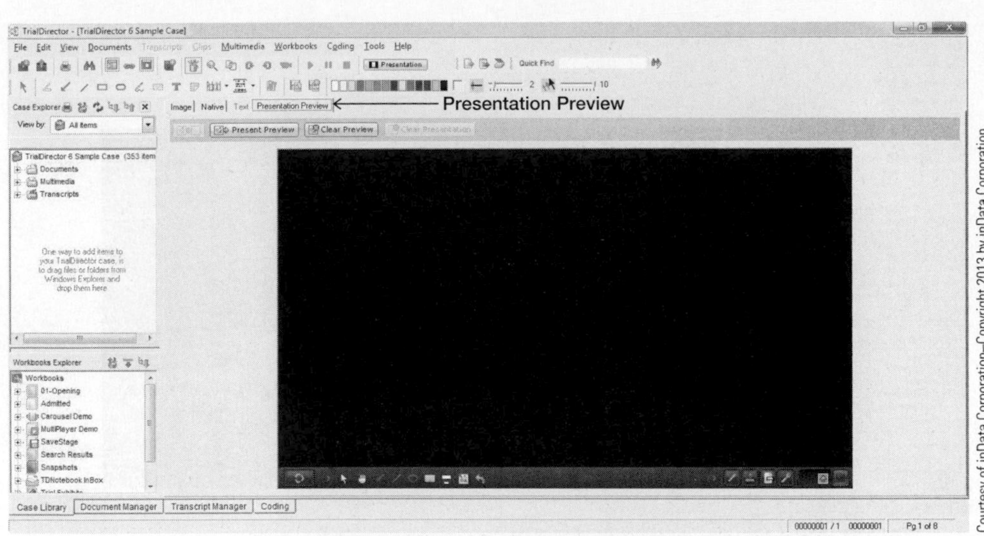

TRIALDIRECTOR EXHIBIT 16

four documents in the four quadrants of the screen. In TrialDirector, the zones are used as follows:

Zones 1 & 2 split the display vertically.
Zones 3 & 4 split the display horizontally.
Zones 5, 6, 7, & 8 split the display into quadrants.
Zone 9 uses the full display. This is the default zone. If you do not choose a zone, your images will display using the full screen. In Presentation Preview, you can drag and drop a document in any of the nine areas. The following diagram shows where to drop a document to display it in a specific zone.

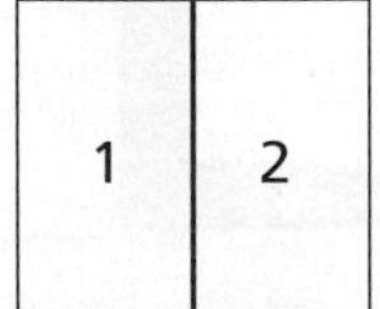

3
4

5
6
7
8

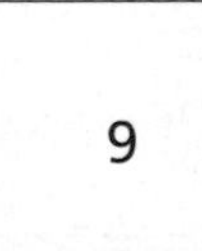

6. Zones may also be selected by clicking the corresponding Function (or F key) on your keyboard. For example, to place an image on the left side of the screen (Zone 1), you would click the F1 key. You may also change the zone by using the Select Zone/Zone Indicator at the bottom far right of the Presentation toolbar.
7. ***Click the plus sign next to Documents to see all the documents. Scroll down to DEMO0066. Click the plus sign next to DEMO0066. Place your cursor on DEMO0066 and drag it to the center of the Presentation Preview screen and then release the cursor.*** The document should appear in the center of the screen (see TrialDirector Exhibit 17).
8. ***Place your cursor over the upper right corner of the document;*** the +, −, and × symbols will appear (see TrialDirector Exhibit 17). ***Place your cursor over the + symbol and practice dragging it to other zones. Click the small − to return the document to the center of the screen. Place your cursor on the + symbol and drag it to Zone 1 (left side). Place your cursor on DEMO0067 in the Case Explorer and drag it to Zone 2 (right side of the Presentation Preview screen) and then release the cursor.*** Your screen should now look like TrialDirector Exhibit 18.
9. It is possible to select a portion of an image and enlarge it to emphasize it to the audience. A callout is an enlargement of a portion of an image displayed

TRIALDIRECTOR EXHIBIT 17

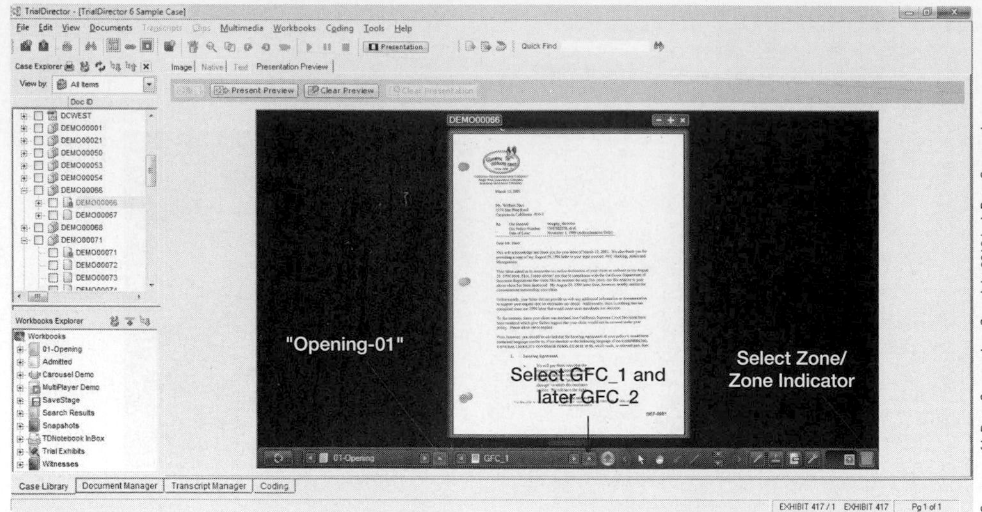

TRIALDIRECTOR EXHIBIT 18

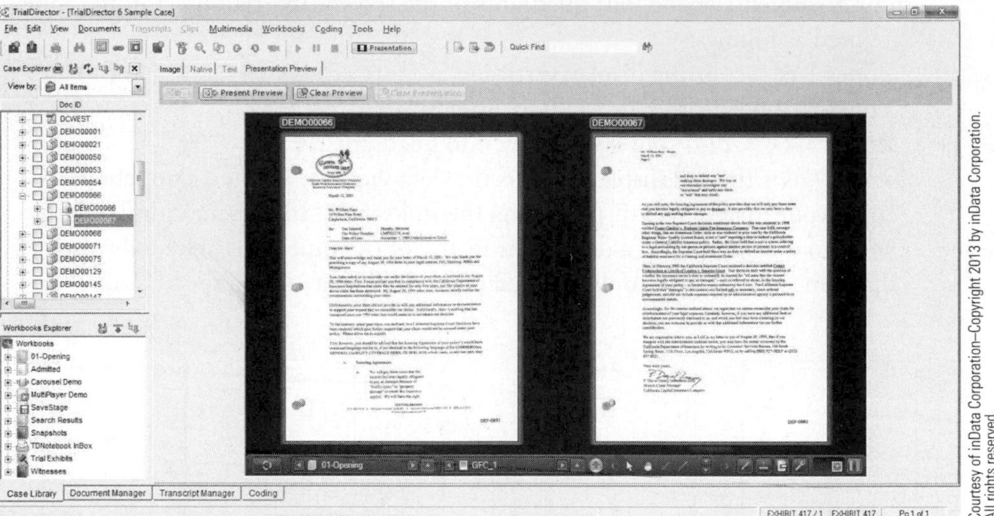

over the image of the complete document. You will first select a text document, so ***select document DEMO0053 and drag it to the center of the screen. Click the Callout Zoom Type icon at the bottom of the screen (see TrialDirector Exhibit 19), then select Projection Zoom. Then place your cursor over the portion of the document, as noted in TrialDirector Exhibit 19. Click and drag your cursor until the entire section is included within the box.*** When you release, the callout will appear over the image of the complete document (see TrialDirector Exhibit 19). You can move the callout by clicking on it and dragging it to the desired location.

10. You can show other forms of evidence in Presentation mode. ***Click Clear Preview to clear the screen*** (see TrialDirector Exhibit 19).

11. We want to display deposition testimony and attached exhibit we prepared in Lesson 3. ***Click the + sign next to Transcripts and then click the + sign next to King, Stacey (Vol. 01)-11/09/2007 [MPEG - 1 Video]. Click and drag SK-2007 to the center of the screen and then release the cursor. After the file has loaded, click the play button (a right facing arrow in a circle). The video clip will appear and Exhibit 417 will appear then disappear*** (see TrialDirector Exhibit 20).

TRIALDIRECTOR EXHIBIT 19

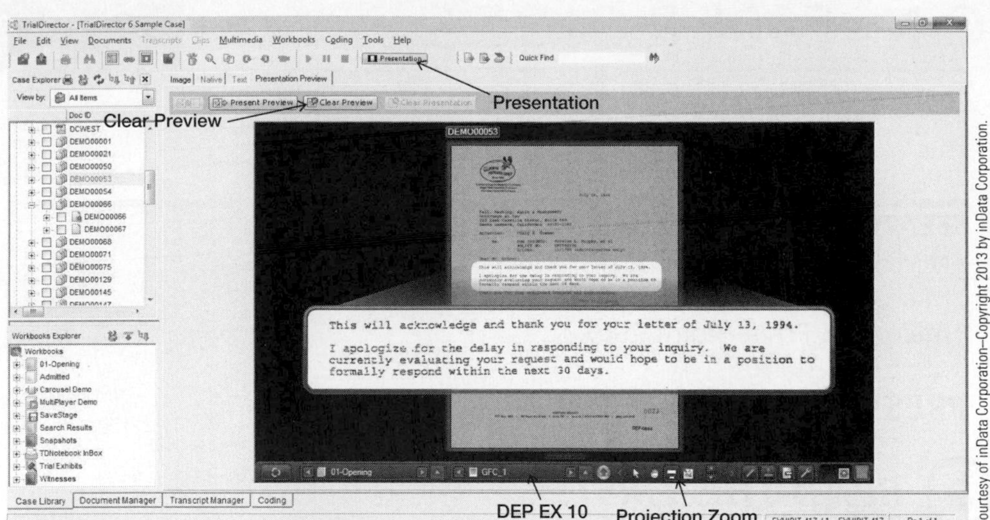

TRIALDIRECTOR EXHIBIT 20

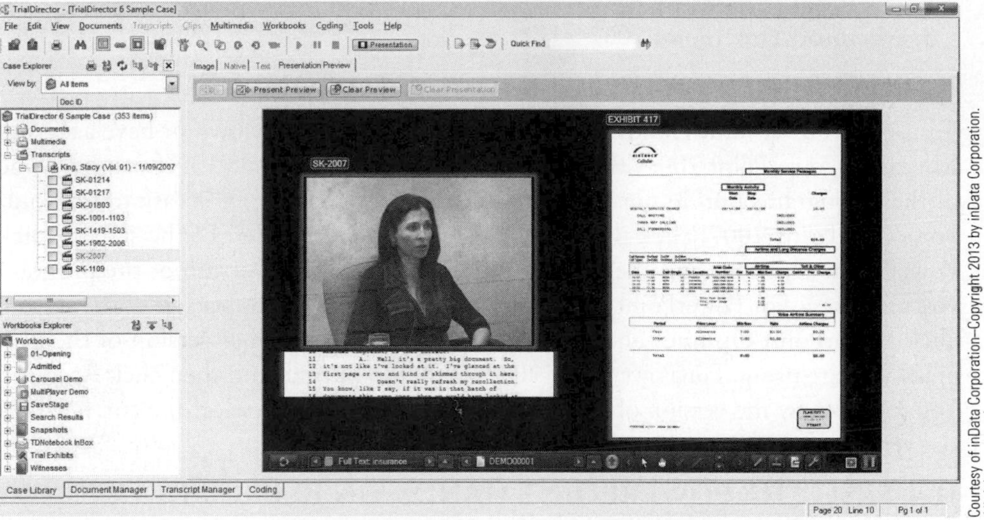

12. ***Click File, then click Exit.*** When prompted to **"Quit TrialDirector 6?,"** ***click Yes.***

This concludes the TrialDirector Hands-On Exercises.

HANDS-ON EXERCISES

FEATURED SOFTWARE
Microsoft PowerPoint 2013
Microsoft PowerPoint 2010
Microsoft PowerPoint 2007

PRESENTATION SOFTWARE

READ THIS FIRST!

1. Microsoft PowerPoint 2013
2. Microsoft PowerPoint 2010
3. Microsoft PowerPoint 2007

I. DETERMINING WHICH TUTORIAL TO COMPLETE

To use the PowerPoint Hands-On Exercises, you must already own or have access to Microsoft PowerPoint 2007, PowerPoint 2010, or PowerPoint 2013. If you have one of these programs but do not know the version you are using, it is easy to find out. For PowerPoint 2007, click the Office button in the upper left of the screen, click PowerPoint Options, and then click Resources to see what version of the program you are using. For PowerPoint 2010, click the File tab in the upper left of the screen, click PowerPoint Options, and then click Resources to see what version of the program you are using. For PowerPoint 2013, click the File tab and then click Account. You must know the version of the program you are using and select the correct tutorial version or the tutorials will not work correctly.

II. USING THE POWERPOINT HANDS-ON EXERCISES

The PowerPoint Hands-On Exercises in this section are easy to use and contain step-by-step instructions. They start with basic skills and proceed to intermediate and advanced levels. If you already have a good working knowledge of PowerPoint, you may be able to proceed directly to the intermediate and advanced exercises. To truly be ready for using presentation software in the legal environment, you must be able to accomplish the tasks and exercises in the more advanced exercises.

III. ACCESSING THE DATA

Some of the advanced PowerPoint Hands-On Exercises use documents on the Premium Website. To access these files, go to your CengageBrain account and click the link for Premium Website for Cornick's *Using Computers in the Law Office*, seventh edition. A new window will open. Under Book Level Resources, click the link for Data Files: PowerPoint and then click the link to the desired lesson. When prompted, click Open.

IV. INSTALLATION QUESTIONS

If you have installation questions regarding installing the exercise data file from the Premium Website, you may contact Technical Support at http://cengage.com/support.

HANDS-ON EXERCISES

MICROSOFT POWERPOINT 2013

Number	Lesson Title	Concepts Covered
BASIC LESSONS		
Lesson 1	Creating a Presentation	Selecting a presentation design, entering text, entering speaker's notes, and saving a file
Lesson 2	Creating Additional Slides	Inserting a new slide; selecting a slide layout; viewing a slide in Slide Show, Outline, and Slide Sorter views; and creating additional slides
INTERMEDIATE LESSONS		
Lesson 3	Creating a Graph	Creating and entering data in a chart
ADVANCED LESSON		
Lesson 4	Finalizing the Presentation	Creating transition effects, creating animation effects, and viewing a final presentation

HANDS-ON EXERCISES

GETTING STARTED

Overview

Microsoft PowerPoint 2013 is a presentation graphics program. It allows you to create presentations, charts, graphs, tables, and much more. PowerPoint 2013 is an easy-to-use program. Note that you will be creating a presentation for an opening statement presentation.

Introduction

Throughout these lessons and exercises, information you need to operate the program will be designated in several different ways:

- Keys to be pressed on the keyboard are designated in brackets, in all caps, and in bold (e.g., press the **[ENTER]** key).
- Movements with the mouse pointer are designated in bold and italics (e.g., ***point to File and click***).
- Words or letters that should be typed are designated in bold (type **Training Program**).
- Information that is or should be displayed on your computer screen is shown in bold, with quotation marks (e.g., **"Press ENTER to continue."**).
- Specific menu items and commands are designated with an initial capital letter (e.g., click Open).

BASIC LESSONS

LESSON 1: CREATING A PRESENTATION

In this lesson, you will start PowerPoint 2013, select a background design for the opening statement presentation, enter the first slide, view your slide, and save your presentation.

1. Start Windows. After it has loaded, ***double-click the Microsoft PowerPoint button, point to Programs or All Programs, click Microsoft Office, and then click Microsoft PowerPoint 2013.***

2. When PowerPoint 2013 opens, it gives you several ways to start a presentation: using a template, a theme, a recent presentation, or a blank presentation. ***Click Blank Presentation.***
3. A blank title screen should now be displayed.
4. ***Click "Click to add title."*** Notice that you are now allowed to type your own title. Type **OPENING STATEMENT** (see PowerPoint 2013 Exhibit 1).

POWERPOINT 2013 EXHIBIT 1

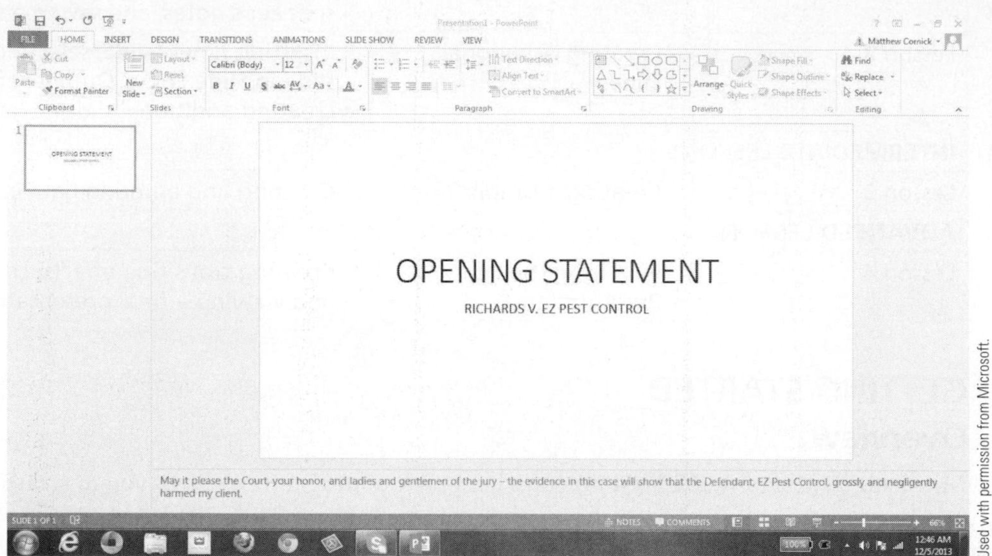
OPENING STATEMENT
RICHARDS V. EZ PEST CONTROL
May it please the Court, your honor, and ladies and gentlemen of the jury – the evidence in this case will show that the Defendant, EZ Pest Control, grossly and negligently harmed my client.

5. ***If the text is not centered, on the Home ribbon tab, click the Center icon in the Paragraph group. Click "Click to add subtitle."*** Type **RICHARDS V. EZ PEST CONTROL** (see PowerPoint 2013 Exhibit 1).
6. ***If the text is not centered, on the Home ribbon tab, click the Center icon in the Paragraph group.***
7. The slide is now created.
8. To view your slide, ***click the Slide Show icon in the lower right of your screen*** (see PowerPoint 2013 Exhibit 1). *Note:* You will see four icons in the lower right of the screen (for Normal view, Slide Sorter view, Reading view, and Slide Show view). The Slide Show icon is all the way to the right. Remember, if you point to any icon and hold the mouse pointer there for a second, the title of the icon will be displayed.
9. You should now see your slide displayed full screen on your computer. This is how your audience will see your slide.
10. Press **[ESC]** to return to editing your presentation.
11. At the bottom of the screen, under the current slide, ***click NOTES***. Now, under the slide, it says **"Click to add notes."** This is the Speaker's Notes section of the screen. Speaker's Notes are not shown in Slide Show view, but they can be printed so that the presenter has talking points from which to speak.
12. ***Click anywhere in the Speaker's Notes section.*** Now, type **May it please the Court, your honor, and ladies and gentlemen of the jury – the evidence in this case will show that the Defendant, EZ Pest Control, grossly and negligently harmed my client** (see PowerPoint 2013 Exhibit 1.)

13. ***Click the Slide Show icon in the lower right of the screen again.*** Notice that speaker's notes do not appear.
14. Press **[ESC]** to return to editing your presentation.
15. It is a good idea to save your presentation often. To save your presentation, ***click the File tab and then click Save; then click Computer; then click My Documents.***
16. Type **Richards Opening Statement and** ***then click Save*** to save the file in the default directory. Be sure to remember where the file is saved so that you can retrieve it in the next lesson.

This concludes Lesson 1. To exit PowerPoint, ***click the File tab and then click Close.*** To go directly to Lesson 2, stay at the current screen.

LESSON 2: CREATING ADDITIONAL SLIDES

In this lesson, you will add more slides to the presentation you created in Lesson 1, and you will look at the presentation using several views. If you did not exit PowerPoint from Lesson 1, go to Step 3.

1. Start Windows. When it has loaded, ***double-click the Microsoft Office PowerPoint 2013 icon on the desktop*** to start PowerPoint 2013 for Windows. Alternatively, ***click the Start button, point to Programs or All Programs, and then click the Microsoft PowerPoint 2013 icon (or point to Microsoft Office and then click Microsoft PowerPoint 2013).***
2. When PowerPoint 2013 opens, it gives you several ways to start a presentation: using a template, a theme, a recent presentation, or a blank presentation. ***Under Recent, click Richards Opening Statement.***
3. You should have the "Richards Opening Statement" slide on your screen. Notice in the lower left of the screen that it says **"SLIDE 1 of 1."** This shows you what slide number you are on.
4. To create a new slide, ***on the Home ribbon tab, click the down arrow next to New Slide in the Slides group*** (see PowerPoint 2013 Exhibit 2). Notice that the program offers you a number of different layouts.
5. ***Click the Title and Content option.***
6. A new slide is displayed on your screen. The top part of the slide should say **"Click to add title"** and the bottom section of the slide (next to a bullet) should say **"Click to add text."** There should also be graphics in the center of the screen.
7. ***Click*** **"Click to add title."** Type **Reasons for Lawsuit** (see PowerPoint 2013 Exhibit 2).
8. ***On the Home ribbon tab, click the Center icon in the Paragraph group.***
9. ***Click*** **"Click to add text."** Type **Recovery of damages from EZ Pest for negligence and breach of contract** and press the **[ENTER]** key. Notice that an additional bullet has been created.
10. Type **EZ Pest's Termite Inspection Report failed to find four massive termite colonies** and then press the **[ENTER]** key.
11. Type **Sherry Richards purchased the home based on the favorable termite report by EZ Pest Control** and press the **[ENTER]** key.
12. The slide is now created (see PowerPoint 2013 Exhibit 2).
13. To view your slide, ***click the Slide Show icon.***

HANDS-ON EXERCISES

14. You should now see your slide displayed full screen on your computer. With the slide running in Slide Show view, press the **[Page Up]** key and notice that the first slide is now shown on your screen. Press the **[Page Down]** key and notice that you are back at the second slide.

POWERPOINT 2013 EXHIBIT 2

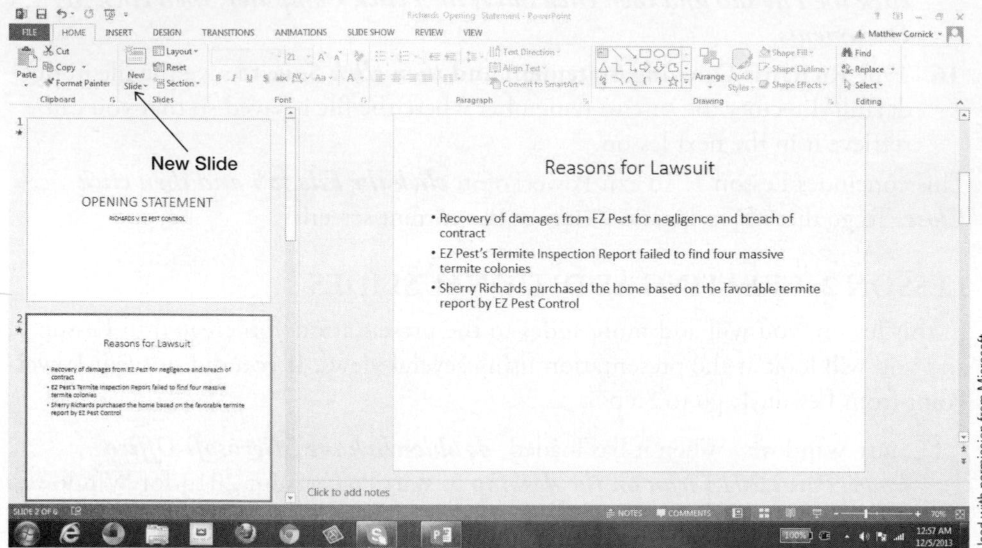

15. Press the **[ESC]** key to return to Normal view.
16. You will now look at your presentation using other views. ***Click the VIEW tab, and then in the Presentation Views group, click Outline View.***
17. The Outline view is now displayed; notice that you can read the words on both of your slides (see PowerPoint 2013 Exhibit 3).

POWERPOINT 2013 EXHIBIT 3

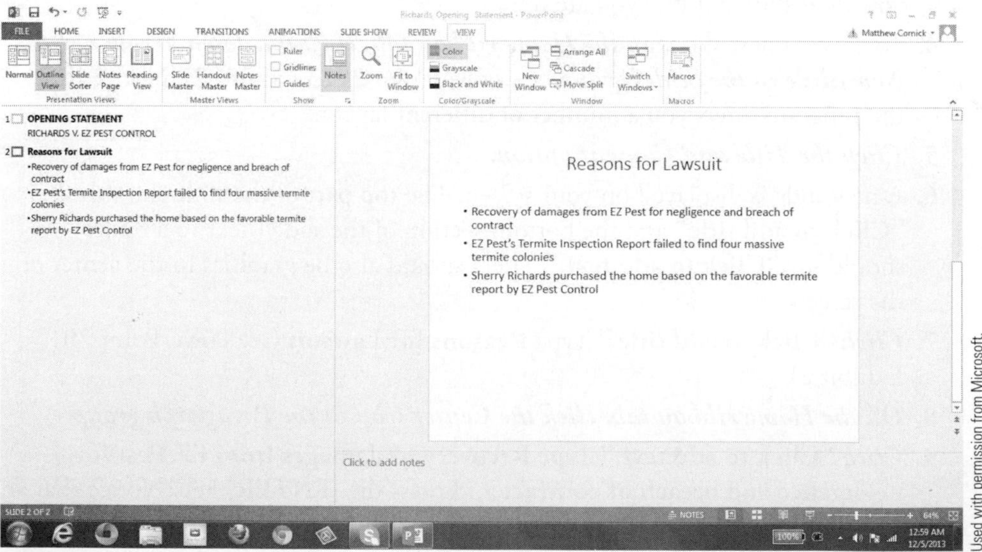

18. In the Presentation Views group, ***click Normal*** to go back to the Slides view.
19. You will now view your slides using the Slide Sorter view. ***Click the Slide Sorter view icon.***
20. Notice that you can see all your slides on the screen at the same time (see PowerPoint 2013 Exhibit 4). This is helpful for getting an overview of your presentation and arranging and rearranging your slide order.

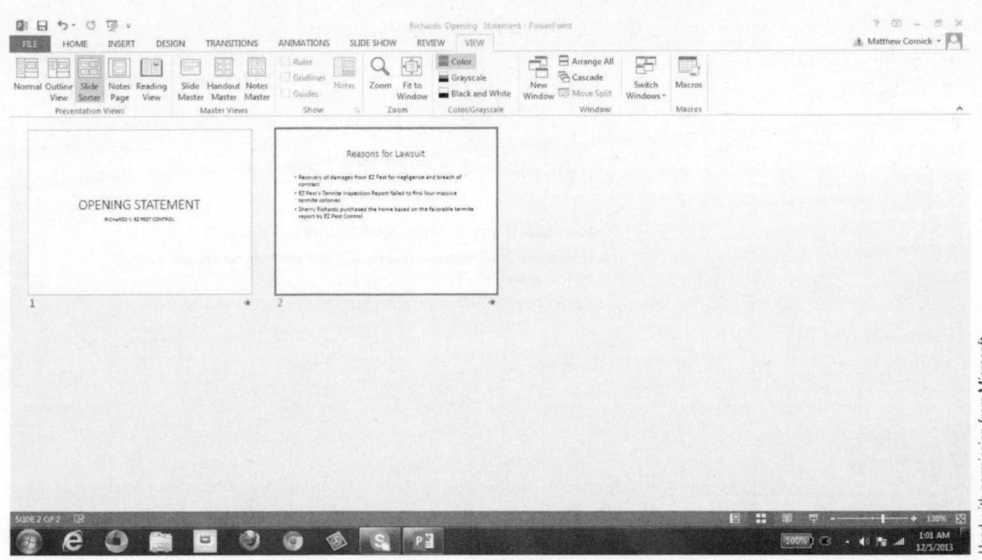

POWERPOINT 2013 EXHIBIT 4

HANDS-ON EXERCISES

21. While you are in Slide Sorter view, ***point to the second slide, click and drag the mouse pointer (holding down the mouse button) to the left of the first slide, and then release the mouse button.*** Notice that the order of the slides is now changed.
22. Press **[CTRL]+[Z]** to undo the move and put the slides back into their original order.
23. ***Click Normal*** (see PowerPoint 2013 Exhibit 1).
24. You should now have the "OPENING STATEMENT" slide on your screen. ***Click the [PAGE DOWN] key to go the second slide.***
25. You are now ready to create another slide. ***On the Home ribbon tab, click the down arrow next to New Slide in the Slides group. Click the Two Content option.***
26. A new slide should now be displayed on your screen. The top of the slide should say **"Click to add title"** and there should be two columns (left and right) that say **"Click to add text."** There should also be some icons in the middle of each of the two columns.
27. ***Click*** **"Click to add title."** Type **Undisputed Facts of the Case** (see PowerPoint 2013 Exhibit 5).
28. ***On the Home ribbon tab, click the Center icon in the Paragraph group.***
29. ***In the left column, Click*** **"Click to add text."** Type **July 2006–Sherry Richards, age 65, purchases house** and press the **[ENTER]** key.
30. Type **November 2007–Massive Formosan termite colonies found dating back 5 years** and press the **[ENTER]** key.
31. Type **December 2007–Cost to repair termite damage $158,000**.
32. Your presentation now has three slides in it.
33. To save your presentation, ***click the Save icon on the Quick Access toolbar.*** (It looks like a floppy disk and is in the upper left of the screen.)

This concludes Lesson 2. To exit PowerPoint, ***click the File tab and then click Close.*** To go to Lesson 3, stay on the current screen.

POWERPOINT 2013 EXHIBIT 5

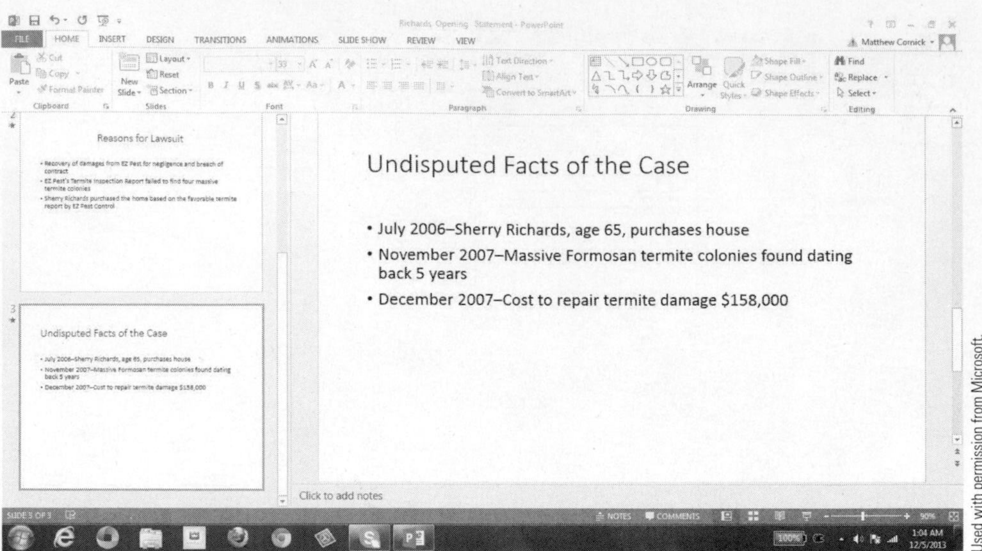

INTERMEDIATE LESSON

LESSON 3: CREATING A GRAPH

In this lesson, you will add a slide with a graph into the training program presentation. If you did not exit PowerPoint from Lesson 2, go to Step 4.

1. Start Windows. When it has loaded, ***double-click the Microsoft Office PowerPoint 2013 icon on the desktop*** to start PowerPoint 2013 for Windows. Alternatively, ***click the Start button, point to Programs or All Programs, and then click the Microsoft PowerPoint 2013 icon (or point to Microsoft Office and then click Microsoft PowerPoint 2013).*** You should be in a clean, blank document.
2. When PowerPoint 2013 opens, it gives you several ways to start a presentation: using a template, a theme, a recent presentation, or a blank presentation. ***Under Recent, click Richards Opening Statement.***
3. You should have the "Richards Opening Statement" slide on your screen. Push the **[PAGE DOWN]** key until you are on the third slide, "Undisputed Facts of the Case."
4. You are now ready to create another slide. ***On the Home ribbon tab, click the down arrow next to New Slide in the Slides group.***
5. ***Click the Title and Content option.*** A new slide is displayed on your screen.
6. The top part of the slide should say **"Click to add title"** and the bottom section of the slide should say **"Click to add text."**
7. ***Click*** **"Click to add title."** Type **Value of Richards Home.** ***From the Home ribbon tab, click the Center icon in the Paragraph group.***
8. Notice that, in the lower middle of the new slide, there are six graphical icons. ***Click the Insert Chart icon*** (it is in the middle on the first row—it looks like a multicolored vertical bar chart).
9. The "Insert Chart" window is displayed (see PowerPoint 2013 Exhibit 6). ***Click Column under Templates on the left side of the window. Then, click the 3-D Clustered Column chart*** (see PowerPoint 2013 Exhibit 6—it is the fourth chart from the left).
10. ***Click OK.***

POWERPOINT 2013 EXHIBIT 6

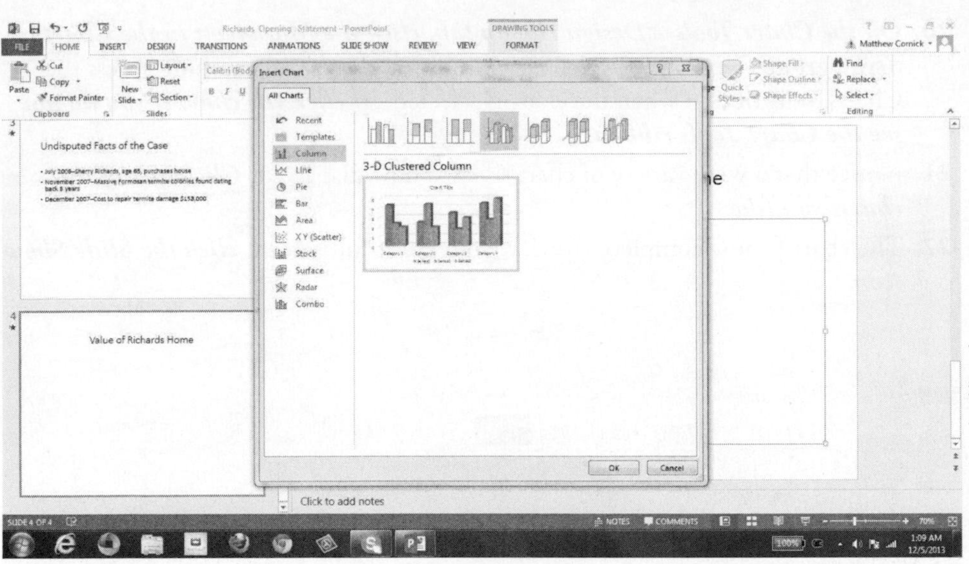

11. A default chart and a default spreadsheet are displayed.
12. You will now add some data and new titles, and also delete some data.
13. Type over the existing data in the spreadsheet for columns A and B as set out in PowerPoint 2013 Exhibit 7 (do not do anything with columns C and D yet).
14. You will now delete columns C and D, as they are not necessary. ***Point to cell C1 and (holding the mouse pointer down) drag to the right so that cell D5 is highlighted.***
15. ***Right-click in the highlighted area, point to Delete, and then click Table Columns.***
16. Your spreadsheet and chart should look similar to PowerPoint 2013 Exhibit 7.

POWERPOINT 2013 EXHIBIT 7

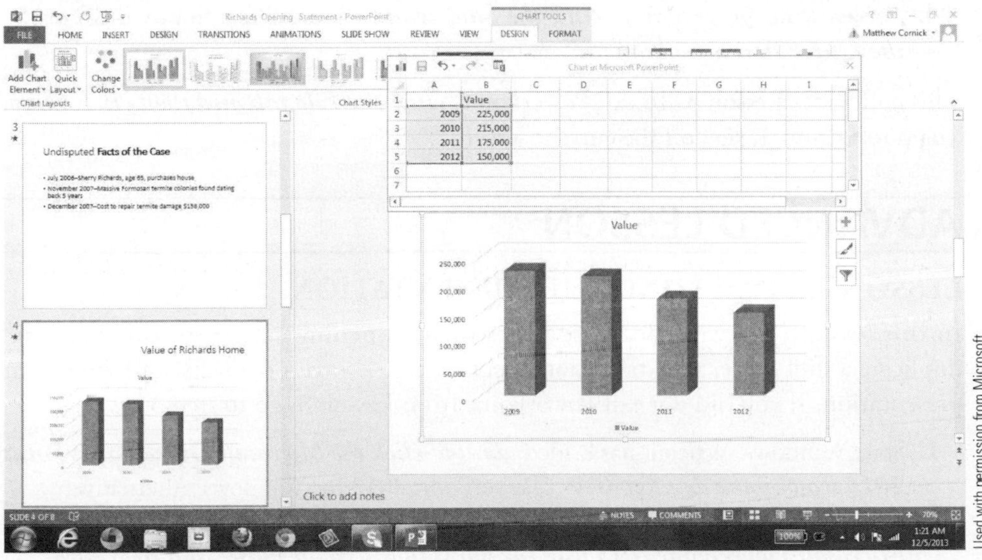

17. ***In the spreadsheet window, click the Close icon*** (the "X" in the upper right corner; see PowerPoint 2013 Exhibit 7).
18. The chart should now be displayed (see PowerPoint 2013 Exhibit 8).
19. PowerPoint 2013 gives you many premade chart styles and colors to choose from.

20. ***On the Chart Tools – Design ribbon tab, click the More icon in the Chart Styles group*** (see PowerPoint 2013 Exhibit 8). *Note:* You can only access the Chart Tools ribbon when the chart is selected, so ***click the chart if you do not see the Chart Tools ribbon.***
21. Notice that a wide variety of chart styles is now displayed. ***Click any of the charts you like.***
22. The chart is now complete. To view your chart full screen, ***click the Slide Show icon.***

POWERPOINT 2013 EXHIBIT 8

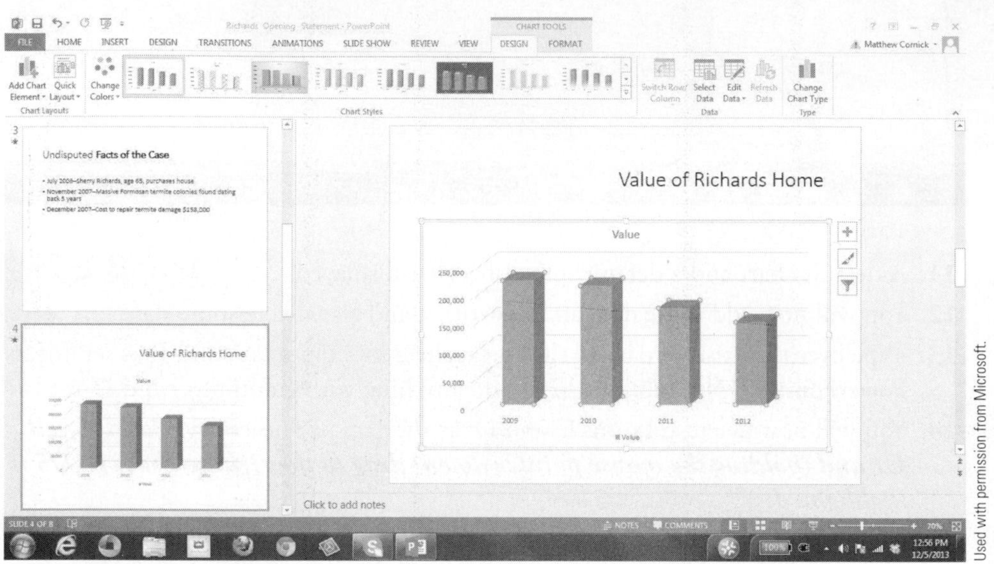

Used with permission from Microsoft.

23. Press the **[ESC]** key.
24. To save your presentation, ***click the Save icon*** (it looks like a floppy disk) ***on the Quick Access toolbar.***

This concludes Lesson 3. To exit PowerPoint, ***click the File tab and then click Close.*** To go to Lesson 4, stay on the current screen.

ADVANCED LESSON

LESSON 4: FINALIZING THE PRESENTATION

In this lesson, you will add more slides to the opening statement presentation, duplicate a slide, enter slide transition effects, create animation effects, and show your presentation. If you did not exit PowerPoint from Lesson 3, go to step 3.

1. Start Windows. When it has loaded, ***double-click the Microsoft Office PowerPoint 2013 icon on the desktop*** to start PowerPoint 2013 for Windows. Alternatively, ***click the Start button, point to Programs or All Programs, and then click the Microsoft PowerPoint 2013 icon (or point to Microsoft Office and then click Microsoft PowerPoint 2013).*** You should be in a clean, blank document.
2. When PowerPoint 2013 opens, it gives you several ways to start a presentation: using a template, a theme, a recent presentation, or a blank presentation. ***Under Recent, click Richards Opening Statement.***
3. You should have the "Opening Statement" slide on your screen. Push the **[PAGE DOWN]** key until you are at the fourth slide, which is the bar chart.

4. You are now ready to create another slide. ***On the Home ribbon tab, click the down arrow next to New Slide in the Slides group.***
5. ***Click the Title and Content option.*** A new slide should be displayed on your screen.
6. The top part of the slide should say **"Click to add title"** and the bottom section of the slide should say **"Click to add text."**
7. ***Click*** **"Click to add title"** and then type **7788 SW 52nd Street**. ***On the Home ribbon tab, click the Center icon in the Paragraph group.***

POWERPOINT 2013 EXHIBIT 9

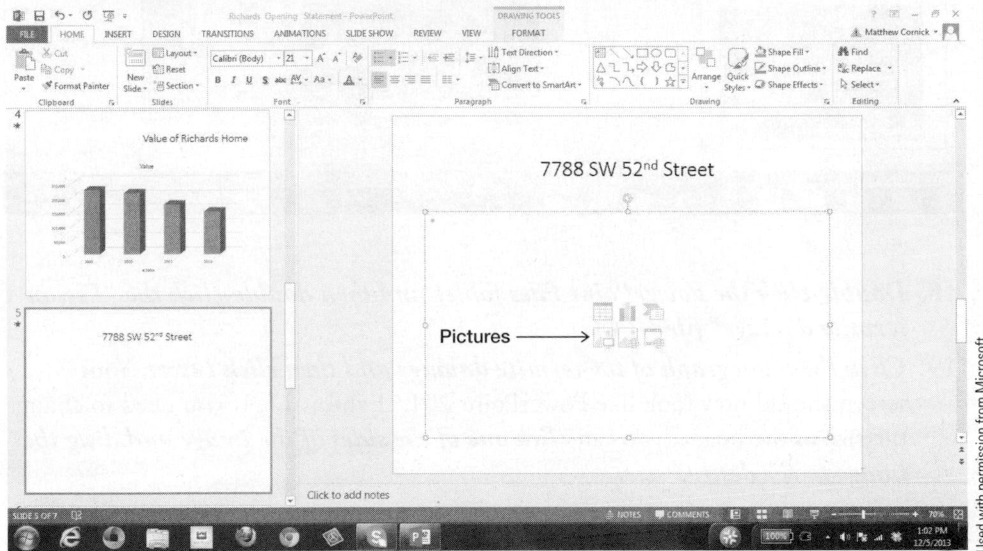

Used with permission from Microsoft.

8. ***In the lower box, where it says*** **"Click to add text,"** ***click Pictures.*** (It is the first icon on the bottom left; see PowerPoint 2013 Exhibit 9.) You will now add a photograph to the presentation.
9. The "Insert Picture" window should now be displayed. Navigate to your CengageBrain account and locate the data files.
10. ***Double-click the PowerPoint Files folder and then double-click the "Lesson 4 house" file (JPEG).***
11. ***Click the photograph of the house and then click Insert.*** Your screen should now look like PowerPoint 2013 Exhibit 10. If you need to change the size of the image, you can ***click one of the sides of the image and drag the image to the desired size.***
12. You will now add another slide. ***On the Home ribbon tab, click the down arrow next to New Slide in the Slides group.***
13. ***Click the Title and Content option.*** A new slide should be displayed on your screen.
14. The top part of the slide should say **"Click to add title"** and the bottom section of the slide should say **"Click to add text."**
15. ***Click*** **"Click to add title"** and type **Termite Damage**. ***On the Home ribbon tab, click the Center icon in the Paragraph group.***
16. ***In the lower box, where it says*** **"Click to add text,"** ***click Pictures*** (It is the first icon on the bottom left; see PowerPoint 2013 Exhibit 9.) You will now add another photograph to the presentation.
17. The "Insert Picture" window should now be displayed. Navigate to your CengageBrain account and locate the data files.

POWERPOINT 2013 EXHIBIT 10

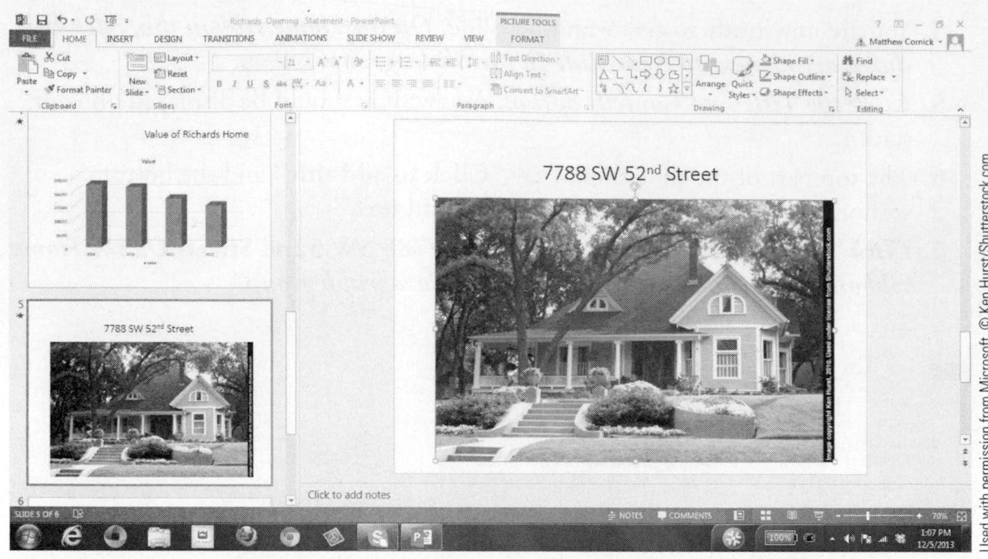

18. ***Double-click the PowerPoint Files folder and then double-click the "Lesson 4 termite damage" file (JPEG).***
19. ***Click the photograph of the termite damage and then click Insert.*** Your screen should now look like PowerPoint 2013 Exhibit 11. If you need to change the size of the image, you can ***click one of the sides of the image and drag the image to the desired size.***

POWERPOINT 2013 EXHIBIT 11

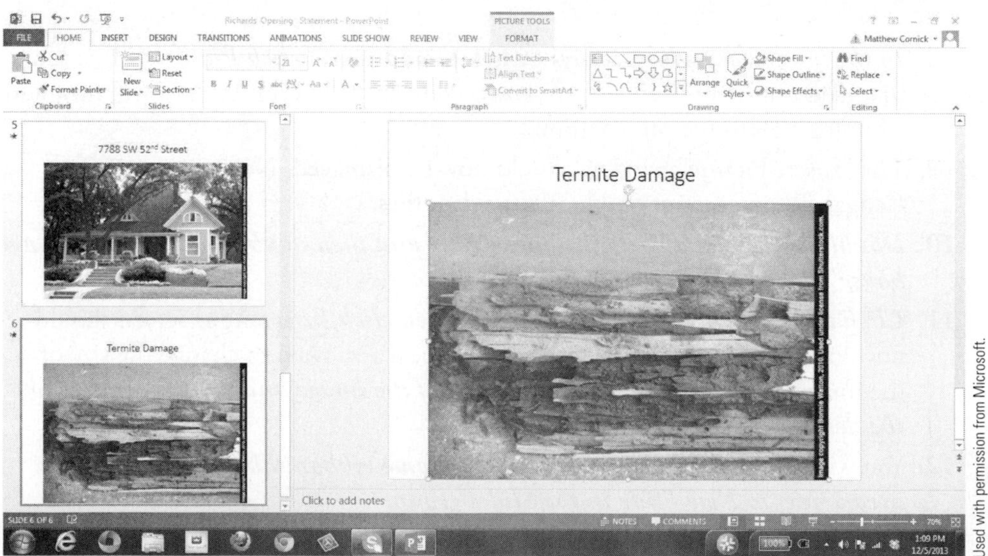

20. Now that you have created all your slides, you are ready to begin finalizing the presentation.
21. ***Click the Slide Sorter view at the bottom left of the screen.*** Notice that you can see all six of your slides on the screen.
22. You will now enter transition effects (effects that take place when you move from one slide to another) and animation effects (effects that take place during display of a single slide).
23. ***Click the first slide, "Richards Opening Statement."***

24. ***Click the TRANSITIONS ribbon tab.*** You should see the Transition to This Slide group (see PowerPoint 2013 Exhibit 12).

POWERPOINT 2013 EXHIBIT 12

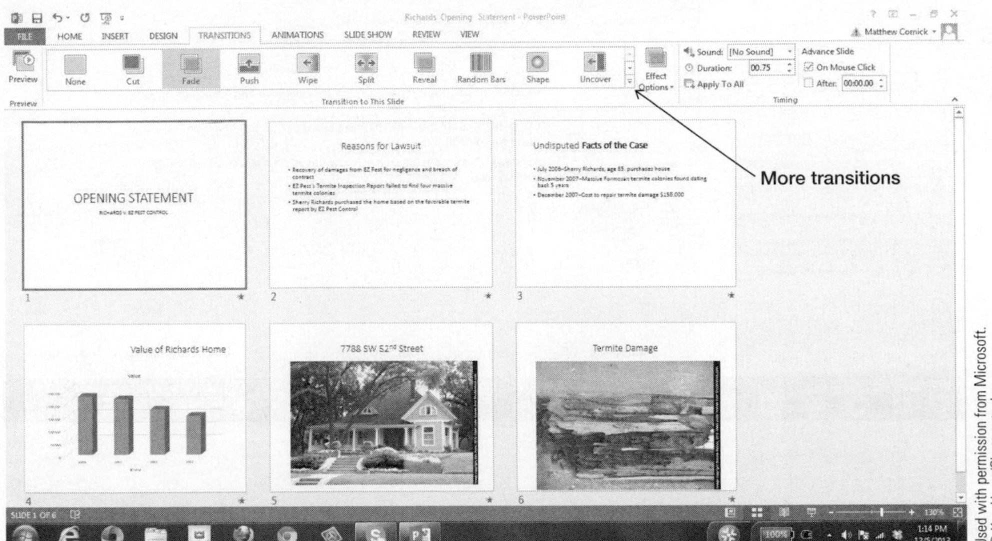

Used with permission from Microsoft.
© Ken Hurst/Shutterstock.com.
© BONNIE WATTON/Shutterstock.com.

25. ***Click the More down arrow in the Transition to This Slide group*** (see PowerPoint 2013 Exhibit 12). Notice that many types of slide transitions are available.
26. Press the **[ESC]** key to make the "More transitions" list disappear.
27. ***Click the Fade transition effect in the Transition to This Slide group; then click the Effect Options and click Smoothly.*** Notice that after you selected it, your slide displayed the transition effect. Fade Smoothly is a professional-appearing transition effect that is not distracting, so it is a good one to use in the legal setting.
28. ***Click Apply To All in the Timing group.*** This will apply the Fade Smoothly effect to all the slides in the presentation. Notice that little symbols now appear under all your slides in the slide sorter; this shows that they have transition effects associated with them.
29. Notice that in the Timing group, under Advance Slide, **"On Mouse Click"** is selected. This means that the slide moves to the next slide only when the mouse is clicked. You could set it to move to the next slide automatically after a given amount of time, but the current selection is fine for this presentation.
30. ***Click the Slide Show icon at the bottom right of the screen*** to see your presentation, including the transition effects. ***Click the mouse button to proceed through the presentation and back to the Slide Sorter screen.***
31. You will now create an animation effect that determines how the slides with bullet points appear on the screen.
32. ***Double-click the second slide, "Reasons for Lawsuit."***
33. ***Click anywhere in the lower half of the screen.***
34. ***On the Animations ribbon tab, click Fade; then click the Effect Options and click By Paragraph*** (see PowerPoint 2013 Exhibit 13).
35. Repeat this same process for slide 3.
36. You are now ready to view your presentation. Press the **[PAGE UP]** key to go to the first slide in the presentation.
37. ***Click the Slide Show icon at the bottom right of the screen.***

HANDS-ON EXERCISES

POWERPOINT 2013 EXHIBIT 13

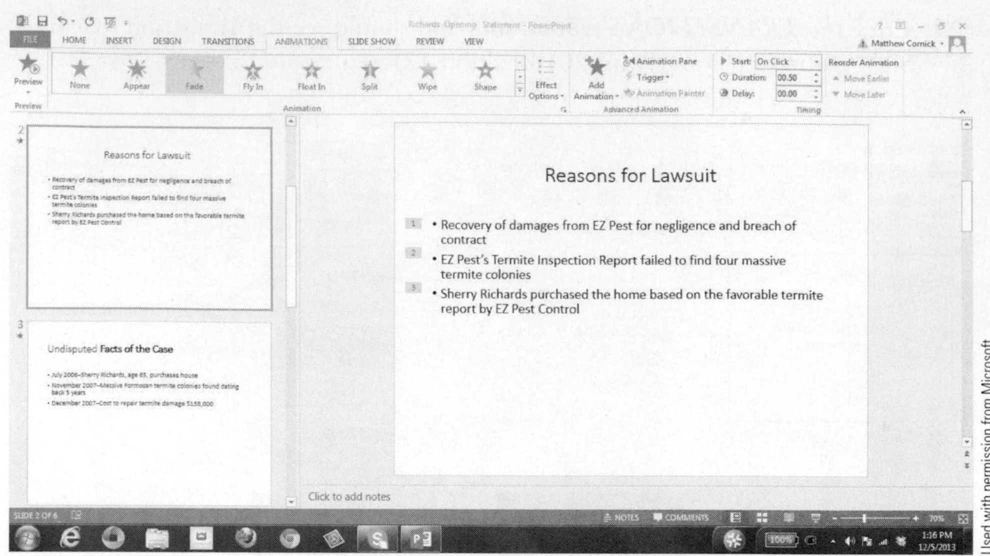

38. Your first slide is now shown full-screen size. To proceed to the next slide, press the **[SPACE BAR]** or ***click the left mouse button.*** Keep pressing the **[SPACE BAR]** or ***clicking the left mouse button*** to proceed with the presentation. Notice on the slides with bullets that you must press the **[SPACE BAR]** or ***click the mouse*** to go to the next bullet; this is the animation effect you created.
39. When you get to the end of the presentation, press the **[SPACE BAR]** or ***click the left mouse button*** to go back to editing the presentation.
40. To print your presentation, ***click the File tab, click Print, select your Printer and Settings, and then click Print.***
41. To save your presentation, ***click the Save icon*** (it looks like a floppy disk) ***on the Quick Access toolbar.***
42. ***Click the File tab and then click Close.***

This concludes the PowerPoint 2013 Hands-On Exercises. To exit PowerPoint, ***click Close.***

HANDS-ON EXERCISES

MICROSOFT POWERPOINT 2010

Number	Lesson Title	Concepts Covered
BASIC LESSONS		
Lesson 1	Creating a Presentation	Selecting a presentation design, entering text, entering speaker's notes, and saving a file
Lesson 2	Creating Additional Slides	Inserting a new slide; selecting a slide layout; viewing a slide in Slide Show, Outline, and Slide Sorter views; and creating additional slides
INTERMEDIATE LESSON		
Lesson 3	Creating a Graph	Creating and entering data in a chart
ADVANCED LESSON		
Lesson 4	Finalizing the Presentation	Creating transition effects, creating animation effects, and viewing a final presentation

GETTING STARTED

Overview

Microsoft PowerPoint 2010 is a presentation graphics program. It allows you to create presentations, charts, graphs, tables, and much more. PowerPoint 2010 is an easy-to-use program. Please note that you will be creating a presentation for an opening statement presentation.

Introduction

Throughout these lessons and exercises, information you need to operate the program will be designated in several different ways:

- Keys to be pressed on the keyboard are designated in brackets, in all caps, and in bold (e.g., press the **[ENTER]** key).
- Movements with the mouse pointer are designated in bold and italics (e.g., ***point to File and click***).
- Words or letters that should be typed are designated in bold (type **Training Program**).
- Information that is or should be displayed on your computer screen is shown in bold, with quotation marks (e.g., **"Press ENTER to continue."**).
- Specific menu items and commands are designated with an initial capital letter (e.g., click Open).

BASIC LESSONS

LESSON 1: CREATING A PRESENTATION

In this lesson, you will start PowerPoint 2010, select a background design for the opening statement presentation, enter the first slide, view your slide, and save your presentation.

1. Start Windows. After it has loaded, ***double-click the Microsoft PowerPoint 2010 icon on the desktop*** to start the program. Alternatively, ***click the Start button, point to Programs or All Programs, click Microsoft Office, and then click Microsoft PowerPoint 2010.***

2. A blank presentation should be on your screen. ***Click the File tab in the upper left corner of the screen and then click New.*** The "New Presentation" window should now be displayed.
3. ***On the left side, under Available Templates and Themes, click Themes. Scroll down and select Paper. Click Create.***
4. A blank title screen should now be displayed.
5. ***Click "Click to add title."*** Notice that you are now allowed to type your own title. Type **OPENING STATEMENT** (see PowerPoint 2010 Exhibit 1).

POWERPOINT 2010 EXHIBIT 1

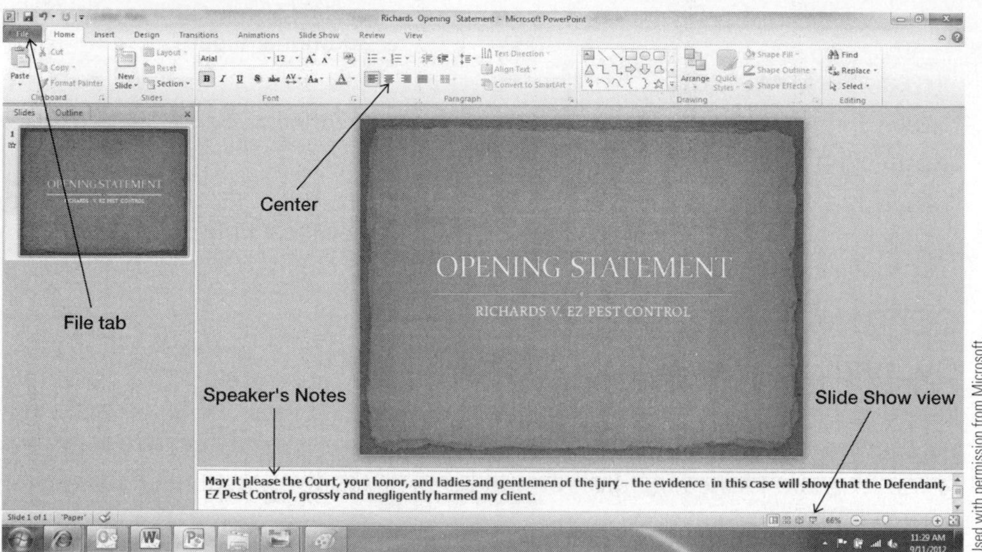
Center
OPENING STATEMENT
RICHARDS V. EZ PEST CONTROL
File tab
Speaker's Notes
Slide Show view
May it please the Court, your honor, and ladies and gentlemen of the jury – the evidence in this case will show that the Defendant, EZ Pest Control, grossly and negligently harmed my client.

6. ***On the Home ribbon tab, click the Center icon in the Paragraph group.***
7. ***Click "Click to add subtitle."*** Type **RICHARDS V. EZ PEST CONTROL** (see PowerPoint 2010 Exhibit 1).
8. ***On the Home ribbon tab, click the Center icon in the Paragraph group.***
9. The slide is now created.
10. To view your slide, ***click the Slide Show icon in the lower right of your screen*** (see PowerPoint 2010 Exhibit 1). *Note:* You will see four icons in the lower right of the screen (for Normal view, Slide Sorter view, Reading view, and Slide Show view). The Slide Show icon is all the way to the right. Remember, if you point to any icon and hold the mouse pointer there for a second, the title of the icon will be displayed.
11. You should now see your slide displayed full screen on your computer. Notice that the dark background with the light-colored letters makes your slide very readable. This is how your audience will see your slide.
12. Press **[ESC]** to return to editing your presentation.
13. Notice that at the bottom of the screen, under the current slide, it says **"Click to add notes."** This is the Speaker's Notes section of the screen. Speaker's Notes are not shown in Slide Show view, but they can be printed so that the presenter has talking points from which to speak.
14. ***Click anywhere in the Speaker's Notes section.*** Now, type **May it please the Court, your honor, and ladies and gentlemen of the jury – the evidence in this case will show that the Defendant, EZ Pest Control, grossly and negligently harmed my client** (see PowerPoint 2010 Exhibit 1).

15. ***Click the Slide Show icon in the lower right of the screen again.*** Notice that speaker's notes do not appear.
16. Press **[ESC]** to return to editing your presentation.
17. It is a good idea to save your presentation often. To save your presentation, ***click the File tab and then click Save.***
18. Type **Richards Opening Statement and** ***then click Save*** to save the file in the default directory. Be sure to remember where the file is saved so that you can retrieve it in the next lesson.

This concludes Lesson 1. To exit PowerPoint, ***click the File tab and then click Exit.*** To go directly to Lesson 2, stay at the current screen.

LESSON 2: CREATING ADDITIONAL SLIDES

In this lesson, you will add more slides to the presentation you created in Lesson 1, and you will look at the presentation using several views. If you did not exit PowerPoint from Lesson 1, go to Step 3.

1. Start Windows. When it has loaded, ***double-click the Microsoft Office PowerPoint 2010 icon on the desktop*** to start PowerPoint 2010 for Windows. Alternatively, ***click the Start button, point to Programs or All Programs, and then click the Microsoft PowerPoint 2010 icon (or point to Microsoft Office and then click Microsoft PowerPoint 2010).*** You should be in a clean, blank document.
2. ***Click the File tab and then click Open.*** The "Open" window should now be displayed. ***Navigate to the folder where the file is located. Click Richards Opening Statement and then click Open.*** Alternatively, if you click the File tab, recently used files appear on the right side of the menu. Locate your file and then ***click it.***
3. You should have the "OPENING STATEMENT" slide on your screen. Notice in the lower left of the screen that it says **"Slide 1 of 1."** This shows you what slide number you are on.
4. To create a new slide, ***on the Home ribbon tab, click the down arrow next to New Slide in the Slides group.*** Notice that the program offers you a number of different layouts.
5. ***Click the Title and Content option.***
6. A new slide is displayed on your screen. The top part of the slide should say **"Click to add title"** and the bottom section of the slide (next to a bullet) should say **"Click to add text."** There should also be graphics in the center of the screen.
7. ***Click*** **"Click to add title."** Type **Reasons for Lawsuit** (see PowerPoint 2010 Exhibit 2).
8. ***On the Home ribbon tab, click the Center icon in the Paragraph group.***
9. ***Click*** **"Click to add text."** Type **Recovery of damages from EZ Pest for negligence and breach of contract** and press the **[ENTER]** key. Notice that an additional bullet has been created.
10. Type **EZ Pest's Termite Inspection Report failed to find four massive termite colonies** and then press the **[ENTER]** key.
11. Type **Sherry Richards purchased the home based on the favorable termite report by EZ Pest Control** and press the **[ENTER]** key.
12. The slide is now created (see PowerPoint 2010 Exhibit 2).
13. To view your slide, ***click the Slide Show icon.***

HANDS-ON EXERCISES

POWERPOINT 2010 EXHIBIT 2

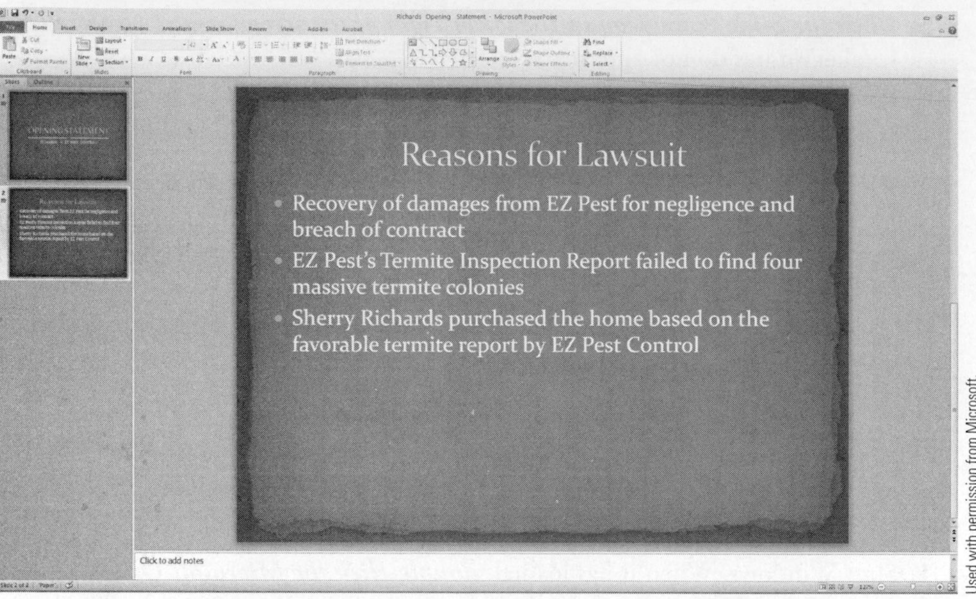

14. You should now see your slide displayed full screen on your computer. With the slide running in Slide Show view, press the **[Page Up]** key and notice that the first slide is now shown on your screen. Press the **[Page Down]** key and notice that you are back at the second slide.
15. Press the **[ESC]** key to return to Normal view.
16. You will now look at your presentation using other views. Notice on the left side of the screen that small versions of both of your slides are displayed (see PowerPoint 2010 Exhibit 2). Notice that, just above the slides, the Slides tab is selected.
17. ***Click the Outline tab just to the right of the Slides tab.***
18. The Outline view is now displayed; notice that you can read the words on both of your slides (see PowerPoint 2010 Exhibit 3).

POWERPOINT 2010 EXHIBIT 3

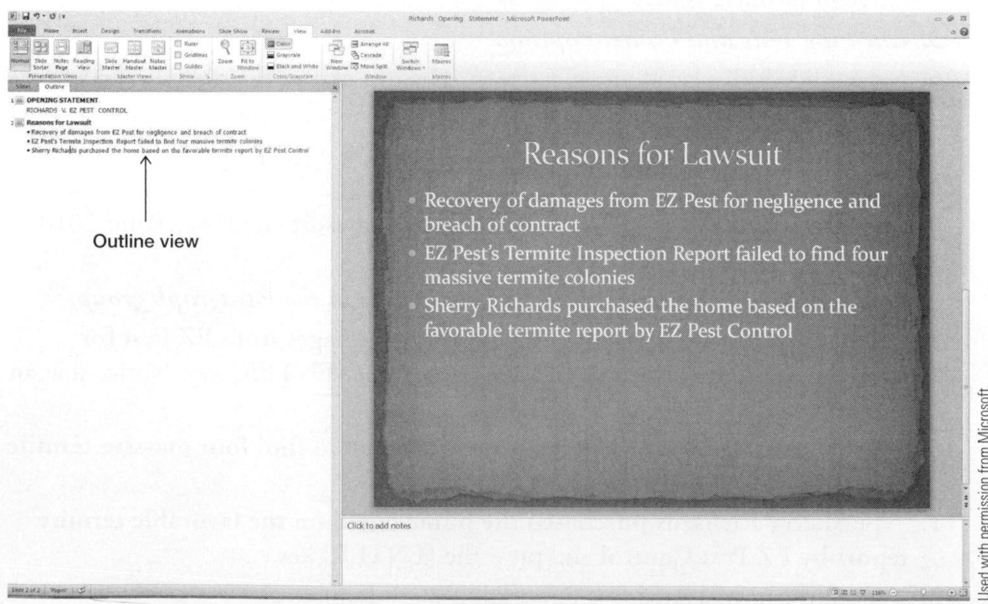

19. ***Click the Slides tab just to the left of the Outline tab*** to go back to the Slides view.
20. You will now view your slides using the Slide Sorter view. ***Click the Slide Sorter view icon.*** The Slide Sorter view icon is at the bottom right of the screen; it is the second of the four "View" icons and has a picture of four small squares (see PowerPoint 2010 Exhibit 1).
21. Notice that you can see all your slides on the screen at the same time (see PowerPoint 2010 Exhibit 4). This is helpful for getting an overview of your presentation and arranging and rearranging your slide order.

POWERPOINT 2010 EXHIBIT 4

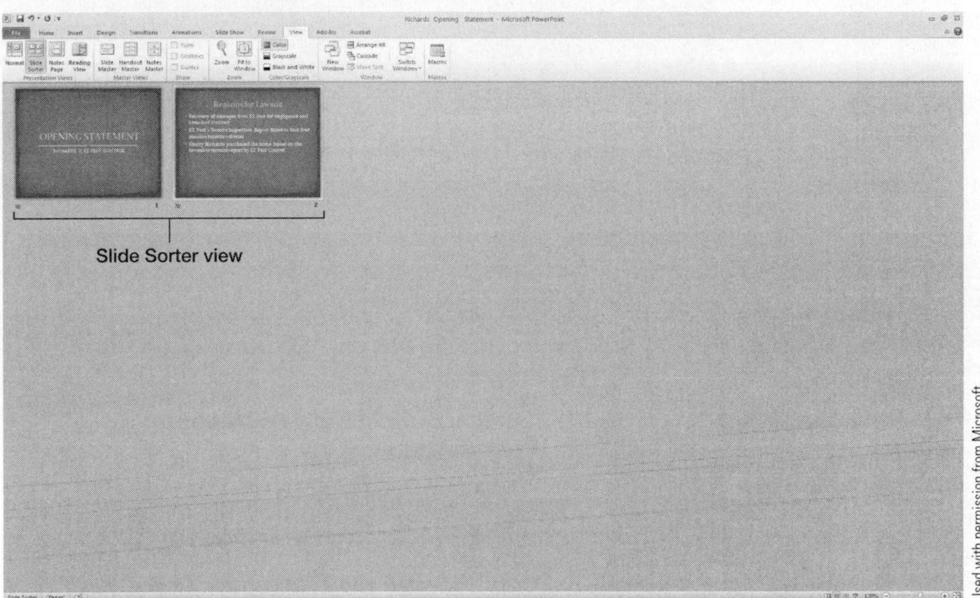

Used with permission from Microsoft.

HANDS-ON EXERCISES

22. While you are in Slide Sorter view, ***point to the second slide, click and drag the mouse pointer (holding down the mouse button) to the left of the first slide, and then release the mouse button.*** Notice that the order of the slides is now changed.
23. Press **[CTRL]+[Z]** to undo the move and put the slides back into their original order.
24. ***Click the Normal view icon in the lower right of your screen*** (see PowerPoint 2010 Exhibit 1).
25. You should now have the "OPENING STATEMENT" slide on your screen. If you are not there, use the **[PAGE UP]** key to go there.
26. You are now ready to create another slide. ***On the Home ribbon tab, click the down arrow next to New Slide in the Slides group. Click the Title and Content option.***
27. A new slide should now be displayed on your screen. The top of the slide should say **"Click to add title"** and there should be two columns (left and right) that say **"Click to add text."** There should also be some icons in the middle of the screen.
28. ***Click*** **"Click to add title."** Type **Undisputed Facts of the Case** (see PowerPoint 2010 Exhibit 5).
29. ***On the Home ribbon tab, click the Center icon in the Paragraph group.***

POWERPOINT 2010 EXHIBIT 5

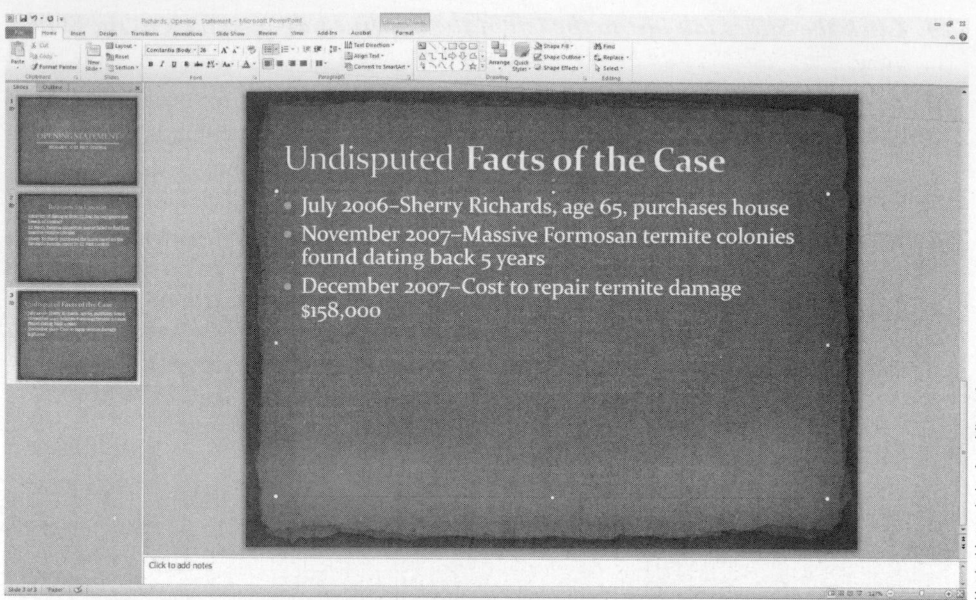

30. *Click* **"Click to add text."** Type **July 2006–Sherry Richards, age 65, purchases house** and press the **[ENTER]** key.
31. Type **November 2007–Massive Formosan termite colonies found dating back 5 years** and press the **[ENTER]** key.
32. Type **December 2007–Cost to repair termite damage $158,000**.
33. Your presentation now has three slides in it.
34. To save your presentation, ***click the Save icon on the Quick Access toolbar.*** (It looks like a floppy disk and is in the upper left of the screen.)

This concludes Lesson 2. To exit PowerPoint, ***click the File tab and then click Exit.*** To go to Lesson 3, stay on the current screen.

INTERMEDIATE LESSON

LESSON 3: CREATING A GRAPH

In this lesson, you will add a slide with a graph into the training program presentation. If you did not exit PowerPoint from Lesson 2, go to Step 4.

1. Start Windows. When it has loaded, ***double-click the Microsoft Office PowerPoint 2010 icon on the desktop*** to start PowerPoint 2010 for Windows. Alternatively, ***click the Start button, point to Programs or All Programs, and then click the Microsoft PowerPoint 2010 icon (or point to Microsoft Office and then click Microsoft PowerPoint 2010).*** You should be in a clean, blank document.
2. ***Click the File tab and then click Open.*** The "Open" window should now be displayed. ***Navigate to the folder where the file is located. Click Richards Opening Statement and then click Open.*** Alternatively, if you click the File tab, recently used files appear on the right side of the menu. Locate your file and then ***click it.***
3. You should have the "OPENING STATEMENT" slide on your screen. Push the **[PAGE DOWN]** key until you are on the third slide, "Undisputed Facts of the Case."

4. You are now ready to create another slide. ***On the Home ribbon tab, click the down arrow next to New Slide in the Slides group.***
5. ***Click the Title and Content option.*** A new slide is displayed on your screen.
6. The top part of the slide should say **"Click to add title"** and the bottom section of the slide should say **"Click to add text."** In addition, there are a number of graphical icons in the middle of the screen; one of them is a bar chart.
7. ***Click*** **"Click to add title."** Type **Value of Richards Home.** ***From the Home ribbon tab, click the Center icon in the Paragraph group*** (see PowerPoint 2010 Exhibit 6).

POWERPOINT 2010 EXHIBIT 6

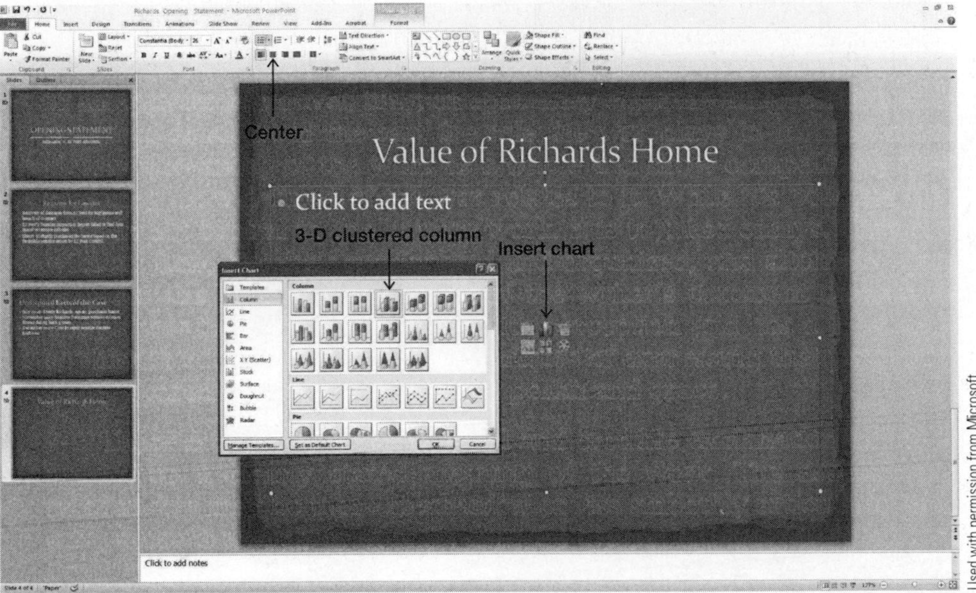

8. Notice that, in the lower middle of the new slide, there are six graphical icons. ***Click the Insert Chart icon*** (it is in the middle on the first row—it looks like a multicolored vertical bar chart).
9. The "Insert Chart" window is displayed (see PowerPoint 2010 Exhibit 6). ***Click Column under Templates on the left side of the window. Then, click the 3-D Clustered Column chart*** (see PowerPoint 2010 Exhibit 6—it is on the first row, fourth chart from the left).
10. ***Click OK.***
11. A default chart is displayed on the left and a default spreadsheet is displayed on the right (see PowerPoint 2010 Exhibit 7).
12. You will now add some data and new titles and also delete some data.
13. Type over the existing data in the spreadsheet for columns A and B as set out in PowerPoint 2010 Exhibit 8 (do not do anything with columns C and D yet).
14. You will now delete columns C and D, as they are not necessary. ***Point to cell C1 and (holding the mouse pointer down) drag to the right so that cell D5 is highlighted.***
15. ***Right-click in the highlighted area, point to Delete, and then click Table Columns.***
16. Your spreadsheet and chart should look similar to PowerPoint 2010 Exhibit 8.

POWERPOINT 2010 EXHIBIT 7

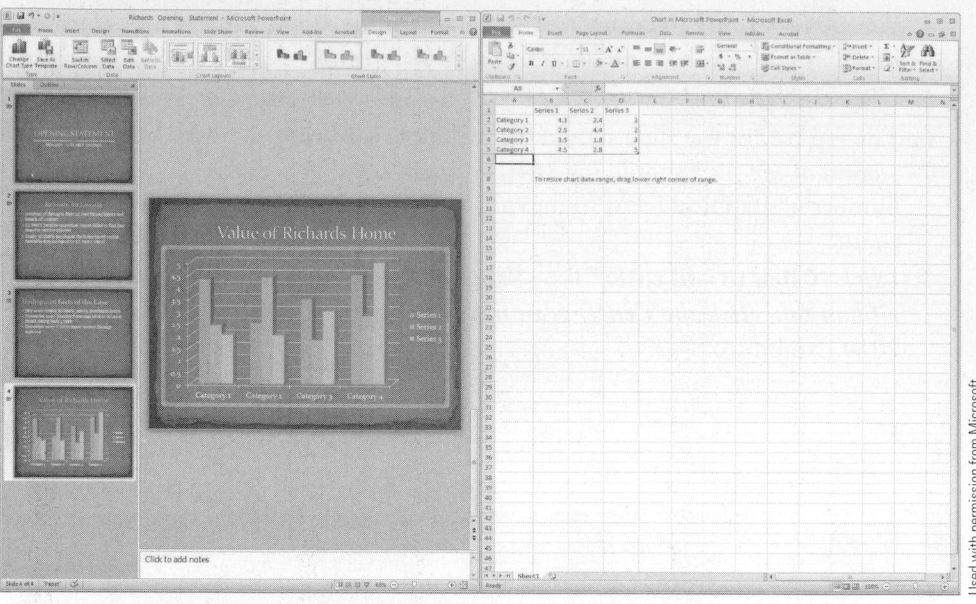

Used with permission from Microsoft.

POWERPOINT 2010 EXHIBIT 8

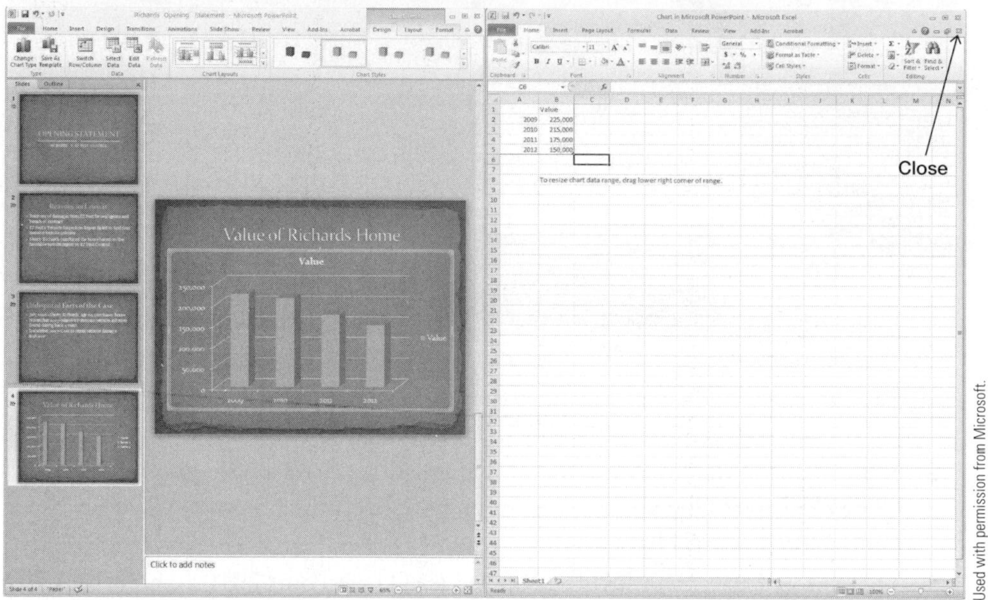

Used with permission from Microsoft.

17. ***In the spreadsheet window, click the Close icon*** (the "X" in the upper right corner; see PowerPoint 2010 Exhibit 8).
18. The chart should now be displayed (see PowerPoint 2010 Exhibit 9).
19. PowerPoint 2010 gives you many premade chart styles and colors to choose from.
20. ***On the Chart Tools – Design ribbon tab, click the More icon in the Chart Styles group*** (see PowerPoint 2010 Exhibit 9). *Note*: You can only access the Chart Tools ribbon when the chart is selected, so ***click the chart if you do not see the Chart Tools ribbon.***
21. Notice that a wide variety of chart styles is now displayed. ***Click any of the charts in the last row;*** these are the 3-D sculpted options.
22. The chart is now complete. To view your chart full screen, ***click the Slide Show icon.***

POWERPOINT 2010 EXHIBIT 9

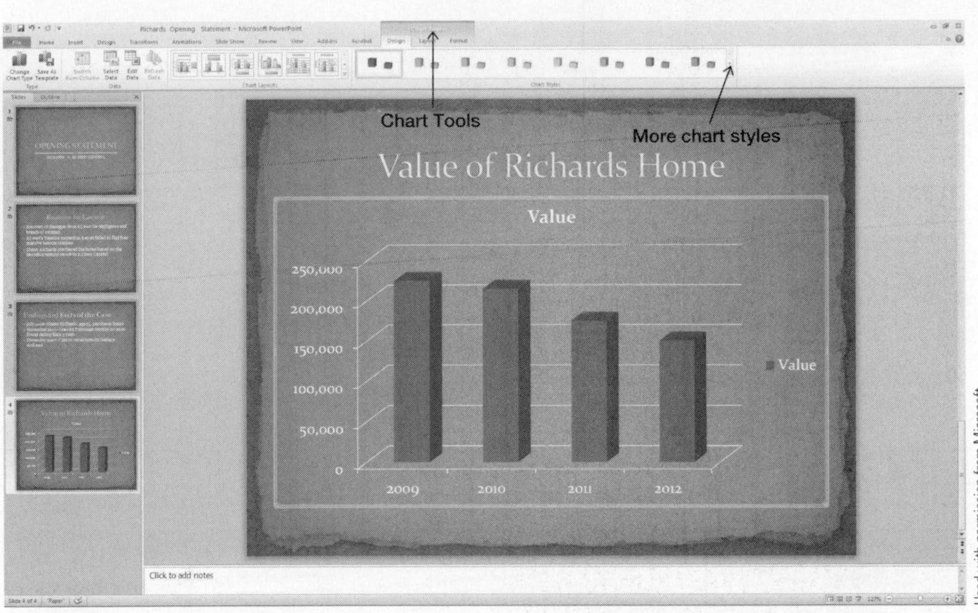

HANDS-ON EXERCISES

23. Press the **[ESC]** key.
24. To save your presentation, ***click the Save icon*** (it looks like a floppy disk) ***on the Quick Access toolbar.***

This concludes Lesson 3. To exit PowerPoint, ***click the File tab and then click Exit.*** To go to Lesson 4, stay on the current screen.

ADVANCED LESSON

LESSON 4: FINALIZING THE PRESENTATION

In this lesson, you will add more slides to the opening statement presentation, duplicate a slide, enter slide transition effects, create animation effects, and show your presentation. If you did not exit PowerPoint from Lesson 3, go to step 3.

1. Start Windows. When it has loaded, ***double-click the Microsoft Office PowerPoint 2010 icon on the desktop*** to start PowerPoint 2010 for Windows. Alternatively, ***click the Start button, point to Programs or All Programs, and then click the Microsoft PowerPoint 2010 icon (or point to Microsoft Office and then click Microsoft PowerPoint 2010).*** You should be in a clean, blank document.
2. ***Click the File tab and then click Open.*** The "Open" window should now be displayed. ***Navigate to the folder where the file is located. Click Richards Opening Statement and then click Open.***
3. You should have the "OPENING STATEMENT" slide on your screen. Push the **[PAGE DOWN]** key until you are at the fourth slide, which is the bar chart.
4. You are now ready to create another slide. ***On the Home ribbon tab, click the down arrow next to New Slide in the Slides group.***
5. ***Click the Title and Content option.*** A new slide should be displayed on your screen.
6. The top part of the slide should say **"Click to add title"** and the bottom section of the slide should say **"Click to add text."**
7. ***Click*** **"Click to add title"** and then type **7788 SW 52nd Street**. ***On the Home ribbon tab, click the Center icon in the Paragraph group.***

POWERPOINT 2010 EXHIBIT 10

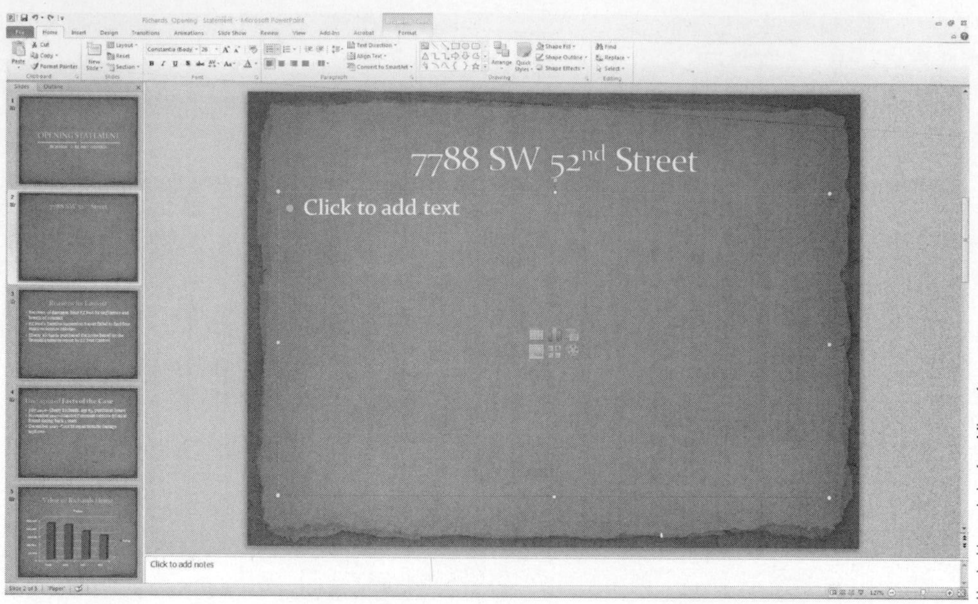

Used with permission from Microsoft.

8. ***In the lower box, where it says* "Click to add text," *click Insert Picture from File.*** (It is the first icon on the bottom left; see PowerPoint 2010 Exhibit 10.) You will now add a photograph to the presentation.
9. The "Insert Picture" window should now be displayed. Navigate to your CengageBrain account and locate the data files on the Premium Website.
10. ***Double-click the PowerPoint Files folder, then double-click the "Lesson 4 house" file (JPEG).***
11. ***Click the photograph of the house and then click Insert.*** Your screen should now look like PowerPoint 2010 Exhibit 11. If you need to change the size of the image, you can ***click one of the sides of the image and drag the image to the desired size.***
12. You will now add another slide. ***On the Home ribbon tab, click the down arrow next to New Slide in the Slides group.***

POWERPOINT 2010 EXHIBIT 11

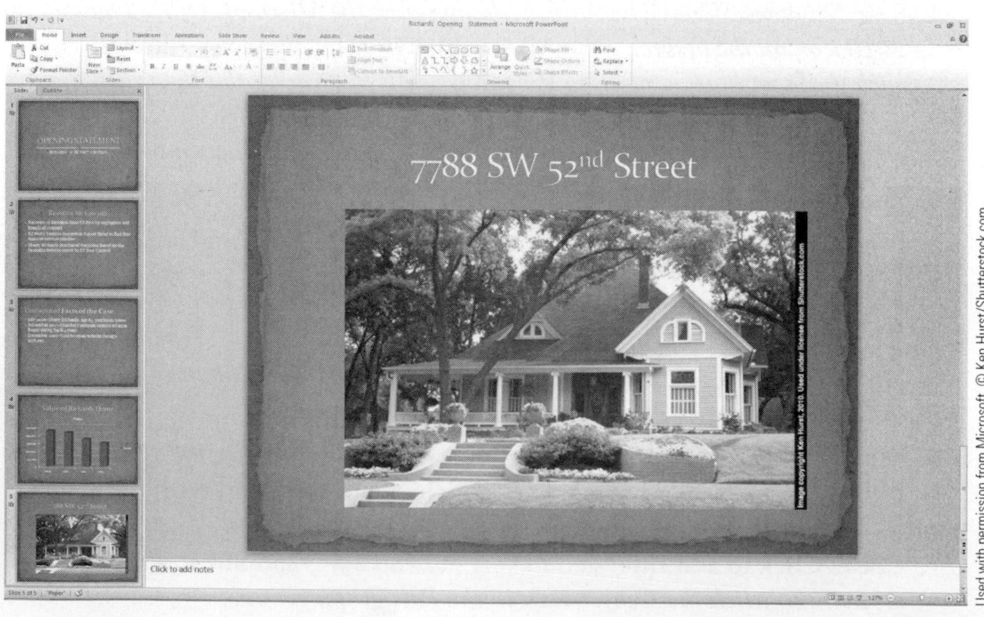

Used with permission from Microsoft. © Ken Hurst/Shutterstock.com.

13. ***Click the Title and Content option.*** A new slide should be displayed on your screen.
14. The top part of the slide should say **"Click to add title"** and the bottom section of the slide should say **"Click to add text."**
15. ***Click*** **"Click to add title"** and type **Termite Damage**. ***On the Home ribbon tab, click the Center icon in the Paragraph group.***
16. ***In the lower box, where it says "Click to add text," click Insert Picture from File.*** (It is the first icon on the bottom left; see PowerPoint 2010 Exhibit 10.) You will now add a photograph to the presentation.
17. The "Insert Picture" window should now be displayed. Navigate to your CengageBrain account and locate the data files on the Premium Website.
18. ***Double-click the PowerPoint Files folder and then double-click the "Lesson 4 termite damage" file (JPEG).***
19. ***Click the photograph of the termite damage and then click Insert.*** Your screen should now look like PowerPoint 2010 Exhibit 12. If you need to change the size of the image, you can ***click one of the sides of the image and drag the image to the desired size.***

POWERPOINT 2010 EXHIBIT 12

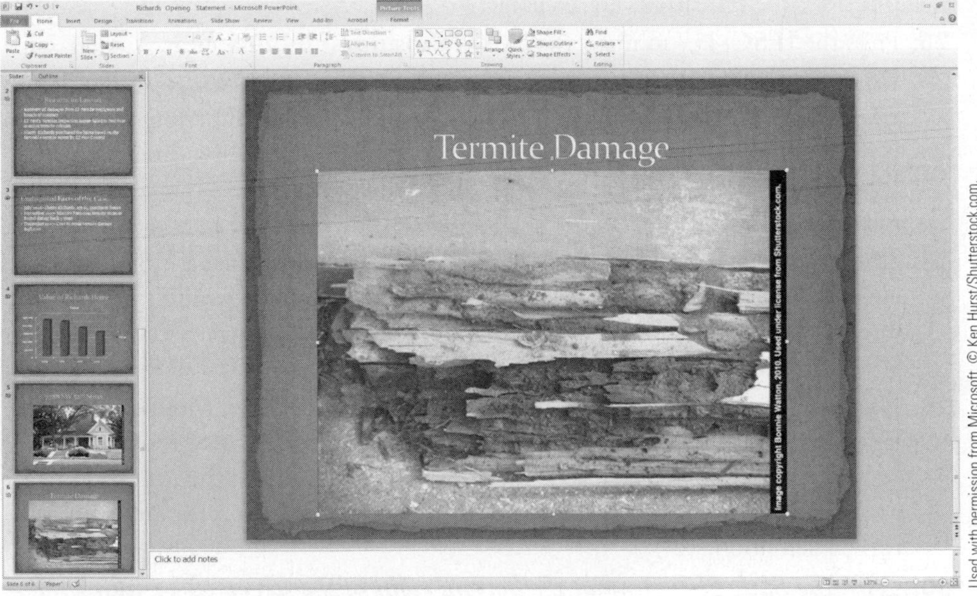

20. Now that you have now created all your slides, you are ready to begin finalizing the presentation. Press **[CTRL]+[HOME]** to go to the first slide in the presentation.
21. ***Click the Slide Sorter view at the bottom left of the screen.*** Notice that you can see all six of your slides on the screen.
22. You will now enter transition effects (effects that take place when you move from one slide to another) and animation effects (effects that take place during display of a single slide).
23. ***Click the first slide,*** "OPENING STATEMENT".
24. ***Click the Transitions ribbon tab.*** You should see the Transition to This Slide group (see PowerPoint 2010 Exhibit 13).

POWERPOINT 2010 EXHIBIT 13

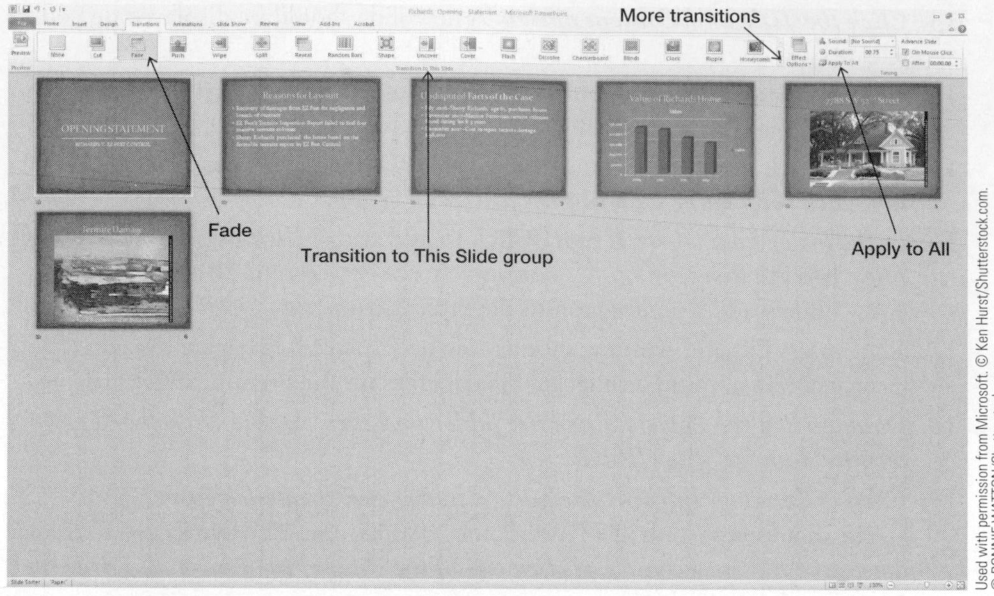

25. ***Click the More icon in the Transition to This Slide group.*** Notice that many types of slide transitions are available.
26. Press the **[ESC]** key to make the "More transitions" list disappear.
27. ***Click the Fade transition effect in the Transition to This Slide group; then click the Effect Options and click Smoothly.*** Notice that after you selected it, your slide displayed the transition effect. Fade Smoothly is a professional-appearing transition effect that is not distracting, so it is a good one to use in the legal setting.
28. ***Click Apply To All in the Timing group.*** This will apply the Fade Smoothly effect to all the slides in the presentation. Notice that little symbols now appear under all your slides in the slide sorter; this shows that they have transition effects associated with them.
29. Notice that in the Timing group, under Advance Slide, **"On Mouse Click"** is selected. This means that the slide will automatically move to the next slide only when the mouse is clicked. You could set it to move to the next slide automatically after a given amount of time, but the current selection is fine for this presentation.
30. ***Click the Slide Show icon at the bottom right of the screen*** to see your presentation, including the transition effects. ***Click the mouse button to proceed through the presentation and back to the Slide Sorter screen.***
31. You will now create an animation effect that determines how the slides with bullet points appear on the screen.
32. ***Double-click the second slide, "Reasons for Lawsuit."***
33. ***Click anywhere in the lower half of the screen.***
34. ***On the Animations ribbon tab, click Fade; then click the Effect Options and click By Paragraph*** (see PowerPoint 2010 Exhibit 14).
35. Repeat this same process for slide 3.

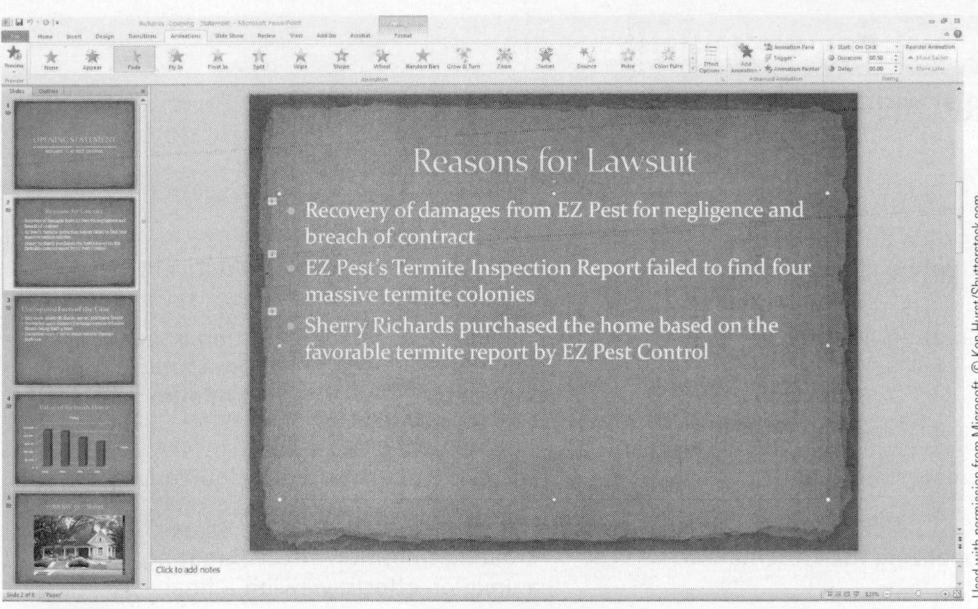

POWERPOINT 2010 EXHIBIT 14

36. You are now ready to view your presentation. Press the **[PAGE UP]** key to go to the first slide in the presentation.
37. ***Click the Slide Show icon at the bottom right of the screen.***
38. Your first slide is now shown full-screen size. To proceed to the next slide, press the **[SPACE BAR]** or ***click the left mouse button***. Keep pressing the **[SPACE BAR]** or ***clicking the left mouse button*** to proceed with the presentation. Notice on the slides with bullets that you must press the **[SPACE BAR]** or ***click the mouse*** to go to the next bullet; this is the animation effect you created.
39. When you get to the end of the presentation, press the **[SPACE BAR]** or ***click the left mouse button*** to go back to editing the presentation.
40. To print your presentation, ***click the File tab, point to Print, and then click Print.***
41. To save your presentation, ***click the Save icon*** (it looks like a floppy disk) ***on the Quick Access toolbar.***
42. ***Click the File tab and then click Close.***

This concludes the PowerPoint 2010 Hands-On Exercises. To exit PowerPoint, ***click the File tab and then click Exit.***

HANDS-ON EXERCISES

MICROSOFT POWERPOINT 2007

Number	Lesson Title	Concepts Covered
BASIC LESSONS		
Lesson 1	Creating a Presentation	Selecting a presentation design; entering text; entering speaker's notes; saving a file
Lesson 2	Creating Additional Slides	Inserting a new slide; selecting a slide layout; viewing a slide in Slide Show, Outline, and Slide Sorter views; creating additional slides
INTERMEDIATE LESSON		
Lesson 3	Creating a Graph	Creating a chart; entering data in a chart
ADVANCED LESSON		
Lesson 4	Finalizing the Presentation	Creating transition effects; creating animation effects; viewing a final presentation

GETTING STARTED

Overview

Microsoft PowerPoint 2007 is a presentation graphics program. It allows you to create presentations, charts, graphs, tables, and much more. PowerPoint 2007 is easy to learn and easy to use. Note that you will be creating a presentation for an opening statement.

Introduction

Throughout these lessons and exercises, information you need to type into the software will be designated in several different ways:

- Keys to be pressed on the keyboard are designated in brackets, in all caps, and in bold (e.g., press the **[ENTER]** key).
- Movements with the mouse pointer are designated in bold and italics (e.g., ***point to File on the menu bar and click***).
- Words or letters that should be typed are designated in bold (e.g., type **Training Program**).
- Information that is or should be displayed on your computer screen is shown in bold, with quotation marks (e.g., **"Press ENTER to continue."**).
- Specific menu items and commands are designated with an initial capital letter (e.g., click Open).

BASIC LESSONS

LESSON 1: CREATING A PRESENTATION

In this lesson, you will start PowerPoint 2007, select a background design for the opening statement presentation, enter the first slide, view your slide, and save your presentation.

1. Start Windows. After it has loaded, ***double-click the Microsoft PowerPoint 2007 icon on the desktop*** to start the program. Alternatively, ***click the Start button, point to Programs or All Programs, click Microsoft Office, and then click Microsoft Office PowerPoint 2007.***
2. A blank presentation should appear on your screen. ***Click the Office button in the upper left corner of the screen and then click New.*** The "New Presentation" window should now be displayed.
3. ***On the left side, under Templates, click Installed Themes. Scroll down and select Paper. Click Create.***
4. A blank title screen should now be displayed.
5. ***Click* "Click to add title."** Notice that you are now allowed to type your own title. Type **OPENING STATEMENT** (see PowerPoint 2007 Exhibit 1).
6. ***On the Home ribbon tab, click the Center icon in the Paragraph group.***
7. ***Click* "Click to add subtitle."** Type **RICHARDS V. EZ PEST CONTROL** (see PowerPoint 2007 Exhibit 1).
8. ***On the Home ribbon tab, click the Center icon in the Paragraph group.***
9. The slide is now created.
10. To view your slide, ***click the Slide Show icon in the lower right of the screen*** (see PowerPoint 2007 Exhibit 1). *Note:* You will see three icons in the lower right of the screen (for Normal view, Slide Sorter view, and Slide Show view). The Slide Show icon is all the way to the right. Remember, if you point to any icon and hold the mouse pointer there for a second, the title of the icon will be displayed.
11. You should now see your slide displayed full screen on your computer. Notice that the dark background with the light-colored letters makes your slide very readable. This is how your audience will see your slide.
12. Press the **[ESC]** key to return to editing your presentation.

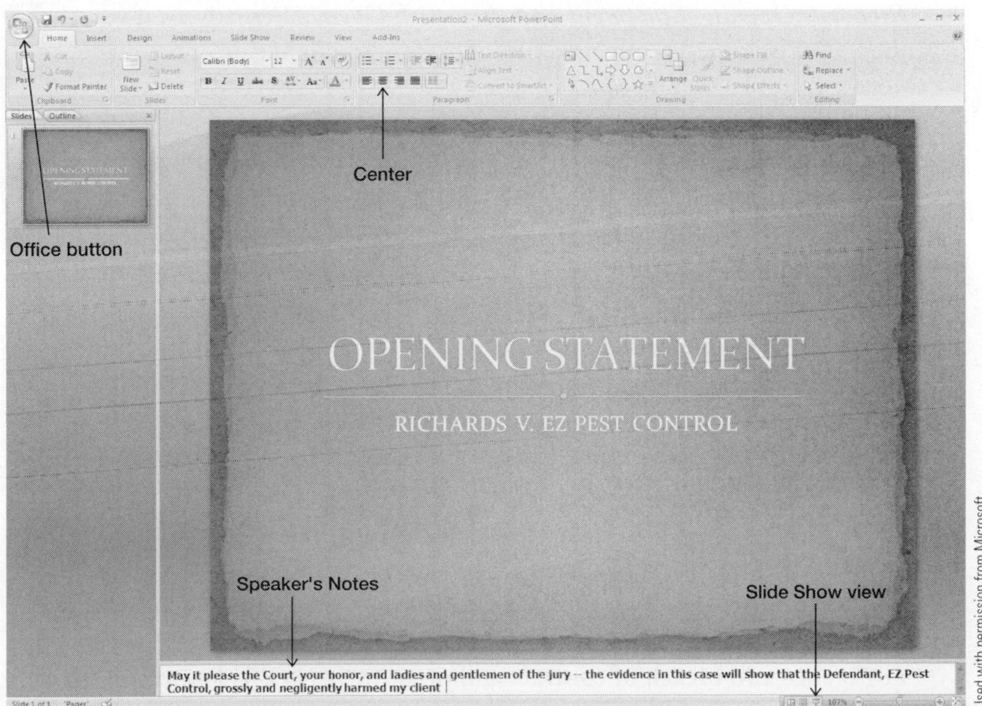
Center
Office button
OPENING STATEMENT
RICHARDS V. EZ PEST CONTROL
Speaker's Notes
Slide Show view
May it please the Court, your honor, and ladies and gentlemen of the jury -- the evidence in this case will show that the Defendant, EZ Pest Control, grossly and negligently harmed my client

POWERPOINT 2007 EXHIBIT 1

13. Notice that at the bottom of the screen, under the current slide, it says **"Click to add notes."** This is the Speaker's Notes section of the screen. Speaker's Notes are not shown in Slide Show view, but they can be printed so that the presenter has talking points to which to refer.
14. ***Click anywhere in the Speaker's Notes section.*** Type **May it please the Court, your honor, and ladies and gentlemen of the jury—the evidence in this case will show that the Defendant, EZ Pest Control, grossly and negligently harmed my client** (see PowerPoint 2007 Exhibit 1).
15. ***Click the Slide Show icon in the lower right of the screen again.*** Notice that the speaker's notes do not appear.
16. Press the **[ESC]** key to return to editing your presentation.
17. It is a good idea to save your work often. To save your presentation, ***click the Office button and then click Save.***
18. Type **Richards Opening Statement** ***and then click Save*** to save the file in the default directory. Be sure to remember where the file is saved so that you can retrieve it for the next lesson.

This concludes Lesson 1. To exit PowerPoint, ***click the Office button and then click Exit PowerPoint.*** To go to Lesson 2, stay at the current screen.

LESSON 2: CREATING ADDITIONAL SLIDES

In this lesson, you will create additional slides for the opening statement presentation you created in Lesson 1, and you will look at the presentation using several views. If you did not exit PowerPoint from Lesson 1, go to Step 3 in the following instructions.

1. Start Windows. ***Double-click the Microsoft Office PowerPoint 2007 icon on the desktop*** to start PowerPoint 2007 for Windows. Alternatively, ***click the Start button, point to Programs or All Programs, and then click the Microsoft PowerPoint 2007 icon (or point to Microsoft Office and then click Microsoft Office PowerPoint 2007).*** You should be in a clean, blank document.
2. ***Click the Office button and then click Open.*** The "Open" window should now be displayed. Navigate to the folder where the file is located. ***Click Richards Opening Statement and then click Open.*** Alternatively, if you click the Office button, recently used files appear on the right side of the menu. Locate your file, then ***click it.***
3. You should have the "OPENING STATEMENT" slide on your screen. Notice in the lower left of the screen that it says **"Slide 1 of 1."** This shows you what slide number you are on.
4. To create a new slide, ***on the Home ribbon tab, click the down arrow next to New Slide in the Slides group.*** Notice that the program offers a number of different layouts.
5. ***Click the Title and Content option.***
6. A new slide is displayed on your screen. The top part of the slide should say **"Click to add title"** and the bottom section of the slide (next to a bullet) should say **"Click to add text."** There should also be graphics in the center of the screen.
7. ***Click*** **"Click to add title."** Type **Reasons for Lawsuit** (see PowerPoint 2007 Exhibit 2).
8. ***On the Home ribbon tab, click the Center icon in the Paragraph group.***
9. ***Click*** **"Click to add text."** Type **Recovery of damages from EZ Pest for negligence and breach of contract** and press the **[ENTER]** key. Notice that an additional bullet has been created.

10. Type **EZ Pest's Termite Inspection Report failed to find four massive termite colonies** and then press the **[ENTER]** key.
11. Type **Sherry Richards purchased the home based on the favorable Termite Inspection Report by EZ Pest Control** and press the **[ENTER]** key.
12. The slide is now created (see PowerPoint 2007 Exhibit 2).

POWERPOINT 2007 EXHIBIT 2

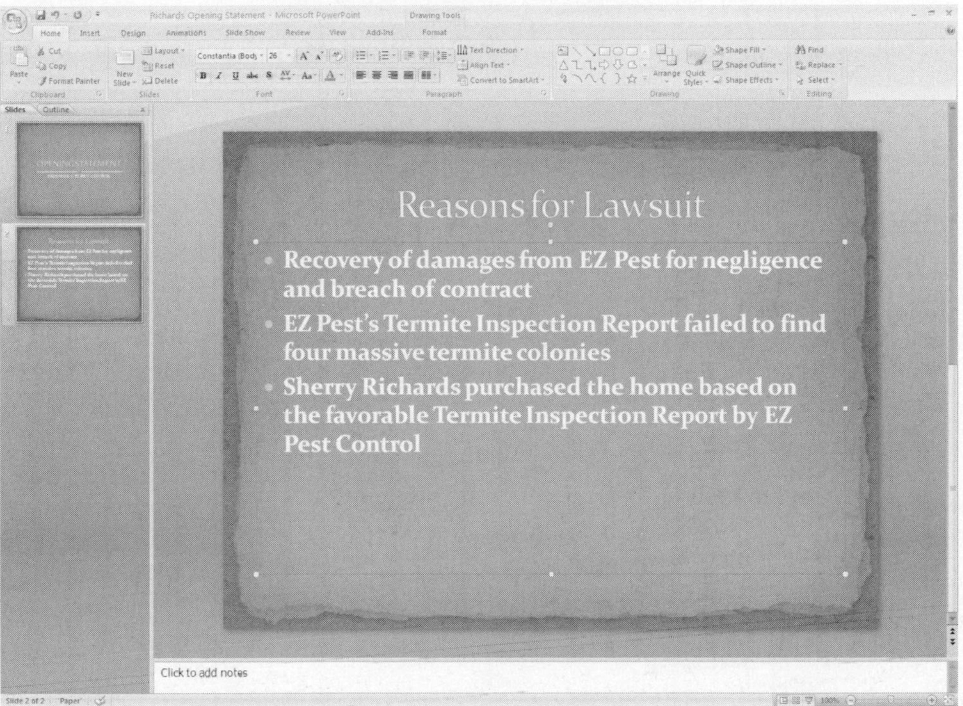

Used with permission from Microsoft.

13. To view your slide, ***click the Slide Show icon.***
14. You should now see your slide displayed full screen on your computer. With the slide running in Slide Show view, press the **[PAGE UP]** key and notice that the first slide is now shown on your screen. Press the **[PAGE DOWN]** key and notice that you are back at the second slide.
15. Press the **[ESC]** key to return to Normal view.
16. You will now look at your presentation using other views. Notice on the left side of the screen that small versions of both of your slides are displayed (see PowerPoint 2007 Exhibit 2). Notice, just above the slides, that the Slides tab is selected.
17. ***Click the Outline tab just to the right of the Slides tab.***
18. The Outline view is now displayed; notice that you can read the words on both of your slides (see PowerPoint 2007 Exhibit 3).
19. ***Click the Slides tab just to the left of the Outline tab*** to go back to the Slides view.
20. You will now view your slides using the Slide Sorter view. ***Click the Slide Sorter view icon.*** The Slide Sorter view icon is at the bottom right of the screen; it is the second of the three View icons, and has a picture of four small squares (see PowerPoint 2007 Exhibit 1).
21. Notice that you can now see all your slides on the screen at the same time (see PowerPoint 2007 Exhibit 4). This is helpful for getting an overview of your presentation and arranging and rearranging the slide order.

POWERPOINT 2007 EXHIBIT 3

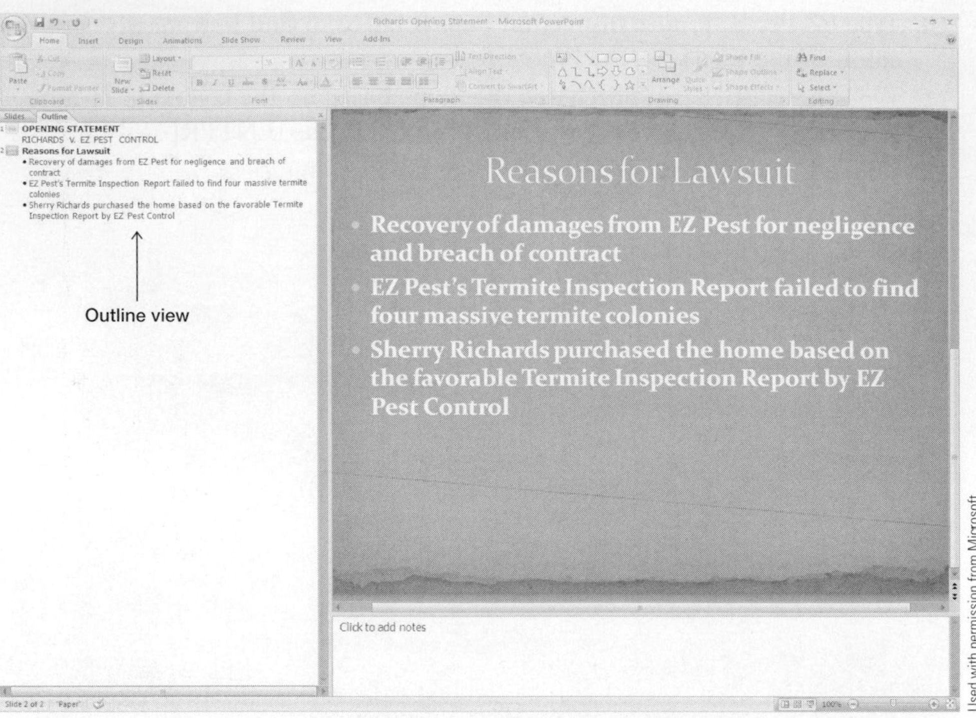

Used with permission from Microsoft.

POWERPOINT 2007 EXHIBIT 4

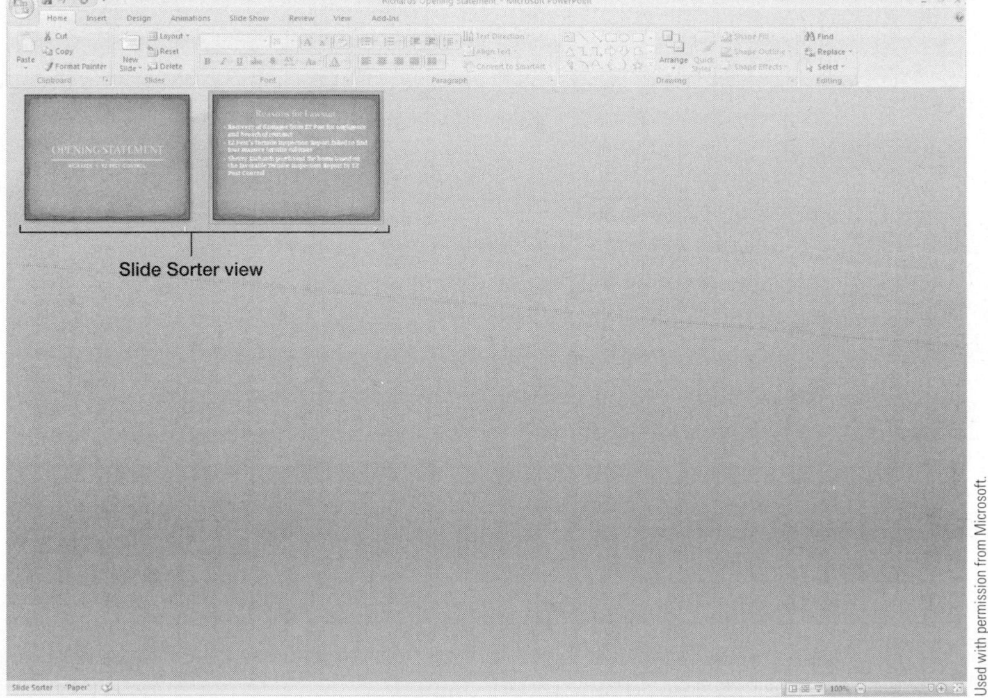

Used with permission from Microsoft.

22. While you are in Slide Sorter view, ***point to the second slide, click it, and (holding down the mouse button) drag the mouse pointer to the left of the first slide. Release the mouse button.*** Notice that the order of the slides has been changed.
23. Press **[CTRL]+[Z]** to undo the move and put the slides back into their original order.

24. ***Click the Normal view icon in the lower right of your screen*** (see PowerPoint 2007 Exhibit 1).
25. You should now have the "OPENING STATEMENT" slide on your screen. If you are not there, use the **[PAGE DOWN]** key to go there.
26. You are now ready to create another slide. ***On the Home ribbon tab, click the down arrow next to New Slide in the Slides group. Click the Title and Content option.***
27. A new slide is displayed on your screen. The top part of the slide should say **"Click to add title"** and the bottom section of the slide (next to a bullet) should say **"Click to add text."** There should also be graphics in the center of the screen.
28. ***Click*** **"Click to add title."** Type **Undisputed Facts of the Case** (see PowerPoint 2007 Exhibit 5).

POWERPOINT 2007 EXHIBIT 5

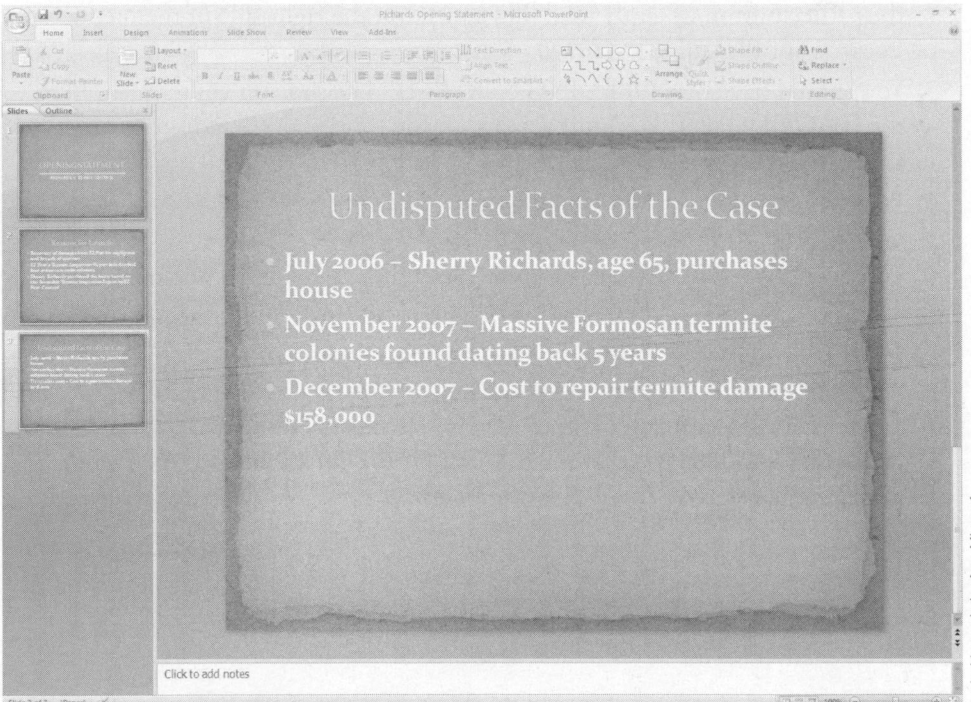

29. ***On the Home ribbon tab, click the Center icon in the Paragraph group.***
30. ***Click*** **"Click to add text."** Type **July 2006 – Sherry Richards, age 65, purchases house** and press the **[ENTER]** key.
31. Type **November 2007 – Massive Formosan termite colonies found dating back 5 years** and press the **[ENTER]** key.
32. Type **December 2007 – Cost to repair termite damage $158,000**.
33. Your presentation now has three slides in it.
34. To save your presentation, ***click the Save icon on the Quick Access toolbar.*** (It looks like a floppy disk and is in the upper left of the screen.)

This concludes Lesson 2. To exit PowerPoint, ***click the Office button and then click Exit PowerPoint.*** To go to Lesson 3, stay at the current screen.

INTERMEDIATE LESSON

LESSON 3: CREATING A GRAPH

In this lesson, you will add a slide with a graph to the opening statement presentation. If you did not exit PowerPoint after completing Lesson 2, go to Step 4 in the following instructions.

1. Start Windows. ***Double-click the Microsoft Office PowerPoint 2007 icon on the desktop*** to start PowerPoint 2007 for Windows. Alternatively, ***click the Start button, point to Programs or All Programs, and then click the Microsoft PowerPoint 2007 icon (or point to Microsoft Office and then click Microsoft Office PowerPoint 2007***). You should be in a clean, blank document.
2. ***Click the Office button and then click Open.*** The "Open" window should now be displayed. Navigate to the folder where the file is located. ***Click Richards Opening Statement and then click Open.*** Alternatively, if you click the Office button, recently used files appear on the right side of the menu. Locate your file and then ***click it.***
3. You should have the "OPENING STATEMENT" slide on your screen. Push the **[PAGE DOWN]** key until you are on the third slide, "Undisputed Facts of the Case."
4. You are now ready to create another slide. ***On the Home ribbon tab, click the down arrow next to New Slide in the Slides group.***
5. ***Click the Title and Content option.*** A new slide is displayed on your screen.
6. The top part of the slide should say **"Click to add title"** and the bottom section of the slide should say **"Click to add text."** In addition, there are a number of graphical icons in the middle of the screen; one of them is a bar chart.
7. ***Click* "Click to add title."** Type **Value of Richards Home** and then press the **[ENTER]** key (see PowerPoint 2007 Exhibit 6). ***On the Home ribbon tab, click the Center icon in the Paragraph group.***

POWERPOINT 2007 EXHIBIT 6

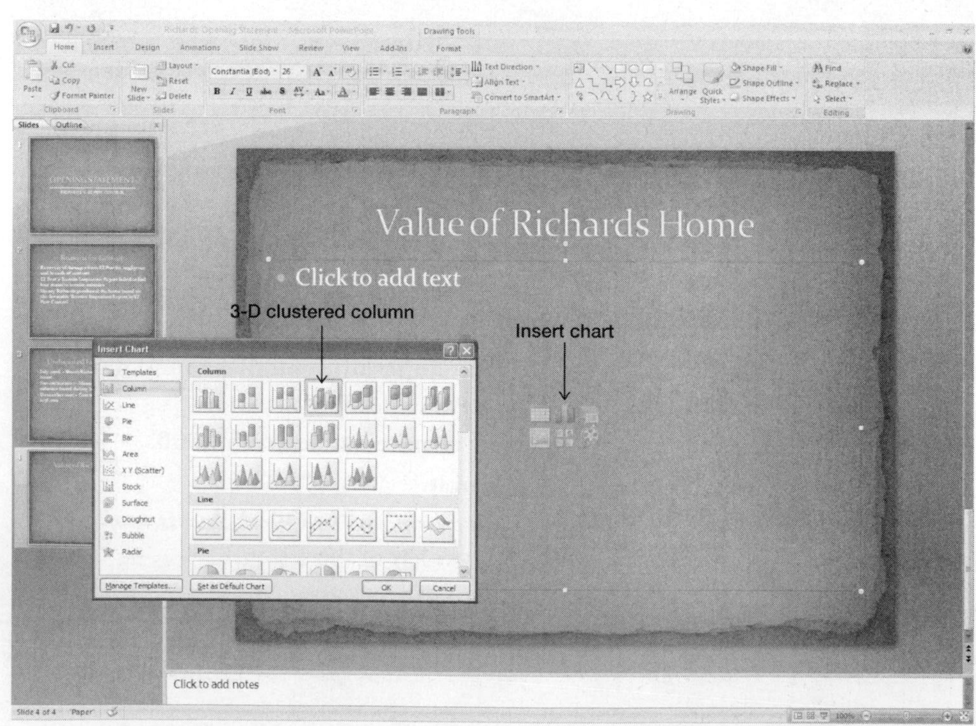

8. Notice that, in the lower middle of the new slide, there are six graphical icons. ***Click the Insert Chart icon*** (it is in the middle on the first row—it looks like a multicolored vertical bar chart).
9. The "Insert Chart" window is displayed (see PowerPoint 2007 Exhibit 6). ***Click Column under Templates on the left side of the window and then click the 3-D Clustered Column chart*** (e.g., see PowerPoint 2007 Exhibit 6—it is on the first row, fourth chart from the left).
10. ***Click OK.***
11. A default chart is displayed on the left and a default spreadsheet is displayed on the right (see PowerPoint 2007 Exhibit 7).

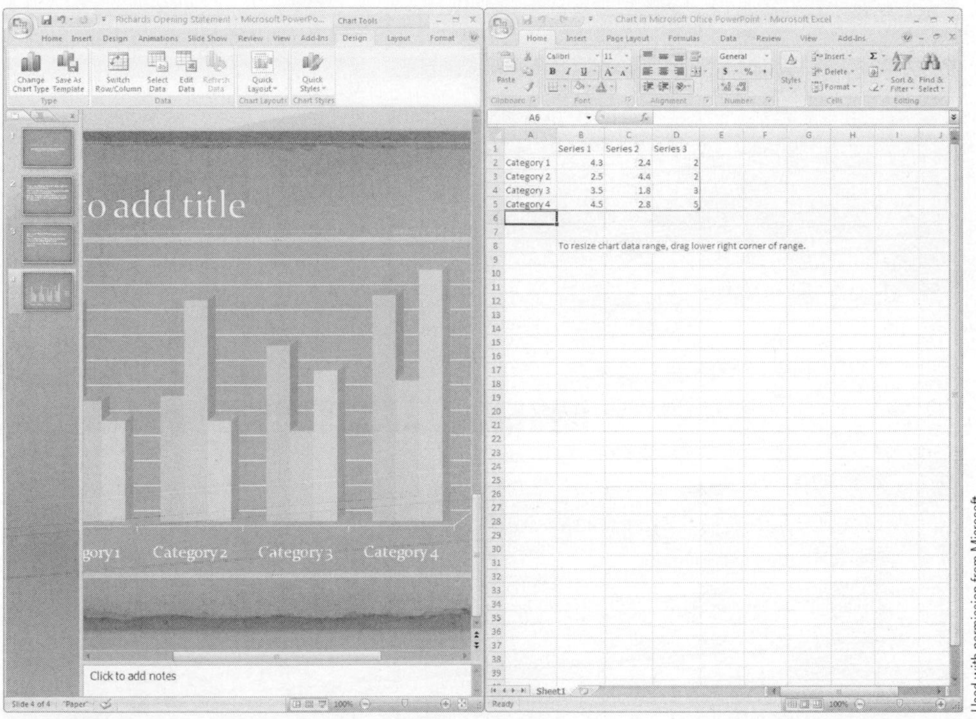

POWERPOINT 2007 EXHIBIT 7

HANDS-ON EXERCISES

12. You will now add some data and new titles and also delete some data.
13. Type over the existing data in the spreadsheet for columns A and B as follows (do not do anything with columns C and D yet):

	A	B	C	D
	2009	2010	2011	2012
Value	225,000	215,000	175,000	150,000

14. You will now delete columns C and D, because they are not necessary. ***Point to cell C1 and (holding the mouse pointer down) drag to the right so that cell D5 is highlighted.***
15. ***Right-click in the highlighted area, point to Delete, and then click Table Columns.***
16. A Microsoft Office Excel window will appear saying that the worksheet contains one or more invalid references; ***click OK.***
17. Your spreadsheet and chart should look similar to PowerPoint 2007 Exhibit 8.
18. ***In the spreadsheet part of the "Chart" window, click the Close icon*** (the X in the upper right corner; see PowerPoint 2007 Exhibit 8).

POWERPOINT 2007 EXHIBIT 8

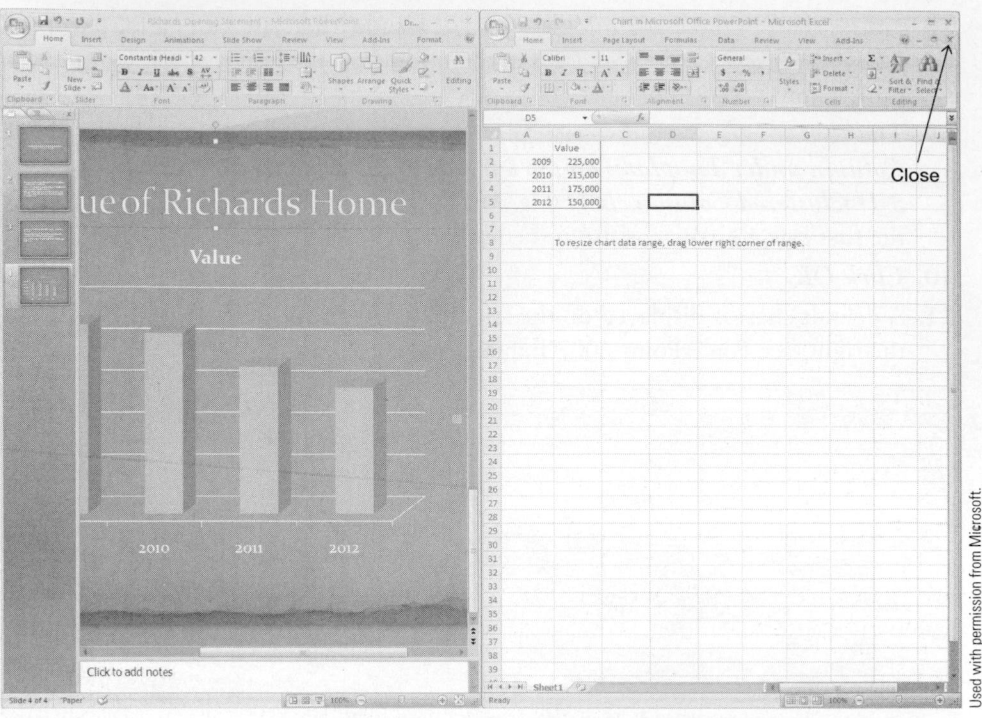

POWERPOINT 2007 EXHIBIT 9

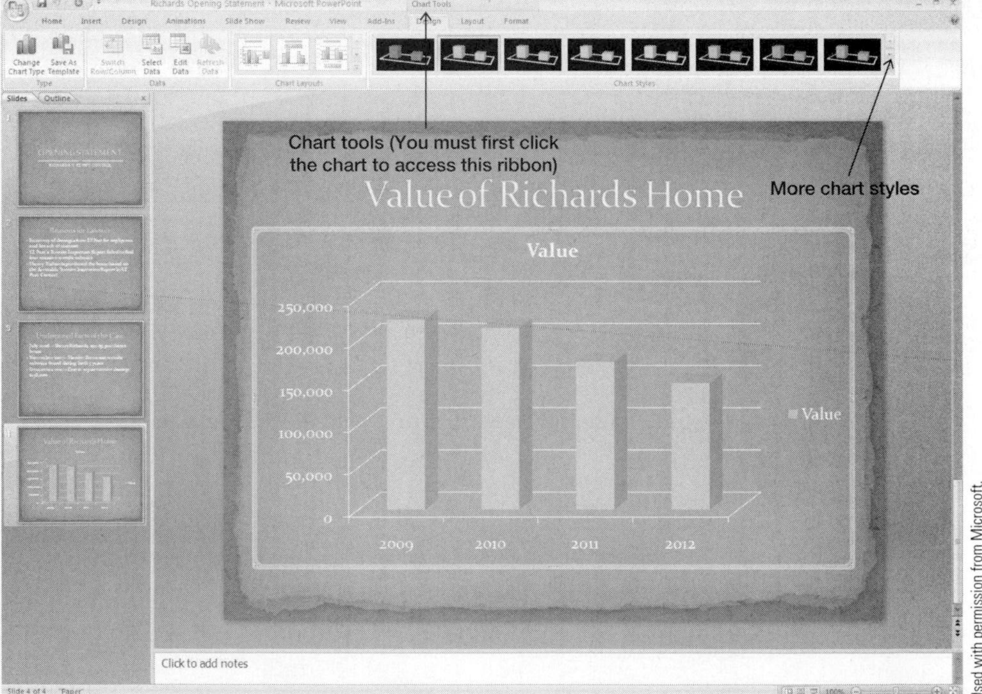

19. The chart should now be displayed (see PowerPoint 2007 Exhibit 9).
20. PowerPoint 2007 offers many premade chart styles and colors to choose from.
21. ***On the Chart Tools – Design ribbon tab, click the More icon in the Chart Styles group*** (see PowerPoint 2007 Exhibit 9). *Note*: You can access the Chart Tools ribbon only when a chart is selected, so ***click the chart if you do not see the Chart Tools ribbon***.
22. A wide variety of chart styles is now displayed. ***Click any of the charts in the last row;*** these are the 3-D sculpted options.

23. The chart is now complete. To view your chart full-screen, ***click the Slide Show icon.***
24. Press the **[ESC]** key.
25. To save your presentation, ***click the Save icon*** (it looks like a floppy disk) ***on the Quick Access toolbar.***

This concludes Lesson 3. To exit PowerPoint, ***click the Office button and then click Exit PowerPoint.*** To go to Lesson 4, stay at the current screen.

ADVANCED LESSON

LESSON 4: FINALIZING THE PRESENTATION

In this lesson, you will add more slides to the opening statement presentation, duplicate a slide, enter slide transition effects, create animation effects, and show your presentation. If you did not exit PowerPoint from Lesson 3, go to step 3 in the following instructions.

1. Start Windows. ***Double-click the Microsoft Office PowerPoint 2007 icon on the desktop*** to start PowerPoint 2007 for Windows. Alternatively, ***click the Start button, point to Programs or All Programs, and then click the Microsoft PowerPoint 2007 icon (or point to Microsoft Office and then click Microsoft Office PowerPoint 2007***). You should be in a clean, blank document.
2. ***Click the Office button and then click Open.*** The "Open" window should now be displayed. Navigate to the folder where the file is located. ***Click Richards Opening Statement and then click Open.***
3. You should have the "OPENING STATEMENT" slide on your screen. Push the **[PAGE DOWN]** key until you are at the fourth slide, which is the bar chart.
4. You are now ready to create another slide. ***On the Home ribbon tab, click the down arrow next to New Slide in the Slides group.***
5. ***Click the Title and Content option.*** A new slide should be displayed on your screen.
6. The top part of the slide should say **"Click to add title"** and the bottom section of the slide should say **"Click to add text."**
7. ***Click*** **"Click to add title"** and then type **7788 SW 52nd Street**.
8. ***In the lower box, where it says*** **"Click to add text,"** ***click Insert Picture from File.*** (It is the first icon on the bottom left; see PowerPoint 2007 Exhibit 10.) You will now add a photograph to the presentation.
9. The "Insert Picture" window should now be displayed. Navigate to your CengageBrain account and locate the data files on the Premium Website.
10. ***Double-click the PowerPoint Files folder, double-click the PowerPoint 2007 folder, and then double-click the "Lesson 4 house" (JPEG).***
11. ***Click the photograph of the house and then click Insert.*** Your screen should now look like PowerPoint 2007 Exhibit 11. If you need to change the size of the image, ***click one of the sides of the image and drag the image to the desired size.***
12. You will now add another slide. ***On the Home ribbon tab, click the down arrow next to New Slide in the Slides group.***
13. ***Click the Title and Content option.*** A new slide should be displayed on your screen.

POWERPOINT 2007 EXHIBIT 10

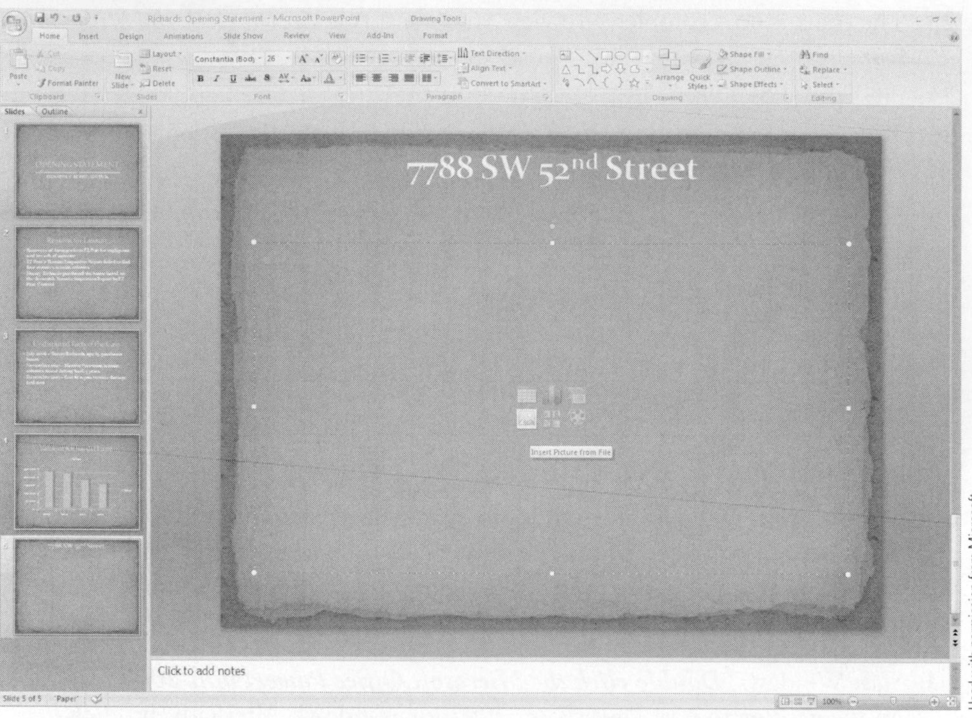

Used with permission from Microsoft.

POWERPOINT 2007 EXHIBIT 11

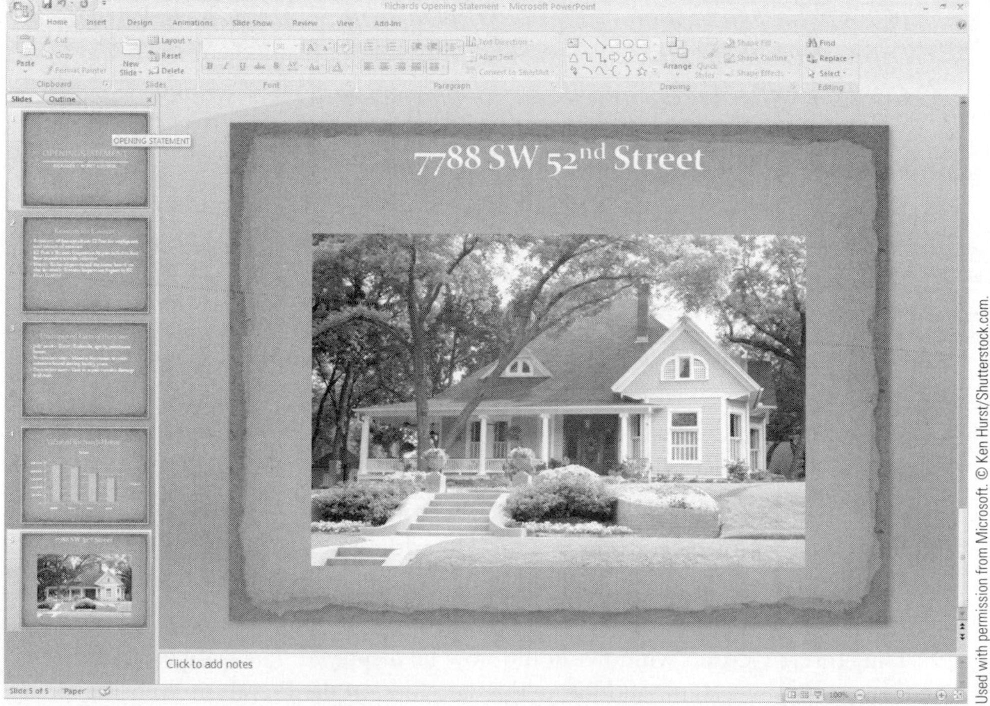

Used with permission from Microsoft. © Ken Hurst/Shutterstock.com.

14. The top part of the slide should say **"Click to add title"** and the bottom section of the slide should say **"Click to add text."**
15. ***Click*** **"Click to add title"** and type **Termite Damage**.
16. ***In the lower box, where it says*** **"Click to add text,"** ***click Insert Picture from File.*** (It is the first icon on the bottom left; see PowerPoint 2007 Exhibit 10.) You will now add another photograph to the presentation.
17. The "Insert Picture" window should now be displayed. Navigate to your CengageBrain account and locate the data files on the Premium Website.

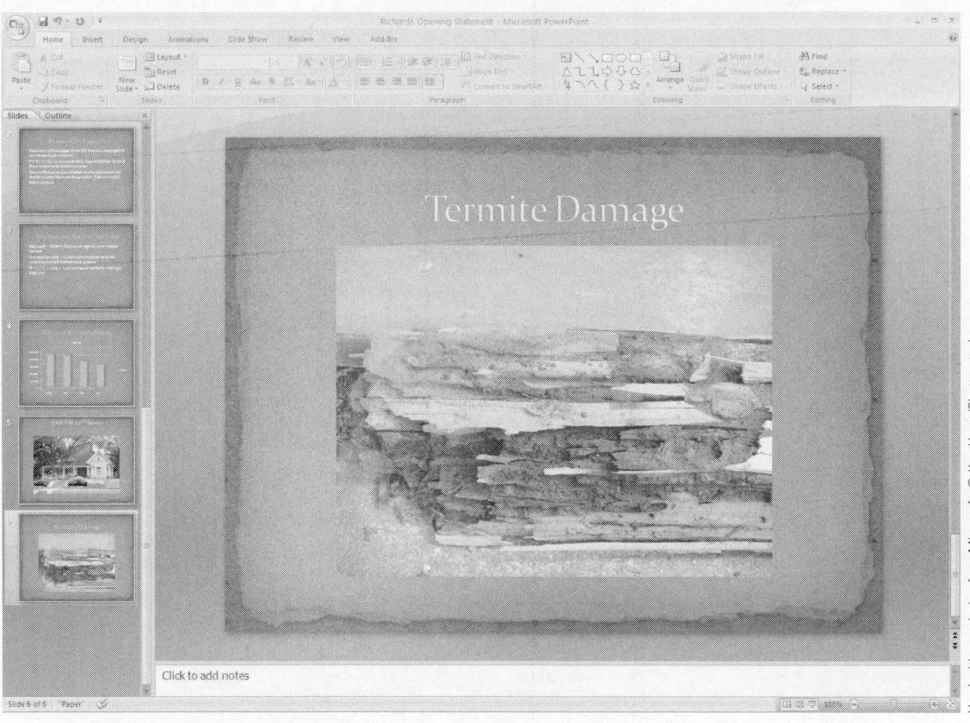

POWERPOINT 2007 EXHIBIT 12

18. ***Double-click the PowerPoint Files folder, double-click the PowerPoint 2007 folder, and then double-click the "Lesson 4 termite damage" (JPEG) file.***
19. ***Click the photograph of termite damage and then click Insert.*** Your screen should now look like PowerPoint 2007 Exhibit 12. If you need to change the size of the image, ***click one of the sides of the image and drag the image to the desired size.***
20. Now that you have created all your slides, you are ready to begin finalizing the presentation. Press **[CTRL]+[HOME]** to go to the first slide in the presentation.
21. ***Click the Slide Sorter view icon at the bottom right of the screen.*** Notice that you can see all six of your slides on the screen.
22. You will now apply transition effects (effects that take place when you move from one slide to another) and animation effects (effects that take place during display of a single slide).
23. ***Click the first slide,*** "OPENING STATEMENT"
24. ***Click the Animations ribbon tab.*** You should see the Transition to This Slide group (see PowerPoint 2007 Exhibit 13). On the left side of the Transition to This Slide group are the various transition choices. To the right are the settings available for each transition.
25. ***On the Animations ribbon tab, click the More icon in the Transition to This Slide group.*** Notice that many types of slide transitions are available.
26. Press the **[ESC]** key to make the "More transitions" list disappear.
27. ***On the Animation ribbon tab, click the Fade Smoothly transition effect in the Transition to This Slide group***. Notice that after you selected it, your slide displayed the transition effect. Fade Smoothly is a professional-appearing transition effect that is not distracting, so it is a good one to use in the legal setting.
28. ***On the Animations ribbon tab, click the down arrow next to Transition Speed: Fast and then click Medium.***

POWERPOINT 2007 EXHIBIT 13

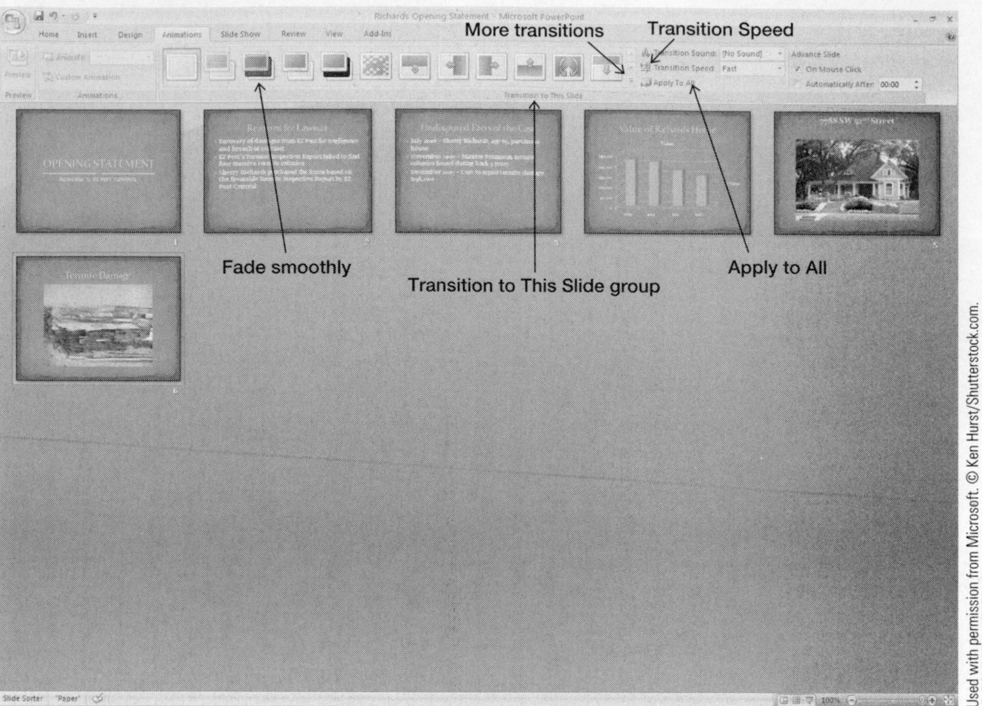

29. ***On the Animations ribbon tab, click Apply to All in the Transition to This Slide group***. This will apply the Fade Smoothly effect to all the slides in your presentation. Notice that little symbols now appear under all your slides in the slide sorter; this shows that they have transition effects associated with them.
30. Notice that in the Transition to This Slide group, under Advance Slide, "On Mouse Click" is selected. This means that the presentation will automatically move to the next slide only when the mouse is clicked. You could set it to move to the next slide automatically after a given amount of time, but the current selection is fine for this presentation.
31. ***Click the Slide Show icon at the bottom right of the screen*** to see your presentation, including the transition effects. ***Click the mouse button to proceed through the presentation and go back to the Slide Sorter screen.***
32. You will now create an animation effect that determines how the slides with bullet points appear on the screen.
33. ***Double-click the second slide, "Reasons for Lawsuit."***
34. ***Click anywhere in the lower half of the screen.***
35. ***On the Animations ribbon tab, click the down arrow next to Animate: No Animation*** (see PowerPoint 2007 Exhibit 14).
36. ***Under Fade, click By 1st Level Paragraphs***. Notice that the animation effect is then demonstrated.
37. Repeat this same process for slide 3.
38. You are now ready to view your presentation. Press the **[PAGE UP]** key to go to the first slide in the presentation.
39. ***Click the Slide Show icon at the bottom right of the screen.***

**POWERPOINT 2007
EXHIBIT 14**

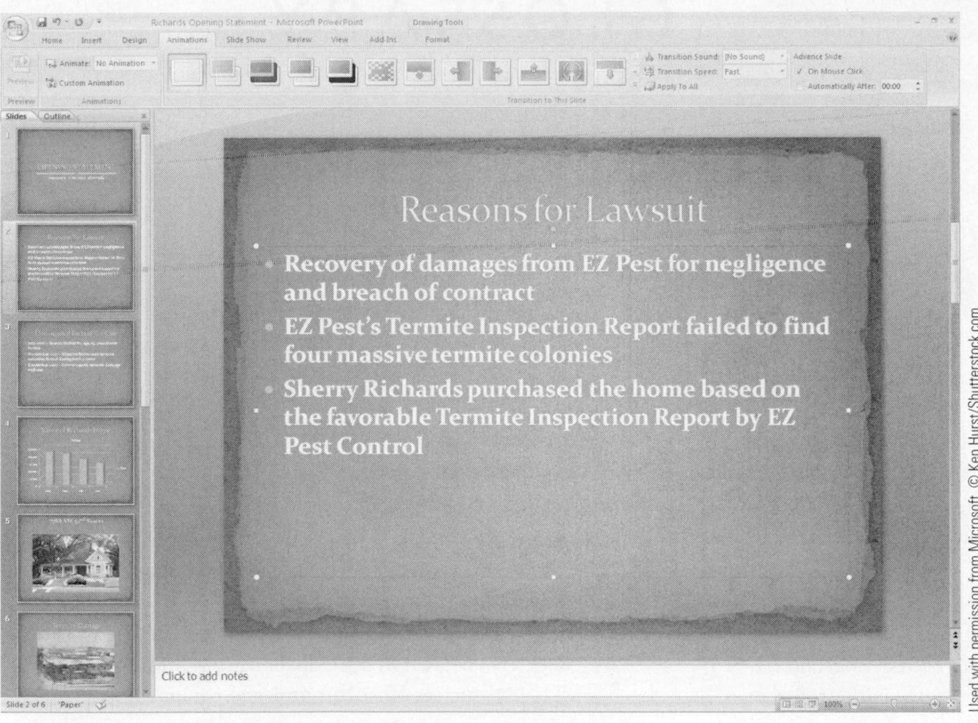

40. Your first slide is now shown at full-screen size. To proceed to the next slide, press the **[SPACE BAR]** or ***click the left mouse button.*** Keep pressing the **[SPACE BAR]** or clicking the left mouse button to proceed with the presentation. Notice that, on the slides with bullets, you must press the **[SPACE BAR]** or click the mouse to go to the next bullet; this is the animation effect you created.

41. When you get to the end of the presentation, press the **[SPACE BAR]** or ***click the left mouse button*** to go back to editing the presentation.

42. To print your presentation, ***click the Office button, point to Print, and click OK.***

43. To save your presentation, ***click the Save icon*** (it looks like a floppy disk) ***on the Quick Access toolbar.***

44. ***Click the Office button and then click Close.***

This concludes the PowerPoint 2007 Hands-On Exercises. To exit PowerPoint, ***click the Office button and then click Exit PowerPoint.***

GLOSSARY

absolute cell reference A cell address in a spreadsheet program formula that does not change when it is copied to a new location.

access rights Network security measure that limits a user's access to only those directories and programs that the user is authorized to use.

access time The amount of time it takes to transfer data between a storage device and RAM.

accessible data Data that have not been deleted and can be accessed without the use of special tools and/or software.

activity hourly rate A fee based on hourly rates that vary depending on the type of service or activity performed and the degree of difficulty of the activity.

aged accounts receivable report A report showing all cases that have outstanding balances due and how much these balances are past due.

analytical litigation support programs A type of software that helps legal professionals analyze a case from a number of different perspectives and draw conclusions about cause-and-effect relationships between facts and evidence in a case.

antivirus and antispyware utilities Programs that attempt to prevent virus and spyware programs from getting into the computer system; most also function to locate and remove any viruses or spyware that do manage to get into the computer.

application service provider (ASP) A company that provides software or a service application through the Internet directly to the user's computer.

application software Instructions (programs) that tell the computer to perform a specific function or task, such as word processing.

arithmetic operators Symbols that tell a spreadsheet how to compute values. Examples include addition signs, subtraction signs, and multiplication signs.

attorney or paralegal hourly rate A fee based on the attorney's or paralegal's level of expertise and experience in a particular area.

automatic page numbering Word-processor feature that automatically numbers the pages of a document for the user; also renumbers pages as material is moved, added, or deleted.

auxiliary storage device A device that stores information so that it can be retrieved for later use. Auxiliary storage devices retain data after power to the computer has been turned off. Auxiliary storage devices include flash drives, hard disk drives, and others.

background The design on which the other elements of the presentation (words, clip art, etc.) are placed.

backing up Making a copy of a user's computer files.

backup utility Program that creates a copy of a user's hard disk or other storage device. The backup copy can be restored if the hard disk is damaged or lost.

bar code scanner Device that reads the special lines of bar codes. Can be used to track documents in litigation, or physical objects such as office furniture and equipment.

bar/column graph A graph consisting of a sequence of bars that illustrate numerical values.

Bates stamp Marks a page with a sequential number and then automatically advances to the next number.

billable hour Sixty minutes of legal services.

billing The process of issuing invoices (bills) to collect monies for legal services performed and for expenses incurred.

blended hourly rate fee A single hourly rate that is set by taking into account the mix of attorneys working on the matter.

blog A website with information contained in posts (writings resembling diary or journal entries) that are arranged in reverse chronological order.

bookmark A tool that enables a user to quickly and easily go back to a website or web page.

Boolean logic search A computer search that allows a search request to include or exclude words, or use other search criteria, so that the search is either refined or broadened.

cable modem A data modem that is designed to work over cable TV lines.

calendaring A generic term used to describe the function of recording appointments for any type of business; includes personal information management.

case management A legal term that usually encompasses functions such as docket control, deadlines, things to do, contact information by case, case notes, document assembly, document tracking by case, integrated billing, and email.

case retainer A fee that is billed at the beginning of a matter, is not refundable to the client, and is usually paid at the beginning of the case as an incentive for the office to take the case.

case type productivity report A report showing which types of cases (e.g., criminal, personal injury, bankruptcy, etc.) are the most profitable.

cash advance Unearned monies that are paid before services are rendered, to cover the attorney's future fees and expenses.

cell An intersection between a row and a column in a spreadsheet.

cell address The row and column location of a cell, usually expressed with column identifier first and row identifier second.

cell pointer The cursor in a spreadsheet program.

cell width The number of characters that can be viewed in any given cell in a spreadsheet program.

central processing unit (CPU) The part of a computer that contains the processor chip and main memory. The CPU organizes and manipulates information, in addition to coordinating with peripheral devices.

centralized word-processing system A system in which all the word-processing documents for an organization are input or typed in a single location or by one department (i.e., a word-processing department).

cite checking Doing research to verify that a case or statute is still valid and that the decision has not been overturned or the statute repealed.

clawback The ability to have privileged material that has been produced inadvertently returned with no waiver of privilege.

client hourly rate A fee based on a single hourly charge for the client, regardless of which attorney works on the case and what she or he does on the case.

client/server network A network that uses a server (or servers) to enhance the function and meet the needs of the other computers on the network.

clip art Predrawn art.

cloud Refers to the ability to access information residing on remote computers.

cloud computing The ability to use one computer to access information stored on a different computer or server.

column An area that extends down a page vertically.

comment Word-processor feature that allows a user to annotate and create notes in a document without changing the text of the document.

compare documents Word-processor feature that allows a user to compare and contrast two documents, either side by side or by blacklining (usually through the creation of a third document showing differences).

compression utility Program that reorganizes a file so that the file takes up less room when it is saved. Many large files that are downloaded from the Internet are routinely compressed to reduce the time needed for the download.

computer An electronic device that accepts input data, processes data, outputs data, and stores data electronically; types include desktop, laptop, handheld, tablet, and file server.

computer virus A destructive computer program that may be designed to delete data, corrupt files, or do other damage; may also be self-replicating, using an "infected" computer to transmit itself to other computers.

computer-aided transcription (CAT) A process that automatically deciphers a court reporter's notes and converts them into a computer-readable format.

computer-assisted legal research (CALR) Research method in which computers are used to find and retrieve legal information.

connectors Characters that define or show a relationship between the keywords in a search query.

contingency fee A fee collected if the attorney successfully represents the client; typically a percentage of the total recovery.

data filtering The process of searching and culling the data to find relevant information and reduce the overall size of the dataset.

data value One item of information; the smallest piece of information in a table.

database management system (DBMS) Application software that manages a database by storing, searching, sorting, and organizing data.

database A collection of related data items. Databases are created because the information contained in them must be accessed, organized, and used.

decentralized word-processing system A system in which individuals or separate departments in an organization perform their own word processing.

de-duplication (de-duping) The process of marking or deleting records that are duplicates.

deleted data Data that at one time were active on a computer, but which have since been deleted.

demonstrative evidence All evidence other than testimony.

disaster recovery plan A prewritten plan of action to be followed if a disaster befalls the legal organization.

discovery The pretrial stage of litigation where parties disclose to each other information about their case.

docket control A legal-specific term that refers to entering, organizing, tracking, and controlling all the appointments, deadlines, and due dates for a legal organization.

document abstract litigation support system Software that allows users to enter document abstracts or summaries into a computer and then search and retrieve the information contained in those abstracts or summaries.

document assembly software Powerful computer program that creates standardized templates and forms.

document camera An overhead projector that uses a camera to display hardcopy documents that have not been imaged.

document imaging A system in which documents are scanned into a computer and the documents' actual images (similar to photographs) are retained in the computer.

document management software Program that organizes, controls, distributes, and allows for extensive searching of electronic documents, typically in a networked environment.

double indenting Word-processor feature (also found in other types of programs) that indents text an equal distance from the left and right margins.

DSL (Digital Subscriber Line) A type of digital phone line that allows both data and voice to be transmitted on the same line, simultaneously if desired. Transmission speed is fairly fast.

earned retainer The money the law office or attorney has earned and is entitled to deposit in the office's or attorney's own bank account.

electronic billing Client billing that uses a standard electronic format, using such means as the Internet, and conforms to standard billing codes.

electronic discovery (e-discovery) The process of producing and receiving litigation documents in electronic format.

electronic filing Supplying electronic versions of legal documents to a court, via the Internet or other electronic means, when the court does not require the hard copy of the document.

electronic mail (email) Computerized communication function that enables users to send and receive messages almost instantly.

electronically stored information (ESI) The term used by the Federal Rules of Civil Procedure to refer to all electronic data, including writings, drawings, graphs, charts, photographs, sound recordings, images, and other data compilations stored in any medium from which information can be obtained or translated.

encryption Process of running a message through an encoder that uses an encrypting key to alter the characters in the message. Unless the person wanting to read the message has the encryption key needed to decode it, the message appears unreadable.

endnote Material that is printed at the end of a chapter or document; marked in text by a numbered referent.

evidence display system Technology that provides networked computer monitors to a judge, jury, court reporter, clerk, attorneys, and the public.

exchangeable image file (EXIF) Metadata embedded within a JPEG file (digital photograph).

expense slip A record of each expense item a firm incurs on behalf of the client.

extranet A secure web-based site that allows clients to access information about their cases and collaborate with the legal professionals who are providing legal services to them.

field A column in a table that contains a category of information.

File Transfer Protocol (FTP) A tool or standard for transferring electronic files over the Internet.

Find a Case by Party Name A Westlaw feature that allows a user who knows the name of at least one party to retrieve a case without knowing the case citation or entering a search query.

Find by Citation A Westlaw feature that allows a user to immediately retrieve a specific case or statute by entering its citation.

firewall Security measure that allows users from inside an organization to access the Internet but keeps outside users from entering the computer or LAN.

flat fee A fee for specific legal services that is billed as a fixed amount.

footer Text that appears at the bottom of each page of a document.

footnote Material that is printed at the bottom of a page; marked in text by a numbered referent.

form Setup that allows a user to view, enter, and edit data in a custom format designed by the user.

formulas Expressions used in spreadsheet programs to automatically perform calculations on other values.

full-text retrieval litigation support system Software that enables a user to search (and retrieve information from) the full text of documents stored in the system.

function command A predefined calculation used in a spreadsheet program to speed up the process of entering complex formulas.

geolocation The ability to track the precise location of a device, and by implication, its owner.

geotagging Geographical metadata embedded in an electronic file.

gigahertz (GHz) Measure of the clock speed of a computer.

hard disk drive A reliable and fast auxiliary storage device that stores data on a rigid magnetic disk; may be built into the computer (internal) or a freestanding peripheral device (external).

hardware The physical equipment of a computer system, as opposed to programs or software.

harvesting data The process of collecting ESI from the client's information systems.

header A title or heading that appears at the top of each page of a document.

Headnotes and Key Numbers Westlaw feature that classifies each legal issue in a case and allows users to search and retrieve other cases with similar Headnotes and Key Numbers.

hourly rate fee A fee for legal services that is billed to the client by the hour at an agreed upon rate.

image format A file structure that shows an image of a document as if it were being viewed in the original application, without the need to use or even have the original application.

imaging Scanning a document into a computer so the user can see an exact picture of the document on the computer.

inaccessible data Data that can be accessed only with the use of special tools and/or software.

individual search engine Search engine that compiles its own searchable database.

in-house computerized litigation support system A litigation support system set up by the firm's or attorney's own staff on their own computer(s).

input Data or information that is entered or transferred into a computer (including by keyboard, mouse, scanner, voice, etc.).

input devices Devices used to enter information into a computer; include the mouse, keyboards, scanners, voice recognition devices, digital cameras, and others.

instant messaging (IM) Communication function that allows users to converse in real time with other users who are using the same IM program. As soon as a user connects to the Internet, the user will know which of his or her colleagues are signed on and be able to send them messages.

Internet service provider (ISP) Supplies users with Internet services such as the World Wide Web, email, listservs, newsgroups, and others.

Internet One of the world's largest computer networks; actually a "network of networks." It allows hundreds of millions of users around the world to share information.

intranet An internal network designed to provide and disseminate information to internal staff; most mimic the look and feel of the World Wide Web.

invisible Web Term for the large portion of the World Wide Web that is not accessible to search engine spiders. This includes PDF files, password-protected sites, some databases, documents behind firewalls, and other data/sites.

KeyCite Westlaw feature that allows users to determine if a case, statute, or other document is good law and enables users to expand their research by finding other sources that have cited the reference.

landscape A method of printing that arranges data across the width of a page.

legacy data Data created with obsolete computer media and programs.

legal malpractice An attorney's breach of an ordinary standard of care that a reasonable attorney would have adhered to under the same circumstances.

library gateway A collection of databases and information sites arranged by subject.

license agreement Contract setting out the user's rights and restrictions on how a piece of software can be used.

line graph A graph that plots numerical values as a time line.

listserv An electronic mailing list that allows people on the list to send messages to and receive messages from everyone on the list via email.

litigation hold An order suspending destruction or disposal of all relevant hard-copy and electronically stored information, instituted when a party reasonably anticipates litigation.

litigation support service provider A company that, for a fee, sets up a litigation support system and enters all documents necessary for a case.

litigation support software Program that assists attorneys and paralegals in organizing, storing, retrieving, and summarizing the information that is gathered during the litigation of a lawsuit.

local area network (LAN) A multiuser system linking computers that are in close proximity for the purpose of communication.

Locate in Result A Westlaw command that allows a user to search the retrieved documents for particular terms, whether or not those terms appeared in the user's original search.

macro Word-processor feature that records the user's keystrokes, saves those keystrokes, and then allows the user to play those keystrokes back.

magnetic tape system Storage device that records data on magnetic tape.

main memory The part of the CPU that stores information that the computer is processing. Main memory consists of read-only memory and random-access memory.

management reports Reports used to help managers analyze whether the office is operating in an efficient, effective, and profitable manner.

memory chips Parts of a computer that store or hold information.

merging The process of combining a form with a list of variables to automatically produce a document; sometimes called document generation.

metadata Electronically stored information that may identify the origin, date, author, usage, comments, or other information about a file; "data about data."

metasearch engine Search engine that does not crawl the Web or compile its own database, but instead sends the user's search request to a number of different individual search engines and then eliminates duplicates and sorts the sites retrieved.

modem A device that allows computers in different locations to communicate using a telephone line.

monitor Screen that displays computer output.

mouse An input device used to move the cursor on the monitor. The cursor moves in the same direction as the mouse is moved.

native format A file structure as defined by the original application in which the file was created.

Natural Language A query/search technique that uses plain English, without the need for complex connectors or syntax, to search for documents.

network operating system System that handles communication tasks between the computers on a network.

normal view PowerPoint screen that shows the slide that is being created, an outline of the total presentation, and speaker's notes for the slide currently displayed.

objective/bibliographical coding System in which only basic information about documents (document number, document name, date, author, recipient, and so forth) is recorded in a document abstract database. The coder makes no subjective characterizations about the document.

offline No longer connected to the Internet; in relation to fee-based CALR services, no longer connected to the information service and thus not accruing charges (except possibly for printing or downloading).

online Connected to the Internet; in relation to fee-based CALR services, connected to the service and incurring charges.

operating account Bank account used by a law firm for the deposit of earned fees and payment of law firm expenses.

operating system software (program) A set of instructions that tell the computer how to operate its own circuitry and manage its components; also controls how the computer communicates with input, output, and auxiliary storage devices. Allows the user to manage the computer.

optical character recognition (OCR) A technology that allows the text of documents to be read or scanned into a computer so the text of the document can be searched or brought into a word processor to be edited.

optical storage devices Devices that use laser beams to write data onto small plastic disks. Optical storage devices can record hundreds of megabytes of data on a single disk.

output Information or computer results that are produced or transmitted from a computer to a user as a result of the computer's operations (including to monitor, printer, etc.).

output device Peripheral device that provides a user with the data a computer has generated, accessed, or manipulated.

paperless office Firm in which all hard-copy documents are converted into electronic form(s) for storage, processing, and distribution.

password Code entered into a computer system or software that acts as a key, allowing the user to access the system and the information it contains.

peer-to-peer network A computer network in which each computer acts as both a server and a client.

peripheral devices Pieces of equipment that are connected to a computer to perform specific functions, such as storing information (auxiliary storage devices), inputting information (input devices), outputting information (output devices), and communicating with other computers (communication devices).

personal information manager (PIM) System that consolidates a number of different tasks into one computer program. Most PIMs handle or provide functions for calendaring, things to do, a contact database that tracks names and addresses of people, note-taking, email, and other tasks.

phishing A type of Internet fraud; "phishers" send fraudulent emails, in which they impersonate legitimate senders, in hopes of gaining personal information from responders.

pie chart A chart that represents each value as a piece or percentage of a whole (a total "pie").

podcast An audio or video recording that is posted on the Internet and made available for users to download so they can listen or watch it on a computer or mobile computing device.

Portable Document Format (PDF) A file format developed by Adobe Systems, Inc., for sharing files independently of the application that created the file or the computer's operating system.

portal A "jumping-off" spot for many things on the Web, offering searching, hierarchical directories, news, sports, shopping, entertainment, and much more.

portrait A method of printing that arranges data down the length of a page.

power-on password Password that the computer immediately prompts the user to enter after the machine has been turned on, but before the computer has completely booted the operating system software. If the user does not know the password, the system will not start and the computer will be unusable.

pre-billing report A rough draft compilation of billings.

predictive coding Computer software applications that use sophisticated algorithms to enable the computer to determine the relevance of documents, based on interaction with a person with knowledge of the case.

primary file A file that contains the information that remains the same (the constant) in a document that is used more than once; usually referred to as a *form* or *template* in a merge document.

processor chip The part of the computer that performs the actual arithmetic computations and logic functions.

project management software Application program that allows the user to track the sequence and timing of the separate activities of a larger project or task.

proximity search A computer search that scans a database for words that are in a given proximity to one another.

pure retainer A fee that obligates the office to be available to represent the client throughout the agreed upon time period.

query Statement that extracts data from a table based on criteria designed by the user. A query allows a user to search for and sort only the information the user is looking for at that time.

random-access memory (RAM) A part of main memory that is temporary and volatile in nature; it is erased every time the computer's power is turned off. Application programs and data are loaded into RAM when the computer is processing the data.

read-only memory (ROM) A part of main memory that contains permanent information a computer uses to operate itself. ROM can be read, but cannot be written to.

real-time transcription System through which an attorney or paralegal connects a computer with the appropriate software to the court reporter's transcription machine, so that within seconds of the testimony being spoken, a rough-draft version of the transcript appears on the computer screen.

record A collection of fields that are treated as a unit. It is essentially one row in a table.

recurring entry A calendar entry that must be done regularly or often.

relative cell reference A cell address in a spreadsheet program formula that automatically changes to reflect its new location when it is copied.

removable drive A small portable device that stores a large amount of data; often used to transfer information between computers.

report Function that extracts and prints data from a table or query as designed by the user. Whereas forms are designed to be used on the screen, reports are designed to be printed.

ResultsPlus A Westlaw feature that automatically includes other documents related to a user's search, such as legal texts, treatises, and law review articles; no additional search is needed to retrieve these supplementary materials.

retainer for general representation A retainer typically used when a client such as a corporation or school board requires continuing legal services throughout the year.

root expander A character that enables a legal information system to retrieve multiple words with the same root.

row An area that extends across a page horizontally.

RSS A group of formats that are used to publish and distribute news feeds, blogs, and podcasts.

rule-based entry A method of entering events in a case management system so that entering one event automatically triggers creation of a list of subsequent calendaring events, based on a rule that was programmed into the application.

SaaS (Software as a Service) Software applications that are hosted in the cloud instead of on the user's computer.

safe harbor A provision of the FRCP providing that parties who act in good faith but inadvertently destroy ESI as a routine part of their information systems handling are not subject to sanctions for that destruction.

sampling data The process of testing data to determine if it is appropriate for production.

search query An instruction to an information service to search a specific database for the occurrence of certain words and combinations of words. Searches can be limited by restricting the query terms, by searching only in specific databases, and by searching only in certain parts of a document (such as the title, synopsis, headnote, etc.).

secondary file The file that contains the information that varies (the *variable*) in a merge document.

single-user system A computer that can accommodate only one person at a time and is not linked to other systems or computers.

single-word search A computer search that scans a database for matches to a single word.

slide show view PowerPoint screen used during a presentation or when the user wants to preview how the audience will actually see the slide. Only the current slide is shown on the screen. The program interface, menus, outline view, and speaker's notes are not shown.

slide sorter view PowerPoint screen that shows the slides in the presentation, but in a greatly reduced format; typically used to review and/or change the order of slides.

slide transition Effects that control how the program proceeds from one slide to another.

social media Online platforms that enable people to communicate easily to share information and resources, including text, audio, video, and images.

soft deletions Information that has been deleted and is not available to the user, but which nonetheless has not been overwritten; can often be fully restored, with complete integrity, by forensic experts.

software Computer programs that instruct the computer hardware how to function and perform tasks.

sound card A device that enhances the sounds that come out of a computer and/or enables speakers attached to a computer to function. Nearly all computers now come with a sound card.

spam Unwanted or unsolicited email messages that are sent to many recipients; the electronic equivalent of junk mail.

specialty search engine Search engine that searches only in specific topical areas or sites.

speech recognition The ability of a computer to understand spoken words.

spoliation The destruction of relevant documents (or other materials) in litigation.

spreadsheet A computerized version of an accountant's worksheet or ledger page.

spreadsheet software Programs that calculate and manipulate numbers using labels, values, and formulas.

spyware A general term for software that tracks a user's movement on the Internet for advertising and marketing purposes, collects personal information about the user, or changes the configuration of the user's computer without the user's consent.

stacked column graph A graph that depicts values as separate sections in a single or stacked column.

storage Retention of electronic information for future use (using storage devices such as hard disks, CD-ROMs, DVDs, flash drives, and other media).

statute of limitations A law that sets a limit on the length of time a party has to file a suit. If a case is filed after the statute of limitations has run (expired), the claim is barred and is dismissed as a matter of law.

storage capacity The maximum amount of data that can be stored on a device.

Stored Communications Act Federal statute prohibiting most internet service providers from releasing an individual's information to a third party.

style A named set of formatting characteristics that users can apply to text.

subject directory A site maintained by a staff of people who select sites to include in the directory.

subjective coding Entering information in a document abstract program about what the document means, including what case issues the document is relevant to or notes about the document.

subject-specific database A database devoted to a single subject or area.

super wildcard search A computer search that scans a database for derivatives of a word, using variations both in front of and in back of the root word.

table A collection of related information stored in rows and columns.

table of authorities Automated word-processor feature that allows the program to generate an accurate list of case and statute citations (authorities), along with the page number(s) on which each cite appears.

Terms and Connectors A search technique that uses Boolean logic and operators/ connectors to connect query terms.

text Descriptive data, such as headings and titles, used for reference purposes in a spreadsheet.

TIFF (Tagged Image File Format) A vendor-neutral file structure that produces image format documents.

timekeeper Anyone who bills for time, including partners, associates, and paralegals.

timekeeper productivity report A report showing how much billable and nonbillable time is being spent by each timekeeper.

timekeeping Tracking time for the purpose of billing clients.

timeslip A slip of paper or computer record that records information about the legal services legal professionals provide to each client.

track changes Word-processor feature that allows reviewers to make or recommend changes to a document; these changes can later be either accepted or rejected by the original author.

trial presentation programs Presentation graphics programs specifically designed to meet the needs of trial attorneys.

trust or escrow account A bank account, separate and apart from a law office's or attorney's operating bank account, where unearned client funds are deposited.

unearned retainer Money that is paid up front by the client as an advance against the attorney's future fees and expenses. Until the money is actually earned by the attorney or law office, it actually belongs to the client.

uniform resource locator (URL) The address of a web page.

universal character A character that represents one letter or number; enables a legal information service to retrieve words with minor variations.

utility software Instructions that help users with the housekeeping and maintenance tasks a computer requires; helps manage either the hardware or software aspects of a computer.

value billing A type of fee agreement that is based not on the time required to perform the work, but on the basis of the perceived value of the services to the client.

values Numbers that are entered into a spreadsheet program for the purpose of making calculations.

video adapter card Piece of hardware that acts as an interface between the monitor and the computer.

videoconferencing A private broadcast between two or more remote locations, with live image transmission, display, and sound. Uses data communications to conduct long-distance, face-to-face meetings.

virtual law office Law office that exists without a permanent physical location.

Voice over Internet Protocol (VoIP) Functionality that allows users to make telephone calls using a broadband Internet connection instead of a regular phone line.

web browser The interface or program that allows the user to see web pages.

"what if" analysis A feature of spreadsheets that allows the user to build a spreadsheet and then change the data to reflect alternative planning assumptions or scenarios.

wide area network (WAN) A multiuser system linking computers that may be located thousands of miles apart.

Wi-Fi A system that provides wireless access to the Internet.

wildcard search A computer search that scans a database for derivatives of a word.

Windows A graphical operating system developed by Microsoft for IBM-compatible computers. Various versions of Windows include Windows XP, Windows Vista, and Windows 7.

wireless modem Modems that many mobile phones and handheld computers now use to connect to the Internet.

wireless networking System that allows computers on the network to communicate with each other using wireless antennas coordinated through a wired access point.

word-processing software Program used to edit, manipulate, and revise text to create documents.

World Wide Web An Internet system, navigation tool, and graphical/multimedia interface that retrieves information using links to other web pages. To access the Web, a user needs a web browser program.

INDEX

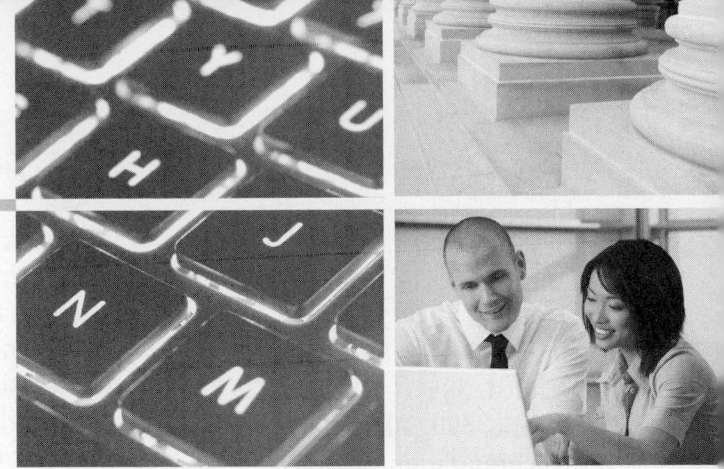

C

M

Y

Z

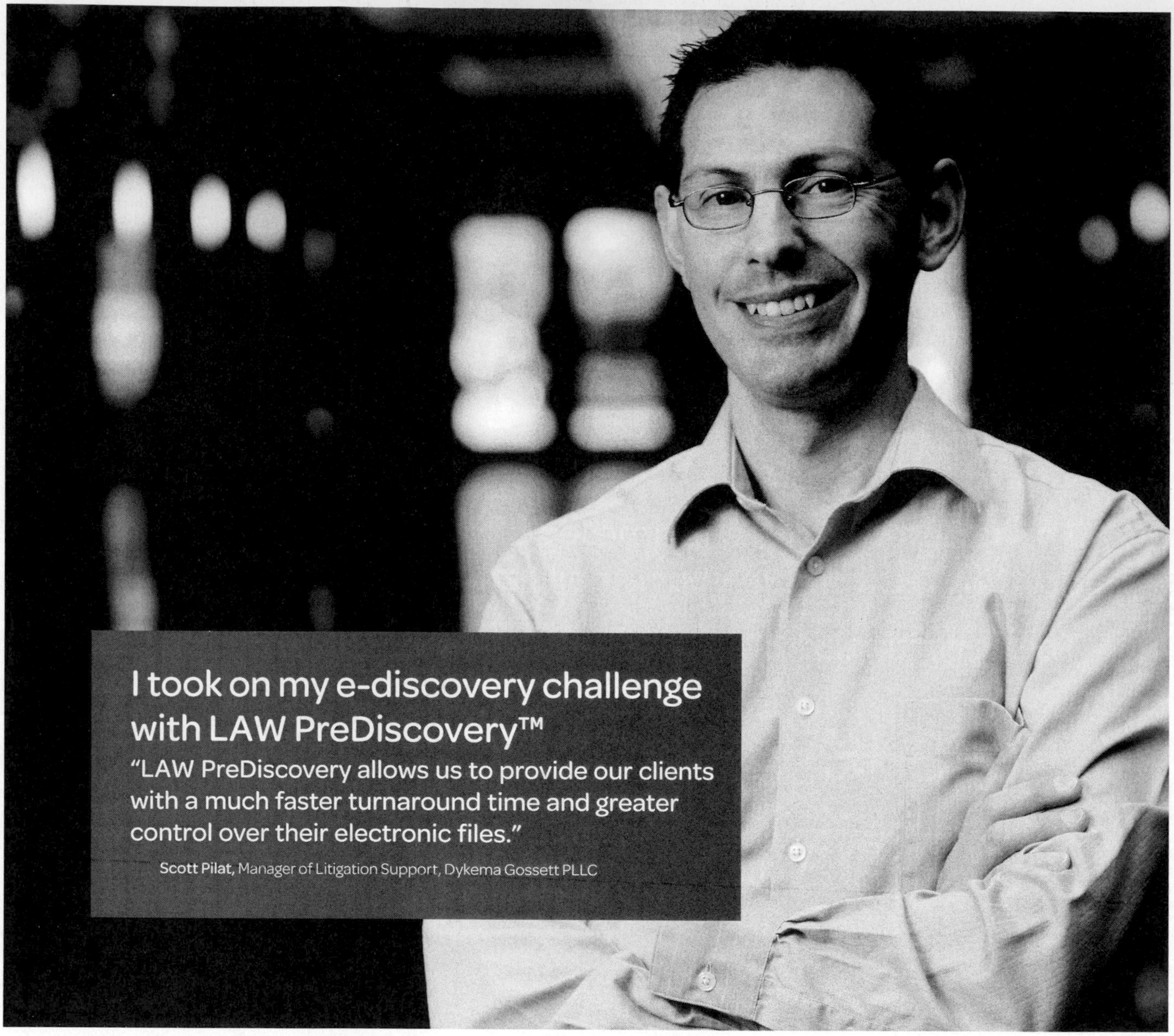

The Challenge: **Controlling soaring electronic discovery expenses.**

Dykema historically relied on outside vendors for electronic discovery processing. But as e-discovery demands and expenses grew, the firm brought processing back in-house and soon began saving their clients money while generating unexpected revenue for the firm.

Manage your daunting data collections quickly and efficiently and reduce initial processing costs with LAW PreDiscovery™ software. And best of all, LAW PreDiscovery usually pays for itself within two months.

LexisNexis®   Read Scott's story at **www.lexisnexis.com/LAWchallenge**

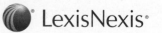